Louisiana Family Law Treatise

Louisiana Family Law Treatise

Monica Hof Wallace

Dean Marcel Garsaud, Jr. Distinguished Professor of Law
Loyola University New Orleans
College of Law

Sandi S. Varnado

William L. Crowe, Sr. Distinguished Professor of Law
Loyola University New Orleans
College of Law

Carolina Academic Press
Durham, North Carolina

Library of Congress Cataloging-in-Publication Data

Names: Wallace, Monica Hof, author. | Varnado, Sandi S., author.
Title: Louisiana family law treatise / Monica Hof Wallace, Sandi S. Varnado.
Description: Durham, North Carolina : Carolina Academic Press, 2025. |
Includes bibliographical references and index.
Identifiers: LCCN 2025000971 | ISBN 9781531033361 (paperback) | ISBN
9781531033378 (ebook)
Subjects: LCSH: Domestic relations—Louisiana.
Classification: LCC KFL94 .W35 2025 | DDC 346.76301/5—dc23/eng/20250114
LC record available at https://lccn.loc.gov/2025000971

Carolina Academic Press
700 Kent Street
Durham, North Carolina 27701
Telephone (919) 489-7486
www.cap-press.com

Printed in the United States of America

To the countless Loyola students who supported us as teachers and whose probing questions, analyses of cases, and critical eyes inspired us to write this treatise, this book is dedicated to you.

Contents

Acknowledgments

Monica Hof Wallace

This treatise would not have been possible but for the friendship and co-authorship of Professor Sandi Varnado. A civil law treatise on the family laws in Louisiana seemed much too big of a project, so I began writing articles in the hope that they could one day be combined in a comprehensive treatise. Without the encouragement of Professor Varnado and assistance in getting this book to the finish line, this manuscript would not have been possible.

For all of those students and faculty members acknowledged in the articles referenced herein, you deserve the same recognition here for being the back on which this treatise was built. I would especially like to thank Michelle Paré Ricca and Ryan Simoneaux, both of whom spent countless hours updating, proofreading, and ensuring consistency in formatting among the various chapters. Any mistake or omission is my own. Thank you as well to Andrew Ates, who proofread the manuscript.

Thank you to my dear friends, Chip LoCoco and Brooke Tigchelaar, who offered to contribute chapters to the treatise, namely Interdiction and Domestic Violence in Families, respectively. Your dedication to the law is admirable, and I am lucky to be able to phone-a-friend with vexing legal questions.

I would also like to thank the administration at the College of Law, the donors of the Dean Marcel Garsaud, Jr. Distinguished Professorship, and the Alfred J. Bonomo, Sr. and Rosaria Sarah LaNasa Families for providing me with funds to hire research assistants to make this book a reality.

To my countless colleagues not only at Loyola but across the state, with whom I have discussed many issues contained in this treatise, your thoughtfulness and shared intellect make the research deeper and more meaningful. To my countless research assistants who have provided family law updates to me for years, I could not have compiled this work without you. To my friends and colleagues in the practicing bar, especially those who attend the Loyola Family Law CLE, you have raised my attention to issues that need to be addressed to better protect children and families. And to the students who make this work fun and possible, this one's for you.

I would be remiss if I did not thank my husband, Todd, and my two wonderful children, Jack and Grace, for supporting me and allowing me weekend and holiday time to work—I finished it!

Sandi Varnado

I would like to thank my friend and co-author, Professor Monica Wallace, for inviting me to contribute to this treatise. I learned so much about Louisiana Family Law and hope that those who read the treatise will, too. I never would have tackled such a project without Professor Wallace's encouragement and support, and I am grateful to have collaborated on it with her.

I am thankful to the many students, practitioners, judges, and professors who have shared their knowledge of family law over the years. Learning from you all has been a true blessing. Special thanks goes to Randy Trahan, whose influence goes back decades. He taught me, mentored me, and has always been a source of support as I have navigated my career. I would like to echo Professor Wallace in her thanks of Chip LoCoco, Brooke Tigchelaar, Michele Paré Ricca, Ryan Simoneaux, and Andrew Ates. Additionally, I am very appreciative of one of my former students, Katherine DeBlanc, who contributed to the Domestic Violence chapter, and current research assistants, Amelia Sylvest and Kaylin Guillory Makowsky, for their editing and proofreading efforts.

I would also like to thank the administration at the College of Law, as well as the donors of the Kathryn Venturatos Lorio Distinguished Professorship and the William L. Crowe, Sr. Distinguished Professorship, for providing me with the funds needed to focus on this project.

This treatise has been a labor of love for many years, and I am grateful for every person who has had a hand in its completion. I especially appreciate my family's patience as I completed my work.

About the Authors

Monica Hof Wallace is the Dean Marcel Garsaud, Jr. Distinguished Professor of Law at Loyola University New Orleans College of Law. Professor Wallace joined the law faculty in 2002 after practicing at the New Orleans firm of Correro Fishman Haygood Phelps Walmsley & Casteix (now Fishman Haygood et al). Professor Wallace graduated first in her class at Loyola College of Law and while attending law school, served on the Law Review and as Chairman of the Moot Court Program. After graduation, Professor Wallace served as a law clerk for the Honorable Jacques L. Wiener, Jr. of the United States Fifth Circuit Court of Appeals and the Honorable Barry Ted Moskowitz of the United States District Court for the Southern District of California.

Professor Wallace is a frequent speaker, author, and consultant in the areas of family law, successions, donations, trusts, and community property, all of which she teaches at the College of Law. She also lectures on family law for Barbri nationally. Professor Wallace is the author of casebooks in family law, successions and donations, and probate and trusts, as well as the Louisiana Civil Law Treatise on Successions and Donations. Professor Wallace is an active member of the Louisiana Law Institute, currently serving on the Marriage-Persons Committee and the Successions and Donations Committee. Professor Wallace also designed, developed, and fundraised for the Loyola Advocacy Center, over which she served as Director at its inception. She is a member of many professional organizations, including the Louisiana State Bar Association, the Louisiana Law Institute, and the St. Thomas More Inn of Court, and she is an active Fellow of the Louisiana Bar Foundation.

Professor Wallace is a three-time recipient of the Professor of the Year award, and she has twice received the University Senate award for Excellence in Teaching and once for Excellence in Research. She was named a CityBusiness Leader in Law, received the Louisiana Youth Seminar's No Man Is An Island award, and was honored with the Gillis Long Poverty Law Center Public Service Award.

Sandi Varnado is the Professor Varnado is the William L. Crowe, Sr. Distinguished Professor of Law. She is the author of Louisiana Law of Persons: Cases and Readings, Louisiana Successions & Donations, and Louisiana Community Property and is the co-author of both Sale, Lease, and Advanced Obligations and Louisiana Law of Obligations. She has published articles on issues of family law and decedent's estates and has presented her scholarship at local and national professional conferences. Professor Varnado regularly teaches numerous civil law courses including Family Law Seminar, Successions & Donations, Community Property, Obligations I, Obligations II, Civil

Law of Persons, and Sales & Leases. She has also taught Comparative Estate Law (as part of the Loyola study abroad programs in Vienna, Austria and Spetses, Greece) and United States Family Law at the University of Silesia in Katowice, Poland. Professor Varnado is heavily involved in Loyola's Supplemental Bar Prep Program and is a lecturer for BARBRI. She has served on numerous committees of and on the Council of the Louisiana State Law Institute.

Professor Varnado has been selected as Favorite Professor of the Year on three occasions (2013, 2016, and 2021). She has also received the University Senate Award for Excellence in Advising (2015) and the University Senate Award for Excellence in Teaching (2021).

Prior to joining the faculty of the Loyola New Orleans College of Law, she clerked for the Honorable James L. Dennis of the United States Court of Appeals for the Fifth Circuit and thereafter, practiced law at Baker, Donelson, Bearman, Caldwell & Berkowitz, P.C., focusing her practice on construction law, labor and employment law, and commercial litigation. In law school, she served as Articles Editor of Volume 66 of the Louisiana Law Review, was on the Chancellor's List each semester of her studies, and received the CALI award in eleven classes; upon graduation, she was ranked second in her class and was inducted into the Order of the Coif. Prior to her legal career, Professor Varnado taught high school social studies and English for eight and a half years in Mississippi and Louisiana.

Louisiana Family Law Treatise

Chapter 1

Natural and Juridical Persons*

§ 1:1 Introduction

Book I of the Louisiana Civil Code begins by defining two types of persons: natural and juridical.[1] In their simplest form, natural persons are human beings, and juridical persons are entities.[2] A "person," in its technical legal sense, signifies a subject of rights and duties. Prior to the comprehensive revision in 1987, the Civil Code distinguished persons based on their status, with corresponding rights and responsibilities based on one's status as a woman, a slave, or an illegitimate, just to name a few.[3] Today, Title I of Book I has been simplified and defines persons as either natural or juridical, with a distinction made for natural persons who reach the age of majority.[4] Although the law of personality is descriptive and does not invoke traditional legal challenges, it is noteworthy because it generates rights, responsibilities, and abilities, either actively or passively, to enjoy rights and engage in obligations.

---

* This chapter was derived from the following article: Monica Hof Wallace, *A Primer on Natural and Juridical Persons in Louisiana*, 64 Loy. L. Rev. 407 (2018). The authors wish to thank the Loyola Law Review for its assistance on the initial work for this chapter.

1. La. Civ. Code Ann. art. 24.

2. La. Civ. Code Ann. art. 24 ("A natural person is a human being. A juridical person is an entity to which the law attributes personality, such as a corporation or a partnership.").

3. *See generally* La. Civ. Code bk. I, tit. I, chps. 1–2, arts. 1–19 (1808). Persons were distinguished in at least thirteen different ways, and one's status affected one's rights and obligations. *See* Jeanne Louise Carriere, From Status to Person in Book I, Title 1 of the Civil Code, 73 Tul. L. Rev. 1263 (1999), for an excellent discussion of the meaning and history of personality.

4. La. Civ. Code Ann. arts. 24, 27–29 (natural persons who reach the age of 18 have the capacity to make juridical acts, while all natural persons, no matter the age, have general legal capacity).

§ 1:2 Natural Persons

Natural personality begins at live birth and ends at death.[5] Personality has retroactive effect from the moment of conception if the unborn child is later born alive.[6] Natural personality begins and ends at definable moments for most human beings—conception and death. However, because children are conceived outside of the womb, and because people disappear or are kept alive by life-sustaining measures, the law must carefully define birth and death.

The importance of natural personality should not be understated. "Natural persons enjoy general legal capacity to have rights and duties."[7] Natural personality, however, does not automatically confer capacity to make juridical acts. To make binding juridical acts, one must be emancipated[8] or reach the age of majority, which in Louisiana is the age of 18, assuming the major is not incapacitated for other reasons, such as interdiction or continuing tutorship.[9]

§ 1:3 Natural Persons—Commencement of Natural Personality

When a child is born alive, natural personality exists. A child that is stillborn has no natural personality, "except for ... actions resulting from its wrongful death."[10] Live birth is necessary for natural personality to commence, but the child need not be capable of living on their own.[11] Once live birth occurs, the law provides that the child possessed natural personality from the moment of conception.[12] The moment of conception, however, is less clear.

5. La. Civ. Code Ann. art. 25.

6. La. Civ. Code Ann. art. 26.

7. La. Civ. Code Ann. art. 27.

8. *See* La. Civ. Code Ann. bk. I, tit. VIII, chp. 2, for a discussion on emancipation.

9. La. Civ. Code Ann. arts. 28–29. Special legislation exists on a minor's ability to contract marriage, *see* La. Child. Code Ann. art. 1545, and a minor's ability to make donations *inter vivos* and *mortis causa*, *see* La. Civ. Code Ann. art. 1476.

10. La. Civ. Code Ann. art. 26. The 1987 revision codified this jurisprudential rule. *See* Danos v. St. Pierre, 402 So. 2d 633 (La. 1981); La. Civ. Code Ann. art. 26 cmt. (d) (rev. 1987).

11. *See generally* In re P.V.W., 424 So. 2d 1015, 1016 (La. 1982) (finding that "a newborn infant whose brain was irreversibly damaged at birth and who was in a comatose state" was born alive and had natural personality). In the Digest of 1808, viability was a prerequisite for natural personality. *See* La. Civ. Code art. 6 (1808). The Civil Code of 1825 contained no prerequisite of viability, providing rather: "When the child is born alive, though it may have been extracted by force from its mother's womb, and may have lived but an instant, provided the fact of its living be ascertained, it inherits the successions opened in its favor since its conception, and transmits them accordingly." La. Civ. Code art. 950 (1825); *see also* La. Civ. Code art. 956 (1870). The Vital Statistics Laws provide a definition of "live birth" as "birth in which the child shows evidence of life after complete birth. A birth is complete when the child is entirely outside the mother, even if the umbilical cord is uncut and the placenta still attached. The words 'evidence of life' include heart action, breathing, or movement of voluntary muscles." La. Stat. Ann. § 40:32.

12. La. Civ. Code Ann. art. 26.

Prior to January 1, 1988, conception "in the mother's womb" was necessary for natural personality.[13] Act 125 of 1987 eliminated that language, and now article 26 provides that "an unborn child shall be considered a natural person ... from the moment of conception."[14] Comment (a) to article 26 reflects that the provision is new but does not change the law. Comment (b), however, suggests a change in the law when it provides that "[a]n 'unborn child' may be a person even if it is in a test tube (rather than its mother's womb)."[15] Removing the language "in the mother's womb" and replacing it with the term "conception" certainly connotes a change in the law given the timing of the revision—when in vitro fertilization was gaining wider use.[16]

Whether natural personality begins in the test tube or in the mother's womb is further complicated by the provisions of the Human Embryo Statute. The Human Embryo Statute, contained in the Louisiana Revised Statutes and passed one year after the revision to article 26, provides that an in vitro fertilized ovum has juridical personality until it is implanted in the womb, "or at any other time when rights attach to an unborn child in accordance with the law."[17] When reading comment (b) to article 26 in conjunction with Section 123 of the Human Embryo Statute, the status of an in vitro fertilized human ovum as a natural or juridical person is unclear. Although an in vitro fertilized ovum has juridical capacity (the effect of which may give the in vitro ovum sufficient rights), the existence of natural personality before it is implanted in the womb is debatable.[18]

Other legislation, found in various sections of the Human Embryo Statute and in the Civil Code, provides some answers on the ability of unborn children to receive donations. Section 133 of the Human Embryo Statute provides: "Inheritance rights will not flow to the in vitro fertilized ovum as a juridical person, unless the in vitro fertilized ovum develops into an unborn child that is born in a live birth, or at any other time when rights attach to an unborn child in accordance with law."[19] The negative inference suggests that inheritance rights *will flow* to an in vitro fertilized ovum once

---

13. La. Civ. Code Ann. art. 29 (1870).

14. La. Civ. Code Ann. art. 26.

15. La. Civ. Code Ann. art. 26 cmt. (b) (rev. 1987). The meaning of the word "conception" likewise affects article 940, in chapter 5 entitled "Loss of Succession Rights," which provides that "an unborn child conceived at the death of the decedent and thereafter born alive shall be considered to exist at the death of the decedent." La. Civ. Code Ann. art. 940.

16. The first in vitro babies were born in Louisiana in 1985. Maki Somosot, *State's First Test-Tube Triplets Celebrate 30th Birthday, Houma Today* (July 29, 2015, 10:30 PM), https://www.houmatoday.com/story/news/2015/07/30/states-first-test-tube-triplets-celebrate-30th-birthday/27140903007/.

17. La. Stat. Ann. § 9:123.

18. Other sections of the Human Embryo Statute have references to the in vitro fertilized ovum as both a juridical person and a natural person. *Compare* La. Stat. Ann. § 9:125 ("An in vitro fertilized ovum as a juridical person is recognized as a separate entity apart from the medical facility or clinic where it is housed or stored."), *and* La. Stat. Ann. § 9:129 ("A viable in vitro fertilized ovum is a juridical person which shall not be intentionally destroyed...."), *with* La. Stat. Ann. § 9:126 ("An in vitro fertilized human ovum is a biological human being which is not property of the physician which acts as an agent of fertilization, or the facility....").

19. La. Stat. Ann. § 9:133.

it is determined that the child was later born alive. In contrast, Article 1474 of the Civil Code provides that to receive a donation *inter vivos*, the "unborn child must be in utero at the time the donation is made," and to receive a donation *mortis causa*, the "unborn child must be in utero at the time of the death of the testator."[20] The right to receive the donations, in both cases, occurs "only if the child is born alive."[21]

According to the revision comment to article 1474, if any conflict exists between article 1474 and section 133 of the Human Embryo Statute, article 1474 should prevail.[22] Therefore, an in vitro fertilized ovum, if not yet implanted in the mother's womb, has no capacity to receive a donation *inter vivos* or *mortis causa*. The in vitro fertilized ovum is classified as a juridical person but will have no inheritance rights unless and until the ovum is implanted in the mother's womb. So, if the donor dies and leaves a will naming his "nieces and nephews" as legatees and one of his nieces is fertilized in vitro, but not yet placed in the mother's womb, that child, if later born alive, has no capacity to receive from the donor. If the unborn child had been placed in the mother's womb at the time of the donor's death and was later born alive, she would have the capacity to receive because once implanted and later born alive, the in vitro fertilized ovum enjoys capacity to receive.[23]

In 2001, the Louisiana Legislature expanded the inheritance rights of a certain group of unborn children. With the enactment of Louisiana Revised Statutes Section 9:391, children who are conceived *after* the death of a parent and are later born alive have rights to inherit from the deceased parent even though the child had no personality—either natural or juridical—at the time of the parent's death.[24] The statute permits a parent to authorize in writing the use of his or her gametes by the surviving spouse for the purpose of conceiving a child after his or her death.[25] In such a case, the child will be considered the child of the deceased parent as long as the child is born alive to the surviving spouse within three years of the death of the decedent.[26] Even though the child was not conceived, either in utero or in vitro, at the time of the parent's death, specific legislation allows the child to have all rights as a natural person and child of the deceased parent.[27]

---

20. La. Civ. Code art. 1474.

21. La. Civ. Code Ann. art. 1474.

22. La. Civ. Code Ann. art. 1474 cmt.

23. *See* Tyler v. Lewis, 78 So. 477 (La. 1918) (allowing a grandchild who was in her mother's womb at the death of the grandfather to take pursuant to a testament that left "all [to] my grandchildren" because the child was born 172 days after her grandfather's death and natural personality existed when the child was in utero); *see also* Kathryn Venturatos Lorio, Successions & Donations § 9:2, *in* 10 Louisiana Civil Law Treatise 264–72 (2d ed. 2009).

24. La. Stat. Ann. § 9:391.1. See John Randall Trahan, *Successions & Donations*, 64 La. L. Rev. 315, 317–22 (2004) for a discussion of the original bill and its amendments.

25. La. Stat. Ann. § 9:391.1(A).

26. La. Stat. Ann. § 9:391.1.

27. The revised statute specifically exempts any law to the contrary, which would include Civil Code Article 1474. See John Randall Trahan, *Successions & Donations*, 64 La. L. Rev. 315 (2004) for a discussion of the statute.

Although Louisiana has been progressive in recognizing the rights of in vitro fertilized ova as juridical persons, with legislation now elevating the rights of posthumously conceived children, the law creates a potential problem for children who are conceived in vitro prior to a parent's death, but not implanted into the womb. For example, assume a couple, with the aid of a fertility clinic, fertilizes the wife's human ova and places the embryos in a state of cryopreservation. If the husband dies before the embryos are implanted into the wife, the child later born to the wife may not have capacity to receive property from the deceased father, because at the time of the father's death, the child was not yet in utero.[28] If the couple had merely stored the husband's gametes, and not yet fertilized the ovum, the statute on posthumously conceived children may apply, giving the child rights to inherit from the deceased father.[29]

§ 1:4 Natural Persons— Termination of Natural Personality

Termination of natural personality occurs at death, which can be established in one of two ways: (1) a doctor's certification of death; or (2) a judicial declaration of death.[30] A doctor may certify death based on the statutory provision found in Louisiana Revised Statutes Section 9:111, in which a person is considered dead if, in the opinion of a licensed physician, "the person has experienced an irreversible cessation of spontaneous respiratory and circulatory functions."[31] If, however, artificial means of support prevent a determination that respiratory and circulatory functions have ceased, then death occurs at "irreversible total cessation of brain function."[32] Death occurs "when the relevant functions [have] ceased."[33]

In circumstances when a person has disappeared and no body has been found, a doctor's certification of death is unavailable. The law therefore permits a court to issue a judicial declaration of death in three instances. First, under Louisiana Civil Code Article 30, when a person has disappeared under circumstances when "death seems certain," a judge can issue a declaration of death even though no body has been found.[34]

---

28. *See* La. Civ. Code Ann. art. 1474 ("To be capable of receiving by donation *mortis causa*, an unborn child must be in utero at the time of the death of the testator.").

29. *See* La. Stat. Ann. § 9:391.1.

30. *See* La. Stat. Ann. § 9:111(A) (doctor's certification of death); La. Civ. Code Ann. arts. 30, 54 & La. Stat. Ann. § 9:1441–43 (judicial declarations of death).

31. La. Stat. Ann. § 9:111(A). The physician must be licensed in the state of Louisiana and must base his or her opinion on "ordinary standards of approved medical practice."

32. La. Stat. Ann. § 9:111(A). A pronouncement of death by the coroner may be based on observations and information from other medical personnel on the scene who have firsthand knowledge of the condition of the deceased. La. Stat. Ann. § 9:111(B).

33. La. Stat. Ann. § 9:111(A).

34. La. Civ. Code Ann. art. 30. Death must be proved by a preponderance of the evidence. La. Civ. Code Ann. art. 30 cmt. (b) (rev. 1990).

In the only reported case to rely on article 30,[35] the court judicially declared the death of a resident of a mental health facility for purposes of a wrongful death claim.[36] The 33-year-old resident of the facility went missing due to lack of adequate supervision. He was completely dependent on the facility and on the administration of anti-seizure medication, he was legally blind, and he had the intelligence of a three-year-old. The court applied the statutory presumption of death, noting the inherent inconsistency in having to prove that "death seems certain" by a preponderance of the evidence, but found that circumstantial evidence negated any hypothesis other than death.[37] The article 30 "death seems certain" standard would also be appropriate in a mass casualty situation, such as a plane crash or bombing, when proof is available that the individual was at the location where the casualty took place.[38]

Second, under the law of absent persons, a court can judicially declare the death of an absent person after the passage of five years.[39] "Absent person" is a legal term of art that describes a person "who has no representative in this state and whose whereabouts are not known and cannot be ascertained by diligent effort."[40] After the passage of five years, an interested party can petition the court to have the absent person declared dead, and the court will judicially declare the date of death.[41]

The last instance in which a court can judicially declare death is based on a presumption of death for military personnel. If a person is on active duty in the United States armed forces and has been reported missing under circumstances where the

35. One other case mentioned article 30 in the context of stowaways on a ship who were allegedly thrown overboard, but the court did not apply the statutory presumption of death. *See* Thornhill v. Otto Candies Inc., No. CIV. A. 94-1479, 1994 WL 532591, *1 n.3 (E.D. La. Sept. 28, 1994). Prior to the enactment of article 30, courts nonetheless considered whether it should apply a presumption of death based solely on the facts as presented. *See, e.g.*, Bennett v. Equitable Life Assurance Society of United States, 156 So. 290, (La. 1934) (refusing to apply a presumption of death for a wife to collect life insurance proceeds when a husband disappeared from his home at the age of 47 while suffering from pulmonary tuberculosis to seek work elsewhere, having been absent and unheard from for seven years).

36. *See* Jones v. State ex rel. Department of Health & Hospitals, 95-1130 (La. App. 3 Cir. 3/27/96), 671 So. 2d 1074.

37. Jones, 671 So. 2d at 1078.

38. *See, e.g.*, Chiaramonte v. Chiaramonte, 435 N.Y.S.2d 523, 525 (1981) ("[T]he general rule that death is presumed to occur at the end of an unexplained absence of five years does not apply where the absentee met his death in a perilous occurrence. In such a case, death is presumed to have occurred on the date of the accident.").

39. La. Civ. Code Ann. art. 54. "If the absence began between August 26, 2005, and September 30, 2005, and was related to Hurricane Katrina or Rita, the absent person" can be declared dead "after the passage of two years" as long as the absent person is not currently charged with a felony offense. *Id.*

40. La. Civ. Code Ann. art. 47; *see* In re Boyd, 98-0052 (La. App. 1 Cir. 12/28/98), 723 So. 2d 1107 (discussing "reasonable diligence" in locating the absentee).

41. La. Civ. Code Ann. art. 54. The law of absent persons contains a comprehensive scheme to deal with the succession and property rights of the absent person. *See* La. Civ. Code Ann. bk. I, tit. III, for the rules on absent persons.

armed service to which the soldier was attached accepts the presumption of death, Louisiana law likewise presumes death and a judicial declaration of death is available.[42]

Termination of natural personality results in the opening of the deceased's succession and the transmission of his estate to his heirs.[43] The decedent's marriage is dissolved,[44] and any community property regime in existence is terminated.[45] The decedent loses various other rights, including the right to custody, the right to be a tutor, and the right to make or receive donations *inter vivos* or *mortis causa*. Unless the right is strictly personal, the decedent's heirs or representatives will have the ability to bring and defend actions, enforce or perform obligations, and transfer or receive property on behalf of the decedent's estate.

For example, in Louisiana, after termination of natural personality, an individual is no longer a "patient" for purposes of a medical malpractice action. In *Gayden v. Tenet Healthsystem Memorial Medical Center, Inc.*, the decedent's surviving family members could not bring a malpractice suit against a hospital that allegedly failed to properly refrigerate and preserve the patient's body after death.[46] The court found that natural personality ceased at death.[47]

Additionally, after the termination of natural personality, the decedent can no longer be a proper party in litigation. In *Rainey v. Entergy Gulf States, Inc.*, the court concluded that any judgment rendered for or against a dead person was a nullity, so it was not permitted to render a decision until the proper plaintiffs were substituted for the decedent.[48] In the personal injury action on behalf of the decedent against her former employer, the court found that the decedent's children were the proper plaintiffs. When the decedent died, her right and her action to enforce an obligation against her former employer transmitted directly to her children.[49]

42. La. Stat. Ann. § 9:1441.

43. La. Civ. Code Ann. arts. 871, 934.

44. La. Civ. Code Ann. art. 101.

45. La. Civ. Code Ann. art. 2356.

46. Gayden v. Tenet Healthsystem Memorial Medical Center, Inc., 2004-0807 (La. App. 4 Cir. 12/15/04), 891 So. 2d 734.

47. Gayden, 891 So. 2d at 736; *see also* La. Civ. Code Ann. art. 25.

48. Rainey v. Entergy Gulf States, Inc., 2001-2414 (La. App. 1 Cir. 6/25/04), 885 So. 2d 1193.

49. Rainey, 885 So. 2d at 1203–04.

§ 1:5 Natural Persons— Effects of Natural Personality on Unborn Children

For children born alive, natural personality commences at the moment of conception, entitling the child to legal rights and duties, including the right of inheritance,[50] and the right to bring claims under the worker's compensation laws[51] and social security laws.[52] In addition, the child born alive may bring claims in tort for prenatal injuries that caused damage to the child[53] or for the personal injuries of the parent.[54] Because natural personality commences only when a child is born alive, whether an action exists to protect a stillborn child has been the subject of controversy. For personal actions in tort and property actions for support, the Louisiana Supreme Court has provided much-needed guidance.

Parents of an unborn child who is stillborn can sue for the child's wrongful death, but not for the child's survival action or for damages based on bystander mental anguish. In 1981, in *Danos v. St. Pierre*, the Louisiana Supreme Court concluded that Article 2315 of the Civil Code permits recovery for the wrongful death of a child even if the child never enjoys natural personality.[55] Article 26 of the Civil Code was later enacted to codify this jurisprudential rule.[56] Then, in *Wartelle v. Women's & Children's Hospital, Inc.*, parents of a stillborn child sued not only for wrongful death, but for survival and bystander mental anguish due to the hospital's failure to monitor the child's fetal heart tones.[57] The trial court awarded the parents damages based on the child's wrongful death but dismissed the survival action and bystander claims because the child was not born alive.[58] The Louisiana Supreme Court affirmed.[59]

The court examined Article 26 of the Civil Code, which specifically provides that an unborn child is a natural person "for whatever relates to its interests from the moment of conception" if the child is born alive.[60] The only exception to the live birth require-

---

50. La. Civ. Code Ann. arts. 940, 1474; *see also* Tyler v. Lewis, 78 So. 477 (La. 1918) (The court allowed a grandchild who was in her mother's womb at the death of the grandfather to take pursuant to a testament that left "all [to] my grandchildren" because the child was born 172 days after her grandfather's death and natural personality existed when the child was in utero.).

51. *See* Eason v. Alexander Shipyards, 47 So. 2d 114, 118 (La. Ct. App. 1950).

52. *See* La. Stat. Ann. § 9:391.1 cmt.; *see also* Astrue v. Capato ex rel. B.N.C., 566 U.S. 541 (2012).

53. *See* Cooper v. Blanck, 39 So. 2d 352 (La. Ct. App. 1923); Vicknair v. Hibernia Building Corporation, 468 So. 2d 695 (La. Ct. App 4 Cir. 1985); Bunch v. Mercy Hospital, 404 So. 2d 520 (La. Ct. App. 4 Cir. 1981); *see also* Vincent R. Johnson, *Tort Liability for Prenatal Injury*, 24 Tul. L. Rev. 435 (1950).

54. *See* Badie v. Columbia Brewing Co., 77 So. 768 (La. 1918).

55. Danos v. St. Pierre, 402 So. 2d 633, 638 (La. 1981).

56. La. Civ. Code Ann. art. 26 (added by Act 125 of the 1987 Regular Legislative Session).

57. Wartelle v. Women's & Children's Hospital, Inc., 97-0744 (La. 12/02/97), 704 So. 2d 778.

58. Wartelle, 704 So. 2d 778.

59. Wartelle, 704 So. 2d 778.

60. La. Civ. Code Ann. art. 26.

ment is an action resulting from the child's wrongful death.[61] The court was faced with whether this exception could extend to survival and bystander causes of action. In both the survival and bystander tort statutes, the victim is described as a "person," and because the child was not born alive, it did not acquire natural personality.[62] Because the unborn child had no rights, the court concluded that it could not transmit any rights.[63] The majority opinion was met with a strong dissent, authored by Justice Lemmon, who argued that the live birth exception for wrongful death should extend to survival and bystander claims.[64] Justice Lemmon explained that a viable full-term fetus could experience pain, as could the laboring mother who could sense the pain of her soon-to-be born child, and recovery against the tortfeasor should not be affected simply because the child failed to live for an instant.[65]

Outside of tort claims, the Louisiana Supreme Court has also concluded that the mother of an unborn child can sue to establish filiation and to obtain support from an alleged father *before* the child is born. In *Malek v. Yekani-Fard*, a pregnant woman filed suit to establish the paternity of the alleged father and to seek natal and prenatal expenses and support.[66] The trial court dismissed the suit as premature because the child had yet to be born.[67] The Louisiana Supreme Court reversed, concluding that parental filiation, support, and heirship are property rights of the unborn child.[68] At the time of conception, the child is capable of acquiring rights, and according to Planiol, "this personality is admitted only in the interest of the child."[69] Because Louisiana recognizes an unborn child's rights in property matters, the court found no reason to await birth to prove paternity and seek support.[70]

Based on *Wartelle* and *Malek*, legal recognition can be given to an unborn child without live birth when necessary to protect its interests.[71] For example, parents are able to acknowledge paternity of the child prior to birth.[72] In the context of tort, whether this recognition will ever extend to survival and bystander claims based on the death of an unborn fetus remains to be seen, although Justice Lemmon's dissent in *Wartelle*

---

61. La. Civ. Code Ann. art. 26 cmt. (d) (rev. 1987).

62. *See* Wartelle, 704 So. 2d at 780, 784; La. Civ. Code Ann. art. 2315.1 (survival action) ("If a person who has been injured by an offense or quasi offense dies...."); *see also* La. Civ. Code Ann. art. 2315.6 (bystander mental anguish) ("To recover for mental anguish or emotional distress under this Article, the injured person must suffer such harm....").

63. Wartelle, 704 So. 2d at 781.

64. Wartelle, 704 So. 2d at 786 (Lemmon, J., dissenting).

65. Wartelle, 704 So. 2d at 786.

66. Malek v. Yekani-Ford, 422 So. 2d 1151 (La. 1982).

67. Malek, 422 So. 2d at 1152.

68. Malek, 422 So. 2d at 1154.

69. Malek, 422 So. 2d at 1153 (quoting Planiol, Civil Law Treatise, Vol. I, Pt. 1, § 367, p. 245).

70. Malek, 422 So. 2d at 1154–55 (Marcus, J., dissenting) (believing that property rights only accrue to the child once the child is born alive).

71. *See* Roy Edward Blossman, *An Unborn Child's Right to Prove Filiation:* Malek v. Yekani-Ford, 44 La. L. Rev. 1777 (1984) (discussing the potential problems with the *Malek* decision and other states' treatment of the issue).

72. *See* Malek, 422 So. 2d at 1154.

provides a well-reasoned path to do so. Notably, legal recognition will not be given to an unborn child if such recognition will result in a detriment to the child. For example, the husband of the mother cannot disavow paternity of a child prior to birth,[73] and prescription does not accrue against an unborn child for medical malpractice actions until the child is born alive.[74]

§ 1:6 Juridical Persons

Juridical persons are entities "to which the law attributes personality."[75] Entities such as corporations, partnerships, and associations are all juridical persons.[76] Although less intuitive, ships, goods subject to civil forfeiture, and in vitro fertilized ovum are also juridical persons.[77] The community of acquets and gains, however, is not a legal entity that has personality.[78]

"The personality of a juridical person is distinct from [the personality] of its members."[79] Juridical persons can be private persons or public persons, depending on the rule of law that governs the person. "The state and its political subdivisions have dual personality" and act as both private and public persons.[80] When the state acts in its sovereign capacity for protection of the public, it acts as a public person, but when it performs under a contract, it acts as a private person.

Juridical persons, as long as they are in existence, have the capacity to make and receive donations. Article 1470 of the Civil Code provides that "[a]ll persons have the capacity to make and receive donations ... except as expressly provided by law."[81] No express provision of law prevents a juridical person from making or receiving donations. In 1964, however, the Fourth Circuit held that "persons" in the context of article 1470 referred only to natural persons.[82] In *Succession of Shepard*, an agency of the United States government was prohibited from accepting a testamentary bequest due to lack of capacity to inherit a donation *mortis causa*.[83] This holding has been criticized by courts and commentators alike,[84] and later courts have limited the holding, finding

73. *See* La. Civ. Code Ann. art. 189.

74. Bailey v. Khoury, 2004-0620, p. 22 (La. 1/20/05), 891 So. 2d 1268, 1282–83.

75. La. Civ. Code Ann. art. 24.

76. *See* La. Civ. Code Ann. art. 24 cmt. (b) (rev. 1987).

77. *See* La. Stat. Ann. § 40:2601 (civil forfeiture); § 9:123 (in vitro fertilized ovum); Cactus Pipe & Supply Co., Inc. v. M/V Montmartre, 756 F.2d 1103, 112 (5th Cir. 1985) (ship).

78. Andrea Carroll & Richard D. Moreno, Matrimonial Regimes § 6.4, *in* 16 Louisiana Civil Law Treatise 524 n.47 (4th ed. 2017).

79. La. Civ. Code Ann. art. 24.

80. La. Civ. Code Ann. art. 24 cmt. (c) (1987 rev.).

81. La. Civ. Code Ann. art. 1470.

82. Succession of Shepard, 156 So. 2d 287, 291 (La. Ct. App. 4 Cir. 1963).

83. Succession of Shepard, 156 So. 2d at 291.

84. *See, e.g.*, Kathryn Venturatos Lorio, Successions & Donations § 9:2, *in* 10 Louisiana Civil Law Treatise 264–72 (2d ed. 2009); Peter S. Title, Louisiana Real Estate Transactions § 11:39, *in* 1 La. Prac. Series (2d ed. 2017); Charles G. Gladney, *Donations—Capacity of United States Government to Accept*

that unincorporated associations,[85] corporations,[86] and agencies of municipal corporations[87] have the ability to receive donations. If a group exists without any organization or legal power, it would not qualify as a juridical person and would not be capable of making or receiving a donation.[88]

§ 1:7 Human Embryo Statute

The Human Embryo Statute, found in Louisiana Revised Statutes Sections 9:121–:133, was added by Act 964 of 1986. The Human Embryo Statute provides legal status, rights, and governing rules for the in vitro fertilized human ovum.[89] The policy of the law is embodied in § 122, which prohibits the sale of human ovum or the farming of human ovum for research purposes, and defines its use as solely for the support and development of an in utero embryo.[90] Any viable in vitro fertilized human ovum is a juridical person and cannot be destroyed, even by the sperm and egg donors.[91] If, however, an in vitro fertilized ovum fails to develop over a 36-hour period, it is not considered a juridical person and is non-viable.[92]

Should the in vitro fertilization patients renounce, by notarial act, their rights to the fertilized ovum, the ovum can be adopted in accordance with the facility's procedures.[93] If the ovum has been cryopreserved but the patients choose not to allow adoption,

---

Donations Mortis Causa under Louisiana Law, 24 La. L. Rev. 918, 920–21 (1964); Lord v. Dist. VIII Baptist Convention, 391 So. 2d 942, 943 (La. Ct. App. 2 Cir. 1980).

85. *See* Lord, 391 So. 2d at 943–44 (unincorporated association is a person and may acquire property through donation *inter vivos*); *see also* La. Stat. Ann. § 9:1051 (corporations unauthorized by law may acquire and possess estates).

86. La. Stat. Ann. § 12:207(B)(4).

87. Succession of Quillou, 221 So. 2d 651, 652 (La. Ct. App. 4 Cir. 1969) (affirming that an agency of the City of New Orleans is treated as a corporation and has the capacity to receive donations).

88. *See, e.g.*, Succession of Fisher, 103 So. 2d 276, 283–84 (La. 1958); Carr v. Hart, 57 So. 2d 739, 740–41 (La. 1952); Succession of Hardesty, 22 La. Ann. 332, 333 (1870). See Kathryn Venturatos Lorio, Successions & Donations § 9:2, *in* 10 Louisiana Civil Law Treatise 264–72 (2d ed. 2009), for a detailed discussion of the capacity of juridical persons to make and receive donations.

89. For a critique of the statute, see Sarah A. Weber, *Dismantling the Dictated Moral Code: Modifying Louisiana's In Vitro Fertilization Statutes to Protect Patients' Procreative Liberty*, 51 Loy. L. Rev. 549 (2005) (suggesting changes to the statute); Dian K. Yang, *What's Mine Is Mine, but What's Yours Should Also Be Mine: An Analysis of State Statutes That Mandate the Implantation of Frozen Preembryos*, 10 J.L. & Pol'y 587, 593–96 (2002) (questioning the constitutionality of Louisiana's statutes); Kevin U. Stephens, Sr., M.D., *Reproductive Capacity: What Does the Embryo Get?*, 24 S.U. L. Rev. 263, 268–71 (1997) (raising unanswered questions in Louisiana's Human Embryo Statute); Robert J. Muller, Davis v. Davis: *The Applicability of Privacy and Property Rights to the Disposition of Frozen Preembryos in Intrafamilial Disputes*, 24 U. Tol. L. Rev. 763, 769–70 (1993) (criticizing Louisiana's statute for failing to address IVF simply as a medical procedure).

90. La. Stat. Ann. § 9:122.

91. La. Stat. Ann. § 9:129.

92. La. Stat. Ann. § 9:129. An exception exists if the ovum is cryopreserved.

93. La. Stat. Ann. § 9:130. Patients may also renounce their rights in favor of another married couple. No compensation is permitted, and adoption shall occur when the married couple executes a notarial act of adoption and birth occurs.

the fertilized ovum cannot be discarded; rather, it must remain frozen indefinitely.[94] Although seemingly in conflict with the Civil Code, the statute provides that once the child is born alive, it receives inheritance rights as a juridical person—i.e., *before* it is implanted in the womb.[95] Further, if the ovum is adopted by another couple, the couple is recognized as the legal parents of the ovum, and no inheritance rights are retained from the in vitro fertilization patients.[96] The physician, hospital, or clinic that acts in good faith in collecting, caring for, or transferring the human ovum has immunity against actions relating to succession rights or inheritance.[97]

The in vitro fertilized human ovum is "a separate entity apart from the medical facility ... where it is housed,"[98] and it is not the property of the physician, the facility, or the sperm and egg donors.[99] The sperm and egg donors, if expressing their identity, will have rights as parents, but the personality of the ovum remains.[100] Finally, the best interest of the in vitro fertilized ovum will apply to any disputes over the fertilized ovum.[101]

Only one Louisiana court has cited the Human Embryo Statute in a reported decision. Although the case was ultimately dismissed on jurisdictional grounds, the court provided some discussion of the Human Embryo Statute, pointing out internal conflicts within the statute. The dispute between Nick Loeb and Sophia Vergara began when Mr. Loeb sought to bring two embryos to term with the use of a surrogate.[102] Mr. Loeb and Ms. Vergara had cryopreserved two embryos in California, their relationship had ended, and the agreements with the fertility center did not provide what happened to the embryos in the event of a breakup.[103] When Ms. Vergara refused to allow Mr. Loeb access the embryos, he created a Louisiana trust and orchestrated a lawsuit by the two human embryos against Ms. Vergara, using the Human Embryo Statute to provide them standing to sue.[104] As beneficiaries, the embryos sought an order of the court prohibiting their destruction and permitting their transfer, continued development, and birth with another woman.[105] The case was removed to federal court and dismissed on jurisdictional grounds because the embryos were conceived and stored in California,

94. *See* La. Stat. Ann. § 9:129.

95. La. Stat. Ann. § 9:133; *see* Section 1:3 of this chapter.

96. La. Stat. Ann. § 9:133; *see also* La. Civ. Code Ann. art. 214.

97. La. Stat. Ann. § 9:132.

98. La. Stat. Ann. § 9:125. The in vitro fertilized ovum, as its own entity, can sue or be sued.

99. La. Stat. Ann. § 9:126. If the donors fail to express their identity, the physician is deemed the temporary guardian until adoptive implantation can occur. A court can appoint a curator to protect the rights of the fertilized ovum. *Id.*

100. *See* La. Stat. Ann. § 9:126.

101. La. Stat. Ann. § 9:131.

102. Loeb v. Vergara, 2020-0261, p. 6 (La. App. 4 Cir. 1/27/21), 313 So. 3d 346.

103. Vergara, 313 So. 3d at 354.

104. *See* Human Embryo #4 HB-A v. Vergara, No. CV 17-1498, 2017 WL 3686569 (E.D. La. Aug. 25, 2017).

105. The case was originally filed in the 24th Judicial District Court, Parish of Jefferson. Human Embryo #4 HB-A v. Vergara, No. 767-189, 2016 WL 7239128 (La. Dist. Ct. Dec. 7, 2016). It was removed by the defendant to the United States District Court for the Eastern District of Louisiana. Human Embryo #4 HB-A v. Vergara, 2017 WL 3686569 (E.D. La. Aug. 25, 2017).

and neither Mr. Loeb nor Ms. Vergara had significant ties to Louisiana. Mr. Loeb then established domicile in Louisiana and filed a separate suit for custody of the human embryos on behalf of himself and the human embryos.[106]

The trial court concluded that it did not have subject matter jurisdiction over the custody matter under the Uniform Child Custody Jurisdiction and Enforcement Act (UCCJEA).[107] On appeal, among other issues, the court considered the interplay between the UCCJEA and the Human Embryo Statute, a *res nova* issue, to determine whether it had subject matter jurisdiction over the embryos' custody. Finding definitions of "child" and "person" in the UCCJEA, it turned to the Human Embryo Statute to address the legal status of an embryo to determine whether the UCCJEA would apply. The court compared section 123 of the statute, which provides juridical personality to an in vitro fertilized human ovum, to Civil Code Article 24, which describes juridical persons as entities, rather than human beings. It further found an inconsistency within the statute, which describes an in vitro fertilized human ovum "as a biological human being."[108]

Turning first to the legislation and finding no clear answers, the court examined the legislative intent of the UCCJEA and the Human Embryo Statute. Found still "in a position of ambiguity," the court explained that the Human Embryo Statute may describe embryos as human, but it stopped short of referring to them as children. Referencing statements made at a legislative committee meeting, the Human Embryo Statute creates a third group of persons—as compared to natural persons and juridical persons that are entities—the IVF ovum that exists as a juridical person.[109] While the third category of juridical person is not clearly defined, according to the court, it did not mean that a human embryo is a child as contemplated within the UCCJEA. Finally, the court relied on jurisprudence from other states interpreting the UCCJEA, all of which concluded that the UCCJEA does not apply to unborn children. Affirming the trial court, the Fourth Circuit concluded that the UCCJEA does not apply to embryos or unborn children, thereby dismissing Mr. Loeb's petition for custody.[110]

106. After the federal case was dismissed, Mr. Loeb, on behalf of himself and the human embryos, filed a custody suit in the 25th Judicial District Court, Parish of Plaquemines, seeking full custody of the embryos. Ms. Vergara removed the case to the United States District Court for the Eastern District of Louisiana, and the court granted Mr. Loeb's motion to remand. Loeb v. Vergara, 326 F. Supp. 3d 295 (E.D. La. 2018).

107. Loeb, 313 So. 3d at 385.

108. Loeb, 313 So. 3d at 387 (citing La. Stat. Ann. § 9:126).

109. Loeb, 313 So. 3d at 389.

110. Loeb, 313 So. 3d at 392; see also A. Brooke Reedy, *Uneggspected: Louisiana's Scrambled Approach to Ownership of Frozen Embryos*, 83 La. L. Rev. 373 (2022).

Chapter 2

Absent Persons*

§ 2:1 Introduction

Title III of Book I of the Louisiana Civil Code, "Of Absent Persons," provides a regime to deal with the rights of a person who has disappeared and whose disappearance affects his rights or the rights of others. The law provides for the appointment of a curator to represent the absent person when he owns property in Louisiana and is unknown to be dead or alive.[1] The curator will maintain and may dispose of the absent person's property while awaiting his return.[2] After the passage of five years, the curator can seek a judicial declaration of the absent person's death, from which succession rights will flow to his heirs.[3] If the absent person reappears, the law gives the absent person the right to reacquire his property and inheritance from his heirs and other gratuitous transferees.[4]

---

* This chapter was derived from the following article: Monica Hof Wallace, *A Primer on Absent Persons in Louisiana*, 64 Loy. L. Rev. 423 (2018). The authors wish to thank the Loyola Law Review for its assistance on the initial work for this chapter.

1. La. Civ. Code Ann. art. 47.
2. La. Stat. Ann. § 13:3437(A).
3. La. Civ. Code Ann. arts. 54–55.
4. La. Civ. Code Ann. art. 57.

In Louisiana, the law of absent persons underwent a comprehensive revision in 1990.[5] During this revision, Louisiana imported the common law presumption of death, which allows transfer of ownership of property to the absent person's heirs, rather than a gradual transfer of rights from the absent person to his heirs.[6] The early law governing absent persons had a two-tiered system for the transfer of property.[7] When a person was absent for a period of five years, his heirs were placed into provisional possession of the absent person's estate.[8] If the absence lasted 30 years from provisional possession or 100 years from the absent person's birth, the heirs could assume absolute possession.[9]

The two-tiered system was abandoned in 1948 in favor of absolute possession after the passage of 30 years.[10] In 1978, the time period for absolute possession was shortened to 10 years,[11] and shortened again to seven years in 1986.[12] In Act 989 of 1990, the legislature revised, amended, and reenacted the title on absent persons, recognizing a presumption of death after the passage of five years. Once presumed dead, a court could issue a judgment declaring death, thereby commencing the succession and permitting the transfer of ownership to the absent person's heirs.

§ 2:2 Absent Person, Generally

An absent person in Louisiana is "one who has no representative in this state and whose whereabouts are not known and cannot be ascertained by diligent effort."[13] "Representative" may include those who have been given authority to represent another under the Civil Code articles on representation and mandate.[14] Absent persons have been referred to as the "living dead" because there is no clear evidence as to whether the person is dead or alive; neither a representative nor a body can be found.[15] Either an

---

5. *See* Act No. 989, 1990 La. Acts 2417–54.

6. Jeanne L. Carriere, *The Rights of the Living Dead: Absent Persons in the Civil Law*, 50 La. L. Rev. 901, 906–07 (1990). Almost all common-law states recognize, either in a statute or the common law, the presumption of death once a person is absent for a period of years. *Id.* at 906. Professor Carriere explains the problems with Louisiana's prior law of "non-functional presumption of death" because the effects of death did not follow from it. *Id.* at 926–32.

7. This system was inspired by French law. *See* 1 M. Planiol, Traité Élémentaire de Droit Civil Nos. 616–36 (La. St. L. Inst. trans., 1959).

8. La. Civ. Code Ann. art. 57 (1948). Provisional possession was permitted before the passage of five years when there was a strong presumption that the absent person died. La. Civ. Code Ann. art. 60 (1948).

9. La. Civ. Code Ann. art. 70 (1978).

10. Act No. 343, 1948 La. Acts 833.

11. Act No. 457, 1978 La. Acts 1132.

12. Act No. 270, 1986 La. Acts 565–66.

13. La. Civ. Code Ann. art. 47.

14. *See* La. Civ. Code arts. 2985-3000; *see also* Certain Underwriters at Lloyd's, London v. Alliance Drilling Consultants, L.L.C., 23-265, p. 6 (La. App. 3 Cir. 12/20/23), 377 So. 3d 459, 468 (noting that the term "legal representative" in a contract includes those given authority under representation and mandate).

15. Jeanne L. Carriere, *The Rights of the Living Dead: Absent Persons in the Civil Law*, 50 La. L. Rev. 901, 901 (1990).

effort to find the absent person must be made or evidence must be submitted to show it would be futile to try.[16]

In efforts to locate the absent person, courts have required "reasonable diligence" in the search.[17] In *In re Boyd*, reasonable diligence included searching the telephone book and placing missing person ads in newspapers for three days in the last two cities where the absent person was known to have lived.[18] Although the court recognized that a search in additional cities or the use of a private investigator might be preferable, it was not necessary for "reasonable diligence."[19] As search engines proliferate in a Post-Information Age society, a more rigorous standard for reasonable diligence will likely result. People finders, broad-based searches, and online help services are readily available and cost-efficient to ensure that the absent person's due process rights are protected. Ultimately, however, if there is strong evidence that the person is dead, a proceeding for a judicial declaration of death under article 30 should follow.[20]

An "absent person" is different from an "absentee" as defined in the Code of Civil Procedure.[21] An "absentee" is a person who is either a nonresident, a domiciliary who has departed the state without leaving an agent, a person whose whereabouts are unknown, or a person who may be dead.[22] The Code of Civil Procedure contains a host of articles on attorneys appointed to represent absentee defendants or absentee heirs.[23] These attorneys represent absentee defendants or heirs in particular civil proceedings and do not have the same powers and authority as the curator over an absent person's property. Although attorneys can be appointed over absentees who are absent persons, not all absentees qualify as an "absent person" under Title III of the Civil Code. The curator of an absent person has rights of administration and disposition and is generally related to the absent person, while an attorney appointed to represent an absentee notifies and represents the absentee in the civil suit without a broad grant of power.

16. La. Civ. Code Ann. art. 47 cmt. (f).

17. The standard of "reasonable diligence" comes from the Code of Civil Procedure, which provides that "the attorney shall use reasonable diligence to communicate with the defendant and inform him of the pendency and nature of the action or proceeding. . . ." La. Code Civ. Proc. Ann. art. 5094.

18. In re Boyd, 98-0052, pp. 6–7 (La. App. 1 Cir. 12/28/98), 723 So. 2d 1107, 1109.

19. In re Boyd, 723 So. 2d at 1109–10.

20. La. Civ. Code Ann. art. 47 cmt. (f). Under article 30, "[w]hen a person has disappeared under circumstances such that his death seems certain, his death is considered to have been established even though his body has not been found." La. Civ. Code Ann. art. 30.

21. *See* La. Code Civ. Proc. Ann. art. 5251(1); *see also* Jessica G. Braun, Handbook on Louisiana Family Law 1407–08 (2022–23).

22. La. Code Civ. Proc. Ann. art. 5251(1).

23. La. Code Civ. Proc. Ann. art. 5091 *et seq*; *see also* La. Child. Code Ann. art. 1023.

§ 2:3 Curator Appointed Over Property

Any interested party can petition the court to have a curator appointed over the property of an absent person on a showing that the absent person owns property in this state and that there is a necessity for appointment.[24] "Property" includes corporeals and incorporeals, movables and immovables, and "necessity" can be shown by the need to protect the absent person, the petitioner, or a third party.[25] On appointment, the curator has the power of administration and the power of disposition over the absent person's property.[26]

Permitting a curator to administer and dispose of an absent person's property raises questions of due process. The United States Supreme Court, in early decisions, explained that to administer an absent person's property within the confines of the Constitution, states needed to expressly grant jurisdiction to their courts, provide the absent person with notice and an opportunity to prove his whereabouts, allow the passage of a reasonable time before a presumption of death applied, and provide a safeguard for the absent person should he reappear.[27] Louisiana law meets those requirements by providing courts with jurisdiction, requiring "reasonable diligence" to find the absent person before appointing a curator to manage his property, mandating a five-year absent period before a judicial declaration of death can be issued, and giving rights to the absent person upon reappearance.[28]

Further, Louisiana courts have recognized the importance of due process before disposing of an absent person's property. In two consolidated cases, the Fourth Circuit concluded that to deprive an absent person of property, the Constitution mandates the appointment of an attorney to represent him.[29] In the consolidated cases of *Succession of Haydel* and *Succession of Hart*, the court annulled a trial court judgment that declared William Hart dead and placed his heirs in possession of his estate because no attorney or curator had been appointed to represent Mr. Hart.[30] Mr. Hart's estate con-

---

24. La. Civ. Code Ann. art. 47; *see also* Succession of Butler, 117 So. 127 (La. 1928) (finding that it was improper to appoint a curator over a person who was absent because the person owned no property at the time of his absence).

25. La. Civ. Code Ann. art. 47 cmts. (b), (d). Necessity can be shown by the pending administration of a succession. *See* Middle Tennessee Council, Inc., Boy Scouts of America v. Ford, 274 So. 2d 173, 176 (La. 1973).

26. La. Civ. Code Ann. art. 48.

27. Scott v. McNeal, 154 U.S. 34, 42 (1894); Cunnius v. Reading School District, 198 U.S. 458, 473 (1905). *See* Jeanne L. Carriere, *The Rights of the Living Dead: Absent Persons in the Civil Law*, 50 La. L. Rev. 901, 910–14 (1990), for a discussion of these cases.

28. *See generally* La. Civ. Code Ann. art. 47 *et seq.*

29. Succession of Haydel, 96-0528 (La. App. 4 Cir. 12/27/96), 685 So. 2d 701. Although courts have discretion to appoint a curator to *manage* the absent person's property, courts have no discretion *to dispose* of property without the appointment of a curator to give notice to the absent person. *Id.* The United States Supreme Court has required "notice reasonably calculated, under all circumstances, to apprise interested parties of the pendency of the action and afford them an opportunity to present their objections" before depriving a person of his interest in property. Mennonite Board of Missions v. Adams, 462 U.S. 791, 795 (1983).

30. *See* Succession of Haydel, 685 So. 2d 701.

sisted solely of an interest in his grandfather's estate. Mr. Hart's heirs filed a petition to have him declared dead due to his absence for five years. On the same day the petition was filed, the trial court issued an ex parte judgment declaring him dead and placing his heirs in possession of his estate.[31] The appellate court reversed, stating:

> [C]onstitutional due process mandates than an absentee be represented by an appointed attorney or curator during proceedings to have the absentee declared dead and his succession opened pursuant to La. C. C. arts. 54 *et seq.* When a party files a petition to declare an absent person dead, the party shall request the trial court to appoint an attorney to represent the absentee under La. C.C.P. art. 5091. The attorney shall use reasonable diligence to represent the absent person and defend the absent person's interests.[32]

If a curator had been appointed to represent the absent person during the pendency of the proceedings, an appointed attorney would have been unnecessary at the time the heirs were placed in possession of his estate. The absent person's due process rights of notice and an opportunity to be heard would have been protected by the curator, rather than an appointed attorney.

Other unique issues arise when the absent person is a spouse in community. During the community, the curatorship is limited to the absent person's separate property,[33] and in most cases, the spouse will be named curator.[34] The spouse of the absent person "is entitled to a judgment decreeing [a] separation of property,"[35] or the spouse can seek authority from a court to act during the absence.[36] Although generally either spouse can manage community property alone, when concurrence of the absent spouse is needed for the other spouse to act,[37] the court in a summary proceeding may authorize the other spouse to act without concurrence on a showing that the action is in "the best interest of the family."[38] The court may also order the other spouse to manage, alienate, encumber, or lease community property over which the absent spouse had exclusive authority, if it is in the best interest of the family.[39] If the other spouse does not seek a separation of property during the spouse's absence, the community property regime will terminate at the judgment declaring death.[40]

---

31. Succession of Haydel, 685 So. 2d at 702.

32. Succession of Haydel, 685 So. 2d at 705.

33. La. Civ. Code Ann. art. 48.

34. The spouse not judicially separated is given preference as curator. La. Stat. Ann. § 13:3433.

35. La. Civ. Code Ann. art. 2374(B).

36. La. Civ. Code Ann. arts. 2346–2349, 2355–2355.1; *see also* Andrea B. Carroll & Richard Moreno, Matrimonial Regimes § 5.8, *in* 16 Louisiana Civil Law Treatise 416 (4th ed. 2013).

37. Concurrence of both spouses is needed for various actions, including the alienation, encumbrance, or lease of community immovables, as well as the donation of community property. *See* La. Civ. Code Ann. arts. 2347–2349.

38. La. Civ. Code Ann. art. 2355.

39. La. Civ. Code Ann. art. 2355.1.

40. *See* La. Civ. Code Ann. art. 51.

§ 2:4 Curator Appointed Over Property—Procedure for Appointment of a Curator

The procedure for appointment of a curator is similar in many respects to the procedure for the appointment of a tutor or a succession representative. An interested person may petition for the appointment of a curator for an absent person in the district court of the parish where the absent person was domiciled at the commencement of his absence.[41] Venue is non-waivable and therefore jurisdictional.[42] Evidence of the absent person's domicile, his ownership of property in Louisiana, and any other fact to show jurisdiction may be established through affidavits and submitted with the petition.[43] The applicant for curator must provide notice to the absent person's spouse not judicially separated, descendants, parents, and brothers or sisters and their descendants,[44] as well as to any person requesting notice of the application.[45]

The court will then order a descriptive list of the absent person's property and set the matter for hearing.[46] Oppositions can be filed and presented at the hearing.[47] Without opposition, the court will appoint the applicant if an appointment of curator is necessary[48] and the applicant is qualified.[49] If an opposition is filed, the court must give preference in the following order to the absent person's: (1) spouse not judicially separated;

41. La. Stat. Ann. § 13:3421(A). If the absent person was not domiciled in Louisiana when his absence commenced, the petition can be filed in the parish where his immovable property is situated, or if the absent person owned no immovable property in Louisiana, where the movable property is situated. La. Stat. Ann. § 13:3421(B). Venue is non-waivable. La. Stat. Ann. § 13:3421(C). Additionally, if two or more petitions are filed, the first-filed petition shall proceed and other petitions shall be stayed. La. Stat. Ann. § 13:3422. During the pendency of appointment, the court may appoint a provisional curator. La. Stat. Ann. § 13:3445.

42. La. Stat. Ann. § 13:3421(C); Miles v. Our Lady of the Lake Regional Medical Center, 2001-2272, p. 5 (La. App. 1 Cir.10/2/02), 836 So. 2d 136, 138–39 (holding that a judgment appointing a curator over an absent person rendered in a court without proper venue lacked subject matter jurisdiction and was therefore an absolute nullity).

43. La. Stat. Ann. § 13:3423(A). "No fact that is at issue in a contradictory proceeding to appoint a curator for an absent person may be proved by affidavit," and the court may require further evidence even in light of an undisputed affidavit. La. Stat. Ann. § 13:3423(C)–(D).

44. La. Stat. Ann. §§ 13:3425, 3433. Notice shall be by registered or certified mail, and the applicant must publish his request in the parish where the petition was filed. La. Stat. Ann. § 13:3425.

45. La. Stat. Ann. § 13:3426.

46. La. Stat. Ann. §§ 13:3427, 3429.

47. La. Stat. Ann. § 13:3428.

48. La. Stat. Ann. § 13:3429.

49. La. Stat. Ann. § 13:3431 ("In proceedings for appointment of a curator for an absent person, no person may be appointed who is: (1) Under 18 years of age; (2) Interdicted, or who, on contradictory hearing, is proved to be mentally incompetent; (3) A convicted felon, under the laws of the United States or of any state or territory thereof; (4) A nonresident of the state who has not appointed a resident agent for the service of process in all actions and proceedings with respect to the curatorship, and caused such appointment to be filed in the curatorship proceeding; (5) A corporation not authorized to perform the duties of curator in this state; (6) A person indebted to the absent person, except a spouse in community, unless he discharges the debt prior to the appointment; (7) An adverse party to a suit to which the absent person is a party; or (8) A person who, on contradictory hearing, is proved to be incapable of performing the duties of curator, or to be otherwise unfit for appointment.").

(2) descendants; (3) parents; and (4) brothers and sisters and their descendants.[50] The curator must furnish security[51] and take an oath to faithfully discharge his duties before receiving letters of curatorship.[52] At the time judgment is rendered, the court must also appoint an undercurator to oversee the actions of the curator.[53]

§ 2:5 Curator Appointed Over Property—Powers and Obligations of the Curator

Like both the tutor in tutorship proceedings and the succession representative in succession proceedings, the curator in an absent person proceeding is given a broad grant of power, subject to court approval, and limited only by expressly prohibited actions. The curator must "take possession of, preserve, and administer the absent person's property," with court approval when needed.[54] The curator must act prudently, and, with court approval, can perform all functions to administer and dispose of the absent person's property.[55] Court approval is also needed to compromise a claim, continue the business of the absent person, place the absent person's property in trust, or perform a contract of the absent person.[56] This grant of power is broad and can empower the curator to act without further court approval for purposes of a particular business or function.[57]

The curator must also enforce all obligations in favor of the absent person and represent the absent person in civil matters.[58] The curator must act as a prudent administrator and will be personally responsible for damages due to his failure to act.[59] Curators are prohibited from acquiring property of the absent person or making donations of the absent person's property.[60] Annually, and at termination of the curatorship, the curator must file an accounting of the absent person's property.[61] For his work, the curator is entitled to reasonable compensation.[62]

---

50. La. Stat. Ann. § 13:3433.

51. La. Stat. Ann. § 13:3434. Security can include bonds or mortgages. Security may be unnecessary in small curatorships. La. Stat. Ann. § 13:3444.

52. La. Stat. Ann. § 13:3435.

53. La. Stat. Ann. § 13:3436.

54. La. Stat. Ann. § 13:3437.

55. La. Stat. Ann. § 13:3438. The activities over which court approval is needed include, but are not limited to, lease, sale, purchase, exchange, borrow, loan, mortgage, deposit, and investment. La. Stat. Ann. § 13:3438(1). These activities mirror those of the succession and tutorship articles.

56. La. Stat. Ann. § 13:3438(2)–(5); *see also* La. Stat. Ann. § 13:3440 (procedure to seek court approval). In *Burns v. Van Loan*, in which the administrator sold the absent person's property without proper authority, the court adjudicated title to the heirs of the absent person, overruling the purchaser's pleas of acquisitive prescription. Burns v. Van Loan, 1877 WL 8011, at *3 (La. 1877).

57. La. Stat. Ann. § 13:3440(D).

58. La. Stat. Ann. § 13:3437.

59. La. Stat. Ann. § 13:3437.

60. La. Stat. Ann. § 13:3439. Court approval can be obtained for the curator to acquire the property of the absent person. La. Stat Ann. § 13:3439(A).

61. La. Stat. Ann. § 13:3443.

62. La. Stat. Ann. § 13:3442.

Curators and undercurators can be removed or can resign on several bases. An interested party can seek removal of the curator or undercurator for failing to discharge his duties, mismanaging the absent person's property, becoming disqualified, or if removal is in the best interest of the absent person.[63] A curator or undercurator can resign for any reason the court deems sufficient, and a successor curator or undercurator must be named simultaneously.[64]

§ 2:6 Curator Appointed Over Property— Effects on the Absent Person

Even though a curatorship has been established over the property of the absent person, the absent person retains full legal capacity to make juridical acts.[65] The curatorship over an absent person is distinct from the curatorship over an interdicted person, as the interdicted person loses his capacity to act.[66] Even after a person is declared absent, he can sell or donate his property, notwithstanding the curator's right to do the same.[67] Third parties who acquire rights in the absent person's immovable property, however, are protected by the public records doctrine.[68] Any conflicting claims of ownership are governed by the first act filed in the registry of the parish where the immovable property is located.[69] For movable property, delivery takes the place of registration.[70]

An absent person's marriage is terminated by the judgment declaring the absent person dead.[71] Although the absent person is presumed dead after the passage of five years, there is no legal authorization for the spouse to remarry unless the absent spouse has been judicially declared dead.[72] Any marriage during the first five years of absence without a declaration of death would be absolutely null.[73] Although not express in any codal provision, if the absent person reappears after death has been declared, his marriage will have terminated and all rights flowing therefrom will have ended.[74] The

63. La. Stat. Ann. § 13:3432(B). Disqualification is provided for in La. Stat. Ann. § 13:3431.

64. La. Stat. Ann. § 13:3432(C).

65. La. Civ. Code Ann. art. 49.

66. *See* La. Civ. Code Ann. art. 395.

67. *See* La. Civ. Code Ann. art. 49.

68. *See* La. Civ. Code Ann. art. 49 & cmt. (b).

69. La. Civ. Code Ann. art. 49.

70. La. Civ. Code Ann. art. 49 cmt. (b).

71. Marriage is terminated upon the death of either spouse. La. Civ. Code Ann. art. 101.

72. Although article 101 provides that a marriage terminates upon "[t]he issuance of a court order authorizing the spouse of a person presumed dead to remarry," the court order referenced in the article applies only to military personnel. La. Civ. Code Ann. art. 101 & cmt. (e) (citing La. Stat. Ann. § 9:301 (1990)).

73. An existing marriage is an impediment to marriage and results in an absolutely null marriage. La. Civ. Code Ann. arts. 88, 94.

74. Some states have "Enoch Arden" provisions, which make clear that marriages remain dissolved even though the absent spouse may reappear. Louisiana does not have a general provision, except in the case of military personnel. *See* Jeanne L. Carriere, *The Rights of the Living Dead: Absent Persons in the Civil Law*, 50 La. L. Rev. 901, 963–66.

widow's reliance on the declaration of death to remarry should pretermit any challenge to a subsequent marriage.

The absent person will retain rights as a successor until the time the absent person is presumed dead or has been declared dead.[75] One who is an absent person for five years is presumed dead.[76] If the absent person is presumed dead or has been declared dead at the time a succession would have been opened in his favor, the estate of the deceased will devolve as if the absent person had predeceased the decedent.[77] A declaration of death is not required for accretion to take place in favor of other successors.[78] However, a declaration of death is needed to open the absent person's succession.[79]

When carefully considering the succession rights of absent persons, an interesting issue arises. In the title on "Absent Persons," article 58 makes clear that a person presumed or declared dead cannot be a successor to a third party's estate,[80] leading to the reverse assumption that during the first five years of absence, prior to being presumed or declared dead, the absent person can be a successor. His curator, in his absence, will appear on his behalf and accept any rights of succession. Conversely, in the title on "Natural and Juridical Persons," article 31 requires that a person who claims a right that has accrued to another person must prove that the other person existed at the time the right accrued.[81] Absent persons, by definition, cannot be proven to be dead or alive.[82] Arguably, the curator appointed for an absent person cannot prove that the absent person existed at the time the right accrued to him, as is required under article 31. Articles 58 and 31 were passed in the same Act in 1990, but no reported case has addressed the issue.[83]

Because the law protects property of the absent person for the first five years of his disappearance in the hopes that he returns, rights to a succession that accrue during these five years should belong to the absent person through the curator. The curator can prove his existence as an "absent person," but no absent person's existence can be certain. In fact, the absent person may have predeceased the decedent during the

75. *See* La. Civ. Code Ann. art. 52 cmt.

76. La. Civ. Code Ann. art. 54. This provision was taken in part from the Greek Civil Code. La. Civ. Code Ann. art. 54 cmt. (a).

77. La. Civ. Code Ann. art. 58.

78. La. Civ. Code Ann. art. 58 cmts. (b)–(c).

79. La. Civ. Code Ann. art. 55. The succession shall be opened on the date of death established in the judgment. *Id.* A presumption of death will not suffice. *See* 4 C. Aubry & C. Rau, Cours De Droit Civil Français § 590 (La. St. L. Inst. trans., 1971).

80. *See* La. Civ. Code Ann. art. 58.

81. This provision was taken in part from the Greek Civil Code. La. Civ. Code Ann. art. 31 cmt. (a). Article 31 and its source provisions (articles 37 and 38 of the Greek Civil Code) were meant to replace the commorientes presumptions. *See* La. Civ. Code Ann. art. 935 cmt. (g). Under the Greek system, a person not presumed dead or declared dead is considered alive and capable of being a successor.

82. *See* 1 M. Planiol, Traité Élémentaire de Droit Civil No. 619 (La. St. L. Inst. trans., 1959).

83. Under prior law, if the absent person disappeared before the opening of a succession to which he was a successor, he would be excluded. *See* Fields v. McAdams, 15 So. 2d 246, 248–49 (La. Ct. App. 1 Cir. 1943) (because curatrix could not prove that her absent spouse was alive when his parents died, as the only heir, the absent spouse could not take in his parents' successions).

first five years of his absence; if the date of the absent person's death becomes known, a judgment declaring death can be amended.[84] But because article 31 appears in the general articles on natural and juridical persons and article 58 applies specifically to absent persons, the maxim that a specific law governs over a general one should apply.[85] Furthermore, the Greek Civil Code, under which a person not presumed dead or declared dead can be a successor, influenced both revisions (natural persons and absent persons) in Louisiana.[86] As a result, the absent person should have a right to successions that open in his favor during the first five years of his absence.

§ 2:7 Termination of Curatorship

Termination of the curatorship, either of right or by declaration of death, ends all rights of the curator over the absent person's property.[87] Either the absent person or his successors will have rights to the property remaining at termination. The curator must file a final accounting of his management, and the curator must restore the property to the absent person or his successors.[88]

§ 2:8 Termination of Curatorship—Termination of Right

The curatorship over an absent person's property terminates, without the necessity of getting a judgment, "when the absent person appoints a person to represent him in the state, when his whereabouts become known, or when he dies."[89] The representative or the absent person may appear anywhere in the world, and once a representative has been appointed to act on the absent person's behalf or the status of the absent person is known, the curatorship shall terminate.[90] Once the curator has knowledge of the termination, he must file a notice in the curatorship proceeding that his authority has ended.[91] If the curator performs any acts of administration or disposition after the termination, third parties will be protected unless notice of the termination has been filed in the curatorship proceedings.[92]

---

84. La. Civ. Code Ann. art. 56.

85. A general rule of statutory construction provides that a specific statute controls over a more general statute. Burge v. State, 2010-2229, p. 5 (La. 2/11/11), 54 So. 3d 1110, 1113; *see also* A.N. Yiannopoulos, Civil Law System: Louisiana and Comparative Law, A Coursebook: Texts, Cases and Materials 239, 257–58 (2d ed. 1999).

86. *See* La. Civ. Code Ann. art. 31 cmt. (a); La. Civ. Code Ann. art. 54 cmt. (a).

87. *See* La. Civ. Code Ann. arts. 50–51.

88. La. Civ. Code Ann. art. 52; La. Stat. Ann. § 13:3443.

89. La. Civ. Code Ann. art. 50.

90. La. Civ. Code Ann. art. 50 cmt. (b).

91. La. Civ. Code Ann. art. 53.

92. La. Civ. Code Ann. art. 53.

§ 2:9 Termination of Curatorship— Termination by Declaration of Death

The curatorship over an absent person's property also terminates when a court issues a judgment declaring the absent person's death.[93] Once an absent person has been missing for a period of five years, the absent person is presumed to be dead.[94] Once presumed dead, any interested party can petition the court for a judgment declaring the absent person dead.[95] In the absence of heirs, the curator must seek the declaration of death after the absent person is presumed dead.[96] In the event that heirs exist but refuse to seek the declaration of death, the curator should be permitted to seek the declaration as well.

In its declaration of death, the court must determine the date on which the absence commenced and the date of death of the absent person.[97] The absence commences on the date the court determines the person left their last known domicile, and the date of death, without other knowledge, occurs five years thereafter.[98] The date of death set by the court will result in termination of the marriage and the community, if one exists, and the opening of the absent person's succession.[99] If, however, clear and convincing new evidence establishes a date of death different than the date established by the court, the judgment shall be amended reflecting the new date of death.[100] Succession rights will flow in accordance with the amended date of death; successors and beneficiaries could change as a result of the amended date of death.[101] The Code does not prescribe rules in the event of an amendment, but the rules governing good faith possessors of property would likely apply.

Once the judgment declaring the death of the absent person is filed in the curatorship proceeding, third parties are on notice that the curatorship has terminated.[102] Any acts thereafter performed by the curator can be declared null.[103]

---

93. La. Civ. Code Ann. art. 51.

94. La. Civ. Code Ann. art. 54. In the wake of Hurricanes Katrina and Rita, the time period for a presumption of death was shortened to two years "[i]f the absence commenced between August 26, 2005, and September 30, 2005, and was related to" either hurricane, and the absent person was not currently charged with a felony offense under United States or Louisiana law. *Id.*

95. La. Civ. Code Ann. art. 54.

96. La. Civ. Code Ann. art. 51.

97. La. Civ. Code Ann. art. 54.

98. In re Boyd, 98-0052, p. 5 (La. App. 1 Cir. 12/28/98), 723 So. 2d 1107, 1110.

99. La. Civ. Code Ann. arts. 55, 2356. The date of death can also affect rights to life insurance proceeds and wrongful death claims. *See* Ledet v. Dep't of Health & Hum. Res., 465 So. 2d 98, 101 (La. Ct. App. 4 Cir. 1985).

100. La. Civ. Code Ann. art. 56. Those previously recognized as successors are bound to restore the estate to the new successors but may keep any gathered fruits of the property. La. Civ. Code Ann. art. 56. If they are unable to restore the property in kind, they are bound to restore its value, and there is no recourse against third parties. La. Civ. Code Ann. art. 56 cmt. (c).

101. *See* La. Civ. Code Ann. art. 56 cmts. (b)–(c).

102. La. Civ. Code Ann. art. 53 cmt. (c).

103. *See* La. Civ. Code Ann. art. 53 cmt. (c).

§ 2:10 Reappearance of Absent Person

An absent person, upon reappearance, is entitled to recover his property and inheritance in the condition that it exists when he returns.[104] If the absent person reappears during the curatorship, the curatorship terminates and the curator must return the property to the absent person.[105] This property would include any inheritance acquired by the curator during the curatorship. If the absent person appears after being declared dead, the absent person can recover his property in the condition in which he finds it from his successors and their transferees by gratuitous title.[106] If the absent person was presumed dead or declared dead when a succession would have opened in his favor, he can also recover his inheritance in the condition in which he finds it from those who succeeded in his default and from their transferees by gratuitous title.[107] Additionally, nothing prevents the absent person from seeking rights of an omitted heir against transferees of immovable property by onerous title as long as the interest is asserted within two years of a final judgment of possession from which the absent person was omitted.[108]

Under the right of restitution, the property must be returned in the condition in which it exists, which could include real rights in favor of third parties.[109] The absent person is also entitled to recover from his successors the net proceeds of things alienated and the diminution in value of things encumbered.[110] The Code does not provide whether a successor will be responsible to the absent person for the value of the proceeds if, at the time of reappearance, the successor had consumed the proceeds. At that point, the policy of protecting the absent person should be outweighed by the reasonable acts of the successor, in disposing of the property and enjoying the proceeds, after the absent person is declared dead and believing that he is the rightful owner.[111]

The revision comments make clear that the ability of the absent person to recover fruits of the property acquired during his absence is governed by the rights of accession by good and bad faith possessors.[112] Although the absent person may recover his property and inheritance, he generally will be unable to recover fruits generated

---

104. A specific provision exists for the reappearance of military personnel who are presumed dead. *See* La. Stat. Ann. § 9:1442.

105. La. Civ. Code Ann. arts. 50, 57.

106. La. Civ. Code Ann. art. 57.

107. La. Civ. Code Ann. art. 59.

108. La. Civ. Code Ann. art. 59 cmt. (d); La. Stat. Ann. § 9:5630.

109. La. Civ. Code Ann. arts. 57, 59 cmt. (c).

110. La. Civ. Code Ann. arts. 57, 59.

111. Articles 2304 and 2305 of the Civil Code, by analogy, support protecting the good faith "owner" of a thing not owned. When the thing not owned is destroyed, damaged, or cannot be returned, the person who received the thing in good faith is only bound to restore its value if the loss was caused by his fault. La. Civ. Code Ann. art. 2304. A person in bad faith is bound to restore its value even if the loss was not caused by his fault. La. Civ. Code Ann. arts. 2304–2305. Professor Carriere disagrees; she concludes that heirs would be encouraged to spend the money on something other than property, thereby stripping the absentee of protection. Jeanne L. Carriere, *The Rights of the Living Dead: Absent Persons in the Civil Law*, 50 La. L. Rev. 901, 955.

112. La. Civ. Code Ann. art. 57 cmt. (c).

from the property.[113] The shift in policy to protect the successor or transferee over the absent person is present here. The successors and gratuitous transferees are considered possessors of the property and, if in good faith, are entitled to keep the fruits they have gathered.[114] Additionally, with respect to improvements made on immovable property by a good faith possessor, the absent person may not demand their demolition and removal and is bound to pay either the cost of material and workmanship, the current value, or the enhanced value of the immovable.[115]

"For purposes of accession, a possessor is in good faith when he possesses by virtue of an act translative of ownership and does not know of any defects in his ownership."[116] An "act translative of ownership" is an act sufficient to transfer property, such as a sale, exchange, or donation.[117] Any legatee through a valid donation *mortis causa* will be a good faith possessor, unless he knows of a defect in his ownership. Because an intestate heir continues the possession of the decedent, if the decedent possessed the property pursuant to an act translative of ownership, so too does the intestate heir.[118] Therefore, the ability of the intestate heir to retain the fruits of the absent person's property depends on the nature of the absentee's possession—either good or bad faith.

If the successors or gratuitous transferees are in bad faith, they are bound to restore the fruits gathered or their value but have a claim for reimbursement of expenses.[119] The absent person may also demand from the bad faith possessors the removal of improvements made on immovable property and reimbursement for any damage that he has sustained.[120]

Although the right of the absent person to prove his ownership is a petitory action and is not subject to liberative prescription,[121] the right of the successor to assert acquisitive prescription against the absent person should be available.[122] Because the absent person has the right to reacquire his property upon return and thereby void title in his successors, ownership should only be permitted through 30-year acquisitive prescription without just title. The interest of the successor after 30 years of uninterrupted possession should outweigh any interest in restitution otherwise available to the absent person.

---

113. La. Civ. Code Ann. art. 57 cmt. (c).

114. La. Civ. Code Ann. art. 486; *see also* La. Civ. Code Ann. art. 57 cmt. (c); La. Civ. Code Ann. art. 59 cmt. (c).

115. La. Civ. Code Ann. art. 496.

116. La. Civ. Code Ann. art. 487.

117. La. Civ. Code Ann. art. 487 cmt. (b) (quoting La. Civ. Code art. 503 (1870)).

118. La. Civ. Code Ann. art. 936; *see also* La. Civ. Code Ann. art. 487 cmt. (f).

119. La. Civ. Code Ann. art. 486.

120. La. Civ. Code Ann. art. 497. If the absent person does not demand removal, he may keep the improvements, but is bound to pay either the current value of the materials and workmanship, or the enhanced value of the immovable. *Id.*

121. *See* La. Civ. Code Ann. art. 481; A.N. Yiannopoulos, Property § 10:12, *in* 2 Louisiana Civil Law Treatise 571 (5th ed. 2015).

122. Early treatise writers agree. *See* Jeanne L. Carriere, *The Rights of the Living Dead: Absent Persons in the Civil Law*, 50 La. L. Rev. 901, 957–58.

In the realm of a possessor's rights and obligations, it is noteworthy that the possessor's rights to fruits and improvements are asserted only against the *owner* of the thing, not against other possessors.[123] Therefore, the rights of a possessor presuppose that the absent person was the owner of the thing he now wishes to reclaim from the possessor. What transpires if the absent person was simply a possessor of the thing (not the owner) when he became absent and now he has reappeared? If acquisitive prescription has not accrued, then both parties are possessors of the same character.[124] If the true owner is unknown, the absent person may claim that he is the "provisional owner" of the thing and exercise rights as owner until the true owner is established.[125]

§ 2:11 Presumption of Death for Military Personnel

Louisiana has specialized statutes to deal with the absence of military personnel. If a person is on active duty in the military and has been reported missing in action, he can be presumed dead when the armed services accepts the presumption of death.[126] The person seeking to prove death need not offer evidence of death; he need only a certified copy of an official certificate of the armed services or the soldier's service records indicating the armed services has accepted the presumption of death.[127] The succession can then be opened in the same manner as any other deceased person.[128] If the soldier presumed dead is alive, and he demands return of his property within 30 years from the date of the judgment of possession, his heirs or legatees must then return the property they still own, subject to all encumbrances, and pay him the value of any property alienated and any amount of encumbrances placed on the property.[129] The heirs or legatees must also return a share of the annual revenues of his property.[130]

---

123. La. Civ. Code Ann. arts. 486, 526.

124. *See* La. Civ. Code Ann. art. 936.

125. *See* La. Civ. Code Ann. art. 3423; *see also* A.N. Yiannopoulos, Property § 10:12, *in* 2 Louisiana Civil Law Treatise 691 (5th ed. 2015).

126. La. Stat. Ann. § 9:1441.

127. La. Stat. Ann. § 9:1443; *see also* Pierce v. Gervais, 425 So. 2d 922 (La. Ct. App. 4 Cir. 1983).

128. La. Stat. Ann. § 9:1442. The succession may be opened in the parish where the service member was domiciled at the time of entering the armed service. *Id.*

129. La. Stat. Ann. § 9:1442(B).

130. La. Stat. Ann. § 9:1442(B). If the service member returns within five years, the heirs of legatees must return two-thirds; after five but within seven years, they must return one-half; and after seven years, they need not return any. *Id.*

Chapter 3

Marriage*

* This chapter was derived from the following article: Monica Hof Wallace, *A Primer on Marriage in Louisiana*, 64 Loy. L. Rev. 557 (2018). The authors wish to thank the Loyola Law Review for its assistance on the initial work for this chapter.

§ 3:1 Introduction

Louisiana recognizes marriage as a legal relationship[1] created by civil contract.[2] While marriage is a nominate contract, with its own, specific rules, parties may rely on general contract principles in resolving questions unanswered by the more specific laws governing marriage.[3] Unlike ordinary contracts, however, the marriage contract "creates a social status that affects not only the contracting parties, but also their posterity and the good order of society."[4] Therefore, certain laws governing marriage cannot be contractually altered by the parties.[5]

As in any state, parties must meet certain prerequisites to contract a marriage. To validly marry in Louisiana, the parties must be free from any legal impediment to marry, which includes (1) being married to someone else, (2) being too closely related, or (3) being under the age of 16, or being 16 or 17 and marrying a person three or more years older.[6] The parties must also freely consent to take one another as spouses at a

1. La. Civ. Code Ann. art. 86. As of the time of publication, the Louisiana Civil Code continues to define marriage as between a man and a woman. *Id.* This code article is unconstitutional in light of *Obergefell v. Hodges*, 135 S. Ct. 2584 (2015). Marriage between members of the same sex is permitted under Louisiana law. *See* Robicheaux v. Caldwell, 791 F.3d 616 (5th Cir. 2015).

2. La. Civ. Code Ann. art. 86. The use of "civil" to modify "contract" indicates that Louisiana law, rather than ecclesiastical law, applies. *See* Katherine Shaw Spaht, *The Last One Hundred Years: The Incredible Retreat of Law from the Regulation of Marriage*, 63 La. L. Rev. 243, 251 (2003).

3. *But see* Wederstrandt v. Kol, 2022-01570 (La. 6/27/23); 366 So. 3d 47, 52–53 (refusing to apply general principles of contract nullity to a marriage contract).

4. La. Civ. Code Ann. art. 86 cmt. (c); Stallings v. Stallings, 148 So. 687, 688 (La. 1933).

5. Rhodes v. Miller, 179 So. 430, 433 (La. 1938) ("[The marriage contract] creates a social status or personal relation which affects not only the contracting parties, but also their posterity and the good order of society. The status or relation thus created has always been subject to legislative control, independent of the will of the parties."); *see also, e.g.*, Holliday v. Holliday, 358 So. 2d 618, 620 (La. 1978) (courts will not enforce an agreement in a prenuptial agreement to waive the obligation of interim support to a spouse); Favrot v. Barnes, 332 So. 2d 873, 875 (La. Ct. App. 4 Cir. 1976) (courts will not enforce an agreed upon sexual obligation between spouses).

6. *See* Section 3:10. Being of the same sex was a legal impediment to marriage prior to 2015 when the United States Supreme Court nationalized same-sex marriage in *Obergefell v. Hodges*, 135 S. Ct. 2584 (2015). *See* Section 3:3.

marriage ceremony.[7] No physical consummation is necessary.[8] If one or more of the prerequisites is missing, the marriage can be declared null.[9]

Louisiana also requires parties to meet other ceremonial formalities, which include, among others, obtaining a marriage license and having witnesses present, but, even if the parties fail to comply with certain technical formalities, the marriage remains valid and cannot be declared null.[10] More detail on marriage prerequisites, nullity of marriage, incidents of marriage, and other related topics are presented in the sections below.

§ 3:2 The 1987 Revision to the Law of Marriage

As part of an ongoing effort to revise the Louisiana Civil Code, the Marriage-Persons Committee of the Louisiana State Law Institute performed a comprehensive revision of the law on marriage, which resulted in Act 886 of 1987. Specifically, the Law Institute Committee and the Law Institute Council deliberated and recommended revisions to Title IV of Book I, "Husband and Wife," which included the law on entry into, nullity of, and the personal effects of marriage. Act 886 of 1987 ultimately revised Civil Code Articles 86 through 136 and several corresponding sections in the Revised Statutes. While the legislature retained much of the law on marriage, it also made some notable changes, as discussed in the article *Revision of the Law of Marriage: One Baby Step Forward.*[11]

§ 3:3 2015 Changes to Same-Sex Marriage

On June 26, 2015, the United States Supreme Court decided the case of *Obergefell v. Hodges*, which nationalized the confection and recognition of same-sex marriage.[12] In a 5-to-4 decision, the Court concluded that the right to marry is a fundamental right inherent in the concept of liberty, and under the Due Process and Equal Protection Clauses of the Fourteenth Amendment, same-sex couples may not be deprived of that right.[13] The Court also required all states to recognize same-sex marriages validly performed in other states.[14]

---

7. La. Civ. Code Ann. art. 87; *see also* Section 3:14. Prior to 1902, first cousins were permitted to marry in Louisiana. Prior to 1972 and 1975, respectively, "white persons" could not marry "Indians" or "colored and black" persons. *See* Katherine Shaw Spaht & John Randall Trahan, Family Law in Louisiana § 3.7, at 73 (2009). Prior to 1970 and 1972, respectively, widows could not marry within ten months of the dissolution of their marriage, and adulterers could not marry their paramour. *See id.*

8. La. Civ. Code Ann. art. 87 cmt. (a).

9. The marriage will either be absolutely null or relatively null, which corresponds to void or voidable marriages under the common law. *See* Section 3:20.

10. *See* Section 3:16.

11. *See* Katherine Shaw Spaht, *Revision of the Law of Marriage: One Baby Step Forward*, 48 La. L. Rev. 1131, 1132 (1988).

12. Obergefell v. Hodges, 135 S. Ct. 2584 (2015).

13. Obergefell, 135 S. Ct. at 2604–05.

14. Obergefell, 135 S. Ct. at 2607–08.

This shift in the law of marriage began several years earlier when targeted challenges were made across the country to state same-sex marriage bans. The United States Supreme Court, exactly two years before the *Obergefell* decision, on June 26, 2013, decided *United States v. Windsor*[15] and *Hollingsworth v. Perry*,[16] which, in large part, predicted the ultimate decision in *Obergefell*. A firestorm of legislative and judicial changes spread across the country, which is chronicled in *Marriage Equality: The "States" of the Law Post-*Windsor *and* Perry.[17]

At the time of the *Windsor* and *Perry* decisions, Louisiana had an express prohibition against same-sex marriage[18] and recognizing same-sex marriages performed in other states.[19] Louisiana had also enacted a Defense of Marriage Act in its constitution.[20] Similar to the plethora of litigation taking place across the country, the case of *Robicheaux v. Caldwell* was filed in the United States District Court for the Eastern District of Louisiana, challenging Louisiana's ban on same-sex marriage.[21] The trial court initially denied the plaintiffs' relief, upholding Louisiana's same-sex marriage ban.[22] Plaintiffs then appealed to the United States Court of Appeals for the Fifth Circuit.[23] The Fifth Circuit issued its opinion just five days after the Supreme Court's edict in *Obergefell*, finding Louisiana's laws prohibiting same-sex marriage unconstitutional.[24]

The Louisiana Supreme Court spoke next in the case of *Costanza v. Caldwell*, which involved a challenge to the same-sex marriage ban by a woman who sought to adopt

---

15. United States v. Windsor, 570 U.S. 744 (2013).

16. Hollingsworth v. Perry, 570 U.S. 693 (2013).

17. Monica Hof Wallace & Christopher Gerald Otten, *Marriage Equality: The "States" of the Law Post-*Windsor *and* Perry, 16 Loy. J. Pub. Int. L. 215 (2014).

18. La. Civ. Code Ann. art. 89.

19. La. Civ. Code Ann. art. 3520(B), *declared unconstitutional by* Robicheaux v. Caldwell, Nos. 13-5090 C/W, 14-97, 14-327, 2015 WL 4090353 (E.D. La. July 2, 2015).

20. La. Const. Ann. art. XII, § 15, *declared unconstitutional by* Robicheaux, 2015 WL 4090353. In 2004, the legislature passed, and the electorate approved, Louisiana's version of the federal Defense of Marriage Act, which provided:

> Marriage in the state of Louisiana shall consist only of the union of one man and one woman. No official or court of the state of Louisiana shall construe this constitution or any state law to require that marriage or the legal incidents thereof be conferred upon any member of a union other than the union of one man and one woman. A legal status identical or substantially similar to that of marriage for unmarried individuals shall not be valid or recognized. No official or court of the state of Louisiana shall recognize any marriage contracted in any other jurisdiction which is not the union of one man and one woman.

Id. In 2005, the Louisiana Supreme Court upheld the act in the face of a constitutional challenge under the single object requirement of the state constitution. *See generally* Forum for Equal. PAC v. McKeithen, 2004-CA-2477, 2004-CA-2523 (La. 1/19/05), 893 So. 2d 715.

21. *See generally* Robicheaux v. Caldwell, 2 F. Supp. 3d 910 (E.D. La. 2014), *rev'd*, 791 F.3d 616 (5th Cir. 2015).

22. *See* Robicheaux, 2 F. Supp. 3d at 927–28.

23. *See generally* Robicheaux v. Caldwell, 791 F.3d 616 (5th Cir. 2015).

24. On July 1, 2015, the Fifth Circuit held that the Louisiana laws violated the fundamental right to marry, and it remanded the case to the district court. *See* Robicheaux, 791 F.3d at 618–19. On July 2, 2015, the United States District Court for the Eastern District of Louisiana likewise declared the laws unconstitutional and granted the plaintiffs' relief. *Robicheaux*, 2015 WL 4090353.

her wife's biological child.[25] The district court granted the adoption, declaring the Louisiana marriage laws unconstitutional, and the State appealed.[26] The State argued that stepparent adoption was not available because Louisiana law did not recognize the marriage of the two women, who were wed in California.[27] The Louisiana Supreme Court, in a brief opinion, held that, in light of the *Obergefell* decision and the subsequent actions of the Louisiana federal court in *Robicheaux*, the issues had been resolved and "the State of Louisiana may not bar same-sex couples from the civil effects of marriage."[28] The appeal was dismissed.

Immediately thereafter, the Marriage-Persons Committee of the Louisiana State Law Institute began the task of considering revisions to the unconstitutional provisions of the Civil Code and suggesting answers to significant questions left unanswered by *Obergefell*. On November 6, 2015, the reporter for the Committee presented to the Louisiana State Law Institute Council a proposal to revise the laws that were rendered obsolete or on which the courts would need guidance.[29] After a lengthy discussion, the Council voted to have the Committee prepare a report to the legislature, on which the Council would vote at a later meeting. The legislature could then decide how to address the issues. Because discussion of the same-sex marriage issues was slated for that day, the Council considered the proposal prepared by the Committee and voted on various revisions to the laws of marriage and other related matters.[30]

On February 12, 2016, the reporter returned to the Council with the work that was completed in November of 2015, along with a draft report to the legislature.[31] The Council passed the motion to adopt the report, and the reporter forwarded it to the Louisiana Speaker of the House and President of the Senate.[32] No bill was introduced by the legislature in the 2016 Regular Session, but to assure the Council that its input was requested, Senator Jean-Paul "J.P." Morrell submitted Senate Resolution 143, which was subsequently adopted by the Senate:

> [U]rge and request the Marriage-Persons Committee of the Louisiana State Law Institute to study, and the Louisiana State Law Institute to make, annual comprehensive and ongoing recommendations to the Legislature regarding state law post *Obergefell v. Hodges*, including but not limited to recommendations in the form of proposed legislation for revisions to laws governing fami-

---

25. Costanza v. Caldwell, 2014-2090 (La. 7/7/15), 167 So. 3d 619.

26. *See* In re Adoption of N.B., 14-314 (La. App. 3 Cir. 2014), 140 So. 3d 1263.

27. *See* In re Adoption of N.B., 140 So. 3d at 1265.

28. *See* Costanza, 167 So. 3d at 621. Three justices concurred in the opinion with reasons, and one justice dissented. *See id.* at 622–24 (Knoll, Weimer & Guidry, J.J., concurring & Hughes, J., dissenting).

29. Louisiana State Law Institute, Minutes of the Meeting of the Council, at 1 (Nov. 6–7, 2015) (on file with the Louisiana State Law Institute).

30. Louisiana State Law Institute, Minutes of the Meeting of the Council, at 1 (Nov. 6–7, 2015) (on file with the Louisiana State Law Institute).

31. Louisiana State Law Institute, Minutes of the Meeting of the Council, at 6 (Feb. 12–13, 2016) (on file with the Louisiana State Law Institute).

32. Louisiana State Law Institute Marriage-Persons Committee, Same-Sex Marriage Report to the Legislature (Mar. 16, 2016) (on file with the Louisiana State Law Institute).

lies, persons, community property, successions, immovable property, the rights of third parties, procedure, and the stability and validity of transactions.[33]

In response to S. Res. 143, the reporter came before the Council on January 20, 2017, and requested that the Council submit a bill to the legislature with many of the same changes that had been adopted in November of 2015, along with some new changes that were needed to address problems raised by the jurisprudence.[34] The Council agreed and approved various changes to the laws of marriage and related matters that it had considered previously.[35] It also addressed new issues related to community property and its retroactivity, given the retroactive validity of same-sex marriages.[36] Because the 2017 Regular Session focused on fiscal matters, no bill on same-sex marriage was introduced.

In the 2018 Regular Session, Senator Morrell introduced Senate Bill 98.[37] In line with the work of the Marriage-Persons Committee shortly after the *Obergefell* opinion, the bill performed various "clean-ups" to the verbiage in the Civil Code. The definition of marriage was changed to a civil contract "between two natural persons," rather than "between a man and a woman."[38] Where the law referred to a "husband and wife," the verbiage was changed to "spouses."[39] Where the law used "father and mother," the language was changed to "parents."[40] The only substantive change dealt with community property. The bill proposed a new statute to be placed in Title 9, which provided as follows:

> Same-sex couples married on or before June 26, 2015, may enter into a matrimonial agreement without court approval until the expiration of one-year from August 1, 2018.... For same-sex couples married on or before June 26, 2015, the application of the legal regime of the community of acquets and gains shall be without prejudice to the rights of third parties validly acquired before August 1, 2018.[41]

Enacting this statute was not intended to affect the validity of any contract entered into by same-sex couples before June 26, 2015; instead, it would allow same-sex couples to opt out of the regime extrajudicially, just like couples who move to Louisiana.[42]

---

33. S. Res. 143, 2016 Leg., Reg. Sess. (La. 2016).

34. *See* Louisiana State Law Institute, Minutes of the Meeting of the Council, at 3–6 (Jan. 20–21, 2017) (on file with the Louisiana State Law Institute).

35. *See* Louisiana State Law Institute, Minutes of the Meeting of the Council, at 3–6 (Jan. 20–21, 2017) (on file with the Louisiana State Law Institute).

36. Louisiana State Law Institute, Minutes of the Meeting of the Council, at 3–5 (Jan. 20–21, 2017) (on file with the Louisiana State Law Institute).

37. S.B. 98, 2018 Leg., Reg. Sess. (La. 2018).

38. S.B. 98, 2018 Leg., Reg. Sess. at 2 (La. 2018).

39. S.B. 98, 2018 Leg., Reg. Sess., at 2 (La. 2018).

40. S.B. 98, 2018 Leg., Reg. Sess., at 2 (La. 2018).

41. S.B. 98, 2018 Leg., Reg. Sess. (La. 2018).

42. *See* S.B. 98, 2018 Leg., Reg. Sess. (La. 2018); *see also* La. Civ. Code Ann. art. 2329.

Because third parties could be affected by the retroactive creation of a community property regime, the law was drafted to protect those third parties.[43]

The bill was referred to the Judiciary A Committee. On March 26, 2018, Senator Morrell presented the bill, and a representative from the Louisiana Family Forum testified against the bill.[44] The debate lasted 16 minutes, and the bill failed by a 4-to-1 vote. To date, no additional legislation has been introduced or passed. As a result, courts are still without guidance on the issue of community property. In addition, the law, as reflected in our Civil Code and related statutes, remains unconstitutional.

§ 3:4 Gifts in Contemplation of Marriage

Prospective spouses and third parties who celebrate them often present gifts prior to and in contemplation of an upcoming marriage. Whether these gifts are completed donations in the absence of a future marriage depends on whether a condition is placed on the gift. The law permits donors to place a condition on a gift, provided the condition is not "contrary to law or good morals."[45] In the event the condition is not fulfilled, the donation can be dissolved.[46]

Because the donation of an engagement ring is conditioned on a future marriage, it can be dissolved if that marriage does not take place.[47] When the condition of a future marriage can no longer be fulfilled (*e.g.*, when the former fiancé marries someone else), the donation is dissolved as of right.[48] If the couple could still marry but have simply broken the engagement, the donation may be dissolved only by consent of the parties or by judicial decree.[49] Therefore, the donor may be required to seek judicial intervention to have the gift returned.[50] Further, even if the donor initially refuses to

43. For example, if immovable property was transferred without the consent of the other now-community spouse, in violation of article 2347, the transaction would still be valid. *See* La. Civ. Code Ann. art. 2347.

44. The Louisiana Family Forum argued that "compliance with the law is very different than redefinition." Senator Morrell urged that Louisiana must abide by the law of the Supreme Court even if its citizens do not agree. He pointed out that the Louisiana State Law Institute is a nonpartisan body that can make changes to the Code when the law from the United States Supreme Court changes. Finally, he highlighted economic development, which could suffer when a state fails to follow the rule of law. Louisiana State Senate Broadcast Archives, https://senate.la.gov/s_video/videoarchive.asp?v=senate/2018/03/032618JUDA_0 (last visited Apr. 6, 2024).

45. La. Civ. Code Ann. art. 1528.

46. *See* La. Civ. Code Ann. arts. 1562–1563.

47. State v. Rubin, 04-1588, p. 2 (La. App. 3 Cir. 4/6/05), 899 So. 2d 187, 189; Glass v. Wiltz, 551 So. 2d 32, 32–33 (La. Ct. App. 4 Cir. 1989); Decuers v. Bourdet, 120 So. 880 (La. Ct. App. 1929). Former article 1740 provided: "Every donation made in favor of marriage falls, if the marriage does not take place." La. Civ. Code Ann. art. 1740 (1952) (amended and reenacted by Act No. 619, 2004 La. Acts 2082, presently La. Civ. Code art. 1736).

48. *See* La. Civ. Code Ann. art. 1562.

49. La. Civ. Code Ann. art. 1562.

50. La. Civ. Code Ann. art. 1562; *see* Glass, 551 So. 2d 32 (fiancé sued to seek return of the engagement ring).

accept return of the gift under the belief that the engagement is not over, the gift is still subject to the condition of marriage and can be dissolved if the marriage does not take place.[51] Actions to dissolve a donation for failure of a condition prescribe five years from the date the donee fails to fulfill the condition.[52]

Gifts made in the hope that marriage will follow, rather than on the condition of marriage itself, should be classified as manual gifts valid upon delivery.[53] Gifts such as promise rings or objects that the parties expect they may share in the future are not conditioned on the promise of marriage but only on the hope that marriage will be in the parties' future.[54] Once delivered, these gifts are completed manual donations, even absent a later marriage.

Third parties also present gifts to prospective spouses in preparation for an upcoming marriage. Chapter 2 of Title II of the Civil Code directly addresses these rules and provides that "[t]he donation shall be made subject to the suspensive condition that the prospective marriage shall take place."[55] Wedding shower gifts made to the couple are not completed gifts until the marriage takes place and are subject to return by the donee in the absence of the future marriage.[56]

§ 3:5 Breach of the Promise to Marry

Louisiana recognizes the claim for breach of the promise to marry, but recovery is rare. A successful claimant may recover pecuniary damages, and in some cases, nonpecuniary damages, as well. The latter is derived from article 1998 in the Title on "Conventional Obligations or Contracts," which permits one damaged by such a breach to recover damages for a nonpecuniary loss in certain scenarios. If a contract, like the agreement to marry, is intended to gratify a nonpecuniary interest, the obligor can be liable in damages for his nonperformance if he knew or should have known that his failure to perform would cause a nonpecuniary loss.[57] Additionally, regardless of the nature of the contract, these damages may be recovered when the obligor intended, through his breach, to aggrieve the feelings of the obligee.[58] The action is strictly per-

51. *See* Daigle v. Fournet, 141 So. 2d 406, 408 (La. Ct. App. 4 Cir. 1962).

52. La. Civ. Code Ann. art. 1564.

53. *See* La. Civ. Code Ann. art. 1543.

54. *See generally* Fortenberry v. Ellis, 217 So. 2d 792 (La. Ct. App. 4 Cir. 1969) (finding that the gift of a stereo was not given in contemplation of marriage).

55. La. Civ. Code Ann. art. 1736. For a discussion of the revision to the chapter entitled "Donations Inter Vivos Made in Contemplation of Marriage by Third Persons," *see generally* Andrea Carroll & Richard D. Moreno, Matrimonial Regimes § 8:10, *in* 16 Louisiana Civil Law Treatise 884 (4th ed. 2013).

56. *See* La. Civ. Code Ann. art. 1736.

57. La. Civ. Code Ann. art. 1998. Nonpecuniary loss is damage of a moral nature that does not affect the tangible part of a person's patrimony. La. Civ. Code Ann. art. 1998 cmt. (b); *see also* Saúl Litvinoff, The Law of Obligations § 6.4, *in* 6 Louisiana Civil Law Treatise 158 (1999) (discussing nonpecuniary loss in the context of a promise to marry and noting that recovery has been related to a pecuniary loss).

58. La. Civ. Code Ann. art. 1998.

sonal and therefore not heritable by the heirs,[59] but if the claim has been reduced to judgment, it can be enforced against the decedent's estate.[60] Because the action sounds in contract, the 10-year prescription that bars a demand in contract applies to a breach of the promise to marry.[61]

The first case to recognize the claim for breach of the promise to marry was *Morgan v. Yarborough* in 1850.[62] The Louisiana Supreme Court explained that a promise of marriage is distinct from a marriage contract; therefore, it need not be in writing, and an action will lie when a breach of that promise causes damage.[63] The unchastity of the plaintiff was a defense to the action, although more recent cases have expanded the defense to include fault generally.[64] Since inception of the claim, few courts have awarded damages for a breach.[65]

Courts have resisted awarding damages unless the plaintiff can demonstrate freedom from fault and sufficient proof of damage. No court, however, has addressed or adopted a definition of fault.[66] For example, in one case, the plaintiff was denied recovery for failing to present sufficient evidence of damage caused by the breach,[67] and in another, the plaintiff was denied recovery for ending the relationship when the donor was attempting to reconcile.[68]

---

59. La. Civ. Code Ann. art. 1766.

60. *See* Johnson v. Levy, 47 So. 422, 424 (La. 1907).

61. *See* Smith v. Braun, 37 La. Ann. 225, 226, 228 (La. 1885).

62. Morgan v. Yarborough, 5 La. Ann. 316 (La. 1850). *See generally* Levy, 47 So. at 424 (discussing the claim of breach of contract to marry and subsequent remedies); Kuck v. Johnson, 38 So. 559 (La. 1905) (discussing an award for breach of contract to marry in the context of the sale of a judgment).

63. Morgan, 5 La. Ann. at 322. The defendant attempted to prove the "unchaste character" of the plaintiff to excuse his breach of the promise. *Id.* at 321. The court did not find that the evidence was sufficient to prove his defense, but it recognized that, if proven, the unchaste nature of the plaintiff would have excused the breach. *See id.* at 321–33.

64. *See* Katherine Shaw Spaht, *The Last One Hundred Years: The Incredible Retreat of Law from the Regulation of Marriage*, 63 La. L. Rev. 243, 269 (2003).

65. *See generally* Levy, 47 So. at 422. In *Levy*, a suitor proposed to the plaintiff, she became pregnant with his child, and he ended the relationship. *Id.* at 422–24. He was murdered shortly thereafter by the plaintiff's father. *Id.* at 424. The jury awarded the plaintiff $20,000 in damages, which was subsequently reduced by half by the appellate court. *Id.*; *see also* Kuck, 38 So. 559 (discussing an award for breach of contract to marry in the context of the sale of a judgment); Braun, 37 La. Ann. 225 (affirming an award for breach of the contract to marry).

66. *See* Spaht, *supra* note 64, at 269–70.

67. *See* Glass v. Wiltz, 551 So. 2d 32 (La. Ct. App. 4 Cir. 1989). In *Glass*, the groom who broke the engagement sued to recover the engagement ring. *Id.* at 32. The bride reconvened, seeking damages for the breach of the promise to marry. *Id.* While the groom was entitled to recover the ring, the bride was unable to recover because she failed to prove any damage she suffered due to the breach of the promise to marry. *See id.* at 33.

68. *See* Daigle v. Fournet, 141 So. 2d 406 (La. Ct. App. 4 Cir. 1962). In *Daigle*, the plaintiff sued to recover the engagement ring given to his fiancée, and she reconvened for breach of the promise to marry. *Id.* at 407. The court denied the fiancée's request for damages for breach of the contract to marry because she broke off the engagement when he was making "serious" efforts at reconciliation. *Id.* at 408.

In a notable case, *Sanders v. Gore*, the Louisiana Third Circuit Court of Appeal denied recovery for breach of a promise to marry because the parties were married to other people at the time the promise was made.[69] The court dismissed the action on an exception of no cause of action, concluding that no matter how the action was styled, any damages arising from the promise when the parties are already married is unenforceable as against public policy.[70] The concurrence and dissents challenged the notion that an action for breach of the promise to marry, when the parties are already married, is contrary to public policy—considering the ease with which parties can get divorced in today's society.[71] Getting divorced to remarry someone else is not condemned by the law; yet, by finding no cause of action for breach of the promise to marry, the court in effect condemned one party to suffer pecuniary damages, while the other party was rewarded with immunity.[72] At the end of the day, however, the majority agreed that enforcing a promise to marry when the other party is knowingly married to another runs afoul of societal mores and, regardless of the attitudinal changes to marriage and divorce, should be discouraged by the state.[73]

§ 3:6 Marital Torts

The ability of spouses to sue one another or a third person for the breakdown of a marriage is severely limited in Louisiana. Louisiana law prevents spouses from suing one another except in specifically enumerated situations.[74] A spouse may only sue the other spouse for: (1) causes of action pertaining to contracts or involving the matrimonial regime; (2) restitution of separate property;[75] (3) divorce or nullity of marriage; or

69. Sanders v. Gore, 95-660 (La. App. 3 Cir. 7/10/96), 676 So. 2d 866. Mrs. Sanders and Mr. Gore agreed to marry during the course of their three-year affair, while both were married to other people. *Id.* at 868. Mr. Gore represented Mrs. Sanders in her divorce from her husband of 21 years. *Id.* Mr. Gore proposed to Mrs. Sanders, but several months later told Mrs. Sanders that he was "too weak" to leave his wife and that their relationship was over. Sanders, 676 So. 2d at 868. Mrs. Sanders sought damages arising from the breach of the promise to marry, which included nonpecuniary losses, the cost of gifts given to him in contemplation of marriage, and the costs of remodeling her home to be their matrimonial domicile. *Id.* She also sought damages for intentional infliction of emotional distress. *Id.* at 868–69.

70. Sanders, 676 So. 2d at 873.

71. Sanders, 676 So. 2d at 875–78 (Yelverton, J., concurring in part and dissenting in part); *id.* at 881 (Cooks, J., dissenting).

72. Contracts with concubines are no longer against public policy, and a married paramour and a concubine can acquire real property as co-vendees. Sanders, 676 So. 2d at 877 (Yelverton, J., concurring in part and dissenting in part). Ultimately, Judge Yelverton concurred in the holding, finding that the institution of marriage should transcend the freedom of contract. *Id.* at 878.

73. Sanders, 676 So. 2d at 875. *See* Spaht, *supra* note 64, at 271, for a discussion of the *Sanders* case and its impact on marriage.

74. *See* La. Stat. Ann. § 9:291.

75. La. Stat. Ann. § 9:291; *see also* Eckhardt v. Reveley, 2004-0288, pp. 3–4 (La. App. 4 Cir. 7/21/04), 881 So. 2d 128, 130–31 (concluding that prescription on the restitution claim continued to accrue during the marriage and was not suspended); Heathcock v. Neuenhaus, 05-954, pp. 3–4 (La. App. 5 Cir. 4/25/06), 930 So. 2d 1013, 1014 (concluding that the wife could have filed suit against the husband during the marriage to recover money loaned pursuant to a promissory note); Hinds v. Hinds, 04-

(4) causes of action pertaining to spousal or child support or custody while the spouses are living separate and apart.[76] Although courts have described these four enumerated exceptions as exclusive, not illustrative,[77] the right to sue a spouse under domestic abuse laws, such as seeking a protective order[78] or damages caused by domestic abuse,[79] are nonetheless available.[80]

As a result, tort actions between spouses are unavailable until the spouses are divorced.[81] The cause of action that one spouse might have against the other is not destroyed by interspousal immunity; rather, once the spouses obtain a judgment of divorce, they are placed "in the same situation with respect to each other as if no marriage had ever been contracted between them."[82] Suits between spouses have been prohibited on the theory that a lawsuit would "disrupt domestic tranquility"; however, once the couple is divorced, the policy reasons for such immunity become moot.[83] Liberative prescription is thus suspended between the spouses during the marriage.[84]

While rare, Louisiana has recognized the tort of fraudulent inducement to marry.[85] Tort claims against third parties who contribute to the breakdown of the marriage, like alienation of affection or criminal conversation, have been eliminated in Louisiana, as has been the practice in most jurisdictions.[86]

1358, pp. 3–4 (La. App. 3 Cir. 3/9/05), 897 So. 2d 890, 892 (concluding that "'restitution of separate property' does not contemplate an eviction proceeding as it is inconsistent with the mutual duties of married persons and the interspousal immunity statute").

76. La. Stat. Ann. § 9:291; *see also* Robert C. Lowe, Louisiana Divorce § 5:18, *in* 1 Louisiana Practice Series 403–04 (2023).

77. Heathcock, 930 So. 2d at 1014.

78. La. Stat. Ann. §§ 46:2131 *et seq.*; La. Stat. Ann. §§ 9:361 *et seq.*

79. La. Civ. Code art. 2315.8.

80. La. Stat. Ann. § 9:291 cmt. (c).

81. *See* La. Stat. Ann. § 9:291 cmt. (d).

82. Duplechin v. Toce, 497 So. 2d 763, 765 (La. Ct. App. 3 Cir. 1987) (internal quotation marks omitted) (quoting Gremillion v. Caffey, 71 So. 2d 670, 674 (La. Ct. App. 1 Cir. 1954)).

83. Duplechin, 497 So. 2d at 765.

84. Duplechin, 497 So. 2d at 765.

85. *See* Section 3:7.

86. *See* Section 3:8. *See generally* Laura Belleau, *Farewell to Heart Balm Doctrines and the Tender Years Presumption, Hello to the Genderless Family*, 24 J. Am. Acad. Matrim. Law. 365 (2012). *But see* Rodriguez v. Lemus, 810 S.E.2d 1 (N.C. Ct. App. 2018) (retaining torts of alienation of affection and criminal conversation); Fitch v. Valentine, 959 So. 2d 1012 (Miss. 2007) (retaining tort of alienation of affection).

§ 3:7 Marital Torts— Fraudulent Inducement to Marry

Although acts of fraud by one party to induce another to marry will not provide the basis for annulment of the marriage, the wronged party may have a claim in tort. At least one Louisiana court has permitted a spouse to seek damages as a result of the other spouse's fraud in inducing her to marry knowing that the marriage would be null. In *Holcomb v. Kincaid*, Mr. Kincaid married Ms. Holcomb before receiving a final judgment of divorce from his first wife.[87] The divorce was finalized two weeks after the null marriage, but he concealed this fact until Ms. Holcomb filed for divorce 12 years later. She sought damages for embarrassment, humiliation, mental suffering, lost wages, and retirement pay. As the claim of fraudulent inducement to marry was *res nova* in Louisiana, the court considered decisions from other jurisdictions.[88] It concluded that nothing in the Civil Code prevented recognition of the claim under the general tort principle found in article 2315.[89] The holding was limited, however, to the instance where one person fraudulently induced the other person to enter into a null marriage.

Whether the claim of fraudulent inducement to marry could be extended to cases in which one spouse induced the other to marry based on a misrepresentation essential to the marriage contract is unclear. Although the *Holcomb* court's holding was limited, it opened the door to additional claims under the general principles of tort law.[90] However, because Louisiana does not permit annulment or divorce based on fraud surrounding the essentials of the marriage contract,[91] it is unlikely that a court would extend tort liability to cover acts between spouses that would fail to nullify the marriage or result in divorce. Even in *Bhati v. Bhati*, a case in which a woman sued her ex-husband for damages on the basis of his bigamy that she discovered post-divorce, the court did not allow recovery.[92] It affirmed the trial court's grant of the ex-husband's summary judgment motion, explaining that article 96, which grants civil effects to good faith spouses, provides the exclusive remedy for damages in the context of a putative marriage.

---

87. Holcomb v. Kincaid, 406 So. 2d 650 (La. Ct. App. 2 Cir. 1981).

88. Holcomb, 406 So. 2d at 651.

89. Holcomb, 406 So. 2d at 652.

90. Other jurisdictions have extended this claim. *See, e.g.*, Miller v. Miller, 956 P.2d 887 (Okla. 1998) (permitting suit for fraudulent inducement to marry based on misrepresentations that plaintiff was the father of her unborn child); Humphreys v. Baird, 90 S.E.2d 796 (Va. 1956) (finding for plaintiff after defendant induced plaintiff to leave employment and enter into marriage while defendant was married to another woman).

91. Some states permit annulment if the fraud relates to an essential element of the marital relationship, such as pregnancy by another man or impotence. *See, e.g.*, Miss. Code Ann. § 93-7-3 (West, Westlaw through 2023 Legis. Sess.); N.C. Gen. Stat. § 51-3 (West, Westlaw through S.L. 2023-133). Of those states that permit a claim for fraudulent inducement to marry, grounds for annulment or divorce based on fraud also exist. *See, e.g.*, Tenn. Code Ann. § 36-4-101 (West, Westlaw through 2023 Legis. Sess.).

92. Bhati v. Bhati, 103 So. 3d 1290, 1291–92 (La. App. 3 Cir. 2012).

§ 3:8 Marital Torts—Other Heart Balm Actions

Louisiana courts have considered and rejected other heart balm actions for alienation of affection, seduction, criminal conversation, and intentional and negligent infliction of emotional distress, all of which arise as a result of a sexual relationship between a spouse and a third party. The Louisiana Supreme Court first considered such a claim in *Moulin v. Monteleone* in 1927.[93] The court rejected alienation of affection as a valid claim in Louisiana because the remedy is punitive and not authorized by the civil law.[94] It further noted that the concept originated as a common-law remedy based on the obsolete idea that the wife was the chattel of the husband.[95] The court explained that no person has a property right in the affections of another.[96]

Mindful that the state of the law and society have developed, courts have continued to reject alienation claims, explaining: "The mere seduction and loss of one's spouse due to the seduction or affair cannot be the basis for the action. There must be proof that defendant violated some legal duty to plaintiff, so that plaintiff is in fact the victim and not just the jilted party."[97] As a result, plaintiffs began to assert the torts of intentional and negligent infliction of emotional distress, urging that the claim is distinguishable from the alienation cause of action.

Undoubtedly, the claim for infliction of emotional distress, whether negligent or intentional, has been successful in non-marital situations.[98] But, emotional distress based on allegations of adultery alone has not sufficed to recover damages; the claim would simply be an alienation of affection claim in disguise.[99] Therefore, courts have explained that when suing the paramour for emotional distress caused by the breakdown of a marriage, the plaintiff must prove not only that the extreme and outrageous conduct of the paramour caused severe emotional distress, which the defendant desired or knew would be substantially certain to follow from his conduct, but also that the paramour violated some legal duty to the plaintiff.[100] In every instance in which the tort has been raised, however, the plaintiff has been unsuccessful in pleading facts to show the breach of a legal duty necessary to survive an exception of no cause of action.[101]

93. Moulin v. Monteleone, 115 So. 447 (La. 1927).

94. Moulin, 115 So. at 448–49.

95. Moulin, 115 So. at 450.

96. Moulin, 115 So. at 451.

97. *See* Scamardo v. Dunaway, 94-545, p. 8 (La. App. 5 Cir. 2/15/95), 650 So. 2d 417, 420; *see also* Greene v. Roy, 604 So. 2d 1359, 1362 (La. Ct. App. 3 Cir. 1992) (recognizing that the law in Louisiana has rejected any cause of action by a spouse for the intentional alienation of the other spouse's affection).

98. Scamardo, 650 So. 2d at 420–21.

99. *See generally* Moulin, 115 So. 447; Butler v. Reader, 573 So. 2d 1159 (La. Ct. App. 5 Cir. 1991). *See also* Price v. Fuerst, 09-545, p. 2 (La. App. 3 Cir. 11/4/09), 24 So. 3d 289, 290; Scamardo, 650 So. 2d at 420.

100. Scamardo, 650 So. 2d at 420–21; Greene, 604 So. 2d at 1363–64.

101. *See* Price, 24 So. 3d at 290 (dismissing claim for intentional infliction of emotional distress when it was based solely on an allegation of an extramarital affair between the plaintiff's wife and her

The only case in which a breach of duty may have been present involved an affair between a judge and a spouse.[102] In *Viator v. Miller*, after divorcing his wife, the husband learned that she had been having a decade-long affair with her boss, who was also a judge.[103] The judge had presided over their divorce and had ordered the husband to pay child support for a child who was born during the marriage and could have been the biological child of the judge.[104] The husband sued the judge, alleging various tort theories of recovery, including intentional infliction of emotional distress.[105] The court explained that any damages that arose from the sexual relationship between the wife and the judge were not recoverable, but that a claim may exist if the judge breached a duty when he knowingly rendered a judgment against the husband for child support of a child that the judge believed to be his.[106] Had he known, the husband could have disavowed the child at the time of the divorce proceeding, but he did not.

The court considered whether Louisiana would recognize a claim for emotional distress due to "misrepresented paternity," and concluded that the decision could wait for another day.[107] As no paternity test had been performed to determine whether the husband or the judge was the father of the child, the court remanded the matter to allow the husband to establish the paternity of the child.[108] Regardless of the ultimate outcome, parties can rest assured that a claim for intentional or negligent infliction of emotional distress will not survive based on the underlying fact of adultery; some breach of duty must be present before a court will consider granting relief.[109]

---

lawyer); Viator v. Miller, 2004-1199, pp. 8–9 (La. App. 3 Cir. 4/27/05), 900 So. 2d 1135, 1142 (finding that plaintiff was unable to allege facts sufficient to support a claim for intentional or negligent infliction of emotional distress in connection with his wife's affair with a judge for whom she worked); Scamardo v. Dunaway, 96-1036, pp. 3–4 (La. App. 5 Cir. 4/29/97), 694 So. 2d 1041, 1042 (dismissing action because plaintiff failed to allege facts sufficient to meet the heightened burden after the court permitted the plaintiff to amend his petition); Greene, 604 So. 2d at 1364 (implicitly recognizing the claim for intentional infliction of emotional distress but ultimately dismissing the plaintiff's claim because the plaintiff failed to allege facts to show intent to cause emotional distress).

102. Viator, 900 So. 2d at 1142.

103. Viator, 900 So. 2d at 1138.

104. Viator, 900 So. 2d at 1138.

105. Viator, 900 So. 2d at 1138.

106. Viator, 900 So. 2d at 1142–43.

107. Viator, 900 So. 2d at 1144–45.

108. Viator, 900 So. 2d at 1146.

109. *See generally* Price v. Fuerst, 09-545 (La. App. 3 Cir. 11/4/09), 24 So. 3d 289; Viator, 900 So. 2d at 1135; Scamardo, 694 So. 2d at 1041; Greene, 604 So. 2d at 1359.

§ 3:9 Proof of Marriage

One who claims benefits from a marriage has the burden of establishing that the marriage existed; once a marriage is shown to exist, the burden then shifts to those who object to its validity.[110] The fact of marriage can be proven through direct and circumstantial evidence.[111] Marriage is presumed when spouses live together and have a general and consistent reputation in the community of being married.[112] While illicit cohabitation and blatant disregard for the strictures of marriage will not be tolerated, the law supports recognizing marriages when circumstances suggest that the prerequisites have been met. This presumption, however, can be overcome by positive testimony that, notwithstanding cohabitation and the birth of children, no marriage ceremony took place.[113]

§ 3:10 Absence of a Legal Impediment

As do all 50 states, Louisiana prohibits certain persons from entering into a marriage. Those who are already married, those who are too closely related, and certain minors cannot validly contract marriage in Louisiana.[114] Louisiana also prohibited the marriage of same-sex couples until 2015 when the United States Supreme Court struck down state marriage bans.[115] Same-sex marriage is now permitted in Louisiana, notwithstanding the language in the Civil Code to the contrary.[116]

---

110. Succession of Giordano, 194 So. 577, 578 (La. 1940). *See generally* Gaines v. City of New Orleans, 73 U.S. 642 (1867).

111. Mazzei v. Gruis, 55 So. 555, 556 (La. 1911).

112. *See, e.g.*, Succession of Tyson, 172 So. 772, 777 (La. 1937); Douglas v. Shepard, 193 So. 264, 266 (La. Ct. App. 2 Cir. 1939); Howard v. Ingle, 180 So. 248, 251 (La. Ct. App. 2 Cir. 1938); Cunningham v. Jordan Drilling Co., 138 So. 689, 690 (La. Ct. App. 2 Cir. 1932).

113. *See generally* Honore v. Jones, 156 So. 191 (La. 1934) (parties admitted they had no marriage ceremony and no mutual agreement to marry under the common-law marriage statute of Texas); Succession of Dotson, 11 So. 2d 488 (La. 1942) (denying existence of marriage even though parties lived together and had four children because wife produced insufficient evidence to show that a marriage ceremony took place, and she subsequently married another man without trying to get a divorce). *See also* Eames v. Woodson, 46 So. 13 (La. 1908); Succession of Hubee, 20 La. Ann. 97 (1868); Succession of Stiles, 11 Teiss. 208 (La. Ct. App. 1914).

114. La. Civ. Code Ann. arts. 88, 90, 90.1. *See* Sections 3:11–3:13.

115. *See* Section 3:3.

116. *See* La. Civ. Code Ann. art. 89, editor's note; Robicheaux v. Caldwell, 791 F.3d 616, 618–19 (5th Cir. 2015).

§ 3:11 Absence of a Legal Impediment— Prior Marriage

"A married person may not contract another marriage."[117] A marriage with a person who is already married is absolutely null. It cannot be ratified even after the prior marriage is dissolved, and it can be attacked collaterally or directly, by the parties or any interested person.[118] Because the bigamous marriage is null from its inception, the non-bigamous party may enter into a valid marriage immediately without having the bigamous marriage declared null.[119] A party who enters into a bigamous union under the good faith belief that neither party is already married may be entitled to the civil effects of a valid marriage under the putative marriage doctrine.[120]

A marriage is terminated by death, divorce, a judicial declaration of nullity, or a court order authorizing the spouse of a person presumed dead to remarry.[121] Therefore, if one spouse's marriage has not been properly terminated, any subsequent marriage is null.[122] A divorce is not final until the signing of the judgment, so any subsequent marriage is null if entered into before the divorce judgment is signed.[123]

A relatively null marriage produces civil effects until a declaration of nullity is obtained, so a final judgment of nullity is necessary to terminate the marriage and remove any legal impediment to a subsequent marriage.[124] A marriage can also be terminated by a doctor's certification of death[125] or by a judicial declaration of death,[126] either of which will permit a subsequent, valid marriage. The court order authorizing the person whose spouse is presumed dead to remarry applies only to persons on active duty in the military who are presumed dead.[127]

---

117. La. Civ. Code Ann. art. 88. Under prior law, if a party guilty of adultery married the accomplice in adultery, the new marriage could be declared an absolute nullity. *See* Rhodes v. Miller, 179 So. 430, 431–32 (La. 1938) (citing old Louisiana Civil Code Article 161, which was repealed in 1990).

118. La. Civ. Code Ann. art. 88 cmt. (b). Parol evidence is permitted to prove a prior undissolved marriage. *See* Oliphant v. La. Long Leaf Lumber Co., 112 So. 500, 502 (La. 1927).

119. La. Civ. Code Ann. art. 88 cmt. (c).

120. La. Civ. Code Ann. art. 96; *see also* Section 3:22.

121. La. Civ. Code Ann. art. 101.

122. Putative spouse status can be given to the good faith spouse. La. Civ. Code Ann. art. 96; *see generally* Galbraith v. Galbraith, 396 So. 2d 1364 (La. Ct. App. 2 Cir. 1981) (marriage one day before divorce judgment was signed was invalid but parties were in good faith); Farrell v. Farrell, 275 So. 2d 489 (La. Ct. App. 1 Cir. 1973) (divorce rendered in open court but not signed until two years later, after spouse contracted another marriage); Bhati v. Bhati, 12-707 (La. App. 3 Cir. 12/5/12), 103 So. 3d 1290 (ex-wife could not obtain damages for ex-husband's bigamy because she had already been compensated for a marriage that was never legally perfected).

123. Note that an appeal from a judgment granting or denying a divorce suspends the execution of the judgment. La. Code Civ. Proc. Ann. art. 3942.

124. La. Civ. Code Ann. art. 97.

125. *See* La. Stat. Ann. § 9:111.

126. *See* La. Civ. Code Ann. arts. 30, 54; La. Stat. Ann. § 9:301; *see also* La. Stat. Ann. § 9:1441.

127. La. Stat. Ann. §§ 9:301, :1441.

§ 3:12 Absence of a Legal Impediment— Too Closely Related

Parties who are too closely related, as defined by law, are not permitted to marry. Ascendants and descendants may not marry one another, and collateral relations within the fourth degree,[128] whether related by the whole or half blood, may not marry.[129] This prohibition applies whether the persons are related by blood or by adoption.[130] Therefore, parents and grandparents cannot marry children or grandchildren, siblings cannot marry siblings, aunts and uncles cannot marry nephews or nieces, and first cousins cannot validly contract marriage in Louisiana.[131]

Relationship prohibitions on marriage stem from scientific and moral objections, but these objections become more attenuated when the parties are related only by adoption.[132] A court in Louisiana can therefore authorize the marriage of collateral relations within the fourth degree if they are unrelated by blood and legally related only by adoption.[133] When hearing the request, courts consider whether family harmony will be preserved or impeded by the union.[134] For example, if a parent adopted an unrelated, orphaned boyfriend or girlfriend of one of their own children to provide care and ensure health insurance coverage for that child, the two children would be related as siblings by adoption. A court could permit the two, related by adoption only, to wed if family harmony would be preserved.[135]

Even though prohibited under Louisiana law, at least one court has recognized a marriage between first cousins validly contracted in a jurisdiction that permits marriages between first cousins.[136] Additionally, by special legislation, Louisiana also recognizes marriages between collaterals "within the fourth degree" who are 55 years of age or older and whose marriage was entered into on or before December 31, 1992.[137] Act 7 of 1993 explained that the legislation sought to legalize "collaterals *in* the fourth

128. Article 901 of the Civil Code describes how to count degrees in the collateral line: "In the collateral line, the number of degrees is equal to the number of generations between the heir and the common ancestor, plus the number of generations between the common ancestor and the deceased." La. Civ. Code Ann. art. 901.

129. La. Civ. Code Ann. art. 90. Marriages between collaterals entered into before September 11, 1981 are legal. La. Civ. Code Ann. art. 90 cmt. (b); *see also* Act No. 886, 1987 La. Acts 2438.

130. La. Civ. Code Ann. art. 90(B).

131. *See* La. Civ. Code Ann. art. 90; State v. Guiton, 24 So. 784, 785 (La. 1898) (holding that a half-niece was within the prohibited degrees of kinship).

132. La. Civ. Code Ann. art. 90(B).

133. La. Civ. Code Ann. art. 90(B).

134. La. Civ. Code Ann. art. 90 cmt. (e).

135. La. Civ. Code Ann. art. 90 cmt. (e); *see also* Israel v. Allen, 577 P.2d 762, 765 (Colo. 1978) (finding state statute that prohibited marriage between a brother and a sister related by adoption to be unconstitutional); State ex rel. Miesner v. Geile, 747 S.W.2d 757, 758 (Mo. Ct. App. 1988) (permitting uncle and niece related only by adoption to marry).

136. *See* Ghassemi v. Ghassemi, 2007-1927 (La. App. 1 Cir. 10/15/08), 998 So. 2d 731; *see also* Section 3:24.

137. La. Stat. Ann. § 9:211.

degree" and the title of the section provides that it applies to "Relations *of* the fourth degree."[138] Although the text of the section permits marriage between collaterals "*within* the fourth degree," it was likely intended to permit marriages only between first cousins after the spouses exceeded child-birthing age.[139] Given Louisiana's longstanding laws on marriage and its criminal law on incest,[140] marriages between second- or third-degree collateral relations related by blood, no matter when contracted, would not be permitted.

Notably absent from the law is a prohibition when the parties are related only by marriage. For example, after the marriage to a blood or adopted relative has ended, former spouses of parents or grandparents can marry stepchildren or step-grandchildren. In other words, former stepparents can marry their former stepchildren. Additionally, within the collateral line, former spouses can marry former in-laws within what could be considered prohibited degrees of kinship, such as former sisters- and brothers-in-law, aunts and uncles, and first cousins related only by marriage. Moreover, even during the marriage of their parents, children from each spouse's prior relationship (i.e., un-adopted stepchildren) can marry, because they are not related by blood or adoption.

§ 3:13 Absence of a Legal Impediment—Underage (Legal Impediment)

In 2019, the Louisiana Legislature added an additional impediment to marriage—the impediment of age. Prior to 2019, minors under the age of 18 were unable to contract a valid marriage without parental or judicial consent, but it was unclear whether a marriage entered into by a minor was absolutely null, relatively null, or valid as long as the minor had general legal capacity. By Act 401 of 2019, minors under the age of 16 can no longer contract marriage, even with parental consent.[141] Further, minors who are 16 or 17 cannot contract marriage with a person of the age of majority when there is an age difference of three or more years between the two.[142] In other words, a 16-year-old cannot marry a 20-year-old, as the age difference creates a legal impediment.

For minors who are 16 or 17 and marry someone less than three years their senior, it remains unclear whether the marriage is relatively null or is valid as long as the minor had general legal capacity. What is clear, though, is that marriages of minors under the

---

138. Act No. 7, 1993 La. Acts 9 (emphasis added).

139. Act No. 7, 1993 La. Acts 9 (emphasis added).

140. La. Stat. Ann. § 14:89. Crime against nature, or incest, is:

> The marriage to, or sexual intercourse with, any ascendant or descendant, brother or sister, uncle or niece, aunt or nephew, with knowledge of their relationship. The relationship must be by consanguinity, but it is immaterial whether the parties to the act are related to one another by the whole or half blood.

La. Stat. Ann. § 14:89. The crime is punishable by imprisonment and fines. *See id.*

141. La. Civ. Code Ann. art. 90.1.

142. La. Civ. Code Ann. art. 90.1.

age of 16 or of minors 16 or 17 who marry someone three or more years their senior are absolutely null.[143]

§ 3:14 Ceremony

Parties must express their consent to marry at a ceremony in front of a third-party officiant.[144] Louisiana does not permit parties to create a common-law marriage in the state,[145] although courts will recognize a common-law marriage validly entered into in another state.[146] There are several ceremonial formalities that the parties and the officiant must meet, some of which are mandatory, and others, although technically required, will not invalidate the marriage if missing. The mandatory provisions of marriage are found in the Civil Code, and those requirements that do not affect the validity of marriage are found in the Revised Statutes.

§ 3:15 Ceremony— Mandatory Formalities

The mandatory formalities for a valid ceremony are two-fold: (1) the parties must be physically present at a ceremony, and (2) the ceremony must be conducted by a third-party officiant who is qualified or who the parties reasonably believe to be qualified.[147] If no ceremony is held or if these mandatory formalities are not met, the marriage is absolutely null.[148]

First, "a marriage may not be contracted by procuration."[149] Neither party can be absent from the ceremony, and no representative can stand in to represent a party.[150] Therefore, marriage over internet channels or by closed-circuit television is not permitted. By observing both parties expressly consenting to marry, the officiant ensures that the third requirement of marriage—free consent of the parties—is met.[151] Although impermissible if contracted in Louisiana, a marriage by procuration has been validated by courts when the marriage was valid under the laws of the state or country where celebrated. For example, Louisiana courts validated the marriage of a couple by proxy

---

143. La. Civ. Code Ann. art. 90.1.

144. La. Civ. Code Ann. art. 91.

145. *See generally* Succession of Marinoni, 148 So. 888 (La. 1933); Clements v. Folse ex rel. Succession of Clements, 2001-1970 (La. App. 1 Cir. 8/14/02), 830 So. 2d 307; State v. Williams, 96-652 (La. App. 3 Cir. 2/5/97), 688 So. 2d 1277; Liberty Mut. Ins. Co. v. Caesar, 345 So. 2d 64 (La. Ct. App. 3 Cir. 1977).

146. Brinson v. Brinson, 96 So. 2d 653, 660 (La. 1957); *see also* Section 3:42.

147. *See* La. Civ. Code Ann. arts. 91–92; *see also* La Civ. Code Ann. art. 92 cmt. (b).

148. La. Civ. Code Ann. art. 94.

149. La. Civ. Code Ann. art. 92.

150. *See* La. Civ. Code Ann. art. 92 cmt. (b).

151. La. Civ. Code Ann. art. 92 cmt. (b). For an interesting discussion on allowing marriage by procuration, *see generally* Andrea B. Carroll, *Reviving Proxy Marriage*, 76 Brook. L. Rev. 455 (2011).

under Texas law while the husband was in prison,[152] as well as the marriage of a couple by proxy under Turkish law while one spouse remained in Louisiana.[153]

Second, the ceremony must be performed by a third-party officiant who is qualified or reasonably believed by the parties to be qualified.[154] To be qualified to perform the marriage ceremony, the person must be a state judge, a state justice of the peace, or a clergyman of any religious sect who is authorized by the religion to perform marriages.[155] State judges and justices of the peace have specific territorial limitations, which are generally tied to the jurisdiction of the court,[156] and religious leaders must register with the clerk of court before performing the ceremony.[157] Judges of the courts of the United States are not generally authorized to perform marriages in Louisiana. Several specific provisions of law, however, have given federal judges limited authority to perform marriages during specified time frames.[158] As the time frames set forth in these provisions have long passed, these provisions should be repealed.

Even if the officiant is not qualified to perform the marriage ceremony, the ceremonial requirement can be met if the parties "reasonably believe" that the officiant is qualified.[159] The parties may reasonably believe that any member of the class of persons generally recognized as having the authorization to perform marriage ceremonies is qualified, whether or not properly registered to do so.[160] Reliance on a reasonable belief will prevent the invalidity of marriages for reasons beyond the control of the parties.[161] Parties necessarily have a reasonable belief that religious leaders, whether authorized by their religion or registered with the state, will be qualified. Friends and family, not otherwise authorized or ordained to perform ceremonies, do not qualify as valid officiants and are unlikely to be believed to be qualified by the soon-to-be spouses.

Proof that an authorized officiant performed a ceremony can be established through documentary evidence, such as the marriage license or marriage certificate, and through the testimony of witnesses. In the absence of evidence of a ceremony, marriages have nevertheless been validated based solely on documentary evidence of the

152. *See* Morris v. Morris, No. 2009-2069, 2010 WL 2342659, at *2 (La. App. 1 Cir. 6/11/10).

153. United States ex rel. Modianos v. Tuttle, 12 F.2d 927, 929 (E.D. La. 1925); *see also* La. Att'y Gen. Op. No. 1950–52, pp. 108–09 (1950); *see* Section 3:42.

154. La. Civ. Code Ann. art. 91.

155. La. Stat. Ann. § 9:202. Clergy includes, but is not limited to, priests, ministers, rabbis, and clerks of the Religious Society of Friends. La. Stat. Ann. § 9:202(1).

156. *See* La. Stat. Ann. § 9:203. For example, a justice of the Louisiana Supreme Court can perform marriage ceremonies within the state, while a judge of a district court can only perform marriages within the district.

157. La. Stat. Ann. §§ 9:202, 204. The religious leader must supply "an affidavit stating his or her lawful name, denomination, and address." La. Stat. Ann. § 9:204. The affidavit must be deposited with the clerk of court of the parish where the religious leader "will principally perform marriage ceremonies, or, in the case of Orleans Parish, with the office of the registrar of vital records." *Id.*

158. La. Stat. Ann. § 9:203(E); *see also* La. Stat. Ann. §§ 9:202, :204.

159. La. Civ. Code Ann. art. 91.

160. La. Civ. Code Ann. art. 91 cmt. (c).

161. La. Civ. Code Ann. art. 91 cmt. (c).

marriage license, proof of cohabitation, and the contents of a subsequent marriage license indicating that the parties had been divorced.[162] To the contrary, proof of an unofficial ceremony that fails to meet the prerequisites of law, even if followed by long cohabitation and the birth of several children, will not result in a valid marriage.[163]

§ 3:16 Ceremony— Other Ceremonial Formalities

The law requires the parties to meet other ceremonial formalities, none of which, if absent, will render the marriage null.[164] For example, Louisiana law requires the parties to obtain a marriage license,[165] but a marriage without a marriage license is still valid.[166] If the parties intend to enter into a covenant marriage, the application for the marriage license must include a declaration of their intent, but a marriage without the declaration, while not a covenant marriage, is still a valid marriage.[167] If a minor age 16 or 17 seeks to marry, the application must include written consent of the minor's parents, tutor, or custodian, and the juvenile court.[168] An officiant who knowingly performs a ceremony of a minor when the officiant does not have the necessary consent and authorization will be permanently deprived of his right to perform future marriage ceremonies,[169] but the marriage may still be valid.[170]

---

162. *See* Allen v. Allen, 254 So. 2d 489, 490 (La. Ct. App. 3 Cir. 1971).

163. Sesostris Youchican v. Texas & P. Ry. Co., 86 So. 551, 552 (La. 1920) (finding that a marriage ceremony performed in accordance with Native American tribe custom was not recognized in Louisiana); *see also* Succession of Cusimano, 138 So. 95, 96 (La. 1931) (finding that the lack of a marriage ceremony resulted in an invalid marriage).

164. La. Civ. Code Ann. art. 91 cmt. (a).

165. La. Stat. Ann. § 9:205. Specific provisions provide the details governing marriage licenses. *See generally* La. Stat. Ann. §§ 9:221–:228. The license is valid for thirty days from the date it was issued. La. Stat. Ann. § 9:235. The license can be reissued if the parties surrender the expired license to the issuing official. La. Stat. Ann. § 9:236. A medical certificate is no longer required to obtain the license. La. Stat. Ann. §§ 9:229–:233 (repealed 1988) (medical certificates containing proof of blood tests were required to screen for venereal disease and HIV/AIDS). After the acceptance of same-sex marriage in Louisiana, the application for a marriage license was changed to allow applicants to choose "bride," "groom," or "spouse," at their option. La. Stat. Ann. §§ 9:245, 40:55. *See* Application for Marriage License: State of Louisiana, Orleans Parish, La. Dep't Health, http://ldh.la.gov/assets/oph/Center-RS/vitalrec/OrleansMarriageApplication.pdf (last visited Jan. 5, 2024), for a current version of the application for marriage.

166. La. Civ. Code Ann. art. 91 cmt. (a); Succession of Jene, 173 So. 2d 857, 861 (La. Ct. App. 4 Cir. 1965).

167. La. Stat. Ann. § 9:224(C).

168. *See* La. Stat. Ann. § 9:225(A)(2); La. Child. Code Ann. art. 1545.

169. La. Child. Code Ann. art. 1550.

170. The marriage of a 16- or 17-year-old minor may be relatively null because the minor lacks consent to contract marriage, but only the minor can seek to have the marriage annulled. *See* Delpit v. Young, 25 So. 547, 548 (La. 1899). Ultimately, the minor can confirm the relatively null marriage after reaching the age of majority. La. Civ. Code art. 95; *see also* Section 3:19.

The officiant is instructed not to perform the ceremony until he has received a license authorizing him to do so[171] and 24 hours have passed since the license was issued.[172] This delay may be waived by any judge or justice of the peace, or any authorized officiant in Orleans Parish for nonresident parties, upon application of the parties giving serious and meritorious reasons for the waiver.[173] Any person can file an opposition to a marriage, which can result in a hearing if the person presents a sufficient reason to suspend the permission to marry.[174]

Present at the marriage ceremony must be two competent witnesses of full age, who must sign the marriage certificate with the parties and the officiant.[175] Ultimately, marriage licenses and certificates are held by the Office of the State Registrar and Vital Records and by the entity that issued the marriage license.[176]

Courts have consistently validated marriages when a technical requirement has been unmet.[177] Failing to meet a combination of these technical requirements, with knowledge of the law and blatant disregard thereof, however, may cause a court to invalidate an otherwise valid marriage. In *Malek v. Yekani-Fard*, a couple married in the Islamic Center of New Orleans without obtaining a marriage license or a medical certificate.[178] Two weeks later, the woman married another man to obtain a "green card" to allow her to work legally in the state.[179] Prior to both alleged marriages, the woman had called the clerk of court's office and learned of the necessary prerequisites for a valid marriage.[180] The court found the first marriage to be invalid, explaining that

---

171. La. Stat. Ann. § 9:205.

172. La. Stat. Ann. § 9:241. Prior law required a 72-hour delay. La. Stat. Ann. § 9:241 (1988). *But see* In re State ex rel. Goodwin, 39 So. 2d 731, 733 (La. 1949) (finding marriage that was in violation of the 72-hour delay valid).

173. La. Stat. Ann. § 9:242. Any violation of the delay, without a valid waiver, may result in revocation of the officiant's authority to perform marriage ceremonies. La. Stat. Ann. § 9:243.

174. *See* La. Stat. Ann. §§ 9:261–:263.

175. *See* La. Stat. Ann. §§ 9:244–:245. *But see* Tennison v. Nevels, 2006-2124, p. 2 (La. App. 1 Cir. 6/8/07), 965 So. 2d 425 (finding that marriage of parties with witnesses who were minors was valid); Parker v. Saileau, 213 So. 2d 190, 192 (La. Ct. App. 3 Cir. 1968) (finding that marriage without the proper number of witnesses and in violation of the delay was valid); Russell v. Taglialavore, 153 So. 44 (La. Ct. App. 2 Cir. 1934) (finding that marriage with only one of three witnesses who signed act of celebration was valid).

176. La. Stat. Ann. §§ 9:251–:256. Penalties are imposed for failure to complete marriage certificates or falsifying information on the license or certificate. La. Stat. Ann. §§ 9:254, :256.

177. *See, e.g.*, Tennison, 965 So. 2d at 427 (validating marriage even though witnesses were minors); Parker, 213 So. 2d at 192 (validating marriage even though number of witnesses was improper and delay was not honored); Landry v. Bellanger, 45 So. 956 (La. 1908) (validating marriage even though there was no license and the proper number of witnesses were not present); Clemons v. Diable, 2022-0493 (La. App. 1 Cir. 01/10/23), 2023 WL 142549 at *5–6 (validating marriage even though marriage license was not filed and holding that "[t]here is no Louisiana statute, nor any jurisprudence, which states that an exchange of vows and/or rings is a requirement for a valid marriage.").

178. Malek v. Yekani-Fard, 451 So. 2d 669, 671–72 (La. Ct. App. 1 Cir. 1984). A medical certificate is no longer required to obtain a marriage license. La. Stat. Ann. §§ 9:229–:233 (repealed 1988).

179. Malek, 451 So. 2d at 672.

180. Malek, 451 So. 2d at 672–73.

"[a]lthough the failure to follow every formal requirement for a valid marriage does not necessarily invalidate it, ... no attempt was made to follow any of the forms or solemnities prescribed by law."[181]

§ 3:17 Consent

As in any contract, the parties to a marriage must freely consent to wed.[182] "Consent is not free when given under duress or when given by a person incapable of discernment."[183] Under prior law, consent was also not free when there was a "mistake respecting the person."[184] "Mistake respecting the person" was interpreted to mean a mistake in the physical identity of a person,[185] rather than in the qualities of the person, and in the revision of 1987, was eliminated as obsolete.[186]

While error and fraud are vices of consent under general contract law, they do not appear in the Civil Code under marriage.[187] Only duress and incapacity of discernment are included in the Civil Code as vices that can vitiate a marriage contract under Lou-

---

181. Malek, 451 So. 2d at 672–73.

182. *See* La. Civ. Code Ann. art. 2031.

183. La. Civ. Code Ann. art. 93.

184. La. Civ. Code art. 91 (1825).

185. *See* Verneuille v. Verneuille, 438 So. 2d 615, 617 (La. Ct. App. 4 Cir. 1983) (concluding that an annulment was inappropriate because "mistake respecting the person" did not include a circumstance when a man married a woman based on her false statement that she was carrying his child). *See generally* Delpit v. Young, 25 So. 547 (La. 1899).

186. Act No. 886, 1987 La. Acts 2409. Marriage where one partner has had sex reassignment surgery raises a potential issue in the context of consent to marry if the sex reassignment surgery was never disclosed to the other partner. Under Louisiana law, a new birth certificate can be issued to a transgender individual once sex reassignment surgery is complete. *See* La. Stat. Ann. § 40:62. Whether the partner who marries a transgender person without knowledge of the sex reassignment can have the marriage annulled based on error has been left unanswered. Error is no longer expressly included as a vice of consent for marriage, as prior laws' provisions regarding "mistake respecting the person" were eliminated and rendered obsolete; today, those obsolete provisions could be reinvented in the context of error to annul a marriage when the gender of a party has changed. No Louisiana court has yet to consider the issue.

187. La. Civ. Code Ann. art. 93. *But see* Katherine Shaw Spaht, *Revision of the Law of Marriage: One Baby Step Forward*, 48 La. L. Rev. 1131, 1145 (1988) (arguing that Civil Code Article 93 does not declare that the reasons for defective consent are exclusive and the general articles on error could be applied). Prior to the revision in 1987, consent was vitiated when there was a "mistake respecting the person." *See* La. Civ. Code Ann. art. 91 (repealed and reenacted by Act 886 of 1987). This phrase was interpreted by the courts narrowly to mean mistake regarding the physical identity of the person and was suppressed in the revision as unnecessary. *See generally* Delpit, 25 So. 547. If a party's consent was affected by a true mistake involving the physical identity of the person, the general articles on error should permit annulment of the marriage. *See* Katherine Shaw Spaht, *Revision of the Law of Marriage: One Baby Step Forward*, 48 La. L. Rev. 1131, 1145 (1988); *see also* Emily Latham, Comment, *Recognizing Error and Fraud in the Contract of Marriage in Louisiana*, 66 La. L. Rev. 563 (2006) (discussing vices of consent in a marriage context and arguing that error and fraud should be included as grounds for annulment of marriage).

isiana law.[188] The Civil Code articles on conventional obligations provide the specifics on duress,[189] which can be applied in the marriage context.

§ 3:18 Consent— Duress and Incapacity of Discernment

Duress is defined in the articles on conventional obligations and includes "a reasonable fear of unjust and considerable injury to a party's person, property, or reputation."[190] To determine whether the fear is reasonable, courts must consider the age, health, disposition, and other personal circumstances of the party claiming duress.[191] Duress includes both executed and threatened violence, provided "the threat is pending at the time consent is given."[192] Threats need not only be directed against the party to the marriage; duress can also occur when threats are directed against an ascendant or descendant of the party.[193] Threats of criminal prosecution may likewise amount to duress if the charges are not warranted by the facts.[194] If, however, the threatened charges are warranted by the facts, duress may not be found.[195] For example, if a man consented to marry a woman because her parent threatened to tell the authorities that he was guilty of the rape of his daughter, the man would be acting under duress if the rape had no basis in fact. Conversely, if the man had sex with the under-aged daughter, the father's alleged threats would be based in fact because of his daughter's age and the criminal laws on rape;[196] in such a case, consent to marry would be unaffected by duress.

Beyond duress, a person who is incapable of discernment cannot freely consent.[197] A person incapable of discernment may include one who suffers from a mental infirmity, is under the influence of alcohol or drugs, or is too young to understand the consequences of the marriage.[198] Ignorance of the law is not enough to render consent unfree, but insanity may be.[199] "Too young to understand the consequences of marriage" contemplates the age to marry, which is discussed in the following section.

---

188. *See* La. Civ. Code Ann. art. 1959.

189. La. Civ. Code Ann. arts. 1959–1963.

190. La. Civ. Code Ann. arts. 1959–1963; *see also* La. Civ. Code Ann. art. 93 cmt. (b) ("Threats to reputation or fortune might be sufficient to invalidate a marriage under this Article.").

191. La. Civ. Code Ann. art. 1959.

192. La. Civ. Code Ann. art. 93 cmt. (b); *see also* Quealy v. Waldron, 52 So. 479, 480 (La. 1910).

193. La. Civ. Code Ann. art. 1960. The court has discretion to consider threatened injury to persons other than ascendants or descendants. *Id. See generally* Lacoste v. Guidroz, 16 So. 836 (La. 1985).

194. *See* La. Civ. Code Ann. art. 1962. *See generally* Grundmeyer v. Sander, 143 So. 45 (La. 1932).

195. *See generally* La. Civ. Code Ann. art. 1962; Lacoste, 16 So. at 838.

196. *See* La. Stat. Ann. §§ 14:41–:43.

197. La. Civ. Code Ann. art. 93.

198. La. Civ. Code Ann. art. 93 cmt. (d).

199. La. Civ. Code Ann. art. 93 cmt. (c)

§ 3:19 Consent—Underage (Consent)

Even though the age and circumstances of certain minors operate as a legal impediment to marriage,[200] other minors who are 16 or 17 (and are not marrying a person three years their senior) may be too young to understand the consequences of marriage.[201] Arguably, simply being under the age of 18 makes them "incapable of discernment," which necessitates the need for parental and court approval to marry.[202] On the other hand, some 16- and 17-year-olds may be capable of discernment in fact.

To protect minors, the court may only authorize the marriage when there is a "compelling reason" to wed and only after conducting separate hearings in chambers with the minor and their prospective spouse.[203] In no case, however, can the judge authorize the marriage of a minor under the age of 16 or the marriage of a minor 16 or 17 who is marrying a person three or more years their senior.[204] The judge must inquire into the best interest of the minor, the potential existence of human trafficking, sexual assault, domestic violence, coercion, duress, or undue influence.[205] Although no court has defined "compelling reason," pregnancy of the minor is one consideration.[206]

The law further requires that minors seeking a marriage license must present a valid birth certificate as well as written consent and judicial authorization.[207] Further, celebrants, other than judges or justices of the peace, who marry minors without necessary consent and judicial authorization will forever be deprived of their right to perform marriage ceremonies.[208] If the minor presents a false birth certificate to the clerk issuing the license or no license is issued at all, however, the minor may still have a valid marriage. Only the minor can seek to annul the marriage as relatively null based on his lack of discernment due to age, and once reaching the age of majority, the minor will no longer have the action to annul, as the minor confirmed the marriage after reaching the age of consent.[209]

---

200. La. Civ. Code Ann. art. 90.1; *see also* Section 3:13.

201. *See* Katherine Shaw Spaht, *Revision of the Law of Marriage: One Baby Step Forward*, 48 La. L. Rev. 1131, 1146 (1988).

202. La. Child. Code Ann. art. 1545.

203. La. Child. Code Ann. art. 1547; La. Child. Code Ann. art. 1548.

204. La. Civ. Code Ann. art. 90.1.

205. La. Child. Code Ann. art. 1548. Article 1548 of the Children's Code provides a complete list of factors the court must consider when determining the minor's best interest, along with required questions the judge must ask during the inquiry.

206. La. Child. Code Ann. art. 1548.

207. La. Stat. Ann. § 9:225 (declared unconstitutional as applied in Viet Anh Vo v. Gee, 301 F. Supp. 3d 661 (E.D. La. 2017)). Officials are prohibited from issuing marriage licenses to minors who do not satisfy the age requirements. La. Stat. Ann. § 9:221.

208. La. Child. Code Ann. art. 1550.

209. La. Civ. Code Ann. art. 95. Because a relatively null marriage is a marriage until it is declared null, the minor is emancipated by marriage and has the procedural capacity to sue to annul it; the right to bring the action does not belong to the minor's parents. Delpit v. Young, 25 So. 547, 548 (La. 1899); *see* La. Civ. Code Ann. art. 367.

§ 3:20 Nullity of Marriage

A marriage that fails to meet the necessary codal prerequisites is null. Rather than file a petition for divorce, those parties whose marriage is defective must file a petition to legally annul the marriage, a process that is distinct from a religious annulment. The marriage is either absolutely null or relatively null depending on the defect.[210] The significance of the marriage prerequisites from a societal standpoint drives the action in nullity.

A marriage is absolutely null when contracted without a valid ceremony, by procuration, or in violation of an impediment.[211] Marriages without a ceremony or burdened with a legal impediment violate the public order and are considered no marriage at all.[212] In other words, an absolutely null marriage is devoid of effect from the moment of inception. Because of the potential prejudice that could befall a spouse who in good faith enters into an absolutely null marriage unknowingly, Louisiana grants the civil effects of marriage to a good faith putative spouse in an absolutely null marriage.[213]

In contrast, if a spouse did not freely consent to marriage at the ceremony, the marriage is relatively null.[214] A marriage lacking consent is treated as a valid marriage until declared null by a court.[215] Because consent between the spouses is required to protect the parties to the marriage contract, rather than the public as a whole, the marriage can be confirmed or challenged by the party whose consent was lacking.[216]

§ 3:21 Nullity of Marriage— Absolutely Null Marriage

Marriages contracted in violation of an impediment, without a valid ceremony, or by procuration are absolutely null—the common law equivalent of a void marriage.[217] An absolutely null marriage is void *ab initio* and cannot be cured by confirmation after removal of the impediment.[218] Although no judicial declaration of nullity is required, either party to the marriage or any other interested party can bring an action to annul

---

210. La. Civ. Code Ann. arts. 94–95.

211. La. Civ. Code Ann. art. 94. The causes for nullity are exclusive. Wederstrandt v. Kol, 2022-01570 (La. 6/27/23), 366 So. 3d 47, 52, *reh'g denied*, 2022-01570 (La. 9/8/23), 370 So. 3d 457.

212. La. Civ. Code Ann. art. 2030.

213. La. Civ. Code Ann. art. 96; *see also* Section 3:22.

214. La. Civ. Code Ann. art. 95.

215. La. Civ. Code Ann. art. 95.

216. La. Civ. Code Ann. art. 2031.

217. La. Civ. Code Ann. art. 94. *See also* Section 3:32. By acts of the legislature, all marriages between collateral relations contracted prior to September 11, 1981, have been validated. *See* Act No. 886, 1987 La. Acts 2438; Act No. 647, 1981 La. Acts 1244.

218. Succession of Minvielle, 15 La. Ann. 342 (La. 1860) ("[T]he nullity ... is absolute, and cannot be cured by ratification."); Farrell v. Farrell, 275 So. 2d 489, 492 (La. Ct. App. 1 Cir. 1973). Confirmation is the process through which an individual cures a relative nullity. *See* La. Civ. Code Ann. art. 1842.

the absolutely null marriage.[219] The nullity may be raised in a direct action or collaterally, either as a claim or as a defense to the claim of another.[220] One who is in an absolutely null marriage is free to marry without seeking a declaration of nullity,[221] although it is common for parties to seek a declaration to formally announce their status or for the purpose of obtaining incidental relief.[222] The action to annul an absolutely null marriage does not prescribe.[223]

The Louisiana Supreme Court in *Wederstrandt v. Kol* held that the grounds to annul an absolutely null marriage are those exclusively enumerated in Article 94 of the Civil Code.[224] The plaintiffs in *Kol* were the parents of a married woman who was killed in a car accident. The parents filed a petition against the daughter's husband to have the marriage declared absolutely null, alleging that she married her husband "for the sole purpose of evading federal immigration laws to obtain permanent resident status for defendant."[225] The husband argued that the exclusive methods to declare a marriage absolutely null appear in article 94, which does not incorporate general principles of nullity found in the obligations articles, specifically article 2030. The trial court, appellate court, and Supreme Court agreed that the obligations articles on general principles of nullity do not apply to marriage contracts.[226] The Court noted the policy implications of nullifying marriage contracts for "illicit or immoral purposes," which "would require courts to engage in the distasteful task of interpreting for what purposes a marriage contract could be considered 'illicit' or—perhaps even more troublesome—'immoral.'"[227]

---

219. La. Civ. Code Ann. art. 94. Even a bigamist may assert the nullity of a marriage. La. Civ. Code Ann. art. 94 cmt. (c); *see also* Clark v. Clark, 192 So. 2d 594, 597 (La. Ct. App. 3 Cir. 1966). Although parties generally attack the validity of their own marriages, other entities, such as the Internal Revenue Service and insurance companies, can attack absolutely null marriages. *See, e.g.*, Prieto v. Succession of Prieto, 115 So. 911, 912 (La. 1928) (allowing potential heirs to decedent who contracted a bigamist marriage to bring an action); Burrell v. Burrell, 154 So. 2d 103, 105 (La. Ct. App. 1 Cir. 1963) (finding that an action for a judicial declaration of nullity is not restricted to only the prejudiced spouse).

220. La. Civ. Code Ann. art. 94 cmt. (c).

221. In *Gaines v. Relf*, a famous Louisiana successions case that reached the United States Supreme Court, the Court found the plaintiff to be the legitimate child of her deceased father because her mother's alleged undissolved marriage at the time that she married plaintiff's father was an absolutely null marriage itself. Gaines v. Relf, 53 U.S. 472, 595 (1851). Plaintiff's mother was therefore recognized as having entered into a valid marriage with plaintiff's father, even though no declaration of nullity of the first marriage had issued. *Id.*

222. Incidental relief, which includes spousal support, child support, child custody and visitation, community property, and use of the community movables and immovables, may be available to a good faith spouse of an absolutely null marriage. *See* Section 3:27.

223. Succession of Gabisso, 44 So. 438, 441 (La. 1907).

224. Wederstrandt v. Kol, 2022-01570 (La. 6/27/23), 366 So. 3d 47, 52, *reh'g denied*, 2022-01570 (La. 9/8/23), 370 So. 3d 457.

225. Wederstrandt, 366 So. 3d at 49.

226. Wederstrandt, 366 So. 3d at 52. Article 2030 provides grounds for nullity involving contracts in general: "A contract is absolutely null when it violates a rule of public order, as when the object of a contract is illicit or immoral. A contract that is absolutely null may not be confirmed." La. Civ. Code Ann. art. 2030.

227. Wederstrandt, 366 So. 3d at 54.

An absolutely null marriage produces no civil effects for either the parties or the children of the marriage, with one notable exception.[228] If either spouse to the marriage was in good faith when the marriage was contracted, the marriage will be deemed putative, the spouse(s) in good faith will receive the civil effects of the marriage, and the children will be deemed children of the marriage, also enjoying the civil effects.[229]

§ 3:22 Nullity of Marriage—Absolutely Null Marriage—Good Faith Putative Spouses

A party who enters into an absolutely null marriage under the mistaken belief that the marriage is valid may nonetheless receive the benefits of a valid marriage if the party contracted the marriage in good faith.[230] The putative marriage rule may apply when one spouse is already married, when the spouses are related within the prohibited degrees of kinship, when a spouse is underage, or when no valid marriage ceremony took place.

Good faith has been defined by jurisprudence as the "honest and reasonable belief" that no legal impediment to the marriage exists.[231] A party must be in good faith at the time the party enters into the marriage, and such good faith can arise from an error of fact[232] or an error of law.[233] As a general rule, the good faith of a party who enters into a null marriage is presumed.[234] As such, a presumption exists as to the validity of the

---

228. La. Civ. Code Ann. art. 96; Burrell, 154 So. 2d at 106 (finding that spouses who both knew of the impediment to marriage did not reap any civil effects and their children were not legitimate); Succession of Virgin, 24 La. Ann. 485 (La. 1872) (finding that children were illegitimate and could not inherit from parents where both spouses were in bad faith).

229. La. Civ. Code Ann. art. 96; *see also* Section 3:27.

230. La. Civ. Code Ann. art. 96. *See generally* Monica Hof Wallace, *The Pitfalls of a Putative Marriage and the Call for a Putative Divorce*, 64 La. L. Rev. 71 (2003); Christopher L. Blakesley, *The Putative Marriage Doctrine*, 60 Tul. L. Rev. 1 (1985).

231. La. Civ. Code Ann. art. 96 cmt. (d).

232. *See* Succession of Pigg, 84 So. 2d 196 (La. 1955) (putative wife relied on husband's fraudulent divorce from first wife); Succession of Marinoni, 164 So. 797, 805–06 (La. 1935) (putative wife relied on husband's assurance, and he was a lawyer); Jones v. Squire, 69 So. 733, 736 (La. 1915) (putative wife believed husband who told her that the clerk who issued the marriage license told him that if her first husband was missing for ten years that the parties could validly marry); Alfonso v. Alfonso, 99-261 (La. App. 5 Cir. 7/27/99), 739 So. 2d 946 (putative wife relied on false divorce papers presented from husband's divorce in Mexico).

233. *See* Funderburk v. Funderburk, 38 So. 2d 502, 504 (La. 1949) (putative wife relied on a null divorce obtained in a court of improper venue); Succession of Buissière, 5 So. 668, 670 (La. 1889) (putative wife was told that marriage between an uncle and a niece was valid if contracted in Mississippi); Jones v. Equitable Life Ins. Co., 173 So. 2d 373, 377 (La. Ct. App. 1 Cir. 1965) (putative wife had no knowledge that it was illegal for her to contract marriage with her spouse because she was his accomplice in adultery); Saacks v. Saacks, 96-736, pp. 7–8 (La. App. 5 Cir. 1/28/97), 688 So. 2d 673, 676 (putative wife believed her marriage in Mexico was invalid under Mexican law); Succession of Lynch v. United States, 17 F. Supp. 674, 676 (W.D. La. 1936) (wife was in good faith believing that a conviction and sentence of her husband to the penitentiary gave her a divorce).

234. La. Civ. Code Ann. art. 96 cmt. (d).

second marriage.[235] The burden of proof rests with the party attacking the second marriage to prove its invalidity.[236] The presumption of good faith, however, is not available to a spouse who was in bad faith or whose prior undissolved marriage is the cause of the nullity; instead, that spouse must affirmatively prove their own good faith.[237]

Good faith is a subjective, fact-intensive inquiry, although the objective element of reasonableness permeates the analysis. What constitutes good faith is relative and "depends ultimately upon the facts and circumstances in each individual case."[238] In light of the wide variation in facts, a body of case law has developed interpreting the broad limits of good faith.[239]

§ 3:23 Nullity of Marriage—Absolutely Null Marriage—Good Faith Putative Spouses—Previous Undissolved Marriage

When examining good faith in the context of bigamy, courts have considered whether a spouse, who knows that his intended spouse had been previously married, has a duty to investigate the prior marriage to determine whether it was actually dissolved. Courts have generally rejected one spouse's sheer reliance on the other spouse's word that the divorce was final, especially when there is reasonable suspicion that an impediment exists.[240] Courts have said that "a party alleging good faith cannot close her ears to information or her eyes to suspicious circumstances" and "[s]he must not act blindly or without reasonable precautions."[241]

With that said, failure to conduct an independent investigation will not preclude a finding of good faith when other circumstances are present to support the conclusion that no impediment existed. For example, in *Gathright v. Smith*,[242] the court found the putative husband to be in good faith even though he failed to investigate his wife's prior undissolved marriage because he had not received any information to cast doubt on the validity of his marriage and his wife's children had concealed from him the true facts of her first marriage.[243] Similarly, in *Succession of Chavis*,[244] the court found the putative wife to be in good faith without an investigation because others told her that her husband had divorced his first wife, his first wife lived in the same city and never

235. *See* Gathright v. Smith, 368 So. 2d 679, 683 (La. 1978); Lands v. Equitable Life Assurance Soc'y of U.S., 120 So. 2d 74, 77 (La. 1960).

236. *See* La. Civ. Code Ann. art. 96 cmt. (d).

237. La. Civ. Code Ann. art. 96 cmt. (d); Gathright, 368 So. 2d at 683.

238. Succession of Chavis, 29 So. 2d 860, 863 (La. 1947).

239. *See* Section 3:21.

240. *See, e.g.*, Schafer v. Schafer, 379 So. 2d 864, 866–67 (La. Ct. App. 4 Cir. 1980); Succession of Hopkins, 114 So. 2d 742, 744–45 (La. Ct. App. 1 Cir. 1959).

241. Hopkins, 114 So. 2d at 744 (internal citations and quotation marks omitted).

242. Gathright v. Smith, 368 So. 2d 679 (La. 1978).

243. Gathright, 368 So. 2d at 685.

244. Succession of Chavis, 29 So. 2d 860 (La. 1947).

asserted herself as his spouse, and she had no reasonable suspicion of the impediment to marriage.[245]

To the contrary, in *Succession of Taylor*,[246] the court failed to find good faith for a wife who did not investigate her husband's claim that he was divorced because she had information to show that his claim was false.[247] Not only did his first wife tell her that there had been no divorce, but two friends cautioned her that he had not been divorced.[248] Based on this evidence, the court concluded that she had a duty to investigate her intended husband's marital status before getting married, which she had not done.[249]

Courts have considered a spouse's education and age when assessing good faith. For spouses who marry at a young age, are illiterate or uneducated, or rely on promises of divorce by an "older, wiser" spouse, courts have found good faith when entering into a null second marriage.[250] If, however, the spouse seeking putative status could have located the first spouse with ease or had an understanding of the legal process of divorce, courts are less likely to find good faith.[251]

Courts have also recognized good faith when the putative spouse relied on an invalid divorce judgment from the first marriage. Putative spouses have relied on: judgments

---

245. Succession of Chavis, 29 So. 2d at 864; *see also* Smith v. Smith, 10 So. 248, 248–49 (La. 1891) (both putative wife and former husband believed they were validly divorced); In re Succession of Jones, 2008-1088, p. 11 (La. App. 3 Cir. 4/22/09), 6 So. 3d 331, 338–39 (putative wife believed that husband was divorced, and statements made by husband's children that "we still have a mother" failed to contain any "certain or authoritative knowledge" that there was an impediment to her marriage).

246. Succession of Taylor, 2 So. 581 (La. 1887).

247. Succession of Taylor, 2 So. at 583–84.

248. Succession of Taylor, 2 So. at 584.

249. Succession of Taylor, 2 So. at 584; *see also* Prieto v. Succession of Prieto, 115 So. 911, 913 (La. 1928) (husband knew that wife had a living husband who she had never divorced and therefore could not be found in good faith); Succession of Hopkins, 114 So. 2d 742, 745 (La. Ct. App. 1 Cir. 1959) (wife was not in good faith because she had been told about husband's first wife and read letters from his daughter); Succession of Glover, 153 So. 496, 497 (La. Ct. App. 1934) (wife should have investigated intended husband's marital status because she had reasons to believe his assertions that he was divorced were false); Jackson v. Swift & Co., 151 So. 816, 818 (La. Ct. App. 2 Cir. 1934) (wife was not in good faith because lawyer advised her that her divorce to her first husband was not final); Hunter v. Richardson, 346 F. Supp. 123, 125 (M.D. La. 1972) (wife was not in good faith because she knew her husband had been previously married and failed to inquire whether marriage had been terminated); Schafer v. Schafer, 379 So. 2d 864, 866 (La. Ct. App. 4 Cir. 1980) (wife was not in good faith because she was aware that her husband's foreign divorce from his first wife was "clouded").

250. *See, e.g.*, Eddy v. Eddy, 271 So. 2d 333, 335 (La. Ct. App. 2 Cir. 1987) (wife was 16 when she married, and her husband told her that he would get a divorce and subsequently told her he actually got a divorce); Succession of Barbier, 296 So. 2d 390, 392 (La. Ct. App. 4 Cir. 1974) (wife was 16 and husband swore to her family he was unmarried and the family did some investigation); Succession of Primus, 131 So. 2d 319, 320 (La. Ct. App. 1 Cir. 1961) (wife who was illiterate and thirteen when married was told by her husband that he would get a divorce); Tillison v. Tillison, 129 So. 2d 522 (La. Ct. App. 1 Cir. 1961) (wife was illiterate and saw what she thought were divorce papers).

251. *See* Rebouche v. Anderson, 505 So. 2d 808, 812–13 (La. Ct. App. 2 Cir. 1987) (noting that even though wife was of low intelligence, she was thirty years old when she left her legal husband, knew how to find him, and was aware of the procedural requirements to obtain a divorce).

of divorce against a spouse who was falsely alleged to be missing;[252] preliminary judgments of divorce that were never finalized;[253] and, out-of-state judgments of divorce that were falsified.[254] Although errors of law as to the propriety of a prior divorce judgment are not likely to impugn the good faith of a putative spouse, the unique facts and circumstances of each case give the courts great discretion when assessing good faith.

§ 3:24 Nullity of Marriage—Absolutely Null Marriage—Good Faith Putative Spouses—Too Closely Related

Parties who are related within the prohibited degrees for marriage may obtain the civil effects of marriage if the spouses believed in good faith that the marriage was valid when contracted.[255] If, for example, the parties were unaware of their blood relationship at the time of the marriage, the putative spouse rule would give effect to their null marriage. Because the prohibited degrees of relations extend only as far as first cousins, it is unlikely that parties would be unaware of their blood relationship. Rather, parties are more likely to suffer from an error of law as to the general validity of marriages between certain blood relatives.

To give effects to null marriages between prohibited relations, courts have required the error of law to be actual and excusable.[256] In *Succession of Buissière*, a young girl married her uncle in Mississippi under the belief that a marriage between an uncle and a niece could be validly contracted there.[257] The woman was a minor, brought over from France by her parents for purposes of the marriage, and she lived as the man's wife and bore his two children.[258] The court recognized her status as putative wife because she was in good faith, even though her good faith lacked a legal foundation.[259]

---

252. Succession of Pigg, 84 So. 2d 196, 197 (La. 1955); Funderburk v. Funderburk, 38 So. 2d 502, 503 (La. 1949).

253. Prince v. Hopson, 89 So. 2d 128, 129–30 (La. 1956) (parties relied on a preliminary default judgment of divorce); *see also* Smith v. Smith, 10 So. 248, 249 (La. 1891) (spouses relied on an out-of-state divorce decree, which may have been entered into without jurisdiction over the parties); Farrell v. Farrell, 275 So. 2d 489, 492 (La. Ct. App. 1 Cir. 1973) (spouses relied on a divorce decree rendered in open court, but unsigned by the judge until two years later); Galbraith v. Galbraith, 396 So. 2d 1364, 1369 (La. Ct. App. 2 Cir. 1981) (spouses relied on a divorce rendered in open court, but without having a signed judgment).

254. *See, e.g.*, Mara v. Mara, 452 So. 2d 329, 332 (La. Ct. App. 4 Cir. 1984) (married couple relied on false divorce in an Alabama divorce scam); Tillison, 129 So. 2d at 524 (prior to second marriage, wife received what she thought were divorce papers from Mississippi, which she signed and returned).

255. A marriage between first cousins that is valid in the state where contracted will be valid in Louisiana. *See* Section 3:12.

256. Chandler v. Hayden, 105 So. 80, 81 (La. 1925); Succession of Buissière, 5 So. 668, 669 (La. 1889).

257. Buissière, 5 So. at 669.

258. Buissière, 5 So. at 669.

259. Buissière, 5 So. at 670.

Several years later, in *Chandler v. Hayden*, a woman who married her first cousin, with knowledge of their familial relationship, sought putative spouse status, claiming that she was unaware that marriage between first cousins was prohibited in Louisiana.[260] The court rejected her request, finding that her error of law was neither actual nor excusable because she had been made aware that it was against the law for first cousins to marry.[261]

§ 3:25 Nullity of Marriage—Absolutely Null Marriage—Good Faith Putative Spouses—Underage

As for the impediment of age, parties who unknowingly marry a minor 16 or 17 years old who is three or more years their junior or marry a minor under the age of 16 may nonetheless be in good faith and entitled to the civil effects of the marriage. Indeed, minors themselves could operate under an error of law and likewise be entitled to the civil effects of marriage. The law provides a special exception for marriages that are null due to the impediment of age—even if neither party is in good faith when they enter the marriage, it produces civil effects in favor of the children of the parties.[262] In other words, even if a minor under the age of 16 marries knowing that the law forbids the marriage, any child born of that absolutely null marriage will nevertheless enjoy the civil effects of the marriage. If the parties to the marriage are in bad faith, however, the other civil effects of marriage will remain unavailable.[263]

§ 3:26 Nullity of Marriage—Absolutely Null Marriage—Good Faith Putative Spouses—No Marriage Ceremony

Whether parties can obtain putative spouse status without a marriage ceremony has been the subject of debate. Article 96 of the Civil Code permits spouses who "contract" a marriage in good faith to enjoy its civil effects.[264] Originally, the Louisiana Supreme Court concluded that civil effects were only available to a marriage actually contracted, denying putative spouse status in an alleged marriage where the parties simply obtained a marriage license but failed to appear before any officiant to perform a ceremony.[265] Just four years later, however, in *Succession of Marinoni*, the court awarded civil

---

260. Chandler, 105 So. at 81.

261. Chandler, 105 So. at 81.

262. La. Civ. Code Ann. art. 96.

263. La. Civ. Code Ann. art. 96.

264. La. Civ. Code Ann. art. 96.

265. *See* Succession of Cusimano, 138 So. 95 (La. 1931). In *Cusimano*, the parties only obtained a marriage license and did not appear before any official. *Id.* at 96. The court concluded, "As there was no marriage contracted by [the alleged spouses], even a void one, the status that existed between

effects to the child of an absolutely null union even though the parties failed to have a ceremony.[266] In *Marinoni*, the putative wife was a young foreign-born woman who was ignorant of the laws and customs of the United States, and her putative husband was an older attorney who told her that getting a marriage license and having their marriage blessed by a priest at a later date would constitute a valid marriage.[267] Even without a ceremony, the court deemed the young woman a putative wife, and therefore her daughter was declared legitimate.[268]

Courts have been critical of the *Marinoni* decision, expressing concern that giving the status of married to spouses who do not attempt a marriage ceremony will ultimately sanction common-law marriage in Louisiana. *Marinoni* has been limited to its facts[269] but nonetheless remains good law.[270]

At least one court has applied *Marinoni*, without so stating, by awarding civil effects without a formal marriage ceremony to a woman who believed she was married after obtaining a license and visiting an officiant.[271] The husband challenged the status of the parties as married, claiming that no ceremony was attempted and the parties knew they were not married.[272] The court found the wife's story to be more credible because she had been given a wedding ring, they lived as married for 40 years, and they had children during that time.[273]

In light of *Marinoni* and the cases that have followed, putative spouse status may be available without a marriage ceremony in limited circumstances. Absent unique circumstances akin to *Marinoni*, a putative spouse must demonstrate that some form of marriage ceremony took place—simply obtaining a marriage license will not suffice.[274]

---

them cannot be deemed that of a putative marriage...." *Id.*; *see also* Succession of Rossi, 214 So. 2d 223, 227 (La. Ct. App. 4 Cir. 1968) (stating that some kind of ceremony should take place for a putative marriage to exist).

266. Succession of Marinoni, 164 So. 797, 804 (La. 1935). The parties did secure a marriage license. *Id.*

267. Succession of Marinoni, 164 So. 797 (La. 1935). The putative wife was born in Italy, emigrated to the United States at thirteen, and was married at 17. *Id.* at 802–03. She was unable to read English and understood very little English. *Id.* at 803.

268. Marinoni, 164 So. at 812–13.

269. Succession of Rossi, 214 So. 2d 223, 227 (La. Ct. App. 4 Cir. 1968) (distinguishing *Marinoni* on its facts and opining that some kind of ceremony should take place for a putative marriage to exist).

270. *See* La. Civ. Code Ann. art. 96 cmt. (e); *see also* David Gruning, *Mapping Society Through Law: Louisiana Civil Law Recodified*, 19 Tul. Eur. & Civ. L.F. 1, 21 (2004).

271. *See* Thomason v. Thomason, 2000-522, p. 5 (La. App. 3 Cir. 12/6/00), 776 So. 2d 553, 556–57. The putative husband and wife lived together as a married couple for forty years and had children during that time. *See generally id.*

272. Thomason, 776 So. 2d at 554.

273. *See generally* Thomason, 776 So. 2d at 554.

274. Note that the presumption of validity of a marriage does not apply for a relationship that begins in open concubinage. *See* Succession of Rossi, 214 So. 2d 223 (La. Ct. App. 4 Cir. 1968). While a presumption of marriage may arise from cohabitation and a general reputation that the parties are married, from the beginning, the relationship must be based on a ceremonial marriage. *See generally id.*; *see also* Eldon E. Fallon, Louisiana Practice: Trial Handbook for Louisiana Lawyers § 21:8 (3d ed. 2017).

§ 3:27 Nullity of Marriage—Absolutely Null Marriage—Civil Effects

The good faith putative spouse is entitled to civil effects from the marriage, which are not limitless. Civil effects include filial, financial, contractual, and property rights, all derived under state law.[275] In fact, the civil effects provide the exclusive remedy to the aggrieved spouse when the marriage is invalid.[276] The request for civil effects can be made at the death of a spouse[277] or incidental to a proceeding for a declaration of nullity of the putative marriage.[278] In connection with the request for a declaration of nullity, the court can award incidental relief that would be permitted incidental to a petition for divorce.[279]

§ 3:28 Nullity of Marriage—Absolutely Null Marriage—Civil Effects—Children

As long as one of the parties to the null marriage is in good faith, any child born during that marriage is treated as born of a valid marriage.[280] Conversely, if neither party to the null marriage is in good faith, a child born of the union is considered to be born outside of marriage and will receive no civil effects as a result of the null marriage, with one notable exception. For a child born of an absolutely null marriage due to the impediment of age, even if the minors who marry are in bad faith, the children are entitled to the civil effects of the marriage.[281] Keep in mind, however, that any child may establish filiation to his biological parents, which will entitle the child to rights, including support and inheritance, as any child of a marriage would receive.[282]

Courts are keenly aware of the troublesome nature of this rule when a child, through no fault of his own, is born into an absolutely null marriage when neither spouse is

---

275. Courts have construed civil effects to encompass rights derived from state law, but not rights derived from federal law. Concern has arisen that defining "spouse" under a federal statute as anything other than a legal spouse would impair the uniform application of the federal statute, depending on each state's laws. *See* United States v. Robinson, 40 F.2d 14, 16 (5th Cir. 1930). Therefore, putative spouses in Louisiana have been denied benefits under federal statutes—namely, the Federal Employers' Liability Act. *See* Beebe v. Moormack Gulf Lines, 59 F.2d 319, 320 (5th Cir. 1932) (noting that federal law does not permit a second recovery by a wife entitled to the effects of marriage under state law).

276. *See* Bhati v. Bhati, 2012-707, p. 2 (La. App. 3 Cir. 12/5/12), 103 So. 3d 1290, 1291 (denying a claim for damages due to a spouse's bigamy because receiving civil effects from the invalid marriage is the proper relief).

277. La. Civ. Code Ann. art. 101.

278. La. Civ. Code Ann. arts. 151–152.

279. La. Civ. Code Ann. arts. 151–152.

280. *See generally* Succession of Chavis, 29 So. 2d 860 (La. 1947); Farrell v. Farrell, 275 So. 2d 489 (La. Ct. App. 5 Cir. 1973); Melancon v. Sonnier, 157 So. 2d 577 (La. Ct. App. 3 Cir. 1963).

281. La. Civ. Code Ann. art. 96.

282. *See* La. Civ. Code Ann. art. 197.

in good faith. In *Burrell v. Burrell*, the mother of three children born during a null marriage sought child support from her alleged spouse.[283] The court denied the request because the mother and her alleged spouse knew that the mother was still married to another man.[284] No civil effects flowed to either party; consequently, no civil effects flowed to the children either.[285] The children were, however, born during the ongoing, valid marriage between the mother and another man.[286] The court applied the legal presumption that the husband of the mother is the father of all children born during the marriage, resulting in the legal husband bearing responsibility for the children, absent a timely disavowal action.[287]

Without an existing presumed father (as in the *Burrell* case), a child born to an absolutely null union when neither spouse is in good faith would be denied rights from his biological father because the child is not considered to be born of a marriage. Under the law of filiation, however, the child can file a paternity action to prove his biological relationship and secure legal rights vis-à-vis his father.[288] Because no time restrictions limit the child's right to bring the paternity action, except in the case of succession rights to the alleged father's estate,[289] the child is less likely to be prejudiced by this rule.

Further, the adoption of a child by a spouse in a putative marriage is unaffected by the nullity of marriage. In *In re Koonce*, a good faith putative husband learned that his marriage was null and sought to set aside an adoption decree under which he had adopted the children of his putative spouse.[290] The court rejected his demand, finding that the stepparent adoption was unaffected by the status of his marriage as putative.[291]

283. Burrell v. Burrell, 154 So. 2d 103 (La. Ct. App. 1 Cir. 1963).
284. Burrell, 154 So. 2d at 105.
285. Burrell, 154 So. 2d. at 108.
286. Burrell, 154 So. 2d at 104–05.
287. Burrell, 154 So. 2d at 105.
288. La. Civ. Code Ann. art. 197.
289. La. Civ. Code Ann. art. 197.
290. In re Koonce, 380 So. 2d 140 (La. Ct. App. 1 Cir. 1979).
291. In re Koonce, 380 So. 2d at 142.

§ 3:29 Nullity of Marriage—Absolutely Null Marriage—Civil Effects—Support and Other Rights

A putative spouse is entitled to the incidents of marriage, including fidelity, support, and assistance.[292] As a result, a putative spouse is entitled to seek spousal support, both interim and final,[293] and can also seek the marital portion.[294] In either case, the putative spouse entitled to seek relief must meet the codal requirements for receiving support.[295] For example, for final spousal support, the spouse must demonstrate a need, the ability of the other spouse to pay, and freedom from fault.[296] Although a putative spouse may be in good faith in contracting a null marriage, that spouse may nonetheless be guilty of fault in the breakdown of the putative marriage, which could negate an award of final support.[297]

An interesting issue surrounding the timing of fault in a putative marriage has not yet been addressed by the jurisprudence. For a spouse to receive final support after a divorce, the spouse must be free from fault in the breakdown of the marriage prior to the filing of a proceeding to terminate the marriage.[298] Because no judicial proceeding to declare its nullity is necessary for an absolutely null marriage, the law does not make clear when support-preclusive fault must occur in the context of a putative marriage. In other words, without a "proceeding to terminate the marriage," when must fault occur to prevent an incidental award of final spousal support? When no proceeding is filed, it would be reasonable to preclude final spousal support if the fault occurred prior to the time when civil effects terminate under article 96.[299] Civil effects terminate either when good faith ends or, in the case of a prior undissolved marriage, when the innocent spouse remarries or the marriage is declared null by a court.[300] In any event, any later occurring fault should not prevent support to the good faith spouse in need.

---

292. Cortes v. Fleming, 307 So. 2d 611, 616 (La. 1973); La. Civ. Code Ann. art. 98.

293. La. Civ. Code Ann. art. 98; Galbraith v. Galbraith, 396 So. 2d 1364, 1370 (La. Ct. App. 2 Cir. 1981) (concluding that when both parties are in good faith, alimony is permitted under the same rules as alimony after divorce; even a good faith spouse to the putative marriage could commit fault sufficient to preclude an award of alimony).

294. Smith v. Smith, 10 So. 248, 251 (La. 1891); La. Civ. Code Ann. art. 2432.

295. La. Civ. Code Ann. arts. 151–52. A putative spouse can receive interim periodic support regardless of good or bad faith, but only a good faith putative spouse can receive final periodic support. *Id.*

296. *See* La. Civ. Code Ann. art. 112.

297. Galbraith, 396 So. 2d at 1370. The *Galbraith* court concluded that final support was permitted even when both of the spouses were in good faith in contracting the invalid marriage, but one judge expressed concern that the decision unnecessarily expanded the rights permitted to putative spouses. *Id.* at 1370 (Jones, J., concurring in part and dissenting in part).

298. La. Civ. Code Ann. art. 111 cmt. (c).

299. *See* Section 3:31; *see also* Thomason v. Thomason, 2000-522 (La. App. 3 Cir. 12/6/00), 776 So. 2d 553 (finding that the community property regime terminated when civil effects ended).

300. La. Civ. Code Ann. art. 96.

Incidental to the putative marriage, a spouse can also sue as a surviving spouse under the wrongful death statute.[301] Courts have recognized the putative spouse's rights under an insurance policy as the widow of the putative husband,[302] as a survivor under state worker's compensation laws,[303] and as a widow to federal social security benefits.[304] The putative spouse can also seek the marital portion[305] and general rights of inheritance, with community property rights being the most controversial.[306]

§ 3:30 Nullity of Marriage—Absolutely Null Marriage—Civil Effects—Community Property

A putative spouse is entitled to a share of the community of acquets and gains that exists during the putative marriage.[307] Generally, the community property regime terminates retroactively to the date of filing of the petition for divorce upon which the divorce is granted.[308] Because neither a divorce action nor an action in nullity is required to end an absolutely null marriage, the Civil Code does not specify when the putative community terminates.

Courts have concluded that the putative community terminates when the civil effects end. In *Thomason v. Thomason*, the putative wife believed her marriage was valid, even though the ceremony was defective.[309] The court concluded that her good faith, and hence her civil effects, ended when the putative husband filed an answer to

301. King v. Cancienne, 316 So. 2d 366, 366 (La. 1975).

302. Jones v. Equitable Life Assurance Soc'y, 173 So. 2d 373, 373 (La. Ct. App. 1 Cir. 1965).

303. Jones v. Powell Lumber Co., 101 So. 135, 136 (La. 1924). *See generally* Fulton Bag & Cotton Mills v. Fernandez, 159 So. 339 (La. Ct. App. 1935) (recognizing that although a putative wife is entitled to recover under worker's compensation laws, when the putative wife is in a contest against the legal spouse who is still dependent on the common spouse, the award must be made in favor of the legal spouse, and the good faith putative spouse cannot recover); Jackson v. Swift & Co., 151 So. 816 (La. Ct. App. 2 Cir. 1934) (recognizing that a bad faith putative spouse is not entitled to recover under worker's compensation laws).

304. *See* Hunter v. Richardson, 346 F. Supp. 123 (M.D. La. 1972) (finding that the wife was not in good faith and therefore did not qualify as a widow based on the facts); Kimball v. Folsom, 150 F. Supp. 482 (W.D. La. 1957) (finding that the wife was in good faith and was entitled to benefits).

305. Smith v. Smith, 10 So. 248, 251 (La. 1891).

306. Zanders v. Zanders, 434 So. 2d 1213 (La. Ct. App. 1 Cir. 1983); Succession of Navarro, 24 La. Ann. 298 (La. 1872); *see also* Section 3:30.

307. *See* Thomason v. Thomason, 2000-522 (La. App. 3 Cir. 12/6/00), 776 So. 2d 553 at 555–57 (finding that the community property regime terminated when the civil effects ended, not upon the filing of an action for nullity because no nullity action was necessary); Mara v. Mara, 513 So. 2d 1220, 1222 (La. Ct. App. 4 Cir. 1987) (finding that the right to community property includes an interest in the putative spouse's pension plan).

308. La. Civ. Code Ann. art. 159.

309. Thomason, 776 So. 2d at 555.

her petition for divorce, claiming that the couple was never validly married.[310] When her civil effects ended, the putative community terminated as well.[311]

In *Thomason*, the civil effects ended when the putative spouse was no longer in good faith.[312] However, civil effects can continue even after good faith ends, when the marriage is absolutely null due to the other spouse's proper undissolved marriage.[313] In that case, the putative community terminates at the innocent spouse's remarriage or when the marriage is pronounced null by a court.[314] Although the term "pronounced null" has not been interpreted by the courts, it would seem that "pronouncement" occurs at the judgment of nullity. The community would therefore terminate on the date of remarriage or on the date of the final judgment of nullity, rather than retroactively to the filing of the petition for nullity.

One of the most controversial rights of the putative spouse is the right of inheritance at the death of the common spouse when the legal spouse is still alive. When a good faith spouse enters a putative marriage, the putative community begins, coterminous with the legal regime.[315] A spouse in good faith at inception of the putative marriage is entitled to a share of the putative community and may also be entitled to the legal usufruct under Article 890 of the Civil Code.[316] By contrast, a spouse in bad faith at inception of the putative marriage will not receive a share of the putative community at death or divorce, nor will the spouse receive the legal usufruct under Article 890 of the Civil Code over any property inherited by descendants.[317] The good faith putative spouse, however, may be faced with a claim by the legal spouse for a share of the putative community, as the legal regime is technically still in existence.

The Louisiana Supreme Court, in several cases, has articulated the inheritance rights of the legal and putative spouses at the death of the common spouse. In *Patton v. Cities of Philadelphia & New Orleans*, a husband left his legal wife in New York and represented himself as a widow to a woman in Louisiana who would later become his putative wife.[318] After the husband's death, his children and both the legal and putative wives claimed rights to property acquired during the putative community property regime, which overlapped with the legal regime.[319] The court concluded that the

---

310. Thomason, 776 So. 2d at 556–57.

311. Thomason, 776 So. 2d at 556–57; *see also* Mara, 513 So. 2d at 1222 (La. Ct. App. 4 Cir. 1987) (finding that putative community terminated when spouses discovered defect).

312. Thomason, 776 So. 2d at 556–57.

313. La. Civ. Code Ann. art. 96.

314. La. Civ. Code Ann. art. 96.

315. *See generally* Monica Hof Wallace, *The Pitfalls of a Putative Marriage and the Call for a Putative Divorce*, 64 La. L. Rev. 71 (2003).

316. *See* La. Civ. Code Ann. art. 96; *see also* A.N. Yiannopoulos, Personal Servitudes § 7.4, *in* 3 Louisiana Civil Law Treatise 437 (5th ed. 2011).

317. *See* La. Civ. Code Ann. art. 96. A surviving spouse is entitled to a usufruct over the decedent's share of the community property when the decedent dies intestate and leaves descendants. La. Civ. Code Ann. art. 890.

318. Patton v. Cities of Philadelphia & New Orleans, 1 La. Ann. 98, 101 (La. 1846).

319. Patton, 1 La. Ann. at 101.

legal and putative wives should each receive one-half of the property, and his children should receive nothing.[320] The legal spouse was entitled to one-half as a spouse in community, and because the husband, acting in bad faith, deceived his putative wife, she was entitled to the husband's half of the property in recompense for the grievous wrong he committed against her.[321] The effect of this decision prevented his innocent children (who were also forced heirs) from inheriting a share of his property.

In a subsequent decision, *Prince v. Hopson*,[322] the Louisiana Supreme Court criticized its decision in *Patton*, which also involved a dispute over property acquired during a putative marriage. The *Prince* case was factually distinguishable from *Patton* because the common spouse in *Prince* was in good faith when he married his putative wife.[323] In fact, both of the legal spouses entered into putative marriages with the good faith belief that his divorce from his first wife had been finalized.[324] Because the common spouse was in good faith at the time of his death, the court concluded that it could not deny him, and therefore his heirs, the civil effects of his marriage.[325] The court therefore awarded one-half of the property to his legal successor, a child from his first marriage.[326] As to the remaining one-half of the property, the court recognized that both the legal and putative spouses had a valid claim to the half, and finding no other appropriate solution, awarded each of the wives one-quarter of the property.[327]

In 2022, the Louisiana Supreme Court overruled *Prince v. Hopson* with its decision in *Succession of Burns* because *Prince* "abrogates the rights given to good faith spouses in Louisiana Civil Code Article 96."[328] Like *Prince*, the common spouse in *Succession of Burns* was in good faith, mistakenly believing that he had received a final judgment of divorce from his former wife in Arkansas.[329] Following the common spouse's death, the surviving putative wife filed to open her late husband's succession; however, the legal spouse—who had been physically separated from the decedent for over forty years—intervened in the succession and sought to be recognized as the legal spouse.[330] Finding the Arkansas divorce had never been finalized, the trial court followed the *Prince* formula and granted one-fourth of the community to the decedent's legal wife,

---

320. Patton, 1 La. Ann. at 106.

321. Patton, 1 La. Ann. at 106.

322. Prince v. Hopson, 89 So. 2d 128 (La. 1956), *overruled by* Succession of Burns, 2022-263 (La. 12/9/22), 354 So. 3d 1197.

323. *See generally* Prince, 89 So. 2d 128. In *Prince*, the husband was married to his first wife for 12 years and filed for divorce. *Id.* at 129. Although he received a preliminary judgment of divorce, a final decree was never entered. *Id.* at 129–30. He later married his putative wife under the mistaken belief that his first marriage had been terminated, and he stayed married to his putative wife for 21 years until his death. *Id.* at 130, *overruled* by Succession of Burns, 2022-263 (La. 12/9/22), 354 So. 3d 1197.

324. *See* Prince, 89 So. 2d at 129–30.

325. *See* Prince, 89 So. 2d. at 133.

326. Prince, 89 So. 2d at 132.

327. Prince, 89 So. 2d at 134.

328. Succession of Burns, 354 So. 3d at 1203.

329. Succession of Burns, 354 So. 3d at 1999.

330. Succession of Burns, 354 So. 3d at 1200.

one-fourth to the decedent's putative wife, and granted the decedent's one-half to his heirs.[331] The court of appeal affirmed.[332] The Louisiana Supreme Court reversed, concluding that article 96 entitles good faith spouses to the full civil effects of marriage, including "an *undivided* one-half interest in the community."[333] Thus, the decedent's heirs received the common spouse's one-half interest and the putative spouse received her one-half interest in the community.[334] In addition, the putative spouse received the surviving spouse usufruct over the decedent's one-half share that was inherited by his heirs.[335] The legal spouse received nothing.

Succession of Burns eliminated the windfall to the legal spouse when the common spouse is in good faith, but the windfall to the legal spouse when the common spouse is in bad faith still remains good law today.[336] Under *Patton*, the legal spouse's rights are elevated over the innocent children when the common spouse is in bad faith, yet, courts do not consider the good or bad faith of the legal spouse, who may be the legal spouse in name only.[337] Additionally, what should be the result if the legal spouse had no knowledge of a putative marriage, believing she was still happily married? Should she have some claim to the property acquired during her ongoing community? These questions remain unanswered.

A putative divorce has been suggested as a way to ameliorate these negative consequences.[338] Instituting a putative divorce at a time when the spouses of the legal marriage sought a divorce or when the common spouse later contracts the putative marriage could create a separate community for the legal and putative spouses and accomplish a just division of ownership.[339] Without adopting the putative divorce, the court in *Succession of Burns* applied its principles but did not address the situation when the legal and common spouse still enjoy an ongoing relationship.[340] In that case, it may be appropriate to award the legal spouse some ownership rights in property acquired during the overlapping legal and putative communities.

---

331. Succession of Burns, 354 So. 3d at 1199.

332. Succession of Burns, 354 So. 3d at 1200.

333. Succession of Burns, 354 So. 3d at 1204.

334. Succession of Burns, 354 So. 3d at 1204.

335. Succession of Burns, 354 So. 3d at 1204.

336. *See, e.g.*, Succession of Fields, 62 So. 2d 495 (La. 1952) (applying *Patton*); Succession of Choyce, 183 So. 2d 457 (La. Ct. App. 2 Cir. 1966) (applying *Patton*).

337. *See* Wallace, *supra* note 314, at 93–94.

338. *See* Wallace, *supra* note 314, at 93–94; Robert A. Pascal, *Persons*, 17 La. L. Rev. 303, 305 (1957).

339. *See* Wallace, *supra* note 314, at 105. If the common spouse in bad faith is still alive, Civil Code Article 96 would prevent him from receiving the civil effects of marriage. *See* La. Civ. Code Ann. art. 96. Application of this article at his death has less appeal. Civil Code Article 96 does not address the situation when both putative spouses are in good faith and a legal spouse has a good faith claim to the property.

340. The legal spouse should have a claim to a share of the putative community if circumstances indicate that the legal spouse still had a relationship with the common spouse. Wallace, *supra* note 314, at 109–14.

§ 3:31 Nullity of Marriage—Absolutely Null Marriage—Duration of Civil Effects

Once in good faith, the spouse receives the civil effects of the marriage as long as that spouse remains in good faith.[341] An exception exists, however, for a spouse who entered a bigamous marriage in good faith, because that spouse is without the power to rectify the null union.[342] Thus, when the cause for the null marriage is one spouse's prior undissolved marriage, the civil effects continue in favor of the other, non-bigamous spouse, even after that spouse is no longer in good faith.[343] Civil effects terminate when the non-bigamous spouse remarries, which is permitted immediately without a declaration of nullity, or upon a declaration of nullity by the court.[344] Even though the bigamous party may be in good faith in contracting the second marriage, his civil effects end simultaneously with his good faith (i.e., when he discovers that his first marriage had not been terminated).[345] The purpose of this exception is two-fold to: (1) deny the spouse whose actions created the impediment the power to end the civil effects by confessing his prior undissolved marriage to the innocent party, and (2) protect the innocent party to the null marriage because that party has no power to rectify the union.[346]

In *Mara v. Mara*, the parties entered into a putative marriage based on the good faith belief that the wife's first marriage had been dissolved by divorce.[347] When the parties learned, during the marriage, that there was no court record of a divorce having been granted, the putative community terminated on that date.[348] The court explained that any assets acquired or liabilities incurred after the date of termination would be the separate property or obligation of each former putative spouse.[349]

Notably, the effective termination date of the community depends on whether the party who seeks the benefits of the putative marriage is the bigamous spouse. For the non-bigamous, good faith spouse, the civil effects of marriage terminate only at remarriage or when the marriage is pronounced null; therefore, the community terminates

341. La. Civ. Code Ann. art. 96.

342. La. Civ. Code Ann. art. 96 cmt. (b).

343. *See* La. Civ. Code Ann. art. 96. Only the spouse with the prior undissolved marriage has the power to rectify the null union, so the good faith spouse receives greater protection. La. Civ. Code Ann. art. 96 cmt. (b).

344. *See* La. Civ. Code Ann. art. 96 & cmt. (b).

345. *See, e.g.*, Evans v. Eureka Grand Lodge, 149 So. 305, 308 (La. Ct. App. 2 Cir. 1933) (finding that once the putative spouse was advised that her marriage was invalid, she could not claim life insurance benefits).

346. *See* Katherine Shaw Spaht, *The Last One Hundred Years: The Incredible Retreat of Law from the Regulation of Marriage*, 63 La. L. Rev. 243, 279 (2003); *see also* La. Civ. Code Ann. art. 96 cmt. (b).

347. Mara v. Mara, 513 So. 2d 1220 (La. Ct. App. 4 Cir. 1987).

348. Mara, 513 So. 2d 1220. At the time, the civil effects of marriage did not continue in favor of the non-bigamous party.

349. Mara, 513 So. 2d 1220; *see also* Thomason v. Thomason, 2000-522, p. 5 (La. App. 3 Cir. 12/6/00), 776 So. 2d 553, 556–57 (finding that putative community terminated when the civil effects ended).

at a date later than the other good faith, bigamous spouse, whose civil effects end at knowledge of the impediment.

§ 3:32 Nullity of Marriage— Relatively Null Marriage

A marriage is relatively null when entered into without a party's free consent.[350] The common-law equivalent of the relatively null marriage is the voidable marriage.[351] Unlike the absolutely null marriage, the relatively null marriage produces civil effects until it is annulled by a court of competent jurisdiction based on the request only of the party whose consent was not free.[352]

As explained above, "consent is not free when given under duress or when given by a person incapable of discernment."[353] Unlike in some jurisdictions, an action to annul a marriage is not available in Louisiana because one spouse has been declared insane during the marriage.[354]

§ 3:33 Nullity of Marriage—Relatively Null Marriage—Challenging a Relatively Null Marriage

The right to challenge a relatively null marriage for lack of consent belongs to the party whose consent was not free.[355] The right is strictly personal and does not pass to the heirs of the non-consenting spouse.[356] Only the non-consenting spouse or his legal representative can file the action to annul for lack of consent during the spouse's lifetime.[357] Courts have rejected pleas by the spouse of a person incapable of understanding to have the marriage annulled on that basis.[358]

The Louisiana First Circuit Court of Appeal, in *Succession of Ricks*, extended the power to challenge a relatively null marriage to a succession representative after the death of the alleged non-consenting spouse.[359] The deceased husband remarried his ex-wife within hours before his death, and his children, in a will contest, alleged that

---

350. La. Civ. Code Ann. art. 95.

351. *See* John DeWitt Gregory et al., Understanding Family Law 50, 66–67 (3d ed. 2005).

352. *See generally* La. Civ. Code Ann. arts. 95, 97.

353. La. Civ. Code Ann. art. 93; *see* Section 3:18.

354. *See* Ryals v. Ryals, 57 So. 904, 905 (La. 1912).

355. *See* La. Civ. Code Ann. art. 95.

356. Succession of Jene, 173 So. 2d 857, 860 (La. Ct. App. 4 Cir. 1965).

357. *See* Stier v. Price, 37 So. 2d 847, 848–50 (La. 1948) (finding that only the insane spouse or his legal representative can bring an action to annul); Succession of Barth, 152 So. 543, 544 (La. 1934) (recognizing the rule from other jurisdictions that a voidable marriage is valid for all purposes until annulled, and it can only be attacked in a direct proceeding during the lifetime of the parties).

358. *See* Stier, 37 So. 2d at 849–50; Ryals, 57 So. at 905.

359. *See* In re Succession of Ricks, 2003-2580, p. 5 (La. App. 1 Cir. 11/10/04), 893 So. 2d 98, 100.

he lacked the mental capacity to consent to the remarriage.[360] The wife argued that the children had no right of action to bring the suit to annul the marriage because the right of action is personal to the spouse and abates on his death.[361] The court disagreed, concluding that the Louisiana Code of Civil Procedure provides that the proper party to sue to enforce the right of the deceased, even if a personal right, belongs to the succession representative.[362] Therefore, the succession representative was the proper party to challenge the marriage as relatively null.[363]

The *Ricks* court, while valiant in its attempt to right a wrong that appears to have been perpetrated by an opportunistic ex-wife, misapplied the law and created a right without a remedy. The right to challenge a relatively null marriage has limitations. The relatively null marriage, similar to the voidable marriage under the common law, can only be challenged by the party whose consent was lacking and only during the life of that party.[364] If the decedent had filed suit to challenge his marriage prior to his death, the succession representative would be the proper party to continue the action.[365] Or, if the law provided that lack of consent rendered a marriage absolutely null, then a challenge after death would be permitted.[366] Neither was the case in *Ricks*.

Furthermore, even if the succession representative was successful in having the marriage declared null after the decedent's death, the marriage was still valid at the time of the decedent's death. A relatively null marriage, by definition, is a marriage until declared null.[367] Therefore, if the succession representative received a declaration of the nullity of the decedent's marriage, it would not retroactively dissolve the decedent's marriage or change his status at death. While there is reason to question the status of a marriage without consent as relatively null (rather than absolutely null), it is nonetheless a marriage until declared null as the Civil Code currently provides.[368]

In fact, during the 1987 revision of the law on marriage, the Marriage-Persons Committee of the Law Institute originally suggested that the right to challenge the relatively null marriage should belong to the party whose consent was not free "or his legal representative."[369] The Committee wanted to be clear that a person who was incapable of discernment, and would therefore lack procedural capacity to bring the action to annul, could have a legal representative bring the action on his behalf.[370] The Council

360. In re Succession of Ricks, 893 So. 2d at 98–99.

361. In re Succession of Ricks, 893 So. 2d at 99. The trial court agreed with the ex-wife and granted her exception of no right of action. *Id.* at 99.

362. *See* In re Succession of Ricks, 893 So. 2d at 100.

363. In re Succession of Ricks, 893 So. 2d at 100.

364. La. Civ. Code Ann. art. 95; Succession of Barth, 152 So. at 544; Morris v. Godwin, 148 A.3d 63, 70 (Md. Ct. Spec. App. 2016).

365. *See, e.g.*, Morris, 148 A.3d at 71.

366. La. Civ. Code Ann. art. 94. *See generally* Succession of Marinoni, 164 So. 797 (La. 1935).

367. La. Civ. Code Ann. art. 95.

368. La. Civ. Code Ann. art. 95.

369. *See* Katherine Shaw Spaht, *Revision of the Law of Marriage: One Baby Step Forward*, 48 La. L. Rev. 1131, 1154–55 (1988).

370. *See* Spaht, *Revision of the Law of Marriage: One Baby Step Forward*, 48 La. L. Rev at 1154.

expressed concern that the language was too broad and could be used to permit an executor or administrator to bring the action after death, the result ultimately reached by the *Ricks* court.[371] Because the Committee believed that the curator could bring the action on the interdict's behalf without the need for the additional "or his legal representative" clause, the clause was ultimately left out.[372]

§ 3:34 Nullity of Marriage—Relatively Null Marriage—Confirming a Relatively Null Marriage

While a marriage can be relatively null at inception for lack of consent, the party who lacked consent can later confirm the marriage "after recovering his liberty or regaining his discernment."[373] Once facts establish that the marriage has been confirmed, the party no longer has the right to annul the marriage.[374] While divorce would be available, the action in nullity would not.[375]

Prior law required "cohabiting together" as the only means to validate a relatively null marriage.[376] In the 1987 revision, the broader term "confirm" replaced the narrow construction.[377] As a result, the general obligations principles on confirming a relatively null contract are applicable to the marriage contract.[378] Parties can implicitly confirm a relatively null union by living together as spouses or holding themselves out as married, or parties can expressly confirm the marriage to cure its relative nullity.[379]

Jurisprudence on the issue of cohabitation or confirmation has been fact-driven, but having sexual intercourse or freely living together as spouses, even for a short time, will likely be sufficient to confirm a marriage.[380] It is necessary, however, that confirmation occurs after the duress has ceased or the person has regained his under-

---

371. *See* Spaht, *Revision of the Law of Marriage: One Baby Step Forward*, 48 La. L. Rev at 1155.

372. *See* Spaht, *Revision of the Law of Marriage: One Baby Step Forward*, 48 La. L. Rev at 1155; *see also* La. Code Civ. Proc. Ann. arts. 684, 4262, 4555.

373. La. Civ. Code Ann. art. 95.

374. *See* La. Civ. Code Ann. art. 95.

375. *See* La. Civ. Code Ann. art. 95.

376. La. Civ. Code Ann. art. 95 cmt. (c). Courts have also interpreted acts of sexual intercourse to constitute "cohabitation" as that term is used in the marriage context. State v. Brown, 108 So. 2d 233, 235 (La. 1959); Ford v. Ford, 292 So. 2d 275, 277 (La. Ct. App. 2 Cir. 1974).

377. La. Civ. Code Ann. art. 95 cmt. (c).

378. *See* La. Civ. Code Ann. art. 95 cmt. (c). Confirmation under article 1842 can be express or tacit. *See* La. Civ. Code Ann. art. 1842.

379. *See* La. Civ. Code Ann. art. 1842.

380. Thompson v. Thompson, 87 So. 250, 250 (La. 1921) (cohabitating as husband and wife for three days); Boutterie v. Demarest, 52 So. 492, 495 (La. 1910) (consummating the marriage); Taylor v. Castille, 318 So. 2d 106, 107, 109 (La. Ct. App. 3 Cir. 1975) (cohabitating as husband and wife for fifteen days).

standing.[381] In other words, if the non-consenting spouse cohabitates while still under duress or while still incapable of understanding his actions, the marriage remains subject to annulment.

Just as confirmation eliminates the right to annul a relatively null marriage, so too would the passage of time. Article 2032 of the Civil Code provides that an action to annul a relatively null contract prescribes "five years from the time the ground for nullity either ceased, as in the case of incapacity or duress, or was discovered, as in the case of error or fraud."[382] Because consent to wed is not free when given by a person under duress or one who lacks capacity (incapable of discernment),[383] the right to bring the annulment action, when there has been no confirmation, prescribes five years from the time the duress or incapacity ended.[384]

§ 3:35 Nullity of Marriage— Actions Incidental to Null Marriages

When a party seeks a declaration of nullity,[385] the court is authorized to award the party incidental relief just as it would in a petition for divorce.[386] When the cause for nullity is lack of consent and the marriage is relatively null, the right to incidental relief is based on the existence of the marriage. When the marriage is absolutely null, however, the court must be given the power to award incidental relief, such as in the case of a good faith putative spouse who is entitled to the civil effects of marriage.

The Civil Code contains two articles dealing with incidental relief: article 151 authorizes interim relief pending the final nullity judgment, and article 152 authorizes final relief after the judgment of nullity.[387] A party is only entitled to final incidental relief if the party is in good faith and therefore entitled to the civil effects of marriage.[388] If the party is unable to prove good faith, interim relief is available, but it will terminate on the declaration of nullity.[389] Even if a party is not entitled to the civil effects of marriage

381. *See* Fowler v. Fowler, 60 So. 694, 695 (La. 1913) (finding that husband who cohabitated with wife for 20 days was still operating under the threat of duress).

382. *See* La. Civ. Code Ann. art. 2032.

383. *See* La. Civ. Code Ann. art. 95.

384. *See* La. Civ. Code Ann. art. 2032. Because error and fraud are not likely vices of consent for the contract of marriage, the discovery portion of article 2032 does not apply.

385. A party must seek a declaration of nullity when the marriage is relatively null. *See* La. Civ. Code Ann. art. 95. When a marriage is absolutely null, a party may seek an action to recognize the nullity if the party seeks civil effects or incidental relief as a result of the null marriage. *See generally* La. Civ. Code Ann. art. 94.

386. *See generally* La. Civ. Code Ann. arts. 151–152.

387. La. Civ. Code Ann. arts. 151–152.

388. *See* La. Civ. Code Ann. art. 152.

389. *See* La. Civ. Code Ann. art. 152 ("Incidental relief granted pending declaration of nullity to a party not entitled to the civil effects of marriage shall terminate upon the declaration of nullity.").

due to a lack of good faith, that party may be able to seek child custody, visitation, and support as a natural result of parenthood, regardless of the null marriage.[390]

While article 151 states the general proposition that incidental relief permitted in a divorce petition is also available in a petition for a declaration of nullity of marriage, undesirable consequences may flow from this general rule as it relates to interim spousal support.[391] Because interim spousal support is available to either spouse in a valid marriage regardless of fault, interim support is arguably available to either spouse in a putative setting.[392] Permitting a bad faith spouse in a putative marriage to receive interim spousal support, however, directly conflicts with the Civil Code's mandate that spouses must be in good faith when contracting the marriage to receive *any* civil effects of marriage.[393] A spouse in bad faith could lure an unsuspecting, wealthy spouse into an invalid marriage to later receive the civil effect of interim support. While the obligation of support owed during marriage should permit parties to a valid marriage to receive interim support regardless of fault, the right to receive interim support should not be afforded to a bad faith spouse when there is no marriage at all due to the actions of the bad faith spouse. No published opinion has considered the issue or has permitted a bad faith putative spouse to receive interim support.

§ 3:36 Incidents and Effects of Marriage

Chapter 3 of Title IV in Book I sets forth the duties owed between married persons and the general authority married persons share over their family. While the litigation surrounding these provisions is scant, the law sets forth general principles of public order that inform other family laws.

---

390. *See id. But see* Section 3:28 (noting that if both parties are in bad faith, the child will be considered to have been born outside of marriage and must establish filiation).

391. *See* La. Civ. Code Ann. art. 151.

392. The comments to article 152 take this position. *See* La. Civ. Code Ann. art. 152 cmt. (b) ("This [Article] and Article 151 govern claims for incidental relief pendente lite, which a party may be granted irrespective of the nature of the alleged nullity, and of whether he was in good or bad faith in contracting the marriage.").

393. *See* La. Civ. Code Ann. art. 96. The "civil effect" of interim support stems from the obligation of support that spouses owe during marriage. *See* Cortes v. Fleming, 307 So. 2d 611, 616 (La. 1973).

§ 3:37 Incidents and Effects of Marriage— Mutual Duties of Married Persons

"Married persons owe each other fidelity, support, and assistance."[394] Fidelity contains both a positive and a negative aspect, including the spouse's duty to refrain from adultery and the obligation to submit to the reasonable and normal sexual desires of the other spouse.[395] Support contemplates providing the other spouse with the necessities of life, which include "food, clothing, and shelter," as well as other conveniences, such as "telephones, appliances, and automobiles."[396] Assistance is distinct from support and focuses on the "personal care to be given to an ill or infirm spouse."[397]

Spouses, by contract, cannot derogate from these rules.[398] For example, in *Boudreaux v. Boudreaux*, the spouses entered into a post-nuptial agreement where the husband agreed to pay spousal support to the wife regardless of her fault at the time of divorce.[399] The husband testified that he signed the agreement in an attempt to save his marriage, not as part of a separation agreement.[400] The court found the agreement absolutely null as violating public policy because it undermined the duty of fidelity owed to a spouse in a marriage.[401]

These obligations are directive in nature and frame the general duties owed to one's spouse. Although one spouse may not sue during marriage to enforce these rights,[402] they provide the basis from which other rights and duties are derived. For example, the negative duty of fidelity, or adultery, is a ground to terminate the marriage,[403] and interim spousal support cannot be waived pending divorce because it derives from the duty of support.[404] Additionally, breach of a marital duty, if rising to the level of cruel treatment, could amount to fault that would prevent one spouse from receiving final spousal support. To receive final spousal support, a party must be in need and must be free from

394. La. Civ. Code Ann. art. 98.

395. La. Civ. Code Ann. art. 98 cmt. (b); *see also* Von Bechman v. Von Bechman, 386 So. 2d 910, 911–12 (La. 1980); Currier v. Currier, 599 So. 2d 456, 458 (La. Ct. App. 2 Cir. 1992). *See generally* Dean v. Dean, 579 So. 2d 1124 (La. Ct. App. 2 Cir. 1991); Shenk v. Shenk, 563 So. 2d 1000 (La. Ct. App. 4 Cir. 1990).

396. La. Civ. Code Ann. art. 98 cmt. (c).

397. La. Civ. Code Ann. art. 98 cmt. (c).

398. La. Civ. Code Ann. art. 98 cmt. (e); *see also* Favrot v. Barnes, 332 So. 2d 873, 875 (La. Ct. App. 4 Cir. 1976), *rev'd in part on other grounds*, 339 So. 2d 843 (La. 1976).

399. Boudreaux v. Boudreaux, 98-791, p. 4 (La. App. 3 Cir. 6/2/99), 745 So. 2d 61, 63.

400. Boudreaux, 745 So. 2d at 63. The court noted that the promise to pay spousal support after a divorce can be the subject of a contract, but those agreements were made after the parties had separated during the pendency of a divorce action to end the marriage. The agreement in *Boudreaux* was made during the marriage, unassociated with divorce.

401. Boudreaux, 745 So. 2d at 63.

402. La. Stat. Ann. § 9:291. Under prior law, a breach of these obligations could lead to a judicial separation. *See* Katherine Shaw Spaht, *The Last One Hundred Years: The Incredible Retreat of Law from the Regulation of Marriage*, 63 La. L. Rev. 243, 293 (2003).

403. La. Civ. Code Ann. art. 103(2).

404. *See* Holliday v. Holliday, 358 So. 2d 618, 620 (La. 1978).

fault prior to filing the proceeding to terminate the marriage.[405] Fault that can bar final spousal support includes a breach of the duty of fidelity, support, or assistance.[406]

§ 3:38 Incidents and Effects of Marriage—Mutual Authority Over the Family

The Civil Code contains a chapter on parental authority that sets forth the rights and duties that govern the relationship between parents and children. Prior to the revision of the chapter on parental authority in 2015, the Code provided that while a minor child remained under the authority of his mother and father, if a dispute arose among them, the father's decision would prevail.[407] This "father-knows-best" provision was rooted in the Civil Code of 1870, but it was tempered by the passage of article 99 in 1987 in the chapter entitled "Incidents and Effects of Marriage."[408] Article 99 provides that "[s]pouses mutually assume the moral and material direction of the family, exercise parental authority, and assume the moral and material obligations resulting therefrom."[409] Although no reported case examined the effect that article 99 had on the father-knows-best provision, it appears that the article tacitly repealed the provision.[410] Regardless, after the wholesale revision of the chapter on parental authority, the "father-knows-best" provision was repealed, and it is now clear that parents mutually enjoy authority over the family.[411] The parties, rather than a court, are free to resolve any disagreement that arises between them.

405. La. Civ. Code Ann. art. 111.

406. Fault includes "misconduct" that would have amounted to "one of the previously existing fault grounds for legal separation or divorce." La. Civ. Code Ann. art. 111 cmt. (c). Because a violation of one spouse's marital duties could have been a ground for separation under prior law, it can amount to misconduct sufficient to preclude final spousal support. *See* Section 3:27.

407. La. Civ. Code Ann. art. 216 (vacated by 2015 La. Acts 260).

408. La. Civ. Code Ann. art. 9.

409. La. Civ. Code Ann. art. 9.

410. La. Civ. Code Ann. art. 9.

411. Act No. 260, 2015 La. Acts 1794, 1806.

§ 3:39 Incidents and Effects of Marriage— Suits Between Spouses & Interspousal Immunity

With limited exceptions, spouses are not permitted to sue one another during marriage.[412] Interspousal immunity from suit exists to promote stability within a family.[413] The immunity is procedural in nature, however, and does not negate a substantive claim that may be available after the marriage has terminated, as liberative prescription is suspended between the spouses during the marriage.[414]

The first exception exists for causes of actions pertaining to contracts or actions arising out of the "Matrimonial Regimes" Title of the Civil Code.[415] The second exception exists for claims for restitution of a spouse's separate property.[416] The third exception exists for suits for divorce or for a declaration of nullity of the marriage, and the fourth for claims of support, either spousal or child, and custody of a child while the spouses are living separate and apart.[417] Procedurally, spouses are therefore able to file a suit for support and custody without having to add a claim for divorce.[418] The exceptions listed in the statute are exclusive, not illustrative.[419]

Spouses must consider the implication of liberative prescription in claims that are permitted under these exceptions. Because prescription is suspended between the spouses during marriage, once the spouses are divorced, prescription will begin to run at that time on any claims between them.[420] If the spouses are separate in property, though, courts have determined that prescription does run between them for claims involving restitution of a spouse's separate property.[421] For example, in *Heathcock v. Neuenhaus*, a former wife sued to enforce payment on a note that her former husband had signed during their marriage and on which no payments due had been made.[422] He claimed that the five-year prescriptive period from the date payment was due had already run.[423] She insisted that prescription was suspended during her marriage, and

412. *See* La. Stat. Ann. § 9:291.

413. Smith v. S. Farm Bureau Cas. Ins. Co., 174 So. 2d 122, 124 (La. 1965).

414. La. Civ. Code Ann. art. 3469. *See generally, e.g.*, Duplechin v. Toce, 497 So. 2d 763 (La. Ct. App. 3 Cir. 1986).

415. *See* La. Civ. Code Ann. bk. III, tit. VI (2024) ("Matrimonial Regimes").

416. La. Stat. Ann. § 9:291. *See, e.g.*, Heathcock v. Neuenhaus, 05-954 (La. App. 5 Cir. 4/25/06), 930 So. 2d 1013.

417. La. Stat. Ann. § 9:291.

418. *See generally* Johnson v. Johnson, 2014-0564 (La. App. 1 Cir. 12/23/14), 168 So. 3d 641.

419. Wilkinson v. Wilkinson, 323 So. 2d 120, 125 (La. 1975); Heathcock, 930 So. 2d at 1014; *but see* fns. 77–80.

420. Schexnayder v. Schexnayder, 451 So. 2d 1192, 1193 (La. Ct. App. 5 Cir. 1984).

421. Heathcock, 930 So. 2d at 1014; Eckhardt v. Reveley, 2004-0288, p. 2 (La. App. 4 Cir. 7/21/04), 881 So. 2d 128, 131.

422. Heathcock, 930 So. 2d at 1013–14.

423. Heathcock, 930 So. 2d at 1013–14.

she had filed her claim within five years from her divorce.[424] The court sided with the former husband and concluded that because the parties were separate in property, the former wife's claim fell under the exception for "restitution of separate property," and she was required to file within five years from when payment was due.[425] As the five years had long passed, her claim, brought after the marriage had ended, was dismissed.[426] For spouses who are separate in property, having notes due on demand, when there is no intent by the spouses to pay the debt during marriage, would preserve a spouse's right to collect in the event of divorce.

§ 3:40 Covenant Marriage

Parties seeking to be wed in Louisiana are presented with the option of entering into a covenant marriage.[427] Furthermore, couples who are already married have the ability to convert their traditional marriage into a covenant marriage.[428] In 1997, Louisiana was the first state to enact covenant marriage legislation, and it did so primarily in an attempt to strengthen marriage and help curb the steep rise in divorce rates.[429] The law did not have the impact many had hoped, however, with only slightly more than 1% of couples who married in Louisiana opting for a covenant marriage in the first ten years after the law passed.[430] That number has declined since.[431]

---

424. Heathcock, 930 So. 2d at 1013–14.

425. Heathcock, 930 So. 2d at 1014.

426. Heathcock, 930 So. 2d at 1014; *see also* Eckhardt, 881 So. 2d at 131 (prescription ran against the spouses who were separate in property).

427. La. Stat. Ann. § 9:272. The law defines covenant marriage as "a marriage entered into by one male and one female who understand and agree that the marriage between them is a lifelong relationship." *Id.* Post-*Obergefell*, the constitutionality of this provision is subject to challenge. *See generally* Obergefell v. Hodges, 135 S. Ct. 2584 (2015).

428. *See* La. Stat. Ann. § 9:275.

429. *See* La. Stat. Ann. § 9:272; Cynthia Samuel, *Letter from Louisiana: An Obituary for Forced Heirship and Birth Announcement for Covenant Marriage*, 12 Tul. Eur. & Civ. L.F. 183, 189–90 (1997); Katherine Shaw Spaht, *What's Become of Louisiana Covenant Marriage Through the Eyes of Social Scientists*, 47 Loy. L. Rev. 709, 710–11 (2001) [hereinafter Spaht, *Social Scientists*]; Katherine Shaw Spaht, *Covenant Marriage Seven Years Later: Its as Yet Unfulfilled Promise*, 65 La. L. Rev. 605, 619–20 (2005) [hereinafter Spaht, *Unfulfilled Promise*]. Few states have followed Louisiana's lead and adopted covenant marriage. *See* Ariz. Rev. Stat. Ann. §§ 25-901 to -906 (West, Westlaw through 2018 Legis. Sess.); Ark. Code Ann. §§ 9-11-801 to -808 (West, Westlaw through 2023 Legis. Sess.). For a discussion of the genesis and early years of covenant marriage, *see* Steven L. Nock et al., Covenant Marriage: The Movement to Reclaim Tradition in America (2008).

430. From 1997 through 2007, the Department of Health and Hospitals reported that in the 11-year period after the creation of covenant marriages, 390,893 total marriage licenses were issued and only 4,112 of those, or 1.05%, were for covenant marriages. Matthew Hinton, *Covenant Marriages Get an 'I don't' from Louisiana Couples*, Times Picayune (Aug. 10, 2009), http://www.nola.com/news/index.ssf/2009/08/covenant_marriages_get_an_i_do.html. For discussions of why one author believes covenant marriage did not take hold in Louisiana, *see* Spaht, *Unfulfilled Promise*, *supra* note 428, at 615–20, and Spaht, *Social Scientists*, *supra* note 428.

431. According to records obtained from the Louisiana Department of Health, in 2014, with 31,408 marriage licenses issued, only 186 were for covenant marriages, amounting to 0.6%. In 2015,

Covenant marriages differ from standard marriages in certain respects; most notable are the requirements of counseling and restrictions on procuring a divorce.[432] Furthermore, certain additional formalities, above what is required to perfect a standard marriage, must be followed to perfect a valid covenant marriage.[433]

First, the parties seeking to be wed must undergo premarital counseling which "emphasizes the nature and purposes of marriage and the responsibilities thereto."[434] Second, the parties must execute a declaration of intent, in which they evince their desire to enter into a covenant marriage.[435] The declaration of intent appears as two separate documents: the recitation and the affidavit.[436] The recitation is a document that is signed by both parties and contains a declaration that the parties are entering into a covenant marriage. The recitation provides that the couple has "chosen each other carefully and disclosed to one another everything which could adversely affect the decision to enter into the marriage."[437] It further provides that the couple has received premarital counseling, read the Covenant Marriage Act, and agreed "to be bound by Louisiana law on Covenant Marriages."[438] The affidavit consists of an attestation by the parties that they have received premarital counseling concerning the seriousness of covenant marriage and that they have read the Covenant Marriage Act.[439] The parties must also procure an attestation, signed by their counselor, confirming that the parties have undergone premarital counseling.[440] Once perfected, these documents must be filed with the official who issues the marriage license.[441]

Once a covenant marriage is created, it is governed by the codal provisions applicable to traditional marriages as well as those Code articles particular to covenant marriages.[442] Parties to a covenant marriage may seek annulment under the Civil Code articles governing absolutely and relatively null marriages.[443] However, fraud might

---

the figured remained at 0.6%; it dropped to 0.4% in years 2016 and 2017, and by 2018, it further dropped to 0.2% of total marriage licenses.

432. *See* La. Stat. Ann. §§ 9:272–:273, :307; *see also* Chapter 4.

433. La. Stat. Ann. § 9:272. For a more detailed explanation of how to perfect a valid covenant marriage, see Jessica G. Braun, Handbook on Louisiana Family Law 33 (2018); Spaht, *Unfulfilled Promise*, *supra* note 428, at 612–15; Katherine Shaw Spaht & John Randall Trahan, Family Law in Louisiana § 3.7, at 67 (2009).

434. La. Stat. Ann. § 9:272. The law does not prescribe the specific type of counseling or counselor required.

435. La. Stat. Ann. § 9:273.

436. La. Stat. Ann. § 9:273.

437. La. Stat. Ann. § 9:273.

438. La. Stat. Ann. § 9:273.

439. La. Stat. Ann. § 9:273.

440. La. Stat. Ann. § 9:273. The counselor's attestation may be made a part of the affidavit, or it may be attached to it. Braun, *supra* note 432.

441. La. Stat. Ann. §§ 9:272–:273. The marriage license must also contain a declaration that the couple intends to contract a covenant marriage. La. Stat. Ann. § 9:272.

442. La. Stat. Ann. § 9:274; *see also* La. Stat. Ann. § 9:293.

443. La. Stat. Ann. § 9:272.

also exist as an additional ground for the annulment of a covenant marriage based on the Declaration of Intent signed by the parties before entering into the marriage.[444]

§ 3:41 Change of a Married Person's Name

In Louisiana, "marriage does not change the name of either spouse."[445] A married person, however, is permitted to use the surname of either or both spouses.[446] While a spouse can change a name on a driver's license and social security card, the legal name of a spouse is not changed on the spouse's birth certificate as a result of marriage.[447] Additionally, a woman can choose to "use her maiden name, her present spouse's name, or a hyphenated combination."[448] If she has been widowed, divorced, or remarried, a woman may still "use her maiden name, the surname of her deceased or former spouse, the surname of her present spouse, or any combination thereof."[449]

Currently, the law only permits a woman to use her former spouse's surname. If a married couple uses a hyphenated surname made up of both of their individual surnames and the parties divorce or one party dies, no legislation specifically permits the man to continue using the hyphenated name, although no law prohibits its use either. The gender-specific statute is ripe for an equal protection challenge if facts arise.

§ 3:42 Conflicts of Laws and Validity of Marriage

Parties must meet the mandatory prerequisites of Louisiana law to validly contract marriage in the state, but marriages validly entered into in other states may be recognized in Louisiana, as well.[450] If the marriage was "valid in the state where contracted, or in the state where the parties were first domiciled as husband and wife," Louisiana recognizes the marriage as valid "unless doing so would violate a strong public policy of the state" whose law applies under general conflicts-of-law provisions governing the status of natural persons.[451] The general conflicts rule provides that "[t]he status of a

444. *See* Katherine Shaw Spaht, *Louisiana's Covenant Marriage: Social Analysis and Legal Implications*, 59 La. L. Rev. 63, 91–92 (1998) (arguing that the signed declaration transforms a suppression of the truth into a misrepresentation, which could be the basis for a finding of fraud in contracting the covenant marriage).

445. La. Civ. Code Ann. art. 100; La. Code Civ. Proc. Ann. art. 3947.

446. La. Code Civ. Proc. Ann. art. 3947.

447. La. Civ. Code Ann. art. 100 cmt. (b).

448. La. Stat. Ann. § 9:292.

449. La. Stat. Ann. § 9:292.

450. The term *states* includes other countries. *See, e.g.*, Ghassemi v. Ghassemi, 2007-1927, p. 10 n.13 (La. App. 1 Cir. 10/5/08), 998 So. 2d 731, 739 n.13.

451. La. Civ. Code Ann. art. 3520(A); *see also* La. Civ. Code Ann. art. 3519. Subsection (B) of article 3520 was rendered unconstitutional by *Robicheaux v. Caldwell*, 2 F. Supp. 3d 910 (E.D. La. 2014), *rev'd*, 791 F.3d 616 (5th Cir. 2015).

natural person ... [is] governed by the law of the state whose policies would be most seriously impaired if its law were not applied to the particular issue."[452]

There is a general policy favoring the marriage of persons validly entered into in other states.[453] As a result, a person who seeks to invalidate the marriage must prove: (1) the law that applies is from a state other than where the parties were married or first domiciled as spouses; and (2) that law would invalidate the marriage for strong public policy reasons.[454] So, if the parties were married overseas and moved to Louisiana, Louisiana would recognize the marriage as valid, unless the party challenging the marriage could prove that the marriage violated a strong public policy of the state that is most closely aligned to the parties and the policies at play, which is not the state where the parties were married or first domiciled.

Louisiana courts have repeatedly concluded that common-law marriages from a state that sanctions common-law marriage will be recognized in Louisiana, even though a common-law marriage cannot be contracted in Louisiana.[455] Louisiana courts have also recognized a marriage by proxy that was valid under the laws of another country or state, even though it would be absolutely null if contracted in Louisiana.[456] In 2008, a Louisiana appellate court concluded for the first time that marriages between first cousins validly entered into in Iran would be valid in Louisiana, even though the marriage would be invalid if contracted in Louisiana.[457] The court concluded that validating the marriage was not a violation of a strong public policy of the state because it found "a clear distinction between the marriage of first cousins and marriages contracted by more closely-related collaterals, *i.e.*, uncle and niece, aunt and nephew, and siblings."[458]

---

452. La. Civ. Code Ann. art. 3519. The law further provides that consideration must be given to:

> [T]he strength and pertinence of the relevant policies of [each] state in light of: (1) the relationship of each state, at any pertinent time, to the dispute, the parties, and the person whose status is at issue; (2) the policies referred to in Article 3515; and (3) the policies of sustaining the validity of obligations voluntarily undertaken, of protecting children, minors, and others in need of protection, and of preserving family values and stability.

Id.

453. *See* La. Civ. Code Ann. art. 3520 cmt. (b).

454. La. Civ. Code Ann. art. 3520 cmt. (b).

455. *See, e.g.*, La. Civ. Code Ann. art. 87 cmt. (d); Brinson v. Brinson, 96 So. 2d 653, 656 (La. 1957); Bloom v. Willis, 60 So. 2d 415, 417 (La. 1952); Fritsche v. Vermilion Par. Hosp. Serv. Dist., 2004-1192, pp. 1–4 (La. App. 3 Cir. 2/2/05), 893 So. 2d 935, 937–38; State v. Williams, 96-652, p. 6 (La. App. 3 Cir. 2/5/97), 688 So. 2d 1277, 1281.

456. *See* Morris v. Morris, 2009-2069, 2010 WL 2342659 (La. App. 1 Cir. 6/11/10) (valid marriage of an incarcerated man by proxy under Texas law); United States ex rel. Modianos v. Tuttle, 12 F.2d 927, 929 (E.D. La. 1929) (valid marriage of man present in Louisiana and represented by proxy in Turkey to a Turkish woman resulted in wife becoming an American citizen).

457. *See* Ghassemi v. Ghassemi, 2007-1927 (La. App. 1 Cir. 10/15/08), 998 So. 2d 731, 743–44.

458. *Id.* The court noted that marriages between first cousins were permitted in Louisiana prior to 1902, and even after 1902, the legislature repeatedly ratified marriages between first cousins that had been contracted in violation of the prohibition. *See* Ghassemi, 998 So. 2d at 744. The court further noted that the criminal incest (crime against nature) statute does not include first cousins, but is limited to siblings, aunt/nephew, and uncle/niece relationships. Ghassemi, 998 So. 2d at 748.

Chapter 4

Divorce[*]

* This chapter was derived from the following article: Monica Hof Wallace, *A Primer on Divorce in Louisiana*, 64 Loy. L. Rev. 617 (2018). The authors wish to thank the Loyola Law Review for its assistance on the initial work for this chapter.

§ 4:1 Introduction

In Louisiana, a marriage can be terminated by the death of either spouse, a divorce, a judicial declaration of nullity when the marriage itself is relatively null, or the issuance of a court order authorizing the spouse of a person presumed dead to remarry.[1] Death terminates a marriage as of the date provided on a doctor's certification of death or provided in a judicial declaration of death.[2] Judicial declarations of nullity, which are necessary when a marriage is relatively null, likewise terminate a marriage and are discussed in the chapter on marriage.[3] A special provision exists that provides for termination of a marriage when a court order is issued authorizing the spouse of a service member who is presumed dead to remarry.[4] Even if the service member is later found to be alive, the judgment authorizing the spouse to remarry has the effect of terminating the marriage regardless.[5] For service members, it appears that the judicial declaration of death authorized in the title on absent persons is not necessary if the spouse of the service member wishes only to remarry.[6]

This Chapter focuses on the final cause for termination of a marriage: divorce. Louisiana provides both fault and no-fault options, which are explored in detail below.

§ 4:2 Historical Perspective on Divorce

Like most United States jurisdictions, Louisiana's divorce laws have seen a slow shift away from a fault-based model toward one in which allegations of fault are unnecessary. The waiting periods to obtain a no-fault divorce have also changed, with the extended seven years of living separate and apart decreasing to only six months or one year, depending on whether the couple has minor children of the marriage.[7] It appears that the Louisiana Legislature reached its tipping point on reducing the waiting periods for divorce, having rejected a proposed 2017 amendment to reduce the no-fault waiting period for all divorces to six months, regardless of whether the couple has minor

1. La. Civ. Code Ann. art. 101.

2. *See* La. Stat. Ann. § 9:111. A judgment of divorce rendered against a deceased person is a nullity. Pierce v. Gervais, 425 So. 2d 922, 923 (La. Ct. App. 4 Cir. 1983).

3. *See* Chapter 3, Section 3:32. Judicial declarations of nullity, although unnecessary, are sometimes also sought when a marriage is absolutely null because the parties seek relief incidental to the nullity action.

4. *See* La. Stat. Ann. §§ 9:301, 9:1441.

5. La. Stat. Ann. § 9:301(B).

6. *See* La. Civ. Code Ann. art. 54. A declaration of death under the absent persons articles, or a no-fault divorce if the parties lived separate and apart before military service began, may be a quicker option than awaiting the military presumption of death. *See* Pierce v. Gervais, 425 So. 2d 922, 924 (La. Ct. App. 4 Cir. 1983).

7. For an excellent discussion of the development of the marriage and divorce laws, *see* Katherine Shaw Spaht & John Randall Trahan, Family Law in Louisiana §§ 7.2–7.8 (2009), and David W. Gruning, Family and Obligation: The Louisiana Civil Law of Persons 171–74 (1990).

children.[8] Cognizant of the changing landscape of divorce and the ease of entering into and getting out of marriage, Louisiana was one of a few states to adopt a covenant marriage law in an attempt to strengthen the weakened bond.[9] Enacting a covenant marriage law, however, did not have the effect that many thought.[10] Indeed, covenant marriages account for less than 1% of marriages in Louisiana.[11]

The cause of action for divorce first entered the Louisiana Civil Code in 1827.[12] Prior to 1827, spouses could only seek a separation from bed and board (legal separation) and only when the other spouse was at fault. The initial divorce legislation provided that a divorce could be obtained for the same reasons as a separation from bed and board—all of which were fault-based grounds. For adultery or conviction of an infamous crime, the separation and divorce judgments could be rendered at the same time; in any other instance of fault, a judgment of separation was required, followed by a period of living apart, before the divorce could be granted.[13] Initially, spouses had to live apart for two years without reconciliation after obtaining a judgment of separation before a spouse could petition for and obtain a judgment of divorce.[14] In 1857, Act 149 reduced that period to one year.[15] In addition, only the spouse who obtained the separation (the innocent spouse) could obtain the divorce.[16] Because a separation judgment was only permitted based on the fault of the other spouse, a spouse who was free from fault could choose not to seek a divorce, and the other spouse would be without a remedy—the parties would remain married.[17]

In 1898, the legislature made it possible for the at-fault spouse to obtain a divorce.[18] Although the at-fault spouse could not file for a separation from bed and board, if the other spouse obtained the judicial separation, the at-fault spouse could seek a divorce

---

8. House Bill 136 of the 2017 Regular Session sought to amend the time periods for all no-fault divorces to six months. It failed to pass the House with a 42–55 vote. H.B. 136, 2017 Leg., Reg. Sess. (La. 2017).

9. *See* Chapter 3, Section 3:40.

10. *See* Chapter 3, Section 3:40.

11. From 1997 through 2007, the Department of Health and Hospitals reported that in the 11-year period, 390,893 marriage licenses were issued and only 4,112 (1.05%) were for covenant marriages. According to records obtained from the Louisiana Department of Health, in 2014, with 31,408 marriage licenses issued, only 186 were for covenant marriages, amounting to 0.6%. In 2015, the figure remained at 0.6%; it dropped to 0.4% in years 2016 and 2017, and by 2018, it further dropped to 0.2% of total marriage licenses.

12. Katherine Shaw Spaht, *The Last One Hundred Years: The Incredible Retreat of Law from the Regulation of Marriage*, 63 La. L. Rev. 243, 301 n.371 (2003). Beginning in 1803, the legislature passed specific laws declaring certain individuals to be divorced, but divorce as a general matter was not yet provided for in the law. Katherine Shaw Spaht & John Randall Trahan, Family Law in Louisiana §§ 7.2 (2009).

13. Katherine Shaw Spaht & John Randall Trahan, Family Law in Louisiana § 7.2 (2009).

14. Katherine Shaw Spaht & John Randall Trahan, Family Law in Louisiana § 7.2 (2009).

15. Act No. 149, 1857 La. Acts 137.

16. Act No. 149, 1857 La. Acts 137.

17. Act No. 149, 1857 La. Acts 137. Articles 138 and 139 of the Code of 1870 provided the specific fault grounds.

18. Act No. 25, 1898 La. Acts 34.

upon showing that the parties had lived apart without reconciliation for two years from the judgment of separation.[19] By 1979, that period had been reduced to one year.[20]

The advent of no-fault divorce in Louisiana took place in 1916. Either spouse could obtain a divorce, without regard to fault, on proof that the spouses had lived separate and apart continuously for seven years or more.[21] Opposition by one spouse was no longer relevant. By 1932, the time period had been reduced to four years of living separate and apart continuously;[22] in 1938, it was reduced to two years;[23] in 1979, to one year;[24] and in 1990, to six months.[25] In 2006, in the first extension of time for living separate and apart, the legislature required parties with minor children of the marriage to live separate and apart continuously for one year before obtaining a no-fault divorce.[26]

During the advent of and initial amendments to no-fault divorce, separation from bed and board remained available. To obtain a judgment of separation, the plaintiff had to prove fault.[27] In 1956, proving fault became unnecessary, and either spouse could obtain a judgment of separation if the spouses voluntarily lived separate and apart without reconciliation for one year.[28] In 1977, this time period was reduced to six months if the spouses attested to "irreconcilable differences" between them.[29]

By 1990, the legislature determined that separation from bed and board was no longer necessary, and it was eliminated.[30] In its place, the legislature enacted Article 102 of the Civil Code along with a specific set of procedural requirements that, in large part, mimicked the separation-then-divorce scheme, which had existed in the law for over a century. A spouse could file the petition for divorce (much like filing for separation), but the spouse could not obtain a judgment of divorce until the time period of living separate and apart had passed.[31] The legislature also pared down the fault-based divorces, leaving only adultery and felony conviction and sentence of death or imprisonment at hard labor.[32] The legislature retained what is considered to be the

---

19. Act No. 25, 1898 La. Acts 34.

20. Act No. 360, 1979 La. Acts 1005. The waiting period to get a divorce after a judgment of separation was reduced to one year and 60 days in 1932. Act No. 56, 1932 La. Acts 265.

21. Act No. 269, 1916 La. Acts 557.

22. Act No. 31, 1932 La. Acts 217.

23. Act No. 430, 1938 La. Acts 1091.

24. Act No. 360, 1979 La. Acts 1005.

25. Act No. 1009, 1990 La. Acts 2507.

26. Act No. 743, 2006 La. Acts 2661.

27. *See* Act No. 269, 1916 La. Acts 557.

28. Act No. 303, 1956 La. Acts 626.

29. Act No. 735, 1977 La. Acts 2002.

30. Act No. 1009, 1990 La. Acts 2507. Legal separation was eliminated because it served as a legal step in the process of getting the divorce, rather than as a vehicle to encourage reconciliation. *See* Katherine Shaw Spaht & John Randall Trahan, Family Law in Louisiana § 7.14 (2009).

31. Act No. 1009, 1990 La. Acts 2507; Katherine Shaw Spaht & John Randall Trahan, Family Law in Louisiana § 7.14 (2009); *see also* discussion Section 4:12.

32. Act No. 1009, 1990 La. Acts 2507.

simplest option for divorce—filing the petition for divorce after already having lived separate and apart for the requisite time period.[33]

These four options for divorce (two fault-based and two no-fault) remained relatively unchanged until 2014 when the legislature added two new fault-based divorce grounds when abuse by one spouse of a spouse or a child of one of the spouses occurs during the marriage.[34] Additionally, in 2006, the legislature bifurcated the time periods to obtain a no-fault divorce: 180 days of living separate and apart continuously if there are no minor children of the marriage and 365 days if there are.[35]

§ 4:3 Louisiana Civil Code Article 102

Article 102 of the Louisiana Civil Code was enacted in 1990 after Louisiana eliminated separation from bed and board. A legal separation is no longer available in Louisiana unless the parties contract a covenant marriage.[36] Pursuant to article 102, unless the parties have contracted a covenant marriage, "a divorce shall be granted upon the motion of a spouse when either spouse has filed a petition for divorce and upon proof that the requisite period of time ... has elapsed from the service of the petition, or from the execution of written waiver of the service."[37]

A separate section in the Code of Civil Procedure provides the procedural requirements for an Article 102 divorce.[38] As compared to the Article 103(1) divorce, discussed in Section 4:9 below, in a 102 divorce either spouse can file, *at any time*, a petition with a verified affidavit requesting that a divorce be granted after the requisite time period of living separate and apart has passed.[39] All that is required is a declaration that the plaintiff seeks to be divorced from the defendant, along with allegations of jurisdiction and venue.[40] Other allegations of marital breakdown, fault, or living separate and apart for a period of time are not necessary.[41]

The petition is served on the other spouse or service is waived, and the parties must then live separate and apart continuously for either 180 or 365 days from the date of service or written waiver of service before either party can request a judgment of di-

33. *See* Act No. 1009, 1990 La. Acts 2507.

34. Act No. 316, 2014 La. Acts 1882.

35. Act No. 743, 2006 La. Acts 2661, *amended by* Act No. 604, 2010 La. Acts 2198 & Act No. 316, 2014 La. Acts 1882. Before the legislature adopted divorce based on abuse, when parties had minor children of the marriage and abuse was present, the 180-day waiting period, rather than the 365-day period, applied to requests for a no-fault divorce. *Id.* Once the abuse-based divorce was enacted, that particular rule was eliminated. *See* Act No. 316, 2014 La. Acts 1882.

36. *See* La. Stat. Ann. § 9:309 (separation from bed and board in a covenant marriage). The legislature passed transitional provisions to address parties who had a legal separation at the time it was repealed. *See* La. Stat. Ann. §§ 9:383–:384.

37. La. Civ. Code Ann. art. 102.

38. *See* La. Code Civ. Proc. Ann. arts. 3951 *et seq.*

39. *See* La. Code Civ. Proc. Ann. art. 3951.

40. *See* La. Civ. Code Ann. art. 102 cmt. (b).

41. La. Civ. Code Ann. art. 102 cmt. (b).

vorce.[42] No answer need be made, and no citation will issue.[43] Only after the requisite time period has passed can either spouse—the spouse who filed the petition or the spouse who was served with the petition—file a rule to show cause to set the matter for hearing.[44] This process is unique because the defendant can request relief based solely on the plaintiff's prayer in the original petition. The rule to show cause is the "sole means" by which a final judgment of divorce may be obtained under article 102.[45] Failure to use the procedural rule to show cause to obtain the divorce can result in reversal on appeal.[46] At the hearing on the rule, oppositions to the Article 102 procedure or allegations of reconciliation can be raised, and if none are present, the court must grant the divorce.[47]

§ 4:4 Louisiana Civil Code Article 102—Living Separate and Apart

Living separate and apart continuously is a quintessential element in a no-fault divorce.[48] It must be alleged in the rule to show cause and again by affidavit at the hearing on the rule.[49] This double attestation is intended to prevent collusion by spouses who may wish to get divorced before the statutory waiting period. If the spouses have no minor children of the marriage, they must live separate and apart continuously for 180 days after service of the divorce petition or written waiver of service before filing the rule.[50] If the spouses have minor children of the marriage, the waiting period is

42. La. Civ. Code Ann. art. 103.1. When there are no minor children of the marriage, the applicable time period is 180 days. La. Civ. Code Ann. art. 103.1(1). When there are minor children of the marriage at the time the rule to show cause is filed in accordance with article 102, the applicable time period is increased to 365 days. La. Civ. Code Ann. art. 103.1(2).

43. La. Civ. Code Ann. art. 102 cmt. (c); *see also* Jefferson Cmty. Health Care Ctr., Inc. v. Roby, 2015-198, p. 3 (La. App. 5 Cir. 11/19/15), 180 So. 3d 585, 587 (finding that citation is not necessary in divorce actions under article 102).

44. La. Code Civ. Proc. Ann. art. 3952; La. Civ. Code Ann. art. 102 cmt. (d) (noting that the waiting period is "not waivable").

45. La. Civ. Code Ann. art. 102 cmt. (g).

46. *See* Parker v. Parker, 95-1373, p. 3 (La. App. 3 Cir. 4/3/96), 671 So. 2d 1143, 1145 (reversing the trial court's divorce judgment because no rule to show cause had ever been filed).

47. La. Civ. Code Ann. art. 102 cmt. (c); Simmons v. Simmons, 34,942, p. 2 (La. App. 2 Cir. 8/22/01), 795 So. 2d 448, 450 (quoting Borel v. Borel, 624 So. 2d 1279 (La. Ct. App. 3 Cir. 1993)) ("The word 'shall' as used in article 102 is mandatory and requires the trial court to grant a divorce upon proof that 180 days have elapsed since the date of original separation.... Its effects take place, automatically, by operation of law (absent reconciliation) on proof by the moving spouse that the delay period expired."); *see also* Champion v. Champion, 618 So. 2d 1181, 1182 (La. Ct. App. 3 Cir. 1993).

48. Living separate and apart is a requirement for both the Article 102 and Article 103(1) divorce. As a result, the jurisprudence may apply to both. *See* discussion Section 4:10.

49. La. Code Civ. Proc. Ann. arts. 3952, 3956.

50. La. Civ. Code Ann. art. 103.1.

extended to 365 days.[51] Any judgment in an Article 102 divorce that is rendered before the time periods have elapsed is an absolute nullity.[52]

Because having minor children of the marriage extends the time period for living separate and apart, a woman's pregnancy necessitates a closer look. The Code provides that the 365-day waiting period applies "when there are minor children of the marriage at the time the rule to show cause is filed in accordance with Article 102."[53] On the date the rule to show cause is filed, if the wife is pregnant, the child born to the wife will be presumed to be the child of the husband as provided in the Civil Code chapter on filiation.[54] As a result, the spouses must wait the full 365 days of living separate and apart, even though they expected to file the rule to show cause after 180 days of living separate and apart when the divorce was initially filed.

Filing an Article 102 divorce petition can precede the spouses' living separate and apart.[55] In other words, parties have the option of filing for an Article 102 divorce while they are still residing together, even though the time clock does not begin to tick until the spouses begin living separate and apart.[56] If the divorce is filed while the spouses are residing together, service of the petition should be made personally on the defendant-spouse to prevent any objections based on improper notice.

Living separate and apart, for purposes of obtaining a final divorce, requires that the parties live apart in such a manner that members of the community are aware of the separation.[57] For example, in *Lemoine v. Lemoine*, the wife appealed an Article 102 divorce judgment by arguing that she and her husband did not live separate and apart continuously for the required 180 days.[58] The court disagreed, finding that the spouses occupied separate residences, even though they did "interact intermittently" during the time period.[59] The court concluded that because others were aware of the separation and the separation was visible to the community, even though they had intermittent sexual encounters, the divorce was properly granted.[60] The court also made clear

51. La. Civ. Code Ann. art. 103.1.

52. *See* La. Code Civ. Proc. Ann. art. 3953; *cf.* Nelson v. Nelson, 42,697, pp. 8–9 (La. App. 2 Cir. 12/5/07), 973 So. 2d 148, 153–54 (concluding that if a 103(1) divorce is filed prematurely, it is not absolutely null because the dilatory exception of prematurity can be waived).

53. La. Civ. Code Ann. art. 103.1.

54. La. Civ. Code Ann. art. 185 ("The husband of the mother is presumed to be the father of a child born during the marriage or within 300 days from the date of termination of the marriage.").

55. La. Civ. Code Ann. art. 102 cmt. (a).

56. Robert C. Lowe, Louisiana Divorce § 6:20, *in* 1 Louisiana Practice Series 429.

57. Lemoine v. Lemoine, 97-1626, p. 8 (La. App. 3 Cir. 7/1/98), 715 So. 2d 1244, 1248 (citing Billac v. Billac, 464 So. 2d 819 (La. Ct. App. 5 Cir. 1985)).

58. Lemoine, 715 So. 2d at 1246.

59. Lemoine, 715 So. 2d at 1248. *But see* Woods v. Woods, 27,199, pp. 1–2 (La. App. 2 Cir. 8/23/95), 680 So. 2d 134, 136–37 (Hightower, J., concurring) (raising the issue of whether living in the garage apartment, traveling together, and doing home projects together gave the outward appearance to the community that the parties were still married and should have defeated the living separate and apart element).

60. Mrs. Lemoine also challenged the ruling of the trial court that there was no reconciliation between the parties, drawing a distinction between reconciliation and simply living separate and

that the issue of living separate and apart is not substantively different from failing to reconcile, so facts tending to show reconciliation are often considered as well.[61]

§ 4:5 Louisiana Civil Code Article 102— Fault Not Relevant

While a determination of fault may be necessary for incidents of a no-fault divorce (particularly final spousal support), this need does not preclude an Article 102 divorce from being granted. Issues of fault need not be decided by the trial court, either together with or prior to the hearing on the rule to show cause filed pursuant to article 102. Courts have consistently concluded that once the mandates of the no-fault divorce have been met, and there has been no reconciliation, a divorce can be granted, even if issues of fault remain.[62] The unilateral no-fault divorce was intended to be a streamlined procedure for divorce that parties may select to use.[63] The inherent requirements are few, the time delays are brief, and the demands on the court are minimal.[64]

If a litigant alleges a fault-based ground for divorce—even if the ground was raised before a no-fault ground was added—courts will award the no-fault divorce without considering fault, provided all of the mandates for the no-fault divorce are met.[65] Further, when a movant is entitled to a divorce after meeting the codal requirements, issues of fault in matters incidental to divorce should be dealt with in the incidental matter.[66]

---

apart. Lemoine, 715 So. 2d at 1248–49. The court explained that its analysis focused on whether the parties lived separate and apart continuously for the required time period without reconciliation and noted that there is no substantive difference between living separate and apart and failing to reconcile. *Id. But see* Woods, 680 So. 2d at 137 (Hightower, J., concurring) (questioning whether the court should have considered living separate and apart differently than reconciliation).

61. Lemoine, 715 So. 2d at 1249; *see also* Rivette v. Rivette, 2004-1630 (La. App. 3 Cir. 4/6/05), 899 So. 2d 873 (considering whether the parties lived together at some period of time sufficient to amount to reconciliation); *see also* discussion in Section 4:10.

62. *See, e.g.*, Vernon v. Vernon, 624 So. 2d 1295, 1298 (La. Ct. App. 3 Cir. 1993); Champion v. Champion, 618 So. 2d 1181, 1182–83 (La. Ct. App. 3 Cir. 1993); Borel v. Borel, 624 So. 2d 1279 (La. Ct. App. 3 Cir. 1993); Watters v. Watters, 607 So. 2d 948, 949 (La. Ct. App. 4 Cir. 1992); Napoli v. Napoli, 543 So. 2d 98, 100 (La. Ct. App. 1 Cir. 1989).

63. Vernon, 624 So. 2d at 1297 (citing Watters, 607 So. 2d 948).

64. Watters, 607 So. 2d at 949–50.

65. Watters, 607 So. 2d at 949–50. In *Watters*, the husband filed an Article 102 divorce, and the wife answered and filed a reconventional demand alleging adultery. The husband filed a rule to show cause, and at the hearing, the wife asked that her right to litigate the adultery claim be reserved. The court denied her request and granted the husband's divorce under article 102. The wife appealed, contending that the trial court erred because issues of fault were still pending. The appellate court disagreed, explaining that the wife could still litigate her claims of fault if the findings were necessary, but because the divorce had been granted, finding fault for purposes of an immediate divorce was unnecessary. *Id. See also* Martin v. Trushyna, 2019-79 (La. App. 5 Cir. 11/13/19), 283 So. 3d 1083 (suggesting that there is no absolute right to a fault-based divorce when the requirements of article 102 have been met).

66. *See* La. Civ. Code Ann. art. 105 ("In a proceeding for divorce or thereafter, either spouse may request a determination of custody, visitation, or support of a minor child; support for a spouse; injunctive relief; use and occupancy of the family home or use of community movables or immovables; or use of personal property.").

In *Martin v. Trushyna*, the Louisiana Fifth Circuit Court of Appeal held that spouses in a pending divorce proceeding have no right to present evidence of fault when both an Article 102 divorce petition and a fault-based divorce petition have been filed and the requirements for the Article 102 divorce are met.[67] In *Martin*, the wife filed an Article 102 petition for divorce and later filed an abuse-based divorce petition under articles 103(4) and 103(5). The district court's decision not to hear evidence of fault did not preclude the wife from later seeking incidental relief for the alleged abuse.[68]

Under the law prior to 1998, awaiting a hearing on fault created problems for litigants receiving interim spousal support. For example, in *Vernon v. Vernon*, the wife's hearing to determine final spousal support was set after the rule to show cause hearing for the Article 102 divorce.[69] She urged the court to continue the hearing on the divorce to the date of her final spousal support trial so that her interim support would not be interrupted while she awaited her hearing on final support.[70] The court declined, recognizing that her interim support would end at the judgment of divorce and viewing the situation as one that should be dealt with by the legislature.[71] Just a few years later, the legislature remedied the problem, allowing interim support to continue past the judgment of divorce if the request for final support was pending at the time the divorce judgment was granted.[72] In 2018, the legislature removed the requirement that a request for final support be pending.[73] Now, in all cases, when interim support is granted, it continues for 180 days following the judgment of divorce to allow the economically disadvantaged spouse sufficient time to transition from the marital relationship.[74]

§ 4:6 Louisiana Civil Code Article 102—Procedural Requirements

A Louisiana court has jurisdiction over an action for divorce if, at the time of filing, one or both of the spouses are domiciled in Louisiana.[75] If a spouse establishes and maintains a residence in a parish of Louisiana for a period of six months, a rebuttable presumption arises that the parish of residence is the spouse's domicile.[76] These jurisdictional rules apply not only to the Article 102 divorce but to the Article 103 divorce, as well.

67. Martin v. Trushyna, 2019-79 (La. App. 5 Cir. 11/13/19), 283 So. 3d 1083, 1089.

68. Martin, 283 So. 3d at 1089; *see also* discussion Section 4:20.

69. Vernon v. Vernon, 624 So. 2d 1295, 1298 (La. Ct. App. 3 Cir. 1993).

70. Vernon, 624 So. 2d at 1298.

71. Vernon, 624 So. 2d at 1298; *see also* Borel, 624 So. 2d at 1283.

72. *See* 1997 La. Acts 1078 (enacting La. Civ. Code Ann. arts. 111, 113 & cmts.).

73. Act No. 265, 2018 La. Acts.

74. Act No. 265, 2018 La. Acts. Interim support can continue past the 180 days for good cause shown. La. Civ. Code Ann. art. 113.

75. La. Code Civ. Proc. Ann. art. 10(A)(7).

76. La. Code Civ. Proc. Ann. art. 10(B).

An Article 102 divorce proceeding is a summary proceeding.[77] It is conducted without citation and without all of the formalities required in ordinary proceedings.[78] A petition for an Article 102 divorce has two specific requirements: the petition must contain allegations of jurisdiction and venue, and the petition must be verified by the affidavit of the petitioner.[79] If the requirements of jurisdiction and venue are not met, any final judgment of divorce rendered in accordance with article 102 will be an absolute nullity.[80]

Because the filing of the petition for divorce under article 102 is only the initial step, and the divorce action is not viable until the passage of time required by article 103.1, no answer is required.[81] Even though no answer is required and citation does not issue, notice by the clerk of court or a deputy clerk is required.[82] Service of the notice and accompanying petition can be made on the party,[83] or the party may expressly waive service and the accompanying notice by a written waiver executed after the filing of the petition.[84] If such a waiver occurs, the time periods imposed by article 103.1 will run from the date of execution of the waiver.[85]

The rule to show cause is the only procedural mechanism to obtain a final judgment of divorce under article 102;[86] a motion for summary judgment or judgment on the pleadings may not be used.[87] The rule to show cause must allege proper service of the initial petition for divorce, that the requisite period of time in accordance with article 103.1 or more has elapsed since service, and that the spouses have lived separate and apart continuously for that requisite period of time.[88] The rule to show cause must be verified by the affidavit of the mover and must be served on the defendant, the

77. Hightower v. Schwartz, 2014-0431, p. 3 (La. App. 4 Cir. 10/15/14), 151 So. 3d 903, 904 ("[T]here is no doubt, that a divorce proceeding under article 102 is a summary proceeding.").

78. La. Code Civ. Proc. Ann. art. 2591.

79. La. Code Civ. Proc. Ann. art. 3951; *see also* La. Civ. Code Ann. art. 102 & cmt. (b) ("The petition need not allege marital breakdown, fault on the part of the other spouse, living separate and apart for a period of time, or any other basis for the plaintiff's demand.").

80. La. Code Civ. Proc. Ann. art. 3953.

81. La. Civ. Code Ann. art. 102 cmt. (c); Morrow v. Morrow, 595 So. 2d 367, 368 (La. Ct. App. 2 Cir. 1992).

82. Notice of suit in an Article 102 divorce action is statutorily directed. La. Stat. Ann. § 13:3491. However, notice signed by the clerk is not mandatory, and the absence of such notice will not render a judgment of divorce invalid for that reason alone. La. Stat. Ann. § 13:3493 (superseding Johnston v. Johnston, 94-1167 (La. App. 3 Cir. 3/8/95), 653 So. 2d 40).

83. Service must be requested within 90 days after the filing of the petition unless waived. La. Code Civ. Proc. Ann. art. 3955.

84. La. Code Civ. Proc. Ann. art. 3957.

85. La. Civ. Code Ann. art. 102.

86. La. Civ. Code Ann. art. 102 cmt. (g).

87. La. Civ. Code Ann. art. 102 cmt. (g); *see also* Cobb v. Cobb, 96-436, pp. 5–6 (La. App. 5 Cir. 11/26/96), 685 So. 2d 342, 344–45. In *Cobb*, a judgment of divorce, rendered in a summary proceeding, was deemed an absolute nullity because the judgment was based on a motion to set a pretrial conference that did not contain the statutorily required information sufficient to substitute for the legislatively mandated rule to show cause. *Id.* at 344–45.

88. La. Code Civ. Proc. Ann. art. 3952.

defendant's attorney of record, or the duly appointed curator for the defendant prior to granting the divorce, unless the defendant waives service.[89]

Either spouse may file the rule to show cause and obtain the final judgment of divorce.[90] Neither article 102 nor Article 3952 of the Code of Civil Procedure specifically states the number of days before the hearing on the rule to show cause that the rule must be served on the opposing party.[91] Article 966 of the Louisiana Code of Civil Procedure requires a 10-day period between notice and a summary judgment hearing,[92] and this time period has been deemed applicable to an Article 102 divorce because of its summary nature.[93] Any final judgment of divorce rendered pursuant to a rule to show cause filed before the requisite time period of living separate and apart will be absolutely null.[94]

At the rule to show cause hearing, the opposing spouse may raise any defenses or procedural deficiencies in the Article 102 divorce. Because no answer is required in an Article 102 divorce, a defense can be raised for the first time at the hearing on the rule, which could be unexpected by the moving party. Such was the case in *Hightower v. Schwartz*.[95] Mr. Hightower raised the defense of reconciliation for the first time at the hearing on the rule, and Mrs. Hightower objected because she had no notice of the defense nor adequate time to refute the allegations.[96] The trial court sustained her objection but allowed Mr. Hightower to proffer evidence of reconciliation.[97] He did not.[98] On appeal, the court recognized that procedurally, because the Article 102 divorce does not require an answer, an affirmative defense cannot be pled and therefore cannot be waived for failure to plead.[99] From a policy standpoint, though, the court was concerned that reconciliation—raised for the first time at the hearing—could serve to

---

89. La. Code Civ. Proc. Ann. art. 3952. The district court rules provide an excellent checklist when seeking a judgment in an Article 102 divorce. *See* Appendix 27.0A: La. C.C. Art. 102 Divorce Checklist, Louisiana Supreme Court (2024), https://www.lasc.org/rules/dist.ct/Title_IV/APPENDIX_27.0A.pdf.

90. La. Civ. Code Ann. art. 102. The article's reference to "the motion of a spouse" makes clear that the defendant in the divorce petition may file the rule and obtain the divorce if the defendant presents the requisite evidence. *See* Bishop v. Bishop, 98-59, p. 4 (La. App. 5 Cir. 5/27/98), 712 So. 2d 697, 700.

91. Hirstius v. Hirstius, 618 So. 2d 423, 425 (La. Ct. App. 5 Cir. 1993) (noting lack of guidance but concluding that six days was insufficient notice).

92. Hirstius, 618 So. 2d at 425.

93. Hirstius, 618 So. 2d at 425 ("Inasmuch as an Art. 102 hearing is summary in nature, a similar ten-day period seems appropriate. In any event, a notice of six days or less is not enough, particularly if the opposing party has filed an exception to the Art. 102 petition.").

94. *See* La. Code Civ. Proc. Ann. art. 3953; *see also* Shewbridge v. Shewbridge, 28,981, p. 2 (La. App. 2 Cir. 12/11/96), 685 So. 2d 418, 420.

95. Hightower v. Schwartz, 2014-0431 (La. App. 4 Cir. 10/15/14), 151 So. 3d 903.

96. Hightower, 151 So. 3d at 904.

97. Hightower, 151 So. 3d at 904.

98. Hightower, 151 So. 3d at 904.

99. Hightower, 151 So. 3d at 904.

extinguish the divorce action.[100] Ultimately, the court did not have to decide the issue because, although Mrs. Hightower opened the door to evidence of reconciliation when she testified that the parties had lived separate and apart "without reconciliation," Mr. Hightower failed to proffer any evidence of reconciliation. The court therefore affirmed the judgment of divorce. [101]

Failure to receive notice and prepare for a reconciliation defense can be a serious concern for litigants at a rule to show cause hearing. Because of the unique nature of the article 102 proceeding, the hearing is an appropriate time to raise the defense; no responsive pleadings are required before that hearing. Certainly, a litigant could make the same argument about procedural deficiencies that are raised for the first time at the rule hearing, but those challenges seem less troublesome because the documents ordinarily speak for themselves. Courts may consider continuing the hearing to allow both sides to adequately prepare for any unexpected defenses.

Using the exception of *lis pendens* when there are competing divorce claims has been given attention by the Louisiana Supreme Court. In *Gamble v. Gamble*, the Court held that a divorce proceeding and any ancillary relief, such as spousal support, involve the same transaction or occurrence within the context of an exception of *lis pendens* pursuant to Article 531 of the Louisiana Code of Civil Procedure.[102] *Gamble* involved two competing divorce petitions that were separately filed by each spouse in different venues.[103] The husband filed his petition for divorce first in Caddo Parish making no ancillary demands, but reserving the right to do so in the future. The wife filed her petition in Orleans Parish a few days thereafter, requesting a partition of community property and other incidental relief.[104] The husband then amended his petition in Caddo, raising some of the same incidental actions as the wife. Each party filed exceptions of *lis pendens* in their preferred courts.[105] The wife's exception in Caddo Parish was overruled, but the husband's exception in Orleans Parish was sustained, dismissing her action. The wife appealed and the Fourth Circuit reversed, concluding that *lis pendens* did not apply to the incidental relief because the wife requested incidental relief before the husband.[106]

The Louisiana Supreme Court reversed again and reinstated the trial court's ruling, declaring that the first party to file a petition for divorce may have any subsequent petitions for divorce or incidental matters—arising out of the same transaction or

---

100. Before the institution of the Article 102 divorce, reconciliation was raised as an affirmative defense, in a motion to dismiss or in a peremptory exception of no cause of action, all of which occurred in ordinary proceedings. Hightower, 151 So. 3d at 905.

101. Hightower, 151 So. 3d at 906–07.

102. Gamble v. Gamble, 2022-00102 (La. 4/20/22), 336 So. 3d 452, 454, *reh'g denied*, 2022-00102 (La. 6/22/22), 339 So. 3d 643; La. Code Civ. Proc. Ann. art. 531.

103. *See generally*, Gamble, 336 So. 3d 452.

104. Gamble, 336 So. 3d 452.

105. Gamble, 336 So. 3d 452.

106. Gamble, 336 So. 3d at 452–453.

occurrence—dismissed under the *lis pendens* exception.[107] Even though defendants in a divorce action are not required to assert claims for ancillary matters in the action for divorce, if they choose to assert ancillary matters before the conclusion of the divorce, the spouse who filed the divorce first can rely on *lis pendens* to have the second suit dismissed.

§ 4:7 Louisiana Civil Code Article 102— Procedural Requirements— Abandonment

Special rules for abandonment and voluntary dismissal apply in an Article 102 divorce. Under Louisiana Code of Civil Procedure Article 3954, the Article 102 divorce is deemed abandoned "if the rule to show cause ... is not filed within two years of service of the original petition or written waiver of service of the original petition."[108] This two-year period is only applicable to Article 102 divorce actions; divorce actions filed under article 103 are subject to the general three-year abandonment provision.[109] Although the Article 102 petition is deemed abandoned without formal order after the passage of two years, any party or interested person may file an ex parte motion with the trial court, and the trial court must then enter an order of dismissal as of the date of abandonment.[110]

It is not necessary that a final judgment of divorce is entered within two years of filing of the divorce petition or written waiver of service; only *filing* the rule to show cause is statutorily required.[111] In *Sharp v. Sharp*, Mrs. Sharp filed an Article 102 divorce petition and, seven months later, filed a rule to show cause.[112] The hearing was set shortly thereafter, but no further action was taken to obtain the judgment of divorce.[113] Mr. Sharp died 10 years later, and Mrs. Sharp sought unpaid interim spousal support

107. Gamble, 336 So. 3d. at 454.

108. La. Code Civ. Proc. Ann. art. 3954. When the article was originally passed, the abandonment period was one year. *See* Act No. 1009, 1990 La. Acts 2507.

109. *See* La. Code Civ. Proc. Ann. art. 561; *see also* Kenneth Rigby & Katherine Shaw Spaht, *Louisiana's New Divorce Legislation: Background and Commentary*, 54 La. L. Rev. 19, 82–83 (1993); Sharp v. Sharp, 2005-1046, p. 7 (La. App. 1 Cir. 6/28/06), 939 So. 2d 418, 422 ("[T]he legislature was aware of the general abandonment rule at the time article 3954 was enacted, and by making it applicable to article 102 divorces, manifested its intent that that provision control in those cases. If the legislature wanted the general abandonment rule to come into effect in situations such as the one presently before this court, or if it wanted to enact other provisions to resolve a situation where abandonment can occur following the timely filing of the rule to show cause, it could have provided for same, but it failed to do so.").

110. La. Code Civ. Proc. Ann. art. 561.

111. *See* Sharp, 939 So. 2d at 421; *see also* Simons v. Simons, 96-832, p. 2 (La. App. 5 Cir. 4/9/97), 694 So. 2d 999, 1000.

112. Sharp v. Sharp, 2005-1046 (La. App. 1 Cir. 6/28/06), 939 So. 2d 418, 421.

113. Sharp, 939 So. 2d at 421.

payments from his estate.[114] His succession representative argued that the divorce had long been abandoned, relying on the general abandonment article that requires three years without "any step in its prosecution or defense."[115] The court concluded that the rule to show cause had been timely filed, and the general abandonment article did not apply in an Article 102 divorce context, as the more specific statute controlled over the more general.[116] As a result, Mrs. Sharp was able to collect spousal support arrearages because the marriage did not terminate until Mr. Sharp's death.[117] The dissent persuasively argued that the general abandonment period should have applied after Mrs. Sharp filed her rule to show cause, but not before.[118]

While article 102 contains its own rules on abandonment, two well-established exceptions under the general abandonment article still apply in an Article 102 divorce context.[119] First, when a plaintiff is prevented, by circumstances beyond his control, from filing the rule to show cause within the two-year period, the period may be suspended.[120] Second, under a theory of estoppel, if a defendant takes any action inconsistent with the intent to treat the case as abandoned, he waives the right to plead abandonment.[121] Therefore, the jurisprudence interpreting the exceptions to the general abandonment article should apply in the context of an Article 102 divorce.

The two-year abandonment period for an Article 102 divorce is important when considering the effect on the community property regime. A spouse's community property regime is terminated "retroactively to the date of filing of the petition in the action in which the judgment of divorce is granted."[122] For an Article 102 divorce, the community could terminate up to two years prior to the divorce judgment, or longer, if extensions are permitted. In light of the retroactive effect on property, a shortened abandonment period should prevent a spouse from threatening divorce and the consequences that could result therefrom for an extended period of time.[123]

---

114. Sharp, 939 So. 2d at 420.

115. *See* La. Code Civ. Proc. Ann. art. 561(A).

116. Sharp, 939 So. 2d at 421–22.

117. Mrs. Sharp was subject to the general five-year prescriptive period for seeking alimony arrearages. Sharp, 939 So. 2d at 422.

118. Sharp, 939 So. 2d at 423–24 (Kuhn, J., dissenting).

119. Exceptions inherent in Louisiana Code of Civil Procedure Article 561 are applicable to Louisiana Code of Civil Procedure Article 3954. *See* Sibley v. Sibley, 1997-1912, p. 2 (La. App. 1 Cir. 12/28/98), 724 So. 2d 275, 277.

120. Sibley, 724 So. 2d at 277 (suspending the two-year abandonment period because the trial court and appellate court were considering an Article 103 divorce in the same case).

121. Sibley, 724 So. 2d at 277. Note that abandonment provisions are to be interpreted liberally in favor of maintaining the action. *Id.*; Sharp, 939 So. 2d at 421.

122. La. Civ. Code Ann. art. 159. Spouses are permitted to terminate the community sooner under articles 2374–75.

123. Obtaining a judgment of separation of property from the outset of the proceeding could eliminate any uncertainty.

§ 4:8 Louisiana Civil Code Article 102— Procedural Requirements— Voluntary Dismissal

A special rule likewise applies when a spouse seeks to voluntarily dismiss an Article 102 divorce petition.[124] A judgment of voluntary dismissal in an Article 102 divorce action must be rendered on joint application of the parties and payment of all costs, or on contradictory motion of the plaintiff.[125] A judgment of dismissal will be without prejudice to any separation of property decree that terminates the community property regime.[126]

A special rule for dismissal is needed in the Article 102 divorce context because either spouse can file the rule to show cause.[127] If one spouse no longer wants to get divorced but the other spouse now desires the divorce, the spouse who did not file the petition can still file the rule. As a result, the other spouse must join in the petition to dismiss, or it must be brought into court contradictorily before the court will authorize a dismissal.

§ 4:9 Louisiana Civil Code Article 103(1)

Louisiana Civil Code Article 103(1) is the second no-fault divorce option and provides an alternative to the Article 102 divorce.[128] In contrast to article 102, article 103(1) allows spouses to obtain an immediate divorce when the parties have already lived separate and apart for the required period of time.[129] The Article 103 divorce is a simpler, less costly option, but it can only be filed *after* the parties have been physically separated for either 180 or 365 days continuously; it is only "immediate" in the sense that the spouses do not have to wait any length of time after the petition is filed, like they would in an Article 102 divorce. If a spouse wishes to file a no-fault divorce *before* having lived separate and apart for the required time period, the only option is an Article 102 divorce.[130] Under article 102, the time period to live separate and apart will begin to run after service or waiver of service of the petition. By necessity, obtaining the judgment of divorce will take longer.

---

124. *See* La. Code Civ. Proc. Ann. art. 3958.

125. La. Code Civ. Proc. Ann. art. 3958.

126. La. Code Civ. Proc. Ann. art. 3958.

127. *See* La. Code Civ. Proc. Ann. art. 3952.

128. La. Civ. Code Ann. art. 103(1) ("Except in the case of a covenant marriage, a divorce shall be granted on the petition of a spouse upon proof that: (1) The spouses have been living separate and apart continuously for the requisite period of time, in accordance with Article 103.1, or more on the date the petition is filed.").

129. La. Civ. Code Ann. art. 103 & cmt. (a).

130. *See* Parker v. Parker, 95-1373, p. 4 (La. App. 3 Cir. 4/3/96), 671 So. 2d 1143, 1145 (failing to grant a 103(1) divorce because the parties had only lived apart three and a half months at the time the petition was filed).

If, after filing an Article 102 divorce petition, the spouses live separate and apart for the requisite time period to then obtain an Article 103(1) divorce, the Article 102 petition could be amended to seek an Article 103(1) divorce, but this route may have a significant impact on the community property regime. As the community property regime terminates retroactive to the filing of the petition on which the divorce is granted,[131] the regime would terminate when the Article 103(1) claim was added (at a later date), not when the Article 102 divorce was originally filed.[132]

§ 4:10 Living Separate and Apart

Article 103(1) requires that parties live separate and apart continuously for a period of either 180 days or 365 days or more *on the date the petition is filed.*[133] If there are no minor children of the marriage, the spouses must live separate and apart continuously for 180 days; if there are minor children of the marriage on the date the petition is filed, the spouses must remain separate and apart continuously for 365 days.[134] Because having minor children of the marriage extends the time period for living separate and apart, a woman's pregnancy will necessitate a longer waiting period. If the wife is pregnant at the time either spouse files the Article 103(1) petition, the child born to the wife will be presumed to be the child of the husband as provided in the Civil Code chapter on filiation.[135] As a result, even if the wife is not pregnant at the time the parties separate, and a spouse therefore expects to file the Article 103(1) divorce at the end of 180 days, that spouse must wait the full 365 days if, at the time of filing, she is pregnant.[136]

Because no court filing is initially made when the spouses begin living separate and apart, the separation contemplated by article 103(1) must be voluntary on the part of at least one of the spouses.[137] When a spouse evidences an intent to terminate the marital association and the spouses physically separate, the statutorily required separation period begins to run; this occurs regardless of the cause of the initial physical separation.[138]

---

131. La. Civ. Code Ann. art. 159.

132. *See* Warner v. Warner, 2002-1380, p. 6 (La. App. 1 Cir. 8/13/03), 859 So. 2d 146, 150; *see also* Gray v. Gray, 463 So. 2d 14 (La. Ct. App. 5 Cir. 1985); Naquin v. Naquin, 572 So. 2d 1075 (La. Ct. App. 5 Cir. 1990); Andrea Carroll & Richard D. Moreno, Matrimonial Regimes § 7:2, *in* 16 Louisiana Civil Law Treatise 559 (4th ed. 2013). Obtaining a judgment of separation of property could eliminate the issue. *See* La. Civ. Code Ann. art. 2374.

133. La. Civ. Code Ann. art. 103(1).

134. La. Civ. Code Ann. art. 103.1.

135. La. Civ. Code Ann. art. 185 ("The husband of the mother is presumed to be the father of a child born during the marriage or within three hundred days from the date of termination of the marriage.").

136. *See* Section 4:4.

137. La. Civ. Code Ann. art. 103 & cmt. (c); Adams v. Adams, 408 So. 2d 1322, 1325 (La. 1982); Nelson v. Nelson, 42,697, p. 4 (La. App. 2 Cir. 12/5/07), 973 So. 2d 148, 151.

138. Nelson, 973 So. 2d at 151 (citing Gibbs v. Gibbs, 30-367 (La. App. 2 Cir. 4/8/98), 711 So. 2d 331); Tarbutton v. Tarbutton, 51,486, p. 5 (La. App. 2 Cir. 5/2/17), 217 So. 3d 1281, 1285.

The Louisiana Supreme Court, in *Adams v. Adams*, explained the need for voluntary separation in an Article 103(1) divorce.[139] In *Adams*, the wife filed for divorce after the parties had lived separate and apart continuously for over two years.[140] The trial court denied the divorce because the couple initially separated when the husband was committed to a mental hospital.[141] On appeal, the wife argued that the law only required the parties to live apart for one year; the law provided no requirement that the separation be voluntary.[142] The husband argued that the separation must be voluntary by both spouses, which cannot exist when the separation begins due to the institutional commitment of one spouse.[143] The court rejected both approaches, explaining that the separation contemplated by the statute must be voluntary on the part of at least one of the spouses, which can be established when the spouse evidences an intent to end the marital association.[144] Because the wife in *Adams* told individuals close to her husband that she was separating from him permanently, and because she filed for a separation (available at the time), she evidenced her intent to end the marriage, and the divorce should have been granted.[145]

Intent to end the marriage can be implied by the conduct of the spouse leaving, even without an express communication to the other spouse.[146] For example, in *Elliott v. Elliott*, the husband moved in with his parents, but according to the wife, he "left because of his father's health, his own health, and work-related pressures."[147] The trial court felt constrained to grant the Article 103(1) divorce, explaining, "I have no discretion in this matter once it is proven to me as the judge of this court that the parties have lived separate and apart for a year and one party asked for a divorce...."[148] The court understood the need for one party to leave freely and voluntarily, and the court could find no evidence to the contrary.

In addition, in *Gibbs v. Gibbs*, the husband initially moved to Texas to find work, but after a few months, he decided not to return to his marriage.[149] He came home infrequently, never stayed overnight, and had no sexual contact with his wife.[150] When the husband filed for divorce under article 103(1), his wife argued that she had no knowledge of his intent to live separate and apart for purposes of a divorce.[151] The trial court found, and the appellate court affirmed, that the husband evidenced his intent to

139. Adams v. Adams, 408 So. 2d 1322, 1322 (La. 1982).
140. Adams, 408 So. 2d at 1323.
141. Adams, 408 So. 2d at 1323.
142. Adams, 408 So. 2d at 1324.
143. Adams, 408 So. 2d at 1324.
144. Adams, 408 So. 2d at 1327.
145. Adams, 408 So. 2d at 1328.
146. *See generally* Gibbs v. Gibbs, 30-367 (La. App. 2 Cir. 4/8/98), 711 So. 2d 331.
147. Elliott v. Elliott, 458 So. 2d 634, 635 (La. Ct. App. 3 Cir. 1984).
148. Elliott, 458 So. 2d. at 635–36.
149. Gibbs, 711 So. 3d 331.
150. Gibbs, 711 So. 2d at 332.
151. Gibbs, 711 So. 2d at 332.

terminate the marriage by his infrequent, short visits and his failure to have conjugal relations with his wife.[152]

Similarly, in *Dunn v. Dunn*, the husband filed an Article 103(1) divorce petition after living separate and apart from his wife due to her having a quadruple bypass that required a three-week hospital stay and a prolonged recovery thereafter.[153] The husband alleged that his wife manifested an intent to terminate the marriage before her surgery by alerting him that she would not be returning to the marital domicile upon her discharge and, instead, would be staying with her sister.[154] The wife alleged that her surgery was a matter of medical necessity and that she did not manifest an intent to terminate the marriage until after her discharge from the hospital.[155] Ultimately, while finding the facts of the case "unique," the court determined that the husband believed that his wife wanted to terminate the marriage and took her conduct as evidence of her intent.[156] It pointed to her request that her husband deliver her van and personal items to the hospital as additional evidence.[157] The appellate court affirmed the trial court's grant of the divorce.[158]

Based on *Elliott*, *Gibbs*, and *Dunn*, a spouse's intent to end the marriage can be implied by that spouse's actions without communicating his intent directly to the other spouse. Notwithstanding the difficulty in determining implied intent, it is troublesome that one spouse need not express an intent to the other spouse to end their marriage. While one spouse may be hoping for and working towards reconciliation, the other spouse can say nothing, stay away, and then file for divorce. Because a no-fault divorce is relatively quick to obtain, the requirement of express communication to the other spouse seems to be more appropriate.

For military personnel, separation resulting from military service will not be considered living separate and apart,[159] but if the separation occurred prior to and independent of the spouse's departure into the armed services, the time while in the service is properly considered living separate and apart for purposes of a divorce.[160]

Furthermore, living separate and apart contemplates living in separate residences, not simply different rooms in the same house.[161] And separation by the spouses should

---

152. Gibbs, 711 So. 2d at 332.

153. Dunn v. Dunn, 53,665 (La. App. 2 Cir. 1/13/21), 309 So. 3d 969, 971.

154. Dunn, 309 So. 3d 969 at 973.

155. Dunn, 309 So. 3d 969 at 973.

156. Dunn, 309 So. 3d 969 at 973.

157. Dunn, 309 So. 3d 969 at 973.

158. Dunn, 309 So. 3d 969 at 973–74.

159. *See, e.g.*, De Maupassant v. Clayton, 38 So. 2d 791 (La. 1949); Pierce v. Gervais, 425 So. 2d 922, 925 (La. Ct. App. 4 Cir. 1983).

160. Pierce, 425 So. 2d at 925 (citing Gardner v. Gardner, 125 So. 2d 463 (La. Ct. App. 2 Cir. 1960); Davis v. Watts, 23 So. 2d 97 (La. 1945)).

161. *See, e.g.*, Singleton v. Rogers, 106 So. 781 (La. 1926) (finding that separate rooms in one house was not sufficient); Billac v. Billac, 464 So. 2d 819, 821 (La. Ct. App. 5 Cir. 1985) (finding that separate rooms in one house was not sufficient); Succession of LeJeune, 59 So. 2d 446, 449 (La. 1952) (finding insufficient evidence where the husband occupied the outside apartment because he was ill, but the

be visible in the community such that others are aware of the separation.[162] For example, living in different apartments, even in the same building, has been held sufficient because the apartments were autonomous and others in the community were aware of the separation.[163] Ultimately, once the parties have been living separate and apart continuously without reconciliation for the required time period, the court has no discretion and must grant the divorce.[164]

§ 4:11 Living Separate and Apart—Fault Not Relevant

As discussed in Section 4:5 above, relative to an Article 102 divorce, fault is not relevant when granting an Article 103(1) divorce.[165]

§ 4:12 Living Separate and Apart—Procedural Requirements

In contrast to a divorce obtained under article 102, a divorce pursuant to article 103 is an ordinary proceeding where citation must issue and ordinary delays apply.[166] To initiate proceedings, a party must file a petition for divorce.[167] In the petition, the movant must allege proper jurisdiction and provide the specific grounds for divorce.[168] Because the divorce is based on living separate and apart continuously at the time suit is filed, facts supporting continuous separation must be alleged in the petition.[169]

---

wife cooked him meals and he acted as a handyman for the home); *cf.* Riley v. Riley, 501 So. 2d 814, 815 (La. Ct. App. 4 Cir. 1986) (finding that living in autonomous separate apartments in the same building was sufficient).

162. Riley, 501 So. 2d at 815; Boyd v. Boyd, 348 So. 2d 121, 122 (La. Ct. App. 4 Cir. 1977); LeJeune, 59 So. 2d at 449. *But see* Woods v. Woods, 27,199, pp. 1–2 (La. App. 2 Cir. 8/23/95), 660 So. 2d 134, 136–37 (Hightower, J., concurring) (noting that living in the garage apartment and participating in family activities looked to the community like the parties were still married).

163. *See* Riley, 501 So. 2d at 815.

164. Williams v. Williams, 491 So. 2d 732, 735 (La. Ct. App. 2 Cir. 1986); Saunders v. Saunders, 422 So. 2d 245, 246 (La. Ct. App. 4 Cir. 1982); Brady v. Brady, 388 So. 2d 57, 58 (La. Ct. App. 1 Cir. 1980).

165. *See* Section 4:5; *see also* Roy v. Florane, 119 So. 2d 849, 854 (La. 1960); Ogea v. Ogea, 378 So. 2d 984, 991 (La. Ct. App. 3 Cir. 1979).

166. Nelson v. Nelson, 42,697, p. 4 (La. App. 2 Cir. 12/5/07), 973 So. 2d 148, 151; Rando v. Rando, 31-366, p. 4 (La. App. 2 Cir. 12/9/98), 722 So. 2d 1165, 1167.

167. *See* La. Civ. Code Ann. art. 103.

168. *See* La. Civ. Code Ann. art. 103. The grounds for divorce enumerated in article 103 are: (1) continuous physical separation for at least 180 days where there are no minor children of the marriage or 365 days where there are minor children of the marriage; (2) adultery; (3) conviction of a felony; (4) during the marriage, the other spouse physically or sexually abused the spouse seeking divorce or a child of one of the spouses, regardless of whether the other spouse was prosecuted for the act of abuse; and (5) after a contradictory hearing or consent decree, a protective order or an injunction was issued during the marriage, in accordance with law, against the other spouse to protect the spouse seeking the divorce or a child of one of the spouses from abuse. *Id.*

169. *See* La. Civ. Code Ann. art. 103 cmt. (a).

A hearing in an Article 103(1) divorce is not required unless the judge so directs.[170] As is common in family law proceedings, the plaintiff must submit with the petition a verified affidavit attesting to the truth of the factual allegations in the petition.[171] When the defendant does not waive formal citation and service but instead files an answer, the proceeding moves forward as an ordinary proceeding.[172] At the trial, the plaintiff must present a prima facie case to support the judgment of divorce, as with any other civil proceeding.

Default judgments are appropriate in Article 103(1) proceedings.[173] Although judgments on the pleadings and summary judgments are not available in divorce proceedings as a general rule, they are available in a 103(1) divorce proceeding when both spouses are represented by counsel and both counsel jointly agree to the facts and the proposed judgment, which is also verified by each spouse.[174] The process can be quick and efficient, as the court may sign the judgment in chambers without a formal hearing.[175]

While a divorce judgment rendered under article 102 is an absolute nullity if the required time period has not passed at the time of filing the rule to show cause, a distinction has been made with the 103(1) divorce.[176] Generally, if the petition under 103(1) is filed prematurely, courts refuse to grant the divorce, finding that living separate and apart before filing is a jurisdictional requirement.[177] However, in *Nelson v. Nelson*, the court explained in dicta that it would grant an Article 103(1) divorce based on a prematurely filed petition.[178] The court distinguished the Article 103(1) divorce from the Article 102 divorce, explaining that the dilatory exception of prematurity is available in an Article 103(1) divorce, unlike in an Article 102 divorce, and that exception can be waived.[179] In *Nelson*, the wife never challenged the prematurity of the husband's divorce

170. Robert C. Lowe, Louisiana Divorce § 6:36, *in* 1 Louisiana Practice Series (2023).

171. Robert C. Lowe, Louisiana Divorce § 6:36, *in* 1 Louisiana Practice Series (2023). The affidavit and petition must be submitted with an original and at least one copy of a proposed final judgment. *Id.*

172. *See* Nelson, 973 So. 2d at 151.

173. A defendant in an Article 103(1) divorce action may waive citation, service of process, all legal delays, notice of trial, and appearance at trial, so long as the defendant acknowledges, by sworn affidavit, receipt of a certified copy of the petition. A judgment of default may be entered against the defendant two days (exclusive of holidays) thereafter in open court or by written motion mailed to the court. A hearing on the motion is not required unless the judge directs otherwise. La. Code Civ. Proc. Ann. art. 1702. Note too that the notice requirements for default judgments generally do not apply to motions for default judgments involving a 103(1) or a 103(5) divorce. La. Code Civ. Proc. Ann. art. 1702(F)(3). For an excellent discussion of the procedure followed in an Article 103(1) divorce, see Robert C. Lowe, Louisiana Divorce § 6:36, *in* 1 Louisiana Practice Series (2023).

174. La. Code Civ. Proc. Ann. art. 969.

175. *See* La. Code Civ. Proc. Ann. art. 969.

176. Nelson, 973 So. 2d at 153–54.

177. *See, e.g.*, Canatella v. Canatella, 11-618, pp. 6–7 (La. App. 5 Cir. 3/13/12), 91 So. 3d 393, 396; Parker v. Parker, 95-1373, p. 4 (La. App. 3 Cir. 4/3/96), 671 So. 2d 1143, 1145; Williams v. Williams, 491 So. 2d 732, 734–35 (La. Ct. App. 2 Cir. 1986).

178. Nelson, 973 So. 2d at 154.

179. Nelson, 973 So. 2d at 154.

petition and even acknowledged that by the time of the hearing that the parties had been living separate and apart for the required time period. Thus, the court concluded that no prejudice would befall the wife, even if the filing had been premature.[180]

§ 4:13 Adultery-Based Divorce

Unlike the no-fault divorces under articles 102 and 103, fault-based divorces (including adultery by a spouse) are immediate.[181] Adultery divorce is considered "immediate" in that no statutory waiting period is required before a court can issue the judgment of divorce; the parties are only constrained by the procedural time delays required in any lawsuit.[182] Additionally, fault-based divorces like adultery may be filed at any time until a final judgment of divorce is rendered, even if the adulterous conduct occurs after physical separation or after one spouse has filed a divorce petition.[183] Therefore, a spouse waiting to obtain a judgment of divorce under article 102 may be entitled to an immediate adultery divorce provided that the spouse can prove that the other spouse committed adultery.[184]

§ 4:14 Adultery-Based Divorce— Actions Constituting Adultery

Adultery in Louisiana is not limited to sexual intercourse. Although the jurisprudence does not define adultery per se, the Louisiana Supreme Court has equated adultery to some degree of sexual connection.[185] Guilty parties often attempt to limit the definition of adultery to traditional coitus, but the jurisprudence has taken a contrary position. For example, Louisiana law recognizes homosexual adultery, which by definition does not include coitus.[186] Additionally, the commission of non-coital acts, such as oral sex or sexual activities short of intercourse, can constitute adultery.

180. Nelson, 973 So. 2d at 154.

181. La. Civ. Code Ann. art. 103(2).

182. *See* La. Code Civ. Proc. Ann. arts. 3941 *et seq.*

183. Morgan v. Morgan, 2022-0472 (La. App. 4 Cir. 12/13/22), 353 So. 3d 1026, 1034 (finding that the timing relative for fault in a judgment of divorce is distinct from fault for the purposes of incidental relief like final spousal support).

184. Morgan, 353 So. 3d at 1034

185. *See* Simon v. Duet, 148 So. 250, 251 (La. 1933) ("It must be alleged that the offending party was guilty of adultery, or was guilty of having sexual connection or intercourse, which mean the same thing.").

186. *See* Menge v. Menge, 491 So. 2d 700, 702 (La. Ct. App. 5 Cir. 1986); Adams v. Adams, 357 So. 2d 881, 882 (La. Ct. App. 1 Cir. 1978) ("Like heterosexual adultery, the commission of acts of homosexual adultery, alleged as a ground for separation (or divorce), may be established by indirect or circumstantial evidence.").

§ 4:15 Adultery-Based Divorce— Sufficiency of Evidence

Allegations of adultery must be expressly set forth in the petition for divorce; it will not suffice to simply set out conduct from which adultery could be inferred.[187] The spouse alleging adultery bears the burden of proof,[188] and the accused spouse's innocence of immoral acts is presumed.[189] Thus, the alleging spouse must prove by a preponderance of the evidence facts and circumstances that "lead fairly and necessarily to the conclusion that adultery has been committed as alleged in the petition, i.e., the proof must be so convincing as to exclude any other reasonable hypothesis but that of guilt of adultery."[190] To meet the burden of proof, the plaintiff may rely on direct or circumstantial evidence.[191]

Several factors are considered in the analysis, including the "propensity of the parties to commit adultery, the amount of time the parties spent together, whether there was an obvious amorous relationship between the parties, whether other persons were present when the alleged illicit rendezvous occurred, and whether the association between the parties is open or surreptitious."[192] The evidence must be viewed "in light of experiences and observations of life,"[193] which can lead to an inference that people "do what comes naturally when they have the opportunity."[194] The burden of proof, however, is not satisfied by evidence that the other spouse had the *opportunity* to commit adultery.[195] The fact that one spouse is alone with another person, even staying together overnight,[196] does not create the presumption that adultery has been committed.[197]

---

187. Simon v. Duet, 148 So. 250, 251 (La. 1933).

188. Sibley v. Sibley, 96-1544, p. 2 (La. App. 1 Cir. 11/10/04), 693 So. 2d 1270, 1271.

189. Sibley, 693 So. 2d at 1271.

190. Marcotte v. Marcotte, 2004-293, p. 2 (La. App. 3 Cir. 11/10/04), 886 So. 2d 671, 673 (citing Lewis v. Lewis, 446 So. 2d 995, 997 (La. Ct. App. 3 Cir. 1984)); *see also* Tidwell v. Tidwell, 49,512, p. 2 (La. App. 2 Cir. 11/19/14), 152 So. 3d 1045, 1047; Bennett v. Bennett, 97-1150, p. 3 (La. App. 5 Cir. 7/28/98), 716 So. 2d 454, 456; Arnoult v. Arnoult, 96-730, p. 4 (La. App. 5 Cir. 2/12/97), 690 So. 2d 101, 102.

191. Tidwell, 152 So. 3d at 1047; *see also* Massa v. Thompson, 56 So. 2d 422, 423 (La. 1952) (finding that the wife failed to prove adultery by a preponderance of the evidence).

192. Sibley, 693 So. 2d at 1271; *see also* Emfinger v. Emfinger, 550 So. 2d 754, 759 (La. Ct. App. 2 Cir. 1989) ("[Adultery] cannot be proved by second hand gossip or allegations of 'community knowledge.'").

193. Bennett, 716 So. 2d at 456.

194. Menge v. Menge, 491 So. 2d 700, 702 (La. Ct. App. 5 Cir. 1986); Everett v. Everett, 345 So. 2d 586, 590 (La. Ct. App. 4 Cir. 1977).

195. Wynn v. Wynn, 513 So. 2d 489, 491 (La. Ct. App. 2 Cir. 1987); *see also* Bennett, 716 So. 2d at 456 (finding no adultery where surveillance showed that man and woman were together on three separate occasions, and on one occasion throughout the night); Sibley, 693 So. 2d at 1274 (reversing trial court's finding of adultery because there was no evidence of sexual touching or hugging, only staying overnight).

196. Wynn, 513 So. 2d at 491; *see also* Bennett, 716 So. 2d at 456; Sibley, 693 So. 2d at 1274.

197. *See* Hermes v. Hermes, 287 So. 2d 789, 790 (La. 1973); Marcotte, 886 So. 2d at 673; Bennett, 716 So. 2d at 456.

A trial court's findings concerning evidence of adultery, a factual issue, depend heavily on credibility evaluations, which are entitled to "very substantial weight on review."[198] Factual findings will not be disturbed on appeal unless they are clearly wrong—when there is no reasonable basis in the record to support them.[199] In a close case, the court found adultery based on the testimony of two different men, who were admitted drug users convicted of various offenses and who testified about having sex with the defendant.[200] The defendant-wife denied the allegations and offered the testimony of character witnesses.[201] The appellate court affirmed the finding of adultery based on the deference given to the trial court when making credibility determinations, recognizing that it may have reached a different result.[202]

Frequently, parties will present the testimony of private investigators hired by one spouse to watch the other.[203] A prima facie case can be established on a private investigator's testimony alone,[204] although most courts prefer corroboration with facts, circumstances, and the direct testimony of other witnesses.[205] The prima facie case cannot be made on the admission of the adulterous spouse alone, as courts are concerned about untrustworthy confessions.[206]

How far courts will extend the definition of adultery remains to be seen. One case that reached the outer limits pronounced adultery based on two encounters with evidence of hugging and kissing.[207] Two private investigators testified to seeing the couple get out of a steamy car and remain alone in a dark home for two hours after a night of drinking.[208] The wife and her paramour testified to what happened on both occasions, yet the court granted the divorce based on adultery.[209] The decision was met with a

---

198. Pearce v. Pearce, 348 So. 2d 75, 78 (La. 1977); McFall v. Armstrong, 10-1041, pp. 5–6 (La. App. 5 Cir. 9/13/11), 75 So. 3d 30, 35.

199. Arceneaux v. Domingue, 365 So. 2d 1330, 1333 (La. 1978).

200. Poole v. Poole, 2008-1325, pp. 5–8 (La. App. 3 Cir. 4/1/09), 7 So. 3d 806, 808, 810–12.

201. Poole, 7 So. 3d at 811.

202. Poole, 7 So. 3d at 812.

203. *See, e.g.*, Arnoult v. Arnoult, 690 So. 2d at 101–02.

204. Hermes, 287 So. 2d at 791; *cf.* Larocca v. Larocca, 606 So. 2d 53, 55 (La. Ct. App. 3 Cir. 1992) (noting the trial court's reliance on "the rule that uncorroborated testimony of private investigators cannot be the basis of a judgment of adultery").

205. Arnoult, 690 So. 2d at 102 (citing McCartan v. Filkins, 64 So. 717 (La. 1914)); *see also* Bennett, 716 So. 2d at 456; Tampira v. Tampira, 539 So. 2d 981, 982–83 (La. Ct. App. 4 Cir. 1989).

206. Bonura v. Bonura, 505 So. 2d 143, 145 (La. Ct. App. 4 Cir. 1987) (quoting Ogea v. Ogea, 378 So. 2d 984, 992 (La. Ct. App. 3 Cir. 1979)) ("This evidence, standing alone, is deemed untrustworthy because of the possibility that spouses may prove adultery by confessions, thereby being granted an immediate divorce."); *cf.* Tidwell, 152 So. 3d at 1049 (finding that the wife's admissions along with the testimony of private investigators was enough to find adultery).

207. Arnoult, 690 So. 2d at 102.

208. Arnoult, 690, So. 2d at 102.

209. Arnoult, 690 So. 2d at 102–03.

strong dissent.[210] Given the proliferation of online dating and sexual relationships, will the definition of adultery reach even farther?[211]

§ 4:16 Felony Conviction and Sentence Divorce

Commission of a felony resulting in a sentence to death or imprisonment at hard labor is another fault-based ground for divorce.[212] Similar to the divorce based on a spouse's adultery, the felony conviction divorce is "immediate," as there is no statutory waiting period required before a court can grant the divorce.[213] The spouse seeking a divorce on this ground must present evidence of the other spouse's conviction and sentencing.[214] A guilty plea has been found to be the equivalent of a conviction for purposes of a divorce action.[215] All delays for appeal need not expire, nor must the convicted spouse have actually served any portion of the sentence.[216] From a policy standpoint, the irreparable harm to the marriage occurs at the initial determination of guilt and sentencing; therefore, the divorce can be obtained without the delays associated with an appeal.[217] The same rationale dictates that a subsequent pardon will not affect the divorce either.[218]

§ 4:17 Abuse-Based Divorce

Reaffirming that domestic violence is a significant problem in Louisiana, the legislature created the Domestic Violence Prevention Commission in 2014 to review and make recommendations regarding existing domestic violence programs and to ensure that laws on domestic violence are properly implemented.[219] At the same time, the legislature added two additional causes of action for immediate divorce when a spouse commits physical or sexual abuse against a spouse or a child of a spouse, based on

---

210. Arnoult, 690 So. 2d at 103 (Gaudin, J., dissenting).

211. *See* Marcotte, 886 So. 2d at 673–74, 679 (finding that phone sex without evidence of a physical sexual relationship was not enough to prove adultery). *But see* Sandi S. Varnado, *Avatars, Scarlet "A"s, and Adultery in the Technological Age*, 55 Ariz. L. Rev. 371 (2013).

212. La. Civ. Code Ann. art. 103(3).

213. *See* La. Code Civ. Proc. Ann. arts. 3941 *et seq.*

214. *See generally* Nickels v. Nickels, 347 So. 2d 510 (La. Ct. App. 2 Cir. 1977).

215. Scheppf v. Scheppf, 430 So. 2d 370, 372 (La. Ct. App. 3 Cir. 1983).

216. Tauzier v. Tauzier, 466 So. 2d 565, 567 (La. Ct. App. 5 Cir. 1985); Nickels, 347 So. 2d at 510. A suspended sentence "does not lessen the impact of a conviction." Kitchen v. Kitchen, 480 So. 2d 494, 495 (La. Ct. App. 5 Cir. 1985).

217. Nickels, 347 So. 2d at 511.

218. Abshire v. Hanks, 44 So. 186 (La. 1907), *overruled on other grounds*, Thomason v. Thomason, 355 So. 2d 908 (La. 1978).

219. *See* La. Stat. Ann. §§ 46:2145–:2147. According to a national survey, "domestic violence inflicts physical, emotional, and financial injury on its victims and exists in every segment of our population. Approximately 32.9% of women and 28.1% of men in the United States have experienced physical violence by an intimate partner in their lifetime." Act No. 663, 2014 La. Acts 2977.

proof of abuse presented at trial or proof of a preexisting protective order or injunction.[220] Although the definition of abuse is not articulated in the article, guidance can be found in the Post Separation Family Violence Relief Act[221] and the Domestic Abuse Assistance Act.[222] In 2015, the legislature amended the article to clarify that the abuse had to occur or that the protective order or injunction had to be issued during the marriage.[223]

Louisiana Civil Code Article 103(4) permits a divorce based on proof of physical or sexual abuse against the spouse or a child of one of the spouses, regardless of whether the other spouse was prosecuted for the act of abuse.[224] Article 103(5) permits a divorce based on the same type of abuse but allows the plaintiff to prove the abuse through a preexisting protective order or injunction that was issued during the marriage, but only if the order or injunction was issued after a contradictory hearing or consent decree.[225] The protective order necessary to secure a divorce under subsection (5) can be a criminal or civil protective order.[226] A spouse petitioning for divorce under article 103(5) may receive a default judgment of divorce.[227]

§ 4:18 Abuse-Based Divorce— Abuse by Proof

The first of the two abuse-based divorces is available when the spouse seeking the divorce proves that the other spouse physically or sexually abused the spouse or a child of one of the spouses during the marriage, regardless of whether there was a prosecution for the abuse.[228] Note that the target of the abuse must be "a child of one of the spouses," not just a child of the marriage between the spouses.[229] As this divorce option is relatively new, there is scant jurisprudence interpreting the law. Questions abound concerning the timing of the abuse. While the article requires the abuse to

---

220. Act No. 316, 2014 La. Acts 1881–82.

221. La. Stat. Ann. § 9:362.

222. La. Stat. Ann. §§ 46:2131–:2143.

223. Act No. 221, 2015 La. Acts 1642–44; *see also* Jessica G. Braun, Louisiana Handbook on Family Law 219 (2022–23). In 2018, a clean-up amendment removed the phrase "in accordance with law" to describe the protective order or injunction as it was unnecessary and superfluous. *See* Act No. 265, 2018 La. Acts.

224. La. Civ. Code Ann. art. 103(4).

225. La. Civ. Code Ann. art. 103(5).

226. La. Civ. Code Ann. art. 103 cmt.

227. A default judgment may be entered provided that the petitioner provides the court with an affidavit containing factual allegations included in the petition, a proposed default judgment with a copy, a certification by the clerk that the record has been examined by the clerk, and a certified copy of the protective order or injunction. If the defendant fails to respond, the judge may then enter a default judgment or direct that a hearing be held. Note, also, that the notice requirements for default judgments do not apply to motions for default judgments involving a 103(1) divorce or a 103(5) divorce. La. Code Civ. Proc. Ann. art. 1702 (F)(3); *see* Section 4:12.

228. La. Civ. Code Ann. art. 103(4).

229. *See* La. Civ. Code Ann. art. 103(4).

occur "during the marriage," would abuse that occurred fifteen years before the divorce filing qualify? Can reconciliation or condonation apply to abuse?[230]

In *Soto v. Sadeghi*, the wife petitioned for an immediate divorce under article 103(4) based on allegations that her husband physically and sexually abused her during their marriage.[231] The trial court denied the wife's request because the only proof of physical or sexual abuse offered by the wife was her own testimony, and she offered no other corroborating evidence in the form of witnesses, medical reports, or emergency room records to support her claim.[232] Under the deferential manifest error standard, the appellate court affirmed.[233]

By contrast, in *Norton v. Norton*, the Fifth Circuit Court of Appeal upheld the trial court's findings of abuse by a preponderance of the evidence.[234] *Norton* involved numerous allegations of abuse in which the wife slapped and clawed her husband several times while intoxicated, at times in front of their children.[235] In its analysis, the court articulated that "Article 103(4) does not require that [Mr. Norton] had to have sought medical attention for his injuries in order to have satisfied his burden of proving physical abuse."[236] Ultimately, "[t]he question of whether a single physical altercation between spouses rises to the level of physical abuse ... presents a mixed question of fact and law that is to be determined by the trier of fact."[237]

---

230. *See* Section 4:25.

231. Soto v. Sadeghi, No. 2016-0471, 2016 WL 7387427 (La. App. 4 Cir. 12/21/16). Plaintiff alleged that her husband forced her to participate in anal sexual intercourse and obtained nude photographs of her from a webcam that had been placed in the couple's bedroom without her permission. Soto, 2016 WL 7387427, at *1–2.

232. Soto, 2016 WL 7387427, at *1, *5; *see also* Ennis v. Ennis, No. 2016-0423, 2017 WL 1900328 (La. App. 1 Cir. 5/8/17) (noting that the husband may have been entitled to a divorce based on the wife's actions of throwing a chair that narrowly missed her husband).

233. Soto, 2016 WL 7387427, at *1, *5; *see also* Ficarra v. Ficarra, 15-368, p. 3 (La. App. 5 Cir. 12/23/15), 184 So. 3d 161, 162; Saacks v. Saacks, 612 So. 2d 925, 926 (La. Ct. App. 4 Cir. 1993) (discussing the deference to a trial court's fact-finding abilities).

234. Norton v. Norton, 21-212 (La. App. 5 Cir. 12/22/21), 335 So. 3d 371, 386.

235. Norton, 335 So. 3d at 374–78.

236. Norton, 335 So. 3d at 383.

237. Norton, 335 So. 3d at 383.

§ 4:19 Abuse-Based Divorce— Abuse by Protective Order

The second of the two abuse-based divorces is available when the spouse presents a protective order or injunction that was issued during the marriage, which protects the spouse or a child of one of the spouses from abuse.[238] Again, the child can be of either spouse and need not be a child of the marriage.[239] The protective order or injunction must be the result of a contradictory hearing or consent decree.[240]

Given the ease with which protective orders and injunctions are issued, concern has arisen that unsuspecting spouses may later discover that agreeing to a protective order in the spirit of conciliation can later result in an immediate divorce, without having to live separate and apart.[241] Further, spouses may be unaware of the financial consequences affecting spousal support when obtaining an abuse-based divorce.[242] For example, an award of attorney's fees, court costs, appeal costs, costs of enforcement and modification proceedings, and evaluation and expert's fees are available when a divorce is granted based on abuse.[243] In addition, when the abuse-based divorce was enacted in 2014, if a spouse was awarded a divorce on this basis, courts were mandated to award final spousal support, and interim support could extend beyond an award of final support if it were greater than the final support award.[244] Further, for final spousal support, the one-third limitation of net income for obligors was eliminated if the divorce was based on abuse.[245]

In 2018, the legislature eliminated the mandatory award of final support as well as the extended interim support when a spouse obtains a divorce based on abuse.[246] The law now provides that a spouse is presumed to be entitled to final spousal support when a divorce is awarded based on any of the fault-based grounds: adultery, felony conviction, or abuse.[247] The exception to the one-third limitation was retained, allowing spouses who obtain a divorce based on abuse to receive awards that exceed one-

---

238. 2014 La. Acts. 316, 616.

239. La. Stat. Ann. § 9:314; La. Civ. Code Ann. art. 2362.1.

240. La. Civ. Code Ann. art. 2362.1.

241. *See* Jessica G. Braun, Louisiana Handbook on Family Law 102 (2018).

242. *See* La. Civ. Code Ann. arts. 112–113; *see also* Section 4:20.

243. La. Stat. Ann. § 9:314; La. Civ. Code Ann. art. 2362.1. The divorce can be based on articles 103(4) or (5) or can be no-fault with proof of domestic abuse.

244. *See* La. Civ. Code Ann. arts. 112–113 (2014) (as amended in 2014 by Act 316 and then repealed in 2018 by Act 265; the law was in effect from August 1, 2014, through August 1, 2018).

245. *See* La. Civ. Code Ann. arts. 112–113 (2014) (as amended in 2014 by Act 316 and then repealed in 2018 by Act 265; the law was in effect from August 1, 2014, through August 1, 2018).

246. Act No. 265, 2018 La. Acts. 922.

247. *See* La. Civ. Code Ann. art. 112. Final spousal support is also available when the party or a child of one of the spouses was a victim of domestic abuse committed by the other party during the marriage, even if a no-fault divorce was granted. *Id.*

third of the obligor's net income.[248] With these modifications, even for the unwitting spouse, the financial consequences of the abuse-based divorce are more palatable.

§ 4:20 Abuse-Based Divorce—Incidental Relief Available with Abuse Divorce

When the legislature enacted two new divorces based on abuse in 2014, it likewise amended the provisions on interim and final spousal support[249] and later added provisions to allow the court to assess court costs, attorney's fees, costs of enforcement and modification proceedings, costs of appeal, evaluation fees, and expert witness fees against the perpetrator of the abuse.[250]

When the changes were initially made in 2014 to the laws on interim support, the interim award terminated no less than 180 days from the judgment of divorce, if a claim for final support was pending at the time of the judgment of an Article 103(4) or (5) divorce and the final support award did not exceed the interim award.[251] In other words, when the interim support award was greater than the final support award (assuming the final support award was not yet decided at the judgment of divorce), the greater interim award continued for at least six months past the judgment of divorce. This allowed the abused spouse to continue to receive a higher interim award even after final support had been awarded.[252]

As to final support, an award of final support was mandatory when the spouse was not at fault prior to filing a petition for divorce and the court determined that the party was a "victim of domestic abuse committed by the other party during the marriage."[253] The court could award periodic payments or a lump sum.[254] Mandatory final support was not conditioned on the spouse obtaining an Article 103(4) or (5) divorce but was broader in scope; it allowed litigants to prove that the spouse had suffered domestic abuse committed during the marriage, even if that spouse sought a no-fault divorce. Further, a factor was added for courts to consider in determining the amount and duration of final support, which included "the existence, effect, and duration of any act of domestic abuse" by the spouse, even if the spouse was not prosecuted for the act.[255]

---

248. La. Civ. Code Ann. art. 112(D). In addition, the one-third limitation does not apply to victims of domestic violence committed during the marriage, even without obtaining an abuse-based divorce. *Id.*

249. Act No. 316, 2014 La. Acts. 1881–84.

250. Act No. 221, 2015 La. Acts. 1643; Act No. 264, 2018 La. Acts. 921.

251. La. Civ. Code Ann. art. 113 (2014).

252. La. Civ. Code Ann. art. 113 (2014). The obligation to pay final support did not begin until the interim award has been terminated. *Id.*

253. La. Civ. Code Ann. art. 112(C) (2014).

254. La. Civ. Code Ann. art. 112(C) (2014).

255. La. Civ. Code Ann. art. 112(B)(9) (2014).

Finally, the one-third limitation that applied to obligors of final spousal support was eliminated for spouses who were victims of domestic abuse during the marriage.[256]

After the legislation was passed, several issues arose, including the question of whether a spouse subject to abuse must show a need for support, given the mandate for support in abuse divorces. Further, some questioned the wisdom of a punitive award that would lead to additional, unnecessary litigation to refute the fact, generating more unstable interactions between the spouses. Spouses may agree to standard protective orders to eliminate friction, but with the possibility that a consent agreement could have detrimental effects on them financially, consent agreements would be less likely. Further, parity between victims of fault was considered. Arguably, spouses who endure any of the fault-based grounds for divorce, like adultery and felony conviction, should be treated similarly to spouses who obtain a divorce based on abuse.

As a result of these concerns, the Marriage-Persons Committee of the Louisiana State Law Institute suggested, and the legislature agreed, that substantive amendments to the law on interim and final support were needed. In 2018, the legislature passed Act 265, which eliminated the mandatory final spousal support for abuse survivors and instead provided a presumption of entitlement to final spousal support for any spouse who obtains a divorce based on fault (which includes adultery, felony conviction, or abuse), or can prove that the spouse or a child was a victim of domestic abuse during the marriage.[257] The law clearly provides that need for support, ability to pay, and pre-filing fault are all relevant considerations in any request for final support.[258] The extended interim support for abuse-based divorces was eliminated in favor of a general extension of interim support for all types of divorces, which now permits interim support to continue in all cases for 180 days from the judgment of divorce.[259] No longer must a claim for final support be pending; interim support is simply tied to the judgment of divorce.[260]

Throughout the revisions, neither domestic violence nor domestic abuse has been defined in the article or in any other section of the Code, although it is present in various statutes with slightly differing definitions.[261] Both the Post-Separation Family Violence Relief Act[262] and the Domestic Abuse Assistance Act[263] include "physical or sexual abuse [as well as] any offense against the person, physical or non-physical as defined in the Criminal Code, except negligent injury and defamation."[264] These broad

256. Act No. 316, 2014 La. Acts 1883.

257. Act No. 265, 2018 La. Acts.

258. Act No. 265, 2018 La. Acts.

259. Act No. 265, 2018 La. Acts.

260. La. Civ. Code Ann. art. 113. Interim support may extend beyond the 180 days from divorce for good cause shown.

261. *See, e.g.*, La. Stat. Ann. § 9:362(4), (6); La. Child. Code Ann. arts. 1103(5), 1565(1); La. Stat. Ann. §§ 46:2121.1(2), :2132(3), :2151(C).

262. *See* La. Stat. Ann. § 9:362.

263. *See* La. Stat. Ann. § 46:2132.

264. La. Stat. Ann. §§ 9:362, 46:2132.

definitions, with an exclusion for reasonable acts of self-defense,[265] would be appropriate in an analysis on the issue of final support.

In 2017, recognizing the need for consistent and comprehensive definitions related to domestic violence, the legislature passed H.R. Con. Res. 79, which asked the Law Institute to study and recommend definitions for "physical abuse" and "sexual abuse" and other related relief that is available under the divorce laws as well as other criminal laws.[266] In response, the Law Institute drafted House Bill 727 of the 2020 Regular Session to provide a single definition of "domestic abuse" throughout the civil law. The bill was deferred as a result of the pandemic and reintroduced as House Bill 159 of the 2021 Regular Session. Ultimately, the bill failed to pass.

Finally, on the issue of attorney's fees and other costs and fees, a provision was added in 2015 to permit an award of fees and costs in any action for divorce under article 103(4) or (5) and in any incidental actions against the abuser.[267] This legislation was originally placed in the "Matrimonial Regimes" Title, article 2362.1, which also classified the obligation as a separate one of the perpetrator.[268] Appropriately, the legislature relocated the court's discretion to assess costs and fees into Title 9, Section 314 of the Civil Code Ancillaries, and kept the classification article in the title on matrimonial regimes in the Civil Code.[269] These additional measures assure survivors of domestic abuse that further financial assistance is available in the event of a divorce.

§ 4:21 Separation and Divorce Under Covenant Marriage

In 1997, the Louisiana State Legislature adopted the Covenant Marriage Act.[270] Covenant marriage exists as an alternative to traditional marriage and requires the parties to obtain premarital counseling and to express their intent to enter into covenant marriage when they apply for a marriage license.[271] The statute proclaims that "[o]nly when there has been a complete and total breach of the marital covenant commitment

---

265. The Post-Separation Family Violence Relief Act contains an exclusion for self-defense used by one parent against the other parent to protect himself or a child from abuse. *See* La. Stat. Ann. § 9:362(4).

266. H.R. Con. Res. 79, 43d Leg., Reg. Sess. (La. 2017). The United Against Domestic Violence Coalition, comprised of the Public Policy Committee of the United Way of Southeast Louisiana, the Louisiana Coalition Against Domestic Violence, and the New Orleans Family Justice Center Alliance, also proposed revisions and enactments of several laws in Louisiana to protect victims. *Id.*

267. Act No. 221, 2015 La. Acts 1643 (amending La. Civ. Code Ann. art. 2362.1).

268. *Id.*

269. Act No. 264, 2018 La. Acts (enacting La. Stat. Ann. § 9:314).

270. Act No. 1380, 1997 La. Acts 2848 (enacting La. Stat. Ann. §§ 9:272 *et seq.*).

271. La. Stat. Ann. §§ 9:272–:275. For two excellent articles chronicling the passage and use of the Covenant Marriage Act, see Katherine Shaw Spaht, *Louisiana's Covenant Marriage: Social Analysis and Legal Implications*, 59 La. L. Rev. 63 (1998), and Katherine Shaw Spaht, *Covenant Marriage Seven Years Later: Its As Yet Unfulfilled Promise*, 65 La. L. Rev. 605 (2005).

may the non-breaching party seek a declaration that the marriage is no longer legally recognized."[272]

A covenant marriage can only be terminated by one of the causes enumerated in Article 101 of the Civil Code, which includes divorce.[273] Louisiana Revised Statutes Section 9:307 provides the exclusive grounds for separation and divorce in a covenant marriage which will be discussed in Sections 4:22 and 4:23.[274] Although separation from bed and board was abolished in 1990,[275] the Covenant Marriage Act reinstated a new version of separation, which applies only to a covenant marriage.[276]

§ 4:22 Separation and Divorce Under Covenant Marriage—Separation in a Covenant Marriage

A spouse to a covenant marriage may choose to pursue a legal separation, called a "separation from bed and board," rather than a divorce; this option does not exist for couples in a standard marriage. A judicial separation from bed and board in a covenant marriage does not dissolve the bond of marriage.[277] The separated husband and wife are not free to marry again, but it does put an end to their conjugal cohabitation.[278] Spouses judicially separated retain that status until they either reconcile or divorce.[279]

Once the parties experience marital difficulties, which would be prior to filing a petition for legal separation, the parties must attend counseling in an attempt to preserve the marriage.[280] While counseling may be required before a judicial separation can be rendered, it is not a prerequisite to a spouse filing a petition for separation to seek support and custody awards.[281] In *Johnson v. Johnson*, the wife filed a petition for separation and in the alternative for divorce of her covenant marriage, and she requested custody

---

272. La. Stat. Ann. § 9:272(A).

273. La. Stat. Ann. § 9:272(C); La. Civ. Code Ann. art. 101.

274. La. Stat. Ann. § 9:307.

275. Act No. 1009, 1990 La. Acts 2505.

276. Act No. 1009, 1990 La. Acts 2505. Some commentators expressed concern that enacting covenant marriage legislation in Louisiana ran contrary to the goal of uniformity in state divorce laws. Katherine Shaw Spaht & Symeon C. Symeonides, *Covenant Marriage and the Law of Conflicts of Law*, 32 Creighton L. Rev. 1085, 1100–20 (1999). This lack of uniformity will result in increased instances of the migratory divorce, i.e., when one or both spouses who entered into a Louisiana covenant marriage seek a divorce in another state. Katherine Shaw Spaht & Symeon C. Symeonides, *Covenant Marriage and the Law of Conflicts of Law*, 32 Creighton L. Rev. 1085, 1100–01 (1999). *See also* Robert C. Lowe, Louisiana Divorce § 6:20, *in* 1 Louisiana Practice Series 420–25, for a discussion of separation from bed and board in a covenant marriage.

277. La. Stat. Ann. § 9:309.

278. La. Stat. Ann. § 9:309.

279. La. Stat. Ann. § 9:309.

280. La. Stat. Ann. § 9:307(A)–(C). "Counseling ... shall not apply when the other spouse has physically or sexually abused the spouse seeking the divorce or a child of one of the spouses." La. Stat. Ann. § 9:307(D). The law does not specify the type of counseling or the counselor the parties must use.

281. Johnson v. Johnson, 2014-0564, p. 7 (La. App. 1 Cir. 12/23/14), 168 So. 3d 641, 645.

and support.[282] The husband filed an exception of no cause of action because the parties had not attended marital counseling.[283] The court recognized that the Covenant Marriage Act requires the couple to receive counseling prior to obtaining a *judgment* of divorce or separation but found no requirement for counseling before obtaining incidentals to divorce, like child custody, child support, and spousal support.[284]

After attending counseling, a spouse may obtain a judgment of separation only upon proof of any of the following:[285] (1) the other spouse committed adultery;[286] (2) the other spouse committed a felony and was sentenced to death or imprisonment at hard labor;[287] (3) the other spouse abandoned the matrimonial domicile for a period of one year and constantly refuses to return;[288] (4) the other spouse physically or sexually abused the spouse seeking the divorce or a child of one of the spouses;[289] (5) the spouses have been living separate and apart continuously without reconciliation for a period of two years; or (6) on account of habitual intemperance[290] of the other spouse, or excesses, cruel treatment,[291] or outrages of the other spouse, if such habitual

---

282. Johnson, 168 So. 3d at 642.

283. Johnson, 168 So. 3d at 642.

284. Johnson, 168 So. 3d at 645.

285. La. Stat. Ann. § 9:307.

286. La. Stat. Ann. § 9:307; *see also* Sections 4:13–15. The jurisprudence interpreting adultery applies to adultery committed in both a covenant marriage and a standard marriage.

287. La. Stat. Ann. § 9:307; *see also* Section 4:16. The jurisprudence interpreting the meaning of a commission of a felony applies to both a covenant marriage and a standard marriage.

288. Abandonment requires proof that one of the parties withdrew from the marital domicile without lawful cause to do so, and that the withdrawing party constantly refused to return. Clary v. Clary, 341 So. 2d 628, 628 (La. Ct. App. 4 Cir. 1977); Chamblee v. Chamblee, 340 So. 2d 378, 381 (La. Ct. App. 4 Cir. 1976). As such, a party "cannot merely prove [that the] spouse left the common dwelling and then rely on the spouse's failure to prove a case [based on marital] fault." Bergeron v. Bergeron, 372 So. 2d 731, 733 (La. Ct. App. 4 Cir. 1979). Constructive abandonment, when one spouse prevents the other from entering the marital home, can likewise qualify as abandonment. *See* Quinn v. Quinn, 412 So. 2d 649, 652 (La. Ct. App. 2 Cir. 1982).

289. La. Stat. Ann. § 9:307. As the jurisprudence under articles 103(4) and (5) develops, it will apply to the covenant marriage laws, as well. Consideration of the jurisprudence under the Post-Separation Family Violence Relief Act and the Domestic Abuse Assistance Act would also be appropriate.

290. Habitual intemperance references constant and repetitive alcohol or drug use. *See generally* Michelli v. Michelli, 93-2128 (La. App. 1 Cir. 5/5/95), 655 So. 2d 1342; Crifasi v. Crifasi, 94-0962 (La. App. 4 Cir. 1/19/95), 650 So. 2d 347; Roland v. Roland, 519 So. 2d 1177 (La. Ct. App. 1 Cir. 1987). One commentator noted that "[t]here may be a question as to whether a gambling addiction is habitual intemperance or cruel treatment." Katherine Shaw Spaht, *Louisiana's Covenant Marriage: Social Analysis and Legal Implications*, 59 La. L. Rev. 63, 120 n.401 (1998) (citing Olivier v. Abunza, 76 So. 2d 528 (1954)); *see also* Halley v. Halley, 480 So. 2d 869 (La. Ct. App. 2 Cir. 1985).

291. Mental cruelty can include the refusal of sexual relations or sexual excess, failure to adequately perform housecleaning and the preparation of meals, religious fervor and constant proselytizing, harassment beyond mere nagging and griping, serious monetary irresponsibility, or an accumulation of such offenses. *See generally* Von Bechman v. Von Bechman, 386 So. 2d 910 (La. 1980); Mudd v. Mudd, 20 So. 2d 311 (La. 1944); Lamb v. Lamb, 460 So. 2d 634 (La. Ct. App. 3 Cir. 1984) (finding that because of couple's financial ability to afford a maid, wife's ineptitude in cleaning and preparing meals did not constitute fault); Minella v. Minella, 97-1264 (La. Ct. 5 App. 5/27/98), 713 So. 2d 816; Daigle v. Breaux, 477 So. 2d 798 (La. Ct. App. 5 Cir. 1985); Roussel v. Roussel, 96-682 (La. App. 5 Cir. 1/28/97), 688 So. 2d 160; Wagner v. Wagner, 96-1420 (La. App. 4 Cir. 12/18/96), 686 So. 2d 946; Guillory v.

intemperance or such ill-treatment is of such a nature as to render their living together insupportable.[292]

The judgment of separation from bed and board terminates the community regime retroactive to the filing of the original petition on which the judgment of separation is rendered.[293] As is the case for standard marriages, if the spouses reconcile, the community is reestablished as of the date of filing the original petition, unless the spouses execute a matrimonial agreement providing otherwise prior to reconciliation.[294] This matrimonial agreement does not require court approval.[295]

Jurisdiction to render a separation from bed and board in a covenant marriage is more narrow than jurisdiction to grant a divorce in both covenant marriages and standard marriages.[296] For jurisdiction to render a legal separation, one or both of the spouses must be domiciled in Louisiana (necessary for divorce) and the ground for separation must be committed in or must have occurred in Louisiana or while the matrimonial domicile was in Louisiana (not required for divorce).[297] The action for separation must be brought in a parish where either party is domiciled or in the parish of the last matrimonial domicile; the venue is non-waivable and is therefore jurisdictional.[298] Consequently, a judgment of separation rendered by a court of improper venue is an absolute nullity.[299] Further, judgments on the pleadings and summary judgments are not available in an action for legal separation.[300]

Guillory, 626 So. 2d 826 (La. App. 2 Cir. 1993); Allen v. Allen, 94-1090 (La. 12/12/94), 648 So. 2d 359, *on remand*, 25,281 (La. App. 2 Cir. 4/5/95), 653 So. 2d 169 (finding proof insufficient because of mitigating circumstances). *But see* Butts v. Butts, 426 So. 2d 302 (La. Ct. App. 4 Cir. 1983). *See, e.g.*, Simon v. Simon, 96-876 (La. App. 5 Cir. 5/14/97), 696 So. 2d 68 (stating that spousal fussing does not ordinarily support a finding of cruel treatment).

292. These grounds are similar to the former article 138, and therefore the jurisprudence interpreting that article could be instructive. La. Civ. Code Ann. art. 138 (repealed 1991); *see* Katherine Shaw Spaht, *Louisiana's Covenant Marriage: Social Analysis and Legal Implications*, 59 La. L. Rev. 63, 108–09 (1998) (discussing some of the differences between the covenant marriage law and the former divorce and separation laws).

293. La. Stat. Ann. § 9:309(B)(1). The retroactive effect is "without prejudice to the liability of the community for the attorney's fees and costs incurred by the spouses in the action in which the judgment is rendered, or to the rights validly acquired [during the time] between commencement of the action and recordation of the judgment." *Id.*

294. La. Stat. Ann. § 9:309(B)(2).

295. La. Stat. Ann. § 9:309(B)(2). The reestablishment of the community is "effective toward third persons only upon filing notice of the reestablishment for registry" and will not "prejudice the rights of third persons validly acquired prior to filing notice of the reestablishment nor shall it affect a prior community property partition between the spouses." La. Stat. Ann. § 9:309(B)(3).

296. *See* Katherine Shaw Spaht, *Louisiana's Covenant Marriage: Social Analysis and Legal Implications*, 59 La. L. Rev. 63, 112 (1998).

297. La. Stat. Ann. § 9:308(B)(1)(a). If the cause for separation occurred outside of Louisiana while one or both spouses were domiciled outside of Louisiana, then jurisdiction can also be proper if the person requesting the separation was domiciled in Louisiana prior to the time the cause of action accrued and is domiciled in Louisiana at the time the action is filed. La. Stat. Ann. § 9:308(B)(1)(b).

298. La. Stat. Ann. § 9:308(B)(2)–(3).

299. La. Stat. Ann. § 9:308(B)(3).

300. La. Stat. Ann. § 9:308(C).

In connection with a proceeding for separation, a court may award a spouse incidental relief available in a proceeding for divorce, which could include spousal support, claims for contributions to education, child custody, visitation rights, child support, injunctive relief, and possession and use of a family residence or community movables or immovables.[301] Because spousal support requires the claimant spouse to be free from fault prior to a "proceeding to terminate the marriage," the relevance of the petition for separation in the context of spousal support has been considered, albeit in dicta. In *Shirley v. Shirley*, the court noted that a judgment of separation does not dissolve the bond of marriage because the spouses "are not at liberty to remarry," so that a petition for judgment of separation is not a "proceeding to terminate the marriage."[302] As the marital bond and duties subsist even with a judicial separation, fault that occurs during the separation but before a petition for divorce would likely trigger the support bar under article 111.

§ 4:23 Separation and Divorce Under Covenant Marriage—Divorce in a Covenant Marriage

Divorce in a covenant marriage can be more complicated and time-consuming than divorce in a standard marriage.[303] The first five grounds for divorce are the same as the grounds for separation as set forth in Section 4:22 above—the first four are based on fault and the fifth is a no-fault option. The sixth and last ground for divorce is another no-fault option that applies after the spouses have received a judgment of separation.[304] If a judgment of separation was entered, either spouse can obtain a divorce following one additional year of living separate and apart continuously from the date the judgment of separation was signed.[305] That time is extended to one year and six months if there is a minor child of the marriage.[306] If, however, the separation was granted based on abuse, then the spouse need only wait one year, even if there is a minor child of the marriage.[307] Unlike in legal separation, there is no option for divorce based on habitual intemperance, excesses, cruel treatment, or outrages that render living together insupportable.[308]

---

301. La. Stat. Ann. § 9:308(D).

302. Shirley v. Shirley, 48-635, p. 14 (La. App. 2 Cir. 10/16/13), 127 So. 3d 935, 943 n.5 (internal quotation marks omitted).

303. Katherine Shaw Spaht, *Louisiana's Covenant Marriage: Social Analysis and Legal Implications*, 59 La. L. Rev. 63, 107–108 (1998).

304. *See* La. Stat. Ann. § 9:307(A)(6).

305. La. Stat. Ann. § 9:307(A)(6). Reconciliation during the separation extinguishes the divorce option and thereby restarts the clock. La. Civ. Code Ann. art. 104.

306. La. Stat. Ann. § 9:307(A)(6).

307. La. Stat. Ann. § 9:307(A)(6).

308. *See* Katherine Shaw Spaht, *Louisiana's Covenant Marriage: Social Analysis and Legal Implications*, 59 La. L. Rev. 63, 120 & n.392 (1998) (citing La. Civ. Code Ann. art. 138(3) (repealed Jan. 1, 1991)).

Couples in a covenant marriage must rely on the covenant divorce provisions if the suit is filed in Louisiana, but a spouse could obtain a divorce outside of the covenant marriage contract if the spouses are domiciled elsewhere. In *Blackburn v. Blackburn*, the parties entered into a covenant marriage in Louisiana and, during their marriage, moved to Alabama.[309] The husband filed suit for divorce in Alabama, and the wife asked the Alabama court to enforce the covenant marriage contract and apply Louisiana law.[310] The trial court declined and issued a judgment of divorce based on Alabama law.[311] The appellate court agreed, explaining that the authority of the court to grant a divorce is purely statutory, and, given that both parties were domiciled in Alabama, it could find no reason to apply the laws of a state other than Alabama.[312] Whether the result would change if one spouse was still domiciled in Louisiana is a more difficult question. Traditional choice of law questions, including the relationship of the parties to the state and their expectations, would affect the analysis.[313]

309. Blackburn v. Blackburn, 180 So. 3d 16, 17 (Ala. Civ. App. 2015).

310. Blackburn, 180 So. 3d at 17.

311. Blackburn, 180 So. 3d at 17. The court granted the divorce based on incompatibility and also noted that Alabama considered and rejected covenant marriage in its state. *Id.* at 19–20.

312. Blackburn, 180 So. 3d at 19–20; *see also* Katherine Shaw Spaht & Symeon C. Symeonides, *Covenant Marriage and the Law of Conflicts of Law*, 32 Creighton L. Rev. 1085, 1109 n.127 (1999) (noting that Louisiana would cease being an interested state in the marriage if neither party retained a domicile in Louisiana).

313. *See* Katherine Shaw Spaht & Symeon C. Symeonides, *Covenant Marriage and the Law of Conflicts of Law*, 32 Creighton L. Rev. 1085, 1109 (1999) (suggesting that a choice of law analysis would often lead to an application of Louisiana law).

§ 4:24 Defenses to Divorce

The only defense to divorce in the Civil Code is reconciliation.[314] The jurisprudence has also applied the common law defenses of connivance,[315] justification,[316] and mental illness[317] as defenses to marital fault, either for the purpose of divorce or to prevent an award of alimony. Recrimination is not a defense to divorce in Louisiana.[318] The next two sections discuss the most common defenses, reconciliation, and mental illness.

§ 4:25 Defenses to Divorce—Reconciliation

Reconciliation of the parties extinguishes the cause of action for divorce.[319] In other words, if a spouse files an Article 102 divorce and the parties thereafter reconcile, the cause of action is extinguished and the spouse will need to file a new petition to re-urge a divorce.[320] Essentially, reconciliation will erase any time that the parties have lived separate and apart. Further, if the divorce is based on the fault of one spouse and the parties reconcile, the spouse can no longer seek a divorce based on the act that gave rise to the original claim of divorce, although the act can be used in a later divorce petition

---

314. La. Civ. Code Ann. art. 104.

315. Schwartz v. Schwartz, 103 So. 438, 440 (La. 1925). In *Schwartz*, the wife was involved in entrapping the husband by sending her husband to two parties with women, booze, and dancing to cause her husband to commit adultery so that she could obtain a divorce. The court denied her petition for divorce. The court found that connivance involves conduct by the other spouse that indicates intent to have his spouse transgress, or at least intent to allow the spouse to do so "undisturbed and unprevented." *Id.* at 439–40; *see also* Bourgeois v. Chauvin, 1 So. 679, 681 (La. 1887).

316. Firstly v. Firstly, 427 So. 2d 76, 77 (La. Ct. App. 4 Cir. 1983). Justification involves a reasonable reaction to the fault of the other spouse, which, if considered alone, would constitute fault. In *Firstly*, the husband abused the wife throughout the marriage, and after one of the incidents, she shot her husband twice. *Id.* The husband urged that her fault should preclude an award of alimony. *Id.* The court found that her actions were justified in light of the husband's history of physical abuse against his wife. *Id.*

317. *See* Cory v. Cory, 395 So. 2d 937 (La. Ct. App. 2d Cir. 1981). In *Cory*, a wife with diminished brain capacity was brought to Louisiana by her sister who initiated interdiction proceedings. The husband previously cared for his wife in California, where the couple had resided for many years. The court found that the husband had not abandoned his wife, and she was not entitled to separation on grounds of abandonment. Cory, 395 So. 2d at 937–40; *see also* Poitevent v. Poitevent, 152 So. 2d 256 (La. Ct. App. 4 Cir. 1963) (recognizing that insanity at the time of abandonment constitutes a defense to separation on that ground).

318. Ogea v. Ogea, 378 So. 2d 984, 991 (La. Ct. App. 3 Cir. 1979); Thomason v. Thomason, 355 So. 2d 908, 911 (La. 1978).

319. La. Civ. Code Ann. art. 104.

320. *See* Schiro v. Farrell, 13-635, pp. 9–10 (La. App. 5 Cir. 12/19/13), 131 So. 3d 997, 1001–02 (finding that the wife's Article 102 divorce should have been filed as a new matter under a new case number because her original petition was extinguished by reconciliation of the spouses).

to corroborate evidence of later fault.[321] Reconciliation is an affirmative defense that must be proven by the defendant by a preponderance of the evidence.[322]

Although the Code provides no definition of reconciliation, courts have explained that reconciliation is the forgiveness of a spouse, or at least the willingness to ignore the past behavior of a spouse, and the resumption of the common life together as spouses.[323] To establish reconciliation, spouses must exhibit a mutual intent to resume their marital relationship voluntarily.[324] Whether the spouses intend to restore or renew their marital relationship is a question of fact that must be determined by the trial judge from the totality of the circumstances.[325]

Isolated acts of sexual intercourse alone will not constitute reconciliation but will be one factor to consider.[326] Separated couples that interact or even cohabite periodically may not have a present intent to resume married life on a permanent basis.[327] For example, in *Woods v. Woods*, the husband urged reconciliation to defeat his wife's request for a no-fault divorce.[328] Rather than claiming that he and his wife resumed their sexual relationship, he asserted that they had attended social events and special occasions, acting affectionately and forgivingly at these events.[329] The wife testified that it was her intent to end the marriage, and she had acted in good faith to ease the pain of divorce on her husband and children.[330] The court granted the divorce, rejecting the defense of reconciliation.[331]

---

321. *See* Bercier v. Bercier, 431 So. 2d 31, 32 (La. Ct. App. 1 Cir. 1983); Gilberti v. Gilberti, 338 So. 2d 971, 974 (La. Ct. App. 4 Cir. 1976); Bloodworth v. Bloodworth, 306 So. 2d 812, 814 (La. Ct. App. 3 Cir. 1975); Virgadamo v. Virgadamo, 250 So. 2d 460, 462 (La. Ct. App. 4 Cir. 1971).

322. Ogea v. Ogea, 378 So. 2d at 990; Brown v. Brown, 260 So. 2d 66, 68 (La. Ct. App. 4 Cir. 1972).

323. Bishop v. Bishop, 98-59, p. 7 (La. App. 5 Cir. 5/27/98), 712 So. 2d 697, 700; Woods v. Woods, 27,199, p. 1 (La. App. 2 Cir. 8/23/95), 660 So. 2d 134, 135.

324. Jordan v. Jordan, 394 So. 2d 1291, 1292 (La. Ct. App. 1 Cir. 1981); Bishop, 712 So. 2d at 700; Woods, 660 So. 2d at 135; Garrett v. Garrett, 324 So. 2d 494, 496 (La. Ct. App. 2 Cir. 1975).

325. Woods, 660 So. 2d at 135 (citing Jordan, 394 So. 2d 1291; Halverson v. Halverson, 365 So. 2d 600 (La. Ct. App. 1 Cir. 1978)); Millon v. Millon, 352 So. 2d 325, 327 (La. Ct. App. 4 Cir. 1977).

326. Eppling v. Eppling, 537 So. 2d 814, 819 (La. Ct. App. 5 Cir. 1989); Whipple v. Smith, 428 So. 2d 1114, 1116 (La. Ct. App. 1 Cir. 1983); Garrett, 324 So. 2d at 496 (La. Ct. App. 2 Cir. 1975); *see also* Ogea, 378 So. 2d at 990–91 (La. Ct. App. 3 Cir. 1979) (reviewing shift in the law from sex-based to intent-based reconciliation); Katherine Shaw Spaht & John Randall Trahan, Family Law in Louisiana § 8.2, 180–81 (2009). Early jurisprudence tended to treat a single act of sexual intercourse as conclusive evidence of reconciliation. This practice, however, discouraged meetings between spouses that could lead to reconciliation, so it was later abandoned.

327. Woods, 660 So. 2d at 136.

328. Woods, 660 So. 2d at 135.

329. Woods, 660 So. 2d at 135–36.

330. Woods, 660 So. 2d at 135–36. Letters that she wrote after their encounters corroborated her testimony.

331. Woods, 660 So. 2d at 136. The concurring opinion pointed out the inconsistency in the court's judgment when it appeared in the community that the couple remained together—traveling, doing home projects—all while the husband lived in the garage apartment on the property. *Id.* at 136–37 (Hightower, J., concurring). But, because the husband did not assign error in this aspect of the trial court's decision, the appellate judge concurred in the decision of the majority. *Id.*

Likewise, in *Lemoine v. Lemoine*, the spouses traveled together out of town on four separate occasions, stayed together at the marital home on four other occasions, and had sexual relations during some of these occasions.[332] The husband never intended to return to the home, had a separate residence, and never moved his possessions back into the home.[333] Similar to the conclusion in *Woods*, the court rejected the defense of reconciliation.[334]

If, however, the spouses attempt to reconcile, even if the reconciliation is ultimately unsuccessful, the result is nonetheless reconciliation.[335] Courts consider not only the subjective intent of the spouses but also the outward appearance of reconciliation, including reestablishing a single marital domicile, attending social events together, and having sexual intercourse.[336] As "living separate and apart continuously" considers the outward appearance of separation to the community, so too does reconciliation.[337] The husband in *Jordan v. Jordan* admitted that when he initially moved back into the marital home, he intended to "patch up the marriage."[338] He moved his personal effects back home, the spouses occupied the same bedroom, had sexual intercourse, and attended social events together.[339] His subjective intent, coupled with the objective indicia of marital association, led the court to find reconciliation.[340]

Reconciliation that is induced by fraud or deceit will not suffice as a true reconciliation, but there will come a point, based on the length and quality of the parties' interactions, when reconciliation occurs as a matter of law.[341] In *Hickman v. Hickman*, the wife feigned reconciliation to circumvent a prior order depriving her of temporary custody of the couple's children.[342] Based on this scheme to defeat the award of custody to her husband, the court was reluctant to find reconciliation. Ultimately, though, when faced

---

332. Lemoine v. Lemoine, 97-1626, p. 3 (La. App. 3 Cir. 7/1/98), 715 So. 2d 1244, 1245–46.

333. Lemoine, 715 So. 2d at 1246.

334. Lemoine, 715 So. 2d at 1249; *see also* Noto v. Noto, 09-1100, p. 8 (La. App. 5 Cir. 5/11/10), 41 So. 3d 1175, 1180 (finding no reconciliation where the spouses vacationed together after the husband confessed his infidelity).

335. Jordan v. Jordan, 394 So. 2d 1291, 1293 (La. Ct. App. 1 Cir. 1981). The husband disputed the reconciliation, calling it only an "attempted reconciliation." *Id.* The couple, however, moved in together, and at the time it was the husband's intention to "patch up the marriage," so the court concluded that reconciliation had occurred. *Id.*

336. *See* Jordan, 394 So. 2d at 1292; *see also* Bishop, 712 So. 2d at 700–01 (noting that husband admitted that he did not want to reconcile even though the wife moved back into the home); Whipple v. Smith, 428 So. 2d 1114, 1117 (La. Ct. App. 1 Cir. 1983) (noting that the husband was living in an apartment with another woman); Orihuela v. Orihuela, 15-460, p. 7 (La. App. 5 Cir. 12/23/15), 184 So. 3d 182, 186 (noting that the spouses spent a considerable amount of time together and wife expressed her intent to reconcile in text messages).

337. Lemoine, 715 So. 2d 1244, 1248.

338. Jordan, 394 So. 2d at 1293.

339. Jordan, 394 So. 2d. at 1292.

340. Jordan, 394 So. 2d. at 1292.

341. Hickman v. Hickman, 227 So. 2d 14, 16 (La. Ct. App. 3 Cir. 1969); *see also* Garrett, 324 So. 2d at 496 (La. Ct. App. 2 Cir. 1975) (holding that if one spouse "entices" the other in hopes of dissolving that spouse's cause of action, then the court should find a lack of intent to reconcile).

342. Hickman, 227 So. 2d at 16.

with overwhelming factual evidence of reconciliation[343] and testimony by the husband that he was aware of her plan but wanted to work to try to save the marriage,[344] the court found reconciliation as a matter of law.[345]

Finally, courts have found that reconciliation can be based on a suspensive condition, such as the end of a spouse's adulterous affair.[346] Fulfilling the condition indicates the spouse's intent to reconcile, but when the spouse fails to fulfill the condition, the spouse lacks the intent necessary to reconcile.[347]

In light of the more recent divorces available for physical or sexual abuse, reconciliation as a defense has become an issue. On one hand, can reconciliation from abuse ever be permitted given the dynamics of an abusive relationship? On the other hand, if those who have suffered domestic abuse are never free to reconcile, could they hold unwieldy power over a former abuser who has sought help? Under prior law, when cruelty was a ground for separation, courts construed cohabitation after physical abuse as reconciliation but allowed previous acts of violence to corroborate subsequent acts of violence to demonstrate, in some instances, the justification for the spouse's abandonment of the marital home.[348]

The degree of abuse may govern whether a court will consider application of the defense of reconciliation, given the more recent understanding of the psychological effects on battered spouses. Conditional reconciliation may also be an avenue for courts to permit reconciliation from abuse but only if the spouse successfully fulfills the conditions of reconciliation, which could include abuse counseling and treatment.

---

343. Hickman, 227 So. 2d. at 15–16. During husband and wife's 78-day reconciliation period, they:

> [S]lept in the same bed and bedroom, lived as husband and wife and engaged in marital relations; in general, were with each other continuously in private and public, and frequently indulged in public displays of affection, by kissing, holding hands, etc., when meeting or together; were friendly and pleasant in conversation, both in public and in private; ate meals at the family home together; went together to pick up the children after work daily; engaged in family recreational activities, including picnics, church activities and horseback riding for the children; went on a family vacation out of state together; each day rode to and from work with each other; shared their lunch hour with each other almost daily during the work week; deposited their pay checks in the same joint bank account and drew checks on that account for the family expenses and obligations.

Id.

344. Hickman, 227 So. 2d at 17.

345. Hickman, 227 So. 2d at 16. The court hinted that if the fraudulent reconciliation was complete within a few hours or days, the result may be different.

346. Tablada v. Tablada, 590 So. 2d 1357, 1359 (La. Ct. App. 5 Cir. 1991). In *Tablada*, the parties agreed "that marital counseling and the cessation of defendant's adulterous affair were conditions of reconciliation, and that defendant failed to make such efforts." *Id.* Thus, the defendant was deemed to lack "the requisite intent to reconcile." *Id.* Accordingly, the court found no reconciliation. *Id.*

347. Tablada, 590 So. 2d at 1359.

348. *See., e.g.*, Gilberti v. Gilberti, 338 So. 3d 971, 974 (La. Ct. App. 4 Cir. 1976); *see also* Thomas v. Thomas, 2017-0760, p. 9 (La. App. 4 Cir. 2/21/18), 238 So. 3d 515, 522 (noting that abandonment due to domestic violence in the home was not fault to bar final spousal support).

§ 4:26 Defenses to Divorce— Mental Disorder

Preexisting mental illness has been used as a defense to allegations of adulterous conduct and could likewise be argued to excuse any type of marital fault. This defense is based on the premise that actions normally construed as fault that contribute to the termination of the marriage are excused when involuntarily induced by a preexisting mental illness.[349] However, to suffice as an excuse, the mental illness must have caused the behavior that would otherwise constitute marital fault.[350] Thus, the burden of proof is twofold: (1) the spouse's mental illness must have existed before the conduct occurred; and (2) the spouse's mental illness must have caused the conduct.[351]

In *Seltzer v. Seltzer*, the wife argued that her on-going acts of adultery should be excused because of her preexisting mental illness.[352] Medical testimony confirmed that she did suffer from a preexisting mental illness prior to committing adultery.[353] However, by all reports, during the period when she admitted to engaging in an extra-marital affair, her mental condition was "markedly improved"; medical testimony indicated that she was making significant progress and was not currently suffering from the psychosis as she had been prior to the extra-marital affair.[354] Even more telling, she admitted seeking a supportive relationship because she was lonely.[355] Recognizing the availability of the defense, the court nonetheless found that the wife's acts of adultery were not caused by her mental illness but were committed voluntarily.[356]

Conversely, in *Courville v. Courville*,[357] the wife was legally excused from a claim of cruel treatment based on her preexisting mental condition.[358] She suffered from schizophrenia, which caused her to sink into periods of depression and made her so aggressive that it was difficult for her to get along with others.[359] Based on testimony from lay and expert witnesses, the court found that her actions, which would have otherwise constituted cruelty, were excused by her mental condition.[360]

---

349. Seltzer v. Seltzer, 584 So. 2d 710, 712 (La. Ct. App. 4 Cir. 1991) (citing Eppling v. Eppling, 537 So. 2d 814 (La. Ct. App. 5 Cir. 1969); Kaplan v. Kaplan, 453 So. 2d 1218, 1221 (La. Ct. App. 2 Cir. 1984)).

350. Seltzer, 584 So. 2d at 712; Credeur v. Lalonde, 511 So. 2d 65, 66 (La. Ct. App. 3 Cir. 1987).

351. *See generally* Seltzer, 584 So. 2d 710.

352. Seltzer, 584 So. 2d at 712.

353. Seltzer, 584 So. 2d at 713.

354. Seltzer, 584 So. 2d at 713.

355. Seltzer, 584 So. 2d at 713.

356. Seltzer, 584 So. 2d at 713.

357. Courville v. Courville, 363 So. 2d 954 (La. Ct. App. 3 Cir. 1978).

358. Courville, 363 So. 2d at 956. The separation from bed and board suit filed against Mrs. Courville alleged that her actions constituted cruel treatment toward her husband. *Id.*

359. Courville, 363 So. 2d. at 957. At one point, she was committed to a state hospital, where she received care for her condition for several months. *Id.*

360. Courville, 363 So. 2d. at 957; *see also* Kaplan v. Kaplan, 453 So. 2d 1218 (La. Ct. App. 2 Cir. 1984) (wife was excused from fault due to her mental illnesses of acute depression and anxiety); Morrison v. Morrison, 395 So. 2d 909 (La. Ct. App. 2 Cir. 1981) (wife's actions excused due to her mental condition and paranoia); Bettencourtt v. Bettencourtt, 381 So. 2d 538 (La. Ct. App. 4 Cir. 1980)

§ 4:27 Effects of Divorce

Divorce has many effects. To start, the marriage is terminated.[361] A divorce likewise terminates the community regime retroactively to the filing of the divorce petition on which the judgment is granted.[362] In connection with a divorce petition, the court can consider incidental relief that arises from the marriage, such as injunctive relief,[363] spousal support,[364] the use of the former family home and other community movables and immovables,[365] and claims for contribution to education and training.[366] The court can also consider rights of custody,[367] visitation,[368] and child support.[369] The court may permit hearings to be conducted in chambers.[370]

Termination of a marriage likewise ends parental authority over children and begins the regime of tutorship.[371] A divorce also revokes legacies or other testamentary provisions to the former spouse when the decedent "is divorced from the legatee after the testament is executed and at the time of his death, unless the testator provides to the contrary."[372] Similarly, divorce revokes benefits payable to a former spouse under a life insurance policy, or pension, profit-sharing, retirement, or similar plans as long as

---

(wife did not abandon the domicile when she left to be admitted to hospital for preexisting mental condition); Gipson v. Gipson, 379 So. 2d 1171 (La. Ct. App. 2 Cir. 1980) (wife not at fault due to her history of mental illness).

361. La. Civ. Code Ann. art. 101.

362. La. Civ. Code Ann. art. 159 ("The retroactive termination of the community shall be without prejudice to rights of third parties validly acquired in the interim between the filing of the petition and recordation of the judgment."). Once terminated, the spouses have the right to demand partition of the former community at any time, La. Civ. Code Ann. art. 2369.8, and absent agreement, a spouse may demand judicial partition, La. Stat. Ann. § 9:2801. For a comprehensive discussion of the effects of termination on community property, *see* Andrea Carroll & Richard D. Moreno, Matrimonial Regimes § 7:2, *in* 16 Louisiana Civil Law Treatise 598–689 (4th ed. 2013).

363. *See* La. Stat. Ann. §§ 9:371 *et seq.*

364. La. Civ. Code Ann. arts. 111–117.

365. La. Stat. Ann. § 9:374.

366. La. Civ. Code Ann. arts. 121–124. *See generally* La. Civ. Code Ann. art. 105. Not all incidental relief must be associated with a divorce action. Spouses may sue one another for spousal support or support of a child while the spouses are living separate and apart, even without a pending divorce petition. La. Stat. Ann. § 9:291.

367. *See* La. Civ. Code Ann. arts. 131–135; La. Stat. Ann. §§ 9:331 *et seq.*

368. *See* La. Civ. Code Ann. arts. 136–137; La. Stat. Ann. §§ 9:331–:333, :341–:348.

369. La. Stat. Ann §§ 9:315 *et seq.*

370. "[T]he court by local rule, and only in those instances where good cause is shown, may provide that only with mutual consent, civil hearings before the trial court in divorce proceedings may be held in chambers." La. Stat. Ann. § 9:302(A). "A motion for hearing in chambers ... may be made by either party or upon the court's own motion." La. Stat. Ann. § 9:302(B). "Such hearings shall include contested and uncontested proceedings and rules for spousal support, child support, visitation, injunctions, or other matters provisional and incidental to divorce proceedings." La. Stat. Ann. § 9:302(A). Additionally, such hearings "shall be conducted in the same manner as if taking place in open court. The minute clerk and court reporter shall be present if necessary to perform the duties provided by law." La. Stat. Ann. § 9:302(C).

371. La. Civ. Code Ann. art. 246. *See* Chapters 9–10.

372. La. Civ. Code Ann. art. 1608(5).

the divorce occurs after the spouse is designated as a beneficiary, the parties remain divorced at the time of death, and no property settlement provides otherwise.[373] Termination of marriage may, under certain facts, also give rise to revocation of donations due to ingratitude.[374]

Although marriage does not change the surname of a spouse (so court action is not needed to regain one's maiden name at divorce),[375] a spouse should change the name on his or her social security card, driver's license, and any other form of identification or registration, all in accordance with the regulations for each agency or entity. A married woman is permitted to retain the surname of her spouse even after their divorce and her remarriage.[376]

§ 4:28 Appeal

A judgment of divorce is a final judgment.[377] An appeal from a judgment granting or refusing a divorce can be taken only within thirty days from either the expiration of the time for applying for a new trial or from the date of the court's refusal to grant a new trial, in accordance with Article 2087(A) of the Code of Civil Procedure.[378] The appeal suspends the execution of the judgment for claims relating to the annulment, divorce, or any partition of community property or settlement of claims arising from the matrimonial regime[379] but not for custody, visitation, or support.[380]

373. La. Stat. Ann. § 9:2449.1 (retirement plans); § 22:911.1 (life insurance).

374. *See* La. Civ. Code Ann. arts. 1556–1560; Whitman v. Whitman, 31,814 (La. App. 2 Cir. 3/31/99), 730 So. 2d 1048.

375. La. Civ. Code Ann. art. 100; La. Code Civ. Proc. Ann. art. 3947.

376. La. Stat. Ann. § 9:292. Because this statute is gender-specific, it would not survive an equal protection challenge.

377. Tarbutton v. Tarbutton, 51,486, p. 4 (La. App. 2 Cir. 5/2/17), 217 So. 3d 1281, 1285.

378. La. Code Civ. Proc. Ann. arts. 2087(A), 3942(A). "The delay for applying for a new trial shall be seven days, exclusive of legal holidays, … [which] commences to run on the day after the clerk has mailed, or the sheriff has served, the notice of judgment." La. Code Civ. Proc. Ann. art. 1974. *But see* Tarbutton, 217 So. 3d at 1285 (considering the appeal of the litigant's divorce even though it was untimely because she appeared pro se). It is not necessary to post an appeal bond. Post v. Post, 376 So. 2d 1275, 1276 (La. Ct. App. 2 Cir. 1979).

379. La. Code Civ. Proc. Ann. art. 3942(B).

380. La. Code Civ. Proc. Ann. art. 3943.

Chapter 5

Spousal Support*

* This chapter was derived from the following article: Sandi S. Varnado, *A Primer on Claims of Spouses in Louisiana*, 68 Loy. L. Rev. 263 (2022). The authors wish to thank the Loyola Law Review for its assistance on the initial work for this chapter.

§ 5:1 Introduction

Louisiana law provides spouses with three potential claims seeking financial support against one another. First, a spouse may make a claim for support during the marriage pursuant to the reciprocal duties of support that spouses owe to one another.[1] Second, a spouse may make a claim for spousal support, which may be interim spousal support (during the pendency of a divorce action)[2] or final spousal support (after the termination of the marriage).[3] Finally, a spouse may make a claim for the financial contributions made during the marriage to the education or training of the other spouse (in a proceeding for divorce or thereafter).[4]

Although spouses may not sue one another as a general rule,[5] among other exceptions, they are allowed to do so to seek spousal support while the parties are living separate and apart[6] or in a proceeding for divorce or thereafter.[7]

§ 5:2 Claim for Support Owed During the Marriage

By operation of law, the contract of marriage creates the reciprocal duty of support for the spouses as detailed in Louisiana Civil Code Article 98.[8] Note that Louisiana law imposes this duty on spouses *during* their marriage, regardless of any impending separation or divorce.[9] As such, it is distinguishable from interim spousal support (the claim to which arises during the pendency of a divorce action) and final spousal support (the claim to which arises upon the termination of the marriage).

This duty of support covers the necessities of life—food, clothing, and shelter.[10] With regard to shelter, one court has interpreted this duty to foreclose one spouse from evicting the other spouse from the matrimonial domicile that was the separate property of the spouse seeking the eviction.[11] The duty of support also extends to the cost of modern conveniences like telephones, appliances, and automobiles.[12]

---

1. La. Civ. Code Ann. art. 98.
2. La. Civ. Code Ann. arts. 105, 111, 113–117.
3. La. Civ. Code Ann. arts. 105, 111–112, 114–117.
4. La. Civ. Code Ann. art. 121.
5. La. Stat. Ann. § 9:291.
6. La. Stat. Ann. § 9:291.
7. La. Civ. Code Ann. art. 105.
8. La. Civ. Code Ann. art. 98.
9. *See, e.g.*, Chi v. Pang, 94-284, p. 3 (La. App. 3 Cir. 10/5/94), 643 So. 2d 411, 413.
10. Bernhardt v. Bernhardt, 283 So. 2d 226, 229 (La. 1973).
11. Purdy v. Purdy, 331 So. 2d 868, 869 (La. Ct. App. 2 Cir. 1976).
12. La. Civ. Code Ann. art. 98 cmt. (c) (rev. 1987).

Like most reciprocal duties imposed on spouses,[13] the duty of support is a rule of public order. This means that generally the parties may not contractually avoid it.[14] However, courts have allowed spouses who opted out of the community property regime to agree on an allocation of expenses during the marriage and even to allocate the everyday and usual expenses of the marriage to one spouse alone, finding that such an arrangement did not violate article 98.[15]

§ 5:3 Claim for Spousal Support

In addition to claims for support during an intact marriage, Louisiana law also allows for spouses to assert claims for spousal support against each other. The sections that follow will explore several topics: the historical development of spousal support in Louisiana, the two types of spousal support (interim support and final support), the time limitations on spousal support claims, the means of modifying, terminating, and extinguishing spousal support, and the parties' freedom to contract for spousal support.

§ 5:4 Claim for Spousal Support— The Historical Development of Spousal Support in Louisiana

Louisiana first codified the concept of spousal support (formerly called "alimony") in Article 160 of the Louisiana Civil Code of 1870.[16] At that time, the law allowed a spouse to obtain a separation from bed and board and/or divorce only on grounds of the other spouse's fault,[17] so alimony, likewise, was tied to fault. In its original form, only a wife could obtain alimony from her at-fault husband.[18] Preeminent French scholar Marcel Planiol insinuated that alimony was a duty of the at-fault husband to make pecuniary amends to the wife for his fault, such that the wife would be restored to the means and resources of which she had been deprived because of his fault.[19] Any

13. Louisiana law provides two other reciprocal duties as well. First is the duty of fidelity, which provides that spouses may not commit adultery (i.e., the negative duty of fidelity) and that they submit to the "reasonable and normal sexual desires" of the other spouse (i.e., the positive duty of fidelity). La. Civ. Code Ann. art. 98 (b) (rev. 1987). *See, e.g.*, Von Bechman v. Von Bechman, 386 So. 2d 910 (La. 1980). Second is the duty of assistance. While this duty arguably falls within the scope of the duty of support, it also includes the personal care to be given to an ill or infirm spouse. La. Civ. Code Ann. art. 98 cmt. (c) (rev. 1987).

14. La. Civ. Code Ann. art. 7; *see* Favrot v. Barnes, 332 So. 2d 873, 875 (La. Ct. App. 4 Cir. 1976) (rejecting the idea that parties, by a premarital understanding, can repeal or amend the nature of marital obligations set forth in the Louisiana Civil Code), *rev'd on other grounds*, 339 So. 2d 843 (La. 1976).

15. *See* Gereighty v. Domingue, 17-339, p. 17 (La. App. 5 Cir. 5/30/18), 249 So. 3d 1016, 1030.

16. Player v. Player, 110 So. 332, 332–33 (La. 1926).

17. La. Civ. Code arts. 138–139 (1870); McAlpine v. McAlpine, 94-1594, p. 4 (La. 9/5/96), 679 So. 2d 85, 88.

18. McAlpine, 679 So. 2d at 88; Player, 110 So. at 332.

19. McAlpine, 679 So. 2d at 87 (quoting Planiol, Civil Law Treatise, Vol. I, No. 1259, pp. 696–97 (La. State Law Institute Translation 1959) ("Divorce having destroyed the marriage, no effects of it

alimony award was paid from the husband's property, and it could not exceed one-third of his income.[20]

In 1916, Louisiana enacted Act 269, which recognized no-fault divorce, allowing either spouse to obtain a divorce on proof of living separate and apart for a certain period of time.[21] To address the no-fault divorce scenario, article 160 was amended to remove the husband's fault as a prerequisite for alimony; instead, it required the wife to prove that she was not at fault.[22] This amendment also made alimony payable from the husband's earnings, as well as his property.[23] In 1979, the legislature again amended article 160 to allow either spouse who had not been at fault to assert a claim for alimony.[24] This amendment served to remove the unconstitutional gender-bias from the article.[25]

Under current law, the request for spousal support commonly arises in connection with a divorce proceeding (fault or no-fault based) or thereafter. Spousal support is one of the many incidents of marriage that a party may request.[26] The request may also arise in a proceeding for the declaration of nullity of a marriage.[27] In a pending proceeding, the court may award a party the same incidental relief afforded in a divorce proceeding,[28] and after a declaration of nullity, "a party entitled to civil effects of marriage may seek the same relief as a divorced spouse."[29]

Either spouse in the proceeding may seek spousal support, and such support may be one of two types—interim periodic support or final periodic support (discussed, in turn, in Sections 5:5–5:13 below).[30] One may assert a claim for both, either, or neither of these types of spousal support, but the decision to award spousal support lies

should continue. Upon what idea is founded persistence of the obligation of support between two persons who have nothing in common? Its basis is found in a principle already mentioned more than once. Whatever act of man causes damage to another obliges him by whose fault it happened to repair it, says Art. 1382. As long as the marriage lasted it gave each of the spouses an acquired position upon which each could count. The community of life permitted the spouse without means to share the welfare of the other. Suddenly through no fault of the spouse in question, he or she finds himself or herself devoid of resources and plunged into poverty. It is manifestly in such a case as this that the guilty party should be made to bear the consequences of his wrongful acts.")).

20. McAlpine, 679 So. 2d at 88; Player, 110 So. at 332.

21. McAlpine, 679 So. 2d at 88. The time period changed several times, from as many as seven years separate and apart to as few as 180 days separate and apart. *Id.*

22. McAlpine, 679 So. 2d at 88.

23. Player, 110 So. at 332.

24. Lovell v. Lovell, 378 So. 2d 418, 421 (La. 1979).

25. Smith v. Smith, 382 So. 2d 972, 974 (La. Ct. App. 1 Cir. 1980); Lovell, 378 So. 2d at 421.

26. La. Civ. Code Ann. art. 105. Others include custody, visitation, or support of a minor child; injunctive relief, use and occupancy of the family home, or use of community movables or immovables; or use of personal property. *Id.*

27. La. Civ. Code Ann. arts. 151–152.

28. La. Civ. Code Ann. art. 151.

29. La. Civ. Code Ann. art. 152. Even a spouse not entitled to civil effects of marriage may be awarded custody, child support, or visitation, and the declaration of nullity has no effect on such awards. *Id.*

30. La. Civ. Code Ann. art. 111.

within the sole discretion of the court.[31] Summary proceedings may be employed for the original spousal support awards, as well as for subsequent modifications and/or termination of spousal support.[32]

In proceedings involving a claim for spousal support, both parties must provide to the court a copy of their most recent federal tax returns, a verified income statement that shows gross income and adjusted gross income, as well as documentation of current and past earnings.[33] Pay stubs or employer statements generally qualify as suitable documentation. If a spouse has an ownership interest in a business, the last three years of state and federal income tax returns with all attachments and schedules, the most recent profit/loss statement, balance sheets, financial statements, quarterly sales tax reports, personal and business bank account statements, receipts, and expenses should qualify as suitable documentation.[34]

In the event that a party alleges that the other party is hiding or underreporting income, the court will admit evidence of redirected income[35] and deferred income,[36] and in the event that the income claimed is inconsistent with the spouse's lifestyle, the court will admit evidence of that spouse's standard of living and assets both before and after the establishment of a spousal support order.[37] When a spouse's income cannot be sufficiently established from the foregoing, courts may admit evidence of wage and earnings surveys distributed by government agencies for the purpose of imputing income.[38]

31. La. Civ. Code Ann. art. 111.

32. La. Code Civ. Proc. Ann. art. 2592.

33. La. Stat. Ann. § 9:326(A).

34. La. Stat. Ann. § 9:326(A).

35. Redirected income might include loans to that spouse by a business they own or payments (in the form of wages or salary) by that spouse or a business they own to someone related to that spouse. La. Stat. Ann. § 9:326(B).

36. Deferred income might include recent reductions in the distribution of income from the spouse's business to the spouse.

37. La. Stat. Ann. § 9:326(B).

38. La. Stat. Ann. § 9:326(C).

§ 5:5 Claim for Spousal Support— Interim Spousal Support

The first type of spousal support that a party may seek is interim spousal support (previously known as *alimony pendente lite*). Recognition of this type of support predated its codification,[39] which happened in Article 146 of the Louisiana Civil Code of 1870.[40] That article provided: "If the wife has not a sufficient income for her maintenance during the suit for separation, the judge shall allow her a sum for her support proportioned to the means of the husband."[41]

Under current law, the claim is gender-neutral, and the spouse in need will seek support from the other spouse who has the ability to pay[42] when the parties are physically separated with or without a pending divorce action.[43] The foundation of this type of spousal support is the mutual duty of support imposed on spouses.[44] As one court explained: "A spouse's right to claim interim periodic support is grounded in the statutorily imposed duty on spouses to support each other during marriage and thus provides for the spouse who does not have sufficient income for his or her maintenance during the period of separation."[45] Thus, this type of spousal support serves to preserve the status quo, i.e., to allow spouses to adjust to the new normal of living apart without suffering unnecessary economic detriment.[46] Stated another way, interim spousal support preserves parity in the levels of maintenance and support and avoids unnecessary financial dislocation until a final determination of support can be made.[47]

39. Player v. Player, 110 So. 332, 332–33 (La. 1926); Malony v. Malony, 1844 WL 1608, at *1 (La. 1844) (an interlocutory decree ordering defendant to pay $10 per month alimony pendente lite).

40. As one court noted, this type of alimony has been in the Louisiana Civil Code since its inception. Cassidy v. Cassidy, 477 So. 2d 84, 85 (La. 1985).

41. La. Civ. Code art. 148 (1870).

42. The terminology change was made in the 1997 revisions to the articles via Act 1078. 1997 La. Sess. Law Serv. Act 1078 (H.B. 2053) (West).

43. La. Stat. Ann. § 9:291; La. Civ. Code Ann. art. 113.

44. *See* La. Civ. Code Ann. art. 98.

45. Hogan v. Hogan, 49,979, p. 16 (La. App. 2 Cir. 9/30/15), 178 So. 3d 1013, 1022.

46. La. Civ. Code Ann. art. 113 cmt. (b) (rev. 1997).

47. Rodriguez v. Rodriguez, 2020-0171, p. 3 (La. App. 1 Cir. 11/6/20), 315 So. 3d 913, 916–17 (citing Lambert v. Lambert, 2006-2399, p. 10 (La. App. 1 Cir. 3/23/07), 960 So. 2d 921, 928).

§ 5:6 Claim for Spousal Support— Interim Spousal Support— Role of Fault

It is important to note that a spouse's fault is irrelevant to a court's determination of interim spousal support.[48] This is because interim spousal support is awarded while the marriage is still intact, and as mentioned above, spouses are statutorily bound to support each other during their marriage pursuant to Louisiana Civil Code Article 98.[49] Thus, the relevant inquiry is the continued existence of the marriage,[50] and fault plays no role in the determination of interim spousal support.[51]

§ 5:7 Claim for Spousal Support— Interim Spousal Support—Considerations for Interim Spousal Support

Either party may move for interim spousal support.[52] In deciding whether to award it, the court considers the moving party's needs, the other party's ability pay, any interim or final child support obligation,[53] and the parties' standard of living during the marriage.[54] The length of the marriage is irrelevant.[55] The party claiming interim support bears the burden of proving entitlement to it,[56] and the court may consider the entire financial condition of the spouses in making its decision.[57]

A judgment awarding an interim spousal support allowance is retroactive to the date of judicial demand except for good cause shown.[58] A court determines whether there is good cause shown on a case-by-case basis.[59] In *Cabral v. Cabral*, the court

48. La. Civ. Code Ann. art. 111.

49. Larson v. Larson, 16-695, p. 2 (La. App 5 Cir. 10/25/17), 229 So. 3d 1043, 1048; Holly v. Holly, 2018-207, pp. 2–3 (La. App. 3 Cir. 9/26/18), 255 So. 3d 1158, 1160.

50. Short v. Short, 09-639, p. 9 (La. App. 5 Cir. 3/23/10), 33 So. 3d 988, 994; Hall v. Hall, 08-706, p. 4 (La. App. 5 Cir. 2/10/09), 4 So. 3d 254, 257.

51. Lightell v. Lightell, 17-327, p. 8 (La. App. 5 Cir. 12/13/17), 234 So. 3d 244, 250.

52. Prior to the 2018 revision to article 113, the court could award interim spousal support upon the motion of a party or when a demand for final spousal support was pending. Under current law, a party must simply move for interim spousal support. La. Civ. Code Ann. art. 113 cmt. (c) (rev. 2018).

53. This consideration was inserted by the legislature in 2014. 2014 La. Acts No. 616, § 1.

54. La. Civ. Code Ann. art. 113(A).

55. Galbraith v. Galbraith, 382 So. 2d 1042, 1043 (La. Ct. App. 2 Cir. 1980) ("Neither the brevity of the marriage nor the wife's capacity to earn a gainful wage are factors to be considered in setting alimony pendente lite").

56. Molony v. Harris, 2009-1529, pp. 3–4 (La. App. 4 Cir. 10/14/10), 51 So. 3d 752, 757.

57. Curry v. Curry, 19-49, p. 4 (La. App. 5 Cir. 2/12/20), 292 So. 3d 128, 132; Huger v. Huger, 2022-0410, p. 14 (La. App. 4 Cir. 12/14/22), 367 So. 3d 705, 712.

58. La. Stat. Ann. § 9:321(A).

59. Roan v. Roan, 38,383, pp. 21–22 (La. App. 2 Cir. 4/14/04), 870 So. 2d 626, 639 (citing Piccione v. Piccione, 2001-1086 (La. App. 3 Cir. 5/22/02), 824 So. 2d 427, 433 ("good cause" must be determined

found good cause to delay commencement where the payor was unable to work while recovering from surgery for a malignant tumor.[60] In cases like this, the court will set the date on which the award commences but in no case will the award commence before the date of judicial demand.[61]

§ 5:8 Claim for Spousal Support—Interim Spousal Support—Considerations for Interim Spousal Support—Needs of Claimant

The first step in an interim spousal support claim is for the claimant to demonstrate need, i.e., the amount sufficient to maintain the claimant in a standard of living comparable to that enjoyed while living with the other spouse during the marriage.[62]

To assess the claimant's needs, courts look at the claimant's means and their expenses. In considering the claimant's means, one court considered the child support received by the claimant for a child of a previous marriage to be part of her income and also imputed full-time earning capacity to the claimant despite the fact that she did not work full-time due to court-ordered attendance at Alcoholics Anonymous meetings.[63] In considering the claimant's expenses, those incurred during the marriage are appropriate for consideration on a claim for interim spousal support, but they must be reasonable.[64] Thus, a claimant must show that they lack sufficient income to maintain that standard of living.[65]

As to the standard of living, this "relates to facts as they have existed during the time that the parties were living together and as they actually exist at the time the litigation commences, not to the future possibilities and capabilities."[66] With regard to the claimant's ability to maintain themselves in that standard of living, a heavily litigated issue is whether the earning capacity of the claimant should be considered. Courts have consistently held that the claimant may not establish their needs by arbitrarily refusing to work.[67] They have also routinely considered the earning capacity of the claimant spouse where the claimant was the primary wage earner during the marriage, where

---

on a case-by-case basis and must constitute, if not a compelling reason, certainly a reason of such significance and gravity that "it would be inequitable to deny an extension of such support.")).

60. Cabral v. Cabral, 503 So. 2d 144 (La. Ct. App. 5 Cir. 1987).

61. La. Stat. Ann. § 9:321(E).

62. King v. King, 51,942, pp. 4–5 (La. App. 2 Cir. 4/11/18), 247 So. 3d 973, 977.

63. Molony v. Harris, 2009-1529, pp. 3–4 (La. App. 4 Cir. 10/14/10), 51 So. 3d 752, 757.

64. Rockett v. Rockett, 51,453, p. 9 (La. App. 2 Cir. 6/21/17), 223 So. 3d 1227, 1233.

65. Note, though, that courts have specified that the claimant need not be practically destitute to qualify for spousal support. Loyacano v. Loyacano, 358 So. 2d 304 (La. 1978).

66. La. Civ. Code Ann. art. 113 cmt. (b) (rev. 1997).

67. *See, e.g.*, Fairchild v. Fairchild, 537 So. 2d 1260, 1260–62 (La. Ct. App. 4 Cir. 1989); Richard v. Richard, 577 So. 2d 110, 112 (La. Ct. App. 1 Cir. 1991); LeBlanc v. LeBlanc, 405 So. 2d 1187, 1188–89 (La. Ct. App. 1 Cir. 1981).

the claimant spouse was regularly employed during the marriage and has the capability of securing employment, or where neither spouse was employed.[68] However, interim spousal support is not foreclosed for a claimant who does not accept the first available job regardless of the circumstances or the income to be earned.[69]

Courts employ one of three different rationales in deciding whether to consider the claimant's earning capacity. First, some courts refuse to consider the claimant's earning capacity where the claimant spouse was not the primary wage earner and was not regularly employed during the marriage.[70] Courts reason that the status quo of the parties during the marriage precludes a consideration of future possibilities or capabilities, and parties should continue in the roles that they held during the marriage until they are divorced.[71] Second, some courts simply state that, given the permissive "may" in Louisiana Civil Code Article 113, the court is vested with the discretion to consider all relevant factors, which may or may not include earning capacity.[72] Finally, some courts reason that if the claimant is able to work for their own support, interim spousal support is inappropriate.[73]

In *Rodriguez v. Rodriguez*, the court awarded interim spousal support to a 56-year-old wife who had little formal education and limited English language skills and who suffered from medical issues.[74] She had been unemployed for most of the marriage, and even when employed, only earned minimum wage. Although the district court refused to award her interim support, insisting that she had exaggerated her medical issues and could work, the appellate court reversed, instead focusing on her continued unemployment during the marriage. Even assuming that she could return to work, the appellate court found that her income earning potential at minimum wage would be insufficient to meet her expenses.[75]

In some interim spousal support claims, litigants have raised the issue of whether a claimant should be forced to deplete assets to meet their needs. In making that determination, courts apply a rule of reasonableness and have considered the relative financial

---

68. *See, e.g.*, Evans v. Evans, 49,160, p. 6 (La. App. 2 Cir. 6/25/14), 145 So. 3d 1093, 1096; Brar v. Brar, 2001-0370, p. 7 (La. App. 3 Cir. 10/3/01), 796 So. 2d 810, 815.

69. Whipple v. Whipple, 424 So. 2d 263, 268 (La. Ct. App. 1 Cir. 1982).

70. *See, e.g.*, Evans, 145 So. 3d at 1096; Braswell v. Braswell, 494 So. 2d 1333, 1338 (La. Ct. App. 2 Cir. 1986); Clayton v. Clayton, 431 So. 2d 1082, 1084 (La. Ct. App. 2 Cir. 1983); Arrendell v. Arrendell, 390 So. 2d 927 (La. Ct. App. 2 Cir. 1980); Harrington v. Campell, 413 So. 2d 297, 302 (La. Ct. App. 3 Cir. 1982); Cortinez v. Cortinez, 414 So. 2d 830, 831–32 (La. Ct. App. 4 Cir. 1982).

71. Evans, 145 So. 3d at 1096.

72. *See, e.g.*, Wester v. Wester, 564 So. 2d 799, 804 (La. Ct. App. 3 Cir. 1990); Hardee v. Hardee, 551 So. 2d 846, 848 (La. Ct. App. 3 Cir. 1989); Kirkpatrick v. Kirkpatrick, 41,851, p. 5 (La. App. 2 Cir. 1/24/07), 948 So. 2d 390, 394.

73. *See, e.g.*, Smith v. Smith, 382 So. 2d 972, 974 (La. Ct. App. 1 Cir. 1980); Lovell v. Lovell, 378 So. 2d 418, 421 (La. 1979); Jones v. Jones, 612 So. 2d 240, 241–42 (La. Ct. App. 4 Cir. 1992); Daigle v. Daigle, 96-541, p. 3–4 (La. App. 3 Cir. 11/6/96); 689 So. 2d 478, 480; Morris v. Morris, 413 So. 2d 285 (La. Ct. App. 3 Cir. 1982).

74. Rodriguez v. Rodriguez, 2020-0171, pp. 7–8 (La. App. 1 Cir. 11/6/20), 315 So. 3d 913, 919–20.

75. Rodriguez, 315 So. 3d at 919.

positions of the parties, the type of asset under consideration, and the consequences of its liquidation. As explained by the Louisiana Supreme Court:

> [I]n determining the rate at which a spouse may be required to deplete his or her assets, it may be pertinent to consider the mental and physical health of the parties, their age and life expectancy, the parties' other financial responsibilities, the relative ability, education and work experience of the parties, and the potential effect of any contemplated depletion of assets upon the children of the marriage. The problem is of such a nature as to be insusceptible of solution by any exact formula or monetary index, and the court should proceed with great caution and due regard for the probable long range effects of any depletion contemplated.[76]

Typically, though, a court will not require the claimant to deplete assets to meet their needs except to the extent that those assets can be invested such that they will generate income without the risk of loss of capital.[77] In *Sonfield v. Deluca*, therefore, the Louisiana Supreme Court refused to allow the claimant's $92,000 worth of equity in her home (a non-liquid asset) to serve as a basis to terminate her existing spousal support award.[78] To do otherwise, it found, would force the claimant to sell her home and exhaust the equity for her support until such time as she again needed to be totally dependent upon her former spouse.

§ 5:9 Claim for Spousal Support— Interim Spousal Support—Considerations for Interim Spousal Support—Other Spouse's Ability to Pay

Once the claimant demonstrates the need for interim spousal support, the court will then assess the other spouse's ability to pay.[79] In other words, the claimant's needs are limited only by the other spouse's ability to pay.[80] Thus, the court must assess the payor's "means." Obviously, a court will consider the payor's income from labor or services performed.[81] However, the term "means" extends beyond income to any resource from which the wants of life may be supplied.[82] As a result, courts have considered the payor's physical property, income from such property, and earning capacity.[83] They have also

76. Loyacano, 358 So. 2d at 311.

77. *See, e.g.*, Arceneaux v. Arceneaux, 426 So. 2d 745, 747 (La. Ct. App. 3 Cir. 1983); Thomas v. Thomas, 281 So. 2d 471, 473 (La. Ct. App. 4 Cir. 1973); Patton v. Patton, 37,401, pp. 6–8 (La. App. 2 Cir. 9/24/03), 856 So. 2d 56, 60–61.

78. Sonfield v. Deluca, 385 So. 2d 232, 235 (La. 1980).

79. Hight v. Hight, 2017-0566, pp. 5–6 (La. App. 4 Cir. 12/13/17), 234 So. 3d 1143, 147.

80. McFall v. Armstrong, 10-181, p. 4 (La. App. 5 Cir. 10/12/10), 50 So. 3d 904, 907.

81. Rockett v. Rockett, 51,453, pp. 9–12 (La. App. 2 Cir. 6/21/17), 223 So. 3d 1227, 1233–34.

82. Curry v. Curry, 19-49, pp. 5–6 (La. App. 5 Cir. 2/12/20), 292 So. 3d 128, 133–34.

83. Rockett, 223 So. 3d at 1233–34.

considered social security benefits,[84] veterans' benefits,[85] retirement income,[86] profitability of a corporation (where payor owned 50% of a Subchapter S corporation that reported profit from income and interest),[87] and draws against future commissions.[88] In a recent case, the court considered the expenses of a husband paid by his parents as an income source to be considered as part of his means.[89] In *Goldberg v. Goldberg*, the court ordered a wife who inherited more than $1 million from her parents to pay interim spousal support to her husband who earned $160,000 per year during the marriage, despite the fact that the wife had never worked during the marriage.[90] In *Huger v. Huger*, the court considered the husband's time spent at an island in Maine and on his yacht in Turks and Caicos.[91] In *Sykes v. Sykes*, a husband failed to carry his burden of proof that he lacked the means to pay interim spousal support.[92] He testified that he was not employed regularly, working only a day occasionally. He claimed that he had tried to secure employment with no success, which he attributed to his lack of education and skill. The court stated that to be excused from his spousal support obligation, he would have to show absolute unemployability, i.e., that he had exhausted every possibility to find employment.[93]

Once the court determines the means of the payor, it will also consider the payor's reasonable expenses. For example, in *Alexander v. Alexander*, the court declined to award interim spousal support to a wife whose husband was paying considerable community debts.[94] It reasoned that because he alone was paying these debts, this expense would preclude him from having the sufficient means to pay the requested support.[95]

In a case where the amount the claimant needs to maintain the prior standard of living exceeds the other party's ability to pay, the court will fix interim spousal support at a sum that will be just and fair to all parties involved.[96] Where there is not enough money for both, the court will not allow one spouse to live better than the other.[97]

---

84. Prestenback v. Prestenback, 2008-0457, pp. 12–13 (La. App. 1 Cir. 11/18/08), 9 So. 3d 172, 181.
85. Vassallo v. Vassallo, 540 So. 2d 1300, 1302–03 (La. Ct. App. 5 Cir. 1989).
86. Vassallo, 540 So. 2d at 1302.
87. Dagley v. Dagley, 96-1796, pp. 4–5 (La. App. 4 Cir. 5/21/97), 695 So. 2d 521, 523.
88. Gravois v. Gravois, 495 So. 2d 315 (La. Ct. App. 4 Cir. 1986).
89. Curry, 292 So. 3d at 133–34.
90. Goldberg v. Goldberg, 96-2145, p. 8 (La. App. 4 Cir. 7/23/97), 698 So. 2d 63, 67–68.
91. Huger v. Huger, 2022-0410, p. 14 (La. App. 4 Cir. 12/14/22), 367 So. 3d 705, 712.
92. Sykes v. Sykes, 308 So. 2d 816, 817 (La. Ct. App. 4 Cir. 1975).
93. Sykes, 308 So. 2d at 817.
94. Alexander v. Alexander, 2002-683, p. 10 (La. App. 3 Cir. 11/13/02), 831 So. 2d 1060, 1067.
95. Alexander, 831 So. 2d at 1067; *see also* Cabral v. Cabral, 503 So. 2d 144, 147 (La. Ct. App. 5 Cir. 1987); Stansbury v. Stansbury, 258 So. 2d 170, 172–73 (La. Ct. App. 1 Cir. 1972).
96. Lambert v. Lambert, 2006-2399, p. 11 (La. App. 1 Cir. 3/23/07), 960 So. 2d 921, 929.
97. Arrendell v. Arrendell, 390 So. 2d 927, 930 (La. Ct. App. 2 Cir. 1980); Rodriguez v. Rodriguez, 2020-0171, p. 3 (La. App. 1 Cir. 11/6/20), 315 So. 3d 913, 917; Rockett, 223 So. 3d at 1234.

Unlike final spousal support discussed in Sections 5:11–5:13 below, there is no statutory maximum on the amount of interim spousal support.[98] However, in *Martello v. Martello*, the appellate court found an abuse of discretion by the trial court that set interim spousal support at 64% of the payor's income, particularly in light of the fact that after paying child support, the payor would only have $886.83 left for his own expenses.[99]

§ 5:10 Claim for Spousal Support— Interim Spousal Support—Duration of Interim Spousal Support

In its original form, *alimony pendente lite* terminated at the judgment of divorce.[100] However, beginning in 1997, the termination of interim spousal support was not necessarily aligned with the divorce judgment. Article 113 of the Louisiana Civil Code, at that time, provided a general rule that an award of interim spousal support terminated upon the rendition of a divorce judgment, but several exceptions existed to complicate the general rule.[101] First, if a claim for final spousal support was pending when the divorce judgment was rendered, the interim spousal award would terminate at the rendition of the judgment awarding or denying final spousal support or 180 days from the rendition of the divorce judgment, whichever came first, but it could be extended for good cause.[102] Second, if a claim for final spousal support was pending when the divorce judgment was rendered on grounds of abuse or protective order and the final spousal support award was equal to or less than the interim spousal support award, the interim spousal support award would terminate no less than 180 days from the rendition of the divorce judgment.[103] Determining whether final support was "pending" when prayed for in the petition or when a motion was pending before a court led to uncertainty and confusion.

In 2018, article 113 was amended to provide the current version of the law, which is straightforward and simplifies the pre-amendment rules. Under current law, interim spousal support terminates 180 days from the rendition of a judgment of divorce as a general rule,[104] and thus, in most instances, the duration of an interim spousal support award is not discretionary.[105] The current law provides a uniform set of rules for all interim support awards, and it ties the duration of the award solely to the judgment of

98. *Compare* La. Civ. Code Ann. art. 112(D) (providing for a maximum final spousal support award of one-third of the obligor's net income, absent abuse), *with* La. Civ. Code Ann. art. 113 (no maximum interim spousal support award provided).

99. Martello v. Martello, 2006-0594, p. 9 (La. App. 1 Cir. 3/23/07), 960 So. 2d 186, 194–95.

100. Wascom v. Wascom, 96-0125, p. 4 (La. 4/8/97), 691 So. 2d 678, 680.

101. La. Civ. Code Ann. art. 113 (1997).

102. La. Civ. Code Ann. art. 113 (1997).

103. La. Civ. Code Ann. art. 113 (1997).

104. La. Civ. Code Ann. art. 113.

105. La. Civ. Code Ann. art. 113 cmt. (c) (rev. 2018).

divorce as opposed to the demand for final spousal support.[106] Note that the amendment is prospective only because the change to the article is substantive.[107]

However, an interim spousal support award may be extended for good cause.[108] Good cause is determined on a case-by-case basis.[109] As explained by one court, good cause must constitute a significant or grave reason such that it would be inequitable to deny an extension of support.[110] Another court provided that an extension must be genuinely needed, for a legitimate purpose, and "not calculated to cause hardship or to obtain as much spousal support as possible for as long as possible."[111]

In *LaRocca v. LaRocca*, the court extended interim spousal support in favor of a 64-year-old wife who had been out of the workforce for 10 years during the marriage and who had only two years of junior college study in interior design, rejecting the payor's argument that an extension should only be granted to a disabled claimant or one who cannot find work due to forces preventing such.[112] In *Hogan v. Hogan*, the court extended interim spousal support because the payor engaged in financial gamesmanship and withheld support to an extent that the court labeled outrageous and extreme, leaving the claimant destitute in the process.[113] Similarly, in *Bernstein v. Bernstein*, the court found good cause to extend interim spousal support where the trial on the issue took place two years after the date of demand, mainly due to the payor's actions.[114] During that time, the payor failed to meet many obligations. He failed to pay child support, did not produce information necessary to determine spousal support (causing continuances), and did not pay attorney's fees, court costs, and expert fees incurred because of those continuances. All of this resulted in the claimant having to file motions for contempt, take advances on community property funds, and secure loans to support herself and the children. Had the court not granted the extension, the interim spousal support award would have terminated more than a year before trial.[115]

---

106. La. Civ. Code Ann art. 113 cmt. (c) (rev. 2018).
107. Hanna v. Hanna, 53,210, pp. 6–7 (La. App. 2 Cir. 11/20/19), 285 So. 3d 116, 120.
108. La. Civ. Code Ann. art. 113.
109. Piccione v. Piccione, 2001-1086, pp. 9–10 (La. App. 3 Cir. 5/22/02), 824 So. 2d 427, 433.
110. Piccione, 824 So. 2d at 433.
111. Roan v. Roan, 38,383, pp. 21–22 (La. App. 2 Cir. 4/14/04), 870 So. 2d 626, 639.
112. LaRocca v. LaRocca, 14-255, pp. 10–11 (La. App. 5 Cir. 10/29/14), 164 So. 3d 207, 213–14.
113. Hogan v. Hogan, 49,979, pp. 25–26 (La. App. 2 Cir. 9/30/15), 178 So. 3d 1013, 1027.
114. Bernstein v. Bernstein, 2019-1106, pp. 16–17 (La. App. 4 Cir. 2/10/21), 313 So. 3d 413, 425.
115. Bernstein, 313 So. 3d at 425.

§ 5:11 Claim for Spousal Support— Final Spousal Support

Final spousal support (formerly known as permanent periodic alimony)[116] is the other type of spousal support recognized by Louisiana law. Unlike spouses in an intact marriage, former spouses have no duty to support one another.[117] As such, some earlier opinions characterized final spousal support awards as a "pension"[118] or a "pure gratuity" awarded in the court's discretion.[119] Thus, a claim for final spousal support differs from one for interim spousal support.

The obligation to pay final spousal support does not begin until the termination of an interim spousal support award or upon the entry of the judgment of divorce when no interim support has been awarded.[120]

§ 5:12 Claim for Spousal Support— Final Spousal Support—Role of Fault

As has been the case from the inception of final spousal support claims, fault plays a very important role. Per the Louisiana Civil Code, one must be free from fault prior to the filing of the divorce action[121] to be awarded final spousal support.[122] Whether a claimant was at fault is a question of fact.[123] In assessing fault in the context of final spousal support, as a general rule, the claimant bears the burden of proving no fault.[124] Of course, proving a negative is not the easiest burden to satisfy. One court found that the claimant satisfied her burden by offering her own testimony that she was not at fault and the testimony of others who stated that she performed her fair share of the

116. The terminology change was made in the 1997 revisions to the articles via Act 1078. 1997 La Acts No. 1078, § 1, eff. Jan. 1, 1998.

117. Barber v. Barber, 2009-0780, p. 5 (La. App. 1 Cir. 5/7/10), 38 So. 3d 1046, 1050.

118. Player v. Player, 110 So. 332, 333 (La. 1926) ("As the marriage is forever dissolved, there is no obligation arising from it. The law accords, not alimony in such a case, but a pension, to the unfortunate spouse who has obtained the divorce. This pension becomes revocable in case it should become unnecessary, and in case the wife should contract a second marriage").

119. Fortier v. Gelpi, 197 So. 138, 140 (La. 1940).

120. La. Civ. Code Ann. arts. 111, 113(B).

121. This timing provision was inserted in the 1997 revision to the articles. *See* Jones v. Jones, 34,822, p. 2 (La. App. 2 Cir. 6/20/01), 793 So. 2d 243, 245. It is a recognition that for fault to bar final spousal support, it should be directly related to and a substantial cause of the dissolution of the marriage. *See* Brown v. Brown, 50,833, p. 7 (La. App. 2 Cir. 8/10/16), 200 So. 3d 887, 893 ("A spouse may be awarded final periodic support when he or she is in need of support and is free from fault prior to the filing of a petition for divorce, based on the needs of that party and the ability of the other party to pay.").

122. La. Civ. Code Ann. arts. 111–112(A).

123. Barnett v. Barnett, 15-766, p. 6 (La. App. 5 Cir. 5/26/16), 193 So. 3d 460, 466; Matthews v. Matthews, 15-499, p. 5 (La. App. 5 Cir. 12/23/15), 184 So. 3d 173, 176.

124. Hutson v. Hutson, 39,901, p. 6 (La. App. 2 Cir. 8/9/05), 908 So. 2d 1231, 1235.

household duties, the couple rarely argued, and they never saw her nag her husband.[125] In the event that a spouse agrees to pay final support, this constitutes a judicial admission that the payee spouse is free from fault,[126] and, in such a situation, the issue cannot be raised later.[127]

This general rule—that the claimant bears the burden of proving lack of fault—carries two noteworthy exceptions under which the law provides that a spouse is presumed to be entitled to final spousal support.[128] First, when a judgment of divorce is granted due to the fault of one spouse,[129] the other spouse is presumed to be entitled to final spousal support.[130] Second, when one spouse is guilty of domestic abuse of the other spouse or a child of either of them, the victim spouse is presumed to be entitled to final spousal support.[131] Like any presumption, these are rebuttable.[132] In both instances, the burden of proof shifts to the non-claimant to rebut the presumption, and that burden is met by proving that the claimant was at fault.[133]

The first issue that arises in assessing fault is its definition. Fault has a different interpretation in the context of final spousal support than it does in the context of divorce. To be at fault for divorce purposes, one must commit adultery,[134] be convicted of a felony carrying a sentence of death or life imprisonment,[135] perpetrate abuse,[136] or perpetrate or threaten abuse sufficient to give rise to a protective order or injunction.[137]

---

125. Hutson, 908 So. 2d at 1236.

126. *See, e.g.*, Vesper v. Vesper, 469 So. 2d 458, 460 (La. Ct. App. 3 Cir. 1985).

127. *See* Shows v. Shows, 345 So. 2d 975, 977 (La. Ct. App. 2 Cir. 1977); Mitchell v. Mitchell, 539 So. 2d 839, 842 (La. Ct. App. 3 Cir. 1989), *reversed on other grounds*, 541 So. 2d 831 (La. 1989).

128. La. Civ. Code Ann. art. 112(C).

129. The Louisiana Supreme Court developed this burden-shifting mechanism in the context of divorces granted on the basis of the non-claimant's adultery, *see* Lagars v. Lagars, 491 So. 2d 5 (La. 1986); but until 2018, it was only in the jurisprudence. The 2018 amendment to article 112 (Paragraph C) via Act 265 codified this mechanism and explicitly extended it to situations when a divorce is granted on any fault-based ground, not just adultery. 2018 La. Sess. Law Serv. Act 265 (H.B. 125) (West). It also specifically allows the court to make a finding of abuse, regardless of the grounds on which the divorce was granted, and it extends the presumption to the victim, as well.

130. La. Civ. Code Ann. art. 112(C).

131. La. Civ. Code Ann. art. 112(C).

132. *See* La. Civ. Code Ann. art. 112 cmt. (c) (rev. 1997).

133. La. Civ. Code Ann. art. 112(C). The non-claimant can also rebut the presumption by proving claimant's lack of need or their own inability to pay. La. Civ. Code Ann. art. 112 cmt (a) (rev 2018).

134. Of course, adultery includes sexual intercourse during the marriage with someone other than a spouse, but the concept is not that limited. Louisiana cases have extended it to other sexual contact, as well. *See, e.g.*, Menge v. Menge, 491 So. 2d 700, 701–02 (La. Ct. App. 5 Cir. 1985); Bonura v. Bonura, 505 So. 2d 143, 144 (La. Ct. App. 4 Cir. 1987). To prove adultery, one may offer (1) direct evidence or (2) circumstantial evidence that leads fairly and necessarily to the conclusion that adultery has been committed. Lyons v. Lyons, 33,237, p. 7 (La. App. 2 Cir. 10/10/00), 768 So. 2d 853, 858.

135. A guilty plea to the crime will suffice as a "conviction." Scheppf v. Scheppf, 430 So. 2d 370, 372 (La. Ct. App. 3 Cir. 1983). Additionally, one is still convicted even if the appeals process has not been exhausted. Nickels v. Nickels, 347 So. 2d 510, 511 (La. Ct. App. 2 Cir. 1977).

136. La. Civ. Code Ann. art. 103(4).

137. La. Civ. Code Ann. art. 103(5).

These grounds qualify as fault for purposes of final spousal support as well,[138] but they are not the exclusive grounds of fault in this context.

When it comes to fault for final spousal support, the list of conduct that qualifies is much broader. Fault in this context has been defined as "serious misconduct which is a cause of the marriage's dissolution."[139] It has also been expressed as "conduct or substantial acts of commission or omission by a spouse violative of his or her marital duties or responsibilities."[140] It has been equated with the fault grounds that previously existed for separation from bed and board under former law[141] and includes cruel treatment or outrages, abandonment, habitual intemperance or excess, public defamation, an attempt on the other's life, fugitive status, and intentional non-support.[142] Additionally, courts have decided that violations of the marital duties of fidelity, support, and assistance also constitute fault.[143] That said, one seeking final spousal support need not be perfect to be free from legal fault.[144]

Cruel treatment is commonly asserted as fault in litigation involving final spousal support. To succeed in proving this ground, one must show (1) cruelty occurred; and (2) it rendered marital life insupportable.[145] A continued pattern of mental harassment, nagging, and griping can qualify as fault.[146] However, friction or dissatisfaction in the marital relationship or incompatibility of the spouses,[147] complaints and criticism,[148] and mere bickering and fussing will not suffice,[149] even where one spouse says extremely harsh things. For example, in *Rusk v. Rusk*, while fighting about money, the wife told her husband that she "should blow his head off."[150] Although the couple owned guns, the husband failed to show that he believed his wife's words were any more than baseless comments made in the heat of an argument or that the wife had the capacity or ability to harm him.[151] By contrast, in *Cauthron v. Cauthron*, the court denied a

138. Gitschlag v. Gitschlag, 593 So. 2d 1331, 1335 (La. Ct. App. 1 Cir. 1991).

139. Anderson v. Anderson, 2002-1226, p. 3 (La. App. 3 Cir. 3/5/03), 839 So. 2d 1091, 1094.

140. Simon v. Davis, 96-876, pp. 6–7 (La. App. 5 Cir. 5/14/97), 696 So. 2d 68, 72; Guillory v. Guillory, 2008-1375 (La. App. 3 Cir. 4/1/09), 7 So. 3d 144, 144.

141. Allen v. Allen, 94-1090, p. 8 (La. 12/12/94), 648 So. 2d 359, 362.

142. Rusk v. Rusk, 2012-176, p. 7 (La. App. 3 Cir. 6/6/12), 102 So. 3d 193, 199.

143. *See* Guillory, 7 So. 3d at 147 (explaining that "fault" contemplates conduct or substantial acts of commission or omission by a spouse violative of his or her marital duties or responsibilities and that those spousal obligations include fidelity, support, and assistance); *see also* Stockton v. Stockton, 2023-0145 (La. App. 1 Cir. 10/18/23), 377 So. 3d 282 (failing to sleep under the covers with husband, be intimate with him, and go with him to the fishing camp did not constitute a breach of her duties because their lack of intimacy was not only her responsibility); Tucker v. Tucker, 23-23 (La. App. 3 Cir. 6/8/22), 344 So. 3d 808.

144. *See* Matthews, 184 So. 3d at 177.

145. Robert C. Lowe, Divorce § 8:175, *in* 1 La. Prac. Divorce § 8:175 (2021).

146. Adkins v. Adkins, 42,076, p. 4 (La. App. 2 Cir. 4/11/07), 954 So. 2d 920, 923.

147. Adkins, 954 So. 2d at 923.

148. *See* Allen, 648 So. 2d at 362; *see generally* Lyons, 768 So. 2d at 859.

149. King v. King, 48,881, p. 9 (La. App. 2 Cir. 2/26/14), 136 So. 3d 941, 947; Anderson, 839 So. 2d at 1093.

150. Rusk, 102 So. 3d at 196.

151. Rusk, 102 So. 3d at 199.

wife's claim for final spousal support due to her cruel treatment.[152] She exhibited a cavalier attitude toward her husband's health and refused to accompany him to Mexico for surgery. The court found this was the final straw leading to the dissolution of the marriage.[153] Other examples of conduct that amounts to cruel treatment include persistently refusing to engage in sexual intercourse without justification,[154] engaging in intimate relations with someone other than a spouse (even if not adulterous under the legal definition of that term),[155] and continuously or habitually failing to perform household chores over a long period of time.[156]

Abandonment and habitual intemperance have likewise been the subject of litigation to prevent final spousal support. In *King v. King*, the husband alleged that the claimant's abandonment[157] precluded her from an award of final spousal support.[158] The court disagreed, determining that while she did withdraw from the common dwelling,[159] she had lawful cause to do so, given the payor's lack of support and communication with her following her cancer diagnosis, as well as his steps to end the marriage and eliminate her access to a bank account and television and internet service while she was undergoing difficult medical treatments.[160] Further, the payor never requested that she return, and therefore, he could not prove that she constantly refused to return, which is another necessary element of an abandonment claim.[161]

In *Rodrigue v. Rodrigue*, the court considered whether a wife's drinking qualified as habitual intemperance rendering the marriage insupportable.[162] It explained that the inquiry is one of the extent and habitualness of consumption rather than amount consumed and that the other spouse's reaction must be considered.[163] Under the facts

152. Cauthron v. Cauthron, 2012-0913, p. 2 (La. App. 1 Cir. 2/15/13), 113 So. 3d 232, 233.

153. Cauthron, 113 So. 3d at 234–35.

154. Jergins v. Jergins, 451 So. 2d 1336, 1338 (La. Ct. App. 1 Cir. 1984), *but see* Tucker, 334 So. 3d at 814 (holding the absence of sexual relations was caused by mutual abstention when husband withdrew from wife and moved into a spare bedroom).

155. Slaughter v. Slaughter, 436 So. 2d 1352 (La. Ct. App. 3 Cir. 1983).

156. Carter v. Carter, 316 So. 2d 829 (La. Ct. App. 3 Cir. 1984); *but see* Lamb v. Lamb, 460 So. 2d 634 (La. Ct. App. 3 Cir. 1984) (where a wife's failure to perform chores was not fault given the spouses' financial standing allowing them to dine out and hire a maid).

157. King, 136 So. 3d at 941. In addition to the traditional notions of abandonment, constructive abandonment also constitutes fault. This is where a spouse, without lawful cause, prevents the other spouse from entering the matrimonial domicile. *See, e.g.*, Kriger v. Kriger, 397 So. 2d 21, 23 (La. Ct. App. 2 Cir. 1981); Guillory v. Guillory, 626 So. 2d 826, 830 (La. Ct. App. 2 Cir. 1993) (citing Quinn v. Quinn, 412 So. 2d 649 (La. Ct. App. 2 Cir. 1982)).

158. King, 136 So. 3d at 948.

159. If both parties agree to the withdrawal, there are no grounds for abandonment. Gitschlag v. Gitschlag, 593 So. 2d 1331, 1335 (La. Ct. App. 1 Cir. 1991).

160. King, 136 So. 3d at 948.

161. The one asserting abandonment has the burden to show the other's withdrawal; once successful, the one who withdrew has the burden to show lawful cause justifying the abandonment. Robert C. Lowe, Divorce § 8:175, *in* 1 La. Prac. Divorce § 8:177 (2021).

162. Rodrigue v. Rodrigue, 424 So. 2d 1185, 1187–88 (La. Ct. App. 1 Cir. 1982).

163. Rodrigue, 424 So. 2d at 1187–88.

of the case, the husband also drank, and the two of them consented to, participated in, and encouraged the other's drinking.[164]

The second issue that arises in assessing fault is its timing. To bar final spousal support, the claimant's fault must have occurred before the filing of a proceeding to terminate the marriage.[165] In other words, the conduct in question must be an independent, contributory, or proximate cause of the breakup of the marriage.[166] In *Matthews v. Matthews*, the court determined that while the claimant's daily marijuana use to increase her appetite (because of anorexia) could constitute habitual intemperance or excess (i.e., fault), the consumption must be to such an extent that it substantially interferes with the person's marital duties or inflicts great mental anguish upon the other.[167] In this instance, her husband knew of her habit prior to and during the marriage, and she fulfilled her marital duties.[168] Thus, the claimant's marijuana use was not a proximate cause of the dissolution of the marriage.[169] Courts have also held that when a spouse does not find out about the other spouse's fault until after the filing of the divorce petition, the conduct will not bar spousal support.[170]

Note, too, that if the parties reconcile after the act of fault, the fault is extinguished under the rationale that the spouse not at fault condoned it.[171] Of course, if the conduct continues post-reconciliation, the pre-reconciliation fault is revived to show a pattern of conduct constituting fault.[172]

The spouse alleged to be at fault can defend against a finding of fault in several ways. Health concerns have excused a spouse's behavior, and a spouse who is provoked may be justified in reasonably responding to the other spouse's fault. For example, in *Barnett v. Barnett*, the court noted that the reason for the claimant's failure to keep or clean the house was her health issues, and therefore, her conduct did not amount to legal fault.[173] In *Anderson v. Anderson*, the court explained that if alcoholism or dependency is an illness over which the alcoholic has no control, this may excuse what would otherwise be considered fault, assuming, of course, that the illness caused the behavior constituting fault.[174]

A frequently litigated issue is whether the conduct of an alleged at-fault spouse was simply a justifiable response to the other's initial acts. For example, a spouse who

---

164. Rodrigue, 424 So. 2d at 1187–88.

165. La. Civ. Code Ann. arts. 111–112(A).

166. Bowes v. Bowes, 2000-1062, p. 4 (La. App. 4 Cir. 8/15/01), 798 So. 2d 996, 999.

167. Matthews, 184 So. 3d at 174.

168. Matthews, 184 So. 3d at 178.

169. Matthews, 184 So. 3d at 179.

170. Henry v. Henry, 2008-692, p. 3 (La. App. 3 Cir. 12/10/08), 999 So. 2d 255, 257.

171. Hamsa v. Hamsa, 95-737, p. 4 (La. App. 5 Cir. 1/17/96), 668 So. 2d 1209, 1211; *see also* Noto v. Noto, 09-1100, p. 7 (La. App. 5 Cir. 5/11/10), 41 So. 3d 1175, 1180 ("The effect of reconciliation is to 'wipe the slate clean' and make the issue of fault of the parties prior to the reconciliation moot as to any cause of action subsequent to the reconciliation.").

172. Bloodworth v. Bloodworth, 306 So. 2d 812, 814 (La. Ct. App. 3 Cir. 1975).

173. Barnett, 193 So. 3d at 469.

174. Anderson v. Anderson, 379 So. 2d 795, 796 (La. Ct. App. 1 Cir. 1979).

suspects infidelity may become quarrelsome or hostile (even to the point of cruel treatment) or may become a habitual substance abuser, and courts have determined that this is a reasonable reaction, not fault.[175] In *Miller v. Miller*, despite telling her husband that she did not love or like him, the wife was not at fault, given her reasonable suspicion that he was having an affair.[176] In such situations, the suspicion of adultery causes the breakup, not the claimant's reaction.[177] In *Jergins v. Jergins*, the court found the wife justified in occasionally refusing sexual relations when it was because of her husband's drunkenness.[178] Similarly, "[i]n the domestic violence context in particular, the court should consider the potentially responsive nature of a victim's response."[179] In other words, abuse is a provocative act, and a spouse's response, which might otherwise constitute fault, may be deemed a justifiable response. In *Smith v. Smith*, a court awarded final spousal support to a wife who threw boiling water on her husband because her conduct was a reasonable or justifiable response to her husband's provocative act.[180]

§ 5:13 Claim for Spousal Support— Final Spousal Support—Considerations for Final Spousal Support

In addition to freedom from fault, a claimant must be in need of support to obtain final spousal support.[181] In determining need for support, the court will evaluate the needs of the claimant and the payor's ability to pay.[182]

The claimant must prove his or her needs, which include the basic necessities of life, like food, shelter, clothing, transportation, medical and drug expenses, utilities, household maintenance, and income tax liability generated by alimony payments.[183] However, courts differ on whether the "in need of support" language in articles 111 and 112 equate to "necessitous circumstances."[184] In some instances, television and internet

175. *See, e.g.*, Diggs v. Diggs, 2008-1271, p. 4 (La. App. 3 Cir. 4/1/09), 6 So. 3d 1030, 1033.
176. Miller v. Miller, 2013-1043, pp. 8–9 (La. App. 3 Cir. 4/2/14), 161 So. 3d 690, 696.
177. Lyons, 768 So. 2d at 859.
178. Jergins, 451 So. 2d at 1338.
179. La Civ. Code Ann. art. 112 cmt. (c) (rev. 2018).
180. Smith v. Smith, 08-575 (La. App. 5 Cir. 1/12/10), 31 So. 3d 453, 454.
181. La Civ. Code Ann. art. 111.
182. La Civ. Code Ann. art. 112(A).
183. Stowe v. Stowe, 49,596, pp. 1–3 (La. App. 2 Cir. 3/4/15), 162 So. 3d 638, 640–41. Prior to January 1, 2019, the payor spouse was allowed a deduction for alimony paid, and the alimony constituted taxable income for the payee spouse. I.R.C. §§ 61(a)(8), 71(a), 215(a) (repealed 2017). That rule was changed pursuant to the Tax Cuts and Jobs Act such that alimony is no longer deductible by the payor nor is it taxable to the payee. 26 U.S.C.A. § 11051. This new rule applies to orders issued or modified after January 1, 2019. 26 U.S.C.A. § 11051(c) 131 Stat. 2090.
184. *Compare* Grissom v. Grissom, 54,775 p. 5 (La. App. 2 Cir. 11/16/22), 351 So. 3d 843, 847 ("The spouse claiming final periodic support is not required to prove necessitous circumstances, only proof of need."), *with* Tucker v. Tucker, 22–23, p. 13 (La. App. 3 Cir. 6/8/22), 344 So. 3d 808, 818 ("'[N]ecessitous circumstance' is synonymous with insufficient means for 'maintenance.' Thus, final periodic

services and lawn maintenance may constitute necessities.[185] In *Anderson v. Anderson*, the hair coloring and dining out of the claimant (who had a history of depression and anxiety) were considered as needs.[186] However, in *Ennis v. Ennis*, the court decided that costs for birthday and Christmas gifts, church donations, vacations, entertainment, and such other expenses were unnecessary for support.[187]

Assuming that the claimant is entitled to final spousal support, the court must determine the amount and duration of the award, considering all relevant factors, including those specifically listed in Louisiana Civil Code Article 112(B). Those factors are:

(1) The income and means of the parties, including the liquidity of such means.

(2) The financial obligations of the parties, including any interim allowance or final child support obligation.

(3) The earning capacity of the parties.

(4) The effect of custody of children upon a party's earning capacity.

(5) The time necessary for the claimant to acquire appropriate education, training, or employment.

(6) The health and age of the parties.

(7) The duration of the marriage.

(8) The tax consequences to either or both parties.

(9) The existence, effect, and duration of any act of domestic abuse committed by the other spouse upon the claimant or a child of one of the spouses, regardless of whether the other spouse was prosecuted for the act of domestic violence.[188]

This list is merely illustrative, and courts are free to consider factors not listed therein.[189]

---

support is awarded to a former spouse in need and is limited to an amount sufficient for maintenance as opposed to continuing an accustomed style of living.").

185. *See* King v. King, 48,881, p. 20 (La. App. 2 Cir. 2/26/14), 136 So. 3d 941, 947, 951 (wherein because the claimant was seriously ill and unable to leave the house often, the court considered television and internet services as a necessary expense).

186. Anderson v. Anderson, 48,027, pp. 10–11 (La. App. 2 Cir. 5/15/13), 117 So. 3d 208, 215.

187. Ennis v. Ennis, 2016-0423, p. 9 (La. App. 1 Cir. 5/8/17), 2017 WL 1900328, at *4; *see also* Tucker, 344 So. 3d 808 (the court refused to consider expenses for lawn care, computer, cell phone, laundry, birthdays, holiday expenses, entertainment, meals away from home, movies, pet expenses, and auto repair and maintenance).

188. La. Civ. Code Ann. art. 112(B). The court must consider "any criminal conviction of the obligor spouse for an offense committed against the claimant spouse during the course of the marriage." La. Stat. Ann. § 9:327(A). Absent a criminal conviction, the court may, in order to assist it in determining the existence and nature of the alleged abuse, order an evaluation of both parties. La. Stat. Ann. § 9:327(B). This evaluation is conducted by an independent, court-appointed mental health professional who is an expert in the field of domestic abuse and who has no familial, financial, or prior medical relationship with either party or their attorneys of record; the mental health professional shall provide a written report of his or her findings to both the court and the parties. *Id.*

189. Rhymes v. Rhymes, 2013-0823, pp. 7–8 (La. 10/15/13), 125 So. 3d 377, 381–82 (given the history of the children's education, the court could consider one parent's role as the homeschooler of

Many of the factors considered for final spousal support awards mirror those employed in the analysis of interim spousal support awards. For example, both require a court to assess the other party's ability to pay and any child support awards.[190] Therefore, analysis of these factors sometimes applies in the context of both interim and final spousal support determinations.[191]

With that said, the rules on interim spousal support and final spousal support differ in some ways. For example, the parties' standard of living during the marriage is clearly a consideration for interim spousal support; while Louisiana Civil Code Article 112 does not address the issue, some courts have decided it is not an appropriate factor to consider for final spousal support.[192] Additionally, while the earning capacity of the claimant is an open question for interim spousal support (as discussed above), Louisiana Civil Code Article 112(B)(3) is clear that the claimant's earning capacity is considered for final spousal support purposes.[193] Note, though, that the parties' earning capacity is assessed in light of the effect that custody of children has upon it.[194] Additionally, many courts take into consideration one spouse's subordination of their own career to attend to the other spouse's, especially if the marriage is one of significant duration.[195]

In addition to the differences in the two sets of rules, the assessment of final spousal support includes factors not considered in the context of interim spousal support. For example, per Louisiana Civil Code Article 112(B)(5), courts must consider the time necessary for the claimant to acquire appropriate education, training, or employment.[196] Thus, while many final spousal support awards are rehabilitative (as opposed to permanent), the time necessary to obtain education or training must be reasonable.[197] One party who has the physical and mental ability to secure employment should not be allowed to avoid employment and remain economically dependent on the other.[198] Also, Louisiana Civil Code Article 112(B)(6)–(8) requires a court to consider the health and age of the parties, the duration the marriage, and the tax consequences

---

the children).

190. La. Civ. Code Ann. art. 112(A), (B)(2); La. Civ. Code Ann. art. 113(A).

191. La. Civ. Code Ann. art. 112(A), (B)(2); La. Civ. Code Ann. art. 113(A).

192. *E.g.*, West v. West, 51,692 (La. App. 2 Cir. 11/15/17), 245 So. 3d 269, 275 (citing Richards v. Richards, 47,492 (La. App. 2 Cir. 9/20/12), 105 So. 3d 77). Prior to the 2006 revision to Louisiana Civil Code Article 112, jurisprudence was in conflict on this question. *See, e.g.*, Gremillion v. Gremillion, 39,588 (La. App. 2 Cir. 4/6/05), 900 So. 2d 262 (court considered the standard of living); Jones v. Jones, 35,502, 35,503 (La. App. 2 Cir 12/5/01), 804 So. 2d 161 (court did not consider the standard of living).

193. La. Civ. Code Ann. art. 112(B)(3).

194. La. Civ. Code Ann. art. 112(B)(4).

195. *See, e.g.*, Politz v. Politz, 2005-2568 (La App. 1 Cir. 8/1/07), 2007 WL 2193547, at *5; Brett v. Brett, 2000-0436, p. 6 (La. App. 1 Cir. 5/30/01), 794 So. 2d 912, 917.

196. La. Civ. Code Ann. art. 112(B)(5).

197. Johnson v. Johnson, 442 So. 2d 901, 903 (La. Ct. App. 3 Cir. 1983).

198. *See* Ballanco v. Ballanco, 538 So. 2d 1100, 1102–03 (La. Ct. App. 5 Cir. 1989); Fountain v. Fountain, 93-2176, pp. 7–8 (La. App. 1 Cir. 10/7/94), 644 So. 2d 733, 739.

to either or both parties, none of which are considered in connection with interim spousal support.[199]

In recent years, domestic abuse has come to the forefront of family law. Among other contexts, it has been considered in connection with final spousal support. Until 2014, domestic abuse was not on the list of fault-based grounds for divorce; it was also not considered in connection with final spousal support determinations.[200] In 2014, the Louisiana Legislature amended Louisiana Civil Code Article 112 to mandate final spousal support to a spouse who had not been at fault prior to the filing of a petition for divorce and who was the victim of domestic abuse committed during the marriage in accordance with the factors set forth in the article.[201] Among the other factors, courts were to consider "[t]he existence, effect, and duration of any act of domestic abuse committed by the other spouse upon the claimant, regardless of whether the other spouse was prosecuted for the act of domestic violence."[202] However, the Louisiana Legislature amended article 112 again in 2018. Under the current version, abuse is retained in the list of factors for consideration, but the provision mandating a final spousal support award for the victim has been deleted.[203] Rather, a spouse who obtains a fault divorce based on the abuse of the other spouse or who is able to prove that a child or the spouse was the victim of domestic abuse during the marriage committed by the other spouse will enjoy a presumption that the spouse is entitled to final spousal support.

As a general rule, the final spousal support award cannot exceed one-third of the payor's net income.[204] No such cap exists when (1) the divorce was rendered on ground of abuse or protective order[205] or (2) the court determines that a party or child of one of the spouses was the victim of domestic abuse committed by the other party

199. La. Civ. Code Ann. art. 112(B)(6)–(8). Note that as of 2019, spousal support is no longer tax-deductible to the obligor or included as income to obligee, unless it was included in a divorce decree that was finalized before 2019. *See* Tax Cuts and Jobs Act, P.L. 115-97.

200. La. Civ. Code Ann. art. 103 (2014); La. Civ. Code Ann. art. 112 (2006).

201. La. Civ. Code Ann. art. 112(B) (2014).

202. La. Civ. Code Ann. art. 112(C)(9) (2014).

203. Remember, though, that article 112(C) now gives the victim of domestic abuse during the marriage a presumption of entitlement to final spousal support as discussed in the section on fault above. Also, remember that this presumption extends to all claimants whose divorces were granted on fault-based grounds or when the court has made a finding of domestic abuse.

204. La Civ. Code. Ann. art. 112(C). Louisiana law offers no guidance on what expenses are appropriate to deduct from gross income to calculate net income. *See* Molony v. Harris, 2009-1529, p. 12 (La. App. 4 Cir. 10/14/10), 51 So. 3d 752, 761. (holding that it is within the trial court's discretion, based on the evidence and testimony before it, to make a determination regarding the spouses' income). Note that prior to 1997, the limitation on final spousal support was calculated using the payor's gross income. *See* La. Civ. Code Ann. art. 112 cmt. (f) (rev. 1997) (citing Slayter v. Slayter, 576 So. 2d 1121 (La. Ct. App. 3 Cir. 1991); Robinson v. Robinson, 412 So. 2d 633 (La. Ct. App. 2 Cir. 1982)).

205. *See* La. Civ. Code Ann. art. 103(4)–(5).

during the marriage.[206] In such instances, the final spousal support may be awarded as a lump sum.[207]

While the term "final spousal support" seems to connote an award that lasts forever, this is not the case. Spousal support awards are never final (even if the award is silent as to its duration) because parties may always move for modification, termination, or extinguishment (as discussed in Sections 5:15–5:18 below).[208]

§ 5:14 Claim for Spousal Support— Time Limitations on Spousal Support Claims

The rules regarding the time limitations to assert a spousal support claim apply to both interim and final spousal support. Ultimately, per Louisiana Civil Code Article 117, a claimant who seeks spousal support after divorce has a peremptive period of three years to do so.[209] A peremptive period must be distinguished from a liberative prescriptive period. Prescription is a mode of barring actions as a result of inaction for a period of time;[210] peremption is a period of time fixed by law for the existence of a right that if not timely exercised, extinguishes the right altogether.[211] While prescriptive periods may be suspended,[212] interrupted,[213] or renounced,[214] the same is not true of peremptive periods.[215] As Louisiana jurisprudence consistently provides, nothing interferes with the running of peremption.[216]

The three-year peremptive period on spousal support claims begins to run from the latest of the following three events: (i) the day the judgment of divorce is signed; (ii) the day a judgment terminating a previous judgment of spousal support is signed (as long as the previous judgment was signed in an action commenced either before the signing of the judgment of divorce or within three years thereafter); or (iii) the day the last spousal support payment is made (if the spousal support obligation is initially performed by voluntary payment within the periods described in (i) or (ii) and no more than three years has elapsed between payments).[217]

206. La. Civ. Code Ann. art. 112(D).

207. La. Civ. Code Ann. art. 112(D).

208. *See, e.g.*, Faucheux v. Faucheux, 11-939, p. 10 (La. App. 5 Cir. 3/27/12), 91 So. 3d 1119, 1126; Harmon v. Harmon, 2012-580, p. 6 (La. App. 3 Cir. 11/7/12), 101 So. 3d 1122, 1126.

209. La. Civ. Code Ann. art. 117.

210. La. Civ. Code Ann. art. 3447.

211. La. Civ. Code Ann. art. 3458.

212. La. Civ. Code Ann. arts. 3467–3473.

213. La. Civ. Code Ann. arts. 3462–3466.

214. La. Civ. Code Ann. arts. 3449–3451.

215. La. Civ. Code Ann. art. 3461.

216. Naghi v. Brener, 2008-2527, p. 1 (La. 6/26/09), 17 So. 3d 919, 920.

217. La. Civ. Code Ann. art. 117.

As explained in the comments to article 117, the general rule is that the three-year peremptive period commences at the signing of the judgment of divorce.[218] However, in the event that an award of spousal support was made before the judgment of divorce or during the peremptive period, the period begins to run anew from the day a judgment terminating that prior judgment of support is signed.[219] That same rule applies if the obligor recognized the obligation by making voluntary payments to the other party, in which case, the period begins to run from the date of the last payment.[220] In *Lacombe v. Lacombe*, the wife's spousal support claim made 10 months after the husband's last voluntary support payment was timely, despite the fact that it was made eight years after the initial divorce petition.[221]

While the three-year peremptive period is an important time limitation, one should note other time limitations that may affect spousal support claims. For example, Louisiana Code of Civil Procedure Article 561 provides that an action is abandoned when the parties fail to take any step in its prosecution or defense in the trial court for a period of three years.[222] Additionally, note that the time period to assert a claim for spousal support differs from the time period to collect *past due* spousal support (also known as "arrearages"). One seeking to collect past due spousal support has a *prescriptive* period of five years.[223]

§ 5:15 Claim for Spousal Support— Modification of Spousal Support

Both interim and final spousal support may be modified as a general rule,[224] and Louisiana Civil Code Article 114 governs both.[225] A judgment modifying a final spousal support judgment is retroactive to the date of judicial demand except for good cause shown,[226] in which case the court may fix the date on which the award commences but in no case may the award commence before the date of judicial demand.[227]

218. La. Civ. Code Ann. art. 117 cmt. (a).

219. La. Civ. Code Ann. art. 117 cmt. (a).

220. *See, e.g.*, Reggio v. Reggio, 14-493 (La. App. 5 Cir. 12/16/14), 166 So. 3d 290; Lacombe v. Lacombe, 11-1178 (La. App. 3 Cir. 2/1/12), 85 So. 3d 721. A "voluntary payment" is one that is not court-ordered. Lacombe, 85 So. 3d at 726. Thus, payments made under an interim order requiring the payor to make the payments pending the trial on the payee's rule for final spousal support did not qualify. *See id.* at 726; Stephens v. Stephens, 49,957, p. 6 (La. App. 2 Cir. 4/9/14), 137 So. 3d 1242, 1246.

221. Lacombe, 85 So. 3d at 726.

222. La. Code Civ. Proc. Ann. art. 561(A).

223. La. Civ. Code Ann. art. 3497.1 (emphasis added).

224. A spousal support award may not be modified if the consent judgment contains a non-modification provision. Bland v. Bland, 97-0329 (La. App. 1 Cir. 12/29/97), 705 So. 2d 1158, 1161.

225. La. Civ. Code Ann. art. 114; *see also* La. Civ. Code Ann. art. 112 cmt. (g) (rev. 1997); La. Civ. Code Ann. art. 113 cmt. (a) (rev. 1997).

226. La. Stat. Ann. § 9:321(C).

227. La. Stat. Ann. § 9:321(E).

The burden of proof rests with the one seeking the modification to show a material change of circumstances of either party—either that the obligor's needs have materially changed or that the obligee's ability to pay has materially changed.[228] Louisiana Civil Code Article 114 specifically states that the subsequent remarriage of the *obligor* spouse (the spouse making payments) shall not constitute a change of circumstance.[229] This is not the case when the *obligee* spouse (the one receiving payments) subsequently remarries, in which case the spousal support obligation is extinguished (as discussed in Section 5:18 below).[230]

Note, though, that a change in circumstances does not automatically result in a modification of spousal support.[231] Instead, such a finding simply shifts the burden to the party opposing the modification.[232] When assessing a request for modification of interim spousal support, the court considers the factors in article 112 (in the case of final spousal support) or article 113 (in the case of interim spousal support).[233]

In *Richards v. Richards*, the trial court awarded spousal support to the wife (along with a child support award) and directed that the spousal support award would terminate if the wife received Social Security disability (SSI) benefits.[234] It also noted that either party could seek modification.[235] Ten years later, the wife began receiving SSI benefits, ending the husband's spousal support obligation. However, about a year later, the youngest child reached majority and graduated from high school, terminating the husband's child support obligation. Thereafter, the wife moved to modify the previous spousal support judgment by having the award reinstated due to the loss of child support as well as her inability to work due to her disability. The court granted the modification based on the wife's acute and devastating financial need and her seriously declining health, finding the loss of child support to be financially catastrophic for her.[236] The court was careful to explain that while the loss of child support alone is not justification for reinstituting final periodic spousal support, it can be considered as a factor in determining the need for final spousal support under appropriate facts, such as those in the case before it.[237]

---

228. La. Civ. Code Ann. art. 114; *see* Williams v. Poore, 2010-1087, p. 2 (La. App. 4 Cir. 1/12/11), 55 So. 3d 953, 955.
229. La. Civ. Code Ann. art. 114 (emphasis added).
230. La. Civ. Code Ann. art. 115.
231. Mizell v. Mizell, 40,601, p. 3 (La. App. 2 Cir. 1/25/06), 920 So. 2d 927, 929.
232. Mizell, 920 So. 2d at 929.
233. La. Civ. Code Ann. art. 114 cmt. (b).
234. Richards v. Richards, 49,260, p. 1 (La. App. 2 Cir. 8/13/14), 147 So. 3d 800, 802.
235. Richards, 147 So. 3d at 805.
236. Richards, 147 So. 3d at 806–07.
237. Richards, 147 So. 3d at 807.

§ 5:16 Claim for Spousal Support—Termination and Extinguishment of Spousal Support

Spousal support awards—interim or final—may be terminated or extinguished.[238] In either scenario, the spousal support award ends. However, a terminated award may be sought again within the three-year peremptive period, but an extinguished spousal support award is lost forever.[239]

§ 5:17 Claim for Spousal Support—Termination and Extinguishment of Spousal Support—Termination of Spousal Support

Termination of a spousal support award is appropriate only if it has become unnecessary.[240] This must be determined by a court, considering the factors in article 112 (in the case of final spousal support) or article 113 (in the case of interim spousal support).[241] The person seeking termination bears the burden of proof.[242] A judgment terminating a spousal support judgment is retroactive to the date of judicial demand except for good cause shown.[243]

In *Williams v. Williams*, the court terminated the husband's spousal support obligation as unnecessary.[244] The wife had settled a personal injury claim, which netted her the sum of $323,724.27, but in the next two years, she had expended all but $40,000 of the proceeds in paying the debts of others, buying gifts, and donating money to charity. The court found that her spirit of charity was admirable, but it also indicated she had sufficient income and means for her support and no longer needed her ex-husband to support her.[245] In *Mitchell v. Mitchell*, the court denied the husband's motion to terminate his spousal support obligation because although he had voluntarily retired, his ex-wife's needs actually increased due to her involuntary reduction in income.[246] Additionally, the husband had disposed of tens of thousands of dollars to buy a truck for himself and gifts for his adult daughter and his second wife (whose income contributed to payment of their expenses).[247] While the husband averred that termination was appropriate, given the marriage to his ex-wife was short and they had no children, the court rejected

238. La. Civ. Code Ann. arts. 114–115.
239. Robert C. Lowe, Divorce § 8:175, *in* 1 La. Prac. Divorce § 8:188 (2021).
240. La. Civ. Code Ann. art. 114.
241. La. Civ. Code Ann. art. 114 cmt. (b).
242. Mizell v. Mizell, 40,601, p. 3 (La. App. 2 Cir. 1/25/06), 920 So. 2d 927, 929.
243. La. Stat. Ann. § 9:321(C)(final support); La. Rev. Stat. Ann. § 9:321(B)(2) (interim support).
244. Williams v. Williams, 2012-0281, p. 1 (La. App. 1 Cir. 11/14/12), 2012 WL 5506669.
245. Williams, 2012 WL 550666, at *6.
246. Mitchell v. Mitchell, 626 So. 2d 571, 572 73 (La. Ct. App. 3 Cir. 1993).
247. Mitchell, 626 So. 2d at 572.

that argument.[248] In *Gray v. Gray*, a husband moved to terminate his spousal support obligation because, among other issues, the wife was receiving financial support from another.[249] The court noted that well-settled jurisprudence provides that "one party's legal obligation to pay alimony is not obviated by the gratuity of another."[250]

§ 5:18 Claim for Spousal Support—Termination and Extinguishment of Spousal Support—Extinguishment of Spousal Support

A spousal support award may also be extinguished on the recipient's remarriage, the death of either party, or a judicial determination that the recipient has cohabited with another person in the manner of married persons.[251] Where the recipient remarries or where either party dies, the obligation to pay spousal support is extinguished automatically, without the need for judicial declaration.[252] Note, too, that even a remarriage of the recipient that is null will terminate the spousal support obligation of the previous spouse.[253]

In *Hamsa v. Hamsa*, the parties had a consent judgment specifying a term for payment of spousal support, and during the term, the wife remarried.[254] The husband filed pleadings to extinguish his support obligation, but the court granted the wife's exception of res judicata, because that the term in the contract of compromise governed, rather than article 115.[255] With that said, this case has been limited to its particular facts.[256] In *Rosenfeld v. Rosenfeld*, the court noted that consent judgments are generally subject to modification and termination.[257] It also noted that the only reason the *Hamsa* court created an exception was that the consent judgment was a lump-sum support

248. Mitchell, 626 So. 2d at 573.

249. Gray v. Gray, 451 So. 2d 579, 586–87 (La. Ct. App. 2 Cir. 1984).

250. *See* Gray, 451 So. 2d at 587; *see also* Shelton v. Shelton, 395 So. 2d 899, 900 (La. Ct. App. 2 Cir. 1981); Herman v. Zatzkis, 632 So. 2d 307, 315 (La. Ct. App. 4 Cir. 1993); *but see* Higginbotham v. White-Higginbotham, 97-1191, p. 6 (La. App. 5 Cir. 5/27/98), 713 So. 2d 832, 835 (finding that the trial judge did not have authority to order husband to pay the mortgage, utilities, insurance, and reasonable expenses related to the family home in which the wife and children continued to live after divorce, absent hearing on fault and alimony after divorce was granted; purpose of payments was to provide financial assistance to the wife, rather than to preserve community asset).

251. La. Civ. Code Ann. art. 115.

252. La. Civ. Code Ann. art. 115.

253. *See, e.g.*, Keeney v. Keeney, 30 So. 2d 549 (La. 1947); La. Civ. Code Ann. art. 115 cmts. (c)–(d). That said, a spouse to a subsequent null marriage may seek spousal support as an incident of that marriage in certain circumstances. *See* La. Civ. Code Ann. art. 96; La. Civ. Code Ann. art. 115 cmt. (d); La. Civ. Code Ann. art. 97.

254. Hamsa v. Hamsa, 05-219, p. 2 (La. App. 5 Cir. 12/27/05), 919 So. 2d 776, 777.

255. Hamsa, 919 So. 2d at 779.

256. Rosenfeld v. Rosenfeld, 11-686, pp. 5–6 (La. App. 5 Cir. 3/13/12), 90 So. 3d 1077, 1080.

257. Rosenfeld, 90 So. 3d at 1080.

judgment that included a significant (13 year) past obligation, and the court could not ascertain what amount of the lump-sum payment was owed for past due obligations and what amount was designated for future support obligations.[258] Thus, in most scenarios, even where a term for the duration of spousal support payments is included in a consent judgment, the recipient's remarriage will extinguish the spousal support obligation automatically unless the judgment provides otherwise.

While extinguishment is automatic in the situations above, a judicial declaration must be obtained when the recipient has cohabited with another person of either sex in the manner of married persons.[259] In *King v. King*, although the wife had been cohabitating with her boyfriend since she and her husband physically separated, she was allowed interim spousal support until the trial court made that determination months later.[260] Thus, the simple fact of the wife's cohabitation with her boyfriend was not sufficient to deny spousal support.

To "cohabitate in the manner of married persons" is defined as living together in a sexual relationship of some permanence; sexual intercourse alone will not suffice.[261] The party seeking extinguishment on this ground bears the burden of proof, and a judgment extinguishing spousal support on these grounds is retroactive to the date of judicial demand.[262] Conception of a child alone will not suffice for a finding of cohabitation.[263] In *Almon v. Almon*, the recipient lived with a man for a year, during which time he contributed to the payment of household expenses, helped with her daughter, and performed repairs.[264] The two engaged in sexual intercourse, but they did not share a bedroom, date, attend events together as a couple, or discuss marriage.[265] The court refused to extinguish the support obligation because the recipient and the live-in man engaged in only random acts of sexual intercourse.[266] In *Ronquille v. Ronquille*, the court denied the husband's motion to terminate permanent spousal support because, although the wife had a sexual relationship with another man who spent at least eight consecutive nights at her home and exercised visitation with his child there, the evidence did not necessarily establish the parties' intent to cohabitate together as married persons.[267] Testimony showed that he did not move his belongings into her home and maintained a separate residence; he also did not contribute financially to her household.[268] By contrast, in *Olsen v. Olsen*, the court granted the husband's motion to extin-

---

258. Rosenfeld, 90 So. 3d at 1080.

259. La. Civ. Code Ann. art. 115 cmt. (e); Almon v. Almon, 05-1848, p. 5 (La. App. 1 Cir. 9/15/06), 943 So. 2d 1113, 1116–17. Under older versions of the law, spousal support terminated when the payor lived in open concubinage with another. Petty v. Petty, 560 So. 2d 629 (La. Ct. App. 4 Cir. 1990).

260. King v. King, 51,942, pp. 5–7 (La. App. 2 Cir. 4/11/18), 247 So. 3d 973, 978.

261. La. Civ. Code Ann. art. 115 cmt. (e).

262. La. Stat. Ann. § 9:321(F).

263. Polk v. Polk, 626 So. 2d 1233, 1237 (La. Ct. App. 4 Cir. 1993).

264. Almon, 943 So. 2d at 1116–18.

265. Almon, 943 So. 2d at 1117–18.

266. Almon, 943 So. 2d at 1118.

267. Ronquille v. Ronquille, 17-207, pp. 4–5 (La. App. 5 Cir. 11/15/17), 233 So. 3d 189, 192–93.

268. Ronquille, 233 So. 3d at 192.

guish spousal support because, although the recipient and the man living with her had separate bedrooms, they had or attempted sexual intercourse on occasion, ate meals together, and discussed marriage.[269] She had also helped him pay his debts and visited him while he was in the hospital.[270] The court determined that this arrangement went beyond friends living together with benefits.[271]

§ 5:19 Claim for Spousal Support— Parties' Freedom of Contract

Louisiana law grants spouses the freedom to enter into a matrimonial agreement before or during marriage as to all matters that are not prohibited by public policy.[272] These contracts—like all contracts in Louisiana—have the effect of law for the parties.[273] With that said, if the agreement violates public policy, it is absolutely null,[274] and therefore, as a general rule, it is deemed never to have existed.[275] Persons are not allowed by juridical acts to derogate from laws enacted for the public interest.[276]

§ 5:20 Claim for Spousal Support— Parties' Freedom of Contract—Waiver of Spousal Support by Contract

One common topic included within a matrimonial agreement is spousal support. Many times, parties will, by contract, waive their rights to spousal support. It is important to note that, for this topic, the law differentiates between final and interim spousal support. Spouses may not waive interim spousal support, which is a matter of public policy,[277] but they may waive final spousal support, which is not.[278]

The public order nature of interim spousal support was explained in *Holliday v. Holliday*, wherein the court noted that although marriage is a contract, it is more than that.[279] Marriage creates a legal relationship which carries with it a duty of support; this,

269. Olsen v. Olsen, 12-737, pp. 7–8 (La. App. 5 Cir. 3/13/13), 113 So. 3d 274, 279.
270. Olsen, 113 So. 3d at 279.
271. Olsen, 113 So. 3d at 280.
272. La. Civ. Code Ann. art. 2329.
273. La. Civ. Code Ann. art. 1983.
274. La. Civ. Code Ann. art. 2030.
275. La. Civ. Code Ann. art. 2033.
276. La. Civ. Code Ann. art. 7.
277. La. Civ. Code Ann. art. 116 cmt.
278. La. Civ. Code Ann. art. 116.
279. Holliday v. Holliday, 358 So. 2d 618, 619 (La. 1978).

in turn, is the basis for the obligation to pay interim spousal support.[280] These duties are of public order, and as such, may not be waived by the parties.[281]

By contrast, final spousal support is not a matter of public order. Spouses are not bound to support one another permanently after the marriage terminates.[282] As explained in *McAlpine v. McAlpine*, final spousal support is not a duty by a spouse to a spouse; after all, the marriage has terminated such that they are no longer spouses.[283] As such, final spousal support protects the private recipient.[284] Accordingly, parties are allowed to modify the rules of the Louisiana Civil Code.[285] They may do so before or during the marriage and also after divorce as long as the waiver is clear and unequivocal, and they follow the requisite form requirements.[286] Matrimonial agreements may be nullified on the same grounds as any contract.[287]

In most instances, the waiver of interim spousal support and the waiver of final spousal support are included in the same contract and, in many instances, in the same provision of that document.[288] When litigated, courts will sever them, thereby invalidating the waiver of interim spousal support and enforcing the waiver of final spousal support.[289]

§ 5:21 Claim for Spousal Support—Parties' Freedom of Contract—Other Topics of Contractual Agreement

Parties may make other agreements regarding spousal support. For example, in *Ellefson v. Ellefson*, the parties agreed to a specific amount in spousal support.[290] Although that amount could have exceeded the statutory limit, the court upheld the agreement as not in violation of public policy.[291] In *Aldredge v. Aldredge*, the parties agreed that spousal support could be modified without a change of circumstances,

280. Holliday, 358 So. 2d at 620.

281. Favrot v. Barnes, 332 So. 2d 873, 875 (La. Ct. App. 4 Cir. 1976).

282. Barber v. Barber, 2009-0780, p. 5 (La. App. 1 Cir. 5/7/10), 38 So. 3d 1046, 1050 (citing McAlpine v. McAlpine, 94-1594, p. 9 (La. 9/5/96), 679 So. 2d 85, 90).

283. McAlpine, 679 So. 2d at 87 (quoting 1 Planiol, Civil Law Treatise, Vol. I, No. 1259 (La. State Law Institute Translation 1959)).

284. McAlpine, 679 So. 2d at 87.

285. La. Civ. Code Ann. art. 116; La. Civ. Code Ann. art. 116 cmt.

286. La. Civ. Code Ann. art. 116. These agreements must be in authentic act or act under private signature duly acknowledged by the obligee. *Id.*; La. Civ. Code Ann. art. 2331. *See also* Vincent v. Vincent, 2005-1175, p. 2 (La. App. 4 Cir. 1/10/07), 949 So. 2d 535, 542–43 (Cannizzaro, J., concurring in part and dissenting in part).

287. McAlpine, 679 So. 2d at 93.

288. *See, e.g.*, Barber, 38 So. 3d at 1050.

289. Barber, 38 So. 3d at 1050 (citing La. Civ. Code Ann. art. 2034).

290. Ellefson v. Ellefson, 616 So. 2d 221, 222 (La. Ct. App. 5 Cir. 1993).

291. Ellefson, 616 So. 2d at 222.

and the court upheld the contract.[292] In *Boudreaux v. Boudreaux*, the parties agreed that the recipient would receive final spousal support unconditionally, even if at fault, but the court struck this agreement as in violation of public policy.[293] Note that some courts have upheld such agreements when the parties enter them in anticipation of or after the dissolution of the marriage, as opposed to at the inception of the marriage in contemplation of divorce.[294]

Parties can also contractually agree when spousal support will terminate. While the Civil Code provides, as a default rule, that the obligation to pay spousal support extinguishes on the remarriage of the recipient, the death of either party, or a judicial determination that the recipient has cohabitated with another person in the manner of married persons,[295] parties may provide otherwise. In *Romero v. Romero*, the parties agreed that final spousal support would terminate on the earlier of the recipient's death or remarriage.[296] Later, the husband moved the court to terminate his spousal support obligation on the grounds that his ex-wife was living with another man, but the court denied his request, reasoning that termination was only appropriate in the instances to which the parties had contractually agreed.[297] In *Gibson v. Gibson*, the parties agreed that spousal support would terminate when the recipient obtained her master's degree, and the court upheld that agreement.[298] In *Waites v. Waites*, the parties agreed that the husband would pay the wife's spousal support until her remarriage, his disability, or her agreement to terminate the agreement at any time, and the court upheld the agreement.[299]

§ 5:22 Awards for Contribution to Education or Training

In addition to claims for support, spouses may also assert claims for reimbursement for their financial contributions to the education or training expenses of the other spouse when such contributions increased the recipient spouse's earning power, to the extent that the claimant spouse did not benefit from that earning power during the marriage. Such claims are typically asserted in a divorce proceeding or thereaf-

292. Aldredge v. Aldredge, 477 So. 2d 73, 75 (La. 1985).

293. Boudreaux v. Boudreaux, 98-791, p. 4 (La. App. 3 Cir. 6/2/99), 745 So. 2d 61, 63; *see also* Williams v. Williams, 99-1101, p. 6 (La. App. 3 Cir. 4/12/00), 760 So. 2d 469, 469; Daigle v. Daigle, 2006-346, pp. 4–5 (La. App. 3 Cir. 9/27/06), 940 So. 2d 891, 891.

294. *See, e.g.*, Cason v. Cason, 38,974, pp. 5–6 (La. App. 2 Cir. 10/27/04), 886 So. 2d 628, 632; Aufrichtig v. Aufrichtig, 34,909, pp. 3–4 (La. App. 2 Cir. 8/22/01), 796 So. 2d 57, 60–61; *but see* Taylor v. Taylor, 33,959, pp. 7–8 (La. App. 2 Cir. 11/1/00), 772 So. 2d 891, 896.

295. La. Civ. Code Ann. art. 115.

296. Romero v. Romero, 509 So. 2d 681, 683–84 (La. Ct. App. 3 Cir. 1987).

297. *See also* Burns v. Burns, 2012-128, pp. 4–5 (La. App. 3 Cir. 9/20/12), 94 So. 3d 941, 943–44.

298. Gibson v. Gibson, 464 So. 2d 914, 916 (La. Ct. App. 4 Cir. 1985).

299. Waites v. Waites, 2017-499, pp. 5–8 (La. App. 4 Cir. 10/10/18), 256 So. 3d 539, 543–45.

ter[300] but may also be asserted in the wake of an action for the declaration of nullity of the marriage.[301]

To succeed on a claim for contributions to a spouse's education or training, one must prove several things. First, the claimant must prove the financial contributions to the spouse's education or training that were made during their marriage.[302] These include direct expenses for educational or training costs paid by the claimant for the other spouse (such as tuition, books, and school fees), as well as contributions to the living expenses of the supported spouse.[303] Transportation costs for commuting are not included.[304] Second, the claimant must prove that the contributions led to the spouse's increased earning power.[305] In *Shaheen v. Khan*, the court denied the husband's claim for contributions to the wife's education, in part, because she received no benefit from the degree.[306]

Finally, the claimant must prove that he or she did not enjoy the benefit of the spouse's increased earning power during the marriage.[307] If the claimant reaped the benefits during the marriage, which could happen by way of an improved standard of living or an accumulation of community property,[308] an award is not appropriate.[309] For example, in *Bourgeois v. Bourgeois*, the parties divorced three years after the husband graduated from law school.[310] After his graduation, the couple had moved into a nicer apartment, purchased a replacement vehicle for the wife and one for the husband, and paid for the wife to obtain cosmetic surgery and upgrade her engagement ring. The court found that the wife had already benefitted from her husband's education.[311]

In deciding a claim for contributions to a spouse's education or training, courts will assess three factors: (1) the claimant's expectation of a shared benefit when the contributions were made, (2) the degree of detriment suffered by the claimant in making the contributions, and (3) the magnitude of the benefit the other spouse received.[312] Courts tend to focus, in part, on the length of the marriage post-education or training. Typically, the longer the spouses are married after the education or training is completed, the more likely that the claimant will have already benefitted.[313] Framed

300. La. Civ. Code Ann. art. 121.

301. La. Civ. Code Ann. arts. 124, 151.

302. La. Civ. Code Ann. art. 121.

303. La. Civ. Code Ann. art. 121 cmt. (d).

304. La. Civ. Code Ann. art. 121 cmt. (d).

305. La. Civ. Code Ann. art. 121.

306. Shaheen v. Khan, 2013-998, p. 13 (La. App. 5 Cir. 5/21/14), 142 So. 3d 257, 265.

307. La. Civ. Code Ann. art. 121.

308. *See, e.g.*, Clemons v. Clemons, 42-129, 42-130, pp. 9–10 (La. App. 2 Cir. 5/09/07), 960 So. 2d 1068, 1074.

309. La. Civ. Code Ann. art. 121.

310. Bourgeois v. Bourgeois, 2000-2149, p. 2 (La. App. 1 Cir. 5/10/02), 818 So. 2d 1005, 1007.

311. Bourgeois, 818 So. 2d at 1010–11.

312. Barrow v. Barrow, 27-714, p. 13 (La. App. 2 Cir. 2/28/96), 669 So. 2d 622, 629.

313. La. Civ. Code Ann. art. 121 cmt. (e).

another way, courts typically grant awards in cases where the parties divorce shortly after the graduation of the recipient spouse.[314] For example, in *McConathy v. McConathy*,[315] the award was appropriate where the parties separated during the final year of the husband's schooling, and in *Shewbridge v. Shewbridge*, the same was true where the parties separated a year after the husband obtained his commercial pilot's license.[316] By contrast, in *Earle v. Earle*, the parties divorced six years after the husband graduated from law school, and the court determined that by that time, the wife had received sufficient benefit from her husband's education and denied her claim.[317]

The considerations set forth in article 121 ensure that the award is granted only when equity dictates, typically in cases where the contributing spouse failed to realize benefits from the contribution due to the timing of the divorce.[318] In other words, one who supports the other spouse through school or training only to be divorced by that spouse shortly thereafter is the most likely recipient of this type of award.

Ultimately, then, the court has discretion to make such an award,[319] and if it does so, it will use the *De La Rosa* formula to determine the amount.[320] Louisiana courts have set forth this formula as: "working spouse's financial contributions to joint living expenses and educational costs of student spouse less one-half (working spouse's financial contributions plus student spouse's financial contributions less cost of education) equals equitable award to working spouse."[321]

If the court decides to make an award for contributions to education or training, it may be in addition to a sum for support and community property received in a partition,[322] making it an independent claim in Louisiana.[323] As a result, rules governing support do not apply, making fault irrelevant to this claim.[324] Additionally, any award for contributions to education or training does not terminate on the remarriage or death of either party.[325] Furthermore, these awards cannot be modified.[326] While an award for reimbursement for contributions to education or training differs from a support award in many ways, both may be awarded in installment payments.[327] The law allows installment payments because the court may make the award early in the

314. La. Civ. Code Ann. art. 121 cmt. (c).

315. McConathy v. McConathy, 25-542 (La. App. 2 Cir. 2/23/94), 632 So. 2d 1200, 1202–06.

316. Shewbridge v. Shewbridge, 31-170, pp. 1, 7 (La. App. 2 Cir. 10/28/98), 720 So. 2d 780, 781–84.

317. Earle v. Earle, 43-925, pp. 12–13 (La. App. 2 Cir. 12/03/08), 998 So. 2d 828, 836–37.

318. La. Civ. Code Ann. art. 121 cmt. (c).

319. La. Civ. Code Ann. art. 121 cmt. (b).

320. *See* McConathy, 632 So. 2d at 1204–05 (citing DeLaRosa v. DeLaRosa, 309 N.W.2d 755 (Minn. 1981), and adopting the formula used by the Minnesota court to calculate the amount of award to be granted under article 121).

321. McConathy, 632 So. 2d at 1205.

322. La. Civ. Code Ann. art. 121.

323. La. Civ. Code Ann. art. 121 cmts. (c), (f).

324. La. Civ. Code Ann. art. 121 cmt. (c).

325. La. Civ. Code Ann. art. 123.

326. La. Civ. Code Ann. art. 123 cmt. (c).

327. La. Civ. Code Ann. art. 123; La. Civ. Code Ann. 123 cmt. (c).

defendant's career, when the spouse has not yet realized the benefits of his education or training.[328] Note, however, that in cases of installment payments, the judgment is still a money judgment for a specified sum, not an open-ended award, like a spousal support award.[329]

Louisiana law provides that a claim for reimbursement for contributions to education or training has a prescriptive period of three years, which begins to run on the date of the signing of the divorce judgment or declaration of nullity of the marriage.[330] By contrast, an action to make arrearages of installment payments of this award executory prescribes in five years.[331] In such a case, the court shall, except for good cause shown, award attorney's fees and costs to the prevailing party.[332]

Claims for contributions to education or training are strictly personal to each party[333] prior to the rendition of a judgment.[334] However, once a court makes the award, it does not terminate on either party's death.[335] If either spouse dies while an action for such a claim is pending, the action dies with that spouse.[336]

328. La. Civ. Code Ann. art. 123; La. Civ. Code Ann. 123 cmt. (b).

329. La. Civ. Code Ann. 123 cmt. (c).

330. La. Civ. Code Ann. art. 124.

331. La. Civ. Code Ann. art. 3497.1.

332. La. Stat. Ann. § 9:375.

333. The rules for heritable and strictly personal obligations can be found in Louisiana Civil Code Articles 1765–66. La. Civ. Code Ann. arts. 1765–66.

334. La. Civ. Code Ann. art. 122.

335. La. Civ. Code Ann. art. 123.

336. La. Civ. Code Ann. 123 cmt. (c).

Chapter 6

Child Custody*

* This chapter was derived from the following article: Monica Hof Wallace, *A Primer on Child Custody in Louisiana*, 65 Loy. L. Rev. 1 (2019). The authors wish to thank the Loyola Law Review for its assistance on the initial work for this chapter.

§ 6:1 Early History of Custody Law in Louisiana

Louisiana derived its early laws on custody from the patriarchal traditions of Europe. In early Roman law, the father had absolute control over his children and their property.[1] English feudal law also vested control of the children in the father, in large part to ensure that property was kept in the family and passed down through generations.[2] In France, although the father was the primary property holder, custody was awarded to the spouse who was not at fault in the divorce, absent any unusual circumstances.[3]

Drawing from these traditions, Louisiana adopted a paternal preference for provisional custody but awarded permanent custody to the innocent spouse, regardless of gender.[4] In the Louisiana Civil Code of 1870, provisional custody was granted to the father unless there was "strong reason[] to deprive him of it."[5] For permanent custody determinations, however, the law required the children to be placed under the care of the parent who obtained the separation or divorce, unless the "greater advantage of the

1. 1 William Blackstone, Commentaries on the Laws of England 451 (George Sharswood ed., 1860).

2. *See* 1 William Blackstone, Commentaries on the Laws of England 451 (George Sharswood ed., 1860); Lois E. Hawkins, *Joint Custody in Louisiana*, 43 La. L. Rev. 85, 85–86 (1982).

3. Lois E. Hawkins, *Joint Custody in Louisiana*, 43 La. L. Rev. 85, 86–87 (1982).

4. *See* La. Civ. Code art. 146 (1870).

5. La. Civ. Code art. 146 (1870). The full text of Civil Code Article 146 provided:

> If there are children of the marriage, whose provisional keeping is claimed by both husband and wife, the suit being yet pending and undecided, it shall be granted to the husband, whether plaintiff or defendant, unless there should be strong reasons to deprive him of it, either in whole or in part, the decision whereof is left to the discretion of the judge.

La. Civ. Code art. 146 (1870). Article 146 was derived from the Projet du Gouvernment, which contained no limitations at all: "If there are children of the marriage whose provisional administration is claimed by both husband and wife, it shall be granted to the husband, whether he be plaintiff or defendant." Projet du Gouvernment, bk. I, tit. VI, art. 32 (1800); *see also* Lois E. Hawkins, *Joint Custody in Louisiana*, 43 La. L. Rev. 85, 87 n.12 (1982).

children" required otherwise.[6] Ultimately, courts awarded custody to the spouse who was not at fault in the dissolution of the marriage.[7]

§ 6:2 Early History of Custody Law in Louisiana— The Revision of 1888 and the Shift to Maternal Preference

In 1888, the Louisiana State Legislature changed course for provisional custody and replaced the paternal preference with a maternal preference.[8] This revision paralleled the shift in feudal culture, where a person's status was less dependent on property ownership.[9] Additionally, women were being recognized as the primary caregivers of the home and the children, while the men were away earning income.[10] The "tender years doctrine," which recognized the need for a nursing mother to sustain the child and the unique ability of a mother to provide love, attention, and affection to a young child, further advanced the maternal preference rule.[11]

The laws governing permanent custody, however, were not amended. Permanent custody was unaffected by a paternal or maternal preference rule. Rather, courts were directed to award permanent custody to the parent that obtained the separation or divorce.[12] Despite the Code's mandate, courts awarded permanent custody in line with provisional custody, which favored the mother, particularly if the children were of tender years.[13] Courts began focusing on the child's best interest and found that cus-

6. La. Civ. Code art. 157 (1870). Civil Code Article 157 provided:

> In all cases of separation, the children shall be placed under the care of the party who shall have obtained the separation, unless the judge shall, for the greater advantage of the children, and with the advice of the family meeting, order that some or all of them shall be intrusted [sic] to the care of the other party.
>
> In all cases of divorce the minor children shall be placed under the tutorship of that party who shall have obtained the divorce.

La. Civ. Code art. 157 (1870).

7. Lois E. Hawkins, *Joint Custody in Louisiana*, 43 La. L. Rev. 85, 87 (1982). For more information on the development of Louisiana Civil Code Article 156, *see id.* at 87, n. 16.

8. Act No. 124, 1888 La. Acts 185. Article 146 was amended to replace "husband" with "wife" in granting custody; the rest of the article remained the same. *Id.*

9. Lois E. Hawkins, *Joint Custody in Louisiana*, 43 La. L. Rev. 85, 88 (1982).

10. Lois E. Hawkins, *Joint Custody in Louisiana*, 43 La. L. Rev. 85, 88–89 (1982).

11. *See, e.g.*, Black v. Black, 18 So. 2d 321, 323 (1944) ("They are both girls of tender years and need a mother's constant care and attention."); *see also* Allan Roth, *The Tender Years Presumption in Child Custody Disputes*, 15 J. Fam. L. 423, 425 (1976).

12. La. Civ. Code art. 157 (1888).

13. *See, e.g.*, Bursha v. Lane, 29 So. 712, 715 (La. 1901) (father obtained separation, but wife was awarded custody of the five-year-old child); Laplace v. Briere, 92 So. 881, 883 (La. 1922) (father had been given temporary custody, but wife was awarded permanent custody of minor child after the court found that there was "no reason for saying that it would be for the greater advantage of the child to intrust [sic] it to the [father]")

tody with the mother generally met that interest.[14] In 1921, the legislature amended article 157 on permanent custody to give the judge discretion to award permanent custody of a child to the parent who did not obtain the separation or divorce, but only "for the greater advantage of the children."[15]

Although the "best interest of the child" standard was not yet codified in Louisiana, it was used by the courts to mitigate a rigid application of the provisional and permanent custody rules.[16] Even though courts evaluated several factors to determine the best custody award for a child, a preference for the mother persisted. Very few situations defeated the preference for the mother.[17] The best interest standard was inextricably linked to the maternal preference rule because society considered it to be in the best interest of a child to be nurtured by his mother.

14. *See, e.g.*, Abreo v. Abreo, 281 So. 2d 693, 697 (La. 1973) ("In keeping with the law's aim to promote the child's welfare, the decisions have recognized that the child's best interest is served when custody is awarded to the mother, especially when the child is of tender years."); Estes v. Estes, 258 So. 2d 857, 860 (La. 1972) (finding that both parents could provide a good home for the children, but custody with the mother was in the ultimate best interest of the children).

15. Act No. 38, 1921 La. Acts 42; *see also* La. Civ. Code art. 157 (rev. 1921).

16. Brewton v. Brewton, 105 So. 307, 309 (La. 1925) (court used discretionary power to award custody of the child to the mother, due in part to the child's tender years).

17. A mother was denied custody when she was mentally or morally unfit to care for the children. *See* Richard v. Richard, 359 So. 2d 696, 697 (La. Ct. App. 1 Cir. 1978); Poole v. Poole, 189 So. 2d 75, 83–84 (La. Ct. App. 1 Cir. 1968). A mother was also denied custody when she failed to provide a wholesome atmosphere for the children, or when she abandoned the home and failed to seek custody of the children. Nethken v. Nethken, 292 So. 2d 923, 926 (La. Ct. App. 1 Cir. 1974) (reasoning that the mother would "routinely [leave] the house in the morning and return[] late at night to minimize the contact with her husband and children ..." and "was unable to discipline the older children ... and could control the younger children only with rather harsh restraints"); Ard v. Ard, 28 So. 2d 461, 462 (La. 1946) (holding that "[f]or a mother to deliberately abandon her children of very tender ages, to make no effort to secure their legal custody ... and to be generally disinterested in them ... are factors that combine to strongly indicate that she is ... unsuited for their custody").

§ 6:3 Early History of Custody Law in Louisiana— The Revision of 1979 and Equal Rights to Parents

By the early 1970s, the feminist and civil rights movements influenced courts to discard presumptions based on gender that resulted in unequal treatment.[18] Although Louisiana courts continued to uphold the constitutionality of the maternal preference rule,[19] the legislature saw fit to amend the provisions on permanent custody to permit awards to either parent, in line with the best interest of the child.[20] Confusion continued, however, because courts were unclear as to whether the amendments eliminated or codified the maternal preference rule.[21]

Therefore, in 1979, the legislature again amended the Code to clarify that the best interest of the child was the sole consideration in awarding custody and that parents had equal rights to custody.[22] The legislature also abrogated the maternal preference rule in provisional custody cases, granting custody to either parent, all determined by the best interest of the child.[23] Courts recognized that these amendments eliminated any legal preference in favor of the mother.[24]

---

18. *See, e.g.*, Orr v. Orr, 440 U.S. 268, 283 (1979) (finding that statute allowing alimony to be paid only to women violated the Equal Protection Clause); Frontiero v. Richardson, 411 U.S. 677, 682 (1973) (finding that classifications based on gender are inherently suspect); Reed v. Reed, 404 U.S. 71, 76–77 (1971) (finding that statute preferring men over women as administrators was unconstitutional).

19. *See* Broussard v. Broussard, 320 So. 2d 236, 238 (La. Ct. App. 3 Cir. 1975).

20. Act No. 448, 1977 La. Acts 1196 ("In all cases of separation and divorce, permanent custody of the child or children shall be granted to the husband or the wife, in accordance with the best interest of the child or children.").

21. *See, e.g.*, Abreo v. Abreo, 281 So. 2d 695, 697 (La. 1973) (granting custody to the mother even though both parents were fit because the mother's right to custody is paramount); Welch v. Welch, 307 So. 2d 737, 738 (La. Ct. App. 2 Cir. 1975) (applying maternal preference as a rebuttable presumption); Brackman v. Brackman, 322 So. 2d 314, 317 (La. Ct. App. 2 Cir. 1975) (applying the maternal preference rule in determining what is in the best interest of the child and finding the preference to be less important "when the children remain[] away from the mother for a substantial period of time").

22. Act No. 718, 1979 La. Acts 1962, 1963–64 ("In all cases of separation and divorce, and changes of custody after an original award, permanent custody of the child or children shall be granted to the husband or wife, in accordance with the best interest of the child or children, *without any preference being given on the basis of the sex of the parent* ...") (emphasis added); *see also* Lois E. Hawkins, *Joint Custody in Louisiana*, 43 La. L. Rev. 85, 87 n.12 (1982).

23. Act No. 718, 1979 La. Acts 1962, 1963 ("If there are children of the marriage, whose provisional keeping is claimed by both husband and wife ... it shall be granted to the husband or the wife, in accordance with the best interest of the children.").

24. Burch v. Burch, 398 So. 2d 84, 86 (La. Ct. App. 3 Cir. 1981); Thornton v. Thornton, 377 So. 2d 417, 420 (La. Ct. App. 2 Cir. 1979).

§ 6:4 Early History of Custody Law in Louisiana— The Revision of 1981 and the Institution of Joint Custody

With the best interest of the child as the governing consideration in child custody cases, courts across the country began to consider alternatives to custody in one parent alone. "Joint custody," "divided custody," "split custody," and "co-parenting" were all labels used to describe parents' legal rights to the child as well as their physical time with the child.[25] These arrangements were urged by parents and accepted by many courts to meet the best interest of the child. Louisiana likewise recognized the need to provide alternatives to sole custody, and in 1981, amended the provisional and permanent custody articles to provide for joint custody.[26]

Joint custody, as it was first enacted into the Code, could only be awarded if both parents agreed, it was in the best interest of the child, and both parents were domiciled

---

25. Lois E. Hawkins, *Joint Custody in Louisiana*, 43 La. L. Rev. 85, 93 (1982); *see also* Mel Morgenbesser & Nadine Nehls, Joint Custody: An Alternative for Divorcing Families 30 (1981). "No consensus of opinion has arisen concerning alternative custody arrangements." Lois E. Hawkins, *Joint Custody in Louisiana*, 43 La. L. Rev. 85, 93 (1982).

26. Act No. 283, 1981 La. Acts 600–02. Article 146, the new provisional custody article, provided:

> A. If there are children of the marriage whose provisional keeping is claimed by both husband and wife, the suit being yet pending and undecided, it shall be granted to the husband or the wife in accordance with the best interest of the children, or, if both husband and wife agree to joint custody and the court deems it in the best interest of the children, the court may award joint custody. In all cases, the court shall inquire into the fitness of both the mother and father and shall award custody to such parent or to both parents, if they agree to joint custody, as the court finds will in all respects be in accordance with the best interest of the child or children. Such custody hearing may be held in private chambers of the judge.
>
> B. An award of joint custody shall be made only when both husband and wife are domiciled in the state of Louisiana. If either parent changes his or her domicile to another state, the other may petition for sole custody. For purposes of this Article "joint custody" shall mean the husband and wife may share the physical custody of children of the marriage and shall enjoy the natural cotutorship of such children in accordance with Article 250.

Act No. 283, 1981 La. Acts 600. Article 157, the new permanent custody article, provided:

> A. In all cases of separation and divorce, and change of custody after an original award, permanent custody of the child or children shall be granted to the husband or the wife, or to both jointly by agreement of both the husband and wife, in accordance with the best interest of the child or children; however, an award of joint custody may be granted only when the husband and wife are both domiciled in the state of Louisiana. If either parent changes his or her domicile to another state, the other may petition for sole custody.
>
> No preference shall be given on the basis of the sex of the parent in cases where custody is awarded to only one parent. Such custody hearing may be held in private chambers of the judge.
>
> In all cases in which the custody of the child or children is awarded to one parent, the parent with legal custody shall of right become the natural tutor or tutrix of said child or children to the same extent and with the same effect as if the other party had died. In all cases in which the custody of the child or children is awarded jointly to both parents, they may share the physical custody of the child or children and shall be entitled to become the natural cotutors of such child or children in accordance with Article 250.

Act No. 283, 1981 La. Acts 600–01.

in Louisiana.[27] Joint custody was not permitted if the parents failed to agree, even if the best interest of the child indicated otherwise.[28] Additionally, if either parent changed domicile, the other parent could seek sole custody.[29] As persists today, joint custody ultimately resulted in some form of shared physical custody and co-tutorship of the child, although the concept of a "domiciliary parent" had yet to be developed.[30]

The 1981 amendments brought substantial and important changes in Louisiana custody law but lacked the details necessary to guide the parties and the court. The best interest of the child standard was vague and undefined, and it previously had been conflated with the now-repealed maternal preference. The method by which parents could agree to joint custody was not specified in the new articles, leading to confusion about whether joint custody agreements could be verbal, express, or tacit.

Because joint custody was a new concept in Louisiana, its advantages and disadvantages were greatly disputed. On the one hand, joint custody was preferred to sole custody because it allowed the child to have a continuing, regular relationship with both parents and prevented the courts from having to name a "winner" and a "loser" in the custody dispute. Because joint custody allowed parents to share the burdens of decision-making, emotional support, and physical care of the child, the parents could also pursue their individual goals and develop new relationships.[31] On the other hand, with the adoption of joint custody, doubts arose as to how it would function and its potential disadvantages to the child and the parents. One common argument against joint custody focused on the unsettling effects of being shuttled between two homes and answering to divided authority.[32] Before joint custody was written into the Civil Code, Louisiana courts historically rejected divided custody arrangements based on the idea that children should not be subjected to a division of authority.[33] Concern arose that parents, who had dissolved their marriage due to conflict, would be unlikely to cooperate with one another in child-rearing.[34]

Notwithstanding the ongoing discussion surrounding the propriety of joint custody, the legislature quickly remedied the shortcomings of articles 146 and 157 by defining joint custody through an implementation plan, much of which still exists today. Act

---

27. Act No. 283, 1981 La. Acts 600.

28. Act No. 283, 1981 La. Acts 600.

29. Act No. 283, 1981 La. Acts 600.

30. *See* Section 6:5.

31. *See* Mel Roman & William Haddad, The Disposable Parent: The Case for Joint Custody 104, 117 (1978).

32. *See* Lois E. Hawkins, *Joint Custody in Louisiana*, 43 La. L. Rev. 85, 94 (1982). This argument was referred to as the "yo-yo" argument.

33. *See* Woods v. Woods, 253 So. 2d 230, 232 (La. Ct. App. 2 Cir. 1971); Ogden v. Ogden, 220 So. 2d 241, 243–44 (La. Ct. App. 1 Cir. 1969); Bowlin v. Bowlin, 222 So. 2d 637, 638 (La. Ct. App. 2 Cir. 1969).

34. *See, e.g.*, H. Jay Folberg & Marva Graham, *Joint Custody of Children Following Divorce*, 12 U.C.D. L. Rev. 523, 549 (1979).

307 of 1982 rewrote articles 146 and 157, adopting the same rules for provisional or permanent custody.[35]

---

35. Act No. 307, 1982 La. Acts 804–07. Amended article 146 provided:

A. If there are children of the marriage whose provisional custody is claimed by both husband and wife, the suit being yet pending and undecided, custody shall be awarded in the following order of preference, according to the best interest of the children:

(1) To both parents jointly. The court, shall, unless waived by the court for good cause shown, require the parents to submit a plan for implementation of the custody order, or the parents acting individually or in concert may submit a custody implementation plan to the court prior to issuance of a custody decree. Such plan may include such considerations as the following:

(a) Domiciliary arrangements for the child or children.

(b) Rights of access and communication between the respective parents and the child or children.

(c) Child support, if appropriate to the economic circumstances of the parents.

(d) Any other matter deemed in the best interest of the child or children.

(2) To either parent. In making an order of custody to either parent, the court shall consider, among other factors, which parent is more likely to allow the child or children frequent and continuing contact with the noncustodial parent, and shall not prefer a parent as custodian because of that parent's sex. The burden of proof that joint custody would not be in a child's best interest shall be upon the parent requesting sole custody.

(3) If to neither parent, to the person or persons in whose home the child has been living in a wholesome and stable environment.

(4) To any other person or persons deemed by the court to be suitable and able to provide an adequate and stable environment.

B. Before the court makes any order awarding custody to a person or persons other than a parent without the consent of the parents, it shall make a finding that an award of custody to a parent would be detrimental to the child and the award to a nonparent is required to serve the best interest of the child. Allegations that parental custody would be detrimental to the child, other than a statement of that ultimate fact, shall not appear in the pleadings.

C. There shall be a rebuttable presumption that joint custody is in the best interest of a minor child unless:

(1) The parents have agreed to an award of custody to one parent or so agree in open court at a hearing for the purpose of determining the custody of a minor child of the marriage; or

(2) The court finds that joint custody would not be in the best interest of the child.

For the purpose of assisting the court in making a determination whether an award of joint custody is appropriate, the court may direct that an investigation be conducted.

D. For purposes of this Article, "joint custody" shall mean the parents shall share the physical custody of children of the marriage, subject to any plan of implementation effected pursuant to Paragraph A of this Article, and shall enjoy the natural cotutorship of such children in accordance with Article 250. Physical care and custody shall be shared by the parents in such a way as to assure a child of frequent and continuing contact with both parents. An award of joint custody obligates the parties to exchange information concerning the health, education, and welfare of the minor child; and, unless allocated, apportioned, or decreed, the parents or parties shall confer with one another in the exercise of decision-making rights, responsibilities, and authority.

E. Any order for joint custody, or any plan of implementation effected pursuant to Paragraph A of this Article, may be modified or terminated upon the petition of one or both parents or on the court's own motion, if it is shown that the best interest of the child requires modification or termination of the order. The court shall state in its decision the reasons for modification or termination of the joint custody order if either parent opposes the modification or termination order.

Most notably, the amendments provided a rebuttable presumption that joint custody was in the best interest of the child.[36] The presumption could be overcome in one of two ways: (1) if the parents agreed to sole custody; or (2) if joint custody was not in the best interest of the child.[37] Absent a parental agreement for sole custody, the presumption that joint custody was in the best interest of the child could be rebutted by evidence that it was, in fact, not in the best interest of the child—a circular proposition at best.[38] At this point, no factors were articulated to help courts determine the best interest of the child, but the courts were permitted to "direct ... an investigation."[39]

The amended articles also required that parents with joint custody submit a custody implementation plan, which could include the living arrangements of the child, access and communication rights of the parents, support for the child, and any other matter deemed to be in the child's best interest.[40] An award of joint custody obligated the parents to exchange information regarding the child and to confer with one another when making decisions.[41] If disputes arose following the decree, the parties had to return to court to enforce their version of the plan or to petition for sole custody.[42] In the revision, the legislature clearly recognized the need for frequent, continuing contact with both parents and provided guidance to litigants on how to achieve that result.[43]

Finally, the revision provided for an award of custody to a nonparent for the first time in Louisiana's history.[44] Nonparent custody had been recognized in the juris-

---

> F. Any order for the custody of a minor child of a marriage entered by a court in this state or in any other state, subject to jurisdictional requirements, may be modified at any time to an order of joint custody in accordance with the provisions of this Article.
>
> G. A custody hearing may be held in private chambers of the judge.
>
> H. Notwithstanding any other provision of law, access to records and information pertaining to a minor child, including but not limited to medical, dental, and school records, shall not be denied to a parent because the parent is not the child's custodial parent.

Act No. 307, 1982 La. Acts 804–06. Amended article 157 provided:

> A. In all cases of separation and divorce, and change of custody after an original award, permanent custody of the child or children shall be granted to the parents in accordance with Article 146.
>
> B. If subsequent to the granting of a divorce or separation one of the parties to the marriage dies and is survived by a minor child or children of the marriage, the parents of such deceased party may have reasonable visitation rights to the child or children of the marriage during their minority, if the court in its discretion finds that such visitation rights would be in the best interests of the child or children.

Act No. 307, 1982 La. Acts 804–06. For a complete discussion of the revision, see generally Richard C. Guerriero, Jr., *Louisiana's New Joint Custody Law*, 43 La. L. Rev. 759 (1983).

36. *See* Act No. 307, 1982 La. Acts 804–06.
37. Act No. 307, 1982 La. Acts 805.
38. Act No. 307, 1982 La. Acts 805.
39. Act No. 307, 1982 La. Acts 805.
40. Act No. 307, 1982 La. Acts 804.
41. Act No. 307, 1982 La. Acts 804–05.
42. Act No. 307, 1982 La. Acts 804.
43. Act No. 307, 1982 La. Acts 804.
44. Act No. 307, 1982 La. Acts 805.

prudence when both parents were unfit, unwilling, or unable to accept custody.[45] The amended articles set a clear standard for nonparent custody: the court must find that parental custody would be detrimental to the child.[46]

As the best interest of the child was paramount in the award of joint custody, the legislature in 1983 amended article 146 again to provide the following list of factors to assist the court in making its determination:

(a) The love, affection, and other emotional ties existing between the parties involved and the child.

(b) The capacity and disposition of the parties involved to give the child love, affection, and guidance and continuation of the education and raising of the child in its religion or creed, if any.

(c) The capacity and disposition of the parties involved to provide the child with food, clothing, medical care, and other material needs.

(d) The length of time the child has lived in a stable, satisfactory environment, and the desirability of maintaining continuity.

(e) The permanence, as a family unit, of the existing or proposed custodial home or homes.

(f) The moral fitness of the parties involved.

(g) The mental and physical health of the parties involved.

(h) The home, school, and community record of the child.

(i) The reasonable preference of the child, if the court deems the child to be of sufficient age to express preference.

(j) The willingness and ability of each of the parents to facilitate and encourage a close and continuing parent-child relationship between the child and the other parent.

(k) The distance between the respective residences of the parties.

(l) Any other factor considered by the court to be relevant to a particular child custody dispute. However, the classification of persons according to race is neither relevant nor permissible.[47]

The parent seeking sole custody had the burden to rebut the presumption that joint custody was in the best interest of the child.[48] Shortly after the revision, courts began considering the illustrative list of factors, and over time, a certain set of facts emerged

45. *See, e.g.*, Deville v. LaGrange, 388 So. 2d 696, 698 (La. 1980); Jones v. Jones, 415 So. 2d 300, 302 (La. Ct. App. 2 Cir. 1982); *see also* Wood v. Beard, 290 So. 2d 675, 676–77 (La. 1974).

46. Act No. 307, 1982 La. Acts 804–05.

47. La. Civ. Code Ann. art. 146 (rev. 1984). The second sentence of factor (*l*) was added in response to the United States Supreme Court decision in *Palmore v. Sidoti*, 466 U.S. 429 (1984), which found that private biases based on race violated the Fourteenth Amendment of the United States Constitution; *see also* Katherine Shaw Spaht, *Persons*, 45 La. L. Rev. 467, 477 (1984).

48. La. Civ. Code Ann. art. 146 (rev. 1984); *see also* Owen v. Gallien, 477 So. 2d 1240, 1245 (La. Ct. App. 3 Cir. 1985); Lake v. Robertson, 452 So. 2d 376, 380 (La. Ct. App. 3 Cir. 1984).

that would generally rebut the presumption of joint custody. Those included severe disagreement over basic issues related to the child,[49] the distance between the parents,[50] child care arrangements made by the parent,[51] or the parent's inability to encourage a relationship between the child and the other parent.[52]

§ 6:5 Early History of Custody Law in Louisiana—The Revision of 1993

The next significant revision to the custody articles took place in 1993. Shortly before, in 1990, the legislature re-designated articles 146 and 157 as articles 131 and 134, respectively.[53] No substantive changes to the articles were made.

In Act 261 of 1993, effective January 1, 1994, the substance of articles 131 and 134 was redistributed among articles 131 through 135.[54] The classification of custody as provisional and permanent was abolished, and the rules governing a temporary award of custody were moved into the Code of Civil Procedure.[55] The overarching factor, "the best interest of the child," appeared first in article 131, making it clear that in all custody cases—initial awards or modification—the court's paramount concern is the child's best interest.[56] The two articles that followed set forth the descending order of custody, with parental custody preferred.

The rebuttable presumption in favor of joint custody was suppressed. Instead, first preference was given to parental agreement, unless the best interest of the child required otherwise.[57] When the parents could not agree or if their agreement was not in the child's best interest, the court was mandated to award joint custody.[58] The shift

49. Kincaide v. Kincaide, 444 So. 2d 651, 652 (La. Ct. App. 1 Cir. 1983) (holding that "because of irreconcilable differences between the parents concerning the child's attending a private religious school and other matters, joint custody would not be in the best interest of the child").

50. *See* Lachney v. Lachney, 446 So. 2d 923, 926 (La. Ct. App. 3 Cir. 1984) (stating that parents living in separate states made a joint custody plan unfeasible).

51. Robicheaux v. Robicheaux, 446 So. 2d 979, 980 (La. Ct. App. 3 Cir. 1984) (the father traveled frequently and left the child in the care of his elderly mother, who was not able to adequately care for the child).

52. *See* Price v. Price, 451 So. 2d 1187, 1191 (La. Ct. App. 1 Cir. 1984) (placing the child in the father's custody because living with his mother and her new husband created a rift between the child and his father). For a discussion of these and other cases post-revision, see Katherine Shaw Spaht, *Persons*, 45 La. L. Rev. 467, 477–78 (1984).

53. Act No. 1008, 1990 La. Acts 2498, 2505; Act No. 1009, 1990 La. Acts 2505, 2528.

54. Act No. 261, 1993 La. Acts 610, 611–22.

55. *See* La. Code Civ. Proc. Ann. art. 3945; *see also* Act No. 1204, 1995 La. Acts 3486.

56. Act No. 261, 1993 La. Acts 610, 611. Louisiana Civil Code Article 131 provided, in part, "In a proceeding for divorce or thereafter, the court shall award custody of a child in accordance with the best interest of the child." *Id.*

57. Act No. 261, 1993 La. Acts 610, 613. The first paragraph of then-Louisiana Civil Code Article 132 provided: "If the parents agree who is to have custody, the court shall award custody in accordance with their agreement unless the best interest of the child requires a different award." *Id.*

58. Act No. 261, 1993 La. Acts 610, 613. The second paragraph of then-Louisiana Civil Code Article 132 provided:

away from a rebuttable presumption of joint custody was not an attempt to weaken the arrangement where parents share child-rearing; rather, it respected the agreement of the parents, absent any harmful effects on the child, to make custody decisions without interference by the state.[59] If the parents were unable to agree, joint custody would be mandated, rather than just presumed.[60]

Act 261 of 1993 also placed a higher burden of proof on the parent seeking sole custody. Under prior law, the parent seeking sole custody had to rebut the presumption that joint custody was in the best interest of the child by a preponderance of the evidence.[61] Under the revision, the parent seeking sole custody had to prove by clear and convincing evidence—highly probable or much more probable than not—that an award of sole custody was in the child's best interest.[62] Focus shifted from the joint custody arrangement—considering the parents' relationship with one another—to whether sole custody in one parent was best for the welfare of the child.[63]

The second article that set forth the order of custody permitted an award of custody to nonparents only in the face of "substantial harm" to the child.[64] The substantial harm standard replaced the two-pronged test under prior law, which required that parental custody be "detrimental" to the child and that nonparent custody serve the best interest of the child.[65] The revision raised the evidentiary bar from "detrimental" to "substantial harm" for the nonparent who sought to remove the parent's paramount right to custody.[66] As reflected in article 131, any award of custody had to consider the best interest of the child.

After the revision, article 134 contained the factors to determine the child's best interest. The illustrative list of factors provided a guide to use in all custody and visitation cases, rather than their former, limited use to rebut the presumption of joint custody.[67] The factors looked substantially similar to former article 146, with three

---

> In the absence of agreement, or if the agreement is not in the best interest of the child, the court shall award custody to the parents jointly; however, if custody in one parent is shown by clear and convincing evidence to serve the best interest of the child, the court shall award custody to that parent.

Act No. 261, 1993 La. Acts 610, 613.

59. Kenneth Rigby, *1993 Custody and Child Support Legislation*, 55 La. L. Rev. 103, 107–09 (1994).

60. La. Civ. Code Ann. art. 132.

61. *See* Section 6:4.

62. Act No. 261, 1993 La. Acts 610, 613.

63. Kenneth Rigby, *1993 Custody and Child Support Legislation*, 55 La. L. Rev. 103, 110 (1994).

64. Act No. 261, 1993 La. Acts 610, 613. Then Louisiana Civil Code article 133 provided:

> If an award of joint custody or of sole custody to either parent would result in substantial harm to the child, the court shall award custody to another person with whom the child has been living in a wholesome and stable environment, or otherwise to any other person able to provide an adequate and stable environment.

Act No. 261, 1993 La. Acts 610, 613.

65. La. Civ. Code Ann. art. 146(B) (1990); *see also* La. Civ. Code Ann. art. 133 (rev. 1994); La. Civ. Code Ann. art. 131(B) (rev. 1993).

66. Kenneth Rigby, *1993 Custody and Child Support Legislation*, 55 La. L. Rev. 103, 111 (1994).

67. *Compare* La. Civ. Code Ann. art. 146 (1990), *with* La. Civ. Code art. 134 (1994).

notable exceptions. First, the capacity of a parent to raise his child "in his religion or creed, if any" was replaced with the capacity to give "spiritual guidance."[68] Second, the "moral fitness" of the parents could be considered only "insofar as it affects the welfare of the child."[69] Third, a twelfth factor was added to consider "the responsibility for the care and rearing of the child previously exercised by each party."[70]

The details of joint custody were moved from article 131 and were further defined in the Louisiana Revised Statutes Section 9:335 mandated a joint custody implementation order when joint custody was ordered, except for good cause shown.[71] Additionally, Act 261 adopted the term "domiciliary parent" to describe the parent with whom the child primarily resides and required the court to name a domiciliary parent in the decree of joint custody.[72] The domiciliary parent was given the authority to make all decisions regarding the welfare of the child, unless restrictions were placed on that parent's authority in the implementation order.[73] The non-domiciliary parent could challenge major decisions of the domiciliary parent in a judicial proceeding, but the decision of the domiciliary parent was presumed to be in the child's best interest.[74] Because the roles of the parents were better defined under the revised law, a successful joint custody plan was not contingent on parental agreement.[75]

Act 261 of 1993 did not define joint custody as an equal sharing of physical custody of the child.[76] The focus of custody was on the best interest of the child. However, after enacting Act 261, the legislature passed Act 905 of 1993, which amended article 131 to provide, "[t]o the extent it is feasible, physical custody of the children shall be shared equally."[77] The effective date of Act 905 was August 15, 1993.[78] Article 131, however, was being amended and re-designated by Act 261, effective January 1, 1994.[79] Although the law was clear between August 15, 1993 and December 31, 1993, as of January 1, 1994, the changes to article 131 adopted in Act 905, which had been approved *after* Act 261, were not included in the revised law.[80] To rectify the apparent conflict, the Louisiana State Law Institute transferred the language of the shared custody provision, with some

---

68. *Compare* La. Civ. Code Ann. art. 146(C)(2)(b) (1990), *with* La. Civ. Code Ann. art. 134(2) (1994).

69. *Compare* La. Civ. Code Ann. art. 146(C)(2)(f) (1990), *with* La. Civ. Code Ann. art. 134(6) (1994).

70. *Compare* La. Civ. Code Ann. art. 146(C)(2) (1990), *with* La. Civ. Code Ann. art. 134(12) (1994).

71. *See* Act No. 261, 1993 La. Acts 610, 625.

72. Act No. 261, 1993 La. Acts 610, 625.; *see also* Kenneth Rigby, *1993 Custody and Child Support Legislation*, 55 La. L. Rev. 103, 117 (1994).

73. Act No. 261, 1993 La. Acts 610, 625.

74. Act No. 261, 1993 La. Acts 610, 625.

75. *See* Kenneth Rigby, *1993 Custody and Child Support Legislation*, 55 La. L. Rev. 103, 113 (1994).

76. Act No. 261, 1993 La. Acts 610, 625.

77. Act No. 905, 1993 La. Acts 2534.

78. Act No. 905, 1993 La. Acts 2535.

79. Act No. 261, 1993 La. Acts 610, 638.

80. *See* La. Stat. Ann. § 9:335 historical and statutory notes.

modification, into Louisiana Revised Statutes Section 9:335.[81] The best interest of the child was still the primary consideration, but when equal sharing is "feasible and in the best interest of the child," it can be ordered in a joint custody arrangement.[82]

The law of custody has remained relatively consistent since the revision of 1993. In 2018, the legislature passed Act 412 at the urging of domestic violence victims advocates.[83] This act amended the general articles on custody to include references to various domestic violence laws to highlight the application of specific statutes that affect custody when domestic abuse is present.[84] Additional revisions have been made to the articles and statutes on visitation, which are discussed in the sections below.[85]

§ 6:6 Types of Custody Proceedings

Louisiana provides several methods to petition for custody. In fact, custody actions are treated as independent causes of actions, not simply actions incidental to divorce.[86] Although custody is often requested in a petition for divorce, it can be awarded in several other actions, including annulment of marriage, paternity actions, voluntary relinquishment of custody, writ of habeas corpus, or simply by petition when the parties are unmarried.[87] The petition for custody, whether incidental to divorce or not, is governed substantively by the best interest of the child standard.[88]

81. *See* La. Stat. Ann. § 9:335; *see also* Kenneth Rigby, *1993 Custody and Child Support Legislation*, 55 La. L. Rev. 103, 120 (1994). The Louisiana State Law Institute is authorized to resolve "conflict[s] between two or more legislative acts affecting the same subject matter." La. Stat. Ann. § 24:252(B) (2019).

82. La. Stat. Ann. § 9:335(A)(2)(b).

83. *See* 2018 La. Sess. Law Serv. Act 412 (S.B. 291) (West, Westlaw through 2018 Reg. Sess.).

84. *See* 2018 La. Sess. Law Serv. Act 412 (S.B. 291) (West, Westlaw through 2018 Reg. Sess.).

85. *See* Sections 6:46–6:52.

86. La. Civ. Code Ann. art. 131 cmt. (e); *see also* Pylant v. Pylant, 45,378, p. 6 (La. App. 2 Cir. 6/23/10), 41 So. 3d 1282, 1285 (concluding that a consent judgment of custody was "a legally independent, valid and enforceable judgment, which survived the abandonment of [the] divorce action").

87. *See* Sections 6:7–6:13.

88. *See* La. Civ. Code Ann. art. 134.

§ 6:7 Types of Custody Proceedings— Custody Incidental to Divorce

In a proceeding for divorce, either spouse may request a determination of custody or visitation of a minor child.[89] Generally, the request is placed in the petition for divorce or in the answer to the petition, and a hearing on custody is requested in a contradictory motion or rule to show cause.[90] If the parties plan to file an Article 103(1) no-fault divorce,[91] no divorce petition is initially filed, but the spouses may need a resolution regarding custody while living separate and apart. Although generally spouses may not sue one another during the marriage, Louisiana law permits spouses who are living separate and apart to institute a suit for custody and support of their minor children.[92]

§ 6:8 Types of Custody Proceedings— Custody Incidental to an Annulment of Marriage

Custody can be awarded when a party seeks a declaration of nullity of a marriage, whether it is relatively or absolutely null.[93] In the case of a marriage that is relatively null, which is given the effects of marriage until declared null, the right of custody is ultimately based on the existence of the marriage.[94] For an absolutely null marriage, which is considered no marriage at all, the right of custody stems from the putative marriage doctrine. As a general rule, this doctrine allows for the filiation of children born of the absolutely null marriage as long one of the spouses contracted the marriage in good faith.[95] In most instances, if neither party to the marriage is in good faith, the

---

89. La. Civ. Code Ann. art. 105.

90. *See* La. Code Civ. Proc. Ann. arts. 2592(8), 2593; *see also* Jessica G. Braun, Handbook on Louisiana Family Law 1174–75 (2019).

91. La. Civ. Code Ann. art. 103(1).

92. La. Stat. Ann. § 9:291.

93. La. Civ. Code Ann. arts. 151–152. Louisiana Civil Code Article 151 pertains to incidental relief, while Louisiana Civil Code Article 152 pertains to permanent relief. *See id.*

94. La. Civ. Code Ann. art. 97 ("A relatively null marriage produces civil effects until it is declared null."). *See also*, Chapter 3, Section 3:32 for a discussion of relatively null marriages.

95. La. Civ. Code Ann. art. 96 ("An absolutely null marriage nevertheless produces civil effects in favor of a party who contracted it in good faith for as long as that party remains in good faith.... When the cause of the nullity is an impediment of age, the marriage produces civil effects in favor of a child of the parties. When the cause of the nullity is another reason, a marriage contracted by a party in good faith produces civil effects in favor of a child of the parties."); *see also* Gaines v. Hennen, 65 U.S. 553, 556 (1860) (interpreting Louisiana law to mean that when either parent contracted a marriage in good faith, the children born of the second marriage are legitimate); Melancon v. Sonnier, 157 So. 2d 577, 581–82 (La. Ct. App. 3 Cir. 1963) (finding that the child of a marriage contracted in good faith by at least one of the parties is legitimate as to both of the parties). All rights and obligations that flow between parents and children, including the rights of inheritance, will apply to children born of a putative marriage. Succession of Jene, 173 So. 2d 857, 861 (La. Ct. App. 4 Cir. 1965). *But see* Patton v. City of Philadelphia, 1 La. Ann. 98, 106 (1846) (denying child of absolutely null marriage his inheritance from bad faith putative spouse, even though the other spouse was in good faith). *See also* Chapter 3, Section

children are not considered born of the marriage.[96] Regardless, in all scenarios, the child's biological parents are allowed to seek custody simply as a result of parenthood.[97]

Without marriage, proof of parenthood may be necessary to obtain custody.[98] Maternity is proven by evidence "that the child was born of a particular woman."[99] With a child's birth certificate, the fact of birth to a particular woman is not difficult to prove.[100] However, proof of paternity can be more difficult. A man can formally acknowledge a child in an authentic act, in which case the Code presumes his paternity and provides him with a limited right of custody and visitation (as well as the obligation of child support).[101] For this presumption of paternity to apply, however, the child cannot be "filiated to another man."[102] If the child is filiated to another man, the father must timely file suit to avow the child[103] or the child must timely file a paternity action against the father.[104]

For example, in *Burrell v. Burrell*, a woman and man entered into a marriage knowing that the woman's prior marriage had never been dissolved.[105] Three children were born of the bigamous union, and the man was registered on the birth certificates based on the unlawful union.[106] The court concluded that because the marriage was entered into in bad faith, it produced no civil effects as to either party or the children of the marriage.[107] Rather, the children were deemed the children of the mother and her legal husband, even though he was not the biological father of the children.[108] The registration on the birth certificate could not operate as a formal acknowledgment because the children were already filiated to another man—the mother's legal husband.[109]

Although *Burrell* predates several revisions to the articles on filiation, under the law today, the result would likely remain the same. A tutor on behalf of the children could sue to establish their paternity to the biological father (from which child custody and support would flow),[110] but the father would remain unable to avow the children for

---

3:21 for a discussion of absolutely null marriages. "Good faith" is defined as "an honest and reasonable belief that there exists no legal impediment to a marriage." La. Civ. Code Ann. art. 96 cmt. (d).

96. Succession of Virgin, 24 La. Ann. 485, 486 (1872); Burrell v. Burrell, 154 So. 2d 103, 104–05 (La. Ct. App. 1 Cir. 1963). An exception is that when the cause of the nullity is an impediment of age, the marriage produces civil effects in favor of the parties' children regardless of the parents' good faith. La. Civ. Code Ann. art. 96.

97. *See* La. Civ. Code Ann. art. 152 cmt. (e).

98. *See* Chapter 8 for a detailed discussion of biological filiation.

99. La. Civ. Code Ann. art. 184.

100. *See* La. Civ. Code Ann. art. 184 cmt. (b).

101. La. Civ. Code Ann. art. 196.

102. La. Civ. Code Ann. art. 196.

103. La. Civ. Code Ann. art. 198.

104. La. Civ. Code Ann. art. 197.

105. Burrell v. Burrell, 154 So. 2d 103, 105 (La. Ct. App. 1 Cir. 1963).

106. Burrell, 154 So. 2d at 104.

107. Burrell, 154 So. 2d at 108.

108. Burrell, 154 So. 2d at 107.

109. *See* Burrell, 154 So. 2d at 108.

110. La. Civ. Code Ann. art. 197.

purposes of custody because his action would be perempted.[111] When a child is filiated to another man, the biological father has only one year from the birth of the child to bring the action to avow the child, with a limited exception when the mother in bad faith deceives him regarding paternity.[112] If the parties to the null marriage are both in bad faith, the biological father will only have one year from the birth of the child to file his action to avow because he would naturally know of his paternity.[113]

Ultimately, in cases of both parents' bad faith, the child may be the only person with the right to prove biological filiation. Assuming the biological father's right to avow ended,[114] only a tutor on behalf of the child could file a paternity action.[115] Naturally, the mother would be the tutor of the child, and if she no longer wanted the biological father in the child's life, she would not bring the action. Another person, possibly related to the biological father, could petition a court to be a named tutor for the purpose of filing suit on behalf of the child to establish the father's paternity, but usurping the natural tutor would be contrary to law.[116] The tutorship of right belongs to the mother of an unacknowledged child or a child acknowledged without her consent, so another person should be unable to bring suit without the mother's consent,[117] even if the best interest of the child would be served by establishing paternity.

§ 6:9 Types of Custody Proceedings— Custody Incidental to a Paternity Action

When an unmarried man seeks to establish his paternity of a child without marrying the mother, he will either sign a formal acknowledgment that he is the father,[118] or he will file an avowal action to receive a judgment of paternity from a court.[119] The formal acknowledgment may be made solely by authentic act and will trigger a presumption in his favor that he is the father of the child only for purposes of custody, visitation, and child support.[120] Therefore, once the man executes the formal acknowledgment, he can present it to a court in a request for custody, even though he will not have full filial rights.[121] If the man institutes an avowal action to establish his paternity of a child, he may also seek custody in his petition, and he will have full filial rights.[122]

111. La. Civ. Code Ann. art. 198.
112. La. Civ. Code Ann. art. 198.
113. *See* La. Civ. Code Ann. art. 198.
114. La. Civ. Code Ann. art. 198.
115. La. Civ. Code Ann. art. 197.
116. La. Civ. Code Ann. art. 256.
117. La. Civ. Code Ann. art. 256.
118. *See* La. Civ. Code Ann. art. 196. The child must not be filiated to another man. *Id.*
119. La. Civ. Code Ann. art. 198. There are strict time requirements for filing the avowal action. *See id.*
120. La. Civ. Code Ann. art. 196. The presumption in favor of the child is unlimited. *See id.*
121. Full filial rights would include, among others, the man's right to inherit from the child. La. Civ. Code Ann. art. 196.
122. La. Civ. Code Ann. art. 198.

Additionally, if a tutor files an action on behalf of the child to establish paternity of the biological father, the father can reconvene for custody of the child if he is adjudged to be the father.[123] Notably, even if genetic tests prove that a man is the father, genetic tests alone do not convey filiation sufficient to receive custody.[124]

§ 6:10 Types of Custody Proceedings— Custody When the Parents Are Unmarried

Custody is routinely requested when parents are unmarried. Although the provisions governing custody of children appear in the Civil Code under Title V, "Divorce," they are equally applicable when the parties are not and were never married.[125] Ultimately, an action for custody without divorce can be instituted by a petition or rule for custody that is treated as an ordinary or summary proceeding, as the case may be.[126]

§ 6:11 Types of Custody Proceedings— Writ of Habeas Corpus

The habeas corpus writ is an extraordinary remedy at law that can be invoked to obtain the custody of minor children. Under Article 3821 of the Louisiana Code of Civil Procedure, the writ is a remedy that enables an individual to command a person who currently has physical custody of a child to produce the child and provide the authority for that custody to the court.[127] Proceeding by writ is appropriate only when brought by a person currently without custody who claims the child is detained by another without a legal right.[128]

The child must be physically produced at the proceeding on the writ.[129] If the child is not present, "a full and satisfactory explanation" must be given "as to why the minor could not or should not be produced; and if the custody [has] been transferred to another to state particularly to whom, at what time, for what cause, and by what authority"

123. La. Civ. Code Ann. art. 197.

124. State in Interest of P.P., 23-38 (La. App. 3 Cir. 06/21/23), 368 So. 3d 250.

125. *See, e.g.*, In re C.A.C., 2017-0108, pp. 4–5 (La. App. 4 Cir. 11/2/17), 231 So. 3d 58, 63 (showing the application of custody articles to same-sex, unmarried partners); Jones v. Coleman, 44,543, p. 1 (La. App. 2 Cir. 7/15/09), 18 So. 3d 153, 155 (showing the application of custody articles to unmarried parents).

126. La. Code Civ. Proc. Ann. arts. 851, 2592.

127. La. Code Civ. Proc. Ann. art. 3821.

128. *See* Griffith v. Roy, 269 So. 2d 217, 222 (La. 1972); State ex rel. Fazzio v. Triolo, 101 So. 211, 212 (La. 1924) ("The writ of habeas corpus properly issues at the instance of one who claims to be entitled to the custody of a child, to test his right to such custody, and to obtain possession of the minor, if it appear that he is entitled thereto.").

129. State ex rel. Collins v. Collins, 111 So. 2d 306, 308 (La. 1959).

the transfer was made.[130] The issuance of the writ forces individuals to present themselves to the court, along with the minor, whether or not they reside in Louisiana.[131]

The writ has been used in custody disputes between divorced parents.[132] The writ has also been permitted between parents during marriage, as long as they are actually living separate and apart.[133] As such, interspousal immunity from suit does not prevent one spouse from proceeding against the other under the writ of habeas corpus.[134]

Upon issuance of the writ, the court determines custody by taking into consideration "[t]he welfare of the child as well as the rights of the parents."[135] These proceedings essentially serve as an inquiry concerning "matters in which the state has an interest" but which involve private rights.[136] Ultimately, courts should "order the child placed in the custody of a proper person," whether that person is the parent or not.[137]

§ 6:12 Types of Custody Proceedings—Temporary Custody

Louisiana law permits an ex parte award of temporary custody in limited circumstances and only upon a showing of "immediate and irreparable injury" to the child.[138] Temporary custody is distinguishable from interim custody because interim custody contemplates an adversarial hearing after which a court needs additional evidence

130. Collins, 111 So. 2d at 308.

131. The long-arm statute can be used to serve out-of-state defendants. La. Stat. Ann. §§ 13:3201–:3207.

132. State ex rel. Jagneaux v. Jagneaux, 18 So. 2d 913 (La. 1944) (husband successfully maintained habeas corpus proceeding against his ex-wife to obtain custody of children born weeks after the wife left her husband); State ex rel. Billington v. Sacred Heart Orphan Asylum, 98 So. 406, 407 (La. 1923) (habeas corpus writ brought by mother against asylum where father had placed the child when they divorced); *see also* Snider v. Snider, 474 So. 2d 1374, 1376 (La. Ct. App. 2 Cir. 1985), *writ denied*, 478 So. 2d 903 (La. 1985); Mendivel v. Simpson, 247 So. 2d 182 (La. Ct. App. 3 Cir. 1971).

133. Stelly v. Montgomery, 347 So. 2d 1145, 1148 (La. 1977) (quoting State ex rel. Lasserre v. Michel, 30 So. 122, 125 (La. 1901)) ("We do not think that either husband or wife should be driven to the necessity of instituting an action of separation from bed and board or divorce, to have the matter of the legal custody of the children judicially inquired into. Actions of separation or divorce should not be forced; nor do we think that where husband and wife are, as a matter of fact, living apart, the spouse out of the possession of the children of the marriage, and claiming the legal right to have such possession, should be driven to force or to fraud to obtain the same.... It is right, proper, and legal for the party entitled to the possession of the child to obtain the same under the sanction of judicial proceedings.") (internal quotation marks omitted).

134. Stelly, 347 So. 2d at 1147.

135. State ex rel. Jagneaux v. Jagneaux, 18 So. 2d 913, 914 (La. 1944).

136. State ex rel. Aucoin v. Aucoin, 139 So. 645, 646 (La. 1932) (internal quotation marks omitted) (quoting State ex rel. Lasserre v. Michel, 30 So. 122 (La. 1901)).

137. Blaine v. Granger, 616 So. 2d 860, 861 (La. Ct. App. 3 Cir. 1993) (quoting Wood v. Beard, 290 So. 2d 675, 677 (La. 1974)) ("The welfare of the child, and not simply the enforcement of a parental right to the possession of the child, is of primary concern to the court.").

138. La. Code Civ. Proc. Ann. art. 3945.

or additional time before making a final award of custody.[139] Temporary custody is governed specifically by Article 3945 of the Louisiana Code of Civil Procedure and mandates specific rules under penalty of nullity.[140] A court is permitted to grant an ex parte order of temporary custody only if it clearly appears from verifiable facts that "immediate and irreparable injury will result to the child before the adverse party ... can be heard in opposition."[141] The applicant's attorney, or the applicant if unrepresented, must certify in writing that efforts have been made to notify the opposing party or, alternatively, that reasons exist such that notice should not be required.[142]

Because of the ex parte nature of the order, it expires by operation of law within 30 days of being signed and can be extended only once for 15 days on a showing of good cause.[143] During the duration of the temporary order, provisions requiring visitation by the adverse party, for "not less than 48 hours during any 15-day period," must be provided unless "immediate and irreparable injury will result to the child as a result of such visitation."[144]

The rule to show cause hearing to determine whether the adverse party should be awarded custody or visitation must be set within 30 days of the ex parte order of temporary custody.[145] Any ex parte order that fails to comply with these provisions shall be deemed null and void.[146]

---

139. *See* Ventura v. Rubio, 2000-0682, pp. 16–18 (La. App. 4 Cir. 3/16/01), 785 So. 2d 880, 892–93 (discussing temporary and interim custody orders). In *Ventura*, the court was concerned that many temporary or interim orders are issued without any explanation of the court's reasoning. *See id.* at 890. Without an adequate record for review, a reviewing court is unable to conduct a proper review to determine whether the trial court abused its discretion. As a result, temporary and interim orders effectively operate as permanent orders, "thereby denying the parties a timely and appropriate adjudication of the issues." *Id.* at 890–91. To remedy the problem, the court mandated that the trial court have a court reporter or transcription of the proceedings leading up to the interim order, set the matter for a final hearing before concluding the interim one, and refuse to extend or enter new interim orders before the final trial on the merits. *Id.* at 892.

140. La. Code Civ. Proc. Ann. art. 3945.

141. La. Code Civ. Proc. Ann. art. 3945(B)(1).

142. La. Code Civ. Proc. Ann. art. 3945(B)(2).

143. La. Code Civ. Proc. Ann. art. 3945(C). No considerable case law has developed the meaning of "good cause" in this context.

144. La. Code Civ. Proc. Ann. art. 3945(C)(2).

145. La. Code Civ. Proc. Ann. art. 3945(D). The custody judgment, as a result of the rule to show cause, becomes a final custody judgment.

146. La. Code Civ. Proc. Ann. art. 3945(E); Stroud v. Stroud, 43,003, pp. 11–12 (La. App. 2 Cir. 12/14/07), 973 So. 2d 865, 871–72 (reversing award of ex parte temporary custody order, finding no verified, specific facts showing irreparable harm or any efforts to give notice to opposing party); Varner v. Varner, 2022-1166 (La. App. 1 Cir. 02/24/23), 361 So. 3d 528 (holding the judgment on appeal was null and void because the judgment maintained ex parte custody beyond 45 days, which violates the provisions of La. C.C.P. art. 3945); Tabuchi v. Lingo, 588 So. 2d 795, 799 (La. Ct. App. 2 Cir. 1991) ("It is well-settled that an ex parte custody order granted by a trial judge without notice, service of pleadings, and without affording a hearing to the parent having custody of the child is null and without effect.") (citing McManus v. McManus, 528 So. 2d 696 (La. Ct. App. 2 Cir. 1988)).

The showing of immediate and irreparable injury to obtain a temporary order of custody is a high burden to meet and is within the sound discretion of the trial court. For example, in *Wilson v. Paul*, the maternal grandparents sought an ex parte order of temporary custody of their seven-year-old grandson.[147] Because of the parents' drug use, association with criminals, and ongoing violent relationship, the court found irreparable harm sufficient to justify a temporary sole custody award to the grandparents.[148] Courts have likewise found irreparable injury sufficient to award temporary custody of the child when the parent has substance abuse issues,[149] abandons the child,[150] or permits any form of abuse.[151] The trial court is vested with considerable discretion, and the interlocutory ruling is used as a vehicle to protect and serve the best interest of the child.[152]

In the event the court denies an ex parte request for temporary custody, it shall allocate time between the parents, "unless immediate or irreparable injury will result."[153] As an aside, this mandate should also apply to nonparents who have cared for the child and are seeking temporary custody. In *Trettin v. Trettin*,[154] the father sought an ex parte order of temporary custody three weeks after the court entered an interim award of joint custody pending a complete custody trial.[155] The court denied his motion and, as

---

147. Wilson v. Paul, 2008-382, p. 1 (La. App. 3 Cir. 10/1/08), 997 So. 2d 572, 573.

148. Wilson, 997 So. 2d at 574–75. Custody in the father was not considered because he tested positive for drug use during the proceedings. Wilson, 997 So. 2d at 574.

149. *See generally, e.g.*, Vidrine v. Vidrine, 2017-722 (La. App. 3 Cir. 5/21/18), 245 So. 3d 1266 (holding that the best interest of the child was served by naming his father as the domiciliary parent and modifying the parties' physical custodial schedule because the mother frequently drove with the minor child in her vehicle after she had been drinking, had developed a substance abuse problem, had anger management issues, mismanaged the child's medical needs, and was unable to exercise her physical custodial rights because of her alcohol addiction); Beene v. Beene, 43,845 (La. App. 2 Cir. 10/22/08), 997 So. 2d 169 (holding that the immediate and irreparable harm standard was met and that it was proper to award the father sole custody of his child when the mother had a history of substance abuse). *But see* Szwak v. Szwak, 49,939 (La. App. 2 Cir. 4/15/15), 163 So. 3d 911 (holding that mother's actions of driving while intoxicated and child's breaking of his femur while riding an ATV under mother's care did not constitute immediate and irreparable harm to satisfy the requirements for an ex parte order of temporary custody); Trettin v. Trettin, 37,260 (La. App. 2 Cir. 3/17/03), 839 So. 2d 1272 (holding that allegations of mother's excessive alcohol use and eating disorder did not represent an immediate and irreparable harm to the children required for an ex parte order of temporary custody).

150. *See generally* In re Custody of Landry, 95-0141 (La. App. 1 Cir. 10/6/95), 662 So. 2d 169 (noting that abandonment by the mother is often enough to award temporary custody).

151. *See generally* K.P. v. T.F.P., 2009-146 (La. App. 3 Cir. 10/7/09), 81 So. 3d 1 (abuse by live-in boyfriend enough to show irreparable harm). *But see* Trettin, 839 So. 2d at 1276 (finding no irreparable harm based on allegations of mother's drinking and eating disorder).

152. *See generally* Trettin v. Trettin, 37,260 (La. App. 2 Cir. 3/17/03), 839 So. 2d 1272; La. Code Civ. Proc. Ann. art. 2083(A); La. Civ. Code Ann. art. 131.

153. La. Code Civ. Proc. Ann. art. 3945(F).

154. Trettin, 839 So. 2d at 1272.

155. *Id.* at 1274.

required by Article 3945 of the Louisiana Code of Civil Procedure, awarded custody to the parents in accordance with its original interim order.[156]

The *Trettin* court also discussed the ability to appeal temporary orders.[157] Because an ex parte temporary order is not a final judgment, it is not immediately appealable.[158] Rather, it is an interlocutory ruling that can be appealed only if it causes irreparable injury.[159] Under prior law, courts found that for provisional custody orders, any irreparable injury necessary to appeal the interlocutory ruling was not present; rather, the proper procedural remedy for a party who objected to a provisional order was to seek an immediate trial on the rule for custody.[160] After the 1993 changes on custody, true "provisional custody" was replaced with final judgments of custody that are only considered "provisional" in the sense that the custody order can be altered due to a material change of circumstance.[161] The only court-ordered "provisional" custody that remains today exists under article 3945 for ex parte custody, under which immediate and irreparable injury must be shown.[162] Because an ex parte order of custody must be followed by an adversarial rule to show cause, the remedy for a party who objects to the ex parte order is to seek an adversarial hearing, after which an appealable final custody judgment will be entered.[163]

156. Trettin, 839 So. 2d at 1274.

157. Trettin, 839 So. 2d at 1275.

158. *See* La. Code Civ. Proc. Ann. arts. 1841, 208.

159. Trettin, 839 So. 2d at 1276.

160. Trettin, 839 So. 2d at 1274.

161. Trettin, 839 So. 2d at 1274.

162. Trettin, 839 So. 2d at 1274–75. *But see* Poole v. Poole, 41,960 (La. App. 2 Cir. 1/24/07), 948 So. 2d 382 (viewing an order that prohibited the parties from seeking a modification for one year as interlocutory in nature).

163. Trettin, 839 So. 2d at 1275; Coutee v. Hill, 43,292, pp. 5–6 (La. App. 2 Cir. 3/26/08), 978 So. 2d 1252, 1255 (denying appeal of an ex parte order of custody and noting that the "proper procedural vehicle" is a summary rule for the determination of custody). Courts have found that interim judgments of custody that have been in place for a period of years can only be modified upon a showing of a material change of circumstances. Chandler v. Chandler, 48,891, pp. 5–6 (La. App. 2 Cir. 12/13/13), 132 So. 3d 413, 417; *see also* Lawson v. Lawson, 48,296 (La. App. 2 Cir. 7/24/13), 121 So. 3d 769. *But see* Chandler, 48,891, p. 2; 132 So. 3d at 421 (Caraway, J., concurring) (arguing that the material change of circumstances test should not apply to an interim order and that the article 134 best-interest factors will suffice to make a proper determination).

§ 6:13 Types of Custody Proceedings—Voluntary Transfer of Custody in Juvenile Court

Louisiana provides a procedure in juvenile court under which parents can voluntarily transfer custody of a child to another responsible adult to provide care for the child.[164] In a voluntary transfer of custody proceeding, the juvenile court transfers custody of a child from a parent or parents to a nonparent.[165] Custody disputes among parents, on the other hand, are handled in civil matters by the district court.[166] When the parents transfer custody in juvenile court, they retain "residual parental rights," which include the "right of visitation, consent to adoption, right to determine religious affiliation, responsibility of support, and the right of inheritance from the child."[167]

The parents who wish to transfer custody must file a petition in the juvenile court in the parish where the parents reside or where the person to whom the transfer will be made resides.[168] The parents must affirm that they are "knowingly and voluntarily transferring custody," provide the "factual basis for the transfer of custody," and "set forth the nature, duration, and extent of the transfer of custody, including any terms and conditions."[169] The person accepting custody must execute an "Affidavit of Acceptance" stating that he knowingly and voluntarily accepts custody of the child under the conditions as agreed to by the parties.[170] The voluntary transfer of custody can move forward without a parent joining in the petition, but notice of the proceedings must be

164. *See* La. Child. Code Ann. arts. 1510-1523. The "Voluntary Transfer of Custody" statute actually permits transfer of custody not only to an individual, but to an agency or institution. The focus of this section, however, is on parents transferring custody of a child to another individual, not on agency or institutional custody. The juvenile court has "exclusive jurisdiction" to conduct proceedings relating to a parent's voluntary relinquishment of custody with two exceptions: (1) "[T]he district court may hear proceedings where custody is being determined by a writ of habeas corpus ..."; and (2) "the district court may determine custody which is incidental to the determination of cases pending in courts with civil jurisdiction." Medus v. Medus, 410 So. 2d 1261, 1264–65 (La. Ct. App. 3 Cir. 1982).

165. *See* La. Child. Code Ann. art. 1520; *see also* State ex rel. D.S.C., 2000-1697, pp. 1–3 (La. App. 3 Cir. 4/4/01), 782 So. 2d 1178, 1179–80. In *State ex rel. D.S.C.*, the court found that the parents' voluntary transfer of custody to the children's paternal grandfather was proper despite the paternal grandmother's emergency petition for temporary custody. State ex rel. D.S.C., 782 So. 2d at 1180. The court concluded that granting temporary custody to the paternal grandfather fell within the parents' wishes, and should that ever change, it would be revocable under articles 1522 and 1523 of the Louisiana Children's Code. *Id.*

166. *See* Lebo v. Lebo, 2004-0444, pp. 3–4 (La. App. 1 Cir. 6/25/04), 886 So. 2d 491, 493 (stating that "[t]he authority to modify a custody order is reserved to the courts pursuant to La. C.C. art. 131 *et seq.* for contested matters and La. Ch. C. art. 1510 *et seq.* for uncontested matters").

167. La. Child. Code Ann. arts. 116(24), 1511(3).

168. La. Child. Code Ann. arts. 1512–1514.

169. La. Child. Code Ann. art. 1515. The petition must contain additional allegations as set forth in the article and the accompanying form. *Id.*

170. La. Child. Code Ann. art. 1516.

served on the parent, or a curator must be appointed to accept service and represent the parent's interests.[171]

After a hearing, the court must render a written judgment that grants or denies the transfer of custody.[172] In preparation for the hearing, the court may make any orders that it deems necessary to protect the best interest of the child, including but not limited to a home study, the physical or mental examination of any party, and the appointment of counsel.[173] If, at any point, the parties wish to dismiss the proceedings and return the child to the parents, the court must be notified and may render an ex parte dismissal or order a hearing.[174] Otherwise, any modification or enforcement of the judgment transferring custody must be by order of the court on the motion of any party.[175] In the event the parents wish to revoke their consent without the agreement of the custodian, the court must conduct a contradictory hearing with the custodian to determine whether to dismiss the transfer of custody, with paramount consideration on the best interest of the child.[176]

In *In re C.L.S.*, the natural parents of C.L.S. voluntarily transferred custody to the child's great-aunt and then subsequently to the Strothers, a childless couple who were seeking to adopt.[177] The parents visited C.L.S. infrequently, and after approximately one year, the relationship between the couples deteriorated.[178] The natural parents attempted to regain custody of C.L.S., but the juvenile court terminated their parental rights, finding that they had abandoned C.L.S., and awarded custody to the Strothers.[179] The natural parents appealed.[180] The appellate court reversed on termination of parental rights but affirmed on custody.[181] The court concluded that the Strothers could not prove any of the grounds for termination of parental rights under the Children's Code.[182] On the issue of custody, because the natural parents had voluntarily

171. La. Child. Code Ann. art. 1517.

172. La. Child. Code Ann. arts. 1519–1520. Although a hearing is preferred, the court may waive a hearing. La. Child. Code Ann. art. 1519.

173. La. Child. Code Ann. art. 1518.

174. La. Child. Code Ann. art. 1522.

175. La. Child. Code Ann. art. 1522. "If the court is concerned about the child's protection upon the return [to the parents], the court may decide to refer the case for an investigation as a potential child in need of care...." La. Child. Code Ann. art. 1522 cmt.

176. La. Child. Code Ann. art. 1523. *See generally* In re K.R.W., 03-1372 (La. App. 5 Cir. 5/26/04), 875 So. 2d 903; In re C.L.S., 94-531 (La. App. 3 Cir. 11/2/94), 649 So. 2d 532; State ex rel. D.S.C., 2000-1697 (La. App. 3 Cir. 4/4/01), 782 So. 2d 1178.

177. *See* In re C.L.S., 649 So. 2d at 534–35. The natural parents did not want the child to be placed in foster care. *Id.*

178. In re C.L.S., 649 So. 2d at 535.

179. In re C.L.S., 649 So. 2d at 536.

180. In re C.L.S., 649 So. 2d at 536.

181. In re C.L.S., 649 So. 2d at 540.

182. In re C.L.S., 649 So. 2d at 537. Although placing C.L.S. in the physical custody of her natural parents would be "nefarious and detrimental" to her welfare, the court found that the parents' actions did not amount to abandonment of their child pursuant to article 1015(9) of the Louisiana Children's Code. *Id.*

transferred custody, the court was required to conduct a best interest analysis to decide whether to return the child to her natural parents.[183] Based on the testimony of the child psychologist,[184] the appellate court agreed with the juvenile court that it was in the child's best interest to remain in the custody of the Strothers, who could offer her a "caring, loving, stable, and safe environment."[185]

§ 6:14 Types of Custody Proceedings— Provisional Custody by Mandate

Provisional custody by mandate allows a parent, tutor, or a grandparent with custody, without the need for court intervention, to transfer custody of a child to another person for a limited period of time.[186] Provisional custody by mandate differs significantly from a full transfer of custody or adoption due to its temporary nature and because no court order is required.[187] The legislative scheme allows a parent to retain legal custody while choosing a worthy temporary substitute to care for the child until the mandate is revoked, renounced, or expires, or until a court appoints a tutor for the child.[188]

The scheme for provisional custody by mandate is found in Louisiana Revised Statutes Sections 9:951–:962.[189] The law is divided into two chapters.[190] Chapter 3 applies to persons having parental authority, which includes parents during marriage and ascendants awarded custody during marriage.[191] Chapter 3A applies to a tutor or a grandparent with custody after parental authority terminates.[192] It can also apply when a "third person other than an ascendant is awarded custody of the child during parental authority."[193]

---

183. In re C.L.S., 649 So. 2d at 538; *see also* La. Child. Code Ann. art. 1523.

184. In re C.L.S., 649 So. 2d at 539. According to the report of a child psychologist furnished during the trial, C.L.S. faced a "70% to 80% chance of being abused if she [was] returned to the custody of her natural parents." *Id.*

185. In re C.L.S., 649 So. 2d at 539.

186. La. Stat. Ann. §§ 9:951–:952, :961.

187. La. Stat. Ann. § 9:951 cmt. (c).

188. La. Stat. Ann. § 9:952; *see also* Lebo v. Lebo, 2004-0444, p. 2 (La. App. 1 Cir. 6/25/04), 886 So. 2d 491, 492 (father, who was the named domiciliary parent, executed a power of attorney in favor of his wife, the child's stepmother, who cared for the child while the father was deployed on military duty).

189. La. Stat. Ann. §§ 9:951–:962.

190. The division occurred in 2015 when the law on parental authority was revised. In the 2015 revision, ascendants who were given custody of a child during the marriage of the parents were given parental authority. Although parents are typically the only persons who exercise parental authority, the law was amended to provide for the reality that grandparents are raising grandchildren, often through legal custody awards as requested by the parents or awarded by a court during the marriage of the child's parents. Act No. 260, 2015 La. Acts 1794.

191. La. Stat. Ann. §§ 9:951–:954.

192. La. Stat. Ann. §§ 9:961–:962.

193. La. Stat. Ann. § 9:951 cmt. (a); La. Civ. Code Ann. art. 234.

Overall, the law sets forth those persons who are permitted to confer provisional custody,[194] those persons to whom provisional custody may be conferred,[195] the powers that are and may be associated with provisional custody,[196] and the methods of dissolution and termination of provisional custody.[197] Grandparents with custody, either during the parents' marriage or after it has ended, can confer the mandate.[198] Prior to 2016, the authority had been provided to parents alone[199] Additionally, when the parents are unmarried, or when a marriage between the parents ends, the child's natural tutor or a tutor with custody is likewise given the right to confer the mandate.[200]

Section 954 of the law provides a form for the act.[201] The law suggests that the form should be authentic, which requires a notary and two witnesses, but the form is merely "suggested" and nothing in the law requires an authentic form.[202] A public act, an act under private signature, or a letter that expressly conveys the transferred power to the provisional custodian is enough to create the mandate.[203] As a limited grant, the length of the mandate is not permitted to exceed one year from its date of execution.[204] Although no court has considered the effect of a mandate that is conferred for more than one year, the law contemplates that it must be re-conferred at the end of each year to be a valid transfer of custody.[205] Regardless of the term stipulated, the provisional custody ends when revoked by the person who conferred the mandate, when the mandatary resigns or renounces the mandate, 15 days after the death of the person conferring the mandate, or when a court appoints a tutor.[206] The provisional custodian must accept the mandate, but the statute does not require the acceptance to be in writing.[207]

The provisional custody by mandate can include the power to consent to and authorize medical care, enroll the child in school, discipline the child in a "reasonable manner," and undertake any other act that is "necessary for the shelter, support, and general welfare of the child."[208] Although not made express in the suggested statutory

---

194. *See* La. Stat. Ann. §§ 9:951, :961.

195. *See* La. Stat. Ann. §§ 9:951, :961.

196. La. Stat. Ann. § 9:953.

197. La. Stat. Ann. § 9:952.

198. La. Stat. Ann. §§ 9:951, :961. Prior law required the parents, during marriage, to act jointly to confer the mandate. La. Stat. Ann. § 9:951 cmt. (a).

199. La. Stat. Ann. § 9:961 cmt. (b) (2015).

200. La. Stat. Ann. § 9:961. The tutor with authority only over the property of the minor would not have the authority to confer the mandate. La. Stat. Ann. § 9:961 cmt. (a).

201. *See* La. Stat. Ann. § 9:954.

202. La. Stat. Ann. § 9:954.

203. Wooley v. City of Baton Rouge, 211 F.3d 913, 920 (5th Cir. 2000).

204. La. Stat. Ann. § 9:952.

205. In *Wooley v. City of Baton Rouge*, the court raised, but did not consider, the effect of an act that transferred custody until the young child reached the age of 18. Wooley, 211 F.3d at 920 n.27.

206. La. Stat. Ann. § 9:952. Although section 952 speaks to "a person having parental authority," section 961 makes this section applicable to tutors who do not have parental authority. La. Stat. Ann. § 9:961.

207. Wooley, 211 F.3d at 920 (citing La. Civ. Code art. 2988 (rev. 1997)); La. Stat. Ann. § 9:954 cmt.

208. La. Stat. Ann. § 9:953.

form, agreeing to serve as the provisional custodian necessarily includes liability for the acts of the minor.[209] It may not, however, include the ability to file suit on behalf of the minor, as that right lies with a tutor that must be authorized by a court.[210]

A provisional custodian who maintains the care, custody, and control of the child after the one-year period expires must seek either another provisional custody grant or permanent custody of the child, or risk losing custody to the grantor of the mandate.[211] In *Peters v. Allen Parish School Board*,[212] a mother left her two young children with Mr. Peters, a former boyfriend, when she moved and got married.[213] About one year after she left, she signed a provisional custody by mandate in favor of Mr. Peters.[214] Mr. Peters cared for the children like a father but did not seek legal custody of the children or an extension of the provisional custody.[215] About four years after she left, the mother went to the children's middle school and removed them, leaving the state.[216] The children were distraught and, as a result of her neglect, were eventually placed in foster care.[217] They subsequently ran away to find and live with Mr. Peters.[218] Mr. Peters sued the school for releasing the children to their mother.[219] The court absolved the school from liability, recognizing that Mr. Peter's provisional custody by mandate expired by its own terms one year after it was issued, and he did not take any legal steps to formalize custody.[220] At the time the mother arrived at the school, she was the proper custodian, even though she ultimately neglected the children.[221]

While provisional custodians maintain the status quo once they begin caring for a minor, the law only permits a one-year temporary custody without court intervention.[222] If the parent issuing the mandate leaves the child with the provisional custodian after the mandate ends, the custodian should seek an extension of the mandate by the

---

209. Article 2318 of the Louisiana Civil Code provides: "The father and mother are responsible for the damage occasioned by their minor child, who resides with them or who has been placed by them under the care of other persons, reserving to them recourse against those persons." La. Civ. Code Ann. art. 2318. Under provisional custody, when the parent has placed the child "under the care of" the provisional custodian, the parents could nonetheless be liable for any damage occasioned by the minor, with the right to sue the provisional custodian for the minor's acts while under his care and control. *See id.*

210. La. Code Civ. Proc. Ann. art. 683; *see also* Jones v. Allen Par. Corr. Ctr., No. 06-0056, 2008 WL 762077, at *5 (W.D. La. Mar. 20, 2008) (finding that the grandmother, who was the provisional custodian, was not the proper plaintiff to sue to enforce a right of an unemancipated minor because she had not been appointed by a court as a tutor for the minor child).

211. *See generally* Peters v. Allen Par. Sch. Bd., 2012-201 (La. App. 3 Cir. 10/3/12), 99 So. 3d 1117.

212. Peters, 99 So. 3d 1117.

213. Peters, 99 So. 3d at 1118.

214. *See* Peters, 99 So. 3d at 1118.

215. *See* Peters, 99 So. 3d at 1118, 1121.

216. Peters, 99 So. 3d at 1118–19.

217. *See* Peters, 99 So. 3d at 1119.

218. Peters, 99 So. 3d at 1119.

219. Peters, 99 So. 3d at 1119–20.

220. Peters, 99 So. 3d at 1121–22.

221. Peters, 99 So. 3d at 1121–22.

222. La. Stat. Ann. § 9:952.

parent, or if the parent is no longer a part of the child's life, seek legal custody. Without a court award of custody, the provisional custodian's rights will end, vesting custody back in the parent, which may not be in the child's best interest.

The Louisiana Attorney General has provided several opinions regarding the propriety and use of provisional custody by mandate. First, the parent need not be a Louisiana domiciliary to confer provisional custody on a Louisiana citizen.[223] Second, the provisional custody by mandate confers rights on the custodian on which a school district can rely.[224] For example, provisional custody by mandate can be used to enroll a child in a school district where the provisional custodian resides, rather than the district of the parent's residence.[225] And, once a parent has executed a valid provisional custody by mandate, local school boards are free to communicate only with the provisional custodian, even if the parents attempt to retain some rights, such as the ability to attend field trips, take part in parent-teacher conferences, sign forms, and pick up report cards for the child.[226]

§ 6:15 Custody Hierarchy

Prior to the revision of 1993, joint custody to the parents was presumed, as the arrangement would naturally be in the best interest of the child.[227] The inquiry was largely directed to the quality of the relationship between the parents and their willingness to encourage the child to have a close relationship with the other parent.[228] Following the revision, the sole focus was the best interest of the child.[229] As a result, the preference for court-ordered joint custody was replaced with the preference for parental agreement, even if the parents agreed to sole custody or nonparent custody.[230]

If the parents cannot reach an agreement or if the agreement is not in the best interest of the child, then custody must be awarded to the parents jointly.[231] If one parent can provide clear and convincing evidence that custody in that parent alone would serve the best interest of the child, then the court must award sole custody.[232] Last in the custody hierarchy is custody to a nonparent, which will only be granted when the nonparent can prove substantial harm to the child.[233] Each step in the custody hierarchy must be considered amidst the backdrop of the United States Constitution, which

223. *See, e.g.*, La. Att'y Gen. Op. No. 97-352 (1997).

224. *See* La. Att'y Gen. Op. No. 97-352 (1997).

225. *See, e.g.*, La. Att'y Gen. Op. No. 97-306 (1997).

226. *See* La. Att'y Gen. Op. No. 00-415 (2000).

227. *See* Section 6:4.

228. *See* Section 6:4.

229. Evans v. Lungrin, 97-0541, p. 7 (La. App. 3 Cir. 12/22/99), 708 So. 2d 731, 735–736.

230. La. Civ. Code Ann. art. 132.

231. La. Civ. Code Ann. art. 132.

232. La. Civ. Code Ann. art. 132; *see also* Harrell v. Harrell, 2017-0561, p. 7 (La. App. 1 Cir. 12/5/17), 236 So. 3d 704, 709; Griffith v. Latiolais, 2010-0754, p. 17 (La. 10/19/10), 48 So. 3d 1058, 1070.

233. La. Civ. Code Ann. art. 133; *see also* McCormic v. Rider, 2009-2584, pp. 2–3 (La. 2/12/10), 27 So. 3d 277, 279; In re C.A.C., 2017-0108, pp. 16–17 (La. App. 4 Cir. 11/2/17), 231 So. 3d 58, 69.

gives parents a constitutionally protected interest in the care, custody, and control of their children.[234]

§ 6:16 Custody Hierarchy— Constitutional Right of Parents to Custody

Parents have enjoyed the longstanding tradition of nurturing and rearing their children. This tradition has roots in natural law, the United States Constitution, and more modern-day state statutes. The basis of this parental right is found in the Due Process Clause of the Fourteenth Amendment, which provides that no state shall "deprive any person of life, liberty, or property, without due process of law."[235] While the Due Process Clause ensures fair process, it has long been held to include a substantive component providing "heightened protection against government interference with certain fundamental rights and liberty interests."[236]

The freedom of personal choice in matters of family life has historically been recognized as a fundamental liberty interest protected by the Fourteenth Amendment.[237] This interest has been further defined to encompass the special right of parents to the care, custody, and control of their children.[238] As a result, state statutes or policies that infringe on parents' rights have been struck down.[239]

The importance of this constitutionally protected right is reflected in Louisiana jurisprudence. Justice Tate, in his concurring opinion in *State ex rel. Paul v. Peniston*,[240] explained:

> The right of a parent to his child existed before governments or other social institutions of mankind. This natural right proceeds from our Creator and exists independently of the state; the state ... does not in my humble opinion possess the power to take away in favor of a stranger the God-given right of a

234. *See* Troxel v. Granville, 530 U.S. 57, 65 (2000); *see also* Susan E. Lawrence, *Substantive Due Process and Parental Rights: From* Meyer v. Nebraska *to* Troxel v. Granville, 8 J.L. & Fam. Stud. 71, 100 (2006).

235. U.S. Const. amend. XIV.

236. Washington v. Glucksburg, 521 U.S. 702, 720 (1997).

237. Santosky v. Kramer, 455 U.S. 745, 753 (1982) (citing over 50 years of United States Supreme Court precedent).

238. Troxel v. Granville, 530 U.S. 57, 66 (2000); *see also* Stanley v. Illinois, 405 U.S. 645, 651 (1972); Meyers v. Nebraska, 262 U.S. 390, 400 (1923).

239. *See, e.g.*, Santosky, 455 U.S. at 758 (striking down a New York statute that permitted the state to terminate parental rights under a "fair preponderance of the evidence" standard of proof, rather than the more stringent clear and convincing standard); Troxel, 530 U.S. at 75 (striking down a Washington state statute that permitted a court to grant visitation of a child, over the parent's objection, upon a showing that visitation was in the child's best interest); Stanley, 405 U.S. at 658 (concluding that "all Illinois parents," including unwed fathers, "are constitutionally entitled to a hearing on their fitness before their children are removed from their custody").

240. State ex rel. Paul v. Peniston, 105 So. 2d 228 (La. 1958).

> parent to his child, in the absence of the parent's forfeiture or abandonment of such right or of positive detriment to the child.[241]

Louisiana's laws of custody reflect the paramount right of parents on issues involving their children. The court must honor the parental choice of custody unless that choice runs afoul of the child's best interest.[242] For a parent to be denied joint custody of their child, the other parent must prove by the heightened burden of clear and convincing evidence that sole custody in their favor alone will serve the child's best interest.[243] Finally, to deprive the parents of custody, a nonparent must prove substantial harm to the child if custody were to rest with the parents.[244]

Louisiana's grandparent visitation rules, rather than its custody rules, have been the subject of constitutional challenges. Visitation for grandparents appears in both the revised statutes and the Civil Code. Louisiana Revised Statutes Section 9:344 permits grandparent visitation with a grandchild if their child is deceased, interdicted, or incarcerated, as long as it serves the best interest of the child.[245] Several courts have upheld the constitutionality of the statute under the due process challenge that the statute violates a parent's fundamental right to make decisions regarding the care, custody, and control of their children.[246] Specifically, in *Galjour v. Harris*, the court found the visitation statute to be narrowly tailored so that it did not infringe on the parents' liberty interest to raise their children without unnecessary interference.[247]

In 2012, the Louisiana Legislature amended Article 136 of the Civil Code, which permitted a grandparent to seek reasonable visitation with a grandchild if it was in the child's best interest.[248] Per that revision, extraordinary circumstances such as death, incarceration, or interdiction were no longer prerequisites for a grandparent to seek visitation. The article was amended again in 2018, with due concern over constitutional issues, to permit a grandparent to seek reasonable visitation when it is in the best interest of the child, only when married parents have filed for divorce or when the parents are unmarried and not living together as though they are married.[249] Are these limitations enough to protect the article from a facial constitutional challenge? Louisiana Revised Statutes Section 9:344 contains more significant limitations and now applies

---

241. State ex rel. Paul, 105 So. 2d at 232.

242. La. Civ. Code Ann. art. 132.

243. La. Civ. Code Ann. art. 132.

244. La. Civ. Code Ann. art. 132.

245. La. Stat. Ann. § 9:344 (2019); Galjour v. Harris, 2000-2696, p. 11 (La. App. 1 Cir. 3/28/01), 795 So. 2d 350, 358.

246. Garner v. Thomas, 2008-1448, p. 15 (La. App. 4 Cir. 05/28/09), 13 So. 3d 784, 792; *see also* Babin v. McDaniel, 2005-2455 (La. App. 1 Cir. 03/24/06), 934 So. 2d 69; Galjour, 795 So. 2d at 358.

247. Galjour, 795 So. 2d at 358.

248. La. Civ. Code Ann. art. 136 (2012). The court is required to hold a contradictory hearing before awarding the grandparent visitation "to determine whether the court should appoint an attorney to represent the child." *Id.*

249. La. Civ. Code Ann. art. 136. The article applies to unmarried parents, but if the parents are unmarried and cohabitating in the manner of married persons, then La. Stat. Ann. § 9:344 will apply. *See also* Section 6:49.

when the parents of the child are married and have not filed for divorce or when the parents are living together.[250] With these recent changes, a constitutional claim may still be imminent.

Harkening back to the United States Supreme Court's mandate in *Troxel v. Granville*, a visitation statute that is "breathtakingly broad" may permit a court to disregard the decision of a parent in favor of what the court believes is in the child's best interest, rather than giving the parent the right to make decisions regarding the rearing of their child.[251] While grandparents naturally may enjoy a closer relationship with a grandchild than other relatives, a showing of best interest alone, without due deference given to the parent's decision to limit or prevent visitation, will run afoul of the parent's constitutional guarantees.

§ 6:17 Custody Hierarchy— Parental Agreement

Article 132 of the Civil Code provides that "[i]f the parents agree who is to have custody, the court shall award custody in accordance with their agreement unless ... the best interest of the child requires a different award."[252] In other words, if the parents can agree on custody, the court must consider whether their proposal is in the child's best interest before accepting their agreement. The parents need not agree to joint custody; they can agree to custody in one parent or custody in a third person, provided the agreement serves the best interest of the child.[253]

Courts have various tools at their disposal to encourage parents to agree. The court can require parents to "mediate their differences ... for a period not to exceed 30 days."[254] The court can also require the parents to attend a court-approved seminar to educate the parties of the needs of children while adjusting to the divorce.[255] Evaluations of the parties or the child that are conducted by a licensed mental health professional can also be ordered by the court, which can give the parents an unbiased view of the child's behavior and relationship with the parents.[256] The court can appoint an attorney to represent the child if, after a contradictory hearing, it determines that doing so is in the best interest of the child.[257]

The preference for parental agreement supports "the God-given" constitutionally protected right of parents to care and control their children.[258] A parent's obligation

250. *See* La. Stat. Ann. § 9:344.

251. *See* Troxel v. Granville, 530 U.S. 57, 67 (2000).

252. La. Civ. Code Ann. art. 132.

253. *See* La. Civ. Code Ann. art. 132 cmt. (b).

254. La. Stat. Ann. § 9:332(A). *See* Section 6:53.

255. La. Stat. Ann. § 9:331.2.

256. La. Stat. Ann. §§ 9:331, 331.3. *See* Section 6:54.

257. La. Stat. Ann. § 9:345.

258. State ex rel. Paul v. Peniston, 105 So. 2d 228, 232 (La. 1958) (Tate, J., concurring); *see also* Kenneth Rigby, *1993 Custody and Child Support Legislation*, 55 La. L. Rev. 103, 108 (1994) ("During

to parent his child does not expire at the end of marriage—it exists as a result of parenthood—and the court must allow the parent to make choices in the best interest of the child.

Parents have broad discretion over provisions in their agreement. Courts have explained that "a bilateral contract ... signed by the parties and accepted by the court ... has binding force from the voluntary acquiescence of the parties, not from the court's adjudication."[259] Courts will uphold an agreement of custody as long as the provisions are in the best interest of the child and do not violate public policy.[260] For example, courts have upheld agreements to pay for college after the child reaches the age of majority.[261] The agreement must be valid under general contract principles, and if so, the court will enforce the free consent of the parents.[262]

Some courts have upheld agreements by parents to apply the heightened *Bergeron* standard to subsequent custody modifications while others have not. Generally, when the court issues a consent decree in accordance with the parents' agreement, any subsequent modification of custody will require the party seeking the modification to prove "a material change of circumstance[] since the original decree was entered, and ... that the proposed modification is in the best interest of the child."[263] When the court issues a considered decree after a hearing during which parental fitness is examined, any subsequent modifications require the party to prove a heightened evidentiary standard known as the *Bergeron* standard. The *Bergeron* standard requires the proponent of the change to prove the heavy burden that "continuation of the present custody is so deleterious to the child as to justify a modification of the custody decree, or ... that the harm likely to be caused by a change of environment is substantially outweighed by its advantages to the child."[264]

The Louisiana Second Circuit Court of Appeal, in *Adams v. Adams*, upheld a stipulation in a joint custody agreement that "any action to modify custody would be gov-

---

the marriage, the decisions of the parents with respect to their children, absent serious harmful effects to the children, are not reviewable by the state. This provision reflects the view that, in the marriage-terminating and post-marriage periods, the agreement of the parents as to custody, absent harm to the child, should continue to be respected.").

259. Gray v. Gray, 37,884, p. 3 (La. App. 2 Cir. 12/12/03), 862 So. 2d 1097, 1099.

260. The cause of one's obligation is unlawful if it "would produce a result prohibited by law or against public policy." La. Civ. Code Ann. art. 1968.

261. Gray, 862 So. 2d at 1098.

262. Gray, 862 So. 2d at 1099. The court in *Gray* construed "monies necessary for the college education of the minor children" to be tuition at any Louisiana state supported college, textbook and lab expenses, dormitory fees, spending money, meal ticket, laundry allowance, transportation allowance, but not funds for a car, fraternity or sorority expenses, entertainment or "beer-drinking" expenses. *Id.* at 1100; *see also* Miller v. Miller, 44,163, p. 6 (La. App. 2 Cir. 1/14/09), 1 So. 3d 815, 818–19 (setting aside a provision related to the payment of college expenses for vagueness and ambiguity); Headrick v. Headrick, No. 2006-2292, 2007 WL 2684886, *5 (La. App. 1 Cir. 9/14/07) (upholding a percentage of college expenses to be paid by each parent).

263. Evans v. Lungrin, 97-0541, 97-0577, pp. 12–13 (La. 2/6/98), 708 So. 2d 731, 738.

264. Bergeron v. Bergeron, 492 So. 2d 1193, 1200 (La. 1986) (internal quotation marks omitted).

erned by the heavy burden applicable to considered decrees as set forth in *Bergeron*."[265] In a modification request years after the agreement, one parent challenged the provision as unenforceable.[266] The court disagreed, explaining that parties are free to contract for any object that is not a violation of public policy, and it could find no policy reason to infringe on the freedom of contract.[267] In fact, the court concluded that the agreement supported the policies that underlie *Bergeron*, including the "protection against harm done to children by custody litigation and threats thereof, changes in custody, continued parental conflict, and erroneous judgments."[268] One judge dissented from the majority, arguing that an agreement to impose the *Bergeron* standard negates "the opportunity for a judicial assessment of parental fitness" and is therefore against public policy.[269]

The Louisiana Fifth Circuit Court of Appeal in *Rodriguez v. Wyatt* agreed with the *Adams* dissent.[270] Again, the parents in an agreement stipulated to the *Bergeron* standard for any subsequent modifications.[271] The court disagreed with the majority opinion in *Adams* and concluded that "parties cannot shield themselves from custody modifications by stipulating to *Bergeron* in cases where there has been no judicial assessment of parental fitness."[272] The court left open the question of whether parties, who enter into an agreement after a judicial assessment of parental fitness, can agree to the heightened *Bergeron* standard.[273] The Louisiana Supreme Court has not yet spoken on this issue.

Courts will not uphold a provision in a parental agreement that it deems to be unlawful or against public policy.[274] An agreement that permanently negates the requirement to pay child support is contrary to the nonwaivable duty of support that fathers and mothers owe to their minor children and will not be upheld.[275] Further, an agreement by parents to share the status of domiciliary parent, as co-domiciliaries, is no longer permitted.[276] In 2015, the Louisiana Supreme Court settled a circuit split and concluded that co-domiciliary parents are not permitted under the statu-

265. Adams v. Adams, 39,424, p. 1 (La. App. 2 Cir. 4/6/05), 899 So. 2d 726, 727.

266. *See* Adams, 899 So. 2d at 728.

267. Adams, 899 So. 2d at 730.

268. Adams, 899 So. 2d at 730.

269. Adams, 899 So. 2d at 732 (Gaskins, J., dissenting).

270. *See* Rodriguez v. Wyatt, 11-82, pp. 11–12 (La. App. 5 Cir. 12/12/11), 102 So. 3d 109, 116.

271. *See* Rodriguez, 102 So. 3d at 116.

272. Rodriguez, 102 So. 3d at 116. *Compare* Poole v. Poole, 41,220, p. 4 (La. App. 2 Cir. 3/22/06), 926 So. 2d 60, 63 (refusing to apply the *Bergeron* standard to an agreement that was entered into after the court took evidence of parental fitness of one of the parties but that contained no stipulation regarding the *Bergeron* standard), *with* Long v. Long, 28,763, pp. 4–5 (La. App. 2 Cir. 12/11/96), 684 So. 2d 1099, 1101 (applying the *Bergeron* standard to an agreement that was entered into after the court began a hearing on parental fitness and that contained a provision stipulating to the *Bergeron* standard).

273. Rodriguez, 102 So. 3d at 116.

274. La. Civ. Code Ann. art. 1968.

275. Durfee v. Durfee, 44,281, pp. 4–5 (La. App. 2 Cir. 5/13/09), 12 So. 3d 984, 988.

276. *See* Hodges v. Hodges, 2015-0585, p. 18 (La. 11/23/15), 181 So. 3d 700, 711 ("We hold that R.S. 9:335 precludes the designation of 'co-domiciliary parents' in a joint custody arrangement.").

tory scheme, and the failure to name a single domiciliary parent is permitted in only two instances—when good cause is shown or when there is a joint implementation order to the contrary.[277] Parties can therefore outline who is to have decision-making authority over major decisions, like education, healthcare, religion, and travel and leave day-to-day decision-making to the parent with whom the child is residing at the time.[278] This may be particularly useful in a shared custody arrangement because there is not one parent with whom the child primarily resides, the statutory definition of a domiciliary parent.[279]

§ 6:18 Custody Hierarchy—Court-Ordered Joint Custody

In the absence of an agreement by the parents, or if their agreement is not in the best interest of the child, the court must award joint custody as a general rule.[280] A court will deviate from joint custody in the parents when there is a history of family violence or clear and convincing evidence is presented that sole custody in one parent is in the best interest of the child.[281] Prior to 1994, Louisiana law provided a rebuttable presumption that joint custody was in the best interest of the child, but that presumption was abandoned in the revision of 1993 in favor of a custody hierarchy, with joint custody ranking after the agreement of the parents, with focus on the best interest of the child.[282]

Louisiana Revised Statutes Section 9:335 provides detailed requirements for an award of joint custody. When the court awards joint custody, it must "render a joint custody implementation order except for good cause shown."[283] No particular form is

277. *See* Hodges, 181 So. 3d at 711.

278. *See* Ehlinger v. Ehlinger, 2017-1120 (La. App. 1 Cir. 5/29/18), 251 So. 3d 418, 426 (concluding that to meet the requirements of *Hodges*, an implementation order without a domiciliary parent named should "at a minimum allocate the legal authority and responsibility for major decisions, such as medical care, elective surgery, dental or orthodontic care, and school and/or preschool choices"); Coody v. Coody, 2020-071 (La. App. 3 Cir. 11/12/20), 307 So.3d 1093 (affirming trial court that issued an implementation order granting father the authority to make decisions regarding the children's medical needs and extracurricular activities because doing so diffused animosity and improved communication between the parents as well as communication between the father and the children).

279. Hodges, 181 So. 3d at 720 (Hughes, J., dissenting) (arguing that shared custody necessitates a finding of co-domiciliaries); *see also* La. Stat. Ann. § 9:335 ("The domiciliary parent is the parent with whom the child shall primarily reside. . . .").

280. La. Civ. Code Ann. art. 132.

281. La. Civ. Code Ann. art. 132; *see also* La. Stat. Ann. § 9:364(A) ("There is created a presumption that no parent who has a history of perpetrating family violence . . . shall be awarded sole or joint custody of children.").

282. *See* Section 6:4; *see also* Simmons v. Hodges, 2022-589, p. 10 (La. App. 3 Cir. 03/08/23), 358 So. 2d 251, 258 (finding equal sharing of time was neither feasible nor in the best interest of the child because of the parents' inability to agree on a custody arrangement and their refusal to "bend an inch").

283. La. Stat. Ann. § 9:335(A)(1).

mandated,[284] but it must provide for three things: (1) the allocation of physical custody of the child; (2) the allocation of legal authority and responsibility of the parents (i.e., legal custody); and (3) the duties of an evacuating parent.[285] The trial court is vested with a great deal of discretion when establishing the particulars of joint custody and can be overturned only when there is an abuse of that discretion.[286]

§ 6:19 Custody Hierarchy— Court-Ordered Joint Custody— Physical Custody

In allocating physical custody between the parents, the goal is "frequent and continuing contact with both parents."[287] Under prior law, equal physical custody was presumed to be in the best interest of the child.[288] After the 1993 revision, equal time is preferable, but only "[t]o the extent it is feasible and in the best interest of the child."[289] Only when it can be shown that 50-50 shared physical custody is both feasible and in the best interest of the child, can such an arrangement be ordered; otherwise, if both prongs are not met, then the court should institute a custody arrangement that ensures each parent has frequent and continuing contact with the child.[290]

---

284. Hodges v. Hodges, 2015-0585, p. 18 (La. 11/23/15), 181 So. 3d 700, 711; Caro v. Caro, 95-0173, p. 2 (La. App. 1 Cir. 10/6/95), 671 So. 2d 516, 518.

285. La. Stat. Ann. § 9:335(A)(2) (stating that the implementation order must include a provision that says when a parent evacuates with the child for an emergency or disaster, if the parties' exercise of custody becomes impossible, they must remain in contact regarding the child's safe evacuation, location during and after the emergency or disaster, and an interim custody plan until the order custody can be resumed).

286. Thompson v. Thompson, 532 So. 2d 101, 101 (La. 1988); *see also* Bergeron v. Bergeron, 492 So. 2d 1193, 1196 (La. 1986).

287. La. Stat. Ann. § 9:335(A)(2)(a); *see also, e.g.*, Bridges v. Bridges, 09-742, pp. 6–7 (La. App. 5 Cir. 2/9/10), 33 So. 3d 914, 918–19 (finding that custody every other weekend, six weeks over the summer, and alternating holidays ensured frequent and continuing contact with the child); Schaeffer v. Schaeffer, 40,562, p. 4 (La. App. 2 Cir. 10/26/05), 914 So. 2d 631, 634 (finding that physical custody of the child for approximately 109 days per year was sufficient to afford the non-domiciliary parent frequent and continuing contact with the child); Aucoin v. Weaver, 2020-364, p. 6 (La. App. 1 Cir. 11/06/20), 315 So. 3d 296, 300 (finding that custody of approximately 82% of the custodial time to one parent and only 18% to the other was not frequent and continuing contact with the child).

288. La. Civ. Code Ann. art. 131(D) (1992). *See also* Section 6:3.

289. La. Stat. Ann. § 9:335(A)(2)(b); *see also, e.g.*, Molony v. Harris, 2010-1316, p. 18 (La. App. 4 Cir. 2/23/11), 60 So. 3d 70, 81–82 (finding that a 50-50 split, one week on and one week off, was in the best interest of the child because both parents worked at home and had "flexibility in their work schedules to accommodate [the child's] needs"); Semmes v. Semmes, 45,006, p. 11 (La. App. 2 Cir. 12/16/09), 27 So. 3d 1024, 1031–32 (failing to award father "equal time" because of his "unwillingness to communicate" with the mother); Evans v. Lungrin, 97-0541, p. 15 (La. 2/6/98), 708 So. 2d 731, 739 (holding that equal, four-month alternating arrangement was not in the best interest of the child because the parents lived in different states and the child was very young).

290. *See* Penn v. Penn, 09-213, pp. 9–10 (La. App. 5 Cir. 10/27/09), 28 So. 2d 304, 310; Beadle v. Beadle, 2020-264 (La. App. 1 Cir. 12/30/20), 318 So. 3d 902.

With a focus on the child's best interest, substantial time, rather than strict equality of time, is required under the legislative scheme.[291] In *Schaeffer v. Schaeffer*, the mother argued that alternating weekends, two weeks each month over the summer, and alternating holidays made her a "mere visitor" in her child's life and did not constitute frequent and continuing contact.[292] The court disagreed, concluding that her physical custody schedule, which amounted to 109 days per year, was sufficient to afford the mother substantial time as well as frequent and continuing contact with her child.[293]

On the other hand, in *Wilson v. O'Neal*, the father made the same arguments based on a physical custody schedule of every other weekend, nine days over the summer, and some holiday time.[294] The court found that 67 days per year, and in some cases 11-day spans when the child would not see the father, did not amount to frequent and continuing contact with the father.[295] The court amended the order to award the father every other Wednesday night and concluded that in all other respects, the schedule was affirmed.[296] With an award of 26 more days, the court determined that 93 days, without long spans away from the father, reached the threshold of frequent and continuing contact.[297]

While each decision is fact-specific, in general, courts consider every other weekend, one day during the alternating week, and the sharing of the summer and holidays to be a typical physical custody schedule for the non-domiciliary parent.[298] Courts are more likely to award an equal sharing of time when the parents live a short distance from one another, live near the child's school, and are able to co-parent effectively with one another.[299]

If a joint custody order provides that each parent shall have physical custody for an equal or approximately equal amount of time, this is referred to as "shared custody."[300] If the joint custody order specifies that each parent is designated the domiciliary par-

---

291. Brewer v. Brewer, 39,647, p. 9 (La. App. 2 Cir. 3/2/05), 895 So. 2d 745, 750; McKenzie v. Cuccia, 2004-0112, p. 5 (La. App. 4 Cir. 6/23/04), 879 So. 2d 335, 339; *see also* Ellinwood v. Breaux, 32,730, p. 5 (La. App. 2 Cir. 3/1/00), 753 So. 2d 977, 980; Nichols v. Nichols, 32,219, p. 8 (La. App. 2 Cir. 9/22/99), 747 So. 2d 120, 125.

292. Schaeffer v. Schaeffer, 40,562, p. 2 (La. App. 2 Cir. 10/26/05), 914 So. 2d 631, 633.

293. *See* Schaeffer, 914 So. 2d at 634; *see also* Nichols, 747 So. 2d at 126 (finding that physical custody one week a month during the school year, two weeks during the summer, and one-half of all holiday periods was sufficient custodial time to the non-domiciliary parent). *But see* Ellinwood, 753 So. 2d at 980 (noting that in some cases, granting the non-domiciliary parent less than 100 days of custody has been grounds for reversal).

294. Wilson v. O'Neal, 50,711, pp. 6–7 (La. App. 2 Cir. 4/13/16), 193 So. 3d 207, 211–12.

295. Wilson, 193 So. 3d at 214.

296. *See* Wilson, 193 So. 3d at 214.

297. Wilson, 193 So. 3d at 211–12.

298. *See* Schaeffer, 914 So. 2d at 633.

299. Swope v. Swope, 521 So. 2d 656, 659 (La. Ct. App. 1 Cir. 1988); *see also* Meylian v. Meylian, 478 So. 2d 218, 220–22 (La. Ct. App. 3 Cir. 1985); Peyton v. Peyton, 457 So. 2d 321, 323 (La. Ct. App. 2 Cir. 1984); Duhe v. Duhe, 451 So. 2d 1198, 1202 (La. Ct. App. 5 Cir. 1984).

300. La. Stat. Ann. § 9:315.9.

ent of at least one child, this is referred to as "split custody."[301] These designations are significant for purposes of child support.[302] Physical custody is only one aspect of joint custody; the joint implementation order must also provide for legal custody—decision-making authority over the child as well as certain duties of evacuating parents.[303]

§ 6:20 Custody Hierarchy— Court-Ordered Joint Custody— Legal Custody

Legal custody, as compared to physical custody, gives the parents the authority and responsibility to make decisions regarding the child. Joint custody, by its very nature, gives both parents decision-making authority, but equal decision-making authority is not generally permitted under the statute. In a joint custody decree, the court is required to name a domiciliary parent unless "there is an implementation order to the contrary or for other good cause shown."[304]

The domiciliary parent has the authority to make the final decision affecting the child if the parents disagree "unless the implementation order provides otherwise."[305] Joint custody obligates parents to confer with one another when making decisions,[306] but if the parents disagree, the domiciliary parent's decision will prevail.[307] This authority is not boundless. "All major decisions made by the domiciliary parent concerning the child shall be subject to review by the court on motion of the other parent."[308] The decision of the domiciliary parent is presumed to be in the best interest of the child, but this presumption can be rebutted by the other parent in a court proceeding.[309] Major decisions could include significant medical and dental treatments or surgeries, school

301. La. Stat. Ann. § 9:315.10.

302. *See* La. Stat. Ann. § 9:315.9–.10.

303. La. Stat. Ann. § 9:335(A)(3).

304. La. Stat. Ann. 9:335(B)(1). The court in *Underwood v. Underwood*, 2021-0277 (La. App. 1 Cir. 10/21/21), 332 So. 3d 128, allocated to the father decision-making authority regarding educational decisions, extracurricular activities, and exchange logistics, and allocated to the mother decision making authority regarding the child's medical decisions and general welfare decisions.

305. La. Stat. Ann. 9:335(B)(3). If the non-domiciliary parent does not want the domiciliary parent to have decision-making authority over one or more aspects of the child's life, those limitations can be placed in the joint custody implementation order. *See* La. Stat. Ann. 9:335(A)(3) ("The implementation order shall allocate the *legal authority* and responsibility of the parents.") (emphasis added).

306. St. Germain v. St. Germain, 2019-0067 (La. App. 1 Cir. 9/11/19); 282 So. 3d 282 (trial court ordered sanctions of $300 and attorney's fees and costs of approximately $10,800 against Mother for her refusal to confer with Father and her failure to provide, or timely provide, information about the health, education, and welfare of their minor child).

307. *See* La. Stat. Ann. § 9:335(B)(3); *see also* La. Stat. Ann. § 9:336 ("Joint custody obligates the parents to exchange information concerning the health, education, and welfare of the child and to confer with one another in exercising decision-making authority.").

308. La. Stat. Ann. 9:335(B)(3).

309. *See* La. Stat. Ann. 9:335(B)(3).

choice, and international travel, but would not include decisions regarding minor issues such as bedtime, curfew, or chores.[310]

If no domiciliary parent is named in the joint custody order and there is no implementation order to the contrary, then the parents enjoy the rights and responsibilities as outlined in the Civil Code title on parental authority.[311] Until the comprehensive revision of the chapter on parental authority in 2015, the law contained the "father-knows-best provision" that identified the father as the decision-maker and administrator of the minor's estate.[312] As a result, the father had the ultimate decision-making authority for the child.[313] The revision provides for equal authority stating, "The father and mother who are married to each other have parental authority over their minor child during the marriage."[314] Therefore, today, the failure to name a domiciliary parent results in equal decision-making authority over the child.

The designation of "co-domiciliary" parents was born after the revision of 1993, when parties did not want to designate a domiciliary parent and courts were reluctant to choose one parent over the other when physical custody was shared. The designation had no basis in the law but had been agreed on by parents and ordered by some courts.[315]

The law on joint custody requires the court to "designate a domiciliary parent except when there is an implementation order to the contrary or for other good cause shown."[316] Some courts construed the law to give a court discretion *not* to designate a domiciliary parent when an exception applied,[317] while others viewed the law as less restrictive, permitting a court to name co-domiciliaries when an exception applied.[318]

---

310. *See* Gutierrez v. Bruno, 2019-1537 (La. App. 1 Cir. 8/5/20), 310 So. 3d 560 (enforcing domiciliary parent's decision that the children attend one school because children were falling behind due to the alternating school schedule); Ehlinger v. Ehlinger, 2017-1120, p. 7 (La. App. 1 Cir. 5/29/18), 251 So. 3d 418, 424.

311. La. Stat. Ann. § 9:335(C). *See generally* Title VII of Book I of the Louisiana Civil Code on parental authority; *see also* Chapter 9.

312. *See* La. Civ. Code Ann. art. 216 (repealed by Act No. 260, 2015 La. Acts 1794).

313. *See* La. Civ. Code Ann. art. 216 (repealed by Act No. 260, 2015 La. Acts 1794).

314. La. Civ. Code Ann. art. 221.

315. *See* Hodges v. Hodges, 14-1575, pp. 9–10 (La. App. 1 Cir. 03/06/15), 166 So. 3d 348, 354–55 (permitting co-domiciliaries); *see also* Distefano v. Distefano, 14-1318 (La. App. 1 Cir. 01/22/15), 169 So. 3d 437 (permitting co-domiciliaries); Stewart v. Stewart, 11-1334 (La. App. 3 Cir. 03/07/12), 86 So. 3d 148 (permitting co-domiciliaries); *cf.* Hanks v. Hanks, 13-1442 (La. App. 4 Cir. 04/16/14), 140 So. 3d 208 (co-domiciliaries not permitted); Molony v. Harris, 10-1316 (La. App. 4 Cir. 02/23/11), 60 So. 3d 70 (co-domiciliaries not permitted); Ketchum v. Ketchum, 39,082 (La. App. 2 Cir. 09/01/04), 882 So. 2d 631 (co-domiciliaries not permitted).

316. La. Stat. Ann. § 9:335(B)(1).

317. Molony, 60 So. 3d at 82 (reversing the trial court's designation of co-domiciliary parents because there was no authority in the law to do so); Ketchum, 882 So. 2d at 639 (finding that there was no authority in the law for the trial court to designate "co-domiciliary" parents).

318. Stewart, 86 So. 3d at 155 ("If a designation of co-domiciliary parents is in the best interest of the child, then we see no reason to reverse such a decision of the trial court."); *see also* Beaudion v. Beaudion, 11-53, pp. 10–11 (La. App. 5 Cir. 12/29/11), 83 So. 3d 355, 361 (finding "good cause shown" to name co-domiciliaries based on the trial court's determination that shared custody is in the best interest of the children); St. Philip v. Montalbano, 2012-1090 (La. App. 4 Cir. 01/09/13), 108 So. 3d 277.

The Louisiana Supreme Court spoke on the issue in 2015 and concluded that courts could only designate a *single* domiciliary parent.[319]

In *Hodges v. Hodges*, the Louisiana Supreme Court settled the circuit split, concluding that "the plain language of La. R.S. 9:335 manifests the legislature's clear intent to establish a custodial system in which a child has a domiciliary parent and no more than one such parent.... Although each parent can share physical custody, the court can only designate a single domiciliary parent."[320] The court tipped its hat to the appellate courts, recognizing that the well-intentioned designation of co-domiciliary parents was used as a panacea to provide both parents with shared legal and physical custody.[321] That desire, the court explained, can be accomplished through the exceptions to the statute, when there is an implementation order to the contrary or for other good cause shown.[322] It explained that courts could choose not to designate a domiciliary parent at all and instead allocate the authority of each parent in the implementation order.[323]

For example, a court could give one parent the authority to make final decisions regarding major aspects of the child's life, such as education, religion, healthcare, or travel, and the other parent could make final decisions regarding the others.[324] As is customary when co-parenting and as legislated by other states, the court could authorize daily decision-making authority to be permitted by the parent with whom the child is residing at the time.[325] Daily decision-making can only involve minor decisions, though, as legal authority to make major decisions must be allocated between the parents.[326]

In *Hodges*, the court did not thoroughly discuss the second exception of "good cause shown."[327] This exception could be used to permit the court to issue a consent judgment based on the parents' agreement not to designate a domiciliary parent. Without a named domiciliary parent, the parents would enjoy equal rights. Section 9:335 of the Revised Statutes incorporates Title VII of Book I of the Civil Code, which includes the articles on parental authority and gives both parents equal rights to the authority over

---

319. Hodges, 181 So. 3d at 706.

320. Hodges v. Hodges, 2015-0585, p. 8 (La. 11/23/15), 181 So. 3d 700, 706.The court conducted a detailed analysis of the lower court decisions that found both for and against co-domiciliary status. *Id.* at 706–09.

321. Hodges, 181 So. 3d at 708.

322. Hodges, 181 So. 3d at 708–09.

323. Hodges, 181 So. 3d at 708–09.

324. *See* Ehlinger v. Ehlinger 2017-1120, p. 10 (La. App. 1 Cir. 2018), 251 So. 3d 418, 426. Note that when allocating decision-making-authority between the parents, any reference to domiciliary parent in the court order is improper. Jenkins v. Jenkins, 2023-0087 (La. App. 1 Cir. 06/02/23); 370 So. 3d 61, 79.

325. *See, e.g.*, Ga. Code Ann. § 19-9-1 (West, Westlaw through 2023 Reg. Sess.); W. Va. Code Ann. § 48-9-207 (West, Westlaw through 2023 Reg. Sess.); N.M. Stat. Ann. § 40-4-9.1 (West, 2024).

326. *See* Condon v. Condon, No. 2023-0572 (La. App. 1 Cir. 2/23/24); 2024 WL 741372 (finding that a consent judgment which split custody on a week-on-week-off schedule with each parent designated as the domiciliary parent when the child was in their custody violated the edict of *Hodges*).

327. *See generally* Hodges, 181 So. 3d 700.

their child.[328] *Hodges* involved a considered decree of custody and recognized that an exception for good cause shown would prevent the designation of a single domiciliary parent.[329] Although naming the parents co-domiciliaries in a consent judgment runs afoul of the court's edict, not naming one, which would have the same practical effect,[330] would seem to comport with the statute[331] and the court's holding in *Hodges*.[332] Indeed, the very purpose of a child custody case is to protect the child's emotional, physical, material and social health;[333] preventing parental strife, when the parents are in agreement, should be good cause to depart from the statute. If and when parental agreement ends, a single domiciliary parent could be named at that time.

Joint custody has been awarded beyond two-parent relationships. Courts have awarded joint custody among three individuals, which has included parents and nonparents. In *McCormic v. Rider*, the Louisiana Supreme Court affirmed the district court's grant of joint custody to the grandmother who was also the adoptive mother, the biological mother, and biological father, naming the biological mother as domiciliary parent.[334] Additionally, in *Cerwonka v. Baker*, joint custody was awarded to the biological mother, biological father, and legal father, and the court named the legal father as domiciliary parent because he could best communicate and facilitate access to the biological parents.[335] Courts have also awarded joint custody to a parent and a nonparent (most often grandparents) on finding that joint custody in both parents or

328. La. Stat. Ann. § 9:335(C); *see* La. Civ. Code Ann. art. 221.

329. Hodges, 181 So. 3d at 708–09.

330. The result is only the same *after* the revision of the title on parental authority, which vested equal decision-making authority in both parents. *See* La. Civ. Code Ann. art. 221. Prior to the revision, the result of not naming a domiciliary parent would place the father in the superior position as decision maker and administrator. La. Civ. Code Ann. art. 216, *repealed by* Act No. 260, 2015 La. Acts 1794. *See also* Chapter 9.

331. The statute defines the domiciliary parent as "the parent with whom the child ... primarily reside[s]." La. Stat. Ann. § 9:335(B)(2). When custody is shared, the child resides equally with each parent, so naming a domiciliary parent results in a legally inconsistent result. Hodges, 181 So. 3d 700, 719–20 (Hughes, J., dissenting).

332. Hodges, 181 So. 3d at 711 (majority opinion) ("We hold that La. R.S. 9:335 precludes the designation of 'co-domiciliary parents' in a joint custody arrangement. It is unnecessary and contrary to the plain language of La. R.S. 9:335 to designate both parents as 'co-domiciliary parents' in order to allocate parental responsibility. For example, when a court wishes to depart from the default rule that the sole domiciliary parent has superior decision-making authority, a court can make different provisions for decision making within the joint custody implementation order.").

333. Hodges, 181 So. 3d at 702.

334. McCormic v. Rider, 2009-2584, pp. 2–4 (La. 2/12/10), 27 So. 3d 277, 279–280.

335. Cerwonka v. Baker, 2006-856, pp. 6–7 (La. App. 3 Cir. 11/02/06), 942 So. 2d 747, 752–53; *see also* C.M.H. v. D.M., No. 2013-1477, 2013 WL 6858331, at *1-3 (La. Ct. App. 1 Cir. Dec. 27, 2013) (awarding joint custody to adoptive parents/great-grandparents and biological mother/nonparent); Whitman v. Williams, 2008–1133, pp. 1–4 (La. App. 3 Cir. 02/04/09), 6 So. 3d 852, 853–854 (awarding joint custody between the mother, father, and maternal aunt/nonparent with the maternal aunt designated as the domiciliary parent); Smith v. Tierney, 2004–2482, p. 17 (La. App. 1 Cir. 2/16/05), 906 So. 2d 586, 596 (awarding joint custody between the paternal grandparents/nonparents and the biological mother).

sole custody in one parent alone would cause substantial harm to the child,[336] a topic discussed in more detail below. Because joint custody is preferred when the parents cannot agree, courts have successfully crafted joint custody arrangements that ensure parents' constitutional rights are protected, with the best interest of the child being paramount.

§ 6:21 Custody Hierarchy— Court-Ordered Sole Custody

A court can award sole custody to one parent if that parent proves by clear and convincing evidence that sole custody is in the best interest of the child.[337] Prior to the 1993 revision, a party was required to rebut the presumption of joint custody with a preponderance of the evidence that joint custody was not in the child's best interest.[338] Not only was the burden elevated to clear and convincing evidence, but the focus shifted to whether sole custody was in the child's best interest, rather than whether joint custody was not.[339]

Understandably, after the revision, sole custody awards declined. Courts could still rely on pre-revision cases, but they were required to apply the heightened burden of proof. Although generally the reasons for awarding sole custody have remained the same, the incidence of successful awards is lower. Of course, the unique factual circumstances of each case will dictate the outcome, but courts are more likely to award sole custody upon a showing of egregious acts by a parent, proof of abuse, or unreasonable interference from third parties. Practical considerations, like the physical distance between the parties' residences or a parent who travels excessively, can also warrant a sole custody award.[340] Furthermore, animosity between the parents resulted in an award of sole custody before the revision. After the revision, however, without focus on the

336. Doyal v. Doyal, 22-769 (La. App. 3 Cir. 05/17/23); 2023 WL 3490464 (unpublished) (awarding joint custody to mother and uncle); Howard v. Oden, 44,191, p. 1 (La. App. 2 Cir. 2/25/09), 5 So. 3d 989, 991 (awarding joint custody to mother and paternal grandfather); Rupert v. Swinford, 95-0395, p. 9 (La. App. 1 Cir. 10/06/95), 671 So. 2d 502, 507–08 (awarding joint custody to father and maternal grandmother, granting visitation to the mother, and naming the grandmother domiciliary custodian); Schloegel v. Schloegel, 584 So. 2d 344 (La. Ct. App. 4 Cir. 1991) (awarding joint custody to father and maternal grandmother); Tierney, 906 So. 2d at 594 (awarding joint custody to mother and paternal grandparents); Robert v. Gaudet, 96-2506, p. 2 (La. App. 1 Cir. 03/27/97), 691 So. 2d 780, 781 (awarding joint custody to mother and paternal grandparents, with paternal grandparents being named domiciliary custodians); In re Landrum, 97-826, pp. 7–8 (La. App. 3 Cir. 12/10/97), 704 So. 2d 872, 876 (awarding mother and maternal grandfather joint custody, with grandfather named domiciliary custodian).

337. La. Civ. Code Ann. art. 132.

338. *See* Section 6:4.

339. *See* Kenneth Rigby, *1993 Custody and Child Support Legislation*, 55 La. L. Rev. 103, 109–10 (1994) (describing the changes in the burden of proof for sole custody awards).

340. *See* Verret v. Verret, 34,982, pp. 7–8 (La. App. 2 Cir. 05/09/01), 786 So. 2d 944, 949 (sole custody was appropriate because one parent lived in Florida and the other in Louisiana).

child's best interest, animosity between the parents alone is generally not sufficient to award sole custody.[341]

Egregious acts by one parent can result in sole custody to the other parent, typically where the actions of a parent are serious, ongoing, and relative to the child's best interest. For example, in *Hawthorne v. Hawthorne*, the court awarded sole custody to the father because the mother had a personality disorder that manifested itself in prolonged fits of rage and serious irrational behaviors.[342] Similarly, in *Stevens v. Stevens*, the court awarded sole custody to the father because the mother was a habitual drug abuser and subjected the child to harmful living arrangements.[343] Last, in *Fairbanks v. Beninate*, the court saw "no other option but to award sole custody" to the father because the mother intentionally prevented him from ever seeing his child, refused to comply with court orders, and resorted to "nefarious allegations" against the father.[344]

Abuse of the child at issue will certainly preclude the abuser any award of custody, but abuse against others can, as well, result in a sole custody award to the other parent.[345] For example, in *Harper v. Harper*, the court awarded sole custody to the mother based on evidence that the father was physically abusive toward his children of a prior marriage, and he had not attempted to establish a relationship with the child whose custody was at issue.[346] The court concluded that it was highly probable that sole custody with the mother was in the child's best interest.[347] In addition, instances of abuse within a family that do not involve the child can lead to a change in domiciliary status even if the evidence is insufficient to result in sole custody to one parent.[348]

It is noteworthy when considering abuse that for a child that has been adjudged in need of care, the heightened burden of proof for sole custody does not apply, and the best interest test will permit an award of sole custody. For example, in *State ex rel.*

---

341. *Cf.* Coody v. Coody, 20-071, (La. App. 3 Cir. 11/12/20), 307 So. 3d 1093.

342. Hawthorne v. Hawthorne, 96-89, p. 17 (La. App. 3 Cir. 05/22/96), 676 So. 2d 619, 627.

343. Stevens v. Stevens, 2007-1133, p. 8 (La. App. 1 Cir. 11/02/07), 978 So. 2d 916, 921; *see also* Johnson v. Butler, No. 10-1502, 2011 WL 1264146, at *3 (La. Ct. App. 3 Cir. Apr. 6, 2011) (granting sole custody to mother because father had never been a big part of the child's life and was of questionable moral character).

344. Fairbanks v. Beninate, 2020-206, pp. 22–23 (La. App. 5 Cir. 12/23/20), 308 So. 3d 1222, 1237–38.

345. *See* La. Stat. Ann. § 9:364(A). The Domestic Abuse Assistance Act provides a presumption that a parent who has a history of perpetrating family violence shall not be awarded sole or joint custody. *Id.*; *see also* La. Stat. Ann. § 46:2135(A)(5).

346. Harper v. Harper, 33,452, pp. 1, 6 (La. App. 2 Cir. 06/21/00), 764 So. 2d 1186, 1187, 1190.

347. Harper, 764 So. 2d at 1190; *see also* Wyatt v. White, 626 So. 2d 816, 818–19 (La. Ct. App. 2 Cir. 1993) (applying preponderance of the evidence standard and awarding sole custody to father because mother's boyfriend, who she intended to marry, had physically abused the child); Galeano v. Galeano, 444 So. 2d 658, 659 (La. Ct. App. 1 Cir. 1983) (applying preponderance of the evidence standard and awarding sole custody to the mother because there were "serious allegations of improper sexual conduct" against the father by an older child).

348. *See* McGee v. McGee, 552 So. 2d 576, 578–80 (La. Ct. App. 2 Cir. 1989) (modifying the original joint custody order that named mother as domiciliary parent to name the father as domiciliary parent due to the violent domestic disputes between the mother and the stepfather).

V.B., the court awarded sole custody to the father, over the mother's objection, after the three children had been taken into state custody because of neglect and violence between the parents.[349] Although the parents had been violent toward one another during the marriage, for the year the children were in state custody, the father underwent anger management and parenting counseling, while the mother was inconsistent in her treatment.[350] The court found that the Children's Code applied, rather than Civil Code Article 132, due to the health and safety concerns surrounding a child in need of care.[351] Custody would therefore be awarded "on such terms and conditions as deemed in the best interest of the child."[352] The court found that sole custody in the father was in the children's best interest because he had completed his counseling and genuinely sought to improve his parenting skills.[353]

Interference by third parties can also result in an award of sole custody to one parent. Interference can be exerted by someone close to one parent, which can ultimately harm the relationship with the other parent, who then seeks sole custody as a result. For example, in *Dooley v. Dooley*, the children's stepmother spoke disparagingly about the mother to the three children, harassed the children, and subverted the mother's authority.[354] The father delegated all of the decisions regarding his children to his new wife.[355] The mother was successful in seeking sole custody of the three children because the father had not demonstrated the capacity to foster a relationship with his children due in part to the permitted interference by the stepmother.[356]

Prior to the revision, sufficient animosity and rancor between the parents could result in an award of sole custody because the parents could not work together to the extent required in a joint custody arrangement. When the focus of the analysis shifted to the best interest of the child, rather than rebutting the presumption of joint custody, courts recognized that the actions of the parents alone would not be sufficient to award sole custody.[357] Post-revision, in *D.R.S. v. L.E.K.*, the trial court awarded sole custody to the mother, finding that "[t]he evidence of continued and unreasonable conflict is clear

349. *See* State ex rel. V.B., 2009-653, pp. 1–3 (La. App. 3 Cir. 11/04/09), 24 So. 3d 281, 281–83.

350. State ex rel. V.B., 24 So. 3d at 283.

351. State ex rel. V.B., 24 So. 3d at 282. Louisiana Children's Code Article 681 provides that when a child has been adjudicated in need of care, the child's health, welfare, and safety is the paramount concern, so the court can place the child in the custody of a parent or other person deemed to be in the best interest of the child. La. Child. Code Ann. art. 681(A)(1).

352. State ex rel. V.B., 24 So. 3d at 282 (quoting La. Child. Code Ann. art. 681(A)(1)(2009)).

353. *See* State ex rel. V.B., 24 So. 3d at 283–84.

354. Dooley v. Dooley, 2010-785, p. 3 (La. App. 3 Cir. 02/02/11), 55 So. 3d 985, 986.

355. Dooley, 55 So. 3d at 989.

356. *See* Dooley, 55 So. 3d at 989; *see also* S.J. v. S.M., 505 So. 2d 897, 898–99 (La. Ct. App. 2 Cir. 1987) (applying preponderance of the evidence standard and awarding sole custody to mother based in part on paternal grandparents who caused the four-year-old child to make false allegations of sexual abuse toward the stepfather in an attempt to help the father receive custody).

357. *See* Yelverton v. Yelverton, 621 So. 2d 36, 39–40 (La. Ct. App. 2 Cir. 1993) (finding that proof of animosity between parents is sufficient to overcome the presumption of joint custody); *see also* Cahanin v. Cahanin, 533 So. 2d 27, 27 (La. Ct. App. 4 Cir. 1988) (finding that the animosity level and inability to communicate rendered a joint custody arrangement unworkable).

and convincing evidence that the[] parents are not able to jointly parent the child."[358] The appellate court reversed because the trial court provided no explanation as to why sole custody was in the best interest of the child.[359] Because the evidence relied on by the trial court surrounded the parents' actions, rather than the child's best interest, the court conducted a de novo review and awarded joint custody to the parents.[360]

To use parental animosity to secure sole custody, a parent must prove by clear and convincing evidence that the animosity has a detrimental *effect* on the child. From a practical standpoint, it may be difficult to prevail because the animosity generally involves both parents, and neither would appear justified to receive sole custody. With proper attention placed on the effects of this animosity on the child, however, an award of sole custody can be proper.[361]

§ 6:22 Custody Hierarchy— Court-Ordered Nonparent Custody

Last in the custody hierarchy is custody to a nonparent, which requires the nonparent to prove substantial harm to the child if custody is awarded to a parent.[362] Upon a showing of substantial harm, the court may award custody to "another person with whom the child has been living in a wholesome and stable environment" or "to any other person able to provide an adequate and stable environment."[363] The best interest of the child analysis must be done, as is required in any custody case.[364]

Prior to 1982, Louisiana law governing nonparent custody developed jurisprudentially, permitting the deprivation of parental custody only when "the parent is unable or unfit, having forfeited parental rights."[365] The Louisiana Supreme Court explained that a simple best interest test was not sufficient, and courts should refrain from com-

---

358. D.R.S. v. L.E.K., 2009-1274, p. 7 (La. App. 3 Cir. 03/10/10), 33 So. 3d 428, 433.

359. D.R.S., 33 So. 3d at 433.

360. D.R.S., 33 So. 3d at 433; *see also* Griffith v. Latiolais, 2010-0754, p. 18 (La. 10/19/10), 48 So. 3d 1058, 1071 (reversing an award of sole custody to the mother because it was based mostly on the father's bad behavior toward the mother, rather than the best interest of the child); Walet v. Caulfield, 2002-2009, p. 11 (La. App. 1 Cir. 06/27/03), 858 So. 2d 615, 623 (concluding that proof that the mother and father had strong animosity toward one another did not provide by clear and convincing evidence that an award of sole custody to the mother was in the child's best interest).

361. *See* Whitmore v. Stamp, No. 2012-2069, 2013 WL 2490337, at *3 (La. Ct. App. 1 Cir. June 7, 2013) (finding that the trial court inappropriately concluded that sole custody could be awarded based on animosity between the parents but finding sufficient effects on the best interest of the child to affirm the sole custody award).

362. La. Civ. Code Ann. art. 133.

363. La. Civ. Code Ann. art. 133. "The use of the singular 'person' ... is intended to rule out any inference that this article might require the awarding of joint custody between nonparents." La. Civ. Code Ann. art. 133 cmt. (c). Joint custody with parents is permitted but not required. *Id.*; *see also* Street v. May, 35,589, p. 11 (La. App. 2 Cir. 12/5/01), 803 So. 2d 312, 318 (stating that the use of the singular "'person' ... does not exclude the designation of several persons").

364. La. Civ. Code Ann. art. 131.

365. Wood v. Beard, 290 So. 2d 675, 677 (La. 1974).

paring the home of the parent with the nonparent to determine who can provide greater advantages to the child.[366] In 1982, the legislature codified the jurisprudential rule in a two-part statutory test under which the nonparent was required to show that parental custody was "detrimental" to the child and that divesting the parent of custody was required to serve the child's best interest.[367]

During the 1993 revision, terminology was changed to require the nonparent to prove that parental custody would result in "substantial harm" to the child.[368] It does not appear that there was any intent to change the law when the phrase "substantial harm" replaced the word "detrimental," and it is clear that the primary right of parental custody remained.[369] Therefore, for a nonparent to receive custody over a parent, the nonparent must prove that: (1) custody to the parent would cause substantial harm to the child; and (2) custody to the nonparent is in the best interest of the child.[370] When applying the two-pronged test of article 133, the best interest of the child factors set forth in article 134 are not considered until *after* a finding of substantial harm.[371] Again, merely showing that the nonparent is in a better position to raise the child than the parent is not enough to deprive the natural parent of custody.[372]

Although a difficult burden to meet, nonparents have been successful in proving the presence of substantial harm to the child. "Substantial harm" has been recognized to include unfitness, neglect, abuse, and any other circumstance, such as prolonged separation of the child from his natural parents, that would cause the child to suffer substantial harm.[373] Courts have considered a parent's drug use or alcohol abuse, the

---

366. Wood, 290 So. 2d at 677; *see also* State ex rel. Rothrock v. Webber, 161 So. 2d 759, 764 (La. 1964).

367. Act No. 307, 1982 La. Acts 804, 805. One court concluded that the statutory language was significantly different and permitted broader application than the jurisprudential rule. Boyett v. Boyett, 448 So. 2d 819, 822 (La. Ct. App. 2 Cir. 1984).

368. Act No. 261, 1993 La. Acts 610, 614.

369. The jurisprudence has used the terms "substantial harm" and "detrimental" interchangeably. *See, e.g.*, McCormic v. Rider, 2009-2584, p. 2 (La. 02/12/10), 27 So. 3d 277, 279; Smith v. Tierney, 2004-2482, p. 7 (La. App. 1 Cir. 2/16/05), 906 So. 2d 586, 590; Wilson v. Paul, 2008-382, p. 2 (La. App. 3 Cir. 10/01/08), 997 So. 2d 572, 574; Dalferes v. Dalferes, 98-1233, 98-1234, p. 2 (La. App. 4 Cir. 11/18/98), 724 So. 2d 805, 806.

370. *See* La. Civ. Code Ann. art. 133; *see also* La. Civ. Code Ann. art. 131.

371. Duplessy v. Duplessy, 12-69, p. 6 (La. App. 5 Cir. 06/28/12), 102 So. 3d 209, 213; Black v. Simms, 2008-1465, p. 5 (La. App. 3 Cir. 06/10/09), 12 So. 3d 1140, 1143.

372. Creed v. Creed, 94-268, p. 8 (La. App. 3 Cir. 12/21/94), 647 So. 2d 1362, 1366. In *Creed*, the court explained that the grandparent's ability to provide a more stable lifestyle, standing alone, could not be used to deprive the mother of custody. *Id.* The mother's "unfortunate economic status" and "marginal lifestyle" did not amount to substantial harm. *Id.* The *Creed* decision is also interesting because the grandparents did not petition for custody and were not even parties to the litigation, yet the trial court granted them custody of the child. *Id.* at 1364 n.1.

373. Doyal v. Doyal, 22-769 (La. App. 3 Cir. 05/17/23); 2023 WL 3490464 (unpublished); Neathery v. Neathery, 51,388, p. 3 (La. App. 2 Cir. 2/17/17), 216 So. 3d 251, 253; Ramirez v. Ramirez, 13-166, p. 16 (La. App. 5 Cir. 08/27/13), 124 So. 3d 8, 17; Bowden v. Brown, 48,268, p. 8 (La. App. 2 Cir. 5/15/13), 114 So. 3d 1194, 1200; Jones v. Coleman, 44,543, p. 8 (La. App. 2 Cir. 7/15/09), 18 So. 3d 153, 159; Teague v. Teague, 44,005, 44,006, p. 13 (La. App. 2 Cir. 11/25/08), 999 So. 2d 86, 95; Smith v.

child living in substandard or dangerous living conditions, the parent's sexual promiscuity or deviance, and the loss of a strong emotional bond with a nonparent caregiver when finding substantial harm, all on a case-by-case basis.[374]

Nonparents can be awarded sole or joint custody.[375] When joint custody is awarded, it can be shared with another nonparent or with the parent.[376] In a custody contest between two nonparents, only the best interest of the child analysis is necessary, as a showing of substantial harm is used when a nonparent seeks custody from a parent.[377] When a nonparent seeks custody against another nonparent, the status of one as a blood relative does not elevate that nonparent in a custody analysis.[378] Nor is there a preference for the nonparent with whom the child has been living when another nonparent can provide an adequate and stable environment.[379] Further, the designation in a will of a tutor for the child does not elevate the nonparent in a custody dispute, which must be based on the child's best interest.[380]

Joint custody between a nonparent and a parent can raise a more difficult question. If the nonparent must prove that custody in the parent will result in substantial harm to the child, then how can the parent ultimately end up with joint custody? The answer lies in relativity—in the temporal sense, not the kinship sense. If a parent is unfit for

---

Tierney, 2004-2482, p. 7 (La. App. 1 Cir. 2/16/05), 906 So. 2d 586, 590; Mills v. Wilkerson, 34,694, p. 6 (La. App. 2 Cir. 3/26/01), 785 So. 2d 69, 73–74.

374. *See, e.g.*, Weicks v. Stromberg, 2023-1004 (La. App. 1 Cir. 3/22/24); 388 So. 3d 398 (awarding sole custody to maternal grandparents after the death of the mother because the father lived an unstable life, lacked credibility, and did not address his mental health issues); Duplessy v. Duplessy, 12-69 (La. App. 5 Cir. 06/28/12), 102 So. 3d 209 (awarding sole custody to the child's brother, who acted as the child's father, in a contest against the adoptive parent, who functioned like a grandparent, due to the strong relationship with the brother and marginal living conditions of the father); Martin v. Dupont, 32,490 (La. App. 2 Cir. 12/08/99), 748 So. 2d 574 (awarding sole custody to a man who was led to believe he was the child's father because the mother's boyfriend was dangerous, he tried to induce the child to drink whiskey, he beat the neighbor's dog, the child was malnourished while living with the mother, the mother's residence was filthy and without food, and the mother and her boyfriend were sexually explicit in the presence of the child); Dalferes v. Dalferes, 98-1233, 98-1234 (La. App. 4 Cir. 11/18/98), 724 So. 2d 805 (awarding sole custody to the child's aunt, who the child had been living with for the past five years because the mother had no plans to care for the child, had mental problems, had put the child in harm's way with men, and had no permanent address); Teague, 999 So. 2d at 95 (awarding custody to grandparents because parents were drug users). See *Merritt v. Merritt* for several cases in which nonparent custody was permitted. Merritt v. Merritt, 550 So. 2d 882, 891 n.1 (La. Ct. App. 2 Cir. 1989).

375. *See* La. Civ. Code Ann. art. 133.

376. *See* La. Civ. Code Ann. art. 133 cmt. (c).

377. *Compare* La. Civ. Code Ann. art. 133, *with* La. Civ. Code Ann. art. 134.

378. Knisely v. Knisely, 2005-1015, p. 6 (La. App. 3 Cir. 3/1/06), 924 So. 2d 423, 427 (awarding custody to the child's stepmother who had raised him for eight years in a contest against the paternal grandmother, who was named tutrix in deceased father's will); In re Tuccio, 95-0302, p. 6 (La. App. 1 Cir. 11/16/95), 665 So. 2d 531, 534 (denying paternity tests on the basis that the status as a grandparent of the child does not affect the right to nonparent custody).

379. Cathey v. Ogea, 2012-563, p. 5 (La. App. 3 Cir. 8/22/12), 98 So. 3d 953, 957 (awarding custody of one child to the maternal relative, even though the child had been living with another relative and his two siblings for a short time).

380. Knisely v. Knisely, 2005-1015, p. 6 (La. App. 3 Cir. 3/1/06), 924 So. 2d 423, 427.

sole custody (or for joint custody with the other parent), it may be less demanding on the parent to share custody with the nonparent. The parent will still be a part of the child's life and have the opportunity to participate in decision-making, but the nonparent, who is already involved in the child's life, will remain a constant source of love and direction.

Therefore, in cases where joint custody is awarded to a parent and a nonparent, courts must find that substantial harm would result if joint custody is awarded to both parents or if sole custody is awarded to either parent.[381] By concluding that an award of sole custody to one parent would result in substantial harm to the child, the court is not deciding that the parent is prevented from serving as a joint custodian with the nonparent.[382] Then, the court must consider what serves the child's best interest.

The Louisiana Supreme Court considered an interesting custody dispute between two parents and a nonparent grandmother. In *McCormic v. Rider*, the grandmother had adopted the child as an infant, and the unmarried mother and father who sought custody were required to prove substantial harm if custody remained with the grandmother, because the grandmother enjoyed the paramount right of custody as a parent by adoption.[383] The trial court determined that sole custody in the grandmother would cause substantial harm to the child.[384] It then concluded that a joint custody arrangement with the grandmother and biological parents would serve the child's best interest as they had all lived together for several years.[385]

Courts before and after *McCormic* have ordered joint custody between a parent and a nonparent when the standards of article 133 are met.[386] Grandparents are most often the nonparents who seek custody, but "nonparent" encompasses any relative or

---

381. Black v. Simms, 2008-1465, p. 3 (La. App. 3 Cir. 6/10/09), 12 So. 3d 1140, 1142 (citing Rupert v. Swinford, 95-0395 (La. App. 1 Cir. 10/06/95), 671 So. 2d 502); *cf.* In re Landrum, 97-826, p. 6 (La. App. 3 Cir. 12/10/97), 704 So. 2d 872, 875. In *In re Landrum*, the court concluded that an express finding of substantial harm to the child if the father was awarded sole custody was not necessary before it awarded joint custody to the mother and grandmother. *See* 704 So. 2d at 875. This decision has been criticized and is not an accurate interpretation of Louisiana Civil Code Article 133. *See* Black, 12 So. 3d at 1142.

382. La. Civ. Code Ann. art. 133 cmt. (c); Black, 12 So. 3d at 1142 (*citing* Rupert, 95-0395; 671 So. 2d 502). *See generally* In re C.A.C., 2017-0108 (La. App. 4 Cir. 11/2/17), 231 So. 3d 58.

383. McCormic v. Rider, 2009-2584, pp. 1–3 (La. 2/12/10), 27 So. 3d 277, 278–79.

384. McCormic, 27 So. 3d at 278–79. Evidence was adduced that the grandmother tethered the child to his bed, regularly medicated the child without him being evaluated and assessed, and whipped the child. McCormic, 27 So. 3d at 280 (Johnson, J., concurring).

385. McCormic, 27 So. 3d at 279 (majority opinion). The court designated the mother as domiciliary parent. *Id.* Other courts have also awarded tripartite joint custody. *See* Whitman v. Williams, 2008-1133, p. 4 (La. App. 3 Cir. 2/4/09), 6 So. 3d 852, 854 (awarding joint custody to the mother, father, and father's maternal aunt, with domiciliary status given to the aunt); Smith v. Tierney, 2004-2482, pp. 3, 17 (La. App. 1 Cir. 2/16/05), 906 So. 2d 586, 588, 596 (awarding joint custody between the mother and paternal grandparents, who had raised the child since her birth).

386. *See, e.g.*, Schloegel v. Schloegel, 584 So. 2d 344, 345, 346–47 (La. Ct. App. 4 Cir. 1991) (awarding joint custody to father and maternal grandmother because father's prior drug use was detrimental to the child); *see also* Rupert v. Swinford, 95-0395 (La. App. 1 Cir. 10/6/95), 671 So. 2d 502 (awarding custody to the father and maternal grandmother because of the father's involvement in drugs and

nonrelative.[387] In fact, courts have awarded custody to grandparents even when they are not a party to the action.[388] Awarding custody to a nonparent without discovery and a hearing promotes judicial efficiency, but it raises serious policy concerns. Although courts are required to consider the best interest of the child, without the nonparents as parties to the litigation, no other litigant has prepared, and no court has considered, the parental fitness of the nonparents.

Awarding custody to a parent who is not filiated to the child also implicates the article 133 burden of proof, unless the court can construe the request for custody as a timely avowal action. In *Jackson v. McNeal*, the court awarded custody to the alleged father of the child, who was not married to the mother, even though the man did not specifically request a judgment of paternity.[389] The mother appealed, claiming that the heightened burden of proof under article 133 should apply because the man was not adjudged to be the father.[390] Relying on supreme court precedent involving filiation for purposes of tort claims, the court found that allegations in the petition that the child was "his son" and the "minor child" of the parties were sufficient to put the mother on notice that he was claiming filiation, even though he did not request a declaration of paternity in his petition.[391] The court found sufficient evidence that the man was the father of the child, so the best interest of the child standard applied.[392] Not only must the father prove paternity for the best interest standard to apply, but the avowal action must be timely.[393]

---

failure to care for the child's health needs); Merritt v. Merritt, 550 So. 2d 882 (La. Ct. App. 2 Cir. 1989); Robert v. Gaudet, 96-2506 (La. App. 1 Cir. 3/27/97), 691 So. 2d 780; In re Landrum, 704 So. 2d 872.

387. *See generally* Black v. Simms, 2008-1465 (La. App. 3 Cir. 6/10/09), 12 So. 3d 1140 (nonparent challenger was a lesbian former partner); Whitman, 6 So. 3d 852 (nonparent challenger was a maternal aunt).

388. Creed v. Creed, 94-268, p. 2 n.1 (La. App. 3 Cir. 12/21/94), 647 So. 2d 1362, 1364 n.1; Schloegel, 584 So. 2d at 348 ("Grandparents of a minor child need not be parties to an action for child custody to be awarded to them."); Stuckey v. Stuckey, 276 So. 2d 408, 411 (La. Ct. App. 2 Cir. 1973).

389. *See* Jackson v. McNeal, 2015-0067, p. 5 (La. App. 1 Cir. 7/13/15), 180 So. 3d 376, 379.

390. Jackson, 180 So. 3d at 377–78.

391. Jackson, 180 So. 3d at 380.

392. Jackson, 180 So. 3d at 381. The "child was born while [the parents] were in a relationship," albeit unmarried, "the child was given the same first, middle, and last name" as the father, and the father testified that he was indeed the child's father. *Id.*

393. In *Jackson*, the child was not filiated to another man, so the father could institute the action at any time. Jackson, 180 So. 3d at 379 (citing La. Civ. Code Ann. art. 198). If the child is presumed to be the child of another man, peremptive time periods to file the avowal action will apply. Jackson, 180 So. 3d at 379 (citing La. Civ. Code Ann. art. 198). *See* Chapter 8.

§ 6:23 Custody Hierarchy— Custody of Children of Same-Sex Couples

Same-sex couples face unique challenges in a custody dispute. After the United States Supreme Court's recognition of marriage equality in 2015,[394] Louisiana courts are beginning to recognize the difference between an uninvolved nonparent seeking custody of a child and a person acting as a parent but biologically unrelated to the child. While Louisiana has not yet taken the step to adopt de facto parentage, the law has evolved to address the needs of the child in a nontraditional family arrangement. Furthermore, the law of filiation must be revised to address the parentage of same-sex married couples who have children through assisted reproductive technology and, by nature, do not always share a biological connection to the child. While adoption by the nonbiological parent is an option,[395] legal presumptions would better protect the rights of parents and the child, whether or not they share a biological connection to the child.[396]

When both spouses in a same-sex marriage are recognized parents by adoption, the provisions of article 132 apply just as they would to a heterosexual married couple.[397] By contrast, when one spouse is a parent to the child biologically or by adoption, and the other spouse functions as a parent in name only, without a valid adoption, the latter has no rights to the child.[398] The other spouse is therefore treated as a nonparent, even though the nonparent may have assumed the role of parent to the child for many years. In such a scenario, the provisions of article 133 will apply, and the nonparent must prove substantial harm to the child to deprive the parent of custody. Joint custody between the parent and nonparent same-sex couple is permitted if the nonparent can

---

394. Obergefell v. Hodges, 135 S. Ct. 2584 (2015).

395. *But see* In re Dennis, 55,851 (La. App. 2 Cir. 7/17/24), 2024 WL 34334184 (rejecting same-sex stepparent adoption). *See also* Chapter 8, Section 8:26.

396. Some Louisiana courts have applied the presumptions of paternity to same-sex married couples. *See, e.g.*, Chaisson v. State, 2017-0642, p. 2 (La. App. 4 Cir. 3/7/18), 239 So. 3d 1074, 1076 (applying the marital presumption of article 185 to a child conceived and born in Louisiana to a lesbian couple legally married in New York); Boquet v. Boquet, 2018-798, p. 1 (La. App. 3 Cir. 4/10/19), 269 So. 3d 895, 897 (applying the marital presumption of article 185 to a child of a lesbian couple married in Louisiana); *but see* In re Dennis, 55,851 (La. App. 2 Cir. 7/17/24), 2024 WL 34334184; *Foret v. Serrano*, 23-1034 (La. App. 1 Cir. 4/30/24), WL 2050131; *See also* Chapter 8, Section 8:26.

397. *See* Palazzolo v. Mire, 2008-0075, pp. 35–36, 38 (La. App. 4 Cir. 1/7/09), 10 So. 3d 748, 768–70 (granting the biological parent sole custody of the child in a custody dispute with the adoptive same-sex parent based on the best interest of the child).

398. Louisiana law does not permit unmarried persons to jointly adopt (often referred to as second parent adoptions). *See* La. Child. Code Ann. art. 1221; In re C.A.C., 2017-0108, p. 4 (La. App. 4 Cir. 11/2/17), 231 So. 3d 58, 74 n.1 (same-sex partner could not have adopted biological child of partner without biological parent relinquishing parental rights because the parties were not married); Ferrand v. Ferrand, 16-7, p. 9 n.16 (La. App. 5 Cir. 8/31/16), 221 So. 3d 909, 918 n. 16 (same). Post-2015, when same-sex couples in Louisiana were permitted to marry, adoption by the same-sex married partner (stepparent adoption) is now permitted. La. Child. Code Ann. art. 1221; *but see* 55,851 (La. App. 2 Cir. 7/17/24), 2024 WL 34334184. Louisiana will also give full faith and credit to an out-of-state adoption by a same-sex parent. *See* Palazzolo, 10 So. 3d at 770.

prove that an award of sole custody to the parent would cause substantial harm to the child and joint custody with the nonparent is in the best interest of the child.[399]

Prior to the legalization of same-sex marriage, courts were reluctant to award custody to the nonparent same-sex partner. In 2009, in *Black v. Simms*, a lesbian couple each gave birth to one child using the same donor's sperm.[400] Ms. Simms gave birth to a daughter, and Ms. Black gave birth to a son.[401] When the couple split up, the daughter was six years old and had lived with her two mothers since birth; the family had also moved in with the parents of Ms. Black two years before the women's separation.[402] Ms. Simms moved out with the child and refused to allow Ms. Black or her parents to see her.[403] One year later, Ms. Black sought custody.[404] She argued that severing the ties of a parent-child relationship, as well as the relationship with the child's brother and grandparents, would cause substantial harm to the child.[405] Applying article 133, the court disagreed, finding that denying the obvious love and affection the Blacks have for the child may be harsh and inconsiderate but does not rise to the level of substantial harm.[406]

Prior to *Obergefell*, courts also refused to issue a consent judgment of custody based on an agreement by a parent to share custody with her nonparent same-sex partner. In *In re Melancon*, a biological mother and her same-sex partner used artificial insemination to have a child.[407] They lived together in the nonparent partner's home.[408] The biological mother consented to joint custody with her partner, but the trial court refused to issue a consent judgment of custody, stating that the nonparent must plead and prove that the award of sole custody to the parent (with whom she wanted to share joint custody) would cause substantial harm to the child under article 133.[409] The nonparent argued that article 132 applied, because the court was asked to issue a judgment in accordance with the agreement of the parents.[410] The court disagreed.[411] Ultimately, because no allegations of harm were present, the court sua sponte raised the exception of no cause of action and dismissed the case.[412] The appellate court affirmed.[413]

---

399. *See generally* In re C.A.C., 231 So. 3d 58; Ferrand, 221 So. 3d 909; Black v. Simms, 2008-1465 (La. App. 3 Cir. 6/10/09), 12 So. 3d 1140.

400. Black, 12 So. 3d at 1141.

401. Black, 12 So. 3d at 1141.

402. Black, 12 So. 3d at 1141.

403. Black, 12 So. 3d at 1141.

404. Black, 12 So. 3d at 1141.

405. Black, 12 So. 3d at 1141.

406. Black, 12 So. 3d at 1145.

407. In re Melancon, 2010-1463, p. 3 (La. App. 1 Cir. 12/22/10), 62 So. 3d 759, 763, *abrogated by* In re J.E.T., 2016-0384 (La. App. 1 Cir. 10/31/16), 211 So. 3d 575.

408. In re Melancon, 62 So. 3d at 763,

409. In re Melancon, 62 So. 3d at 763.

410. In re Melancon, 62 So. 3d at 763.

411. In re Melancon, 62 So. 3d at 763.

412. In re Melancon, 62 So. 3d at 764.

413. In re Melancon, 62 So. 3d at 764.

Both the *Black* and *Melancon* decisions have been limited, if not abrogated, post-*Obergefell*. The Louisiana Supreme Court has made clear that in all custody determinations—even between a parent and a nonparent—the paramount goal and primary consideration must be the best interest of the child.[414] The Louisiana Supreme Court has likewise recognized the right of a parent to consent to custody with a nonparent,[415] and other Louisiana courts have observed that substantial harm can befall a child who is separated from a loving parent, no matter the sex.[416]

For example, in *In re J.E.T.*, the court refused to nullify a stipulated judgment of joint custody between an unmarried lesbian couple, one parent and one nonparent, when their relationship ended when the child was 11 years old.[417] The biological parent argued that the stipulated judgment was null because the court at the time had not determined that custody in her alone would cause substantial harm to the child.[418] The court disagreed, finding ample authority for a parent to consent to joint custody with a nonparent without implicating the article 133 burden of substantial harm.[419] It refused to nullify the stipulated judgment and found no material change of circumstance to modify the arrangement.[420]

Without an agreement of custody or a valid adoption by the nonparent, courts must apply article 133 to a same-sex couple, mindful of the constitutionally protected right of the parent. The court did just that in *In re C.A.C.*, which involved the breakup of a lesbian couple, who co-parented a child carried by one of the partners.[421] The other partner did not adopt the child.[422] The women were not married but had lived together in a committed relationship for 18 years, and at the time of their separation, their daughter was seven.[423] The women both raised the child as mothers, the child treated both women as mothers, and there was documentary evidence that the biological mother expected her partner to be involved in the child's life forever.[424]

---

414. Tracie F. v. Francisco D., 2015-1812, p. 2 (La. 3/15/16), 188 So. 3d 231, 235.

415. Tracie F., 188 So. 3d at 243. *See generally* Bowden v. Brown, 48-286 (La. App. 2 Cir. 5/15/13), 114 So. 3d 1194 (awarding custody of the four children in a consent judgment to the grandmother based on the agreement of the parents who were still married).

416. *See* In re C.A.C., 2017-0108, p. 15 (La. App. 4 Cir. 11/2/17), 231 So. 3d 58, 68; Ferrand v. Ferrand, 16-7, p. 11 (La. App. 5 Cir. 8/31/16), 221 So. 3d 909, 920; Bowden, 114 So. 3d at 1200.

417. *See* In re J.E.T., 2016-0384, pp. 2, 19 (La. App. 1 Cir. 10/31/16), 211 So. 3d 575, 578, 588.

418. In re J.E.T., 211 So. 3d at 582.

419. In re J.E.T., 211 So. 3d at 584. The court also found that *In re Melancon* was not controlling because the petition for custody was filed by the nonparent in *Melancon*, rather than the parent in *J.E.T.*, and the *Melancon* decision involved a direct appeal, while the request in *J.E.T.* was attacking a judgment rendered 10 years before. In re J.E.T., 211 So. 3d at 584–85.

420. *See* In re J.E.T., 211 So. 3d at 588.

421. *See generally* In re C.A.C., 231 So. 3d 58.

422. In re C.A.C., 231 So. 3d at 73 (Broussard, J., concurring in part & dissenting in part).

423. In re C.A.C., 231 So. 3d at 61, 63 (majority opinion).

424. *See* In re C.A.C., 231 So. 3d at 62. The biological mother signed a Domestic Partnership Agreement, which contemplated joint custody in the event of the parties' separation, a power of attorney in which she granted her partner unlimited rights over the child, and a testament which left her

When the couple broke up, the biological mother asserted her constitutionally protected right to limit physical custody of the child with a nonparent, her former partner.[425] The former partner sought joint custody; the trial court applied article 133 and awarded joint custody with liberal custodial time in favor of the nonbiological mother.[426] On appeal, the Fourth Circuit affirmed, finding significant factual differences from the *Black v. Simms* case and recognizing "the difficulty in applying art. 133 to cases that present a factual anomaly to the traditional family situation."[427] The court explained:

> The difficulty in applying La. C.C. art. 133 to same-sex custody contests is that article 133 presupposes an issue regarding the fitness of one or both parents exists, thus creating a threat of "harm to the child."
>
> ...
>
> ... These articles were fashioned to manage circumstances in which a parent or parents become unable or unwilling to properly parent the child and an extended family member or other concerned adult seeks custody. In same-sex relationships the third party is much more likely to be a co-parent from the child's point of view than in situations where a grandparent or other extended family member seeks custody. The third party life partner was there when the child was born and has established a bond that, to the child, is indistinguishable from that shared with the biological parent.[428]

The court concluded that substantial harm to the child would result if she was separated from either of her mothers, and the award of joint custody was in the child's best interest.[429] The court made clear that the biological mother was not an unfit parent and the other mother was not a typical third party envisioned by article 133.[430] Joint custody was appropriate given the unique factual circumstances and the best interest of the child.[431]

The Louisiana Supreme Court took a different approach in the 2021 case of *Cook v Sullivan*.[432] There, an unmarried lesbian couple began living together as romantic partners in 2002. Seven years later, one of them gave birth to a child conceived by intercourse with a male friend after failed attempts at assisted reproductive technology. The child was given a hyphenated last name of the women's respective last names, and the three of them lived together as a family until 2013 when the women ended their relationship. For a few years thereafter, the women shared custody of the child, but in

---

partner as trustee of the trust in favor of her daughter and instructed both extended families to be involved in the child's life. *Id.* at 62.

425. In re C.A.C., 231 So. 3d at 63.
426. In re C.A.C., 231 So. 3d at 64.
427. In re C.A.C., 231 So. 3d at 68.
428. In re C.A.C., 231 So. 3d at 69.
429. In re C.A.C., 231 So. 3d at 70–71.
430. In re C.A.C., 231 So. 3d at 71.
431. In re C.A.C., 231 So. 3d at 71.
432. Cook v. Sullivan, 2020-01471 (La. 9/30/21); 330 So. 3d 152.

2016, the biological mother unilaterally terminated that arrangement. The nonparent then sought parentage, custody, and support.

The trial court decided that "disputes between same-sex individuals who are living in the same household and where one of them conceives a child through assisted reproduction methods or adopts a child are clearly distinguishable from a traditional third-party dispute with a biological parent."[433] Instead of applying article 133, the trial court invoked the doctrine of psychological/de facto parent and applied its own test below to determine whether the nonparent should be treated as a legal parent:

1) The parties entered into and engaged in assisted reproduction measures, voluntarily and jointly planned, which resulted in conception by one of the parties;
2) The parties resided in the same household before and for a substantial time after the birth of the child sufficient to form a parental bond;
3) The non-biological parent engaged in full and permanent responsibilities and caretaking of the child without expectations or compensation;
4) The non-biological parent acknowledged publicly and held [herself] out to be a parent of the child;
5) The non-biological parent established a bonded and dependent relationship with the child of a parental nature; and
6) The biological parent supported and fostered the bonded and dependent relationship between the child and non-biological parent.[434]

The trial court determined that the nonparent was a legal parent and that substantial harm would result if the relationship between the child and non-biological parent was not re-established; it awarded joint custody to the two women.[435]

The appellate court reversed. While it "commended the trial court for its detailed reasons for judgment and recognized its effort to formulate a ruling that it believed to be both fair to [the non-biological parent] and in the best interest of the child," the appellate court also acknowledged that "it is not the judiciary's role to fill in gaps left by the legislature."[436] As such, it employed an article 133 analysis and explained that "the substantial harm standard of Article 133 requires a finding by the court that sole custody to [the biological mother] would result—future tense—in substantial harm to the child."[437] Finding none, the court granted sole custody to the biological mother.[438]

433. Cook, 330 So. 3d at 155.

434. Cook, 330 So. 3d at 155.

435. Cook, 330 So. 3d at 155.

436. Cook, 330 So. 3d at 156 (internal citations omitted).

437. Cook, 330 So. 3d at 156 (internal citations omitted).

438. Cook, 330 So. 3d at 156–57. The court did recognize that the biological mother's decision to remove the other woman from the child's life "may seem callous and controversial," but it also recognized that "her decision is protected under the laws of the United States and Louisiana as a fundamental liberty interest of a parent in the absence of substantial harm or neglect." *Id.* at 156.

The Louisiana Supreme Court agreed. While noting the state legislature's silence on the issue of children of same-sex relationships, the court also pointed out that "Louisiana has neither statutorily nor jurisprudentially recognized the in loco parentis, de facto parent, or psychological parent status in custody contests between a parent and nonparent."[439] Therefore, the court applied article 133, found no substantial harm, and affirmed the court of appeals.

Louisiana courts have also begun to address cases involving custody of children of transgender parents. The court in *Ferrand v. Ferrand* considered a cisgender biological mother and her female transgender partner who identified as a man.[440] The couple had twins through artificial insemination during their relationship.[441] The couple had been together for seven years when the twins were born, and they presented themselves as a married couple, sharing the same last name and co-parenting the children.[442] The children called the transgender father "Daddy," and he was active in the children's lives.[443] The mother moved out of the home when the children were four years old, and the transgender father became the primary caregiver for approximately two years, until the mother removed his name from the birth certificate, changed the children's last names, and prevented the father from seeing them.[444] In a suit for custody, the father presented expert testimony that the children would suffer emotional problems without the presence of their father.[445] The trial court dismissed his petition for custody, finding no evidence that the biological mother was "unable, unfit, neglectful, abusive, unwilling, or that she abandoned her rights" such that her constitutionally protected right should be overridden.[446]

In a comprehensive opinion, the Fifth Circuit vacated the decision of the trial court and ordered a custody evaluation to be performed to determine whether the children would suffer substantial harm if sole custody were granted to the mother.[447] The court conducted a thorough examination of the law in several southern states governing nonparent custody, suggesting that a more malleable standard may be needed given the changing nature of the American family.[448] Without opining on what standard may be appropriate, and cognizant that article 133 undeniably applies to a nonparent seeking custody, the court recognized the need to know the impact of a sole custody award on the children given the test of substantial harm.

439. Cook, 330 So. 3d at 158–59.

440. Ferrand v. Ferrand, 16-7, p. 6 (La. App. 5 Cir. 8/31/16), 221 So. 3d 909.

441. Ferrand, 221 So. 3d at 916.

442. Ferrand, 221 So. 3d at 916.

443. Ferrand, 221 So. 3d at 916.

444. Ferrand, 221 So. 3d 909, 917.

445. Ferrand, 221 So. 3d at 918.

446. Ferrand, 221 So. 3d at 918.

447. Ferrand, 221 So. 3d at 939.

448. *See* Ferrand, 221 So. 3d at 928–38. The court discussed the doctrines of in loco parentis, psychological parent, and de facto parent, which allow courts to consider the child's best interest in light of the changing demographics of the family. *See* Ferrand, 221 So. 3d at 922–24.

Some Louisiana courts acknowledge that disputes between same-sex couples who raise a child together as parents are more akin to heterosexual divorcing parents than a typical parent–nonparent relationship.[449] Still, a natural parent has rights protected by the Constitution,[450] and those rights must be balanced against the best interest of the child.[451] Louisiana's law on nonparent custody strikes a principled balance by requiring the nonparent to prove substantial harm to the child if custody would be vested solely in the biological parent. Once a court determines that a child will experience substantial harm or detrimental consequences if the nonparent is denied custody, it should permit custody to the nonparent. The current issue, though, is that the highest court in the state is requiring future harm to the child and has found no substantial harm to children who are removed from the lives of the nonparent with whom they have had a relationship.[452] Courts should keep in mind the changing nature of the family and the best interest lens under which each particular set of facts and circumstances should be viewed. Justice Griffin, in her concurrence in *Cook*, emphasized this by stating: "The nuclear family concept that has influenced our laws regarding custody and visitation of children is not always reflected in the real life factual circumstances in the cases that come before our courts."[453] She recognized that the biological mother in that case is not an unfit mother, and the nonparent is not the third party envisioned by the legislature in its enactment of article 133.[454] She ended by placing the burden on the legislature "to address these important policy issues of child custody and visitation rights involving same-sex relationships."[455]

Although article 133 is a "dual part" analysis—first, the nonparent must prove substantial harm to the child if custody is awarded to the parent, and second, the nonparent must prove that custody with the nonparent is in the best interest of the child—can one prong really be examined without considering the other?[456] Whether the children would suffer substantial harm necessitates looking at their best interest. Indeed, integrating these prongs is most desirable when the nonparent is acting as a parent. Determining that a nonparent is a psychological or de facto parent, as compared to a nonparent who has never functioned as a parent, could assist in a finding of substantial harm. In fact, a doctrine that differentiates between a nonparent who is welcomed by

449. In re C.A.C., 2017-0108 (La. App. 4 Cir. 11/2/17), 231 So. 3d 58.

450. In re C.A.C., 2017-0108, p. 15 (La. App. 4 Cir. 11/2/17), 231 So. 3d 58, 70; Tracie F. v. Francisco D., 2015-1812, p. 14 (La. 3/15/16), 188 So. 3d 231, 242.

451. *See* Ferrand, 221 So. 3d at 919 (noting that the right of a parent is not unconditional).

452. Cook v. Sullivan, 2020-01471 (La. 9/30/21), 330 So. 3d 152.

453. Cook, 330 So. 3d at 160.

454. Cook, 330 So. 3d at 160.

455. Cook, 330 So. 3d at 160.

456. Ferrand, 221 So. 3d at 922 ("In light of the Supreme Court's recent emphasis in *Tracie F. v. Fran[c]isco D.* that the best interest of the child is the principal consideration in all child custody determinations, including initial custody contests between parents and nonparents, however, the legal question arises—may a trial judge rule on whether a nonparent has met his burden of proving substantial harm under La. C.C. art. 133 without also considering the best interest of the child, as provided in La. C.C. art. 134?").

the parent to function as another parent and a nonparent who functions only as a close relative or friend of the child better protects the wishes of the parent, the expectations of the parties, and the best interest of the child.

§ 6:24 Best Interest of the Child Factors

The hallmark consideration in an award of custody is the best interest of the child.[457] Courts use the enumerated factors found in Article 134 of the Civil Code to make its determination. When applying these factors, the court should not perform a mechanical application of the factors but should decide each case in light of those applicable to the unique factual circumstances of each case.[458] "These factors are not exclusive but are provided as a guide to the court, and the relative weight given to each factor is left to the discretion of the court."[459] Further, courts can consider the conduct of the parents both before and during the marriage in assessing best interest.[460]

Trial courts have inherent power to determine a child's best interest; as a result, courts can tailor custody and visitation orders to minimize any negative consequences on the child.[461] Courts are required to weigh and balance the factors favoring or opposing custody based on the evidence presented, and the court is not bound to give more weight to one factor over another.[462] Additionally, the court is not permitted to apply any presumption or preference based solely on the gender of the parent.[463]

On appellate review, the trial court's determination of custody is afforded great weight, and its discretion will not be disturbed on review in the absence of a clear showing of abuse of discretion because the trial court is in a better position to evaluate

457. La. Civ. Code Ann. art. 131; *see also* Orrill v. Orrill, 2008-0400, p. 4 (La. App. 4 Cir. 2/4/09), 5 So. 3d 279, 282 (stating the best interest of the child is the "principal substantive criterion for granting and changing custody"); Lee v. Davis, 579 So. 2d 1130, 1132 (La. Ct. App. 2 Cir. 1991); Schloegel v. Schloegel, 584 So. 2d 344, 346 (La. Ct. App. 4 Cir. 1991).

458. Noland v. Noland, 2016-641, p. 5 (La. App. 3 Cir. 4/26/17), 218 So. 3d 215, 220; Dunklin v. Dunklin, 46-885, p. 5 (La. App. 2 Cir. 2/29/12), 86 So. 3d 741, 744; Thibodeaux v. O'Quain, 2009-1266, p. 3 (La. App. 3 Cir. 3/24/10), 33 So. 3d 1008, 1012; Martello v. Martello, 2006-0594, p. 5 (La. App. 1 Cir. 3/23/07), 960 So. 2d 186, 191; Verret v. Verret, 34-982, p. 15 (La. App. 2 Cir. 5/9/01), 786 So. 2d 944, 953; Breaux v. Breaux, 96-214, pp. 3–4 (La. App. 3 Cir. 7/17/96), 667 So. 2d 1106, 1108.

459. Langford v. Langford, 49,080, p. 3 (La. App. 2 Cir. 4/9/14), 138 So. 3d 101, 104; *see also* La. Civ. Code Ann. art. 134 cmts. (a)–(b); C.M.J. v. L.M.C., 2014-1119, p. 17 (La. 10/15/14), 156 So. 3d 16, 29; Turner v. Turner, 455 So. 2d 1374, 1377 n.2 (La. 1984). In *Veronie v. Mireles*, the court considered the mother's alleged intellectual deficiencies but did not deem them concerning. 2022-105 (La. App. 3 Cir. 6/8/22), 44 So. 3d 210.

460. Hargrove v. Hargrove, 29,590, p. 3 (La. App. 2 Cir. 5/9/97), 694 So. 2d 645, 647.

461. Lucky v. Way, 51,706, p. 31 (La. App. 2 Cir. 9/1/17), 245 So. 3d 110, 129; *see also* Duplessy v. Duplessy, 12-69, p. 13 (La. App. 5 Cir. 6/28/12), 102 So. 3d 209, 216.

462. Moreau v. Moreau, 2015-0564, p. 6 (La. App. 4 Cir. 11/18/15), 179 So. 3d 819, 823; Martello v. Martello, 2006-0594, p. 5 (La. App. 1 Cir. 3/23/07), 960 So. 2d 186, 191; Luplow v. Luplow, 41,021, p. 5 (La. App. 2 Cir. 2/28/06), 924 So. 2d 1135, 1140; Romanowski v. Romanowski, 2003-0124, p. 4 (La. App. 1 Cir. 2/23/04), 873 So. 2d 656, 659; Hill v. Hill, 34,104, pp. 2–3 (La. App. 2 Cir. 1/24/01), 777 So. 2d 1263, 1265.

463. Hill, 777 So. 2d at 1266; Dubois v. Dubois, 532 So. 2d 360, 361 (La. Ct. App. 3 Cir. 1988).

the credibility of the witnesses.[464] Even the trial court's failure to include an analysis of the article 134 factors has not been deemed an abuse of discretion, because "no exhaustive analysis of La. Civ. Code art. 134 is required under the law."[465]

Through the comprehensive revision of the laws on custody in 1993 until the year 2018, the best interest of the child factors remained the same. In 2018, the legislature enacted Act 412, adding two new factors and expounding on two existing factors, all with a focus on potential abuse that could affect a child.[466] Best interest is now defined in 14, rather than 12, factors, but the factors remain illustrative, so any fact having a bearing on the child should be considered in the court's analysis.

§ 6:25 Best Interest of the Child Factors—Factor 1: The Potential for the Child to Be Abused

In 2018, the legislature renumbered the existing best interest of the child factors and added a new first factor: "The potential for the child to be abused, as defined by Children's Code Article 603(2), which shall be the primary consideration."[467] Article 603(2) defines abuse expansively and includes attempted or actual mental or physical injury, exploitation or overwork, and involvement in sexually related activities.[468] Any form of abuse performed or tolerated by the parent will be a factor affecting the custody of a child, and the Post-Separation Family Violence Relief Act,[469] as well as the Domestic Abuse Assistance Act,[470] provide mandatory, nonwaivable restrictions on custody and visitation.[471] This factor contemplates abuse not yet attempted or performed, but the potential that the child could be abused by the person seeking custody or other people in the company of that person.[472]

---

464. La. Civ. Code Ann. art. 134 cmt. (b).

465. Stewart v. Stewart, 2011-1334, p. 6 (La. App. 3 Cir. 3/7/12), 86 So. 3d 148, 154.

466. Act No. 412, 2018 La. Acts.

467. La. Civ. Code Ann. art. 134(A)(1).

468. La. Child. Code Ann. art. 603(2).

469. *See generally* La. Stat. Ann. §§ 9:361–:369.

470. *See generally* La. Stat. Ann. §§ 46:2131–:2143.

471. Paragraph B of article 134 was added to include direct reference to the Post-Separation Family Violence Relief Act and the Domestic Abuse Assistance Act when abuse, as defined by those acts and other criminal laws, are present. *See* La. Civ. Code Ann. art. 134(B).

472. *Cf.* Wilson v. Brown, 54,699 (L. App. 2 Cir. 8/10/22, 345 So. 3d 513 (finding the child's complaints of being "hurt all the time" and the mother and her boyfriend "being mean to him" to possibly be indications of poor parenting skills but not necessarily abuse even though they admitted to using corporal punishment to discipline child).

§ 6:26 Best Interest of the Child Factors—Factor 2: The Love, Affection, and Other Emotional Ties Between Each Party and the Child

When evaluating the child's best interest, courts can consider the love, affection and emotional ties between the party and the child.[473] Courts generally do not spend a great deal of time on this factor because both parties are seeking custody and thus genuinely love the child.[474] If there is evidence that one party has abdicated parenting responsibilities to another or has little interest in the child, this factor can favor the other party.[475] A custody evaluation can help determine whether one party has stronger emotional ties with the child. Courts consider the emotional connection that exists at the time custody is determined, even if the connection changed due to the acts of another party.[476] Courts have also recognized that a parent's mode of discipline can affect the emotional ties with the child, particularly when the discipline is not age-appropriate.[477]

---

473. La. Civ. Code Ann. art. 134(A)(2); *see also, e.g.*, Bourque v. Bourque, 03-1254, p. 12 (La. App. 5 Cir. 3/30/04), 870 So. 2d 1088, 1096 (finding that father played an important role in child's life by fishing, hunting, and attending church services with him); Masters v. Masters, 35,477, p. 5 (La. App. 2 Cir. 10/2/01), 795 So. 2d 1271, 1276 (determining that child's establishment of a support system in father's community, despite the mother constantly trying "to thwart father-daughter relationship," was sufficient to establish that love, affection, and other emotional ties weighed in the father's favor).

474. *See, e.g.*, Hobbs v. Hobbs, 42,353, pp. 8–9 (La. App. 2 Cir. 8/15/07), 962 So. 2d 1148, 1153 (weighing factor equally because both parents equally loved the child); Greene v. Taylor, 2001-1137, p. 10 (La. App. 3 Cir. 2/27/02), 809 So. 2d 1187, 1194 (weighing factor equally because "the children show[ed] their affection to both parents"); In re Marriage of Blanch, 2010-1686, p. 16 (La. App. 4 Cir. 9/28/11), 76 So. 3d 557, 568 (noting that the court-appointed evaluator determined that both parents genuinely loved the child).

475. *See* Cortez v. Cortez, No. 2011-1485, 2012 WL 1079201, at *6 (La. Ct. App. 1 Cir. Mar. 29, 2012) (weighing factor against the mother because she abdicated her parenting responsibilities to her sister-in-law when her husband was not home); Griffith v. Latiolais, 2009-0824, pp. 11, 22 (La. App. 3 Cir. 3/3/10), 32 So. 3d 380, 388, 395 (weighing factor in mother's favor because father had only a "passing interest" in child and saw custody award as "nothing more than victory over his former lover").

476. *See* Palazzolo v. Mire, 2008-0075, p. 47 (La. App. 4 Cir. 1/7/09), 10 So. 3d 748, 775 (finding that a disruption of the maternal or paternal bond that once existed between the party and the child affects the "emotional ties" and tends to be detrimental in weighing this factor, even when the other parent is responsible for the disruption); *see also* Harang v. Ponder, 2009-2182, pp. 14–15 (La. App. 1 Cir. 3/26/10), 36 So. 3d 954, 965 (finding that sufficient evidence was presented showing that a "material change in circumstances" had occurred because the child was older, "had developed a closer and more loving relationship with his father," and it was in child's "best interest to expand his relationship with his father," who testified that his bonding with child had drastically increased over time).

477. *See, e.g.*, Bergeron v. Clark, 2002-493, p. 7 (La. App. 3 Cir. 10/16/02), 832 So. 2d 327, 331 (finding that mother's discipline for toddler was not age appropriate, and as a consequence, her emotional connection suffered).

§ 6:27 Best Interest of the Child Factors—Factor 3: The Capacity and Disposition of Each Party to Give the Child Love, Affection, and Spiritual Guidance and to Continue the Education and Rearing of the Child

Courts also consider the capacity and disposition of the parties to give love, affection, spiritual guidance, and a good education to the child. Because those vying for custody generally show sincere love and affection for the child,[478] courts tend to focus on whether a party attends church[479] and whether a party has some special ability or has shown an inability to assist in the educational rearing of the child.[480]

Consideration of a party's religious preference has the potential to interfere with the Free Exercise Clause of the First Amendment, so courts are careful in their discussion. Generally, courts have recognized the custodial parent's authority to make decisions relative to the child's religious upbringing.[481] However, parents cannot force their religious affiliation on the noncustodial or nondomiciliary parent or prevent the parent from introducing a different religious affiliation to the child, absent some negative effect on the child's best interest.[482]

The Third Circuit, in the only comprehensive discussion of the issue, protected the religious interests of a nondomiciliary parent when those interests conflicted with the domiciliary parent. In *D.R.S. v. L.E.K.*, the trial court granted the mother sole custody

---

478. *But see* Cortez v. Cortez, No. 2011-1485, 2012 WL 1079201, at *6 (La. Ct. App. 1 Cir. Mar. 29, 2012) (weighing factor against the mother because she avoided parenting responsibility).

479. *See generally* Schneider v. Schneider, 2012-1241 (La. App. 3 Cir. 6/20/13), 115 So. 3d 1279 (finding that emotional ties to one's church are strong considerations); Crowsen v. Crowsen, 32,314, p. 6 (La. App. 2 Cir. 9/22/99), 742 So. 2d 107, 111 (La. App. 2 Cir. 1999) (favoring the father because he was the child's "only exposure to organized religion" before and after the divorce).

480. *See, e.g.*, Greene v. Taylor, 2001-1137, p. 10 (La. App. 3 Cir. 2/27/02), 809 So. 2d 1187, 1194 (weighing factor against mother because of child's consistent tardiness at school while in mother's custody and mother's inability to assist the child in completing the child's home assignments); Hobbs v. Hobbs, 42,353, pp. 5–6 (La. App. 2 Cir. 8/15/07), 962 So. 2d 1148, 1152 (weighing factor in favor of mother because she was an educator); Palazzolo v. Mire, 2008-0075, p. 48 (La. App. 4 Cir. 1/7/09), 10 So. 3d 748, 776 (weighing factor in favor of mother that had home schooled the child and continued to assist the child with school work); Richard v. Richard, 2009-0299, p. 17 (La. App. 1 Cir. 6/12/09), 20 So. 3d 1061, 1073 (weighing factor in favor of father because of mother's unrealistic expectations for special needs child and the fact that mother was distracted by new marriage and baby).

481. Pardue v. Pardue, 285 So. 2d 552, 554–55 (La. Ct. App. 1 Cir. 1978) (noting that the mother, as legal tutrix of the children, was charged with responsibility for their religious training and the children preferred her choice of religion, so the father's visitation had to comply with those wishes); *see also* Reynier v. Reynier, 545 So. 2d 663, 664–65 (La. Ct. App. 5 Cir. 1989) (finding that the father was required to take his daughter to her religious training when she was visiting him on Sunday mornings and was not to talk about his religion because it was scary for the child).

482. D.R.S. v. L.E.K., 2009-1274, pp. 9–10 (La. App. 3 Cir. 3/10/10), 33 So. 3d 428, 433. *But see* Reynier, 545 So. 2d at 665 (stopping the father from discussing religion with the child). *See also* Linda D. Elrod, Child Custody Practice and Procedure § 6:21 (2013).

with the sole authority to decide the children's religion.[483] The Third Circuit reversed the award of sole custody to the mother because she had not met her clear and convincing burden of proof.[484] The court awarded the parents joint custody and found it necessary to address the issue of religious preference because it named the mother as the domiciliary parent.[485] The court pointed to the Children's Code, which defines "residual parental rights" as those rights provided to a parent without custody, which includes the right to determine religious affiliation.[486] The court also considered a Fifth Circuit case in which a mother attempted to restrict the father's visitation rights based on the asserted religious beliefs of the children.[487] The Fifth Circuit recognized the importance of both parents in the life of a child and the "realistic necessity" that a child needs to learn to interact with others of different religious backgrounds.[488] Ultimately, the court in *D.R.S. v. L.E.K.* balanced the rights of the parents to further the best interest of the child when it concluded:

> Though the custodial or domiciliary parent may raise the child in a legitimate religion of his/her own choosing, that parent may not force that religion or religious affiliation upon the noncustodial parent or preclude the noncustodial parent from pursuing his/her own religious affiliation and sharing same with the child provided doing so does not negatively affect the best interests of the child.[489]

Undoubtedly, the best interest of the child, even in religious disagreements, remains the primary consideration. And, while spiritual guidance provided by a parent can be a catalyst to receiving custody, it cannot be used as a sword to minimize the religious rights of the other parent.

---

483. D.R.S, 33 So. 3d at 433.

484. D.R.S., 33 So. 3d at 433.

485. D.R.S., 33 So. 3d at 433.

486. La. Child. Code Ann. art. 116(24) (defining "residual parental rights" as "those rights and responsibilities remaining with the parents after the legal transfer of custody of their child, including but not necessarily limited to right of visitation, consent to adoption, *right to determine religious affiliation*, responsibility of support, and the right of inheritance from the child") (emphasis added).

487. *See generally* Becnel v. Becnel, 98-593 (La. App. 5 Cir. 03/25/99), 732 So. 2d 589.

488. Becnel, 732 So. 2d at 595; *see also* Susan Higginbotham, *"Mom, Do I Have to Go to Church?": The Noncustodial Parent's Obligation to Carry Out the Custodial Parent's Religious Plans*, 31 Fam. L. Q. 585, 596 (1997) (noting that "curtailing" the noncustodial parent's visitation with a child "in order to further the religious wishes of a custodial parent is not in harmony with [the] goal" of maintaining a healthy relationship with the noncustodial parent).

489. D.R.S., 33 So. 3d at 434.

§ 6:28 Best Interest of the Child Factors—Factor 4: The Capacity and Disposition of Each Party to Provide the Child with Food, Clothing, Medical Care, and Other Material Needs

The best interest of the child also involves the capacity and disposition of each party to provide for the child, namely food, clothing, medical care, and any other material needs. Although custody cannot be determined solely by comparing the parents' financial abilities, it may be considered when weighing the parents' respective abilities to provide.[490] Therefore, courts have considered the income and job stability of the parties[491] and have favored the party who historically provided for the child's material needs.[492]

Public policy would dictate that no factor should weigh against a party in a custody contest simply because the party has a lower income and will need an award of child support if custody is awarded. At least one court, however, noted that the mother's dependency on child support and public assistance weighed against her.[493]

---

490. Millet v. Andrasko, 93-0520, p. 7 (La. App. 1 Cir. 3/11/94), 640 So. 2d 368, 371; *see also* Boyd v. Boyd, 26,292, p. 7 (La. App. 2 Cir. 12/7/94), 647 So. 2d 414, 417–18 (noting that one parent's greater material wealth is not a factor when the other parent's home is adequate).

491. *See, e.g.*, Hobbs v. Hobbs, 42,353, p. 5 (La. App. 2 Cir. 8/15/07), 962 So. 2d 1148, 1151 (favoring the father who made more money and was a better financial manager than the mother who had filed for bankruptcy); Greene v. Taylor, 2001-1137, pp. 10–11 (La. App. 3 Cir. 2/27/02), 809 So. 2d 1187, 1194 (favoring the father who had a steady job when compared to the mother who was remarried and no longer working while caring for her and her new husband's children); *cf.* Griffith v. Latiolais, 2009-0824, p. 11 (La. App. 3 Cir. 3/3/10), 32 So. 3d 380, 389 (finding that though the father was in a superior financial position, he had shown that he was more willing to use that situation to get his way rather than to financially support his child, and mother was the party actually providing food, clothing, medical care, and other material needs).

492. *See* L.E.P.S. v. R.G.P., 2008-1349, p. 19 (La. App. 3 Cir. 6/3/09), 11 So. 3d 633, 645 (finding that both parties had the financial means to provide for the children, but favoring the mother who had been the party to take care of those needs on a day-to-day basis).

493. *See* Bergeron v. Clark, 2002-493, pp. 7–8 (La. App. 3 Cir. 10/16/02), 832 So. 2d 327, 331 (favoring the father because the mother was dependent on child support payments and public assistance to provide for the child and her other two children).

§ 6:29 Best Interest of the Child Factors—Factor 5: The Length of Time the Child Has Lived in a Stable, Adequate Environment, and the Desirability of Maintaining Continuity of that Environment

Factor five is often considered the most debated among the factors. When courts consider the length of time the child has lived in a stable and adequate environment, it considers whether it is desirable to maintain that living environment. Change is difficult for a child, and stability can help to ameliorate any negative feelings the child may have about the separation of his parents. Courts have analyzed this factor pragmatically, considering the size of the house and room available for the child,[494] as well as whether the home is a loving and caring home.[495] In a modification request, courts have also focused on whether the home environment is stable and whether the physical custody arrangement is beneficial to the child.[496] When the child is flourishing in his current environment, any change of custody is less likely, but if changes in physical custody are stressful on the child, this factor can be used to modify physical custody to create more stability for the child.[497]

---

494. *See* Greene v. Taylor, 2001-1137, p. 11 (La. App. 3 Cir. 2/27/02), 809 So. 2d 1187, 1194 (weighing factor in favor of father who had moved into a three-bedroom home where the children would have their own room as compared to the mother who lived in a one-bedroom apartment where the mother, her new husband, and the children shared a room); *see also* Palazzolo v. Mire, 2008-0075, p. 49 (La. App. 4 Cir. 1/7/09), 10 So. 3d 748, 776.

495. *See* Schneider v. Schneider, 2012-1241, pp. 14–15 (La. App. 3 Cir. 6/20/13), 115 So. 3d 1279, 1287–88 (reversing the trial court, which found the factor determinative of the case, because there was no evidence that the mother provided a home where the child was bombarded with negative feelings about his father, and all evidence pointed to a loving and caring family home); Hoskins v. Hoskins, 36,031, p. 4 (La. App. 2 Cir. 4/5/02), 814 So. 2d 773, 780 ("[Factors four and five] are relatively equal, even though the mother has moved many times over the past few years. She is currently married and more stable than she was before, and she has stable and suitable housing. The father also has stable and suitable housing, but he did move, requiring the child to change schools."); Thibodeaux v. O'Quain, 2009-1266, p. 7 (La. App. 3 Cir. 3/24/10), 33 So. 3d 1008, 1014 (finding that the mother's idea of stability amounted to control and prevented the child from having fun, thereby weighing the factor in favor of the father); *see also* Rogers v. Stockmon, 34,327, p. 5 (La. App. 2 Cir. 11/1/00), 780 So. 2d 386, 389.

496. *See, e.g.*, Holland v. Spellman, 10-982, pp. 14–15 (La. App. 5 Cir. 6/14/11), 71 So. 3d 996, 1004 (rejecting father's request to modify physical custody of child despite shortcomings of mom because child was happy and "living in a warm, stable, and loving environment with his mother at his grandmother's house"); Chandler v. Chandler, 45,308, p. 10 (La. App. 2 Cir. 5/19/10), 37 So. 3d 569, 576 (rejecting father's proposed change to shared equal custody because the "child ha[d] flourished under the current custody arrangement … [and] benefited greatly from stability and continuity under existing custody decree"); Ketchum v. Ketchum, 39,082, p. 9 (La. App. 2 Cir. 9/1/04), 882 So. 2d 631, 638 (rejecting a father's request to alternate physical custody on a week-to-week basis because the young child was thriving under the present custody arrangement); Lee v. Lee, 34,025, p. 9 (La. App. 2 Cir. 8/25/00), 766 So. 2d 723, 728 ("Stability of environment is an important factor to be taken into account in considering changes in custody. A change from a stable environment should not be made absent a compelling reason.").

497. *See, e.g.*, Griffith v. Latiolais, 2009-0824, p. 23 (La. App. 3 Cir. 3/3/10), 32 So. 3d 380, 395 (weighing this factor in favor of the mother because child had lived with the mother his entire life,

§ 6:30 Best Interest of the Child Factors—Factor 6: The Permanence, as a Family Unit, of the Existing or Proposed Custodial Home or Homes

The permanence of the existing or proposed custodial home requires the court to consider the continuity of the child's family unit, specifically siblings. When examining the permanence of the home, courts focus on the amount of time the child has lived in the home[498] and whether the parent has maintained a stable home life.[499] When examining the permanence of the "family unit," courts look beyond immediate family and have favored custody to a parent who has a large extended family near the custodial home.[500] For example, in *Trahan v. Kingrey*, the court emphasized that it was in the best interest of the child for him to remain in Houma, as he had approximately 91 relatives living in or around the area, instead of moving to West Virginia with his mother.[501]

Whether to separate siblings in a custody dispute has been a recurring issue. In 1969, the Louisiana Supreme Court in *Tiffee v. Tiffee* set forth the "family solidarity rule":

> The separation of children of a family, though sometimes necessary, is a custodial disposition that courts seek to avoid. Normally, the welfare of these children is best served by leaving them together, so they can have the full benefit of companionship and affection. When feasible, a court should shape its orders to maintain family solidarity.[502]

The court reaffirmed the family solidarity rule in 1999, in *Howze v. Howze,* when it reversed the award of split custody of two boys who were five years apart in age.[503]

---

child's emotional problems arose when the father disrupted that environment, and the mother still offered stability to child); Lemoine v. Lemoine, 2009-861, p. 10 (La. App. 3 Cir. 12/16/09), 27 So. 3d 1062, 1068 (weighing factor in favor of the mother's request for a change in physical custody because the "resultant upheaval in [the child's] life and constant change of domicile" was not in his best interest); Miller v. Miller, 32,506, p. 4 (La. App. 2 Cir. 6/16/99), 743 So. 2d 221, 224 (rejecting a modification request because the children were living in a safe and nurturing environment).

498. *See, e.g.*, Ketchum v. Ketchum, 39,082, p. 9 (La. App. 2 Cir. 9/1/04), 882 So. 2d 631, 638 (maintaining primary physical custody in the home where the child was born and lived since that date because of the importance of permanence to a young child); Flanagan v. Flanagan, 36,852, p. 8 (La. App. 2 Cir. 3/5/03), 839 So. 2d 1070, 1075 (denying a modification of custody because the father had maintained the custodial home for his three daughters for the past six years and maintaining continuity was in their best interest).

499. *See* Masters v. Masters, 35,477, p. 6 (La. App. 2 Cir. 10/2/01), 795 So. 2d 1271, 1276 (weighing the factor in father's favor because he maintained his residence in Ouachita Parish, while the mother had moved repeatedly in and out of state, and had failed to move back to Ouachita Parish as she claimed).

500. *See* Trahan v. Kingrey, 2011-1900, pp. 14–15 (La. App. 1 Cir. 5/4/12), 98 So. 3d 347, 355 (weighing the factor in favor of the father because the father and child had strong ties to Louisiana as their home, with over 90 relatives nearby, rather than moving to West Virginia with his mother); *see also* Bonnecarrere v. Bonnecarrere, 2011-0061 (La. App. 1 Cir. 7/1/11), 69 So. 3d 1225.

501. Trahan, 98 So. 3d at 361–62.

502. Tiffee v. Tiffee, 223 So. 2d 840, 843 (La. 1969). The Louisiana Supreme Court reversed the lower court's split custody of two sisters, ages six and seven, and reinstated the original custody in favor of the mother with reasonable visitation by the father. *Id.*

503. Howze v. Howze, 99-0996, p. 3 (La. 5/14/99), 735 So. 2d 619, 621.

The court explained that "the age gap is not so large as to preclude the children from sharing some similar interests and from deriving great benefit and comfort from living together as part of a family."[504] Of course, courts must only apply the family solidarity rule if it is in the best interest of the children. To determine whether keeping siblings together is in the children's best interest, courts have considered the age of the siblings,[505] the age difference between the siblings,[506] the sex of the siblings,[507] and the consanguinity of the siblings.[508] In some circumstances, separation of siblings has been deemed to be in the best interest of the children.[509] Courts will consider any fact that affects the child's best interest, and to aid in its analysis, courts have relied on the testimony of experts and have been sensitive to any emotional or physical concerns within the family.[510]

---

504. Howze, 735 So. 2d at 621.

505. *See, e.g.*, Roberie v. Roberie, 33,168, pp. 7–8 (La. App. 2 Cir. 12/8/99), 749 So. 2d 849, 854 (determining that teenage boys benefit from companionship and affection, just as younger boys).

506. *See, e.g.*, Tiffee, 223 So. 2d at 843 (refusing to separate sisters one year apart in age); Howze, 735 So. 2d at 621 (refusing to separate brothers who were approximately five years apart); Walker v. Walker, 38, 982, pp. 3–4 (La. App. 2 Cir. 8/18/04), 880 So. 2d 956, 959–60 (separating brothers who were seven and one-half years apart and who preferred to live with different parents); Lee v. Davis, 579 So. 2d 1130, 1133–34 (La. Ct. App. 2 Cir. 1991) (refusing to separate two sisters who were six years apart).

507. *See* Guidry v. Guidry, 2007-1272, p. 8 (La. App. 3 Cir. 3/5/08), 979 So. 2d 603, 608 (separating a son who was 15 and a daughter who was 14 to live with their father and mother, respectively, in light of the troubled relationship the son had with the mother; the parents lived one block from one another, and the children attended the same school). Same-sex siblings are less likely to be separated. *See, e.g.*, Tiffee, 223 So. 2d 840; Howze, 735 So. 2d at 621; Roberie, 749 So. 2d 849.

508. It does not appear that the family solidarity rule applies with the same vigor in half-sibling cases as it applies to full-blooded siblings; regardless, the best interest of the child overarches any analysis. *See, e.g.*, Cathey v. Ogea, 2012-563, pp. 9–10 (La. App. 3 Cir. 8/22/12), 98 So. 3d 953, 959 (awarding custody of an infant half-sibling to a different relative than was raising the other half-siblings because it would be best for one child's financial and health needs, but awarding visitation with the half-siblings); McKinley v. McKinley, 631 So. 2d 45, 50 (La. Ct. App. 2 Cir. 1994) (refusing to separate brother from two half-sisters, even though custodian of half-sister was not the biological father of the boy); *see also* Street v. May, 35,589 (La. App. 2 Cir. 12/5/01), 803 So. 2d 312; Mills v. Hardy, 2002-1062 (La. App. 3 Cir. 3/26/03), 842 So. 2d 443.

509. Daughtery v. Cromwell, 501 So. 2d 955, 956 (La. Ct. App. 2 Cir. 1987).

510. *See* Winzor v. Winzor, 2003-329, p. 11 (La. App. 3 Cir. 10/1/03), 856 So. 2d 107, 115 (refusing to separate three children because the middle and youngest of the children suffered mental and physical problems and would rely on the older child); Price v. Price, 451 So. 2d 1187, 1191 (La. Ct. App. 1 Cir. 1984) (separating the brother and sister to preserve the father-son relationship).

§ 6:31 Best Interest of the Child Factors—Factor 7: The Moral Fitness of Each Party, Insofar as It Affects the Welfare of the Child

The moral fitness of a party has long been a consideration in custody awards, but the focus has shifted toward the effects on the child, rather than simply the parent's behavior. To explain, the predecessor to factor seven instructed courts to consider "the moral fitness of the parties involved."[511] Because the focus at that time was the parent's immoral behavior, parents who lived in "open and public adultery" were considered morally unfit to maintain custody of children.[512] To soften the harsh result of this rule, the Louisiana Supreme Court created the "reformation rule," which permitted a parent to retain custody of a child if the parent reforms or abstains "from any previous course of open indiscretion and probable immorality."[513]

Over the course of the following two decades, courts applied the reformation rule liberally, and the focus began to shift to the effect the parent's immorality had on the children.[514] The legislature recognized that shift when, during the 1993 revision, it added the phrase "insofar as it affects the welfare of the child" to the morality factor.[515] After the revision, the statutory provision fell in line with the fundamental purpose of custody awards—to serve the best interest of the child, rather than to regulate human behavior.[516] Today, the reformation rule has little use because, regardless of whether the

511. La. Civ. Code Ann. art. 131(C)(2) (rev. 1992); *see also* La. Civ. Code Ann. art. 134 cmt. (f).

512. Monsour v. Monsour, 347 So. 2d 203 (La. 1977); Hilderbrand v. Hilderbrand, 391 So. 2d 577, 579–80 (La. Ct. App. 4 Cir. 1980).

513. Fulco v. Fulco, 254 So. 2d 603, 606 (La. 1971).

514. See Albarado v. Toler, 495 So. 2d 355, 358 (La. Ct. App. 3 Cir. 1986) for a development of the law after the creation of the reformation rule.

515. Act No. 261, 1993 La. Acts 610, 616.

516. La. Civ. Code Ann. art. 134 cmt. (f); *see* Stephenson v. Stephenson, 404 So. 2d 963, 966 (La. 1981) (upholding award of custody to wife whose past adulterous behavior was not shown to have any detrimental effect on the children); Cleeton v. Cleeton, 383 So. 2d 1231, 1236 (La. 1980) (same); *see also* Monsour, 347 So. 2d at 205 (primary consideration was welfare of child, not past misconduct of custodian). *But see* Bagents v. Bagents, 419 So. 2d 460, 462 (La. 1982) (upholding change of custody from mother who had lived in open concubinage in the custodial home). The rule embodied in this article should apply not only to past misconduct, as in the cases just cited, but also to continuing immorality that does not harm the child. *See* Rollins v. Rollins, 521 So. 2d 647, 649 (La. Ct. App. 1 Cir. 1988), *writ denied*, 522 So. 2d 573 (La. 1988) (joint custody not modified where there was no showing that mother's discreet illicit relationship had detrimental effect on child); Montgomery v. Marcantel, 591 So. 2d 1272, 1274 (La. Ct. App. 3 Cir. 1991) (change of custody to sole custody to wife due to father's living in concubinage reversed in absence of evidence of detrimental effect on child); Peters v. Peters, 449 So. 2d 1372, 1375 (La. Ct. App. 2 Cir. 1984) (upholding judgment refusing to take child from custody of mother who was living in concubinage with man she planned to marry); Peyton v. Peyton, 457 So. 2d 321, 324–25 (La. Ct. App. 2 Cir. 1984) (upholding equal joint custody award where both parents were engaged in discreet sexual relationships that had no adverse effect on the child).

parent's immoral behavior occurred before or at the time of the custody determination; instead, the focus remains on the effect the behavior has on the child.[517]

Courts apply this factor to various parental behaviors. As discussed in detail below, sexual relationships[518] and parental alienation[519] are consistently relevant in evaluating the moral fitness of a parent. So, too, are substance abuse[520] and criminal convictions.[521] Activities can range in severity from lack of judgment to sociopathic qualities, all of which can affect a custody award depending on the specific factual circumstances present in each case.

The effect of a parent's sexual lifestyle on a child receives considerable discussion in the jurisprudence. Courts consider the effect a parent's out-of-wedlock acts have on a child. As society's opinions on sexuality have changed, so too has the case law.

One of the first cases to consider the effect of a parent's sexual preference on a child was *Scott v. Scott*, decided in 1995.[522] In *Scott*, the parents initially had a joint custody agreement with the mother named as the domiciliary parent.[523] When the mother moved back to Louisiana to live with another woman, the father filed a rule to change custody.[524] The father argued that her lesbian relationship and open displays of affection had a detrimental effect on their two boys.[525] To determine whether a parent's sexual lifestyle is cause for affecting custody, the court set forth a four-part analysis: "(1) whether the children were aware of the illicit relationship, (2) whether sex play occurred in their presence, (3) whether the furtive conduct was notorious and brought embarrassment to the children, and (4) what effect the conduct had on the family home life."[526]

---

517. *See* Weaver v. Weaver, 2001-1656, pp. 6–7 (La. App. 3 Cir. 5/29/02), 824 So. 2d 438, 443 (noting that the reformation rule does not apply to absolve the mother's eight-year history of having seven boyfriends who lived or slept overnight at her residence in the presence of her young daughter).

518. *See, e.g.*, Crowson v. Crowson, 32,314, pp. 7–8 (La. App. 2 Cir. 9/22/99), 742 So. 2d 107, 112 (extramarital relationships); Richard v. Richard, 2009-0299 (La. App. 1 Cir. 6/12/09), 20 So. 3d 1061 (homosexual relationship); Scott v. Scott, 95-0816 (La. App. 1 Cir. 12/15/95), 665 So. 2d 760 (homosexual relationship).

519. *See, e.g.*, England v. England, 2017-0493 (La. App. 4 Cir. 3/2/18), 238 So. 3d 1064 (finding that mother's frivolous claims of child abuse that alienated the children from their father justified sole custody to father); Lucky v. Way, 51,706 (La. App. 2 Cir. 09/01/17), 245 So. 3d 110 (finding that parental alienation by mother contributed to an award of sole custody to father); Percle v. Noll, 93-1272 (La. App. 1 Cir. 3/11/94), 634 So. 2d 498, 501 (finding mother morally unfit because she hid children from father).

520. *See* L.E.P.S. v. R.G.P., 2008-1349, p. 20 (La. App. 3 Cir. 6/3/09), 11 So. 3d 633, 646; Fernandez v. Pizzalato, 2004-1676, p. 19 (La. App. 4 Cir. 4/27/05), 902 So. 2d 1112, 1124; Long v. Dossett, 98-1160, p. 23 (La. App. 3 Cir. 4/28/99), 732 So. 2d 773, 786; Gill v. Dufrene, 97-0777, p. 10 (La. App. 1 Cir. 12/29/97), 706 So. 2d 518, 523.

521. *See* L.E.P.S., 11 So. 3d at 646.

522. *See generally* Scott v. Scott, 95-0816 (La. App. 1 Cir. 12/15/95), 665 So. 2d 760.

523. Scott, 665 So. 2d at 762.

524. Scott, 665 So. 2d at 762.

525. The boys were approximately nine and six years of age at the time of the divorce and custody hearing. *See* Scott, 665 So. 2d at 762.

526. Scott, 665 So. 2d at 766.

After a review of each factor, the court concluded that domiciliary custody should be changed to the father based on the mother living with her girlfriend, concerns that the children had experienced embarrassment, and the "indiscreet displays of affection beyond mere friendship."[527] The court reaffirmed a statement made in a prior case that the mere fact of homosexuality will not deprive a parent of joint custody, but went on to say, "It is the opinion of this court that under such facts, primary custody with the homosexual parent would rarely be held to be in the best interests of the child."[528]

Almost 15 years later, in *Richard v. Richard*, the court modified a custody agreement to name the father as domiciliary parent even though he was in an openly gay relationship.[529] Upon the parents' divorce, the father moved in with his male partner and agreed to give domiciliary status of the four-year-old child to the mother.[530] Four years later, out of concern for the child's safety due to the mother's new husband and the father's relocation back to Louisiana, the father sought a change of custody requesting that he be named domiciliary parent of his now eight-year-old son.[531]

The court considered several factors to determine the child's best interest, and when focusing on the issue of the father's sexuality, applied the principles set forth in *Scott*.[532] The court noted that the father lived with his partner, who was actively involved in the child's life, the child knew that his father was gay, and there was no evidence that the child was embarrassed or that the men engaged in inappropriate contact in front of the child.[533] The court affirmed the trial court's decision to name the father as the domiciliary parent, regardless of "[w]hether personal feelings and moral judgments would incline individuals to consider otherwise."[534]

The *Scott* four-factor test predated the decision of the United States Supreme Court in *Obergefell v. Hodges*[535] that legalized same-sex marriage, so its continued application is not clear.[536] While the *Scott* test was crafted in a case involving homosexuality, it can be applied to any sexual orientation to the extent that the conduct causes embarrassment to the child and affects the child's family life. Indeed, when considering the best interest of the child, a parent's sexual conduct that reasonably causes distress to a child

527. Scott, 665 So. 2d at 766. The father admitted to sexual activity with his fiancée while the children were sleeping, but the two did not spend the night together. *Id.* at 765.

528. Scott, 665 So. 2d at 766; *see also* Lundin v. Lundin, 563 So. 2d 1273, 1277 (La. Ct. App. 1 Cir. 1990) (reversing the trial court's grant of sole custody to the mother and awarding joint custody with more custodial time to the father because the indiscreet displays of affection could affect the child's gender identity, which was not in his best interest).

529. Richard v. Richard, 2009-0299, pp. 16–17 (La. App. 1 Cir. 6/12/09), 20 So. 3d 1061, 1072–73.

530. Richard, 20 So. 3d at 1063–64.

531. Richard, 20 So. 3d at 1064.

532. Richard, 20 So. 3d at 1072.

533. Richard, 20 So. 3d at 1072.

534. Richard, 20 So. 3d at 1072–73.

535. *See generally* Obergefell v. Hodges, 135 S. Ct. 2584 (2015).

536. *See* Ferrand v. Ferrand, 16-7, p. 12 (La. App. 5 Cir. 8/31/16), 221 So. 3d 909, 921 (noting the dearth of Louisiana case law on custody of a child of a same-sex couple since the Supreme Court's decision).

and affects the child's daily living should be considered regardless of the parent's sexual orientation.

The concepts of parental alienation and parental alienation syndrome have also been discussed as an element of moral fitness, as well as a part of factor 12, the willingness to facilitate a relationship with the other party discussed in Section 6:36.[537] Although often confused, parental alienation is not the same as parental alienation syndrome, the latter of which has generated more controversy. Parental alienation involves a wide scope of behaviors by the alienating parent, whether conscious or unconscious, that disturbs the relationship between the child and the other parent.[538] By contrast, parental alienation syndrome occurs when a child is preoccupied with deprecation and criticism of a parent that is unjustified or exaggerated.[539] Parental alienation focuses on the parent's behavior alone, and parental alienation syndrome requires the child to be an active participant with the alienating parent.[540]

One Louisiana court comprehensively discussed parental alienation syndrome. In *Palazzolo v. Mire*, the court did not decide whether to recognize the disorder per se, but it considered the facts and the opinions of the experts to determine that the child was an "alienated child."[541] One expert opined that it would be best for an alienated parent to receive sole custody to begin to repair the damage to the relationship, while another expert opined that the alienating parent should receive sole custody because the child's alienation was not due solely to the alienating parent's tactics but the unwavering preference of the nine-year-old child.[542] The court concluded that the presence of alienation favored the alienated parent for the moral fitness and willingness to facilitate a close relationship factors but ultimately granted sole custody to the alienating parent with visitation to the other parent due to other factors.[543]

---

537. *See* Hilkirk v. Johnson, 2015-0577, p. 38 (La. App. 4 Cir. 12/23/15), 183 So. 3d 731, 752–53; Palazzolo v. Mire, 2008-0075, pp. 40–46 (La. App. 4 Cir. 1/7/09), 10 So. 3d 748, 771–75.

538. Sandi S. Varnado, *Inappropriate Parental Influence: A New App for Tort Law and Upgraded Relief for Alienated Parents*, 61 DePaul L. Rev. 113, 120 (2011).

539. Sandi S. Varnado, *Inappropriate Parental Influence: A New App for Tort Law and Upgraded Relief for Alienated Parents*, 61 DePaul L. Rev. 113, 116–17 (2011). The syndrome was coined by Dr. Richard Gardner in the 1980s and has generated controversy in the mental health and legal fields. Although the existence of parental alienation syndrome is controversial, there is little doubt that parental alienation has existed for years. *Id.* at 117 n.12.

540. Sandi S. Varnado, *Inappropriate Parental Influence: A New App for Tort Law and Upgraded Relief for Alienated Parents*, 61 DePaul L. Rev. 113, 117 n.2 (2011).

541. Palazzolo v. Mire, 2008-0075, p. 40 (La. App. 4 Cir. 1/7/09), 10 So. 3d 748, 771 ("[T]he classic alienated child is one that unjustifiably turns against the alienated parent solely as a result of the alienating parent's hostile actions, parenting tactics, and programming.").

542. Neither of the experts based their decision on parental alienation syndrome, although both recognized that alienation was present. Palazzolo, 10 So. 3d at 774–75.

543. Palazzolo, 10 So. 3d at 775–77. The parents in the *Palazzolo* case had a 24-year-long lesbian relationship. Palazzolo, 10 So. 3d at 750, 762. The alienating parent was the biological mother who changed her lifestyle after the breakdown of the relationship, and the alienated parent was the adoptive mother who was still living as a lesbian. *Id.*

In *White v. Kimrey*, the court likewise discussed parental alienation syndrome when a father sought a change of custody because of the alienating acts of the mother.[544] For the three years that the mother had domiciliary custody of the child, she intentionally undermined the father-daughter relationship, made relentless false allegations of sexual abuse, and constantly refused to allow the father to exercise his court-ordered visitation rights.[545] One expert diagnosed the situation as parental alienation syndrome because the mother was programming the child to be negative about the father.[546] If left with the mother, the child was at-risk for developing more serious emotional problems. When considering the best interest factors, the court recognized that the alienation impacted the mother's moral fitness as well as her willingness to facilitate a relationship with the father, and it named the father as the domiciliary parent.[547]

Although not always couched in terms of "parental alienation syndrome," courts recognize the damaging results possible when a parent partakes in any alienating behavior.[548] Even without using the term, courts understand alienating behavior when presented with it.[549] Whether the actions are discussed in the context of moral fitness or facilitating a relationship, alienating acts will have a bearing on custody.[550]

---

544. White v. Kimrey, 37,408 (La. App. 2 Cir. 5/14/03), 847 So. 2d 157.

545. White, 847 So. 2d at 163.

546. White, 847 So. 2d at 163 ("Dr. Baker further testified in effect that the mother was programming the child to be negative as regards the father. He diagnosed the situation as parental alienation syndrome, which is harmful to the child. He further related that the accepted method of treatment for parental alienation syndrome is to give the child to the parent not causing the alienation.").

547. White, 847 So. 2d at 163–64.

548. *See* Hilkirk v. Johnson, 2015-0577, p. 38 (La. App. 4 Cir. 12/23/15), 183 So. 3d 731, 752 (considering parental alienation to favor the father because the mother's negative and hostile attitude toward the father caused the child's negative view and alienation to her father).

549. *See* England v. England, 2017-0493, p. 8 (La. App. 4 Cir. 3/2/18), 238 So. 3d 1064, 1070 (the mother brought four frivolous claims of abuse against the father and subjected children to several "welfare checks" by the police while they were with their father; court determined that actions were detrimental to the children and awarded the father sole custody and supervised visitation to the mother); Lucky v. Way, 51,706, p. 21 (La. App. 2 Cir. 9/1/17), 245 So. 3d 110, 124 (emotional abuse by mother was an attempt to alienate child from his father; court awarded sole custody to the father with supervised visitation to the mother).

550. *See* Watts v. Watts, 2008-0834, p. 7 (La. App. 4 Cir. 4/8/09), 10 So. 3d 855, 860 (designating the mother as domiciliary parent because of the alienating behavior of the father and his new wife); Masters v. Masters, 35,477, p. 3 (La. App. 2 Cir. 10/2/01), 795 So. 2d 1271, 1274 (finding that the mother's perjury and coaching of the child to falsely allege sexual abuse bore negatively on her moral fitness); Goodwin v. Goodwin, 618 So. 2d 579, 586 (La. Ct. App. 2 Cir. 1993) ("[T]o intentionally damage a child's relationship with his father and to use children as instrumentalities to inflict pain on a former spouse is a serious shortcoming in the area of moral fitness."); *see also* Winzor v. Winzor, 2003-329, p. 9 (La. App. 3 Cir. 10/1/03), 856 So. 2d 107, 114 (noting the harmfulness of alienating statements made by the maternal grandparent, but refusing to impute the actions to the mother seeking to maintain custody).

§ 6:32 Best Interest of the Child Factors—Factor 8: The History of Substance Abuse, Violence, or Criminal Activity of Any Party

The history of substance abuse, violence, or criminal activity of a party was added as a new factor in 2018.[551] Although each of these actions could have been considered under other factors, they are now express. Presumably, though, crimes or violence that occurred in the past, which have been resolved by the person seeking custody, should not prevent an award of custody. Likewise, the history of an addict or alcoholic who has recovered and been clean for years should not affect custody.

§ 6:33 Best Interest of the Child Factors—Factor 9: The Mental and Physical Health of Each Party

The mental and physical health of the parties is another factor that courts consider when assigning custody. In 2018, this factor was amended to include a specific situation that could negatively affect a parent's mental health; namely, "evidence that an abused parent suffers from the effects of past abuse by the other parent" cannot prevent the abused parent from gaining custody.[552]

In assessing health, courts have considered the drug and alcohol use of a parent[553] and the physical ailments or impairments of a parent,[554] as well as the mental health of a parent.[555] In what was considered a "close case," the mother's emotional and physical health issues that caused her to deal with the children in a "stringent manner" impacted a trial court's decision to name the father as the primary domiciliary parent.[556]

The interdiction of a parent impacts the threshold question of fitness and can preclude an award of joint custody with that parent. In a custody dispute between a mother and a father, who had been interdicted due to a massive head injury, the court

551. Act No. 412, 2018 La. Acts.

552. Act No. 412, 2018 La. Acts.

553. *See generally* Molony v. Harris, 2010-1316 (La. App. 4 Cir. 2/23/11), 60 So. 3d 70 (mother's alcohol dependence basis for a motion to change custody that was ultimately denied); Brown v. Brown, 2005-1346 (La. App. 3 Cir. 3/1/06), 925 So. 2d 662 (mother's former drug use considered when maintaining sole custody with the father).

554. *See* Hargrove v. Hargrove, 29,590, pp. 7–8 (La. App. 2 Cir. 5/9/97), 694 So. 2d 645, 649 (mother's diagnosis of scleroderma, a potentially debilitating disease, contributed to a material change in circumstances, but was not enough to conclude that the mother was unable to care for the child); Gill v. Dufrene, 97-0777, pp. 12–13 (La. App. 1 Cir. 12/29/97), 706 So. 2d 518, 524 (considering the fact that the mother, who was deaf, turned off her hearing aid at night, which could affect her ability to hear the child cry out or the telephone).

555. *See* Watson v. Watson, 45,652, p. 6 (La. App. 2 Cir. 8/11/10), 46 So. 3d 218, 222 (considering father's mental health due to his pornography problem); Hobbs v. Hobbs, 42,353, pp. 4, 9 (La. App. 2 Cir. 8/15/07), 962 So. 2d 1148, 1151, 1153 (mother's depression resulted in weighing factor seven in father's favor, but did not preclude an award of joint custody because it was being treated).

556. *See* Luplow v. Luplow, 41,021, pp. 13–14 (La. App. 2 Cir. 2/28/06), 924 So. 2d 1135, 1144.

found that joint custody was inappropriate due to the father's interdiction alone.[557] The trial court awarded the mother sole custody, relying on the fact that the father could not make decisions regarding his children without the aid of his curator (the children's grandfather).[558] The appellate court affirmed, recognizing that an award of joint custody to the mother and father would effectively be an award of custody between a parent and a nonparent because the father's decision-making authority over himself—and therefore the children—rests with his curator, a nonparent.[559]

§ 6:34 Best Interest of the Child Factors—Factor 10: The Home, School, and Community History of the Child

Closely aligned with the permanence of the existing or proposed family home is the home, school, and community history of the child. When analyzing this factor, courts generally consider how long a child has resided in the home, what school the child is attending, the child's success in the school, and the involvement of the child in the community, including family relationships and extracurricular activities.

In *Leblanc v. Leblanc*, the trial court based its decision on the home and community history of the child.[560] The father filed a motion to modify custody to name him as the domiciliary parent because the mother was moving to a nearby city with her new husband.[561] Because both parents were equal in the other best interest factors, the court focused on the home and community history of the child.[562] The trial court modified custody and named the father as the domiciliary parent, focusing on the fact that the child had lived in the same parish his entire life and had extended family from both sides and close family friends in the parish, the loss of which would be a significant change in his life.[563] The appellate court reversed, finding that the father was unable to show a material change of circumstances simply based on the fact that the mother was moving.[564]

While this factor has relevance in any child custody determination, unless the child is a newborn, it is generally not a factor that is dispositive of custody. At the time when a child has a significant history in a home or with a school, the child is old enough to

557. Breaux v. Breaux, 96-214, pp. 4–6 (La. App. 3 Cir. 7/17/96), 677 So. 2d 1106, 1108–1109.

558. Breaux, 677 So. 2d at 1109.

559. Breaux, 677 So. 2d at 1108–09.

560. *See generally* Leblanc v. Leblanc, 2006-1052 (La. App. 3 Cir. 2/14/07), 951 So. 2d 500. The child was a preschooler and "did not have a significant school history yet." Leblanc, 951 So. 2d at 507.

561. Leblanc, 951 So. 2d at 505.

562. Because the move was less than 150 miles within the state, the relocation statute was not applicable. Leblanc, 951 So. 2d at 505.

563. Leblanc, 951 So. 2d at 503–04.

564. Leblanc, 951 So. 2d at 506–07. One judge on the panel dissented, arguing that deference should have been given to the trial court. Leblanc, 951 So. 2d at 508 (Genovese, J., dissenting).

establish a preference, which is generally given greater weight in the custody analysis.[565] In fact, if children have successfully moved and assimilated well, then this factor carries less weight.[566]

§ 6:35 Best Interest of the Child Factors—Factor 11: The Reasonable Preference of the Child, If the Court Deems the Child to Be of Sufficient Age to Express a Preference

Once a child is of an age and maturity to express a preference regarding custody, the court will give that preference weight. A child's preference, however, is not dispositive in deciding custody. The weight to be placed on the desires of a child varies from case to case. Indeed, a child's wishes may not be in the child's best interest.[567] Although a court should consider the child's wishes in awarding custody, it should not disregard the overwhelming evidence if the desired custody is contrary to the child's best interest.[568] Stability and continuity can be more important considerations than the wishes of the child. But, "where the parents are relatively equally balanced in terms of caring for the child, the preference of a mature and grounded teenager ... is entitled to great weight," notwithstanding instability.[569] The court's ultimate task is to determine what is in the child's best interest; the child's preference can be persuasive but not dispositive.

To determine the child's preference, the judge may interview the child, but before doing so, the judge must first determine the child's competency to testify. Judges may also choose not to question the child at all.[570] If the judge uses an interview to discover

565. *See, e.g.*, Palazzolo v. Mire, 2008-0075, p. 50 (La. App. 4 Cir. 1/7/09), 10 So. 3d 748, 777.

566. *See* L.E.P.S. v. R.G.P., 2008-1349, p. 19 (La. App. 3 Cir. 6/3/09), 11 So. 3d 633, 646 (triplet girls had successfully moved from Slidell to Jonesville, so making new friends in Arizona, where their mother was moving, should not be problematic).

567. *See* Jones v. Jones, 46,315, p. 8 (La. App. 2 Cir. 4/13/11), 63 So. 3d 1074, 1078 (12-year-old's desire to live with father was not in his best interest); Richardson v. Richardson, 2001-0777, pp. 12, 15 (La. App. 1 Cir. 9/28/01), 802 So. 2d 726, 733, 735 (12-year-old's desire to remain in Louisiana with friends and family was insufficient to show it was in his best interest to stay in state); Simmons v. Simmons, 554 So. 2d 238, 243 (La. Ct. App. 3 Cir. 1989)(preference of nine-year-old alone was insufficient to modify custody).

568. *See* L.E.P.S. v. R.G.P., 2008-1349 (La. App. 3 Cir. 6/3/09), 11 So. 3d 633 (refusing to follow preference of 13-year-old triplets who wanted to remain with their father and grandmother because their mother was moving to Arizona, even though the father had a drug problem and criminal problems involving carnal knowledge of a 15-year-old).

569. Mulkey v. Mulkey, 2012-2709, p. 16 (La. 5/7/13), 118 So. 3d 357, 368 (testimony of mature 14-year-old child convinced the court to change custody to child's father).

570. *See* In re C.M.M., 42,238, p. 18 (La. App. 2 Cir. 5/9/07), 957 So. 2d 330, 340 (in a termination of parental rights case, no reversible error when trial court refused to question the children); Bourque v. Bourque, 03-1254, p. 5 (La. App. 5 Cir. 3/30/04), 870 So. 2d 1088, 1091–92 (not error for trial court to refuse to question 11-year-old because the child was very anxious and stressed to choose one parent over the other).

the child's preference, he must conduct what is referred to as a "*Watermeier* hearing" based on the landmark *Watermeier v. Watermeier*[571] decision.

In *Watermeier*, the child's father challenged the interview of his five-year-old son by the judge in chambers without a record being made and over the objection of his counsel.[572] The Fifth Circuit concluded that the judge could not conduct an in-chambers interview of the child without a record being made, but it did set forth a detailed procedure under which a judge could interview a child as follows:[573]

> [T]he interview must be conducted in chambers outside of the presence of the parents, but in the presence of their attorneys, with a record being made by the court reporter. The judge shall first determine his competency as "a person of proper understanding" by interrogating the child with appropriate questions. The attorneys shall be allowed to participate in the competency examination by asking questions and registering appropriate but only necessary objections. If the judge determines that the child is not a competent witness as outlined above, he shall immediately terminate the interview.
>
> However, if the judge determines that the child is competent, he may continue the interview in the presence of the attorneys as observers only. They shall not participate by asking questions, or cross-examining or registering objections, as we deem this would upset, distract and possibly intimidate the child to a degree that would undermine his willingness to give any useful information.[574]

The *Watermeier* court further explained that this procedure need not be followed if the parties agree to an alternate procedure.[575] In other words, the trial court "may examine the child ... on or off the record, and with or without parents or counsel being present" as long as the parties agree.[576] Failure to follow this procedure without the consent of the parties is reversible error unless the party challenging has suffered no prejudice.[577] Furthermore, excluding testimony from a child without first conducting a *Watermeier* hearing can also be reversible error.[578] However, if the child is older, at least one court has concluded that a parent's due process rights could be violated if

571. *See generally* Watermeier v. Watermeier, 462 So. 2d 1272 (La. Ct. App. 5 Cir. 1985), *writ denied*, 464 So. 2d 301 (La. 1985); *see also* Lisa Carol Rogers, *Child Custody: The Judicial Interview of the Child*, 47 La. L. Rev. 559 (1987).

572. Watermeier, 462 So. 2d at 1273.

573. Watermeier, 462 So. 2d at 1275.

574. Watermeier, 462 So. 2d at 1275. Some courts permit the attorneys to submit a list of questions to the judge.

575. Watermeier, 462 So. 2d at 1275.

576. Watermeier, 462 So. 2d at 1275.

577. *See, e.g.*, In re Custody of Landry, 95-0141, p. 8 (La. App. 1 Cir. 10/6/95), 662 So. 2d 169, 173 (interviewing the children without the attorneys present and without a record was reversible error). *But see* Osborne v. McCoy, 485 So. 2d 150, 153 (La. Ct. App. 2 Cir. 1986) (failing to make a record of the child's testimony was not reversible error because of the lack of prejudice to the challenger).

578. *See* Raney v. Wren, 98-0869, pp. 9–10 (La. App. 1 Cir. 11/6/98), 722 So. 2d 54, 60 (failure to examine the child's competence when the record contains evidence that the child was competent is error).

they were *not* permitted to hear the child's testimony. For example, in *Fuge v. Uiterwyk*, the mother was sequestered during her 14- and 16-year-old sons' testimony.[579] There, the court concluded that the children, who the court described as "bright and capable young men," needed no protection from the presence of their parents during questioning, and on balance, the trial court's sequestration order violated the mother's due process rights.[580]

The level of competency, under a literal reading of the factor, suggests that the child must be of "sufficient age." Courts, however, have made clear that a person's age alone is not the test of their competency, but whether that person has "proper understanding."[581] The test of proper understanding comes from both the Louisiana Code of Evidence as well as Title 13 under "Competency of Witnesses." Article 601 of the Louisiana Code of Evidence provides: "Every person of proper understanding is competent to be a witness except as otherwise provided by legislation."[582] Title 13 of the Louisiana Revised Statutes, "Courts and Judicial Procedure," likewise provides: "The competent witness in any civil proceeding in court or before a person having authority to receive evidence shall be a person of proper understanding."[583]

As a result, no specific age has been deemed a "sufficient age." "[C]ompetency and maturity, not age, are the true determining factors."[584] Courts have permitted children as young as seven years old to testify[585] and have rejected the testimony of five- and six-year-olds as being of "tender age" and "not capable" of expressing a reasonable preference.[586] Between the ages of eight and 12, cases conflict and hinge on the understanding and maturity of the child.[587] Some states give greater weight to a child's preference if the child is over the age of 12, but Louisiana has no definable age-based rule.[588] In most cases, though, the preference of a child over the age of 12 will be considered, even

---

579. Fuge v. Uiterwyk, 94-1815, p. 6 (La. App. 4 Cir. 3/29/95), 653 So. 2d 707, 712.

580. Fuge, 653 So. 2d at 712. *But see* Lyons v. Lyons, 571 So. 2d 220, 221 (La. Ct. App. 3 Cir. 1990) (testimony of 14-year-old child allowed, and parent rightfully excluded from courtroom during child's testimony).

581. Watermeier, 462 So. 2d at 1274.

582. La. Code Evid. Ann. art. 601.

583. La. Stat. Ann. § 13:3665.

584. Bandy v. Bandy, 07-849, p. 14 (La. App. 3 Cir. 12/5/07), 971 So. 2d 456, 465.

585. *See* Osborne v. McCoy, 485 So. 2d 150, 153 (La. Ct. App. 2 Cir. 1986); *see also* Rodgers v. Rodgers, 26,093, p. 5 (La. App. 2 Cir. 9/21/94), 643 So. 2d 764, 767 (eight-year-old allowed to testify if *Watermeier* was followed); Raney v. Wren, 98-0869, pp. 9–10 (La. App. 1 Cir. 11/6/98), 722 So. 2d 54, 60 (decision to exclude competent nine-year-old's testimony was error).

586. *See, e.g.*, Bowden v. Brown, 48,268 (La. App. 2 Cir. 5/15/13), 114 So. 3d 1194 (children ages five and seven years old); In re S.I.G., 39,704 (La. App. 2 Cir. 3/2/05), 895 So. 2d 773 (children ages five and three); Alfonso v. Cooper, 2014-0145 (La. App. 4 Cir. 7/16/14), 146 So. 3d 796 (six-year-old child); Dykes v. Dykes, 488 So. 2d 368, 371 (La. Ct. App. 3 Cir. 1986) (five-year-old child); In re Fox, 504 So. 2d 101 (La. Ct. App. 2 Cir. 1987) (six-year-old child).

587. *See, e.g.*, Hensgens v. Hensgens, 94-1200 (La. App. 3 Cir. 3/15/95), 653 So. 2d 48 (eight-year-old); Richardson v. Richardson, 2009-609 (La. App. 3 Cir. 11/18/09), 25 So. 3d 203 (seven- and four-year-old children).

588. Prior Louisiana law contained a provision with particularized rules for determining the competency of children under the age of 12 to testify in criminal cases, but that was repealed in favor of a

though it will not always be followed.[589] Courts recognize, however, that the preference of a mature teenager can be given great weight in a determination of custody.[590]

Additionally, several criminal cases exist that apply "proper understanding" in the context of children and perform a fact-based inquiry to determine whether the child is competent to testify.[591] Children as young as four have been permitted to testify in a criminal case.[592] While no reported civil case has allowed a child that young to testify as to his preference regarding custody, the tests are substantially similar, so reliance on criminal cases may be appropriate.

§ 6:36 Best Interest of the Child Factors—Factor 12: The Willingness and Ability of Each Party to Facilitate and Encourage a Close and Continuing Relationship Between the Child and the Other Party

This factor can be considered one of the most important factors because when joint custody is ordered, which is most common, the law seeks to maintain continuing and frequent contact with both parents.[593] Therefore, the parent that is willing to encourage a close and continuing relationship between the child and the other parent will have the upper hand in a custody determination. In 2018, this factor was amended to make clear that one party need not be willing or able to facilitate a close relationship between the child and the other party when "objectively substantial evidence of specific abuse, reckless, or illegal conduct has caused one party to have reasonable concerns for the child's safety or well-being while in the care of the other party."[594]

---

general test of "proper understanding." *See* La. Stat. Ann. § 15:469, *repealed by* Act No. 515, 1988 La. Acts 1085.

589. *See, e.g.*, Jones v. Jones, 46,315, p. 7 (La. App. 2 Cir. 4/13/11), 63 So. 3d 1074, 1078 (12-year-old child; did not agree with preference); Sebren v. Sebren, 46,076, p. 6 (La. App. 2 Cir. 12/15/10), 56 So. 3d 1032, 1034 (12-year-old child; followed his preference); Bandy v. Bandy, 07-849 (La. App. 3 Cir. 12/5/07), 971 So. 2d 456 (12-year-old child; followed his preference); Stroud v. Stroud, 43,003, p. 10 (La. App. 2 Cir. 12/14/07), 973 So. 2d 865, 871 (12, almost 13, but did not agree with preference).

590. *See* Wages v. Wages, 39,819, p. 8 (La. App. 2 Cir. 3/24/05), 899 So. 2d 662, 667 (16-year-old child); Mulkey v. Mulkey, 2012-2709, pp. 15–16 (La. 5/7/13), 118 So. 3d 357, 367–68 (14-year-old child); Fuge v. Uiterwyk, 94-1815 (La. App. 4 Cir. 3/29/95), 653 So. 2d 707 (14- and 16-year-old child)

591. *See, e.g.*, State v. Pierce, 11-320, p. 17 (La. App. 5 Cir. 12/29/11), 80 So. 3d 1267, 1278 (7-year-old child); State v. Linson, 94-0061, pp. 6–7 (La. App. 1 Cir. 4/7/95), 654 So. 2d 440, 444 (7- and 8-year old children); State v. Doss, 522 So. 2d 1274, 1279 (La. Ct. App. 5 Cir. 1988), *writ denied*, 530 So. 2d 563 (La. 1988) (6- and 8-year old children).

592. *See* State v. Arnaud, 412 So. 2d 1013, 1018 (La. 1982) (the four-year-old child of a rape victim was found to be competent to testify); Doss, 522 So. 2d at 1279 (affirming trial court's decision that children, ages eight and six, were competent to testify in aggravated rape proceeding and not in violation of any statute or precedent).

593. *See* La. Stat. Ann. § 9:335.

594. Act No. 412, 2018 La. Acts.

Issues of parental alienation, explored above under factor seven and related to the moral fitness of the parent as it affects the child, are present in this factor as well.[595] For example, in *Orrill v. Orrill*, the court believed that the mother created a "fear" in her son surrounding his father's drinking and showed her unwillingness to facilitate a close relationship between the child and his father by unnecessarily involving the police when the son was staying with his father.[596] The court believed her actions amounted to "parental alienation" and named the father as the domiciliary parent, with custodial time with the mother only on the weekends.[597] In *England v. England*, the mother orchestrated situations to fabricate mistreatment by the father and consistently sent state workers to check on the father when the children were present.[598] The court awarded the father sole custody and the mother supervised visitation until she sought counseling by a mental health professional.[599] Even without terming the actions "parental alienation," courts will recognize a parent's efforts to undermine the parent-child relationship when considering this factor in custody determinations.[600]

Courts have considered not only the parent's willingness to facilitate a close relationship with the other parent but the willingness of other persons in the parent's life to do so, as well. In *McAlister v. McAlister*, even though the court recognized the mother's constant need to discredit the father, it also relied on the fact that the mother lived with her own father (the child's grandfather), who "loathed" the child's father, when it granted custody to the child's father.[601]

Under this factor, courts may also consider "a party's willingness to make travel arrangements and facilitate electronic communications" for the child to maintain a close relationship with the other parent.[602] For example, courts have looked favorably on a parent's willingness to live closer to the other parent to assure a child's continuing relationship with the parent. In *Steinebach v. Steinebach*, the mother was willing to stay in Louisiana, rather than move to Arizona with her parents, after the father moved to Florida, to avoid the need to transport the child a greater distance.[603] The court found that this factor favored the mother in her decided willingness to facilitate a relationship between the child and his father.[604]

---

595. *See* Section 6:31.

596. Orrill v. Orrill, 2008-0400, p. 12 (La. App. 4 Cir. 2/4/09), 5 So. 3d 279, 286.

597. Orrill, 5 So. 3d at 281, 286, 288; *see also* Guidry v. Guidry, 2007-1272, pp. 6–8 (La. App. 3 Cir. 3/5/08), 979 So. 2d 603, 607–09 (father and son's negative attitude toward the mother necessitated that daughter's custody remain with mother).

598. England v. England, 2017-0493, pp. 5, 8 (La. App. 4 Cir. 3/2/18), 238 So. 3d 1064, 1068, 1070.

599. England, 238 So. 3d at 1069.

600. *See* Verret v. Verret, 34,982, pp. 15–16 (La. App. 2 Cir. 5/9/01), 786 So. 2d 944, 953.

601. McAlister v. McAlister, 2008-1008, pp. 6–7 (La. App. 1 Cir. 9/19/08), 2008 WL 4287571.

602. La. Civ. Code Ann. art. 134 cmt. (rev. 2012).

603. Steinebach v. Steinebach, 2007-38, p. 8 (La. App. 3 Cir. 5/2/07), 957 So. 2d 291, 297.

604. Steinebach, 957 So. 2d at 297.

§ 6:37 Best Interest of the Child Factors—Factor 13: The Distance Between the Respective Residences of the Parties

Distance is a consideration that focuses on the daily welfare of the child and the practicalities of the child's relationship with each parent post-divorce. The legislature, under prior law, highlighted the importance of this factor when it enacted a special provision that eliminated the presumption of joint custody if one parent moved out-of-state.[605] As the presumption was repealed in the revision, so too was the special rule, but this factor remained to assist in determining not only the type of custody but the allocation of physical custody, as well.

When the parties live a sufficient distance from one another, equal sharing of time is not feasible. Joint custody mandates "frequent and continuing contact" with both parents but suggests that "to the extent it is feasible and in the best interest of the child" the parents should share equal physical custody.[606] As a matter of practicality, distance will play a significant role when allocating physical custody. When the parties live across state lines or at a distance that will involve significant travel time for the child, the court disfavors an equal sharing of time.

For example, when one parent lived in Texas and the other in Louisiana, the court explained that the distance between the parties' residences disfavored an equal sharing of time; rather, having one domiciliary parent with the other enjoying reasonable weekend and holiday time would be in the child's best interest.[607] Additionally, in *Elliot v. Elliot*, the parents shared joint custody with the father as domiciliary parent, and the mother moved to Texas, about five hours away from the children.[608] The father alleged a change of circumstances to modify her custodial time because it would involve up to 12 hours of travel for the children in a 48-hour window of time.[609] Recognizing that an interstate move is not a per se change of circumstance to warrant a modification of custody,[610] the court nonetheless found that the facts warranted a reduction in the mother's custodial time because of the significant distance between the parties and its effects on the children's extracurricular activities.[611]

---

605. *See* La. Civ. Code Ann. art. 134 cmt. (h).

606. La. Stat. Ann. § 9:335.

607. *See* Goldberg v. Goldberg, 2010-0452, 2010 WL 3903687, at *9–10 (La. Ct. App. 3 Cir. Oct. 6, 2010); see also Tripp v. Gener, No. 55,132-CA (La. App. 2 Cir. 04/26/23); 362 So. 3d 1265, 1274 (finding that shared custody with parents living in Webster Parish, Louisiana and Miami, Florida was not in the best interest of the child).

608. Elliot v. Elliot, 2010-0755, p. 3 (La. App. 1 Cir. 9/10/10), 49 So. 3d 407, 409–10.

609. Elliot, 49 So. 3d at 413.

610. *See* Bonnecarrere v. Bonnecarrere, 2009-1647, p. 7 (La. App. 1 Cir. 4/14/10), 37 So. 3d 1038, 1044.

611. Elliot, 49 So. 3d at 415–16; *see also* Doyle v. Doyle, 465 So. 2d 167 (La. Ct. App. 3 Cir. 1985); Lachney v. Lachney, 446 So. 2d 923 (La. Ct. App. 3 Cir. 1983).

§ 6:38 Best Interest of the Child Factors—Factor 14: The Responsibility for the Care and Rearing of the Child Previously Exercised by Each Party

The consideration of care and rearing previously exercised by each party is relatively new, inserted into the Civil Code in the revision of 1993. While the factor is a relatively recent addition to the Code, Louisiana courts have considered it in the past.[612] This factor, in particular, is especially relevant when determining which party should be the domiciliary parent, an intuitive concept as that parent has already been caring for the child and is likely the decision-maker for the child. In fact, one court suggested that a change in domiciliary status from a parent who has been the child's caregiver since birth could "greatly disrupt [the child] emotionally, developmentally, and academically, which would absolutely not be in the [the child's] best interest."[613]

The comments to Article 134 of the Civil Code provide a list of duties to assist a court in determining which party bears the responsibility for the child:

> (1) preparing and planning meals for the child; (2) bathing, grooming, and dressing him; (3) purchasing, cleaning, and caring for his clothes; (4) obtaining and providing medical care, including nursing and trips to physicians; (5) arranging for social interaction among the child's peers after school, e.g. transporting the child to friends' houses or to girl or boy scout meetings; (6) arranging alternative care, e.g. baby-sitting, day-care, etc.; (7) putting the child to bed at night, attending to the child in the middle of the night, waking the child in the morning; (8) disciplining him, including teaching him general manners and toilet training; (9) obtaining and providing education (religious, cultural, or social) for the child; and (10) teaching him elementary skills, e.g. reading, writing and arithmetic.[614]

In a traditional household, this factor will generally favor the mother, and when the child is of a young age, courts still consider the natural, maternal bond that exists with the child.[615] Although a maternal preference rule no longer exists, the realities of this factor, when the mother stays home with the child, will favor the mother. Even when the mother works outside of the home, if she is the parent with the primary respon-

612. La. Civ. Code Ann. art. 134 cmt. (i); Brackman v. Brackman, 322 So. 2d 314, 317 (La. Ct. App. 2 Cir. 1975) (in a best interest analysis, considering the desire to continue the children "in the care of the parent, who, in a normal situation, has provided the degree of continuous care and affection which creates such a close bond that it would be harmful to the children to alter that relationship"); *see also* Edwards v. Edwards, 556 So. 2d 207, 209 (La. Ct. App. 2 Cir. 1990); Quinn v. Quinn, 412 So. 2d 649, 654–55 (La. Ct. App. 2 Cir. 1982); Nale v. Nale, 409 So. 2d 1299, 1302 (La. Ct. App. 2 Cir. 1982).

613. In re Marriage of Blanch, 2010-1686, pp. 19–20 (La. App. 4 Cir. 9/28/11), 76 So. 3d 557, 570 (child had been in the care of the mother since birth for seven and a half years).

614. La. Civ. Code Ann. art. 134 cmt. (i).

615. *See, e.g.*, In re Marriage of Blanch, 76 So. 3d at 569–70; Nale, 409 So. 2d at 1302; Edwards, 556 So. 2d at 209.

sibility for a young child, as long as she is still in the position to do so, this factor will favor the mother.[616]

The court performed an analysis of primary caregiving in the case of *Cortez v. Cortez*, which involved the custody of a one-year-old child.[617] The majority awarded joint custody with domiciliary status to the father, even though he had been on duty for the National Guard during six months of the child's first year of life.[618] The mother, while periodically caring for the child, had relied on the father's relatives during his absence and had feigned an illness, which led to serious credibility problems with the court.[619] The majority found that the mother avoided primary caregiving for the child.[620] The majority was met with a strong dissent, which challenged factually the mother's alleged abdication of responsibility, noting that for most of the first year of the child's life, the mother was caring for the child.[621] The dissent discounted any credibility determination because it was not pertinent to the best interest of the child.[622] As is true for every factor, the particular facts generate the outcome, and the trial court is vested with a great deal of discretion in evaluating each witness and each factor.

§ 6:39 Best Interest of the Child Factors— Application of the Best Interest of the Child Factors

The article 134 factors are not exclusive and serve as a guide for the court in determining the best interest of the child.[623] The inquiry is fact-intensive and requires a court to weigh and balance factors to reach the paramount goal of a decision that meets the best interest of the child.[624] The plain language of article 134 illustrates that "the court is not bound to make a mechanical evaluation of all factors listed"; rather, "[e]ach

616. *See* Chauvin v. Chauvin, 2010-1055, p. 12 (La. App. 1 Cir. 10/29/10), 49 So. 3d 565, 574–75.

617. *See generally* Cortez v. Cortez, No. 2011-1485, 2012 WL 1079201 (La. Ct. App. 1 Cir. Mar. 29, 2012).

618. Cortez, 2012 WL 1079201, at *1–2.

619. Cortez, 2012 WL 1079201, at *4–6.

620. Cortez, 2012 WL 1079201, at *6–7.

621. Cortez, 2012 WL 1079201, at *9–13 (Hughes, J., dissenting).

622. Cortez, 2012 WL 1079201, at *9.

623. La. Civ. Code Ann. art. 134 cmts. (a)–(c). Comment (a) provides that "the factors are simply provided as a guide ... in making the fundamental finding as to what disposition is in the best interest of the child." La. Civ. Code Ann. art. 134 cmt. (a). Comment (b) provides that the list of factors provided in article 134 is "nonexclusive, and the determination as to the weight to be given each factor is left to the discretion of the trial court." La. Civ. Code Ann. art. 134 cmt. (b). Comment (c) states that "[t]he illustrative nature of the listing of factors contained in [article 134] gives the court freedom to consider additional factors." La. Civ. Code Ann. art. 134 cmt. (c).

624. *See* Stephens v. Stephens, 2002-0402, p. 4 (La. App. 1 Cir. 6/21/02), 822 So. 2d 770, 774; Martello v. Martello, 2006-0594, p. 5 (La. App. 1 Cir. 3/23/07), 960 So. 2d 186, 191; Bergeron v. Bergeron, 44,210, p. 11 (La. App. 2 Cir. 3/18/09), 6 So. 3d 948, 955 (overruled on other grounds); Semmes v. Semmes, 45,006, p. 5 (La. App. 2 Cir. 12/16/09), 27 So. 3d 1024, 1029; McCorvey v. McCorvey, 2005-

case should be decided on its facts in light of these factors."[625] Courts should consider the totality of the circumstances in each case, and absent a clear showing of abuse of discretion, an award of custody by a trial court should not be disturbed.[626]

In *Turner v. Turner*, the Louisiana Supreme Court discussed the nonexclusive nature of the article 134 factors.[627] The court explained that while the factors provide guidance to courts, "other factors" fall within the scope of the article to meet the child's best interest.[628] The "other factors" that impacted the court's decision involved the parents' unwillingness and inability to share the responsibility of child-rearing that, in the court's opinion, would serve only to stunt the children's development.[629] The court denied joint custody, recognizing that "[t]he trial judge sits as a sort of fiduciary on behalf of the child, and must pursue actively that course of conduct which will be of greatest benefit to the child" and "as a lookout for the child, the court is obligated to consider additional factors."[630] Post-*Turner*, courts continue to recognize that the factors are intended to encompass all aspects of the child's life, both physical and emotional, and that a fundamental role of the trial judge is to ensure the best interest of the child.[631]

2577, p. 18 (La. App. 3 Cir. 11/2/05), 916 So. 2d 357, 370; Ellinwood v. Breaux, 32,730, p. 2 (La. App. 2 Cir. 3/1/00), 753 So. 2d 977, 979.

625. Breaux v. Breaux, 96-214, p. 4 (La. App. 3 Cir. 7/17/96), 677 So. 2d 1106, 1108.

626. Mayeux v. Mayeux, 93-1603, p. 3 (La. App. 3 Cir. 6/1/94), 640 So. 2d 686, 687 (citing State in the Interest of Sylvester, 525 So. 2d 604 (La. Ct. App. 3 Cir. 1988)); Theriot v. Huval, 413 So. 2d 337, 340 (La. Ct. App. 3 Cir. 1982) (citing Stephenson v. Stephenson, 404 So. 2d 963 (La. 1981)); In re L.M.M., 17-345, p. 15 (La. App. 5 Cir. 10/25/17), 230 So. 3d 301, 310 (citing Stephens v. Stephens, 02-402 (La. App. 1 Cir. 6/21/02), 822 So. 2d 770, 774); Henry v. Sullivan, 2016-0564, p. 10 (La. App. 1 Cir. 7/12/17), 223 So. 3d 1263, 1271 (citing Martello v. Martello, 2006-0594, p. 5 (La. App. 1 Cir. 3/23/07), 960 So. 2d 186, 191–92).

627. Turner v. Turner, 455 So. 2d 1374, 1379 (La. 1984). Act No. 261 of 1993 amended and reenacted Section 3 of Chapter 2 of Title V of Book I of the Civil Code, comprised of Civil Code articles 131–158, to consist of articles 131–136. The substance of previous article 146 can be found in current article 134. Act No. 261, 1993 La. Acts 610.

628. Turner, 455 So. 2d at 1380.

629. Turner, 455 So. 2d at 1380 ("Based on the extensive history of the litigation in this matter ... it is clear that the parties are unable to settle their differences amicably, or to insulate the children from their battles."); *see also* Goldman v. Logue, 461 So. 2d 469, 473 (La. Ct. App. 5 Cir. 1984) (emphasizing that parents could not put aside their differences and cooperate in matters affecting the well-being of their child).

630. Turner, 455 So. 2d at 1379–80; *see also* McManus v. McManus, 2013-699, p. 8 (La. App. 3 Cir. 12/11/13), 127 So. 3d 1093, 1098.

631. McManus, 127 So. 3d at 1098; Gautreau v. Gautreau, 96-1548, p. 6 (La. App. 3 Cir. 6/18/97), 697 So. 2d 1339, 1345; Breaux, 677 So. 2d at 1108; *see also* Krotoski v. Krotoski, 454 So. 2d 374, 376 (La. Ct. App. 4 Cir. 1984) (in determining that it would be in the best interest of the child to reside with her mother, the court considered the fact that the child was approaching puberty, and it would be beneficial for a young girl to be with a same-sex parent).

§ 6:40 Best Interest of the Child Factors—Exceptions to Immediate Application of the Best Interest of the Child Factors

When article 134 was amended in 2018, Paragraph B was added, which forms an exception to immediate application of the best interest of the child factors. Before reaching a best interest analysis, Paragraph B requires the application of the Post-Separation Family Violence Relief Act (PSFVRA)[632] or a Revised Statutes section that provides for restrictions on visitation[633] when there exists either (1) a history of committing family violence as defined by the PSFVRA; or (2) domestic abuse, which includes sexual abuse, as defined by the Domestic Abuse Assistance Act and related criminal laws.[634] These restrictions are mandated even if the party did not seek relief under the applicable domestic violence statutes available to the party.[635]

The PSFVRA provides a "presumption that no parent who has a history of perpetrating family violence shall be awarded sole or joint custody of children."[636] Recall that "a history of perpetrating family violence" may be found if the court finds that one incident of family violence has resulted in serious bodily injury or the court finds more than one incident of family violence."[637] The PSFVRA also contains a provision if both parents have a "history of perpetrating family violence" and two provisions on restricted visitation until a treatment program is completed by the parent.[638] Louisiana Revised Statutes Section 341 on visitation likewise restricts visitation when a court finds "that a parent has subjected his or her child to physical abuse, or sexual abuse or exploitation, or has permitted such abuse or exploitation."[639] While these restrictions on custody and visitation applied before the addition of Paragraph B to article 134, the direct reference in the Code was likely intended to alert lawyers and judges alike of the mandate.

---

632. *See* La. Stat. Ann. § 9:364.

633. *See* La. Stat. Ann. § 9:341.

634. La. Civ. Code Ann. art. 134(B).

635. Even before the enactment of this section, at least one court recognized that pleading domestic violence would implicate the Act, even if the Act was not specifically pled. *See* Melancon v. Russel, 18-48, pp. 6–7 (La. App. 5 Cir. 10/17/18), 258 So. 3d 955, 960. *See also* Duran v. Rose, 2022-0300 (La. App. 4 Cir. 9/15/22), 366 So. 3d 484 (applying the PSFVRA even though relief was not sought under it and holding that the district court erred in awarding the parties joint custody because there was no evidence the father completed a treatment program, that he was not abusing alcohol or illegal drugs, or that the best interests of the children required him to be custodial parent).

636. La. Stat. Ann. § 9:364.

637. La. Stat. Ann. § 9:364.

638. La. Stat. Ann. § 9:364.

639. La. Stat. Ann. § 9:341.

§ 6:41 Visitation

Louisiana's law on visitation is found in Articles 136 and 137 of the Civil Code, with more specific provisions found in Title 9 of the Revised Statutes,[640] the Children's Code,[641] and other specialized acts.[642] Visitation is a term of art that should be used only when a parent or nonparent does not have custody.[643] Joint custodians share physical custodial time, even if the child lives primarily with one custodian. To say that parents share joint custody and the non-domiciliary parent enjoys visitation with the child is technically incorrect. When parents or nonparents enjoy custody, visitation could apply, if permitted by law, to a non-custodian.

The current law of parental visitation had its genesis in the Louisiana Supreme Court case of *Maxwell v. LeBlanc*. The *Maxwell* case concerned the visitation rights of the father of an acknowledged child.[644] The mother and father lived together but never married, and after they separated, the child remained with her mother.[645] The father paid weekly child support payments and continued to visit the child multiple times per week.[646] When the mother remarried, she rejected the child support payments and denied the father visitation rights.[647] He filed suit but was denied visitation by the trial and appellate courts, in part because of the child's illegitimacy.[648] In a comprehensive opinion, the Louisiana Supreme Court reversed the lower courts, recognizing visitation as a species of custody, which emanates from the natural right that parents enjoy with respect to their children.[649] The court explained that without forfeiting the right of access by conduct or risk of harm to the child, a parent of a child should enjoy visitation with his child.[650]

In 1988, the law of visitation entered the Civil Code,[651] and in the comprehensive revision of 1993, current article 136 was enacted.[652] The first paragraph of article 136 provided the law on parental visitation, the second paragraph provided the law on nonparent visitation, and the third introduced two revised statutes on visitation, which

640. *See* La. Stat. Ann. §§ 9:332, :341–:348.

641. *See* La. Child. Code Ann. arts. 1264–1269.

642. *See* Post-Separation Family Violence Relief Act, La. Stat. Ann. §§ 9:364–:369; Domestic Abuse Assistance Act, La. Stat. Ann. §§ 46:2131–:2143; Military Parent and Child Custody Protection Act, La. Stat. Ann. §§ 9:359–:359.13.

643. *See e.g.*, Granger v. Granger, 2009-272, pp. 2–3 (La. App. 3 Cir. 11/10/09); 25 So.3d 162, 164.

644. Maxwell v. LeBlanc, 434 So. 2d 375, 376 (La. 1983).

645. Maxwell, 434 So. 2d at 376.

646. Maxwell, 434 So. 2d at 376.

647. Maxwell, 434 So. 2d at 376.

648. Maxwell, 434 So. 2d at 376.

649. Maxwell, 434 So. 2d at 376–77.

650. Maxwell, 434 So. 2d at 377. The *Maxwell* court set forth factors for the court to consider in an award of visitation, which are today included in Louisiana Civil Code Article 134. *Id.* at 378.

651. *See* Act No. 817, 1988 La. Acts 2104 (enacting article 146.1, which was redesignated as article 132).

652. Act No. 261, 1993 La. Acts 610.

in some cases supersede the provisions of the article.[653] The structure of the article is similar today, although grandparents are now treated separately as a subset of nonparents.[654] Even though the provisions are found in the Title on Divorce, they are applied to situations outside of marriage as well.[655] Each provision of the article and the revised statutes are discussed in the following sections.

§ 6:42 Visitation—Parental Visitation

The law of parental visitation is found in the first paragraph of Article 136, which provides that parents who are not granted custody of a child are entitled to reasonable visitation with the child unless the court conducts a hearing and finds that visitation is not in the child's best interest.[656] The Louisiana Supreme Court in *Maxwell* explained, "The right of visitation for a non-custodial parent is a natural right with respect to his children, and this right is enforceable in a civil action when the custodial parent denies visitation access."[657] The right is constitutionally protected but is subservient to the child's best interest after a hearing on the issue.[658]

---

653. Act No. 261, 1993 La. Acts 610. Article 136, as originally enacted, provided:

A. A parent not granted custody or joint custody of a child is entitled to reasonable visitation rights unless the court finds, after a hearing, that visitation would not be in the best interest of the child.

B. Under extraordinary circumstances, a relative, by blood or affinity, not granted custody of the child may be granted reasonable visitation rights if the court finds that it is in the best interest of the child. In determining the best interest of the child, the court shall consider:

(1) The length and quality of the prior relationship between the child and the relative.

(2) Whether the child is in need of guidance, enlightenment, or tutelage which can best be provided by the relative.

(3) The preference of the child if he is determined to be of sufficient maturity to express a preference.

(4) The willingness of the relative to encourage a close relationship between the child and his parent or parents.

(5) The mental and physical health of the child and the relative.

C. In the event of a conflict between this Article and R.S. 9:344 or 345, the provisions of the statute shall supersede those of this Article.

Act No. 261, 1993 La. Acts 610.

654. *See* La. Civ. Code Ann. art. 136.

655. *See, e.g.*, State ex rel. Satchfield v. Guillot, 2002-0150 (La. App. 3 Cir. 6/26/02), 820 So. 2d 1255; La. Stat. Ann. § 9:344(B).

656. La. Civ. Code Ann. art. 136(A). The law restates the test as established by the Louisiana Supreme Court in *Maxwell v. Leblanc*, 434 So. 2d 375, 376 (La. 1983). La. Civ. Code Ann. art. 136 cmt. (b).

657. Maxwell, 434 So. 2d at 376; *see also* Roshto v. Roshto, 39 So. 2d 344, 345 (La. 1949); Johnson v. Johnson, 39 So. 2d 340, 342–43 (La. 1949); Pierce v. Pierce, 35 So. 2d 22, 23 (La. 1948); Jacquet v. Disimone, 143 So. 710, 711 (La. 1932); Evans v. Terrell, 27,615, p. 6 (La. App. 2 Cir. 12/6/95), 665 So. 2d 648, 652; Oglesby v. Oglesby, 25,974, p. 6 (La. App. 2 Cir. 8/17/94), 641 So. 2d 1027, 1031.

658. Maxwell, 434 So. 2d at 377. A parent not granted custody is "entitled to reasonable visitation rights unless the court finds, after a hearing, that visitation would not be in the best interest of the child." Bauer v. Mena, 22-234 (La. App. 5 Cir. 5/31/22), 2022 WL 2182792. As a result, an order will be vacated if no contradictory hearing with testimony, evidence, or cross-examination is held. *Id.*

The parental right of visitation is not limitless.[659] The trial court has great discretion in determining whether visitation by a noncustodial parent would be in the best interest of the child.[660] Because each analysis is fact-intensive, decisions regarding visitation are made on a case-by-case basis.[661] Absent conclusive evidence that visitation by the noncustodial parent would endanger the child's physical, mental, moral or emotional health, the parent is entitled to reasonable visitation rights.[662] The party seeking to restrict a parent's access to the child bears the burden of proof.[663] A decision at the trial court level will not be disturbed absent an abuse of discretion.[664]

Courts may deny visitation altogether or restrict visitation by time or by access. A denial or termination of a parent's visitation rights will only be warranted if the parent has forfeited his right of access to the child or if the exercise of visitation would be harmful to the child.[665] Because of the strict standard to deny a parent visitation, courts will often limit (rather than deny) visitation to meet the best interest of the child. Limitations can take many forms depending on the unique factual circumstances and may include supervised visitation,[666] limits on contact with others who associate with

---

659. Tracie F. v. Francisco D., 15-224, p. 57 (La. App. 5 Cir. 9/21/15), 174 So. 3d 781, 815, *aff'd but criticized*, 2015-1812 (La. 3/15/16), 188 So. 3d 231; Leeper v. Leeper, 44,777, p. 6 (La. App. 2 Cir. 9/23/09), 21 So. 3d 1006, 1010; Hawthorne v. Hawthorne, 96-89, p. 22 (La. App. 3 Cir. 5/22/96), 676 So. 2d 619, 630; Pendergrass v. Pendergrass, 94-1165, 94-1629, p. 6 (La. App. 4 Cir. 1/26/96), 667 So. 2d 1213, 1216; Duvalle v. Duvalle, 27,271, p. 7 (La. App. 2 Cir. 8/23/95), 660 So. 2d 152, 157.

660. Dearmon v. Dearmon, 96-222, p. 3 (La. App. 3 Cir. 11/13/96), 682 So. 2d 1006, 1007; Fountain v. Fountain, 93-2176, p. 3 (La. App. 1 Cir. 10/7/94), 644 So. 2d 733, 737; Steagall v. Steagall, 442 So. 2d 732, 735 (La. Ct. App. 1 Cir. 1983).

661. Leeper, 21 So. 3d at 1010; Hawthorne, 676 So. 2d at 630.

662. Palazzolo v. Mire, 2008-0075, p. 53 (La. App. 4 Cir. 1/7/09), 10 So. 3d 748, 778; *see also* Becnel v. Becnel, 98-593, p. 4 (La. App. 5 Cir. 3/25/99), 732 So. 2d 589, 592; Adkins v. Adkins, 29,088, p. 5 (La. App. 2 Cir. 1/31/97), 687 So. 2d 1109, 1113.

663. Percle v. Noll, 93-1272 (La. App. 1 Cir. 3/11/94), 634 So. 2d 498, 502.

664. Smith v. Smith, 44,663, p. 9 (La. App. 2 Cir. 8/19/09), 16 So. 3d 643, 649; Fountain, 644 So. 2d at 737; Steagall, 442 So. 2d at 735.

665. Maxwell, 434 So. 2d at 377; *see also* Leeper, 21 So. 3d at 1011 (court refused to force the child to visit his mother in prison and found it was best for him to continue his relationship with her through mail correspondence); C.F.C. v. J.D.C., 539 So. 2d 47, 49 (La. Ct. App. 4 Cir. 1988) (circumstances suggested the father more likely than not had sexually abused his children, warranting a forfeiture of his visitation rights); Franz v. Franz, 230 So. 2d 450, 452 (La. Ct. App. 4 Cir. 1970) (mother was an alcoholic who was not getting help). *But see* Roshto v. Roshto, 39 So. 2d 344, 344–45 (La. 1949) (father did not forfeit his right to visitation because he was away on military duty and was then denied access to the child); Jacquet v. Disimone, 143 So. 710, 711 (La. 1932) (divorce judgment in favor of mother did not divest father of fatherhood, and thus, father was still entitled to visitation under reasonable regulations).

666. *See* England v. England, 2017-0493, p. 8 (La. App. 4 Cir. 3/2/18), 238 So. 3d 1064, 1070 (ordering supervised visitation because mother was fabricating stories of abuse against father); Coleman v. Coleman, 47,080, p. 11 (La. App. 2 Cir. 2/29/12), 87 So. 3d 246, 254 (ordering supervised visitation because of father's past drug abuse and personality disorders); Dooley v. Dooley, 10-785, p. 10 (La. App. 3 Cir. 2/2/11), 55 So. 3d 985, 991 (ordering supervised visitation due to actions of second spouse); Bandy v. Bandy, 07-849 (La. App. 3 Cir. 12/5/07), 971 So. 2d 456 (ordering supervised visitation due to dad's drug use and testimony of 12-year-old child that he was afraid of his father); Bradford v. Bradford, 30,128, p. 4 (La. App. 2 Cir. 12/23/97), 704 So. 2d 440, 442 (holding that supervised visitation

the parent,[667] denial of overnight visitation,[668] or other limits on time. Drug abuse by a parent, even after rehabilitation, will often result in restrictions on visitation.[669] Sexual abuse by a parent or by others associated with the parent will likewise result in restrictions on visitation.[670] Even without abuse, limitations may be warranted if the parent has not been a part of the child's life or the parent's lifestyle is not in the child's best interest.[671] Courts may order a parent to attend therapy before lifting limitations on visitation.[672] In older cases, restrictions on visitation were imposed due to a parent's extramarital relationships.[673] Today, the fact that a parent is living outside of marriage with another person will be less likely to result in restrictions on visitation; however,

---

was warranted between the father and daughter, who suffered from sexual abuse, because the daughter expressed fear of continuing unsupervised visitation with her father); Percle v. Noll, 93-1272 (La. App. 1 Cir. 3/11/94), 634 So. 2d 498, 502 (ordering supervised visitation because mother had hidden the children from their father for several years).

667. *See* Sorrells v. Sorrells, 2015-500, p. 16 (La. App. 3 Cir. 11/4/15), 178 So. 3d 288, 297 (trial court required that the children should not have contact with the mother's new husband when they were with her because of his prior sexual abuse crime; the court relied on visitation principles even though the parents were granted joint custody). *Compare* Becnel v. Becnel, 98-593, p. 8 (La. App. 5 Cir. 3/25/99), 732 So. 2d 589, 595 (restriction on stepmother not being in presence of children was lifted because no allegations of harm were present; the court relied on visitation principles even though the parents were granted joint custody), *with* Coleman, 87 So. 3d at 255 (child ordered to not be in the presence of mother's adult child because of his drug and alcohol abuse and criminal history).

668. *See generally* Noe v. Noe, 93-1316 (La. App. 3 Cir. 5/4/94), 640 So. 2d 537 (refusing to reinstate unsupervised and overnight visitation to a father because he admitted to molesting his two older daughters from a previous marriage as well as two other minors).

669. Coleman, 87 So. 3d at 254 (ordering supervised visitation because of father's past drug abuse and personality disorders); Teague v. Teague, 44,005, p. 22 (La. App. 2 Cir. 11/25/08), 999 So. 2d 86, 98 (prohibiting father from living in the same home as his children or from being alone with the children due to his chronic drug abuse).

670. Noe, 640 So. 2d 537 (refusing to reinstate unsupervised and overnight visitation to a father because he admitted to molesting his two older daughters from a previous marriage as well as two other minors); Thompson v. Thompson, 559 So. 2d 4, 6 (La. Ct. App. 1 Cir. 1990) (refusing to allow mother's current husband to be present during visitation because he committed sexual misconduct against his own daughter). *But see* Bourque v. Bouillion, 95-909, p. 5 (La. App. 3 Cir. 10/18/95), 663 So. 2d 491, 494 (finding error in suspending father's visitation privileges due to allegations of sexual abuse without any proof of allegations).

671. Palacios v. Palacios, 608 So. 2d 243, 244 (La. Ct. App. 5 Cir. 1992) (limiting visitation by noncustodial father to only be allowed in the presence of the child's maternal grandfather because the father had not developed a relationship with his four-year-old son); Reed v. Hargroder, 525 So. 2d 661, 663 (La. Ct. App. 3 Cir. 1988) (father's visitation could be restricted to the residence of the child's paternal grandparents because of the father's lifestyle and past emotional issues); Gordy v. Langner, 502 So. 2d 583, 591 (La. Ct. App. 3 Cir. 1987) (mother's visitation was subject to restrictions because of her disruptive behavior and poor parenting skills).

672. *See, e.g.*, England v. England, 2017-0493, pp. 9–10 (La. App. 4 Cir. 3/2/18), 238 So. 3d 1064, 1071 (ordering supervised visitation until mother sought professional therapy, but court was not permitted to name specific therapist).

673. *See, e.g.*, Larroquette v. Larroquette, 293 So. 2d 628, 629–30 (La. Ct. App. 4 Cir. 1974) (concluding that the father's visitation privileges were allowed but only in places outside of his home, and overnight visits were not allowed because father had a concubine); Shipp v. Shipp, 165 So. 189, 191 (La. 1935) (holding that the father would be allowed visitation if he could show that the safety, welfare, and well-being of the children would not be in jeopardy due to his extramarital relationship).

if exposure to the other person would be undesirable for the child's best interest, then restrictions would be warranted.

Although the preference of the child does not control the analysis, it is certainly considered.[674] For example, in *Bandy v. Bandy* the court found that it was in the best interest of the child that the father's visits be reduced and supervised.[675] The 12-year-old son testified that he was afraid of his father, knew he was a drug addict, and did not want to be a part of the chaos at his father's home.[676] Furthermore, in *Fuge v. Uiterwyk*, three teenaged sons testified in a post-divorce proceeding that their father beat them with a broomstick, drove his boat and automobile while drinking alcohol, and ridiculed their mother.[677] Their testimony led the appellate court to reverse the trial court's order that the children must visit their father in Florida.[678]

As an aside, because the term *visitation* has been used to describe one parent's physical custodial time when the parents have been awarded joint custody, courts have relied on the jurisprudence interpreting visitation when awarding joint custody.[679] In an award of joint custody, restrictions on one parent's physical custodial time may be necessary, but these restrictions should not be termed "supervised visitation" or "restricted visitation" as the term *visitation* should be reserved to situations when a parent is *not* awarded custody.[680]

§ 6:43 Visitation—Parental Visitation—Mandatory Limits on Parental Visitation

Louisiana law also provides mandatory limitations on visitation in specific instances. The court is given no discretion to award visitation when the circumstances are so egregious that a child's best interest will never be served by permitting visitation with the person. The first mandate is found in Civil Code Article 137, which denies a parent visitation rights in the case of the child's conception through that parent's commission of a sex offense or the parent's intentional criminal conduct that resulted in the death of the other parent.[681] Paragraph A provides that "if the child was conceived through the

674. Lawson v. Lawson, 311 So. 2d 624, 628 (La. Ct. App. 3 Cir. 1975).

675. *See generally*, Bandy v. Bandy, 07-849 (La. App. 3 Cir. 12/5/07), 971 So. 2d 456.

676. Bandy, 971 So. 2d at 464 (child felt unsafe and afraid of his father and testified that he did not want to be around his father's drug use, and father spoke negatively about child's mother); *see also* Lawson, 311 So. 2d at 628 (children desired visitation with their mother but only when her abusive partner was not around).

677. Fuge v. Uiterwyk, 94-1815, p. 7 (La. App. 4 Cir. 3/29/95), 653 So. 2d 707, 712.

678. Fuge, 653 So. 2d at 714 (testimony of children was entitled deference in light of teacher's testimony that children were highly intelligent and honest).

679. *See, e.g.*, Sorrells v. Sorrells, 2015-500 (La. App. 3 Cir. 11/4/15), 178 So. 3d 288; Coleman v. Coleman, 47,080 (La. App. 2 Cir. 2/29/12), 87 So. 3d 246; Becnel v. Becnel, 98-593 (La. App. 5 Cir. 3/25/99), 732 So. 2d 589.

680. *See* La. Civ. Code Ann. art. 136(A).

681. La. Civ. Code Ann. art. 137. The sex offenses in question are set forth in Louisiana Revised Statutes Section 15:541.

commission of sex offense as provided by R.S. 15:541, the parent who committed the sex offense shall be denied visitation rights and contact with the child."[682] Paragraph B provides that a relative seeking visitation rights or contact with the child shall not be allowed those rights "if the court determines … that the intentional criminal conduct of the relative resulted in the death of the parent of the child."[683]

The second mandate is found in Louisiana Revised Statutes Section 9:341 and provides that "[w]henever the court finds by a preponderance of the evidence that a parent has subjected his or her child to physical abuse, or sexual abuse or exploitation, or has permitted such abuse or exploitation of the child, the court shall prohibit visitation."[684] Only when the parent can prove that visitation will not cause "physical, emotional, or psychological damage to the child" can the court allow visitation in such scenarios.[685] Even then, safeguards must be put into place to "minimize any risk of harm to the child."[686]

In *Hollingsworth v. Semerad*, the father abused the step-mother, inflicted bruises on the child, and abused alcohol.[687] The trial court ordered supervised visitation with the father but allowed the supervisor to be a friend or relative of the father.[688] Relying on section 9:341, the appellate court amended the order and required a third-party supervisor who was not a friend or relative of the father because it was in the child's best interest.[689] Moreover, in *W.M.E. v. E.J.E.*, in the face of evidence that the father had sexually abused the daughter, the court terminated his visitation with his daughter altogether.[690] The court also suspended visitation with his son even though there was

682. La. Civ. Code Ann. art. 137(A). The Louisiana Children's Code provides for the termination of parental rights where there is a conviction or commission of a sex offense as defined in R.S. 15:541 by that natural parent which resulted in the conception of the child. La. Child. Code Ann. art. 1015.1.

683. La. Civ. Code Ann. art. 137(B). The Louisiana Children's Code provides for the termination of parental rights in certain situations that involve criminal conduct by a parent towards the other parent: (1) conviction of murder of the child's other parent and (2) unjustified intentional killing of the child's other parent. La. Child. Code Ann. art. 1015(1)–(2).

684. La. Stat. Ann. § 9:341(A) (rev. 1994). Section 341 was passed in 1993 and contains substantially the same language as article 133 prior to 1993. Act No. 261, 1993 La. Acts 610. Section 341 eliminated the conflict between former article 133 and section 574 of Title 9. *See* In re A.D., 628 So. 2d 1288, 1290 (La. Ct. App. 3 Cir. 1993).

685. La. Stat. Ann. § 9:341(A).

686. La. Stat. Ann. § 9:341(A). The abusive parent is to pay all costs. Also, if the court authorizes restricted visitation, the parent with restricted visitation rights must not remove the child from the jurisdiction of the court absent court approval and a showing of good cause. La. Stat. Ann. § 9:341(B)–(C).

687. Hollingsworth v. Semerad, 35,264, pp. 3–4 (La. App. 2 Cir. 10/31/01), 799 So. 2d 658, 659–60.

688. Hollingsworth, 799 So. 2d at 661.

689. Hollingsworth, 799 So. 2d at 665. *But see* Evans v. Terrell, 27,615, p. 7 (La. App. 2 Cir. 12/6/95), 665 So. 2d 648, 652 (allowing supervised visitation because there was no definitive finding that the mother abused the child despite unexplained bruises on the child's body); Landry v. Thomas, Nos. 2011-CW-1571, 2011-CW-0587, 2011-CW-1852, 2011 WL 6780138, at *5–6 (La. Ct. App. 1 Cir. Dec. 21, 2011) (allowing supervised visitation with the father due to insufficient evidence of sexual abuse).

690. W.M.E. v. E.J.E., 619 So. 2d 707, 709–10 (La. Ct. App. 3 Cir. 1993) (recognizing that termination was mandatory under the law and applying Louisiana Civil Code Article 133, the predecessor to Louisiana Revised Statutes Section 9:341).

no evidence that he had sexually abused the son.[691] Recognizing that no mandatory law required termination of visitation with a child who was not abused, the court explained that parents are only entitled to visitation if it is in the child's best interest; in this case, visitation with his son was not in the child's best interest.[692]

The third mandate, the Post-Separation Family Violence Relief Act (PSFVRA), is found in Title 9, sections 361 through 369 of the Revised Statutes. The PSFVRA provides immediate remedies to parents and children who have suffered family violence by suspending an abusive parent's access to a child pending completion of a program designed to inhibit further abuse.[693] The act was designed to protect victims of family violence "when domestic disputes arise in the course of separation and divorce."[694] The legislature created the PSFVRA because findings show that issues of family violence do not end when the spouses separate or divorce.[695] To the contrary, the violence often escalates, and the abuse may continue in the form of visitation and custody disputes.[696] The Act serves specifically to address "the issues of child custody and visitation and how they are affected by family violence during legal separation and divorce."[697]

Courts may award relief under the PSFVRA in domestic abuse cases even if not specifically requested in the pleadings,[698] and if a history of perpetrating family violence is proven, the application of the PSFVRA is mandated.[699] The Act defines family violence generally as physical or sexual abuse committed by one parent against the other parent or the children, not including acts of self-defense.[700] A history of perpetrating family violence can be based on one incident of family violence that resulted in serious bodily injury or more than one incident of family violence.[701] The PSFVRA will not apply in cases with only one incident of family violence that does not result in serious bodily

691. W.M.E., 619 So. 2d at 710.

692. W.M.E., 619 So. 2d at 710.

693. *See* La. Stat. Ann. § 9:364; Folse v. Folse, 98-1976, p. 10 (La. 6/29/99), 738 So. 2d 1040, 1045–46.

694. Slayton v. Slayton, 05-1529, p. 3 (La. App. 3 Cir. 5/3/06), 929 So. 2d 865, 868.

695. La. Stat. Ann. § 9:361.

696. La. Stat. Ann. § 9:361.

697. State ex rel. S.D.K., 04-218, p. 5 (La. App. 5 Cir. 5/26/04), 875 So. 2d 887, 890.

698. Melancon v. Russel, 18-48, pp. 6–7 (La. App. 5 Cir. 10/17/18), 258 So. 3d 955, 960 (trial court applied the PSFVRA because of the allegations of violence in the pleadings, even though the Act, specifically, was not pled); Dufresne v. Dufresne, 08-215, pp. 8, 11 (La. App. 5 Cir. 9/16/08), 992 So. 2d 579, 586–87 (trial court awarded relief under the PSFVRA even though wife's initial allegations did not include domestic violence; based on the evidence adduced at the fault hearing, the wife moved to amend her pleadings, which was granted).

699. Lewis v. Lewis, 34,031, p. 3 (La. App. 2 Cir. 11/3/00), 771 So. 2d 856, 859.

700. La. Stat. Ann. § 9:362(4). Any offense against the person as defined in the Criminal Code of Louisiana can also be a basis of "family violence." *See* Hollingsworth v. Semerad, 35,264, pp. 10–11 (La. App. 2 Cir. 10/31/01), 799 So. 2d 658, 663 (acts against stepmother did not trigger the PSFVRA when child did not live with father).

701. Hollingsworth, 799 So. 2d at 663; *see also, e.g.*, Dufresne, 992 So. 2d at 585 (multiple acts of domestic violence during the marriage). *But see* Smith v. Smith, 44,663, pp. 9–10 (La. App. 2 Cir. 8/19/09), 16 So. 3d 643, 648 (minor incidences that were provoked by other parent or for which the parent sought counseling were not enough to invoke the PSFVRA).

injury.[702] In determining whether there is a history of family violence, courts should consider "the entire chronicle of the family ... [s]uch factors as the number, frequency, and severity of the incidents will be relevant as well as whether the violence occurred in the presence of the children, and to what extent there existed provocation for any violent act."[703]

Section 363 of the Act prevents a spouse or parent from being ordered to participate in mediation if that spouse, parent, or child has been the victim of family violence.[704] Section 364 of the Act provides for "a presumption that no parent who has a history of perpetrating family violence ... shall be awarded sole or joint custody of children."[705] The presumption can be overcome by showing by a preponderance of the evidence that the parent has successfully completed a court-monitored domestic abuse intervention program,[706] is not abusing drugs or alcohol, and that the best interest of the child requires that parent's participation in the child's life.[707]

The Act also provides that when "both parents have a history of perpetrating family violence, custody shall be awarded solely to the parent who is less likely to continue to perpetrate family violence."[708] In *Morrison v. Morrison*, the court found that, although both spouses had a history of family violence, the wife was less likely to perpetuate violence, so sole custody would be awarded to her under the condition that she participate in and complete a treatment program.[709] The husband was granted supervised visitation but only after he completed a treatment program, as well.[710]

---

702. Petsch v. Petsch, 2001-0491, p. 3 (La. App. 1 Cir 06/22/01), 809 So. 2d 222, 224 (getting pushed out of the car did not inflict serious bodily injury).

703. Smith, 16 So. 3d at 650; *see also* Michelli v. Michelli, 93-2128, p.10 (La. App. 1 Cir. 05/05/95), 655 So. 2d 1342, 1349; Morrison v. Morrison, 97-0295, p. 3 (La. App. 1 Cir. 09/19/97), 699 So. 2d 1124, 1126.

704. La. Stat. Ann. § 9:363 (applying in any separation, divorce, child custody, visitation, child support, alimony, or community property proceeding).

705. La. Stat. Ann. § 9:364(A).

706. Section 362 of the act states:

> "Court-monitored domestic abuse intervention program" means a program, comprised of a minimum of 26 in-person sessions, that follows a model designed specifically for perpetrators of domestic abuse. The offender's progress in the program shall be monitored by the court. The provider of the program shall have all of the following:
>
> (a) Experience in working directly with perpetrators and victims of domestic abuse.
>
> (b) Experience in facilitating batterer intervention groups.
>
> (c) Training in the causes and dynamics of domestic violence, characteristics of batterers, victim safety, and sensitivity of victims.

La. Stat. Ann. § 9:362(3); *see also* D.O.H. v. T.L.H., 2001-174, pp. 5–6 (La. App. 3 Cir. 10/31/01), 799 So. 2d 714, 718 (finding six sessions of anger management training with a clinical psychologist met the prerequisite for overcoming the presumption against custody).

707. La. Stat. Ann. § 9:364(B).

708. La. Stat. Ann. § 9:364(D).

709. Morrison, 699 So. 2d at 1127; *see also* Hicks v. Hicks, 98-1527 (La. App. 3 Cir. 5/19/99), 733 So. 2d 1261.

710. Morrison, 699 So. 2d at 1127.

If the court finds that a parent has a history of perpetrating family violence, and custody is therefore denied, the court should allow supervised visitation on the condition that the parent completes a court-monitored domestic abuse intervention program.[711] Unsupervised visitation is only allowed if the violent parent can show that he has completed a treatment program, is not abusing alcohol and drugs, poses no danger to the child, and that visitation is in the best interest of the child.[712]

The Act contains a specific provision dealing with sexual abuse. If a court finds, by clear and convincing evidence, that a parent has sexually abused his child, visitation and contact shall be prohibited until the court finds by a preponderance of the evidence that the abusive parent has participated and successfully completed a treatment program designed for such sexual abusers and that supervised visitation is in the child's best interest.[713] When the PSFVRA was originally enacted, the allegations of sexual abuse had to be proven by the lower preponderance of the evidence standard. The Louisiana Supreme Court found the provision unconstitutional because the lower burden of proof violated the parent's due process rights as a result of the parent's total loss of contact with the child.[714] The statute was thereafter amended to raise the standard to clear and convincing evidence.[715] Today, the clear and convincing standard of proof under the PSFVRA is greater than the standard articulated in section 9:341, as noted above, which requires proof by a preponderance when a parent subjects his child to physical or sexual abuse. Undoubtedly, in the context of sexual abuse, the standards are different. Although section 341 has not been challenged on constitutional grounds, at least one court refused to extend the reasoning of the Louisiana Supreme Court to the standard of visitation in section 341, creating a disparity between the statutes when sexual abuse of a child is at issue in a custody proceeding.[716]

The Act also contains a specific provision outlining visitation with an incarcerated parent. Section 364.1 provides that if a court authorizes visitation with an incarcerated parent, that order shall include "restrictions, conditions, and safeguards as are necessary to protect the mental and physical health of the child and minimize the risk of

711. La. Stat. Ann. § 9:364.

712. La. Stat. Ann. § 9:364(C); *see also* Morrison, 699 So. 2d at 1127 (determining that father was not eligible for supervised visitation because he had not completed the requisite treatment program).

713. La. Stat. Ann. §§ 9:341(B), :364(F). A contradictory hearing must be held before visitation can be allowed. La. Stat. Ann. § 9:341(B); *see also* C.L.S. v. G.J.S., 2005-1419, pp. 33–36 (La. App. 4 Cir. 2007), 953 So. 2d 1025, 1041–42 (finding that the mother had the burden of proof of clear and convincing evidence that the child was sexually abused and the father was the perpetrator of the abuse, and determining that a lack of physical evidence did not mean that the daughter did not suffer sexual abuse because there was other strong evidence including the sexualized behavior exhibited by the young child).

714. In re A.C., 93-1125, p. 2 (La. 10/17/94), 643 So. 2d 743, 745.

715. Act No. 888, 1995 La. Acts 562.

716. Bourque v. Bouillion, 95-909, pp. 4–5 (La. App. 3 Cir. 10/18/95), 663 So. 2d 491, 494 (declining to extend the holding of *In re A.C.* because the father only lost unsupervised visitation, rather than a total loss of access to the child).

harm to the child."[717] The statute provides a host of factors that a court must consider before ordering supervised visitation with an incarcerated parent.[718]

Under the PSFVRA, a court may appoint a licensed mental health professional with "current and demonstrable training and experience working with perpetrators and victims of family violence" to conduct an evaluation.[719] Further, all child visitation orders and judgments issued under the PSFVRA must contain an injunction and a Uniform Abuse Prevention Order.[720] Violations of the injunctions are punishable as contempt of court and will result in termination of all court-ordered visitation.[721] All court costs, attorney's fees, evaluation fees, medical and psychological care for the abused spouse or children, and expert witness fees must be paid by the family violence perpetrator.[722]

The provisions of the PSFVRA do not affect the remedies provided in the Domestic Abuse Assistance Act, the Louisiana Criminal Code, or the Children's Code.[723] However, any case under the Domestic Abuse Assistance Act may also impose the remedies available in the PSFVRA.[724] Finally, public funds allocated to programs involved in pro-

---

717. La. Stat. Ann. § 9:364.1(A).

718. *See* La. Stat. Ann. § 9:364.1(B).

> (1) The length and quality of the prior relationship between the child and the parent; (2) whether the child is in need of guidance, enlightenment, or tutelage which can best be provided by the parent; (3) the preference of the child if he is determined to be of sufficient maturity to express a preference; (4) the willingness of the relative to encourage a close relationship between the child and his parent or parents, including the willingness of the child's custodial parent, caretaker, or legal guardian to voluntarily take the child to the incarcerated parent's place of incarceration for supervised visitation; (5) the mental and physical health of the child and parent; (6) the length of time that the child lived with the parent prior to the parent's incarceration; (7) the desirability of maintaining the continuity of the relationship between the child and the incarcerated parent; (8) the costs of travel and other expenses incurred by visitation at the place of incarceration, and who will bear the responsibility for such costs; (9) the effect upon the child of supervised visitation in the place of incarceration and the feasibility, if any, of alternative or additional use of technology pursuant to R.S. 9:357; (10) other testimony or evidence and the court may consider applicable.

La. Stat. Ann. § 9:364.1(B). These factors are not exclusive. *See* Loya v. Loya, 17-555, p. 7 (La. App. 5 Cir. 2/21/18), 239 So. 3d 1048, 1053 (denying contact with father in prison because not in the best interest of the child).

719. La. Stat. Ann. § 9:365.

720. La. Stat. Ann. § 9:366(A).

721. La. Stat. Ann. § 9:366(B).

722. La. Stat. Ann. § 9:367. These provisions were found to be constitutional. In re A.C., 1993-1125 (La. 1/27/94), 643 So. 2d 719.

723. La. Stat. Ann. § 9:368.

724. La. Stat. Ann. § 9:368. Section 2131 of the Domestic Abuse Assistance Act states the purpose:

> [The Domestic Abuse Assistance Act was created in recognition of] the complex legal and social problems created by domestic violence.... The legislature further finds that previous societal attitudes have been reflected in the policies and practices of law enforcement agencies and prosecutors which have resulted in different treatment of crimes occurring between family members.... It is the intent of the legislature to provide a civil remedy for domestic violence which will afford the victim immediate and easily accessible protection.

La. Stat. Ann. § 46:2131. Section 2132(4) defines "family members" as spouses, former spouses, parents and children, stepparents, stepchildren, foster parents, and foster children, other ascendants,

viding for the victims of domestic violence must not be used to assist the perpetrator of the family violence.[725]

§ 6:44 Visitation—Nonparent Visitation

Nonparent visitation requires a distinctly different analysis than parental visitation. As the parent's interest in the care, custody, and control of his child "is perhaps the oldest of the fundamental liberty interests recognized by this Court," a nonparent's request to visit with a child must tread lightly on these constitutionally protected interests.[726] The Constitution has long protected parents in their ability to decide with whom their child should associate, which at times can be at odds with family members close to the child who wish to visit with the child. State statutes address these family dynamics under the backdrop of primal parental rights. After a discussion of the development of the law on nonparent visitation, the current state of the law as applied to grandparents and other nonparents will be presented. Although constitutional challenges still loom, the constitutionality of the law of nonparent visitation will be addressed, as will be the application of the rules by the jurisprudence.

§ 6:45 Visitation—Nonparent Visitation—Historical Development

The basis of nonparent visitation is found in article 136 and Louisiana Revised Statutes Section 9:344, which were added in 1993. Article 136, when originally enacted, required all nonparents to prove "extraordinary circumstances" to receive visitation with a child.[727] Visitation also had to be reasonable and in the best interest of the child.[728] The Code provided guidance to determine the child's best interest, which included several factors:

(1) The length and quality of the prior relationship between the child and the relative.

(2) Whether the child is in need of guidance, enlightenment, or tutelage which can best be provided by the relative.

(3) The preference of the child if he is determined to be of sufficient maturity to express a preference.

---

and other descendants. "Family member" also means the other parent or foster parent of any child of the offender. La. Stat. Ann. § 46:2132(4); *see also* Buchanan v. Langston, 36,520, p. 6 (La. App. 2 Cir. 9/18/02), 827 So. 2d 1186, 1190 (holding that the PSFVRA provides similar relief as the Domestic Abuse Assistance Act and Louisiana Children's Code art. 1570(F)).

725. La. Stat. Ann. § 9:369.

726. Troxel v. Granville, 530 U.S. 57, 65 (2000).

727. Act No. 261, 1993 La. Acts 610. Originally, the only nonparents who could seek visitation were relatives by blood or affinity. In 1995, former stepparents and stepgrandparents were added to the list. Act No. 176, 1995 La. Acts 539.

728. *See* Act No. 261, 1993 La. Acts 610.

(4) The willingness of the relative to encourage a close relationship between the child and his parent or parents.

(5) The mental and physical health of the child and the relative.[729]

Section 9:344 was also enacted in 1993 to provide specific circumstances when grandparents and siblings could seek visitation with a child without having to prove "extraordinary circumstances."[730] As grandparents and siblings are naturally closer to the child, the legislature saw fit to carve out circumstances under which it would be easier for them to receive visitation rights.[731]

Section 9:344 was drafted to apply when parents are married or living together without marriage. Grandparents were given the right to seek reasonable visitation of the minor if the grandparent's married child died, was interdicted, or was incarcerated.[732] Grandparents were also given the right to seek visitation if the grandparent's unmarried child was living together with the other parent of the child and either died or was incarcerated.[733] As for siblings of the minor, they were given the right to seek reasonable visitation if the parents were married and one died or was incarcerated.[734] In all cases, the grandparent or sibling had to prove that visitation was in the child's best interest.[735] Note that for siblings, they could not seek visitation when a married parent was interdicted, unlike grandparents.

In 1999, a provision was added to section 9:344 to allow grandparents and siblings to seek visitation of the child when the child's married parents legally separated or lived apart for a period of six months, even without a divorce, death, interdiction, or incarceration.[736]

In 2012, significant revisions were made. The Legislature amended article 136 to elevate grandparents in the visitation laws.[737] Under the amendment, grandparents could

---

729. Act No. 261, 1993 La. Acts 610.

730. Act No. 261, 1993 La. Acts 610.

731. *See* Act No. 261, 1993 La. Acts 610; *see also* Janway v. Jones, 47-203, p. 6 (La. App. 2 Cir. 03/30/12), 88 So. 3d 713, 717 (finding that the legislature made it less difficult for grandparents who do not have to show extraordinary circumstances under section 9:344); Wood v. Wood, 2002-0860, p. 8 (La. App. 1 Cir. 9/27/02), 835 So. 2d 568, 573 (finding that "the legislature made the determination, rather than the court, that the death, incarceration, or interdiction of a parent qualified as 'extraordinary circumstances'"); Galjour v. Harris, 2000-2696, p. 7 (La. App. 1 Cir. 3/28/01), 795 So. 2d 350, 355 (explaining that the grandparent is relieved of showing extraordinary circumstances when proceeding under section 9:344).

732. La. Stat. Ann. § 9:344(A) (1993); *see also* Fontenot v. Granger, 2007-1588, p. 3 (La. App. 3 Cir. 6/4/08), 985 So. 2d 859, 861 (applying article 136(B), rather than section 9:344(A), to a request for grandparent visitation because the parties were divorced before the death of the parent). Incarceration was added as an extraordinary circumstance in 1999. *See* Act No. 1352, 1999 La. Acts 3633.

733. La. Stat. Ann. § 9:344(B) (1993). Incarceration was added as an extraordinary circumstance in 1999. *See* Act No. 1352, 1999 La. Acts 3633.

734. La. Stat. Ann. § 9:344(C) (1993). Incarceration was added as an extraordinary circumstance in 1999. *See* Act No. 1352, 1999 La. Acts 3633–34.

735. La. Stat. Ann. § 9:344(A)–(C) (1993).

736. Act No. 1352, 1999 La. Acts 3633.

737. *See* Act No. 763, 2012 La. Acts 3110.

obtain reasonable visitation without having to prove "extraordinary circumstances," upon proof that visitation is in the best interest of the child.[738] Before making this determination, the court must to hold a contradictory hearing to determine whether to appoint an attorney for the child.[739]

Although grandparents no longer had to prove extraordinary circumstances, "any other relative, by blood or affinity, or a former stepparent or step-grandparent" had to prove extraordinary circumstances to request visitation.[740] In addition, a finding that a parent abuses a controlled dangerous substance was expressly included as an extraordinary circumstance.[741] The five factors used to analyze the child's best interest remained the same.

Section 344 was also amended in 2012. For parents who were married and separating without divorce, grandparents and siblings now had to prove "extraordinary circumstances."[742] According to the testimony given when the bill was amended, a grandparent would need to show extraordinary circumstances because the parents, although separated, were still married, so the court must be more protective of the parent's decision-making authority.[743] The amendment also required the court to consider the article 136(D) factors when determining the child's best interest.[744]

In 2014, article 136 was amended again to remove the phrases "not granted custody" from both provisions on nonparent visitation.[745] In other words, nonparents need not be denied custody to have visitation with a child. Although the language was likely used, as it is for parental visitation, to make clear that visitation can only be awarded to a person who does not have custody, the court in *Francis v. Francis* interpreted the phrase to mean "having been denied custody" and therefore dismissed the grandpar-

---

738. In the 2012 revision, the law provided:

> A grandparent not granted custody of a child may be granted reasonable visitation rights if the court finds that it is in the best interest of the child. Before making this determination, the court shall hold a contradictory hearing as provided for in R.S. 9:345 in order to determine whether the court should appoint an attorney to represent the child.

Act No. 763, 2012 La. Acts 3110. In the 2018 revision, the word "reasonable" was no longer used to describe the "visitation," but the best interest of the child is still paramount. *See* La. Civ. Code Ann. art. 136(B)(1) (2019).

739. La. Civ. Code Ann. art. 136(B) (rev. 2012).

740. La. Civ. Code Ann. art. 136(C) (rev. 2012).

741. La. Civ. Code Ann. art. 136(C) (rev. 2012).

742. *See* Act No. 763, 2012 La. Acts 3110. The term "legal separation" was also removed from Paragraph D. Extraordinary circumstances expressly included a determination by a court that the parent is abusing a dangerous controlled substance. *Id.*

743. Louisiana House of Representatives, Civil Law and Procedure meeting archives, May 14, 2012 found at https://house.louisiana.gov/H_Video/VideoArchivePlayer?v=house/2012/May_2012/0514_12_CL (bill discussion begins at 21 minutes, 30 seconds).

744. *See* Act No. 763, 2012 La. Acts 3110.

745. Act No. 586, 2014 La. Acts 2765.

ents' request for visitation because they had never been denied custody.[746] *Francis* was legislatively overruled by the amendment to article 136.

Finally, in 2018, the Legislature amended article 136 to clarify that it should be applied when the parents are unmarried or divorcing, and section 9:344 should be applied when the parents are married or living together.[747] At the same time, the Legislature removed the caveat that the visitation be "reasonable," and it amended the five factors courts consider when awarding visitation by adding in a consideration of the parents' fundamental constitutional rights and removing the willingness of a relative to encourage a close relationship with the parent.[748]

§ 6:46 Visitation—Nonparent Visitation—Current Law

Current law continues to bifurcate visitation for grandparents from other relations.

Grandparents

There are three ways for grandparents to receive visitation: (1) pursuant to Children's Code Articles 1264–69, when a child is adopted;[749] (2) pursuant to Civil Code Article 136, when the married parents have filed for divorce, or when the parents are not married and not living together as married persons; [750] or (3) pursuant to Section 344 of Title 9, when the parents are married and have not filed for divorce or are unmarried but living together.[751]

Under Children's Code Article 1264, when a parent dies and the child is later adopted (often by a stepparent), the natural parents of the deceased parent may have limited visitation.[752] Prior to 2023, the deceased parent had to be married at the time of death for the article to apply, but that requirement was eliminated.[753] In addition, when a

---

746. *See generally* Francis v. Francis, 2011-2116 (La. App. 1 Cir. 6/13/12), 97 So. 3d 1091. In *Francis*, the father's rights were terminated, and the child was adopted by the mother's new husband. *Id.* at 1093. Because the mother and the adoptive father were the child's new parents, the court concluded that there had been no custody dispute in which a court determined that the parents should not be awarded custody, and the custody was awarded to a nonparent under article 133. *Id.* at 1096. As a result, the court concluded that the grandparents did not have the right of action for visitation since they did not meet the requirement of having been denied custody. *Id.*

747. *See* Act No. 383, 2018 La. Acts 1192; *see also* Louisiana State Senate, Judiciary A meeting archives, April 3, 2018, found at http://senate.la.gov/video/videoarchive.asp?v=senate/2018/04/040318JUDA_0 (bill discussion begins at 12 minutes, 30 seconds); Louisiana House of Representatives, Civil Law and Procedure meeting archives, April 24, 2018, found at https://house.louisiana.gov/H_Video/VideoArchivePlayer?v=house/2018/apr/0424_18_CL (bill discussion begins at 53 minutes, 30 seconds).

748. *See* Act No. 383, 2018 La. Acts 1192.

749. La. Child. Code Ann. arts. 1264–69.

750. La. Civ. Code Ann. art. 136.

751. La. Stat. Ann. § 9:344.

752. La. Child. Code Ann. art. 1264. The article also applies when both parents die and the child is thereafter adopted. *See* O'Brien v. Shepley, 451 So. 2d 82 (La. App. 5 Cir. 1984).

753. 2024 La. Act No. 92, effective Aug. 1, 2023.

parent loses the right to object to the adoption by law, the parents of that parent, i.e., grandparents, may also have limited visitation.[754] Note that when a parent surrenders their child for adoption—as opposed to losing the right to object—the grandparent has no right to seek visitation under these articles.[755] The request for visitation is made in the adoption proceeding, and the grandparents bear the burden of proving unreasonable denial of visitation with the child and that limited visitation would be in the child's best interest.[756] The constitutionality of these articles is subject to challenge.[757]

Under article 136, grandparents need only prove that visitation is in the best interest of the child.[758] The court must hold a contradictory hearing to determine whether it should appoint an attorney for the child.[759] To determine whether visitation is in the best interest of the child, the court is required to consider only the five factors listed in the article, the first of which requires the court to consider the fundamental rights of the parents to determine the care, custody, and control of their children.[760] Notably, there is a presumption in the article that a fit parent will act in the child's best interest.[761]

Under section 9:344, grandparents must prove that visitation is in the best interest of the child and must also prove that the parent (who is the grandparent's child) either died, is incarcerated, or is interdicted.[762] For parents who are simply living together, rather than are married, the grandparents must prove that visitation is in the best interest of the child and that the parent (who is the grandparent's child) either died or is incarcerated.[763] Finally, if the parents are married but have lived separate and apart for six months or more, the grandparents must prove extraordinary circumstances and that visitation is in the child's best interest.[764] The five factors included in article 136(D) must be considered by the court.[765]

Siblings

As for siblings of the minor, there are two ways to receive visitation: (1) pursuant to Civil Code Article 136, when the married parents have filed for divorce or when the parents are not married and not living together as married persons;[766] or (2) pursuant

754. La. Child. Code Ann. art. 1264; *see also* La. Child. Code Ann. art. 1265.

755. Popwell v. State, 43,848 (La. App. 2 Cir. 12/3/08), 998 So. 2d 841; State in the Interest of Robinson, 517 So. 2d 477 (La. App. 1 Cir. 1987),

756. La. Child. Code Ann. arts. 1266–67.

757. In re Porter, No. 55,433 (La. App. 2 Cir. 11/15/23); 375 So. 3d 594, *writ denied*, 379 So. 3d 33 (La. 2/14/24) (refusing to consider the constitutionality of articles 1264 and 1267 because the trial court had not ruled on the merits of visitation).

758. La. Civ. Code Ann. art. 136(B).

759. La. Civ. Code Ann. art. 136(C).

760. La. Civ. Code Ann. art. 136(D).

761. La. Civ. Code Ann. art. 136(D).

762. La. Stat. Ann. § 9:344(A).

763. La. Stat. Ann. § 9:344(B).

764. La. Stat. Ann. § 9:344(D).

765. La. Stat. Ann. § 9:344(D). Extraordinary circumstances expressly include a determination by a court that the parent is abusing a dangerous controlled substance. *Id.*

766. La. Civ. Code Ann. art. 136.

to section 9:344, when the parents are married and have not filed for divorce or are unmarried but living together.[767] Under article 136, full, half, or stepsiblings must prove extraordinary circumstances and that visitation is in the best interest of the child.[768] Just like the process for grandparents, the court must hold a contradictory hearing to determine whether it should appoint an attorney for the child.[769] To determine whether visitation is in the best interest of the child, the court is required to consider only the five factors listed in the article.[770]

Under section 9:344, siblings can seek visitation if the child's parent either died or is incarcerated, and the sibling can prove that visitation is in the best interest of the child.[771] Like the article, siblings in section 9:344(C) include "siblings of a minor child or children of the marriage," which should include full, half, or stepsiblings.[772] In addition, siblings can seek visitation if the child's parents are married but have lived separate and apart for six months or more, and the sibling can prove extraordinary circumstances and that visitation is in the child's best interest.[773] The five factors included in article 136(D) must be considered by the court.[774]

Other relations

Other relatives by blood or marriage, and former stepparents and stepgrandparents have only way one way to receive visitation: pursuant to Civil Code Article 136, when the parents have filed for divorce, or when the parents are not married and not living together as married persons.[775] Just like grandparents and siblings, other relations must prove extraordinary circumstances and that visitation is in the best interest of the child.[776] The court must also hold a contradictory hearing to determine whether it should appoint an attorney for the child,[777] and the court is required to consider only the five factors listed in the article.[778]

767. La. Stat. Ann. § 9:344.
768. La. Civ. Code Ann. art. 136(B)(2).
769. La. Civ. Code Ann. art. 136(C).
770. La. Civ. Code Ann. art. 136(D).
771. La. Stat. Ann. § 9:344(B).
772. La. Stat. Ann. § 9:344(C).
773. La. Stat. Ann. § 9:344(D).
774. La. Stat. Ann. § 9:344(D). Extraordinary circumstances expressly include a determination by a court that the parent is abusing a dangerous controlled substance. *Id.*
775. La. Civ. Code Ann. art. 136.
776. La. Civ. Code Ann. art. 136(B)(2).
777. La. Civ. Code Ann. art. 136(C).
778. La. Civ. Code Ann. art. 136(D).

§ 6:47 Visitation—Nonparent Visitation—Constitutionality

Since 2000, visitation of a child has been analyzed under the framework articulated by the United States Supreme Court in *Troxel v. Granville* to adequately protect a parent's liberty interest when considering visitation by a nonparent.[779] Brad Troxel and Tommie Granville had two daughters.[780] After the couple ended their relationship, Brad moved in with his parents, who were involved in the care of their granddaughters.[781] Brad died tragically, but his parents maintained regular contact with the young girls.[782] Approximately six months after Brad's death, Tommie limited contact with the Troxels to one day each month.[783] The Troxels then filed a petition for visitation under the Washington statute, which provided: "Any person may petition the court for visitation rights at any time, including, but not limited to, custody proceedings. The court may order visitation rights for any person when visitation may serve the best interest of the child whether or not there has been any change of circumstances."[784] After the Washington Supreme Court found that the statute unconstitutionally infringed on the mother's right to rear her children, the Troxels appealed to the United States Supreme Court.[785]

In a plurality opinion authored by Justice O'Connor, the Court held that the Washington statute infringed on the fundamental rights of parents to make decisions regarding the care, custody, and control of their children.[786] Cognizant of the special relationship grandparents and other relatives have with a child, the Court was troubled that "any person" could petition the court for visitation with the child "at any time."[787] It found the statute to be "breathtakingly broad," without any presumption of validity or weight given to the parent's estimation of what would be in the child's best interest.[788]

The Court took issue with the fact that the Troxels had not alleged that the children's mother was unfit.[789] Without a challenge to the parent's fitness, the law provides a presumption that the parent will act in the best interest of the child.[790] Furthermore, the Court noted that the mother never intended or sought to completely restrict the Trox-

779. *See generally* Troxel v. Granville, 530 U.S. 57 (2000).
780. Troxel, 530 U.S. at 60.
781. Troxel, 530 U.S. at 60.
782. Troxel, 530 U.S. at 60.
783. Troxel, 530 U.S. at 60.
784. Troxel, 530 U.S. at 60.
785. Troxel, 530 U.S. at 63.
786. Troxel, 530 U.S. at 67, 72.
787. Troxel, 530 U.S. at 67.
788. Troxel, 530 U.S. at 67.
789. Troxel, 530 U.S. at 68.
790. Troxel, 530 U.S. at 68–69. The Court also took issue with the fact that at the trial court level, the burden was wrongly placed on Granville to disprove why the visitation was not in her children's best interest because "the court's presumption failed to provide any protection for Granville's fundamental constitutional right to make decisions concerning rearing her own daughters." *Id.* at 69–70.

els from visiting their grandchildren; she only sought to shorten the visitation.[791] The Court saw no reason for the state to "inject itself into the private realm of the family" to question a fit mother's decision.[792] It therefore affirmed that the grant of visitation to the Troxels "was an unconstitutional infringement on Granville's fundamental right to make decisions concerning the care, custody, and control of her two daughters."[793]

Even before the United States Supreme Court's ruling in *Troxel*, the constitutionality of Louisiana's laws on visitation was questioned. In *Reinhardt v. Reinhardt*, a mother sought to terminate the visitation rights of her children's paternal relatives, arguing that article 136(B) infringed on her fundamental rights as a parent.[794] It was not clear what paternal relatives were seeking visitation, but these relatives bore the burden of proving extraordinary circumstances and the best interest of the child.[795] The court applied strict scrutiny and found compelling reasons for the state to protect children from divorced families, which was met by a narrowly drawn statute that furthered visitation with extended family under restrictive circumstances.[796] By requiring the nonparent to prove extraordinary circumstances and the best interest of the child, the statute was narrowly drawn. Because no automatic grant of visitation was allowed and the court conducted an appropriate balancing of interests, the provision was constitutional.[797]

The first Louisiana case, post-*Troxel*, to consider the constitutionality of section 9:344 was *Galjour v. Harris*.[798] The court compared the Louisiana statute to the Washington statute at issue in *Troxel* and found the Louisiana statute to be "more narrowly drawn."[799] The court focused on the nonparent having to prove extraordinary circumstances, which could be in the nature of a death, interdiction or incarceration of the parent, as well as having to show reasonableness and best interest of the child.[800] A balance must be struck between state interests and constitutional protections afforded to the parent, the court explained, and the statute met that balance.[801] Further, as applied to the facts of the case, the court was satisfied that the trial court went to great lengths to accede to the conditions on visitation imposed by the parent.[802] Given the length and

791. Troxel, 530 U.S. at 71. The mother told the Troxels that they would be permitted to visit their grandchildren for one short visit per month, as well as special holidays. *Id.*

792. Troxel, 530 U.S. at 68.

793. Troxel, 530 U.S. at 68, 72. The Court did not consider "whether the Due Process Clause requires all nonparent visitation statutes to include a showing of harm or potential harm to the child as a condition precedent to granting visitation." Troxel, 530 U.S. at 73.

794. Reinhardt v. Reinhardt, 97-1889, p. 2 (La. App. 1 Cir. 9/25/98), 720 So. 2d 78, 79.

795. Reinhardt, 720 So. 2d at 80.

796. Reinhardt, 720 So. 2d at 80.

797. Reinhardt, 720 So. 2d at 80 (holding that article 136(B) was "narrowly drawn to further visitation with the extended family, but only under set, restrictive circumstances").

798. *See generally* Galjour v. Harris, 2000-2696 (La. App. 1 Cir. 3/28/01), 795 So. 2d 350.

799. Galjour, 795 So. 2d at 355.

800. Galjour, 795 So. 2d at 355.

801. Galjour, 795 So. 2d at 358; *see also* Wood v. Wood, 2002-0860, p. 8 (La. App. 1 Cir. 9/27/02), 835 So. 2d 568, 573.

802. Galjour, 795 So. 2d at 358.

quality of the relationship between the grandparents and the child, the court affirmed the award of visitation.[803]

After the *Galjour* decision, during its 2001 session, the Louisiana State Legislature passed a House Concurrent Resolution to further study the effects of *Troxel* to ensure that Louisiana's laws adequately protect the fundamental rights of parents.[804] The legislature requested that the Louisiana State Law Institute make specific recommendations for revisions to state laws to ensure their constitutionality.[805] Consequently, in its 2003 session, the legislature passed another House Concurrent Resolution, which reported that, according to the Law Institute, Louisiana's statutes on visitation were constitutional on their face but may be unconstitutional as applied to a particular litigant.[806]

Litigants continue to challenge the constitutionality of Louisiana's statutes, both facially and as applied to the facts of each case. Although no court has struck down a visitation statute on its face, courts have scrutinized the awards of visitation to ensure that primary parental rights are protected.[807] For example, in *Barry v. McDaniel*, the court awarded visitation to grandparents after the death of their daughter, even though the parent articulated several instances when the grandparents ignored their requests, for example, to refrain from discussing her mother's illness and death, follow bedtime routines, and call them during a visitation.[808] The appellate court nonetheless affirmed the visitation schedule,[809] noting that the trial court made specific rulings to give deference to the parents' preferences while allowing the child to continue her relationship with her grandparents.[810] The concurring opinion in *Barry* cautioned that the decision "comes perilously close to being an unconstitutional application of grandparents' rights."[811]

Each case rises and falls on its own set of facts, but as visitation time with a nonparent increases, the potential for infringement on the parent's right to make decisions for

---

803. Galjour, 795 So. 2d at 358.

804. H.R. Con. Res. 68, 27th Leg., Reg. Sess. (La. 2001); *see also* Wood, 835 So. 2d at 572.

805. H.R. Con. Res. 68, 27th Leg., Reg. Sess. (La. 2001).

806. H.R. Con. Res. 38, 29th Leg., Reg. Sess. (La. 2003). The Resolution requested an additional study and recommendation for revision to the visitation statutes based on statements made in the report. H.R. Con. Res. 38, 29th Leg., Reg. Sess. (La. 2003); *see also* Barry v. McDaniel, 2005-2455, p. 8 n.7 (La. App. 1 Cir. 3/24/06), 934 So. 2d 69, 75 n.7 (noting legislative activity).

807. *See, e.g.*, Broussard-Scher v. Legendre, 2010-1164, pp. 6–7 (La. App. 3 Cir. 3/23/11), 60 So. 3d 1292, 1295 (concluding that article 136(B) did not infringe on the parent's rights to make decisions regarding the child); Babin v. Babin, 2002-0396, pp. 7–8 (La. App. 1 Cir. 7/30/03), 854 So. 2d 403, 408–09 (rejecting constitutional challenge to section 9:344 and affirming award of grandparent visitation); Garner v. Thomas, 2008-1448, p. 15 (La. App. 4 Cir. 5/28/09), 13 So. 3d 784, 792 (affirming grandparent visitation after recognizing the constitutional presumption in favor of the parent's wishes).

808. Barry v. McDaniel, 2005-2455, pp. 13–14 (La. App. 1 Cir. 3/24/06), 934 So. 2d 69, 78–79. The grandparents were proceeding under Louisiana Revised Statutes Section 9:344. *Id.* at 71.

809. The visitation schedule ordered by the trial court consisted of one weekend per month and one week over the summer. Barry, 934 So. 2d at 72. The order also outlined certain details regarding the visitation arrangement. *Id.*

810. Barry, 934 So. 2d at 78.

811. Barry, 934 So. 2d at 79 (Whipple, J., concurring).

the child increases as well. Now, after the revisions of 2012 and 2018, grandparents in some cases need not show extraordinary circumstances before an award of visitation is possible.[812] Grandparents must still prove that the visitation is in the best interest of the child (and in some cases that it is reasonable), but without the additional hurdle of extraordinary circumstances, the statute is subject to further scrutiny. To date, challenges to both article 136(B) and Section 9:344 continue, and visitation awards to grandparents are still being affirmed.[813]

§ 6:48 Visitation—Nonparent Visitation—Application

Louisiana courts recognize the protection afforded to parents when a nonparent seeks visitation. If the parents are married, have never been separated or divorced, no custody litigation has ever been instituted regarding a child, and there has been no allegation that the parents' care of the child is inadequate, grandparents have no cause of action for visitation.[814] For example, in *Droddy v. Porter*, the court sanctioned the grandparent and his lawyer for frivolous filings because visitation was not warranted by existing law.[815]

Courts apply the presumption that fit parents act in the best interest of their children. While the presumption is strong, "there is no mandate that this presumption is not able to be overcome."[816] It is the burden of the party seeking visitation to prove: (1) extraordinary circumstances, if needed, to justify visitation; (2) that the amount of visitation is reasonable;[817] and (3) that visitation is in the child's best interest, despite a parental preference against visitation.[818] Article 136(D) lists factors the court must consider when evaluating whether visitation is in the best interest of the child.[819]

First, as to extraordinary circumstances that are not provided by law,[820] courts look for "a highly unusual set of facts that are not commonly associated with a particular

812. *See* Section 6:46.

813. *See* McGovern v. McGovern, 15-737 (La. App. 5 Cir. 3/30/16), 189 So. 3d 503 (affirming award of grandparent visitation without directly considering constitutionality of amended article 136(B)); Rogers v. Pastureau, 2012-2008 (La. App. 1 Cir. 4/26/13), 117 So. 3d 517 (affirming award of grandparent visitation and finding § 9:344 constitutional).

814. Droddy v. Porter, 2019-0633 (La. App. 1 Cir. 12/27/19); 292 So. 3d 925, 929; Lingo v. Kelsay, 94-1038 (La. App. 3 Cir. 3/1/95); 651 So. 2d 499, 500.

815. Droddy, 292 So. 3d at 929.

816. Broussard-Scher v. Legendre, 2010-1164, p. 11 (La. App. 3 Cir. 3/23/11), 60 So. 3d 1290, 1298.

817. Note that the term "reasonable" was eliminated from the grandparent visitation provision in Louisiana Civil Code Article 136(B) in the 2018 revision. *Compare* La. Civ. Code Ann. art. 136(B), *with* Act No. 763, 2012 La. Acts 3110. "Reasonable visitation" still appears in the provision on parental visitation, however. La. Civ. Code Ann. art. 136(A).

818. *See* La. Civ. Code Ann. art. 136; La. Stat. Ann. § 9:344.

819. *See* La. Civ. Code Ann. art. 136(D).

820. *See, e.g.*, La. Stat. Ann. § 9:344; Fontenot v. Granger, 2007-1588, p. 7 (La. App. 3 Cir. 6/4/08), 985 So. 2d 859, 863; Stracener v. Joubert, 2005-1121, p. 6 (La. App. 3 Cir. 3/1/06), 924 So. 2d 430, 435; Ray v. Ray, 94-1478, p. 3 (La. App. 3 Cir. 5/3/95), 657 So. 2d 171, 173.

thing or event."[821] Extraordinary circumstances have been found following the death or incarceration of a parent, even when § 9:344 does not apply.[822] Extraordinary circumstances were also found when a stepgrandparent acted as the child's primary caregiver, provided for the child financially, and stepped in as the mother of the child when the biological mother of the child was absent.[823] In addition, when a grandparent was present in the delivery room, lived with the child while the parents lived with others, and remained the primary caregiver of the child, the court found those circumstances extraordinary.[824]

Courts have failed to find extraordinary circumstances when the circumstances are not unique enough to justify interference with a parent's right to make decisions regarding their child.[825] For example, in *State ex rel. Satchfield v. Guillot*, even though the grandparents played a central role in the child's early life, after the remarriage of the father and issues surrounding the actions of the grandparents, the father opposed the child's visitation with his parents.[826] The court found insufficient circumstances to overcome the will of a fit parent and determined that a lack of visitation with the grandparents would not be detrimental to the child.[827] In addition, in *Sterling v. Shirley*, a fourth cousin was denied visitation even though she was the trustee over a trust for the child and wanted the child to maintain a relationship with the relatives of her deceased father.[828] Because the mother could independently choose to continue those relationships and the fourth cousin was a distant relative, the court did not find extraordinary circumstances.[829]

If a court determines that extraordinary circumstances are present, either by way of unusual facts or application of section 9:344, the court must consider the factors set forth in article 136(D). The first factor simply echoes the mandate of *Troxel v. Granville* in that the court must consider "[a] parent's fundamental constitutional right to make decisions concerning the care, custody, and control of their own children and the traditional presumption that a fit parent will act in the best interest of their children."[830] The

821. Huber v. Midkiff, 2002-0664, p. 2 (La. 2/7/03), 838 So. 2d 771, 778 (Weimer, J., concurring); Broussard-Scher, 60 So. 3d at 1296.

822. *See* Fontenot, 985 So. 2d at 863 (finding extraordinary circumstances as a result of death); Stracener, 924 So. 2d at 435 (finding extraordinary circumstances as a result of death); Lindsey v. House, 29,790, p. 4 (La. App. 2 Cir. 9/24/97), 699 So. 2d 1190, 1192 (finding extraordinary circumstances as a result of incarceration).

823. Henry v. Henry, 97-0366, p. 4 (La. App. 1 Cir. 11/7/97), 704 So. 2d 793, 796.

824. Broussard-Scher, 60 So. 3d at 1296.

825. *See* Flack v. Dickson, 2003-5, p. 6 (La. App. 3 Cir. 4/30/03), 843 So. 2d 1261, 1265; State ex rel. Satchfield v. Guillot, 2002-0150, p. 14 (La. App. 3 Cir. 6/26/02), 820 So. 2d 1255, 1265; Shaw v. Dupuy, 2006-0546, p. 8 (La. App. 1 Cir. 2/9/07), 961 So. 2d 5, 9.

826. Satchfield, 820 So. 2d at 1257.

827. Satchfield, 820 So. 2d at 1265.

828. Sterling v. Shirley, 2002-0915, p.4 (La. App. 3 Cir. 12/11/02), 832 So. 2d 1179, 1182.

829. Sterling, 832 So. 2d at 1182.

830. La. Civ. Code Ann. art. 136(D)(1).

prior section discusses the constitutionality of nonparent visitation under Louisiana law.

The second factor considers "the length and quality of the prior relationship between the child and the relative."[831] In *Ray v. Ray*, the court relied on the fact that the mother and child previously lived with the great-grandfather and that the great-grandfather made an effort to keep in contact with the child but was prevented from doing so by the child's mother.[832] In *Garner v. Thomas*, the court considered the "intense babysitting and nurtur[ing] of the children" as evidence supporting the factor.[833]

Under the third factor, courts must consider "whether the child is in need of guidance, enlightenment, or tutelage which can best be provided by the relative."[834] This factor favors a mentoring figure in the child's life and has been relied on to ensure that a child has a connection to an absent parent's family members.[835] In *Ray*, the child's father was deceased and the great-grandfather and aunt were the child's only connection to the father; this factor favored visitation.[836] If, on the other hand, the needs of the child are being met, such that the relative requesting visitation cannot specifically provide any unmet needs, then this factor will weigh against visitation.[837]

The fourth factor concerns the preference of the child,[838] and the fifth concerns the mental and physical health of the child and the relative.[839] The final factor is typically satisfied, absent evidence suggesting otherwise. For health to be an issue, the ailments must not merely exist but must have an effect on the best interest of the child.[840] In *Henry v. Henry*, attempts were made to call into question the mental health of the child and the relative, but the court determined that "this did not constitute 'problems' such

831. La. Civ. Code Ann. art. 136(D)(2).

832. Ray v. Ray, 94-1478, p. 4 (La. App. 3 Cir. 5/3/95), 657 So. 2d 171, 173–74.

833. Garner v. Thomas, 2008-1448, p. 17 (La. App. 4 Cir. 5/28/09), 13 So. 3d 784, 793; *see also* McGovern v. McGovern, 15-737, p. 8 (La. App. 5 Cir. 3/30/16), 189 So. 3d 503, 508 (discussing visitation and holding that the trial court did not abuse its discretion in awarding the maternal grandmother visitation).

834. La. Civ. Code Ann. art. 136(D)(3).

835. Ray, 657 So. 2d at 174.

836. Ray, 657 So. 2d at 174.

837. *See* Henry v. Henry, 97-0366, pp. 5–6 (La. App. 1 Cir. 11/7/97), 704 So. 2d 793, 797 (finding that this factor did not support visitation by a stepgrandmother who acted as a primary caregiver for a part of the child's life because she was not meeting any unmet need); *see also* Lindsey v. House, 29,790, p. 4 (La. App. 2 Cir. 9/24/97), 699 So. 2d 1190, 1192 (finding that the child needs to be familiar with two sides of the family).

838. La. Civ. Code Ann. art. 136(D)(4). Courts have not considered the preference of the child because of his young age. *See* Henry, 704 So. 2d at 797; McMillin v. McMillin, 2008-502, p. 5 (La. App. 3 Cir. 3/25/09), 6 So. 3d 414, 418. The general principles that apply under Louisiana Civil Code Article 134 would apply in a visitation context.

839. La. Civ. Code Ann. art. 136(D)(5).

840. Henry, 704 So. 2d at 798.

that the best interest of the child had been, or would be, affected."[841] In *Ray*, the court noted that the great-grandfather was 67 years old but was in excellent health.[842]

Prior to 2018, article 136(D) also required the court to assess the "willingness of the relative to encourage a relationship between the child and his parent or parents."[843] Because the article provides that the court shall consider *only* the factors provided therein, one might assume that it is no longer relevant. However, analysis of such facts is still important, as it can be included within the umbrella of the first factor, i.e., the parent's fundamental constitutional right to parent their own children.[844] In the scheme of primary parental rights, interference in the child's relationship with the parent could alone thwart any claim for nonparent visitation. For example, in *Henry v. Henry*, while the step-grandmother established extraordinary circumstances to justify a request for visitation, this factor proved to be the most problematic for her and ultimately resulted in a denial of visitation.[845] The step-grandmother interfered in the mother's new marriage and portrayed herself in public documents as the child's mother.[846] As the step-grandmother's relationship with the child's mother deteriorated and the litigation began, she spoke to the child about the dispute, which upset the mother.[847]

Additionally, in *Janway v. Jones*, the grandparents interfered with the relationship between the child and her father.[848] The grandparents emailed the child's teacher disparaging the child's father, called the father's place of employment and attempted to have him fired, and took things from the child's father's home without permission.[849] Because the evidence suggested "that the grandparents [were] attempting to interfere and sabotage the relationship that [the father] had with his daughter," the court denied visitation.[850]

As a final note, not only must the factors weigh in favor of visitation, but the visitation must be reasonable. In *Stracener v. Joubert*, the mother objected to the amount of visitation with the child's paternal grandparents.[851] The court considered the joint custody arrangement that the parents had agreed to before the father's death, which included less time than the grant of visitation to the grandparents.[852] Considering the parent's constitutional right to privacy in child-rearing and the excessive amount of

841. Henry, 704 So. 2d at 798.

842. Ray, 657 So. 2d at 174.

843. La. Civ. Code Ann. art. 136(D)(4) (2014).

844. La. Civ. Code Ann. art. 136(D)(4) (2014).

845. Henry, 704 So. 2d at 797.

846. Henry, 704 So. 2d at 797–98.

847. Henry, 704 So. 2d at 798.

848. Janway v. Jones, 47,203, p. 10 (La. App. 2 Cir. 3/30/12), 88 So. 3d 713, 719.

849. Janway, 88 So. 3d at 715.

850. *Compare* Janway, 88 So. 3d at 719, *with* Rogers v. Pastureau, 2012-2008, p. 19 (La. App. 1 Cir. 4/26/13), 117 So.3d 517, 530 (awarding visitation and noting that the grandparents did not ever interfere or disregard the rights of the parents).

851. *See generally* Stracener v. Joubert, 2005-1121 (La. App. 3 Cir. 3/1/06), 924 So. 2d 430.

852. Stracener, 924 So. 2d at 436.

visitation awarded to the grandparents, the court found the visitation to be unreasonable and significantly reduced the schedule of visitation set forth by the trial court.[853]

§ 6:49 Modification of Custody and Visitation

Custody and visitation of a child are always subject to modification to meet the child's best interest.[854] As a result, no judgment awarding custody or visitation bars a subsequent action to modify.[855] Further, a court maintains continuing jurisdiction to modify prior awards.[856] Notably, a judgment modifying custody is effective when ordered by the court and is not retroactive to the date of judicial demand.[857] Allowing modifications ensures that the law's overriding principle—the best interest of the child—is met.[858]

Modifications of custody, even when warranted on the facts, may nevertheless be difficult for the child, as change is not always easy. Because custody is never final, and modifications may be difficult, the law requires the proponent of change to prove: (1) a material change of circumstance affecting the welfare of the child after the original custody decree was entered; and (2) a change of custody is in the best interest of the child.[859] In Louisiana, this two-pronged test is elevated when the original custody order was entered after a court considered evidence of parental fitness. In that case, the proponent of change must prove "that the continuation of the present custody is so deleterious to the child as to justify a modification of the custody decree," or "by clear and convincing evidence that the harm likely to be caused by a change of environment is substantially outweighed by its advantages to the child."[860]

To determine which standard applies, courts must first analyze whether the initial award of custody was made pursuant to a considered decree or a consent decree (also referred to as stipulated decree). A *considered decree* is "an award of permanent custody in which the trial court receive[d] evidence of parental fitness to exercise care, custody,

853. Stracener, 924 So. 2d at 436; *see also* McMillin v. McMillin, 2008-502, p. 8 (La. App. 3 Cir. 3/25/09), 6 So. 3d 414, 420 (finding the visitation schedule unreasonable in part because of the three-hour distance between the grandparent's and the mother's home).

854. *See* Messner v. Messner, 122 So. 2d 90 (La. 1960); Willis v. Willis, 24 So. 2d 378, 380 (La. 1945); State ex rel. Bush v. Trahan, 51 So. 216, 219 (La. 1909); Kleiser v. Kleiser, 619 So. 2d 178, 179–80 (La. Ct. App. 3 Cir. 1993).

855. Kleiser, 619 So. 2d at 179 (citing Benoit v. Lestremau, 603 So. 2d 269 (La. Ct. App. 5 Cir. 1992)).

856. Dupuy v. Dupuy, 2000-2744, p. 5 (La. App. 1 Cir. 3/28/01), 808 So. 2d 562, 565.

857. Searles v. Searles, 2023-0112 (La. App. 1 Cir. 08/31/23), 371 So. 3d 1088, 1094 (concluding that an order awarding child support can be retroactive to the date of judicial demand but a change in child custody cannot be; when a change in custody changes the amount in child support due, the change in support can only begin once the custody arrangement changes).

858. Falgout v. Dealers Truck Equip. Co., 98-3150, p. 9 (La. 10/19/99), 748 So. 2d 399, 406; *see also* Harvey v. Harper, 22-744, p. 10 (La. App. 3 Cir. 3/01/23), 358 So. 3d 988, 996.

859. Evans v. Lungrin, 97-0541, p. 13 (La. 2/6/98), 708 So. 2d 731, 738. Courts consistently remind that the material change of circumstances must have occurred *after* the original decree. *See, e.g.*, Belcher v. Pace, 54,397, pp. 16–18 (La .App. 2 Cir. 4/13/22), 337 So. 3d 178, 185–86.

860. Bergeron v. Bergeron, 492 So. 2d 1193, 1200 (La. 1986) (citation omitted).

and control of the children."[861] The considered decree occurs when the court awards custody because the parents cannot agree on custody or when their agreement is not in the best interest of the child.[862] A *consent* or *stipulated decree*, on the other hand, occurs when the parents consent to a custodial arrangement or the award is entered by default, and no evidence of parental fitness is presented to the court.[863] A plan agreed on by the parents is preferred over a court-ordered plan, but in either case, the best interest of the child is paramount.[864]

The Louisiana Supreme Court recognizes the inherent power courts have when making any modification of custody. In 1986, in *Bergeron v. Bergeron*, the court noted:

> The child has at stake an interest of transcending value in a custody modification suit—his best interest and welfare—which may be irreparably damaged not only by a mistaken change in custody but also by the effects of an attempted or threatened change of custody on grounds that are less than imperative. The consequences to the mental and emotional well being and future development of the child from an erroneous judgment, unjustified litigation, threat of litigation, or continued interparental conflict are usually more serious than similar consequences in an ordinary civil case.[865]

Because of the discretion afforded a trial court, findings "will not be set aside on appeal unless they are manifestly erroneous or clearly wrong."[866] The heightened abuse of discretion rule applies.[867]

Once the burden of proof for modification is satisfied, the parent or nonparent must still meet the burden of proof for the award of custody requested.[868] For example, evidence can be sufficient to show a material change of circumstance since the entry of a consent order but insufficient to meet the clear and convincing standard of proof for

861. Evans, 708 So. 3d at 738.

862. La. Civ. Code Ann. art. 132.

863. Evans, 708 So. 2d at 738; Odom v. Odom, 606 So. 2d 862, 866 (La. Ct. App. 2d Cir. 1992) (finding that the *Bergeron* standard does not apply when a prior award of custody was uncontested, but not consented to, by a parent).

864. Haik v. Haik, 94-563, p. 9 (La. App. 5 Cir. 12/14/94), 648 So. 2d 1015, 1020.

865. Bergeron, 492 So. 2d at 1200.

866. Caples v. Caples, 47,491, p. 10 (La. App. 2 Cir. 7/25/12), 103 So. 3d 437, 443; Harvey v. Harper, 22-744 (La. App. 3 Cir. 3/01/23), 358 So. 3d 988.

867. McCormic v. Rider, 2009-2584, p. 4 (La. 2/12/10), 27 So. 3d 277, 280; Atkins v. Atkins, 47,563, p. 4 (La. App. 2 Cir. 9/26/12), 106 So. 3d 614, 616; Glover v. Tooley, 25,988, p. 5 (La. App. 2 Cir. 8/17/94), 641 So. 2d 1032, 1035.

868. Molony v. Harris, 2010-1316, pp. 9–10 (La. App. 4 Cir. 2/23/11), 60 So. 3d 70, 77; White v. Kimry, 37,408, pp. 4–5 (La. App. 2 Cir. 5/14/03), 847 So. 2d 157, 160.

an award of sole custody.[869] Likewise, a nonparent who seeks a modification to request custody must also prove substantial harm to the child.[870]

Modification of visitation is treated differently than a modification of custody.[871] Courts have concluded that, because a change in visitation is not as substantial as a change in physical custody, the proponent of change need only prove that modification is in the child's best interest.[872] No showing of a material change of circumstance or the elevated *Bergeron* standard is necessary.

§ 6:50 Modification of Custody and Visitation—Considered Decrees

When a court awards custody after considering evidence of parental fitness, the party who seeks to modify the decree must meet a heightened standard, referred to as the *Bergeron* standard. Rather than simply require a material change of circumstance that meets the child's best interest, the *Bergeron* standard requires the proponent to demonstrate that "continuation of the present custody is so deleterious to the child as to justify a modification of the custody decree," or "by clear and convincing evidence that the harm likely to be caused by a change of environment is substantially outweighed by its advantages to the child."[873] The standard is disjunctive. The first prong permits change due to deleterious effects on the child in the present custody arrangement, while the second prong permits change under a weighing analysis when a parent can show by the heightened clear and convincing evidentiary standard that the child's best interest warrants the change.[874]

Before considering the modification request, a court must determine whether the *Bergeron* standard applies. The burden lies with the party who claims that *Bergeron*

869. *See* Molony, 60 So. 3d at 81 (reversing the trial court's award of sole custody to the father because, although he was able to show a sufficient change of circumstances since the consent decree, he was not able to show highly probable evidence that sole custody was in the best interest of the child); White v. Kimry, 37,408, p. 12 (La. App. 2 Cir. 5/14/03), 847 So. 2d 157, 164.

870. Robert v. Gaudet, 96-2506, p. 6 (La. App. 1 Cir. 3/27/97), 691 So. 2d 780, 783; *see also* Tracie F. v. Francisco D., 15-224, p. 27 (La. App. 5 Cir. 9/21/15), 174 So. 3d 781, 798 (noting that a custody action brought by a nonparent may only arise when a threat of substantial harm looms).

871. *Cf.* Olavarrieta v. Robeson, 22-158, p. 1 (La. App. 5 Cir. 7/06/22), 345 So. 3d 1103, 1106 (father alleged his motion for modification of physical custody was a request for a change in visitation, but court held father was seeking a modification of joint custody because the parents had shared joint custody and, therefore, visitation is not at issue).

872. *See* Moore v. Moore, 47,947, p. 17 (La. App. 2 Cir. 3/6/13), 111 So. 3d 1120, 1129; Piccione v. Piccione, 2009-300, p. 3 (La. App. 3 Cir. 10/7/09), 20 So. 3d 576, 578; Acklin v. Acklin, 29,193, p. 3 (La. App. 2 Cir. 2/26/97), 690 So. 2d 869, 871; Bennett v. Bennett, 95-152 (La. App. 3 Cir. 05/31/95), 657 So. 2d 413; Reynier v. Reynier, 545 So. 2d 663, 665 (La. Ct. App. 5 Cir. 1989).

873. Mulkey v. Mulkey, 2012-2709, p. 11 (La. 5/7/13), 118 So. 3d 357, 365; Bergeron v. Bergeron, 492 So. 2d 1193, 1200 (La. 1986). To prove a matter by clear and convincing evidence, one must demonstrate that the existence of a disputed fact is highly probable, or much more probable than its nonexistence. State ex rel. Manuel v. Manuel, 619 So. 2d 871, 875 (La. Ct. App. 3 Cir. 1993).

874. *See* Mulkey, 118 So. 3d at 361.

applies, and that party must show that the court considered parental fitness when it issued the prior custody award.[875] Introducing the transcript of the prior proceeding can satisfy that burden.[876] If the record is silent on the issue of whether custody was litigated, the court presumes that the award was uncontested, and *Bergeron* does not apply.[877] If the record fails to contain a transcript of the hearing, the court endeavors to determine the context of the hearing, but in the absence of any evidence, *Bergeron* does not apply.[878] If the hearing takes place for a period of time, but the parties agree in a consent judgment, *Bergeron* may apply.[879] Finally, even if evidence of parental fitness was taken, some courts have concluded that an interim order is not subject to *Bergeron* because the order is not a "final, considered decree" given after the trial court has examined all of the pertinent evidence.[880]

For example, in *Howze v. Howze*, the transcript from the trial, which did include evidence of parental fitness, was not contained in the appellate record.[881] However, the minutes and the language of the judgment, which included statements like "after conclusion of the trial," allowed the appellate court to infer that both parties put on testimony and evidence and to conclude that the judgment was a considered decree.[882] The heavy burden of *Bergeron* applied.[883]

When a considered decree has been entered, the *Bergeron* standard applies to changes in both legal and physical custody.[884] It can likewise apply in disputes between

---

875. Ogelsby v. Ogelsby, 25,974, p. 4 (La. App. 2 Cir. 8/17/94), 641 So. 2d 1027, 1030; Odom v. Odom, 606 So. 2d 862, 865 (La. Ct. App. 2 Cir. 1992). Some courts have even affirmed trial court rulings as long as they reflect an implicit finding of material change of circumstances. *See, e.g.*, House v. House, 2020-355 (La. App. 3 Cir. 5/26/21), 318 So. 3d 386. Courts have also held that the *Bergeron* standard applies to modify a prior considered decree even where an intervening consent judgment exists. *See, e.g.* Paille v. Newell, 2019-1694 (La. App. 1 Cir. 7/08/20), 2020 WL 3840756 (holding that *Bergeron* standard applies to the original considered custody decree even though subsequent consent decree was entered).

876. *See, e.g.*, Odom, 606 So. 2d at 865.

877. Tennessee v. Campbell, 28,823, p. 7 (La. App. 2 Cir. 10/30/96), 682 So. 2d 1274, 1278 (finding that *Bergeron* did not apply when the record failed to contain a transcript of the initial hearing); Ogelsby, 641 So. 2d at 1030 (finding that *Bergeron* did not apply when judgment referred to "evidence adduced and stipulations" but also mentioned coming to trial "by consent"); *see also* Norris v. Norris, 604 So. 2d 107 (La. App. 2 Cir. 1992); Odom, 606 So. 2d at 865; Stevens v. Stevens, 340 So. 2d 584, 587 (La. App. 1 Cir. 1976).

878. *See, e.g.*, Howze v. Howze, 2017-0358, p. 5 (La. App. 1 Cir. 9/28/17), 232 So. 3d 606, 609; Poole v. Poole, 41,220, p. 4 (La. App. 2 Cir. 3/22/06), 926 So. 2d 60, 63; Tennessee, 682 So. 2d at 1278.

879. *See, e.g.*, Cherry v. Cherry, 2004-0002, pp. 6–7 (La. App. 4 Cir. 2/2/05), 894 So. 2d 1208, 1213 (three days of trial before consent determined to be a considered decree); Long v. Long, 28,763, pp. 4–5 (La. App. 2 Cir. 12/11/96), 684 So. 2d 1099, 1101 (finding *Bergeron* applied where trial started but recessed and over two weeks, contentious discussions continued).

880. McManus v. McManus, 2013-699, p. 10 (La. App. 3 Cir. 12/11/13), 127 So. 3d 1093.

881. Howze, 232 So. 3d at 609.

882. Howze, 232 So. 3d at 609.

883. Howze, 232 So. 3d at 609.

884. Melton v. Johnson, No. 2018-0403, 2018 WL 657104, at *4 (La. Ct. App. 1 Cir. Dec. 12, 2018); Granger v. Granger, 2009-272, pp. 4–5 (La. App. 3 Cir. 11/10/09), 25 So. 3d 162, 165; Howze, 232 So. 3d at 610–11; *see also* Davenport v. Manning, 95-2349, p. 4 (La. App. 4 Cir. 6/5/96), 675 So. 2d 1230, 1232.

parents and nonparents.[885] In other words, requests for a change in the domiciliary status of a parent or nonparent will require application of the *Bergeron* standard even though joint custody remains the same.[886] When visitation, rather than custody, is at issue, courts may "tweak" visitation schedules even though the evidence does not satisfy the *Bergeron* standard.[887] Courts should not apply the flexible standard for visitation, however, if the modification contemplates changes in physical or legal custody, even though the litigants may refer to the nondomiciliary person's physical custodial time as "visitation."[888]

The *Bergeron* standard is difficult to meet and is designed to prevent disruption of considered custody arrangements.[889] Due to the heavy burden, courts can be reluctant to find that modification is justified. Because of the fact-driven nature of a modification request, it would be difficult to capture the multitude of changes that could justify a modification under any standard. Situations that have justified a change in custody under *Bergeron* have included a child coming of school age,[890] the deterioration of

885. *See, e.g.*, Sheppard v. Hood, 605 So. 2d 708, 712 (La. Ct. App. 2 Cir. 1992) (finding that mother who was seeking a change of custody from grandparents was unable to prove *Bergeron*; even though she enjoyed the paramount parental right to custody, that right was already protected in the initial determination of custody); *see also* Bragg v. Home, 33,857 (La. App. 2 Cir. 6/21/00), 764 So. 2d 1177; Noe v. Noe, 93-1316 (La. App. 3 Cir. 5/4/94), 640 So. 2d 537; Miller v. Andrasko, 93-0520, p. 6 (La. App. 1 Cir. 3/11/94), 640 So. 2d 368, 371.

886. Silbernagel v. Silbernagel, 10-267, pp. 10–11 (La. App. 5 Cir. 5/10/11), 65 So. 3d 724, 730 (changing domiciliary parent from co-domiciliaries to father because the drive between the parties' homes on the highway placed the child in danger and his growing maturity amounted to a material change in the circumstances since the original decree, and it would have been deleterious to the child to continue this custody plan); *see also* Moffett v. Moffett, 21-594 (La. App. 3 Cir. 02/23/22), 2022 WL 534410 (reversing award of domiciliary parent to father because of child's preference to live with mother and desire to attend school in Baton Rouge, and father's on-call work requirements).

887. *See* Howze, 232 So. 3d at 609–10; *see also* Mason v. Mason, 2016-287, p. 15 (La. App. 3 Cir. 10/5/16), 203 So. 3d 519, 529; Brantley v. Kaler, 43,418, pp. 6–7 (La. App. 2 Cir. 6/4/08), 986 So. 2d 188, 191.

888. *See* Howze, 232 So. 3d at 611; DeSoto v. DeSoto, 2004-1248, p. 3 (La. App. 3 Cir. 2/2/05), 893 So. 2d 175, 177.

889. A.E.B. v. J.B.E., 99-2668, p. 7 (La. 11/30/99), 752 So. 2d 756, 761.

890. *See, e.g.*, Melton v. Johnson, No. 2018-CU-0403, 2018 WL 6571044 (La. Ct. App. 1 Cir. Dec. 12, 2018); Freeman v. Johnson, 51,550, p. 14 (La. App. 2 Cir. 6/21/17), 225 So. 3d 524, 532–33; *see also* Shaffer v. Shaffer, 2000-1251, p. 5 (La. App. 1 Cir. 9/13/00), 808 So. 2d 354, 357 (finding coming of school age to be a material change of circumstances to modify a stipulated judgment).

communication,[891] excessive punishment,[892] poor living conditions,[893] discontinuity and instability,[894] and abuse,[895] just to name a few.

The child's preference as to which parent should have custody, in and of itself, is generally not enough to justify a change under *Bergeron*.[896] Nor is the remarriage of the noncustodial parent or the stability of that parent's new household a compelling reason to uproot a child from his present environment.[897] Further, the custodial parent's romantic relationships alone do not justify a change under *Bergeron* unless there is proof of other factors that have a detrimental or direct effect on the welfare of the child.[898] Whether a fact alone or with others satisfies the heavy *Bergeron* standard is an extremely fact-intensive analysis that is left within the province of the trier of fact, only to be reversed on an abuse of discretion.

Can parties agree to opt-out of the *Bergeron* standard for future modifications when it would otherwise apply? At least one Louisiana court has said yes.[899] Can parties agree to opt in to the *Bergeron* standard for future modifications when they consent to custody? Courts have gone both ways. Even though the parties are stipulating to custody—and the lower standard would apply in a modification request—some courts have concluded that no public policy consideration is undermined by allowing the parties to freely contract into the *Bergeron* standard.[900] "In fact, ... their agreement is supported by the very policies which underlie the *Bergeron* burden of proof—protec-

---

891. *See, e.g.*, Welborne v. Welborne, 29,479, p. 7 (La. App. 2 Cir. 5/7/97), 694 So. 2d 578, 583 (changing custody from joint to sole in mother because of daughter's "strained relationship" with her father); *see also* Hughes v. Talton, 14-17, p. 11 (La. App. 5 Cir. 10/15/14), 181 So. 3d 10, 16.

892. *See, e.g.*, Ard v. Ard, 628 So. 2d 1221, 1223 (La. Ct. App. 3 Cir. 1993) (changing custody from father to mother because father of children with psychological problems made them sniff their wet sheets after bed-wetting, lay face-down on the floor after unruly behavior, and stand on their toes—whipping them if they lost their balance).

893. *See, e.g.*, Hull v. Hull, 542 So. 2d 205, 207 (La. Ct. App. 3 Cir. 1989) (changing custody from mother to father due in part to the crowded living conditions in the home).

894. Nielsen v. Nielsen, No. 55,447 (La. App. 2 Cir. 11/22/23); 375 So. 3d 1042 (changing custody from joint to sole custody with mother because of father's transient lifestyle and failure to care for children financially or emotionally); Hodgkin v. Hodgkin, 54,559 (La. App. 2 Cir. 6/29/22), 342 So. 3d 420 (changing custody from father to mother because of the following: father divorced his second wife, the child's primary caretaker; father moved his new girlfriend and her three children into his home; father received orders that he would be deployed for six months; child would likely be relocated to different state in the future; and child would likely withdraw from his therapy for autism).

895. *See, e.g.*, Kiefer v. Yellon, 94-218, pp. 6–7 (La. App. 5 Cir. 11/16/94), 646 So. 2d 1073, 1076 (sexual abuse); Lawrence v. Lawrence, 50,799, p. 4 (La. App. 2 Cir. 5/25/16), 197 So. 3d 198, 201 (physical force).

896. Bergeron v. Bergeron, 492 So. 2d 1193, 1203 (La. 1986); Monteleone v. Monteleone, 591 So. 2d 1228, 1235 (La. Ct. App. 4 Cir. 1991).

897. Monteleone, 591 So. 2d at 1235; Bailey v. Bailey, 527 So. 2d 1030, 1034 (La. Ct. App. 2 Cir. 1988); Tolar v. Tolar, 569 So. 2d 267, 270 (La. Ct. App. 2 Cir. 1990).

898. *See, e.g.*, Montgomery v. Marcantel, 591 So. 2d 1272, 1273–74 (La. Ct. App. 3 Cir. 1991); Plunkett v. Plunkett, 576 So. 2d 100, 104 (La. Ct. App. 2 Cir. 1991).

899. Bagwell v. Bagwell, 48,913 (La. App. 2 Cir. 1/15/14), 132 So.3d 426.

900. Adams v. Adams, 39,424, pp. 6–7 (La. App. 2 Cir. 4/6/05), 132 So. 3d 426; Long v. Long, 28,763 (La. App. 2 Cir. 12/11/96), 684 So. 2d 1099.

tion against harm done to children by custody litigation and threats thereof, changes in custody, continued parental conflict, and erroneous judgments."[901] On the other hand, some courts have concluded that allowing the *Bergeron* standard to apply to a consent judgment when the evidence has not been evaluated by the judge would "erode the definition of considered decree and the policy reasons for the rule as examined by the *Bergeron* court."[902] The Louisiana Supreme Court has yet to decide.

§ 6:51 Modification of Custody and Visitation—Consent (or Stipulated) Decrees

When the original custody decree is a stipulated decree—the parties consented to the custodial arrangement and no evidence of parental fitness was taken—the party seeking a modification need not prove the heightened *Bergeron* standard, but rather must prove that: (1) a material change of circumstances has occurred since the original custody decree was entered; and (2) the proposed modification is in the best interest of the child.[903] This standard is often referred to as the *Evans* standard, based on the Louisiana Supreme Court case *Evans v. Lungrin*.[904]

Ultimately, if there is no material or significant change in circumstances, no modification of custody can be made.[905] Likewise, if the proposed modification is not in the best interest of the child, no modification may occur.[906] From a policy standpoint, the heavy burden of proof from *Bergeron* is inapplicable because no court has reviewed the facts and made a determination of custody.[907] Some courts conclude that a material change is not necessary for the court to alter the days of physical custodial time from the original stipulated judgment.[908]

---

901. Adams, 899 So. 2d at 730.

902. Rodriguez v. Wyatt, 11-82, p. 12 (La. App. 5 Cir. 12/12/11), 102 So. 3d 109, 116 (citation and internal quotation marks omitted).

903. Evans v. Lungrin, 97-0541, p. 13 (La. 2/6/98), 708 So. 2d 731, 738.

904. *See generally* Evans, 708 So. 2d 731.

905. Kingston v. Kingston, 2011-1629, pp. 6–7 (La. App. 1 Cir. 12/21/11), 80 So. 3d 774, 778; Bonnecarre v. Bonnecarre, 2009-1647, p. 7 (La. App. 1 Cir. 4/14/10), 37 So. 3d 1038, 1044; Bingham v. Bingham, 42,140, p. 3 (La. App. 2 Cir. 4/4/07), 954 So. 2d 842, 844; *see* McLaren v. Childress, 53,521, p. 11 (La. App. 2 Cir. 7/22/20), 300 So. 3d 906, 913; Barrett v. Barrett, 20-266 (La. App. 5 Cir. 2/24/20), 314 So. 3d 1023 (although the father's blindness created difficulties in his ability to assist in transporting the children, it did not constitute a material change in circumstances to warrant a modification). Courts are flexible in allowing claims for modification even in the face of inartful pleading. *See, e.g.*, Beem v. Beem, 2020-0897 (La. App. 1 Cir. 4/20/21), 324 So. 3d 682, 687 (affirming the trial court's designation of father as domiciliary parent was appropriate even though he failed to use the phrase "change in circumstances" because his pleading sufficiently stated a cause of action for designation of domiciliary parent).

906. *See* Fuller v. Fuller, 54,098 (La. App. 2 Cir. 07/21/21), 324 So. 3d 1103 (denying modification because it was not in the child's best interest—mother's repeated actions to damage the relationship between father and the children).

907. *See generally* Evans, 708 So. 2d 731.

908. Gerace v. Gerace, 2005-1300, pp. 3–4 (La. App. 3 Cir. 4/5/06), 927 So. 2d 622, 624 (concluding that time spent with each parent in a joint custody award need only be in the best interest of the child).

A myriad of factual circumstances can amount to a material change.[909] When custody is uncontested by default because the parent did not make an appearance, a material change must be proven, rather than the heightened *Bergeron* standard.[910] While the change that precipitates a request must occur after the last custody order was rendered, some courts recognize that evidence of actions prior to the last custody order may be admissible to show effects on the child in the best interest analysis, even though they may not be used to establish a material change.[911]

§ 6:52 Modification of Custody and Visitation— Parent Seeking Modification of Custody Awarded to a Nonparent

When a parent seeks to modify custody that has been awarded to a nonparent, courts have struggled with the appropriate legal standard to apply given the parent's primary right to custody. In 2016, the Louisiana Supreme Court settled a split among the circuits, concluding that, in an action by a parent to modify a stipulated joint custody arrangement in favor of a nonparent, the parent bears the burden of proof and must satisfy the *Evans* standard, i.e., must show a material change of circumstance since the original custody decree was entered and the proposed modification is in the best interest of the child.[912]

Various schools of thought existed in the appellate courts when a parent sought custody from a nonparent. Some circuits placed the burden of proof on the parent to demonstrate first that the parent's rehabilitation to be presently fit eliminates the "substantial harm" to the child that existed when the nonparents were initially granted custody (the standard under article 133), and second, that there has been a material

---

But see Cetodal v. Cetodal, 2005-1524, p. 7 (La. App. 1 Cir. 11/4/05); 927 So. 2d 433, 437 (finding that both a material change and best interest must be shown to modify physical custodial time).

909. *See, e.g.*, Lawrence v. Lawrence, 50,799, p. 4 (La. App. 2 Cir. 5/25/16), 197 So. 3d 198, 201 (inability of parents to work together under the existing agreement was enough to amount to a material change); Odom v. Odom, 606 So. 2d 862, 866 (La. Ct. App. 2 Cir. 1992) (evidence of one parent not allowing the children to have any contact with the other parent was found to constitute a material change of circumstances); Bagwell v. Bagwell, 48,913, p. 7 (La. App. 2 Cir. 1/15/14), 132 So. 3d 426, 431 (relocation of the parent amounted to a material change of circumstance); Yepez v. Yepez, 2021-04777, pp. 11–13 (La. App. 1 Cir. 12/22/21), 340 So. 3d 36, 42–44 (mother's inability to facilitate and encourage a relationship between the child and the father and the mother's mishandling of finances that materially affected the child).

910. *See, e.g.*, Odom, 606 So. 2d at 864 (finding that *Bergeron* did not apply to mother who was represented by curator ad hoc when custody was initially rendered because the custody was not contested by the curator).

911. *See* Bowden v. Brown, 48, 268, p. 12 (La. App. 2 Cir. 5/15/13), 114 So. 3d 1194, 1202 (finding that facts predating a stipulated judgment of custody by married parents to the maternal grandmother were relevant in a subsequent modification request); Touchet v. Touchet, 36,881 (La. App. 2 Cir. 1/29/03), 836 So. 2d 1149 (finding that mother's prior criminal conduct affected her ability to encourage the child's relationship with the father).

912. *See generally* Tracie F. v. Francisco D., 2015-1812 (La. 3/15/16), 188 So. 3d 231.

change in the adequate and stable environment in which the child is living with the nonparents.[913] Yet others, while still placing the burden of proof on the parent seeking to modify, required the parent to prove only a material change of circumstances that met the best interest of the child.[914] Still others rejected the idea that the parent bears any burden of proving a material change of circumstance or that a change is in the best interest if the child, finding that parental primacy would otherwise be violated.[915] Rather, the burden of proof was placed on the nonparent to retain custody: once the parent sought to modify custody in the nonparent, the nonparent had to show that a custody award to the parent would continue to result in substantial harm to the child.[916]

The Louisiana Supreme Court in *Tracie F. v. Francisco D.* concluded that the established *Evans* standard for modification applied to parents, which both preserved the parental rights of primacy and followed Civil Code Article 131 and its interpretive jurisprudence.[917] In *Tracie F.*, the biological father sought to modify a stipulated judgment that awarded joint custody to him and to the child's maternal grandmother. The trial court awarded sole custody to the father, but the appellate court vacated the award, finding that the father must demonstrate rehabilitation to eliminate any substantial harm. The Louisiana Supreme Court reversed, concluding that the parent must show only a material change of circumstance since the original custody order and that modification is in the best interest of the child.[918] In *dicta*, the Louisiana Supreme Court noted that its analysis may not apply when a parent has relinquished custody, either voluntarily or involuntarily, as regaining custody may deserve a different standard than expanding custody:[919]

> We are not presented with a custody contest between a biological parent who has voluntarily relinquished custody or whose parental rights have otherwise been terminated; such a contest represents a separate class of cases which differs from the one which we presently decide. There is a distinction between the efforts of a parent to *expand* custodial rights and the efforts of a parent to *regain* custodial rights.[920]

Just two years later in *In re L.M.M., Jr.*, the Louisiana Supreme Court applied its statements in *dicta* to a parent who was seeking to regain rights after the State of Mississippi appointed a guardian for the minor when he was removed from the custody

913. Jones v. Coleman, 44,543, p. 19 (La. App. 2 Cir. 7/15/09), 18 So. 3d 153, 164.

914. Tracie F., 188 So. 3d 231, 241 (citing Dalme v. Dalme, 09-524 (La. App. 3 Cir. 10/14/09), 21 So. 3d 477, 479–80).

915. Cutts v. Cutts, 2006-33, p. 5 (La. App. 3 Cir. 5/24/06), 931 So. 2d 467, 471; Tennessee v. Campbell, 28,823, p. 10 (La. App. 2 Cir. 10/30/96), 682 So. 2d 1274, 1279; *see also* Mills v. Wilkerson, 34,694, p. 5 (La. App. 2 Cir. 3/26/01), 785 So. 2d 69, 73.

916. Cutts, 931 So. 2d at 470; Tennessee, 682 So. 2d at 1279; *see also* Mills, 785 So. 2d at 73.

917. Tracie F., 188 So. 3d at 245.

918. Tracie F., 188 So. 3d at 245.

919. Tracie F., 188 So. 3d at 246.

920. Tracie F., 188 So. 3d at 246.

of his natural parents.[921] Noting that "this is not, as in *Tracie F.*, a situation wherein a parent seeks to *expand* existing custodial rights, but rather one in which the parent is seeking to *regain* such rights," the court applied Children's Code Article 724, which supplied the appropriate standard for parents seeking to terminate a guardianship.[922]

Appellate courts have applied the *Tracie F.* standard to parents seeking to regain custody from a nonparent, noting:

> Why should a parent be prejudiced in the future when they make a decision that is in the best interest of the child to be in the care of a nonparent?... Stipulating to sole custody in favor of a nonparent preserves and fosters the longstanding jurisprudence that repetitive custody litigation is harmful to children.[923]

Courts in same-sex custody cases have also applied *Tracie F.* standard for disputes between parents and nonparents.[924] In *D.A.B. v. C.G.W.*, the biological mother and her partner consented to joint custody, naming the biological mother as the domiciliary parent.[925] When the biological mother sought to modify custody, naming her as the sole custodian, the trial court concluded that the nonparent had the burden of proving that substantial harm would result to the child to retain custody.[926] The appellate court reversed, concluding that the standard in *Tracie F.* applied to a modification of custody, and finding on de novo review that the biological mother met the two-pronged standard.[927]

§ 6:53 Court-Ordered Mediation

Once custody or visitation is before the court, it may order the parties to mediate their differences.[928] The court will first seek agreement by the parties to name the mediator; however, if the parties cannot agree, the court will appoint one.[929] Once the court issues an order requiring the parties to mediate, it may stay any further determination of custody or visitation, although the stay cannot exceed 30 days from the issuance of the court's order of mediation.[930]

---

921. In re L.L.M., Jr., 2017-1988 (La. 6/27/18); 319 So. 3d 231.

922. In re L.L.M., Jr., 319 So. 3d at 241.

923. Smith v. Harmon, 2021-772 (La. App. 3 Cir. 4/6/22), 337 So. 3d 912, 918 (quoting the trial court); *see also* Harvey v. Harper. 2022-744 (La. App. 3 Cir. 3/1/23); 358 So. 3d 988.

924. D.A.B. v. C.G.W., No. 2023-548 (La. App. 3 Cir. 3/27/24), 2024 WL 1289824; In re J.E.T., 16-384 (La. App. 1 Cir. 10/31/16), 211 So. 3d 575.

925. D.A.B., 2024 WL 1289824.

926. D.A.B., 2024 WL 1289824, at *3.

927. D.A.B., 2024 WL 1289824, at *4.

928. La. Stat. Ann. § 9:332. The decision to order mediation is within the discretion of the trial court. *See* Angelette v. Callais, 2010-2279, p. 6 (La. App. 1 Cir. 5/6/11), 68 So. 3d 1122, 1126.

929. La. Stat. Ann. § 9:332(A). The duties and the qualifications of the mediator are found in Louisiana Revised Statutes Sections 9:333 and 9:334, respectively. *See generally* La. Stat. Ann. §§ 9:333–:334.

930. La. Stat. Ann. § 9:332(A).

Before mediation begins, the court has the option to require the parties to pay in advance for mediation.[931] If costs are not paid in advance and mediation is successful, the court may apportion the costs of mediation between the parties.[932] If costs are not paid in advance and the mediation is unsuccessful, however, the court must tax the costs of mediation as court costs.[933] The cost of mediation is always subject to approval by the court.[934]

If the parties reach an agreement during mediation, the mediator must prepare a written, signed, and dated agreement that will be submitted to the court for its approval and, if approved, the agreement is incorporated into a subsequent consent judgment.[935] If the parties are unable to reach an agreement or if no agreement can be reached within the 30-day stay, evidence of conduct or statements made in mediation (that are not otherwise discoverable) are inadmissible in any proceeding in the trial court.[936] In other words, even if disclosed during mediation, such evidence will not be admissible unless it satisfies the rules of evidence at trial.

Mediation can be mandated before or after an initial award of custody, as long as the 30-day stay is honored. For example, in *Edwards v. Edwards*, the Louisiana Third Circuit Court of Appeal enforced a mediation order after an initial award of custody was granted.[937] In the original order that granted the parents joint custody, the trial court also ordered that if the parties were unable to agree on living and schooling arrangements for the child, they must mediate at least six months prior to the child attending kindergarten.[938] If the parties were unable to agree on a mediator, the parties were required to have the court appoint one.[939] Six months before the child started kindergarten, without having sought mediation, the mother filed for a change of custody in the venue where she was then living.[940] The trial court in the new venue did not enforce the mediation order, finding that it was against public policy.[941] The Third Circuit reversed, concluding that the mediation mandate authorized by Louisiana Revised Statutes Section 9:332 should have been followed, and the court in the new venue should have enforced the mediation order of the original court or transferred the case to the original court.[942]

931. La. Stat. Ann. § 9:332(A).
932. La. Stat. Ann. § 9:332(A).
933. La. Stat. Ann. § 9:332(A).
934. La. Stat. Ann. § 9:332(A).
935. La. Stat. Ann. § 9:332(B).
936. La. Stat. Ann. § 9:332(C).
937. *See* Edwards v. Edwards, 99-994, p. 4 (La. App. 3 Cir. 12/22/99), 755 So. 2d 331, 334.
938. Edwards, 755 So. 2d at 333.
939. Edwards, 755 So. 2d at 334.
940. *See* Edwards, 755 So. 2d at 333.
941. Edwards, 755 So. 2d at 335.
942. Edwards, 755 So. 2d at 335.

§ 6:54 Use of Expert Witnesses

Trial courts must make difficult, fact-based findings when ruling on custody. Expert witnesses can be a vital tool to assist the court in determining what is in the child's best interest. The written findings by the expert, as well as those conveyed through testimony, can play a significant role in a trial court's fact-finding process. As such, the admissibility of an expert's report and testimony is critical and can depend on the type of expert used. Although the most commonly used experts in custody cases are custody evaluators, other experts may also testify during the proceeding. Mental health experts retained by either party, as well as treating physicians or therapists of a party, commonly participate in custody trials, even when a custody evaluator has been appointed and will also testify.[943] In 2024, the legislature, on recommendation of the Law Institute, bifurcated the law on custody and mental health evaluators, because prior to the revision, they were both covered by the same provision of law, even though custody and mental health evaluations are different.

Section 9:331 provides courts with discretion to appoint an independent mental health evaluator,[944] and section 9:331.3 provides courts with discretion to appoint an independent child custody evaluator.[945] The evaluations can be ordered for a party or the child when "good cause [is] shown."[946] The two statutes are very similar, although the custody evaluator must follow specific guidelines and have specific experience performing evaluations under the supervision of a court-ordered evaluator.[947] In either case, when domestic abuse is an issue, the mental health or the custody evaluator must have training and experience working with victims of domestic abuse.[948]

Trial courts most frequently use custody evaluators in highly contentious custody battles.[949] Even one instance of domestic violence has been enough to warrant the

---

943. *See generally* Griffith v. Latiolais, 2010-0754 (La. 10/19/10), 48 So. 3d 1058 (expert testimony was heard by the mother's therapist, the child's treating therapist and co-parenting counselor, the doctors who performed the psychological evaluations of the parties and the minor children, and the court-appointed custody evaluator at the custody trial).

944. La. Stat. Ann. § 9:331. However, this statute does not provide courts with authority to order a party to seek counseling as a result of a custody or visitation proceeding. *See* England v. England, 2017-0493, pp. 5–7 (La. App. 4 Cir. 3/2/18), 238 So. 3d 1064, 1074–76 (Lobrano, J., concurring in part & dissenting in part).

945. La. Stat. Ann. § 9:331.3.

946. La. Stat. Ann. §§ 9:331(A), 331.3(A).

947. La. Stat. Ann. §§ 9:331.3(A), (B).

948. La. Stat. Ann. §§ 9:331(D), 331.3(D).

949. *See generally* Huber v. Midkiff, 2002-0664 (La. 2/7/03), 838 So. 2d 771. In *Huber*, "[t]he [trial court] appointed [a custody evaluator] and ordered all parties to participate in any interview and/or testing conducted by the evaluator ... to determine the most appropriate domiciliary and visitation arrangements [for the child]." *Id.* at 774. There had been allegations by the father that the child's mother was abusing/mistreating the child. *Id.* In her report, the custody evaluator noted that "[t]he central issue [was] more about control." *Id.*; *see also* Griffith, 48 So. 3d at 1060 (several experts were needed because custody battle was "highly acrimonious"); Lucky v. Way, 51,706, p. 29 (La. App. 2 Cir. 9/1/17), 245 So. 3d 110, 128 (expert needed in "protracted litigation" where parties could not agree on important issues regarding the child).

appointment of a custody evaluator to understand the basis of the conflict.[950] Ultimately, trial courts have great discretion to appoint a custody evaluator given the permissive language of the statute.[951] As such, refusal to grant a motion seeking appointment of an evaluator is not reversible error, provided the trial court did not abuse its discretion.[952]

Custody or mental health evaluators are appointed by a court to help determine the appropriate custody arrangement and to sort through allegations, factual inconsistencies, and conflicts that necessarily occur when a court is tasked with determining the legal and physical custody of a child.[953] Evaluators must be "licensed mental health professionals," defined as "a person who possesses at least a master's degree and who holds a current unrestricted license in counseling, social work, psychology, or marriage and family counseling."[954] Further, mental health professionals who only review the work of other mental health professionals or who simply assist in the preparation of an evaluation without actually interviewing the parties may also be permitted to testify.[955]

In *Bourque v. Bourque*, a trial court refused to grant a father's request for an independent psychological evaluation.[956] The trial judge explained in his reasons for judgment that to order such an evaluation would be "nothing more than an abdication of his responsibilities, which often proves expensive to the parties."[957] In essence, the judge felt that he was in the best position to independently evaluate the situation as a neutral third party—a decision the appellate court commended him for making.[958] Because of

---

950. *See* Ellis v. Ellis, 50,378, p. 11 (La. App. 2 Cir. 11/18/15), 184 So. 3d 752, 759.

951. Both statutes provide that "[a] court *may* order...." La. Stat. Ann. §§ 9:331(A), 331.3(A) (emphasis added).

952. *See, e.g.*, Elliott v. Elliott, 2010-0755, pp. 5–6 (La. App. 1 Cir. 9/10/10), 49 So. 3d 407, 411; Silbernagel v. Silbernagel, 06-879, pp. 11–12 (La. App. 5 Cir. 4/11/07), 958 So. 2d 13, 20; C.L.S. v. G.J.S., 2005-1419, p. 37 (La. App. 4 Cir. 3/7/07), 953 So. 2d 1025, 1043; Bourque v. Bourque, 03-1254, p. 4 (La. App. 5 Cir. 3/30/04), 870 So. 2d 1088, 1091.

953. Costs of custody evaluation can be allocated to one parent alone if the custody dispute results entirely from one parent's behavior or mental health. Kott v. Kott, 2020 0873 (La. App. 1 Cir. 04/16/21), 324 So. 3d 165.

954. La. Stat. Ann. §§ 9:331(A)(C), 331.3(A).

955. *See* Raney v. Wren, 98-0869, p. 13 (La. App. 1 Cir. 11/6/98), 722 So. 2d 54, 62. The trial court heard testimony of a clinical psychologist who reviewed the custody evaluation and personality tests taken by the parties but did not interview the parties. *Id.* The court also heard testimony of a social worker who assisted the court-appointed clinical psychologist in his evaluation and in preparing the expert report for the court. *Id.* Although she did not administer the test herself, she was admitted as an expert in the field of social work, and her testimony was considered in the trial court's award of custody. *See id.*

956. Bourque, 870 So. 2d at 1091. At trial, a licensed clinical social worker was admitted as an expert and testified regarding his opinions and assessment of the child. *Id.* at 1090–91. The expert had been retained by the mother and met with her and the child 15 times, whereas he only met with the father five times in preparing his evaluation. *Id.* The father requested an independent psychological evaluation, which the trial court denied, explaining that the mother's expert would be weighed with the other evidence at trial. *Id.*

957. Bourque, 870 So. 2d at 1091.

958. Bourque, 870 So. 2d at 1091. On review, the appellate court explained, "We commend the trial judge for retaining his responsibility to evaluate the case himself, based on the evidence presented to him rather than turning it over to an independent evaluator." *Id.*; *see also* Elliott v. Elliott, 2010-0755,

the broad discretion granted to trial courts, a decision to order a custody evaluation and to rely on the recommendation of the evaluator is difficult to attack and overturn.

The evaluator must examine the lives and circumstances of the child and the parties to evaluate the best custody arrangement for the best interest of the child. Mental health and custody evaluations may require home visits, mental health assessments, and psychological testing when appropriate.[959] A custody evaluation may also include interviews of all parties involved, the child whose custody is at issue, as well as any non-parties who play a crucial role in the child's daily life.[960]

Note, however, that revisions made in 2022 prohibit ex parte communications by the litigants or their attorneys with the evaluators when they are court-appointed.[961] All oral communication with the professional shall be by teleconference or meeting in which each party to the proceeding participates; all written communication to the mental health professional, along with any attachments thereto, shall be provided contemporaneously to all parties to the litigation or their attorneys of record.[962] Exceptions exist when authorized by law or court order, by the agreement of the parties, or when communication is initiated by the professional for the purpose of conducting the court-ordered evaluation.[963]

The professional performing the evaluation must provide all parties involved with a copy of the expert report.[964] The court shall not be provided a copy of the report because the reports are subject to various evidentiary restrictions.[965] Failure to furnish the expert report to either party will result in a violation of that party's due process rights, constituting reversible error.[966] For example, in *Fuge v. Uiterwyk*, the Louisiana Fourth Circuit Court of Appeal reversed the trial court because it refused to allow

---

p. 6 (La. App. 1 Cir. 9/10/10), 49 So. 3d 407, 411 (finding no good cause to order an evaluation because the court could render a decision on the issue of physical custodial periods without the input of a mental health evaluator).

959. The most common test administered to parents engaged in a custody dispute is the Minnesota Multi-Phased Personality Inventory-2 (MMPI-2). However, various experts note that this test "must be administered with more than just a single interview." Raney v. Wren, 98-0869, p. 13 (La. App. 1 Cir. 11/6/98), 722 So. 2d 54, 62. Likewise, it is also often noted that the results of the test tend to display a "guarded profile," which is common for individuals involved in a custody dispute. Expert Report & Affidavit, Wurtzel v. Wurtzel, No. 552-615, 2003 WL 25277014 (24th J.D.C. La. Feb. 13, 2003), 1999 WL 34002369.

960. Non-parties may include such individuals as grandparents, neighbors, treating physicians of the parties, the child's school teacher, or anyone else who plays a significant role in either the parties or child's day-to-day lives. *See* Guidelines for Child Custody Evaluations in Family Law Proceedings, Am. Psychol. Ass'n, https://www.apa.org/practice/guidelines/child-custody (last visited May 27, 2024) ("Psychologists ... frequently make contact with members of extended family, friends and acquaintances and other collateral sources when the resulting information is likely to be relevant.").

961. La. Stat. Ann. §§ 9:331(E), 331.3(I).

962. La. Stat. Ann. §§ 9:331(E), 331.3(I).

963. La. Stat. Ann. §§ 9:331(E), 331.3(I).

964. La. Stat. Ann. §§ 9:331(B), 331.3(F).

965. La. Stat. Ann. §§ 9:331(F), 331.3(J).

966. Fuge v. Uiterwyk, 94-1815, p. 6 (La. App. 4 Cir. 3/29/95), 653 So. 2d 707, 712.

the parties access to the report of the examining mental health professional.[967] The court noted that the trial judge's ultimate determination relied heavily on the expert report because there existed "no other credible supportive evidence" to form the basis of the judgment.[968] Therefore, "[w]ithout the opportunity to review the report, and to cross-examine the psychiatrist, [the opponents] were denied fundamental due process."[969] If admitted into evidence, counsel should ensure that the report is filed into the record to support the trial court's findings of fact in the event of an appeal.

Although there are no specific requirements regarding the contents of a custody evaluation, the evaluator can use the Association of Family and Conciliation Courts' Guidelines for Parenting Plan Evaluations in Family Law Cases.[970] A few general topics and issues are standard, as they appear in many expert reports of custody evaluators.[971] The report should include the names of the parties, the children, and any other individuals with whom the evaluator met and whose interviews form the basis of the report.[972] It should also explain any tests administered or methodologies used to assess the parties. The Model Standards of Practice for Child Custody Evaluations warn that evaluators should be prepared to defend their decisions concerning chosen methodologies.[973] Other topics and information contained within the report may include the relationship between the parties, personal histories of each party,[974] psychological statuses of all parties involved,[975] information revealed in interviews with third parties, facts obtained via review of various relevant documents,[976] and finally, the evaluator's conclusions and recommendations.

---

967. Fuge, 653 So. 2d at 712.

968. Fuge, 653 So. 2d at 712.

969. Fuge, 653 So. 2d at 712; *see also* Barker v. Barker, 2014-0775, p. 6 (La. App. 1 Cir. 11/7/14), 167 So. 3d 703, 706 (holding that "[w]ithout allowing the parties an opportunity to review the report and cross examine [the expert] violates the mandate in La. R.S. 9:331(B) and constitutes a denial of due process").

970. La. Stat. Ann. § 9:331.3(A).

971. *See, e.g.*, La. Dist. Ct. R. app. 24.13 (West, Westlaw through Dec. 15, 2023) (Court-Specific Rules Concerning Mental Health Evaluations in Family Law Proceedings).

972. *See* Report or Affidavit of J. Steven York, Ph.D., Lagarde v. Lagarde, No. 614-018 (24th J.D.C. La. July 26, 2006), 2006 WL 3892976 (listing every individual the evaluator met with, detailing the number of times he met with each, along with the purpose of the meeting).

973. David A. Martindale, The Model Standards of Practice for Child Custody Evaluations, 45 Fam. Ct. Rev. 70, 79 (2007). In *Raney v. Wren*, MMPI-2 tests were administered by the custody evaluator to both parents, and a clinical psychologist retained by the father testified as an expert regarding the particular methodology used and his experiences with the use of the particular test. Raney v. Wren, 98-0869, p. 13 (La. App. 1 Cir. 11/6/98), 772 So. 2d. 54, 62.

974. Personal histories of all parties include their family, social, and mental health histories. *See generally* Expert Report & Affidavit, Wurtzel v. Wurtzel, No. 552-615, 2003 WL 25277014 (24th J.D.C. La. Feb. 13, 2003), 1999 WL 34002369.

975. This includes test results, prior mental or physical health issues as revealed by interviews, or medical records from prior treating physicians of the examined party. *See generally* Expert Report & Affidavit, Wurtzel v. Wurtzel, No. 552-615, 2003 WL 25277014 (24th J.D.C. La. Feb. 13, 2003), 1999 WL 34002369.

976. Pertinent documents in performing a custody evaluation can include, but are not limited to, emails from the parties and non-parties expressing concern or relaying information pertinent to the

While it is preferable to have live testimony of the evaluator, subject to cross-examination by the parties, the law does not require it. Sections 331 and 331.3 provide that the mental health professional shall serve as a witness, subject to cross-examination by a party, but the failure of a party to call the expert is not reversible error.[977] When the custody evaluator does not testify in the custody proceeding, the report may be considered inadmissible hearsay.[978] Absent objection by a party, however, an expert report has been considered by a court even without live testimony of the expert.[979]

In *Verret v. Verret*, after a thorough review of the expert report, the trial court determined that the expert's findings and recommendations were inconsistent.[980] On appeal, the father argued that the court was in error for rejecting the recommendations without the evaluator being given a chance to address the court's concerns on the witness stand.[981] The Second Circuit disagreed, explaining that the trial court had a sufficient basis for rejecting the recommendations after considering the expert report and all of the testimony and evidence adduced at trial, as well as the demeanor of the parties and witnesses.[982] In fact, neither party called the expert to testify.[983] Presumably, no party objected at trial when the report was introduced into evidence without the expert present. If met with a hearsay objection, the report of the expert would be properly excluded.

Before the evaluator can testify, the court must first qualify the expert based on his "knowledge, skill, experience, training, or education" in the subject matter.[984] Failure to timely object to a proposed expert's qualifications will operate as a waiver of the right, and may not be asserted collaterally on appeal.[985] The subject of the expert's testimony

---

custody determination, letters from the parties or non-parties to the same effect, copies of medical records of any of the parties, results of any forensic examination, etc.

977. La. Stat. Ann. §§ 9:331(B), 331.3(H); *see also* Verret v. Verret, 34,982, pp. 12–13 (La. App. 2 Cir. 5/9/01), 786 So. 2d 944, 951–52 (explaining that either party could have called the evaluator as a witness, but their failure to do so did not result in reversible error when the trial judge chose not to adopt the evaluator's recommendations).

978. *See* Mimms v. Brown, 2002-1681, p. 13 (La. App. 4 Cir. 9/3/03), 856 So. 2d 36, 43–44.

979. Verret, 786 So. 2d at 952.

980. Verret, 786 So. 2d at 951.

981. Verret, 786 So. 2d at 952.

982. Verret, 786 So. 2d at 952. The trial judge noted in his reasons for judgment that his observation of the parties revealed the "obvious hostility of the father toward the mother and his attempts to limit the child's contact with her." *Id.*

983. Verret, 786 So. 2d at 952.

984. La. Code Evid. Ann. art. 702(A) provides:

> A witness who is qualified as an expert by knowledge, skill, experience, training, or education may testify in the form of an opinion or otherwise if: (1) The expert's scientific, technical, or other specialized knowledge will help the trier of fact to understand the evidence or to determine a fact in issue; (2) The testimony is based on sufficient facts or data; (3) The testimony is the product of reliable principles and methods; and (4) The expert has reliably applied the principles and methods to the facts of the case.

985. La. Code Evid. Ann. art. 103 provides:

> Error may not be predicated upon a ruling which admits or excludes evidence unless a substantial right of the party is affected, and … [w]hen the ruling is one admitting evidence, a timely

is typically limited to the report prepared by the expert and submitted to the parties and the court. The credibility of the expert's testimony can be examined and tested by any party challenging the conclusions reached by the expert.[986] Both parties are given a chance to cross-examine or confront the evaluator on any perceived inconsistencies or contested issues of fact contained within the report.[987] The expert testimony of an evaluator regarding the child's preferences and feelings, based on the evaluation and interactions with the child, will serve to remedy any judicial error in not allowing the child to testify.[988]

When two professionals evaluate the parties and assist the court in its custody determination, their recommendations and reasons may conflict.[989] Trial judges must resolve conflicting expert testimony and make credibility determinations by examining and assessing the underlying bases for each expert's recommendations.[990] The effect and weight to be given to the expert testimony are within the broad discretion of the trial judge.[991] In *Orill v. Orill*, the court addressed conflicting reports and commended an evaluator for her consistent cross-validation of all information provided to her by each party as well as from other parties she interviewed.[992]

Because trial judges are in the best position to make credibility determinations of parties and witnesses, great deference is given to their determinations in child custody cases and will not be disturbed absent clear abuse of discretion.[993] Although court-appointed experts spend significant time inquiring into the lives and well-being of all parties involved, oftentimes, the trial judge will ultimately spend more time with the parties throughout the case. Therefore, consistent observation of the parties' behavior and demeanor toward one another leaves the judge in the best position to weigh the evidence presented, given the credibility of each party. Because the ultimate decision-

---

objection or motion to admonish the jury to limit or disregard appears of record, stating the specific ground of objection....

986. *See* Leard v. Schenker, 2006-1116, p. 3 (La. 6/16/06), 931 So. 2d 355, 357.

987. *See* Fuge v. Uiterwyk, 94-1815, p. 6 (La. App. 4 Cir. 03/29/95), 653 So. 2d 707, 712.

988. *See* Fernandez v. Pizzalato, 2004-1676, pp. 17–18 (La. App. 4 Cir. 4/27/05), 902 So. 2d 1112, 1123.

989. Orrill v. Orrill, 2008-0400, p. 7 (La. App. 4 Cir. 2/4/09), 5 So. 3d 279, 284 ("[R]esolution of conflicts in expert testimony, are factual issues to be resolved by the trier of fact...."). This may happen when parties feel comfortable with different mental health professionals and display inconsistent behavior. It can also often be the result of the number of times the expert meets with each party; the more frequently the evaluator is able to observe a person's behavior and demeanor, the more accurate their understanding of that individual will be.

990. Moreau v. Moreau, 2015-0564, p. 7 (La. App. 4 Cir. 11/18/15), 179 So. 3d 819, 824; Orrill, 5 So. 3d at 284.

991. McFall v. Armstrong, 10-1041, p. 8 (La. App. 5 Cir. 9/13/11), 75 So. 3d 30, 36–37.

992. Orrill, 5 So. 3d at 284 (explaining that the other evaluator merely accepted as true what each party told her and made recommendations accordingly, without further inquiry into the allegations).

993. A.E.B. v. J.B.E., 99-2668, p. 7 (La. 11/30/99), 752 So. 2d 756, 776 ("[T]he determination of the trial judge in custody matters is entitled to great weight, and his discretion will not be disturbed on review in the absence of a clear showing of abuse."); *see also* Prejean v. Prejean, No. 11-1571, 2012 WL 1521522, at *4 (La. App. 3 Cir. May 2, 2012).

making authority remains with the judge, the law provides there is no presumption in favor of the child custody evaluator's findings.[994]

The weight given to expert testimony depends on the professional qualifications of the evaluator, the expert's experience, and the facts upon which the opinion is based.[995] Trial judges may, and oftentimes do, substitute their own judgment and common sense "when such a substitution appears warranted upon the record as a whole."[996] Such justification permits trial courts to refuse to adopt a custody evaluator's recommendations. In *Goodwin v. Goodwin*, the court refused to adopt the evaluator's recommendations, and it explained that after eight days of observing the parties' interactions, as well as testimony as to their extreme animosity, the court-appointed expert "did not realize the intensity of hatred involved" when he recommended joint custody.[997]

The most frequently appealed judgments in child custody cases are those in which the trial court fails to adopt the recommendation of the court-appointed custody evaluator.[998] However, unless the appellate court can find no factual basis for the trial court's judgment, it will be upheld.[999] Furthermore, as long as the findings of fact and the reasons for judgment are provided in sufficient detail, as evidenced by the record, appellate courts are reluctant to disturb the trial court's judgment.[1000]

In *Fernandez v. Pizzalato*, the appellate court highlighted the importance of detailed judicial findings and reasons for judgment when considering a trial court's custody award that was in complete disregard of the custody evaluator's recommendations.[1001] The appellate court reversed the award of custody because the trial judge gave the evaluator's recommendations no weight in the judgment.[1002] The trial court gave no reasons for its decision to discredit the expert, even though the court selected that particular

---

994. La. Stat. Ann. § 9: 331.3(G).

995. Verret v. Verret, 34,982, p. 11 (La. App. 2 Cir. 5/9/01), 786 So. 2d 944, 951.

996. Verret, 786 So. 2d at 951 (citing Curtis v. Curtis, 34,317 (La. App. 2 Cir. 11/1/00), 773 So. 2d 185); *see also* Goodwin v. Goodwin, 618 So. 2d 579 (La. Ct. App. 2 Cir. 1993) (noting that the trial court rejected the findings and recommendations of the experts after evaluating the evidence and testimony as a whole).

997. Goodwin, 618 So. 2d at 585–86 (opting not to adopt the recommendations of the court-appointed evaluator, a licensed clinical social worker, who conducted comprehensive evaluations of the child and both parents).

998. *See generally* Moreau v. Moreau, 2015-0564 (La. App. 4 Cir. 11/18/15), 179 So. 3d 819; Molony v. Harris, 2010-1316 (La. App. 4 Cir. 02/23/11), 60 So. 3d 70; Kees v. Kees, 2008-0124 (La. App. 4 Cir. 08/13/08), 992 So. 2d 568; Fernandez v. Pizzalato, 2004-1676, p. 21 (La. App. 4 Cir. 4/27/05), 902 So. 2d 1112; Goodwin, 618 So. 2d 579; McKenzie v. Cuccia, 2004-0112 (La. App. 4 Cir. 06/23/04), 879 So. 2d 335; Verret, 786 So. 2d at 944.

999. *See* La. Civ. Code Ann. art. 134 cmt. (b) ("A trial court's custody award will not be disturbed absent a manifest abuse of discretion."); Bergeron v. Bergeron, 492 So. 2d 1193, 1196 (La. 1986); A.E.B. v. J.B.E., 99-2668, p. 7 (La. 11/30/99), 752 So. 2d 756, 776.

1000. *See* Fernandez, 902 So. 2d at 1125.

1001. *See* Fernandez, 902 So. 2d at 1125.

1002. Fernandez, 902 So. 2d at 1125. (noting that the custody evaluation was both "extremely comprehensive and thorough").

evaluator, making it unlikely that the expert was unqualified to render an opinion.[1003] Detailed findings of fact and reasons for judgment are prudent and can be necessary if the case is pursued on appeal.

§ 6:55 Use of Parenting Coordinators

A common non-expert used by the court in custody cases is a parenting coordinator.[1004] The Association of Family and Conciliation Courts (AFCC) Task Force on Parenting Coordination defines parenting coordination as:

> [A] child-focused alternative dispute resolution process in which a mental health or legal professional with mediation training and experience assists high conflict parents to implement their parenting plan by facilitating the resolution of their disputes in a timely manner, educating parents about children's needs, and with prior approval of the parties and/or the court, making decisions within the scope of the court order or appointment contract.[1005]

The parenting coordination model stemmed from an idea developed by AFCC, "an interdisciplinary and international association of professionals dedicated to developing, refining, and practicing constructive resolution of family conflict."[1006] Realizing the need for a more tailored approach to resolving problems with high-conflict families, the AFCC presented the concept as "assessment-based parenting coordination" at its first Custody Evaluation Symposium in 1994.[1007] In 2000, the American Bar Association also recognized the need for a model to help reduce the impact of high-conflict custody cases on children,[1008] and by 2001, 14 states had implemented some form of a parenting coordination model.[1009]

In light of the growing acceptance of the model, the AFCC appointed a Task Force on Parenting Coordination ("Task Force").[1010] The Task Force discussed a need for model standards of practice; however, because the parenting coordinator role was so new, it simply laid out various issues that arose and how jurisdictions with parenting coordi-

---

1003. Fernandez, 902 So. 2d at 1125.

1004. La. Stat. Ann. § 9:358.1.

1005. AFCC Task Force on Parenting Coordination, *Guidelines for Parenting Coordination*, 44 Fam. Ct. Rev. 164, 165 (2006).

1006. *About*, Ass'n of Family & Conciliation Courts of La., https://www.afcc-la.org/ (last visited Jan. 17, 2024). "AFCC members are the leading practitioners, researchers, teachers and policymakers in the family court arena." *About AFCC*, Ass'n of Family & Conciliation Courts, https://www.afccnet.org/About/About-AFCC (last visited May 27, 2024).

1007. Sharon Press, *Family Court Services: A Reflection on 50 years of Contributions*, 51 Fam. Ct. Rev. 48, 51 (2013).

1008. Sharon Press, *Family Court Services: A Reflection on 50 years of Contributions*, 51 Fam. Ct. Rev. 48, 51 (2013).

1009. Sharon Press, *Family Court Services: A Reflection on 50 years of Contributions*, 51 Fam. Ct. Rev. 48, 51 (2013).

1010. Sharon Press, *Family Court Services: A Reflection on 50 years of Contributions*, 51 Fam. Ct. Rev. 48, 51 (2013).

nation models resolved them.[1011] The Task Force published its approach in "Parenting Coordination: Implementation Issues" in 2003.[1012] Then, in 2005, the AFCC published "Guidelines for Parenting Coordination," which provided specific and detailed recommendations for training parenting coordinators as well as best practices.[1013]

Leading the way in parenting coordination legislation, Oklahoma enacted the first parenting coordination statute in 2001, which served as a model for other states.[1014] Idaho and Oregon followed in 2002, and Colorado, Texas, and North Carolina in 2005.[1015] Louisiana joined in 2007, followed by South Dakota in 2008 and Florida in 2009.[1016] Although the Task Force set out recommendations for best practices, it also encouraged states to define guidelines that would work for them, which has resulted in many similarities among these states.[1017]

Louisiana Revised Statutes Section 9:358.1 sets out the general provisions for appointment of a parenting coordinator.[1018] According to the statute, the court may appoint a parenting coordinator either on motion of a party or the court.[1019] The appointment may only be made for good cause shown and only if the court had previously entered a judgment establishing child custody.[1020] In other words, no parenting coordinator can be appointed before a court awards child custody.

The first limitation of Revised Statutes Section 9:358.1 requires that an existing custody order be in place.[1021] The custody order may be a considered decree or an order

---

1011. Sharon Press, *Family Court Services: A Reflection on 50 years of Contributions*, 51 Fam. Ct. Rev. 48, 51 (2013).

1012. *See generally* AFCC Task Force on Parenting Coordination, *Parenting Coordination: Implementation Issues April 30, 2003*, 41 Fam. Ct. Rev. 533 (2003).

1013. AFCC Task Force on Parenting Coordination, *Guidelines for Parenting Coordination*, 44 Fam. Ct. Rev. 164 (2006).

1014. Leta S. Parks et al., *Defining Parenting Coordination with State Laws*, 49 Fam. Ct. Rev. 629, 629 (2011).

1015. Leta S. Parks et al., *Defining Parenting Coordination with State Laws*, 49 Fam. Ct. Rev. 629, 630 (2011).

1016. Leta S. Parks et al., *Defining Parenting Coordination with State Laws*, 49 Fam. Ct. Rev. 629, 630 (2011).

1017. Leta S. Parks et al., *Defining Parenting Coordination with State Laws*, 49 Fam. Ct. Rev. 629 (2011).

1018. *See* La. Stat. Ann. § 9:358.1.

1019. La. Stat. Ann. § 9:358.1(A).

1020. La. Stat. Ann. § 9:358.1(A).

1021. *See* La. Stat. Ann. § 9:358.1(A); La. Stat. Ann. § 9:358.1 cmt. (b); *see also* Broussard-Scher v. Legendre, 2010-1164, p. 12 (La. App. 3 Cir. 3/23/11), 60 So. 3d 1290, 1298 (holding that the trial court lacked authority to appoint a parenting coordinator in a proceeding filed by the grandmother seeking visitation with the grandchild because the trial court had not previously entered a judgment establishing child custody); Griffith v. Latiolais, 2010-0754, p. 19 (La. 10/19/10), 48 So. 3d 1058, 1071–72 (reversing the trial court's order that the parties continue co-parenting counseling sessions because the counseling was "outside the parameters of La. Stat. Ann. § 9:358.1" in several ways, one of which being that the trial court initially ordered co-parenting counseling before it issued a judgment establishing custody).

based on a joint stipulation, but it cannot be an ex parte custody order.[1022] The comments to § 9:358.1 explain that "the purpose of this limitation is to prevent the court from using the parenting coordinator process as a means of abdicating responsibility to make the initial custody determination."[1023]

The second limitation permits appointment only when good cause is shown.[1024] According to the statute, "good cause" may include the inability or unwillingness of either or both parties "to collaboratively make parenting decisions without assistance of others or insistence of the court."[1025] Additionally, good cause may include:

> [A]n inability or unwillingness to comply with parenting agreements and orders or a determination by the court that either or both parties have demonstrated an ongoing pattern of unnecessary litigation, refusal to communicate or difficulty in communicating about and cooperation in the care of children, and refusal to acknowledge the right of each party to have and maintain a continuing relationship with the children.[1026]

However, a showing of good cause is not necessary if there is a joint motion of the parties; in that case, the court *shall* appoint a parenting coordinator.[1027]

The appointment of a parenting coordinator is also limited to an initial one-year term, which may be extended for additional one-year terms for good cause shown.[1028]

1022. La. Stat. Ann. § 9:358.1 cmt. (b).

1023. La. Stat. Ann. § 9:358.1 cmt. (b).

1024. La. Stat. Ann. § 9:358.1(A); *see also* La. Stat. Ann. § 9:358.1 cmt. (c).

1025. La. Stat. Ann. § 9:358.1 cmt. (c).

1026. La. Stat. Ann. § 9:358.1 cmt. (c); *see also* Hanks v. Hanks, 2013-1442, p. 33 (La. App. 4 Cir. 4/16/14), 140 So. 3d 208, 229 (recommending appointment of a parenting coordinator upon remand); Molony v. Harris, 2010-1316, pp. 20–21 (La. App. 4 Cir. 2/23/11), 60 So. 3d 70, 82–83 (finding that the presence of several factors supported appointment of a parenting coordinator); Palazzolo v. Mire, 2008-0075, p. 54 (La. App. 4 Cir. 1/7/09), 10 So. 3d 748, 779 (upon remand for determination of visitation rights, recommending use of parenting coordinator because several factors for good cause were present); Griffith v. Latiolais, 2010-0754, p. 20 (La. 10/19/10), 48 So. 3d 1058, 1071–72 (holding not only that the trial court had appointed a parenting coordinator outside the confines of Louisiana Revised Statutes Section 9:358.1, but also that "good cause had not been shown sufficient to require a parenting coordinator for such an extensive length of time" because the record did not show an "inability or unwillingness to comply with the parenting agreements and orders ... [or] an ongoing pattern of unnecessary litigation, refusal to communicate[,] [or] difficulty in communicating about and cooperation in the care of [the child]"); Tracie F. v. Francisco D., 15-224, p. 61 (La. App. 5 Cir. 9/21/15), 174 So. 3d 781, 817, *aff'd but criticized*, 2015-1812 (La. 3/15/16), 188 So. 3d 231 (remanding matter and encouraging trial court and parties to consider appointment of a parenting coordinator); Council v. Livingston, 2016-1228, 2017 WL 4161681, *10–11 (La. App. 4 Cir. 9/20/17) (finding that the trial court did not abuse its discretion by refraining from appointing a parenting coordinator because the judge found the parties communicated with each other).

1027. *See* La. Stat. Ann. § 9:358.1(A) & cmt. (d).

1028. La. Stat. Ann. § 9:358.1(B); *see also* Griffith v. Latiolais, 2010-0754, pp. 19–20 (La. 10/19/10), 48 So. 3d 1058, 1071–72 (holding that the trial court's order allowing the parties to see the parenting coordinator for two years, and to continue seeing him for an indefinite period after the issuance of the final custody judgment, to be outside the parameters of La. Stat. Ann. § 9:358.1).

Termination of the appointment likewise occurs for good cause shown, upon motion of the court or of a party, or upon request of the parenting coordinator.[1029]

Another limitation on the appointment of a parenting coordinator arises when "a party has a history of perpetrating family violence," in which case no parenting coordinator shall be appointed absent good cause shown.[1030] "Family violence" is defined in the PSFVRA to include "physical or sexual abuse and any offense against the person as defined in the Criminal Code of Louisiana, except negligent injuring and defamation, committed by one parent against the other parent or against any of the children."[1031] Per the statute, "The court may find a history of perpetrating family violence if the court finds that one incident of family violence has resulted in serious bodily injury or the court finds more than one incident of family violence."[1032]

Louisiana Revised Statutes Section 9:358.1 also outlines responsibility for costs of parenting coordinators, requiring each party to pay a portion.[1033] The court may apportion the fee according to the parties' ability to pay; if the parties have an approximately equal ability to pay, they will typically pay the costs of their time spent with the parenting coordinator and split the costs of any time that the parenting coordinator spent otherwise.[1034] In any case, the portion that each party is required to pay must be specified in the order of appointment.[1035] Importantly, if a party has been granted pauper status or is unable to pay the apportioned cost, no parenting coordinator shall be appointed at all.[1036]

Louisiana Revised Statutes Section 9:358.3 lists the qualifications that a parenting coordinator must possess[1037] as well as the type of training needed.[1038] To remain qualified, a parenting coordinator must receive 20 hours of continuing education every two years.[1039]

The authority and duties of a parenting coordinator are outlined in Louisiana Revised Statutes Section 9:358.4. Parenting coordinators are required to "assist the

---

1029. La. Stat. Ann. § 9:358.8 & cmt. In this instance, "good cause" may include various factors, such as "nonpayment of fees, the process has exhausted itself, safety concerns, a lack of reasonable progress despite the best efforts of the parties, one of the parties is a perpetrator of family violence, or the parenting coordinator is unable or unwilling to serve." *Id.*

1030. La. Stat. Ann. § 9:358.2.

1031. La. Stat. Ann. § 9:362(4). This statute also points out that "family violence does not include reasonable acts of self-defense utilized by one parent to protect himself or herself or a child in the family from the family violence of the other parent." *Id.*

1032. La. Stat. Ann. § 9:364.

1033. La. Stat. Ann. § 9:358.1(C).

1034. La. Stat. Ann. § 9:358.1 cmt. (f).

1035. La. Stat. Ann. § 9:358.1 cmt. (f).

1036. La. Stat. Ann. § 9:358.1(C); *see also* Griffith, 48 So. 3d at 1071 (holding that the trial court erred in appointing a parenting coordinator despite the fact that one of the parties was unable to pay her apportioned cost).

1037. La. Stat. Ann. § 9:358.3(A).

1038. La. Stat. Ann. § 9:358.3(B).

1039. La. Stat. Ann. § 9:358.3(C).

parties in resolving disputes and in reaching agreements regarding children in [the parties'] care."[1040] The statute provides a non-exclusive list of issues that may arise, including physical schedules, health management, education, religion, travel, communication, interactions, and general child-rearing.[1041] When the parties are unable to reach an agreement with the parenting coordinator's help, the parenting coordinator may make a recommendation in a report to the court which then decides the issue.[1042] While parenting coordinators assist the court and the parties with daily issues that parents alone are unable to resolve, they should not facilitate an agreement that would change legal custody or significantly change physical custody or visitation that could result in a change in child support.[1043]

A parenting coordinator is considered a "mandatory reporter"[1044] who must report to the proper department or agency[1045] any cause to believe that "a child's physical or mental health or welfare is endangered as a result of abuse or neglect."[1046] The parenting coordinator has an obligation to provide the reports to the court, the parties, and their attorneys.[1047] However, the parenting coordinator cannot be called as a witness in the child custody proceeding unless the court permits the coordinator to do so because other capable mental health experts involved in the proceeding will testify or furnish a report touching on any conflicts or tension between the parties.[1048] Therefore, if a court-appointed custody evaluator, or even an examining or treating mental health professional, is available to testify or submit a report, the need for the parenting coordinator's testimony does not rise to the requisite standard.[1049] Parenting coordinators

---

1040. La. Stat. Ann. § 9:358.4(A).

1041. *See generally* La. Stat. Ann. § 9:358.4(A).

1042. La. Stat. Ann. § 9:358.4(C).

1043. La. Stat. Ann. § 9:358.4(B).

1044. La. Child. Code Ann. art. 603(17)(h).

1045. See article 610 of the Louisiana Children's Code for proper procedure. *See generally* La. Child. Code Ann. art. 610; *see also* La. Child. Code Ann. art. 609(A)(1)(a) ("[A]ny mandatory reporter ... shall report in accordance with [La. Child. Code Ann.] Article 610.").

1046. La. Child. Code Ann. art. 609(A)(1)(a). For purposes of article 609, "the pregnancy of a child under the age of 13 years shall constitute cause to consider whether the child has been abused." La. Child. Code Ann. art. 609(A)(1)(b).

1047. La. Stat. Ann. § 9:358.5(B); *see also* Schneider v. Schneider, 2012-1241, p. 7 (La. App. 3 Cir. 6/20/13), 115 So. 3d 1279, 1284 (holding that "the trial court erred in requiring the parenting coordinator to report directly to the court").

1048. La. Stat. Ann. § 9:358.5(A). Comment (a) specifies that "a judge should not authorize the issuance of a subpoena to a parenting coordinator unless the calling party demonstrates a need for the testimony and that evidence cannot be adduced from other sources," and that "the court may not call the parenting coordinator as a witness on its own motion." La. Stat. Ann. § 9:358.5 cmt. (a); *see also* Carollo v. Carollo, 2013-0010, pp. 10–11 (La. App. 1 Cir. 5/31/13), 118 So. 3d 53, 61 (finding no error in the trial court's decision to exclude the parenting coordinator's testimony).

1049. The general purpose of the parenting coordinator is to "assist[] parents ... to implement a parenting plan by facilitating the resolution of their disputes in a timely manner and by reducing their child-related conflict so that the children may be protected from the impact of that conflict," as well as "[to] assist[] the parties in promoting the best interests of the children by reducing or eliminating child-related conflict through the use of the parenting coordination process." La. Stat. Ann. § 9:358.1 cmt. (a).

cannot communicate with the court ex parte, except in an emergency situation,[1050] and the parties must cooperate with the coordinator by providing requested information.[1051] Finally, parenting coordinators are protected by a limitation on personal liability for any loss arising from the exercise of their official duties as long as the loss was not caused by gross negligence or willful or wanton misconduct.[1052]

The parenting coordinator model has been criticized for improper delegation of judicial authority because of the fact-finding and decision-making that parenting coordination may entail.[1053] Some states have responded by implementing parenting coordination procedures that allow for the court to review and approve a parenting coordinator's recommendations, as well as provide an opportunity for a dissatisfied party to object.[1054] Louisiana has avoided this issue by limiting the role of parenting coordinator, who can only make recommendations to the court and only when the parties are unable to reach an agreement.[1055]

Some have also argued that parenting coordination infringes on a parent's constitutional rights.[1056] No Louisiana court has entertained the issue. However, in *Barnes v. Barnes*,[1057] the Oklahoma Supreme Court considered the argument that the Oklahoma Parenting Coordinator Act was unconstitutional because it required "nothing more than a best-interest determination to infringe on a parent's fundamental right to make child-rearing decisions and in treating a divorced parent differently than a married parent."[1058] There, the court found that the act was constitutional, noting that neither the order nor the statute itself gave the parenting coordinator authority to hear and decide any more than limited issues that aid in communication between the parties and enforcement of the court's order.[1059]

While courts across Louisiana may handle the use of parenting coordinators differently, their use undoubtedly eases judicial involvement on specific, ministerial issues over which the parties simply need third-party help to reach an agreement. When the parties are unable to reach an agreement, the court must still decide the issue and can consider the recommendation of the parenting coordinator, who is knowledgeable

---

1050. La. Stat. Ann. § 9:358.6.

1051. La. Stat. Ann. § 9:358.7.

1052. La. Stat. Ann. § 9:358.9.

1053. Christine A. Coates et al., *Parenting Coordination for High-Conflict Families*, 42 Fam. Ct. Rev. 246, 248 (2004).

1054. Christine A. Coates et al., *Parenting Coordination for High-Conflict Families*, 42 Fam. Ct. Rev. 246, 249–50 (2004).

1055. Leta S. Parks et al., *Defining Parenting Coordination with State Laws*, 49 Fam. Ct. Rev. 629, 635 (2011).

1056. *See* Christine A. Coates et al., *Parenting Coordination for High-Conflict Families*, 42 Fam. Ct. Rev. 246, 251 (2004).

1057. *See generally* Barnes v. Barnes, 107 P.3d 560 (Okla. 2005).

1058. Christine A. Coates et al., *Parenting Coordination for High-Conflict Families*, 42 Fam. Ct. Rev. 246, 251 (2004); *see also generally* Barnes, 107 P.3d at 563.

1059. Barnes, 107 P.3d at 565; *see also* Christine A. Coates et al., *Parenting Coordination for High-Conflict Families*, 42 Fam. Ct. Rev. 246, 251–52 (2004).

about the parties' interactions and daily life. Nonetheless, the parties still receive needed judicial oversight, which may be necessary in a hotly contested child custody matter.

§ 6:56 Drug Testing in Custody or Visitation Proceedings

A court "may order a party in a custody or visitation proceeding to submit to specified drug tests and the collection of hair, urine, tissue, and blood samples" upon good cause shown after a contradictory hearing.[1060] The refusal to submit to testing can be considered by the court, and the rules for the admissibility of the testing reports are governed by the blood and tissue sampling statutes found in Louisiana Revised Statutes Sections 9:397.2 and 397.3, rather than the general rules of evidence.[1061] Both the order for and results of the drug test are confidential and are not admissible in any other proceeding.[1062]

§ 6:57 Psychological Parent, De Facto Parent, or In Loco Parentis

The doctrines of psychological parent, de facto parent, or in loco parentis provide needed assistance when considering a custody dispute between a parent and a non-parent who has functioned as a parent in the child's life. Louisiana has yet to formally adopt, either legislatively or jurisprudentially, these doctrines per se,[1063] but as the nature of the family unit has changed, so too has the need to incorporate principles embodied in these doctrines to better provide for the best interest of a child.[1064] In particular, same-sex unions when one parent is not filiated to the child, either biologically or through adoption, obviate the need for a deeper consideration of the effect on a child when a person who has functioned as a parent is removed from the child's life. Although few in number, courts in Louisiana have applied current law in a way that

---

1060. La. Stat. Ann. § 9:331.1; *see also* Hogan v. Hogan, 49,979, p. 6 (La. App. 2 Cir. 9/30/15), 178 So. 3d 1013, 1017 (reasoning that drug testing was proper when mother alleged that father had issues with alcohol; the mother was also concerned as to the safety of the children while in their father's care, particularly because of the people with whom he associated); Richardson v. Richardson, 2007-0430, pp. 17–18, 22 (La. App. 4 Cir. 12/28/07), 974 So. 2d 761, 773, 776 (holding that suspicion that both parties to a custody action were habitual drug users was sufficient to warrant random drug testing).

1061. *See* La. Stat. Ann. § 9:331.1; *see also* Richardson, 974 So. 2d at 771 (rejecting the use of drug test results that were simply read into the record without following the prerequisites of the Revised Statutes).

1062. L.E.P.S. v. R.G.P., 2008-1349, p. 14 (La. App. 3 Cir. 06/03/09), 11 So. 3d 633, 642–43. Costs can be taxed against any parties as may be equitable. *Id.*

1063. Cook v. Sullivan, 2020-01471 (La. 9/30/21), 330 So. 3d 152, 158–59.

1064. *See generally* Sandi S. Varnado, *The Ever-Changing Face of the Family in the Mirror of Law: A Comparative Study*, 84 La. La. Rev. 990 (2024) (discussing the changing face of the family nationally and in Louisiana).

protects parental autonomy but expands the definition of "substantial harm" when a parent-figure is the nonparent seeking custody.

In two cases from the Fifth Circuit, one that involved grandparent custody and the other a same-sex partner seeking custody, the court examined the law of other states on the issue of psychological, de facto, or "in loco parentis."[1065] In *Ferrand v. Ferrand*, the court considered a custody dispute between the biological mother, Paula, and her former partner, Vincent.[1066] Vincent identified as a male but was biologically female.[1067] The couple conceived twins through artificial insemination during their relationship.[1068] After the breakdown of their relationship,[1069] Vincent sought custody of the minor children, Caitlin and Vincent II.[1070] The trial court denied his petition because Vincent, as neither the children's biological parent nor the legal parent, failed to meet the burden of proof required under Louisiana Civil Code Article 133—that granting sole custody to Paula would result in substantial harm to the children.[1071] Vincent appealed.

On appeal, mindful of the burden on a nonparent seeking to remove custody from a parent, the Fifth Circuit began with the paramount, constitutionally protected right of parents to the "companionship, care, custody, and management" of their child.[1072]

1065. *See generally* Tracie F. v. Francisco D., 15-224 (La. App. 5 Cir. 9/21/15), 174 So. 3d 781; Ferrand v. Ferrand, 16-7 (La. App. 5 Cir. 8/31/16), 221 So. 3d 909.

1066. Ferrand, 221 So. 3d at 913.

1067. Ferrand, 221 So. 3d at 913.

1068. Ferrand, 221 So. 3d at 916. Vincent and Paula's relationship began seven years before they decided to have children. Vincent paid for Paula to undergo in vitro fertilization treatment, which resulted in Paula's pregnancy with the twins. Vincent was present at the hospital when the children were born; he and Paula both shared the same last name and wore wedding bands. The couple represented themselves as a couple to the hospital staff. Vincent signed the birth certificate as the children's father. Vincent was an active caregiver of the children, sharing child-rearing duties with Paula, and known as "Daddy" to the two children. *Id.*

1069. When the children were four years old, Paula began a relationship with a former boyfriend, who she eventually married. During the two-year time frame that Paula dated her soon-to-be husband, Vincent was the children's primary caregiver. Vincent testified that during that period, Caitlin slept at Paula's apartment six times and Vincent II only four times. Vincent also testified that during that time Paula provided virtually no support for the children and that she essentially "walked away." Paula also had two children from a previous relationship that were living with the father, as well. Ferrand, 221 So. 3d at 916–17.

1070. Ferrand, 221 So. 3d at 914.

1071. Ferrand, 221 So. 3d at 918. During the custody hearing, the court heard testimony from Dr. Marianne Walsh, an expert in psychology retained by Vincent to evaluate the then nine-year-old twins. *Id.* at 917. Dr. Walsh testified that in her opinion the children had a "'secure bond' with their father, Vincent. *Id.* She further testified that without regular contact with their father, the children would suffer "emotional problems" and that "[t]his healthy relationship with their father is crucial to their psychological and emotional well-being. And his constant daily presence in their lives is also vital to their well-being." *Id.* at 918. Despite this testimony from Dr. Walsh, the trial judge found that Vincent failed to prove that Paula was "'unable, unfit, neglectful, abusive, unwilling, or that she abandoned her rights' to justify the court's interference with Paula's constitutional rights to parent her biological children." *Id.* The judge concluded that Vincent failed to meet his burden of proving by clear and convincing evidence that substantial harm would result to the children if custody remained with Paula. *Id.*

1072. Ferrand, 221 So. 3d at 919.

The court then espoused, "[T]hat right is not unconditional"; rather, each case must be viewed in light of its own facts, considering the "overarching and overriding concern for the best interest of the child as well as the parent's concomitant rights and responsibilities."[1073]

As article 133 governed the analysis, the nonparent, Vincent, was required to prove that an award of custody to the natural parent, Paula, would cause substantial harm to the children; upon a finding of substantial harm, the court would then determine if an award of custody to Vincent was required to serve the children's best interests.[1074] Traditionally, substantial harm "includes parental unfitness, neglect, abuse, abandonment of rights, and is broad enough to include 'any other circumstances, such as prolonged separation of the child from its natural parents, that would cause the child to suffer substantial harm.'"[1075] Under the dual-pronged analysis, the best interest of the child factors are not considered until after substantial harm has been found.[1076]

The Fifth Circuit questioned the efficacy of that approach, recognizing that the "overarching inquiry" in any custody dispute is the child's best interest.[1077] As the Louisiana Supreme Court had yet to consider a case factually analogous to Vincent's, in which the nonparent has *parented* the child in a non-traditional family unit since the child's birth, the court undertook an analysis of other southern states.[1078]

In all states, the nonparent seeking custody or visitation bears the burden of proof, and as always, the best interest of the child is paramount.[1079] Several southern states have applied one or more of the doctrines to recognize the bonds formed between legal nonparents and children.[1080] The common thread among the doctrines is the nonpar-

---

1073. Ferrand, 221 So. 3d at 919; *see also* McCormic v. Rider, 2009-2584, p. 3 (La. 2/12/10), 27 So. 3d 277, 279.

1074. *See* Black v. Simms, 08-1465, p. 5 (La. App. 3 Cir. 6/10/09), 12 So. 3d 1140, 1143; *see also* Duplessy v. Duplessy, 12-69, pp. 5–6 (La. App. 5 Cir. 06/28/12), 102 So. 3d 209, 212–13.

1075. Ramirez v. Ramirez, 13-166, p. 16 (La. App. 5 Cir. 08/27/13), 124 So. 3d 8, 17.

1076. *See* Duplessy, 102 So. 3d at 213; *see also* Gill v. Bennett, 2011-886 (La. App. 3 Cir. 12/7/11), 82 So. 3d 383; Leblanc v. Guillory, 2010-164 (La. App. 3 Cir. 5/5/10), 38 So. 3d 490.

1077. Tracie F. v. Francisco D., 2015-1812, p. 2 (La. 3/15/16), 188 So. 3d 231, 235; *see also* La. Civ. Code Ann. art. 134 (rev. 1992); La. Civ. Code Ann. art. 131(A) (rev. 1992); Act No. 718, 1979 La. Acts 1962–64.

1078. Ferrand, 221 So. 3d at 922. The court also noted the drastically changing dynamics of American families. *Id.* at 921. "Same-sex couples are raising more than two million children in the United States." *Id.* (citing Garrett Cain, *"Don't Talk to [Legal] Strangers": Louisiana's Parentage Policy and the Burdens It Places on Same-Sex Parents and Their Children*, 16 Loy. J. Pub. Int. L. 167, 169 (2014)). In the landmark case of *Obergefell v. Hodges*, the United States Supreme Court held that "the right to marry is a fundamental right inherent in the liberty of the person, and under the Due Process and Equal Protection Clauses of the Fourteenth Amendment, couples of the same-sex may not be deprived of that right and that liberty." Obergefell v. Hodges, 135 S. Ct. 2584, 2604 (2015). Inherent in the liberty interest of the individual is the decision to start a family.

1079. *See generally* Troxel v. Granville, 530 U.S. 57 (2000).

1080. Ferrand, 221 So. 3d at 923. Kentucky and Oklahoma distinguished a traditional nonparent (a grandparent or stepparent) from a nonparent who the natural parent intended to be a second parent to the child. *See* Ramey v. Sutton, 362 P.3d 217, 221–22 (Okla. 2015) (holding that a biological mother's former same-sex partner had standing to seek custody and visitation under the Uniform

ent assumes caretaking responsibilities that are typical of a natural parent. As such, severing the bond with the nonparent acting as a parent should not be at the expense of the child's well-being.[1081]

Although Louisiana has yet to adopt a doctrine, the Fifth Circuit pointed out that the Louisiana Supreme Court recognized the concept of a "psychological parent" in the context of an adoption proceeding.[1082] In *In re J.M.P.*, the Court explained that "'[t]he best interests of the child' must draw its meaning from the evolving body of knowledge concerning child health, psychology and welfare that marks the progress of a maturing society."[1083] The court further noted, "Whether any adult becomes the psychological parent of a child is based on day-to-day interaction, companionship, and shared experiences ... neither the biological relation nor the fact of legal adoption is any guarantee that an adult will become the psychological parent of a child."[1084] Ultimately, in *Ferrand* the Fifth Circuit vacated the judgment that denied custody to Vincent and ordered a mental health evaluation of the parties.[1085]

Just one year later, the Fourth Circuit in *In re C.A.C.* considered a similar case involving a same-sex couple in a custody dispute.[1086] Two women in a long-term relationship started a family using in vitro fertilization and parented the child for seven years before their relationship dissolved.[1087] The biological mother refused to grant the

---

Custody Jurisdiction and Enforcement Act, where the couple had not had the opportunity to take advantage of the legal protections of marriage before their relationship ended; the nonparent partner had been intimately involved in the conception, birth, and parenting of the child at the biological mother's request; and the biological mother and the nonparent partner had made a conscious decision to have a child and co-parent as a family); *see also* Mullins v. Picklesimer, 317 S.W.3d 569 (Ky. 2010) (finding that a mother waived her superior right as natural parent to sole custody of a child in favor of a joint custody arrangement with her same-sex nonparent partner, and thus the nonparent partner was entitled to shared custody of the child following dissolution of the relationship between the mother and her partner, where the mother and the partner had jointly decided to start a family; a sperm donor had been selected based in part on the nonparent partner's characteristics; and the mother had encouraged, fostered, and facilitated an emotional and psychological bond between the nonparent partner and the child). Mississippi jurisprudence has stated that "parentage should not be limited to biology." Ferrand, 221 So. 3d at 922 ("*See* Griffith v. Pell, 881 So. 2d 184 (Miss. 2004) (finding that the ex-husband had standing to seek custody and/or visitation of a child born before the marriage, where the ex-husband had acted in loco parentis by assuming status and obligations of a parent before and during the marriage).").

1081. *See, e.g.*, Ramey, 362 P.3d at 221; Bethany v. Jones, 378 S.W.3d 731 (Ark. 2011); Davis v. Vaughn, 126 So. 3d 33, 38 (Miss. 2013); Mason v. Dwinnell, 660 S.E.2d 58, 71 (N.C. App. 2008); Marquez v. Caudill, 656 S.E.2d 737 (S.C. 2008); Griffith, 881 So. 2d 184.

1082. Ferrand, 221 So. 3d at 937.

1083. In re J.M.P., 528 So. 2d 1002, 1013 (La. 1988).

1084. In re J.M.P., 528 So. 2d at 1013

1085. Ferrand, 221 So. 3d at 939.

1086. *See generally* In re C.A.C., 2017-0108 (La. App. 4 Cir. 11/2/17), 231 So. 3d. 58.

1087. In re C.A.C., 231 So. 3d at 61, 63. Both women were involved in the selection of the sperm donor, the pregnancy, and the birth of the child. The child referred to one as "Mom" and the other as "Bae" and the women executed a Domestic Partnership Agreement as well as Last Will and Testaments that provided for continued co-parenting of the child. *Id.* at 61–64.

non-biological mother rights of custody over the child, and the lawsuit ensued. The trial court awarded joint custody, and the biological mother appealed.[1088]

The Fourth Circuit, citing the *Ferrand* decision, recognized that a parent's constitutional right is "neither absolute nor perpetual," and that even though a nonparent bears a heavy burden of proof, it is nonetheless attainable.[1089] Proof of substantial harm, along with the best interest analysis, adequately protects the parent's rights but is limited because of its application to a traditional family. The court explained: "The 'substantial harm' envisioned in article 133 is the threat of abuse or neglect of the child by an unfit parent and is inapplicable under the facts and circumstances of this case."[1090] Rather, the court noted the expansive meaning of "substantial harm," finding it "more inclusive," "not precise," and akin to "detrimental" in the jurisprudence.[1091]

While article 133 may have been passed to protect the rights of parents in traditional families, the court recognized that the demographics of our society have changed, and the law must react to the factual circumstances present before it. While article 133 presupposes that the third party seeking custody will be less likely to have a parent-child bond than the natural parent, in a same-sex relationship, the third party may be more "like a co-parent from the child's point of view than in situations [involving] a grandparent or other extended family members."[1092] Thus, separation from the nonparent who in words and actions lived as the child's parent would cause substantial harm.[1093] The Fourth Circuit therefore affirmed the award of joint custody between the parent and the nonparent.[1094]

Neither the court in *Ferrand* nor the court in *In re C.A.C.* found the need to adopt the psychological, de facto, or in loco parentis doctrines by name to reach its result. Those doctrines, in theory, provided the underpinnings to allow "substantial harm" to be interpreted to include separation from a person who acted in all respects as the parent. In both cases, the nonparent acted as the primary caregiver—feeding, clothing, and caring for the child as though the child was biologically her own.

A few years later in *Cook v. Sullivan*,[1095] a trial court applied the doctrine of psychological parent to give a non-biological same-sex parent joint custody with the biological parent. The Second Circuit reversed, and the Supreme Court affirmed noting:

1088. In re C.A.C., 231 So. 3d at 61.

1089. In re C.A.C., 231 So. 3d at 67.

1090. In re C.A.C., 231 So. 3d at 68.

1091. In re C.A.C., 231 So. 3d at 68.The court cited the Louisiana Supreme Court case *McCormic v. Rider*, which permitted a tripartite custody arrangement with parents and nonparents because it served the best interest of the child. *Id.* (citing McCormic v. Rider, 2009-2584 (La. 2/2/10), 27 So. 3d 277).

1092. In re C.A.C., 231 So. 3d at 69.

1093. In re C.A.C., 231 So. 3d at 70.

1094. In re C.A.C., 231 So. 3d at 70, 72.

1095. Cook v. Sullivan, 2020-01471 (La. 9/30/21), 330 So. 3d 152.

> Notwithstanding the United States Supreme Court's decision in *Obergefell*, which held that, under the Due Process and Equal Protection Clauses of the Fourteenth Amendment, couples of the same sex may not be denied the fundamental right to marry and start a family, the Louisiana Legislature has remained silent on the issue of children of same sex relationships. Likewise, Louisiana has neither statutorily nor jurisprudentially recognized the in loco parentis, *de facto* parent, or psychological parent status in custody contests between a parent and nonparent. The current law in Louisiana governing all custody disputes between a parent and nonparent is found in La. Civ. Code art. 133, relevant to an "[a]ward of custody to a person other than a parent; order of preference."[1096]

Justice Griffin concurred to specifically urge the legislature to address the important policy issues that affect same-sex couples, given the problematic application of article 133 to two fit individuals raising a child as parents.[1097]

Undoubtedly, the law recognizes that biology is not dispositive of parentage. Louisiana presumes the husband of the mother is the father of the children born or conceived during the marriage, regardless of biology,[1098] and after the passage of time, that presumption becomes irrebuttable, even if another man is proven to be the father.[1099] Further, a husband who consents to his wife's use of donor sperm to conceive a child cannot later disavow that child, even though that child will not be biologically related to the father.[1100] Both parents—heterosexual or homosexual, biological or non-biological—who consent to have a child and raise that child in a family unit with two parents contributing to one household, should enjoy custody of that child in the event of a separation, provided it serves the child's best interest.

The Louisiana Supreme Court has repeatedly emphasized that the "paramount goal and primary consideration in all custody determinations is the best interest of the child."[1101] Along with the changing nature of the family must be an expanded understanding of the law to best promote the child's best interest. Even without, as of yet, an express acceptance of the psychological, de facto, or in loco parentis doctrines, the law can be interpreted to protect children who will suffer solely for the sake of biology.

1096. Cook, 330 So. 3d at 158–59.

1097. Cook, 330 So. 3d at 160 (Griffin, J., concurring).

1098. La. Civ. Code Ann. art. 185.

1099. *See* La. Civ. Code Ann. arts. 187, 189; State v. Walker, 97-0330, pp. 2–3 (La. 10/21/97), 700 So. 2d 496, 498; Modisette v. Phillips, 31,905, pp. 6–7 (La. App. 2 Cir. 5/5/99), 736 So. 2d 983, 987.

1100. *See* La. Civ. Code Ann. art. 188.

1101. Ferrand, 221 So. 3d at 938 (citing Tracie F. v. Francisco D., 15-1812 (La. 03/15/16), 188 So. 3d 231, 234).

§ 6:58 Relocating a Child's Residence

The process in Louisiana for relocating the principal residence of a child is found in a comprehensive statute. Historically, prior to the 1997 enactment of a statute, Louisiana courts, like many state courts, struggled with what was then termed post-custody "removal."[1102] The foundation of Louisiana's relocation statute can be traced back to jurisprudence from as early as the 1950s and 1960s.[1103] During this time, courts questioned their jurisdiction to modify previous custody judgments after the parent awarded custody removed the child from the state.[1104] At first, courts exercised their discretion and generally allowed parents to remove their children from Louisiana post-custody order, provided the removing parent was the custodial parent and had a justifiable reason for the removal.[1105] In fact, prior to 1968, removal was only prohibited on one occasion and only because the custodial parent failed to provide any reason for wanting to remove the minor children from Louisiana.[1106]

Regardless, removal determinations were complicated. Courts were faced with balancing the right of custodial parents to travel freely and relocate against the right of the noncustodial parents to conveniently exercise physical custody and visitation, while ensuring the best interest and welfare of the children. Ultimately, those rights conflicted. To illustrate, the Second Circuit, in *Broomfield v. Broomfield*, permitted the custodial mother to remove the children from Louisiana, finding removal to another state for better employment opportunities a good and sufficient reason for relocation.[1107] The court further indicated that any impairment the relocation had on the noncustodial parent's visitation rights was "subordinate to the rights of the custodial parent to be reasonably unrestricted in selecting a place of residence for economic and justifiable personal reasons."[1108] Based on that rationale, courts focused primarily on the rights of the custodial parents while incidentally considering the effects removal had on the children.

By the mid-1970s, Louisiana courts began recognizing the correlation between relocation and modification of custody, so focus began to shift to the interests of the children. For example, in *Lloyd v. Lloyd*, after the custodial mother removed the children to Florida, the noncustodial father challenged the relocation by seeking to change the court-ordered custody from geographically unrestricted to geographically

---

1102. *See, e.g.*, Wilmot v. Wilmot, 65 So. 2d 321, 327 (La. 1953); Sachse v. Sachse, 150 So. 2d 772 (La. Ct. App. 1 Cir. 1963); Pattison v. Pattison, 208 So. 2d 395 (La. Ct. App. 4 Cir. 1968).

1103. *See* Pattison, 208 So. 2d at 396.

1104. *See* Pattison, 208 So. 2d at 396.

1105. *See* Pattison, 208 So. 2d at 396. The Fourth Circuit reversed the lower court that had required the custodial parent, who moved to New York with her children, to return to Louisiana or be held in contempt. *Id.* The Fourth Circuit held that where the mother moved to New York to live with her new husband in such a "highly mobile society," she could not be "confined to a certain geographical area." *Id.*

1106. Pattison, 208 So. 2d at 396 (citing *Sachse*, 150 So. 2d 772).

1107. Broomfield v. Broomfield, 283 So. 2d 839, 840–41 (La. Ct. App. 2 Cir. 1973) (holding that a court may allow the custodial parent to move from Louisiana to another state where the custodian has a good reason for living in the other state and such course is consistent with the welfare of the child).

1108. Broomfield, 283 So. 2d at 841.

restricted.[1109] The Second Circuit found such a "serious change in custodial care" akin to a custody modification that would change custody from one parent to the other.[1110] Acknowledging the link between removal and modification of custody for the first time in Louisiana, the Second Circuit found that such a change warranted application of the burden that applied to modify custody arrangements.[1111] To prevail, the father had to prove that changes in the conditions of custody were in the child's best interest.[1112]

Courts continued to consider relocation, and by 1993, the First Circuit in *Hertzak v. Hertzak* articulated a test for removal cases, which was later codified in the relocation statute.[1113] Proper removal required the custodial parent to show: (1) a good faith reason for the move; and (2) that the move was in the best interest of the child.[1114] When applying this test in *Hertzak*, because there was no proof that relocation was *not* in the best interest of the children, the court permitted the custodial parent's relocation to Texas even though the father's rights necessarily would be impaired.[1115] Going forward, the focus in relocation cases shifted to the best interest of the child, rather than the best interest of the custodial parent.[1116]

In 1997, Louisiana became the first state to enact a relocation statute based on the American Academy of Matrimonial Lawyers' Proposed Model Relocation Act.[1117] In Senate Bill 1508,[1118] Senator Arthur Lentini proposed guidelines for parents seeking to move their children within or outside of the state of Louisiana after a custody or visitation order was in place.[1119] At its inception, Louisiana's relocation statute sought

---

1109. Lloyd v. Lloyd, 313 So. 2d 854, 857 (La. Ct. App. 2 Cir. 1975). The mother was awarded custody of their two daughters, and the father was awarded custody of the son. *Id.*

1110. Lloyd, 313 So. 2d at 857.

1111. Lloyd, 313 So. 2d at 857. At the time, the standard that applied to a custody modification was two-fold. The court required the father to prove (1) a deleterious situation, and (2) that change in the conditions of custody would be in the best interest of the child. *See id.*

1112. Lloyd, 313 So. 2d at 857.

1113. *See* Hertzak v. Hertzak, 616 So. 2d 727, 729 (La. Ct. App. 1 Cir. 1993); *see also* La. Stat. Ann. § 9:355.10 (rev. 1997).

1114. Hertzak, 616 So. 2d at 729. In a recent case, a parent argued that the mother's reason to relocate was not in good faith because her new employment was not "ironed out," Nevertheless, the Third Circuit determined that the proof of success upon relocation is not necessary; the mere opportunity for success is sufficient. Wingate v. Wingate, 21-472 (La. App. 3 Cir. 01/26/22), 333 So. 3d 848. *See also* Carranza v. Carranza, 2018-971 (La. App. 3 Cir. 6/5/19), 276 So. 3d. 1028 (finding military mother's desire to relocate in good faith given her orders from the United States Army).

1115. Hertzak, 616 So. 2d. at 730.

1116. Pittman v. Pittman, 94-952, pp. 5–8 (La. App. 5 Cir. 3/15/95), 653 So. 2d 1211, 1213–14 (denying the mother's relocation request because even though her new husband's prospects of a job were good and sufficient reason for the move, the relocation was nonetheless not in the best interest of the children, based on testimony by the court-appointed child psychologist).

1117. Laura Caviness Cocus, *Louisiana's Restrictive Relocation Laws: Jeopardizing Stability in Custodial Arrangements for the Sake of Geographical Proximity Between Divorced Parents*, 53 Loy. L. Rev. 79, 88 (2007).

1118. S.B. 1508, 1997 Leg., Reg. Sess., at 1 (La 1997), http://www.legis.la.gov/Legis/ViewDocument.aspx?d=53546.

1119. Digest of the Senate Bill as It Left the Senate: S.B. 1508, 1997 Leg., Reg. Sess., at 1 (La. 1997), http://www.legis.la.gov/Legis/ViewDocument.aspx?d=550962.

to establish a comprehensive procedure to assist divorced parents awarded custody of their children who later decided to move or relocate to a different state, often in the face of the noncustodial parent's objections.[1120]

The relocation statute, then entitled "Moving the Child's Residence Within or Outside of the State," applied to parents with primary custody or equal physical custody[1121] and to an intended move out of state or an in-state move 150 miles from the domicile of the primary custodian.[1122] The relocation of the child's residence had to be for a period of 60 days or more, which was not temporary.[1123]

The statute provided due process to the other parent in the form of notice and an opportunity to be heard. The parent seeking relocation had to provide notice by mail to the other parent of his intent to move, which included reasons for the move and the various details surrounding the new residence.[1124] To prevent relocation, the other parent could object within 20 days of receipt of the notice by initiating a summary proceeding.[1125] The statute adopted the burden first articulated in the jurisprudence, which required the relocating parent to prove that relocation was made in good faith and in the best interest of the child.[1126] A host of factors provided guidance to the court in making relocation decisions.[1127]

In 2003, the statute was amended to carve out a provision for parents with equal physical custody. To relocate, a parent with equal physical custody was required to obtain court authorization after a contradictory hearing or the written consent of the other parent with equal physical custody.[1128] All other custodians could relocate if the other parent failed to timely object to the relocation.[1129] Further, the amendment increased the time to object from 20 days to 30 days after receiving notice.[1130]

In 2008, the law was amended again to require all parents to obtain either court authorization after a contradictory hearing or the written consent of the other parent before relocating.[1131] The onus to object no longer rested with the non-relocating par-

1120. Digest of the Senate Bill as It Left the Senate: S.B. 1508, 1997 Leg., Reg. Sess., at 1 (La. 1997), http://www.legis.la.gov/Legis/ViewDocument.aspx?d=550962.

1121. Act No. 1173, 1997 La. Acts 2258; La. Stat. Ann. § 9:355.1 (rev. 1997). "Equal physical custody" was defined as "parents share equal parental authority of the child absent a court order to the contrary," and "parent entitled to primary custody" was defined as "a parent designated by a court order as the sole custodian or primary or domiciliary custodian within a joint custody arrangement." *Id.* The statute also applied to any parent in the absence of a court order or agreement between the parties. La. Stat. Ann. § 9:355.1(3) (rev. 1997).

1122. La. Stat. Ann. § 9:355.1 (rev. 1997). If there was no custody order, then the move had to be 150 miles from the domicile of the other parent. *Id.*

1123. La. Stat. Ann. § 9:355.1(4)(c) (rev. 1997).

1124. *See* La. Stat. Ann. § 9:355.4 (rev. 1997).

1125. La. Stat. Ann. § 9:355.7–.8 (rev. 1997).

1126. La. Stat. Ann. § 9:355.13 (rev. 1997).

1127. *See* La. Stat. Ann. § 9:355.4 (rev. 1997).

1128. La. Stat. Ann. § 9:355.1 (rev. 2003). *Id.*

1129. La. Stat. Ann. § 9:355.7–.8 (rev. 2003).

1130. La. Stat. Ann. § 9:355.7–.8 (rev. 2003).

1131. Act No. 751, 2008 La. Acts 2897–98.

ent; rather, the parent seeking relocation had to affirmatively seek court approval or the written consent of the other parent.[1132]

The legislature comprehensively amended the statute in 2012, changing its title to "Relocating a Child's Residence," reducing the geographic threshold to 75 miles, reverting back to the bifurcated treatment of equal physical custodians versus other custodians, and expanding the notice requirements to any person recognized as a parent and any other person awarded custody or visitation under a court order, among others.[1133] The revision comment explains that the geographic threshold decreased "in recognition of the likelihood that weekday visitation and the general ability to participate in the child's daily life [was] substantially affected by a distance of more than 75 miles."[1134] For the first time, the law requires notice to persons without custody orders, such as parents established by filiation or avowal actions, presumptions, or formal acknowledgments, or those with orders of visitation.[1135] The amendment broadened the scope of the statute by removing the term *parents* and replacing it with *persons*, acknowledging the nonparent influence in custody.[1136]

The bifurcated treatment of objections remained, with equal physical custodians protected by mandatory, express consent or a contradictory court hearing before relocation is permitted, and with all others required to timely object within 30 days of notice to prevent relocation.[1137] Any objection must be made in writing to the relocating parent, who will then initiate a summary proceeding with the court.[1138] Parents and nonparents who have been awarded custody enjoy the right to object to the relocation,[1139] while nonparents who enjoy visitation cannot object to the relocation but can seek a revised visitation schedule.[1140] The burden of proof remained the same as did the expansive factors that a court must consider in a hearing to oppose relocation.[1141] The legislature also clarified that the court need not make a finding on each of the factors in any relocation contest.[1142] Finally, the revision explained that a proposed relocation is not automatically a basis for a custody modification, but actual relocation or any change in the child's principal residence, even one below the geographical threshold,

1132. Act No. 751, 2008 La. Acts 2897–98. Note, though, that at least one appellate court has held that even though La. R.S. 9:355.4(B) mandates court authorization prior to relocating, the statute does not require a relocating parent to file a petition; the statute only requires that a contradictory hearing be held, which may be instituted by the other parent. Langston v. Langston, 54,611 (La. App. 2 Cir. 05/25/22), 340 So. 3d 1272.

1133. Act No. 627, 2012 La. Acts 2755.

1134. La. Stat. Ann. § 9:355.2 cmt. (a). A number of other states have lower thresholds. *Id.* (listing Alabama, Maine, and Oregon, which have a 60-mile distance, and Florida, which has a 50-mile distance).

1135. La. Stat. Ann. § 9:355.4 & cmt. (c).

1136. *See* La. Stat. Ann. § 9:355.3.

1137. La. Stat. Ann. § 9:355.7.

1138. *Id.*; La. Stat. Ann. § 9:355.9.

1139. La. Stat. Ann. § 9:355.7–.8.

1140. La. Stat. Ann. § 9:355.8.

1141. La. Stat. Ann. § 9:355.10, .14.

1142. La. Stat. Ann. § 9:355.14 cmt. (a).

may constitute a change of circumstances warranting modification.[1143] Speculation on the negative impact a move may have on children, however, will generally be insufficient to seek a modification.[1144]

§ 6:59 Relocating a Child's Residence—Application

The relocation statute applies when there is a custody or visitation order issued on or after August 15, 1997, or a custody or visitation order issued before August 15, 1997, if the "order does not expressly govern the relocation of the child."[1145] A proposed relocation triggers application of the statute when one of the following exists: (1) intent to establish principal residence outside of the state; (2) intent to establish principal residence within the state at least 75 miles from the domicile of the other parent, absent a custody order; (3) intent to establish principal residence within the state at least 75 miles from the principal residence of the child at the time of the custody order, if one exists; or (4) intent to establish principal residence within the state at least 75 miles from anyone entitled to object, absent a principal residence or where there is shared equal physical custody.[1146] The statute does not apply when the parties have entered into an express written agreement for the child's relocation,[1147] violence or abuse is present,[1148] or the move is within a distance shorter than the geographic threshold.[1149] The straight-line or "as the crow flies" method of measurement is the most uniform method to measure distances and has been applied in at least one relocation case.[1150]

In the same way that the former relocation statutory language only applied to restrict the movement of the custodial or domiciliary parent, leaving the non-custodian and nondomiciliary parent free to relocate at will,[1151] the relocation statute only applies to restrict the movement of the person with legal decision-making authority over the

1143. La. Stat. Ann. § 9:355.17; *see also* Masters v. Masters, 33,438, p. 6 (La. App. 2 Cir. 4/5/00), 756 So. 2d 1196, 1200 (finding that the trial court erred in modifying custody because the mother only expressed her intent to move; court did not give the mother the opportunity to remain in Louisiana).

1144. Hensgens v. Hensgens, 94-1200, pp. 8–9 (La. App. 3 Cir. 3/15/95), 653 So. 2d 48, 53 (evidence that mother's move would negatively impact the children was pure speculation and therefore, before the children actually moved with mother, the issue of modification was not ripe for adjudication).

1145. La. Stat. Ann. § 9:355.2.

1146. La. Stat. Ann. § 9:355.2.

1147. La. Stat. Ann. § 9:355.2(D)(1).

1148. La. Stat. Ann. § 9:355.2(D)(2); Cormier v. Cormier, 2021-234 (La. App. 3 Cir. 10/20/21), 330 So. 3d 681. The language relating to abuse is expansive but specifically excludes harassment. La. Stat. Ann. § 9:355.2 cmt. (f).

1149. *See* Major v. Major, 2002-2131, p. 6 (La. App. 1 Cir. 2/14/03), 849 So. 2d 547, 551.

1150. Holley v. Holley, 17-325, p. 14 (La. App. 5 Cir. 11/20/17), 232 So. 3d 717, 727.

1151. Laura Caviness Cocus, *Louisiana's Restrictive Relocation Laws: Jeopardizing Stability in Custodial Arrangements for the Sake of Geographical Proximity Between Divorced Parents*, 53 Loy. L. Rev. 79, 87 (2007).

child.[1152] The relocation statute is first triggered where there is a proposed or manifested intent to relocate, even if the party entitled to object resides out-of-state. In *Bullock v. Bullock*, the mother and primary custodian of the minor children who wished to move from Louisiana to Alabama argued that the relocation statute did not apply because the father resided outside of Louisiana, in Mississippi.[1153] The Fourth Circuit, after examining the text of the statute, concluded that the relocation statute applied even though neither parent would be a resident of Louisiana.[1154] The court explained that relocation is triggered when there is "a change in the principal residence of a child for a period of 60 days or more" regardless of the parties' geographic locations.[1155] Although the statute has been amended since *Bullock*, relocation is still defined as a "change in the principal residence of a child for a period of 60 days or more,"[1156] and any out-of-state move triggers application of the statute.[1157]

Once the relocation statute is triggered and an objection is made, the analysis by the court is fact-driven.[1158] The Louisiana Supreme Court has explained that the burden is heavy on the parent seeking relocation, and the guiding fundamental principle in any relocation analysis is the best interest of the child.[1159] The statute requires the court to consider the 12 listed factors when conducting its analysis.[1160] The court is free to weigh some factors more heavily than others.[1161] While the court must consider the 14 factors, the court is "not required to expressly analyze each factor in its oral or written reasons

1152. La. Stat. Ann. § 9:355.3 cmt. (a). The comment indicates that, generally, the person with legal decision-making authority over the child is the sole custodian, domiciliary parent, natural tutor, both parents if married, or both persons with shared equal physical custody. *Id.*; *see also* In re J.E.T., 2016-0384, p. 18 (La. App. 1 Cir. 10/31/16), 211 So. 3d 575, 587.

1153. Bullock v. Bullock, 98-0206, p. 1 (La. App. 4 Cir. 1/29/98), 706 So. 2d 671, 672.

1154. Bullock, 706 So. 2d at 672.

1155. Bullock, 706 So. 2d at 672; *see also* Nelson v. Land, 2001-1073, p. 2 (La. App. 1 Cir. 11/9/01), 818 So. 2d 91, 92 (applying the relocation statute when a domiciliary parent sought to relocate from Louisiana to New York and the nondomiciliary parent resided in California).

1156. La. Stat. Ann. § 9:355.1(2).

1157. La. Stat. Ann. § 9:355.2(B)(1).

1158. *See generally* Dragon v. Dragon, 2022-0076 (La. App. 1 Cir. 8/30/22), 2022 WL 3754615; Higgins v. Higgins, 2021-182 (La. App. 3 Cir. 10/6/21), 2021 WL 4572025; Merrells v. Dotray, 299 So. 3d 208 (La. App. 2 Cir. 7/8/20), 299 So. 3d 208; Gautreaux v. Gautreaux, 2019-1486 (La. App. 1 Cir. 7/23/20), 309 So. 3d 362.

1159. Curole v. Curole, 2002-1891, pp. 4–5 (La. 10/15/02), 828 So. 2d 1094, 1096; *see also* Narcisse-Thomas v. Thomas, 2023-0463 (La. App. 4 Cir. 5/3/24), 390 So. 3d 890 (denying relocation to Jacksonville, Florida because the father could not relocate and his relationship with the children would suffer); Bridges v. Bridges, 2020-300 (La. App. 1 Cir. 11/10/20), 316 So. 3d 17 (denying relocation to Dubai because parent failed her burden of proving it was in the children's best interest—instability in the Middle East, children's medical and mental health issues, difficulty of father to travel to Dubai, and loss of the relationship between the children and family); Carranza v. Carranza, 2018-971 (La. App. 3 Cir. 6/5/19), 276 So.3d 1028 (referring to the relocating parent's burden as "very heavy" and allowing military mother with order to relocate children).

1160. *See* La. Stat. Ann. § 9:355.14.

1161. Gathen v. Gathen, 2010-2312, p. 10 (La. 5/10/11), 66 So. 3d 1, 8.

for judgment."[1162] However, appellate review is easier when the trial court articulates reasons for its decision.[1163] Because the trial court is in the best position to judge the credibility of the witnesses and consider the wide array of facts, the trial court's factual determinations are entitled to great weight and will not be overturned absent an abuse of discretion.[1164] Any error of law is subject to *de novo* review.[1165]

§ 6:60 Uniform Child Custody Jurisdiction and Enforcement Act

The Uniform Child Custody Jurisdiction and Enforcement Act (UCCJEA) was passed in Louisiana in 2006[1166] to supplant the Uniform Child Custody Jurisdiction Act (UCCJA) that was passed in 1978.[1167] The former UCCJA was designed to avoid jurisdictional competition and conflict among states and to promote cooperation and the exchange of information among states.[1168] Jurisprudence decided under the UCCJA remains relevant after the Act was amended and reenacted as the UCCJEA. All 50 states have enacted the UCCJEA, and it applies to both domestic and international cases.[1169] The Act has provided for uniformity and predictability with the best interest of the child at its center.

The Louisiana Code of Civil Procedure confers subject matter jurisdiction over a proceeding to obtain the legal custody of a minor who is in this state.[1170] The UCCJEA provides a more specific, second tier of analysis for jurisdiction when the parties or the child reside in separate states.[1171] Jurisdiction under the UCCJEA must be proper at the time the petition is filed, whether that petition requests initial custody or a modification of custody.[1172] The UCCJEA sets forth explicit rules for initial jurisdiction, juris-

---

1162. Gathen, 66 So. 3d at 9; Simpson-Mitchell v. Mitchell, 55,652 (La. App. 2 Cir. 2/28/24), 382 So. 3d 453, 467.

1163. Gathen, 66 So. 3d at 10. The court noted that either party could have requested that the findings of facts and reasons be in writing. *Id.* at 9.

1164. Gathen, 66 So. 3d 1, 9; Hernandez v. Jenkins, 2012-2756, p. 9 (La. 6/21/13), 122 So. 3d 524, 529.

1165. *See* Smith v. Smith, 44,663, p. 18 (La. App. 2 Cir. 08/19/09), 16 So. 3d 643, 654 (applying de novo review because the trial court committed legal error when it applied the factors in article 136 rather than the relocation factors).

1166. *See* La. Stat. Ann. § 13:1801.

1167. *See* La. Stat. Ann. §§ 13:1700 *et seq.* (1978, as amended).

1168. UCCJA, Prefatory Note, 9 U.L.A. 116; *see also* Christopher L. Blakesley, *Comparativist Ruminations from the Bayou on Child Custody Jurisdiction: The UCCJA, the PKPA, and the Hague Convention on Child Abduction*, 58 La. L. Rev. 449, 476 (1998).

1169. La. Stat. Ann. § 13:1805; Guzman v. Sartin, 2009-1677, p. 4 (La. App. 1 Cir. 12/23/09), 31 So. 3d 426, 429; *see generally* Harm v. Lake-Harm, 16 F.4th 450 (5th Cir. 2021).

1170. La. Code Civ. Proc. Ann. art. 10(5). Additionally, the UCCJEA does not apply to unborn children. Loeb v. Vergara, 2020-0261 (La. App. 4 Cir. 1/27/21), 313 So. 3d 346.

1171. Albitar v. Albitar, 16-167, p. 18 (La. App. 5 Cir. 6/30/16), 197 So. 3d 332, 345.

1172. *See* Wootten v. Wootten, 49,001, p. 7 (La. App. 2d Cir. 5/14/14), 138 So. 3d 1253, 1257.

diction to modify, and temporary emergency jurisdiction.[1173] These distinctions are the starting point for any custody or visitation dispute that crosses the Louisiana state line.

§ 6:61 Uniform Child Custody Jurisdiction and Enforcement Act—Initial Jurisdiction

The UCCJEA provides four grounds, in preferential order, for a Louisiana court to exercise jurisdiction in an initial child custody determination: (1) Louisiana is or was the child's home state; (2) the child and a parent have a significant connection with Louisiana and there is substantial evidence relating to the child in Louisiana; (3) other courts decline to exercise jurisdiction because Louisiana is the appropriate forum; and (4) no other court will exercise jurisdiction, so Louisiana will do so by default.[1174] These limitations on a court exercising jurisdiction further the UCCJEA's purposes, which include "avoiding jurisdictional competition, assuring that custody litigation takes place in the state with which the child and his family have the 'closest connection' and where relevant evidence is located, promoting a stable home environment, deterring abductions, and encouraging cooperation among the courts of different states."[1175]

First, a Louisiana court may exercise initial jurisdiction over a child custody proceeding if it is the "home state" of the child on the date the action is commenced.[1176] "Home state" is defined as "the state in which a child lived with a parent or a person acting as a parent for at least six consecutive months immediately before the commencement of a child custody proceeding."[1177] For a child less than six months of age, the home state is the state in which the child lived with a parent or a person acting as a parent since the child's birth.[1178] Further, if the state was the child's home state within the last six months but the child is absent from the state and a parent or a person acting as a parent still lives in the state, home state jurisdiction still applies.[1179] In other words, for the first six months, if the child is absent from his home state but a parent still remains in the state, that state maintains its classification as the child's home state. Once the child is absent from his home state with a parent for a period of six months, the new state will become the child's home state. The law also provides that Louisiana can be the child's home state if it had been the child's home state within 12 months

1173. *See* La. Stat. Ann. §§ 13:1813–:1822.

1174. La. Stat. Ann. § 13:1813.

1175. Stelluto v. Stelluto, 2005-0074, p. 8 (La. 6/29/05), 914 So. 2d 34, 39; *cf.* Harvey v. Harvey, 2109-1635 (La. App. 1 Cir. 5/11/20), 303 So. 3d 357.

1176. La. Stat. Ann. § 13:1813(A)(1); *see also* McNeil v. Stern, 2023-314 (La. App. 3 Cir. 09/27/23); 371 So. 3d 1187, *writ denied*, 376 So. 3d 847 (La. 1/10/24); Veronie v. Mireles, 22-105 (La. App. 3 Cir. 06/08/22), 344 So. 3d 210; Harvey, 303 So. 3d 357.

1177. La. Stat. Ann. § 13:1802(7)(a).

1178. La. Stat. Ann. § 13:1802(7)(a); *see* McNeil, 371 So. 3d 1187 (finding that Louisiana was the home state of a child who was three months old, even though the child was born in Texas, because the mother spent fifty-one of the sixty-one days in Louisiana, consistently provided an Abbeville address, and applied for Louisiana Medicaid).

1179. La. Stat. Ann. § 13:1813(A)(1).

before the proceeding, and the child is absent from the state due to a forced emergency evacuation.[1180] When evaluating time periods for purposes of home state jurisdiction, a proceeding commences on the date the action is filed, rather than the date service of process is made on the defendant.[1181] In addition, the Louisiana Supreme Court has concluded that the notice of relocation to a nonresident defendant does not require service pursuant to the long-arm statute but instead only requires notice "'reasonably calculated to give actual notice.'"[1182]

Home state is the preferred choice of jurisdiction in a custody action because the court is usually in the best position to exercise "continuity of control" over the child and access evidence involving the child.[1183] As a result, other state courts should defer to the home state. For example, in *Sergeant v. DeRung*, the court concluded that Louisiana lacked jurisdiction to make an initial child custody determination because the 11-month-old child was born in Minnesota and had resided there since his birth, with the exception of a 17-day period.[1184] The child's father argued that because the child was conceived in Louisiana, had visited Louisiana, and because he filed the petition when the child was only four months old, Louisiana could exercise jurisdiction.[1185] The court disagreed, finding the home state of the child to be Minnesota.[1186] Given that Minnesota had not declined to exercise jurisdiction, the Louisiana court lacked subject matter jurisdiction over the action.[1187]

Louisiana courts will exercise home state jurisdiction even if the person caring for the child is not the parent, provided that person is "acting as a parent."[1188] In *State ex rel. A.U.M.*, the court found Louisiana to be the home state of the child because the child was living in Louisiana under the care of his mother's adult cousin.[1189] Even though the adult cousin was not a biological parent, she fit the definition of a "person acting as a parent" because the incarcerated mother placed the child in her cousin's care upon her incarceration.[1190]

1180. La. Stat. Ann. § 13:1813(A)(1).

1181. *See* Martinez v. Reed, 490 So. 2d 303, 306 (La. Ct. App. 4 Cir. 1986) (finding that Louisiana could exercise jurisdiction where the mother filed a petition within six months of the child being removed from Louisiana, even though service was not made until after the six months had passed).

1182. Cochran v. Forman, 2020-1400 (La. 3/09/21), 312 So. 3d 263, citing La. Stat. Ann. § 13:1808.

1183. *See* Cancienne v. Cancienne, 02-378, p. 4 (La. App. 5 Cir. 10/29/02), 831 So. 2d 484, 486; *see also* Devillier v. Smith, 95-0846, p. 3 (La. App. 1 Cir. 11/09/95), 665 So. 2d 71, 73.

1184. Sergeant v. DeRung, 2016-1203, pp. 6–7 (La. App. 4 Cir. 3/8/17), 213 So. 3d 423, 427; *compare also* McNeil, 371 So. 3d 1187.

1185. Sergeant, 213 So. 3d at 424, 427.

1186. Sergeant, 213 So. 3d at 427.

1187. Sergeant, 213 So. 3d at 427. *But see* Hero v. Hero, 97-2799, p. 2 (La. App. 4 Cir. 5/27/98), 714 So. 2d 868, 870 (finding that Louisiana was the child's home state even though the child was living in Wisconsin with the mother because the child had just been removed from Louisiana when the grandparents' visitation petition was filed); State ex rel. A.U.M., 46,082, p. 5 (La. App. 2 Cir. 2/16/11), 62 So. 3d 185, 189 (finding that Louisiana was the child's home state).

1188. *See* La. Stat. Ann. § 13:1802(7)(a), (13) (defining person acting as a parent).

1189. State ex rel. A.U.M., 62 So. 3d at 187, 189.

1190. State ex rel. A.U.M., 62 So. 3d at 187, 189.

Second, Louisiana courts may acquire jurisdiction to make an initial child custody determination when there is no home state of the child,[1191] the child and at least one parent or person acting as parent has a significant connection (other than mere presence) in Louisiana, and there is substantial evidence concerning the child's care, protection, training, and personal relationships in Louisiana.[1192] Referred to as the "significant connection/substantial evidence test," jurisdiction can be conferred based on the relationships the child and the parents have with a state. When a home state of the child exists, however, jurisdiction is appropriately left with the home state unless that state declines to exercise it.[1193]

When a court assumes jurisdiction because of its connection to the parties, the interests of the child, not merely the convenience of the parties, should be of paramount concern. In *Amin v. Bakhaty*, the mother moved from Egypt to Louisiana with the child and within one month filed a petition for custody.[1194] As Louisiana was not the child's home state, the court evaluated the child's connections. The child's only connection with Louisiana was the presence of the mother's family.[1195] Even though no other state had home state jurisdiction, the court could not assume jurisdiction based on significant connections because even though there were contacts with Louisiana, they were not "sufficient maximum contacts," which were essential for jurisdiction.[1196]

"The significant connection standard requires proof that Louisiana ha[s] the strongest connection to the child when the suit is filed."[1197] Evidence of the child's and parent's residence outside the state of Louisiana and the duration of the out-of-state residency is relevant to this analysis.[1198] Likewise, the child's place of birth and the res-

1191. La. Stat. Ann. § 13:1813. Jurisdiction is also available if the court of the home state declines to exercise jurisdiction on the ground that Louisiana is a more appropriate forum (forum non conveniens).

1192. La. Stat. Ann. § 13:1813(A)(2).

1193. *See* Stelluto v. Stelluto, 2005-0074, pp. 1–4 (La. 6/29/05), 914 So. 2d 34, 42–44 (Weimer, J., dissenting) (disagreeing with majority that permitted jurisdiction in Louisiana due to significant connections even though California was the child's home state).

1194. Amin v. Bakhaty, 2000-2710, p. 2 (La. App. 1 Cir. 5/11/01), 812 So. 2d 12, 17.

1195. Amin, 812 So. 2d at 27–28.

1196. Amin, 812 So. 2d at 27–28; *see also* Martin-Creech v. Armstrong, 42,649, p. 9 (La. App. 2 Cir. 9/12/07), 965 So. 2d 624, 629 (finding that four months in Louisiana was not enough given child's connections in Virginia). *But see* Gill v. Bennett, 2011-886, p. 4 (La. App. 3 Cir. 12/7/11), 82 So. 3d 383, 387 (finding significant connections when child, child's mother, and grandmother moved to Louisiana, and father was a long-time resident of Louisiana).

1197. *See* Martin-Creech, 965 So. 2d at 629 ("[T]he choice of the optimum jurisdiction under the UCCJL focuses on the strength of connections between the child and the competing states, more akin to a personal jurisdiction analysis.").

1198. *See* Cormier v. Cormier, 2021-234 (La. App. 3 Cir. 10/20/21), p. 4–5, 330 So. 3d 681, 684 (trial court concluding and court of appeal affirming that significant connection to Louisiana was lacking given "the fact that the child and her mother have lived the past six consecutive months in the state of Missouri."); *see also* Martin-Creech, 965 So. 2d at 629 (holding that the parental figures' and child's "four-month period in Louisiana prior to [the] action [was] insufficient to satisfy the connection requirement of the UCCJL when compared to the connections of the child with the State of West

idence of the child's extended family must be considered under the connection test.[1199] However, "[t]he law and jurisprudence require more than just the fact that one parent continues to reside in this state."

The third and fourth bases of jurisdiction are less common. Louisiana can exercise jurisdiction if other courts with jurisdiction decline to hear the matter because Louisiana is the more appropriate forum,[1200] or by default when no other state has subject matter jurisdiction over the action.[1201]

Finally, Louisiana can exercise jurisdiction temporarily when an emergency arises.[1202] A Louisiana court can exercise temporary emergency jurisdiction over a proceeding if the child is present in the jurisdiction, and the child has been abandoned or the child, sibling, or parent is subject to or threatened with abuse.[1203] Temporary jurisdiction can become final if no other state has jurisdiction and Louisiana becomes the home state of the child.[1204] If a child custody proceeding was initiated in another state, a Louisiana court can allow the litigant to obtain relief from the state having jurisdiction, while the temporary order issued in Louisiana will remain in effect.[1205] Once the Louisiana court becomes aware that another state has jurisdiction, it must communicate with the court of that state immediately "to resolve the emergency, protect the safety of the parties and the child, and determine a period for the duration of the temporary order."[1206]

§ 6:62 Uniform Child Custody Jurisdiction and Enforcement Act—Jurisdiction to Modify

Louisiana Revised Statutes Section 13:1815 limits the conditions under which a Louisiana court can modify the decisions of a court in another state. The statute provides that a court in Louisiana cannot modify a child custody determination from another state unless the Louisiana court has either home state or significant connection jurisdiction and either (1) the court of the other state determines that it no longer has "exclusive continuing jurisdiction" or that Louisiana is a more appropriate forum, or

Virginia," which included the fact that the child was born in West Virginia and the child's mother, father, and maternal grandmother all resided in West Virginia).

1199. *See* Martin-Creech, 965 So. 2d at 629.

1200. La. Stat. Ann. § 13:1813(A)(3).

1201. La. Stat. Ann. § 13:1813(A)(4); *see also* Amin, 812 So. 2d at 19.

1202. *See* La. Stat. Ann. § 13:1816.

1203. La. Stat. Ann. § 13:1816(A).

1204. La. Stat. Ann. § 13:1816(B).

1205. La. Stat. Ann. § 13:1816(C).

1206. La. Stat. Ann. § 13:1816(D); *see also, e.g.*, Brunt v. Abernathy, 2011-705, p. 6 (La. App. 3 Cir. 11/2/11), 79 So. 3d 425, 429 (concluding that temporary jurisdiction applied, but remanding because there was no evidence that the trial court communicated with the court of another state that may have jurisdiction); State ex rel. J.W., 43,163, pp. 10–11 (La. App. 2 Cir. 2/13/08), 975 So. 2d 841, 847 (finding that the trial court had emergency jurisdiction to protect the child but was required to determine the appropriate jurisdiction under the UCCJA).

(2) the Louisiana court or the court of the other state determines that the child, the parents, and any person acting as a parent no longer reside in the other state.[1207]

For example, in *Otwell v. Otwell*, the court reversed the trial court's modification of custody because there was no evidence that the Georgia court made any determination that it no longer had continuing jurisdiction or that "Louisiana would be a more convenient forum."[1208] The mother argued that because the children had resided in Louisiana for more than one year, Louisiana was their home state and, thus, the trial court had subject matter jurisdiction to modify custody.[1209] The court disagreed, pointing out the express terms of the statute and finding that the Georgia court made no determination that Louisiana was a more appropriate forum. Consequently, the Georgia court maintained continuing exclusive jurisdiction.[1210]

When a child resides in Louisiana for an extended period of time, it is natural for a parent to seek modification of a custody order in Louisiana. But, once a custody order is in place from another jurisdiction, the Louisiana court can only exercise jurisdiction to modify if the court that issued the initial order determines that it no longer has continuing exclusive jurisdiction or that Louisiana is a more appropriate forum.[1211] The Louisiana court must seek guidance from the other state court unless no parties reside in the other state.[1212]

A court in Indiana provided guidance to a Louisiana court in *Gill v. Bennett*.[1213] In *Gill*, a child was born outside of marriage in Indiana while the father resided in Louisiana.[1214] Prior to the father's knowledge of his paternity, the child's maternal grandmother obtained an order of permanent guardianship from an Indiana court.[1215] Subsequently, after the father's paternity was established, the grandmother, mother, and child moved to Louisiana.[1216] When the relationship between the parties crumbled, the father sought custody of the child.[1217] The grandmother objected to jurisdiction in Louisiana due to her order of permanent guardianship in Indiana, which required the father to litigate custody there.[1218] The Louisiana court disagreed. First, the court

---

1207. La. Stat. Ann. § 13:1815.

1208. Otwell v. Otwell, 2010-1176, p. 4 (La. App. 3 Cir. 2/9/11), 56 So. 3d 1232, 1235.

1209. Otwell, 56 So. 3d at 1233.

1210. Otwell, 56 So. 3d at 1235; *see also* Brunt v. Abernathy, 2011-705, p. 5 (La. App. 3 Cir. 11/2/11), 79 So. 3d 425, 428–29 (refusing to exercise jurisdiction because the court in Oklahoma did not determine that Louisiana was the more appropriate forum); Hughes v. Fabio, 07-1008, p. 7 (La. App. 4 Cir. 3/25/08), 983 So. 2d 946, 951 (refusing to exercise jurisdiction to modify because Massachusetts initially decided custody, the father still lived in Massachusetts, and the child was only living in Louisiana pursuant to a temporary order).

1211. La. Stat. Ann. § 13:1815(1).

1212. La. Stat. Ann. § 13:1815(2).

1213. *See generally* Gill v. Bennett, 2011-886 (La. App. 3 Cir. 12/7/11), 82 So. 3d 383.

1214. Gill, 82 So. 3d at 385.

1215. Gill, 82 So. 3d at 385.

1216. Gill 82 So. 3d at 385.

1217. Gill 82 So. 3d at 385.

1218. Gill 82 So. 3d at 386.

recognized that the permanent guardianship order constituted a child custody determination in Indiana, so the Indiana court had continuing exclusive jurisdiction over the custody matter.[1219] However, the Indiana court declined jurisdiction under the UCCJEA, finding that Louisiana was a more appropriate forum given the residence of the child, mother, grandmother (permanent guardian), and father, all of whom lived in Louisiana.[1220] Because the father was a long-time resident of and had substantial connections in Louisiana, Louisiana could assume jurisdiction.[1221]

§ 6:63 Uniform Child Custody Jurisdiction and Enforcement Act—Exclusive, Continuing Jurisdiction

Louisiana Revised Statutes Section 13:1814 provides for exclusive, continuing jurisdiction in Louisiana once a Louisiana court has made an initial child custody determination[1222] or has appropriately modified another state court's order of custody.[1223] Exclusive, continuing jurisdiction will remain in Louisiana until (1) a Louisiana court determines that neither the child, nor the child and one parent (or a person acting as a parent) have a significant connection with Louisiana and substantial evidence is no longer available in Louisiana concerning the child's welfare; or (2) a Louisiana court or the court of the other state determines that the child, the child's parents, and any person acting as a parent do not presently reside in Louisiana.[1224] In other words, either state court can make a determination about the parties' presence in Louisiana, but only a Louisiana court can evaluate the parties' connections to the state. Finally, even when a Louisiana court determines that it has maintained exclusive, continuing jurisdiction, it nonetheless may decline to exercise its jurisdiction if it determines that it is an inconvenient forum and that a court of another state is a more appropriate forum.[1225]

Exclusive, continuing jurisdiction cannot be conferred by consent of the parties.[1226] Rather, the provisions of the UCCJEA govern, and Louisiana courts can exercise exclusive, continuing jurisdiction until one of two events occur. First, if a Louisiana court

1219. Gill, 82 So. 3d at 387.

1220. Gill, 82 So. 3d at 387. The court also noted that it conferenced with the Louisiana court, which is appropriate under the UCCJEA. *See* La. Stat. Ann. § 13:1810; *see also* Spears v. McClaine, 2023-0664 (La. App. 4 Cir. 1/10/24); 381 So. 3d 119, 130 (finding that Texas was the more appropriate forum and declining continuing jurisdiction in Louisiana)

1221. Gill, 82 So. 3d at 387.

1222. La. Stat. Ann. § 13:1813.

1223. La. Stat. Ann. § 13:1815.

1224. La. Stat. Ann. § 13:1814. Temporary emergency jurisdiction is an exception to exclusive, continuing jurisdiction. *See* La. Stat. Ann. § 13:1816.

1225. La. Stat. Ann. § 13:1815; *see* Spears v. McClaine, 2023-0664 (La. App. 4 Cir. 1/10/24), 381 So. 3d 119, 128.

1226. Spears, 381 So. 3d at 127; Hebert v. Hebert, 2018-499 (La. App. 3 Cir. 3/27/19), 269 So. 3d 831, 833; Wootten v. Wootten, 49,001, p. 12 (La. App. 2 Cir. 5/14/14), 138 So. 3d 1253, 1260; Holdsworth v. Holdsworth, 621 So.2d 71 (La. App. 2d Cir. 1993).

determines that the child and one parent (or a person acting as a parent) no longer have a significant connection with the state, exclusive, continuing jurisdiction will end.[1227] The jurisprudence applying the significant connection/substantial evidence test for purposes of initial jurisdiction would apply here as well. And at least one court has concluded that "[t]he law and jurisprudence require more than just the fact that one parent continues to reside in this state" to establish a substantial connection.[1228]

Second, exclusive, continuing jurisdiction will also end when either state court determines that "the child, the child's parents, and any person acting as a parent" are no longer residents of the state of Louisiana.[1229] Notably, the law considers residency, which is not to be confused with domicile, for a person "may reside in several places but may not have more than one domicile."[1230] At least one Louisiana court has addressed the issue of residency in the context of the UCCJEA. In *Burst v. Schmolke*, a married mother tragically died in a car crash with her toddler in the backseat; the child survived.[1231] After the mother's death, the child's maternal grandparents lived with the child and father to support him in raising the child.[1232] However, the father's relationship with the child's grandparents deteriorated, and the grandparents filed for and were granted visitation rights.[1233] When the child was five years old, the father and his new wife moved to North Carolina with the child.[1234] The father thereafter filed a petition for declaratory judgment requesting a declaration that the Louisiana court no longer had jurisdiction because he and his family were no longer Louisiana residents.[1235] The court concluded that the father and the child were North Carolina residents for purposes of the UCCJEA even though the father was still registered to vote in Louisiana and continued to operate a business in Louisiana.[1236] Because it needed to determine whether North Carolina would accept jurisdiction, the trial court stayed the proceedings.[1237] On appeal, the Fourth Circuit agreed with the opinion on residency but remanded the

1227. La. Stat. Ann. § 13:1814(A)(1).

1228. Hebert, 269 So. 3d at 834 (also noting La. Stat. Ann. § 13:1814(B)).

1229. La. Stat. Ann. § 13:1814(A)(2). For purposes of UCCJEA, courts of foreign countries are treated like other states in the United States so long as "the child custody law of a foreign country [does not] violate[] fundamental principles of human rights." La. Stat. Ann. § 13:1805.

1230. La. Civ. Code Ann. art. 39; *see, e.g.*, Gauthier v. Benson, 95-1730 (La. App. 4 Cir. 1/11/96), 667 So. 2d 1181, 1183, writ denied, 96-0275 (La. 2/9/96), 667 So. 2d 545 ("Residence" is not a specific legal term. It is in common usage and has a variety of meanings. One may have a residence in a home, institution, town, city, parish, state, country, continent, etc. The term is nebulous and has no precise meaning. In contrast, domicile is where one makes his habitual residence. Domicile should not be confused with residence. Residence and domicile are not synonymous, and a person can have several residences but only one domicile.").

1231. Burst v. Schmolke, 2010-1036, p. 1 (La. App. 4 Cir. 4/6/11), 62 So. 3d 829, 831.

1232. Burst, 62 So. 3d at 831.

1233. Burst, 62 So. 3d at 831.

1234. Burst, 62 So. 3d at 831.

1235. Burst, 62 So. 3d at 834.

1236. Burst, 62 So. 3d at 831. The maternal grandparents also argued that the child currently was living in Louisiana, even though the child was living with the father in North Carolina and attending school there. *See id.*

1237. Burst, 62 So. 3d at 837.

matter so that the court could rule on the issue of exclusive, continuing jurisdiction to prevent a further stalemate on jurisdiction.

§ 6:64 Uniform International Child Abduction Prevention Act

On August 15, 2007, the Louisiana State Legislature passed the Uniform International Child Abduction Prevention Act.[1238] This legislation was prompted by the Uniform Child Abduction Prevention Act (UCAPA), which was drafted in 2006 by the National Conference of Commissioners on Uniform State Laws (NCCUSL) and approved for recommendation to the states.[1239]

The NCCUSL drafted the Uniform Act to deter domestic and international child abductions by parents or those acting on behalf of a parent either before or after a child custody decree has been entered.[1240] A study commissioned by the Office of Juvenile Justice and Delinquency Prevention found that over 250,000 children were abducted in one year with 78% of those children abducted by a family member; approximately one-third of the abductions were international.[1241] UCAPA "is premised on the general principle that preventing an abduction is in a child's best interest."[1242] The Act therefore allows courts to impose prevention measures when there is a credible risk of abduction of a child.[1243]

Today, 15 states and the District of Columbia have enacted their own versions of UCAPA.[1244] Louisiana was one of the first states to adopt a version of the Act in 2007, but its version is narrower than the Uniform Act. The Louisiana Act only applies when

---

1238. Act No. 369, 2007 La. Acts 2065–71 (enacted as La. Stat. Ann. § 13:1851 *et seq.* (2019)).

1239. Unif. Child Abduction Prevention Act (Nat'l Conference of Comm'rs on Unif. State Laws 2006) (available at https://www.uniformlaws.org/viewdocument/final-act-33?CommunityKey=c8a53ebd-d5aa-4805-95b2-5d6f2a648b2a&tab=librarydocuments).

1240. Unif. Child Abduction Prevention Act 1 (available at https://www.uniformlaws.org/viewdocument/final-act-33?CommunityKey=c8a53ebd-d5aa-4805-95b2-5d6f2a648b2a&tab=librarydocuments).

1241. Unif. Child Abduction Prevention Act 1 (available at https://www.uniformlaws.org/viewdocument/final-act-33?CommunityKey=c8a53ebd-d5aa-4805-95b2-5d6f2a648b2a&tab=librarydocuments).

1242. Unif. Child Abduction Prevention Act 1 (available at https://www.uniformlaws.org/viewdocument/final-act-33?CommunityKey=c8a53ebd-d5aa-4805-95b2-5d6f2a648b2a&tab=librarydocuments).

1243. *See also* La. Stat. Ann. § 13:1857. Jurisdictional statutes, like the Uniform Child Custody Jurisdiction and Enforcement Act, La. Stat. Ann. § 13:1801 *et seq.*, and the Parental Kidnapping Prevention Act, 28 U.S.C. § 1738A, also help to deter abductions by specifying the appropriate state to adjudicate custody.

1244. Alabama, Colorado, District of Columbia, Florida, Kansas, Louisiana, Maryland, Michigan, Mississippi, Nebraska, Nevada, New Mexico, Pennsylvania, South Dakota, Tennessee, and Utah have enacted the Uniform Child Abduction Prevention Act. Child Abduction Prevention Act, Unif. Law Comm'n, https://www.uniformlaws.org/committees/community-home?CommunityKey=c8a53ebd-d5aa-4805-95b2-5d6f2a648b2a (last visited Jan. 30, 2024).

an abduction occurs "beyond the territorial limits of the United States," hence its name, "International Child Abduction Prevention Act." [1245] The original Senate Bill did not limit the Act to international abductions. Amendments were proposed by the House Committee and adopted by the House and the Senate to limit its scope to international abductions and to require a court to consider all of the factors as provided in the statute when determining whether a credible risk of abduction exists.[1246]

Under the Act, the court on its own motion or a party in a child custody determination can order or request abduction prevention measures if there is a credible risk of abduction of the child.[1247] To determine whether a credible risk of abduction exists, the Act sets forth several factors to guide courts.[1248] These include the more obvious risk factors, such as previous abduction attempts, previous threats of abduction, or recent activities that indicate a planned abduction,[1249] but also the less obvious factors, such as quitting one's job, closing bank accounts, or lacking "strong familial, financial, emotional, or cultural ties to the United States."[1250] If a court determines that a credible risk exists, it can issue an order imposing abduction prevention measures or, in certain cases, a warrant to take custody of the child.[1251]

The court has vast discretion regarding the extent of the abduction prevention order.[1252] The order may include travel restrictions, prohibitions of travel, and surrender of the child's passport, among others.[1253] If a court finds the need to prevent imminent abduction, it can issue an ex parte warrant to take physical custody of the child.[1254] If the ex parte warrant is granted, the respondent must be given the "opportunity to be heard at the earliest possible time ... but not later than the next judicial day unless a hearing on that day is impossible."[1255] If the court finds, after a hearing, that the peti-

---

1245. La. Stat. Ann. §§ 13:1851–:1852. Abduction is defined as "the wrongful removal or wrongful retention of a child beyond the territorial limits of the United States." La. Stat. Ann. § 13:1852(1).

1246. Official Journal of the House of Representatives of the State of Louisiana, 23rd Day's Proceedings, 2007 Leg., 33rd Reg. Sess., at 853 (Report of the Committee on Civil Law and Procedure); Official Journal of the House of Representatives of the State of Louisiana, 31st Day's Proceedings, 2007 Leg., 33rd Reg. Sess., at 1174–75; Official Journal of the Senate of the State of Louisiana, 34th Day's Proceedings, 2007 Leg., 33rd Reg. Sess., at 1177–78; *see also* N.J. Law Revision Comm'n, Final Report Relating to Uniform Child Abduction Prevention Act 3–4. (2008), https://static1.squarespace.com/static/596f60f4ebbd1a322db09e45/t/5e84d47fecaa9066345c5234/1585763455889/ucapaFR122208+%28remote%29.pdf.

1247. La. Stat. Ann. § 13:1854. The party who fears abduction must file in a court that has jurisdiction to make a child-custody determination. La. Stat. Ann. § 13:1855.

1248. La. Stat. Ann. § 13:1857.

1249. La. Stat. Ann. § 13:1857.

1250. La. Stat. Ann. § 13:1857. The court must consider all of the factors and evidence. La. Stat. Ann. § 13:1857(A).

1251. La. Stat. Ann. §§ 13:1858(B), :1859(A).

1252. *See* La. Stat. Ann. § 13:1858(B).

1253. La. Stat. Ann. § 13:1858(C). The court is directed to give due consideration to the custody and visitation rights of the parties and to consider the age of the child, the potential harm to the child, and the difficulties that may ensue if the child is abducted. La. Stat. Ann. § 13:1858(B).

1254. La. Stat. Ann. § 13:1859(A).

1255. La. Stat. Ann. § 13:1859(B).

tioner sought an ex parte warrant for the purpose of harassment or in bad faith, the court may award the respondent costs and fees.[1256] Any abduction prevention order will be effective until the time provided by the court in the order, the emancipation of the child, the child's majority, or the time in any subsequent order by a court with jurisdiction, whichever occurs first.[1257]

In *Mohsen v. Mohsen*, the only Louisiana decision to apply the Act, the court vacated the trial court's order to surrender the child's passport, finding that reliance on only one abduction factor was in error.[1258] In *Mohsen*, the child's mother sought international visitation so that the child could spend 12 days with her maternal grandparents in Nicaragua.[1259] The trial court denied her request[1260] and ordered surrender of the child's passport, concluding that Nicaragua was not a signatory to the Hague Convention.[1261] Until the mother could offer proof that "the United States had recourse in the event of an abduction," the court would not authorize a visit.[1262] Because the father feared that the mother might travel with the child to Nicaragua even though the court denied her motion, the court ordered surrender of the child's passport.[1263] The First Circuit vacated that portion of the trial court's decision, finding that the Act requires a consideration of all factors to determine "whether there [is] a credible risk of abduction of the child, thereby justifying the surrender of the child's passport."[1264]

1256. La. Stat. Ann. § 13:1859(G).

1257. La. Stat. Ann. § 13:1860.

1258. Mohsen v. Mohsen, 2008-1703, pp. 8–9 (La. App. 1 Cir. 12/23/08), 5 So. 3d 218, 224.

1259. Mohsen, 5 So. 3d at 220.

1260. Mohsen, 5 So. 3d at 220. The court denied the mother's motion for international visitation because she did not provide any evidence in support of her motion; she did not even attend the hearing. Mohsen, *Id.* at 221.

1261. Mohsen, 5 So. 3d at 220.

1262. Mohsen, 5 So. 3d at 223–24.

1263. Mohsen, 5 So. 3d at 224.

1264. Mohsen, 5 So. 3d at 224.

Chapter 7

Child Support*

* This chapter was derived from the following article: Monica Hof Wallace, *A Primer on Child Support in Louisiana*, 69 Loy. L. Rev 131 (2022). The authors wish to thank the Loyola Law Review for its assistance on the initial work for this chapter.

§ 7:1 Introduction

The Civil Code contains only two articles on child support, both of which are found in Title V of Book I on Divorce. Article 141 gives the court authority to order either or both parents to pay interim or final child support based on the child's needs and the ability of the parents to pay.[1] An award of child support is not limited to proceedings incidental to divorce, as the obligation to support a child is derived from parenthood alone.[2] Even though the article is found in the title on divorce, when the parents of a child separate, whether married or not, child support may still be awarded based on the needs of the child and the ability of the parent to pay support.[3]

Article 142 provides the standard for a court to apply when child support is modified or terminated.[4] Modification is permitted when a material change of circumstances occurs from the time of the last award, and termination is permitted when support becomes unnecessary.[5] Although the two code articles provide express authorization for child support, the details governing child support are found in the Revised Statutes Sections 9:315 through 315.47 with additional provisions scattered throughout Title 9's general provisions in the chapter on divorce.[6]

§ 7:2 Historical Background

Louisiana's current child support laws originated from years of legislative, judicial, and societal mandates for parental support of children. Child support focuses on the general proposition that parents, whether married or unmarried, have an obligation to support their children. This obligation is not unique. Since the beginning of western legal tradition, society has imposed an obligation to care for children. In classical Byzantium, Emperor Justinian created legislation to permit children of unwed fathers to seek support from their fathers.[7] The French derived the obligation of support from the contract of marriage, providing, "Married persons contract together, by the single act of marriage, the obligation of nourishing, supporting, and bringing up their children."[8] Few laws, though, allowed recovery for the financial support of a child.[9]

1. La. Civ. Code Ann. art. 141.

2. *See* La. Civ. Code Ann. art. 224; *see also* La. Civ. Code Ann. art. 141, cmt (i) (referencing La. Civ. Code art. 227 (1870), which was amended and reenacted as article 224 in Act No. 260, 2015 La. Acts 1812–28).

3. *See* La. Stat. Ann. § 9:291; La. Civ. Code Ann. art. 141.

4. *See* La. Civ. Code Ann. art. 142.

5. La. Civ. Code Ann. art. 142.

6. *See generally* La. Stat. Ann. §§ 9:315–315.47; *see also* La. Stat. Ann. §§ 9:303, 304.1, 311, 311.1, 313.

7. Kathryn Venturatos Lorio, *Roman Sources and Constitutional Mandates: The Alpha and Omega of Louisiana Laws on Concubine and Natural Children*, 56 La. L. Rev. 317, 322 (1995); Ferdinand Mackeldey, Handbook of the Roman Law 410 (Moses A. Dropsie ed. & trans., 1883).

8. Code civil [C. civ.] [Civil Code] art. 203 (Fr.).

9. The Elizabethan Poor Laws created a tax system that allowed a parish to recover money spent on a single mother and her child when they were destitute, but the parish could only recover from a relative, such as the father, and only what was needed to prevent destitution. No private right of action

Louisiana law, derived from French law, used the contract of marriage as the legal basis on which to enforce child support. Article 227 of the Civil Code of 1870 provided, "Fathers and mothers, by the very act of marrying, contract together the obligation of supporting, maintaining, and educating their children."[10] As early as 1909, the Louisiana Supreme Court recognized that this obligation exists even without marriage.[11] Instead, the high court held that child support arises "from the fact of the paternity," that it "exists in favor of children born out of wedlock," and "[h]ence, the dissolution of the marriage does not dissolve the obligation of support."[12]

Child support awards, initially termed alimony, were governed generally by statute, but the judiciary was given the role of balancing the child's needs with the obligor's ability to pay.[13] Much discretion was given to the trial court, resulting in awards that were often inconsistent and inadequate.[14] Louisiana was not alone in these problems. Other states likewise suffered from a lack of legislation, resulting in inadequate awards and disparate results.[15]

The federal government intervened in an attempt to create consistency and accuracy in child support awards and to improve the collection of child support dollars for the benefit of the child. In 1975, the Child Support Enforcement Act (CSEA) was enacted by Congress.[16] The goal of the program was to establish paternity and child support orders and to collect child support through a federal, state, and local partnership.[17] The CSEA required every state to establish a child support enforcement system to

---

by the mother for support of the child was permitted. During the American colonization, state laws resembled the Poor Laws, and state statutes failed to provide private claims for individuals. Drew D. Hansen, *The American Invention of Child Support: Dependency and Punishment in Early American Child Support Law*, 108 Yale L.J. 1123, 1134 (1999) (citing 43 Eliz. c. 2 (Eng. 1601)); *see also* James Schouler, A Treatise on the Law of the Domestic Relations, 342–43 (4th ed. 1889) ("The Stat. 43 Eliz. may be considered as having been ... re-enacted in many of our States....").

10. La. Civ. Code art. 227 (1870).

11. State v. Seghers, 124 La. 115, 116 (La. 1909).

12. Seghers, 124 La. at 116 (citations omitted); *see also* Marcel Planiol, 1 Treatise on the Civil Law § 1681, at 40 (La. State L. Inst. trans., 12th ed. 1959); Green v. Scott, 29,197, p. 2 (La. App. 2 Cir. 1/22/97), 687 So. 2d 655, 656; In re EWB, 441 So. 2d 478, 483 (La. Ct. App. 2 Cir. 1983); Pierce v. Pierce, 397 So. 2d 62, 64 (La. Ct. App. 2 Cir. 1981).

13. Articles 227 and 230 were the basis for awards of child support. Article 227, cited above, set forth the general obligation of parents to support and educate their children. La. Civ. Code Ann. art. 227. Article 230 governed the scope of the obligation, which is defined as "what is necessary for the nourishment, lodging, and support of the person who claims it," as well as education. La. Civ. Code Ann. art. 230.

14. Christopher L Blakesley, *Louisiana Family Law*, 52 La. L. Rev. 607, 608–09 (1992).

15. *See generally* Donna Schuele, *Origins and Development of Paternal Child Support*, 27 J. Fam. L. 807 (1989) (detailing nineteenth century developments in the law of child support throughout the United States).

16. *See* U.S. Child Support Enforcement Act of 1975, 42 U.S.C. §§ 651–69 (1997) (originally in title IV–D of the SSA).

17. U.S. Child Support Enforcement Act of 1975, 42 U.S.C. §§ 651–69 (1997) (originally in title IV–D of the SSA).

implement these goals locally.[18] Each state created or designated a special state agency to collect child support payments and report its results to the federal government.[19] The CSEA marked the first major advancement in child support legislation.

The next significant legislation was the Child Support Enforcement Act of 1984,[20] followed by the Family Support Act of 1988.[21] These Acts ultimately mandated the use of child support guidelines to ensure an accurate calculation of a child support award.[22] Using standardized guidelines led to a rebuttable presumption that the calculated award was appropriate, and following the guidelines became a more desirable and meaningful process.[23]

As required by law, the Louisiana Legislature created the Office of Family Services—Support Enforcement Services to establish paternity and child support orders, to collect child support, and to report to the federal agency.[24] The office, now called the Department of Children and Family Services (DCFS)—Child Support Enforcement (CSE), is a division of Family Support.[25] Since its inception, the office has worked in partnership with the federal government to improve child support collection. DCFS operates under legislature-mandated guidelines, which are reviewed every four years.[26] The guidelines were first enacted in 1989,[27] and they were not comprehensively reviewed again until 2001.[28] Since 2001, they were reviewed in 2004 and every four years thereafter.[29]

---

18. U.S. Child Support Enforcement Act of 1975, 42 U.S.C. §§ 651–69 (1997) (originally in title IV-D of the SSA).

19. U.S. Child Support Enforcement Act of 1975, 42 U.S.C. §§ 651–69 (1997) (originally in title IV-D of the SSA).

20. *See* U.S. Child Support Enforcement Amendments of 1984, Pub. L. No. 98-378, 98 Stat. 1305; 42 U.S.C. §§ 601, 652–669b (1984 and Supp. 1991).

21. *See* Family Support Act of 1988, Pub. L. No. 100-485, 102 Stat. 2343.

22. *See* Guillot v. Munn, 1999-2132, p. 5 (La. 3/24/00), 756 So. 2d 290, 295.

23. *See* Guillot, 756 So. 2d at 295; Jane C. Venohr & Robert G. Williams, *The Implementation and Periodic Review of State Child Support Guidelines*, 3 Fam. L.Q. 7 (1999) (chronicling the development of child support guidelines in the United States).

24. *See generally* La. Dept. of Child. & Fam. Serv., https://www.dcfs.louisiana.gov/ (last visited May 28, 2024) (website hosted by Dept. of Child. & Fam. Serv. to facilitate the collection of child support orders).

25. Fam. Support, La. Dept. of Child. & Fam. Serv., www.dss.state.la.us/page/family-support (last visited May 28, 2024).

26. La. Stat. Ann. § 9:315.16.

27. Act No. 9, 1989 La. Acts 2563–75 (codified as amended at La. Stat. Ann. §§ 9:315–315.14 (Supp. 1990)).

28. The review process took place in two stages, in 1999 and 2000. First, in 1999, the legislature directed the Department of Social Services and the Louisiana District Attorneys' Association to conduct a comprehensive review and make recommendations in 2000. A resolution was passed in 2000 that requested continued study of the recommendations. As a result, Act No. 182 of the 2001 Regular Legislative Session was passed. *See* Katherine Shaw Spaht, *The Two "ICE" of the 2001 Louisiana Child Support Guidelines: Economics and Politics*, 62 La. L. Rev. 709, 714–15 (2002).

29. *See* La. Stat. Ann. § 9:315.16, as originally enacted Act No. 1082, 2001 La. Acts 2275. ("The guidelines set forth in this Part shall be reviewed by the legislature not less than once every four

Louisiana follows the income shares model, which is used by the majority of states.[30] This model bases support on the total net income earned by the parents and the needs of the child; the goal is to find an appropriate level of support so a child can receive the same share of parental income that the child would have received if the parents were living together.[31] Considering the parents' income, a published schedule provides a base level of child support, which is intended to capture amounts needed for food, clothing, and shelter of the child.[32] To this base amount, further expenses are added, which reflect additions for child care, private schooling, medical expenses, and other extraordinary needs of the child.[33] Each parent will share in these expenses in proportion to the share of income each contributes to the family.[34] To carry out the income shares model, worksheets have been promulgated by the legislature, the details of which will be fully discussed in sections that follow.[35]

§ 7:3 Duty of Support Generally

Louisiana recognizes two distinct types of support available to children: the unilateral support that parents owe to their minor children[36] and the reciprocal support that parents and children owe to one another, regardless of age.[37] Parental support for minor children results from the obligation that all parents owe to their minor children because of the minor's incapacity. In 2015, the legislature extended the unilateral duty that parents owe to minor children to also include adult children with an intellectual or physical disability, who are unmarried and incapable of self-support, as long as the disability manifested itself before the age of majority.[38] Louisiana law does not

---

years."). In 2004, a child support review committee was constituted to participate in the review process. *See* Act No. 249, 2004 La. Acts 1304–05.

30. Diana Cross, *Preserving Continuity and Fairness: The Louisiana Supreme Court Limits Deviation from Child Support Guidelines*, 47 Loy. L. Rev. 885, 891 (2001). Other methods include the Percentage of Obligor Method, the Melson Formula, and a hybrid approach between the income shares model and the percentage of obligor model. For a description of all four methods, see *id.* at 890–92. For a detailed discussion of the 2001 review of the child support guidelines, see Katherine Shaw Spaht, *The Two "ICE" of the 2001 Louisiana Child Support Guidelines: Economics and Politics*, 62 La. L. Rev. 709, 714–15 (2002).

31. *See* Guillot, 756 So. 2d at 295.

32. *See* La. Stat. Ann. § 9:315.19.

33. La. Stat. Ann. §§ 9:315.3–315.6. Deductions for income of the child are subtracted. La. Stat. Ann. § 9:315.7.

34. La. Stat. Ann. § 9:315.

35. See discussion Sections § 7:42–45.

36. *See* La. Stat. Ann. §§ 9:315–315.47. In 2015, the legislature passed the Adult Children with Disabilities Act, which permits child support to be paid to an adult child with an intellectual or physical disability that manifested itself before the child reached the age of majority. *See* La. Stat. Ann. § 9:315.22(E), as relocated to § 9:315.22.1.

37. La. Civ. Code Ann. arts. 236–39. The reciprocal support extends to all ascendants and descendants, as well. *See* La. Civ. Code Ann. art. 237.

38. La. Stat. Ann. § 9:315.22(E), as enacted by Act No. 379, 2015 La. Acts 2132–34, and as relocated to § 9:315.22.1.

currently address child support owed by parents who are minors, but the issue is being studied.[39] The unilateral duty is governed by the comprehensive set of laws known as the Child Support Guidelines.[40] By contrast, the reciprocal support obligation between parents and children continues beyond a child's minority and arises simply because of the parent-child relationship.[41] This support, however, is more limited in nature and is not governed by the Child Support Guidelines.[42]

The Child Support Guidelines are found in Title 9 of the Louisiana Revised Statutes.[43] The support of a child is a joint duty shared by both parents, in accordance with their resources.[44] In fact, the child is a creditor to both parents, and the debt is enforceable by the other parent, who is given a right of action against the non-custodial parent to pay support for the child's upbringing.[45]

A parent's duty of support is legally owed and cannot be renounced or permanently suspended.[46] The obligations are continuous and cannot be escaped.[47] When a parent proves that he is not only unemployed but unemployable, the obligation of support may be suspended during the period of unemployment.[48] Likewise, an incarcerated parent's child support obligation may be suspended during the period of incarceration.[49]

Although the discretion of the court is more carefully guided since passage of the Child Support Guidelines, the overarching concern surrounding the needs of the child and the ability of parents to pay continues to infuse the awards. Children who enjoyed

---

39. 2024 La. House Concurrent Resolution 28.

40. La Civ. Code Ann. arts. 236–39. *See* Chapter 9 for a detailed discussion of the alimentary obligation.

41. Marcel Planiol, 1 Treatise on the Civil Law § 1681, at 40 (La. State L. Inst. trans., 12th ed. 1959).

42. La. Civ. Code Ann. arts. 236–39. This support is referred to as an "alimentary obligation" and flows from the parent to the child *and* from the child to the parent. The obligation, however, includes only the necessities of life when the relative cannot meet his or her needs through other means. La. Civ. Code Ann. art. 237; *see also* Section 7:9.

43. La. Stat. Ann. §§ 9:315–315.47.

44. *See* La. Stat. Ann. § 9:315(A).

45. Dubroc v. Dubroc, 388 So. 2d 377, 379–80 (La. 1980); *see also* State of Louisiana v. Tassin, 22-350 (La. App. 5 Cir. 2/27/23), 359 So. 3d 527 (child support can be awarded even when the parties are married but living separately); State in Interest of Johnson v. Johnson, 22-566 (La. App. 5 Cir. 5/24/23), 366 So. 3d 807 (same).

46. Dubroc, 388 So. 2d at 380. "A parent may discharge this duty by either (1) providing support in kind as a domiciliary parent or (2) paying money for obtaining the support, maintenance, and education as a nondomiciliary parent." Sharp v. Moore, 47,888, p. 4 (La. App. 2 Cir. 2/27/13), 110 So. 3d 1232, 1234.

47. *See* Walder v. Walder, 105 So. 300, 302 (La. 1925). In *Walder*, the court held an agreement null and void because it relieved a father from all legal obligations of support to his children, noting that these obligations cannot be escaped. *Id.* at 301–02.

48. *See* Rutherford v. Rutherford, 452 So. 2d 432, 435 (La. Ct. App. 3 Cir. 1984); *see also* Chaudoir v. Chaudoir, 446 So. 2d 951, 953 (La. Ct. App. 3 Cir. 1984). Note that under the Louisiana Civil Code, "[t]he masculine gender comprehends the two sexes, ... the words he, his and such like, are applicable to both males and females." La. Civ. Code Ann. art. 3506(1). Throughout this chapter, the use of the masculine pronoun includes the feminine.

49. La. Stat. Ann. § 9:311.1.

a higher standard of living before divorce are entitled to that same standard of living after divorce.[50] While difficult to achieve in all circumstances, the goal of child support is for children to be shielded from the economic consequences of divorce or separation of their parents.

§ 7:4 Duty of Support Generally—Stepparents

Stepparents do not have an obligation to support a step-child, except and to the extent that expenses for the step-child are classified as community obligations.[51] For example, absent a matrimonial agreement a child support obligation from a previous marriage is a community obligation, which can be satisfied from the community property of the subsequent marriage or the separate property of the spouse who incurred the obligation.[52] During the 1950s, the Louisiana Supreme Court considered now-repealed Civil Code Article 2403[53] and its Spanish origins, and concluded that even though the support debt existed prior to the second marriage, it was a debt of the current community because the debt was legal in nature and not contractual.[54] The court concluded that responsibility fell only on the community interest of the spouse who owed the prior support obligation.[55]

Two decades later, the Louisiana Supreme Court was presented with the question of whether an obligor spouse must furnish an accounting to and reimburse the stepparent

50. *See* Wilmot v. Wilmot, 65 So. 2d 321, 329 (La. 1953) (pre-guidelines case recognizing that children continue to enjoy the activities they enjoyed during the marriage even though in the custody of the less affluent parent); *see also* Dufresne v. Dufresne, 10-963, pp. 11–12 (La. App. 5 Cir. 5/10/11), 65 So. 3d 749, 757 (finding that the inclusion of recreational expenses in the child support award was justified because the standard of living that the child enjoyed with her mother was modest in relation to that enjoyed by her millionaire father and the mother's financial constraints prevented the child from going on school trips); Piccione v. Piccione, 2001-1086, p. 7 (La. App. 3 Cir. 5/22/02), 824 So. 2d 427, 431 (noting that children whose custody is awarded to mother are entitled to the same standard of living as if they reside with their father); Reeves v. Reeves, 36,259, p. 6 (La. App. 2 Cir. 7/24/02), 823 So. 2d 1023, 1027, *on reh'g* (9/12/02) (commenting that children are entitled to support in an amount to maintain them in the lifestyle commensurate with the standard of living the family enjoyed before the marriage terminated); Lamothe v. Lamothe, 262 So. 2d 87, 88 (La. Ct. App. 4 Cir. 1972) (holding that the monthly child support award was not manifestly excessive considering that the minor in question had "enjoyed a standard of living above that customarily afforded to persons of average means" such as being provided with "education in private schools, maid service, substantial clothing allowance . . .").

51. Although this section is dedicated to child support owed by stepparents, payments by the parent spouse for a child's rent, tuition, insurance, hospital bills, and other related expenses are also community obligations of the stepparent. *See* Munson v. Munson, 2000-348, pp. 5–6 (La. App. 3 Cir. 10/4/00), 772 So. 2d 141, 145; Gill v. Gill, 39,406, p. 22 (La. App. 2 Cir. 3/9/05), 895 So. 2d 807, 820.

52. La. Civ. Code Ann. arts. 2362, 2345.

53. La. Civ. Code Ann. art. 2403, *repealed by* Act. No 709, 1979 La. Acts 1857–58 ("[T]he debts contracted during the marriage enter into the partnership or community of gains, and must be acquitted out of the common fund, whilst the debts of both husband and wife, anterior to the marriage, must be acquitted out of their own personal and individual effects.").

54. *See* Fazzio v. Krieger, 76 So. 2d 713, 714–16 (La. 1954).

55. *See* Fazzio, 76 So. 2d at 717.

spouse for support payments made from assets in the community.[56] The court explained that regular month-by-month support payments due during the existence of the second community are properly paid from all of the community funds, not just the incurring spouse's community interest.[57] Further, the support payments—paid with community funds—are not subject to reimbursement by the obligor spouse to the step-parent spouse because the community funds did not increase the value of the obligor's separate property.[58] No reimbursement was due.[59]

In 1980, the matrimonial regime articles underwent a significant revision, and the first court to consider the issue of step-parent support post-revision was *Bagwell v. Bagwell*.[60] In *Bagwell*, the custodial parent asked the court to order an income assignment from the obligor parent and her new spouse, arguing that both are solidarily bound for the support payments.[61] The court held that a step-parent is neither personally nor solidarily obligated to support a spouse's child of a prior marriage.[62] The court did recognize that the obligation impacts the community of the parent and step-parent, because the step-parent's entire share of the community is subject to seizure to satisfy the other spouse's support obligation; however, the step-parent is not personally liable for a share of the support.[63] As a result, the court refused to order a compulsory income assignment against the step-parent.[64]

§ 7:5 Duty of Support Generally—Unborn Children

In light of the 2022 United States Supreme Court decision *Dobbs v. Jackson Women's Health Organization*[65] and a gap in the law protecting women,[66] the Louisiana Legislature enacted Act 439 in its 2023 Regular Session. This act created Louisiana Revised Statute 9:399.2, which allows a biological mother, within a peremptive period of two years from her child's birth, the right to institute an action against the child's bio-

---

56. *See* Connell v. Connell, 331 So. 2d 4, 5 (La. 1976) (per curiam).

57. Connell, 331 So. 2d at 6. The court also distinguished this legal obligation from those that would preexist the second marriage and be contractual, rather than legal, in nature; the latter would be reimbursable on termination of the community. *Id.*

58. Connell, 331 So. 2d at 6. The court applied article 2403, which was repealed in the revision of 1980. *Id.* After the revision, article 2366 addresses reimbursement claims when community property is used to benefit the spouse's separate property. *See* La. Civ. Code Ann. art. 2366.

59. Connell, 331 So. 2d at 6.

60. *See* Bagwell v. Bagwell, 29,756 (La. App. 2 Cir. 8/20/97), 698 So. 2d 746.

61. *See* Bagwell, 698 So. 2d at 747.

62. Bagwell, 698 So. 2d at 748 (Although not solidarily bound, a step-parent's income may be considered in determining the amount of support owed, but only to the extent that the income is used directly to reduce expenses of the obligor parent).

63. *See* Bagwell, 698 So. 2d at 748.

64. Bagwell, 698 So. 2d at 748.

65. Dobbs v. Jackson Women's Health Organization, 597 U.S. 215 (2022).

66. Hearing on H.B. 5 Before the H. Comm. On Civ. L. and Proc. At 2:00 (La. 2023) (statement of Rep. Miller), https://house.louisiana.gov/H_Video/VideoArchivePlayer?v=house/2023/apr/0419_23_CL.

logical father, who has formally acknowledged the child or whose paternity has been proven by clear and convincing evidence, to recover 50% of documented out-of-pocket pregnancy-related medical expenses.[67]

The statute lists only the following out-of-pocket expenses as covered: (1) actual medical expenses, including hospital, testing, nursing, pharmaceutical, travel, or other expenses, incurred by the biological mother for prenatal care, and (2) those medical expenses incurred by the biological mother and child incident to birth. Additionally, it allows the court to authorize, by order, any additional expense on a specific finding that the expense is reasonable and necessary.

§ 7:6 Duty of Support Generally—Children Born Outside of Marriage

Children born outside of marriage are entitled to support from their mother and father, as long as the child is properly filiated to each parent. Filiation is the legal relationship between a child and parent, which can be established by proof of maternity, proof of paternity, or by adoption.[68] Proof of maternity is typically established through proof, by a preponderance of the evidence, that a child is born of a particular woman.[69] A child can prove maternity though documentary evidence, like a birth certificate, scientific evidence, or the testimony of witnesses to the fact of birth.[70]

Traditionally, the law has focused on proving paternity, rather than maternity, for purposes of collecting support. To facilitate proof of paternity, Louisiana recognizes presumptions that attach as a matter of law when the parents are married. When the parents are married and a child is born during the marriage or within 300 days after termination of the marriage, the husband of the mother is presumed to be the father of the child.[71] If this presumption is not timely challenged, it becomes irrebuttable, and the husband is obligated to support the child, even if it is later proven that he is not the biological father.[72]

A presumption of paternity also attaches to a man who marries the mother of the child after the child's birth, if, with the mother's consent, the man formally acknowledges the child as his own via authentic act, as long as the child is not filiated to another man.[73] Again, if this presumption is not timely challenged, it becomes irrebuttable, and

---

67. La. Stat. Ann. § 9:399.2. Notably, the burden of proof to establish paternity by clear and convincing evidence under this statute requires blood and tissue evidence and is higher than the burden of proof by a preponderance of the evidence.

68. La. Civ. Code Ann. arts. 178–79. *See* Chapter 8.

69. La. Civ. Code Ann. art. 184. An exception exists for valid surrogacy contracts, under which the intended mother, not the birth mother, is filiated to the child. *See* La. Stat. Ann. §§ 9:2718–2720.15.

70. La. Civ. Code Ann. art. 184. cmt. (b).

71. La. Civ. Code Ann. art. 185.

72. *See* La. Civ. Code Ann. art. 189.

73. La. Civ. Code Ann art. 195. The acknowledgment can occur before or after the marriage. *Id.*

the husband is obligated to support the child, even if it is later proven that he is not the father.[74]

An additional presumption exists outside of marriage if a man formally acknowledges the child as his own by executing an authentic act attesting to paternity.[75] The child, however, cannot already be filiated to another man.[76] Assuming the formal acknowledgement is not annulled or timely revoked,[77] the child, through the custodial parent, will be entitled to collect support from that man.[78]

The alleged father can also bring an avowal action in court to legally filiate himself to the child.[79] This strictly personal right of action is limited by short peremptive periods if the child is already filiated to another man (for example, as a result of one of the presumptions that arise with marriage) or if the child dies.[80] If the child is not filiated to another man, the father can bring an avowal action without strict time limitations, and a judgment of paternity will also result in an obligation to support the child.[81] The alleged father must prove by a preponderance of the evidence that he is the biological father of the child, and will have full filial rights, including an ongoing obligation of support for the child.[82]

Court action is also available to the child, through a representative, to prove the paternity of the child's biological father.[83] Through a paternity action, if the child can

---

74. *See* La. Civ. Code Ann. art. 195; *see* Wetta v. Wetta, 2021-92, pp. 11–12 (La. App. 3 Cir. 6/2/21), 322 So. 3d 365, 373–74, *writ denied*, 2021-00940 (La. 10/19/21), 326 So. 3d 255 (holding that man who signed an act of acknowledgment knowing he was not the father and then married the mother could not be released of his obligations to the child by revoking the acknowledgment; he did not timely disavow); *but see* Kelley v. Kelley, 55,358 (La. App. 2 Cir. 12/23/23), 376 So. 3d 320, 324 (holding that man who signed act of acknowledgment knowing that he was not the child's father and then married the mother could rescind the act of acknowledgment because it was absolutely null).

75. La. Civ. Code Ann. art. 196.

76. La. Civ. Code Ann. art. 196.

77. *See* La. Stat. Ann. § 9:406 (permitting annulment and revocation of the act of acknowledgement).

78. La. Stat. Ann. § 9:392(5). The presumption created by the acknowledgement, however, does not operate in favor of the man who acknowledges the child, except the man can seek custody and visitation and will be required to pay support. La. Stat. Ann. § 9:392; *see also* La. Stat. Ann. § 9:392.1 ("In child support . . . cases, the acknowledgement of paternity by authentic act is deemed to be a legal finding of paternity and is sufficient to establish an obligation to support the child . . ."). If the man wants reciprocal paternal rights to the child, he will have to file an avowal action. *See* La. Civ. Code Ann. art. 198.

79. La. Civ. Code Ann. art. 198.

80. *See* La. Civ. Code Ann. art. 198 cmt. (d). If the child is filiated to another man, the action must be brought within one year from the birth of the child, unless the mother in bad faith deceived the man regarding his paternity, then the action can be brought within one year of when he learned or should have learned of his paternity, or within 10 years from the child's birth, whichever occurs first. La. Civ. Code Ann. art. 198.

81. La. Civ. Code Ann. art. 198. Whether a father simply signs a formal acknowledgement or brings a court action to avow himself to the child, the same obligation of child support will exist. Only the father's rights will be affected depending on the option he chooses. *Id.*

82. La. Civ. Code Ann. art. 198.

83. La. Civ. Code Ann. art. 197.

prove by a preponderance of the evidence that a living man is the father, the obligation of support will exist.[84]

With the recognition of same-sex marriage in 2015,[85] questions of support by non-biological, same-sex parents have arisen. For same-sex female couples, proof of maternity only filiates the child to the mother who gave birth to the child.[86] As for the non-biological mother, at least one court has interpreted the presumption of paternity of the husband to apply equally to a same-sex female spouse, requiring her to pay child support for children born during the marriage.[87] For same-sex male spouses, who cannot carry a child during the marriage, the presumption of paternity will not apply; adoption[88] or out-of-state surrogacy[89] will be necessary.

Once properly filiated to a parent, the Child Support Guidelines will apply, regardless of whether the child was born of or outside of a marriage. Even prior to the Child Support Guidelines, as distinctions between in and out-of-wedlock children began to disappear, courts applied the same needs/means analysis to children born outside of marriage as to children born during a marriage when making an award of child support.[90]

§ 7:7 Duty of Support Generally—Dual Paternity

Dual paternity is a concept that was first introduced in Louisiana jurisprudence in the 1974 case of *Warren v. Richard*, in which the court allowed a child to recover for the wrongful death of his biological father, while the child was also legally filiated to another man.[91] The jurisprudential concept then spread through the court system, allowing children, regardless of legal presumptions, to establish their biological parentage.[92] Dual paternity was eventually codified in Articles 197 and 198 of the Louisiana

84. La. Civ. Code Ann. art. 197 ("The child can bring this action even if he is presumed to be the child of another man."). The action for child support is not available after the death of the father. *See* Kendrick v. Estate of Barre, 2021-00993, p. 6 (La. 3/25/22), 339 So. 3d 615, 619.

85. *See* Obergefell v. Hodges, 576 U.S. 644 (2015).

86. *See* La. Civ. Code Ann. art. 185.

87. *See* Boquet v. Boquet, 2018-798, p. 6 (La. App. 3 Cir. 4/10/19), 269 So. 3d 895, 900; *but see* In re Dennis, 55,851 (La. App. 2 Cir. 7/17/24), 2024 WL 3434184 (disagreeing with *Boquet*).

88. Married couples may adopt a child. *See* La. Child. Code Ann. art. 1281.9.

89. Surrogacy in this context is not permitted in Louisiana because the married couple must contribute their gametes to conceive the child, thereby excluding same-sex married couples who would need to use donor gametes. *See* La. Stat. Ann. §§ 9:2718–2720.15. Note, too, that the presumptions have not been applied to male sex-sex couples who used surrogacy. *See* Foret v. Serrano, 23-1034 (La. App. 1 Cir. 4/30/24), 395 So. 3d 876.

90. *See* Hoffman v. Lucia, 604 So. 2d 169, 171 (La. Ct. App. 5 Cir. 1992) (concluding that the same standard should apply to legitimate and illegitimate children when determining child support).

91. *See* Warren v. Richard, 296 So. 2d 813, 817 (La. 1974).

92. *See* Smith v. Cole, 553 So. 2d 847, 854 (La. 1989); Griffin v. Succession of Branch, 479 So. 2d 324, 326 (La. 1985); Malek v. Yekani-Fard, 422 So. 2d 1151, 1154 (La. 1982); Succession of Mitchell, 323 So. 2d 451, 456–57 (La. 1975); Dep't of Soc. Servs., Off. of Fam. Support ex rel. Smith v. Williams, 605 So. 2d 7, 9 (La. Ct. App. 2 Cir. 1992); Starks v. Powell, 552 So. 2d 609, 612 (La. Ct. App. 2 Cir. 1989);

Civil Code during the 2005 legislative revision.[93] Article 197 allows a child to "prove paternity even though he is presumed to be the child of another man."[94] Article 198 allows for reciprocal relief when a man wishes to prove his paternal filiation to a child, even if the child is presumed to be the child of another man.[95] Should the action by either the child or the father succeed, the child may have both a legal father and a biological father, thereby resulting in dual paternity.

In the child support context, all parents have a duty and are obligated to support their children.[96] The presumptions of paternity created by law "protect innocent children from the stigma attached to illegitimacy" but were "not intended to shield biological fathers from their support obligations."[97] In fact, presumptions cannot protect biological fathers because they are obligated by nature to provide support for their offspring.[98] In other words, a biological father cannot benefit from a presumption of paternity in favor of another man, such that a biological father could "escape his support obligations merely because others may share ... the responsibility."[99]

The concept of dual paternity raises several issues in the context of child support. First, may both a presumed father and a biological father be ordered to pay support for the same child? Second, how is child support calculated in the event of dual paternity? Finally, may a presumed father recover reimbursement for support paid once he learns that a biological father exists?

A court may indeed order both a presumed father and a biological father to pay support. A biological father always has a civil duty to support his child, and no court has extinguished the presumed legal father's obligation in light of the biological father.[100] Instead, with the best interest of the child in mind, courts have welcomed additional financial support, finding that "a biological father capable of providing support cannot equitably be ignored."[101] So, a presumed father who fails to timely disavow may be

---

Thomas v. Smith, 463 So. 2d 971, 974–75 (La. Ct. App. 3 Cir. 1985); Succession of Levy, 428 So. 2d 904, 910 (La. Ct. App. 1 Cir. 1983).

93. Act No. 192, 2005 La. Acts 1455–59.

94. La. Civ. Code Ann. art. 197.

95. La. Civ. Code Ann. art 198.

96. La. Civ. Code Ann. art 224.

97. Smith, 553 So. 2d at 854.

98. Smith, 553 So. 2d at 854; *see also* Jones v. Rodrigue, 2000-0899, p. 8 (La. App. 1 Cir. 11/3/00), 771 So. 2d 275, 280 (following *Smith*, holding that biological father could be ordered to pay child support retroactive to the date of mother's filing of petition, even during the period when mother's fiancé, who had signed an acknowledgment of paternity, was presumed to be the father; and further that a parent's duty of support is a legal duty that cannot be renounced or suspended).

99. Smith, 553 So. 2d at 854; *see also* Dep't of Soc. Servs. ex rel. Munson v. Williams, 35,550, p. 3 (La. App. 2 Cir. 12/8/99), 747 So. 2d 1245, 1248 (reversing the decision of trial court and holding that the fact that another man is legally presumed to be the father "does not obviate or alter in any way the support obligation owed by the biological father").

100. *See* J.M.Y. v. R.R., 2008-805, p. 4 (La. App. 3 Cir. 12/11/08), 1 So. 3d 725, 728.

101. Smith, 553 So. 2d at 855 n.8; *see* Dep't of Child. & Fam. Servs. ex rel. A.L. v. Lowrie, 2014-1025, p. 17 (La. 5/5/15), 167 So. 3d 573, 585 (finding that a legal father is entitled to have the court consider the income of an alleged biological father).

ordered to pay child support, and his obligation is not extinguished even if another man is conclusively proven to be the biological father of the child.[102]

As to the method of calculating support when there are two fathers, in *State ex rel. Wilson v. Wilson* the Louisiana Second Circuit Court of Appeal applied a "fictional father" model whereby the incomes of the child's presumed and biological fathers were combined to represent a fictional father in the worksheet.[103] Once the fictional father's income was determined, the court added it to the mother's income to create an adjusted monthly gross income.[104] After additions for health insurance premiums, the fictional father was assigned a monthly support obligation of $519.88.[105] Of the roughly $520 due, the biological father was assigned a 65% share based on his share of the total "fictional father" income, resulting in a monthly payment of $339.00.[106] The Second Circuit applauded the district court's ingenuity, finding the calculation to be within "the spirit of the guidelines" to "fairly apportion" the obligations of each parent.[107]

As to the final question, even after discovery of a biological father, Louisiana law does not permit a presumed father, who has been paying child support for another man's child, to recover reimbursement from the mother for payments previously made for the child. In *Gallo v. Gallo*, the Louisiana Supreme Court considered a presumed father's claims for reimbursement from the child's mother under Civil Code Article 2299, which provides that "[a] person who has received payment or a thing not owed to him is bound to restore it to the person from whom he received it."[108] The court explained that the funds were not wrongfully paid because the support payments, although made to the mother, were for the benefit of the child.[109] Therefore, she was not a person who received payment not owed to her and was under no obligation to refund the money.[110] "Fatherhood rests on something more than genes," explained the

102. *See* J.M.Y., 1 So. 3d at 728; *see also* Fontenot v. Thierry, 422 So. 2d 586, 590 (La. Ct. App. 3 Cir. 1982) (concluding that a child may recover child support from its biological father even though it is the presumed legitimate offspring of another man).

103. State ex rel. Wilson v. Wilson, 37,674, p. 4 (La. App. 2 Cir. 9/24/03), 855 So. 2d 913, 915 n.5.

104. Wilson, 855 So. 2d at 915.

105. Wilson, 855 So. 2d at 915 n.5.

106. Wilson, 855 So. 2d at 916.

107. Wilson, 855 So. 2d at 916; *see also* Dep't of Child. & Fam. Servs. ex rel. A.L., 167 So. 3d at 585 (finding that a legal father is entitled to have the court consider the income of an alleged biological father); Dep't of Soc. Servs. ex rel. P.B., 12-838 (La. App. 5 Cir. 4/24/13), 114 So. 3d 1161, 1167 (holding that award of child support in amount of $1,213.00 per month was appropriate under the child support guidelines, where child's biological father was responsible for 86% of amount of support for which "fictional father" was responsible under child support guidelines).

108. Gallo v. Gallo, 2003-0794, p. 10–12 (La. 12/3/03), 861 So. 2d 168, 175–77; La. Civ. Code Ann. art. 2299. Mr. Gallo also relied upon then existing Louisiana Revised Statues § 9:305(B); however, that argument was rejected based on statutory construction and interpretation. Gallo, 861 So. 2d at 175–76.

109. Gallo, 861 So. 2d at 178.

110. Gallo, 861 So. 2d at 178; *see also* D.K.P. v T.G.L., 2009-1385, p. 2 (La. App. 3 Cir. 3/24/10), 33 So. 3d 1006, 1008 (following *Gallo* and not allowing for reimbursement even though a factual determination could be made that the support payments were not used to benefit the child).

court, which went on to state that "[a] concomitant of the obligation of child support is the parental authority the father has over the child."[111]

Whether a court would permit a claim by the presumed father for reimbursement against the biological father seems unlikely but is not foreclosed. Although dual child support can be ordered from a presumed father and a biological father, it is uncertain whether a presumed father, who timely disavows, can collect reimbursement from the biological father for payments made prior to a judgment of disavowal. A claim seems unlikely given dicta by the Louisiana Supreme Court in *Gallo*,[112] and Louisiana Revised Statutes Section 9:402, which provides that disavowal "does not affect any child support payment or arrearages paid, due, or owing prior to the date the disavowal action was filed."[113] Undoubtedly, though, the biological father enjoys a level of unjust enrichment that seems untenable. Although one court found no cause of action under Louisiana law for a legal father to demand reimbursement from one "who has never been established to be the biological father,"[114] the question of reimbursement owed from the established biological father is yet unanswered.

§ 7:8 Duty of Support Generally— College Education

In Louisiana, a parent has no affirmative legal duty to support a child while in college.[115] Generally, child support terminates at the age of majority or emancipation, with three exceptions.[116] If a child is an unmarried, full-time student in good standing in a secondary school or its equivalent and is dependent on either parent, then child support can continue until the child reaches the age of 19 years.[117] Next, if a child has a developmental disability, as defined by statute, and is a full-time student in a secondary school, child support can continue until the child reaches the age of 22 years.[118] Third and finally, without any mention of school, an adult child with an intellectual or physical disability that manifested itself before the age of majority may receive child support indefinitely.[119]

"Secondary school" is not defined by statute, but courts have regarded the term as a school that is more advanced in grade than elementary school but is not a college

111. Gallo, 861 So. 2d at 178–79.

112. Gallo, 861 So. 2d at 176 (noting that even if a disavowal action is available, it does not affect any previously paid child support).

113. La. Stat. Ann. § 9:402.

114. J.M.Y., 1 So. 3d at 728.

115. *See, e.g.*, Miller v. Miller, 44,163, pp. 2–3 (La. App. 2 Cir. 1/14/09), 1 So. 3d 815, 817 ("Although most financially able parents willingly assist their adult children in obtaining a higher education, any duty to do so is a moral rather than a legal one, absent a binding contractual agreement by the parent to pay such support.").

116. *See* La. Stat. Ann. § 9:315.22.

117. La. Stat. Ann. § 9:315.22(C).

118. La. Stat. Ann. § 9:315.22(D). *See* La. Stat. Ann. § 28:451.2 (defining developmental disability).

119. La. Stat. Ann. § 9:315.22(E), as relocated to § 9:315.22.1 (2025).

or university.[120] Secondary schools offer general, technical, vocational, or college-preparatory courses.[121] In *Park v. Park*, the First Circuit found that a vocational-technical school where the child was seeking a high school equivalency diploma qualified as a secondary school.[122] In making its determination, the court gave "due consideration" to both the educational facility and the curriculum taught.[123] Relying on *Parks* and considering both the form and substance of the education, the Fourth Circuit in *Dwyer v. Blanque*, determined that a high school that awarded a child a Certificate of Achievement, rather than a high school diploma, was still a "secondary school" under the statute, such that child support could continue until the age of 19.[124] Finally, in *Summers v. Summers*, the First Circuit concluded that a special school for a major child who functioned at a one-year-old level was also considered a secondary school, such that the father was obligated to pay child support until the child reached the age of 22 years old.[125]

To argue that parents should provide support for college, litigants have relied on the reciprocal support obligation owed between parents and children when in need.[126] Courts have been unwilling, however, to find a major child "in need" as contemplated by the statute simply because he is in college. Under the articles governing reciprocal obligations, a child is "in need" if he is unable to support himself either by gainful

---

120. Park v. Park, 93-0115, p. 6 (La. Ct. App. 1 Cir. 3/30/94), 634 So. 2d 83, 86 (relying on Webster's Ninth New Collegiate Dictionary).

121. Park, 634 So. 2d at 86.

122. Park, 634 So. 2d at 86.

123. Park, 634 So. 2d at 86.

124. Dwyer v. Blanque, 95-2012, p. 6 (La. App. 4 Cir. 4/3/96), 671 So. 2d 567, 570. *See also* Basile v. Basile, 2004-25 (La. App. 3 Cir. 5/12/04), 872 So. 2d 1274 (determining that a "wilderness type experience" whereby children lived in the woods in primitive conditions and were taught by a certified teacher constituted a secondary school).

125. *See* Summers v. Summers, 2003-2562, p. 3 (La. App. 1 Cir. 10/29/04), 897 So. 2d 109, 110 ("[W]e conclude that to limit the definition of 'secondary school' to exclude support for a developmentally disabled child in a special school would lead to an absurd result defeating the purpose of [Louisiana Revised Statutes Section 9:315.22(D)]."). In *Billiot v. Billiot* the court determined that the College Living Experience (CLE) education program attended by the major child with Asperger's Syndrome did not satisfy the requirements of a full-time secondary school, explaining that the substance of the program, not the classification of the institution, was the determining factor in whether or not the program is considered a secondary education. Furthermore, the court cited both *Blanque* and *Summer*, noting that unlike the major child and secondary school in those cases, the CLE has no curriculum with standards against which students' performance is measured, has no academic component, and students do not work toward a measurable goal by receiving a valuable certificate. Because the child in *Billiot* had already obtained a high school diploma, did not attend the CLE full-time, and the CLE did not satisfy the requirements of secondary education, the parent's request for child support and reimbursement for education expenses for the CLE was denied. Billiot v. Billiot, 52,391, p. 9–11 (La. App. 2 Cir. 11/4/18), 262 So. 3d 401, 407–08.

126. La. Civ. Code Ann. art. 237 (formerly article 229, as amended Act No. 260, 2015 La. Acts 1794). Children have also relied on Civil Code Article 224, which obligates parents to continue the education of a child after minority as provided by law. La. Civ. Code Ann. art. 224. Comment (b) makes clear, however, that Louisiana Revised Statutes Section 9:315.22(C) and (D) are the "as provided by law" reference, which includes support for secondary school only. La. Civ. Code Ann. art. 224, cmt. (b).

employment or because he does not have property or other means sufficient for his support.[127] In most cases, although the 18- or 19-year-old will not have sufficient means to support himself, the child is capable of employment and is therefore not "in need."[128] In *Phillips v. Phillips*, a 22-year-old college student argued that, even with part-time employment, she was still left in need, but the court denied her request for additional support, concluding that "[t]he only reason that she is unable to work full-time is that she is attending college."[129]

When the age of majority in Louisiana was 21 years old,[130] courts obligated parents to pay for college education "where the parents [were] financially able to do so, and where the child's desire, ambition, capability, academic background and other circumstances indicate[d] college as a logical and necessary step in the complete education of the child."[131] Today, however, because the age of majority is 18[132] and support is available until age 19 only if the child is in secondary school,[133] court-ordered support for college education is unavailable.

Courts will, however, enforce binding contracts to pay for a major child's college education.[134] In fact, after the child reaches the age of majority, the agreement can only be enforced by the now-major child, unless the agreement is incorporated into a court order and gives the former spouse the right of action.[135] The language in the contract will govern the extent of the support obligation, and when faced with ambiguity, courts

---

127. Dubroc v. Dubroc, 284 So. 2d 869, 870 (La. Ct. App. 5 Cir. 1973).

128. *See, e.g.*, Fisher v. Fisher, 320 So. 2d 326, 329 (La. Ct. App. 3 Cir. 1975) (concluding that a major child may petition for support if he is in necessitous circumstances); Litel v. Litel, 490 So. 2d 741, 743 (La. Ct. App. 3 Cir. 1986) (noting that the duty to provide a college education to a major child does not operate as a natural obligation but instead operates only in a moral sense, much like the duty of exercising gratitude or charity); Vorisek v. Vorisek, 423 So. 2d 758, 765 (La. Ct. App. 4 Cir. 1982) (placing the burden on the three major children to prove their need for support, as the law does not force a parent to contribute to an adult child's education; noting too that a parent's voluntary payments to his major children are not expenses for purposes of determining spousal support); Phillips v. Phillips, 399 So. 2d 1299, 1301 (La. Ct. App. 1 Cir. 1976) (finding that a major child who is in school but capable of working is not, by the mere fact of schooling, in need of support).

129. Phillips, 399 So. 2d at 1300. Addressing the responsibility of a father, the court stated, "While we might be inclined to think a father worthy of the name will always generously support and encourage his child's reasonable educational ambitions, the law wisely leaves his generosity as a matter between him and his own conscience. The law declines to force a parent to contribute to his adult child's education or to give support to his adult child who is capable of self-support." *Id.* at 1301–02.

130. La. Civ. Code art. 37 (1870) (repealed by Act No. 125, 1987 La. Acts 412–18).

131. Pettitt v. Pettitt, 261 So. 2d 687, 689 (La. Ct. App. 2 Cir. 1972); *see also* Fellows v. Fellows, 267 So. 2d 572, 575 (La. Ct. App. 3 Cir. 1972). In dicta in *Hines v. Hines*, the court cited *Pettitt* as authority for the proposition that support can extend to education beyond high school, but the children in that case were only 16 and 13 years old and support for college education was not at issue. Hines v. Hines, 419 So. 2d 971, 972–73 (La. Ct. App. 3 Cir. 1982).

132. La. Civ. Code Ann. art. 29.

133. La. Stat. Ann. § 9:315.22(C).

134. Miller, 1 So. 3d at 819; Gray v. Gray, 37,884, p. 4 (La. App. 2 Cir. 12/12/03), 862 So. 2d 1097, 1100.

135. Jackson v. Jackson, 275 So. 2d 456 (La. Ct. App. 3 Cir. 1973) (right to bring action to collect child support after the child is a major belongs to the child alone); Hogan v. Hogan, 465 So. 2d 73, 78

will construe the contract against the party who prepared it.[136] Careful drafting of provisions governing higher education support are necessary to ensure that the obligation is carried out.[137]

Additionally, under the Child Support Guidelines, a spendthrift trust is now available for high-income-earning parents to save for the child's college education. Under Louisiana Revised Statutes Section 9:315.13(C)(2), if the combined adjusted gross income of the parents exceeds the highest level on the Child Support Guidelines,[138] the court has authority to order that a portion of the child support awarded be placed in a spendthrift trust for the educational or medical needs of the child.[139] The trust must terminate when the child reaches the age of 24, unless the parties agree to a later date.[140]

Some states have passed legislation to permit child support to extend into the college years, recognizing that the economic consequences of divorce on a child do not end at high school.[141] Legislation has varied from general to very specific, placing requirements on the parents and the child in an attempt to strike a balance between support for a child and autonomy of the parents.[142] Although Louisiana has yet to pass legislation mandating support for college, through the use of the spendthrift trust it has provided an option for parents of means to ensure that monies will be available for the child for post-secondary education.[143] And, of course, parents are free to contractually agree to continue support for their children through college.

(La. Ct. App. 5 Cir. 1985) (permitting the ex-spouse the right of action to collect post-majority support because the agreement was incorporated into a court order that gave the ex-spouse the right of action).

136. La. Civ. Code Ann. art. 2056 ("In case of doubt that cannot be otherwise resolved, a provision in a contract must be interpreted against the party who furnished its text. A contract executed in standard form of one party must be interpreted, in case of doubt, in favor of the other party."); Campbell v. Melton, 2001-2578, pp. 6–7 (La. 5/14/02), 817 So. 2d 69, 75.

137. *See* Robert C. Lowe, 1 La. Prac. Divorce 8:11 (2022).

138. Currently, the highest level is $50,000 per month in adjusted gross income. La. Stat. Ann. § 9:315.19.

139. La. Stat. Ann. § 9:315.13(C)(2).

140. La. Stat. Ann. § 9:315.13(C)(2).

141. For a survey of state laws sanctioning higher education support, see Monica Hof Wallace, *A Federal Referendum: Extending Child Support for Higher Education*, 58 U. Kan. L. Rev. 665 (2010).

142. Monica Hof Wallace, *A Federal Referendum: Extending Child Support for Higher Education*, 58 U. Kan. L. Rev. 666–67 (2010).

143. Monica Hof Wallace, *A Federal Referendum: Extending Child Support for Higher Education*, 58 U. Kan. L. Rev. 697 (2010) (suggesting legislation to adequately protect children and parents).

§ 7:9 Duty of Support Generally—Reciprocal Support for Parents and Children

As a corollary to Louisiana's age-based support rules, a family member's difficulty to provide for life's necessities obligates ascendants and, uniquely, descendants to offer financial support. [144] Louisiana Civil Code Article 237 provides that "[d]escendants are bound to provide the basic necessities of life to their ascendants who are in need, upon proof of [the ascendants'] inability to obtain these necessities by other means or from other sources."[145] This obligation is reciprocal and, therefore, binds ascendants to provide descendants with these same necessities.[146] The necessities considered under this article are "limited to the basic necessities of food, clothing, shelter, and health care."[147] The obligation is owed in order of the degree of relationship to the obligee, and if the obligee is married, the obligation owed by his ascendants and descendants is secondary to the obligation owed by his spouse.[148] Any amount of support owed "shall be determined" in accordance with the needs of the obligee and the means of the obligor.[149] A court may subsequently modify the amount of support owed based on a

144. For a detailed discussion of this obligation, *see* Chapter 9, Sections 9:15–9:19.

145. La. Civ. Code Ann. art. 237 (formerly cited as La. Civ. Code Ann. art. 229).

146. La. Civ. Code Ann. art. 237 cmt. a. The obligation imposed by this article continues past a descendant's reaching the age of majority. Ramos v. Ramos, 425 So. 2d 989, 992 (La. Ct. App. 5 Cir. 1983) ("reciprocal alimentary duties of ascendants and descendants, continues past minority, as long as the party seeking it is in need"); Howell v. Howell, 391 So. 2d 1304, 1307 (La. Ct. App. 4 Cir. 1980) ("the obligation of support does not terminate by operation of law when a child reaches the age of majority").

147. La. Civ. Code Ann. art. 237. This article provides only for the basic necessities of life, which are explicitly limited by its terms to "food, clothing, shelter, and health care." La. Civ. Code Ann. art. 237 cmt. (a) (rev. cmt. 2015). *See* Suire v. Miller, 363 So. 2d 945, 948–49 (La. Ct. App. 3 Cir. 1978) (stating that the article is a "less onerous burden" and "does not include education or other special expenses of a minor's rearing").

148. La. Civ. Code Ann. art. 237. The parental obligation of support primes a grandparent's obligation to provide support under article 237. *See* Banquer v. Banquer, 554 So. 2d 790, 793 (La. Ct. App. 5 Cir. 1989) (stating that these provisions, when used to seek support from ascendants, should be "used sparingly and as a last resort; and only when attempts at parental support have been exhausted; and only for the basic necessities of life"); Landeche v. Airhart, 372 So. 2d 598, 600 (La. Ct. App. 4 Cir. 1979) (stating that the paternal obligation primes the obligation of ascendants and setting a three-part test when seeking support from grandparents which requires a showing of: (1) "need" on behalf of the grandchildren; (2) the "ability of the grandparent to pay support;" and (3) that the requesting parent(s) cannot obtain work, "including reasonable extra work ... which would prevent the children from being in need or lessen the amount of that need"); Levy v. Levy, 536 So. 2d 742, 745 (La. Ct. App. 3 Cir. 1988) (finding the nature of the alimentary obligation to differ from a parental obligation and holding that the grandparents owed no duty of support because caring for a child's best interest is "fundamentally a parental responsibility" which "does not shift to the grandparents simply when the father is not supporting his children").

149. La. Civ. Code Ann. art. 238. This article incorporates the provisions of Article 231 of the 1870 Louisiana Civil Code. La. Civ. Code Ann. art. 238 cmt. (a) (rev. cmt. 2015).

material change in circumstances of the obligor or obligee or terminate the support if it becomes unnecessary.[150]

The obligee must prove an inability to obtain the necessities by other means or from other sources,[151] including public assistance,[152] or the obligee's other capital resources and earning capacity.[153] To demonstrate need, one must be able to prove that he is unable to provide for his support, either due to a physical or mental impairment or because one has no means sufficient to meet the basic necessities.[154] If the individual is capable of gainful employment, then he must work, and support is unavailable under article 237.[155]

Although the basic necessities for which an obligation is owed are defined in Civil Code Article 237, the level of necessities required is determined on a case-by-case basis, based on need.[156] When considering the needs of a severely disabled woman, the court in *In re Tutorship of Blanque* noted the additional levels of support that might be necessary in her case.[157] In *Blanque*, "clothing" as a necessity encompassed more than just the articles of clothing themselves, but also included her need for assistance to get dressed.[158] Similarly, the woman's need for "shelter" expanded beyond "a protected environment" to include the additional expense of modifications based on her disabil-

150. La. Civ. Code Ann. art. 239. This article incorporates the provisions of Article 232 of the 1870 Louisiana Civil Code. La. Civ. Code Ann. art. 239 cmt. (rev. cmt. 2015). *See* Hester v. Hester, 2003-1259, p. 4 (La. App. 4 Cir. 4/14/04), 874 So. 2d 859, 861–62 (reducing support award after obligee obtained full-time employment and became eligible to receive health benefits as an employee but still required support because monthly gross pay was insufficient to support a severely disabled adult suffering from Tourette's syndrome, obsessive-compulsive disorder, and Asperger's disease).

151. *See* Banquer, 554 So. 2d at 793 (finding grandchildren were not in need and that the paternal grandparents owed no obligation when grandchildren were provided with the basic necessities by mother and voluntary support from maternal grandparents).

152. La. Civ. Code Ann. art. 237 cmt. (d) (rev. cmt. 2015).

153. La. Civ. Code Ann. art. 237 cmt. (c).

154. *See* Hester, 874 So. 2d at 862 (noting that there is nothing contained in the statute or case law requiring a party to be "completely disabled or entirely unemployable" to qualify for support); Suire v. Miller, 363 So. 2d 945 (La. Ct. App. 3 Cir. 1978) (awarding support to daughter, emancipated through marriage, after showing necessitous circumstances based on her inability to find employment based on her age (16 years old) and lack of education, creating a situation in which she is "almost unemployable").

155. *See* Dubroc v. Dubroc, 284 So. 2d 869, 871 (La. Ct. App. 5 Cir. 1973) (holding that major child, although still in high school, is not entitled to receive support and is not in need as she "is mentally and physically able to work for a living, to secure, for herself, that means of support"); Phillips, 399 So. 2d at 1301–02 (holding major child not in need when college attendance prevented her from working full-time, but was "fully capable of supporting herself within the contemplation of the law").

156. *See* In re Tutorship of Blanque, 97-249, p. 7 (La. App. 5 Cir. 9/30/97), 700 So. 2d 1077, 1080 ("a more restrictive reading of the statute might be given in a different case where the child in question was a more healthy, more self-sufficient adult"); Hester, 874 So. 2d at 861 (requiring, before determining entitlement to support, a court to understand the claimant's necessities and "[e]ach case must be considered on its own facts").

157. *See* In re Tutorship of Blanque, 700 So. 2d at 1081.

158. In re Tutorship of Blanque, 700 So. 2d at 1081.

ity.[159] Because the woman's needs were "far different from and greater than those of a less disabled person," she required and deserved a correspondingly greater award.[160]

Prior law included not only payment for necessities, but alternatively, the obligation to receive the obligee-relative into the home when the obligor-relative was unable to furnish monetary support.[161] In the revision of 2015, this provision was removed.[162]

§ 7:10 Child Support Guidelines Generally

Louisiana follows the income shares model, which uses the percentage of parental net income to assign a share of support required for children in an intact family, while taking into account additional expenses necessary for that particular child.[163] The guidelines were enacted in 1989 to address two issues: inconsistency in the amounts of child support awards and inadequacy of awards granted.[164] Because each parent owes a duty of support and must contribute in proportion to their resources, the income shares model combines the adjusted monthly gross income of both parties to determine the amount of support awarded.[165] By combining the adjusted monthly gross income of both parents, the guidelines attempt to fairly apportion the mutual financial obligation between the parents in an "efficient, consistent, and adequate manner."[166]

Recognizing the adverse impact of inconsistent and inadequate child support awards, Congress enacted the Child Support Enforcement Amendments of 1984, which encouraged states to develop child support guidelines and pursue stronger enforcement actions.[167] Encouragement shifted to a mandate just a few years later when Congress enacted the Family Support Act of 1988, which required states to create a

---

159. In re Tutorship of Blanque, 700 So. 2d at 1081 (In this case, the woman resided in a home specially designed to fit her orthopedic needs). The court also made the same determination with regards to health care and understood that based on the level of disability of the woman, her expenses may be greater than that of a lesser disabled adult.

160. In re Tutorship of Blanque, 700 So. 2d at 1081.

161. La. Civ. Code Ann. art. 233, repealed by Act No. 260, 2015 La. Acts 1794 ("If the person, whose duty it is to furnish alimony, shall prove that he is unable to pay the same, the judge may, after examining into the case, order that such person shall receive in his house, and there support and maintain the person to whom he owes alimony."). The substance of former article 233 was not reproduced elsewhere in the 2015 revision.

162. Act No. 260, 2015 La. Acts 1807.

163. La. Stat. Ann. § 9:315(A). Guidelines for the determination of child support are located in Louisiana Revised Statutes Sections 9:315 through 9:315.20. *See* La. Stat. Ann. §§ 9:315–315.20.

164. Sue Nations, *Louisiana's Child Support Guideline: A Preliminary Analysis*, 50 La. L. Rev. 1057, 1058 (1990); *see also* Stogner v. Stogner, 98-3044, p. 6 (La. 7/7/99), 739 So. 2d 762, 766.

165. Stogner, 739 So. 2d at 766 (citing Hogan v. Hogan, 549 So. 2d 267 (La. 1989)); *see also* Percle v. Noll, 634 So. 2d 498, 503 (La. Ct. App. 1 Cir. 1994) (the amount determined by the guideline formula is presumed to be in the child's best interest).

166. Stogner, 739 So. 2d at 766–67 (citing State ex rel. Travers, 28,022 (La. App. 2 Cir. 12/6/95), 665 So. 2d 625).

167. Sue Nations, *Louisiana's Child Support Guideline: A Preliminary Analysis*, 50 La. L. Rev. 1057, 1057–58 (1990). *See also* Child Support Enforcement Amendments 1984, Pub. L. No. 98-378, § 18(a), 98 Stat. 1305, 1321–22 (1984).

feasible and presumptively correct schedule of child support guidelines.[168] States failing to enact numerical guidelines ran the risk of losing millions of dollars in federal funding through public assistance programs.[169] As a result, the new child support guidelines became effective in Louisiana on October 1, 1989.[170]

§ 7:11 Calculations of Income

The benchmark of the income shares model is the income of both parents. "Gross income" from both parents is used as the starting point to determine the basic child support obligation.[171] Gross income is listed on the first line of the worksheets[172] and includes income from any source, expense reimbursements, or in-kind payments, as well as net self-employment income.[173] The guidelines provide limited exclusions from the comprehensive definition of gross income.[174] If a parent is unemployed or not employed at full capacity, potential income is included as gross income.[175] Further, the court may also consider expense sharing as income.[176] Subtracted from gross income are child and spousal support obligations owed under an order of support, as well as extrajudicial payments of child support for those who are not a party to the proceeding, resulting in an "adjusted gross income."[177] The parties' adjusted gross incomes are combined and then used to calculate each parent's proportionate share of the combined amount.[178] The resulting figure (percentage of combined adjusted gross income) is ultimately used to determine the share of the child support obligation owed by each.

§ 7:12 Calculations of Income— Gross Income: Income from Any Source

The first and most comprehensive definition of gross income includes "income from any source." The statute provides a non-exhaustive list of income sources:

---

168. Sue Nations, *Louisiana's Child Support Guideline: A Preliminary Analysis*, 50 La. L. Rev. 1057, 1058 (1990); Christopher L. Blakesly, *Louisiana Family Law—Child Support*, 52 La. L. Rev. 607, 609 (1992); *see* The Family Support Act of 1988, Pub. L. No. 100-485, § 103, 102 Stat. 2343 (1998).

169. Sue Nations, *Louisiana's Child Support Guideline: A Preliminary Analysis*, 50 La. L. Rev. 1057, 1058 (1990) (citation omitted).

170. *See* Sue Nations, *Louisiana's Child Support Guideline: A Preliminary Analysis*, 50 La. L. Rev. 1057, 1058 (1990) (citing Act No. 9, 1989 La. Acts 2563–75 (codified as amended at Louisiana Revised Statutes Sections 9:315–315.14 (Supp. 1990)); Christopher L. Blakesly, *Louisiana Family Law—Child Support*, 52 La. L. Rev. 607, 609 (1992).

171. *See* La. Stat. Ann. § 9:315.20.

172. La. Stat. Ann. § 9:315.20.

173. La. Stat. Ann. § 9:315(3)(a)–(c).

174. La. Stat. Ann. § 9:315(C)(3)(d).

175. La. Stat. Ann. § 9:315(C)(5)(b).

176. La. Stat. Ann. § 9:315(C)(5)(c).

177. La. Stat. Ann. § 9:315(C)(1).

178. La. Stat. Ann. § 9:315.2(C).

(a) [t]he income from any source, including but not limited to salaries, wages, commissions, bonuses, dividends, severance pay, pensions, interest, trust income, recurring monetary gifts, annuities, capital gains, social security benefits, workers' compensation benefits, basic and variable allowances for housing and subsistence from military pay and benefits, unemployment insurance benefits, disaster unemployment assistance received from the United States Department of Labor, disability insurance benefits, and spousal support received from a preexisting spousal support obligation.[179]

The Louisiana Supreme Court has recognized that the wording "including but not limited to" is inclusive and expansive.[180] For example, even before a military member's "basic and variable allowances for housing and subsistence" were expressly included in the definition, the Louisiana Supreme Court found a servicemember's Basic Allowance for Housing (BAH) and Basic Allowance for Subsistence (BAS) to be income.[181] Shortly thereafter, the legislature amended the definition of "gross income" to conform to the court's 2006 decision.[182]

Because the definition of gross income is inclusive, the categories of income are practically endless. The following represent select categories of income specifically considered by courts.

179. La. Stat. Ann. § 9:315(C)(3)(a). Revised Statutes § 9:315(C)(3)(d) provides an exhaustive list of income sources which are not part of the "gross income" calculation and will be discussed further in Sections 7:24–7:29. *See id.*

180. Dep't of Soc. Servs. ex rel. D.F. v. L.T., 2005-1965, p. 7 (La. 7/6/06), 934 So. 2d 687, 691.

181. La. Stat. Ann. § 9:315(C)(3)(a); Dep't of Soc. Servs. ex rel. D.F., 934 So. 2d at 693–94.

182. Act No. 481, 2006 La. Acts 1920–22.

§ 7:13 Calculations of Income— Gross Income: Income from Any Source— Bonuses

Including bonuses in a party's gross income is within the trial court's discretion.[183] Because bonuses are statutorily part of the definition of income, if bonuses exist, they must be considered.[184] To determine whether to include a bonus as income, though, courts look at the consistency of the bonuses received[185] and the amount of the bonus compared to the recipient's base income.[186] Annual bonuses are routinely included, even if the bonus is not paid monthly and is not guaranteed.[187] When the bonus is irregular and can be classified as "extraordinary overtime," the funds should be excluded from gross income.[188]

§ 7:14 Calculations of Income— Gross Income: Income from Any Source— Recurring Monetary Gifts

Recurring monetary gifts are also included in the statutory list of income items,[189] but courts are unlikely to include them based on the testimony of the opposing party alone. Instead, courts require proof that the monetary gift is provided with some consistency and regularity. The Third Circuit in *Barlow v. Barlow* found that contributions by family and friends of the mother when she needed assistance did not constitute recurring monetary gifts without any evidence but the testimony of the father.[190] In addition, in *Frederick v. Buckingham*, the Second Circuit refused to consider the financial assistance provided by the mother's family as a recurring monetary gift.[191] The aunt and grandmother assisted the single mother with her college expenses and had given

---

183. *See* Patrick v. Patrick, 34,799, pp. 9–11 (La. App. 2 Cir. 4/4/01), 785 So. 2d 169, 175–76 (recognizing the potential problems associated with large year-end bonuses and attributing them as income and providing examples of ways trial courts have used their discretion to set support awards based on bonuses).

184. Earle v. Earle, 43,925, p. 7 (La. App. 2 Cir. 12/3/08), 998 So. 2d 828, 834 (finding that the trial court abused its discretion in failing to consider the bonus received by the obligor parent).

185. *See* Gary v. LeBlanc, 2016-1054, p. 12 (La. App. 3 Cir. 6/7/17), 222 So. 3d 784, 792 (upholding use of year-end bonus in income calculation because bonus was not a large bonus nearly equal to the normal monthly income and there was no evidence presented that the bonuses were sporadic or subject to cancellation).

186. Earle, 998 So. 2d at 834 (recalculating child support obligation and including year-end bonus because it was not so large compared to obligor's salary that he would be in a precarious financial position even if the bonus was not issued again the following year).

187. *See, e.g.*, Herman v. Zatzkis, 632 So. 2d 307, 318 (La. Ct. App. 4 Cir. 1993); Gary, 222 So. 3d at 792.

188. La. Stat. Ann. § 9:315(C)(3)(d)(iii); *see* Section 7:24 Exclusions from Gross Income.

189. La. Stat. Ann. § 9:315(C)(3)(a).

190. Barlow v. Barlow, 2011-1286, p. 15 (La. App. 3 Cir. 4/11/12), 87 So. 3d 386, 395.

191. Frederick v. Buckingham, 44,458, p. 5 (La. App. 2 Cir. 6/24/09), 15 So. 3d 1223, 1226.

her a car while she pursued higher education.[192] The court found that the aid did not qualify as income to the mother because it was provided immediately after the birth of her child.[193]

§ 7:15 Calculations of Income—Gross Income: Income from Any Source—Personal Injury Settlement

Income from a personal injury settlement is not specifically referenced in the list of income items in section 315(C)(3)(a). Courts have, however, considered settlement funds to be income in the child support calculation, but only after the settlement funds have been received by the parent.[194] For example, in *Guidry v. Guidry*, the Third Circuit reversed the trial court's approach to use as income the average of the total amount of settlement funds to be received in five-year intervals, because the parent had not yet collected the funds.[195] Although the Third Circuit approved of classifying the funds as income, it required actual disbursement before the settlement could affect child support.[196]

When settlement funds are paid to one parent in a lump sum, courts are unlikely to classify the funds as income, but the funds could be used by the other parent to request a deviation. For example, in *Department of Social Services ex rel. P.B. v. Reed*, the parent received and immediately used settlement funds to pay down a home loan and bills that accrued while she was not working.[197] The court found no reason to reclassify that capital infusion as income to modify the child support order.[198] Likewise, in *Kelly v. Kelly*, the court refused to consider a lump sum settlement as income, explaining that any interest or return from the settlement funds should be considered as income, but the funds themselves are not recurring.[199] Rather, a lump sum settlement could justify a deviation from the guideline amount.[200] These decisions are in accord with the treatment of other lump sum payments, like life insurance, which courts have considered capital, rather than income, and are excluded from income for child support purposes.[201]

---

192. Frederick, 15 So. 3d at 1226.

193. Frederick, 15 So. 3d at 1226.

194. Guidry v. Guidry, 2008-1166, pp. 3–4 (La. App. 3 Cir. 2/4/09), 6 So. 3d 845, 847.

195. Guidry, 6 So. 3d at 846–47.

196. Guidry, 6 So. 3d at 847.

197. Dep't of Soc. Servs. ex rel. P.B. v. Reed, 16-171, p. 15 (La. App. 5 Cir. 7/27/16), 197 So. 3d 817, 828.

198. Dep't of Soc. Servs. ex rel. P.B., 197 So. 3d at 828 (finding that lump sum settlement funds that were used to pay down a home loan and other expenses that accrued while the parent could not work did not constitute a change in circumstance to justify a modification in child support).

199. Kelly v. Kelly, 1999-2478, pp. 9–10 (La. App. 1 Cir. 12/22/00), 775 So. 2d 1237, 1243–44, *overruled on other grounds by* Salles v. Salles, 2004-1449 (La. App. 1 Cir. 12/2/05), 928 So. 2d 1.

200. Kelly, 775 So. 2d at 1244.

201. Guy v. Guy, 600 So. 2d 771, 773 (La. Ct. App. 5 Cir. 1992).

In the opinion of the authors, if the settlement funds are used to compensate for the recipient's lost wages, however, it may be more appropriate to classify the funds, once received, as income. But if the funds are used to reimburse damage to property, classifying those funds as income would not be appropriate. Pain and suffering damages may be harder to classify, but if those funds are used for basic living expenses, they could provide a substitute for traditional income. Finally, how the personal injury settlement is paid may have an impact on how the funds are treated for child support purposes. Undoubtedly, payments made over time are more likely to be classified as income, while a single lump sum payment looks more like an infusion of capital, which could either generate income or justify a deviation.

§ 7:16 Calculations of Income— Gross Income: Income from Any Source— Capital Gains, Pensions, and Annuities

Capital gains, pensions, and annuities are included in the definition of gross income,[202] but courts have been reluctant to include lump-sum amounts if they are not ongoing sources of income.[203] Although courts have discretion to include the funds as income in the year in which they are received or to distribute the funds over multiple years if the funds are non-recurring,[204] some courts have failed to classify payments as income, relying instead on the other parent to assert community property rights to the funds.[205] If, however, capital gains are produced on a transaction that generates no cash, the capital gains are appropriately excluded from income.[206] To determine whether to include distributions as income, courts generally examine whether the funds are in the

202. La. Stat. Ann. § 9:315(C)(3)(a).

203. *See, e.g.*, Rutland v. Rutland, 13-70, p. 11 (La. App. 5 Cir. 7/30/13), 121 So. 3d 776, 782 (noting that the funds father received from the withdrawal of his pension and capital gains received from the sale of his house were not ongoing sources of income on the date child support was established and therefore the trial court did not abuse its discretion by not including the funds in the award calculation).

204. *See, e.g.*, Robichaux v. Robichaux, 2004-162, p. 7 (La. App. 3 Cir. 6/2/04), 879 So. 2d 279, 283–84 (finding that the trial court properly included divorced father's capital gains, an IRA distribution, and his pension in the year in which the funds were received contrary to the father's argument that they should be distributed among several years).

205. *See, e.g.*, Rutland, 121 So. 3d at 782.

206. Farrar v. Farrar, 2000-1487, pp. 3–4 (La. App. 4 Cir. 7/11/01), 791 So. 2d 796, 798–99 (concluding that father's capital gain income was not to be included in calculating father's gross income for child support purposes because capital gains that occurred after father transferred retirement assets from mutual funds into a retirement annuity created no readily available funds).

control of the recipient,[207] readily accessible to the recipient,[208] and "an ongoing source of income"[209] for the recipient. For example, in *Bullock v. Bullock*, the Third Circuit held that the trial court properly excluded a mother's earnings from her Individual Retirement Account (IRA) because the earnings were not yet available to her and the mother had not withdrawn funds from the account.[210]

§ 7:17 Calculations of Income— Gross Income: Income from Any Source— Trust Income

Trust income is included in the statutory list of gross income items.[211] Even undistributed trust income can be treated as income if a prior history of distributions exists before the filing of the child support proceedings.[212] In *Kern v. Kern*, the Louisiana Fourth Circuit included as the mother's income distributions from her family trust, which provided for the children's support "in their accustomed manners of living."[213] The mother argued that the prior withdrawals were not used for living expenses but were used as a partial down payment on a home.[214] The court explained that the mother was the trustee of the trust and had absolute discretion to distribute funds at any time and for whatever purpose she deemed appropriate, so it should be included as income to her.[215] The court did, however, reverse the trial court's decision to impute additional income to the mother for "undermanaging" the trust fund by failing to invest the principal in higher yielding accounts.[216] Given the inherently personal decisions regarding investment strategy and risk, the court appropriately avoided extending underemployment or unemployment principles to investment choices in trust.

---

207. *See* Melancon v. Melancon, 2007-0576, p. 1 (La. App. 1 Cir. 11/2/07), 2007 WL 3227189 (finding that capital gains that were reinvested back into a closely held company and were never received, neither of which were in the mother's control, were not included in the gross income calculation; court ordered the matter reviewed every six months to determine if any distributions have been received by the mother).

208. Robichaux, So. 2d at 283–84; *see also* Bullock v. Bullock, 98-0263, p. 8 (La. App. 3 Cir. 8/19/98), 719 So. 2d 113, 117.

209. Rutland, 121 So. 3d at 779; *but see* Tuft v. Tuft, 51-293, pp. 11–12 (La. App. 2 Cir. 1/18/17), 2017 WL 4341309 (including the mother's nonrecurring capital gain as income for child support purposes).

210. Bullock, 719 So. 2d at 117; *see also* Jones v. Jones, 628 So. 2d 1304, 1306 (La. Ct. App. 3 Cir. 1993) (refusing to include funds allocated to wife in estate planning agreement, although the accumulated interest, dividends, etc., were taxed as her income).

211. La. Stat. Ann. § 9:315(C)(3)(a).

212. Bagwell v. Bagwell, 35,728, pp. 14–16 (La. App. 2 Cir. 3/8/02), 812 So. 2d 854, 866–67; Kern v. Kern, 2000-1126, pp. 5–6 (La. App. 4 Cir. 4/25/01), 786 So. 2d 193, 197.

213. Kern, 786 So. 2d at 197.

214. Kern, 786 So. 2d at 197.

215. Kern, 786 So. 2d at 197.

216. Kern, 786 So. 2d at 197.

Note, too, that if the child is the named beneficiary of the trust, trust income can also be included as income for the child, which reduces the obligation of the parent.[217] For example, in *Stelly v. Stelly*, distributions of income from a trust were treated as income to the child and used to reduce the child support obligation owed by the parents when the trust was funded with life insurance to benefit the child.[218] The court considered it relevant that the terms of the trust permitted annual distributions for the child's health, education, maintenance, or support, that the trustee had been making distributions to the child, and that the distributions had been reducing the child's basic needs.[219]

§ 7:18 Calculations of Income— Gross Income: Income from Any Source— Social Security Benefits

Social Security benefits are included in the statutory list of gross income.[220] Social Security benefits can relate to retirement as well as to disability and, when paid to a parent, constitute income.[221] Note, however, that "supplemental security income (SSI)" is expressly excluded from a parent's gross income because that benefit is needs-based, rather than funded through earnings, even though both types of disbursements are administered by the Social Security Administration.[222]

Additionally, a Social Security benefit paid to a child because of the earnings of a parent may be considered income of the child at the discretion of the court.[223] If the court chooses to include the benefits as income, the amount can only be credited against the share of child support owed by the parent on whose earnings record the benefit is based.[224] For example, in *Todtenbier v. Todtenbier*, a Social Security Administration payment to a daughter based on her mother's disability and earnings was applied as a credit against the obligation of the mother, rather than as a deduction from

---

217. See Section 7:41 for discussion on deductions for income of a child.

218. Stelly v. Stelly, 2002-113, p. 4 (La. App. 3 Cir. 6/26/02), 820 So. 2d 1270, 1273.

219. Stelly, 820 So. 2d at 1273.

220. La. Stat. Ann. § 9:315(C)(3)(a).

221. *See* Richard v. Richard, 2005-0798, p. 7 (La. App. 4 Cir. 4/12/06), 930 So. 2d 156, 161.

222. La. Stat. Ann. § 9:315(C)(3)(d)(i); *see also* Richard, 930 So. 2d at 161 (excluding the father's supplemental security income benefits from his income for child support purposes and excluding the money mother received from Social Security as a result of their son's learning disability as it was also characterized as supplemental security income). Determining whether benefits are Social Security or SSI is not an easy task, as many people who are eligible for SSI are also eligible for Social Security benefits. *See* U.S. Social Security Administration, https://www.ssa.gov/ssi/text-entitle-ussi.htm (last visited May 28, 2024).

223. La. Stat. Ann. § 9:315.7(D); *see* Section 7:25 for further discussion on Social Security benefits.

224. La. Stat. Ann. § 9:315.7(D). Because of the permissive language in the statute, a court is not required to treat the payments as income of the child. *See* Rougeau v. Rougeau, 2002-484, p. 4 (La. App. 3 Cir. 10/30/02), 829 So. 2d 1125, 1127 (refusing to treat the Social Security funds paid to the child as income).

the basic support obligation of both the mother and father, because the mother was the sole basis for the Social Security benefits.[225] The mandate that the credit be given to the parent on whose earnings the social security benefits are based originated in a 2006 amendment to Section 9:316.7 of the Louisiana Revised Statutes,[226] which legislatively overruled prior cases that allowed the benefits paid to a child to offset the total amount of child support due by both parents.[227]

Keep in mind, though, that the decision to treat a Social Security benefit paid to the child as income of the child is within the sound discretion of the trial court.[228] Some courts have even allowed a credit against arrearages for monthly Social Security benefits that exceed the obligation owed by the parent.[229] Note, however, that after the 2006 amendment, a court must hold an evidentiary hearing before reducing any arrearage with payments made to the child.[230]

§ 7:19 Calculations of Income— Gross Income: Income from Any Source— Lottery or Gaming Proceeds

Lottery or gaming proceeds are not included in the list of income in section 315(C)(3)(a). However, in *Green v. Scott*, the Second Circuit considered lottery proceeds as gross income for purposes of calculating a father's child support obligation, even though the proceeds represented an unearned flow of funds in the nature of a prize.[231] Because the father received his lottery winnings in 20 annual installments, the court analogized the annual payment of the prize to an annuity, trust income, or capital gain—all of which are included in the statutory definition of income.[232] Likewise, in *Bagwell v. Bagwell*, the Second Circuit found that the father's gambling winnings, as offset by proven gambling losses, were properly characterized as gross income for child support purposes.[233]

---

225. *See* Todtenbier v. Todtenbier, 2010-0304, p. 7 (La. App. 1 Cir. 10/27/10), 48 So. 3d 413, 418; Dep't of Child. & Fam. Servs. ex rel. Jones v. Peters, 2014-1800, p. 4 (La. App. 1 Cir. 6/5/15), 174 So. 3d 1200, 1202.

226. Act No. 386, 2006 La. Acts 1606.

227. *See, e.g.*, Camacho v. Camacho, 2006-330, p. 5 (La. App. 3 Cir. 9/27/06), 940 So. 2d 190, 197.

228. Rougeau, 829 So. 2d at 1127 (refusing to treat the Social Security funds paid to the child as income); *see also* Hall v. Hall, 617 So. 2d 204, 205 (La. Ct. App. 3 Cir. 1993) (considering only one-half of the children's benefits as income that would be credited against the child support payment).

229. *See, e.g.*, McCloud v. McCloud, 544 So. 2d 764, 767 (La. Ct. App. 3 Cir. 1989); *see also* Faul v. Faul, 548 So. 2d 957, 961 (La. Ct. App. 3 Cir. 1989).

230. La. Stat. Ann. § 9:315.7(E).

231. Green v. Scott, 29,197, p. 2 (La. App. 2 Cir. 1/22/97), 687 So. 2d 655, 658.

232. Green, 687 So. 2d at 658.

233. Bagwell v. Bagwell, 35,728, pp. 14–16 (La. App. 2 Cir. 3/8/02), 812 So. 2d 854, 861.

§ 7:20 Calculations of Income— Gross Income: Income from Any Source— Spousal Support from a Preexisting Spousal Support Obligation

Included as income is any preexisting spousal support paid to a parent from a former spouse who is not a party to the current child support proceedings.[234] The Second Circuit made clear that current spousal support payments made to the spouse who is a party to the child support proceeding is not included as income for purposes of child support.[235] In many instances, support from a prior spouse will not be an issue. Because spousal support obligations are generally extinguished upon the obligee spouse's remarriage,[236] having a "preexisting spousal support obligation" when there is a subsequent marriage would be rare.[237] By contrast, with no subsequent marriage, preexisting spousal support awards may be more prevalent. When an unmarried parent receives spousal support from a former spouse, those payments constitute income to that parent in child support litigation with the other parent.

§ 7:21 Calculations of Income— Gross Income: Income from Any Source— Military Pay and Benefits

Basic and variable allowances for housing and subsistence from military pay and benefits are included in the statutory definition of gross income.[238] Prior to being included in the statutory definition in 2006, military allowances were included by Louisiana courts when it was clear that the parent financially benefitted from the allowance.[239] Veterans Affairs disability benefits[240] and income from the military reserve[241] are also considered as military allowances that are included in gross income.

Even though qualified military benefits are tax-exempt, they are still included in calculating gross income for child support purposes.[242] Under the guidelines, per

---

234. La. Stat. Ann. § 9:315(C)(3)(a).

235. Laird v. Laird, 52,560, p. 6 (La. App. 2 Cir. 4/10/19), 268 So. 3d 443, 448.

236. *See* La. Civ. Code Ann. art. 115.

237. Parties could contractually agree to ongoing spousal support even in the event of a subsequent marriage.

238. La. Stat. Ann. § 9:315(C)(3)(a) *amended by* Act No. 315, 2006 La. Acts 1488.

239. *See* Dep't of Soc. Servs. ex rel. D.F. v. L.T., 2005-1965, p. 7 (La. 7/6/06), 934 So. 2d 687, 691 (finding that Basic Allowance Housing (BAH) and Basic Allowance Subsistence (BAS) were included in the per month calculation of the father's gross income for calculating child support).

240. *See* Carter v. Carter, 49,517, pp. 5–6 (La. App. 2 Cir. 11/26/14), 155 So. 3d 81, 85 (finding that a VA disability award constituted monthly income and should be imputed as such).

241. *See* Bonnecarrere v. Bonnecarrere, 2009-1647, pp. 10–11 (La. App. 1 Cir. 4/14/10), 37 So. 3d 1038, 1046.

242. *See* Dep't of Soc. Servs. ex rel. D.F., 934 So. 2d at 691–92.

diem allowances that are not subject to federal income tax under the Internal Revenue Code are expressly excluded from gross income.[243] Litigants have argued that military allowances, like per diem allowances, should be excluded because the benefits are tax-exempt. At least one Louisiana court disagreed, concluding that the purposes of the allowances are different and the provisions of the Internal Revenue Code do not control gross income for child support purposes.[244] As such, military allowances were included in gross income.[245]

§ 7:22 Calculations of Income— Gross Income: Expense Reimbursement or In-Kind Payments

The second category of gross income includes expense reimbursements or in-kind payments received in the course of employment:

> (b) [e]xpense reimbursement or in-kind payments received by a parent in the course of employment, self-employment, or operation of a business, if the reimbursements or payments are significant and reduce the parent's personal living expenses. Such payments include but are not limited to a company car, free housing, or reimbursed meals.[246]

The payments must not only be significant (so periodic reimbursement for metered parking may be excluded), but they must also "reduce the parent's personal living expenses."[247] For example, in *Bernstein v. Bernstein*, the father was subject to an agreement under which the business covered the income tax obligations of its shareholders.[248] As such, he did not actually receive the money; instead, it was paid directly to the Internal Revenue Service. Further, the father had no control over the payments or when they were disbursed. Consequently, because the father could not use the money for support purposes, the court refused to consider the payments as part of his income.

243. La. Stat. Ann. § 9:315(d)(ii).

244. *See* Dep't of Soc. Servs. ex rel. D.F., 934 So. 2d at 692.

245. Dep't of Soc. Servs. ex rel. D.F., 934 So. 2d at 693–94.

246. La. Stat. Ann. § 9:315(C)(3)(b); *see* Dejoie v. Guidry, 2010-1542, p. 9 (La. App. 4 Cir. 7/13/11), 71 So. 3d 1111, 1118 (finding that defendant's use of company credit card for personal purchases and free use of company owned vehicles and homes constituted in-kind payments).

247. La. Stat. Ann. § 9:315(C)(3)(b); *see also* Shaw v. Shaw, 30,613, pp. 10–11 (La. App. 2 Cir. 6/24/98), 714 So. 2d 906, 912 (finding that the employer's expenses for uniforms were insignificant and half-priced meals while wearing her uniform were not a benefit received in the course of her employment, so neither should be included as income); *see also* Roberts v. Roberts, 95-1626, p. 9 (La. App. 4 Cir. 6/5/96), 677 So. 2d 1042, 1048 (finding that benefits that father derived from living rent-free in apartment above his business, his receipt of telephone and electrical service from business, and his use of vehicles owed by the business were part of his gross income, even if father's use of business assets did not result in any increase in business expenses).

248. Bernstein v. Bernstein, 2019-1106 (La. App. 4 Cir. 2/10/21), 313 So. 3d 413.

While the language of the statute makes clear that a company car, free housing, and reimbursed meals are the type of payments that would be included as income, Louisiana courts cannot agree on whether insurance premiums paid by an employer on behalf of an employee should be included in gross income. The Second and Third Circuits have concluded that employer-paid health insurance premiums are not to be included in the calculation of gross income.[249] The Third Circuit explained that while gross income does include Social Security and disability payments, it does not include the premiums paid by the employer for obtaining those benefits, so gross income should not include the premiums paid for purchasing health insurance for the employee.[250] Furthermore, health insurance premiums are defined in the statute, which expressly excludes amounts paid by the employer.[251]

On the other hand, the First Circuit expressly disagreed with the Third Circuit and concluded that premiums paid by an employer fit squarely within the definition of "gross income" because the benefit relieves the employee from expending personal funds and thereby reduces the employee's living expenses.[252] Even though the statute defines health insurance premiums to exclude amounts paid by the employer, the court explained that the statutory definition addresses the amount to be paid in child support, not the amount to be included in the parent's gross income.[253] The majority opinion was met with a strong dissent that agreed with the Third Circuit that health insurance premiums paid by the employer should not be included as income of the parent.[254]

Health insurance premiums are defined in the same section of the law that defines gross income,[255] resulting in a conflated view of two different principles. Gross income includes in-kind payments like housing, transportation, or meals because the parent does not have to incur the expense of these items. So, a parent who makes $5,000 per month, but receives a company car and meals worth $1,000, will be treated similarly to a parent who makes $6,000 per month and must purchase a car and food without the employer's help. Both would enjoy $5,000 after meal and car expenses, and both would pay the same share of child support.

The same rationale applies to an employer who pays the employee's share of health insurance. Gross income should include only the employee parent's share of health

---

249. *See* Shaw, 714 So. 2d at 912; Widman v. Widman, 619 So. 2d 632, 634–35 (La. Ct. App. 3 Cir. 1993).

250. Widman, 619 So. 2d at 635.

251. Widman, 619 So. 2d at 635. (relying on the definition of "health insurance premiums" in La. Stat. Ann. § 9:315).

252. Ola v. Ola, 2007-0667, pp. 4–5 (La. App. 1 Cir. 4/16/08), 985 So. 2d 786, 789. The dissent argued that premiums should not be part of the "gross income" calculation because "health insurance premiums" are separately defined in the statute. Ola, 985 So. 2d at 790–92 (Downing, J., dissenting). The majority disagreed, believing that the definition was intended to clarify the phrase in other sections of the child support guidelines, namely Louisiana Revised Statutes §§ 9:315.4, 9:315.8, and 9:315.20. Ola, 985 So. 2d at 790 (majority opinion).

253. Ola, 985 So. 2d at 790.

254. Ola, 985 So. 2d at 791–92 (Downing, J., dissenting).

255. La. Stat. Ann. § 9:315(C).

insurance paid by the employer and not the share attributed to the children. Thus, the benefit of not having to pay health insurance is accounted for with regard to the parent, but the amount of health insurance premium paid by the employer for the child should not be included as income to the parent. Instead, it should only appear as an expense that is included in the child support worksheet.

Confusion and incongruity arise because health insurance premiums, as defined in the statute, expressly exclude any amount paid by the employer. Accordingly, if the employer pays the health insurance premium for the child, it is as though no health insurance is expensed for the child. Some courts, however, have included the child's health insurance premium expense as income to the parent whose employer pays the expense, believing the result is a net-zero.[256] In reality, this practice results in an inappropriately inflated gross income number for that parent, which affects the parent's percentage share of child support. The better practice would be to include health insurance premiums for the child as an expense regardless of who or what entity pays the premium so the expense can be shared between the parents. If the employee parent pays that expense by having the premiums deducted from income, then that parent should receive a credit on the worksheet for that direct payment. Ultimately, the parent's share of child support will be reduced by the direct payments the parent makes for the cost of health insurance for the children.

§ 7:23 Calculations of Income— Gross Income: Self-Employment

The third category of gross income includes self-employment income, from which ordinary and necessary expenses are excluded:

> (c) Gross receipts minus ordinary and necessary expenses required to produce income, for purposes of income from self-employment, rent, royalties, proprietorship of a business, or joint ownership or a partnership or closely held corporation. "Ordinary and necessary expenses" shall not include amounts allowable by the Internal Revenue Service for the accelerated component of depreciation expenses or investment tax credits or any other business expenses determined by the court to be inappropriate for determining gross income for purposes of calculating child support.[257]

For a party who is self-employed, the calculation of gross income can be difficult. Self-employment income is reduced by "ordinary and necessary expenses" to prevent a parent with exclusive control over a company from limiting his own salary and thus, his support obligation.[258] The court, however, is not bound by a party's designation of

256. *See* Ola, 985 So. 2d at 789.

257. La. Stat. Ann. § 9:315(C)(3)(c).

258. Lavigne v. James, 15-19, pp. 4–5 (La. App. 5 Cir. 5/14/15), 170 So. 3d 1163, 1165–66 (citing Scott v. Scott, 43,455, p. 6 (La. App. 2 Cir. 8/13/08), 989 So. 2d 290, 294–95); *see also* Sawyer v. Sawyer, 35,583, p. 6 (La. App. 2 Cir. 11/2/01), 799 So. 2d 1226, 1231 ("One cannot avoid all or part of his child

what expenses are ordinary and necessary, even if the expenses are included in the self-employed party's federal tax return.[259] For example, while ordinary depreciation is a valid expense, accelerated depreciation is not; nor are personal expenses placed on a credit card but deducted as an expense by the business.[260] Ultimately, the party controlling the closely-held business bears the burden of proving that the expenses are both "ordinary" and "necessary."[261]

For example, in *Lavigne v. James*, the defendant argued that the trial court erred in calculating his gross income because it failed to credit him with the ordinary and necessary expenses of his business.[262] At trial, the defendant presented his tax returns, which showed various expenses for a business of which he was self-employed as owner.[263] The expenses included meals, home-related payments—such as the mortgage note, supermarket purchases, and home repairs—and ATM withdrawals, without receipts linking the withdrawals to purchases for the business.[264] The court refused to treat the expenses as ordinary and necessary, finding that the expenditures were not used to produce income for the business but instead were used to personally benefit the defendant.[265]

§ 7:24 Calculations of Income— Exclusions from Gross Income

While the definition of "gross income" is broad, it does contain several exclusions. These exclusions ensure that certain funds earned or received by a parent do not inflate the gross income figure. Each of the exclusions will be addressed in turn.

---

support obligation by exercising exclusive control over a corporation wholly owned by him in order to limit his own salary."); Holleman v. Barrilleaux, 2014-499, p. 4 (La. App. 3 Cir. 11/19/14), 161 So. 3d 789, 792 (finding that trial court erred in failing to include distributions from a privately owned business, which represented the parent's share of the profits).

259. Dejoie v. Guidry, 2010-1542, p. 9 (La. App. 4 Cir. 7/13/11), 71 So. 3d 1111, 1118.

260. Magnon v. Magnon, 2020-143, pp. 6–7 (La. App. 3 Cir. 11/18/20), 307 So. 3d 1151, 1156 (accelerated depreciation and officer salary when the father was the sole officer should not be deducted from gross income); Dejoie, 71 So. 3d at 1119 (holding that straight line depreciation of a business asset required to produce income may be an ordinary and necessary expenses); Guste v. Guste, 2016-0872, pp. 3–4 (La. App. 4 Cir. 4/19/17), 217 So. 3d 542, 544 (holding that straight line depreciation was allowed concerning rental property because Louisiana Revised Statutes Section 9:315(C)(3)(c) excludes only accelerated depreciation); *see also* Thomey v. Thomey, 33,000, p. 3 (La. App. 2 Cir. 4/7/00), 756 So. 2d 698, 701 (finding that self-employed father could not deduct business loan payments in calculating income for determining child support payments).

261. Dejoie, 71 So. 3d at 1118; Lavigne, 170 So. 3d at 1166; Scott, 989 So. 2d at 295.

262. Lavigne, 170 So. 3d at 1165.

263. Lavigne, 170 So. 3d at 1166 (presenting an income of $17,300 and gross business receipts totaling $184,830 in year one and an income of $20,900 and gross business receipts totaling $212,279 in year two).

264. Lavigne, 170 So. 3d at 1166.

265. Lavigne, 170 So. 3d at 1166.

§ 7:25 Calculations of Income— Exclusions from Gross Income—Child Support Received or Public Assistance

First, "[c]hild support received, or benefits received from public assistance programs, including Family Independence Temporary Assistance Plan, supplemental security income, food stamps, and general assistance" are excluded from the calculation of gross income.[266] Supplemental Social Security income benefits should be distinguished from Social Security retirement or disability benefits because the supplemental benefits are excluded from gross income. Supplemental Social Security income is a needs-based, federal cash assistance program, which is funded by general revenues of the United States rather than by the Social Security trust fund.[267] Accordingly, supplemental Social Security income (SSI) is appropriately categorized as "assistance," and therefore excluded from child support calculations.[268]

§ 7:26 Calculations of Income— Exclusions from Gross Income— Per Diem Allowances

Second, "per diem allowances which are not subject to federal income taxation under the provisions of the Internal Revenue Code" are likewise excluded from gross income.[269] The parent receiving per diem allowances bears the burden of proving that the amount was inappropriately included in income.[270] In addition, the Louisiana Supreme Court has made clear that military allowances are not considered per diem allowances, even though they are not subject to federal income taxation.[271]

In *Breaux v. Pickett*, the mother claimed that the trial court erred in including her per diem allowances in its calculation of her gross income.[272] The appellate court disagreed, finding that she failed to prove that the per diem payments were not subject to federal income tax. While the mother testified as to the fact and submitted documentary evidence showing that her employer did not withhold taxes on the per diem

---

266. La. Stat. Ann. § 9:315(C)(3)(d)(i).

267. *See* 42 U.S.C. § 1381 (2012); Supplemental Security Income Home Page—2024 Edition, U.S. Social Security Administration (2024), https://www.ssa.gov/ssi/.

268. Richard v. Richard, 2005-0798, p. 7 (La. App. 4 Cir. 4/12/06), 930 So. 2d 156, 161.

269. La. Stat. Ann. § 9:315(C)(3)(d)(ii).

270. *See* Dep't of Child. & Fam. Servs. ex rel. Alexander v. Alexander, 16-387, p. 11 (La. App. 5 Cir. 12/28/16), 228 So. 3d 1261, 1269 (rejecting father's argument that his income was overstated because it included per diem allowances because father could not prove that the income used by the trial court included per diems).

271. Dep't of Soc. Servs. ex rel. D.F. v. L.T., 2005-1965, p. 7 (La. 7/6/06), 934 So. 2d 687, 691–92 (distinguishing the purposes of the IRC versus the child support guidelines).

272. Breaux v. Pickett, 2022-19 (La. App. 3 Cir. 5/25/22), 340 So. 3d 196, 198–201.

amounts, she did not produce her tax returns as required by Louisiana Revised Statutes Section 9:315.2.

§ 7:27 Calculations of Income—Exclusions from Gross Income—Extraordinary Overtime

Third, excluded from gross income is "[e]xtraordinary overtime including but not limited to income attributed to seasonal work regardless of its percentage of gross income when, in the court's discretion, the inclusion thereof would be inequitable to a party."[273] Key to a court's analysis is the term "extraordinary" as the definition of "gross income" generally includes "income from any source, including … bonuses…."[274] In other words, extraordinary overtime is excluded, but ordinary overtime is included. Once a court determines the overtime is extraordinary, it must also determine whether including the overtime pay would be inequitable to a party.[275]

Louisiana courts have defined extraordinary overtime as overtime that is undertaken on a temporary or limited basis to reach a specific end or that is not guaranteed or continuous.[276] If the income is significant and continuous, then it should be included in the calculation of gross income, even when classified as "overtime."[277] For example, in *Montou v. Montou*, the parent's base salary was $30,000 per year, but during the prior three years, he earned between $13,000 and $18,000 in annual overtime pay.[278] The parent and his supervisor testified that, although overtime hours were not guaranteed, they were hardly a rarity and were par for the job.[279] Overtime hours were so prevalent that the employer had even created a plan to evenly distribute overtime among employees.[280] Because of its consistency and significance, the court did not find the overtime pay to be extraordinary and included it in gross income.[281]

273. La. Stat. Ann. § 9:315(C)(3)(d)(iii).

274. La. Stat. Ann. § 9:315(C)(3)(a).

275. Dep't of Soc. Servs. v. Toledano, 97-1424, p. 3 (La. App. 4 Cir. 5/13/98), 713 So. 2d 679, 681.

276. Walden v. Walden, 2000-2911, p. 6 (La. App. 1 Cir. 8/14/02), 835 So. 2d 513, 519.

277. Montou v. Montou, 96-1463, p. 3 (La. App. 3 Cir. 4/2/97), 692 So. 2d 705, 707; *see* Douthit v. Douthit, 31,713, pp. 2–3 (La. App. 2 Cir. 3/31/99), 732 So. 2d 616, 618; Ezernack v. Ezernack, 2004-1584, pp. 2–4 (La. App. 3 Cir. 4/6/05), 899 So. 2d 198, 200–01.

278. Montou, 692 So. 2d at 706–07.

279. Montou, 692 So. 2d at 707.

280. Montou, 692 So. 2d at 707.

281. Montou, 692 So. 2d at 707; *see also* Douthit, 732 So. 2d at 618 (finding overtime to be ordinary when, based on tax returns, the individual had "consistently worked substantial amounts of overtime" and imputing previous overtime payments into calculation of gross income); Ezernack, 899 So. 2d at 201 (following *Douthit* and imputing prior ordinary overtime income when the court found defendant to have voluntarily ceased working overtime hours "for the express and admitted purpose of avoiding court-ordered [support] payments"); Cole v. Cole, 2013-1442, pp. 13–14 (La. App. 3 Cir. 6/4/14), 139 So. 3d 1225, 1232–33 (finding that an increase in pay from consistent overtime work constituted a material change in circumstances allowing for a modification of the support order); Hagan v. Hagan, 2010-1432, p. 2 (La. App. 3 Cir. 7/27/11), 70 So. 3d 1081, 1083 (excluding from gross income a share

Overtime was not included in gross income in *Walden v. Walden*.[282] During marriage, the father worked a considerable amount of overtime to reach long-term family goals.[283] Once the marriage ended, he ceased working overtime, which was neither required nor guaranteed by his employer and which was not included as an essential part of his job description.[284] Initially, the trial court imputed his prior overtime wages into the calculation of his gross income.[285] The Louisiana First Circuit Court of Appeal reversed, finding that extraordinary overtime is not included in gross income, especially because "the overtime was voluntarily undertaken for a limited goal, and outside of the ordinary full-time job requirements and income."[286] The court explained that if it were to find this type of overtime as anything other than extraordinary, such an interpretation "would require all parents who worked overtime for a limited goal[] to continue to work at the highest level of overtime achieved or be classified as underemployed."[287]

A father's 103 hours of overtime over the course of five months was also not included in his gross income in *Dugue' v Dugue'*.[288] The father performed this work after unprecedented flooding in Baton Rouge in 2016, and the court found that he rarely worked overtime, and when he did, it was not nearly as much as he did during the time period immediately following the 2016 flood. It also found that the father did not earn a significant amount of overtime during most pay periods.

---

of the income earned for refereeing high school basketball games on a seasonal basis because the work was not guaranteed).

282. Walden, 835 So. 2d at 518–19.

283. Walden, 835 So. 2d at 518 (putting his overtime pay towards the purchase of a new home and vehicles for the family).

284. Walden, 835 So. 2d at 518.

285. Walden, 835 So. 2d at 518.

286. Walden, 835 So. 2d at 519.

287. Walden, 835 So. 2d at 519; *see also* Toledano, 713 So. 2d at 681 (finding overtime pay to be extraordinary when it was attributable to a unique work situation, was not an expected or ordinary part of the job, and was not guaranteed in the following years); Pennington v. Pennington, 2011-1022, pp. 6–7 (La. App. 1 Cir. 12/21/11), 80 So. 3d 763, 767 (holding that the individual was not underemployed for terminating his part-time employment and understanding that if the court "were [] to analyze the second job in the context of 'overtime,' based on *Walden*, Mr. Pennington's second job should not be considered" in the child support calculation).

288. Dugue' v Dugue,' 20-292 (La. App. 5 Cir. 3/24/21), 316 So. 3d 170, 173–75.

§ 7:28 Calculations of Income—Exclusions from Gross Income—Gift to Supplement Child Support Payments

Fourth, "[a]ny monetary gift to the domiciliary party when the objective of the gift is to supplement irregular child support payments from the nondomiciliary party" should not be included as income to the domiciliary party.[289] As a result, payments made by the mother's parents to assist the mother because her ex-husband failed to pay his monthly child support were not considered income to the mother.[290] On the other hand, gifts that are not used to supplement irregular child support payments, such as annual gifts made by parents to their children, should be included as income.

§ 7:29 Calculations of Income—Exclusions from Gross Income—Disaster Benefits

Fifth and finally, "[a]ny disaster assistance benefits received from the Federal Emergency Management Agency through its Individuals and Households Program or from any other nonprofit organization qualified as a tax-exempt organization under Section 501(C) of the Internal Revenue Code of 1954, as amended" is excluded from gross income.[291] This provision was passed in December of 2005 after Hurricanes Katrina and Rita. With the prevalence of disasters in Louisiana, any governmental or nonprofit benefit will not affect—one way or the other—the obligation of child support.

§ 7:30 Calculations of Income—Potential Income

When a party is employed at full capacity, actual income is used as gross income.[292] If, however, the party is unemployed or underemployed, then the potential income of the party must be calculated and used in place of, or in addition to, actual gross income.[293] A parent is not voluntarily unemployed or underemployed if the parent is "absolutely unemployable or incapable of being employed"[294] or if the un/underem-

---

289. La. Stat. Ann. § 9:315(C)(3)(d)(iv).

290. *See* Anderson v. Anderson, 11-864, p. 8 (La. App. 5 Cir. 5/31/12), 96 So. 3d 1278, 1282–83.

291. La. Stat. Ann. § 9:315(C)(3)(d)(v).

292. La. Stat. Ann. § 9:315(C)(5)(a).

293. La. Stat. Ann. § 9:315(C)(5)(b).

294. La. Stat. Ann. § 9:315(C)(5)(b); *see* State v. James, 45,955, p. 6–7 (La. App. 2 Cir. 1/26/11), 57 So. 3d 447, 449 (finding obligor voluntarily underemployed when he worked only as a school bus driver but was formerly trained and previously worked as a barber, and position as school bus driver left open hours in the day for part-time employment as a barber); Lopez v. Breaux, 462 So. 2d 1333, 1336 (La. Ct. App. 3 Cir. 1985) (holding that a party "must show that he is absolutely unemployable, not merely that he is unemployed at the time"). A party "shall not" be deemed voluntarily unemployed

ployment "results through no fault or neglect of the party."[295] The guidelines in section 315.11 contain more specific, explanatory provisions to guide courts when parents are voluntarily unemployed or underemployed.

Section 315.11 explains that income-earning potential should be used unless the parent is "physically or mentally incapacitated, or is caring for a child of the parties under the age of five years."[296] Although section 315.11 may be duplicative for parents who are absolutely unemployable due to a physical or mental incapacity, it excepts those parents who are capable of working but are caring for a preschool-aged child of the parties.[297] Notably, the parent must actually be caring for the child for the provision to apply. In *Guidry v. Guidry*, the court declined to apply section 315.11 because the child was in daycare from 9 a.m. to 5 p.m. five days per week.[298] Furthermore, a parent caring for a preschool-aged child conceived of another union does not qualify.[299]

The section also explains how income earning potential is calculated.[300] Generally, the wage earned prior to voluntary unemployment is the best estimate of an obligated party's potential income.[301] If prior work history is unavailable, however, courts can consider the Louisiana Occupational Employment Wage Survey.[302] Finally, in 2016, the legislature added a provision that applies when no evidence of an obligor's prior

---

or underemployed if he is responsible for an adult child with a disability, or if he is or was incarcerated for 180 consecutive days or longer. La. Stat. Ann. § 9:315.11(C)(1)–(2).

295. La. Stat. Ann. § 9:315(C)(5)(b). An involuntary change of employment results from fortuitous events or other circumstances beyond a person's control, such as loss of one's position or illness. Dep't of Child. & Fam. Servs. v. Jones, 14-918, p. 4–5 (La. App. 5 Cir. 4/15/15), 170 So. 3d 297, 299–300 (citing Savage v. Savage, 36-138, p. 4 (La. App. 2 Cir. 6/12/02), 821 So. 2d 603, 606 (allowing for deviation from support guidelines upon determination that, while party voluntarily chose to retire, she did so in good faith to pursue her education full-time to advance her career and increase her income, which would be for the betterment of herself and child)).

296. La. Stat. Ann. § 9:315.11(A)(1).

297. La. Stat. Ann. § 9:315.11(A)(1).

298. Guidry v. Guidry, 2008-1166 (La. App. 3 Cir. 2/4/09), 6 So. 3d 845.

299. Germany v. Germany, 599 So. 2d 350 (La. App. 1 Cir. 1992) (finding La. R.S. § 9:315.9 inapplicable because the mother stayed home to care for an infant child conceived with her subsequent husband).

300. If a parent is voluntarily unemployed or underemployed, then the court must calculate child support "based on a determination of income earning potential." Germany, 599 So. 2d 350. The court may consider the most recently published Louisiana Occupational Employment Wage Survey when determining a party's income earning potential. Germany, 599 So. 2d 350. Section 315.11 contains a list of considerations that the court "shall" consider. La. Stat. Ann. § 9:315.11(A)(1)(a)–(m). If a court determines that evidence is lacking or not presented regarding a party's actual income or income earning potential, there is a "rebuttable presumption that the party can earn a weekly gross amount equal to 32 hours at minimum wage." La. Stat. Ann. § 9:315.11(A)(2).

301. Haverner v. Haverner, 29,785, p. 11 (La. App. 2 Cir. 8/20/97), 700 So. 2d 533, 539–40; Glover v. Glover, 28,493, p 3–4 (La. App. 2 Cir. 6/26/96), 677 So. 2d 659, 660–61 (finding that income earning potential of voluntarily unemployed father, for purposes of fixing child support in divorce proceeding, should have been determined using wages earned at last steady work, rather than using hourly wage for job offered but rejected; further finding that father's limited efforts to find employment provided insufficient evidence that work was not available or was available only at hourly wage, lower than wages earned at last steady work).

302. La. Stat. Ann. § 9:315.11(A)(1).

employability or skills is available.[303] Specifically, and as a last resort, the legislation adopted a rebuttable presumption that a party can earn a weekly gross income based on 32 hours at minimum wage.[304]

Courts consider good faith when assessing whether the party's voluntary unemployment or underemployment should result in imputing income to that party.[305] Voluntary unemployment or underemployment is a question of fact to be assessed by the trial court.[306] For example, if a parent voluntarily reduces his income to spend more time with the children and to realize a greater opportunity for career advancement, a court may not impute income.[307] By contrast, when a parent's pay is reduced due to a pattern of drug abuse, a court may impute earning capability because the parent's voluntary actions resulted in a reduction in income.[308] Note that a court rejected imputing income to a parent for failing to invest funds that belonged to the parent to yield a higher rate of return for the child.[309]

Section 315.11 also includes two other instances when parties are not deemed voluntarily unemployed or underemployed. A party who is caring for an unmarried child with a disability, when the child is incapable of self-support and requires personal care and supervision, cannot have income imputed to him.[310] The court must consider

303. Act No. 218, 2016 La. Acts 968.

304. La. Stat. Ann. § 9:315.11(A)(2) (calculating the minimum wage "according to the laws of his state of domicile or federal law, whichever is higher").

305. Rutland v. Rutland, 13-70 (La. App. 5 Cir. 7/30/13), 121 So. 3d 776 (father was voluntarily underemployed after securing a lower-paying job after his termination for sleeping on the job); Dugue' v. Dugue,' 20-292 (La. App. 5 Cir. 3/24/21), 316 So. 3d 170, 177 (sufficient evidence in the record to support a finding that father's attempts to find meaningful employment, comparable in pay and skills required to previous positions he held, showed that his unemployment or underemployment was not a result of neglect on his part); Anderson v. Anderson, 11-864, p. 8 (La. App. 5 Cir. 5/31/12), 96 So. 3d 1278, 1281 (finding the father to be voluntarily underemployed because he lost his job as a nurse anesthetist because of a drug abuse problem); Savage, 821 So. 2d at 606–07 (When a parent voluntarily terminates his employment, his support obligation may be reduced if he can prove: "1) [that] a change in circumstances occurred; 2) the voluntary change is reasonable and justified; 3) [the parent] is in good faith and not attempting to avoid [his] alimentary obligation; and 4) the action will not deprive the child of continued reasonable financial support."); Curtis v. Curtis, 34,317, pp. 9–11 (La. App. 2 Cir. 11/1/00), 773 So. 2d 185, 192–93 (finding obligor in good faith, although underemployed, when underemployment was not to avoid support obligation, but instead took a lower paying job which allowed him to work days, rather than nights, and afforded him more time with the children and a greater opportunity for future career advancement).

306. Anderson, 96 So. 3d at 1281; Saacks v. Saacks, 05-365, p. 13 (La. App. 5 Cir. 9/26/06), 942 So. 2d 1130, 1138.

307. *See, e.g.*, Curtis, 773 So. 2d at 192–93. *See also* State in Interest of Minor, 2022-815 (La. App. 3 Cir. 9/13/23), 2023 WL 5962190 (unpublished) (even though father earned less at his current job, he was not voluntarily under-employed; his current job required fewer hours but a better overall life situation and more time to see his children).

308. Anderson, 96 So. 3d at 1281. *But see* Kott v. Kott, 2020-0873 (La. App. 1 Cir. 4/16/21), 324 So. 3d 165 (father who had been attorney and real estate agent not underemployed despite now earning $15/hour because he was not allowed to work in the legal field and was facing disciplinary action from the real estate licensing board, all as a result of his substance abuse and criminal activity).

309. Kern v. Kern, 2000-1126, pp. 5–6 (La. App. 4 Cir. 4/25/01), 786 So. 2d 193, 197.

310. La. Stat. Ann. § 9:315.11(C)(1).

the child's particular needs for care, including eligibility for school, public benefits, and services.[311] While the language seems to apply to a parent caring for any disabled child, even a child who is still a minor, the provision mirrors the language that allows continued child support for adult children with disabilities, suggesting that only parents who are caring for adult children are excepted from having income imputed to them.[312] In addition, parents who are incarcerated cannot have income imputed to them.[313] This provision applies when child support is suspended during the obligor's period of incarceration.[314]

§ 7:31 Calculations of Income—Income from Expense Sharing

A court may consider expense sharing when assessing a party's income. In other words, to the extent that a party's direct expenses are reduced due to sharing expenses with a third party, the reduction in actual expenses can be included as income.[315] Income from expense sharing can be derived from the family and friends of a parent or from a subsequent spouse of a parent.[316] Presenting proof of expense sharing has been difficult for some litigants, even in instances where the circumstances clearly showed that expenses were being contributed by another party.[317] Because the abuse of discretion standard applies to the trial court's decision on whether to include income, reversal is rare.[318]

---

311. La. Stat. Ann. § 9:315.11(C)(1).

312. La. Stat. Ann. § 9:315.22(E)(1), as relocated to § 9:315.22.1 (2025).

313. La. Stat. Ann. § 9:315.11(C)(2).

314. La. Stat. Ann. § 9:311.1.

315. La. Stat. Ann. § 9:315(C)(5)(c).

316. *See* Gould v. Gould, 28,996, p. 14 (La. App. 2 Cir. 1/24/97), 687 So. 2d 685, 693 (holding that trial court did not abuse its discretion in finding that the obligor-father did not receive any special benefit from expense sharing by living with his parents, where he paid his parents $300 per month for rent and rent debt accrued during the time he did not pay rent).

317. La. Stat. Ann. § 9:315(C)(5)(c); *see generally* Evans v. Evans, 36,731, pp. 4–5 (La. App. 2 Cir. 11/6/02), 830 So. 2d 591, 593–94 (finding that trial court did not abuse its discretion in failing to include income of mother's fiancé in the child support calculations, given that the extent to which fiancé's income reduced mother's actual expenses was not disclosed by the record); Hutto v. Kneipp, 627 So. 2d 802 (La. Ct. App. 2 Cir. 1993) (finding that the trial court was not required to include income of mother's current husband in child support calculation when mother's husband earned considerably less than mother and parties provided no evidence of their expenses); Dazet v. Price, 16-362, p. 7 (La. App. 5 Cir. 12/7/16), 204 So. 3d 1152, 1156–57 (finding that record was devoid of any request from the court or ex-husband for relevant expense sharing documents).

318. *See* Ficcara v. Ficcara, 11-569, pp. 11–12 (La. App. 5 Cir. 2/14/12), 88 So. 3d 548, 556; Dep't of Soc. Servs. ex rel. Clark v. Ruiz, 04-1064, p. 10 (La. App. 5 Cir. 2/15/05), 898 So. 2d 514, 520 (citing the language of child support statute providing that court may consider as income benefits a party derives from expense sharing with another or other sources is permissive, not mandatory, and it is within the discretion of trial court to include or disallow such alleged "benefits"); Matherne v. Matherne, 571 So. 2d 888 (La. Ct. App. 5 Cir. 1990) (same); *see also* Willis v. Demelo, 14-427, pp. 9–10 (La. App. 5 Cir. 10/15/14), 182 So. 3d 57, 63 (affirming trial court discretion in not considering expense sharing); Harrington v. Harrington, 43,373, p. 15 (La. App. 2 Cir. 8/13/08), 989 So. 2d 838, 847 (finding that in

For example, in *Hagan v. Hagan*, the father testified that he was paying his girlfriend $250 per month to live with her, and it would cost him between $400 and $450 to live alone.[319] The mother asked for $200 to be included as income for expense sharing. Without explaining its reasons, the trial court declined to include any amount for expense sharing, and on appeal the appellate court affirmed, citing deference to the trial court's discretion.[320] Similarly in *Mayo v. Crazovich*, the trial court refused to include income for expense sharing when the father's second wife's income was his primary source of income while the father was starting a new business.[321] The appellate court affirmed the trial court's decision stating, "The extent to which this income reduced which actual expenses of [the father] is not disclosed by the record. We, therefore, cannot say that the trial court abused its discretion...."[322] Both cases appear to warrant expense sharing as income.

Appropriately, the trial court in *Kern v. Kern* included as income an amount for expense sharing because the mother's new spouse paid the note on their new home.[323] The mother argued that she was paying for a home, which she was in the process of selling, and that she planned to reimburse her new husband for half of the payments once she sold her old home.[324] The court understood that if the mother were living alone, she would have to pay the note on the new home—as well as the note on the old home—all by herself.[325] Because the mother's actual expenses were paid by her husband's income, expense sharing had indeed occurred.[326] The appellate court affirmed.[327]

Complexities abound when a parent and the parent's subsequent spouse have commingled funds or business interests.[328] For example, in *LaForge v. LaForge*, the child's father and his new spouse were each co-owners of a trucking business.[329] Each co-owner

---

addition to evidence establishing ex-husband benefited from expense sharing with his new spouse, the court could also consider the two additional children in ex-husband's household).

319. Hagan v. Hagan, 2010-1432, p. 2 (La. App. 3 Cir. 7/27/11), 70 So. 3d 1081, 1083.

320. Hagan, 70 So. 3d at 1083; *see also* Pendergrass v. Pendergrass, 94-1165, pp. 10–11 (La. App. 4 Cir. 1/26/96), 667 So. 2d 1213, 1218 (citing only the permissive language of the statute to hold that the trial court did not error by not including expense sharing in the calculation of a party's income).

321. Mayo v. Crazovich, 621 So. 2d 120, 124 (La. Ct. App. 2 Cir. 1993).

322. Mayo, 621 So. 2d at 124; *see also* Semmes v. Semmes, 45,006, pp. 16–17 (La. App. 2 Cir. 12/16/09), 27 So. 3d 1024, 1034 (refusing to include benefits from expense sharing because there was no direct evidence of a reduction in the former wife's actual expenses).

323. Kern v. Kern, 2000-1126, p. 6 (La. App. 4 Cir. 4/25/01), 786 So. 2d 193, 198.

324. Kern, 786 So. 2d at 198.

325. Kern, 786 So. 2d at 198.

326. Kern, 786 So. 2d at 198.

327. Kern, 786 So. 2d at 198. *See also* McClelland ex rel. Winters v. Broussard, 98-906 (La. App. 3 Cir. 2/3/99), 736 So. 2d 878 (including the income of mother's subsequent husband because of their co-owned accounting business from which neither took a salary and all of the couple's bills were paid).

328. *See* Baas v. Baas, 91-1715, p. 4 (La. App. 4 Cir. 9/29/94), 643 So. 2d 823, 825 (finding that the income of father's second wife was community property and could properly be considered when fixing the father's support obligations); *see also* Lewis v. Lewis, 616 So. 2d 744 (La. Ct. App. 1 Cir. 1993) (finding a marriage contract will not preclude examination of expense sharing benefits derived from subsequent spouse if a court elects to examine it).

329. LaForge v. LaForge, 26,317, p. 4 (La. 2 Cir. 1/25/95), 649 So. 2d 151, 154.

earned income from the business, and expenses of the business were paid from their gross income.[330] The trial court concluded that separation of their personal expenses, which were commingled with the business expenses, would have been extremely difficult and therefore, it did not include any share of the new spouse's income as expense sharing.[331] The appellate court affirmed, finding no abuse of discretion.[332]

§ 7:32 Calculations of Income— Concealed or Underreported Income

In 2009, the legislature passed a provision to help determine actual income when one party receives a benefit from a business that party controls, and the other party believes that income is being concealed or underreported.[333] When one party alleges that income is being concealed or underreported, the court must admit evidence to establish the actual income of the other party, including evidence of any redirected income, deferred income, or the standard of living and assets of the party.[334] The law provides presumptions to assist the party without knowledge of the business activities to ascertain the actual income of the business owner.[335]

Redirected income is shown by evidence of "[l]oans to the obligor by a business in which the obligor has an ownership interest and whether the loans will be repaid."[336] The law creates a presumption that these loans are income of the obligor.[337] The obligor may rebut the presumption if the obligor can demonstrate a history of similar loans, which are being paid, or that were repaid in a timely manner at market interest rates.[338] Similarly, payments of salary or wages to a person related by blood or affinity to the obligor-owner are also considered redirected income.[339] Again, a presumption exists that such payments are the obligor's income, but the presumption can be rebutted with evidence supporting a history of payments or evidence that the payments represent fair market value for services actually performed.[340] The burden of proof to overcome these presumptions lies with the owner of the business.[341]

The statute also considers deferred income as "recent reductions in distributions of income."[342] Here, too, there is a presumption that past distributions of income will

330. LaForge, 649 So. 2d at 154.

331. LaForge, 649 So. 2d at 153–54.

332. LaForge, 649 So. 2d at 154.

333. La. Stat. Ann. § 9:315.1.1 (enacted by Act No. 378, 2009 La. Acts 2620–21).

334. La. Stat. Ann § 9:315.1.1(A).

335. La. Stat. Ann § 9:315.1.1, cmt. (b).

336. La. Stat. Ann. § 9:315.1.1(A)(1)(a).

337. La. Stat. Ann. § 9:315.1.1(A)(1)(a).

338. La. Stat. Ann. § 9:315.1.1(A)(1)(a). Any amount by which a commercially reasonable payment exceeds the amount actually repaid shall be treated as income. *Id.*

339. La. Stat. Ann. § 9:315.1.1(A)(1)(b).

340. La. Stat. Ann. § 9:315.1.1(A)(1)(b).

341. La. Stat. Ann. § 9:315.1.1(A)(1)(b).

342. La. Stat. Ann. § 9:315.1.1(A)(2).

continue.[343] The obligor may rebut this presumption by demonstrating that business conditions justify a reduction in distributions.[344]

Finally, courts are given authority to examine the standard of living and assets of the owner both prior and subsequent to the child support order to determine the actual income of the obligor if the amount claimed as income is inconsistent with the obligor's lifestyle.[345] If the income cannot be sufficiently established, courts are permitted to admit evidence of wage and earnings surveys to establish income.[346]

In *McClanahan v. McClanahan*, the court affirmed that Mr. McClanahan had sufficient income to pay the child and spousal support as ordered by the trial court, noting that he had failed to rebut the presumption of income because of "the opacity of the complicated transactions among his various companies and himself," and his failure to provide "complete and updated financial information."[347] Moreover, the court found that Mr. McClanahan's reported salary of $60,000 per year was inconsistent with his financial records and lifestyle, when considering his documented travel, luxury vacations, personal investments, purchases, sales of real estate, as well as the interim child and spousal support he was paying to his ex-wife.[348]

Similarly, in *Brossett v. Brossett*, the court found that the trial court acted within its discretion when it imputed income of $20,000 per month to a husband with a "cavalier attitude about his unlawful business practices."[349] The husband had concealed and underreported his income, making it nearly impossible to determine his true income.[350] The court evaluated the husband's income tax records, bank statements, deposits, spending, and lifestyle, which together revealed expenditures well in excess of his stated income.[351]

---

343. La. Stat. Ann. § 9:315.1.1(A)(2).

344. La. Stat. Ann. § 9:315.1.1(A)(2).

345. La. Stat. Ann. § 9:315.1.1(A)(3).

346. La. Stat. Ann. § 9:315.1.1(B); *see* State v. Alexander, 2014-615, pp. 1–5 (La. App. 3 Cir. 11/5/14), 150 So. 3d 679, 679–82.

347. McClanahan v. McClanahan, 2014-670, p. 8 (La. App. 5 Cir. 3/25/15), 169 So. 3d 587, 593; *see also* McCorvey v. McCorvey, 2005-889, p. 2 (La. App. 3 Cir. 2/1/06), 922 So. 2d 694, 702 (affirming the trial court child support award in the face of obligor's claims that he had inadequate income because the self-employed spouse had a history of consistently under-reporting and misrepresenting his income, in addition to failing to provide discovery regarding his income); Verges v. Verges, 2001-0208, p. 9 (La. App. 1 Cir. 3/28/02), 815 So. 2d 356 (citing Hudnall v. Hudnall, 2000-0330, p. 8 (La. App. 1 Cir. 5/11/01), 808 So. 2d 641, 647) ("[T]he court will not allow a person to shield their income in order to diminish their liability owed to a child. It is the parties [sic] obligation to be honest and forthcoming regarding the establishment of his/her legitimate income and any diminutions to that income.").

348. McClanahan, 169 So. 3d at 595 (citing Sawyer v. Sawyer, 35,583, p. 6 (La. App. 2 Cir. 11/2/01), 799 So. 2d 1226, 1232) (finding that obligor's luxury vacations, use of private jets, ownership of an extravagant home, vehicles, a pool house and a boat was evidence indicative of greater income than was reported on the obligor's W-2 forms).

349. Brossett v. Brossett, 49,883, p. 5 (La. App. 2 Cir. 6/24/15), 195 So. 3d 471, 475.

350. Brossett, 195 So. 3d at 476.

351. Brossett, 195 So. 3d at 475.

§ 7:33 Calculations of Income—Adjusted Gross Income

Once each parent's gross income has been determined, it is adjusted by subtracting: "(a) [a]mounts for preexisting child support or spousal support obligations *owed* under an order of support to another who is not a party to the proceedings,"[352] or "(b) [a]t the court's discretion, amounts *paid* on behalf of a party's minor child who is not the subject of the action of the court."[353] In other words, these deductions involve payments to former spouses or children who are not parties in or subject to the current proceedings. The resulting amount is each parent's adjusted gross income.

The first possible adjustment to gross income, amounts owed for preexisting support obligations, can be determined with reference to the court order that requires support.[354] Prior to a 2016 amendment, "adjusted gross income" was adjusted by preexisting child or spousal support payments *paid* to another.[355] Because questions surrounded whether parties had to submit proof of payments made in order to adjust income, the legislature amended the section to require simply that the obligation be *owed* to adjust income.[356] Because a trial court is vested with discretion, evidence that a support obligation owed either went entirely unpaid or was paid unreliably was likely to convince a court that an adjustment to the obligor's income is inappropriate.[357] In fact, in *Brossett v. Brossett*, the court refused to adjust the father's income because the child support payments he made for prior children, pursuant to two consent judgments, were inconsistent, sporadic, and unreliable.[358]

The second possible adjustment to gross income requires documentary or testimonial proof that a party made extrajudicial payments for another child, without an order of support.[359] For extrajudicial payments, the trial court is given discretion whether or

352. La. Stat. Ann. § 9:315(C)(1)(a); *see* St. Philip v. Montalbano, 2016-0254, pp. 4–5 (La. App. 1 Cir. 10/16/16), 206 So. 3d 909, 912 (finding that trial court did not abuse its discretion in failing to deduct preexisting child support payments from gross income calculation when no evidence of a support obligation was presented).

353. La. Stat. Ann. § 9:315(C)(1)(b) (emphasis added); *see also* Obligation Worksheets A & B, La. Stat. Ann. § 9:315.20 (Line 1.a).

354. State ex rel. Stockton v. Lafferty, 2001-2110, pp. 5–6 (La. App. 1 Cir. 7/24/02), 835 So. 2d 476, 479 (refusing to deduct child support payments for other children based on the testimony of obligor alone); Stowe v. Stowe, 617 So. 2d 161, 163 (La. Ct. App. 3 Cir. 1993) (finding that the trial court failed to deduct the $200.00 preexisting child support payment the father paid to a former wife and recalculating the father's monthly gross income to reflect the amount).

355. *See* La. Stat. Ann. § 9:315(C)(1), *amended by* Act No. 222, 2016 La. Acts 971.

356. *See* Hearing on H.B. 395 Before the H. Comm. on Civ. L. and Proc. at 1:08 (La. 2016) (statement of Rep. Davis), https://house.louisiana.gov/H_Video/VideoArchivePlayer?v=house/2016/apr/04 04_16_CL.

357. *See, e.g.*, State ex rel. L.P. v. Elmore, 47,908, p. 5 (La. App. 2 Cir. 2/27/13), 110 So. 3d 1240 (finding that the trial court acted within its discretion by not reducing the father's income relative to a younger child for whom the father paid child support pursuant to a Vernon Parish order).

358. Brossett v. Brossett, 49,883, p. 7 (La. App. 2 Cir. 6/24/15), 195 So. 3d 471, 479.

359. La. Stat. Ann. § 9:315(C)(1)(b).

not to adjust the income.[360] While this adjustment could be read to include children who are living with and supported by the obligor, courts consider children living with the obligor to be a guideline deviation factor, rather than an adjustment to income.[361]

For example, in *Timmons v. Timmons*, the father appealed a child support award, arguing that the trial court failed to consider expenses he paid for his daughter from a prior marriage who lived with him.[362] The father argued that if he were paying support, rather than acting as the domiciliary parent, he would be entitled to a reduction in "adjusted gross income" under the guidelines.[363] Because he was paying expenses directly, rather than paying support to another parent, he argued that he should still be entitled to a deduction for those expenditures.[364] The Second Circuit disagreed, finding a legal difference between paying child support to another parent and paying for goods and services to support a child in one's own household.[365] The court concluded that "support paid to another for a nondomiciliary child who is not a party to the proceeding is to be deducted in the initial stages of calculation," while "the support given to a domiciliary child not a party to the proceeding is to be considered in determining whether the court wishes to deviate from the guidelines."[366] Even though this decision occurred before the 2016 amendment to the definition of "adjusted gross income,"[367] the amendment did not disturb its holding.

360. La. Stat. Ann. § 9:315(C)(1)(b); *see* State ex rel. Metcalf v. Samuels, 34,302, p. 2 (La. App. 2 Cir. 12/20/00), 775 So. 2d 1162, 1164–65 (allowing father a downward deviation from the child support guidelines when the minor child was not a party to the proceeding and was living in the father's household). *See also* Guillot v. Munn, 1996-0620, p. 1 (La. App. 2 Cir. 6/21/96), 676 So. 2d 86, 86 (deviation not permitted because there was no evidence of expenses for child born to father's subsequent marriage and no evidence of the extent to which father's present wife contributed to the support of that child); Jackson v. Belfield, 1998-0440, pp. 9–10 (La. App. 4 Cir. 11/25/98), 725 So. 2d 32, 37 (finding that the trial court erred in considering the father's testimony of his support for his son from another relationship when there was no sufficient evidentiary proof of such support).

361. Guillot, 756 So. 2d at 297. The Louisiana Supreme Court has made clear that deviations should be allowed only in limited circumstances so that the function of the guidelines, which is to provide adequacy and consistency in child support awards, is preserved. Guillot, 756 So. 2d at 297.

362. Timmons v. Timmons, 605 So. 2d 1162, 1167–68 (La. Ct. App. 2 Cir. 1992).

363. Timmons, 605 So. 2d at 1167–68.

364. Timmons, 605 So. 2d at 1167–68.

365. Timmons, 605 So. 2d at 1168.

366. Timmons, 605 So. 2d at 1168; Pratt v. Wells, 2002-1032, p. 8 (La. App. 4 Cir. 2/26/03), 840 So. 2d 1230, 1235 (noting that while the amount of extrajudicial support required for the other domiciliary children is not automatically deducted from gross income, it would be an abuse of discretion to fail to even consider it).

367. La. Stat. Ann. § 9:315(C)(1), *amended by* Act No. 222, 2016 La. Acts 971. The amendment did two things: (1) made it clear that the amount "owed" under a preexisting child or spousal support court order can be subtracted from gross income and (2) at the court's discretion, the court can subtract from gross income extrajudicial agreements of child support made between the parents when there is no court order. *See* Hearing on H.B. 212 Before the H. Comm. On Civ. L. and Proc. At 1:08 (La. 2016) (discussion), https://house.louisiana.gov/H_Video/VideoArchivePlayer?v=house/2016/apr/04 04_16_CL.

§ 7:34 Documentation to Prove Parental Income

Documentary evidence of income is essential to setting any child support order, even interim and temporary orders.[368] Revised Statutes § 9:315.2(A) requires that each party provide to the court and to the other party a verified income statement showing gross income and adjusted gross income, together with documentation of current and past earnings.[369] Documentation includes pay stubs or employer statements and a copy of the party's most recent federal tax return.[370] Other documents that are necessary for a court to properly determine income can also be considered.[371]

Courts have ordered support, even without a verified income statement, as long as the record contained sufficient evidence to determine a party's income.[372] For example, in *Collins v. Collins*, personal tax returns, W-2 statements, and the profit and loss statements for the father's medical clinic were sufficient evidence to determine earnings.[373] In *Kern v. Kern*, it was not an abuse of discretion for the trial court to consider only the most recent tax return, rather than averaging income from the past three returns, to determine annual income.[374] In *State in Interest of Washington v. Bourgeois*, it was

---

368. Drury v. Drury, 2001-0877, pp. 7–8 (La. App. 1 Cir. 8/21/02), 835 So. 2d 533, 539 (remanding to trial court because support could not be set in accordance with the law when neither party submitted verified statements, documentation of current and past earnings, copies of most recent tax returns, or other evidence as required by statute); *see also* Clarke v. Clarke, 2016-669, p. 6 (La. App. 5 Cir. 4/12/17), 219 So. 3d 1228, 1232 (vacating support award because there was no evidentiary documentation to support); Dep't of Soc. Servs. ex rel. J.S. v. Smith, 2005-1, p. 6 (La. App. 5 Cir. 4/26/05), 902 So. 2d 516, 519 (vacating order and remanding to trial court because the record did not contain adequate income verification).

369. La. Stat. Ann. § 9:315.2(A).

370. La. Stat. Ann. § 9:315.2(A).

371. The documents required are non-exhaustive. *See* Morris v. Freeman, 2017-565, p. 5 (La. App. 3 Cir. 8/23/17), 226 So. 3d 1126, 1129–30 (holding that statute governing calculation of support does not limit discovery to only the information listed in the statute when discovery requests were relevant to modification of support order and likely to lead to the discovery of admissible evidence).

372. St. Philip v. Montalbano, 2016-0254 (La. App. 1 Cir. 10/16/16), 206 So. 3d 909, 913; Bonnecarrere v. Bonnecarrere, 2009-1647, p. 11 (La. App. 1 Cir. 4/14/10), 37 So. 3d 1038, 1047 (pay stubs from civilian employment and statement from military confirming monthly reserve pay sufficient evidence to determine party's earnings); Riggs v. LaJaunie, 1998-30, p. 3 (La. App. 3 Cir. 10/7/98), 720 So. 2d 114, 116 (finding that tax returns, unchallenged by the other party and verified in their nature, were sufficient verified proof of income); Hosch v. Hosch, 1996-0258, pp. 2–3 (La. App. 4 Cir. 1996), 684 So. 2d 541, 542–43 (upholding trial court's determination of income and support order in absence of verified income statement from either party when it found that court had sufficient evidence to determine gross monthly earnings); *but see* Clarke, 219 So. 3d at 1232 ("[Louisiana Revised Statutes Section] 9:315.2 requires, at the very least, verified income statements showing gross income and adjusted gross income, with documentation of current and past earnings for the parties, and both party's [sic] most recent federal tax return.").

373. Collins v. Collins, 2012-726, p. 4 (La. App. 3 Cir. 12/5/12), 104 So. 3d 771, 775.

374. *See* Kern v. Kern, 2000-1126 (La. App. 4 Cir. 4/25/01), 786 So. 2d 193, 195–96 (holding that it was proper for trial court to set party's income based on the most recent tax return when that party placed into evidence the previous three years of tax returns to show decreasing income and prove a material change in circumstances sufficient to warrant a reduction in support).

within the court's discretion to rely on sworn testimony and a wage survey when the father failed to appear at the hearing or provide any documentation of his income.[375]

Courts may also consider a party's potential income, rather than actual income, if a party fails to provide verified income statements, or if the statements provided reflect an inaccurate picture of a person's income. If the court considers potential income rather than actual income, it must articulate its reasons.[376] Documentation of shared expenses may also be required if either parent has remarried.[377] On request of the court or a party, a parent who has remarried shall provide relevant information regarding the source of payments for their household expenses, as long as the request is filed within a reasonable time prior to the hearing on child support.[378]

A parent who possesses an ownership interest in a business must provide additional documentation to the court and other party including, but not limited to, the last three personal and business state and federal income tax returns, the most recent profit and loss statements, balance sheets, financial statements, quarterly sales tax reports, and personal and business bank account statements, receipts, and expenses.[379] Finally, courts permit parties to stipulate to either party's income or that all documentation available to determine income is before the court.[380]

---

375. State in the Interest of Washington v. Bourgeois, 2022-0931 (La. App. 1 Cir. 3/8/23), 2023 WL 2397373.

376. *Compare* Ventura v. Rubio, 2000-0682, pp. 9–10 (La. App. 4 Cir. 3/16/01), 785 So. 2d 880, 888–89 (finding a setting of child support was arbitrary and an abuse of discretion when the trial court assigned income to a party with no evidentiary basis for doing so), *with* Harris v. Harris, 2007-0966, pp. 5–6 (La. App. 4 Cir. 2008), 976 So. 2d 347, 350–51 (finding no error in trial court's use of income for period immediately prior to becoming voluntarily underemployed, rather than setting support order based on evidence of party's current income).

377. *See* Section 7:31.

378. Failure to timely file a request for evidence of expense sharing shall not be grounds for a continuance. La. Stat. Ann. § 9:315.2(A).

379. This shall include all attachments and schedules, specifically Schedule K-1 and W-2 forms, 1099 forms, and amendments. La. Stat. Ann. § 9:315.2(A).

380. *See* Landry v. Landry, 97-183, pp. 3–4 (La. App. 4 Cir. 11/25/98), 724 So. 2d 271, 272–73 (upholding trial court's finding of defendant's monthly income, after no testimony was taken, when both parties stipulated that all documents required to determine income were before the court); Jones v. Jones, 92-1345 (La. App. 3 Cir. 12/08/93), 628 So. 2d 1304, 1304 (finding that trial court could award child support without receiving any evidence from father because mother presented documentation regarding father's gross income, joint stipulations were entered into the record concerning the gross income of both parties, and father admitted that the reason he failed to submit any evidence was because his attorney misled him to believe that he would have the opportunity at a later date to present such evidence).

§ 7:35 Basic Child Support Amount

Once the adjusted gross income of each party is determined, the income is combined and a percentage share of the combined income is calculated for each party.[381] This percentage share will be used to calculate the child support owed by each party, i.e., the income shares model.[382]

The schedule in § 315.19 provides the basic monthly child support obligation based on the parties' combined adjusted gross income and the number of children subject to the child support order.[383] If the monthly gross income falls between the amounts shown on the schedule, the parties must interpolate to determine the exact figure.[384] The income level on the schedule spans from $1050 to $50,000 per month,[385] and for combined monthly income above $50,000 per month, the award must exceed the highest scheduled amount.[386] However, "in no event shall the lowest basic amount of child support in the schedule be construed as a limitation on the court's authority to deviate under R.S. 9:315.1(C)."[387]

§ 7:36 Additions to and Deductions from the Basic Child Support Amount

Following the assessment of the basic child support obligation, additions and deductions are made to reach the total child support award.[388] While the basic child support figure covers generally food, clothing, and shelter for any child, the additional expenses are necessary to tailor the award for each particular child. Examples of these additions (and deductions) are discussed below.

---

381. La. Stat. Ann. § 9:315.2(C).

382. La. Stat. Ann. § 9:315.8(C).

383. La. Stat. Ann. § 9:315.2(D). Under prior law, the mandatory minimum child support award was $100.00. *See* La. Stat. Ann. § 315.14 (repealed by Acts 2023, No. 24, § 2).

384. La. Stat. Ann. § 9:315.13(B). Although the statute uses the term "extrapolate," the proper term for estimating between two data points is interpolate. *See* Merriam-Webster Dictionary (interpolate: "to estimate values of (data or a function) between two known values").

385. La. Stat. Ann. § 9:315.19. The guidelines are reviewed every four years. La. Stat. Ann. § 9:316.16.

386. La. Stat. Ann. § 9:315.13(C).

387. La. Stat. Ann. § 9:315.2(D). Note that for awards when the combined adjusted gross income falls below the lowest level, a deviation is no longer appropriate and a specific provision directs the court. *See* La. Stat. Ann. § 9:315.13(A).

388. *See* La. Stat. Ann. §§ 9:315.2(E), 9:315.3–315.7; *see also* Genusa v. Genusa, 2009-0917, p. 5 (La. App. 1 Cir. 12/23/09), 30 So. 3d 775, 778 ("These expenses then become a part of the total child support obligation owed by the parents."); Lauve v. Lauve, 2008-0076, p. 9 (La. App. 4 Cir. 8/20/08), 6 So. 3d 184, 190 (adding expenses of sections 9:315.4–315.6 to the basic child support obligation).

§ 7:37 Additions to and Deductions from the Basic Child Support Amount— Child Care Costs

Net child care costs, which are defined as "reasonable costs of child care incurred by a party due to employment or job search, minus the value of the federal income tax credit for child care," are added to the basic child support obligation.[389] Applying the federal income tax credit to the gross child care cost is mandatory, and failure to properly account for it will result in reversible error.[390] At least one court has allowed expenses for net child care costs to remain in place even when a parent is temporarily unemployed, as long as the parent requires child care during the absence from work and the absence from work is only temporary.[391]

In 2014, the legislature amended the statute to extend the cost of reasonable child care expenses to parents who are receiving job training or education to obtain or enhance earning power, unless doing so unreasonably burdens the parent paying child support.[392] Prior to this amendment, the court had no authority to authorize child care expenses based on one party obtaining higher education—even if it "may ultimately enure to the benefit of the children."[393]

In *Campbell v. Campbell*, the simple testimony of an unemployed parent that she planned to return to work as soon as possible was enough for the court to approve the

389. La. Stat. Ann. §§ 9:315(C)(7), 9:315.3. Net childcare costs are determined by subtracting the Federal Credit for Child and Dependent Care Expenses provided in Internal Revenue Form 2441 from the total child care costs. La. Stat. Ann. § 9:315.3(A).

390. *See* Lewis v. Lewis, 624 So. 2d 1211, 1211–12 (La. 1993) (granted writ application and remanded to the trial court with an order to "fix as part of the award net child care costs, which constituted reasonable costs minus a reasonably estimated prospective credit to federal income tax for child care."); Harris v. Harris, 2007-0966 (La. App. 4 Cir. 2008), 976 So. 2d 347, 354–55 (remanding back to trial court for recalculation of support award to conform with guidelines requiring deduction of federal income tax credit from child care costs); Bonnecarrere v. Bonnecarrere, 2009-1647, p. 11 (La. App. 1 Cir. 4/14/10), 37 So. 3d 1038, 1048–49 (remanding to trial court based on failure to add child care expenses or consider tax credit as required by mandatory language of statute); Walden v. Walden, 2000-2911 (La. App. 1 Cir. 8/14/02), 835 So. 2d 513, 521–22 (remanding to trial court for recalculation of support award using net child care costs in conformity with statute when trial court did not consider the federal tax credit).

391. *See* Hargroder v. Hargroder, 96-583, p. 3 (La. App. 3 Cir. 11/6/96), 682 So. 2d 999, 1001 (allowing for child care addition to calculation for temporarily unemployed parent when unemployment was due to medical condition and that medical condition necessitated need for child care; forgoing subtraction of tax credit from expenses when, due to inability to work and nature of tax code, no taxes were due by parent and therefore the tax credit had zero value).

392. La. Stat. Ann. § 9:315.3(B) (2022) (enacted by Act No. 134, 2014 La. Acts 1422).

393. Hamilton v. Hamilton, 97-2909, pp. 6–9 (La. App. 4 Cir. 6/24/98), 716 So. 2d 412, 416–17 (finding that one party's college attendance was not due to employment or job search and stating that "the legislature apparently does not feel that education under these circumstances is an end sufficient to justify the award of the means to attain it.").

cost of after-school daycare.[394] However, in most cases, for those costs to be included, a claimant must provide proof that the child-care expenses are work-, training-, or education-related, as well as evidence of the cost of the child care.[395]

§ 7:38 Additions to and Deductions from the Basic Child Support Amount— Health Insurance Premiums

Next, the cost of the health insurance premiums for the share attributed to the child shall be added to the basic support obligation.[396] To ensure health insurance for all children, the court may order a party to enroll or maintain the child in a health benefits plan, policy, or program.[397] When determining which party shall be required to enroll the child or maintain insurance for the child, the court must consider each party's available health insurance program, employment history, personal income, and any other resources.[398] As noted above in Section 7:21, there is some disagreement about whether the premium paid by a party's employer to provide health insurance for the child should be included in that parent's gross income.[399] Regardless, health insurance premiums that relate to the child *only* should be an addition to the basic child support obligation.

---

394. Campbell v. Campbell, 95-1711, p. 13 (La. App. 1 Cir. 10/10/96), 682 So. 2d 312, 321 (unable to find manifest error in trial court's determination that the "costs were necessitated by [] efforts to obtain employment.").

395. Jackson v. Belfield, 1998-0440, p. 9 (La. App. 4 Cir. 11/25/98), 725 So. 2d 32, 36–37 (refusing to include child care costs because no proof of cost or relationship to work was provided).

396. La. Stat. Ann. § 9:315.4(A). The definition of "health insurance premiums" is as follows:

> "Health insurance premiums" means the *actual amount paid by a party* providing health insurance *on behalf of a child*. It does not include an amount paid by an employer or any amount paid for coverage of any other persons. If more than one dependent is covered by health insurance paid through a lump-sum dependent-coverage premium, and not all of the dependents are the subject of the guidelines calculation, the cost of the coverage will be prorated among the dependents covered before being applied to the guidelines.

La. Stat. Ann. § 9:315(C)(4) (emphasis added).

397. La. Stat. Ann. § 9:315.4(A).

398. La. Stat. Ann. § 9:315.4(A). *See* State v. Redmann, 2020-00338, (La. 7/31/20), 347 So. 3d 649 (affirming trial court decision that father could seek reimbursement against mother for her proportionate share of premiums for the child's health insurance coverage, where father paid his second wife for health insurance coverage on the child through her employer); In re Touchet, 2013-0815, pp. 8–10 (La. App. 1 Cir. 9/13/13), 135 So. 3d 30 (allowing mother to obtain health insurance for the child because she already had a policy of insurance and had begun investigating coverage for the child and father was only speculating); State ex rel. Metcalf v. Samuels, 34,302 (La. App. 2 Cir. 12/20/00), 775 So. 2d 1162, 1162 (requiring father to enroll child under his health insurance plan was appropriate given that his plan provided greater coverage than the mother's).

399. *See* Section 7:22.

§ 7:39 Additions to and Deductions from the Basic Child Support Amount— Extraordinary Medical Expenses

"Extraordinary medical expenses incurred on behalf of the child" are also added to the basic child support obligation.[400] Medical expenses considered "extraordinary" are those that are unreimbursed by medical insurance and exceed $250 per child per calendar year.[401] Ordinary medical expenses, those that are unreimbursed and less than or equal to $250 per child per year, are incorporated into the calculation of support through the schedule of support in Louisiana Revised Statutes Section 9:315.19.[402] Medical expenses may include orthodontia, dental treatment, asthma treatment, physical therapy, treatment for chronic health problems, and professional counseling or psychiatric therapy for diagnosed mental disorders not covered by medical insurance.[403]

"Extraordinary" is not synonymous with unforeseen, unusual, or remarkable; rather, it relates to any unreimbursed, current or future, medical expenses which exceed the statutorily imposed dollar amount of $250 per child per calendar year.[404]

---

400. La. Stat. Ann. § 9:315.5; *see* Bonnecarrere v. Bonnecarrere, 2009-1647 (La. App. 1 Cir. 4/14/10), 37 So. 3d 1038, 1049 (ordering trial court to amend its judgment ordering obligor to pay percentage of "ordinary" medical expenses, which are included in support schedule, rather than "extraordinary" medical expenses). Although costs for extraordinary medical expenses shall be added to the basic support obligation, the statute does not require that the costs be assessed proportionately based on each parent's percentage share of the support obligation. *See* Hall v. Hall, 11-60, p. 6 (La. App. 5 Cir. 5/24/11), 67 So. 3d 635, 640 (holding that payments of extraordinary medical expenses need not be proportionate to the parties' respective child support obligations); Satterfield v. Alline, 2000-2069, p. 6 (La. App. 4 Cir. 12/12/01), 805 So. 2d 309, 312–13 ("allocation of payment of future medical expenses not covered by insurance lies within the discretion of the trial court").

401. La. Stat. Ann. § 9:315.5. Prior to 2004, extraordinary medical expenses were defined as "uninsured expenses over one hundred dollars for a single illness or condition." La. Stat. Ann. § 9:315(C)(3), *amended by* Act No. 251, 2004 La. Acts 1307–08. As a result, a parent could pay numerous co-payments during a year, none of which could be included as additional expenses on the child support worksheet because they did not exceed $100 for each illness. *See* Treitler v. Treitler, 2003-1931, pp. 5–7 (La. App. 4 Cir. 4/7/04), 872 So. 2d 1200, 1204. In Act 251 of the 2004 Regular Legislative Session, the legislature removed the reference to "one hundred dollars for a single illness or condition" in favor of an annual accumulation of uninsured expenses of "$250 per child per year." In 2008, the legislature amended the provision to be clear that "per year" equated to a calendar year.

402. La. Stat. Ann. § 9:315(C)(8).

403. La. Stat. Ann. § 9:315(C)(8).

404. *See* Welborne v. Welborne, 29,479, p. 7 (La. App. 2 Cir. 5/7/97), 694 So. 2d 578, 583 (holding that the court is not precluded from adding "ordinary, noncovered, medical expenses" to the basic child support obligation); Carmouche v. Carmouche, 03-1106, p. 5 (La. App. 5 Cir. 2/23/04), 869 So. 2d 224, 227 (citing to *Welborne* and upholding support order requiring that parties equally share any "uncovered" medical expenses); Treitler, 872 So. 2d at 1204–05 (ordering father to reimburse proportional share of cost of air purifier when evidence showed that purchase was reasonable and necessary in treatment of child's asthma and although prescribed by physician, purchase was not covered by insurance); Satterfield, 805 So. 2d at 312 (stating that ordinary medical expenses are those "covered by a health insurance policy").

After the domiciliary party has paid unreimbursed ordinary medical expenses of $250 per child per calendar year, the remaining medical expenses should be attributed to the parties based on their percentage share. Therefore, any co-payments or deductibles are accounted for in the monthly schedule amount up to $250 per child per calendar year. Once that amount is reached, the parties should share extraordinary medical expenses for the remainder of the year.

For an expense to be included as an extraordinary medical expense, courts have required the parent to show a need for the expense and details concerning the charges.[405] For example, in *Loftin v. Loftin*, the court refused to include expenses of counseling for the child based on the parent's self-serving testimony without the identification of the counselor or the basis for the counseling.[406] In addition, courts have refused to increase child support without clear costs of the medical expense.[407] With adequate evidence of need and cost, medical expenses over $250 should be shared by the parties on a pro-rata basis.

§ 7:40 Additions to and Deductions from the Basic Child Support Amount— Other Extraordinary Expenses

Additional out-of-pocket expenses incurred on behalf of the child can be added to the basic support obligation on agreement of the parties or by order of the court.[408] These expenses include those required for attending a special or private school necessary to meet the needs of the child,[409] for the transportation of the child from one party to the other,[410] and special expenses incurred for child-rearing and intended to enhance the health, athletic, social, or cultural development of a child.[411] Notably, payment of an extraordinary expense for purposes of child support is distinct from the decision to incur the expense, which relies on the rules governing custody. In other

405. *See* Loftin v. Loftin, 2009-0795, p. 5 (La. App. 3 Cir. 2/1/10), 28 So. 3d 1274, 1278–79; Lloyd v. Lloyd, 94-0421, pp. 6–7 (La. App. 1 Cir. 12/22/94), 649 So. 2d 32, 36 (upholding trial court's decision to not increase basic support award for extraordinary medical expenses when no evidence, other than mother's testimony, was presented as to the children's need for braces); Jackson v. Belfield, 1998-0440, p. 9 (La. App. 4 Cir. 11/25/98), 725 So. 2d 32, 37–38 (holding that trial court did not err by failing to add extraordinary medical expenses to basic support calculation when the only evidence offered of child's condition and treatment was mother's testimony).

406. Loftin, 28 So. 3d at 1278–79.

407. Lloyd, 649 So. 2d at 36.

408. La. Stat. Ann. § 9:315.6.

409. La. Stat. Ann. § 9:315.6(1) (describing expenses allowable by statute are those for tuition, registration, books, and supply fees required for attendance).

410. La. Stat. Ann. § 9:315.6(2). *See* Steinebach v. Steinebach, 2007-38, pp. 17–23 (La. App. 3 Cir. 5/2/07), 957 So. 2d 291, 301–04; Porter v. Porter, 35,301, p. 8 (La. App. 2 Cir. 12/19/01), 803 So. 2d 399, 404–05; Jones v. Jones, 92-1345 (La. App. 3 Cir. 12/08/93), 628 So. 2d 1304, 1304.

411. La. Stat. Ann. § 9:315.6(3) (noting expenses include, but are not limited to, camp, music or art lessons, travel, and school sponsored extracurricular activities); *see also* Lehr v. Lehr, 31,181, p. 4 (La. App. 2 Cir. 10/28/98), 720 So. 2d 412, 414–15.

words, even though a domiciliary parent has the authority to make decisions regarding the child, the nondomiciliary parent is not necessarily required to pay for that decision under the Child Support Guidelines.[412]

First, to include special or private school expenses as part of the child support order, the statute requires that the school be necessary "to meet the needs of the child."[413] Prior to 2001, the law required the parent to prove that the school met the "particular educational" needs of the child, which required a greater showing.[414] Now, the "needs of the child" can be met by evidence that the school provides stability or continuity in the child's educational program.[415]

The party seeking to include the expense of private school tuition bears the burden of proving a need that will be met by attendance at that particular school.[416] If the parents agreed initially to send the child to private school, courts are more likely to include expenses of continued private school education.[417] Because the issue is heavily

---

412. *See, e.g.*, Porter, 803 So. 2d at 404 (finding that although mother could decide that child should have a car, father was not required to pay for a share of it); Romig v. Romig, 00-1922, pp. 2–4 (La. App. 5 Cir. 5/30/01), 788 So. 2d 656, 658–69 (recognizing that mother, as sole custodian of the children, is permitted to choose the schools which the children attend, but the issue of payment of a pro-rata share of costs requires a specific showing of need for the child, which mother did not provide).

413. La. Stat. Ann. § 9:315.6(1).

414. La. Stat. Ann. § 9:315.6 (2001 rev. cmt.); *see, e.g.*, Walden v. Walden, 2000-2911 (La. App. 1 Cir. 8/14/02), 835 So. 2d 513, 522.

415. La. Stat. Ann. § 9:315.6 (2001 Revision Comment); *but see* Angelette v. Callais, 2010-2279, pp. 7–9 (La. App. 1 Cir. 5/6/11), 68 So. 3d 1122, 1126–28 (upholding trial court's refusal to add private school tuition to child support calculation when mother enrolled child in private school without consulting father and no evidence of need to attend private school was present).

416. Rabalais v. Rabalais, 2023-164 (La. App. 3 Cir. 10/18/23), 372 So. 3d 970 (requiring father to pay pro-rata share of private school tuition because attendance there greatly enhanced the educational benefits for the children); A.S. v. D.S., 2014-1098, pp. 18–21 (La. App. 4 Cir. 4/8/15), 165 So. 3d 247, 258–59 (finding that mother met her burden of proof that the environment in the private school provided block scheduling and smaller class sizes, which assisted with the child's learning issues, and assisted with social issues); *but see* Short v. Short, 11-3, pp. 11–16 (La. App. 5 Cir. 10/25/11), 77 So. 3d 405, 412–16 (holding that mother failed to meet her burden of showing that children's attendance at private school was necessary to meet their needs because children, who had been homeschooled by mother, did not have a consistent history of attendance at private school that would require their attendance to ensure stability and continuity in their education, mother did not present supporting evidence that private school in which she had enrolled children met their needs, and mother admitted that there were excellent public schools in her area); Dep't of Soc. Servs. ex rel. Anders v. Swords, 2008-0580, pp. 2–4 (La. App. 3 Cir. 11/5/08), 996 So. 2d 1267, 1269–70 (finding that mother's testimony alone as to child's medical condition and school performance was insufficient to establish that child had needs that required attendance in a private school).

417. Flickinger v. Flickinger, 2005-2228, pp. 7–9 (La. App. 1 Cir. 12/28/06), 952 So. 2d 70, 75–76 (including private school tuition because parties had discussed putting child in private school before child was born); Williams v. Williams, 2004-1624, pp. 6–8 (La. App. 4 Cir. 3/16/05), 899 So. 2d 628, 630–33 (upholding trial court's award of support for private school based on party's original agreement and finding continuity of education at private school was in child's best interest); Walden, 835 So. 2d at 522 (finding no error in trial court's award of private school tuition and expenses when parents agreed while married that child should attend private school and obligor-parent failed to offer any evidence that attendance at private school was not in child's best interest); Bertrand v. Bertrand, 637

fact-based and depends on the credibility of the parents either requesting or opposing private school tuition, the decision is highly discretionary.[418] Courts undeniably consider a parent's ability to pay,[419] and, in some cases, they have permitted attendance at a requested private school without the concomitant requirement for the opposing parent to pay a share of the cost.[420] In any event, the trial court has great discretion over whether or not to include private school tuition and expenses as part of the child support calculation, even if it finds private school to be in the child's best interest.[421]

Second, expenses for transportation of the child between the parties can be included as an extraordinary expense.[422] The cost of a vehicle, gasoline, and other related travel expenses incurred to transport the child would be an appropriate addition. The Third Circuit in *Jones v. Jones* rejected a *credit* for the cost of one parent to transport the children to and from the other parent's home.[423] While the court recognized that travel expenses could be *added* to the child support obligation, it concluded that the use of a *credit* against the parent's share of child support was unsupported by the record.[424] Subsequently, the same circuit in *Steinebach v. Steinebach* explained further that the costs of transportation to exercise physical custodial time could be a basis for a deviation from the guidelines, or it could reduce the amount owed by the nondomiciliary parent because extraordinary expenses directly paid by one parent reduce that parent's payment to the domiciliary parent.[425]

Certainly, a deviation from the guidelines is permitted when in the best interest of the child or inequitable to the parties,[426] and one party shouldering the expense of travel may be inequitable to that party. To better apportion transportation expenses between both parents, transportation costs should be included as an addition to the basic child support obligation *before* deducting it as a direct expense of the nondomi-

---

So. 2d 531, 534 (La. Ct. App. 1 Cir. 1993) (assigning share of private school tuition to father because he had agreed with former wife for children to attend private school and continue in that school).

418. *See, e.g.*, Thomas v. Robinson, 15-82, pp. 7–8 (La. App. 5 Cir. 9/23/15), 176 So. 3d 698, 702 (finding that trial judge had to make a credibility determination and did not abuse his discretion).

419. *See* Millet v. Braud, 15-363, pp. 8–9 (La. App. 5 Cir. 11/19/15), 179 So. 3d 849, 854–55 (affirming trial court's refusal to add private school tuition when neither parent had significant disposable income).

420. Romig, 788 So. 2d at 658–69 (recognizing that mother, as sole custodian of the children, is permitted to choose the schools which the children attend, but the issue of payment of a pro-rata share of costs requires a specific showing of need for the child, which mother did not make); Boudreaux v. Boudreaux, 2022-804 (La. App. 3 Cir. 7/5/23); 368 So. 3d 754 (mother not in contempt for failing to pay private school tuition when no court order required her to).

421. *See* Guste v. Guste, 2016-0872 (La. App. 4 Cir. 4/19/17), 217 So. 3d 542, 546 (upholding trial court's decision to exclude private school tuition and fees in the child support calculation because the parties demonstrated the ability to come together to make major education decisions regarding the children and had already paid private school tuition for the year).

422. La. Stat. Ann. § 9:315.6.

423. Jones v. Jones, 92-1345 (La. App. 3 Cir. 12/08/93), 628 So. 2d 1304, 1307.

424. Jones, 628 So. 2d at 1307.

425. Steinebach, 957 So. 2d at 301–04.

426. La. Stat. Ann. § 9:315.1(B).

ciliary parent. That way, both parents share the cost of transportation in their pro-rata shares, even though one parent ultimately pays the cost of travel and receives a credit for the full amount. In the *Steinebach* case, it was unnecessary to include the travel costs as an addition to the basic child support obligation because the mother had no income and the father bore all of the expense.[427]

Third, expenses for other developmental activities can be included as an expense.[428] The guidelines provide examples such as "camp, music, art lessons, travel, and school sponsored extracurricular activities."[429] Prior to the legislation specifically permitting expenses for other developmental activities for the child,[430] courts were reluctant to include these items as an "other extraordinary expense," finding them to be a part of the basic child support obligation.[431] After 2008, expenses for gymnastics, baseball, summer camps, guitar lessons, and the like should be included as an extraordinary expense and shared between the parents pro-rata.

§ 7:41 Additions to and Deductions from the Basic Child Support Amount— Deduction for Child's Income

Income of a child that reduces the basic needs of that child may be considered as a deduction from the basic support obligation.[432] The ability of a child to work does not relieve the parent of a support obligation, but the child's actual earnings may be considered to reduce child support owed by a parent.[433] Two exceptions exist: the income earned while the child is a full-time student,[434] and the benefits received by a child from public assistance programs.[435] If the child is a full-time student, the child's income is not deducted from child support due, regardless of whether the income was earned during the summer or holiday break.[436] Benefits received by the child from public assistance programs include funds from the Family Independence Temporary

427. Steinebach, 957 So. 2d at 301–04.

428. La. Stat. Ann. § 9:315.6(3).

429. La. Stat. Ann. § 9:315.6(3).

430. La. Stat. Ann. § 51:579 (2008) (repealed 2011).

431. *See* Lehr v. Lehr, 31,181, pp. 2–4 (La. App. 2 Cir. 10/28/98), 720 So. 2d 412, 414–15 (reversing the trial court's inclusion of gymnastics and baseball expenses, finding no statutory authority for doing so); Valure v. Valure, 96-1684, pp. 4–5 (La. App. 1 Cir. 6/20/97), 696 So. 2d 685, 688 (refusing to include expenses for dance classes).

432. La. Stat. Ann. § 9:315.7(A).

433. Dep't of Soc. Servs. ex rel. C.J.V. v. Neahtery, 39,796, pp. 4–5 (La. App. 2 Cir. 7/29/05), 909 So. 2d 40, 43 (citing Borden v. Borden, 550 So. 2d 901 (La. Ct. App. 2 Cir. 1989)) (holding that trial court incorrectly determined that minor child was not entitled to child support after having obtained a GED and working full time at $6.25 per hour).

434. La. Stat. Ann. § 9:315.7(B).

435. La. Stat. Ann. § 9:315.7(C).

436. La. Stat. Ann. § 9:315.7(B).

Assistance Programs, food stamps, or other means-tested programs.[437] Like student income, needs-based programs that offer payments to the child do not reduce the amount of support due by the parents for the child.

Social Security benefits received by the child due to a parent's earnings may also be considered as income to the child, but if considered, they must be credited against the obligation of the parent on whose earning record the benefits are based.[438] By Act 386 of 2006, the legislature made clear that Social Security benefits that are received by the child are not credited against the basic child support obligation; rather, they are credited against the amount in child support owed by the parent on whose earning record the benefits are based.[439] Thus, cases that were decided before the 2006 amendment, which credited Social Security benefits against the basic child support obligation, have been legislatively overruled.[440] Nonetheless, trial courts retain their discretion to include the Social Security benefits as income to the child at all.[441]

Notably, if Social Security benefits are received due to the earnings of a parent who has predeceased the child, those benefits should be included as income for the child because the benefits are paid to reduce the needs of the child.[442] Although the 2006 amendment did not address this situation, the general rule governing income of the

---

437. La. Stat. Ann. § 9:315.7(C).

438. La. Stat. Ann. § 9:315.7(D); Dep't of Soc. Servs. ex rel. B.B. v. C.B., 14-360, pp. 5–6 (La. App. 5 Cir. 10/29/14), 164 So. 3d 850, 852–53. *See* Cloud v. Dean, 1015-297, pp. 8–10 (La. App. 3 Cir. 12/16/15), 181 So. 3d 939, 943 (remanding to trial court and ordering that child support arrearages be recalculated by crediting obligor's child support obligation with the amount of Social Security benefits the child received on obligor's behalf); Dep't of Child. & Fam. Servs. ex rel. Jones v. Peters, 2014-1800 (La. App. 1 Cir. 6/5/15), 174 So. 3d 1200, 1202–03 (finding that trial court incorrectly applied Social Security benefits as a deduction from the basic child support calculation, rather than credit towards obligation of parent for whom benefit was received); Tudtenbier v. Tudtenbier, 2010-0301, p. 7 (La. App. 1 Cir. 10/27/10), 48 So. 3d 413, 418 (same); Genusa v. Genusa, 2009-0917 (La. App. 1 Cir. 12/23/09), 30 So. 3d 775, 779–80 (same).

439. Flickinger v. Flickinger, 2005-2228 (La. App. 1 Cir. 12/28/06), 952 So. 2d 70, 74 (applying amended Louisiana Revised Statutes Section 9:315.7 retroactively to credit the parent on whose income the Social Security benefit was paid to the child).

440. *See, e.g.*, Camacho v. Camacho, 2006-330 (La. App. 3 Cir. 9/27/06), 940 So. 2d 190, 192–93 (upholding the trial court's treatment of Social Security benefits that father received on behalf of child as income to the child, and applying it to child's basic child support award, rather than as a credit only to the father's child support obligation, where the mother and father had joint physical custody of the child).

441. Armstrong v. Rayford, 39,653, pp. 7–8 (La. App. 2 Cir. 5/11/05), 902 So. 2d 1214, 1219; Rougeau v. Rougeau, 2002-484 (La. App. 3 Cir. 10/30/02), 829 So. 2d 1125, 1126–27; Phillips v. Phillips, 95-2043, pp. 3–4 (La. App. 1 Cir. 5/10/96), 673 So. 2d 333, 335 (finding no abuse of discretion in trial court's decision not to consider the Social Security benefits received by the children to be income as the decision is discretionary). Note, too, that if a child support arrearage exists, the court must hold an evidentiary hearing before a lump sum payment received by a child is used to reduce an arrearage. *See* State v. Jones, 2011-1520, p. 2 (La. App. 3 Cir. 4/4/12), 87 So. 3d 1014, 1016 (holding Social Security benefits paid on behalf of child that were over and above father's basic child support obligation could not be credited against father's Family Independence Temporary Assistance Programs (FITAP) arrears, where arrearages were owed to the state, not to the child).

442. *See* Corley v. Corley, 600 So. 2d 908, 910 (La. Ct. App. 4 Cir. 1992).

child should apply to account for the increased benefit to the child, which should then be subtracted from the basic child support obligation.[443]

§ 7:42 Total Child Support Obligation

Once additions to and deductions from the basic child support obligation are made, the total child support obligation is determined, from which each party's pro-rata share is calculated.[444] The noncustodial or nondomiciliary party will owe his share as a money judgment of child support to the custodial or domiciliary party, minus any court-ordered direct payments for work-related net child-care costs, health insurance premiums, extraordinary medical expenses, or extraordinary expenses.[445]

Once the obligation is reduced to judgment, the support must be paid until the judgment is modified or terminated by a subsequent judgment or until it is terminated by operation of law.[446] Two exceptions have been recognized by courts: (1) when the evidence shows that the parties have clearly agreed to waive or otherwise modify the court-ordered payments, or (2) when the domiciliary parent has voluntarily placed custody of the children with the nondomiciliary parent.[447] In all orders not being enforced by the Department of Children and Family Services, the court is required to include an immediate income assignment as a part of the order, unless there is a written agreement between the parties[448] or the court finds good cause not to require an immediate income assignment.[449]

The guidelines provide useful worksheets for calculating the total child support obligation whether custody is sole, joint, shared, or split.[450] Worksheet A is used for sole, split, or joint custody that is not shared, and Worksheet B is used for joint, shared custody.

---

443. *See, e.g.*, Corley, 600 So. 2d at 910 (netting the Social Security benefits against the nondomiciliary party's share but determining it would have been more appropriate to net the amount against the basic child support obligation first and then divide the remaining share between the parties).

444. La. Stat. Ann. § 9:315.8.

445. La. Stat. Ann. § 9:315.8(D).

446. Hendrix v. Hendrix, 457 So. 2d 815, 817 (La. App. 1 Cir. 1984).

447. Hendrix, 457 So. 2d at 817.

448. La. Stat. Ann. § 9:303(B)(1) ("'Written Agreement' means a written alternative arrangement signed by both parents, reviewed by the court, and entered into the record of the proceedings.").

449. La. Stat. Ann. § 9:303(B)(2) ("Good cause" may exist when: "(a) there has been no delinquency in payment of child support for the six calendar months immediately preceding the filing of the motion for modification of an existing child support order, (b) the respondent is agreeable to a consent judgment authorizing an automatic ex parte immediate income assignment if he becomes delinquent in child support payments for a period in access of one calendar month, (c) the respondent is not likely to become delinquent in the future, (d) any other sufficient evidence which, in the court's discretion, constitutes good cause.").

450. La. Stat. Ann. § 9:315.20.

§ 7:43 Total Child Support Obligation— Worksheet A

Worksheet A is the most commonly used worksheet for calculating child support. If a party has sole custody, joint custody, or split custody, Worksheet A will allocate the share owed by each party.[451] Split custody occurs when each party is the sole custodial or domiciliary parent of at least one child for whom support is due.[452] When split custody applies, each party computes a theoretical total child support obligation under Worksheet A for the child in the custody of the other parent, and the parent owing the greater amount of child support owes the difference between the two amounts to the other parent.[453] When joint custody is awarded, an adjustment may be available to account for the time that the nondomiciliary party spends with the child, which is not captured by the general guideline amount.[454]

While the calculations under the worksheets appear simply formulaic, litigants and courts have struggled with whether to use Worksheet A versus Worksheet B. The decision can result in a significant shift in the amount of child support owed.[455] As a result, the majority of litigation surrounding the worksheets revolves around whether the joint custodial arrangement amounts to shared custody under Worksheet B or whether the court should instead use Worksheet A and apply a joint custody adjustment that may reduce the child support owed by the obligor. Generally speaking, obligors benefit by using Worksheet B, so obligees prefer to use Worksheet A, even with a joint custody adjustment. Each will be discussed in the following sections.

§ 7:44 Total Child Support Obligation— Joint Custody Adjustment Using Worksheet A

The "joint custody adjustment" used in Worksheet A originated in section 315.8(E) of the Child Support Guidelines with the jurisprudential gloss from the Louisiana Supreme Court case of *Guillot v. Munn*.[456] In *Guillot*, the father of two children sought a reduction in the monthly child support he owed, arguing that he spent 37% of the year with the children as the nondomiciliary, joint custodian.[457] He argued that he should receive a credit on the amount he owed in child support, considering the increased time with and resulting expenses incurred on behalf of the children.[458] Noting that the

451. La. Stat. Ann. § 9:315.20.
452. Nixon v. Nixon, 631 So. 2d 42 (La. Ct. App. 2 Cir. 1994).
453. La. Stat. Ann. § 9:315.10.
454. La. Stat. Ann. § 9:315.8(E); *see* Section 7:44.
455. *See* Section 7:45.
456. Guillot v. Munn, 1999-2132 (La. 3/24/00), 756 So. 2d 290, 297–301.
457. Guillot, 756 So. 2d at 293.
458. Guillot, 756 So. 2d at 293.

issue was *res nova*, the court held that a reduction in the amount due by the nondomiciliary parent may be warranted when the nondomiciliary parent has the children for an "extraordinary" amount of time each year.[459] The court did not define extraordinary but explained that the guidelines presume some typical amount of physical custodial time because the statutory scheme envisions the child having regular contact with both parents.[460] Before making any adjustment, however, the court required an assessment of the economic impact on both parties to assure the domiciliary parent's ability to care for the child financially.[461] The majority was met with two strong dissents.[462]

The year after *Guillot* was decided, the legislature gave specificity to the meaning of "extraordinary" when it enacted section 9:315.8(E). The statute requires the court to consider the period of time that a child spends with the nondomiciliary parent as "a basis for adjustment" of the amount of support paid during that period of custody, but nothing in the statute makes an adjustment mandatory.[463] First, the adjustment only applies to joint custody that is not shared custody.[464] Shared custody occurs when the parents have physical custody "for an approximately equal amount of time."[465] In such cases, Worksheet B will apply.[466] Second, extraordinary time occurs when the obligor has physical custody of the child for more than 73 days, which amounts to 20% of the year.[467] Third, like the Supreme Court warned,[468] a rigid analysis of time cannot be the only basis for adjustment; rather, the court must consider the amount of time the child spends with the nondomiciliary parent, the continuing expenses of the domiciliary party, the financial burdens placed on both parties,[469] the best interest of

---

459. Guillot, 756 So. 2d at 299.

460. Guillot, 756 So. 2d at 300–01.

461. Guillot, 756 So. 2d at 300–01.

462. Guillot, 756 So. 2d at 302–09 (Johnson, J., dissenting) (Victory, J., dissenting).

463. La. Stat. Ann. § 9:315.8(E)(1). The trial court is vested with a great deal of discretion in determining whether a deviation is warranted. The showing which must be made is that a deviation is in the best interest of the child and that a mechanical application of the guidelines would be inequitable to the parties.

464. La. Stat. Ann. § 9:315.8(E).

465. La. Stat. Ann. § 9:315.9(A)(1).

466. La. Stat. Ann. § 9:315.9(B).

467. La. Stat. Ann. § 9:315.8(E)(2). What constitutes a "day" is left to the discretion of the trial court but cannot be less than four hours of physical custody by the nondomiciliary parent. *Id.*

468. *See* Guillot, 756 So. 2d at 300.

469. *See, e.g.*, Jones v. Jones, 38,790 (La. App. 2 Cir. 06/25/04), 877 So. 2d 1061, 1069–70 (upholding denial of deviation when children spent 28% of time with nondomiciliary parent, domiciliary parent's ongoing expenses were unaffected during time spent with nondomiciliary parent, and total support payments were only 11–12% of nondomiciliary parent's income); Farrar v. Farrar, 2000-1487 (La. App. 4 Cir. 7/11/01), 791 So. 2d 796, 799 (upholding refusal to deviate when nothing showed that the child's expenses were reduced during periods with nondomiciliary parent and domiciliary parent's expenses remained constant); Falterman v. Falterman, 97-192, p. 8 (La. App. 3 Cir. 10/8/97), 702 So. 2d 781, 785 (refusing to allow for deviation when father spent 40% of time with the children but the domiciliary parent's ongoing expenses were unaffected and constant during periods of time with the nondomiciliary parent).

the child, and the equities between the parties.[470] The party who seeks the credit bears the burden of proof.[471]

Note that the joint custody adjustment is distinct from a deviation and is referenced on one line at the end of the Worksheet A, permitting "adjustments ... if ordering a credit for a joint custodial arrangement."[472] Distinguishing an adjustment from a deviation is critical because the reasons for a deviation must be made a part of the record,[473] whereas an adjustment is simply within the trial court's discretion.[474] Because the point at which joint custody converts to shared custody is uncertain, it can be difficult to determine whether a child support determination for a joint custodial arrangement should rely on Worksheet A (with or without a joint custody adjustment) or should be characterized as shared custody using Worksheet B.[475]

§ 7:45 Total Child Support Obligation— Worksheet B

Worksheet B is used to determine child support when shared custody exists.[476] "Shared custody" means that each parent has physical custody of the child for "an approximately equal amount of time."[477] An approximately equal amount of time is described in the comments as a percentage, namely 49% to 51%.[478] If shared custody exists, with or without court order, then the basic support obligation is multiplied by one and one-half to account for the increased expense in raising a child between two households sharing equal time.[479] The basic child support obligation is divided between

470. La. Stat. Ann. § 9:315.8(E)(3); *see, e.g.*, Gary v. LeBlanc, 2016-1054, p. 12 (La. App. 3 Cir. 6/7/17), 222 So. 3d 784, 791 (upholding trial court's deviation when no evidence appeared in the record that there was an increased financial burden on the nondomiciliary parent or a decreased burden on the domiciliary parent due to joint custodial time); Hagen v. Hagen, 2011-1130, p. 14 (La. App. 1 Cir. 8/15/12), 110 So. 3d 172, 180 (upholding trial court's downward deviation and allowing for credit to obligor parent, who had custody of two children 40% of the time and the other child 50% of the time, even though combined adjusted gross income exceeded guidelines); Walden v. Walden, 2000-2911 (La. App. 1 Cir. 8/14/02), 835 So. 2d 513, 520–21.

471. La. Stat. Ann. § 9:315.8(E)(4).

472. La. Stat. Ann. § 9:315.20.

473. La. Stat. Ann. § 9:315.1(B)(1).

474. *See* Murphy v. Murphy, 2004-1332, p. 8 (La. App. 3 Cir. 2/2/05), 894 So. 2d 542, 548 (noting that a joint custody adjustment does not require the court to provide oral or written reasons for its decision); *compare* Atkinson v. Atkinson, 2016-0759, pp. 10–11 (La. App. 4 Cir. 2/15/17), 212 So. 3d 631, 637–38 (remanding to trial court for failing to provide written or oral reasons for support deviation that suspended support payments during two summer months when obligor parent had custody).

475. *Compare* Murphy, 894 So. 2d at 548 (applying a one-twelfth joint custody adjustment when father had physical custody approximately 50% of the time), *with* Broussard v. Rogers, 10-593, p. 6 (La. App. 5 Cir. 1/11/11), 54 So. 3d 826, 830 (using Worksheet B for shared custody when father exercised 46% physical custody).

476. La. Stat. Ann. § 9:315.9(B).

477. La. Stat. Ann. § 9:315.9(A)(1).

478. La. Stat. Ann. § 9:315.9 cmt. (a).

479. La. Stat. Ann. § 9:315.9(A)(2).

the parents in proportion to their respective adjusted gross incomes, and then each parent's theoretical child support obligation is cross-multiplied by the actual percentage of time the child spends with the other party to determine each party's share.[480] Each parent's proportionate share of net child care costs and extraordinary adjustments is added to the amount, and any direct payments made by a party are deducted.[481] The parent who owes the greater amount of child support will owe the difference between the two figures to the other parent, but in no event can that amount be higher than the amount that parent would have owed as the domiciliary parent.[482]

No court has established a threshold percentage to apply the rules for shared custody. In fact, courts have considered cases with the same division of time between the parties, with divergent results.[483] Because shared custody requires only "an approximately equal amount of time," regardless of the court order of custody, courts have discretion to determine whether a custody arrangement constitutes shared custody. For example, in *Cole v. Cole*, even though the custody order provided for "shared custody," the court applied Worksheet A without any joint custody adjustment because the father exercised physical custodial time only 39% of the year, and he was unable to prove that his former wife enjoyed a decreased financial burden due to his increased time.[484]

To the contrary, in *Janney v. Janney*, the court found that a father's exercise of 45.3% of physical custodial time, compared to the mother's 54.7%, amounted to an approximately equal amount of time and therefore applied Worksheet B.[485] The court relied on a prior opinion, which found that a 37%–63% split amounted to shared custody because the order of custody so provided.[486] The majority was met with both a concurrence and dissent, which argued that statements made in a custody order should not be determinative of whether the parents have custody an approximately equal amount of time.[487] The dissent insisted that a 10% margin between 45% and 55% was too large to constitute an approximately equal amount of time.[488]

---

480. La. Stat. Ann. § 9:315.9.

481. La. Stat. Ann. § 9:315.9. The court can order each party to pay his or her proportionate share of uninsured medical expenses that are under $250. *Id.*

482. La. Stat. Ann. § 9:315.9(A)(7).

483. *Compare* Mendoza v. Mendoza, 14-954, pp. 4–7 (La. App. 5 Cir. 5/14/15), 170 So. 3d 1119, 1122–23 (court used Worksheet A when father exercised 46% physical custody), *and* Desoto v. Desoto, 2004-1248, pp. 4–7 (La. App. 3 Cir. 2/2/05), 893 So. 2d 175, 178–80 (court used Worksheet A when father exercised 45% physical custody), *with* Broussard v. Rogers, 10-593, p. 6 (La. App. 5 Cir. 1/11/11), 54 So. 3d 826, 830 (court used Worksheet B for shared custody when father exercised 46% physical custody), *and* Janney v. Janney, 2005-0507, pp. 3–6 (La. App. 1 Cir. 7/26/06), 943 So. 2d 396, 398–400 (court used Worksheet B when father exercised 45.3% custody).

484. Cole v. Cole, 2013-1442, p. 14 (La. App. 3 Cir. 6/4/14), 139 So. 3d 1225, 1233.

485. Janney, 943 So. 2d at 398–400.

486. Janney, 943 So. 2d at 400 (citing Westcott v. Westcott, 04-2298, p. 2 (La. App. 1 Cir. 11/4/05), 927 So. 2d 377, 378).

487. Janney, 943 So. 2d at 403 (McDonald, J., concurring) (Hughes, J., dissenting).

488. Janney, 943 So. 2d at 403 (Hughes, J. dissenting).

The structures of the guidelines seem to suggest that Worksheet A is the rule and Worksheet B is the exception, applying the latter only in the limited situation of shared custody, which requires a party to prove that physical custody is approximately equal (49%/51% split). Because one day with the child could comprise four hours or 12 hours,[489] a court should be given discretion to consider the extent of time the party spends with the child, rather than just counting days. And if custody is not "approximately equal," the joint custody adjustment provides the court with ample discretion to adjust the amount of child support owed under Worksheet A.[490] The Third Circuit in *Lea v. Saunders* best explained how the guidelines should function: "[I]f a party exercises physical custody less than 49%, that party cannot rely on the presumption and the mathematical calculations established in La. R.S. 9:315.9 [shared custody] and must bear the burden of proof in accordance with La. R.S. 9:315.8 [joint custody adjustment]."[491]

So, if the court determines that each party exercises equal (50%/50% split) or approximately equal (49%/51% split) physical custody, then "the statute creates a rebuttable presumption that the financial burden is being shared equally without the necessity of the additional proof" that is required when seeking the joint custody adjustment.[492] While courts have not uniformly adopted this approach, several courts have chosen to apply Worksheet A with a joint custody adjustment when the difference in physical custodial time was greater than 2%.[493]

The approach articulated by the *Lea* court is preferable because of the significant reduction in support owed under Worksheet B, which should be applied only to a true 50%/50% shared custody or a slight difference in equal time like a 49%/51% split. To illustrate, consider a hypothetical couple with two children where the adjusted gross income of the parents is $10,000 per month; the petitioner earns 40%, the respondent earns 60%, and only the basic child support obligation is due.[494] If the petitioner has physical custodial time of the children for 55% of the year and the respondent for 45%, then using Worksheet A, the petitioner would be entitled to $1,232 per month.[495] Using Worksheet B, however, the petitioner would only be entitled to $462 per month.[496]

---

489. For purposes of the joint custody adjustment, a "day" can constitute no less than four hours of physical custody of the child. La. Stat. Ann. § 9:315.8(E)(2).

490. La. Stat. Ann. § 9:315.8(E).

491. Lea v. Saunders, 2004-762, p. 10 (La. App. 3 Cir. 12/22/04), 890 So. 2d 764, 769–70 (denying a joint custody adjustment to a father whose physical custodial time equaled 43% because their arrangement did not significantly reduce the domiciliary parent's expenses).

492. Lea, 890 So. 2d at 767.

493. *See* Mendoza, 170 So. 3d at 1122–23 (reviewing several cases).

494. As of the 2025 guidelines, the basic child support obligation for two children with an AGI of $10,000 per month was $2,053. La. Stat. Ann. § 9:315.19.

495. The petitioner's share would be 40% of $2,053 or $821, and the respondent's share would be 60% of $2,053 or $1,232.

496. The base child support of $2,053 would be multiplied by one and one half, which would equal $3,080. The petitioner's 40% would be $1,232 and the respondent's 60% share would be $1,848. The petitioner then multiplies the obligation by the time spent with the other party (45%), which totals $554, and the respondent does the same (multiplied by 55%), which totals $1,016. The obligation owed is the difference between the two figures: $462.

While it might be preferable for the respondent to receive a downward adjustment to his obligation based on increased time spent with the child, that adjustment would be unlikely to drop the amount of child support owed to $462 per month unless the parties truly shared equal (or approximately equal) time.

§ 7:46 Deviation from the Guidelines

The law provides a rebuttable presumption that the amount of child support established through use of the guidelines is the appropriate amount.[497] Accordingly, a court may deviate from the guidelines only if its application "would not be in the best interest of the child or would be inequitable to the parties."[498] Even though any factor that impacts the best interest of the child or affects the equities among the parties can be a valid reason to deviate, the guidelines provide eight reasons why a court may deviate.[499]

If a court deviates, it must provide specific oral or written reasons for the deviation, it must articulate the amount of support under the guidelines without a deviation, and it must state the particular facts and circumstances that warrant the deviation.[500] Failure of the trial court to provide specific oral or written reasons is reversible error.[501] Finally, the Louisiana Supreme Court has made clear that deviations should only occur in "limited circumstances" so that the function of the guidelines may be preserved.[502]

---

497. La. Stat. Ann. § 9:315.1(A).

498. La. Stat. Ann § 9:315.1(B). See Louisiana Revised Statutes Section 9:315.1(C)(1)–(8) for an illustrative list of reasons for which a court may deviate. La. Stat. Ann. § 9:315.1.

499. *See* La. Stat. Ann. § 9:315.1(C)(1)–(8). Subpart (C)(8) is a "catch-all" that allows a court discretion to rely on any factor to deviate.

500. La. Stat. Ann. § 9:315.1(B). *See also* Guillot v. Munn, 1999-2132 (La. 3/24/00), 756 So. 2d 290, 297 ("When deviating from the guidelines, courts must give specific reasons for the deviation, specifying the particular facts and circumstances evidencing that a deviation is warranted."); Curtis v. Curtis, 34,317 (La. App. 2 Cir. 11/1/00), 773 So. 2d 185, 193. Failure of the court to provide oral or written reasoning for deviation from the guidelines is legal error and precludes appellate review of the deviation. Aydelott v. Aydelott, 42,161, p. 4 (La. App. 2 Cir. 5/9/07), 957 So. 2d 350, 353. *See also* Dep't of Soc. Servs. Off. of Fam. Support ex rel. Young v. Jennings, 2000-0814, p. 3 (La. App. 4 Cir. 6/27/01), 790 So. 2d 750, 752 (stating that the trial court failed to comply with the provisions of Louisiana Revised Statutes Section 9:315.1(B)); Dep't of Child. & Fam. Servs. ex rel. A.F. v. Fennidy, 11-547, pp. 6–7 (La. App. 5 Cir. 12/13/11), 82 So. 3d 421, 424–25 (reversing the trial court's support award because the reasons for deviation were not justified by reference to the child support statutes or evidence in the record); Dufresne v. Dufresne, 10-963 (La. App. 5 Cir. 5/10/11), 65 So. 3d 749, 754; State v. Reed, 44,119. pp. 3–4 (La. App. 2 Cir. 1/14/09), 5 So. 3d 269, 271–72.

501. *See* Dep't of Child. & Fam. Servs. ex rel. A.F., 82 So. 3d at 424–25; Kelly v. Kelly, 1999-2478 (La. App. 1 Cir. 12/22/00), 775 So. 2d 1237, 1244.

502. Guillot, 756 So. 2d at 297 (citing Stogner v. Stogner, 98-3044 (La. 7/7/99), 739 So. 2d 762, 767); Lea v. Saunders, 2004-762 (La. App. 3 Cir. 12/22/04), 890 So. 2d 764, 764.

§ 7:47 Deviation from the Guidelines— Income that Falls Outside of the Guidelines

Prior to January 1, 2025, a deviation was appropriate when the parties' combined monthly adjusted gross income was above or below the stated guideline amount.[503] After January 1, 2025, while a court must set child support for families whose adjusted gross income either falls below or exceeds the child support guideline amounts, the amount is no longer considered a deviation.[504] Rather, the guidelines specifically provide rules when income falls outside of its parameters.

The guideline amounts initially ranged from a combined adjusted gross income of $600 to $10,000 per month.[505] In 2001, the schedule was amended to extend the highest guideline amount to $20,000 per month and to impose a statutory minimum award of $100 per month in child support.[506] By 2008, the highest income amount was extended again to $30,000 per month, and the lowest level on the guidelines reflected $0 in monthly adjusted gross income.[507] The statutory minimum child support award of $100 per month remained.[508] In 2016, the highest guideline amount was extended to $40,000 per month.[509] In 2023, and the statutory minimum award of child support was repealed,[510] and in 2024, the highest guideline amount was extended to $50,000 per month.[511]

Prior to January 1, 2024, a deviation was appropriate when the "adjusted gross income of the parties is not within the amount shown on the schedule in [Revised Statutes Section] 9.315.19."[512] At that time, the lowest amount on the guidelines schedule was $0, meaning that in no instance would the combined adjusted gross income of the parties be less than the lowest sum on the schedule. In addition, it is questionable whether a deviation actually occurs when a court sets a support obligation for parents whose combined income is not even on the schedule. As a result, the legislature removed from the deviation factors when income falls outside of the guidelines,[513] and $1050 became the lowest combined income amount on the guidelines.[514] In addition, section 315.13 specifically addresses how a court should award child support when income is below the lowest amount ($1050) or above the highest amount ($50,000).

503. La. Stat. Ann. § 9:315.1(C)(1)–(2).

504. Acts 86 and 448 of 2024 collectively cleaned up the guidelines to make clear that high or low income is no longer considered a deviation, but is simply a function of the guidelines.

505. Act No. 1082, 2001 La. Acts 2275–80, *amended by* La. Stat. Ann. § 9:315.14 (2022).

506. Act No. 1082, 2001 La. Acts 2285.

507. Act No. 585, 2008 La. Acts 2467.

508. Act No. 585, 2008 La. Acts 2467.

509. Act No. 602, 2016 La. Acts 1967.

510. Acts 2023, No. 24, § 2, eff. January 1, 2024.

511. Acts 2024, No. 86, § 1, eff. January 1, 2025.

512. La. Stat. Ann. § 9:315.1(C)(1) (2016).

513. Acts 2024, No. 448, § 2, eff. January 1, 2025.

514. Acts 2024, No. 86, § 1, eff. January 1, 2025.

When the combined adjusted gross income is *below* the lowest level of the guidelines, the court must consider the actual income of the parties, whether a party is voluntarily unemployed or underemployed, and "any other evidence of a parent's ability to pay."[515] When the combined adjusted gross income is *above* the highest level of the guidelines, the court has broad discretion to set the amount of basic child support in line with the best interest of the children and the circumstances of each party, but "in no event shall it be less than the highest amount set forth in the schedule."[516] Because the court is acting with broad discretion, no universal mathematical formula is applied.[517] Instead, the overriding factor in determining is the best interest of the children and the equities of the parties.[518] Although some courts have simply extrapolated upward from the guidelines for above-the-guidelines cases, concern for the needs and lifestyle of the children should be paramount.[519] In fact, one court specifically stated, "[S]imple extrapolation, without considering the child's needs, is not an acceptable method."[520]

Now, for both low- and high-income earners, setting basic support is no longer characterized as a deviation, because the guidelines provide no listed amount from which to deviate. When choosing an amount above or below the guidelines, the trial court need not provide written reasons for its chosen amount.[521] Rather, once the court determines the basic child support amount (which, for high income earners, must exceed the highest amount on the guidelines), it may make adjustments and deviations to that amount in the same way as any other child support analysis.[522] Indeed, a deviation could result in a final child support order in an amount that may be less than

---

515. La. Stat. Ann. § 9:315.13, as amended by Acts 2024, No. 448, § 2, eff. January 1, 2025.

516. La. Stat. Ann. § 9:315.13(C)(1). Note that this statute never referred to the court's calculation as a deviation from the guidelines, which had been inconsistent with section 9:315.1. Rather, the court must use its discretion to set the basic child support calculation. *See* Fontana v. Fontana, 2013-0916, p. 12 (La. App. 4 Cir. 2/12/14), 136 So. 3d 173; Harang v. Ponder, 2009-2182, p. 21 (La. App. 1 Cir. 3/26/10), 36 So. 3d 954, 968 (noting that the trial court had "discretion in setting the base child support award" and not that it made any deviation). Louisiana Civil Code Article 141 provides that "the court may order either or both of the parents to provide an interim allowance or final support for a child based on the needs of the child and the ability of the parents to provide support."

517. *See* Harang, 36 So. 3d at 968; Serrate v. Serrate, 1996-1545, p. 7 (La. App. 1 Cir. 12/20/96), 684 So. 2d 1128, 1133.

518. La. Stat. Ann. § 9:315.13(D) (2025). For high-income earners, *see* Dufresne v. Dufresne, 10-963 (La. App. 5 Cir. 5/10/11), 65 So. 3d 749, 755 (citing Duffel v. Duffel, 2010-274, p. 3 (La. App. 5 Cir. 11/9/10), 54 So. 3d 675, 676). *See* Serrate, 684 So. 2d at 1133 (concluding that there is "no universal mathematical formula that can be applied" when the parties' income exceeds tables and that the court must consider the needs of the child and the circumstances of those who are obligated to pay); Rosenbloom v. Rosenbloom, 1994-1762, p. 6 (La. App. 4 Cir. 4/26/95), 654 So. 2d 877, 880 (holding that "the trial court's procedure of taking a flat percentage of the amount above the guideline's maximum without concern and discretion by the court in balancing the needs and lifestyle of the child clearly leads to an excessive award").

519. *See, e.g.*, Collins v. Collins, 2012-726 (La. App. 3 Cir. 12/5/12), 104 So. 3d 771, 776–77; Holleman v. Barrilleaux, 2014-499 (La. App. 3 Cir. 11/19/14), 161 So. 3d 789, 794; Rosenbloom, 654 So. 2d at 881; Colvin v. Colvin, 1994-2413 (La. App. 1 Cir. 10/6/95), 671 So. 2d 444, 447.

520. Piccione v. Piccione, 2001-1086 (La. App. 3 Cir. 5/22/02), 824 So. 2d 427.

521. *See* Fontana, 136 So. 3d at 185.

522. *Compare* La. Stat. Ann. § 9:315.13, *with* La. Stat. Ann. § 9:315.1(C).

the highest guideline amount.[523] That would be unusual, however, because children are entitled to the same standard of living as if they resided with the obligor parent whenever financially feasible.[524]

In 2008, the legislature provided an additional option to provide support for children of high-income earners: the court may order a portion of an award to "be placed in a spendthrift trust to be used for the educational or medical needs of the child."[525] Unless the parties agree to a later date, the trust must terminate when the child attains the age of 24.[526] Otherwise, its provisions are governed by the Louisiana Trust Code.[527] Directing child support into a spendthrift trust for the child permits the capture of additional funds from high-income earners to extend support of the child into majority, but it should not be used as a mechanism to oversee the expenditures of the domiciliary parent.[528]

§ 7:48 Deviation from the Guidelines— Support of Other Dependents

A deviation is also appropriate to account for "[t]he legal obligation of a party to support dependents who are not the subject of the action before the court and who are in that party's household."[529] This sub-section should not to be confused with the "multiple family"[530] deviation found in subpart (C)(2), which permits deviation when

523. *See* Hagen v. Hagen, 2011-1130 (La. App. 1 Cir. 8/15/12), 110 So. 3d 172, 176–80 (permitting final support at an amount below the highest amount set forth in the schedule because of the amount of time nondomiciliary parent spent with the child, even though the adjusted gross income of parents exceeded the schedule); *but see* Fontana, 136 So. 3d 173 (upholding trial court order exceeding the schedule when parents' adjusted income exceeded the table, basic support obligation was set in accordance with table, and final support order was based on statutory adjustments based on actual expenses—tuition, school expenses, health insurance, etc.—of children).

524. Hagen, 110 So. 3d at 176–80; Dufresne, 65 So. 3d at 755 (citing Langley v. Langley, 2007-754, p. 6 (La. App. 4 Cir. 3/26/08), 982 So. 2d 881, 885)); Duffel, 54 So. 3d at 677–78.

525. La. Stat. Ann. § 9:315.13(B)(2), enacted by Act No. 579, 2008 La. Acts 2416–17, as amended by Act No. 448, § 2 and redesignated as La. Stat. Ann. § 9:315.13(C)(2).

526. La. Stat. Ann. § 9:315.13(C)(2).

527. La. Stat. Ann. § 9:315.13(C)(2).

528. *See, e.g.*, Harang v. Ponder, 2009-2182, p. 21 (La. App. 1 Cir. 3/26/10), 36 So. 3d 954, 966, 970 (affirming trial court's denial of nondomiciliary parent's request to place funds in trust when there was no evidence that child support payments were misused or unnecessary).

529. La. Stat. Ann. § 9:315.1(C)(1) (prior to the amendments by Act 448 of 2024, the support for other dependents deviation was numbered (C)(3)). Any deviation by the court is "expressly discretionary." Frederick v. Buckingham, 44,458, p. 5 (La. App. 2 Cir. 6/24/09), 15 So. 3d 1223, 1226–27 (finding no abuse of discretion in trial court's refusal to deviate when obligor parent "provided inadequate proof" of support obligation for a child living outside the home and also had sole custody of three-year-old son living in the home).

530. "Multiple families is defined as one or more families with children not living in the home of the noncustodial or nondomiciliary parent (obligor parent) who have existing child support orders that reduce such obligor parent's income below the lowest amount in the tables." La. Stat. Ann. § 9:315.1 cmt. (b) (2001).

an obligor already has existing child support orders with multiple families, thereby reducing the obligor's income for another child support order.[531]

Support of other dependents, by contrast, allows the court, in its discretion, to deviate when a party is legally required to support a dependent who is living with that party.[532] The party seeking the deviation bears the burden of establishing that the amount of support under the guidelines without a deviation would be inequitable to that party.[533] As such, evidence of the expenses incurred in support of the dependent who is not subject to the litigation is required.[534]

On the one hand, if an obligor is paying a preexisting child support payment to another person, that amount is deducted from gross income to arrive at the "adjusted gross income" figure.[535] On the other hand, the dependent deviation allows a court to consider an adjustment to the guideline amount of child support when an obligor is supporting a dependent person by caring and hence paying for them to live in their own household, rather than paying out support to another.[536] "Dependent" is not

---

531. La. Stat. Ann. § 9:315.1(C)(2) (prior to the amendments by Act 448 of 2024, the multiple families deviation was numbered (C)(4)).

532. *See, e.g.*, Frederick, 15 So. 3d at 1227 (finding that "any downward deviation" for other dependents living in a party's household is purely within the trial court's discretion); Dep't of Soc. Servs. ex rel. L.B. v. L.B., 2007-127, p. 4 (La. App. 5 Cir. 9/25/07), 968 So. 2d 762, 764.

533. Dep't of Soc. Servs. ex rel. L.B., 968 So. 2d at 764 (upholding juvenile court judge's refusal to deviate from guidelines as it is "well within his discretion" to do so when obligor fails to establish that the amount of support "was not in the child's best interest or was inequitable to him" and finding that there is no restriction limiting application of the statute "only to cases where the household dependent is older than the subject of the action before the court."). *See also* Lambert v. Lambert, 2006-2399, p. 8 (La. App. 1 Cir. 3/23/07), 960 So. 2d 921, 927 ("the parent seeking the deviation … [has] the burden of proving that an application of the child support guidelines would be in the best interest of his child or would be inequitable to him because of his expenses in connection with his obligation to support his other [] children.").

534. *See* Curtis v. Curtis, 34,317, p. 13 (La. App. 2 Cir. 11/1/00), 773 So. 2d 185, 194 (refusing to consider deviation from the guidelines because no evidence was entered "as to the expenses incurred in supporting" obligor's child from second marriage, "nor to the extent to which present wife contributes to the support of that child"); Guillot v. Munn, 1996-0620, p. 1 (La. App. 2 Cir. 6/21/96), 676 So. 2d 86, 86 ("A deviation pursuant to this provision … must be supported by an evidentiary basis."); Greene v. Greene, 634 So. 2d 1286, 1291 (La. Ct. App. 3 Cir. 1994) (upholding trial court's refusal to deviate from guidelines for expenses of providing for daughter in subsequent marriage when no evidence was presented as to the amount contributed for her support).

535. La. Stat. Ann. § 9:315(C)(1)(a). The amount is deducted whether the payment is made pursuant to a court order or by voluntary payment by the party. La. Stat. Ann. § 9:315(C)(1)(a).

536. *See* Lambert, 960 So. 2d at 927 (considering but rejecting obligor's request to deviate even though he was supporting three children from a previous marriage without support from their mother); State ex rel. Metcalf v. Samuels, 34,302, p. 2 (La. App. 2 Cir. 12/20/00), 775 So. 2d 1162, 1165 (awarding a downward deviation because obligor cared for child living in his household); Dep't of Soc. Servs. ex rel. Robert v. Hughes, 08-183, p. 7 (La. App. 5 Cir. 6/19/08), 989 So. 2d 805, 808 (finding that district court erred in deviating from the guidelines when it ordered a reduction in support based on obligor parent's minor children when there was no existing support order, nor did they reside in his home).

defined in the statute and could be interpreted to include not only minor children but other dependent relatives living in the household.[537]

The Child Support Guidelines clearly distinguish between payments given to another for a nondomiciliary child, which are subtracted from gross income,[538] and a credit for the support of a domiciliary child, which is a deviation factor.[539] One court aptly explained this apparent contradiction: "Although there may be no fundamental difference between having to pay child support to another and having to pay for goods and services to support and maintain a child in one's own household, there is a legal difference because the statute clearly distinguishes between the two."[540] Unfortunately, courts appear reluctant to deviate from the guidelines when an obligor is supporting a dependent living in the household,[541] but the difficulty in assessing how much to deviate from the guidelines should not prevent the unfortunate incongruity that results when an obligor rightfully cares for a dependent in the household. Refusing to even consider evidence of a party's financial obligations to dependents in the household would constitute an abuse of discretion.[542]

§ 7:49 Deviation from the Guidelines—Multiple Families

A deviation is also appropriate when an obligor has children in multiple families for which he is paying child support.[543] To rely on the "multiple families" deviation, an obligor must have existing child support orders for children in one or more families for which he owes child support.[544] The multiple families deviation is intended to ameliorate the negative consequence of earlier child support orders depressing the obligor's calculated income in child support proceedings for subsequent children.[545] Because an obligor's preexisting child support orders are subtracted from the obligor's monthly gross income, the income used to calculate child support for later families is necessarily lower, leading to a lesser amount of money awarded to children from later families.

---

537. According to the IRS, the term "dependent" means a "qualifying child" or "qualifying relative." I.R.S. Publication 501 (Dec. 9, 2022).

538. La. Stat. Ann. § 9:315(C)(3)(d)(1).

539. La. Stat. Ann. § 9:315.1(C)(1).

540. Timmons v. Timmons, 605 So. 2d 1162, 1168 (La. Ct. App. 2 Cir. 1992) (emphasis omitted).

541. *But see* Gerage v. McCants, 2023-0294 (La. App. 1 Cir. 11/9/23), 2023 WL 7405225 (affirming the trial court's downward deviation for father because a mechanical application of the guidelines would be inequitable because of his expenses in connection with his obligation to support his other children).

542. Pratt v. Wells, 2002-1032, p. 8 (La. App. 4 Cir. 2/26/03), 840 So. 2d 1230, 1235.

543. La. Stat. Ann. § 9:315.1(C)(2).

544. La. Stat. Ann. § 9:315.1(C)(2); *see also* Dep't of Child. & Fam. Servs. ex rel. A.F. v. Fennidy, 11-547 (La. App. 5 Cir. 12/13/11), 82 So. 3d 421, 424. Prior law also required the obligor to prove that the multiple support orders would reduce his income below the lowest income level on the schedule. La. Stat. Ann. § 9:315.1(C)(4), amended by Acts 2023, No. 24, § 1, eff. Jan. 1, 2024 and Acts 2024, No. 448, eff. Jan 1, 2025.

545. *See* Taylor Gay, Comment, *All in the Family: Examining Louisiana's Faulty Birth Order-Based Discrimination*, 73 La. L. Rev. 295 (2012) for a discussion of the issues involving multiple families.

In 2008, after extensive work by the Louisiana Law Institute, Senate Bill 605 was introduced, which attempted to amend the child support guidelines to treat children of separate households with a common parent equally in the award of child support.[546] Because of the difficulty in achieving equality among children in different jurisdictions with different needs, the proposed law adopted a new worksheet, used complex formulas, and was not well-received. The bill was referred to committee but never heard.[547] As a result, although current law permits courts to make a multiple family deviation, courts have not appeared to do so.[548]

§ 7:50 Deviation from the Guidelines—Extraordinary Medical Expenses

Deviations can be made for the extraordinary medical expenses of a party not accounted for in the guidelines.[549] These extraordinary medical expenses are distinguishable from those included in the calculation of child support. When calculating child support, the *child's* extraordinary medical expenses are assessed. By contrast, the deviation applies when the *parent* has extraordinary medical expenses, or when the *parent* is responsible for the extraordinary medical expenses of another person.[550] The parent seeking the deviation bears the burden of proving present medical expenses.[551]

§ 7:51 Deviation from the Guidelines—Extraordinary Community Debt

Extraordinary community debt of the parties can likewise lead to a deviation.[552] Extraordinary debt alone will not justify a deviation; rather, the debt must be community debt shouldered by one parent.[553] For example, in *Savoie-Moore v. Moore*, the court affirmed a deviation based on extraordinary community debt when the payor parent was juggling the obligations of both child support and community debt, had

546. S.B. 605, 2008 Leg., Reg. Sess. (La. 2008).

547. S.B. 605, 2008 Leg., Reg. Sess. (La. 2008).

548. Dep't of Child. & Fam. Servs. ex rel. A.F., 82 So. 3d at 424–25 (reversing the trial court because no evidence was submitted to show that the multiple support orders would reduce the obligor's income below the lowest income level, even though the appellate court was unclear whether the trial court even used the multiple family deviation); Dep't of Soc. Servs. ex rel. Robert v. Hughes, 08-183, p. 7 (La. App. 5 Cir. 6/19/08), 989 So. 2d 805, 808 (finding that district court erred in deviating from the guidelines when it ordered a reduction in support based on obligor parent's minor children when there was no existing support order).

549. La. Stat. Ann. § 9:315.1(C)(3).

550. La. Stat. Ann. § 9:315.1(C)(3).

551. Cameron v. Cameron, 2007-1091, p. 4 (La. App. 3 Cir. 3/5/08), 2008 WL 585001 (affirming trial court's denial of a deviation because the obligor did not include evidence of present extraordinary medicals, only possible future diagnoses and cost of medical treatment).

552. La. Stat. Ann. § 9:315.1(C)(4).

553. Pratt v. Wells, 2002-1032 (La. App. 4 Cir. 2/26/03), 840 So. 2d 1230, 1236. (deviation for extraordinary community debt was not appropriate where parents were unmarried, and debts were

to borrow money from his parents to cover the debts, and was considering declaring bankruptcy.[554] Payment of extraordinary community debt can also serve as one of many considerations that may justify a deviation from the guidelines.[555] In either case, it falls on the party arguing for a deviation to show that payment of an extraordinary debt causes an inequity to a party or is not in the best interest of the child.[556]

§ 7:52 Deviation from the Guidelines— Disability of a Parent or Adult Child

The last two deviation factors, before the "catch-all" factor, address issues of disability. Deviation is permitted when "[t]he permanent or temporary total disability of a spouse ... diminishes his present and future earning capacity, his need to save adequately for uninsurable future medical costs, and other additional costs associated with such disability, such as transportation and mobility costs, medical expenses, and higher insurance premiums."[557] The parent seeking the deviation must prove the disability through medical records or testimony for a trial court to properly deviate from the guidelines.[558]

In addition to considering the disability of the parent, the guidelines permit a court to consider the financial burden imposed when an obligor is ordered to pay long-term support for an adult child with a disability.[559] The court should consider not only the long-term nature of the support, but the circumstances surrounding the manifestation of the disability.[560]

---

not incurred jointly with the mother); Dep't of Soc. Servs. ex rel. Harrison v. Rodell, 98-0093, pp. 9–10 (La. App. 1 Cir. 5/18/99), 733 So. 2d 1247, 1253 (deviation for extraordinary community debt was not appropriate where parents were unmarried).

554. Savoie-Moore v. Moore, 98-0235, p. 6 (La. App. 4 Cir. 9/16/98), 719 So. 2d 551, 555.

555. Steinebach v. Steinebach, 2007-38 (La. App. 3 Cir. 5/2/07), 957 So. 2d 291, 302 (allowing for deviation based on multiple factors including obligor making community debt payments in excess of $450 per month).

556. *See* Lord v. Lord, 2009-457, p. 7 (La. App. 3 Cir. 11/4/09), 22 So. 3d 1134, 1139 (not allowing deviation for community debt when, although debt was established at trial, obligor made no showing of how the debt created inequity after assuming community debt in original consent judgment).

557. La. Stat. Ann. § 9:315.1(C)(6).

558. *See* Moody v. Moody, 2019-642, 2020 WL 578877, at *4–5 (La. App. 3 Cir. 2/5/20) (mother failed to prove a disability and inability to work to deviate from the guidelines).

559. La. Stat. Ann. § 9:315.1(C)(7).

560. La. Stat. Ann. § 9:315.1(C)(7).

§ 7:53 Deviation from the Guidelines— "Catch-All" Factor

Finally, deviation may be allowed pursuant to "[a]ny other consideration which would make application of the guidelines not in the best interest of the child or children or inequitable to the parties."[561] This "catch-all" factor is very broad and grants much discretion to the court to consider any other consideration. For example, in *Mize v. Mize*, the court set the award based on an upward deviation from the guidelines.[562] In that case, mother had physical custody of the children for essentially 100% of the time; the father kept the children overnight only approximately nine times within an 18-month period despite their joint custody arrangement. Consequently, the mother's expenses were elevated by feeding and entertaining the children on weekends when the father did not do so. The appellate court agreed with the trial court's reasoning that "it would be inequitable to place the burden of virtually all the day-to-day expenses on" the mother.[563]

§ 7:54 Tax Deductions

The basic child support obligations set forth in the schedule "presume that the custodial or domiciliary party has the right to claim the child as a dependent."[564] However, for federal and state income tax purposes, the nondomiciliary party has the right to claim the child as a dependent if the nondomiciliary parent's support obligation equals or exceeds 50% of the total support obligation, and the court makes two findings after a contradictory hearing.[565] First, the court must conclude that no arrearages are owed by the nondomiciliary party.[566] Second, the court must find that the right to claim the child would substantially benefit the nondomiciliary party without signifi-

---

561. La. Stat. Ann. § 9:315.1(C)(8).

562. Mize v. Mize, 2022-0094 (La. App. 1 Cir. 11/4/22), 355 So. 3d 16.

563. Mize, 355 So. 3d at 20.

564. La. Stat. Ann. § 9:315.18(A).

565. La. Stat. Ann. § 9:315.18(B). Prior to 2004, the nondomiciliary party was automatically entitled to the dependency deduction if no arrearages were owed. *See* S.B. 564, 2004 Leg., Reg. Sess. (La. 2004). Courts diverge on whether allocating the tax exemption to the noncustodial parent constitutes a deviation. The Third Circuit opinion concluded that because the schedule presumes that the custodial or domiciliary parent has the right to claim the child as a dependent, any allocation of tax exemptions to the noncustodial or nondomiciliary parent is a deviation from the guidelines for which the court must provide written or oral reasons. *See* Greene v. Greene, 634 So. 2d 1286, 1291–92 (La. Ct. App. 3 Cir. 1994) *amended by* 638 So. 2d 1245 (La. Ct. App. 3 Cir. 1994). However, the First Circuit has opined that "the matter currently before us [on the issue of tax exemptions] does not involve a deviation from the amount of support set forth in the child support guidelines." Dirteater v Dirteater, 2022-0266 (La. App. 1 Cir. 9/16/22), 352 So. 3d 1016, 1021.

566. La. Stat. Ann. § 9:315.18(B)(1)(a); Dep't of Soc. Servs. v. Mason, 09-1088, pp. 6–10 (La. App. 5 Cir. 6/29/10), 44 So. 3d 744, 748–750 (finding order granting nondomiciliary father tax deductions for minor children for two tax years was manifest error when father failed to present records from Louisiana Automated Support Enforcement System or testimony to demonstrate that he was not in arrears in child support).

cantly harming the domiciliary party.[567] The absence of proof can be enough to deny the tax exemption.[568]

If the nondomiciliary parent's request is granted, the child support order must set forth the years that the nondomiciliary party may claim the deduction, require the domiciliary parent to execute all needed forms, and prohibit the nondomiciliary party from claiming the deduction when arrearages are owed on the last day of the year.[569]

Even if the nondomiciliary parent does not pay 50% or more of the child support obligation, the parent can still be entitled to claim a child as a dependent if, after a contradictory motion, the judge finds: (1) the domiciliary party is unemployed and will not file a tax return, (2) the obligor owes arrears, and (3) the obligor's anticipated tax refund can be used to reduce the arrears.[570] Although a nondomiciliary party may meet all of these statutory requirements to claim the tax deductions, courts are still given discretion to allocate the deductions and craft a support order in the best interests of the child and equitable to the parties.[571]

---

567. La. Stat. Ann. § 9:315.18(B)(1)(b); Bickham v. Bickham, 46,264, pp. 9–10 (La. App. 2 Cir. 3/2/11), 58 So. 3d 950, 957–58 (recognizing that the trial court erred in allowing deduction for nondomiciliary parent when no evidence was presented as to substantial benefit to nondomiciliary parent or significant harm to the domiciliary parent, but granting no relief because domiciliary parent did not appeal the judgment); Semmes v. Semmes, 45,006 (La. App. 2 Cir. 12/16/09), 27 So. 3d 1024, 1034–35 (finding no error in allocating tax credit to domiciliary parent when nondomiciliary parent failed to present any evidence regarding significant harm to domiciliary parent or substantial benefit to nondomiciliary parent; only stating that he would benefit more than the other parent because his income was greater); *see also* Dirteater v Dirteater, 2022-0266 (La. App. 1 Cir. 9/16/22), 352 So. 3d 1016 (allowing the father to claim child as dependent in odd-numbered years and finding no merit in mother's argument that while the father earned $64,000 and she only earned $47,500, the harm to her was greater than the benefit to him because the tax deduction represents a larger percentage of her income).

568. *See, e.g.*, Semmes, 27 So. 3d at 1035 (denying the father the exemption because of lack of proof of benefits and harm).

569. La. Stat. Ann. § 9:315.18(B)(2)(a)–(c). Louisiana Revised Statutes Section 9:315.18 (B)(2)(c) applies to child support orders rendered or modified in accordance with the section on or after January 1, 2021. *See* Carter v. Carter, 49,517 (La. App. 2 Cir. 11/26/14), 155 So. 3d 81, 83–84 (finding that the trial court's order alternating annually the dependency deduction between mother and father was not an abuse of discretion in child support modification proceeding where the record was devoid of evidence on the issue).

570. La. Stat. Ann. § 9:315.18(D)(1)–(3).

571. *See* Bickham, 58 So. 3d at 957–58 (upholding award allowing nondomiciliary parent to receive tax credit every third year); Steinebach v. Steinebach, 2007-38 (La. App. 3 Cir. 5/2/07), 957 So. 2d 291, 305 (affirming award of tax credit to nondomiciliary parent until domiciliary parent became employed and thereafter, rotating the tax credit so each parent received it on alternating years; showing of substantial benefit was satisfied because nondomiciliary parent was the only employed parent and paid all daycare expenses, while there would be no harm to domiciliary parent who did not work or pay any daycare expenses); Folse v. Folse, 2001-0946, pp. 5–6 (La. App. 1 Cir. 5/10/02), 818 So. 2d 923, 926 (deciding former husband was entitled to the income tax dependency exemptions for his two children when he was the nondomiciliary parent paying more than 50% of the child support obligation, the wife's only income was from Social Security benefits, wife had not filed an income tax return in three years, and husband benefitted from the deductions while wife was not harmed by allowing husband to use the deductions); Walker v. Walker, 2002-606, pp. 3–4 (La. App. 3 Cir. 12/4/02), 832 So.

§ 7:55 Party Agreement and Stipulations

Even before enactment of the guidelines, courts recognized that parents may enter into a stipulated, or consent, judgment as to the amount of a child support award.[572] The agreements are bilateral contracts accepted by the court due to the voluntary acquiescence of the parties.[573] However, not all such parental agreements will be upheld. For example, in *Vogler v. Ayres*, the parties had executed a consent judgment in 2014, waiving the father's prospective child support obligation.[574] When the mother later attacked the judgment as absolutely null because of this, the court agreed with her. It found that the provision "amounted to a full and complete waiver of prospective child support" which rendered it "null and void as against public policy."[575]

Although contractual in nature between the parties, agreements as to the amount of child support are still subject to modification by a court with proof of a material change in circumstance, regardless of non-modification contractual language to the contrary, because the support of children is a matter of public policy.[576] Although parties are free to waive the need for a party to prove a material change of circumstances for a court to modify the amount of support, the parties cannot—as a matter of public policy—attempt to remove court oversight of support for a child.[577]

The Child Support Guidelines, in Louisiana Revised Statutes Section 315.1(D), provide that courts "may review and approve a stipulation between the parties" and if a review is conducted, "the court shall consider the guidelines . . . to review the adequacy of the stipulated amount. . . ."[578] Read in isolation, paragraph (D) insinuates that review of the parties' stipulated amount is discretionary; however, the Louisiana Supreme Court has concluded otherwise. Because the guidelines must be used "in any proceed-

---

2d 1098, 1101 (reversing trial court ruling in part and allowing former husband to claim federal and state tax dependency deductions every year, where husband was the nondomiciliary parent whose child support obligation exceeded 70%, to wit, 74.5%, of the total child support obligation, and no evidence existed that he owed arrearages to former wife); Warlick v. Warlick, 27,389, p. 9 (La. App. 2 Cir. 9/29/95), 661 So. 2d 706, 713 (awarding two of three dependency tax deductions to nondomiciliary parent where nondomiciliary parent who paid substantial child support, was in higher tax bracket than domiciliary parent, and would need dependency deductions to maintain her paying ability).

572. Aldredge v. Aldredge, 477 So. 2d 73 (La. 1985); *see also* Stogner v. Stogner, 98-3044 (La. 7/7/99), 739 So. 2d 762, 767 (citing Hogan v. Hogan, 549 So. 2d 267 (La. 1989)).

573. Toups v. Kauffman, 2016-0248, pp. 6–7 (La. App. 4 Cir. 11/23/16), 204 So. 3d 1044, 1049 (citing Gebhard v. Gebhard, 2010-1412, p. 6 (La. App. 4 Cir. 02/16/11), 60 So. 3d 717, 721).

574. Vogler v. Ayres, 54,734, pp. 7–10 (La. App. 2 Cir. 8/17/22), 345 So. 3d 1184, 1189–91.

575. Vogler, 345 So. 3d at 1190. *See also* Greene v. Greene, 19-528 (La. App. 5 Cir. 5/28/20), 296 So. 3d 1239 (nullifying consent judgment under which mother paid the children's tuition and other expenses instead of paying monthly child support because the judgment did not follow statutory guidelines, was essentially a waiver of support (was void as a matter of public policy), and was accepted by the hearing officer without proof of the mother's income).

576. Gebhard, 60 So. 3d 717, 721; Durfee v. Durfee, 44,281, pp. 5–7 (La. App. 2 Cir. 5/13/09), 12 So. 3d 984, 988; Ellefson v. Ellefson, 616 So. 2d 221, 224 (La. Ct. App. 5 Cir. 1993).

577. *See* Aldredge, 477 So. 2d at 75.

578. La. Stat. Ann. § 9:315.1(D). In the court's review of the agreement, it may require the parties to submit income statements and documentation.

ing to establish or modify support,"[579] any judicial review must consider the guidelines, even if the parties agree.[580] The Louisiana Supreme Court explained the requirement in *Stogner v. Stogner*:

> [W]e find that the opening sentence's use of the words "court may review and approve the stipulation" in La. R.S. 9:315.1(D) means that although the parents may present a stipulation for consideration, the trial court is not bound to follow it and may choose to use the guidelines instead. In this context, we find that the opening phrase of the second sentence of Paragraph (D), "If the court does review the stipulation," simply means that if the trial court does not categorically reject the proposed stipulation, i.e., it chooses to entertain the stipulation, the trial court "shall consider the guidelines ... to review the adequacy of the stipulated amount." To assume, as the lower courts did herein, that the reviewing role of the trial court was discretionary creates an anomaly that cannot be reconciled with the mandated application of the guidelines to the establishment or modification of child support provided in Paragraph (A) of La. R.S. 9:315.1. Moreover, such a reading would impermissibly find the guidelines inapplicable.[581]

Therefore, parties may enter, and the court may approve, a consent judgment that deviates from the guidelines, but the court must consider the guidelines and specify for the record its reasons for allowing a deviation.[582]

Consideration of the guidelines is necessary at every stage of the proceeding, even for interim stipulated orders. Because the need for immediate and temporary child support is a factor the court may consider when deviating from the guidelines, the court must consider the guideline amount in order to deviate.[583] In any deviation, the court must "give specific oral or written reasons for the deviation, including a finding as to the amount of support that would have been required under a mechanical application of the guidelines...."[584] For example, in *Discua v. Discua*, the trial court ordered interim child support of $700, based on the stipulations of the parties and without reference to the guidelines.[585] Three years later, when the court ordered a final support amount of $1,250 based on the guidelines, the domiciliary parent requested that the greater amount be made retroactive to the date of judicial demand, with credits for the $700 per month already paid.[586] The trial court disagreed, concluding that the interim support ended and the final support began after the hearing in which final support was set.[587] The appellate court reversed, concluding that the interim child support orders

---

579. La. Stat. Ann. § 9:315.1(A).
580. Stogner, 739 So. 2d at 767.
581. Stogner, 739 So. 2d at 767.
582. La. Stat. Ann. § 9:315.1; Stogner, 739 So. 2d at 768.
583. *See* La. Stat. Ann. § 9:315.1(C)(5).
584. La. Stat. Ann. § 9:315.1(B).
585. Discua v. Discua, 2021-0210, p. 10 (La. App. 4 Cir. 11/10/21), 331 So. 3d 992, 998.
586. Discua, 331 So. 3d at 1002.
587. Discua, 331 So. 3d at 1002.

were devoid of any reference to the child support guidelines, did not rely on the income or expense information of the parents, and lacked reasons for making a deviation.[588]

§ 7:56 Standard of Appellate Review

An appellate court will not disturb findings of fact made by the trier of fact unless the trial court abused its discretion or manifestly erred.[589] The child support guidelines specifically provide that guideline deviations "shall not be disturbed absent a finding of manifest error," which is also referred to as the "clearly wrong" standard of review.[590] To reverse a finding under this standard, the appellate court must conduct a two-part inquiry. First, the court must find no reasonable factual basis for the finding made by the trier of fact.[591] Next, the court must determine that the findings are clearly wrong.[592] Ultimately, the appellate court need not consider "whether the trier of fact was right or wrong but whether the conclusion was [] reasonable" in light of the facts reviewed in their entirety.[593] Therefore, if two permissible views of the evidence exist, the "factfinder's choice between them cannot be manifestly erroneous."[594]

The manifest error standard of review also applies to mixed questions of law and fact,[595] but if one or more legal errors affect the fact-finding process, the appellate court is duty bound to conduct a *de novo* review.[596] The appellate court should not, however, conduct a *de novo* review if it only finds an abuse of discretion with respect to the amount of an award; rather, it should lower or raise the amount.[597] Note, too, that in jurisdictions where hearing officers make recommendations to the district court, any

588. Discua, 331 So. 3d at 1005–06.

589. *E.g.,* Larson v. Larson, 16-695, p. 9 (La. App. 5 Cir. 10/25/17), 229 So. 3d 1043, 1051; Dep't of Soc. Servs. ex rel. D.F. v. L.T., 2005-1965 (La. 7/6/06), 934 So. 2d 687, 690; Verberne v. Verberne, 2005-2644, p. 3 (La. App. 1 Cir. 9/27/06), 944 So. 2d 620, 621 (citing Dep't of Soc. Servs. ex rel. D.F., 934 So. 2d 687).

590. La. Stat. Ann. § 9:315.17; A.S. v. D.S., 2014-1098 (La. App. 4 Cir. 4/8/15), 165 So. 3d 247, 253 (reviewing finding of voluntary underemployment under the manifest error-clearly wrong standard of review); Verberne, 944 So. 2d at 622 (finding trial court was not manifestly erroneous in calculation of appellant's annual income); Hensgens v. Hensgens, 2019-485, pp. 5–7 (La. App. 3 Cir. 12/18/19), 287 So. 3d 795, 800–01 (holding that there was no manifest error in trial court including the sale of farm equipment in its calculation of ex-husband's gross income for child support purposes).

591. A.S., 165 So. 3d at 253.

592. A.S., 165 So. 3d at 253; Riggs v. LaJaunie, 1998-30, p. 3 (La. App. 3 Cir. 10/7/98), 720 So. 2d 114, 116.

593. A.S., 165 So. 3d at 253 (quoting Stobart v. Dep't of Transp. & Dev., 617 So. 2d 880, 882 (La. 1993)); Walden v. Walden, 2000-2911 (La. App. 1 Cir. 8/14/02), 835 So. 2d 513, 517 (citing Sistler v. Liberty Mutual Ins. Co. 558 So. 2d 1106, 1112 (La. 1990)).

594. Walden, 835 So. 2d at 517.

595. A.S., 165 So. 3d at 254.

596. Dejoie v. Guidry, 2010-1542 (La. App. 4 Cir. 7/13/11), 71 So. 3d 1111, 1120.

597. Campbell v. Campbell, 95-1711 (La. App. 1 Cir. 10/10/96), 682 So. 2d 312, 316.

party who timely objects to the hearing officer's recommendations is entitled to *de novo* review at the district court.[598]

§ 7:57 Modification or Suspension by the Court

Child support awards are never final; rather, they are subject to modification as the needs of children or the ability of parents to pay change. Louisiana Civil Code Article 142 provides in pertinent part, "An award of child support may be modified if the circumstances of the child or of either parent materially change...."[599] Louisiana Revised Statutes Section 9:311(A)(1) adds a temporal requirement by prohibiting support award modification "unless the party seeking the modification shows a material change in circumstances of one of the parties between the time of the previous award and the time of the rule for modification of the award."[600] Recently, the legislature expounded on the meaning of a material change, adding a second sentence to section 9:311(A)(1): "The material change in circumstances must be *substantial* and *continuing since the last award for support*."[601] This 2018 amendment made clear that previous awards mentioned in the statute referred only to awards of support that had actually been made, rather than motions that had been raised and denied.[602] Unless good cause

598. *See, e.g.*, State ex rel. Harper v. Harper, 52,485, p. 5 (La. App. 2 Cir. 5/20/20), 296 So. 3d 1163, 1167.

599. La Civ. Code Ann. art. 142. Prior to 2001, a support award could be modified if "the circumstances of the child or of either parent materially change...." Until 1998, courts interpreted this to require a "substantial change," but jurisprudence changed with the *Stogner* decision, which held that it was an error of law to require a showing of substantial change and that the law of the time only required "simply showing a change of circumstances...." Stogner v. Stogner, 98-3044 (La. 7/7/99), 739 So. 2d 762, 770 (providing consolidated list of lower court rulings requiring the heightened evidentiary standard of "substantial change"). The phrase "material change in circumstances" was part of the 2001 amendments to legislatively overrule the *Stogner* court's interpretation and defined a material change as "a change in circumstance having real importance or great consequences for the needs of the child or the ability to pay of either party." *See* La. Stat. Ann. § 9:311 cmt. (a) (rev. cmt. 2001). This newest amendment to Louisiana Revised Statutes Section 9.311(A)(1) adding the requirement that the material change be "substantial" would seem to bring pre-*Stogner* caselaw back to relevance.

600. La. Stat. Ann. § 9:311(A)(1). If a previous support award had been made which was not in accordance with the guidelines, then there is no requirement to show a "material change in circumstance" and the court may set a new award concurrent with the guidelines. *See* Sharp v. Moore, 47,888, p. 4 (La. App. 2 Cir. 2/27/13), 110 So. 3d 1232, 1236 (requiring no material change to modify previous consent judgments which were not in accordance with the guidelines); State v. Reed, 44,119 (La. App. 2 Cir. 1/14/09), 5 So. 3d 269, 272 ("[A] previously flawed judgment cannot be used to deny a modification of child support.").

601. La. Stat. Ann. § 9:311(A)(1) (202) (emphasis added). *See* 2018 La. Sess. Law Serv. Acts 379 (S.B. 330). What constitutes a "material change in circumstance" is judicially determined on a case-by-case basis. Dep't of Soc. Servs. v. Burkett, 02-1128, p. 7 (La. App. 5 Cir. 4/29/03), 845 So. 2d 1183, 1188.

602. The legislature adopted the interpretation made by courts that the phrase "previous award" was defined as "the last time an award was actually made," not the last time a motion was considered and denied. Deshotels v. Deshotels, 93-638, p. 6 (La. App. 1 Cir. 6/24/94), 638 So. 2d 1199, 1202 (noting that the best interest of the child would not be served if the court only considers changes made

is shown, any modification to the order of child support will be retroactive to the date of judicial demand. In no case, however, can support be modified before the date of judicial demand.[603]

Specific rules exist when there is an interim support order in place and final support is ordered.[604] When a judgment initially awards or denies final child support, the award is effective on the date the judgment is signed, and it terminates the interim support award on that date.[605] Whether the final support award could be given retroactive application to affect an already existing interim award was decided by the Louisiana Supreme Court in *Vaccari v. Vaccari*.[606] The court concluded that nothing in the law "expressly forbid a court from making a final child support award retroactive when an interim allowance was in place," but the proponent must show good cause for the court to do so.[607] When a payor falsely presents his financial information or otherwise misleads the tribunal in an attempt to avoid the full extent of his obligation, good cause may exist to retroactively apply the final child support award.[608]

With proof of a material change in circumstances, a party has the legal right to demand modification of a child support award, even if a stipulated or consent judgment contains language to the contrary, preventing a future modification of the support order.[609] The burden rests with the moving party to show that a material change

---

between rules; if that were the case, the court could not take into account the "incremental build-up of small changes, which can dramatically change the circumstances"); *see also* Cole v. Cole, 2013-1442 (La. App. 3 Cir. 6/4/14), 139 So. 3d 1225, 1229–30 (using the last date in which child support was set based on use of worksheet for modification, rather than later date of custody order implementation which did not alter child support); Starks v. Starks, 28,237, p. 2 (La. App. 2 Cir. 4/3/96), 671 So. 2d 1224, 1226 (holding that trial court was correct in determining "previous award" was the child support judgment and not the date of a later joint custody implementation that neither modified nor awarded child support); Magown v. Magown, 599 So. 2d 880, 882 (La. Ct. App. 2 Cir. 1992) (finding "previous award" date was the date parties entered into an extra-judicial agreement to reduce child support).

603. La. Stat. Ann. § 9:315.21(A); *see also* State v. Istre, 54,203, p. 5 (La. App. 2 Cir. 4/5/22), 335 So. 3d 1025, 1028 (reversing trial court's modification of child support to the date the parent obtained physical custody of the child, which predated the date of judicial demand); Larson v. Larson, 16-695 (La. App. 5 Cir. 10/25/17), 229 So. 3d 1043, 1052–53 (permitting both a decrease and an increase in child support in the same proceeding because each request was retroactive to the date of judicial demand); Franks v. Franks, 2020-1170 (La. App. 1 Cir. 4/16/21), 323 So. 3d 876, 878–79 (modification of child support not retroactive to date parties began sharing custody because father did not request modification of support obligation when requesting change of custody).

604. La. Stat. Ann. § 9:315.21(B); Vaccari v. Vacarri, 10-2016 (La. 12/10/10), 50 So. 3d 139; *see also* Ledet v. Diapaul, 55,137 (La. App. 2 Cir. 08/23/23), 369 So. 3d 972; St. Philip v. Montalbano, 16-0254 (La. App. 1 Cir. 10/31/16), 206 So. 3d 909.

605. La. Stat. Ann. § 9:315.21(B)(1).

606. Vaccari v. Vacarri, 10-2016 (La. 12/10/10), 50 So. 3d 139.

607. Vacarri, 50 So. 3d 143.

608. Vacarri, 50 So. 3d at 141; see also Ledet v. Diapaul, 55,137 (La. App. 2 Cir. 08/23/23), 369 So. 3d 972 and cases cited within.

609. *See* Barton v. Barton, 2006-2032, p. 8 (La. App. 1 Cir. 8/8/07), 965 So. 2d 939, 943; Megison v. Megison, 94-152, pp. 4–5 (La. App. 5 Cir. 9/14/94), 642 So. 2d 885, 888; In re Spence, 600 So. 2d 782, 784 (La. Ct. App. 5 Cir. 1992) (citing Mitchell v. Mitchell, 543 So. 2d 128 (La. Ct. App. 2 Cir. 1989)); Crowder v. Crowder, 595 So. 2d 810, 812–13 (La. Ct. App. 2 Cir. 1992); Holleman v. Barrilleaux,

in circumstances has occurred.[610] Again, the material change must be "substantial and continuing"[611] and have "real importance or great consequences for the needs of the child or the ability to pay of either party."[612] "Once the moving party proves change in circumstances, a presumption exists that child support obligation must be modified. The burden then shifts to the other party to disprove the change or otherwise overcome the presumption."[613] If a court determines that a motion to modify child support is frivolous and either dismisses it before a hearing or finds insufficient cause to modify, it may order the mover to pay costs and reasonable attorney's fees of the other party.[614]

Finding a "material change of circumstances" is inherently subjective, but courts have identified norms that affect the analysis. Undeniably, trial courts exercise their sound discretion to determine what constitutes a material change warranting modification on a case-by-case basis.[615] By statute, a judgment for past due support alone does not constitute a material change in circumstances sufficient to reduce an award of child support.[616] A party cannot fail to pay child support obligations and then, when a judgment for arrearages is made executory, claim a change in circumstance due to the garnishment of wages to satisfy the judgment.[617]

Courts have generally distinguished between voluntary and involuntary changes in circumstances. As one court explained: "An involuntary change in circumstances results from fortuitous events or other circumstances beyond a person's control, such as loss of one's position or illness. A voluntary change in circumstances generally does not justify a reduction in the support obligation."[618]

The commentary to Civil Code Article 142 describes the durability of obligations in the face of voluntary changes: "[A]ny voluntary act by a parent that renders it difficult or impossible to perform the primary obligation of support and maintenance of his children cannot be countenanced as a ground for release of the parent, in whole or

---

2020-194 (La. App. 3 Cir. 2/10/21), 311 So. 3d 506 (father failed to provide verified income statement to support material change in his ability to pay, and his sale of business without supporting documentation made it difficult to confidently establish actual income).

610. La. Stat. Ann. § 9:311(A)(1). *See also* Cloud v. Dean, 1015-297 (La. App. 3 Cir. 12/16/15), 181 So. 3d 939, 940 (placing burden of proving material change of circumstances with party seeking modification of support order); Dejoie v. Guidry, 2010-1542 (La. App. 4 Cir. 7/13/11), 71 So. 3d 1111, 1116–17; Preis v. Preis, 610 So. 2d 163, 164 (La. Ct. App. 3 Cir. 1992) (citation omitted) ("The party seeking to increase or decrease the amount of the child support . . . bears the burden of proving a [material] change of circumstances since the rendition of the prior judgment fixing the amount of support.").

611. La. Stat. Ann. § 9:311(A)(1).

612. La. Stat. Ann. § 9:311 cmt. (a) (rev. cmt. 2001).

613. Dep't of Soc. Servs. v. Burkett, 02-1128, p. 7 (La. App. 5 Cir. 4/29/03), 845 So. 2d 1183, 1188 (citing La. Stat. Ann. § 9:311(C)(1) (2022)).

614. La. Stat. Ann. § 9:311(E). This provision does not apply when public entities provide support enforcement services. La. Stat. Ann. § 9:311(F).

615. *See, e.g.*, Folse v. Folse, 2001-0946 (La. App. 1 Cir. 5/10/02), 818 So. 2d 923, 925 (citing Stogner, 739 So. 2d at 770).

616. La. Stat. Ann. § 9:311(B).

617. Kirby v. Kirby, 579 So. 2d 508, 518 (La. Ct. App. 4 Cir. 1991).

618. State in Interest of Harper v. Harper, 53,485 (La. App. 2 Cir. 5/20/20), 296 So. 3d 1163, 1167.

in part, from that obligation."[619] Even voluntary retirement by the obligor may not constitute a material change if the obligor has other financial means to meet the needs of the child.[620] Although voluntary unemployment by the obligor parent is generally insufficient to show a material change in circumstances,[621] a reduction may still be warranted if the obligor can show that the voluntary change is reasonable and justified, the parent is in good faith, and the child is not deprived of continued financial support.[622]

One example of voluntary unemployment that nevertheless supported a reduction in support occurred in a case where the obligor father lost his nursing license following a conviction on drug charges.[623] The court explained that the father remained employable by performing manual labor, did not incur additional financial obligations in attempt to avoid his child support obligation, and did not fall into arrears until he lost his job.[624] The court also observed that the reduction would not deprive the child of reasonable financial support.[625]

In addition, in *Fontenette v. Doucet*, the obligor father lost his job as a professional athlete due to an injury that he incurred through no fault of his own.[626] At the time of the hearing, the father was living off "rapidly depleting capital assets" as a full-time college student with zero earned income because he could not secure employment

619. La. Civ. Code Ann. art. 142 cmt. (b) (1993). Note that while imprisonment was seen as a voluntary act insufficient to reduce child support, *see* Toups v. Toups, 97-0620, pp. 3–4 (La. App. 1 Cir. 4/8/98), 708 So. 2d 849, 850 (finding actions resulting in imprisonment are voluntary acts and may not be used as an excuse to escape the financial obligation to support one's children), the legislature enacted Louisiana Revised Statutes Section 9:311.1, effective in 2020, which requires suspension of child support during an obligor's incarceration.

620. *See* Wyatt v. Wyatt, 39,518, pp. 6–7 (La. App. 2 Cir. 4/6/05), 899 So. 2d 788, 792 (finding no material change in circumstances as to justify reduction in father's child support obligation as bank records showed that father had financial resources in addition to his monthly retirement check, father's voluntary retirement was neither reasonable nor justified in light of the obligation he owed to support his child, father's past failure to pay his full child support obligation absent income assignment order suggested that he was not in good faith and that his request for reduction based on his voluntary retirement was an attempt to avoid his obligation to his child, and the record did not establish that the father was unemployable or unable to work).

621. *See, e.g.*, Watson v. Watson, 39,458, pp. 5–6 (La. App. 2 Cir. 3/2/05), 894 So. 2d 1263, 1266–67 (finding no material change in circumstance for reduction in support when father's lower earnings for one year were due to temporary unemployment due to his leaving a long-term job to search for new employment and mother's annual wages increased by approximately $200 per month); *see also* La. Stat. Ann. § 9:315.11(A)(1).

622. *See* Lewis v. Lewis, 2018-0378, p. 8 (La. App. 4 Cir. 10/3/18), 255 So. 3d 1216, 1222; Durfee v. Durfee, 44,281 (La. App. 2 Cir. 5/13/09), 12 So. 3d 984, 989 (citation omitted); Strange v. Strange, 42,281, p. 7 (La. App. 2 Cir. 6/20/07), 960 So. 2d 1223, 1228–29; Savage v. Savage, 36-138 (La. App. 6/12/02), 821 So. 2d 603, 606–07.

623. Dep't of Soc. Servs., Off. of Fam'y Support ex rel. Seals v. Seals, 97-1508 (La. App. 4 Cir. 10/29/97), 701 So. 2d 746. *See also* Harper, 296 So. 3d at 1167 (father's request to modify downward was granted where he lost his license due to his past inconsistent payment of child support, making his termination involuntary, and there was no indication that he was able to return to work in his previous field but chose not to do so).

624. Dep't of Soc. Servs., Off. of Fam'y Support ex rel. Seals, 701 So. 2d at 749.

625. Dep't of Soc. Servs., Off. of Fam'y Support ex rel. Seals, 701 So. 2d at 749.

626. Fontenette v. Doucet, 2015-358, p. 4 (La. App. 3 Cir. 10/7/15), 175 So. 3d 1160, 1163.

in the same field.[627] As a result, the court found a material change in circumstances sufficient to reduce child support.[628]

Inflation alone has been found insufficient to warrant modifying an award, but it can be a factor for a court to consider in the presence of other factors.[629] Loss of spousal expense-sharing has also been found insufficient to garner a change.[630] Simply showing a decrease of income from a personally owned business is likewise insufficient to prove a material change,[631] but proof of a two-fold increase in income may be enough to justify additional support.[632] Significant changes in income or expenses may be enough to constitute a material change.[633]

When the Louisiana Department of Social Services (DSS) is providing child support enforcement services, the rules differ a bit. In that case, a rebuttable presumption that a material change in circumstances exists when a strict application of the child support guidelines would result in at least a 25% change to the existing child support award.[634] Even without a 25% change, though, the court can modify the amount of support

627. Fontenette, 175 So. 3d at 1163.

628. Fontenette, 175 So. 3d at 1163.

629. *See* Young v. Young, 1995-1154, p. 5 (La. App. 3 Cir. 4/17/96), 673 So. 2d 1154, 1156.

630. Reed, 5 So. 3d at 274 (finding no error in trial court's finding that no material change in circumstances existed when father lost $1,000 of imputed income due to expense sharing when current wife filed for bankruptcy and the expense sharing income no longer existed).

631. Hall v. Hall, 11-60 (La. App. 5 Cir. 5/24/11), 67 So. 3d 635, 639; Koch v. Koch, 97-1600, p. 6 (La. App. 4 Cir. 4/22/98), 714 So. 2d 63, 66–67 (finding that father's reduction in income and unpaid wages was a result of voluntary bad investment decisions and did not warrant reduction in child support).

632. Dejoie, 71 So. 3d at 1115 (proof of increase in obligor's income was enough to constitute a material change).

633. Fontenette, 175 So. 3d at 1163 (material change in circumstance shown when father was no longer a professional football player, was a full-time student, and was living off depleting assets); Hernandez v. Hernandez, 11-526, pp. 7–8 (La. App. 5 Cir. 12/28/11), 83 So. 3d 168, 172 (material change of circumstances proven when costs of health insurance, transportation, and tuition had increased and obligor's savings had been depleted); Hudnall v. Hudnall, 2000-0330 (La. App. 1 Cir. 5/11/01), 808 So. 2d 641, 644–45 (material change in circumstances and increase in the father's support obligation warranted because the child had various health and educational problems, and the mother had not attempted to locate less expensive child care because the child care provider and child were very compatible and provider knew all of the child's sign language and how to handle her aggressive behavior); Authement v. Authement, 96-1289, p. 13 (La. App. 1 Cir. 5/9/97), 694 So. 2d 1129, 1136 (finding an increase in support warranted even though one child aged out of child support because the parents' incomes had increased); *but see* Knoepfler v. Knoepfler, 553 So. 2d 1031, 1033 (La. Ct. App. 4 Cir. 1989) (finding that a reduction in child support payable by child's father was not warranted despite the transfer of the children from private to public school when evidence indicated that the cost of living was higher in the area of which mother had moved and mother and new husband were encountering economic difficulties).

634. La. Stat. Ann. § 9:311(C); *see also* Dep't of Soc. Servs., Support Enf't Servs. ex rel. A.M. v. Taylor, 2000-2048, p. 6 (La. App. 1 Cir. 2/15/02), 807 So. 2d 1156, 1161. However, a material change does not exist if the amount of the award was the result of a deviation and there has not been a material change to warrant the deviation. La. Stat. Ann. § 9:311(C)(1). In addition, courts can deny modification even if a 25% change is present if applying the guidelines would not be in the best interest of the child or would be inequitable to the parties. La. Stat. Ann. § 9:311(C)(2).

when a party proves a material change that is "substantial and continuing."[635] Finally, modification may be made every three years without showing a material change of circumstances as long as the existing award differs from the guideline amount.[636]

Other provisions exist within the guidelines that specifically permit modification or suspension in certain factual circumstances. First, a modification is permitted at any time to include a court-ordered award for medical support.[637] Second, modification or suspension is permitted when a joint custodial parent intentionally removes the child from the obligor parent's life.[638] If a joint custodial parent or a parent's agent intentionally secrets a child "with the intent to preclude the other joint custodial parent from knowing the whereabouts of the child sufficiently to allow him to exercise his rights or duties as joint custodial parent," the obligor parent can seek a court order to suspend or modify the obligation of support.[639] The obligor must affirmatively seek relief and cannot rely on the provision as a defense to an action for failure to pay child support or to enforce past due child support.[640] Third, child support is suspended by operation of law if an obligor is incarcerated for 180 consecutive days or more.[641] The details of this provision are covered in a separate section.[642]

As a final note, as a defense in an action to modify, the court may consider the interests of the obligor's subsequent family when the obligor has taken a second job or works overtime to provide for them.[643] In such a scenario, the obligor bears the burden of proof in establishing that the additional income is used to provide for the subsequent family.[644]

---

635. La. Stat. Ann. § 9:311(C)(2).

636. La. Stat. Ann. § 9:311(C)(3). When the best interest of the child requires, the department must request a judicial review of support on its own initiative or upon a party's request. *Id.* The same is true upon any party's incarceration and for awards suspended due to the obligor's incarceration once the incarceration ends. *Id.*

637. La. Stat. Ann. § 9:311(D)(1).

638. La. Stat. Ann. § 9:315.23.

639. La. Stat. Ann. § 9:315.23. *See* Moyer v. Moyer, 2013-212, p. 4 (La. App. 3 Cir. 10/9/13), 123 So. 3d 880, 884 (concluding that mother's repeated violations of custody order, including by leaving the parties' children with her parents while she was out of town without giving the father the opportunity to care for them instead and by relocating the children to another jurisdiction, warranted suspension of father's child support obligation despite contention that the children should not be caused to suffer due to the actions of a parent).

640. La. Stat. Ann. § 9:315.23.

641. La. Stat. Ann. § 9:311.1.

642. *See* Section 7:59.

643. La. Stat. Ann. § 9:315.12.

644. La. Stat. Ann. § 9:315.12.

§ 7:58 Modification or Suspension by the Parties

Louisiana's child support laws contemplate that judgments awarding support generally remain in full effect until the judgment is modified, suspended, or terminated.[645] Courts will, however, enforce an extrajudicial agreement between parents that modifies support awards if the mutual agreement meets the prerequisites for a conventional obligation, does not interrupt the child's maintenance or upbringing, and is in the child's best interest.[646] In *Dubroc v. Dubroc*, the Louisiana Supreme Court considered an agreement by parents to reduce a $250 per month award of child support to $125 per month when the obligor father took custody of one child in his home, while the mother remained the custodian of the other child in her home.[647] After four years of this arrangement, the mother sued the father for delinquent child support.[648] The Supreme Court enforced the parents' agreement, notwithstanding the prior judgment awarding child support at a greater amount, because the parties clearly agreed to the modification and the agreement did not affect the child's upbringing or best interest.[649]

The party asserting the existence of an extrajudicial modification has the burden of proving a clear and specific agreement; merely accepting a reduced payment on behalf of the child will not waive the right to enforce the standing judgment.[650] So, a parent who acquiesces in a lower amount of child support does not inadvertently assent to a modification of the child support judgment by inaction.[651]

---

645. Halcomb v. Halcomb, 352 So. 2d 1013, 1016 (La. 1977).

646. Dubroc v. Dubroc, 388 So. 2d 377, 380 (La. 1980). In *Cahn v. Cahn*, 2022-0801 (La. App. 4 Cir. 6/14/23), 368 So. 3d 717, the parties' text messages did not suffice to prove an extrajudicial modification because they did not evidence a clear and specific agreement between the parties; further, the parties' trial testimony regarding the meaning behind the texts was conflicting, and provided no clarity on the issue.

647. Dubroc, 388 So. 2d at 378.

648. Dubroc, 388 So. 2d at 378.

649. Dubroc, 388 So. 2d. at 380; *see also* State in Interest of Michelli v. Michelli, 2020-1171 (La. App. 1 Cir. 4/16/21), 323 So. 3d 870 (finding the parties extrajudicially modified their consent judgment); Cosey v. Cosey, 2000-0567, pp. 3–4 (La. App. 4 Cir. 5/2/01), 785 So. 2d 1051, 1053. In *Cosey*, the court recognized an agreement between the parties to modify support when their oldest child reached the age of majority pursuant to in globo award. The father made consistent monthly payments which were exactly half the amount ordered before the oldest child reached majority, he maintained both children on his health insurance, and he documented payments of "substantial sums" directly to his oldest child. The credibility of the mother was severely called into question because she took the position that the father had missed and not made all payments, yet the father was able to provide banking statements proving the contrary.

650. Heflin v. Heflin, 44,155, p. 4 (La. App. 2 Cir. 1/14/09), 1 So. 3d 820, 822 (citing Dubroc, 388 So. 2d 377 (La. 1980)); *see also* Lynch v. Lynch, 2023-0608 (La. App. 1 Cir. 11/27/23); 379 So. 3d 706 (refusing to recognize an extrajudicial modification because although the mother admitted to discussing lowering the father's child support amount, they did not come to an agreement); McDaniel v. McDaniel, 2003-1763, pp. 6–7 (La. App. 3 Cir. 5/19/04), 878 So. 2d 686, 690–91 (obligee parent's mere acceptance of reduced support payments not sufficient to show that an extrajudicial agreement had been made between the parties).

651. *See* Halcomb, 352 So. 2d 1013; McDaniel, 878 So. 2d at 690–91.

Not all extrajudicial agreements must be express, however. Courts have recognized "implied agreements" when a child resides with the obligor parent at the request of the other parent for a substantial period of time, during which the obligor-parent provides full financial support.[652] Even though a child support order should be formally modified, courts have suspended child support by implied agreement for the time period that the child lived with and was fully supported by the obligor parent.[653] In *Heflin v. Heflin*, the mother "voluntarily relinquished physical custody" of her daughter to the obligor father after she began having disciplinary issues with her daughter.[654] The father then ceased making support payments but maintained custody of their daughter. Ten years later, the mother filed a petition seeking past due child support.[655] The court found an implied agreement to suspend child support because the mother took no action for 10 years to collect past-due child support, the mother visited with her daughter but never sought custody pursuant to the court order, and the mother previously petitioned the court to modify the original custody agreement to reflect the current arrangement, testifying that it was what they "had pretty much always done."[656] Further, the father provided for all of the food, clothing, and shelter needs of his daughter.[657]

Enforcement of extrajudicial agreements also extends to agreements to *create* child support obligations. For example, in *Thevenot v. Thevenot*, the court concluded that a logical extension of the Louisiana Supreme Court's decision to permit parents to agree to *modify* child support would be to permit parents to agree to *establish* child support.[658] Both parents testified to the existence of an oral agreement and the father's subsequent failure to comply with the agreement.[659] Based on the clear existence of the parties' agreement, the appellate court reversed the trial court and ordered the father to pay arrearages based on the agreement.[660]

§ 7:59 Suspension Due to Incarceration of Obligor

In 2017, the Louisiana Legislature began the process of enacting legislation that would suspend child support due by an obligor during the period of imprisonment. Act 264 of 2017 provided:

---

652. Heflin, 1 So. 3d at 826.

653. Heflin, 1 So. 3d at 825.

654. Heflin, 1 So. 3d at 826.

655. Heflin, 1 So. 3d at 821. In *Heflin*, testimony from each parent conflicted. The mother stated that the father refused to return their daughter after the agreed-on two-week period while the father stated that they agreed he was to maintain custody of their daughter and the mother would begin making support payments to him. During the 10-year period, the mother testified that she had visitation of her daughter two weekends per month, spring break, and alternating major holidays. *Id.*

656. Heflin, 1 So. 3d. at 826.

657. Heflin, 1 So. 3d at 826.

658. Thevenot v. Thevenot, 2003-684, p. 4 (La. App. 3 Cir. 12/23/03), 864 So. 2d 229, 232.

659. Thevenot, 864 So. 2d at 232.

660. Thevenot, 864 So. 2d at 232.

> The legislature finds that the purpose of modifying child support during a person's incarceration is to increase the likelihood of successful reintegration into the workforce and [of] long-term stability after a jail or prison term. Establishing financial stability in the weeks and months following a jail or prison term reduces the risk of recidivism, [thereby] increasing both public safety and the likelihood of consistent payment of child support over time.[661]

Because the administrative work to implement child support suspension would take time, the effective date of the Act was originally set for January 1, 2019.[662] In 2018, the legislature extended the effective date to August 1, 2019,[663] and yet again in 2019, the legislature extended the effective date to August 1, 2020.[664] Finally, in 2021 the legislation was amended and reenacted by Act 339 of the 2021 regular session.[665]

Currently, child support is suspended by operation of law "when the obligor is incarcerated for, or is sentenced to, with or without hard labor, 180 consecutive days or more."[666] "Incarceration" is defined as "a county, parish, state or federal prison or jail, in which the obligor is not permitted to earn wages from employment outside the facility."[667] Probation and parole are not included in the definition of incarceration.[668] Generally, the Department of Children and Family Services receives notification of the obligor's incarceration and will notify the custodial parent. DCFS must also "file an affidavit with the court that has jurisdiction over the child support order."[669] The period of suspension will begin on the date the department files the affidavit with the court.[670] Any suspended child support order will be reinstated "on the first day of the

---

661. 2017 La. Acts 264 (H.B. 680) (discussion of House Bill 426 (which would become Act 264) in the House Committee on Civil Law and Procedure provides some legislative history). *See* Hearing on H.B. 426 Before the H. Comm. on Civ. L. and Proc. (La. 2017), https://house.louisiana.gov/H_Video/VideoArchivePlayer?v=house/2017/may/0509_17_CL.

662. 2017 La. Acts 264 (H.B. 680).

663. 2018 La. Acts 136 (H.B. 576). Legislative history can further be explored in the discussion of House Bill 576 (which would become Act 136) in the House committee hearing. Hearing on H.B. 576 Before the H. Comm. on Civ. L. and Proc. (La. 2018), https://house.louisiana.gov/H_Video/VideoArchivePlayer?v=house/2018/mar/0326_18_CL.

664. 2019 La. Acts 277 (S.B. 185). Senate Bill 185 (which would become Act 277) further delayed implementation. *See* Hearing on S.B. 185 Before the H. Comm. on Civ. L. and Proc. (La. 2019), https://house.louisiana.gov/H_Video/VideoArchivePlayer?v=house/2019/may/0528_19_CL.

665. There was a great deal of discussion about the changes necessitated by federal law in two committee meetings on House Bill 449 (which would become Act 339). Hearing on H.B. 449 Before the H. Comm. on Civ. L. and Proc. at 2:42 (La. 2021), https://house.louisiana.gov/H_Video/VideoArchivePlayer?v=house/2021/may/0511_21_CL; Hearing on H.B. 449 Before the H. Comm. on Civ. L. and Proc. (La. 2021) (meeting continues several days later), https://house.louisiana.gov/H_Video/VideoArchivePlayer?v=house/2021/may/0517_21_CL.

666. La. Stat. Ann. § 9:311.1(A). Suspension due to incarceration will not affect any past due support that accrued prior to the date of suspension. *See* La. Stat. Ann. § 9:311.1(H).

667. La. Stat. Ann. § 9:311.1(B)(2).

668. La. Stat. Ann. § 9:311.1(B)(2).

669. La. Stat. Ann. § 9:311.1(D), (E). The Department of Public Safety and Corrections or the sheriff will provide notice under an interagency agreement.

670. La. Stat. Ann. § 9:311.1(E)(2); *see also* La. Stat. Ann. § 1:2 ("No section of the Revised Statutes is retroactive unless it is expressly stated.").

second full month following the obligor's release from incarceration."[671] Private parties can also use the statute to seek an order's suspension or modification under the law.[672]

Most noteworthy about the new law is the ability of the child or custodial parent to seek the extension of child support past the date of termination to recapture funds from the time period when payments were suspended due to the obligor's incarceration. If the obligor is released from incarceration when the child is still minor, DCFS or a party must petition the court for a hearing to establish the terms of the suspended order, and the court may extend the termination date, "not to exceed the amount of time the child support order was suspended."[673] Based on the mandatory language of the act, every suspended order of child support must be brought before the court at the end of the suspension period. However, if the obligor is released after the child has reached the age of majority, either the custodial party or the child may petition the court to establish an award for support within 24 months from the release. Such an award shall not exceed the amount of time that the order was suspended and must be established using the guidelines.[674]

Whether the act would have retroactive application received some discussion as the bill progressed through the legislative process,[675] and at least one court has concluded that the law is substantive and cannot be applied retroactively.[676]

---

671. La. Stat. Ann. § 9:311.1(G)(1).

672. La. Stat. Ann. § 9:311.1(F). Note that a second statute, Louisiana Revised Statutes Section 9:311.2, which would have addressed the procedure for private litigants, was included in the original House Bill 449 of 2021, which became Act 339. The legislature ultimately removed that section from the bill.

673. La. Stat. Ann. § 9:311.1(G)(3)(a)(i)–(ii).

674. La. Stat. Ann. § 9:311.1(G)(3)(b).

675. *See* Hearing on H.B. 449 Before the H. Comm. on Civ. L. and Proc. (La. 2021) (discussion begins at 33:25), https://house.louisiana.gov/H_Video/VideoArchivePlayer?v=house/2021/may/0517_21_CL.

676. State v. Mazique, 21-243, p. 3 (La. App. 5 Cir. 1/26/22), 336 So. 3d 558, 560. In *Mazique*, the obligor was released from prison on January 1, 2019, before the effective date of the act, so suspension was not appropriate. Because the obligor was imprisoned for 10 years, the court made executory past due child support totaling over $70,000. *Id.*

§ 7:60 Termination of Child Support

Generally, child support terminates when the child reaches the age of majority[677] or when the child is emancipated.[678] Although unlikely, child support can also terminate on a finding by a court that it has become unnecessary.[679] When a child support award applies to only one child, the obligor can automatically cease making payments at the child's majority or emancipation.[680] However, when the child support award is *in globo* for two or more children, the obligation of child support remains until the youngest child subject to the order reaches the age of majority or is emancipated.[681] To reduce the amount due under an *in globo* order, the obligor must seek a modification of the order.[682] Noteworthy is that one or more children reaching the age of majority does not automatically create a material change in circumstances sufficient to modify the order.[683] Ultimately, when the payments legally end—either when one child or the youngest child reaches the age of majority or is emancipated—the obligor may recover support payments made after the obligation terminated.[684]

While these general rules apply broadly, certain extensions of child support are available in specific circumstances, which are covered in the sections following.

---

677. The age of majority in Louisiana is 18 years old. La. Civ. Code Ann. art. 29.

678. La. Stat. Ann. § 9:315.22(A). Emancipation relieves a minor from some or all of the effects of minority. *See* La. Civ. Code Ann. art. 365. Emancipation by marriage or full judicial emancipation releases an obligor from child support. *See* La. Civ. Code Ann. arts. 366–67. For a detailed discussion of emancipation, *see* Chapter 11.

679. La. Civ. Code Ann. art. 142.

680. La. Stat. Ann. § 9:315.22(A).

681. La. Stat. Ann. § 9:315.22(B).

682. *See* Davis v. Davis, 43,490, p. 10 (La. App. 2 Cir. 10/22/08), 997 So. 2d 149, 157 (holding that payor's unilateral one-third reduction in child support payments, after one child reached the age of 19 and graduated from high school, "was improper and contrary to law"); Chambers v. Saucier, 2006-1290, p. 5 (La. App. 3 Cir. 2/7/07), 949 So. 2d 662, 666–67.

683. Henry v. Henry, 2007-284, pp. 4–5 (La. App. 3 Cir. 5/30/07), 958 So. 2d 150, 153–54; Hester v. Hester, 2001-0380, p. 9 (La. App. 4 Cir. 12/12/01), 804 So. 2d 783, 789; Hogan, 465 So. 2d 73 (La. App. 5 Cir. 1985).

684. Fobbs v. Fobbs, 2009-219, p. 4 (La. App. 3 Cir. 11/10/09), 25 So. 3d 168, 171 (providing credit to obligor for overpayment of child support for over one year after his youngest child reached the age of majority); State ex rel. S.L.J. v. Hammond, 32,508, p. 3 (La. App. 2 Cir. 12/8/99), 749 So. 2d 814, 816 (holding that the state had an obligation to reimburse support payments collected through income assignment after the child had reached the age of majority).

§ 7:61 Termination of Child Support—Extension for Students

Child support can extend beyond the age of majority or beyond emancipation for an unmarried child who meets three conditions: (1) "the child is a full-time student in good standing in a secondary school or its equivalent," (2) the child "has not attained the age of nineteen," and (3) the child "is dependent upon either parent."[685] From a policy standpoint, the extension seeks to cover those students who reach the age of majority before graduating from high school or an equivalency; those students may therefore receive child support until their nineteenth birthday.

To determine whether the child is in a secondary school within the meaning of the statute, courts consider the educational facility and the curriculum taught there.[686] Attending a vocational-technical school to obtain a high school equivalency diploma has been interpreted as a secondary school.[687] A less structured "therapeutic boarding school," in which a certified teacher taught the students in the woods in a survival-type of setting, constituted a secondary school, as well.[688] Once a court determines that the child is enrolled in a valid secondary school, the child is presumed to be "in good standing" as long as the child is attending the program, even without evidence of their transcripts.[689]

To extend child support, the child must not only be enrolled in a secondary school, but the child must also be dependent on at least one of the parents.[690] Moving in with a non-parent—even a direct relative—can be sufficient grounds for a court to find the child to be independent of the parents, thereby terminating child support.[691] For example, in *Smith v. Smith*, the parents agreed to emancipate the child so that she could move to Indiana to live with an aunt and uncle.[692] The child attended high school, had not attained the age of 19, and was in need of knee surgery.[693] The trial court found,

---

685. La. Stat. Ann. § 9:315.22(C).

686. Park v. Park, 93-0115 (La. App. 1 Cir. 3/30/94), 634 So. 2d 83, 86; *but see* Dep't of Soc. Servs., Support Enf't Servs. ex rel. A.M. v. Taylor, 2000-2048 (La. App. 1 Cir. 2/15/02), 807 So. 2d 1156, 1166 (even though the evidence did not identify the type of institution, the child was pursuing a high school equivalency, so support should have continued).

687. Park, 634 So. 2d at 86 (suggesting that "secondary school" is more advanced than grade school and offers general, technical, vocational, or college prep courses).

688. *See* Basile v. Basile, 2004-25, pp. 5–6 (La. App. 3 Cir. 5/12/04), 872 So. 2d 1274, 1278.

689. *See* Basile, 872 So. 2d at 1278; *see also* Authement v. Authement, 96-1289 (La. App. 1 Cir. 5/9/97), 694 So. 2d 1129, 1135 (finding "implicitly" that student was in good standing based on her graduating, uncontradicted testimony of her good grades, and a lack of negative testimony regarding her status at the school).

690. La. Stat. Ann. § 9:315.22(C).

691. Smith v. Smith, 44,663, pp. 27, 29 (La. App. 2 Cir. 8/19/09), 16 So. 3d 643, 658–660 (obligor was no longer responsible for child support payments for an emancipated child residing with family members in another state); Authement, 694 So. 2d at 1135 (obligor was not responsible for child support after majority while child lived with boyfriend).

692. Smith v. Smith, 44,663 (La. App. 2 Cir. 8/19/09), 16 So. 3d 643, 659.

693. Smith, 16 So. 3d at 659.

and the appellate court affirmed, that no child support was due because the aunt and uncle were supplying the material needs of the child, so she was no longer dependent on her parents for support.[694]

§ 7:62 Termination of Child Support— Extension for Developmentally Disabled Children

Child support also extends until the age of 22 for a child who has a developmental disability, as long as the child is a full-time student in a secondary school.[695] Even though the child may have reached the age of majority, the domiciliary parent is the appropriate party to seek continued payment of the child support award.[696]

When considering the term "secondary school" in the context of a disabled child, courts broadly interpret the term to envelop a specialized school that meets the needs of that child. For example, in *Summers v. Summers*, the child functioned at a level of less than a one-year-old, and the court interpreted "secondary school" to include the school attended by the child to meet his needs, noting that to hold otherwise "would lead to an absurd result defeating the purpose of [the statute]."[697]

§ 7:63 Termination of Child Support— Extension for Adult Children with a Disability

In 2015, the Louisiana Legislature enacted laws to extend child support, regardless of age and for as long as necessary, for a child who: (1) is unmarried,[698] (2) is incapable of self-support, and (3) "requires substantial care and personal supervision because of an intellectual or physical disability that [] manifested before the child attain[ed] the age of majority."[699] Substance abuse and addiction are expressly excluded from the statute, and the action may be filed at any time by the major child, his tutor, or his

694. Smith, 16 So. 3d at 659. The court encouraged both parents to continue to support their daughter, even though she was living out-of-state, under the nature of a natural obligation. *Id.*

695. La. Stat. Ann. § 9:315.22(D). Developmental disability, as it pertains to this statute, is defined by Louisiana Revised Statutes Section 28:451.2. Pleading requirements are found in La. Stat. Ann. § 9:315.14.

696. La. Stat. Ann. § 9:315.22(D).

697. Summers v. Summers, 2003-2562, p. 3 (La. App. 1 Cir. 10/29/04), 897 So. 2d 109, 110; *but see* Summers, 897 So. 2d at 111 (Fitsimmons, J., concurring) (stating that this holding should be limited to the particular facts of this case and should not "serve as a basis for finding that all special schools may be categorized as secondary schools").

698. The fact that a child was married will not prevent eligibility as long as the child is unmarried at the time of the request. La. Stat. Ann. § 9:315.22 cmt. (c) (2015).

699. La. Stat. Ann. § 9:315.22(E), as relocated to § 9:315.22.1 (2025). The need for "substantial care and personal supervision" is a fact question but does not require the need for around-the-clock care. La. Stat. Ann. § 9:315.22 cmt. (d) (2015). Whether or not the child is institutionalized has no bearing on the court setting or continuing an award for a child under this paragraph.

curator.[700] In determining whether a child support award should be made, the court must consider "the eligibility of the child for public benefits and services and may make orders necessary to promote the best interest of the child."[701] In 2024, the legislature relocated the provision to its own section[702] and made clear that a contradictory motion must be filed before the minor attains the age of majority and a copy of any judgment must be furnished to all counsel and unrepresented parties.[703]

If a child does not qualify under the specific legislation for adult children with a disability, the child may nevertheless be entitled to support under Civil Code Article 237—the alimentary obligation that all parents owe to their children.[704] Further, a disabled child may be entitled to support under the section for developmentally delayed children in a secondary school; once child support terminates for the developmentally delayed child, it can immediately start for that adult child under this section.[705]

§ 7:64 Enforcement of Child Support

The collection of child support dollars for the benefit of the child was the impetus of the federal government's first foray into state child support systems.[706] Over the years, enforcement systems have become more robust, and an arsenal of laws are available to ensure that the funds reach the child. For example, in Louisiana, income assignment orders are mandated unless the parties agree otherwise in writing or the court finds good cause not to require an income assignment order.[707] Because the mandate is subject to exceptions and a great deal of discretion, non-payment continues to plague the child support system.[708]

In the event of non-payment, monetary and non-monetary penalties are available to the obligee. The obligee can seek to make executory the past-due payments of child support, and "[the court] shall, except for good cause shown, award attorney fees and costs to the prevailing party."[709] The amount of attorney's fees and costs awarded is

---

700. La. Stat. Ann. § 9:315.22.1(A)–(B).

701. La. Stat. Ann. § 9:315.22.1(D). A special needs trust may be appropriate for the child. La. Stat. Ann. § 9:315.22.1(D).

702. La. Stat. Ann. § 9:315.22.1 (enacted by 2024 La. Act No. 448, § 2, effective January 1, 2025).

703. La. Stat. Ann. § 9:315.22(D)(2), as amended by 2024 La. Act No. 448, § 2, effective January 1, 2025.

704. La. Stat. Ann. § 9:315.22 cmt. (f).

705. La. Stat. Ann. § 9:315.22 cmt. (g).

706. *See* U.S. Child Support Enf't Act of 1975, 42 U.S.C. §§ 651–69.

707. La. Stat. Ann. § 9:303(A).

708. Parents can agree or the courts can find good cause not to order an income assignment. La. Stat. Ann. § 9:303(A). "Good cause" exists (1) if child support has been paid on time for six months preceding a motion to modify, (2) if the obligor agrees to an automatic income assignment order if he becomes delinquent for more than one month, (3) if the obligor is unlikely to later become delinquent, or (4) for any other good cause. La. Stat. Ann. § 9:393(B)(2). When the Department of Children & Family Services enforces payment, Title 46 applies. *See* La. Stat. Ann. § 9:303(C).

709. La. Stat. Ann. § 9:375(A); *see also* Smith v. Pillow-Smith, 2010-0167, pp. 5, 8 (La. App. 4 Cir. 11/17/10), 52 So. 3d 264, 269–70 (although an obligor may not be in contempt, he must still show good

within the sound discretion of the trial court.[710] However, unless a party can show good cause as to why attorney's fees should not be awarded, the award is mandatory.[711] When support arrears have accumulated, a court has the discretion to allow the obligor to pay the arrearages in monthly payments or in a lump sum.[712] Further, at the request of any interested person, the recorder of mortgages must record the judgment making past-due payments executory, which shall be a judicial mortgage for the amount due.[713]

Civil contempt is also available when the obligor fails to comply with the order of support,[714] and an award for attorney's fees is available to the prevailing party.[715] Criminal contempt arises only when the amount of arrearage is more than $2,500 and the obligation has been outstanding for at least six months.[716] Finally, criminal neglect of family charges are also available for the intentional nonsupport for a child in necessitous circumstances.[717]

---

cause to avoid the imposition of attorney's fees). The prescriptive period to make past due payments executory is 10 years. La. Civ. Code Ann. art. 3501.1.

710. *See, e.g.*, Quinn v. Quinn, 2012-455, p. 7 (La. App. 5 Cir. 2/21/13), 110 So. 3d 1113, 1117 (awarding prevailing party $5,000 in attorney's fees when attorney submitted documentation that actual cost of representation on the motion was greater than $9,000); Derbes v. Derbes, 2006-91, p. 10 (La. App. 5 Cir. 9/26/06), 942 So. 2d 1086, 1091–92 (finding no abuse of discretion in trial court's awarding attorney's fees and costs in the amount of $51,662 when plaintiff actively pursued claim against defendant who made himself unavailable, missed and continued multiple hearings, and failed to respond to "simple" discovery questions regarding employment and finances requiring the filing of multiple motions to compel).

711. *See, e.g.*, Chauvin v. Chauvin, 46,365, p. 10 (La. App. 2 Cir. 6/22/11), 69 So. 3d 1192, 1199 (holding that plaintiff's need to hire an attorney to collect unpaid child support supported an award of attorney's fees); Dettman v. Rablee, 2001-1228, pp. 12–13 (La. App. 1 Cir. 9/28/01), 809 So. 2d 373, 381 (finding no evidence of good cause in the record and holding the trial court erred in its refusal to award attorney's fees based on actions and interactions of both parties; obligor was held in contempt for failure to comply with support order and ordered to pay arrearages); *compare* Guillory v. Guillory, 1997-354, pp. 12–13 (La. App. 3 Cir. 10/29/97), 702 So. 2d 1079, 1086 (good cause existed when defendant made lump sum payment for arrearages two months prior to hearing on rule for contempt seeking payment of arrearages), *with* Harris v. Harris, 505 So. 2d 835, 836–37 (La. Ct. App. 2 Cir. 1987) (finding no error in denying attorney's fees where defendant's failure to pay first month of child support obligation was an "honest misinterpretation of the judgment, rather than an arbitrary or capricious refusal" to pay).

712. *See* Davis v. Davis, 43,490, p. 10 (La. App. 2 Cir. 10/22/08), 997 So. 2d 149, 157; *but see* Vaughan v. Vaughan, 415 So. 2d 483, 485 (La. Ct. App. 1 Cir. 1982) (holding that the statute is mandatory, not discretionary, and monies owed become a vested property right, due in a lump sum).

713. La. Stat. Ann. § 9:323.

714. La. Stat. Ann. § 13:4611(1)(d)(i). For civil contempt, the court may issue "a fine of not more than five hundred dollars, or imprisonment for not more than three months, or both." *Id.*

715. La. Stat. Ann. § 13:4611(1)(g); *see* Lacour v. Lacour, 1999-0913, p. 9 (La. App. 4 Cir. 2/9/00), 763 So. 2d 678, 683 (assessing attorney's fees against obligor who was not found to be in contempt, but was ordered to pay arrearages); Hilbun v. Hilbun, 498 So. 2d 1127, 1128 (La. Ct. App. 3 Cir. 1986) (assessing attorney's fees against obligor based on contempt even though obligor was not in arrears as he paid the amount due on the morning of the rule).

716. La. Stat. Ann. § 14:75. The fines depend on the number of offenses. La. Stat. Ann. § 14:75.

717. La. Stat. Ann. § 14:74. "Whoever commits the offense of criminal neglect of family shall be fined not more than five hundred dollars or be imprisoned for not more than six months, or both, and may be placed on probation...." La. Stat. Ann. § 14:74(D)(1).

Other unique legal remedies include intercepting the obligor's federal tax refund to satisfy arrearages[718] and suspending professional, sporting, and motor vehicle licenses of the non-paying obligor.[719] Once the obligor complies with the order of support, licenses may be reissued.[720]

§ 7:65 Uniform Interstate Family Support Act (UIFSA)

The interstate enforcement of child support is governed by Louisiana's Uniform Interstate Family Support Act (UIFSA).[721] Found in Chapter 13 of the Children's Code, "[t]he primary purpose of UIFSA was to eliminate multiple and inconsistent support orders by establishing a principle of having only one controlling order in effect at any one time" using a concept called "continuing, exclusive jurisdiction," under which the issuing state retains exclusive jurisdiction until certain conditions exist to permit jurisdiction elsewhere.[722]

---

718. *See* La. Stat. Ann. § 9:315.26.

719. La. Stat. Ann. § 9:315.30 (provisions and procedures for judicial suspension of licenses). Licenses include: (a) professional, occupational, business, or industry license; (b) motor vehicle license; and (c) licenses for sporting activities, including fishing and hunting. *See id.*; *see also id.* §§ 37:2952 (trade, occupation, and professional licensing); 32:432(A)–(C) (suspension or denial of driving privileges); 56:647(A)(1) (suspension or denial of hunting and fishing license). The court may suspend an obligor's license for nonpayment of a judgment of child support for an indefinite period of time until compliance with the support order is obtained. *See* La. Stat. Ann. §§ 9:315.31(11), 9:315.34 (procedures for reissuing obligor licenses), 9:315.32(A)(1)(c) ("An order suspending a license to operate a motor vehicle may provide specific time periods for the suspension at the court's discretion."). *See also* Richey v. Richey, 1997-838, pp. 4–5 (La. App. 3 Cir. 12/10/97), 704 So. 2d 343, 345 (finding that trial court did not abuse its discretion in suspending divorced mother's nursing and driver's licenses for failure to pay child support, even though such licenses may have been essential to her ability to pay child support, where she had paid only $20 on $12,645.80 owed, despite making between $12 and $14 hourly when working and having remarried to spouse who made $1,200 per month); Brown v. Taylor, 31,352, pp. 9–10 (La. App. 2 Cir. 2/26/99), 728 So. 2d 1058, 1063 (finding that trial court could order a mother's driver's license surrendered and suspended for willful failure to pay court-ordered child support as a civil, not criminal measure).

720. La. Stat. Ann. § 9:315.34(B)(1). Once the issuing board receives a court order of compliance, they shall issue, reissue, renew, or otherwise extend an obligor's license in accordance with the issuing board's rules. La. Stat. Ann. § 9:315.35. The Department of Children and Family Services is likewise vested with authority to directly seek suspension of an obligor's licenses. *See* La. Stat. Ann. § 9:315.40; *see also* Dep't of Soc. Servs. ex rel. L.P. v. F.P., 2013-894, pp. 6–7 (La. App. 5 Cir. 4/23/14), 140 So. 3d 328, 331 (holding that juvenile court judge erred by ordering the state to return obligor's driver's license which was suspended through action by Department of Children and Family Services and stating, "We are unaware of any provision in the law allowing a juvenile court judge to overrule or rescind the administrative suspension of an obligor's driver's license without requiring compliance with the specific procedures set forth in LSA-9:315.40 *et seq.*").

721. UIFSA was preceded by the Uniform Reciprocal Enforcement of Support Act (URESA), which was repealed at the time of UIFSA's adoption in 1995. *See* 1995 La. Sess. Law Serv. Act 251 (H.B. 1518) La. Child. Code Ann. arts. 1301–42, *repealed by* Act No. 251, 1995 La. Acts 688–714.

722. Jurado v. Brashear, 2000-1306, pp. 4–5 (La. 3/19/01), 782 So. 2d 575, 578. The state was under a congressional mandate to remain eligible for federal funding of child support enforcement. *Id.* at 578 n.4.

Once a Louisiana court issues an initial order of child support, it will maintain "continuing, exclusive jurisdiction" to modify its order,[723] unless (1) at the time of filing the request for modification, all parties involved—obligor, obligee, and child for whom the benefit is awarded—have established residency in another state;[724] (2) the order is not the controlling order;[725] or (3) all parties consent in writing to another state assuming continuing, exclusive jurisdiction.[726] Further, if another state modifies a Louisiana order of child support in accordance with that state's version of UIFSA, then a Louisiana court must recognize the continuing, exclusive jurisdiction of the other state.[727] Ex parte temporary orders do not create continuing, exclusive jurisdiction.[728]

When establishing an initial child support order, a Louisiana court may exercise jurisdiction even if a comparable pleading has been filed in another state or country, as long as (1) the Louisiana proceeding is filed before the expiration of time to challenge the exercise of jurisdiction in the other court, (2) the contesting party challenges the jurisdiction of the other court, and (3) Louisiana is the home state of the child.[729] "Home state" is defined as "the state or foreign country in which a child lived with a parent or a person acting as parent for at least six consecutive months immediately preceding the time of filing...."[730]

When only one tribunal has issued a child support order pursuant to UIFSA, that order controls and must be recognized.[731] When two or more states have issued sup-

---

723. La. Child. Code Ann. art. 1302.2. For the order to be valid, Louisiana must have personal jurisdiction over a nonresident defendant. *Id.*

724. La. Child. Code Ann. art. 1302.5(A)(1). However, jurisdiction will continue to exist if all parties, who reside in another state, consent in a record or in open court that the tribunal of Louisiana may continue to exercise jurisdiction to modify its order. La. Child. Code Ann. art. 1302.5(A)(2). *See* Jurado, 782 So. 2d at 581 (holding that the issuing district court maintained continuing, exclusive jurisdiction to enforce its support order, but no longer maintained continuing, exclusive jurisdiction to modify the support order after all parties had established residency in states other than Louisiana); Martzell v. Wydooghe, 1999-1356, pp. 1–2 (La. App. 4 Cir. 6/16/99), 737 So. 2d 953, 954 (jurisdiction to modify support order remained with tribunal of this state because rule to modify support order was filed while obligor-parent was still a resident of Louisiana and prior to all parties establishing residency outside of state).

725. La. Child. Code Ann. art. 1302.5(B)(2). Determining whether a child support order is the controlling order is governed by Louisiana Children's Code Article 1302.7.

726. La. Child. Code Ann. art. 1302.5(B)(1). *See* Spicer v. Spicer, 2010-1577, p. 6 (La. App. 1 Cir. 3/25/11), 62 So. 3d 798, 802 (finding that Louisiana retained continuing, exclusive jurisdiction over the child support order because one of the parties still resided in Louisiana and not all of the parties signed a written consent filed with the Louisiana tribunal for another state to assume jurisdiction).

727. La. Child. Code Ann. art. 1302.5(C).

728. La. Child. Code Ann. art. 1302.5(E).

729. La. Child. Code Ann. art. 1302.4(A). In the reverse situation—a subsequent filing in another state, which meets the same test—a Louisiana court may not exercise jurisdiction. La. Child. Code Ann art. 1302.4(B); *but see* State v. Lannelongue, 22-220 (La. App. 5 Cir. 2/01/23), 358 So. 3d 899 (holding that the court need not apply art. 1302.4 because the court had authority under UIFSA to establish child support orders—even though a foreign country had issued child support orders—because jurisdictional requirements were not met in the country issuing the initial child support order).

730. La. Child. Code Ann. art. 1301.2(8).

731. La. Child. Code Ann. art. 1302.7(B)(1).

port orders regarding the same child, UIFSA provides specific rules to determine which order controls and must be recognized.[732] Because every state has some version of UIFSA, the statute promotes uniformity of law[733] and permits communication between states to determine the appropriate tribunal to exercise jurisdiction.[734] Louisiana courts may act as an "initiating tribunal" when forwarding proceedings to a tribunal of another state or as a "responding tribunal" when accepting proceedings initiated by other states or foreign countries.[735] When properly applied, UIFSA results in an interstate finding of jurisdiction in which both states' tribunals agree.[736]

Jurisdiction to enforce a child support award is treated differently than jurisdiction to modify an order. A Louisiana court can always enforce its own support order.[737] An out-of-state support order can be enforced in Louisiana by registering the order in a Louisiana court[738] or by sending an income-withholding order directly to the obligor's employer.[739] A support order issued in another state or foreign country can be filed and registered in a Louisiana court and will be "enforceable in the same manner and is subject to the same procedures" as a Louisiana order, even though the Louisiana court may not be able to modify it.[740] Ultimately, the law of the issuing state will govern the "nature, extent, amount and duration" of the order.[741] A Louisiana court will only be able to modify an order issued by the other state pursuant to UIFSA if the other state loses continuing, exclusive jurisdiction and Louisiana has personal jurisdiction

732. La. Child. Code Ann. art. 1302.7(C).

733. La. Child. Code Ann. art. 1309.1.

734. La. Child. Code Ann. arts. 1303.17–1303.18.

735. La. Child. Code Ann. art. 1302.3; *see also* La. Child. Code Ann. arts. 1302.5(B), 1302.6, 1302.11.

736. *See, e.g.*, State v. Hanson, 1998-0570, p. 3 (La. App. 4 Cir. 11/19/98), 725 So. 2d 514, 515 (rejecting jurisdiction in Louisiana over a purported father's request for a paternity test to challenge a judgment obtained by the mother in Iowa, which declared him to be the father and ordered him to pay child support; the purported father had to return to the forum that initially rendered judgment).

737. La. Child. Code Ann. art. 1302.6; *see also* Jurado v. Brashear, 2000-1306, pp. 4–5 (La. 3/19/01), 782 So. 2d 575, 579.

738. La. Child. Code Ann. art. 1306.1 *et seq.*

739. La. Child. Code Ann. art. 1305.1 *et seq.*

740. La. Child. Code Ann. art. 1306.3; Stagg v. Stagg, 1998-556, p. 4 (La. App. 3 Cir. 11/12/98), 721 So. 2d 1097, 1099 (when a Louisiana court receives a pleading from a court in another state to enforce a support order and causes a petition or pleading to be filed, the Louisiana court has very broad authority concerning the manner in which to enforce the support order).

741. La. Child. Code Ann. art. 1306.4; *see* Dep't of Soc. Servs. ex rel. State of Ohio v. Davis, 2001-535, p. 3 (La. App. 3 Cir. 10/31/01), 799 So. 2d 781, 783. In a proceeding to collect and enforce arrearages, the statutes of limitation of either Louisiana or the issuing state or foreign country, whichever is longer, applies. La. Child. Code Ann. art. 1306.4(B). *See* State ex rel. Jackson v. Jackson, 2012-999, p. 3 (La. App. 3 Cir. 2/16/13), 110 So. 3d 597, 598–99 (holding that judgment was unenforceable because it had prescribed under issuing state law prior to filing a Rule to Register and Enforce the Out of State Order); Dep't of Soc. Servs., Off. of Fam. Support ex rel. O'Neal v. Peteet, 2009-1219, p. 6 (La. App. 4 Cir. 5/12/10), 40 So. 3d 1015, 1019 (using Ohio statute of limitation, rather than Louisiana prescriptive period, for collection of arrearages for outstanding support obligations when Ohio's statute of limitation exceeded the two-year prescriptive period allowed under Louisiana law).

over the respondent.[742] In any event, modification—if permitted—cannot include the duration of the award, which is governed by the law of the issuing state throughout the life of the order.[743]

Even without registration, direct enforcement is available to an obligee by sending an income assignment order issued in another state to an employer in Louisiana without having to register the order in a Louisiana court.[744] The obligor's Louisiana employer must immediately provide a copy of the order to the obligor, and the employer must treat the order in the same way as it would an order issued by a Louisiana court.[745] The obligor does have the ability to challenge the validity of an income assignment order that was rendered out-of-state in a Louisiana court.[746] Finally, an obligee can seek enforcement of a Louisiana order against an out-of-state obligor by either registering the order in the other state or by direct enforcement of the order through the obligor's out-of-state employer.[747]

---

742. *See* La. Child. Code Ann. art. 1306.11.

743. La. Child. Code Ann. art. 1306.11(C); Dep't of Child. & Fam. Servs. v. Laflamme, 2020-1299 (La. App. 1 Cir. 6/4/21), 327 So. 3d 999 (finding that New Jersey law governed the duration of the father's child support obligation even though no parties lived in New Jersey; the order was issued there).

744. La. Child. Code Ann. art. 1305.1.

745. La. Child. Code Ann. art. 1305.2.

746. La. Child. Code Ann. art. 1305.6.

747. The litigant would rely on the other state's UIFSA's provisions on registration and direct enforcement.

Chapter 8

Biological Filiation*

* This chapter was derived from the following article: Sandi S. Varnado, *A Primer on Biological Filiation in Louisiana*, 69 Loy. L. Rev. 237 (2022). The authors wish to thank the Loyola Law Review for its assistance on the initial work for this chapter.

§ 8:1 Introduction

Filiation is defined as "the legal relationship between a child and his parent."[1] The law of filiation carries numerous consequences, as many rights and obligations accompany this legal parent-child relationship. The law of filiation has been revised significantly over the years, with the most significant revisions enacted from 2004–2006[2] after a decade of debate and modification by the Louisiana State Law Institute.[3]

The impetus for revision of the law of filiation goes back to the 1960s with the judicial demand to end discrimination against illegitimate children.[4] Historically, Louisiana discriminated against children born outside of marriage, primarily in the world of successions, where the law either denied or severely restricted such child's inheritance rights.[5] The then-existing filiation regime played a significant role in this discrimination because it included an elaborate ranking system for all children born outside of marriage,[6] labeling them as "adulterous bastards"[7] or "natural children."[8] It also outlined the procedural devices that, if certain facts were present, could elevate the child's rank in this hierarchy. Ultimately, the child's label or rank under the filiation scheme determined their rights in the law of intestate succession.

However, in *Levy v. Louisiana*, the United States Supreme Court held that Louisiana, in its wrongful death statute, had no rational basis for discriminating against children born outside of marriage.[9] Other cases followed, and in 1980, the Louisiana Supreme Court decided the landmark case of *Succession of Brown*, in which the lower court denied intestate inheritance rights to four illegitimate heirs of the decedent, due to a higher-ranking adopted illegitimate child of the decedent.[10] The *Brown* court, and numerous cases to follow, determined that Louisiana's distinction between children born of marriage and those born outside of marriage was unconstitutional.[11] Thus,

1. La. Civ. Code Ann. art. 178. This article was first enacted in 2009, but the comment makes clear that the definition contained within it is consistent with that offered by doctrine. La. Civ. Code Ann. art. 178 cmt.

2. *See* Act No. 26, 2004 La. Acts 936–54 (eliminating the terminology of illegitimate and legitimate children); Act No. 192, 2005 La. Acts 1444–59 (revising all of the laws on filiation in the Civil Code); Act No. 344, 2006 La. Acts 1528–35 (implementing legislation that finalized the revision in the Civil Code ancillaries).

3. *See* Katherine S. Spaht, *Who's Your Momma, Who Are Your Daddies: Louisiana's New Law of Filiation*, 67 La. L. Rev. 307, 307 (2007).

4. *See* Harry D. Krause, *Legitimate and Illegitimate Offspring of* Levy v. Louisiana: *First Decisions on Equal Protection and Paternity*, 36 U. Chi. L. Rev. 338, 338 (1969).

5. *See* Kathryn V. Lorio, Successions and Donations § 3:5, in 10 Louisiana Civil Law Treatise (2d ed. 2009).

6. *See generally* La. Civ. Code arts. 180–204 (1870); *see also* Kathryn V. Lorio, Successions and Donations § 3:5, in 10 Louisiana Civil Law Treatise (2d ed. 2009).

7. La. Civ. Code art. 182 (1870), *repealed by* Act No. 607, 1979 La. Acts 1643–47.

8. La. Civ. Code art. 202, *repealed by* Act No. 607, 1979 La. Acts 1643–47.

9. Levy v. Louisiana, 391 U.S. 68, 72 (1968).

10. *See* Succession of Brown, 388 So. 2d 1151 (La. 1980).

11. *See, e.g.*, Succession of Brown, 388 So. 2d at 1154.

the law of filiation needed a total overhaul. Before *Brown* was even rendered, though, the Louisiana Legislature began amending the filiation laws.[12] A thorough revision occurred in 1980 and 1982, and through it, the discrimination against children born outside of marriage in the realm of succession and donation rights ended.[13] However, despite these revisions to inheritance law, the laws of filiation needed further reform.

The Louisiana Legislature finally began to heed the challenge in 2004 by officially removing the terms "illegitimate" and "legitimate" from Louisiana law; it enacted this change by revising article 3506, an article that defines terms of art in the Louisiana Civil Code.[14] Article 3506 now defines "children" as either a child "born of marriage" or "born outside of marriage."[15] More significant revisions followed in 2005, which totally overhauled the Civil Code's chapter on Filiation. The 2005 revision updated the law and aligned it with the recent jurisprudence and other federal standards.[16] For the first time, the Civil Code addressed maternal filiation.[17] The next year, the legislature revised the associated filiation provisions in Louisiana's Revised Statutes to ensure correlation with the Civil Code.[18] The revisions solved many controversial issues (as discussed herein) and also improved the presentation of Louisiana's filiation laws.

Current law provides two avenues to establish filiation between a parent and child: (1) proof of maternity or paternity; or (2) adoption.[19] The sections below explore filiation through proof of maternity or paternity,[20] sometimes referred to as "biological filiation."[21] However, this term is actually a misnomer. While it might seem intuitive to assume that biology is the sole impetus for the filiation of a parent and child, this is not always the case under Louisiana law.[22] Filiation is a question of fact,[23] and the standard of appellate review of facts is manifest error.[24]

12. *See* La. Civ. Code Ann. arts. 208–09 (Supp. 1984).

13. *See* Kathryn V. Lorio, Successions and Donations § 3:5, in 10 Louisiana Civil Law Treatise (2d ed. 2009).

14. *See* La. Civ. Code Ann. art. 3506 cmt.

15. La. Civ. Code Ann. art. 3506(8).

16. *See* Kerry Triche, Handbook on Louisiana Family Law 362 (Thomson Reuters/West 2009).

17. Act No. 192, 2005 La. Acts, 1–2.

18. Act No. 344, 2006 La. Acts 1528–35.

19. La. Civ. Code Ann. art. 179.

20. Filiation by adoption is not covered in this chapter, as it arises from the juridical act of adoption. La. Civ. Code Ann. art. 199.

21. La. Civ. Code Ann. arts. 184–85.

22. *See, e.g.*, State ex rel. C.C., 18-440 (La. App. 5 Cir. 10/12/18), 256 So. 3d 565.

23. Succession of Gussman, 288 So. 2d 665, 668 (La. Ct. App. 3 Cir. 1974).

24. Succession of Pruitt, 96-534, p. 5 (La. App. 5 Cir. 1/15/97), 688 So. 2d 103, 105.

§ 8:2 Maternal Filiation

Historically, maternal filiation in Louisiana was straightforward. Prior to 2005, maternal filiation followed from the child's birth, which was almost always documented.[25] However, because of the increased use of assisted reproductive technology, proving maternity has become more nuanced. In some instances, multiple women are involved in the reproductive process, so Louisiana has had to decide who will be the child's legal mother: the one providing the egg, the one carrying and delivering the child, or the one who intends to be the mother.[26]

§ 8:3 Maternal Filiation—General Rules

Currently, Louisiana law provides that "[m]aternity may be established by a preponderance of the evidence that the child was born of a particular woman, except as otherwise provided by law."[27] Thus, in most cases, the woman who gives birth to a child is, by law, the mother of that child. Any evidence may be used to prove maternity at any time, and this evidence "includes all facts and circumstances establishing that the child was born of a particular woman," for example, witness testimony as "to the fact of the birth, documentary evidence (including formal or informal acknowledgment), and scientific evidence."[28] In *Succession of Gore*, the decedent's purported adopted son petitioned to be appointed as succession administrator, but the decedent's biological daughters excepted, arguing that he had no right of action.[29] While the son had no judicial decree of adoption and thus could not qualify as an adopted child, he did have a birth certificate with the decedent's name listed as his mother.[30] The court cited Louisiana Revised Statutes Section 40:42(A)[31] for the notion that "[e]xcept for delayed or altered certificates, every original certificate on file in the vital records registry is prima facie evidence of the facts therein stated."[32] Because the daughters were unable to offer evidence to controvert that prima facie evidence, their exception was overruled.[33]

---

25. *See* Katherine S. Spaht, *Who's Your Momma, Who Are Your Daddies: Louisiana's New Law of Filiation*, 67 La. L. Rev. 307, 309 (2007).

26. Sandi Varnado, *Who's Your Daddy?: A Legitimate Question Given Louisiana's Lack of Legislation Governing Assisted Reproductive Technology*, 66 La. L. Rev. 609, 630 (2006); *see also* Kerry Triche, Handbook on Louisiana Family Law 365–66 (Thomson Reuters/West 2009); Katherine S. Spaht, *Who's Your Momma, Who Are Your Daddies: Louisiana's New Law of Filiation*, 67 La. L. Rev. 307, 309 (2007).

27. La. Civ. Code Ann. art. 184.

28. La. Civ. Code Ann. art. cmts. (a)–(b).

29. Succession of Gore, 17-68, p. 2 (La. App. 5 Cir. 5/31/17), 223 So. 3d 628, 630.

30. Succession of Gore, 223 So. 3d at 630. According to the son, he had been told by his parents that he had been adopted from his father's sister, but no record of adoption could be found.

31. La. Stat. Ann. § 40:42(A).

32. Gore, 223 So. 3d at 632.

33. Gore, 223 So. 3d at 633.

§ 8:4 Maternal Filiation—Surrogacy Contracts

While birth is typically the determining factor, Civil Code Article 184 contains the qualifier, "except as otherwise provided by law."[34] This signals that Louisiana law recognizes instances in which someone other than the woman who gives birth to the child is the legal mother of that child. This happens in a couple of situations. First, Louisiana allows for a married couple to adopt human embryos created by the gametes of another man and woman.[35] In such a situation, the embryo is implanted into the married woman who then delivers the child. This adoptive mother is the child's legal mother, despite the lack of genetic relation to the child.[36] While included as an exception to general rule, the provision on adoptive embryos actually supports the proposition that birth is determinative of maternity.

Second, Louisiana allows for certain forms of surrogacy contracts, under which the woman who carries and delivers the child is not the legal mother, despite the fact of birth.[37] From a scientific standpoint, a surrogacy relationship can exist in a variety of forms, depending on the surrogate's role and the contributors of sperm and egg.[38] However, Louisiana's surrogacy law is extremely limited in scope. The evolution of Louisiana's surrogacy law has been extremely slow in comparison to that of other states.[39] Prior to 2016, the only form of surrogacy that Louisiana law recognized was one under which a married couple provided the egg and sperm to create a child who would be carried and delivered by a surrogate who was related by blood or affinity to one of them.[40] In other words, only gestational surrogacy arrangements were enforced and only for married couples with viable sperm and egg who were able to secure a relative to serve as the surrogate. Additionally, the law prohibited the surrogate's compensation.[41]

The Louisiana Legislature introduced surrogacy bills in its 2013 and 2014 sessions, but in spite of support in both chambers, Governor Bobby Jindal vetoed them.[42] Both

---

34. La. Civ. Code Ann. art. 184.

35. *See* La. Stat. Ann. § 9:130.

36. La. Stat. Ann. § 9:130.

37. *See* La. Stat. Ann. § 9:2720.

38. For example, a "traditional" surrogacy arrangement involves the surrogate as both the contributor of the egg (to be fertilized by the sperm of a man (either the intended father or a donor)), as well as the one to carry and deliver the child. By contrast, a "gestational" surrogacy arrangement involves the surrogate as only the one to carry and deliver the child; the egg is supplied by another woman—either the intended mother or a donor—and then fertilized by the sperm of a man (either the intended father or a donor). Nayana H. Patel et al., *Insight into Different Aspects of Surrogacy Practices*, J. Hum. Reprod. Scis. July–Sept. 2018, at 212.

39. *See* Guide to State Surrogacy Laws, Am. Progress (Dec. 17, 2007), http://www.americanprogress.org/article/guide-to-state-surrogacy-laws/.

40. La. Stat. Ann. § 40:32; *see also* § 40:34(B)(1)(a)(viii), (B)(1)(h)(v), (B)(1)(i), (B)(1)(j) (repealed by 2016 La. Acts 434).

41. La. Stat. Ann. § 9:130 (1986).

42. Governor Jindal suggested that Louisiana citizens were free to enter informal surrogacy agreements, but such agreements were actually not legally enforceable and did not create a legal relationship

chambers passed subsequent surrogacy legislation in 2016, and Governor John Bel Edwards signed it into law, effective August 1, 2016.[43] Entitled "Gestational Carrier Contracts," the legislation is housed in Louisiana Revised Statutes Sections 9:2718–2720.15.[44]

As was the case under prior law, a contract for a genetic gestational carrier—when the surrogate provides the egg—is absolutely null under the new legislation.[45] Simply put, a traditional surrogacy arrangement, pursuant to which the surrogate supplies the egg which is fertilized by the sperm of the intended father or a donor, renders the contract unenforceable. This rule reflects Louisiana's longstanding disapproval of such contracts, as well as the public policy against allowing a mother to agree to relinquish her biological child in advance of birth.[46] To prevent circumvention of this rule, the law allows a court to order genetic testing,[47] and if it finds a violation, then the surrogate will be the legal parent of the child[48] leaving the other parties no legal protection.[49]

Whereas genetic gestational surrogacy is prohibited, a contract for a gestational carrier—when a woman attempts to carry and give birth to a child born as a result of an in utero transfer of a human embryo to which she makes no genetic contribution[50]—is enforceable.[51] What distinguishes this type of surrogacy agreement is that the intended parents provide the gametes.[52] Of course, this is not the only requirement for these types of contracts, as the statutes set forth many more substantive and formal requirements.

---

between the intended parents and the child. Emily Lane, *Bobby Jindal again vetoes bill allowing for legal surrogacy births in Louisiana*, Nola.com (May 31, 2014), https://www.nola.com/news/politics/article_91d70d5a-2367-5bfc-9285-dd67ac0ae718.html.

43. *See* H.R. 1102, 2016 Leg., Reg. Sess. (La. 2016).

44. *See* La. Stat. Ann. §§ 9:2718–20.15. At the same time, the legislature revised Louisiana Revised Statutes Sections 40:34 and 14:286 and enacted Louisiana Revised Statutes Sections 40:93–96 and 44:4.1. H.R. 1102, 2016 Leg., Reg. Sess. (La. 2016).

45. La. Stat. Ann. § 9:2719. "Genetic gestational carrier" is defined as "the process by which a woman attempts to carry and give birth to a child using her own gametes and either the gametes of a person who intends to parent the child or donor gametes, when there is an agreement to relinquish the custody of and all rights and obligations to the child." La. Stat. Ann. § 9:2718.1(3).

46. La. Stat. Ann. § 9:2719 cmt. (a).

47. "If any party refuses to submit to such tests, the court may resolve the question of filiation against such party or enforce its order if the rights of others and the interest of justice so require." La. Stat. Ann. § 9:2720.14.

48. La. Stat. Ann. § 9:2720.14. The issue of filiation may be raised in a filiation, disavowal, or contestation action. La. Stat. Ann. § 9:2720.14. cmt. (a).

49. La. Stat. Ann. § 9:2719 cmt. (b).

50. An "in utero embryo transfer" is a "medical procedure whereby the genetic mother's egg is fertilized with the sperm of the genetic father, with the resulting embryo transferred into the uterus of the gestational carrier." La. Stat. Ann. § 9:2718.1(5).

51. *See* La. Stat. Ann. § 9:2720.

52. "Intended parents" is defined as a "married couple who each exclusively contribute their own gametes to create their embryo and who enter into an enforceable gestational carrier contract ... with a gestational carrier pursuant to which the intended parents will be the legal parents of the child resulting from an in utero embryo transfer." La. Stat. Ann. § 9:2718.1(6).

First, all of the parties to the gestational carrier contract—the intended parents, gestational carrier, and her spouse (if married)—must undergo various background checks.[53]

Second, the gestational carrier contract must set forth the obligations of the surrogate.[54] To start, she must be between 25 and 35 years old and have given birth to at least one child.[55] Additionally, she must agree to: (1) "become pregnant through in utero embryo transfer, using the gametes of the intended parents" and to deliver the child; (2) seek "reasonable medical evaluation and treatment during the ... pregnancy" and comply with "reasonable medical instructions about prenatal health," as well as "execute medical records releases ... in favor of the intended parents;" (3) certify attendance in at least two counseling sessions, separated by at least 30 days; (4) certify that she will relinquish all rights and duties as the parent of the resulting child;[56] and (5) agree to at least one counseling session after the child's birth but no more than six months thereafter.[57] The contract may not require the surrogate to terminate the resulting pregnancy, and any such provision is absolutely null and unenforceable as against public policy.[58]

Third, the gestational carrier contract must set forth the obligations of the intended parents. They must: (1) acknowledge that the surrogate has sole authority to make medical decisions during the pregnancy, as would a pregnant woman carrying a biological child; (2) agree to accept custody and full parental rights and obligations for the child once born; (3) "agree to be recognized as the legal parents of the child"; and (4) have a valid will or succession plan establishing custody of the child should both intended parents die before the child's birth.[59] A divorce of the intended parents before in utero transfer terminates the contract, but the death of an intended parent does not.[60] The deceased parent will be considered a parent of the resulting child if the child is born within three years of death, and the parent agreed to accept parenthood pursuant to a transfer after death.[61]

Fourth, the surrogate is not allowed to accept compensation, defined as "a payment of money, objects, services, or anything else having monetary value."[62] Any contract violating this rule is absolutely null and unenforceable as against public policy.[63] Nonetheless, the surrogate is allowed "reimbursement of actual expenses."[64] These include:

---

53. La. Stat. Ann. § 9:2720.4.

54. *See* La. Stat. Ann. § 9:2720.2(A).

55. La. Stat. Ann. § 9:2720.1.

56. If the surrogate is married, her spouse must also make this certification. La. Stat. Ann. § 9:2720.2(A)(4).

57. La. Stat. Ann. § 9:2720.2(A).

58. La. Stat. Ann. § 9:2720(D).

59. La. Stat. Ann. § 9:2720.2(B).

60. La. Stat. Ann. § 9:2720.11.

61. La. Stat. Ann. § 9:2720.11.

62. La. Stat. Ann. §§ 9:2720(C), 9:2718.1(1).

63. La. Stat. Ann. § 9:2720(C). Contracts executed outside of Louisiana that provide for compensation are likewise null as violating of public policy. *Id.*

64. La. Stat. Ann. § 9:2718.1(1).

(a) Actual medical expenses, including hospital, testing, nursing, midwifery, pharmaceutical, travel, or other similar expenses, incurred by the gestational carrier for prenatal care and those medical and hospital expenses incurred incident to the birth.

(b) Actual expenses incurred for mental health counseling services provided to the gestational carrier prior to the birth and up to six months after birth.

(c) Actual lost wages of the gestational carrier, not covered under a disability insurance policy, when bed rest has been prescribed for the gestational carrier for some maternal or fetal complication of pregnancy and the gestational carrier, who is employed, is unable to work during the prescribed period of bed rest.

(d) Actual travel costs related to the pregnancy and delivery, court costs, and attorney fees incurred by the gestational carrier.

(e) Payment of a judicially sanctioned settlement or judgment rendered in favor of the gestational carrier or her heirs as a result of her death, loss of reproductive organs or capability, or any other health complication caused by the in utero embryo transfer, pregnancy or resulting childbirth, miscarriage, or termination of pregnancy.[65]

Additionally, the contract must include a preliminary estimate of anticipated expenses and how the parties will allocate them.[66]

Finally, the gestational carrier contract must meet form requirements. Per the statutes, it must be "in writing and signed by the gestational carrier, her spouse if she is married, and both of the intended parents."[67]

Even assuming all of those requirements are met, the contract must still be approved by a court in advance of the in utero embryo transfer.[68] The procedure for approval is detailed in Louisiana Revised Statutes Section 9:2720.3(B), which requires that an obstetrician/gynecologist or reproductive endocrinologist who has treated the intended mother submit a signed affidavit indicating that the in utero embryo transfer with a gestational carrier is medically necessary to assist in reproduction.[69] Before approving, the court must find that all of the following are satisfied: (1) compliance with the requirements of Louisiana Revised Statutes Sections 9:2720–2720.3 and that there is no risk of harm to the child or the gestational carrier after assessing the criminal records, child abuse or neglect complaints, and Louisiana Protective Order Registry; (2) "provisions have been made for all reasonable healthcare and legal expenses associated with the gestational carrier contract until the birth of the child, including

65. La. Stat. Ann. § 9:2720.5(B)(3).

66. La. Stat. Ann. § 9:2720.2(C).

67. La. Stat. Ann. § 9:2720(A).

68. La. Stat. Ann. § 9:2720(B).

69. La. Stat. Ann. § 9:2720.3(B)(4). "'Medically necessary' means that the intended mother has been diagnosed to be infertile, or to have a physical condition such that a pregnancy would create serious risk of death or substantial and irreversible impairment of a major bodily function beyond the risk customary to pregnancy and childbirth." *Id.* § 9:2720.3(B)(5).

responsibility for those expenses if the contract is terminated"; (3) the gestational carrier will receive no compensation other than that specifically allowed by the statute; (4) the parties understand and freely consent to the contract.[70] The court conducts its proceedings in chambers or a closed hearing, and the only attendees are the parties in interest, their attorneys, and officers of the court (unless the court grants a petitioner's request to allow others to be present).[71] To further protect the privacy of the proceedings, the court records and parties' identities are sealed and are only "subject to disclosure, release, or inspection" upon application to the court and in conformity with the confidentiality requirements applicable to adoptions found in the Louisiana Children's Code.[72]

Once the court issues an order permitting the embryo transfer, multiple transfer attempts may be made until a live birth occurs.[73] After the child is born, a post-birth order is requested, which confirms that the intended parents are the legal parents and directs that a new birth certificate be issued naming the intending parents and sealing the original birth certificate.[74] No adoption or additional legal proceeding is necessary.

Other provisions of the legislation provide rules for jurisdiction,[75] termination of the surrogacy contract,[76] remedies,[77] subsequent marriage of the surrogate,[78] post-birth orders,[79] and time limitations.[80] The surrogacy legislation also prompted amendments to the vital statistics law and the criminal code.[81]

§ 8:5 Paternal Filiation

While the maternal filiation rules tie the legal relationship to biology in instances other than assisted reproductive technology, the same is not true of paternal filiation. Paternity cannot be proven by the child's birth. In fact, other than scientific testing, there is no direct proof of the identity of the male participant in a child's conception. As a result, the law relies first on presumptions, most of which apply in the context of marriage and are based on the reciprocal obligation of fidelity between spouses.[82] Additionally, Louisiana law allows filiation between the father and the child by judicial

70. La. Stat. Ann. § 9:2720.5(B).
71. La. Stat. Ann. § 9:2720.7.
72. La. Stat. Ann. § 9:2720.7.
73. La. Stat. Ann. § 9:2720.6.
74. La. Stat. Ann. § 9:2720.13.
75. La. Stat. Ann. § 9:2720.8.
76. La. Stat. Ann. §§ 9:2720.9, 9:2720.11.
77. La. Stat. Ann. § 9:2720.10.
78. La. Stat. Ann. § 9:2720.12.
79. La. Stat. Ann. § 9:2720.13.
80. La. Stat. Ann. § 9:2720.15.
81. *See* La. Stat. Ann. § 40:34(B) (Supp. 2012), *amended by* Act No. 1118, 2001 La. Acts 2371–73; La. Stat. Ann. §§ 40:93–96, *added by* Act No. 494, 2016 La. Acts 1603–15; La. Stat. Ann. § 14:286(B), *amended by* Act No. 562, 2018 La. Acts 1649–63.
82. *See* La. Civ. Code Ann. art. 98.

action.[83] These two avenues differ in that the presumptions operate as a matter of law and may be rebutted,[84] whereas a judicial action requires a successful court proceeding yielding a judgment of paternity.

§ 8:6 Paternal Filiation—Presumptions of Paternity

Louisiana law resorts to presumptions of paternity because outside of scientific testing, a man's participation in conception generally cannot be proven. There are five presumptions of paternity under Louisiana law. Below is a presentation of each presumption, including the methods through which each presumption may be rebutted by certain interested parties.

§ 8:7 Paternal Filiation—Presumptions of Paternity—Marriage Presumption

The first presumption, which is referred to as the strongest presumption in the law,[85] is based on the timing of the marriage of the mother and her husband, who is the presumed father. This presumption provides that "[t]he husband of the mother is presumed to be the father of a child born during the marriage or within three hundred days from the date of the termination of the marriage."[86] In either instance, the presumption hinges on the well-established reciprocal duty of fidelity owed by spouses.[87] The 300-day extension is designed to filiate children who were conceived during the marriage but were actually born outside of marriage.[88] Absent assisted reproductive technology or an extramarital sexual relationship, this presumption aligns with the reality of most married couples: that the husband of the mother is actually the biological father of the child. However, in some instances, this presumption leads to results that conflict with obvious biological facts,[89] i.e., reality, causing the Louisiana Supreme

83. The court may order the mother, child, and alleged father, or the mother's husband or former husband to submit to the collection and testing of blood or tissue samples in any civil action that involves paternity. The court may do so on its own or at the request of a party to the proceeding or a person whose blood or tissue is involved. La. Stat. Ann. § 9:396(A). The details surrounding such tests are set forth in Louisiana Revised Statutes Sections 9:397–397.3. *See* La. Stat. Ann. §§ 9:397–97.3.

84. *See generally* La. Civ. Code Ann. arts. 187–95.

85. La. Civ. Code Ann. art. 185 cmt. (b).

86. La. Civ. Code Ann. art. 185. Note that a marriage terminates not only on divorce but also on the death of either spouse, the issuance of a court order authorizing the spouse of a person who is presumed dead to remarry, or a judicial declaration that it is relatively null. La. Civ. Code Ann. art. 101. An absolutely null marriage is null from its inception and requires no declaration of nullity to be terminated. La. Civ. Code Ann. arts. 2033, 94, 101 cmt. (d).

87. *See* La. Civ. Code Ann. art. 98.

88. *See* Jessica G. Braun, Handbook on Louisiana Family Law 460 (West 2021–2022). Of course, this rule sometimes captures children who are not fathered by the husband, especially if the mother and husband live separate and apart for a significant length of time prior to the termination of the marriage.

89. Robert A. Pascal, *Civil Code and Related Subjects: Persons*, 14 La. L. Rev. 114, 124 (1953).

Court to admit that the presumption is not without its flaws.[90] In these instances, the presumption may be rebutted by the presumed father or his successors (disavowal action), or the mother of the child (contestation and establishment action).[91]

Application of the presumption to same-sex couples is discussed in Section 8.26 on Marriage Equality and Filiation.

§ 8:8 Paternal Filiation—Presumptions of Paternity—Marriage Presumption—Rebuttal by Disavowal Action

The presumed father is the person most likely to rebut the presumption, given the serious legal effects of being responsible for all parental obligations for the child; the avenue by which he does so is a disavowal action.[92] Note, though, that if the presumed father consented to an assisted reproductive technology to create the child, he is prohibited from disavowing that child.[93]

Successfully disavowing a child is sometimes a difficult task.[94] The articles on this action are strictly construed to further the policy of protecting innocent children born during marriage against scandalous attacks on their paternity.[95] To ensure that the proceedings are fair to the child, in an action to disavow paternity, the judge must appoint an attorney to represent the child, and the appointed attorney is not permitted to represent any other party in the litigation.[96] The presumed father must prove by clear and convincing evidence that he is not the biological father of the child.[97] While he may testify on the issue, to meet his burden, that testimony must be corroborated by other evidence, which could include scientific or medical evidence, evidence of physical impossibility due to location at the probable time of conception, the testimony of lay witnesses, or any other admissible evidence.[98]

90. Smith v. Cole, 553 So. 2d 847, 850 (La. 1989).

91. The court may order the mother, child, and alleged father, or the mother's husband or former husband to submit to the collection and testing of blood or tissue samples in any civil action that involves paternity. The court may do so on its own or at the request of a party to the proceeding or a person whose blood or tissue is involved. La. Stat. Ann. § 9:396(A) (2022). The details surrounding such tests are set forth in Louisiana Revised Statutes Sections 9:397–397.3. *See* La. Stat. Ann. §§ 9:397–97.3.

92. *See generally* La. Civ. Code Ann. arts. 187–89.

93. La. Civ. Code Ann. art. 188.

94. Rachel L. Kovach, *Sorry Daddy—Your Time Is Up: Rebutting the Presumption of Paternity in Louisiana*, 56 Loy. L. Rev. 651, 667 (2010).

95. Gallo v. Gallo, 2003-0794, p. 7 (La. 12/3/03), 861 So. 2d 168, 173.

96. La. Code Civ. Proc. Ann. art. 5091.1.

97. La. Civ. Code Ann. art. 187.

98. La. Civ. Code Ann. art. 187 cmt. (b).

The presumed father must file the disavowal action in timely fashion; otherwise, the presumption becomes irrebuttable.[99] Prior to 2016, the liberative prescriptive[100] period was one year, commencing on the day that the presumed father knew or should have known of the birth of the child.[101] This rule led to cases of deception of the presumed father by the child's mother.[102] For example, in *Fontenot v. Fontenot*, a man learned nine years after the children's birth and five years after his divorce from their mother that those children—all born during that marriage—were not his biological progeny.[103] The mother knew all along, but she never informed him.[104] Under the law at that time, his disavowal action had prescribed.[105] As the Louisiana Supreme Court previously explained, the determining factor for commencing prescription is not whether the husband had knowledge of the mother's deceit, but rather if he had knowledge of the child's birth.[106] The law was amended to address such situations.[107] Under current law, a disavowal action is still subject to a liberative prescriptive period of one year, but as a general rule, it begins on the later of the day (1) the child is born or (2) the presumed father knew or should have known that he may not be the biological father of the child, like when he has knowledge of the mother's adultery, for example.[108]

There is an additional exception to the prescription rules in situations where the mother and the presumed father lived separate and apart continuously during the 300 days immediately preceding the birth of the child.[109] In this factual scenario, the husband still enjoys the right to disavow, and his claim has a one-year prescriptive period. However, the period commences only once the husband is notified in writing that a party in interest has asserted that he is the child's father.[110]

In 2013, the Louisiana Supreme Court was called on to interpret this exception in *Pociask v. Moseley*. [111] In that case, the parties physically separated on April 30, 2006,

99. Modisette v. Phillips, 31,905, pp. 6–7 (La. App. 2 Cir. 5/5/99), 736 So. 2d 983, 987.

100. "Liberative prescription is a mode of barring of actions as a result of inaction for a period of time." La. Civ. Code Ann. art. 3447. Prescription must be contrasted with peremption, which is "a period of time fixed by law for the existence of a right. Unless timely exercised, the right is extinguished upon the expiration of the peremptive period." La. Civ. Code Ann. art. 3458. Both refer to the passing of time to preclude claims. However, peremption actually extinguishes rights, whereas prescriptive simply bars the right to exercise it. La. Civ. Code Ann. art. 3458 cmt. (b). Further, peremption may not be renounced, interrupted, or suspended, whereas prescription may. La. Civ. Code Ann. art. 3461, cmt. (c); *see generally* La. Civ. Code Ann. arts. 3449–3451, 3462–3472.

101. La. Civ. Code Ann. art. 189 cmt. (rev. cmt. 2016).

102. La. Civ. Code Ann. art. 189 cmt. (rev. cmt. 2016).

103. Fontenot v. Fontenot, 2000-1057, p. 1 (La. App. 3 Cir. 12/6/00), 774 So. 2d 330, 331.

104. Fontenot, 774 So. 2d at 331.

105. Fontenot, 774 So. 2d at 334.

106. Gallo, 861 So. 2d at 174.

107. La. Civ. Code Ann. art. 189 cmt. (rev. cmt. 2016).

108. La. Civ. Code Ann. art. 189.

109. La. Civ. Code Ann. art. 189.

110. La. Civ. Code Ann. art. 189.

111. Pociask v. Moseley, 2013-0262, p. 6 (La. 06/28/13), 122 So. 3d 533, 537–38.

and the child in question was born more than 300 days later, on March 15, 2007.[112] The presumed father received notice to trigger the one-year prescriptive period under the exception on July 15, 2008, and filed a disavowal action a little over a month later.[113] However, the mother argued that because the presumed father had stayed overnight at the former matrimonial domicile in May of 2006, the requisite 300 days were "interrupted," rendering the exception inapplicable and his action untimely under the general rule in effect at that time.[114]

The Louisiana Supreme Court disagreed.[115] Using the existing jurisprudence for divorce law, it held that "the phrase 'living separate and apart continuously' in the divorce articles and the disavowal action article found in our Civil Code should be read *in pari materia*."[116] In doing so, the court decided that "one overnight visit in the former matrimonial domicile when both parties were present did not interrupt the three-hundred-day time period required for the former husband to live separate and apart continuously from the mother to avail himself of the exception to the running of prescription set forth in Art. 189."[117] As the court pointed out, there was no evidence indicating that the parties did not hold themselves out to the community as living separate and apart; in fact, there were no allegations of cohabitation, sexual relations, or reconciliation that might defeat or interrupt the 300-day requirement.[118]

In any case, the presumed father is allowed to petition a court for an order directing the mother, child, and petitioner himself to submit to the collection of blood or tissue samples, or both, for a determination of paternity.[119] If he does so prior to filing a disavowal action but within his prescriptive period, then his petition will operate to suspend the prescriptive period for one year from the date it is filed.[120] The court may not make a paternity determination based on the test results and conclusions of the experts, but the test results are admissible in any subsequent action filed relating to the filiation of the child.[121]

The disavowal action is heritable.[122] Thus, if the presumed father dies before asserting a timely disavowal action, any of his successors whose interests are adversely

112. Pociask, 122 So. 3d at 535.
113. Pociask, 122 So. 3d at 535.
114. Pociask, 122 So. 3d at 536.
115. Pociask, 122 So. 3d at 543.
116. Pociask, 122 So. 3d at 543.
117. Pociask, 122 So. 3d at 542.
118. Pociask, 122 So. 3d at 542.
119. La. Stat. Ann. § 9:398.2(A)(1). The court may order the mother, child, and alleged father, or the mother's husband or former husband to submit to the collection and testing of blood or tissue samples in any civil action that involves paternity. The court may do so on its own or at the request of a party to the proceeding or a person whose blood or tissue is involved. La. Stat. Ann. § 9:396(A). The details surrounding such tests are set forth in Louisiana Revised Statutes Sections 9:397–397.3. *See* La. Stat. Ann. §§ 9:397–397.3 (2022).
120. La. Stat. Ann. § 9:398.2(A).
121. La. Stat. Ann. § 9:398.2(E).
122. *See* La. Civ. Code Ann. art. 190.

affected may assert it in his stead.[123] In such a situation, the burden of proof remains clear and convincing, and the prescriptive period remains one year.[124] However, the commencement of this prescriptive period hinges on whether prescription had begun to run against the presumed father before his death.[125] If it had, the successor's one-year prescriptive period begins at the death of the presumed father.[126] If not, the successor's one-year period begins on the day the successor is notified in writing that a party in interest has asserted that the deceased husband is the child's father.[127]

"A judgment of disavowal terminates existing child support and visitation orders."[128] It also "terminates the obligation to pay child support and revokes any court order enforcing that obligation."[129] It does not, however, "affect any child support payment or arrearages paid, due, or owing prior to the date" of the filing of the disavowal action.[130] Note that a legal father who does not disavow the child (or break the filial link to the child in some other fashion) will obtain no relief from parental obligations, including child support. For example, in *Gallo v. Gallo*, a husband who learned that he was not the child's biological father sued the mother to recover the child support that he had paid for years.[131] The court denied his claim because he had never disavowed paternity, reiterating: "Fatherhood rests on something more than genes."[132] Similarly, in *J.M.Y. v. R.R.*, the legal father who never disavowed the child brought an action against the alleged biological father for reimbursement of child support that he (the legal father) had paid.[133] The court granted the alleged biological father's exception of no cause of action, noting that even if the child was fathered by him, which had never been proven, this would not extinguish the legal father's obligation to support the child.[134] Simply put, the "legal tie of paternity will not be affected by subsequent proof of the child's actual biological tie."[135]

With that said, while the legal father may not escape his obligations without disavowing the child, that does not necessarily mean that the biological father escapes his obligations. Courts have clearly stated that this presumption "was not intended to shield biological fathers from their support obligations."[136] After all, certain state agencies have the authority to bring an action to determine filiation and fix child support

123. La. Civ. Code Ann. art. 190.
124. La. Civ. Code Ann. art. 187.
125. *See* La. Civ. Code Ann. art. 190.
126. La. Civ. Code Ann. art. 190.
127. La. Civ. Code Ann. art. 190.
128. La. Stat. Ann. § 9:402.
129. La. Stat. Ann. § 9:402.
130. La. Stat. Ann. § 9:402.
131. Gallo, 861 So. 2d at 170.
132. Gallo, 861 So. 2d at 178.
133. J.M.Y. v. R.R., 2008-805, p. 1 (La. App. 3 Cir. 12/11/08), 1 So. 3d 725, 726.
134. J.M.Y., 1 So. 3d at 728; *see also* Chapter 7, Section 7:7.
135. Smith v. Cole, 553 So. 2d 847, 854 (La. 1989).
136. *E.g.*, Dep't of Child. & Fam. Servs. ex rel. A.L. v. Lowrie, 2014-1025, p. 11 (La. 5/5/15), 167 So. 3d 573, 582.

against a biological father, despite this presumption of paternity.[137] Also, as discussed in Section 8:21, biological fathers may become filiated to a child, and in situations where that child already has a legal father, the biological father becomes the child's second father, also referred to as dual paternity.[138] This concept allows a child to seek support from the biological father notwithstanding the existence of the child's legal father.[139]

§ 8:9 Paternal Filiation—Presumptions of Paternity—Marriage Presumption—Rebuttal by Contestation and Establishment Action

Like the presumed father and his successors, the mother of a child may seek to rebut the presumption set forth in article 185. Until 2005, the Louisiana Civil Code did not grant her the right to do so,[140] and jurisprudential efforts to establish such a claim were typically unsuccessful.[141] However, as part of the sweeping 2005 revision, the mother is now allowed to bring a contestation and establishment action to rebut the presumption, provided certain requirements are satisfied.[142] The purpose of this action is "to align more closely biological and legal paternity in instances when the child's status will not be adversely affected by the social stigma" of being born outside of marriage; such is the case only when the contestation action will "establish legally the child as a member of an intact family, whose stability is marked by the marriage of the mother and alleged father."[143]

As such, the threshold requirement for the mother to bring the contestation and establishment action is that the mother must be married to someone who has executed an authentic act acknowledging the child.[144] She must also seek, in the contestation and establishment action, a judgment that her former husband is not the father of the child and that her current husband is the father of the child.[145] In other words, the mother, in using the contestation and establishment action, must simultaneously disprove her

137. *See, e.g.*, Dep't of Soc. Servs. ex rel. Munson v. Washington, 32,550, p. 1 (La. App. 2 Cir. 12/8/99), 747 So. 2d 1245, 1247.

138. Smith v. Jones, 566 So. 2d 408, 410 (La. Ct. App. 1 Cir. 1990).

139. *E.g.*, Dep't of Soc. Servs. ex rel. Williams v. Howard, 2003-2865, p. 3 (La. App. 1 Cir. 12/30/04), 898 So. 2d 443, 444.

140. Lucie R. Kantrow, *Presumption Junction: Honey, You Weren't Part of the Function—A Louisiana Mother's New Right to Contest Her Husband's Paternity*, 67 La. L. Rev. 633, 635 (2007). Louisiana lagged behind many jurisdictions in this regard. *Id.*

141. *See, e.g.*, Leger v. Leger, 2002-428, p. 3 (La. App. 3 Cir. 10/30/02), 829 So. 2d 1101, 1104.

142. *See* La. Civ. Code Ann. arts. 191–94.

143. La. Civ. Code Ann. art. 191 cmt. (b).

144. *See* La. Civ. Code Ann. art. 191. Note that prior to 2016, the mother's husband could acknowledge the child by signing the child's birth certificate. However, in the 2016 legislative session, Act Number 309 amended article 191 to require that the acknowledgement be in the form of an authentic act. *See* Act No. 309, 2016 La. Acts 1145–49.

145. La. Civ. Code Ann. art. 191.

former's husband paternity while proving her present husband's paternity.[146] As such, the mother is the proper party plaintiff, and her former and present husbands are the proper party defendants in such an action.[147] The mother's burden of proof is clear and convincing evidence, and her testimony must be corroborated by other evidence.[148] Any judgment rendered in a contestation and establishment action must decree that the former husband is not the child's father while also decreeing that the present husband is the child's father.[149]

The mother must bring the contestation and establishment action within the two peremptive periods provided in article 193. First, the mother must bring the action within 180 days of the marriage to her current husband; second, the action must be instituted within two years of the child's birth.[150] By keeping the time period short, the mother is encouraged to act quickly, which is in the interest of all parties, particularly the child who may form an emotional attachment to the presumed father otherwise.[151] Unlike the father's disavowal action, nothing in the law addresses the heritability of the mother's action. Given the general premise that obligations are heritable unless they are strictly personal, the mother's action is likely heritable if brought within the peremptive periods available to the mother.[152]

If the mother succeeds in her contestation and establishment action, child custody and visitation orders affecting the former husband are terminated unless the court finds extraordinary circumstances justifying reasonable visitation to him in the child's best interest.[153] Additionally, the judgment terminates the former husband's child support obligation and revokes any court order enforcing that obligation.[154] By contrast, it does not affect any child support payment or arrearages paid, due, or owing prior to the date that the contestation and establishment action was filed.[155]

---

146. La. Civ. Code Ann. art. 191 cmt. (c).

147. La. Stat. Ann. § 9:403(A).

148. La. Civ. Code Ann. art. 192. The court may order the mother, child, and alleged father, or the mother's husband or former husband to submit to the collection and testing of blood or tissue samples in any civil action that involves paternity. The court may do so on its own or at the request of a party to the proceeding or a person whose blood or tissue is involved. La. Stat. Ann. § 9:396(A). The details surrounding such tests are set forth in Louisiana Revised Statutes Sections 9:397– 397.3. *See* La. Stat. Ann. §§ 9:397–97.3.

149. La. Civ. Code Ann. art. 194.

150. La. Civ. Code Ann. art. 193.

151. La. Civ. Code Ann. art. 193 cmt.

152. *See* La. Civ. Code Ann. art. 1765; *see also* Short v. Plantation Management Corp., 99-0899 (La. App. 1 Cir. 12/27/00), 781 So. 2d 46, 53–54 (causes of action related to a nursing home resident's "bill of rights" were heritable).

153. La. Stat. Ann. § 9:403(C)(1).

154. La. Stat. Ann. § 9:403(C)(2).

155. La. Stat. Ann. § 9:403(C)(3).

§ 8:10 Paternal Filiation—Presumptions of Paternity—Dueling Presumptions

When there are "dueling" or "overlapping" presumptions, the law must provide resolution. To illustrate, suppose that Woman gets pregnant in January while married to Spouse 1. In March, Woman and Spouse 1 divorce. In May, Woman marries Spouse 2. In October, Woman gives birth to a child. Under the first presumption, both Spouse 1 and Spouse 2 would be presumed fathers because the child is born during the marriage of Woman and Spouse 2 and born within 300 days of the termination of the marriage of Woman and Spouse 1.

Article 186 resolves the question of paternity in such situations. It provides that if a child is born within 300 days of the termination of one marriage and the mother has remarried before the child's birth, then the prior husband (Spouse 1) is presumed to be the father.[156] If the prior husband or his successor successfully disavows the child, then the current husband (Spouse 2) is automatically presumed to be the child's father,[157] which operates to protect the child from the social stigma of illegitimacy.[158] Some argued that the rule should be the opposite, i.e., that the current husband should be presumed to be the child's father.[159] After all, this would better align with the likely reality that when a man marries a pregnant woman, he is the father of her child. However, crafting the rule this way would require the law to presume that the mother committed adultery during her first marriage.[160]

§ 8:11 Paternal Filiation—Presumptions of Paternity—Dueling Presumptions—Rebuttal by Disavowal Action

The prior husband (the child's first presumed father) may file a disavowal action to rebut this presumption, as may his successors.[161] Note, however, that the current husband must be made a party to the disavowal action filed by the prior husband and must be served with process.[162]

If the prior husband successfully disavows the child, the current husband is presumed to be the child's father as discussed above. With that said, as a matter of fairness, the current husband or his successors may also file a disavowal action.[163] This disavowal action is the same in all respects as the one granted to the prior husband but

156. La. Civ. Code Ann. art. 186.
157. La. Civ. Code Ann. art. 186.
158. La. Civ. Code Ann. art. 186 cmt. (c).
159. Jessica G. Braun, Handbook on Louisiana Family Law 460 (West 2021–2022).
160. La. Civ. Code Ann. art. 186 cmt. (b).
161. *See* La. Civ. Code Ann. arts. 187–90.
162. La. Stat. Ann. § 9:401(A).
163. La. Civ. Code Ann. art. 186, cmt. (d).

for the time limit attached to it. The current husband must file the disavowal action within a peremptive period of one year from the day that the prior husband's judgment of disavowal is final and definitive,[164] which is when it is final and no longer subject to appeal.[165] Like so many time limitations in the parent-child arena, the reason that the period is peremptive is because of the "desirability of a relatively short period of time for resolving paternity, and thus the status of the child."[166]

§ 8:12 Paternal Filiation—Presumptions of Paternity—Dueling Presumptions—Rebuttal by Contestation and Establishment Action

The mother of the child can also rebut the presumption as to either presumed father through a contestation and establishment action, and the time limits are the same.[167]

§ 8:13 Paternal Filiation—Presumptions of Paternity—Marriage + Formal Acknowledgment Presumption

The presumption of paternity when a man marries the mother and acknowledges the child was enacted as part of the 2005 revision to address the circumstances of former Civil Code Article 198. That article recognized the legitimation of a child by the subsequent marriage of the parents if the man formally or informally[168] acknowledged the child.[169] The law changed by creating a presumption of paternity instead and requiring formal acknowledgment by authentic act or signing the birth certificate.[170] In 2016, the article was amended to remove signing the child's birth certificate as a mode of acknowledgment;[171] however, it still applies to birth certificates signed prior to August 1, 2016, the effective date of the amendment.[172]

Like the other presumptions above, the third presumption involves marriage—namely, one occurring after the child is born. This presumption provides that a man who marries the mother of the child and also acknowledges the child by authentic

---

164. La. Civ. Code Ann. art. 186.

165. La. Civ. Code Ann. art. 186 cmt. (d).

166. La. Civ. Code Ann. art. 186 cmt. (e).

167. *See* Sections 8:7 through 8:9 for a discussion on how a mother can rebut the presumption of paternity through a contestation and establishment action.

168. Informal acknowledgment came in several forms, like a writing where the father referred to the child as his or conversations and other similar conduct to that effect. La. Civ. Code Ann. art. 195 cmt. (d).

169. La. Civ. Code Ann. art. 195, cmt. (d).

170. La. Civ. Code Ann. art. 195, cmt. (d).

171. This amendment was a result of Act 309 of the 2016 legislative session. *See* Act No. 309, 2016 La. Acts 1145–49.

172. La. Civ. Code Ann. art. 195, cmt. (b) (rev. cmt. 2016).

act, with the mother's concurrence, is presumed to be the child's father, as long as the child is not filiated to another man.[173] For this presumption to be triggered, the first requirement is that a man must marry the child's mother, meaning that the child must already be born.[174] The second requirement is that this man must execute an authentic act in which he acknowledges the child.[175] The authentic act may be signed either before or after the marriage.[176] The third requirement is that the mother must concur in the acknowledgment by a juridical act, which is a voluntary act intended to cause legal consequences.[177] In many cases, the mother will concur in the father's authentic act of acknowledgment. The fourth and final requirement is that the child cannot be filiated to another man, [178] i.e., the child was not born or conceived during a prior marriage or if so, the presumption was successfully rebutted[179] or another man has not formally acknowledged the child.[180] All four must be satisfied; otherwise, the presumption is inapplicable.[181] Note, however, that if the child is filiated to another man, the child and the biological father may become filiated through an avowal or paternity action, leading to a possible dual paternity scenario.[182]

---

173. La. Civ. Code Ann. art. 195.

174. La. Civ. Code Ann. art. 195; *see* La. Civ. Code Ann. art. 185. If the man marries the mother before the child's birth, the marital presumption of article 185 would be triggered, and he would be the child's presumed father thereunder. *Id.*

175. La. Civ. Code Ann. art. 195. The acknowledgment may be executed before or after the child's birth. La. Civ. Code Ann. art. 195 cmt. (d).

176. La. Civ. Code Ann. art. 195. In child support, custody, and visitation cases, an acknowledgment via authentic act is deemed to be a legal finding of paternity and establishes the obligation to support the child and to establish visitation without the need for a judgment of paternity. La. Stat. Ann. §§ 9:392.1, 9:405.

177. *See* La. Civ. Code Ann. art. 2347 cmt. (c).

178. La. Civ. Code Ann. art. 195.

179. La. Civ. Code Ann. arts. 185–190, 191–94.

180. La. Civ. Code Ann. art. 196.

181. *But see* La. Civ. Code Ann. art. 196 cmt. (b) (rev. cmt. 2016) ("The elimination of signing the birth certificate as a means of accomplishing a formal acknowledgment is intended to have prospective effect only. Formal acknowledgments that were accomplished prior to the effective date of the 2016 revision will therefore remain effective.").

182. *See* Sections 8:21 through 8:23 for a discussion of avowal actions and paternity actions, which may result in dual paternity.

§ 8:14 Paternal Filiation—Presumptions of Paternity—Marriage + Formal Acknowledgment Presumption—Rebuttal by Disavowal Action

Like the prior presumptions, a disavowal action is available to the presumed father or his successors "as provided in Article 187."[183] The disavowal action differs from the others mentioned in one major respect: it has a very short peremptive period of 180 days.[184] The period begins to run from the later of either the date of marriage or the acknowledgment.[185]

§ 8:15 Paternal Filiation—Presumptions of Paternity—Marriage + Formal Acknowledgment Presumption—Rebuttal by Revoking or Annulling the Authentic Act of Acknowledgement

Without a doubt, the marriage + acknowledgment presumption of article 195 may be rebutted by a disavowal action as set forth in Section 8:14. In fact, the 2016 Revision Comment (a) suggests that this is the only avenue to rebut this presumption.[186] However, question has arisen as to whether the revocation or the annulment of the act of acknowledgment suffices to rebut this presumption, as well.

Per Section 9:406 of the Louisiana Revised Statutes, a person who executes an authentic act of acknowledgment[187] is allowed to revoke it without cause within 60 days of its execution.[188] To do so, the person must submit a sworn statement refuting paternity in a judicial hearing for the limited purpose of revoking the acknowledgment, or in a judicial hearing relating to the child wherein the acknowledging person is a party to the proceeding.[189] However, article 195 specifically provides that "[r]evocation of the authentic act of acknowledgment alone is not sufficient to rebut the

183. La. Civ. Code Ann. art. 195.

184. La. Civ. Code Ann. art. 195, cmt. (c) (rev. cmt. 2005).

185. La. Civ. Code Ann. art. 195.

186. La. Stat. Ann. § 9:406 cmt. (rev. cmt. 2016) ("To rebut the presumption paternity by subsequent marriage and formal acknowledgment of the child, a timely disavowal action *must* be brought.") (emphasis added).

187. This language suggests that only the man who executed the acknowledgment may revoke it, making it strictly personal. *See generally* La. Civ. Code Ann. arts. 1765–66. The language of a related statute, Louisiana Revised Statutes Section 9:392, seemingly supports that conclusion. It requires the notary to apprise the mother and alleged father that an "*alleged father who executed* an authentic act of acknowledgment may revoke the act. . . ." La. Stat. Ann. § 9:392(A)(7) (emphasis added). It does not mention anyone else, *id.*, but these provisions should be revised to clearly indicate who may revoke the act of acknowledgment.

188. La. Stat. Ann. § 9:406(A)(1); La. Stat. Ann. § 9:392(A)(7).

189. La. Stat. Ann. § 9:406(A); § 392(A)(7).

presumption of paternity created by this Article."[190] Thus, it is clear that the *revocation* of the act of acknowledgement will not operate to rebut the marriage + acknowledgement presumption.

However, a person who executes an authentic act of acknowledgement[191] may also *annul* it under section 9:406, and the effect of this on the presumption is less clear. Absent a timely revocation, a person who executes the authentic act of acknowledgment may petition the court to annul it.[192] The person bears the burden of proving, by clear and convincing evidence, that the act was induced by fraud, duress, material mistake of fact or error, or that the man is not the biological parent of the child.[193] While the person may testify, the testimony must be corroborated by other evidence.[194] If the court finds a substantial likelihood that the man is not the biological parent of the child, or that the act was induced by fraud, duress, material mistake of fact or error, then the court shall order genetic tests.[195] If these tests lead to an annulment of the acknowledgment and no support order has been established, no further action may be initiated against the man.[196] Article 195 and its comments are silent as to whether an *annulment* of the act of acknowledgment operates to rebut the presumption, but jurisprudence has developed and addressed the issue, generating some interesting legal discussions and a circuit split among Louisiana appellate courts.

To fully explore the question requires analysis of the 1995 Louisiana Supreme Court opinion in *Succession of Robinson*.[197] In that case, a man acknowledged three daughters

---

190. La. Civ. Code Ann. art. 195.

191. Like with revocation of the act of acknowledgment, this language suggests that only the man who executed the acknowledgment may annul it. However, this conclusion is not without question. After all, a related statute, Louisiana Revised Statutes Section 9:392, requires the notary to apprise the mother and the alleged father that, after the 60-day period to revoke the act of acknowledgment has expired, it nonetheless "*may be voided*" upon proof of fraud, duress, material mistake of fact or error, or that the man is not the biological parent of the child. La. Stat. Ann. § 9:392(A)(7)(b) (emphasis added). This terminology and use of passive voice suggests that the action for annulment is not limited solely to the alleged father. Additionally, if the act of acknowledgment is an absolute nullity (as determined by *Succession of Robinson*, 94-2229, p. 4 (La. 5/22/95), 654 So. 2d 682 and progeny), then anyone should be allowed to raise the issue. *See* La. Civ. Code Ann. art. 2030 ("Absolute nullity may be invoked by any person. . . ."). These provisions should be revised to clearly indicate who may annul the act of acknowledgment.

192. La. Stat. Ann. § 9:406(B)(1).

193. La. Stat. Ann. § 9:406(B)(1).

194. La. Stat. Ann. § 9:406(B)(5). The court may order the mother, child, and alleged father, or the mother's husband or former husband to submit to the collection and testing of blood or tissue samples in any civil action that involves paternity. The court may do so on its own or at the request of a party to the proceeding or a person whose blood or tissue is involved. La. Stat. Ann. § 9:396(A). The details surrounding such tests are set forth in Louisiana Revised Statutes Sections 9:397–397.3. *See* La. Stat. Ann. §§ 9:397–397.3.

195. La. Stat. Ann. § 9:406(B)(3). These tests may be ordered pursuant to Louisiana Revised Statutes Section 9:396. *See* La. Stat. Ann. § 9:396.

196. La. Stat. Ann. § 9:406(D)(2).

197. Succession of Robinson, 654 So. 2d 682.

born during their mother's marriage to another man.[198] After his death, the daughters sought to intervene in his succession as forced heirs, and the succession administrator (the man's child born of marriage) moved to compel genetic testing to determine the women's relationship to the decedent. Because the statute for testing allowed it only if "relevant," the court had to determine "whether the validity of the formal acknowledgment depends upon whether decedent was the intervenor's biological father."[199] The court began by recognizing that the Civil Code does not expressly preclude a man with no biological relationship from executing an acknowledgment. Nonetheless, the court held that an acknowledgment made by someone other than the biological parent is absolutely null.[200] To reach its conclusion, the court relied on Louisiana and French jurisprudence, as well as the treatise of renowned civil law scholar Planiol who explained: "A fact cannot be avowed when it has never existed."[201] Because the acknowledgement by a non-biological parent is absolutely null, the court concluded that "it produces no effects."[202] The court's rationale suggests that annulling the act of acknowledgment does not simply rebut the presumption; it bars its application altogether.[203]

This rationale has ultimately led to more courts assessing the parental rights and obligations of men who acknowledged children that were not their biological progeny, creating a circuit split on the use of section 9:406. For example, in cases from the First, Second, and Third Circuit Courts of Appeal, courts have allowed men who are not biological parents to annul their acts of acknowledgments in accordance with the statute, barring the application of the article 195 presumption.[204] However, the First and Third Circuits have ruled to the contrary, refusing to allow the annulment of an acknowledgment to rebut the Article 195 presumption.[205]

---

198. Succession of Robinson, 654 So. 2d 682. This case actually involved the presumption created by formal acknowledgment alone, currently set forth in article 196. However, its rationale applies to the presumption of article 195, as well, when the man has formally acknowledged the child. In fact, the court's discussion cited to cases involving the article 195 presumption.

199. Succession of Robinson, 654 So. 2d at 684.

200. Succession of Robinson, 654 So. 2d at 684.

201. Succession of Robinson, 654 So. 2d at 684 (citing Marcel Planiol, 1 Treatise on the Civil Law § 1490(2) (La. State L. Inst. trans., 12th ed. 1959)).

202. Succession of Robinson, 654 So. 2d at 684.

203. Succession of Robinson, 654 So. 2d at 684. At least one appellate court recognized the parental rights of a man who married the pregnant mother and with her concurrence, formally acknowledged the child, who had no legal father, even though the man was not biologically related to the child. *See, e.g.*, Wesley v. David, 2013-1500, p. 4 (La. App. 1 Cir. 2/18/14), 2014 WL 651784, at *4. In this case, the man was not attempting to annul the act of acknowledgement. Instead, the mother was attempting, through exceptions of no right and no cause of action, to preclude the man's custodial rights. The court explained that the man had not disavowed the child and that a woman's sole avenue to challenging a man's paternity is the contestation and establishment action, which did not apply in the case at issue, given that the woman was not remarried.

204. Barras v. O'Rourke, 2019-0412, pp. 3–5 (La. App. 3 Cir. 12/18/19), 287 So. 3d 817; McKinley v. McKinley, 2022-0132 (La. App. 1 Cir. 9/16/22), 352 So. 3d 1001; Kelley v. Kelley, 55,358 (La. App. 2 Cir. 12/20/23), 376 So. 3d 320.

205. Wetta v. Wetta, 2021-92 (La. App. 3 Cir. 6/2/21), 322 So. 3d 365; Wesley v. David, 2013-1500, p. 4 (La. App. 1 Cir. 2/18/14), 2014 WL 651784, at *4.

In the Third Circuit case of *Wetta v. Wetta*, a man formally acknowledged his wife's child, but during their divorce, he attempted to annul the acknowledgment under section 9:406.[206] The court agreed that absolute nullities are imprescriptible by nature but framed the issue as the relationship between section 9:406 (allowing for revocation and annulment of the acknowledgement) and article 195 (providing for a disavowal action to rebut the presumption).[207] As it stated: "Prior to the 2016 amendment [to article 185] revoking or annulling the act of acknowledgment was enough to rebut the presumption of paternity, but the legislature changed that by amending La. Civ. Code art 195 [to provide that revocation alone will not suffice]."[208] It noted that while the man seemed to suggest that revocation/annulment and disavowal are "two separate and distinct issues before the court," his "goal" was disavowal, not simply revocation or annulment of the acknowledgment.[209] Therefore, the court treated the man's claim as one for disavowal under article 195 and found his claim perempted under the 180-day-period in that article. In rejecting the application of section 9:406, it explained: "If all that was needed to rebut a presumption of paternity was to show the act of acknowledgment was null, there would be no need for a one hundred eighty-day peremptive period. Therefore, even though an authentic act of acknowledgment signed by a man who is not the biological father of the minor child is a nullity that does not prescribe, La. Civ. Code art 195 contains a peremptive period within which to disavow paternity."[210]

The Second Circuit, in *Kelley v. Kelley*, recognized the split among the circuits (and within the Third Circuit).[211] It justified its decision to allow a man to use section 9:406 to annul his act of acknowledgement under similar facts by explaining that "in keeping with the rationale set forth in *Succession of Robinson*, and reiterated in [the First and Third Circuit's opinions], we find that [the man's] acknowledgments are absolute nullities, and as such, productive of no legal effects from their execution."[212] It went on to state that "his right to rescind his acknowledgments has not expired as it is imprescriptible by nature."[213] This court also offered a suggestion to non-biological fathers who want to create a paternal relationship with a child who has no presumptive father: adoption.[214] The majority was met with a dissent, essentially agreeing with the rationale in *Wetta* that article 195 controls the outcome.[215] The dissent noted "The majority fails to recognize that Louisiana law allows for different kinds of paternity. There may be

---

206. Wetta, 322 So. 3d 365.

207. Wetta, 322 So. 3d at 372.

208. Wetta, 322 So. 3d at 372. The court also explained: "Even though the article uses the term 'revocation' when discussing the act of acknowledgment, it is implied that annulment of the act of acknowledgment is also not enough to defeat the presumption." *Id.*

209. Wetta, 322 So. 3d at 372.

210. Wetta, 322 So. 3d at 372.

211. Kelley v. Kelley, 55,358 (La. App. 2 Cir. 12/20/23), 376 So. 3d 320, 324.

212. Kelley, 376 So. 3d at 324.

213. Kelley, 376 So. 3d at 324.

214. Kelley, 376 So. 3d at 324.

215. Kelley, 376 So. 3d at 326 (Pitman, J. dissenting).

biological paternity or presumed paternity or both." Because the father failed to timely disavow, he should remain the legal father.[216]

Some argue that the rationale employed by the *Kelley* court is sound from a civilian legal methodology standpoint. For decades, Louisiana has recognized that acknowledgments based on an untrue recitation of paternity are absolutely null. Likewise, Louisiana law is well-established that an absolute nullity creates no legal effects, and the right to raise it never prescribes. Under a pure legal analysis, the *Kelley* court's approach has appeal. On the other hand, when the parties pair the acknowledgment of a child with a marriage, arguably, the focus of the law changes. Under the article 195 presumption, when the parties marry, the husband has a limited right to escape the obligation to care for the child he acknowledged—the right to disavow. Like the article 195 presumption, the article 185 centers on marriage. Article 185 declares a presumption of paternity of the husband when the child is born during marriage or within 300 days from its termination.[217] If the presumed father does not timely disavow, he is considered the legal father of that child, notwithstanding a lack of biology.[218] Likewise, when a man marries the mother after the birth of the child, the same type of presumption attaches to the husband of the mother under article 195, but the man must also sign a formal acknowledgment, attesting to his biology.[219] Because the man married the mother and acknowledged the child, he only has a short window of 180 days to disavow.[220] Arguably, if the husband fails to meet that time period to disavow under article 195, as is the case under article 185, he should forever be considered the legal father of the child. Marriage elevates the legal relationship of the man to the child, and the acknowledging man should not be allowed to walk away from his obligations to the child.

Another issue that has arisen in the jurisprudence addressing annulment of paternal acts of acknowledgment involves the retroactive application of section 9:406. Originally, the statute required that the petition for annulment be filed within a prescriptive period of two years of its execution.[221] However, that period was repealed in 2016,[222] which has been expressed as a codification of *Succession of Robinson* "in recognition of well-settled law that an absolute nullity is not subject to prescription."[223] As explained by the comment to Louisiana Revised Statutes Section 9:406, "To speak of prescription when a father seeks a declaration of absolute nullity is inappropriate, as absolute nulli-

216. Kelley, 376 So. 3d at 327.

217. La. Civ. Code Ann. art. 185.

218. La. Civ. Code Ann. art. 189; *see* Modisette v. Phillips, 31,905 (La. App. 2 Cir. 5/5/99), 736 So. 2d 983 (concluding that if the presumed father fails to bring a timely disavowal action, the presumption of paternity is irrebuttable even if another man is proven to be the man's biological father).

219. La. Civ. Code Ann. art. 195.

220. La. Civ. Code Ann. art. 195.

221. La. Stat. Ann. § 9:406 (2008).

222. Act No. 309, 2016 La. Acts 1145–49. *See also* La. Stat. Ann. § 9:406 cmt. (rev. cmt. 2016).

223. Barras v. O'Rourke, 2019-0412, pp. 3–5 (La. App. 3 Cir. 12/18/19), 287 So. 3d 817; McKinley v. McKinley, 2022-0132 (La. App. 1 Cir. 9/16/22), 352 So. 3d 1001.

ties are imprescriptible by nature."[224] Thus, under current law, there is no time limitation to annul the acknowledgment.[225] In recent years, several cases have addressed the retroactive effects of the amendment to section 9:406.

In 2019, the Louisiana Third Circuit Court of Appeal confronted the issue in *Barras v. O'Rourke*.[226] In that case, a man acknowledged a child before the revision to section 9:406, but he attempted to annul it post-revision. The child's mother filed an exception of prescription based on the pre-revision version of 9:406 in place at the time of the acknowledgement. The court framed the issue as "whether La.R.S. 9:406(B)(1) is to be applied prospectively only, rendering [the man's] claim prescribed, or retroactively, allowing his action to continue."[227] It noted the general rule that prescriptive periods are treated as procedural laws and applied retroactively, but it also recognized that reviving a prescribed claim is concerning "because a change in the right to plead prescription, once acquired, 'constitutes a substantive change in the law as applied to the defendant,' who would have lost the ability to claim prescription."[228] The court acknowledged the revival of a prescribed cause of action as "an extreme exercise of legislative power," such that "a clear and unequivocal expression of intent by the legislature was needed before the court would interpret such a legislative intent behind a statute."[229] Finding that unequivocal reasoning by the legislature in amending section 9:406, the court held that the amendment applied retroactively and the man's claim not time-barred, allowing him to annul the acknowledgment.[230]

In *McKinley v. McKinley*, the Louisiana First Circuit Court of Appeal reached the same result under similar facts.[231] A man filed a petition to annul his acknowledgments of paternity of his wife's two children,[232] because DNA tests revelated that he was not their biological father; the mother filed an exception of prescription. The acknowledgements were executed pre-revision, while the man's claim was asserted post-revision. The appellate court employed the rationale from *Barras*, and additionally it noted that another statute, setting forth the procedural requirements for executing an authentic act of acknowledgment of paternity, contained no prescriptive period for annulling it,

224. La. Stat. Ann. § 9:406 cmt. (rev. cmt. 2016) (citing La. Civ. Code Ann. art. 2032 and also calling the two-year prescriptive period "illogical").

225. La. Stat. Ann. § 9:406.

226. Barras, 287 So. 3d 817. This case actually involved the presumption created by formal acknowledgment alone, currently set forth in article 196. However, its rationale applies to the presumption of article 195, as well, when the man has formally acknowledged the child.

227. Barras, 287 So. 3d at 819.

228. Barras, 287 So. 3d at 819–20 (citing La. Civ. Code Ann. art. 6 and quoting Chance v. American Honda Motor Co., Inc., 93-2582 (La. 4/11/94), 635 So. 2d 177, 178).

229. Barras, 287 So. 3d at 820.

230. Barras, 287 So. 3d at 820 (citing to La. Stat. Ann. § 9:406 cmt. (rev. cmt. 2016)).

231. McKinley, 352 So. 3d 1001.

232. As to one of the children, the court determined that the man had acknowledged the child by signing the child's birth certificate under pre-revision law, and therefore, without an act of acknowledgement, section 9:406 was not implicated for that child. McKinley, 352 So. 3d at 1003.

either.[233] Therefore, the court held that the amendment applied retroactively to allow the man's claim to annul the acknowledgment.

In December of 2023, the Louisiana Second Circuit Court of Appeals weighed in on the retroactivity issue in *Kelley v. Kelley*.[234] There, a man acknowledged his wife's children under the pre-revision version of section 9:406, but he attempted to annul the acknowledgements in 2022 under the current version of the statute. The court applied the amendment retroactively to allow his claim.[235]

§ 8:16 Paternal Filiation—Presumptions of Paternity—Marriage + Formal Acknowledgment Presumption—Rebuttal by Contestation and Establishment Action

It is technically possible that all of the facts would align to trigger a mother's contestation and establishment action to overcome the presumption by marriage and formal acknowledgment. For example, suppose Woman has a child outside of marriage. She then marries Man 1, who acknowledges the child with her concurrence.[236] However, it turns out that Man 1 is not the father of the child; Man 2 is. If Woman and Man 1 (now Husband 1) divorce and Woman thereafter marries Man 2 (now Husband 2), she may be inspired to pursue a contestation and establishment action to simultaneously break the filial link between the child and Husband 1 and establish a filial link between the child and Husband 2. However, given that all of this would have to occur within the strict peremptive period of two years from the child's birth, it seems very unlikely. The issue has never been confronted by a Louisiana court and based on comment (e) to Louisiana Civil Code Article 191, providing that the contestation action was designed to rebut the presumptions of article 185 and article 186, it seems that the Louisiana Legislature did not consider the possibility.[237]

233. McKinley, 352 So. 3d at 1005 (citing La. Stat. Ann. § 9:393(A)(7)(b)).
234. Kelley v. Kelley, 55,358 (La. App. 2 Cir. 12/20/23), 376 So. 3d 320.
235. Kelley, 376 So. 3d at 324.
236. See Section 8:13.
237. *See* La. Civ. Code Ann. art. 191 cmt. (e).

§ 8:17 Paternal Filiation—Presumptions of Paternity—Formal Acknowledgment Presumption

The presumption created by formal acknowledgment was enacted as part of the 2005 revision to replace former Civil Code Article 203. The previous version of that article created a presumption of paternity when a man executed an authentic act of acknowledgment or signed the registry of the child's birth or baptism.[238] By contrast, in the 2005 revision, the man had to formally acknowledge the child by executing an authentic act or by signing the child's birth certificate.[239] In 2016, the article was amended again to remove acknowledgment via signing the child's birth certificate;[240] however, it still applies to birth certificates signed prior to August 1, 2016, the effective date of the amendment.[241]

Unlike the other presumptions, the formal acknowledgment does not involve marriage. It provides that a man who, by authentic act, acknowledges a child is presumed to be the father of that child, as long as that child is not filiated to another man.[242] Prior to the execution of such an authentic act of acknowledgment of paternity, the notary is required to provide in writing all of its legal ramifications, including how one may challenge or revoke the acknowledgment (discussed in Sections 8:15 and 8:18).[243]

As to what exactly will suffice as an authentic act, the Louisiana Fifth Circuit has held that a consent judgment does not meet the criteria of an authentic act and will not suffice to trigger this presumption.[244] Similarly, the Louisiana Second Circuit has held that the filing of a statement alleging paternity in a request for a Medical Review Panel will not either.[245]

This presumption is unique in that it may be invoked only on behalf of the child in most instances.[246] The acknowledgment does not create a presumption in favor of the man who acknowledges the child except as provided in custody, visitation, and child support cases.[247] In those cases, an acknowledgment via authentic act is "deemed to be a legal finding of paternity" and establishes the "obligation to support the child and to establish visitation without" the need for a judgment of paternity.[248] In other words, for the man to seek custody or visitation, or for the domiciliary parent to seek child

238. La. Civ. Code Ann. art. 203 (Supp. 1997).

239. La. Civ. Code Ann. art. 195 cmt. (d) (rev. cmt. 2005).

240. Act No. 309, 2016 La. Acts 1145–49.

241. La. Civ. Code Ann. art. 196 cmt. (b) (rev. cmt. 2016).

242. La. Civ. Code Ann. art. 196.

243. *See* La. Stat. Ann. § 9:392.

244. Morgan v. Foster, 20-363, p. 11 (La. App. 5 Cir. 4/7/21), 347 So. 3d 963, 969.

245. Flintroy v. State of Louisiana Health Sci. Ctr.-Monroe, 53,777, pp. 11–12 (La. App. 2 Cir. 3/3/21), 315 So. 3d 395, 400–01.

246. La. Civ. Code Ann. art. 196.

247. La. Civ. Code Ann. art. 196.

248. La. Stat. Ann. §§ 9:392.1, 9:405.

support, a formal acknowledgement is sufficient. In other types of situations, like the child's wrongful death and succession, the man does not enjoy the benefit of filiation and would need to file an avowal action.[249] This led preeminent Louisiana family law scholar, Katherine Shaw Spaht, to opine that this presumption does not "operate in the same manner and with the same strength as the other two presumptions."[250]

A question has arisen regarding the biological father's intent to filiate a child. In *Succession of Dangerfield,* the biological father donated immovable property to a woman, whom he declared to be his daughter in the act of donation, which was in authentic form.[251] The court ruled that this document indeed triggered the presumption; it also affirmatively stated that the biological father's intent to filiate the child is not a requirement for a formal acknowledgment.[252]

Questions have also arisen as to the effect of an acknowledgment executed by a man who is not the biological father. As discussed in Section 8:15 relative to the Louisiana Supreme Court in *Succession of Robinson*, when a man other than the biological father acknowledges the child, for purposes of this presumption, the acknowledgment is null, and thus, the presumption is not triggered in the first place.[253]

§ 8:18 Paternal Filiation—Presumptions of Paternity—Formal Acknowledgment Presumption—Rebutting the Formal Acknowledgment Presumption

Like any presumption in Louisiana's law of persons, the one created by a man's formal acknowledgement may be rebutted. The proper means by which to do so is not exactly clear. As discussed in Section 8:15, a person who executes an authentic act of acknowledgment is allowed to revoke it without cause within 60 days of its execution,[254] and absent a timely revocation, the person may petition the court to annul it, as well.[255] In the case of a successful revocation or annulment of the act of acknowledgment, the presumption of article 196 should not apply.

Interestingly, article 196 does not mention a disavowal action to rebut the presumption by formal acknowledgment, as the disavowal action appears to be reserved to the marriage presumptions. However, comment (d) references "the action to rebut the

249. *See* Section 8:22 for a discussion of avowal actions; *see also* Katherine S. Spaht, *Who's Your Momma, Who Are Your Daddies: Louisiana's New Law of Filiation*, 67 La. L. Rev. 307, 322–23 (2007).

250. Katherine S. Spaht, *Who's Your Momma, Who Are Your Daddies: Louisiana's New Law of Filiation*, 67 La. L. Rev. 307, 319 (2007).

251. Succession of Dangerfield, 2016-0293, pp. 4–5 (La. App. 1 Cir. 10/31/16), 207 So. 3d 427, 430.

252. Succession of Dangerfield, 207 So. 3d at 435.

253. Succession of Robinson, 94-2229 (La. 5/22/95), 654 So. 2d 682.

254. La. Stat. Ann. § 9:406(A)(1); La. Stat. Ann. § 9:392(A)(7).

255. La. Stat. Ann. § 9:406(B)(1).

presumption created by this article."[256] What action could that be? The comment also goes on to indicate that there is no limitation on who may rebut the presumption and no applicable time bar to doing so.[257] The accuracy of that statement is debatable.

After all, Article 681 of the Louisiana Code of Civil Procedure provides that "an action can be brought only by a person having a real and actual interest which he asserts[,]"[258] and personal actions are, by default, subject to a 10-year liberative prescriptive period.[259] Furthermore, legislation is a primary source of law in Louisiana, whereas the comments to the code articles are merely persuasive, so comment (d)'s authority has always been questionable.[260] The latest revisions to the law of filiation only heighten the scrutiny surrounding comment (d). Under current law, the presumption of formal acknowledgment is created only by authentic act, and Louisiana Revised Statutes Section 9:406 details how to revoke or annul the authentic act,[261] suggesting that other actions to rebut the presumption may be unavailable.

Additionally, there are questions as to who may revoke or annul the authentic act of acknowledgment. Throughout section 406, the right of action to revoke or to annul belongs to "the person who executed an authentic act of acknowledgement."[262] This language suggests that only the man who executed the acknowledgment may revoke it, making it strictly personal.[263] The language of a related statute, Louisiana Revised Statutes Section 9:392, seemingly supports that conclusion. It requires the notary to apprise the mother and alleged father that an "*alleged father who executed* an authentic act of acknowledgment may revoke the act...."[264] The statute fails to mention anyone else.

On the other hand, section 9:392 requires the notary to apprise the mother and the alleged father that, after the 60-day period to revoke the act of acknowledgment has expired, it nonetheless "*may be voided*" upon proof of fraud, duress, material mistake of fact or error, or that the man is not the biological parent of the child.[265] This terminology and use of passive voice suggests that the action for annulment is not limited solely to the alleged father. Additionally, if the act of acknowledgment is an absolute nullity (as determined by *Succession of Robinson* and progeny), then anyone should be allowed to raise the issue.[266] These provisions should be revised to clearly indicate who may annul the act of acknowledgment.

---

256. La. Civ. Code Ann. art. 196 cmt. (d).

257. La. Civ. Code Ann. art. 196 cmt. (d).

258. La. Code Civ. Proc. Ann. art. 681.

259. La. Civ. Code Ann. art. 3499.

260. *See* La. Civ. Code Ann. arts. 1–5; *but see* In re Succession of Loustalot, 2015-0631, pp. 5–6 (La. App. 1 Cir. 11/6/15), 183 So. 3d 556, 559 (citing the comment with approval).

261. *See* La. Stat. Ann. § 9:406.

262. *See* La. Stat. Ann. §§ 9:406(A)(1) (revoke), 9:406(B)(1) (annul).

263. *See generally*, La. Civ. Code Ann. arts. 1765–66.

264. La. Stat. Ann. § 9:392(A)(7)(a) (emphasis added).

265. La. Stat. Ann. § 9:392(A)(7)(b) (emphasis added). The term "to be voided" in the common law has the same meaning as "to be annulled" in the civil law.

266. *See* La. Civ. Code Ann. art. 2030 ("Absolute nullity may be invoked by any person....").

§ 8:19 Paternal Filiation—Presumptions of Paternity—Three-Party Acknowledgement

In its 2018 session, the Louisiana Legislature enacted Louisiana Civil Code Article 190.1.[267] Like the mother's contestation and establishment action, this article allows for a break in the child's filial link to one man while simultaneously establishing paternity for another man.[268] It aligns paternity by consent. The acknowledgment requires the action of three people—the child's mother, presumed father, and biological father—as well as proof by blood and tissue sampling.[269]

Article 190.1 provides:

> If blood or tissue sampling indicates by a ninety-nine and nine-tenths percentage point threshold probability that the biological father is the father of the child and he is not the husband or former husband presumed to be the father of the child, then the husband or former husband presumed to be the father of the child, the mother, and the biological father of the child may execute a three-party acknowledgment in authentic form declaring that the husband or former husband is not the father of the child and that the biological father is the father of the child.[270]

Per this article, upon obtaining blood or tissue sampling affirming the biological father's paternity, the child's mother, biological father, and presumed father may execute an authentic act attesting both that the presumed father is not the father and that the biological father is the father—otherwise known as a three-party acknowledgment. While the article states that following these steps creates merely a presumption of paternity in favor of the biological father and a presumption against the paternity of the presumed father, that is not actually the case; instead, satisfaction of article 190.1's requirements actually determines paternity. Although the law is not express, the results of the blood and tissue sampling should be attached to the three-party acknowledgment to ensure its validity.

The three-party acknowledgment of paternity carries several effects. For one, it terminates the obligation of the presumed father to pay child support and "revokes any court order enforcing that obligation."[271] However, it does not affect any child support payments paid, due, or owed prior to the date the three-party acknowledgment was executed.[272] Additionally, it allows for the child's birth certificate to be changed to reflect the change in paternity by following the procedure set forth in Louisiana Revised Statutes Section 40:34.5.1.

---

267. Act No. 21, 2018 La. Acts 28–32.
268. La. Civ. Code Ann. art. 190.1.
269. La. Civ. Code Ann. art. 190.1.
270. La. Civ. Code Ann. art. 190.1.
271. La. Stat. Ann. § 9:402.1.
272. La. Stat. Ann. § 9:402.1.

Parties must execute the three-party acknowledgment by the child's tenth birthday and never more than one year from the child's death.[273] The time periods are peremptive.[274]

§ 8:20 Paternal Filiation—Presumptions of Paternity—Limited Presumption

Louisiana law includes another limited presumption. For example, in the legislation permitting a court to order blood and tissue sampling for purposes of paternity, Louisiana Revised Statutes Section 9:397.3(B)(2)(b) provides that a presumption is created when blood or tissue sampling indicates a 99.9% threshold probability that the alleged father is the father of the child.[275] However, this is not actually a presumption of paternity; rather, it is simply proof of paternity.

§ 8:21 Paternal Filiation—By Judicial Action

Besides the presumptions of paternity (which occur as a matter of law), children and their biological fathers may filiate through one of two judicial actions.[276] The first is an avowal action, an action initiated by the biological father to filiate himself to the child. The second is a paternity action, an action initiated by the child, if old enough to have procedural capacity,[277] or their representative to filiate the child to the biological father.

---

273. La. Civ. Code Ann. art. 190.1.

274. La. Civ. Code Ann. art. 190.1.

275. La. Stat. Ann. § 9:397.3(B)(2)(b).

276. In a filiation or paternity proceeding, the child's mother, the husband of the mother, and the biological father, if known, shall be joined as parties "except that joinder is not required of a person whose parental rights have been terminated, or who is deceased, or whose joinder is determined otherwise not to be feasible." La. Stat. Ann. § 9:408. Uncontested proceedings to establish paternity may be proven by affidavits if allowed by the local rule of the court with jurisdiction. La. Stat. Ann. § 9:407. Except for a good cause, a court shall award attorney's fees and costs to the prevailing party in an action seeking to establish paternity. La. Stat. Ann. § 9:398.1. Louisiana Revised Statutes Section 9:399.1 provides information on how and under what circumstances a judgment of paternity may be set aside or vacated by an adjudicated father, the child, or the mother of the child. *See* La. Stat. Ann. § 9:399.1.

277. *See* La. Code Civ. Proc. Ann. arts. 682–83 (providing that only competent majors and competent emancipated minors have capacity to sue and excluding unemancipated minors from procedural capacity).

§ 8:22 Paternal Filiation—By Judicial Action—Avowal Action

The avowal action is the vehicle by which the biological father may filiate to the child.[278] Although it was not codified until the 2005 revision, Louisiana jurisprudence allowed the biological father to avow the child even in the face of a legally presumed father, rationalizing that the biological father may be liable for child support and also that the child may assert paternity to sue for his wrongful death or to inherit from him.[279] As the Louisiana Supreme Court noted, the biological father should be allowed to avow the child, given his obligations to the child and the benefits that the child receives.[280]

Notably, if the biological father successfully established his paternity in an avowal action and the presumed father was no longer able to disavow paternity, the child would have two legal fathers, giving rise to dual paternity. In other words, an avowal action by the biological father did not simultaneously act as a disavowal action by the presumed father, as the two actions are distinct and separate.[281]

The Louisiana Supreme Court first recognized the concept of dual paternity in *Warren v. Richard*.[282] In that case, the court addressed the issue of whether a child born outside of marriage could recover for the wrongful death of the biological father, despite the fact that the child already had a legal father.[283] The court held that the child could have two fathers in Louisiana. As it explained:

> To say that the child ... had no right to recover for her biological father's wrongful death because the law presumed her to be the legitimate child of another man would run counter to the principles established in the decisions of the United States Supreme Court ... and would ignore the existence of the child's biological father.[284]

The court also noted that dual paternity was not novel to Louisiana, as its adoption law already recognized the concept by allowing an adopted child to inherit from both

278. La. Civ. Code Ann. art. 198.

279. *See* T.D. v. M.M.M., 98-0167, p. 3 (La. 3/2/99), 730 So. 2d 873, 876 *overruled on other grounds by* Fishbein v. State ex rel. La. State Univ. Health Scis. Ctr., 04-2482, p. 15–16 (La. 4/12/05), 898 So. 2d 1260, 1270; *see also* Smith v. Cole, 553 So. 2d 847, 851 (La. 1989); Succession of Mitchell, 323 So. 2d 451 (La. 1975); Finnerty v. Boyett, 469 So. 2d 287 (La. App. 2 Cir. 1985); Katherine Shaw Spaht & William Marshall Shaw Jr., *The Strongest Presumption Challenged: Speculations on* Warren v. Richard *and* Succession of Mitchell, 37 La. L. Rev. 59, 79 (1997). *Cf.* Griffin v. Succession of Branch, 479 So. 2d 324 (La. 1985) (children's right to avowal action despite legal paternity of another man); Warren v. Richard, 296 So. 2d 813 (La. 1974) (child's right to recover from biological father despite legal paternity of another man).

280. Griffin, 479 So. 2d at 324.

281. Finnerty, 469 So. 2d at 292.

282. Warren, 296 So. 2d at 815.

283. Warren, 296 So. 2d at 815.

284. Warren, 296 So. 2d at 817.

their biological and adopted families.[285] With that said, the court was "not unmindful of the problems a logical extension of these holdings may create, such as a child in these circumstances recovering from both fathers for support and maintenance, or, conversely, requiring the child to support both fathers in a proper case."[286] Later cases indeed addressed some of these problems. In the world of dual paternity, both men are liable to support the child and may inherit from the child, and the child may inherit from both men.[287] Although the legislature attempted to eliminate the potential for dual paternity through statutory revisions, the Louisiana Supreme Court continued interpreting the law to permit it.[288]

The issue of dual paternity was hotly debated and very contentious in the 2005 revision. Members of the Louisiana State Law Institute, in conjunction with the state legislature, debated whether to codify or overrule the jurisprudence allowing dual paternity.[289] At the time the decision was made, Louisiana became the first state to formally adopt the concept of dual paternity.[290] While the Louisiana Civil Code does not explicitly refer to it, its existence is recognized through the codification of the avowal action and the paternity action.[291] Dual paternity can lead to interesting issues in a legal system that presupposes that a child has only one father. For example, in *Cerwonka v. Baker*, a court awarded joint custody to a mother, legal father, and biological father but named the legal father as the domiciliary parent because he was best at facilitating communication with everyone involved.[292] Further, courts have used creative ways to require child support to be paid from the legal and biological fathers, as well as the mother.[293]

---

285. Warren, 296 So. 2d at 817.

286. Warren, 296 So. 2d at 817.

287. Smith, 553 So. 2d at 854; see also Chapter 9 for a discussion of parental authority and alimentary obligations.

288. *See* Griffin, 479 So. 2d at 326–28; Louisiana State Law Institute Revision of the Louisiana Civil Code of 1870, Book I—Of Persons, Title VII Parent and Child: Policy Issues Before the Marriage-Pers. Comm., La. State L. Inst. Couns. Meeting Oct. 14–15, 1994 (prepared for meeting by Katherine S. Spaht, Rptr., and Kerry Triche, Staff Att'y) ("[D]espite the intention to end dual paternity in 1981 the Louisiana Supreme Court confirmed its concept by its interpretation of the Civil Code articles.").

289. Katherine S. Spaht, *Who's Your Momma, Who Are Your Daddies: Louisiana's New Law of Filiation*, 67 La. L. Rev. 307, 321 (2007) ("Of all the issues presented for deliberation by the Council of the Law Institute that concerned filiation, the most contentious, and the issue that produced the most vacillating results, was 'dual paternity.'").

290. La. Civ. Code Ann. art. 197 cmt. (b); *see also* Sandi Varnado, *Who's Your Daddy?: A Legitimate Question Given Louisiana's Lack of Legislation Governing Assisted Reproductive Technology*, 66 La. L. Rev. 609, 628 (2006).

291. The paternity action is discussed in Section 8:23.

292. *See* Cerwonka v. Baker, 2006-856, pp. 6–7 (La. App. 3 Cir. 11/2/06), 942 So. 2d 747, 752–53.

293. State ex rel. Wilson v. Wilson, 37,674, p. 4 (La. App. 2 Cir. 9/24/03), 855 So. 2d 913, 915 n.5 (applying a "fictional father" model to assess child support against three parents); *see also* Chapter 7, Section 7:7.

Under current law, the avowal action is a strictly personal right of the biological father, such that he is the sole person allowed to assert it.[294] In an avowal action, the biological father bears the burden of proving his paternity by a preponderance of the evidence, and he may use any relevant evidence, such as blood tests,[295] informal acknowledgment, and cohabitation with the mother at the time of conception to do so.[296] Of course, before instituting the avowal action, the biological father may petition the court for an order for blood testing to establish biological paternity.[297] Note, however, that the statute forbids the court from making a paternity determination based on the test results and conclusions of the experts filed in the record in the proceeding to order blood testing.[298] Instead, the test results are admissible in a *subsequent action* filed by a party relating to the child's filiation.[299] This premise is illustrated in *State ex rel. C.C.*, wherein the sister of the biological father was granted custody by the juvenile court judge.[300] The Louisiana Fifth Circuit determined that the juvenile court had committed legal error by allowing DNA results to equate to filiation under Louisiana law when the father had failed to file an action to establish filiation.[301]

Article 198 provides time limitations to file the avowal action, and all of the relevant time periods are peremptive.[302] The man may institute the action at any time as a general rule.[303] For example, in a subsequent appellate review by the Fifth Circuit in *State ex rel. C.C.*, even though the avowal action was filed approximately four years after the child's birth, it was not perempted.[304] No facts existed to trigger the time constraints set forth in article 198, which are discussed below.

When the child has a presumed father, though, the biological father must assert the avowal action within one year of the child's birth, with limited exception.[305] According to comment (e), this one-year period was implemented "to protect the child from the upheaval of such litigation and its consequences in circumstances where the child may actually live in an existing intact family with his mother and presumed father or

294. La. Civ. Code Ann. art. 198. For a detailed explanation of the term "strictly personal," see La. Civ. Code Ann. art. 1766.

295. The court may order the mother, child, and alleged father, or the mother's husband or former husband to submit to the collection and testing of blood or tissue samples in any civil action that involves paternity. The court may do so on its own or at the request of a party to the proceeding or a person whose blood or tissue is involved. La. Stat. Ann. § 9:396(A). The details surrounding such tests are set forth in Louisiana Revised Statutes Sections 9:397–397.3. *See* La. Stat. Ann. §§ 9:397–997.3 A presumption that the man is the father is created when blood or tissue sampling indicates a 99.9% threshold probability that the alleged father is the father of the child. La. Stat. Ann. § 9:397.3(B)(2)(b).

296. La. Civ. Code Ann. art. 198 cmt. (b).

297. La. Stat. Ann. § 9:398.2(A)(2).

298. La. Stat. Ann. § 9:398.2(E).

299. La. Stat. Ann. § 9:398.2(E).

300. State ex rel. C.C., 18-440, pp. 5–9 (La. App. 5 Cir. 10/12/18), 256 So. 3d 565, 568–71.

301. State ex rel. C.C., 256 So. 3d at 572.

302. La. Civ. Code Ann. art. 198.

303. La. Civ. Code Ann. art. 198.

304. State ex rel. C.C., 20-307, p. 10 (La. App. 5 Cir. 3/17/21), 316 So. 3d 154, 163.

305. La. Civ. Code Ann. art. 198.

may have become attached over many years to the man presumed to be his father."[306] The one-year period provides an exception for situations in which the mother in bad faith deceived the biological father regarding his paternity.[307] In such a scenario, the biological father must bring the avowal action within the earlier of one year from the day he knew or should have known of his paternity or 10 years from the child's birth.[308]

The peremptive periods of article 198 were intently argued and discussed in *Kinnett v. Kinnett*, a case in which a married woman gave birth to a child conceived with her paramour.[309] Their last sexual contact was in November 2014, during which the two used contraception.[310] The child was born on August 5, 2015, and allegedly looked like the woman's husband.[311] In September of 2015, the mother told her paramour that she had had sexual intercourse with her husband and had given birth to his child.[312] Over a year later, on December 9, 2016, the mother called her now-former paramour and told him that she had learned, through DNA tests on her two children, that her husband was not actually the father of the child at issue.[313] Additional testing revealed that her ex-paramour was the child's biological father.[314] Once the mother informed her husband of that fact, she filed for divorce in January 2017, and the biological father intervened to establish paternity in February 2017 (approximately 18 months after the child's birth).[315] The presumed father and the mother excepted to the biological father's avowal action on grounds, among others, of peremption.[316] The trial court granted their exception, reasoning that because the child had a presumed father and because the mother did not in bad faith deceive the biological father, the one-year period applied, thereby perempting the avowal action.[317]

The appellate court reversed, holding that the mother in bad faith deceived the biological father, explaining that "there is no set of circumstances wherein a woman—who has had sexual relations with more than one man during the period of possible conception—may have an 'honest belief' that one man, and not the other, is the father."[318] Furthermore, the court held that "a married woman—whose husband is presumed to be the father of her child—who knows that it is possible that another man is the child's biological father has a duty to inform that man of his possible paternity[,]" and failure to do so constitutes bad faith deception.[319] Because of the mother's deception,

306. La. Civ. Code Ann. art. 198 cmt. (e).
307. La. Civ. Code Ann. art. 198.
308. La. Civ. Code Ann. art. 198.
309. Kinnett v. Kinnett, 17-625, pp. 2–3 (La. App. 5 Cir. 8/6/20), 302 So. 3d 157, 163.
310. Kinnett, 302 So. 3d at 163.
311. Kinnett, 302 So. 3d at 164.
312. Kinnett, 302 So. 3d at 164.
313. Kinnett, 302 So. 3d at 164.
314. Kinnett, 302 So. 3d at 165.
315. Kinnett, 302 So. 3d at 165.
316. Kinnett, 302 So. 3d at 165.
317. Kinnett, 302 So. 3d at 165.
318. Kinnett, 302 So. 3d at 181.
319. Kinnett, 302 So. 3d at 179.

the biological father's knowledge of his paternity did not occur until December 9, 2016, making his February 10, 2017 avowal action timely.[320]

The Louisiana Supreme Court granted writ applications[321] and subsequently reversed the appellate court, holding that the mother did not in bad faith deceive the biological father; thus, his avowal action was perempted under the one-year period.[322] The court rejected "the notion that a woman who has sex with more than one man during the period of conception cannot have an honest belief that one man and not the other is the father."[323] As it noted: "[A] credible belief may exist without factual certainty."[324] In the case at bar, the mother believed that her husband was the child's father, given her use of contraception with the biological father and the child's looks mirroring her husband's at birth.[325] The court explained then that "[a] mother who knows another man is possibly the father of her child, can also honestly believe that her husband is the father."[326] Although the mother may have been mistaken, her error did not translate to a finding of bad faith or deception on her part.

An additional peremptive period applies to the avowal action: in every case, the biological father's avowal action must be brought within one year of the child's death.[327] "[A] father who failed during a child's life to assume his parental responsibilities should not be permitted unlimited time to institute an action to benefit from the child's death."[328] In *Udomeh v. Joseph*, the Louisiana Supreme Court confronted the issue of how a biological father must frame his avowal action.[329] In that case, after the death of his child, the man did not file an avowal action but, instead, asserted his paternity in a wrongful death and survival petition within one year of the child's death.[330] The court held that under Louisiana's fact-pleading system, the man's petition contained sufficient facts to assert an avowal action and stated that the requisite facts need not be in a petition that "specifically request[s] a judgment of paternity."[331] Following *Udomeh*, Louisiana courts have liberally construed petitions as stating enough to preserve the claim of paternity as long as they allege that the plaintiff is the child's father.[332]

---

320. Kinnett, 302 So. 3d at 182–87.

321. Kinnett v. Kinnett, 2020-01156, p. 1 (La. 2/9/21), 309 So. 3d 738, 738.

322. Kinnett v. Kinnett, 2020-01156, p. 12 (La. 12/10/21), 332 So. 3d 1149, 1157.

323. Kinnett, 332 So. 3d at 1155.

324. Kinnett, 332 So. 3d at 1155.

325. Kinnett, 332 So. 3d at 1156.

326. Kinnett, 332 So. 3d at 1156. In subsequent litigation, the Louisiana Supreme Court determined that the time limits in article 198 were constitutional. Kinnett v. Kinnett, 23-00060 (La. 6/27/23), 366 So. 3d 24.

327. La. Civ. Code Ann. art. 198.

328. La. Civ. Code Ann. art. 198 cmt. (d).

329. *See* Udomeh v. Joseph, 2011-2839, p.1 (La. 10/26/12), 103 So. 3d 343, 344.

330. Udomeh, 103 So. 3d at 343.

331. Udomeh, 103 So. 3d at 348.

332. Flintroy v. State of Louisiana Health Sci. Ctr. Monroe, 53,777, pp. 11–12 (La. App. 2 Cir. 3/3/21), 315 So. 3d 395, 399 (citing Miller v. Thibeaux, 2014-1107 (La. 1/28/15), 159 So. 3d 426); Caceras v. Work, 2012-1097 (La. App. 4 Cir. 2/27/13), 110 So. 3d 275; Jackson v. McNeal, 2015-0067 (La. App. 1 Cir. 7/13/15), 180 So. 3d 376). *See also* Jackson, 180 So. 3d at 376.

Notably, though, those claims were filed in district courts that had subject matter jurisdiction to determine paternity. In *Thomas v. Ardenwood Properties*, the district court lacked jurisdiction because exclusive jurisdiction for establishing paternity had been granted to the Family Court in that judicial district.[333] However, the appellate court raised the issue of peremption on its own motion and decided that the man's amended petition requesting a judgment of paternity did not relate back to his original petition, which only had asserted—and not requested—his paternity.[334] In *Flintroy v. State of Louisiana Health Science Center*, a man filed a timely request for Medical Review Panel (MRP) with the Division of Administration within a year of his alleged daughter's death.[335] After that body issued its opinion two years later—finding no breach of the standard of care—the man filed a medical malpractice petition three months thereafter.[336] The court held that his request to the MRP did not constitute a paternity claim because the Division of Administration had no authority to decide paternity.[337] Additionally, while a request to the MRP may interrupt prescription, the time bar on an avowal action is peremptive and may not be interrupted.[338]

The constitutionality of the peremptive periods in article 198 has been challenged. In *Leger v. Leger*, the alleged father intervened in the mother's divorce proceeding to determine the paternity of a minor child born during her marriage.[339] Because the intervention was filed more than one year after the child's birth, the trial court sustained the legal father's exception of peremption.[340] After the ruling was affirmed on appeal, the alleged father filed a petition challenging article 198 on constitutional grounds.[341] He argued that the time period was too short, interfered with his rights as a parent, and violated the Equal Protection Clause of the United States Constitution because mothers have more time to establish paternity in the contestation and establishment action.[342] The court rejected his argument, noting that the biological father and the mother are not presented with similar circumstances and that the "nature, interests and consequences" of the parent's respective actions are different.[343] Thus, it upheld the constitutionality of article 198.[344]

---

333. Thomas v. Ardenwood Properties, 2010-0026, p. 2 (La. App. 1 Cir. 6/11/10), 43 So. 3d 213, 214.

334. Thomas, 43 So. 3d at 217–18. Note that two years after the *Thomas* decision, the Louisiana Supreme Court announced in *Udomeh* that the pleading need not specifically request a judgment of paternity. Udomeh, 103 So. 3d at 348.

335. Flintroy, 315 So. 3d at 397.

336. Flintroy, 315 So. 3d at 397.

337. Flintroy, 315 So. 3d at 400. Its authority is limited and extends only to the review of a malpractice claim (and no other civil matters) and to the suspension of prescription (and not peremption). *Id.*

338. Flintroy, 315 So. 3d at 400–01.

339. Leger v. Leger, 2017-270 (La. App. 3 Cir. 12/6/17), 258 So. 3d 624, 625.

340. Leger, 258 So. 3d at 625.

341. Leger, 258 So. 3d at 625.

342. Leger, 258 So. 3d at 626–27.

343. Leger, 258 So. 3d at 631.

344. Leger, 258 So. 3d at 631.

Just a few years later, in *Kinnett v. Kinnett*, both the biological father and attorneys appointed on behalf of the child again raised the constitutionality of article 198.[345] Challenges were made under the Due Process and Equal Protection Clauses of the Fourteenth Amendment.[346] As to the child's challenge, the Louisiana Supreme Court held that the child lacked standing.[347] The court noted article 198 affects the alleged biological father's rights, not the child's.[348] As to the biological father's challenge, the Louisiana Fifth Circuit Court of Appeal on remand decided that the one-year time period under article 198 was an unconstitutional deprivation of the father's due process rights. As the court explained, the father had grasped at the opportunity to parent his child as soon as he learned of his paternity, and he was denied the fundamental vested liberty interest to parent his biological child.[349] The Louisiana Supreme Court reversed again, holding that article 198 is indeed constitutional as applied.[350] As it noted: "On review, we hold, under the factual circumstances presented in this case, that the putative biological father has no fundamental constitutional right to parent a child born to a mother, who was married to and living with another man at the time of the child's conception and birth."[351] The court relied heavily on the United States Supreme Court case of *Michael H. v. Gerald D.*[352] to conclude that legislative policy, rather than constitutional law, should decide whether the paternity of a child born into a marriage should be rebutted.[353] As it explained: "The people of Louisiana, through the Louisiana Legislature, have spoken through the enactment of La. C.C. art. 198, to give a biological father a limited window in which to file a paternity action when there is a legal father," which the court found to be constitutionally permissible.[354]

---

345. Kinnett v. Kinnett, 2020-01156 (La. 12/10/21), 332 So. 3d 1149, 1152–53.

346. Kinnett, 332 So. 3d at 1153.

347. Kinnett, 332 So. 3d at 1157.

348. Kinnett, 332 So. 3d at 1157. The child's claim is governed by article 197, as discussed in Section 8:23.

349. Kinnett v. Kinnett, 17-625, pp. 24–25 (La. App. 5 Cir. 12/28/22), 355 So. 3d 181, 198–99.

350. Kinnett v. Kinnett, 2023-00060 (La. 6/27/23), 366 So. 3d 25.

351. Kinnett, 366 So. 3d at 26.

352. Michael H. v. Gerald D., 491 U.S. 110 (1989).

353. Kinnett, 366 So. 3d at 35.

354. Kinnett, 366 So. 3d at 39–40.

§ 8:23 Paternal Filiation—By Judicial Action—Paternity Action

The other judicial action is the paternity action, the vehicle by which the child, or their legal representative if they are a minor, may filiate to the biological father.[355] Just like the avowal action, the paternity action may be asserted even if the child already has a presumed father,[356] and as such, may lead to dual paternity.

For example, in *Smith v. Cole*, the Louisiana Supreme Court allowed a mother to assert a paternity action against an alleged biological father, notwithstanding that the child in question was the legitimate child of another man.[357] Relying on the concept of dual paternity, the court explained that a biological father is obligated to support his child even if the child is the legitimate child of another man and stated: "Since [the legal father's] failure to disavow paternity would not preclude [the biological father] from bringing an avowal action, it would be unjust to construe the presumption so as to provide [the biological father] with a safe harbor from child support obligations."[358]

In a paternity action, the child bears the burden of proving the biological father's paternity. The standard of proof depends on the timing of the institution of the action. If the child brings the action during the alleged father's lifetime, the standard is a preponderance of the evidence; by contrast, if the child brings the action after the alleged father's death, the standard is elevated to clear and convincing evidence.[359] As explained in comment (d) to article 197, the standard is more onerous after the alleged father's death to protect his estate from fraudulent claims.[360] The Louisiana Supreme Court upheld the constitutionality of the varying burdens of proof in *Sudwischer v. Estate of Hoffpauir*.[361]

All relevant evidence is admissible in the paternity action. Comment (c) to article 197 gives examples such as blood tests,[362] informal acknowledgment, and cohabitation

---

355. La. Civ. Code Ann. art. 197; *see, e.g.*, O'Bannon ex rel. O'Bannon v. Azar, 506 So. 2d 522, 524 (La. Ct. App. 1 Cir. 1987). The filiation action under article 197 must be brough in an ordinary proceeding. La. Stat. Ann. § 9:410.

356. La. Civ. Code Ann. art. 197.

357. Smith v. Cole, 553 So. 2d 847, 848 (La. 1989).

358. Smith, 553 So. 2d at 854.

359. La. Civ. Code Ann. art. 197 cmt. (d).

360. La. Civ. Code Ann. art. 197 cmt. (d) (citing Katherine Shaw Spaht, *Developments in the Law, 1981–1982—Persons*, La. L. Rev. 535, 537 (1982)).

361. Sudwischer v. Estate of Hoffpauir, 705 So. 2d 724, 733 (La. 1991).

362. La. Civ. Code Ann. art. 197 cmt. (c). The court may order the mother, child, and alleged father, or the mother's husband or former husband to submit to the collection and testing of blood or tissue samples in any civil action that involves paternity. The court may do so on its own or at the request of a party to the proceeding or a person whose blood or tissue is involved. La. Stat. Ann. § 9:396(A). The details surrounding such tests are set forth in Louisiana Revised Statutes Sections 9:397–397.3. *See* La. Stat. Ann. §§ 9:397–397.3. A presumption that the man is the father is created when blood or tissue sampling indicates a 99.9% threshold probability that the alleged father is the father of the child. La. Stat. Ann. § 9:397.3(B)(2)(b).

of the mother and father at the time of conception.[363] Cases have further explained that this evidence could also "include the alleged father's acknowledgment of the child in formal writings or in public or private conversations, [supporting] the education of the child as his own," living with the mother "at the time of the child's conception, rearing the child in his home, naming the child in his will, giving the child his surname, and holding the child out in the community as his own."[364]

Much like the avowal action, issues have arisen as to how to frame the paternity action. For example, in *Succession of Morris*, a child received social security benefits on his alleged father's account after averring in his application that he was born out of wedlock.[365] When the child subsequently intervened in the succession of his alleged father's relative, the court had to determine if the previously-filed application for social security benefits sufficed as an "action" to establish paternity.[366] The court focused on Louisiana Code of Civil Procedure Article 421, which provides that "[a] civil action is a demand for the enforcement of a legal right" that "is commenced by the filing of a pleading presenting the demand to a court of competent jurisdiction"[367] to determine that the social security application did not qualify.[368] By contrast, in *Succession of Harrison*, the court held that the alleged child's motion to compel turnover of succession property—in which he alleged the decedent's paternity—and his introduction of filiation evidence during the proceedings constituted the institution of legal proceedings to prove filiation for purposes of the applicable one-year peremptive period.[369] After the passage of Act 96 of 2024, the holding of *Succession of Harrison* has been called into question. The law now provides that the paternity action must be brought in an ordinary proceeding either instituted separately or cumulated in a succession proceeding, but commencing a succession proceeding does not constitute initiating a paternity action for purposes of article 197.[370] Now, a motion in a succession proceeding alone will not constitute a paternity action sufficient to meet the peremptive period.

Under current law, the child may assert the claim at any time as a general rule.[371] However, for succession purposes only, the child has a peremptive period of one year from the alleged father's death.[372] Prior to the 2005 revision, Louisiana Civil Code Article 209 applied and required the child to institute the paternity action by the earlier of their nineteenth birthday and a year from the alleged father's death,[373] both of which

---

363. La. Civ. Code Ann. art. 197 cmt. (c).

364. Ladmirault v. Succession of Humphrey, 2016-0525, p. 4 (La. App. 4 Cir. 12/7/16), 206 So. 3d 987, 989–90; *see also* Jenkins v. Mangano Corp., 2000–0790, p. 3–4 (La. 11/28/00), 774 So. 2d 101, 103.

365. In re Succession of Morris, 13-533, pp. 2–3 (La. App. 5 Cir. 12/12/13), 131 So. 3d 274, 275.

366. In re Succession of Morris, 131 So. 3d at 276.

367. La. Code Civ. Proc. Ann. art. 421.

368. In re Succession of Morris, 131 So. 3d at 276.

369. In re Succession of Harrison, 48,432, p. 7 (La. App. 2 Cir. 11/8/13), 129 So. 3d 681, 685.

370. La. Stat. Ann. § 9:410.

371. La. Civ. Code Ann. art. 197.

372. La. Civ. Code Ann. art. 197.

373. La. Civ. Code Ann. art. 209 (Supp. 1984).

were peremptive periods.[374] A question arose as to whether to apply former article 209 or current article 197 to cases in which the child celebrated their nineteenth birthday prior to the amendment, but the alleged father died after the amendment. Obviously, if courts apply the prior law (article 209), then the claim is barred, but if they apply the current law (article 197), it is not—assuming, of course, that the action is filed within a year of the biological father's death. The legislative act stated that the timing provisions in article 197 applied only to "claims existing or actions pending on its effective date and all claims arising or actions filed on and after its effective date."[375] Until 2022, circuits were split on how to handle this issue.[376]

For example, in *Succession of Pelt*, the Louisiana Third Circuit held that article 197 retroactively applied, allowing a paternity claim that would have been perempted under former article 209 to be made because it was brought within a year of the alleged father's death.[377] The court used four bases for its decision.[378] First, it reasoned that in interpreting identical language on the applicability of a new law, the Louisiana Supreme Court had held that the law applied retroactively.[379] Second, it noted that Louisiana Civil Code Article 870 provides that succession rights are governed by the law in effect at the decedent's death.[380] Third, it pointed to comment (e) of article 197, which explained that the former article led to "a harsh result not justified by any policy consideration."[381] Finally, it explained that applying article 197 would not disrupt any vested rights.[382]

By contrast, in *Succession of James*, the Louisiana First Circuit held that article 209 applied, such that the post-revision claim was perempted.[383] That court explained that article 197 applies only to viable causes of action.[384] Because peremption extinguished the child's claim on their nineteenth birthday, no viable cause of action existed thereafter.[385] Furthermore, the court noted that no legislative intent existed for article 197 to revive an extinguished filiation claim.[386]

---

374. Matherne v. Broussard, 2006-0838, p. 8 (La. App. 1 Cir. 2/14/07), 959 So. 2d 975, 980.

375. Act. No. 192, 2005 La. Acts 1444–59.

376. For a recent and comprehensive discussion of the jurisprudence on this topic, see Emily M. Gauthier, *Let Louisiana's Bastards Beat the Clock: It's Time to Amend Article 197*, 80 La. L. Rev. 1437 (2020).

377. Succession of Pelt, 2017-860, p. 13 (La. App. 3 Cir. 4/11/18), 244 So. 3d 476, 486; *see also* Succession of Younger, 50,876 (La. App. 2 Cir. 9/28/16), 206 So. 3d 1088; In re Succession of Harrison, 129 So. 3d at 685.

378. *See* Succession of Pelt, 244 So. 3d at 481–84.

379. Succession of Pelt, 244 So. 3d at 481–82.

380. Succession of Pelt, 244 So. 3d at 482.

381. Succession of Pelt, 244 So. 3d at 484.

382. Succession of Pelt, 244 So. 3d at 484.

383. In re Succession of James, 2007-2509, p. 8 (La. App. 1 Cir. 8/21/08), 994 So. 2d 120, 125.

384. In re Succession of James, 994 So. 2d at 125.

385. In re Succession of James, 994 So. 2d at 125.

386. In re Succession of James, 994 So. 2d at 125.

In March of 2022, the Louisiana Supreme Court granted an application for supervisory writs in *Succession of Lewis* to address and resolve the circuit split,[387] and in October 2022, it handed down its decision.[388] In *Lewis*, the decedent, John Charles Lewis, had a relationship with another woman during his marriage, allegedly resulting in the birth of two children.[389] One of those children, Cherie Jefferson, filed a paternity action in Mr. Lewis's succession proceedings.[390] After thoroughly discussing the rationale and holdings of numerous, conflicting appellate decisions, the court held that article 197 applies retroactively, and thus, Ms. Jefferson's claim was timely.[391] The court began by noting no ambiguity in the article, and specified that it would constitute a change in the law.[392] Next, the court explained that because the time period is peremptive (and remedial in nature), it should be given retroactive application absent contrary legislative intent, of which the court found none; in fact, the court found that the clear language of the article, combined with article 870 (providing for the applicability of law in effect at a decedent's death to apply), evidenced the legislature's intent for retroactive application of article 197.[393] As the court noted, "[T]he prior law (former La. C.C. art. 209) 'was a harsh result not justified by any policy considerations.'"[394] Therefore, it found that not applying article 197 retroactively would defeat the purpose of enacting the article.[395] Additionally, the court explained that retroactive application of the law would lead to constant results and comport with the legislature's intent to abandon the "harsh and unjustified peremptive period of former [Louisiana Civil Code Article] 209."[396] Finally, the court provided that its decision to apply the article retroactively would not deprive the other potential heirs of a vested right, because such a right did not arise until Mr. Lewis died.[397]

Another issue affecting the retroactive application of article 197 is the interplay between paternity actions and wrongful death/survival actions, i.e., tort claims. Prior to 2005, article 209 allowed a child who had already reached their nineteenth birthday to nonetheless bring a paternity action within a year of that parent's death for the sole purpose of establishing standing to sue under Louisiana Civil Code Article 2315.[398] Under current law (article 197), a child may bring a paternity action at any time, except

---

387. Succession of Lewis, 2022-00079, p. 1 (La. 3/22/22), 334 So. 3d 746.

388. Succession of Lewis, 2022-00079, p. 1 (La. 10/21/22), 351 So. 3d 336.

389. Succession of Lewis, 351 So. 3d at 338.

390. Succession of Lewis, 351 So. 3d at 338.

391. Succession of Lewis, 351 So. 3d at 349–50; *see also* Succession of West, 2022-0570 (La. App. 4 Cir. 1/13/23), 357 So. 3d 430 (court applied the La. Supreme Court's decision in Succession of Lewis to allow alleged child to bring an action to establish filiation with putative father for purposes of succession).

392. Succession of Lewis, 351 So. 3d at 349.

393. Succession of Lewis, 351 So. 3d at 349–50.

394. Succession of Lewis, 351 So. 3d at 349 (quoting La. Civ. Code Ann. art. 197 cmt. (e) (2005)).

395. Succession of Lewis, 351 So. 3d at 349–50.

396. Succession of Lewis, 351 So. 3d at 350.

397. Succession of Lewis, 351 So. 3d at 350.

398. La. Civ. Code Ann. art. 209 (Supp. 1984).

for succession purposes.[399] In *Ratliff v. LSU Board of Supervisors*, the Fourth Circuit reviewed available legal actions for non-filiated alleged children after Charles Ratliff died in May 2007.[400] Six months later, the alleged children sought damages for wrongful death and survival, asserting their status as children, but not seeking filiation.[401] In June of 2008—over one year after Mr. Ratliff's death—the children filed supplemental and amending petitions to establish paternity.[402] The defendants challenged the filiation action as untimely. Both the trial and appellate courts rejected the challenge because the paternity action related back to the timely-filed survival and wrongful death action that alleged the status of the plaintiffs as children, and the original claim for damages provided fair notice to the defendants and arose out of the same facts as the later filed filiation pleading.[403] In *Washington v. Magnolia Manor Nursing Home and Rehabilitation, L.L.C.*, the Louisiana Third Circuit declined to follow *Ratliff* because the court failed to consider article 197, which it deemed should apply.[404] Instead, the *Washington* court determined that as long as the tort petition is filed timely, the filiation claim is timely because the child has no peremptive period within which to assert a paternity claim in a non-succession case.[405]

§ 8:24 Modern Filiation Issues

With the rapid increase in the use of assisted reproductive technology (ART), along with the United States Supreme Court's recognition of marriage equality in *Obergefell v. Hodges*,[406] Louisiana's filiation laws have struggled to keep pace. When applying Louisiana's filiation laws to these scenarios, the potential issues are many, and in some instances, the laws lead to bizarre legal conclusions.[407] Although the Louisiana Legislature created a task force to study the impact of ART decades ago,[408] current legislation on the topic is scant.

399. La. Civ. Code Ann. art. 197.

400. Ratliff v. LSU Bd. of Supervisors, 2009-0012, p. 3 (La. App. 4 Cir. 5/7/10), 38 So. 3d 1068, 1072.

401. Ratliff, 38 So. 3d at 1073.

402. Ratliff, 38 So. 3d at 1073.

403. Ratliff, 38 So. 3d at 1076.

404. Washington v. Magnolia Manor Nursing Home and Rehab., L.L.C., 51,899, p. 9 (La. App. 2 Cir. 3/28/18), 247 So. 3d 156, 162.

405. Washington, 247 So. 3d at 162.

406. Obergefell v. Hodges, 576 U.S. 644 (2015).

407. Sandi Varnado, *Who's Your Daddy?: A Legitimate Question Given Louisiana's Lack of Legislation Governing Assisted Reproductive Technology*, 66 La. L. Rev. 609, 611 (2006).

408. Katherine S. Spaht, *Who's Your Momma, Who Are Your Daddies: Louisiana's New Law of Filiation*, 67 La. L. Rev. 307, 330 (2007).

§ 8:25 Modern Filiation Issues— Assisted Reproductive Technology and Filiation

The Louisiana Criminal Code addresses the use of gametes donated or provided to create human embryos. This law prohibits any person from "knowingly us[ing] a sperm, ovum, or embryo, through the use of assisted reproduction technology, for any purpose other than that indicated by the sperm, ovum, or embryo provider's signature on a written consent form."[409] Likewise, "[n]o person shall knowingly implant a sperm, ovum, or embryo, through the use of [ART], into a recipient who is not the sperm, ovum, or embryo provider, without the signed written consent" of both the provider and recipient.[410] Violators face immediate revocation of their professional licenses.[411] This legislation is aimed at doctors and other professionals working in clinics that perform ART procedures.

However, the aforementioned criminal law does not apply to the use of ova or sperm by the spouse or surviving spouse of a decedent in order to conceive a child, even without a consent form provided by the other spouse.[412] This leads to an interesting conundrum when compared to a civil law that provides for the filial rights of a child born to a surviving spouse after the death of the gamete-providing spouse, but only with the written consent of the gamete-providing spouse. Louisiana Revised Statutes Section § 9:391.1 provides for children who are conceived posthumously through the use of ART.[413] While this statute addresses an important issue, it is limited because it only applies to married couples, and the deceased party must have specifically authorized in writing for their deposited gametes to be used by their surviving spouse.[414] Additionally, the child must be born after the deceased party's death and also within a three-year window thereof.[415] If all of the statutory requirements are satisfied, the child shall be deemed the child of the decedent with all rights, including inheritance.[416] When compared to the criminal law involving the use of sperm or ova, it appears that a spouse can use the other spouse's gametes after death without consent and without fear of criminal penalties, but a child born as a result will not have filial rights to that deceased parent.[417] For a living spouse who did not consent for the other spouse to use their ova or sperm, however, any child born as a result can filiate to the gamete-provider by timely filing a child's paternity action, even though the gamete-provider did not provide consent.

409. La. Stat. Ann. § 14:101.2.

410. La. Stat. Ann. § 14:101.2.

411. La. Stat. Ann. § 14:101.2.

412. La. Stat. Ann. § 14:101.2, as amended by 2024 La. Acts No. 256.

413. La. Stat. Ann. § 9:391.1.

414. La. Stat. Ann. § 9:391.1.

415. La. Stat. Ann. § 9:391.1.

416. La. Stat. Ann. § 9:391.1.

417. *Compare* La. Stat. Ann. § 14:101.2 with La. Stat. Ann. § 9:391.1. If the child is born within one year of the gamete-provider's death, the child could conceivably file a timely paternity action. See La. Civ. Code Ann. art. 197.

The Human Embryo Statute is another piece of legislation, and it provides the legal status, rights, and regulation of an in vitro fertilized human ovum.[418] This law prohibits the sale of a human ovum or the farming of human ova for research purposes, and it also confines the use of such solely for the support and development of an in utero embryo.[419] Any viable in vitro fertilized human ovum is a juridical person and, therefore, cannot be destroyed, even by the gamete donors.[420] If the ovum has been cryopreserved, the fertilized ovum cannot be discarded and must remain frozen indefinitely.[421] If the sperm and egg donors express their identity, they will have rights as parents,[422] but the separate juridical personality of the ovum remains intact.[423] With that said, a viable in vitro fertilized ovum may be adopted for implantation in another person in accordance with the facility's procedures; in such a situation, the in vitro fertilization patients must formally renounce rights to the fertilized ovum by notarial act.[424] Upon the adoption, the adopting couple are the legal parents of the ovum, which retains no inheritance rights from the in vitro fertilization patients.[425] In the event of a conflict surrounding the fertilized ovum, courts must consider the best interest of the in vitro fertilized ovum.[426]

Although Louisiana has taken some steps to legislate in the area of ART, the current law in Louisiana is insufficient. It addresses only the most traditional circumstances—a married couple who desires a child but who is unable to have one via sexual intercourse. However, as recent Louisiana cases demonstrate, ART may assist a variety of people who want children, including single individuals, unmarried couples, and married same-sex couples. Therefore, the lack of relevant ART legislation creates a major hurdle to the right of some individuals to procreate.

It also leads to many unanswered legal questions. Louisiana law is silent on issues that arise when a woman uses donor gametes to become pregnant.[427] This, in turn, means that Louisiana courts have no legislative guidance when it comes to balancing the competing interests of the prospective parents, the donors of sperm and eggs, and the resulting child, whose interests carry the greatest weight.[428] Although donors rarely seek rights to the resulting child, cases across the country show that is not always

418. *See* La. Stat. Ann. §§ 9:121–33; *see also* Chapter 1, Section 1:7.

419. La. Stat. Ann. § 9:122.

420. La. Stat. Ann. § 9:129.

421. *See* La. Stat. Ann. § 9:129.

422. La. Stat. Ann. § 9:126.

423. La. Stat. Ann. § 9:129.

424. La. Stat. Ann. § 9:130.

425. La. Stat. Ann. §§ 9:130, 9:133.

426. La. Stat. Ann § 9:131.

427. Sandi Varnado, *Who's Your Daddy?: A Legitimate Question Given Louisiana's Lack of Legislation Governing Assisted Reproductive Technology*, 66 La. L. Rev. 609, 613 (2006).

428. Sandi Varnado, *Who's Your Daddy?: A Legitimate Question Given Louisiana's Lack of Legislation Governing Assisted Reproductive Technology*, 66 La. L. Rev. 609, 613 (2006).

true.[429] Some donors are demanding the right to interact with their biological children, and the child's "parents" are responding by demanding financial support from such donors.[430] ART allows for numerous people to be involved in a child's conception, but Louisiana law does not address the rights of all of these parties, leaving many unanswered questions, some of which include:

> Who are the "parents" of a child born under these circumstances? What rights, if any, does a donor have to develop a relationship with that child? What obligations, if any, does a donor owe to that child? Most importantly, what rights does the child have? Does such a child have a right to know the identity of his or her biological parents and to demand support from them? Does such a child and his or her intended parent(s) have a right to be protected from unwanted interference from donors, who might seek to claim parental rights?[431]

For example, because Louisiana permits dual paternity, a child born of ART could be filiated to their intended father (the husband of the mother) and also his sperm donor (the biological father).[432] Ultimately, Louisiana faces a number of unresolved legal issues, leaving the courts to decide res novo issues based on the state's public policy and constitutional restraints.

The scarcity of legislative guidance has forced Louisiana's state courts to address sensitive issues without legislative guidance.[433] It seems that in some instances, courts are hesitant to undertake the task. For example, in *Hall v. Fertility Institute of New Orleans*, a man deposited semen at a fertility clinic.[434] He later died of cancer, and his mother and the woman who accompanied him to the clinic both sought possession of his frozen semen.[435] The woman claimed that the deceased had donated it to her by authentic act prior to his death.[436] The court clearly explained that its decision would be limited to the validity of the donation and the public policy behind it.[437] Ultimately, the court decided that the donation could not be set aside on the basis of public policy and found that the woman's proposed artificial insemination was not contra bonos mores.[438]

---

429. Sandi Varnado, *Who's Your Daddy?: A Legitimate Question Given Louisiana's Lack of Legislation Governing Assisted Reproductive Technology*, 66 La. L. Rev. 609, 616 (2006).

430. Sandi Varnado, *Who's Your Daddy?: A Legitimate Question Given Louisiana's Lack of Legislation Governing Assisted Reproductive Technology*, 66 La. L. Rev. 609, 616 (2006).

431. Sandi Varnado, *Who's Your Daddy?: A Legitimate Question Given Louisiana's Lack of Legislation Governing Assisted Reproductive Technology*, 66 La. L. Rev. 609, 612 (2006).

432. Sandi Varnado, *Who's Your Daddy?: A Legitimate Question Given Louisiana's Lack of Legislation Governing Assisted Reproductive Technology*, 66 La. L. Rev. 609, 631 (2006).

433. Kathryn Venturatos Lorio, *Alternative Means of Reproduction: Virgin Territory for Legislation*, 44 La. L. Rev. 1641, 1676 (1984).

434. Hall v. Fertility Inst. of New Orleans, 94-1135, p. 2 (La. App. 4 Cir. 12/15/94), 647 So. 2d 1348, 1349.

435. Hall, 647 So. 2d at 1348–49.

436. Hall, 647 So. 2d at 1348.

437. Hall, 647 So. 2d at 1351.

438. Hall, 647 So. 2d at 1351. The court granted a preliminary injunction in favor of the decedent's mother, however, because determining whether the act of donation was valid would require the trial court to make findings of fact. Hall, 647 So. 3d at 1351.

In *Black v. Simms*, two unmarried women involved in a same-sex relationship were artificially inseminated using the sperm of the same donor.[439] Ms. Simms gave birth to Braelyn, and, a couple of years later, Ms. Black gave birth to Eli.[440] The couple raised the children together in one family unit, with the help of Ms. Black's parents.[441] Eventually, though, the couple ended their relationship.[442] Later, Ms. Simms moved to Lake Charles to be with her new partner.[443] Initially, Ms. Simms and the Black family agreed on visitation of Braelyn; however, after a confrontation, even Ms. Black was precluded from seeing Braelyn.[444] When Ms. Black subsequently sought custody of the child, the court applied the rules on a non-parent seeking custody against a parent.[445] That law provides that the non-parent must show substantial harm to the child by the parent.[446] Although Ms. Black argued that the legislature had been silent on the issue of children raised by same-sex couples and asked the court to act in equity to protect the rights and best interests of the children involved, the court found that Ms. Black had failed to meet the requisite standard to award her custody.[447] This was true despite Ms. Black's argument that she shared a parent-child bond with Braelyn and had been involved in the child's life since she was born.[448] Because Ms. Simms was the biological mother of Braelyn, the court determined that she had the right to direct how the child was raised, even if her choices were harsh and inconsiderate of Braelyn's attachment to Eli and the Black family.[449]

Less than a year after the *Black* case was decided, another Louisiana appellate court addressed a similar set of facts in the case of *In re Melancon*.[450] This case also involved a woman who conceived a child through artificial insemination and wished to share custody of the child with her same-sex partner.[451] The two women signed a consent judgment agreeing to such, but the trial court refused to sign it, citing *Black v. Simms*.[452] On appeal, the Louisiana First Circuit affirmed the lower court's holding,[453] possibly reluctantly, given the concurring judge's opinion that stated: "I am constrained to follow the law as it presently exists in the State of Louisiana.... I further note that if there

439. Black v. Simms, 2008-1465, p. 1 (La. App. 3 Cir. 6/10/09), 12 So. 3d 1140, 1141.

440. Black, 12 So. 3d at 1141.

441. Black, 12 So. 3d at 1141.

442. Black, 12 So. 3d at 1141.

443. Black, 12 So. 3d at 1141.

444. Black, 12 So. 3d at 1141.

445. Black, 12 So. 3d at 1141.

446. La. Civ. Code Ann. art. 133.

447. Black, 12 So. 3d at 1145.

448. Black, 12 So. 3d at 1144.

449. Black, 12 So. 3d at 1145; *see also* Chapter 6, Section 6:23, for a discussion of custody issues for same-sex couples.

450. *See* In re Melancon, 2010-1463 (La. App. 1 Cir. 12/22/10), 62 So. 3d 759.

451. In re Melancon, 62 So. 3d at 763.

452. In re Melancon, 62 So. 3d at 763.

453. In re Melancon, 62 So. 3d at 764.

is going to be any change of the existing law, it should be addressed by the Louisiana State Legislature."[454]

§ 8:26 Modern Filiation Issues— Marriage Equality and Filiation

In 2015, the United States Supreme Court legalized marriage equality in *Obergefell v. Hodges*,[455] yet the Louisiana Legislature has done nothing since then to revise its filiation laws to account for marriage equality.[456] Again, the Louisiana courts are left to make decisions as to how to apply existing and insufficient filiation laws to same-sex married couples. In doing so, they have relied upon the *Obergefell* rationale that the "constellation of benefits" associated with marriage should also apply to same-sex couples.[457]

For example, in *Chiasson v. State*, Ms. Chiasson and Ms. Nelson were legally married in New York in 2011, and Ms. Chiasson gave birth to a child conceived via artificial insemination in New Orleans in 2014.[458] In 2017, after the *Obergefell* decision, Ms. Nelson individually and without the knowledge of Ms. Chaisson applied for an amendment to the child's birth certificate to list her name as a parent.[459] After she provided a copy of the marriage certificate, the Registrar of the Office of Vital Statistics made the amendment.[460] Later that month, Ms. Chiasson filed a petition to restore the original birth certificate and to strike the amended one from the state's vital statistics records.[461] Relying on laws addressing the rights of a heterosexual man to request a birth certificate amendment, Ms. Chiasson argued that the amendment was improper without an affidavit of acknowledgment or court order.[462] The court disagreed, explaining that the

454. In re Melancon, 62 So. 3d at 764 (Pettigrew, J. concurring). *In re Melancon* has been limited in light of the Louisiana Supreme Court's decision in *Tracie F. v. Francisco D.*, 2015-1812 (La. 3/15/16), 188 So. 3d 231, as discussed in *In re Jet*, 2016-0384 (La. App. 1 Cir. 10/31/16), 211 So. 3d 575, 582–85.

455. *See* Obergefell v. Hodges, 576 U.S. 644 (2015).

456. During the 2016 legislative session, the Louisiana Senate passed Resolution 143, in which it urged and requested that the Marriage-Persons Committee of the Louisiana State Law Institute study and make recommendations regarding state law post-*Obergefell*. *See* Louisiana State Law Inst., Annual Report to the Legislature in Response to SR No. 143 of the 2016 Regular Session (2019), https://lsli.org/files/reports/2019/2016%20SR%20143%20SameSex%20Marriage%20Annual%20Report.pdf. That committee offered its recommendations to the Law Institute's Council in January of 2017. The Council approved the project, and the Committee submitted its recommendations to the Louisiana Legislature. Nevertheless, no legislation was proposed during the 2017 session. In the 2018 session, Senate Bill 98 was introduced; this bill proposed defining marriage as "a legal relationship between two natural persons that is created by civil contract." Senate Bill 98 progressed only to the Committee on Judiciary A. The committee made further recommendations in 2019, but no legislation was enacted. To date, this is still true. *See also* Chapter 3, Section 3:3.

457. Obergefell, 576 U.S. at 670.

458. Chaisson v. State, 2017-0642, p. 2 (La. App. 4 Cir. 3/7/18), 239 So. 3d 1074, 1076.

459. Chaisson, 239 So. 3d at 1077.

460. Chaisson, 239 So. 3d at 1077.

461. Chaisson, 239 So. 3d at 1077.

462. Chaisson, 239 So. 3d at 1079.

law relied on by Ms. Chaisson applied only to birth certificates of children born outside of marriage.[463] For children born of marriage, a birth certificate may be amended based on the presumption set forth in Civil Code Article 185 (presumption of the husband of the mother), such that one must show only proof of marriage and that the child was born during the marriage or within 300 days of its termination.[464] Therefore, the court applied the legal presumption to the same-sex marital couple and allowed for the amendment.[465] Although Ms. Chiasson argued that Ms. Nelson had no biological relationship with the child, the court emphasized that the spousal presumption in Civil Code Article 185 is not based on biology but instead on the marriage contract existing at the child's birth, and same-sex couples are entitled to equal protection of the laws.[466]

Similarly, in *Boquet v. Boquet*, Brittany and Nicole Boquet married on December 18, 2015, when Nicole was pregnant, a fact that Brittany well knew.[467] The child was born during their marriage on February 5, 2016.[468] When the couple divorced, Nicole sought child support from Brittany, and Brittany sought to disavow the child, filing the action on April 28, 2017.[469] The trial court found and the appellate court affirmed that Brittany's petition to disavow was untimely, and Brittany, as the spouse of the mother of a child born during their marriage, was presumed to be the child's parent.[470] The court held that a same-sex spouse should be treated the same as an opposite-sex spouse would have been.[471] Because Brittany knew or should have known all along that she was not the biological parent of the child, the one-year prescriptive period began to run on the date of the child's birth.[472] The unresolved question, which the court did not need to address, is whether Brittany could successfully disavow the child had she timely filed, a fact that she certainly could have proven. In most same-sex cases, biology will be absent for one parent, begging the question of whether consent should be the operative analysis.

The First Circuit in *Foret v. Serrano*[473] refused to apply the holdings in *Chaisson* and *Boquet* to two male spouses, concluding that the article 185 presumption does not apply in the absence of a childbearing spouse.[474] Mr. Foret and Mr. Serrano married before the birth of their daughter, who was born using a surrogate. The daughter was biologically the child of Mr. Foret using a gestational carrier from Texas. When the child was almost two years old, Mr. Foret filed for divorce and Mr. Serrano sought custody. Finding that Mr. Serrano was not the parent of the child, the court denied

463. Chaisson, 239 So. 3d at 1079.
464. Chaisson, 239 So. 3d at 1079.
465. Chaisson, 239 So. 3d at 1079.
466. Chaisson, 239 So. 3d at 1081–82.
467. Boquet v. Boquet, 2018-798, p. 1 (La. App. 3 Cir. 4/10/19), 269 So. 3d 895, 897.
468. Boquet, 269 So. 3d at 897.
469. Boquet, 269 So. 3d at 897.
470. Boquet, 269 So. 3d at 897.
471. Boquet, 269 So. 3d at 899–900.
472. Boquet, 269 So. 3d at 900.
473. Foret v. Serrano, 2023-1034 (La. App. 1 Cir. 4/30/24), 2024 WL 2050131.
474. Foret, 2024 WL 2050131 at *4.

him custody. Mr. Serrano appealed, claiming equal protection rights under *Obergefell v. Hodges*. Specifically, he argued that because the child was born during his marriage, the article 185 presumption should apply to him, giving him rights as a legal parent. The court of appeal disagreed, concluding that article 185 requires the presence of a child-bearing spouse, meaning a person capable of birthing the child.[475] Because the presumption does not apply in a heterosexual marriage where a spouse does not give birth to the child, the court concluded that no equal protection violation exists.[476]

The Second Circuit in *In re Dennis*[477] not only refused to apply the holdings in *Chaisson* and *Boquet*, but the court openly disagreed with the holding in *Boquet*, concluding that the article 185 presumption does not apply to two married women because neither can be described as a husband or a father, as the plain language of the article dictates.[478] With the assistance of a sperm donor, Jessica Dennis delivered a child during her marriage to Kristen Dennis, and Kristen filed a petition for a stepparent adoption. The trial court *sua sponte* rejected the petition for stepparent adoption, concluding that article 185 applied and Kristen was a legal parent based on the presumption. The Second Circuit reversed, concluding that Kristen, a woman, does not fit within the plain language of article 185, which applies to the *husband* of the mother, who is deemed the *father* of the child. The court also concluded that Kristen could not adopt the child as a stepparent because the child was born during her marriage to Jessica, ultimately leaving Kristen without any legal remedy to filiate to her child.[479]

Until the Louisiana Legislature amends the state's filiation laws, issues such as these will continue to arise for same-sex married couples, leaving courts to analogize and extend (or not extend) existing laws. Such a result is problematic, particularly in a civil law jurisdiction like Louisiana, where judicial activism is discouraged.[480]

---

475. Foret, 2024 WL 2050131 at *3 (citing Katherine Shaw Spaht, *Who's Your Momma, Who Are Your Daddies? Louisiana's New Law of Filiation*, 67 La. L. Rev. 307, 309 (2007)). The court further explained: "As written, a predicate fact central to the application of the presumption found in Article 185 is the existence of a 'mother....'" *Id.*

476. Foret, 2024 WL 2050131 at *3.

477. In re Dennis, 55,851 (La. App. 2 Cir. 7/17/24), 2024 WL 3434184.

478. 2024 WL 3434184 at *7.

479. 2024 WL 3434184 at *7.

480. Laura Tracy, *Presumption Junction What's That Function: Louisiana Marriage and Parenthood Laws Post-*Obergefell, 81 La. L. Rev. 1524, 1527 (2021).

Chapter 9

Parental Authority and Alimentary Obligation

§ 9:1 Introduction

Louisiana law specifically recognizes the strong ties and the reciprocal obligations and rights of parents and children. Dubbed "the bedrock of the relationship of parents and their children,"[1] the term "parental authority" describes a system of rules governing the relationship of some parents and their children. While the term "parental authority" seemingly suggests that all parents and children are subject to it, its applicability is actually much more limited. Only parents who are *married to each other* enjoy parental authority over their minor children and only while their marriage endures.[2] In addition, a grandparent may also enjoy parental authority if the grandparent is

1. Griffith v. Roy, 269 So. 2d 217, 221 (La. 1972).
2. La. Civ. Code Ann. art. 221 & cmt. (a).

awarded custody during the marriage of the parents.[3] Parents who never marry, as well as those whose marriages terminate,[4] do not enjoy parental authority; instead, the legal regime of tutorship applies to their parent-child relationships.[5] As the Louisiana Supreme Court has cautioned: "It is necessary to be constantly aware of the distinctions of paternal authority, custody, and tutorship."[6]

§ 9:2 History of Parental Authority

Louisiana's law of parental authority finds its genesis in Roman law and Germanic customs; the French *Code civil* and Spanish law, as set forth in *Las Siete Partidas*,[7] influenced it, as well.[8] The following sections discuss the French and Spanish influences, as well as the evolution of Louisiana's law on parental authority—from the Digest of 1808 to the Louisiana Code of 1825 to the Louisiana Code of 1870. Finally, it explores the 2015 comprehensive revision to the law of parental authority in Louisiana.

§ 9:3 History of Parental Authority— Early Sources of Parental Authority

The early sources of Louisiana's parental authority law distinguished between legitimate and illegitimate children. For legitimate children, under Roman law, the concept of "*patria potestas*," a Latin term translated to "power of a father," governed the parent-child relationship. As its name clearly connotes, the power it bestowed, described by the Louisiana Supreme Court as "absolute,"[9] belonged exclusively to the male head of the family, and it extended over the family property (including, among others, the children).[10] The fundamental structure of "*patria potestas*" included the following key aspects: the paternal power never belonged to the mother; it persisted indefinitely regardless of the child's age; a child, in theory, was unable to acquire property for himself, as all property aside from savings, belonged to the male head of the family; and children were incapable of borrowing or making a testament.[11] The French southern

---

3. 2015 La. Acts. 260, enacting La. Civ. Code Ann. art. 234.

4. *See generally* La. Civ. Code Ann. art. 101.

5. La. Civ. Code Ann. art. 221 cmt. (c). *See* Chapter 10 for a detailed exploration of the similarities and differences between parental authority and tutorship.

6. Griffith, 269 So. 2d at 221.

7. Las Siete Partidas is a seven-part Castilian code promulgated around the 13th century.

8. *See* Christopher L. Blakesley, *Comparativist Ruminations from the Bayou on Child Custody Jurisdiction: The UCCJA, the PKPA, and the Hague Convention on Child Abduction*, 58 La. L. Rev. 449, 455–60 (1998) (discussing the historical development of parental authority); Griffith v. Roy, 269 So. 2d 217, 221 (La. 1972).

9. Bosworth v. Beiller, 2 La. Ann. 293, 297 (1847).

10. Thomas W. Tucker, *Sources of Louisiana's Law of Persons: Blackstone, Domat, and the French Codes*, 44 Tul. L. Rev. 264, 267 (1970).

11. Marcel Planiol, 1 Treatise on the Civil Law § 1637, at 15 (La. State L. Inst. Trans., 12th ed. 1959).

provinces, where written law prevailed, largely preserved the Roman concept of "*patria potestas*."[12] Spain also followed this version of parental authority.[13]

By contrast, under Germanic customary law, the concept of "*mundium*," or protection, governed the parent-child relationship.[14] In contrast to "*patria potestas*," the concept of "*mundium*" centered on the person of the child, more specifically on protecting the child, rather than on the power of the father. Additionally, it allowed both the mother and father to hold authority over the child, but the mother's power was subjugated to the father's with regard to managing the child's property.[15] Ultimately, the parents' authority was the mechanism by which parents fulfilled their duties as the family protector,[16] and consequently, it ceased when the child no longer required such protection (typically when the child was emancipated expressly or tacitly).[17] The central and northern provinces of France, where customs prevailed, followed the Germanic customary law of "*mundium*."

Illegitimate children (often referred to as "natural children"), by contrast, were generally not subject to parental authority. Even in Rome, "where the authority of parents was carried further than in any other civilised [*sic*] country," this legal doctrine did not confer power on the father of illegitimate children.[18] As the Louisiana Supreme Court explained:

> The institutes of Justinian declare, that the children whom we have under our power are those which are born in legitimate marriage. The digest has an express provision that natural children cannot be brought under the paternal authority. *(Patriam potestatem.) The 2d law of the 17th title of the 4th Partida*, provides, that natural children are not in the power of the father as legitimate children are, and the Spanish commentators state their law to be in conformity with this provision.[19]

By the time of the French Revolution, the differences in the concepts of "*patria potestats*" and "*mundium*" had lessened,[20] and the liberation of the individual was seen as a

---

12. Marcel Planiol, 1 Treatise on the Civil Law § 1637, at 15 (La. State L. Inst. Trans., 12th ed. 1959).

13. Bosworth, 2 La. Ann. at 297.

14. Thomas W. Tucker, *Sources of Louisiana's Law of Persons: Blackstone, Domat, and the French Codes*, 44 Tul. L. Rev. 264, 271 (1970); Marcel Planiol, 1 Treatise on the Civil Law § 1638, at 16 (La. State L. Inst. Trans., 12th ed. 1959).

15. Thomas W. Tucker, *Sources of Louisiana's Law of Persons: Blackstone, Domat, and the French Codes*, 44 Tul. L. Rev. 264, 271 (1970).

16. Thomas W. Tucker, *Sources of Louisiana's Law of Persons: Blackstone, Domat, and the French Codes*, 44 Tul. L. Rev. 264, 271 (1970).

17. Thomas W. Tucker, *Sources of Louisiana's Law of Persons: Blackstone, Domat, and the French Codes*, 44 Tul. L. Rev. 264, 271 (1970); Marcel Planiol, 1 Treatise on the Civil Law § 1638, at 16 n.1 (La. State L. Inst. Trans., 12th ed. 1959) ("The extinction of the father's power through arriving at a majority that emancipates, unknown to the Romans, was on the contrary, well known to the Germanic races.").

18. Acosta v. Robin, 1829 WL 1559, at *1 (La. 1889).

19. Acosta, 1829 WL 1559, at *1 (emphasis in original).

20. Thomas W. Tucker, *Sources of Louisiana's Law of Persons: Blackstone, Domat, and the French Codes*, 44 Tul. L. Rev. 264, 271 (1970).

principal achievement of the Revolution.[21] Thus, the customs on "*mundium*," seen as more readily adaptable to the new French *Code civil*, carried the day.[22] Under the French *Code civil*, the family was defined narrowly—parents and their cohabiting children.[23] The father essentially served as an administrator, allowing him the usufruct and management of his child's property.[24] He retained very little power other than that he could correct the child, who was also required to live with the father until the child's majority.[25]

Unlike Roman law, the French *Code civil* of 1804 contained no parental authority articles for illegitimate children.[26] As explained by the Louisiana Supreme Court, renowned civil law commentator

> Toullier seems to consider that in tender age the child should be confided to the mother, but that as it advances in life the reasons in favour [*sic*] of her having the possession are not so conclusive. He considers it a question left to the prudence of the magistrate under all the circumstances of the case, and that the right should be conferred on either father or mother, as the interest of the minor may dictate.[27]

§ 9:4 History of Parental Authority— Early Louisiana Law

Louisiana law on parental authority has evolved over the years. This section examines its history from the Louisiana Digest of 1808 to the Louisiana Civil Code of 1825 to the Louisiana Civil Code of 1870.

Louisiana Digest of 1808

The majority of Book I of the Louisiana Digest of 1808 was derived from the French *Projet* and the Code Napoleon.[28] Like "*mundium*," the mother enjoyed parental authority alongside the father under the digest.[29] As the Louisiana Supreme Court explained: "The influence of Christianity had elevated the mother from the almost servile con-

---

21. Thomas W. Tucker, *Sources of Louisiana's Law of Persons: Blackstone, Domat, and the French Codes*, 44 Tul. L. Rev. 264, 271 (1970).

22. Thomas W. Tucker, *Sources of Louisiana's Law of Persons: Blackstone, Domat, and the French Codes*, 44 Tul. L. Rev. 264, 271 (1970).

23. Thomas W. Tucker, *Sources of Louisiana's Law of Persons: Blackstone, Domat, and the French Codes*, 44 Tul. L. Rev. 264, 272 (1970).

24. Thomas W. Tucker, *Sources of Louisiana's Law of Persons: Blackstone, Domat, and the French Codes*, 44 Tul. L. Rev. 264, 272 (1970).

25. Thomas W. Tucker, *Sources of Louisiana's Law of Persons: Blackstone, Domat, and the French Codes*, 44 Tul. L. Rev. 264, 272 (1970).

26. Acosta, 1829 WL 1559, at *2 (noting that while Louisiana law distinguished between legitimate and illegitimate children, no distinction is found in the French Code Civil).

27. Acosta, 1829 WL 1559, at *2.

28. Thomas W. Tucker, *Sources of Louisiana's Law of Persons: Blackstone, Domat, and the French Codes*, 44 Tul. L. Rev. 264, 281 (1970).

29. La. Civ. Code art. 37 (1808).

dition in which the roman law had originally placed her."[30] Additionally, the digest allowed parents to delegate their authority to others, such as teachers, schoolmasters, and other who educated their children.[31] Also similar to the concept of "*mundium*," the regime of parental authority was temporary, ending on the child's majority or emancipation.[32] Children born outside of marriage were not subject to parental authority.[33]

Under the digest, parents had more power than their French counterparts subject to the *Code civil*.[34] In Louisiana, parents' rights included the child's duty to honor and respect them,[35] as well as to obey them[36] and to remain in the family home (at least until puberty).[37] The law also granted parents the right to appoint testamentary tutors for their child,[38] enjoyment over the child's estate[39] (unless acquired by the child's labor and industry while apart from the parents),[40] and protection from suit by the child for advancements.[41] In exchange, the parents' obligations included those to which usufructuaries were subjected (with regard to the child's estate), along with nourishing, maintaining, and educating their child,[42] forced heirship,[43] protection and legal representation of the child,[44] acceptance of donations to the child,[45] and liability for the child's offenses and quasi-offenses.[46] Children were obligated "to be security for their" parents and other ascendants, to deliver them out of prison, by obliging themselves to represent them or to pay for them, as their circumstances may allow.[47] Additionally, the digest provided that children should "redeem" their parents if they have the means, when they are captives, render them all the assistance which their situation may require (if the parents fall into a state of insanity), and not marry as minors without parental consent.[48] Punishment for a child's breach of an obligation was to be "deservedly disinherited."[49]

30. Bosworth v. Beiller, 2 La. Ann. 293, 297 (1847).
31. La. Civ. Code art. 41 (1808).
32. La. Civ. Code art. 37 (1808).
33. La. Civ. Code art. 59 (1808) (providing that these children "belong to no one family, and have no relations").
34. Bosworth, 2 La. Ann. at 284.
35. La. Civ. Code art. 36 (1808).
36. La. Civ. Code art 38 (1808).
37. La. Civ. Code art. 39 (1808).
38. La. Civ. Code art. 40 (1808).
39. La. Civ. Code art. 42 (1808).
40. La. Civ. Code art. 45 (1808).
41. La. Civ. Code. art. 47 (1808).
42. La. Civ. Code art. 43 (1808). *See also* La. Civ. Code art. 46 (1808).
43. La. Civ. Code art. 54 (1808).
44. La. Civ. Code arts. 55–56 (1808). Parents were allowed to justify themselves in an action begun against them for assault and battery. La. Civ. Code art. 56 (1808).
45. La. Civ. Code art. 55 (1808).
46. La. Civ. Code art. 57 (1808).
47. La. Civ. Code art. 58 (1808).
48. La. Civ. Code art. 58 (1808).
49. La. Civ. Code art. 58 (1808).

Louisiana Civil Code of 1825

The amended version of the parental authority regime set forth in the Louisiana Civil Code of 1825 differed in some respects from its predecessor digest, most of which were minor.[50] However, one glaring change was the distinction that the 1825 Code made between fathers and mothers. The 1825 Code provided that "[i]n case of difference between parents, the authority of the father prevails."[51] In 1847, the Louisiana Supreme Court explained the reasoning behind this "father-knows-best" provision[52] as follows:

> The paternal power was one of the main pillars of that wonderful social organization which is the basis of modern civilization, and which gave laws to posterity on which society still rests for its support. Roman legislation placed the safety and welfare of the child under the aegis of paternal affection, and time has borne witness to the profound wisdom of its provision.[53]

Louisiana Civil Code of 1870

The Louisiana Civil Code of 1870 did not alter much with regard to parental authority. In keeping with the "father-knows-best" mentality, the 1870 Code also allowed him—and him alone—to administer the child's estate until the termination of the parental authority regime.[54] Nonetheless, the law still allowed both parents the enjoyment of their child's estate.[55]

§ 9:5 History of Parental Authority—Revisions to Louisiana Law

Louisiana's parental authority saw very few changes after the 1870 Code until a comprehensive revision that was completed in 2015 and effective in 2016. Those changes are discussed in detail below.

Pre-Revision Changes

One change between the 1870 Code and the 2015 Revision was that the parental right of enjoyment did not attach to property donated to the child *inter vivos* unless the donation was by written act that provided for such a right.[56] Another change came with the adoption of Article 99 of the Louisiana Civil Code in 1987. Per that article,

---

50. Many of the changes were merely semantic. *Compare* La. Civ. Code art. 38 (1808) *with* La. Civ. Code art. 235 (1825); La. Civ. Code art. 43 (1808) *with* La. Civ. Code art. 240 (1825); La. Civ. Code art. 46 (1808) *with* La. Civ. Code art. 243 (1825). However, in addition to delegating parental authority, the 1825 Civil Code allowed parents to bind their children as apprentices. La. Civ. Code art. 238 (1825).

51. La. Civ. Code art. 234 (1825).

52. *See* Chapter 3, Section 3:38.

53. Bosworth, 2 La. Ann. at 297.

54. La. Civ. Code art. 221 (1870). *See also* La. Civ. Code art. 222 (1870) for procedural rules to sell or mortgage the minor's property or to take "any other step" that may affect the child's interest.

55. *See* La. Civ. Code art. 223 (1870).

56. La. Civ. Code Ann. art. 226 (2015).

"Spouses mutually assume the moral and material direction of the family, exercise parental authority, and assume the moral and material obligations resulting therefrom."[57] According to the comment, article 99 "states a general principle of equality between the spouses in the moral and material direction of the family."[58] Presumably, that equality would have extended to parental authority, as well, even though the comment to the article did not specifically say this. While no reported cases addressed the issue, scholars opined that article 99 tacitly repealed the father-knows-best provision.[59]

LSLI Comprehensive Revision

For many years, the Marriage-Persons Committee of the Louisiana State Law Institute worked to comprehensively revise the parental authority regime. In 2015, the Louisiana Legislature enacted the Committee's work. Some of the changes in the revision simply modernized the concepts and language employed in the Code articles.[60] Some changes served an organizational function.[61] Others clarified prior law.[62] However, one marked revision was the repeal of the "father-knows-best" provision.[63] Civil law jurisdictions like France and Quebec had long since recognized equal rights for parents during their marriage.[64] Now Louisiana law clearly establishes that both parents share authority over the family equally,[65] and they may together resolve their own disagreements.[66] Likewise, neither parent is favored with regard to administration of the child's property.[67] Finally, as part of the revision, the prior Code articles addressing the parental authority of "illegitimate children" were repealed.

---

57. La. Civ. Code Ann. art. 99.

58. La. Civ. Code Ann. art. 99 cmt.

59. *See* Chapter 3, Section 3:38. *See also* La. Civ. Code Ann. art. 229 cmt. (a) (providing that "[u]pon enactment in 1987, however, C.C. Art. 99 recognized that parental authority was to be exercised equally.").

60. For example, none of the current Code articles provide for parents to bind their children as apprentices.

61. *See, e.g.*, La. Civ. Code Ann. art. 223–226 (compiling the rights and obligations of parental authority over the person of the child, the parental obligation of support and education, the parental liability for offenses and quasi-offenses).

62. For example, article 222 "makes explicit that parental authority includes representation of the child." La. Civ. Code Ann. art. 222 cmt. (a).

63. *See* Chapter 3.

64. Katherine Connell-Thouez, *The Family in Contemporary Civil Law—Comparative Developments in Alimentary Obligations and Parental Authority: Linking Traditional Rights and Responsibilities to Create an Integrated Structure for Solving the Child Care Dilemma*, 60 Tul. L. Rev. 1135, 1151 (1986) (noting the equal authority and access to the courts in case of disagreement) (citing French Civil Code article 372-1 and Quebec Civil Code article 653).

65. *See* Chapter 3.

66. *See* Chapter 3.

67. La. Civ. Code Ann. art. 229.

§ 9:6 Parameters of Parental Authority

Parental authority is commonly considered a regime that is less burdensome to parents than is the similar regime of tutorship,[68] and Louisiana jurisprudence has historically recognized that the duties and responsibilities of married parents and those of tutors "are very different."[69] The current legal regime of parental authority sets forth both the rights and obligations of the parents holding it, as well as the obligations of the child subject to it.[70] Note that "one may not renounce rights deriving from ... paternal authority...."[71]

§ 9:7 Parameters of Parental Authority—Rights and Obligations of the Parents

One right and obligation of parents under this regime is their representation of their child,[72] which means that the parents stand in for the child in legal relations.[73] This includes, among other things, that the parents appear for their minor child in civil suits[74] and act for their minor child in juridical acts.[75] However, parental representation is not without exception, as the law maintains the personal nature of certain juridical acts. For example, only the child may enter into the contract of marriage, and only the child may execute a testament.[76] In addition to representation, parental authority includes the right, upon the parent's death, to designate a tutor for the child[77] via testament or authentic act.[78]

Over the Child's Person

Parents under this regime enjoy the rights and obligations of physical care, supervision, protection, discipline, and instruction of their child,[79] all of which attach to the person of the child.[80] This aligns with parents' constitutionally-protected rights of

---

68. *See, e.g.*, LaPorte v. Clesi, Inc., 197 So. 2d 419 (La. Ct. App. 4 Cir. 1967) (disallowing certain actions of the child's father who had "only the powers of a tutor"). By way of example, parents enjoying parental authority need not qualify or be appointed by a court into the role; this stands in stark contrast to the rules governing tutors. See Chapter 10.

69. In re Monrose, 175 So. 475, 478 (La. 1937).

70. La. Civ. Code Ann. art. 223.

71. Hogan v. Hogan, 549 So. 2d 267, 271–72 (La. 1989).

72. La. Civ. Code Ann. art. 222.

73. La. Civ. Code Ann. art. 222 cmt. (b).

74. La. Civ. Code Ann. art. 222 cmt. (b); *see also* La. Code Civ. Proc. Ann. arts. 683, 732 (detailing rules on procedural capacity of unemancipated minor children subject to parental authority).

75. La. Civ. Code Ann. art. 222 cmt. (a).

76. La. Civ. Code Ann. art. 222 cmt. (a).

77. La. Civ. Code Ann. art. 222.

78. La. Civ. Code Ann. art. cmt. (c).

79. La. Civ. Code Ann. art. 223.

80. La. Civ. Code Ann. art. 223 cmt. (a).

custody and control of their children.[81] "Custody and control" encompasses the ability to make all manner of decisions on their behalf. As one scholar noted:

> Parents' day-to-day authority over their children is thus universally acknowledged and respected.... Parents decide where their children will live, where they will attend school, which doctors will attend them, which medical procedures they will undergo, and every aspect of how they will be raised—their daily schedules, activities, diets, etc. Once an individual is identified as a parent, community actors such as school officials and health care providers afford them the decision-making authority that attend that status.[82]

Of the enumerated rights and obligations mentioned above, physical care is principal, as it embodies the parents' paramount right to custody of their child; practically speaking, it also makes the supervision, protection, and instruction of the child possible.[83] The rights and obligations of supervision and instruction enable parents to perform their obligation of moral and material direction of the child as set forth in Louisiana Civil Code Article 99.[84] While the absence of parental supervision may result in action by the State of Louisiana, no authority exists to protect the child from the lack of moral and material direction.

In addition to what has already been mentioned, parents subject to the legal regime of parental authority owe three obligations to their child.[85] First, parents must support, maintain, and educate their child.[86] Courts have described this duty of support as "one of the strongest obligations the law imposes upon a parent."[87] Louisiana caselaw essentially makes the child a "veritable creditor" of each parent's obligation for the child's upbringing, and it also provides that parents are solidarily liable for the obligation to support the child.[88] This obligation is solidary so that "if one of them has nothing, or if one of them dies, the other is obligated to support alone all the expenses."[89] The duty of maintenance is not simply a monetary obligation but includes the daily care and maintenance that a parent gives by their physical presence and efforts.[90]

---

81. Vivian E. Hamilton, *Adulthood in Law and Culture*, 91 Tul. L. Rev. 55, 68 (2016).

82. Vivian E. Hamilton, *Adulthood in Law and Culture*, 91 Tul. L. Rev. 55, 68 (2016).

83. Vivian E. Hamilton, *Adulthood in Law and Culture*, 91 Tul. L. Rev. 55, 68 (2016).

84. La. Civ. Code Ann. art. 223 cmt (b).

85. Note that the statutes on covenant marriage specifically provide that married parents subject to this regime also owe the duty to maintain, teach, and educate their children in accordance with their capacities, natural inclinations, and aspirations; additionally, these parents must prepare their children for their future. La. Stat. Ann. § 9:298.

86. La. Civ. Code Ann. art. 224. Under prior law, the parents' duty of support was in accordance with their standard of living. *See* La. Civ. Code Ann. art. 224 cmt. (a).

87. Department of Children and Family Services in Interest of Lannelongue-Navarro v. Lannelongue, 22-220 (La. App. 5 Cir. 2/1/23), 358 So. 3d 899, 904.

88. State ex rel. Gilbert v. Gilbert, 34,203-CA (La. App. 2 Cir. 12/20/00), 775 So. 2d 1182.

89. Hogan v. Hogan, 549 So. 2d 267, 271–72 (La. 1989) (citing Marcel Planiol, 1 Treatise on the Civil Law § 1683).

90. Sims v. Sims, 457 So. 2d 163 (La. Ct App. 2 Cir. 1984).

Second, parents are liable for the damage caused by their child "as provided by law."[91] This aspect of parental authority is probably the most litigated. Per Louisiana tort law, parents are responsible for the damage occasioned by their minor child who resides with them or who has been placed by them under the care of other persons.[92] This liability stems from the authority of the parents over their child's person, i.e., the rights to and obligations of physical care, supervision, protection, discipline, and instruction.[93] As the Louisiana Supreme Court noted: "Paternal responsibility is the consequence and offspring of the paternal authority."[94] Phrased conversely, liability is not tied to any fault of the parent's. As one court explained: "[T]he parents' liability is not based upon a presumption of fault for having failed to properly supervise and train the minor. It is absolute liability arising out of the parent-child relationship."[95] In the case of *Turner v. Bucher*, a six-year-old child struck someone with his bicycle on a city sidewalk. The tort victim sued, among other persons, the child's father. The Louisiana Supreme Court decided that the father was not independently negligent and that the child was incapable of legal liability. However, the court also decided that had the child been a person of discernment, his conduct would have qualified as civil negligence and held the father strictly liable for the damage caused by the acts of his child.[96]

Finally, parents must provide moral, social, and material direction for their child,[97] an obligation imposed on them as a result of their marriage.[98] "Moral direction" includes "instruction and exhortation concerning moral obligations and common moral principles;" by contrast, "social direction" is more expansive, extending to teaching acceptable conduct within the broader community.[99] "Material direction" contemplates instruction regarding basic economic matters such as living within one's means.[100]

Over the Child's Property

A final set of parental rights and obligations under the regime of parental authority pertains to the child's property. Note, first, that parents are treated much differently in this regard than their counterparts subject to the legal regime of tutorship.[101] Unlike

91. La. Civ. Code Ann. art. 225. This extends to tutors, as well. *See* La. Civ. Code Ann. art. 2317. Prior to the revision, it did not extend to the father of a child born outside of marriage. In *Tippen v Baker*, the court explained that "an illegitimate child is not subject to paternal authority." Tippen v. Baker, 31,195-CW, p. 2 (La. App. 2 Cir. 1998), 718 So. 2d 617, 619. Thus, because the father had no paternal authority over the child, he was not subject to liability for the child's torts.

92. La. Civ. Code Ann. art. 2318. *See also* Penton v. Castellano, 48,433-CA (La. App. 2 Cir. 10/23/13), 127 So. 3d 944 (father with sole custody held liable for second grade child's conduct in tripping the school disciplinarian which caused injuries).

93. La. Civ. Code Ann. art. 225 cmt.

94. Coats v. Roberts, 35 La. Ann. 891, 892 (La. 1883).

95. Deshotel v. Casualty Reciprocal Exchange, 350 So. 2d 283, 286 (La. Ct. App. 3 Cir. 1977).

96. Turner v. Bucher, 308 So. 2d 270 (La. 1975).

97. La. Civ. Code Ann. art. 226.

98. *See* La. Civ. Code Ann. art. 99.

99. La. Civ. Code Ann. art. 226 cmt. (b).

100. La. Civ. Code Ann. art. 226 cmt. (b).

101. *See, e.g.*, Darlington v. Turner, 202 U.S. 195 (1906) (noting that parental authority and tutorship are "wholly distinct").

tutors, parents enjoying parental authority are not required to take an oath, inventory their child's property, or offer a legal mortgage to protect the child's property. Note, too, that the parental authority laws differentiate between the parents' rights and obligations to *administer* the child's property, on the one hand, and their rights and obligations to *dispose* of the child's property, on the other.[102]

The term "administration" refers to the "preservation or protection of acquired rights or the exploitation of them without changing the substantial character of the minor's patrimony as a whole."[103] As such, acts of administration differ from alienation, encumbrance, and lease,[104] with the latter three more appropriately classified as acts of disposition. The term "disposition" is broadly defined as "any other act that is not administration"[105] and would also include compromising a child's claim, as well as acts incurring an obligation on behalf of the child (all of which should be for the purpose of education, support, or maintenance of the child).[106]

As to administration of a child's property, the regime of parental authority allows each parent that right and obligation.[107] This stands in stark contrast to the pre-revision law under which only the father could administer the child's property (unless the father was an absent person or an interdict).[108] Under current law, either parent may act to administer the child's property without court approval[109] until the regime of parental authority terminates.[110] In their role as administrator, the parents must act prudently,[111] and their administrative acts must be for the child's benefit.[112] A breach of these obligations subjects the parents to liability for damages resulting from fraud, fault, default or neglect,[113] assuming the child asserts an action within the allowable liberative prescription period of five years of his eighteenth birthday.[114]

Like administration, both parents enjoy the right and obligation to dispose of the child's property. Generally, however, they must obtain prior judicial approval before disposal. For example, article 230 provides that "[e]ither parent may alienate, encum-

102. *Compare* La. Civ. Code Ann. art. 229 *with* La. Civ. Code Ann. art. 230; *see also* La. Civ. Code Ann. art. 229 cmt. (c).

103. La. Civ. Code Ann. art. 229 cmt. (c).

104. La. Civ. Code Ann. art. 229 cmt. (c).

105. La. Civ. Code Ann. art. 229 cmt. (c). This distinction between administration and disposition in article 229 "more nearly reflects the classic distinction" between those terms (as contrasted with the regime of tutorship). La. Civ. Code Ann. art. 229 cmt. (c) (citing Katherine Shaw Spaht, Family Law in Louisiana, 714–15 (2000)).

106. La. Civ. Code Ann. art. 229 cmt. (c).

107. La. Civ. Code Ann. art. 229.

108. La. Civ. Code Ann. art. 229 cmt. (a).

109. La. Civ. Code Ann. art. 229 cmt. (c).

110. *See* Section 9:12.

111. La. Civ. Code Ann. art. 229.

112. La. Civ. Code Ann. art. 229 cmt. (b).

113. La. Civ. Code Ann. art. 229.

114. La. Civ. Code Ann. art. 229. *See also* La. Civ. Code Ann. art. 29 (noting that the age of majority is 18). Note, though, that after the regime of parental authority ends and tutorship begins, the child only has four years to assert the action. *See* La. Civ. Code Ann. art. 340.

ber, or lease the property of the child, compromise a claim of the child, or incur an obligation of the child for his education, support, and maintenance only with prior court approval, except as otherwise provided by law."[115] Note that further protections exist when a minor is to be paid funds as the result of a judgment or settlement.[116]

With that said, Louisiana law offers many exceptions to that general rule. For example, parents may perform the following, smaller dispositive acts without court approval:

(1) Alienate any movable property of the minor if the sum to be received does not exceed fifteen thousand dollars.

(2) Encumber any property of the minor as security for his obligation if the secured obligation does not exceed fifteen thousand dollars.

(3) Compromise a cause of action of the minor if the sum or value of the property to be paid or received does not exceed fifteen thousand dollars, excluding court costs, attorney fees, and other expenses.

(4) Make usual or customary donations of the corporeal, movable property of the minor, if the value of the minor's property transferred by the donation does not exceed one thousand dollars and the minor's property donated without court approval during parental authority does not exceed a total of fifteen thousand dollars.

(5) Obligate the minor if the obligation does not exceed fifteen thousand dollars.[117]

Additionally, a parent may expend the fruits of the child's property without prior judicial permission if those fruits are used for: (1) the shared benefit of the family (which consists of parents and children, excluding major children not living in the household);[118] (2) the expenses of the child's household (like electricity, water, rent);[119] or (3) the expenses of the child's property.[120] Significantly, under pre-revision law, the parents were granted a right of enjoyment, a form of usufruct over the property of the

115. La. Civ. Code Ann. art. 230. *See* La. Civ. Code Ann. art. 4501 for the procedural rules on how the parents obtain such approval. This approval procedure mirrors that required for tutors seeking to do the same. *See* Chapter 10.

116. *See* La. Code Civ. Proc. Ann. art. 4521 (allowing the court to order, as a general rule, any of the following or any combination thereof: (1) the funds be paid directly into the registry of the court for the minor's account, to be withdrawn only upon approval of the court and to be invested in certain ways as approved by the court; (2) the funds be invested directly in an interest-bearing investment approved by the court; (3) the funds be placed in trust in accordance with the Louisiana Trust Code to be administered by an individual or corporate trustee as determined by the court; (4) the funds be paid under a structured settlement agreement as approved by the court that provides for periodic payments and is underwritten by a financially responsible entity that assumes responsibility for future payments).

117. La. Stat. Ann. § 9:572.

118. La. Civ. Code Ann. art. 230 cmt. (c). The limitations of "shared benefit of the family" has yet to be explored in Louisiana jurisprudence, raising interesting questions of law. For example, could a parent expend the fruits of the child's property to pay for a family vacation or some other shared and beneficial experience?

119. La. Civ. Code Ann. art. 230 cmt. (c).

120. La. Civ. Code Ann. art. 230.

child.[121] This former right of enjoyment gave to the parents ownership of the fruits of the child's property and allowed them to expend those fruits in their sole discretion.[122] No longer do the parents hold this right of enjoyment, and they are allowed to expend the fruits of the child's property only for the purposes specifically enumerated.[123]

Any juridical act pursuant to which a parent violates the rules on disposition of the child's property is relatively null.[124] Note, however, that the child may not sue the parents during the regime's existence.[125] Consequently, many of the parental authority laws are, to some degree, aspirational.

§ 9:8 Parameters of Parental Authority— Obligations of Children

The legal regime of parental authority also sets forth the obligations that a child owes to their married parents. Recall, of course, that the parents may not sue the child for any breach.[126]

Per the 2015 revision, the first obligation that a child owes is assistance,[127] which, at a minimum, refers to the personal care of an ill or infirm parent.[128] This obligation of assistance also includes cooperating and participating in the daily tasks necessary for the efficient functioning of the family and other responsibilities consistent with the purposes and goals of family life; however, it does not include financial support.[129]

Second, the child is obligated to remain in the family residence; to permanently[130] leave requires the consent of both parents, except as otherwise provided by law.[131] While the rule may seem directed at runaways, it has historically applied in other contexts, as well. For example, in *Prieto v. St. Alphonsus Convent of Mercy*,[132] a 17-year-old girl left home without permission to join a convent to become a nun. The Louisiana

121. La. Civ. Code Ann. art. 230 cmt (d). Prior law provided: "Parents have during marriage the enjoyment of the property of their children until their majority or emancipation. This usufruct is nonalienable and exempt from seizure." La. Civ. Code art. 223 (1870).

122. La. Civ. Code Ann. art. 230 cmt (d).

123. La. Civ. Code Ann. art. 230 cmt (d).

124. La. Civ. Code Ann. art. 230 cmt. (a).

125. La. Stat. Ann. § 9:571(A)–(B). Per this statute, the same is true for tutors.

126. La. Stat. Ann. § 9:571(A)–(B). Per this statute, the same is true for tutors.

127. La. Civ. Code Ann. art. 227. This explicit obligation of assistance is new under the current regime of parental authority. La. Civ. Code Ann. art. 227 cmt. (a).

128. La. Civ. Code Ann. art. 227 cmt. (a). Without the ability to sue for specific performance, this obligation is aspirational.

129. La. Civ. Code Ann. art. 227 cmt. (a).

130. This obligation does not extend to a temporary absence. La. Civ. Code Ann. art. 227 cmt. (b).

131. La. Civ. Code Ann. art. 227. No reported Louisiana cases have discussed what constitutes "except as otherwise provided by law," a phrase that was added in the 2015 Revision to the parental authority articles.

132. Prieto v. St. Alphonsus Convent of Mercy, 27 So. 153 (La. 1900).

Supreme Court granted her mother's *habeus corpus* writ, and the girl was returned to her. The court explained:

> [D]uring his minority, unless sooner emancipated, [a child] is without capacity, under our Code, to leave the parental domicile permanently, and select for himself another domicile or residence. This is a fundamental principle that lies at the very foundation of society, and was intended to support and maintain the exercise of paternal authority in the family and the home, and to guard and protect the children of the family until their minds should become sufficiently cultivated, and their judgments sufficiently matured, to enable them to make judicious and proper selections of places of abode for themselves.[133]

Ultimately, then, this rule protects children from their own immaturity.

Third, a child is obligated to obey their parents in all matters not contrary to law or good morals.[134] This obligation of the child is foundational to the parents' corresponding right and obligation to correct and discipline the child in a reasonable manner.[135] The parental obligation of correction and discipline is deemed essential to comply with parental obligations of care, supervision, protection, and instruction.[136] Additionally, because "acculturation of children occurs principally within the family, the law recognizes the necessity of reasonable discipline by those who love the child to instill character, self-discipline, and virtue."[137]

Corporal punishment of children by their parents is allowed in Louisiana as long as it is reasonable.[138] In *Griffith v. Latiolais*, the Louisiana Supreme Court refused to recognize a provision in the trial court's order that prohibited both divorced parents from corporal punishment of the child, because the court deemed the provision unnecessary.[139] The court explained that while the mother had spanked the child with a wooden spoon on a few occasions, she no longer did so after being counseled to use time outs instead. The court did note, of course, that "if any party uses corporal punishment in an unreasonable manner, that issue will have to be addressed at that time."[140]

Determining what corporal punishment is "reasonable" has generated some litigation. Without a doubt, as one court noted, "[I]t is clear that the right of correction in a 'reasonable manner' does not include what are the grounds for a protective order under the [Domestic Abuse Assistance] Act—'domestic abuse' which is defined, in part, as 'physical ... abuse ... committed by one family member ... against another.'"[141] It seems that defining the parameters of "reasonable" is fact-specific. In *Leal v. Olivier*, a six-feet

133. Prieto, 27 So. at 169.
134. La. Civ. Code Ann. art. 228.
135. La. Civ. Code Ann. art. 228. *See also* La. Civ. Code Ann. art. 223.
136. La. Civ. Code Ann. art. 228 cmt. (b).
137. La. Civ. Code Ann. art. 228 cmt. (b).
138. *See, e.g.,* La. Civ. Code Ann. art. 228; La. Stat. Ann. § 14:18.
139. Griffith v. Latiolais, 10-CJ-0754 (La. 10/19/10), 48 So. 3d 1058.
140. Griffith, 48 So. 3d at 1072.
141. S.L.B. v. C.E.B., 2017 0978, p. 7 (La. App. 4 Cir. 07/27/18), 252 So. 3d 950, 957.

two-inch, 300-pound father hit his 104-pound nine-year-old daughter with a belt four times, which caused visible bruising and pain for at least 24 hours.[142] The appellate court found his discipline to be unreasonable but affirmed the trial court's decision to deny a protective order nonetheless, because he did not routinely use corporal punishment to discipline his daughter.[143] The court did, however, enjoin the father from using excessive corporal punishment to discipline his daughter going forward.[144]

In *Mason v. Hadnot*,[145] the unmarried mother of a preteen child prevented the father from exercising his court-awarded physical time because he had struck the child with a belt 10–15 times on her buttocks. The father sought to hold the mother in contempt as a result, but the court declined to do so, as it deemed the father's punishment unreasonable, fostering the child's fear of visiting her father. Similarly, in *S.L.B. v. C.E.B.*,[146] the court found that a mother who held down her 14-year-old son, slapped and hit him, and caused his bloody nose (in the presence of her other, 12-year-old son) was not exercising "reasonable corporal punishment" as permitted under Louisiana law. Instead, the mother's conduct constituted physical abuse per the Domestic Abuse Assistance Act.

§ 9:9 Suspension, Loss, and Termination of Parental Authority

In some instances, parental authority may be suspended or lost altogether, and in all instances, parental authority is limited in duration and eventually terminates.[147] Note, however, that even when parental authority is suspended or lost, some aspects of it may continue. For example, a parent allowed visitation with the child is allowed to discipline and correct the child and must also support, maintain, and educate the child.[148] These rights and obligations attach to parenthood generally, not just to parents enjoying parental authority.[149]

When a parent is deprived of parental authority over a child, the parent owes no legal responsibility for the child. In other words, "when the law... destroys or suspends the paternal authority over the minor, it, at the same time, destroys or suspends the paternal responsibility."[150] For example, in *Coats v. Roberts*, the child at issue killed

142. Leal v. Olivier, 20-181, p. 6 (La. App. 3 Cir. 11/4/20), 2020 WL 6479294, *6.

143. Leal, 2020 WL 6479294, at *6.

144. Leal, 2020 WL 6479294, at *6–7.

145. Mason v. Hadnot, 2008 CU 2015 (La. App. 1 Cir. 02/13/09), 6 So. 3d 256.

146. S.L.B., 252 So. 3d 950.

147. La. Civ. Code Ann. art. 221 cmt. (b).

148. La. Civ. Code Ann. art. 234 cmt. (d).

149. La. Civ. Code Ann. art. 234 cmt. (d).

150. Coats v. Roberts, 1883 WL 8275, at *2 (La. 1883). *See also* Toca v. Rojas, 93 So. 108, 111 (La. 1921); Simmons v. Sorenson, 71 So. 2d 377 (La. Ct. App. 1 Cir. 1954) (negating parental authority due to military service).

another during military service, and the victim's mother sued the child's father.[151] The Court found that because the father lacked parental authority during the child's military service, the father was not liable. It explained: "The law took the minor from the control and authority of the parent, and placed him under the exclusive control of its officer and in a situation which exposed him to the risk of committing the fault which happened. Why should the father be held responsible?"[152]

§ 9:10 Suspension, Loss, and Termination of Parental Authority— Suspension of Parental Authority

In some instances, parental authority is suspended. Typically, this happens when the state acts to protect a child, allowable because of its "superior right and interest in the statuses of all of its citizens."[153] However, the state may only interfere with parental authority under special laws[154] and cannot "usurp parental authority at its whim."[155] The special laws include when a guardian is appointed for the child pursuant to the Louisiana Children's Code or when a judgment is rendered by public law either removing the child from the parents' care or interfering with either or both parents' authority over the child.[156]

In Louisiana, the only children who have guardians are those who have been adjudged to be in need of care.[157] After this adjudication, the Department of Children and Family Services (DCFS), the child's parent(s), or the child's attorney may request that the court appoint a guardian.[158] Guardianship is intended to be a permanent placement and is employed when neither reunification with the parents nor adoption is in the child's best interest.[159] In such a case, the guardian must exercise the rights and responsibilities of legal custody and has certain authority over the child as detailed in the Children's

---

151. Coats, 1883 WL 8275, at *2.

152. Coats, 1883 WL 8725, at *2.

153. Wood v. Beard, 290 So. 2d 675, 678 (La. 1974) (J. Barham concurrence).

154. Griffith v. Roy, 269 So. 2d 217, 222 (La. 1972).

155. State in Interest of D.E.M., 441 So. 2d 514, 515 (La. Ct. App. 2 Cir. 1983).

156. La. Civ. Code Ann. art. 235 cmt. (b).

157. La. Department of Children & Family Services, https://www.dcfs.louisiana.gov/page/687#:~:text=The%20child%20must%20have%20been,for%20at%20least%206%20months (last visited May 17, 2024). For the grounds for adjudication of a child in need of care, see La. Child. Code Ann. art. 606.

158. La. Department of Children & Family Services, https://www.dcfs.louisiana.gov/page/687#:~:text=The%20child%20must%20have%20been,for%20at%20least%206%20months (last visited May 17, 2024). For the grounds that the movant must prove to have the court appoint a guardian, see La. Child. Code Ann. art. 722.

159. La. Child. Code Ann. art. 718; *see also* La. Child. Code Ann. art. 722.

Code.[160] The guardian is not vicariously liable for the damage caused by the child,[161] and the law of tutorship determines the administration of the child's property.[162]

The state may remove a child from the parents' care in several situations. For example, under the rules on Children in Need of Care, the court may remove a child when "continuation in the home would be contrary to the health, welfare, and safety of the child and the health, welfare, and safety of the child cannot, in the opinion of the court, be adequately secured without removal."[163] Similarly, under the rules for Families in Need of Services, the court may remove a child when "his welfare cannot, in the opinion of the court, be adequately safeguarded without such removal."[164] In each of these cases, parental authority of the parents is suspended while the child is in state custody but may be reinstituted if reunification is appropriate, or may be terminated if adoption is warranted.

§ 9:11 Suspension, Loss, and Termination of Parental Authority— Loss of Parental Authority

In three instances, parental authority is lost during the marriage.[165] The first instance occurs when custody is awarded to the other parent (1) when a rule to show cause is filed while the parents are living separate and apart; (2) after a petition for divorce is filed; or (3) during a proceeding for judicial separation if the parents are in a covenant marriage.[166] When any of these happen, only the parent with custody has parental authority because "[l]egal custody in one spouse cannot co-exist with the parental authority."[167] In *Emancipation of Dupuy*, the court awarded custody of the child to the mother and explained that "[b]y such judgment the father ... was divested of all parental authority over the [child]...."[168] In such scenarios, the custody award in one parent "legally disrupts the other's parental authority and transfers the liability of LSA-C.C. art. 2318 to the custodial parent."[169]

160. La. Child. Code Ann. art. 719(A) (guardian may consent to the child's marriage and enlistment in the armed forces of the United States and is allowed to make other decisions concerning the child, except the right to consent to the child's adoption).

161. La. Child. Code Ann. art. 719(B).

162. La. Child. Code Ann. art. 719(C).

163. La. Child. Code Ann. art. 682.

164. La. Child. Code Ann. art. 780.

165. Article 234 was enacted for the first time as part of the 2015 Revision. La. Civ. Code Ann. art. 234 cmt. (a).

166. La. Civ. Code Ann. art. 234 & cmt. (a).

167. DeVillier v. DeVillier, 543 So. 2d 1142, 1146 (La. Ct. App. 1 Cir. 1989).

168. Emancipation of Dupuy, 199 So. 384, 385 (La. 1940).

169. Wilde v. McMilleon, 513 So. 2d 551, 554 (La. Ct. App. 2 Cir. 1987).

Second, parental authority may be lost in a joint custody implementation order that modifies parental authority.[170] For example, the implementation order could designate a domiciliary parent. In such a case, because the domiciliary parent has authority to make decisions regarding the child, the concept of parental authority is inherently modified.[171] After all, the domiciliary parent has the authority to make all decisions affecting the child as a general rule.[172] Alternatively, the implementation order could specifically delineate each parent's individual authority over the child, and as long as the implementation order is detailed and provides for decision-making by one or both parents, the order modifies parental authority.[173] As to the specificity needed, one court explained that "an implementation order should at a minimum allocate the legal authority and responsibility for major decisions, such as medical care, elective surgery, dental or orthodontic care, and school and/or preschool choices."[174] For example, in *Coody v. Coody*, the appellate court affirmed the trial court's implementation order that granted the father the authority to make decisions regarding the children's health care, sports, band, and extracurricular activities; the mother retained parental authority as to other decisions.[175] Parental authority is lost by the parent who no longer has decision-making authority on those issues.

Third, parental authority is lost when a judgment awards custody of the child to a third person.[176] Courts are reluctant to interfere with a parent's right of custody,[177] but when they do, parental authority terminates. For example, in *Jackson v. Ratliff*, the court awarded custody of the child to the grandmother, upon which "the father's parental authority was taken away."[178] In such a case, the third person enjoys parental authority only if they are the child's ascendant.[179] For other adults, the rules of tutorship govern the relationship between the third person and the child.[180]

170. La. Civ. Code Ann. art. 234.
171. La. Civ. Code Ann. art. 234 cmt. (b).
172. La. Stat. Ann. § 9:335(B).
173. La. Civ. Code Ann. art. 234 cmt. (b).
174. Ehlingher v. Ehlingher, 17-1120 (La. App. 1 Cir. 5/29/18), 251 So. 3d 418, 426.
175. Coody v. Coody, 20-071 (La. App. 3 Cir. 11/12/20), 307 So. 3d 1093.
176. La. Civ. Code Ann. art. 234.
177. State ex rel. Lombardo v. Miller, 94 So. 2d 888, 889 (La. 1957).
178. Jackson v. Ratliff, 84 So. 2d 103 (La. App., Orleans 1955).
179. La. Civ. Code Ann. art. 234.
180. La. Civ. Code Ann. art. 234 cmt. (c).

§ 9:12 Suspension, Loss, and Termination of Parental Authority—Termination of Parental Authority

Parental authority ends when the child attains the age of majority (at 18 years of age),[181] is emancipated,[182] or when the parents' marriage terminates.[183] When the child's parents contract a covenant marriage, parental authority also terminates on the parents' judgment of separation from bed and board.[184] As explained in *Frazer v. Day*, because the father was living separate and apart from his wife and child under a judgment of separation, "the state had superseded" his parental authority.[185] Parental authority also seemingly terminates simultaneously with the termination or surrender of parental rights.[186] It certainly terminates once a child is adopted, and the married adoptive parents thereafter enjoy parental authority.[187]

At termination, the parents must deliver the child's property, and a court may also order the parents to account for their administration of the child's property.[188] In accounting, the parents "must explain what happened to the child's property that is no longer in their possession or under their control and for what purpose any proceeds were expended."[189] In *Lewis v. Lewis*, after attaining majority, a son sued his father to account for $10,000 in damages awarded to the father as administrator for the son while he was a minor.[190] The trial court granted the father's exception of no right of action. On appeal, however, the appellate court reversed, noting: "In the instant case, the [father] is the one who, under article 221, is responsible for an accounting of his minor son's property. The [son] is the former minor who is calling for the accounting. The plaintiff therefore falls within the class of individuals who have a remedy under article 221."[191]

---

181. La. Civ. Code Ann. art. 29.

182. *See* Chapter 11 for a detailed discussion of emancipation.

183. La. Civ. Code Ann. art. 235; *see also* La. Civ. Code Ann. art. 221 cmt. (b).

184. La. Civ. Code Ann. art. 235 cmt. (b).

185. Frazer v. Day, 307 So. 2d 733, 735 (La. 1975). Note, however, that a subsequent reconciliation of the parents reestablishes parental authority. *See, e.g.*, Dooley v. Dooley, 443 So. 2d 630, 631–32 (La. Ct. App. 3 Cir. 1983).

186. For the grounds for involuntary termination of parental rights, see La. Child. Code Ann. arts. 1015, 1015.1. The process for voluntary relinquishment of parental rights may be found in Louisiana Children's Code Articles 1101–1161.

187. M.P.W. v. L.P.W., 2013-0366 (La. App. 1 Cir. 11/1/13), 136 So. 3d 37 (providing that execution of a voluntary act of surrender of parental rights and the subsequent adoption of a child effectually terminates the parental rights and obligations of the surrendering parent, including the surrendering parent's obligation to support the child, and the adopting parent becomes the parent of the child for all purposes).

188. La. Civ. Code Ann. art. 231.

189. La. Civ. Code Ann. art. 231 cmt. (a).

190. Lewis v. Lewis, 469 So. 2d 269 (La. App. 1 Cir. 1985).

191. Lewis, 469 So. 2d at 270.

The child's right to assert an action to enforce the obligation of delivery has no prescriptive period, but the child's action to require the parents to account prescribes five years from the day the child attains the age of majority.[192]

§ 9:13 Delegation of Parental Authority

Clearly, the child's parents enjoy parental authority regime once they are married, as long as they remain married. However, the law also allows them to delegate all or some of their parental authority to others in some circumstances.[193] First, parents may delegate via a contract of mandate under which they grant provisional custody of the child to another natural person for a term of up to a year.[194] Second, parents may delegate if they, through a proceeding in juvenile court, voluntarily grant custody of the child to other responsible adults for the purpose of enabling the child to receive adequate care and treatment.[195] Third, parents may delegate if they expressly grant authority to a person (i.e., a relative, neighbor, or babysitter) with whom the parents place the child. Fourth, parents may delegate by circumstances under which it is customary for a parent to delegate part of their authority, such as when the child sleeps over at a friend's home.[196] Finally, parents implicitly delegate part of their authority to teachers and others for the purpose of educating the child simply by enrolling the child in school.[197] The rights held by the person to whom parental authority is delegated depend on the circumstances surrounding the delegation (whether full or partial). Note, though, that parents who delegate their authority are still liable for their child's offenses or quasi-offenses.[198]

---

192. La. Civ. Code Ann. art. 231 cmt. (c).

193. La. Civ. Code Ann. art. 233.

194. *See generally* La. Stat. Ann. §§ 9:951–954. Regardless of the term stipulated, the mandate of provisional custody terminates upon (1) revocation by a person having parental authority, (2) the mandatary's resignation or renunciation of the mandate, (3) the passage of 15 days after the death of a person with parental authority, or (4) the qualification of a court-appointed tutor or provisional tutor. La. Stat. Ann. § 9:952; *see also* Chapter 6, Section 6:14.

195. This avenue of delegation is governed by Title XV, Chapter 3 of the Children's Code, specifically articles 1510–1523. These articles serve to protect the health and welfare of children and to promote mutual understanding of the rights and responsibilities of the parents and custodians and of any terms or conditions which may be set forth by agreement of the parties. La. Child. Code Ann. art. 1510. They allow parents to petition, in writing, for a juvenile court to transfer custody of their child, La. Child. Code Ann. arts. 1514–1515, to another who executes an affidavit of acceptance of the custody of the child. La. Child. Code Ann. art. 1516.

196. La. Civ. Code Ann. art. 233 cmt. (a).

197. La. Civ. Code Ann. art. 233 & cmt. (b); *see also* La. Stat. Ann. § 17:223 (allowing teachers and principals to discipline minor children who are students at their schools).

198. La. Civ. Code Ann. art. 233 cmt. (c).

§ 9:14 Commentary on Current Parental Authority Regime

While the 2015 revisions to the regime of parental authority achieved the much-needed equality vis-à-vis a minor's married parents, one must question the continued viability of the dichotomy between parental authority and tutorship. This is especially true when a child's parents never married. As noted in Chapter 10 on Tutorship:

> [F]or single parents, does the responsibility to prepare an inventory and file a legal mortgage make sense? Does the parental responsibility for their child's person or property really change when a marriage ends or never even began? It seems unlikely that single parents mismanage their child's property at a greater rate than married parents, such that additional legal requirements are necessary. Is an equal protection challenge looming? Would an extension of parental authority outside of marriage provide fewer burdens to parents without sacrificing protection of the child?[199]

Louisiana would be well-served to take lessons from its civil law counterparts abroad.[200] Some of those jurisdictions have modernized the regime of parental authority by extending it to all parents.[201] In other words, parental authority is enjoyed solely due to parentage, regardless of the parents' marital status.[202] Thus, if the parents never marry or if their marriage terminates, they still enjoy parental authority,[203] which ends instead upon child's majority, marriage, or emancipation.[204] In those jurisdictions,

---

199. *See* Chapter 10, Section 10:30.

200. *See* Chapter 10, Section 10:30.

201. Prof. Frédérique Ferrand, National Report: France, Parental Responsibilities, Commission on European Family Law, https://ceflonline.net/wp-content/uploads/France-Parental-Responsibilities.pdf; Cristina González Beilfuss, National Report: Spain, Parental Responsibilities, Commission on European Family Law, https://ceflonline.net/wp-content/uploads/Spain-Parental-Responsibilities.pdf; Prof. Dr. Nina Dethloff & Prof. Dr. Dieter Martiny, National Report: Germany, Parental Responsibilities, Commission on European Family Law, https://ceflonline.net/wp-content/uploads/Germany-Parental-Responsibilities.pdf (the term parental custody is used in the place of parental authority); Achilles G. Koutsouradis, National Report: Greece, Parental Responsibilities, Commission on European Family Law, https://ceflonline.net/wp-content/uploads/Greece-Parental-Responsibilities.pdf; *but see* Civil Code of Québec, C.C.Q. 1991, c. 64 arts. 597 *et seq.*, 192 *et seq.* (Can.) (parents enjoy parental authority over the care of the minor and are also legal tutors for the purpose of administering the minor's patrimony).

202. Prof. Frédérique Ferrand, National Report: France, Parental Responsibilities, Commission on European Family Law, https://ceflonline.net/wp-content/uploads/France-Parental-Responsibilities.pdf.

203. Prof. Frédérique Ferrand, National Report: France, Parental Responsibilities, Commission on European Family Law 1–4, 11–12, https://ceflonline.net/wp-content/uploads/France-Parental-Responsibilities.pdf; *see also* Bürgerliches Gesetzbuch [BGB] [Civil Code], § 1680, https://www.gesetze-im-internet.de/englisch_bgb/englisch_bgb.html#p6318 (Ger.) (parental custody continues in the surviving parent after the death of one parent).

204. Bürgerliches Gesetzbuch [BGB] [Civil Code], § 1680, https://www.gesetze-im-internet.de/englisch_bgb/englisch_bgb.html#p6318 (Ger.) (parental custody continues in the surviving parent after the death of one parent).

tutorship applies only when a third person is involved.[205] This might happen when both parents are deprived of parental authority over the child due to their deaths, interdiction, or loss of custody.[206]

The modern approach from the aforementioned foreign civil law jurisdictions treats all parents uniformly, and it eliminates the unnecessary change in regime on a parent's death or the parents' divorce.[207] This seems preferable to Louisiana's current regime which shifts from parental authority to tutorship on certain events. In some such scenarios, parents are forced to access the judicial system and are subject to additional burdens, like taking oaths, preparing inventories, and inscribing legal mortgages, that their married counterparts do not endure. Such disparate treatment does not make sense, particularly for widowed or single parents. Even for divorced parents: "While divorced parents may not enjoy a cooperative relationship when acting as administrators, their rights as parents could still be constitutionally protected and procedural safeguards could be put in place to address administrative issues when they disagree."[208]

§ 9:15 Alimentary Obligations

Some obligations between parents and their child continue beyond the termination of parental authority, the child's emancipation, and the child's attaining the age of majority. Per article 236, all children, no matter their age, owe honor and respect to their parents.[209] While this article also implies that the parents will conduct themselves toward their children in such way as to merit honor and respect, the first duty is on the child.[210] Of course, there is no direct sanction for a child's breach of this obligation, but it is "hortatory and instructive as to the conduct of a good child of any age."[211]

205. Code civil [C. civ.] [Civil Code] arts. 373-5, 390 (Fr.); David Gruning, Alain A. Levasseur, John Randy Trahan, Estelle Roy. Traduction du Code civil français en anglais version bilingue. 2015, ffhalshs-01385107f https://shs.hal.science/halshs-01385107/document; Bürgerliches Gesetzbuch [BGB] [Civil Code], § 1773 *et seq.*, https://www.gesetze-im-internet.de/englisch_bgb/englisch_bgb.html#p6318 (Ger.) (the term guardianship is used); Código Civil [C.C.] [Civil Code] arts. 222 *et seq.*, (Spain) (2016), https://www.mjusticia.gob.es/es/AreaTematica/DocumentacionPublicaciones/Documents/Spanish_Civil_Code_(Codigo_Civil_Espanol).PDF (the term guardianship is used); Astikos Kodikas [A.K.] [Civil Code] 11:1589 *et seq.*, (Greece) https://ceflonline.net/wp-content/uploads/Greece-Parental-Responsibilities-Legislation.pdf (the term guardianship is used).

206. *Id.*

207. Note that the Quebec Civil Code has retained a distinction between parental authority and legal tutorship, both of which are imposed on the parents of the minor. However, the role of a legal tutor is to manage the child's patrimony. Civil Code of Québec, C.C.Q. 1991, c. 64 art. 192 (Can.), https://www.legisquebec.gouv.qc.ca/en/document/cs/CCQ-1991?langCont=en#ga:l_two-gb:l_four-h1.

208. *See* Chapter 10, Section 10:30.

209. La. Civ. Code Ann. art. 236 & cmt.

210. Landry v. Himel, 176 So. 627 (La. App. 1 Cir. 1937).

211. La. Civ. Code Ann. art. 236 cmt.

Additionally, certain family members owe to one another a lifetime[212] reciprocal alimentary obligation—the duty to financially support one another when in need.[213] This alimentary obligation is distinct from the parental obligation of support and should not be confused.[214] Parental support is required as a fact of paternity or maternity,[215] and parents bear the first and principal obligation of supporting, maintaining, and educating their children.[216] The alimentary obligation, "a less onerous burden,"[217] is not an extension of parental support,[218] as it is "not nearly as broad."[219]

§ 9:16 Alimentary Obligations— History of Alimentary Obligations

The French *Code civil* included the reciprocal duty of maintenance for necessities between ascendants and descendants.[220] Per one Louisiana judge, the circumstances of relationships at the time of codification drove the alimentary obligation. As he explained:

> At that point in time when [the alimentary obligation] was placed in the Code Napoleon there was surely a great deal more collegiality and familiarity between grandparents and grandchildren than there is today, just as family ties in general were stronger with much more intimate relationships existing among children, parents and grandparents. The latter's obligation to provide some support was counter-balanced by some recognition of their authority, some respect for their opinions and some inclination to heed their advice.[221]

Under French law, any award had to be in proportion to the claimant's needs and the obligor's means,[222] but if the parties' circumstances changed, the award could be

---

212. La. Civ Code Ann. art. 237 cmt. (a). This obligation does not terminate upon reaching majority or upon emancipation. *See, e.g.*, Tolley v. Karcher, 200 So. 4, 6 (La. 1941) ("We find no language in Article 229 which limits to minor children the support which ascendants are obliged to give to needy descendants. To so hold would be nothing short of judicial legislation.").

213. Katherine Connell-Thouez, *The Family in Contemporary Civil Law—Comparative Developments in Alimentary Obligations and Parental Authority: Linking Traditional Rights and Responsibilities to Create an Integrated Structure for Solving the Child Care Dilemma*, 60 Tul. L. Rev. 1135, 1136 (1986).

214. Levy v. Levy, 536 So. 2d 742, 743–44 (La. Ct. App. 3 Cir. 1988).

215. Levy, 536 So. 2d at 744. *See also* Tobin v. Tobin, 323 So. 2d 896 (La. Ct. App. 2 Cir. 1975); Robert C. Lowe, 1 La. Prac. Divorce § 8:3 (citing Demarie v. Demarie, 295 So. 2d 229 (La. Ct. App. 3d Cir. 1974)).

216. Landeche v. Airhart, 372 So. 2d 598, 599–600 (La. App. 4 Cir. 1979).

217. Suire v. Miller, 363 So. 2d 945, 949 (La. App. 3 Cir. 1978).

218. Levy, 536 So. 2d at 744. *See also* Tobin, 323 So. 2d 896; Robert C. Lowe, 1 La. Prac. Divorce § 8:3 (2024) (citing Demarie v. Demarie, 295 So. 2d 229 (La. Ct. App. 3d Cir. 1974)).

219. In re Tutorship of Blanque, 97-249 (La. App. 5 Cir. 09/30/97), 700 So. 2d 1077, 1080.

220. Code civil [C. civ.] [Civil Code] art. 205 (1804) (Fr.) ("Children owe a maintenance to their fathers and mothers, and other ancestors who are in want thereof."); Code civil [C. civ.] [Civil Code] art. 207 (1804) (Fr.) ("The obligations resulting from these regulations are reciprocal."). This duty was even imposed on sons and daughters-in-law. Code civil [C. civ.] [Civil Code] art. 206 (1804) (Fr.).

221. Landeche v. Airhart, 372 So. 2d 598, 599–600 (La. App. 4 Cir. 1979).

222. Code civil [C. civ.] [Civil Code] art. 208 (1804) (Fr.).

modified.[223] In the event that an obligor showed that he was unable to pay, the court could order the obligor to take the claimant into their home and "nourish and maintain" them.[224]

§ 9:17 Alimentary Obligations— History of Alimentary Obligations— Early Louisiana Law

Early Louisiana law was derived from the French *Code civil*, and the alimentary obligation did not see many major changes over the years.

Louisiana Digest of 1808

The Louisiana Digest of 1808 distinguished between the alimentary rights and obligations of legitimate children and those of illegitimate children. Legitimate children were bound to maintain their parents and other ascendants in need, and the ascendants had a reciprocal obligation to their needy descendants.[225] These obligations only extended to the needy relative's "nourishment, lodging and clothing,"[226] and the amount was determined by comparing the needs of the claimant-relative to the circumstances of the payor.[227] If the payor proved an inability to pay, the judge had the discretion to order the payor to take the claimant into their home and "nourish and maintain" them.[228] Alimentary awards could be terminated or modified if the claimant no longer had need, the payor no longer could pay, or either party's circumstances had materially changed.[229] Finally, the alimentary obligation did not terminate on death; instead, ascendants and descendants were reciprocally required to leave a portion of their estate to one another.[230]

The 1808 Digest rules on alimentary obligations differed for illegitimate children. The digest clearly noted that illegitimate children "belong[ed] to no family, and ha[d] no relations,"[231] but recognized "[n]evertheless nature and humanity establish certain reciprocal duties between fathers and mothers and their natural children."[232] While the digest clearly provided a reciprocal obligation of alimony between parents and their

---

223. Code civil [C. civ.] [Civil Code] art. 209 (1804) (Fr.).

224. Code civil [C. civ.] [Civil Code] art. 210 (1804) (Fr.). If the parents choose to receive their child in their home in lieu of paying the alimentary obligation, the judge shall dispense them from the obligation of paying for it elsewhere. Code civil [C. civ.] [Civil Code] art. 211 (1804) (Fr.).

225. La. Civ. Code art. 48 (1808).

226. La. Civ. Code art. 49 (1808).

227. La. Civ. Code art. 50 (1808).

228. La. Civ. Code art. 52 (1808). If a parent chooses to receive their child in their home in lieu of paying the alimentary obligation, the judge shall dispense them from the obligation of paying for it elsewhere. La. Civ. Code art. 53 (1808).

229. La. Civ. Code art. 51 (1808).

230. La. Civ. Code art. 54 (1808).

231. La. Civ. Code art. 59 (1808).

232. La. Civ. Code art. 60 (1808).

natural children when either was in need,[233] the child had to meet certain criteria to pursue a claim for it.[234] First, the child had to have been (a) legally acknowledged by both parents or the parent from whom they claimed alimony; or (b) declared to be their natural children by a judgment duly pronounced.[235] Second, the child had to prove "absolute[] need of said alimony for their support."[236] Beyond special rules to assert the claim in the first place, the amount awarded could "never exceed what is absolutely necessary for their nourishment, lodging and clothing."[237] Additionally, the alimentary obligation terminated when the child could provide for himself by labor or when either parent had "caused him to be learnt an art, trade or profession fit to procure him a sufficient livelihood, unless some continual sickness or infirmity prevents such child from working for his subsistence."[238] Likewise, the child could not assert the claim against the parents' heirs if either parent had provided "during life, for a sufficient maintenance" for the child or had made donations or other advantages to the child that would suffice for that purpose.[239] Aside from these distinctions, the rules applicable to legitimate children applied to natural children, as well.[240]

Louisiana Civil Code of 1825

The Louisiana Civil Code of 1825 instituted only a few changes to the alimentary obligation laws but still differentiated between legitimate and illegitimate children.

As to legitimate children, in addition to the general pronouncement of the alimentary obligation, the 1825 Code explicitly specified that those subject to it "are also bound to render reciprocally all the services which their situation can require, if they should become insane."[241] Second, the 1825 Code inserted into the definition of "alimony"—in addition to nourishment, lodging, and clothing—education for minor children.[242]

As to illegitimate children, the 1825 Code provided that the strict restriction on the amount owed now applied only to children of color, who were limited to "what is absolutely necessary to ensure them their board and lodging, and to unable [*sic*] them to learn to read and write, and a trade."[243] Finally, the Code of 1825 explicitly extended the alimentary obligation to all illegitimate children, specifically including those conceived in adulterous or incestuous unions, whose claim was against their mother and her ascendants.[244]

233. La. Civ. Code art. 61 (1808). Children enjoying this right could even enforce it, after their parent's death, against their parent's heirs. La. Civ. Code art. 62 (1808).

234. La. Civ. Code art. 63 (1808).

235. La. Civ. Code art. 63 (1808).

236. La. Civ. Code art. 63 (1808).

237. La. Civ. Code art. 64 (1808).

238. La. Civ. Code art. 65 (1808).

239. La. Civ. Code art. 65 (1808).

240. La. Civ. Code art. 66 (1808).

241. La. Civ. Code art. 245 (1825).

242. La. Civ. Code art. 246 (1825).

243. La. Civ. Code art. 259 (1825).

244. La. Civ. Code art. 262 (1825).

Louisiana Civil Code of 1870

The Louisiana Civil Code of 1870 made no changes to the alimentary obligation

§ 9:18 Alimentary Obligations— History of Alimentary Obligations— Revisions to Louisiana Law

Louisiana's laws on the alimentary obligation saw very few changes between the Code of 1870 and the comprehensive revision in 2015.

Pre-Revision Changes

One such change was that the duty to supply life's basic necessities applied in all instances, regardless of a child's status as legitimate or illegitimate.[245] Additionally, to assert a claim, the claimant was required to prove that he could not obtain those necessities "by other means or from other sources."[246] Finally, the law extended the definition of "alimony" to provide education for persons of the age of majority if (1) they were a full-time student in good standing in a secondary school, had not attained the age of 19, and were dependent on either parent, or (2) they had not attained the age of 22 and had a developmental disability.[247] For illegitimate children, the Legislature repealed the Code article directed at children of adulterous or incestuous unions.

By 1979, at least one Louisiana judge expressed reservations about the alimentary obligation, calling it "anachronistic."[248] He explained that because attitudes pertaining to and relationships with remote ascendants have changed considerably, "it seems anomalous to saddle" them with responsibility for their descendants "in an age when the family as an institution is threatened and the notion of the grandfather as the family patriarch has been rejected."[249] As a result, he suggested applying the alimentary obligation "sparingly and only where the [descendant is] in dire need and parental responsibility has been exhausted."[250]

LSLI Comprehensive Revision

As part of the parental authority revision, the legislature amended the alimentary obligation articles, effective 2016. While the pre-revision scheme included over a dozen code articles, the revised articles are fewer. As will be discussed in greater detail, some of the changes were significant. For example, under current law, the alimentary

245. La. Civ. Code Ann. art. 229 (2015). Under this article, basic necessities included food, clothing, shelter, and health care. La. Civ. Code Ann. art. 229 (2015).

246. La. Civ. Code Ann. art. 229 (2015).

247. La. Civ. Code Ann. art. 230 (2015). These changes tracked the rules governing child support. *See* Chapter 7, Sections 7:61-7:62.

248. Landeche v. Airhart, 372 So. 2d 598, 601 (La. Ct. App. 4 Cir. 1979) (J. Schott concurrence).

249. Landeche, 372 So. 2d at 601.

250. Landeche, 372 So. 2d at 601.

obligation is strictly personal.[251] Additionally, the current law sets forth a ranking of those who owe the obligation and explicitly details the type of liability among multiple obligors.[252] It also removes the alternative of receiving a claimant into the home to satisfy the obligation and removes education of a minor from the definition of "alimony." Finally, a striking change was the repeal of all articles directed at "illegitimate" children, unifying the rules on the alimentary obligation, without any reference to a child's filial status.

§ 9:19 Alimentary Obligations— Parameters of Alimentary Obligation

Under the current version of the alimentary obligation, all relatives in the direct line (i.e., ascendants and descendants)[253] owe to each other the obligation to provide for the basic necessities of life, including food, clothing, shelter, and health care, for the duration of their lives.[254]

Clearly, the claimant-relative must be in need. For example, in *Rhodes v. Rhodes*, the court ordered the paternal grandparents to pay $100 per month for the grandchildren in necessitous circumstances.[255] Their father was totally disabled, and their mother was on sick leave from her job. One child required medical and rehabilitative assistance, and the others had typical needs. The nourishment, lodging, and support required for the children exceeded the amounts available to them from their parents. By contrast, in *Banquer v. Banquer*, the court denied a mother's claim against her children's paternal grandparents because the children were not in need.[256] The children had never been without the basic necessities of life because the mother had some income and also obtained food stamps, and her parents willingly gave additional financial support. In fact, the children enjoyed attendance at private schools and dance lessons and also other "extras."[257] The *Banquer* court stated that the alimentary obligation "should be used sparingly and as a last resort."[258]

---

251. La. Civ. Code Ann. art. 237.

252. La. Civ. Code Ann. art. 237.

253. La. Civ. Code Ann. art. 901.

254. La. Civ. Code Ann. art. 237 & cmt. (a).

255. Rhodes v. Rhodes, 305 So. 2d 673, 674–76 (La. Ct. App. 2 Cir. 1974). *See also* Jefferson v. Jefferson, 163 So. 2d 74 (La. 1964) (child of 16-year-old unemployed mother, who had no income and lived with her own parents, was in need); Butts on behalf of Walker v. Butts, 428 So. 2d 1165 (La. Ct. App. 5 Cir. 1983) (30-year-old paraplegic entitled to alimentary support from father as well as insurance coverage under his policy).

256. Banquer v. Banquer, 554 So. 2d 790 (La. Ct. App. 5 Cir. 1989).

257. Banquer, 554 So. 2d at 792.

258. Banquer, 554 So. 2d at 793. *See also* Landeche v. Airhart, 372 So. 2d 598 (La. Ct. App. 4 Cir. 1979) (children were not in need because mother was receiving alimony and child support from husband, together with sole and full use of family home and its contents, and mother's medical condition was not serious enough to prevent her from seeking gainful employment).

The alimentary obligation exists regardless of any alleged misconduct by the claimant toward the obligor. For example, in *Tolley v. Karcher*, the claimant's mother attempted to negate her alimentary obligation to her daughter by highlighting the claimant's choice to marry as a minor without the mother's permission.[259] The court rejected the mother's argument, stating: "The mere fact then that plaintiff married, while a minor, without the consent of her mother, is no legal ground for the refusal of her mother to pay her alimony."[260]

Read narrowly, the alimentary obligation includes only the duty to provide for basic necessities; it generally does not include education or other special expenses of rearing a child.[261] For example, in *Phillips v. Phillips*, the court denied a healthy and capable 22-year-old daughter's claim for alimentary support against her father.[262] While the daughter averred that she could not support herself because she could not work full-time due to her college attendance, the court determined that "it is clear that the plaintiff is fully capable of supporting herself within the contemplation of the law."[263] Thus, the court stated, "[S]he is not 'in need'" within meaning of the article and had no right to support from her father.[264] However, in *In re Tutorship of Blanque*, the court awarded support to a severely disabled daughter under a more liberal reading of the law.[265] Her father had argued that the Code articles allowed her only the "most limited form of shelter, clothing, food and health care and not one single thing more."[266] The court disagreed, noting that every case turns on its own facts and that under the ones presented, the claimant needed more. It explained:

> [The claimant] is severely disabled. Thus, where the term clothing might mean just the articles themselves in another case, in this case she must additionally be provided the assistance to dress. While shelter in another case might mean simply a protected environment from the outdoors, in [the claimant's] case the "shelter" or home in which she resides must be specially designed to fit her special orthopedic needs. Health care, as applied to this case because of [the claimant's] mental disability must include activities that might not be included for a less disabled adult. We find the same to be true in all aspects of the [claimant's] day to day activities. [The claimant's] needs or necessities are far different

259. Tolley v. Karcher, 200 So. 4 (La. 1941).

260. Tolley, 200 So. at 7. *See also* Borden v. Borden, 550 So. 2d 901, 903 (La. Ct. App. 2 Cir. 1989) (refusing to terminate child support of a minor based on son's physical and verbal abuse of father and explaining that "[e]ven under the reciprocal support duty [between adult children and parents], conduct of an adult child that might constitute grounds for disinherison ... has been held not to excuse the parent's obligation to support her needy adult child").

261. Suire v. Miller, 363 So. 2d 945 (La. Ct. App. 3 Cir. 1978).

262. Phillips v. Phillips, 339 So. 2d 1299 (La. Ct. App. 1 Cir. 1976).

263. Phillips, 339 So. 2d at 1301.

264. Phillips, 339 So. 2d at 1300–01.

265. In re Blanque, 97-249 (La. App. 5 Cir. 09/30/97), 700 So. 2d 1077.

266. In re Blanque, 700 So. 2d at 1080.

> from and greater than those of a less disabled person. [She] requires and deserves more time and expense.[267]

A claimant seeking to enforce this obligation must prove inability to obtain these necessities from other means or sources.[268] For instance, in *Levy v. Levy*,[269] a woman, whose estranged husband only sporadically paid child support, sued his parents, seeking to enforce their alimentary obligation to her children. The court denied the claim, stating: "The burden of caring for a child's basic needs is fundamentally a parental responsibility."[270] It went on to explain that the burden only shifts to the grandparents if the parents are unable to provide the children's basic necessities. Here, the father was not unable to provide but was simply unwilling to satisfy his child support obligation. The mother was underemployed and thus, had not exhausted her own means of providing for the children. Under such circumstances, the grandparents did not owe an alimentary obligation to the grandchildren; such an obligation is not an extension of support. Note, too, that the alimentary obligation of direct relatives is secondary to any duty of support owed to the claimant by their spouse.[271]

If owed, the relatives' liability is determined based on the order of their degree of relationship to the claimant (with those more closely related being the ones obligated), and it is joint and divisible among the obligors.[272] This obligation is strictly personal, and thus, it may not be enforced by a third person,[273] nor may it be owed by a third person. For example, in *In re Succession of Elie*,[274] the court held that the decedent-son's succession had no obligation to support his mother after his death.

The amount owed is determined in accordance with the needs of the claimant and the means of the obligor,[275] and the obligated relative need not fully deplete his assets in order to do so. For example, in *Elchinger v. Elchinger*, the court held that the alimentary obligation does not require that one dispose of property that is the only source of revenue and cause virtual bankruptcy.[276] Once an award is rendered, it may be modified

267. In re Blanque, 700 So. 2d. at 1081.

268. La. Civ. Code Ann. art. 237. "Other means" could include capital resources or earning capacity, for example. La. Civ. Code Ann. art. 237 cmt. (c). "Other sources" could include public assistance. La. Civ. Code Ann. art. 237 cmt. (c).

269. Levy v. Levy, 536 So. 2d 742 (La. Ct. App. 3 Cir. 1988). *See also* Russell v. Culpepper, 344 So. 2d 1372 (La. 1977) (finding widow not in need because she benefitted from a railroad pension and also had a usufruct of an 815-acre plot that generated funds from mineral rights and leases, crops, timber, lumber, farming, raising livestock, and rented houses).

270. Levy, 536 So. 2d at 745.

271. La. Civ. Code Ann. art. 237.

272. La. Civ. Code Ann. art. 237; *see also* La. Civ. Code Ann. arts. 1788 (joint obligations), 1815–1817 (divisible obligations), 1789 (interplay of joint and divisible obligations).

273. La. Civ. Code Ann. art. 237 & cmt. (f).

274. Succession of Elie, 10-525 (La. App. 3 Cir. 11/03/10), 50 So. 3d 262.

275. La. Civ. Code Ann. art. 238.

276. Elchinger v. Elchinger, 135 So. 2d 347 (La. Ct. App. 4 Cir. 1961).

upon a material change of circumstances of either party and shall be terminated if it becomes unnecessary.[277]

A relative who has fulfilled the alimentary obligation may have a claim for at least partial reimbursement against others who also owe the alimentary obligation. For example, in *Succession of Glaudi*, the court stated that the children who provided services to their needy parent may assert a claim against their siblings for contribution (to the extent of their virile shares). Also, if the parent dies solvent, the claim may be satisfied by an action against the siblings' share in the parent's succession.[278]

---

277. La. Civ. Code Ann. art. 239.

278. Succession of Glaudi, 469 So. 2d 1127 (La. Ct. App. 4 Cir. 1985).

Chapter 10

Tutorship*

* This chapter was derived from the following article: Monica Hof Wallace, *A Primer on Tutorship in Louisiana*, 70 Loy. L. Rev. 291 (2024). The authors wish to thank the Loyola Law Review for its assistance on the initial work for this chapter.

§ 10:1 Introduction

The regime of tutorship mirrors the regime of parental authority in several ways. Because laws must ensure the protection of minors, minors whose parents are married are subject to parental authority,[1] and minors whose parents are unmarried are subject to tutorship.[2] In other words, parents exercise parental authority during their marriage, but at its termination (usually by death or divorce),[3] tutorship begins. In addition, tutorship applies to a minor whose parents were never married.[4]

Article 246 of the Louisiana Civil Code provides that an unemancipated minor is placed under tutorship "after the dissolution of the marriage of his father and mother or the separation from bed and board of either one of them from the other."[5] Outside of a covenant marriage, Louisiana no longer provides married couples with the option of a legal separation, formerly known as a "separation from bed and board."[6] However, a legal separation from another jurisdiction could give rise to the need for tutorship of a minor in Louisiana.[7]

Louisiana recognizes four different types of tutorship: (1) by nature (natural tutorship), (2) by will, (3) by the effect of law (legal tutorship), and (4) by the appointment of the judge (dative tutorship).[8] Tutorship by nature, the most common, takes place as of right, so that the tutor need not be appointed or confirmed in order to serve.[9] Natural tutorship simply begins; court approval is unneeded unless the tutor performs certain actions that the law has deemed deserving of additional oversight.[10] For all of the other tutorships, the tutor must be appointed or confirmed by a court before acting as tutor, and court approval is generally necessary to protect the minor.[11]

1. *See* La. Civ. Code Ann. arts. 221–239.
2. *See* La. Civ. Code Ann. arts. 246–362.
3. *See* La. Civ. Code Ann. art. 101.
4. *See* La. Civ. Code Ann. arts. 256, 261.
5. La. Civ. Code Ann. art. 246.
6. La. Civ. Code art. 138 (1870), *repealed by* Act No. 1009, 1990 La. Acts 2510 cmt. (b).
7. *See* La. Civ. Code Ann. art. 246 editor's note.
8. La. Civ. Code Ann. art. 247.
9. La. Civ. Code Ann. art. 248.
10. *See* La. Civ. Code Ann. arts. 248, 250.
11. La. Civ. Code Ann. art. 248.

Tutorship includes both the care of the person of the minor and the administration of the minor's property,[12] which creates an overlap with the law of custody.[13] Although tutorship over the minor's property can be bifurcated from tutorship over the minor's person,[14] tutorship over the minor's person can never be bifurcated from custody of the minor,[15] creating a possible conflict in the laws of custody and tutorship. For this and other reasons expressed below, the laws of tutorship are in need of revision.

§ 10:2 History

European Law, specifically Roman, Spanish, and French law, heavily influenced the Louisiana law of tutorship, just as it did many other Civil Code concepts.[16] Be it the Spanish acquisition in the latter half of the eighteenth century or the retrocession of the Louisiana territory to France in the early nineteenth century, the laws that prevailed during the Louisiana Purchase in 1803 resulted in the first Digest of Laws enacted in 1808.[17] The effect of the Spanish regime on the modelled Code Napoleon paved the way for the movement from paternal authority over children (an inherently Spanish concept) toward a parental approach, attributed in part to the rise of women in society that occurred during the French Revolution.[18] The first Digest of 1808 contained articles derived from French codified law or other French sources, amounting to arguably 85% of the whole, and the remaining 15% were derived from Spanish sources.[19] These influences shaped the development of tutorship in Louisiana.

---

12. La. Code Civ. Proc. Ann. arts. 4261–62.

13. *See* La. Civ. Code Ann. art. 131.

14. *See* La. Civ. Code Ann. art. 258.

15. *See* La. Civ. Code Ann. art. 258.

16. *See generally* Asya Ostroukh, *The Mystery of the Mixité Around the Title of the Louisiana Digest of the Civil Laws of 1808*, 62 Loy. L. Rev. 725 (2016); Vernon Valentine Palmer, *The French Connection and the Spanish Perception: Historical Debates and Contemporary Evaluation of French Influence on Louisiana Civil Law*, 63 La. L. Rev. 1067 (2003); J.R. Trahan, *The Continuing Influence of le Droit Civil and el Derecho Civil in the Private Law of Louisiana*, 63 La. L. Rev. 1019, 1036–37 (2003); Raphael J. Rabalais, *The Influence of Spanish Laws and Treatises on the Jurisprudence of Louisiana: 1762–1828*, 42 La. L. Rev. 1485 (1982); Rodolfo Batiza, *The Louisiana Civil Code of 1808: Its Actual Sources and Present Relevance*, 46 Tul. L. Rev. 4 (1971); Robert A. Pascal, *Sources of the Digest of 1808: A Reply to Professor Batiza*, 46 Tul. L. Rev. 603 (1971). Much has been written about the development of Louisiana law.

17. A.N. Yiannopoulos, The Civil Codes of Louisiana 4–5 (2000).

18. On the position of women in society, see 15 Encyclopaedia of the Social Sciences 439–51 (Edwin R.A. Seligman et al. eds., 1935).

19. A.N. Yiannopoulos, *Requiem for a Civil Code: A Commemorative Essay*, 78 Tul. L. Rev. 379, 387 (2003).

§ 10:3 History—Spanish Influence

Spanish law, which derived its roots of paternal authority from Roman law, impacted the foundational concept of tutorship in Louisiana.[20] *Las Siete Partidas*, the medieval code of Spain in 1505, was composed of seven parts or "partidas."[21] Title XVI of the sixth *Partida* contained the rules governing the guardianship of minors. It began by referencing the Latin root "tutela," which it defined as "the guardianship which is given and conferred over minors of free condition who are under 14 years of age when they are males and under 12 years, when they are females, as being incapable and not knowing how to defend themselves."[22] Minors were "of free condition" only in the absence of a father's authority; "the [absence] of the mother had no effect on the status of the child."[23] Tutorship[24] began when the child no longer enjoyed paternal authority and continued until the minor reached the age of puberty; after puberty and until the age of majority, the minor was subject to a less stringent regime of curatorship.[25] Louisiana abandoned the two-tiered approach to tutorship in 1830 when the legislature repealed curatorship and extended tutorship until the minor attained the age of majority.[26]

Under the *Partidas*, paternal authority continued with the appointment of the tutor, who had to be at least 25 years old and male.[27] One exception existed: a mother or grandmother of the child could become tutrix if she promised not to marry and she

---

20. Harry R. Sachse, *The Evolution of the Regime of Tutorship in Louisiana*, 16 La. L. Rev. 412, 412–413 (1956).

21. The Law of Las Siete Partidas: Which Are Still in Force in the State of Louisiana (L. Moreau Lislet & Henry Carleton trans., 1820). The quotations of the *Partidas* in this chapter are from the official Moreau Lislet & Carleton translation of 1820 and the more recent translation by Samuel Parsons Scott in 2001. For the more recent translation by Samuel Parsons Scott, see Las Siete Partidas, Volume 5: Underworlds (Robert I. Burns ed., Samuel Parsons Scott trans. 2001).

22. The Law of Las Siete Partidas: Which Are Still in Force in the State of Louisiana 6.16 (L. Moreau Lislet & Henry Carleton trans., 1820). As a civil law author aptly described:

> *Las Siete Partidas*, written in 1256, and promulgated as law in 1343, became the basic law of Spain in 1505. In varying degrees, the *Partidas* was the law of Louisiana from the Spanish acquisition in 1769 to the second quarter of the nineteenth century. In 1820 it was still considered in effect in Louisiana despite the Digest of 1808, and for that reason the Legislature commissioned its translation. The origin of many of the present articles of the Civil Code and the Code of Practice lies in the Partidas.

Harry R. Sachse, *The Evolution of the Regime of Tutorship in Louisiana*, 16 La. L. Rev. 412 n.2 (1956).

23. Harry R. Sachse, *The Evolution of the Regime of Tutorship in Louisiana*, 16 La. L. Rev. 412 (1956).

24. In the *Partidas*, care of the minor is termed "guardianship." Las Siete Partidas, Volume 5: Underworlds 1284–92 (Robert I. Burns ed., Samuel Parsons Scott trans. 2001). Throughout this Chapter, for comparative purposes, the authors refer to the Spanish regime of guardianship as tutorship.

25. *See* Las Siete Partidas, Volume 5: Underworlds 6.16.13 (Robert I. Burns ed., Samuel Parsons Scott trans. 2001); *see also* Harry R. Sachse, *The Evolution of the Regime of Tutorship in Louisiana*, 16 La. L. Rev. 413–14 (1956).

26. 1830 La. Acts 48–49.

27. The Law of Las Siete Partidas: Which Are Still in Force in the State of Louisiana 6.16.4 (L. Moreau Lislet & Henry Carleton trans., 1820). The tutor also had to be "neither dumb, deaf, a lunatic, a prodigal, nor a person of bad morals." *Id.*

renounced protections that the laws granted to women.[28] The promise not to marry was based on the presumption that if she were to marry, the care for her new husband would exceed that of her child, thereby hindering her ability to protect the interests of the child and the child's property.[29] The requirement to renounce special legal protections afforded to women was required so that men could fairly deal and make contracts with her.[30]

Tutors could be appointed by will (in a valid testament), by operation of law (to the nearest relation), or by order of the court (when no relations could accept the tutorship).[31] In all cases, the father could appoint a tutor by testament, and mothers who were widowed and named their children as legatees also had the ability to appoint a tutor by will.[32] If there was no testamentary tutor in place, the law provided for the nearest male relative to be the legal tutor, and in the event that no male relative was available, a male tutor would be appointed by the judge.[33] If, however, the mother was "of good reputation," then she could retain authority over the minor but only if she remained a widow.[34] These overtly paternal measures transitioned to full parental authority in the Louisiana Digest of 1808, which also incorporated provisions of the French *Code civil* (*Code civil*).[35]

Under the *Partidas*, the minor's estate provided his maintenance, but if the tutor used his own property to rear the minor, the minor was bound to reimburse the tutor at termination.[36] At inception, the tutor was required to create a written inventory of the minor's property, under penalty of removal.[37] The tutor was charged with teaching the minor good morals, to read and write, and to earn a living, as well as providing for the minor's needs "in proportion to the amount of the estate he had received from him."[38] A tutor could not donate or alienate immovable property of the minor, and the tutor

---

28. Las Siete Partidas, Volume 5: Underworlds 1285 (Robert I. Burns ed., Samuel Parsons Scott trans. 2001).

29. Las Siete Partidas, Volume 5: Underworlds 1285 (Robert I. Burns ed., Samuel Parsons Scott trans. 2001).

30. Las Siete Partidas, Volume 5: Underworlds 1285 (Robert I. Burns ed., Samuel Parsons Scott trans. 2001).

31. Las Siete Partidas, Volume 5: Underworlds 1284 (Robert I. Burns ed., Samuel Parsons Scott trans. 2001).

32. Las Siete Partidas, Volume 5: Underworlds 1285–86 (Robert I. Burns ed., Samuel Parsons Scott trans. 2001).

33. Las Siete Partidas, Volume 5: Underworlds, 1284, 1287–88 (Robert I. Burns ed., Samuel Parsons Scott trans. 2001).

34. Las Siete Partidas, Volume 5: Underworlds, 1291 (Robert I. Burns ed., Samuel Parsons Scott trans. 2001).

35. Harry R. Sachse, *The Evolution of the Regime of Tutorship in Louisiana*, 16 La. L. Rev. 417–18 (1956).

36. Las Siete Partidas, Volume 5: Underworlds, 1291–92 (Robert I. Burns ed., Samuel Parsons Scott trans. 2001).

37. Las Siete Partidas, Volume 5: Underworlds, 1290 (Robert I. Burns ed., Samuel Parsons Scott trans. 2001).

38. Las Siete Partidas, Volume 5: Underworlds, 1290 (Robert I. Burns ed., Samuel Parsons Scott trans. 2001).

represented the minor in actions for or against him.[39] Overall, the *Partidas* provided the tutor with sole authority to make decisions regarding the minor, under the watchful eye of the judge.[40] The French expanded decision-making authority over the minor, a system that Louisiana ultimately adopted.

§ 10:4 History—French Influence

While French law recognized the father as the authority over a minor's property during marriage, at dissolution of the marriage—when the regime of tutorship[41] began—parental authority prevailed, providing equal rights to the mother to serve as tutor.[42] The French system introduced natural tutorship, which began at the death of either parent, and the role of an undertutor, which oversaw the actions of the tutor.[43] In addition, the French extended decision-making authority over the minor to a family council, which consisted of at least six relations of the minor on the mother's and father's sides.[44] In Louisiana, the family council evolved into the family meeting, which ultimately fell into disuse and was eliminated from the law.[45]

Under French law, when one parent died, tutorship belonged to the surviving parent.[46] While the father had the right to nominate a special counsel to serve at his death, whose role would be to oversee the acts of the surviving mother, if the father failed to do so, then the mother could serve alone.[47] In the absence of natural tutorship, tutorship by will was available to the parent dying last.[48] Without a named tutor by will, tutorship fell by operation of law to the nearest ancestor,[49] and without available ancestors, a tutor was named by a family council.[50]

In all tutorships, an undertutor was appointed, generally by the family council.[51] The tutor had care and control of the "person of the minor" as well as the minor's property.[52]

---

39. Las Siete Partidas, Volume 5: Underworlds, 1290 (Robert I. Burns ed., Samuel Parsons Scott trans. 2001).

40. *See* Harry R. Sachse, *The Evolution of the Regime of Tutorship in Louisiana*, 16 La. L. Rev. 415 (1956).

41. Like the Spanish, the French referred to the regime as "guardianship." *See* Code Civil [C. civ.] [Civil Code] arts. 389–475 (Fr.) (1803). For comparative purposes, the authors refer to the regime as tutorship.

42. Code Civil [C. civ.] [Civil Code] arts. 389–90 (Fr.) (1803).

43. Code Civil [C. civ.] [Civil Code] arts. 390, 420–26 (Fr.) (1803).

44. Code Civil [C. civ.] [Civil Code] arts. 405–19 (Fr.) (1803). "In France the family meeting became so strong that it was referred to as the legislative branch of tutorship, the tutor being the executive." Harry R. Sachse, *The Evolution of the Regime of Tutorship in Louisiana*, 16 La. L. Rev. 419 (1956).

45. Harry R. Sachse, *The Evolution of the Regime of Tutorship in Louisiana*, 16 La. L. Rev. 418 (1956).

46. Code Civil [C. civ.] [Civil Code] art. 390 (Fr.) (1803).

47. *See* Code Civil [C. civ.] [Civil Code] arts. 390–92 (Fr.) (1803).

48. Code Civil [C. civ.] [Civil Code] arts. 397–401 (Fr.) (1803).

49. Code Civil [C. civ.] [Civil Code] arts. 402–404 (Fr.) (1803).

50. Code Civil [C. civ.] [Civil Code] art. 405 (Fr.) (1803).

51. Code Civil [C. civ.] [Civil Code] arts. 420–21 (Fr.) (1803).

52. Code Civil [C. civ.] [Civil Code] art. 450 (Fr.) (1803).

At inception of the tutorship, the tutor, with oversight of the undertutor, was required to take an inventory of the minor's property.[53] The tutor could not borrow from the minor, nor alienate or mortgage the minor's immovable property without authorization from the family council after showing that the other assets were insufficient for the minor's maintenance.[54] In sum, involvement of the family council was necessary for significant actions that affected the minor.[55]

§ 10:5 History—Tutorship in Louisiana

The Digest of 1808 was intended to compile the civil laws already in force in Louisiana, the majority of which were Spanish, but provisions of the French *Code civil* appeared, introducing new ideas and altering the law of tutorship.[56] Even though Louisiana still viewed the husband/father as the head of the family,[57] the movement away from the paternal Spanish regime placed both natural parents into familial control.[58] Louisiana adopted natural tutorship from the French, and the father had no greater rights than the mother when it came to qualifying as a tutor.[59] During marriage, the law considered each parent to be an "advis[o]r" and "restraining influence" on the other, so on the death of one, the natural unit of parental authority ended and the regime of tutorship began.[60] This structure of the law continues today.[61]

One of the biggest changes introduced in the Digest of 1808—and subsequently repealed by the 1960 overhaul of the Civil Code—was the use of the family meeting.[62] Derived from the *Code civil*, its roots trace back to Roman practice, although it was never part of Roman codified law.[63] In France, the family meeting was used to gather important information from loved ones related to the property and education of the

53. Code Civil [C. civ.] [Civil Code] art. 451 (Fr.) (1803).

54. Code Civil [C. civ.] [Civil Code] art. 457 (Fr.) (1803).

55. *See, e.g.*, Code Civil [C. civ.] [Civil Code] arts. 463–464, 467 (Fr.) (1803).

56. *See* Harry R. Sachse, *The Evolution of the Regime of Tutorship in Louisiana*, 16 La. L. Rev. 417 (1956); Civil Code of Louisiana: Revision of 1870 with Amendments to 1947, at 15, (Joseph Dainow ed., 1947); C. Russell Reynolds, *Alfonso el Sabio's Laws Survive in the Civil Code of Louisiana*, 12 J. La. Hist. Ass'n 137, 141–42 (1971).

57. The father was the head of the community of acquets and gains, and the administrator of the minor's assets. Digest of the Civil Laws Now in Force in the Territory of Orleans, with Alterations and Amendments Adapted to Its Present System of Government 58, 336 (1808).

58. Digest of the Civil Laws Now in Force in the Territory of Orleans, with Alterations and Amendments Adapted to Its Present System of Government 52 (1808).

59. Digest of the Civil Laws Now in Force in the Territory of Orleans, with Alterations and Amendments Adapted to Its Present System of Government 58 (1808).

60. Harry R. Sachse, *The Evolution of the Regime of Tutorship in Louisiana*, 16 La. L. Rev. 418 (1956).

61. *See* La. Civil Code Ann. art. 250.

62. La. Civil Code art. 281 (1870); La. Civil Code art. 305 (1825); Digest of the Civil Laws Now in Force in the Territory of Orleans, with Alterations and Amendments Adapted to Its Present System of Government 62 (1808).

63. Harry R. Sachse, *The Evolution of the Regime of Tutorship in Louisiana*, 16 La. L. Rev. 419 (1956).

minor to find outcomes that would serve the best interest of the child. The family meeting enjoyed many powers formerly given to a judge.[64]

The Digest of 1808 departed from the French model in that the family meeting functioned as a reactive body, used to approve or disapprove actions of the tutor.[65] The Digest of 1808 introduced the family meeting, and its use further developed in the 1825 and 1870 Codes.[66] By the mid-twentieth century, sentiment surrounding family meetings had changed, and statutory safeguards and judicial oversight took their place.[67] Ultimately, the legislature shifted discretion to courts to supervise tutorship proceedings.[68]

In addition, the Digest of 1808 adopted the undertutor from French law.[69] Similar to the family meeting, the undertutor provided oversight to ensure that the minor's interests were protected.[70] In every tutorship, the judge had to appoint an undertutor to act for the minor when the minor's and the tutor's interests conflicted.[71] Further duties of the undertutor developed in later revisions, and the ultimate repeal of the family meeting gave the undertutor more purpose.[72]

Provisions of the French system related to the disposition of the property of the minor appeared in the Digest of 1808.[73] The Digest adopted the compulsory sale of all goods of the minor, movable and immovable, to relieve the tutor of the overwhelming administrative duties required for larger estates and of the complications arising from the care of movables.[74] The French *Code civil* required the sale of the minor's movable property, while the Spanish *Partidas* mandated property preservation.[75] By 1811, the legislature repealed these mandates, and a new provision stated "that no property of the [minor], movable or immovable, could be sold without the consent of the under-

64. Harry R. Sachse, *The Evolution of the Regime of Tutorship in Louisiana*, 16 La. L. Rev. 419 (1956).

65. Harry R. Sachse, *The Evolution of the Regime of Tutorship in Louisiana*, 16 La. L. Rev. 420 (1956).

66. Harry R. Sachse, *The Evolution of the Regime of Tutorship in Louisiana*, 16 La. L. Rev. 420 (1956). For a history of the family meeting in Louisiana, see Nathan Greenberg, Comment, *The Family Meeting and its Successor in Louisiana Law*, 25 Tul. L. Rev. 237 (1951).

67. Harry R. Sachse, *The Evolution of the Regime of Tutorship in Louisiana*, 16 La. L. Rev. 429–30 (1956).

68. Leonard Oppenheim, *The Basic Elements of Tutorship in Louisiana*, 44 Tul. L. Rev. 452, 457 (1970).

69. Digest of the Civil Laws Now in Force in the Territory of Orleans, with Alterations and Amendments Adapted to Its Present System of Government 64 (1808).

70. Digest of the Civil Laws Now in Force in the Territory of Orleans, with Alterations and Amendments Adapted to Its Present System of Government 64 (1808).

71. Digest of the Civil Laws Now in Force in the Territory of Orleans, with Alterations and Amendments Adapted to Its Present System of Government 64 (1808).

72. Harry R. Sachse, *The Evolution of the Regime of Tutorship in Louisiana*, 16 La. L. Rev. 300–04 (1956).

73. Harry R. Sachse, *The Evolution of the Regime of Tutorship in Louisiana*, 16 La. L. Rev. 421 (1956).

74. Digest of the Civil Laws Now in Force in the Territory of Orleans, with Alterations and Amendments Adapted to Its Present System of Government 68 (1808).

75. Harry R. Sachse, *The Evolution of the Regime of Tutorship in Louisiana*, 16 La. L. Rev. 421 (1956).

tutor and the five nearest relatives of the [minor]."[76] By 1825, the minor's immovable property could only be sold at a public sale with permission of the judge and the family meeting; movable property, in contrast, was required to be sold unless the judge and the family meeting gave the tutor permission to retain it.[77]

From its inception, the law of tutorship in Louisiana involved the care of the minor's person and administration of his estate.[78] As laws on the custody of a minor developed, an overlap between the law of tutorship and the law of custody occurred.[79] In addition, because a mother could retain custody of her child but refuse to administer the child's estate, the idea of split tutorship began.[80] Without clear answers, courts continue to deal with these competing interests when appointing tutors.[81]

Undoubtedly, the law of tutorship needs comprehensive review and revision. The Louisiana State Law Institute's work to revise Book I of the Civil Code has been fruitful,[82] with the exception of Chapter 1 of Title VIII, "Of Tutorship."[83] While some articles

---

76. Harry R. Sachse, *The Evolution of the Regime of Tutorship in Louisiana*, 16 La. L. Rev. 422 (1956).

77. La. Civ. Code arts. 333–334, 336 (1825).

78. Digest of the Civil Laws Now in Force in the Territory of Orleans, with Alterations and Amendments Adapted to Its Present System of Government 68 (1808) ("The tutor watches over the person of the minor and administers his estate. . . ."); La. Civ. Code art. 327 (1825) ("The tutor shall have the care of the person of the minor, and shall represent him in all civil acts. He shall administer his estate as a prudent administrator would do, and shall be responsible for all damages resulting from a bad administration. . . ."); La. Civ. Code art. 337 (1870) ("The tutor shall have the care of the person of the minor, and shall represent him in all civil acts. He shall administer his estate as a prudent administrator would do, and shall be responsible for all damages resulting from a bad administration.").

79. *See* Section 10:31.

80. *See* Digest of the Civil Laws Now in Force in the Territory of Orleans, with Alterations and Amendments Adapted to Its Present System of Government 52 at 58–60 (1808); La. Civ. Code art. 253 (1870).

81. *See* Section 10:31.

82. Title I (Natural and Juridical Persons) was revised in 1987. *See* Act No. 125, 1987 La. Acts 412–18 (revising Title I of Book I, Natural and Juridical Persons (articles 24 through 29)); Act No. 989, 1990 La. Acts 2417–54 (revising Title I of Book I, Natural and Juridical Persons (articles 30 and 31)). Title II (Domicile) was revised in 2008. *See* Act No. 801, 2008 La. Acts 3046–51 (revising Title II of Book I, Domicile (articles 38 through 46)). Title III (Absent Persons) was revised in 1990. *See* Act No. 989, 1990 La. Acts 2417–54 (revising Title III of Book I, Absent Persons (articles 47 through 59)). Title IV (Husband and Wife) was revised in 1987. *See* Act No. 886, 1987 La. Acts 2409–39 (revising Title IV of Book I, Husband and Wife (articles 86 through 90 and 91 through 100)); Act No. 1009, 1990 La. Acts 2505–29 (revising Title IV of Book I, Husband and Wife (article 101)). Title V (Divorce) was revised in 1990 and 1997. *See* Act No. 1009, 1990 La. Acts 2505–29 (revising Title V, Chapter 1, of Book I, Divorce (articles 102 through 105)); *see also* Act No. 1008, 1990 La. Acts 2498–505 (adding articles 117 through 120 (redesignated as articles 121 through 124)); Act No. 261, 1993 La. Acts (revising Title V, Chapter 1, of Book I, Divorce (articles 131 through 152)); Act No. 1078, 1997 La. Acts 1885–97 (revising Title V, Chapter 2, section 1, of Book I, Spousal Support (articles 111 through 117)); Act No. 265, 2018 La. Acts 922–26 (revising Title V, Chapter 1, of Book I, Divorce (articles 103, 112 through 115)). Title VII (Parent and Child), Chapter 1 (Filiation) was revised in 2009. *See* Act No. 3, 2009 La. Acts 4–9 (revising Title VII of Book I, Parent and Child (article 178, 179, 186, 199, and 200)).

83. Digest of the Civil Laws Now in Force in the Territory of Orleans, with Alterations and Amendments Adapted to Its Present System of Government 58–72 (1808). While the related Chap-

have been repealed or revised,[84] no comprehensive review has been completed, with many of the original articles from the Code of 1870 remaining. Further, many laws that address the substantive nature of tutorship appear in the Louisiana Code of Civil Procedure and should be appropriately relocated to the Civil Code.[85]

§ 10:6 Kinds of Tutorship

The call to tutorship occurs in the hierarchical order presented in the Civil Code. In other words, "[e]ach form of tutorship is invoked only in the absence of a candidate with a higher priority."[86] Tutorship can be a legal charge, as in the case of natural tutorship, or it can be voluntary, in the case of tutorship by will or by law.[87] Whether compulsory or voluntary, tutorship mandates accountability and qualification as provided by law.[88] There are four types of tutorships: (a) by nature; (b) by will; (c) by the effect of law; and (d) by the appointment of the judge.[89] Additionally, every tutorship requires the appointment of an undertutor.[90]

§ 10:7 Kinds of Tutorship—Tutorship by Nature (Natural Tutorship)

Natural tutors are parents of the minor, who derive their rights and obligations from law.[91] As natural parents, no judicial intervention is necessary to obtain the role.[92] However, while a parent's *right* to act as tutor is automatic, that right is inchoate when judicial authorization is required by law.[93]

---

ter 5 of Title VII on Parental Authority of Married Persons was revised in 2015, the revision of the law of tutorship was never completed. *See* La. Civ. Code Ann. arts. 215–35.

84. The law of continuing tutorship was adopted by Act 496 of 1966 as an additional section in the Chapter on tutorship, but the general law of tutorship was not revised. *See* Act No. 496, 1966 La. Acts 1035.

85. *See* Leonard Oppenheim, *The Basic Elements of Tutorship in Louisiana*, 44 Tul. L. Rev. 452 (1970). When the Code of Civil Procedure was enacted in 1960, effective January 1, 1961, changes were made to the duties and powers of the tutor, resulting in substantive laws effecting tutorship landing in the Code of Civil Procedure, rather than the Civil Code. *See id.*

86. Succession of Wetmore, 422 So. 2d 726, 728 (La. Ct. App. 4 Cir. 1982). The nature of tutorship arose as a juridical function to administer the property of a person incapable to do so in his own right. Marcel Planiol, Treatise on the Civil Law 1615 (La. State L. Inst. Trans., 12th ed. 1959).

87. *See* La. Civ. Code Ann. art. 248.

88. *See, e.g.*, La. Code Civ. Proc. Ann. arts. 4261–62.

89. La. Civ. Code Ann. art. 247.

90. La. Civ. Code Ann. art. 273; *see also* La. Code Civ. Proc. Ann. arts. 4202–05.

91. La. Civ. Code Ann. art. 250.

92. La. Civ. Code Ann. art. 250.

93. *See* Griffith v. Roy, 269 So. 2d 217, 225 (La. 1972).

Tutorship begins when parental authority ends.[94] During marriage, the father and mother enjoy parental authority over their minor children.[95] If one parent dies during the marriage, the surviving parent is the natural tutor.[96] In the event that a husband dies while his wife is pregnant, no tutor is appointed for the child until after the child's birth.[97] If necessary, however, while the unborn child is in utero, a court may appoint a curator to preserve the rights of the unborn child, and that person shall be the undertutor to the mother at the child's birth.[98]

Natural tutorship also begins when the parents divorce or, in the rare instance of a covenant marriage, obtain a separation from bed and board.[99] In a divorce or separation, the parent who is awarded custody of the child is his or her natural tutor.[100] A parent without custody does not have natural tutorship.[101] If the parents enjoy joint custody, cotutorship belongs to both parents, which means, as a general rule, that the parents have equal authority, privileges, and responsibilities.[102] Cotutorship, however, does not mandate equal sharing of physical custodial time.[103] Further, cotutors with equal authority need not act together; they may act alone on behalf of the child, unless a court orders or the parties agree otherwise.[104] If one of the parents who shares joint custody dies, "tutorship ... belongs of right to the surviving parent."[105]

Finally, natural tutorship also exists when a child is born outside of marriage.[106] Indeed, those who may qualify as natural tutors for children born outside of marriage extend beyond the natural parent; grandparents or aunts and uncles may also qualify

94. La. Civ. Code Ann. art. 246. For a detailed discussion of parental authority, see Chapter 9.

95. La. Civ. Code Ann. art. 221.

96. La. Civ. Code Ann. art. 250.

97. La. Civ. Code Ann. art. 252.

98. La. Civ. Code Ann. art. 252. The Human Embryo Statute further provides legal recognition to an unborn child both in vitro and in utero to protect the unborn child's interests. La. Stat. Ann. §§ 9:121–9:133; *see also* La. Civ. Code Ann. art. 24 cmt. (c).

99. La. Civ. Code Ann. art. 250. A separation decree from another jurisdiction would also give rise to tutorship in Louisiana. *See* La. Civ. Code art. 246 editor's note. For more on covenant marriage and judicial separation, see Chapter 3.

100. La. Civ. Code Ann. art. 250.

101. *See* La. Civ. Code Ann. art. 250.

102. La. Civ. Code Ann. art. 250.

103. Favaloro v. Cooper, 562 So. 2d 943, 945 (La. Ct. App. 5 Cir. 1990).

104. La. Civ. Code Ann. art. 250. The effect of a domiciliary parent designation is unclear. Act 121 of 2022 added the verbiage that natural tutors who are joint custodians have equal authority "to act alone, on behalf of the child," S. 102, 2022 Leg., Reg. Sess. (La. 2022), but the Code of Civil Procedure does not permit one natural tutor who shares joint custody with another natural tutor to unilaterally bring an action for damages in tort without first qualifying for tutor and giving notice to the other natural tutor. *See* La. Code Civ. Proc. Ann. art. 4061.1; In re Tutorship of Cardenas, 2009-2020, p. 7 (La. App. 1 Cir. 6/11/10), 38 So. 3d 1284, 1289–90.

105. La. Civ. Code Ann. art. 250.

106. La. Civ. Code Ann. art. 256; *see also* La. Civ. Code Ann. art. 221 cmt. (c). Rather than tutorship, fathers and mothers enjoy parental authority over their child during their marriage, with few exceptions. *See* La. Civ. Code Ann. arts. 221, 232, 234.

as natural tutors.[107] If the father has not acknowledged the child or has acknowledged the child without the mother's concurrence, the mother is the tutor as of right.[108] If the mother concurred in the father's acknowledgement, tutorship will generally depend on custody.[109] If the parents are awarded joint custody, the parents will share cotutorship with equal authority to act together or alone and with equal privileges and responsibilities, unless modified by court order or by parental agreement.[110] Without an award of joint custody, the judge will appoint as tutor the parent whose care of the child will serve the child's best interests.[111] In the event the mother dies before the father acknowledges the child, a court will appoint the tutor, giving first consideration to the mother's parents or to the mother's siblings, and second consideration to the father, always considering the best interests of the child.[112] In the event the mother dies after the father acknowledged the child, the father will enjoy natural tutorship.[113] For example, in *Jones v. Willis*, the court rejected the grandparents' attempt to seek tutorship of a child, after the death of their daughter, when the biological father had acknowledged paternity before the child's death.[114]

§ 10:8 Kinds of Tutorship—Tutorship by Will

Tutorship by will occurs when a parent with authority designates a tutor in a valid last will and testament or by a declaration in an authentic act.[115] Generally, the right to appoint a tutor by will belongs exclusively to the parent dying last.[116] For example, if both parents are alive and one parent dies testate, naming a tutor in his testament, the tutor named will not serve because natural tutorship prevails, and the surviving parent will serve as the child's tutor.[117] In that case, the surviving parent has the right to appoint a tutor by will.[118] An exception exists for married parents when one parent has been interdicted and the other parent is named curator; the right to appoint a tutor belongs only to the curator-parent.[119] For a child born outside of marriage, the parent

107. La. Civ. Code Ann. art. 256(B); *see* In re Johnston, 1999-980, p. 4 (La. App. 3 Cir. 2/2/00), 757 So. 2d 738, 740 (recognizing grandfather as natural tutor of child born outside of marriage when the mother died and the father was unidentified).

108. La. Civ. Code Ann. art. 256(A).

109. La. Civ. Code Ann. art. 256(C).

110. La. Civ. Code Ann. art. 256(C); *see also* text accompanying footnote 104 in this section.

111. La. Civ. Code Ann. art. 256(C).

112. La. Civ. Code Ann. art. 256(B); *see* Johnston, 757 So. 2d at 740 (recognizing grandfather as natural tutor of child born outside of marriage when the mother died and the father was unidentified).

113. La. Civ. Code Ann. art. 250.

114. Jones v. Willis, 43,608, p. 12 (La. App. 2 Cir. 9/17/08), 996 So. 2d 364, 370.

115. La. Civ. Code Ann. arts. 257–58, 261. The declaration must be in authentic form: before a notary and two witnesses. La. Civ. Code Ann. art. 257.

116. La. Civ. Code Ann. art. 257.

117. *See* In re Sanches, 619 So. 2d 799, 801 (La. Ct. App. 1 Cir. 1993).

118. La. Civ. Code Ann. art. 257.

119. La. Civ. Code Ann. art. 257; *see also* La. Stat. Ann. § 9:601.

entitled to natural tutorship is allowed to appoint a tutor for the child.[120] Ultimately, the judge must confirm the appointment, ensuring that the appointee is qualified.[121]

If the parents are divorced or legally separated, the right to designate a tutor by will belongs to the parent with custody.[122] If a parent is denied custody, the parent enjoys no right to appoint a tutor by will.[123] If the parents have joint custody, the right to appoint a tutor by will belongs to the parent dying last.[124] A special exception exists for a parent to appoint a tutor over the property that the parent leaves to the child.[125] Even in the face of a natural tutor, the tutor appointed by will can separately administer the portion of the child's property that is attributable to that parent's estate. The appointment of a tutor over the property left to the child should be express in the testament. If both parents appoint a tutor over the property of the minor, then a court must decide which tutor shall administer the portion of the property which is not attributable to either parent's estate.[126] Technically, the tutor named by the parent dying last should administer the remaining property.

If a parent appoints several tutors, the person first mentioned shall be the sole tutor, with the second named tutor called to serve in the case of the death, absence, refusal, or incapacity of the first.[127] Further, the tutor by will is not obligated to accept the tutorship, but the tutor will lose the legacies and advantages made in his favor under the supposition that tutorship would be accepted.[128]

§ 10:9 Kinds of Tutorship—Tutorship by the Effect of Law (Legal Tutorship)

Legal tutors are appointed by a court and are necessary when no natural tutor exists and no tutor by will has been appointed or is available to serve.[129] In such a situation, the judge appoints from among three groups: (1) qualified ascendants in the child's direct line;[130] (2) collaterals by blood within the third degree;[131] and (3) the surviving

120. La. Civ. Code Ann. art. 261.
121. La. Civ. Code Ann. art. 261; *see also* La. Code Civ. Proc. Ann. art. 4231.
122. La. Civ. Code Ann. art. 258.
123. La. Civ. Code Ann. art. 257.
124. La. Civ. Code Ann. art. 258.
125. La. Civ. Code Ann. art. 258.
126. La. Civ. Code Ann. art. 258.
127. La. Civ. Code Ann. art. 262.
128. La. Civ. Code Ann. art. 259.
129. *See* La. Civ. Code Ann. art. 263.
130. La. Civ. Code Ann. art. 263. Ascendants in the direct line are people from whom the child descends, including grandparents and great-grandparents. La. Civ. Code Ann. art. 901.
131. La. Civ. Code Ann. art. 263. Collaterals are those who descend from a common ancestor but not from each other, and the term "by blood" omits collaterals related by marriage only. *Id.* art. 901. Collaterals within the third degree include siblings (second degree) and aunts and uncles (third degree). *See id.*

spouse of the parent dying last, i.e., the child's step-parent.[132] The judge will appoint the tutor in line with the best interests of the minor.[133] No hierarchy exists when legal tutorship is awarded; the best interest of the minor is paramount.[134] The articles in the chapter on tutorship do not provide factors to address the best interest of the minor, nor do they reference the best interest of the child factors from the section on child custody.[135] However, the best interest factors from Louisiana Civil Code Article 134 governing custody can be probative when choosing a legal tutor among relations of the minor.[136]

§ 10:10 Kinds of Tutorship—Tutorship by the Appointment of the Court (Dative Tutorship)

As a final option, dative tutors are appointed by the court from those who are neither entitled to demand nor obliged to accept tutorship.[137] A dative tutor is necessary when no natural tutor exists, there is no tutor appointed by will, and there is no preferred relative to claim legal tutorship.[138] A more distant relative or friend of the minor may be appointed dative tutor in the absence of others entitled to request tutorship or when those persons are excused, refuse the tutorship, or are disqualified.[139]

---

132. La. Civ. Code Ann. art. 263.

133. La. Civ. Code Ann. art. 263. The Code of Civil Procedure requires that an applicant for tutorship mail a copy of the petition for tutorship to all of those included in the list of available relations. *See* La. Code Civ. Proc. Ann. art. 4065.

134. *See* In the Interest of S.L.G., 39,704, p. 4–6 (La. App. 2 Cir. 3/2/05), 895 So. 2d 773, 776–77. Prior law required the court to appoint the applicant with the highest priority of appointment, but that law was repealed. *See* La. Civ. Code arts. 270–72 (1870); *see also* Succession of Scott, 303 So. 2d 897 (La. Ct. App. 1 Cir. 1974) (applying former Louisiana Code of Civil Procedure Article 4067).

135. *See* La. Civ. Code Ann. art. 263.

136. *See* Knisely v. Knisely, 2005-1015, p. 5 (La. App. 3 Cir. 3/1/06), 924 So. 2d 423, 426 (relying on the factors from article 134 when assessing custody and tutorship); In re Custody of Booty, 95-0828, p. 12 (La. App. 1 Cir. 11/9/95), 665 So. 2d 444, 448 (recognizing that whether the laws of custody or tutorship apply, the best interest of the minor is paramount, and citing a custody article); *but see* Succession of Wetmore, 422 So. 2d 726, 729 (La. Ct. App. 4 Cir. 1982) (appointing the legal tutor based on the best interest of the minor without a consideration of the custody factors); S.L.G., 895 So. 2d at 777; In re Dative Tutorship of Moore, 55,047, p. 10–11 (La. App. 2 Cir. 3/1/23), 358 So. 3d 203, 208; Jones v. Willis, 43,608 (La. App. 2 Cir. 9/17/08), 996 So. 2d 364, 370–71.

137. La. Civ. Code Ann. art. 270.

138. La. Civ. Code Ann. art. 270; Odom v. Culverhouse, 505 So. 2d 837, 840 (La. Ct. App. 2 Cir. 1987) (allowing friend who had a close relationship with the child and deceased mother to petition the court to be appointed dative tutor and argue that legal tutors should be excluded or disqualified).

139. *See* Section 10:15.

§ 10:11 Kinds of Tutorship— Role of the Undertutor

In every tutorship, an undertutor is necessary.[140] Once appointed, the duties of the undertutor end when the tutorship terminates.[141] Both the Civil Code and the Code of Civil Procedure contain articles outlining the duties and responsibilities of the undertutor.[142]

Derived from French law, the role of the undertutor is to protect the minor's interests when in conflict with the tutor and to concur (or not) in actions suggested by the tutor before a court.[143] "The undertutor's role is that of a watchdog."[144] The only qualification for an undertutor is that he be "a responsible person."[145] There are no preferences based on the undertutor's relationship to the tutee, as there are for the tutor, and no one is compelled to accept the appointment as an undertutor.[146] Just like the tutor, the undertutor must take an oath to faithfully fulfill the duties of his office.[147] The undertutor need not furnish security.[148] Usually, the appointment of an undertutor is made at the same time the tutor is appointed or confirmed.[149]

Specifically, the undertutor must compel the tutor to file an accounting of the tutee's property whenever the tutor has failed to do so;[150] cause the tutor to record and pro-

140. La. Civ. Code Ann. art. 273. Even when the parents are granted joint custody and serve as cotutors, an undertutor is necessary. *Id.* If, however, the parents agree that one parent will assume the role as tutor, the other parent can serve as undertutor, *see* La. Code Civ. Proc. Ann. art. 4201, which may serve the minor and judicial efficiency more effectively than having the parents serve as cotutors with a third person serving as undertutor. Further, parents who share joint custody can jointly file an action for damages on behalf of a child without first qualifying as tutor. La. Code Civ. Proc. Ann. art. 4061.1 If the claim is compromised, however, the parents must then qualify to receive judicial authorization to compromise the claim. La. Code Civ. Proc. Ann. art. 4265.

141. La. Civ. Code Ann. art. 280.

142. *See* La. Civ. Code Ann. arts. 273–280; La. Code Civ. Proc. Ann. arts. 4201–06.

143. La. Code Civ. Proc. Ann. art. 4202.

144. Succession of Schmolke, 2012-1630, p. 27 (La. App. 4 Cir. 6/13/13), 119 So. 3d 916, 926–27; *see also* Green v. City of Shreveport, 39,066, p. 5 (La. App. 2 Cir. 10/27/04), 888 So. 2d 314, 317 (noting that the duty of an undertutor to the minor is "to exercise a constant supervision or watchdog role over the acts of the tutor"); In re Helm, 2011-0500, p. 9 (La. App. 4 Cir. 11/2/11), 84 So. 3d 601, 605.

145. La. Code Civ. Proc. Ann. art. 4201. No Louisiana court has discussed the qualities of a "responsible person," but in one case, the court affirmed summary judgment in favor of the natural tutor who sought to name his brother as undertutor over the objection of the child's maternal uncle, who had no evidence that the brother was not responsible. In re Sanches, 619 So. 2d 799, 801, 803 (La. Ct. App. 1 Cir. 1993). The court rejected the uncle's argument that a best-interest-of-the-minor analysis was appropriate. *Id.*

146. La. Code Civ. Proc. Ann. art. 4201 cmt. (a).

147. La. Code Civ. Proc. Ann. art. 4201 cmt. (a).

148. La. Code Civ. Proc. Ann. art. 4201 cmt. (c).

149. La. Code Civ. Proc. Ann. art. 4201 cmt. (b); *see* Succession of LeRuth, 569 So. 2d 555, 557 (La. Ct. App. 5 Cir. 1990) (rejecting the argument by the natural tutor that appointing an undertutor was premature because minors did not as yet own property; undertutor was appointed at the same time natural tutor was confirmed of right).

150. La. Code Civ. Proc. Ann. art. 4203.

vide security properly;[151] and apply to the court for appointment of a new tutor when a vacancy in the role of tutor occurs.[152] For natural tutorship, if the undertutor fails or neglects to cause the tutor to inscribe the legal mortgage in favor of the minor, the undertutor will be liable for damages sustained by the minor.[153] When the minor reaches majority or is emancipated, the undertutor is relieved of his duties although liability for any acts while serving as undertutor are unaffected.[154]

The tutorship does not belong to the undertutor when the tutor no longer serves.[155] Nor can the tutor appoint the undertutor to act as his agent; two persons are necessary to protect the minor.[156] The roles of the two are separate, and when a tutor chooses not to act, the undertutor is not permitted to step into the role of tutor.[157] If the undertutor believes sufficient cause exists, the undertutor could seek removal of the tutor and the appointment of another tutor.[158]

The role of an undertutor is limited. The Fourth Circuit Court of Appeal in *In re Tutorship of Washington* refused to allow an undertutor to obtain tutorship funds for his use while visiting with the tutee or to personally inspect property purchased by the tutor for the tutee.[159] The court noted that undertutors have a right not to concur in actions suggested by the tutor, which would result in a contradictory hearing before a court, but nothing in the law provides a separate claim for the undertutor to either inspect property or to request the use of the tutor's funds.[160] In addition, in *Green v. City of Shreveport*, the Second Circuit Court of Appeal concluded that the undertutor of two minor children did not have the authority to pay the estimated costs for an appeal when the tutors failed to timely do so, resulting in the abandonment of the appeal.[161] In fact, the court noted that including the undertutor as a representative party plaintiff when the minor child was represented by a tutor was inappropriate.[162]

---

151. La. Code Civ. Proc. Ann. art. 4204.

152. La. Code Civ. Proc. Ann. art. 4205.

153. La. Civ. Code Ann. art. 278. The claim will prescribe only when the minor's right against his tutor prescribes. *Id.*

154. La. Code Civ. Proc. Ann. art. 4206; *see* Hanks v. Alexander, 157 So. 772, 775 (La. Ct. App. 2 Cir. 1934).

155. La. Code Civ. Proc. Ann. art. 4205.

156. Eby v. McLain, 48 So. 772, 780 (La. 1909); *see also* Bordelon v. Capers, 189 So. 615, 617 (La. Ct. App. 1939).

157. Green, 888 So. 2d at 317.

158. La. Code Civ. Proc. Ann. art. 4234.

159. Tutorship of Washington, 2004-0465, p. 8 (La. App. 4 Cir. 7/20/05), 913 So. 2d 165, 168.

160. Tutorship of Washington, 913 So. 2d at 168.

161. Green, 888 So. 2d at 317.

162. Green, 888 So. 2d at 317.

§ 10:12 Refusal, Excuse, and Disqualification as Tutor

While tutors are chosen in order of preference as detailed in the Code,[163] some may not actually serve because they can refuse the office of tutorship, be legally excused, or be disqualified by law.[164]

When a tutor is appointed by will, he can refuse to accept the appointment as requested by the minor's parent.[165] As noted, if the person appointed refuses the tutorship, he loses all of the legacies and any other advantages, such as the appointment as executor or trustee, which were given to him based on the understanding that he would accept the role of tutorship.[166] Prior to the 1974 revisions aimed at modernizing and furthering gender equality in the Civil Code, a mother was permitted to refuse the tutorship of her children, while the Code required men to accept.[167] The present Code now forbids either parent from refusing the tutorship of their child.[168]

§ 10:13 Refusal, Excuse, and Disqualification as Tutor—Excuse

Parents cannot be excused from the tutorship of their children,[169] but other people may be excused because they hold a certain public office or perform a specific function.[170] For example, the Governor, the secretary of state, the mayor of New Orleans, the collector of customs, judges, military members, public school officials, and ministers are legally excused.[171] Note, however, that if a person who could have been excused accepts the tutorship regardless, that person will not be allowed to be excused on that

---

163. *See* Sections 10:6–11.

164. For the option to refuse tutorship, see La. Civ. Code Ann. art. 259. For the ways in which tutors are excused, see La. Civ. Code Ann. arts. 292–331. For disqualification of a tutor, see La. Code Civ. Proc. Ann. art. 4231(A).

165. La. Civ. Code Ann. art. 259.

166. La. Civ. Code Ann. art. 259.

167. Liz Williams, *Legal Equality for Women*, 1 S. Univ. L. Rev. 116, 123 (1975); *see also* La. Civ. Code Ann. art. 253, *repealed by* Act No. 163, 1974 La. Acts 457–58 ("The mother is not compelled to accept the tutorship of her minor children, but in case she refuses, she shall be bound to fulfill the duties of a tutor, until she has caused a tutor to be appointed. The mother, who refuses the tutorship of her children, retains the superintendence of them, and the care of their education. The tutor, in such a case, is merely entrusted with what concerns the administration of their property.").

168. La. Civ. Code Ann. art. 301.

169. La. Civ. Code Ann. art. 301; Kelley v. Kelley, 3 So. 2d 641, 645 (La. 1941) ("[A]s the father of his minor children, [he] was not only entitled to be appointed their natural tutor, but, under the law, it was his obligation to accept the appointment.").

170. La. Civ. Code Ann. art. 292.

171. La. Civ. Code Ann. art. 292.

basis at a later time.[172] But, if the person accepts a tutorship and the basis for excuse arises thereafter, he may be excused, and another tutor will take his place.[173]

Non-parents may also be excused based on their age, health, and relationship to the minor.[174] Poverty, alone, is not an excuse.[175] Individuals not related to the child by blood or related to the child beyond the fourth degree (beyond first cousins) cannot be compelled to accept the tutorship.[176] Non-parents may be excused if they are 65 years or older; if they were appointed prior to the age of 65, they can be excused at the age of 70.[177] Those with a serious illness that renders them incapable of transacting their own business are also excused and can be discharged if the illness arises after their appointment.[178] A subjective analysis is necessary to assess whether a serious illness will result in an excuse, and the Code's reference to "transacting [his] own business" suggests that a person who cannot care for his estate due to an illness, can neither care for the minor's.[179] The focus seems to be patrimonial, rather than personal, but no court has considered the issue.

If a person has been appointed to two tutorships, then that person can be excused from accepting a third.[180] A parent who has been appointed to one tutorship can be excused from a second, unless it involves his own child.[181] When presenting an excuse, tutors must act swiftly or lose the right to use it; a tutor must present his excuse to the judge within 10 days after the appointment, or after notification of the appointment, unless he has sufficient reason for a further delay.[182] During a proceeding to consider the validity of any excuse, the tutor shall be bound to act provisionally if and until he is discharged.[183]

172. La. Civ. Code Ann. art. 293.
173. La. Civ. Code Ann. arts. 293–94.
174. La. Civ. Code Ann. arts. 295–97.
175. *See* La. Civ. Code Ann. arts. 292–301.
176. La. Civ. Code Ann. art. 295.
177. La. Civ. Code Ann. art. 296.
178. La. Civ. Code Ann. art. 297.
179. La. Civ. Code Ann. art. 297.
180. La. Civ. Code Ann. art. 298.
181. La. Civ. Code Ann. art. 298.
182. La. Civ. Code Ann. art. 299.
183. La. Civ. Code Ann. art. 300.

§ 10:14 Refusal, Excuse, and Disqualification as Tutor—Disqualification

Louisiana Code of Civil Procedure Article 4231(A) provides a variety of grounds to be disqualified from acting as a tutor.[184] Courts must consider whether certain tutors are disqualified,[185] and litigants can challenge the appointment of others because they are disqualified.[186] A tutor is legally disqualified if he is:

(1) Under eighteen years of age;

(2) Interdicted, or, on contradictory hearing, proved to be mentally incompetent;[187]

(3) A convicted felon, under the laws of the United States or of any state or territory thereof;

(4) Indebted to the minor, unless he discharges the debt prior to the appointment;

(5) An adverse party to a suit to which the minor is a party; or

(6) On contradictory hearing, proved to be incapable of performing the duties of the office, or to be otherwise unfit for appointment because of his physical or mental condition or bad moral character.[188]

These grounds serve to exclude those who lack capacity to serve as tutor, those who are unfit to do so, and those whose own interests would conflict with those of the minor.

As a general rule, the grounds for disqualification do not apply to the parent of the minor unless the parent is interdicted (cause 2) is mentally incompetent as determined by a court (cause 2), is incapable of performing the duties of a tutor (cause 6), or is unfit for appointment due to a physical or mental condition or bad moral character (cause 6).[189] Stated otherwise, the minor's parent is not disqualified for being under 18 years of age, a convicted felon, indebted to the minor, or an adverse party in a lawsuit in which the minor is a party.[190] However, a natural parent who has been convicted of a felony

184. La. Code Civ. Proc. Ann. art. 4231(A).

185. A court must appoint a tutor named in a testament or authentic act "unless he is disqualified." La. Code Civ. Proc. Ann. art. 4062.

186. An opposition to the appointment of a legal or dative tutor can be made because "the applicant is disqualified." La. Code Civ. Proc. Ann. art. 4067. There is no provision for an opposition to be filed against a natural tutor, but courts have the power to appoint provisional tutors or separate tutors over the minor's property, which allows the court to protect the interest of the minor if a natural tutor is disqualified. *See* La. Code Civ. Proc. Ann. arts. 4069–70; *see also* Leonard Oppenheim, *The Basic Elements of Tutorship in Louisiana*, 44 Tul. L. Rev. 477–79 (1970).

187. Whether both a full and limited interdict would be disqualified under the law is unclear because the article on disqualification was passed before the bifurcation in the law of interdiction. *Compare* Act No. 573, 1974 La. Acts (La. Code Civ. Proc. Ann. art. 4231), *with* 2000 La. Acts 25 (La. Civ. Code Ann. arts. 389–91). While a full interdict is undoubtedly disqualified, a limited interdict who is unable to care for either his person or his property should also be disqualified from the same in regard to caring for the minor's person or estate.

188. La. Code Civ. Proc. Ann. art. 4231(A).

189. La. Code Civ. Proc. Ann. art. 4231(B).

190. *See* La. Code Civ. Proc. Ann. art. 4231(B).

involving theft or misappropriation of funds, a crime of violence, a sex offense, or any other crime against a minor cannot serve as tutor.[191] As for a minor who has a child, the minor would necessarily be under the regime of parental authority or tutorship but could act as the tutor for his or her minor child.[192] Finally, the grounds for disqualification, other than indebtedness to the minor, apply also to an undertutor.[193]

Any cause for disqualification is a matter of factual proof, and the burden of proof lies with the party seeking to disqualify the tutor.[194] Courts conduct a fact-intensive analysis, most often to determine whether the tutor is incapable of handling the office due to health conditions or general unfitness.[195] When opposing tutors are similarly situated, courts have considered whether the tutor can handle the needs of active children and possesses financial stability but have not disqualified tutors because of their limited financial strength.[196] Further, a tutor is not disqualified simply because another tutor is "more favorably qualified."[197]

For example, in *Succession of Wetmore*, the parent died, leaving the minor in the custody of a non-relative, who sought legal custody and tutorship.[198] The trial court awarded the non-relative custody and tutorship, notwithstanding the opposition of the paternal grandmother and aunt.[199] On appeal, the Fourth Circuit reversed, finding that the trial court inappropriately named a non-relative as tutor when "qualified relatives [were] available for appointment."[200] The Fourth Circuit did not address the conflict between an award of custody and tutorship, relying solely on the law of tutorship.[201] Because tutorship is decided based on an order of priority, the court must look first to a close relative of the minor before moving to a stranger.[202] Because the non-relative could not prove the disqualification of either relative, the Fourth Circuit found that

---

191. La. Code Civ. Proc. Ann. art. 4231(C).

192. *See* La. Code Civ. Proc. Ann. art. 4231(A)(1), (B) (providing that parents who are under the age of eighteen can be tutors).

193. La. Code Civ. Proc. Ann. art. 4236.

194. Succession of Wetmore, 422 So. 2d 726, 729 (La. Ct. App. 4 Cir. 1982); *see also* Succession of Chambers, 357 So. 2d 1367, 1368 (La. Ct. App. 4 Cir. 1978) (finding the disqualification of a father to serve as tutor because of his consistent failure to see the children and provide support); Succession of Quave, 214 So. 2d 260, 263 (La. Ct. App. 4 Cir. 1968) (reversing the trial court when it disqualified a grandparent due to her "poverty, strict religion, age, a lack of recreational activities for the children and the lack of a man in the household" when she was higher in priority to serve than an opponent who was wealthier); *see also* Leonard Oppenheim, *The Basic Elements of Tutorship in Louisiana*, 44 Tul. L. Rev. 477–79 (1970).

195. Quave, 214 So. 2d at 263; Chambers, 357 So. 2d at 1368.

196. Quave, 214 So. 2d at 263; *see also* Succession of Scott, 303 So. 2d 897, 899 (La. Ct. App. 1 Cir. 1974) (noting the financial strength of the chosen tutor); Chambers, 357 So. 2d at 1368 (disqualifying a tutor because of his failure to support the children).

197. Wetmore, 422 So. 2d at 729.

198. Wetmore, 422 So. 2d at 727.

199. Wetmore, 422 So. 2d at 729.

200. Wetmore, 422 So. 2d at 728.

201. *See* Wetmore, 422 So. 2d at 728.

202. Wetmore, 422 So. 2d at 728.

the trial court erred in appointing the non-relative simply because it was in the best interest of the child.[203]

§ 10:15 Appointment of Tutors

In all tutorships, the tutor must qualify for the office as provided by law.[204] Natural tutors need not be appointed because they assume the role of tutor by right.[205] Tutors by will, legal tutors, and dative tutors are all appointed by the court.[206] After qualification, letters of tutorship are issued to the tutor, which evidence the appointment.[207] The Civil Code mandates that the minor's relations apply to the court when it is necessary for a tutor to be appointed.[208] If the minor's relations neglect to do so, they are responsible for damages suffered by the minor.[209]

This section details the respective processes for the appointment of natural tutors as compared to tutors by will, legal tutors, and dative tutors. The option of appointing a separate tutor over the property of the minor is also addressed. Finally, this section ends with the special rules governing the appointment of a provisional tutor, a tutor over small tutorships, and foreign tutors.

§ 10:16 Appointment of Tutors— Natural Tutors

Although natural tutorship takes place of right, the natural tutor still must qualify for the office, with limited exceptions.[210] At the time the natural tutor assumes his duties, which generally occurs when he performs some juridical act on behalf of the minor, the natural tutor must take an oath, prepare an inventory or detailed descriptive list of the minor's property, and inscribe a legal mortgage in favor of the minor or furnish other appropriate security to protect the minor.[211] The court must also consider

203. Wetmore, 422 So. 2d at 729; *see also* Section 10:31.

204. La. Civ. Code Ann. art. 248.

205. La. Civ. Code Ann. art. 248.

206. La. Code Civ. Proc. Ann. arts. 4062–64. Civil Code Article 248 provides that tutors are either confirmed or appointed. La. Civ. Code Ann. art. 248. Although the Code of Civil Procedure provides that the court "shall appoint" tutors by will, legal tutors, and dative tutors, tutors by will and natural tutors (when court authority is needed) are actually confirmed because they assume their role by designation in a testament or by right, respectively. *See id.*; La. Code Civ. Proc. Ann. arts. 4062–64.

207. La. Code Civ. Proc. Ann. art. 4172.

208. La. Civ. Code Ann. art. 308.

209. La. Civ. Code Ann. art. 310. Minors are exempt from this mandate. La. Civ. Code Ann. art. 309.

210. La. Civ. Code Ann. art. 248. For the exceptions, *see* La. Code Civ. Proc. Ann. art. 4061.1 and La. Stat. Ann. § 9:196.

211. La. Code Civ. Proc. Ann. arts. 4061, 4134; *see also* La. Civ. Code Ann. art. 322. Recording an abstract of the inventory or detailed descriptive list in each parish where the minor owns immovable property constitutes a legal mortgage on the property. La. Code Civ. Proc. Ann. art. 4134. Failure to file the legal mortgage prior to the judge signing the order confirming the parent as tutor will not annul the tutorship. *See* In re Tutorship of Watts, 96-0073, p. 5 (La. App. 1 Cir. 9/27/96), 681 So. 2d 74, 77 n.6.

whether the natural tutor is disqualified to serve.[212] If, however, a natural parent fails to qualify before performing an act on behalf of the minor, courts have nonetheless affirmed the actions of the natural tutor because the parent can act "of right" even without being formally confirmed as the tutor.[213]

Understandably, after the death of a spouse, the other spouse may not immediately proceed to court to be confirmed as the natural tutor of their minor child. It is reasonable that confirmation of a natural parent as tutor may never be necessary during the child's minority. However, when parents divorce or separate and a parent is awarded custody of the minor, the court can and should confirm the parent as tutor (or in the case of joint custody, the parents as cotutors) at that time, although failure to do so will not affect the parent's future right to act as tutor.

A special provision allows a natural tutor to perform or discharge any act affecting a right or interest of the minor that involves $10,000 or less received by the minor—exclusive of court costs, attorney's fees, and other expenses—without qualifying.[214] Not only must the right or interest involved amount to $10,000 or less, but a natural tutor also must consent to compromise any claim below that amount for any release to be valid.[215] A similar provision appears in the statutes governing parental authority and allows a parent to alienate or encumber property, compromise a claim, donate property, or obligate the minor without court approval, as long as the property involved is $15,000 or less, excluding court costs, attorney's fees, and other expenses.[216] When the tutorship articles are revised, the sum will likely mirror that of parental authority, and a formal tutorship will not be necessary for natural tutors when the amount involves $15,000 or less. In other words, the different amounts are solely the result of legislative revision in one regime (parental authority) without a concomitant revision in the other (tutorship).

A natural tutor is also permitted to file an action for damages based in tort without first qualifying for office, as provided in Article 4061.1 of the Louisiana Code of Civil Procedure.[217] To rely on this special provision, the natural tutor must be either a

---

212. La. Code Civ. Proc. Ann. art. 4231. Natural parents cannot serve if they are interdicted or mentally incompetent; if they are incapable of performing the duties of the office or otherwise unfit; or if they have been convicted of certain felonies. *Id.*

213. Corcoran v. Alonzo, 99-607, p. 7 (La. App. 5 Cir. 11/10/99), 749 So. 2d 708, 711. Even though a child's mother was never appointed by the court to serve as the tutrix of her minor child upon the death of the child's father, and did not comply with any of the requirements of La. Code Civ. Proc. Ann. art. 4061, the court dismissed a suit by the child's dative tutrix to set aside the mother's settlements of the child's claims against tortfeasors because the mother became the child's natural tutor upon the father's death pursuant to La. Civ. Code Ann. art. 250. Corcoran, 749 So. 2d at 708. Further, the settlements were properly approved by the court. *See* Succession of LeRuth, 569 So. 2d 555 (La. Ct. App. 5 Cir. 1990).

214. La. Stat. Ann. § 9:196.

215. *See* Boudreaux v. Franks, 2012-647, p. 7 (La. App. 3 Cir. 12/19/12), 106 So. 3d 270, 274 (refusing to recognize a minor's settlement when there was no evidence that the minor's tutrix consented to the agreement to compromise).

216. La. Stat. Ann. § 9:572.

217. *See* La. Code Civ. Proc. Ann. art. 4061.1; *see also* In re McCauley, 52,206, pp. 10–11 (La. App. 2 Cir. 9/26/18), 257 So. 3d 255 (refusing to allow non-natural tutor to file a tort action on behalf of the

surviving parent, a parent awarded sole custody of the minor, or the mother of a child born outside of marriage when the father did not acknowledge the child or acknowledged the child without her concurrence.[218] Conspicuously absent are parents who share joint custody or parents who have both acknowledged their child born outside of marriage.[219] Parents who have joint custody must petition jointly as cotutors, but one parent can act alone if they seek to enforce a right of the minor if the other parent "fails or refuses to do so."[220]

In *In re Tutorship of Cardenas*, the mother successfully challenged the appointment of the father as tutor and his wife, the child's step-mother, as undertutor, when the mother and father shared joint custody.[221] The First Circuit Court of Appeal explained that, when parents share joint custody of a minor and they seek to file an action for damages based on tort, they:

> must adhere to the general obligations imposed upon a natural tutor.... In cases where one parent fails or refuses to enforce a particular right or compromise a particular claim of an unemancipated minor, the other parent may, with the permission of the judge, file a petition to be appointed as natural tutor of said minor for this limited purpose.[222]

Because the parents were natural cotutors, they could not avail themselves of the special provision in article 4061.1, and they were required to jointly petition for relief or make a showing that the other parent failed or refused to enforce a right, neither of which occurred.[223] Accordingly, the court set aside the judgment of tutorship.[224]

In *Rice ex rel. CIR v. Cornerstone Hospital*, the federal court applying Louisiana law allowed grandparents to bring a wrongful death claim on behalf of their grandchildren, even though their mother held the role as natural tutor.[225] Relying in part on Louisiana Code of Civil Procedure Article 4061.1, the court explained that the mother was given notice of the lawsuit and failed to respond, leaving the children unrepresented, and a federal rule allowed the court to appoint the grandparents as guardians *ad litem* for the

---

minors when the natural tutor refused to do so); *but see* Rice v. Cornerstone Hospital of W. Monroe, L.L.C., 589 Fed. Appx. 688 (5th Cir. 2014) (permitting a guardian to be appointed in light of the natural tutor's failure to join in a lawsuit on behalf of the minors).

218. La. Code Civ. Proc. Ann. art. 4061.1(A).

219. *See* La. Code Civ. Proc. Ann. 4061.1(C).

220. La. Code Civ. Proc. Ann. art. 4031; *see* Roussell v. Roussell, 96-148 (La. App. 5 Cir. 7/30/96), 678 So. 2d 612 (refusing to appoint father as tutor to bring an action against the minor's therapist when mother refused).

221. In re Tutorship of Cardenas, 2009-2020, p. 7 (La. App. 1 Cir. 6/11/10), 38 So. 3d 1284, 1284. The father was attempting to file a civil action against the mother's father (the children's grandfather). Cardenas, 38 So. 3d at 1285–86.

222. Cardenas, 38 So. 3d. at 1289 (citing La. Code Civ. Proc. Ann. art. 4031).

223. Cardenas, 38 So. 3d. at 1289.

224. Cardenas, 38 So. 3d. at 1289.

225. Rice, 589 Fed. Appx. at 691.

purpose of bringing the suit.[226] Under Louisiana law, the grandparents had no right to act when the mother refused to bring suit because the grandparents were not cotutors with the mother; the mother's decision, or inaction in this case, controlled unless the grandparents had the mother disqualified and had themselves named as tutors.[227] The court in *Rice* relied on federal procedural law to provide the grandparents with the right of action as a guardian or "next friend," a concept not available under Louisiana tutorship law.[228] Its applicability under Louisiana law is questionable when a natural tutor exists.

§ 10:17 Appointment of Tutors—Tutors by Will, Legal Tutors, and Dative Tutors

Non-natural tutors must be confirmed or appointed by the court and must qualify for the office as provided by law.[229] Like natural tutors, these tutors must take an oath, prepare an inventory or detailed descriptive list of the minor's property, and post security, but legal mortgages are only available for natural tutors.[230] Individuals seeking appointment as legal or dative tutors must (1) notify the minor's ascendants, the minor's second and third degree collaterals (siblings, aunts/uncles, nieces/nephews), and the surviving spouse of the minor's parent who died last (surviving step-parent) who reside in Louisiana that a petition for the appointment of a tutor has been filed; (2) provide an affidavit to the court listing the persons who receive notification; and (3) publish notice of the petition for appointment in the parish where the petition was filed.[231] All three steps must be performed under penalty of nullity.[232] An opposition to the appointment can be filed, which shall allege why the applicant is disqualified or

226. Rice, 589 Fed. Appx. at 690–91. The court interpreted Federal Rule of Civil Procedure 17(c) to allow the appointment of a next friend or guardian *ad litem* when a minor's legal representative is unable or refuses to act. *Id.* at 691. Federal Rule Civil Procedure 17(c) provides: "A minor ... who does not have a duly appointed representative may sue by a next friend or by a guardian *ad litem*. The court must appoint a guardian *ad litem*—or issue another appropriate order—to protect a minor or incompetent person who is unrepresented in an act." Fed. R. Civ. P. 17(c)(2).

227. Rice, 589 Fed. Appx. at 690–92.

228. Rice, 589 Fed. Appx. at 690.

229. La. Code Civ. Proc. Ann. arts. 4062–64.

230. La. Code Civ. Proc. Ann. arts. 4061, 4101–02, 4171, 4131–37; *see* Dennis v. Rodriguez, 2007-1582, pp. 5–8 (La. App. 1 Cir. 3/26/08), 985 So. 2d 758, 761–72 (finding that the legal mortgage was not available to minor's aunt because she was not a natural tutor).

231. La. Code Civ. Proc. Ann. art. 4065; *see also* La. Stat. Ann. § 43:203. The notification must be made by registered or certified mail. La. Code Civ. Proc. Ann. art. 4065.

232. Continuing Tutorship of Harris, 2022-1013, pp. 3–4 (La. App. 1 Cir. 2/24/23), 361 So. 3d 1068, 1071–72 (vacating the appointment of a continuing tutrix because procedure was not followed); In re Robertson, 283 So. 2d 834, 836 (La. Ct. App. 2 Cir. 1973) (setting aside the tutorship of an aunt because the procedure was not followed, even though removal of the aunt as tutrix "would border on the 'ridiculous'"); *see also* In re Custody of Booty, 95-0828 (La. App. 1 Cir. 11/9/95), 665 So. 2d 444, 448 n.2; Tutorship of Woodard, 216 So. 2d 132 (La. Ct. App. 2 Cir. 1968).

why the opponent, rather than the applicant, should be appointed tutor.[233] If no oppositions are filed and the applicant is not disqualified, the appointment of the applicant will be made.[234]

§ 10:18 Appointment of Tutors—Separate Tutor over the Minor's Property

In light of exceptional circumstances and for good cause, a court may appoint a bank or other person as a separate tutor of the minor's property.[235] The appointment may be made when tutorship is initially established or, when necessary, during the period of tutorship.[236] The court has discretion to determine when a separate tutor over the property is necessary, and a possible conflict of interest between the minor and the tutor may be enough.[237] In *In re Tutorship of Werling*, the minor's mother, who was the natural tutor, killed the minor's father and was the named beneficiary of a substantial amount of life insurance.[238] Because the minor was the secondary beneficiary of the life insurance, the Fourth Circuit found "exceptional circumstances" and "good cause shown" to appoint a separate tutor over the minor's property to protect the minor's interest in the life insurance.[239]

In addition, parents who share joint custody may appoint a tutor by will, but because tutorship by will belongs only to the parent dying last, the parent who dies first can name a tutor only over the property of the minor attributable to his or her estate.[240] Because these parents are expressly authorized by the Code to appoint a separate tutor over the property, the court should not need to find exceptional circumstances or good cause shown, as both are provided by law.[241]

---

233. La. Code Civ. Proc. Ann. art. 4066. The opposition must meet the same requirements as oppositions in succession proceedings. *See* La. Code Civ. Proc. Ann. art. 2972. There are no statutory or jurisprudential limits on who may oppose the appointment, likely to ensure that the court is aware of all facts that could impact the best interest of the minor.

234. La. Code Civ. Proc. Ann. art. 4067. The appointment can be made 10 days from publication or the date notice is mailed to the minor's relations, whichever period is longer. *Id.*

235. La. Code Civ. Proc. Ann. art. 4069. The idea of a split tutorship was recognized in the Code of 1870 when mothers could retain custody of the child but not administration of the minor's estate. La. Civ. Code art. 253 (1870).

236. La. Code Civ. Proc. Ann. art. 4069 cmt. (b).

237. In re Tutorship of Werling, 518 So. 2d 1177, 1179 (La. Ct. App. 4 Cir. 1988); *see also* In re England, 2016-0933, p. 4 (La. App. 4 Cir. 04/05/17), 215 So. 3d 720, 722 (exercising discretion in refusing to appoint a separate tutor over the minor's property); In re Sanches, 619 So. 2d 799, 802–03 (La. Ct. App. 1 Cir. 1993) (same).

238. Werling, 518 So. 2d at 1178.

239. Werling, 518 So. 2d at 1178.

240. La. Civ. Code Ann. art. 258.

241. *But see* Sanches, 619 So. 2d at 802 n.3 (court did not find exceptional circumstances or good cause shown to name a separate tutor over the property of the minor, even though the deceased parent named her brother as tutor in her testament).

§ 10:19 Appointment of Tutors— Appointment of a Provisional Tutor

Appointment of a provisional tutor is available when necessary for the welfare of the minor or to preserve the minor's property.[242] Provisional tutors can be used to fill a gap in the court's power to protect the minor, most notably when the court is seeking to confirm a permanent tutor or when a vacancy in the role of tutor exists.[243] The provisional tutor has the same authority as the tutor and is subject to the same duties to care for the minor and to preserve the minor's property pending the appointment of a permanent tutor.[244] There is no provision for the appointment of a provisional undertutor.[245]

§ 10:20 Appointment of Tutors— Tutors for Small Tutorships

When the value of the minor's property has a gross value of $50,000 or less, Louisiana law provides simpler rules for tutorship.[246] While the hierarchy of natural, by will, legal, and dative tutors still apply, applicants in a small tutorship need only file a detailed descriptive list, rather than an inventory, and legal and dative tutors may not need to post security.[247] Natural tutors, however, must inscribe the legal mortgage.[248] Finally, no undertutor is necessary in a small tutorship, and court costs are one-half of the court costs generally charged in larger tutorships.[249] Overall, the law governing small tutorships provides a more economical approach in light of the reduced value of the minor's property.

---

242. La. Code Civ. Proc. Ann. art. 4070–73.

243. Leonard Oppenheim, *The Basic Elements of Tutorship in Louisiana*, 44 Tul. L. Rev. 453 (1970).

244. La. Code Civ. Proc. Ann. art. 4073. A special provision in the revised statutes also provides for a provisional tutor when the mother is dead before the child's majority and the father is absent. La. Stat. Ann. § 9:195.

245. La. Code Civ. Proc. Ann. art. 4070 cmt. (c).

246. La. Code Civ. Proc. Ann. arts. 4461–64. When initially enacted, the small tutorship involved $2,000 or less. La. Code Civ. Proc. Ann. art. 4461 cmt. (a). By Act 71 of 1979, the amount increased to $20,000 and by Act 118 of 2013, the amount increased to $50,000. Act No. 71, 1979 La. Acts.

247. La. Code Civ. Proc. Ann. arts. 4462–63.

248. La. Code Civ. Proc. Ann. arts. 4061–62, 4131–37. Failure of the natural tutor in a small tutorship to file the descriptive list in the mortgage records did not invalidate the tutorship. *See* In re Johnston, 1999-980 (La. App. 3 Cir. 2/2/00), 757 So. 2d 738, 740–41.

249. La. Code Civ. Proc. Ann. arts. 4463–64.

§ 10:21 Appointment of Tutors— Foreign Tutors

A foreign tutor is one that has been appointed by a court outside of Louisiana for a minor residing outside of Louisiana.[250] When no tutor has been appointed in Louisiana, the foreign tutor can appear in a Louisiana court without first qualifying as tutor in Louisiana.[251] Court authorization may still be necessary when the minor's property is affected, and to adjudicate the property, the foreign tutor must proceed in the same manner as a tutor appointed by a Louisiana court.[252] The foreign tutor need not take an oath or post security, as those requirements are necessary when individuals qualify as tutor under Louisiana law.[253] Rather, the foreign tutor must seek court authority to act on behalf of the minor when court authorization is necessary, or when the tutor seeks to take possession of the minor's property or remove it from the state.[254] The court may consider appointing an undertutor ad hoc to ensure that the minor's interests are represented.[255] Note that if the minor resides in Louisiana, then the appointment of a tutor must be made in accordance with Louisiana law.[256]

§ 10:22 Duties and Powers of the Tutor

The tutor's duties and powers are set forth in the Louisiana Code of Civil Procedure.[257] While they would be more appropriately placed in the Civil Code, the work of the Tutorship Procedure Committee of the Louisiana State Law Institute has yet to be completed.

The overarching power of the tutor is both personal and patrimonial, extending to the care of the person of the minor and administration of the minor's estate.[258] First, the tutor bears responsibility for the custody and care of the child, as well as for ensuring "that the minor is properly reared and educated in accordance with his station in

250. La. Code Civ. Proc. Ann. art. 4431. The foreign tutor may be termed a guardian under the foreign law. *Id.*

251. La. Code Civ. Proc. Ann. art. 4431. A foreign tutor may nonetheless be appointed as tutor using the same procedure as a resident tutor. La. Code Civ. Proc. Ann. art. 4433. If a foreign tutor is appointed in Louisiana, he must appoint a resident as his agent for service of process. La. Code Civ. Proc. Ann. art. 4433 cmt. (b).

252. La. Code Civ. Proc. Ann. arts. 4431–32.

253. *See* Curtis v. Union Homestead Ass'n, 53 So. 63, 67 (La. 1910).

254. La. Code Civ. Proc. Ann. arts. 4431–32.

255. *See* Curtis, 53 So. at 67.

256. Slade v. Louisiana Power & Light Co., 418 F.2d 125, 126 (5th Cir. 1969) (refusing to allow a guardian, appointed by a Mississippi court, over a minor who resided in Louisiana to bring an action on the children's behalf, as that right belonged to the parents of the children under Louisiana law of tutorship).

257. La. Code Civ. Proc. Ann. arts. 4261–75.

258. La. Code Civ. Proc. Ann. arts. 4261–62. A separate section in this chapter is devoted to the overlap of the care of the minor's person under tutorship and the laws on custody. *See* Section 10:31.

life."[259] As a general rule, expenses for support and education are limited to revenue generated from the minor's property, but if the revenue is insufficient, the tutor may obtain court approval to expend the minor's capital.[260] The personal duties owed by tutors undeniably overlap with custody, which has led to inconsistent application and confusion among courts, and will be discussed in more detail below.[261]

Second, the tutor owes duties to the minor over his patrimonial interests.[262] For example, the tutor must take possession of, preserve, and administer the minor's property, enforce all obligations in favor of the minor, and represent the minor in all civil matters.[263] Note, however, that in *Liebendorfer v. Gayle*, the court refused a request by the natural tutrix to take possession of certain bonds belonging to the minors because the parents had previously agreed that the bonds would be held by the father.[264] The dissenting judge described the duty of the tutor to take possession and preserve the property of the minor as mandatory, such that any prior agreement should give way to the positive law.[265] In all cases, the tutor must act as a prudent administrator and is held personally responsible for damages due to his failure to act.[266] Like parents, tutors are also responsible for the damage occasioned by the minor child.[267]

As a prudent administrator, the tutor cannot self-deal, under penalty of nullity.[268] The tutor is not allowed, in his personal or representative capacity, to make any contracts with the minor.[269] Further, the tutor cannot acquire property of the minor, personally or through a third person, except as otherwise provided by law.[270] For example, when parents and minors own property in common, the parent is permitted to purchase all or some of the minor's share, as long as the price is fixed by experts appointed by the court and the transaction is approved by the court.[271]

259. La. Code Civ. Proc. Ann. art. 4261.

260. La. Code Civ. Proc. Ann. art. 4261.

261. *See* Section 10:31.

262. *See* La. Code Civ. Proc. Ann. art. 4262.

263. La. Code Civ. Proc. Ann. art. 4262. For further protection of the minor, the Code also imposes a duty for any nonresident tutor (or temporary absence from the state) to execute a power of attorney appointing a resident of Louisiana as an agent to receive service of process for any action brought against them in their capacity as tutor. *Id.*; La. Code Civ. Proc. Ann. art. 4273.

264. Liebendorfer v. Gayle, 210 So. 2d 120, 122 (La. Ct. App. 3 Cir. 1968).

265. Liebendorfer, 210 So. 2d at 123–24 (Savoy, J., dissenting); *see also* Leonard Oppenheim, *The Basic Elements of Tutorship in Louisiana*, 44 Tul. L. Rev. 482–83 (1970).

266. La. Code Civ. Proc. Ann. art. 4262.

267. La. Civ. Code Ann. art. 2318.

268. *See* La. Code Civ. Proc. Ann. art. 4263.

269. La. Code Civ. Proc. Ann. art. 4263.

270. La. Code Civ. Proc. Ann. art. 4263.

271. La. Code Civ. Proc. Ann. art. 4361; *see also* La. Code Civ. Proc. Ann. arts. 4362–63.

§ 10:23 Duties and Powers of the Tutor— Duty to Account

The tutor's duty to account is significant. It is the mechanism that allows the minor and the undertutor to review the tutor's administration of the property. Further, the final accounting can alert the minor to act quickly and, within the four-year prescriptive period after his majority, to challenge the actions of the tutor.[272] The final accounting is generally a prerequisite for claims that the minor may have against the tutor.[273]

From the day of the tutor's appointment, an annual account must be filed with the court.[274] In addition, the court can order an accounting to be prepared at any other time when the court recognizes a need or an interested person requests it.[275] Then, at expiration of the tutorship, the tutor should prepare a final account, although there is no absolute duty to do so.[276] When ordered by the court based on a request by the former minor, however, the tutor must prepare a final account.[277] Further, a final account is necessary after a judgment ordering the tutor's removal or accepting his resignation.[278]

Modelled from succession procedure, the accounting must show the minor's property at the beginning of the period; the revenue, receipts, disbursements, and disposition of property during the period; and the minor's remaining property at the end of the period.[279] The annual or interim accounting filed by the tutor must be served on the undertutor.[280] The final accounting also must be served on the former minor and the successor tutor, if applicable.[281] Although the tutor must only serve the former minor with a final accounting, a minor would certainly have the right to review an accounting filed during the tutorship.[282]

---

272. La. Civ. Code Ann. art. 340; *see* Farris v. Kolb, 47,886, pp. 5–6 (La. App. 2 Cir. 2/27/13), 135 So. 3d 674, 676–77 (refusing to dismiss a minor's request for an accounting made within the four-year prescriptive period, even though the minor consented to cancel the tutor's surety bond); Succession of Triola, 2017-301, p. 12 (La. App. 5 Cir. 12/27/17), 236 So. 3d 792, 801 (dismissing claims of former minor against his father because no accounting had been requested nor claim brought within the four-year prescriptive period).

273. Kolb, 135 So. 3d at 676.

274. La. Code Civ. Proc. Ann. art. 4391.

275. La. Code Civ. Proc. Ann. art. 4391.

276. *See* Succession of Jarreau, 289 So. 2d 887, 890 (La. Ct. App. 4 Cir. 1974).

277. La. Code Civ. Proc. Ann. art. 4392.

278. La. Code Civ. Proc. Ann. art. 4392.

279. La. Code Civ. Proc. Ann. arts. 3333, 4393.

280. La. Code Civ. Proc. Ann. art. 4394. The undertutor must also receive notice that the account can be homologated after 10 days from the date of service of the accounting, and any opposition must be filed before homologation. *Id.* For a final account, the former minor and any successor tutor must receive service if the final account is prepared after a removal, resignation, death, or interdiction of the tutor. *Id.*

281. La. Code Civ. Proc. Ann. art. 4394.

282. La. Code Civ. Proc. Ann. art. 4394.

§ 10:24 Duties and Powers of the Tutor—Power to Act

The tutor exercises power over the minor's affairs, with judicial oversight at times.[283] Without the need for court approval, the tutor is allowed to act in his own name as tutor, exercising all procedural rights available to a litigant, and he may also act through a mandatary or attorney in fact in certain circumstances.[284] A tutor can hire a lawyer on behalf of the minor without prior court approval.[285] As it relates to fees for representing the minor, the court will necessarily consider the appropriateness of the fees assessed when it approves the settlement of the minor's claims, but the decision to terminate or modify the terms of a representation agreement do not require court approval.[286] Additionally, the tutor may accept donations made to the minor without court approval, but the tutor cannot make any donations of the minor's property.[287]

Other powers are granted to the tutor only after judicial authorization, the absence of which may render the action null.[288] These powers include: (1) compromising an action or right of action by or against the minor;[289] (2) extending, renewing, or modifying an obligation owed by or to the minor;[290] (3) continuing a business in which the minor has an interest;[291] (4) borrowing money in the minor's name, including mortgaging or pledging property to secure the loan;[292] (5) granting a lease on the property of the minor;[293] (6) placing some or all of the minor's property in a spendthrift

---

283. *See* La. Code Civ. Proc. Ann. art. 4264.

284. La. Code Civ. Proc. Ann. art. 4264.

285. *See* S. Shipbuilding Corp. v. Richardson, 372 So. 2d 1188, 1190–91 (La. 1979); In re Tutorship of Ingraham, 565 So. 2d 1012, 1018 (La. Ct. App. 1 Cir. 1990).

286. Ingraham, 565 So. 2d at 1018 (concluding that concurrence of the undertutor and/or court approval is not needed to enter into a contract for the services of an attorney, to modify the contract, or to terminate the contract).

287. La. Code Civ. Proc. Ann. art. 4275.

288. *See* Green v. City of Shreveport, 39,066 (La. App. 2 Cir. 10/27/04), 888 So. 2d 314. Natural tutors may act on behalf of a minor child without judicial authorization for matters that do not exceed $10,000. La. Stat. Ann. § 9:196.

289. La. Code Civ. Proc. Ann. art. 4265.

290. La. Code Civ. Proc. Ann. art. 4265.

291. La. Code Civ. Proc. Ann. art. 4266. Continuing the business must appear to be in the minor's best interest. *Id.*

292. La. Code Civ. Proc. Ann. art. 4267. Borrowing funds must appear to be in the best interest of the minor, and the funds must be necessary to preserve or administer the minor's property, to pay debts, to pay for expenditures in the regular course of a business, or to pay for the care, maintenance, training, or education of the minor. *Id.* Additional security by the tutor may be required. *Id.*

293. La. Code Civ. Proc. Ann. art. 4268. The lease may extend beyond the term of the tutorship and must appear to be in the best interest of the minor. *Id.* Mineral leases are included as are other contracts affecting the minor's interest in in oil, gas, or other minerals. *Id.*

trust;[294] (7) investing, reinvesting, or withdrawing the minor's funds;[295] (8) selling or exchanging the minor's property;[296] and (9) expending the minor's capital to support and educate the minor.[297]

The tutor must seek court approval in a petition that explains the action affecting the minor's interests, includes the tutor's recommendations and reasons for the request, and attaches the undertutor's written concurrence.[298] If a tutor fails to seek court approval, minors can annul agreements with creditors or other third parties who dealt with a tutor acting without proper authority.[299] For example, in *Deville v. Federal Savings Bank*, the court annulled a loan in favor of a minor and the pledge of the minor's savings account as security for the loan because the tutrix failed to obtain court authorization for either.[300] Because the bank made loans to a tutrix who lacked court authority and a minor who lacked contractual capacity, it could not enforce the loan against the minor's property.[301] As explained by the court, although the tutrix had the power to borrow money for the benefit of the minor, it could only exercise the power with "prior express authorization" by a court.[302]

As for compromising and settling the claims of a minor, the statutory requirements are rigorous because "it is the general policy of our law to protect all minors from the possible consequences of immaturity."[303] The tutor must be appointed and seek court approval before compromising a claim, and the court must determine that the proposed compromise is in the best interest of the minor.[304] In *Succession of Hellmers*,

---

294. La. Code Civ. Proc. Ann. art. 4269.1. The minor must be the sole beneficiary; the trust shall name a trustee; and the trust must terminate at the option of the beneficiary at the age of majority or, if the minor fails to attain the age of majority, at the option of his heirs or legatees. *Id.*

295. La. Code Civ. Proc. Ann. art. 4270. A court may authorize a tutor to open a checking account on behalf of the minor and write checks for the minor's necessary expenses without the need to obtain prior court approval. The account shall not exceed $5,000 a year, except for good cause shown, and all amounts should appear on the accounting. *Id.*

296. La. Code Civ. Proc. Ann. art. 4301. The sale or exchange can be for any purpose, which includes a partition. La. Code Civ. Proc. Ann. art. 4301 cmt. (b); *see also* La. Code Civ. Proc. Ann. arts. 4641–43. The sale shall be for cash, unless a credit sale is authorized, and the tutor may have to post additional security. La. Code Civ. Proc. Ann. arts. 4302-04. The sale may be made at a public or private sale as provided by law. *See* La. Code Civ. Proc. Ann. arts. 4321–42. An exchange for other property or property and cash is also available. La. Code Civ. Proc. Ann. art. 4371.

297. La. Code Civ. Proc. Ann. art. 4261.

298. La. Code Civ. Proc. Ann. art. 4271. Without the undertutor's concurrence, the tutor must file a contradictory motion against him. *Id.*

299. Deville v. Federal Savings Bank of Evangeline Parish, 93-1853 (La. 4/11/94), 635 So. 2d 195, 198; Snowden v. Huey P. Long Memorial Hospital, 581 So. 2d 287 (La. Ct. App. 3 Cir. 1991); Daigle v. Clemco Indus., 593 So. 2d 1282 (La. Ct. App. 1 Cir. 1991), *aff'd*, 613 So. 2d 619 (La. 1993); *but see* Corcoran v. Alonzo, 99-607 (La. App. 5 Cir. 11/10/99), 749 So. 2d 708.

300. Deville, 635 So. 2d at 196.

301. Deville, 635 So. 2d at 198.

302. Deville, 635 So. 2d at 197–98.

303. Johnson v. Ford Motor Co., 707 F.2d 189, 194 (5th Cir. 1983) (internal quotation marks omitted) (quoting State in the Interest of Dino, 359 So. 2d 586, 593 (La. 1978)).

304. *See* Carter v. Fenner, 136 F.3d 1000, 1009 (5th Cir. 1998).

the court rejected the defendant's argument that a father was authorized to settle a claim of his minor son because his petition was brought "individually and on behalf of his minor children" when no tutorship proceeding had been instituted.[305] The court explained that even if the father had been properly confirmed as tutor, court approval was required to compromise the minor's claim, which also did not occur.[306] Although the defendant would receive credit for the payment of funds that the father used to benefit the children, the defendant's payment to the father, in the amount of $1.4 million, did not satisfy its liability to the minor children because court oversight, necessary to protect the interests of the children, was nonexistent.[307]

As for investing, the tutor may acquire and retain every kind of property and investment for the benefit of the minor, and the tutor is charged with exercising the judgment and care that persons "of prudence, discretion, and intelligence exercise in the management of their own affairs."[308] The tutor is not restricted in the type of investment but should consider "the probable income as well as the probable safety of their capital;" the tutor should not speculate but should evaluate the options as the tutor would if the investment involved his own funds.[309] Prudence guides the investment; courts provide an additional review.[310]

Courts not only provide express authorization for actions of the tutor that require judicial oversight and approval, but courts also must approve payments made to the minor.[311] When a minor is to be paid funds pursuant to a judgment or settlement, the court may order that the funds be kept in the court registry, invested in interest-bearing accounts, placed in trust, placed in a structured settlement, or any combination thereof.[312] Courts also permit reasonable compensation to the tutor, which cannot exceed 10% of the annual revenue of the minor's property unless the court finds that

---

305. Succession of Hellmers, 93-2386 (La. App. 4 Cir. 5/26/94), 637 So. 2d 1302, 1307–08 (internal quotation mark omitted); *see also* Bowen v. Smith, 2003-0432 (La. App. 4 Cir. 9/8/04), 885 So. 2d 1, 3–4; Snowden, 581 So. 2d at 289–90; *but see* Corcoran, 749 So. 2d at 711–12 (affirming settlement of minor's claims even though mother had not been confirmed as natural tutor because court had approved the settlement and the party challenging the settlement was the undertutor in the original settlement).

306. Hellmers, 637 So. 2d at 1308.

307. Hellmers, 637 So. 2d at 1308–09. A malpractice claim was brought against the attorney who failed to open the tutorship proceeding for the minors' claims, but it had prescribed. *Id.* at 1305–06; *see also* Bowen, 885 So. 2d 1 (annulling the settlement of a minor's claim because natural tutor did not seek court approval of the compromise).

308. La. Code Civ. Proc. Ann. art. 4269; *see* Leonard Oppenheim, *The Basic Elements of Tutorship in Louisiana*, 44 Tul. L. Rev. 484–89 (1970) (describing the shift toward "the prudent man rule" and discussing its applicability).

309. La. Code Civ. Proc. Ann. art. 4269; *see* Leonard Oppenheim, *The Basic Elements of Tutorship in Louisiana*, 44 Tul. L. Rev. 484–85 (1970) (noting that with the enactment of the Code of Civil Procedure, the restriction on investing the minor's property in equities was lifted).

310. La. Code Civ. Proc. Ann. arts. 4269–70; *see* Leonard Oppenheim, *The Basic Elements of Tutorship in Louisiana*, 44 Tul. L. Rev. 484–89 (1970).

311. La. Code Civ. Proc. Ann. art. 4272.

312. La. Code Civ. Proc. Ann. art. 4521. The court will consider factors to determine whether a structured settlement is in the best interest of the minor. *Id.*

amount to be inadequate.[313] Court approval is pervasive to protect the interest of the minor, but court oversight likewise protects the decisions of the tutor and undertutor from later claims of liability for imprudence.[314]

§ 10:25 Revocation, Resignation, and Removal of Tutor

The law provides specific rules governing the revocation, resignation, and removal of a tutor.[315] Because the tutor may have served for some period of time, the law has an interest in protecting the minor related to any acts performed while under the tutorship. As a result, even though a tutor who has resigned or has been removed no longer has authority (except the duty to provide a final accounting), the tutor remains liable for all acts committed prior to his resignation or removal.[316] Upon the death, removal, or resignation of a tutor, another tutor must be appointed in accordance with the law.[317] The same rule applies for the undertutor.[318] Tutorship is not a heritable right, although a former tutor's succession representative or heirs are responsible for administering the minor's property while the appointment of a new tutor is pending.[319]

Revocation of appointment occurs when the tutor fails to qualify, having never been the tutor.[320] If the tutor, who is not a parent of the minor, fails to qualify (i.e., fails to sign the oath, prepare the inventory or detailed descriptive list, or post security) within 10 days of his appointment, unless that time is extended for good cause shown, the court may revoke the tutor's appointment and appoint another person.[321] The role of the undertutor can likewise be revoked for the same reasons and using the same process.[322] Resignation and removal, on the other hand, apply after a tutor has properly qualified but is being removed, either voluntarily or involuntarily, as tutor.

---

313. La. Code Civ. Proc. Ann. art. 4274; *see* Tutorship of Scott, 142 So. 710, 712 (La. Ct. App. 2 Cir. 1932) (concluding that the annual revenues from which the tutor's 10% compensation was calculated included gross revenues before expenses for taxes, repairs, insurance premiums, and the like).

314. Leonard Oppenheim, *The Basic Elements of Tutorship in Louisiana*, 44 Tul. L. Rev. 491–92 (1970) (noting that court reliance on approvals by tutors and undertutors results in summary approval of their decisions without due regard for their prudence).

315. *See* La. Code Civ. Proc. Ann. arts. 4232–34.

316. La. Code Civ. Proc. Ann. art. 4235. The rule technically does not apply to revocation because the person appointed tutor never assumed the role.

317. La. Code Civ. Proc. Ann. art. 4237.

318. La. Code Civ. Proc. Ann. art. 4237.

319. La. Code Civ. Proc. Ann. art. 4238.

320. La. Code Civ. Proc. Ann. art. 4232.

321. La. Code Civ. Proc. Ann. art. 4232.

322. La. Code Civ. Proc. Ann. art. 4236.

§ 10:26 Revocation, Resignation, and Removal of Tutor—Resignation

A tutor, when authorized by a court, may be allowed to resign from office.[323] The Code of Civil Procedure provides the grounds for resignation:

(1) If subsequent to his appointment as tutor he has been invested with an office or engaged in a service or occupation which excuses him from the obligation of serving as tutor;

(2) If he has reached the age of seventy years;

(3) If because of infirmity he has become incapable of discharging the duties of his office; or

(4) For any other reason which the court in its discretion may deem sufficient.[324]

The first three grounds emanate from the grounds for disqualification[325] but occur after the person has been vested with tutorship. The fourth provides great discretion to the court because "[a] tutor who is unwilling to continue in office is not likely to afford the best care to the minor or his property."[326] In no case, however, can a parent of the minor child resign.[327] Undertutors may likewise resign at any time for any reason, as long as court approval is obtained.[328] The resignation of a tutor or undertutor is effective when a successor has been appointed and qualified, and for the tutor, when the final account has been filed and accepted.[329]

§ 10:27 Revocation, Resignation, and Removal of Tutor—Removal

A court may remove a tutor involuntarily when: (1) the tutor is or has become disqualified; (2) the tutor is a nonresident or is a resident who left the state and did not appoint an agent to represent him;[330] (3) the tutor has become incapable of performing his duties; (4) the tutor has mismanaged the minor's property; (5) the tutor has failed to perform a legal or court-ordered duty; or (6) if removal is in the best interest of the minor.[331]

---

323. La. Code Civ. Proc. Ann. art. 4232.

324. La. Code Civ. Proc. Ann. art. 4233.

325. *See* La. Code Civ. Proc. Ann. art. 4231.

326. La. Code Civ. Proc. Ann. art. 4233 cmt. (b).

327. La. Code Civ. Proc. Ann. art. 4231 cmt. (a).

328. La. Code Civ. Proc. Ann. art. 4236.

329. La. Code Civ. Proc. Ann. arts. 4233, 4236.

330. La. Code Civ. Proc. Ann. art. 4234; *see also* La. Code Civ. Proc. Ann. art. 4273; In re Tutorship of Ingraham, 565 So. 2d 1012, 1019 (La. Ct. App. 1 Cir. 1990) (removing a nonresident for failing to appoint an agent within 10 days from appointment).

331. La. Code Civ. Proc. Ann. art. 4234.

At any point during tutorship, the court may order the tutor to show cause why he should not be removed from office.[332] If the tutor cannot be served, an attorney must be appointed to represent him,[333] and before removal, a contradictory hearing must be held.[334] Any removal is prospective only and does not affect any of the tutor's action before his removal.[335] Undertutors can be removed for the same reasons and using the same process.[336]

The court is given wide discretion to remove a tutor when it is in the best interest of the minor.[337] In *In re Jones*, the court removed a father as cotutor because of his consistent, unsupported opposition to payments being made from a special needs trust to his disabled daughter.[338] Based on facts developed from testimony of the father, the mother, and the third-party trustee, the father sought only to preserve the funds without considering the immediate and pressing needs of the minor.[339] As a result, needless funds of the minor were being used to defend decisions that were in the best interest of the minor.[340] The father was therefore removed.[341]

§ 10:28 Termination and Continuing Tutorship

Tutorship ends when the minor reaches the age of majority or is fully emancipated.[342] Judicial emancipation is available for a minor age 16 years or older,[343] and the minor can petition alone, the tutor can petition alone, or the minor and the tutor can jointly petition to relieve the minor of the effects of minority.[344] Emancipation by marriage likewise occurs when a minor age 16 or 17 marries, whether the marriage is lawful or putative.[345]

---

332. La. Code Civ. Proc. Ann. art. 4234. The court may proceed on its own motion or at the request of an interested party. La. Code Civ. Proc. Ann. art. 4234; *see also* In re McCauley, 52,206 (La. App. 2 Cir. 9/26/18), 257 So. 3d 255, 259 (finding that a defendant in a civil suit brought by the tutrix was an interested party to seek the removal of the tutrix).

333. La. Code Civ. Proc. Ann. art. 4234.

334. La. Code Civ. Proc. Ann. art. 4234; *see also* In re Tutorship of Todd, 198 So. 2d 505, 506 (La. Ct. App. 4 Cir. 1967) (vacating an ex parte removal of a tutrix for failure to conduct a hearing).

335. La. Code Civ. Proc. Ann. art. 4234.

336. La. Code Civ. Proc. Ann. art. 4236.

337. Roussell v. Roussell, 96-148 (La. App. 5 Cir. 7/30/96), 678 So. 2d 612, 614. The manifest error standard therefore applies on appellate review. *Id.*; *see also* In re Continuing Tutorship of J.R., 17-235 (La. App. 2 Cir. 1/3/18), 237 So. 3d 1256, 1259 (removing mother as cotutor due to mental health concerns).

338. In re Jones, 2012-1598 (La. App. 1 Cir. 9/10/13), 2013 WL 4828572.

339. Jones, 2013 WL 4828572.

340. Jones, 2013 WL 4828572.

341. Jones, 2013 WL 4828572.

342. *See* La. Civ. Code Ann. art. 246.

343. La. Civ. Code Ann. art. 366.

344. La. Code Civ. Proc. Ann. art. 3991.

345. La. Civ. Code Ann. art. 367, 367 cmts. (b)–(c).

Tutorship may not end at the age of majority if a person is placed under a continuing tutorship.[346] In 1966, Louisiana adopted a special procedure for persons with intellectual disabilities or mental deficiencies.[347] In 2024, the procedure was expanded to include not only children with intellectual disabilities, but those with limitations in adaptive functioning.[348] A person who is over the age of fifteen and "possesses less than two-thirds of the intellectual or adaptive functioning of a person of the same age with average intellectual or adaptive functioning," may be placed under full or limited continuing tutorship, which shall not end until the tutorship is removed by a court.[349] After the revision of 2024, a continuing tutorship may be full or limited, much like the law of interdiction.[350] Therefore, for an unemancipated minor who has an adaptive functioning level that renders him consistently unable to make reasoned decisions regarding some aspect of his life, a limited continuing tutorship may be appropriate.[351]

In a full continuing tutorship, the legal capacity of the person is relegated to that of a minor, and no interdiction proceeding is necessary.[352] In a limited continuing tutorship, the legal capacity of the person is relegated to that of a minor only with respect to the decree of continuing tutorship.[353] Procedurally, when the person is between the ages of fifteen and eighteen, the rules governing the appointment of a tutor—be it natural, by will, legal, or dative—apply.[354] Once a person reaches the age of majority, a continuing tutorship is no longer available; rather an interdiction may be available, but different procedural requirements apply including service on the person and the appointment of an attorney to represent him.[355] Failure to follow these rules can result in a continuing tutorship that is absolutely null.[356]

The grant of a continuing tutorship confers on the tutor and undertutor the same authority, responsibilities, and privileges as in other tutorships, with one notable

---

346. *See* La. Civ. Code Ann. art. 355.

347. Act No. 496, 1966 La. Acts 1036.

348. Act. No. 123, 2024 La. Acts. After the revision, the court can consider "children functioning at very low levels in the areas of communication, daily living skills, and socialization" as candidates for continuing tutorship. La. Civ. Code Ann. art. 355 cmt. (a) (2024).

349. La. Civ. Code Ann. arts. 354–55. The parents or tutors may petition with written concurrence of the coroner. La. Civ. Code Ann. art. 355.

350. La. Civ. Code Ann. art. 354 and cmt. (a) (2024).

351. La. Civ. Code Ann. art. 354 cmt. (a) (2024).

352. La. Civ. Code Ann. arts. 354, 359. Note that interdiction is nonetheless still available. La. Civ. Code Ann. art. 362.

353. La. Civ. Code Ann. arts. 358.1, 359.

354. La. Civ. Code Ann. art. 356.

355. La. Civ. Code Ann. art. 355 cmt. (b); *see also* Interdiction of Conrad, 17-530 (La. App. 5 Cir. 12/5/17), 2017 WL 6812284. Prior to the revision in 2024, a continuing tutorship was available after the person reached the age of majority, even though the procedural rules for interdiction applied. *See* La. Civ. Code Ann. art. 355 cmt (b) (2024).

356. *See* Conrad, 2017 WL 6812284 (concluding that orders of continuing tutorship from over 30 years before were absolute nullities because at the time the continuing tutorship was instituted, the disabled woman was over the age of eighteen and had not been served with process nor had an attorney been appointed to represent her as required by the interdiction laws); *see also* Continuing Tutorship of M.A., 2020-1190 (La. App. 1 Cir. 12/30/20), 2020 WL 7869244.

exception: continuing tutors are not responsible for the torts of the tutee.[357] Further, a non-profit continuing tutor service program may be appointed as the continuing tutor for an indigent in need if no individual seeks the appointment or meets the qualifications.[358] A continuing tutorship will necessarily extend beyond majority, and the tutee or any person adversely affected by the continuing tutorship can contest its continuing nature.[359] For good cause, the court may modify or terminate the tutorship.[360]

Whether one should pursue continuing tutorship or interdiction is up for debate.[361] When an intellectual deficiency or adaptive functioning gives rise to the need for protection at a young age, a regime directed to a minor seems appropriate. Ultimately, though, interdiction or the alternatives to interdiction can be considered, which are covered in the chapter on interdiction.[362]

§ 10:29 Tutorship Compared

The regime of tutorship overlaps, compares, and dovetails with other legal regimes that affect minors. While duplicating efforts to protect minors is a laudable goal, questions arise when the regimes intersect. Notably, parental authority ends when tutorship begins, but for natural parents, the day-to-day interactions remain the same. Further, as the law governing the custody of minors develops, the regime of tutorship sits idle and neglected, causing confusion when custodians clash or property issues arise. Finally, when the common law concept of guardianship for children in need of care made its entrance into Louisiana law, the law of tutorship appropriately shared its stage.

§ 10:30 Tutorship Compared— Parental Authority

For a minor, when parental authority ends, tutorship begins, keeping the minor always under the authority of a parent or tutor.[363] In many ways, parental authority and tutorship overlap. For example, during marriage, when a parent needs court approval to alienate, encumber, or lease the property of the minor, the law requires the parents to follow the same procedure applicable to tutors.[364] During parental authority,

357. La. Civ. Code Ann. art. 358; *see* Continuing Tutorship of Harris, 2022-1013 (La. App. 1 Cir. 2/24/23), 361 So. 3d 1068 (failure to follow the rules of tutorship in a request for continuing tutorship, filed three days before the minor's birthday, rendered the appointment an absolute nullity).

358. *See* La. Stat. Ann. §§ 9:1031–1034. The appointment of a non-profit service is also available for an indigent adult in need of full or limited interdiction. *See id.*

359. La. Civ. Code Ann. art. 361; *see* In re Franques, 2011-190 (La. App. 3 Cir. 10/5/11), 74 So. 3d 812.

360. La. Civ. Code Ann. art. 361.

361. *See* William Reed Huguet, *The New Law of Interdiction—Clear and Convincing Revision?*, 47 Loy. L. Rev. 1059, 1080–82 (2001).

362. *See* Chapter 12.

363. La. Civ. Code Ann. art. 234.

364. La. Code Civ. Proc. Ann. art. 4501.

parents have rights and obligations,[365] and during tutorship, the tutor has powers and duties.[366] Liability for damage caused by the minor applies to parents and tutors alike.[367] Care of the minor and administration of the minor's property are paramount in both regimes.[368] During the existence of parental authority and tutorship, neither the parent or tutor can sue the minor, nor can the minor sue the parent or tutor.[369]

Unlike a tutor, however, a parent during marriage is entitled to certain benefits from the minor.[370] The law provides that "[a] child owes assistance to his parents" and "shall obey his parents in all matters not contrary to law or good morals."[371] No parallel provisions exist under the regime of tutorship. Further, a parent during marriage may expend the fruits of the minor's property, not just for the child, but for the shared benefit of the family,[372] while the tutor is given no parallel right.

In addition, during marriage, parents act without qualification or appointment, and enjoy administration of the minor's property.[373] Only if the parent seeks to alienate, encumber, or lease the property of the minor or seeks to compromise a claim of the minor does the parent need court authority.[374] No inventory is made of the minor's property, and no legal mortgage protects the minor. Natural tutors, on the other hand—even though they receive tutorship "of right"—must take an oath, make an inventory of the minor's property, and cause a legal mortgage to be inscribed on the minor's property in lieu of security.[375] Further, a judge must determine that the parent is not "disqualified," a consideration never made when the parents are married.[376]

Courts have long recognized that the duties and responsibilities of tutors and parents during marriage "are very different,"[377] which might appropriately capture an elevated level of protection needed for the minor when his parents are no longer a family unit. However, for single parents, does the responsibility to prepare an inventory and file a legal mortgage make sense? Does the parental responsibility for their child's person or property really change when a marriage ends or never even began? It seems unlikely that single parents mismanage their child's property at a greater rate than married

365. La. Civ. Code Ann. art. 223.

366. La. Code Civ. Proc. Ann. arts. 4261–62.

367. La. Civ. Code Ann. art. 2317.

368. *Compare* La. Code Civ. Proc. Ann. art. 4262 (tutorship) *with* La. Civ. Code Ann. art. 229 (parental authority).

369. La. Stat. Ann. § 9:571.

370. *See* La. Civ. Code Ann. arts. 227–28.

371. La. Civ. Code Ann. arts. 227–28.

372. La. Civ. Code Ann. art. 230.

373. La. Civ. Code Ann. arts. 229–31.

374. La. Code Civ. Proc. Ann. art. 4501; *see e.g.*, LaPorte v. Clesi, Inc., 197 So. 2d 419 (La. Ct. App. 4 Cir. 1967) (finding that the father as administrator of the minor's property could not purchase property for the child nor ratify the child's contract for purchase without prior court approval because he had only the powers of a tutor).

375. La. Civ. Code Ann. art. 250; La. Code Civ. Proc. Ann. art. 4061.

376. La. Code Civ. Proc. Ann. art. 4031.

377. In re Monrose, 175 So. 475, 478 (La. 1937).

parents, such that additional legal requirements are necessary. Is an equal protection challenge looming? Would an extension of parental authority outside of marriage provide fewer burdens to parents without sacrificing protection of the child? Louisiana can learn from its civilian counterparts across the globe.

Although Louisiana continues to maintain a distinction between parental authority during marriage and natural tutorship outside of marriage, many civilian jurisdictions have modernized their laws by enlarging parental authority to apply to all parents, whether single, married, or divorced.[378] Since the turn of the century, civil law countries like France have tied parental authority to the act of parentage, regardless of the parents' relationship.[379] Parental authority terminates only when the child reaches the age of majority, is emancipated, or marries, but not when the parents divorce or are unmarried.[380] While a court may determine that only one parent can exercise parental authority after separation, the parents retain parental authority even in light of a separation in fact, legal separation, divorce, or annulment.[381]

Tutorship, on the other hand, applies when a third person steps in to care for a child if, for example, both parents are unable to exercise parental authority because they are deceased, interdicted, or have lost custody of the minor.[382] The more modern approach provides parents with rights as parents, regardless of their marital status, and eliminates the unnecessary change in regime when one parent dies and the other parent's role as the caregiver and administrator for the child never changes.[383] Indeed, placing the onus on a surviving parent after the death of a spouse or on a single parent

378. Frédérique Ferrand, National Report: France, Parental Responsibilities 11–12 (2005), https://ceflonline.net/wp-content/uploads/France-Parental-Responsibilities.pdf; Cristina González Beilfuss, National Report: Spain (2005), https://ceflonline.net/wp-content/uploads/Spain-Parental-Responsibilities.pdf; Nina Dethloff, National Report: Germany (2005), https://ceflonline. net/wp-content/uploads/Germany-Parental-Responsibilities.pdf (the term parental custody is used in the place of parental authority); Achilles G. Koutsouradis, National Report: Greece (2004), https://ceflonline.net/wp-content/uploads/Greece-Parental-Responsibilities.pdf; *but see* Civil Code of Québec, S.Q. 1991, c 64, art 597 (Can.) (parents enjoy parental authority over the care of the minor and are also legal tutors for the purpose of administering the minor's patrimony).

379. Ferrand, *supra* note 378.

380. Ferrand, *supra* note 378, at 1–4, 11–12; *see also* Bürgerliches Gesetzbuch [BGB] [Civil Code], § 1680, https://www.gesetze-im-internet.de/englisch_bgb/englisch_bgb.html#p6318 (Ger.) (parental custody continues in the surviving parent after the death of one parent).

381. Code civil [C. civ.] [Civil Code] art. 373-2 (Fr.); Ferrand, *supra* note 378, at 12; *see also* Ministerio de Justicia, Spanish Civil Code 52 (2016), https://www.mjusticia.gob.es/es/AreaTematica/DocumentacionPublicaciones/Documents/Spanish_Civil_Code_(Codigo_Civil_Espanol).PDF ("[when] parents ... live separately, parental authority [is] exercised by the parent with whom the child lives").

382. Code civil [C. civ.] [Civil Code] art. 373-5 (Fr.); Bürgerliches Gesetzbuch [BGB] [Civil Code], § 1773, https://www.gesetze-im-internet. de/englisch_bgb/englisch_bgb.html#p6318 (Ger.) (the term "guardianship" is used); Spanish Civil Code, *supra* note 381, at 56 (the term "guardianship" is used); Greek Civil Code: Translation of Constatntin Taliadoros 11, https://ceflonline.net/wp-content/uploads/Greece-Parental-Responsibilities-Legislation.pdf (the term "guardianship" is used).

383. Note that the Quebec Civil Code has retained a distinction between parental authority and legal tutor, which are both imposed on the parents of the minor, but the role of legal tutor includes only the management of the child's patrimony. Civil Code of Québec, S.Q. 1991, c 64, art 192 (Can.).

caring for a child to engage the judicial system, prepare an inventory, and inscribe the legal mortgage seems unnecessary. While divorced parents may not enjoy a cooperative relationship when acting as administrators, their rights as parents could still be constitutionally protected, and procedural safeguards could be put in place to address administrative issues when they disagree.

§ 10:31 Tutorship Compared—Custody

The law of custody impacts tutorship because a tutor enjoys custodial rights—the care of the minor's person. The extent to which custody and tutorship overlap has raised substantive and procedural issues for courts. Resolution of these issues should be addressed when the laws of tutorship are revised. A simple resolution could limit tutorship to the administration of the property of the minor and allow the laws of custody to address the care and control of the person of the minor.[384]

The court in *State ex rel. Bannister v. Bannister* first addressed the overlap of custody and tutorship when the natural mother of the child brought habeas corpus proceedings against the child's stepmother, who had been named the child's dative tutor.[385] After the natural parents divorced, custody of the minor child was awarded to the father, who later remarried.[386] After the father's death, his second wife (the child's stepmother) was appointed dative tutor to represent the minor in the father's succession.[387] The action was brought in a court of general jurisdiction, not the dedicated family court. About eight months later, the mother brought habeas corpus proceedings in the family court, naming the stepmother as defendant, and asking for custody of the minor.[388] The stepmother excepted to jurisdiction on the basis that her lawsuit had been first filed in the district court that shares concurrent jurisdiction with the family court on matters relating to minors.[389] On the merits, the stepmother argued that tutorship and legal custody are synonymous because tutorship involves the custody of the minor.[390]

Conceding that tutorship contains some right to custody of the person, the court highlighted the differences, explaining that tutorship primarily concerns the administration of the minor's estate:

> The concept that tutorship, although embracing some incidents of custody, is primarily concerned with the administration of the minor's business affairs

384. *See, e.g.*, Civil Code of Québec, S.Q. 1991, c 64, art[s] 192, 599 (Can.) (legal tutorship for parents involves only the management of the child's patrimony; parental authority involves the care of his well-being).

385. State ex rel. Bannister v. Bannister, 198 So. 2d 196 (La. Ct. App. 1 Cir. 1967).

386. Bannister, 198 So. 2d at 198.

387. Bannister, 198 So. 2d at 198.

388. Bannister, 198 So. 2d at 198. The paternal grandmother likewise brought habeas corpus proceedings in the family court. *Id.*

389. Bannister, 198 So. 2d at 198.

390. Bannister, 198 So. 2d at 198.

> has long been recognized. For example, in *State Ex Rel. Peter v. Stanga*, 161 La. 978, 109 So. 783 [La. 1926], a father seeking custody of his minor child in a proceeding conducted contradictorily with the maternal grandparents, contended that his prior appointment as natural tutor entitled him to custody. The court found the argument without substance on the ground that custody, as distinguished from tutorship, does not involve property rights, consequently the father's appointment as natural tutor conferred upon him no greater right to custody than he possessed by law as parent of the minor.[391]

Applying that reasoning, the court found that the district court had jurisdiction to appoint a tutor to administer the rights of the minor in his father's succession, but the family court had jurisdiction to consider the distinct, albeit related, issue of custody.[392] The stepmother would continue to serve as tutor until she was removed, but the mother could seek custody in the habeas corpus proceeding brought in family court.[393]

After the decision in *Bannister*, the Louisiana Supreme Court confirmed that tutorship and custody are distinct.[394] The court rejected the idea that every award of custody includes tutorship, following the development of the law of tutorship in the Civil Code and the Code of Civil Procedure.[395] While a person awarded custody of a minor may be "of right" the natural tutor, that person has no more than simply a "right," which is inchoate until a court appoints the person as tutor.[396] Stated otherwise, an award of custody is not an award of tutorship.

Particularly as it relates to succession proceedings, courts have used the law of tutorship, rather than the law of custody, to consider which applicant for tutorship would be a better custodian after the death of both parents.[397] The disqualification rules provide an avenue for the court to reject one custodian in favor of another.[398] A tutor is disqualified if he is "incapable of performing the duties" or is "otherwise unfit for appointment because of his physical or mental condition or bad moral character," which allow a court to consider the personal ability of the proposed tutor to raise a child.[399] For example, in *Succession of Quave*, the maternal and paternal grandmothers and a paternal aunt all sought tutorship of three minor children after the death of both parents.[400] When it appointed a tutor, the court did not apply the laws of custody; rather, based

391. Bannister, 198 So. 2d at 198–99.

392. Bannister, 198 So. 2d at 199.

393. Bannister, 198 So. 2d at 199; *see also* Paul v. Cloud, 378 So. 2d 586 (La. Ct. App. 3 Cir. 1979) (considering tutorship and custody separately and thereby awarding tutorship and custody to the decedent's brother, rather than the child's father, because the deceased mother, who had sole custody of the child, appointed her brother as tutor in her will and the court determined that custody in her brother would serve the child's best interest).

394. Griffith v. Roy, 269 So. 2d 217, 223 (La. 1972).

395. Griffith, 269 So. 2d at 223.

396. Griffith, 269 So. 2d at 223–24.

397. *See, e.g.*, Succession of Quave, 214 So. 2d 260 (La. Ct. App. 4 Cir. 1968).

398. *See, e.g.*, Quave, 214 So. 2d 260.

399. La. Code Civ. Proc. Ann. art. 4231(A)(6).

400. Quave, 214 So. 2d at 261.

on the disqualification requirements, the court considered the living conditions, age, and mental and physical health of the applicants, as well as the priority given to legal tutors, which included the personal care of the minor.[401]

Nothing in the law mandates a party to use the tutorship articles rather than the custody articles, or vice versa. Because there are separate venue articles for the two actions,[402] conflicts will necessarily arise. In *Matter of the Custody of Booty*, due to the murder-suicide of the minor's parents, an uncle sought and was awarded ex parte custody from the family court in East Baton Rouge, even though the grandfather was awarded provisional tutorship from a Tangipahoa court.[403] The grandfather challenged the removal of the child from Louisiana pursuant to the custody award, but the court found no error in the award of custody.[404] Because the two proceedings are different, with their own venue articles and requirements, the appointment of a custodian should not void the naming of a tutor or vice versa.[405] Noting that "at some point, the competing interests of the custodian and a provisional tutor must be resolved," the court found no need to do so because the child's best interest was served living with the uncle out of state, away from the tragic death of both parents.[406]

When litigants seek custody and tutorship in the same proceeding, courts apply both laws, with focus on the best interest factors when considering who is best to care for the person of the minor, which is necessarily a part of tutorship.[407] While tutorship includes an aspect of custody, custody does not include administration of the minor's estate, which is reserved to the tutor. After the death of a minor's parents, however, it seems sensible that the minor would reside with different relatives during the initial period of upheaval. Unbeknownst to friends and relatives, these decisions could have jurisdictional and substantive consequences in later proceedings when the care for the minor's person and property are at issue. Adjudicating tutorship and custody in the same proceeding is certainly preferrable but not always possible.[408]

---

401. Quave, 214 So. 2d at 262–63; *see also* Succession of Scott, 303 So. 2d 897 (La. Ct. App. 1 Cir. 1974) (applying tutorship laws, including the law of disqualification, rather than the laws of custody to name a personal caregiver of the minor).

402. *See, e.g.*, In re Custody of Booty, 95-0828 (La. App. 1 Cir. 11/9/95), 665 So. 2d 444.

403. Booty, 665 So. 2d 444.

404. Booty, 665 So. 2d at 447.

405. Booty, 665 So. 2d at 448; *see also* Knisely v. Knisely, 2005-1015 (La. App. 3 Cir. 3/1/06), 924 So. 2d 423, 426 ("While the concept of tutorship of minor children necessarily involves the responsibility of their custody and care, the ultimate test is the children's best interest in accordance with the factors outlined in La. Civ. Code art. 134. That is to say, custody and tutorship are not necessarily the same thing, and, although the appointment of a custodian and a tutor affect each other, the two proceedings are independent of each other, and each proceeding has its own venue article and requirements." (internal citations omitted)); In re Bogues, 236 So. 2d 665 (La. Ct. App. 2 Cir. 1970).

406. Booty, 665 So. 2d at 448.

407. *See* In the Interest of S.L.G., 39,704 (La. App. 2 Cir. 3/2/05), 895 So. 2d 773; *see also* In re Dative Tutorship of Moore, 55,047 (La. App. 2 Cir. 3/1/23), 358 So. 3d 203; Jones v. Willis, 43,608 (La. App. 2 Cir. 9/17/08), 996 So. 2d 364.

408. For example, if the venue articles do not permit filing in the same parish, if the jurisdiction of the court does not include both tutorship and custody, or if the litigant chooses not to request

§ 10:32 Tutorship Compared—Guardianship

The term guardianship is a common law concept, which in other jurisdictions functions much like tutorship. In 2011, the legislature approved a proposal to add a chapter entitled "Guardianship" in the Louisiana Children's Code in Title VI on Child in Need of Care to comply with federal law and to improve the outcomes of children removed from their parents' care.[409]

"Guardianship" is defined as "the judicial placement of a child under the duty and authority of a guardian to make decisions in matters having a permanent effect on the life and development of the child."[410] When a child is removed from his parents' care and placed in state custody, the state is required to submit a "permanent plan" after the child enters foster care.[411] The state's first option is always reunification with the parents, the second option is adoption, and the third is placement with a legal guardian.[412] Guardianship is a viable option when reunification and adoption are unavailable or not in the child's best interest.[413] In response to a call by Congress, Louisiana sought to expand the practice of appointing guardians, who are often relatives of the child, to provide permanence during minority for those children "stranded in the foster care system."[414]

While the common law concept of guardianship, like tutorship, includes both care of the child's person and property, Louisiana elected to give guardians only the care of the child's person.[415] Guardians in Louisiana have legal custody of the child, but do not have rights of administration over the child's property.[416] Unlike parents and tutors, guardians are not liable for any "damage occasioned by the child."[417] Should the guardian desire administrative rights over the child's property, then a separate tutor-

---

both, litigating the matters in the same proceeding is not possible. *See, e.g.*, Knisely, 924 So. 2d at 427 (rejecting argument that tutor named in the parent's will should get custody because of the tutorship designation when litigant did not even request appointment as tutor).

409. *See* La. Child. Code Ann. arts. 718–724.1, 718 cmt. (a); *see also* 42 U.S.C. § 601 (The Adoption and Safe Families Act); 42 U.S.C. § 671 (Fostering Connections to Success and Increasing Adoptions Act). Originally, to comply with the Adoption Assistance and Child Welfare Act of 1980, 42 U.S.C. 1305, Louisiana adopted a limited form of legal guardianship when the parents or tutor made a voluntary transfer of custody. *See* Christopher L. Blakesley, *Louisiana Family Law*, 52 La. L. Rev. 607, 634–35 (1992).

410. La. Child. Code Ann. art. 116(12.1).

411. La. Child. Code Ann. art. 702.

412. La. Child. Code Ann. art. 702; *see* La. Child. Code Ann. art. 603. If a guardian is not available, the law provides further options. La. Child. Code Ann. art. 702.

413. La. Child. Code Ann. art. 719, art. 719 cmt. (a).

414. La. Child. Code Ann. art. 718 cmt (b).

415. La. Child. Code Ann. art. 719 cmt. (a).

416. La. Child. Code Ann. art. 719(A). Guardians also have authority to consent to the child's marriage and to his enlistment in the armed forces of the United States, but they cannot consent to the child's adoption. *Id.*

417. La. Child. Code Ann. art. 719(B).

ship proceeding in the district court would be necessary.[418] Otherwise, the chapter on guardianship provides the laws applicable to those who serve children in need of care as guardians.[419]

§ 10:33 Future Revision

Whether the Romans, the French, the Spanish or any combination thereof shaped the law of tutorship, Louisiana is long overdue to address its deficiencies and to complete a comprehensive review of its law. The substantive law of tutorship, including the duties and powers of a tutor, should be relocated to the Civil Code, and decisions should be made regarding the overlap in custody and tutorship. Whether tutorship should apply only to non-parents is an interesting idea that also deserves exploration. And these suggestions do not even scratch the surface of the procedural issues that also deserve review—such as the venue provisions in tutorship and custody that allow the procedures to proceed independently[420] and the uncertainty of which court should authorize a settlement for a minor.[421] Tutorship has cemented its place in the laws of Louisiana as a protective regime for minors; as the law develops and changes, the best interest of the minor should remain paramount.

---

418. La. Child. Code Ann. art. 719(C) & cmt. (c).

419. *See* La. Child. Code Ann. arts. 718–724.1.

420. *Compare* La. Code Civ. Proc. Ann. art. 4031 (venue for tutorship) *with* La. Code Civ. Proc. Ann. art. 74.2 (venue for custody); *see also* La. Code Civ. Proc. Ann. art. 44 (providing that venue in tutorship is unwaivable).

421. *Compare* La. Code Civ. Proc. Ann. art. 4031 (venue for tutorship) *with* La. Code Civ. Proc. Ann. art. 74 (venue for tort claim); *see also* La. Code Civ. Proc. Ann. art. 4265 (providing that court approval is needed to compromise the claim).

Chapter 11

Emancipation

§ 11:1 Introduction

As explained in Chapters 9 and 10, parental authority and tutorship terminate upon, among other events, a minor child's emancipation, i.e., the child's liberation from the restrictions imposed by the legal status of minority.[1] This freedom is typically reciprocal because in most instances, emancipation relieves the minor child's parents from vicarious liability for that child.[2]

1. *See* Frank L. Maraist, 1A Louisiana Civil Law Treatise, Civil Procedure § 6:3 (2008).

2. *See, e.g.*, La. Civ. Code Ann. art. 2318, 368 cmt. (a) (relieving parents of liability for a child who has been emancipated by marriage or through a judgment of full emancipation, or judgment of limited emancipation that expressly relieves the parents of liability for damages occasioned by their minor children).

§ 11:2 Emancipation

Emancipation is currently quite uncommon under Louisiana law. This is probably because, as of 1972, the age of majority in this state is only 18 years.[3] Under prior law, when the age of majority was 21 years old, emancipation was more prevalent. This is because in such circumstances, a child might leave the family home before majority and need the independence that emancipation provides.

Emancipation in Louisiana was based on French law, derived from a combination of Roman principles. Understanding the history of emancipation law—from its early sources, through its development in Louisiana—informs its application today.

§ 11:3 Emancipation—History of Emancipation

Under ancient Roman law, emancipation served as relinquishment of parental power, but the emancipated child still lacked legal capacity.[4] The Romans also recognized the idea of "*venia aetatis*" or "coming of age," under which minors of a certain age were given anticipated capacity.[5]

The French combined the concepts from ancient Roman law to create its version of emancipation in the *Code civil*.[6] Similar to Roman law, an emancipated minor in France did not attain legal status as an adult.[7] Instead, the French considered an emancipated minor's status to lie somewhere between the incapable minor and the fully capable adult, with renowned civil law scholar, Planiol, comparing emancipation to a training period.[8]

The *Code civil* recognized two forms of emancipation: (1) emancipation by declaration, and (2) emancipation by marriage.[9] Under either form, once the minor was emancipated, their capacity extended primarily to administrative acts; other actions could be achieved only with the involvement of a curator or family council.[10] However, the law made an exception for emancipated minors who entered into a trade, whose

3. La. Civ Code Ann. art. 29.

4. Dane S. Ciolino & Monica Hof Wallace, *Recodifying Emancipation: A Precis of the 2009 Revision of Louisiana Emancipation Law*, 56 Loy. L. Rev. 135, 136 n. 4 (2010).

5. Dane S. Ciolino & Monica Hof Wallace, *Recodifying Emancipation: A Precis of the 2009 Revision of Louisiana Emancipation Law*, 56 Loy. L. Rev. 135, 136 n. 4 (2010).

6. Dane S. Ciolino & Monica Hof Wallace, *Recodifying Emancipation: A Precis of the 2009 Revision of Louisiana Emancipation Law*, 56 Loy. L. Rev. 135, 136 (2010).

7. Dane S. Ciolino & Monica Hof Wallace, *Recodifying Emancipation: A Precis of the 2009 Revision of Louisiana Emancipation Law*, 56 Loy. L. Rev. 135, 136 (2010).

8. Dane S. Ciolino & Monica Hof Wallace, *Recodifying Emancipation: A Precis of the 2009 Revision of Louisiana Emancipation Law*, 56 Loy. L. Rev. 135, 136 (2010).

9. *See* Code civil [C. civ.] [Civil Code] arts. 476–477 (1804) (Fr.) [hereinafter Code Napoleon].

10. Code Napoleon arts. 481, 484 (1804); Dane S. Ciolino & Monica Hof Wallace, *Recodifying Emancipation: A Precis of the 2009 Revision of Louisiana Emancipation Law*, 56 Loy. L. Rev. 135, 137–38 (2010). The family council was an assembly, comprised of six or more relatives, relatives-in-law, or friends of the minor, half from the mother's side and half from the father's side, presided over by the justice of the peace. *Id.* at 136 n. 10 (internal citations omitted).

status was that of a major for all acts relative to that trade.[11] Under neither form could the minor petition for their own emancipation.[12]

Emancipation by Declaration

An emancipation by declaration allowed a person with authority to declare a minor emancipated. In the initial draft of the *Code civil* (i.e., the *Projet du Gourvernement*), one could not declare a child to be emancipated before the child attained the age of 18 years.[13] However, this idea was never universally embraced, and in the final *Code civil*, the emancipation by declaration was allowed once the minor child had attained 15 years of age.[14]

Emancipation by declaration required the father, or in default of him, the mother, to declare the minor's emancipation.[15] The parent had to execute an act of under private signature and present it to a justice of the peace.[16] If neither parent could do so, the family council could recommend emancipation to a justice of the peace who could then declare it; however, this avenue was available only after the child had attained 18 years of age.[17] In neither case was the declarant required to obtain the child's agreement to be emancipated or notify the child of the declaration.[18]

The French acknowledged the possibility that an emancipated minor might overextend his resources.[19] Consequently, the French law allowed courts to reduce the child's excessive obligations upon consideration of the minor's resources, the intentions of parties contracting with the child, and the necessity of the expenses.[20] In case of reduction, the child's emancipation could thereafter be revoked,[21] reinstituting his full incapacity and returning him to the care of an adult until he attained majority.[22]

Emancipation by Marriage

The *Code civil* recognized marriage as tacitly emancipating minors.[23] Because the very idea of marriage inherently conflicts with parental authority, emancipation was

---

11. Code Napoleon art. 487 (1804).
12. Dane S. Ciolino & Monica Hof Wallace, *Recodifying Emancipation: A Precis of the 2009 Revision of Louisiana Emancipation Law*, 56 Loy. L. Rev. 135, 136–137 (2010).
13. Dane S. Ciolino & Monica Hof Wallace, *Recodifying Emancipation: A Precis of the 2009 Revision of Louisiana Emancipation Law*, 56 Loy. L. Rev. 135, 136–137 (2010).
14. Code Napoleon art. 477 (1804).
15. Code Napoleon art. 477 (1804).
16. Code Napoleon art. 477 (1804).
17. Code Napoleon art. 478 (1804).
18. Dane S. Ciolino & Monica Hof Wallace, *Recodifying Emancipation: A Precis of the 2009 Revision of Louisiana Emancipation Law*, 56 Loy. L. Rev. 135, 137 (2010).
19. Dane S. Ciolino & Monica Hof Wallace, *Recodifying Emancipation: A Precis of the 2009 Revision of Louisiana Emancipation Law*, 56 Loy. L. Rev. 135, 138 (2010).
20. Code Napoleon art. 484 (1804).
21. Code Napoleon art. 484 (1804).
22. Code Napoleon art. 486 (1804). Courts could not revoke the emancipation of a minor achieved by marriage. Dane S. Ciolino & Monica Hof Wallace, *Recodifying Emancipation: A Precis of the 2009 Revision of Louisiana Emancipation Law*, 56 Loy. L. Rev. 135, 138 (2010).
23. Code Napoleon art. 476 (1804).

automatic for a minor who married.[24] Such a minor did not need a formal declaration; the emancipation occurred by operation of law.[25]

§ 11:4 Emancipation—History of Emancipation—Early Louisiana Law

Emancipation law in Louisiana law changed several times over the years. This subpart explores its evolution from the Louisiana Digest of 1808 to the Louisiana Civil Code of 1825 to the Louisiana Civil Code of 1870.

Louisiana Digest of 1808

The state's first emancipation laws in the Louisiana Digest of 1808 paralleled that of the French *Code civil* in many ways.[26] Both emancipation by declaration and by marriage were allowed.[27] Unlike minors in France, those in Louisiana could take the initiative and directly petition for emancipation after their parents' death.[28] To do so, like under the *Code civil*, the minor had to be 18 years old, and the emancipation had to be recommended after a family meeting.[29] Similar to French law, Louisiana's rules in the digest contained several provisions to protect emancipated minors, albeit in different ways. First, upon the emancipation, the minor's property had to be invested into movable or immovable property to provide him with a revenue.[30] Second, the minor's obligations could be reduced when the minor had bound himself for more than one year of revenues.[31] Third, the law prohibited the minor from donating property *inter vivos*.[32] Unlike French law, the digest included no mechanisms to revoke the minor's emancipation.[33]

Louisiana Civil Code of 1825

The emancipation laws set forth in the Louisiana Civil Code of 1825 closely mirrored the Digest of 1808 in most ways. However, it added another basis on which a

24. Dane S. Ciolino & Monica Hof Wallace, *Recodifying Emancipation: A Precis of the 2009 Revision of Louisiana Emancipation Law*, 56 Loy. L. Rev. 135, 137 (2010).

25. Dane S. Ciolino & Monica Hof Wallace, *Recodifying Emancipation: A Precis of the 2009 Revision of Louisiana Emancipation Law*, 56 Loy. L. Rev. 135, 137 (2010).

26. Dane S. Ciolino & Monica Hof Wallace, *Recodifying Emancipation: A Precis of the 2009 Revision of Louisiana Emancipation Law*, 56 Loy. L. Rev. 135, 138–139 (2010).

27. La. Civil Code arts. 87–88 (1808). At first, for a minor to be emancipated by marriage, they had to obtain parental or tutorial consent; eventually, the Louisiana Supreme Court held that the marriage of a minor over the age of 18 served to emancipate the minor regardless of consent. Dane S. Ciolino & Monica Hof Wallace, *Recodifying Emancipation: A Precis of the 2009 Revision of Louisiana Emancipation Law*, 56 Loy. L. Rev. 135, 139 (2010).

28. La. Civil Code art. 89 (1808).

29. La. Civil Code art. 89 (1808).

30. La. Civil Code art. 90 (1808).

31. La. Civil Code art. 92 (1808).

32. La. Civil Code art. 95 (1808).

33. Dane S. Ciolino & Monica Hof Wallace, *Recodifying Emancipation: A Precis of the 2009 Revision of Louisiana Emancipation Law*, 56 Loy. L. Rev. 135, 139–40 (2010).

minor could be emancipated—when his parents "ill treat him excessively, refuse to support him, or give him corrupt examples."[34] Under this basis, a minor could directly petition a court for emancipation based on the parents' ill treatment, but even if granted, the minor still enjoyed only administrative powers.[35] The Code of 1825 also inserted means by which a court could revoke the emancipation if the minor had exceeded his power, returning the child to a status of incapacity.[36]

Louisiana Civil Code of 1870

The Louisiana Civil Code of 1870's version of emancipation extended the rights and powers of some emancipated minors. Under the 1870 Code, a minor had several routes to emancipation. First, "emancipation conferring the power of administration" was achieved by (a) a notarial declaration executed by the parents once the child attained 15 years of age; (b) by the judicial petition of the minor or a relative, with the consent of the parents or tutor, after the minor reached the age of 18 years; or (c) by judicial petition of the minor on grounds of his parents' ill treatment, refusal of support, or corrupt examples (with no need for parental or tutorial consent).[37] As its name clearly connotes, this type of emancipation allowed the minor only administrative power; by contrast, the minor did not have the power of disposition.[38]

The second option for emancipation was "emancipation by marriage," which, like the first option, still only allowed the minor to exercise administrative powers in most cases.[39] Once the minor emancipated by marriage attained 18 years of age, however, he was relieved from the disabilities of minority and allowed the full capacity of a major.[40]

The third option, "emancipation conferring majority,"[41] was new. This route was achieved by the minor, who had attained 18 years of age and obtained the consent of their parent or tutor, petitioning the court[42] or by the minor, of any age, petitioning the court on the grounds of ill treatment (which did not require the minor to obtain

34. La. Civ. Code art. 371 (1825).

35. Dane S. Ciolino & Monica Hof Wallace, *Recodifying Emancipation: A Precis of the 2009 Revision of Louisiana Emancipation Law*, 56 Loy. L. Rev. 135, 140 (2010).

36. La. Civ. Code arts. 380–381 (1825).

37. La. Civ. Code arts. 365–368 (1870). *See also* Emancipation of Dupuy, 199 So. 384, 386 (La. 1940) (finding parental consent essential on grounds other than ill treatment).

38. The power of administration generally refers to preserving or exploiting rights without changing the substantial character of the patrimony as a whole, whereas the power of disposition includes anything else. *See, e.g.*, La. Civ. Code Ann. art. 229 cmt. (c). Acts like alienation, encumbrance, and lease constitute acts of disposition. *See id.*

39. La. Civ. Code arts. 365, 379, 384 (1870). *But see* La. Civ. Code art. 380 (1870) (allowing minors emancipated by marriage to appear in courts of justice without a curator and allowing the husband-minor to authorize his wife to appear, as well); La. Civ. Code art. 382 (1870) (allowing minors emancipated by marriage freedom from the assistance of a curator in any act or proceeding).

40. La. Civ. Code art. 382 (1870).

41. In the actual Code of 1870, this type of emancipation is referred to a "emancipation relieving the minor from the time prescribed by law for attaining the age of majority." La. Civ. Code art. 365 (1870). It will be referred to herein as "emancipation conferring majority" for the sake of brevity.

42. La. Civ. Code arts. 385, 387 (1870).

parental or tutorial consent).[43] Unlike the other types of emancipation, emancipation conferring majority allowed minors full capacity, i.e., the power of majority, even in the absence of the minor's trade.[44]

§ 11:5 Emancipation—History of Emancipation—Revisions to Louisiana Law

Until the comprehensive revision to the law of emancipation, which took effect in 2009, this area of law saw only a few changes after the 1870 Code.

Pre-Revision Changes

In 1908, the Louisiana Legislature amended the law of emancipation, as it affected married minors, by dividing them into two different categories, with their rights dependent on the category into which they fell. First were the married majors who had attained at least 18 years; the amended law allowed them the full capacity of a major.[45] By contrast, the law remained the same for the other category—married minors under the age of 18 years—who were still limited to powers of administration only.[46]

In 1972, because the state legislature lowered the age of majority from 21 years to 18 years, changes to the law of emancipation were necessary.[47] No longer was there a need for the division of married minors based on their age, because those who had attained 18 years were now legal adults and no longer needed marriage to emancipate them. No longer was any version of judicial emancipation—either conferring administration or conferring majority—necessary for a minor who had attained 18 years of age. Clearly, such persons were now of the age of majority and had no need to resort to the judiciary for freedom from incapacity; by default, they had full capacity at their eighteenth birthday. Because the law generally allowed only a minor who had attained 18 years to petition for a judicial emancipation anyway, the need for judicial emancipation was now all but negated. The sole exception involved minors aged 15 to 17 years who had suffered ill treatment by their parents who could still petition for judicial emancipation.

A few years later, though, judicial emancipation re-emerged. In 1976, the law changed to allow minors, who had reached their sixteenth birthday and who had

43. La. Civ. Code art. 387 (1870).

44. La. Civ. Code art. 386 (1870).

45. Dane S. Ciolino & Monica Hof Wallace, *Recodifying Emancipation: A Precis of the 2009 Revision of Louisiana Emancipation Law*, 56 Loy. L. Rev. 135, 141 (2010).

46. Dane S. Ciolino & Monica Hof Wallace, *Recodifying Emancipation: A Precis of the 2009 Revision of Louisiana Emancipation Law*, 56 Loy. L. Rev. 135, 141 (2010).

47. Dane S. Ciolino & Monica Hof Wallace, *Recodifying Emancipation: A Precis of the 2009 Revision of Louisiana Emancipation Law*, 56 Loy. L. Rev. 135, 142 (2010).

parental or tutorial consent, to petition for a judicial emancipation.[48] In such a scenario, the judicial emancipation conferred majority upon the child, i.e., full emancipation.[49]

In 1978, the law of emancipation by marriage was amended once again.[50] Recall, of course, that once a child reached the age of 18 years, they were of the age of majority without the need for emancipation. The amended law again divided married minors into two age-based categories: (1) those below 16 years of age; and (2) those who had attained 16 years of age. Like the former split in this version of emancipation, the married minor's rights hinged on the category into which they fell. Married minors below the age of 16 years still enjoyed only administrative powers, whereas those married minors who were 16 and 17 years of age were conferred majority.[51]

LSLI Comprehensive Revision

In 2004, the Louisiana State Law Institute (LSLI) created the Emancipation Committee to revise Louisiana's emancipation law.

Recall that prior to the revision, a minor could obtain emancipation in one of three ways. First, the minor attained emancipation conferring the power of administration by a (a) notarial declaration executed by their parents or tutor once the minor was 15 years old; or (b) the minor's judicial petition on the basis of ill treatment. Second, the minor attained emancipation by marriage, but the extent of their emancipation hinged on their age-based category. Finally, the minor attained emancipation conferring majority by the minor's judicial petition, with parental or tutorial consent, but the minor could only use this option after their sixteenth birthday.

From 2004 to 2008, the Emancipation Committee worked on the revisions. While many legal issues were confronted during this time, two were most prevalent. First, the Committee considered the vicarious liability of the parents/tutors for an emancipated minor's delicts and quasi-delicts. While opinions on this issue varied, the legislature ultimately revised Civil Code Article 2318 to relieve the adults in question of vicarious liability for the torts of an emancipated minor under limited circumstances.[52] Second, the Committee considered the advisability of continuing the emancipation by notarial act. Ultimately, the legislature chose to retain this mode of emancipation, but similar to prior law, this type of emancipation allowed the minor fewer rights.[53]

---

48. Dane S. Ciolino & Monica Hof Wallace, *Recodifying Emancipation: A Precis of the 2009 Revision of Louisiana Emancipation Law*, 56 Loy. L. Rev. 135, 142 (2010).

49. Dane S. Ciolino & Monica Hof Wallace, *Recodifying Emancipation: A Precis of the 2009 Revision of Louisiana Emancipation Law*, 56 Loy. L. Rev. 135, 142 (2010).

50. Dane S. Ciolino & Monica Hof Wallace, *Recodifying Emancipation: A Precis of the 2009 Revision of Louisiana Emancipation Law*, 56 Loy. L. Rev. 135, 142 (2010).

51. Dane S. Ciolino & Monica Hof Wallace, *Recodifying Emancipation: A Precis of the 2009 Revision of Louisiana Emancipation Law*, 56 Loy. L. Rev. 135, 142 (2010).

52. Dane S. Ciolino & Monica Hof Wallace, *Recodifying Emancipation: A Precis of the 2009 Revision of Louisiana Emancipation Law*, 56 Loy. L. Rev. 135, 143 (2010).

53. Dane S. Ciolino & Monica Hof Wallace, *Recodifying Emancipation: A Precis of the 2009 Revision of Louisiana Emancipation Law*, 56 Loy. L. Rev. 135, 143 (2010).

The revisions, effective in 2009, served to modernize, simplify, and clarify Louisiana's emancipation law,[54] and they apply prospectively only.[55]

§ 11:6 Emancipation—Types of Emancipation

After the revision of 2008, the law still provides for three avenues to emancipation, which differ in some respects from prior law. As discussed below, these three avenues are: (1) judicial emancipation; (2) emancipation by marriage; and (3) limited emancipation by authentic act.[56]

§ 11:7 Emancipation—Types of Emancipation—Judicial Emancipation

The first avenue of emancipation of a minor child is a judicial emancipation. As the term implies, a judicial emancipation is obtained by judicial order[57] rendered by a court of competent jurisdiction.[58] The minor child alone, the parents or tutor alone, or the parties jointly may file a petition for judicial emancipation.[59]

To obtain such an order, the minor must be at least 16 years of age or older, and the court must find good cause to grant it.[60] The term "good cause" allows for the exercise of judicial discretion. A court may find that good cause exists, for example, to protect the parents of a minor child who has run away and cannot be found.[61] This serves to protect the parents from liability for the minor child's conduct resulting in damage over which they have no control.[62] Similarly, a court may find that good cause exists when the minor child needs capacity to enter juridical acts, for example, if that child operates

54. Dane S. Ciolino & Monica Hof Wallace, *Recodifying Emancipation: A Precis of the 2009 Revision of Louisiana Emancipation Law*, 56 Loy. L. Rev. 135 (2010).

55. In re Franques, 2011-190 (La. App. 3 Cir. 10/5/11), 74 So. 3d 812. Therein, the court explained:

> Louisiana Civil Code Article 6 provides that "substantive laws apply prospectively only" unless the legislature has declared otherwise. There is no such declaration in this case. Contrarily, the Act states that the effective date of the new emancipation statutes is January 1, 2009.

In re Franques, 74 So. 3d at 814.

56. La. Civ. Code Ann. art. 365.

57. La. Civ. Code Ann. art. 366.

58. For a Louisiana court to exercise jurisdiction over emancipation proceedings, the minor child must be domiciled in this state. La. Code Civ. Proc. Ann. art. 10(A)(2). Furthermore, city courts, justice of the peace courts, and juvenile courts do not have jurisdiction over emancipation proceedings. La. Code Civ. Proc. Ann. arts. 4847(B), 4913(B)(8); La. Child. Code Ann. art. 303.

59. La. Code Civ. Proc. Ann. art. 3991. For a summary of the procedural rules governing judicial emancipation proceedings, see Frank L. Maraist, 1A Louisiana Civil Law Treatise, Civil Procedure § 6:3 (2008). *See also* La. Code Civ. Proc. Ann. arts. 3991–94.

60. La. Civ. Code Ann. art. 366. This type of emancipation is similar to the emancipation conferring majority that existed under prior law. La. Civ. Code Ann. art. 366 cmt. (a).

61. La. Civ. Code Ann. art. 366 cmt. (g).

62. La. Civ. Code Ann. art. 366 cmt. (g).

a business requiring the execution of contracts.[63] Finally, a court may find that good cause exists if the parents act as corrupt examples for a mature and responsible child or if they subject the child to excessive ill treatment or neglect to support the child.[64]

Few recent cases discuss these grounds, but a few older ones do. For example, in *Emancipation of Dupuy*, the court failed to find ill treatment by a mother who refused to cancel the child's contract, which he alleged was not in his best interest.[65] In *Gaston v. Rainach*, the court suggested that parental abandonment would constitute ill treatment but found no proof of the allegation under the facts.[66]

When a court decides to judicially emancipate a minor child, it must determine whether to order a full or limited emancipation.[67] The two differ in the effects of majority conferred on the child. Full judicial emancipation confers all of the effects of majority on the minor child[68] unless otherwise provided by law,[69] whereas, limited judicial emancipation is more tailored to the needs of the minor child and their parents or tutor.[70] In particular, it confers only the effects of majority specified in the judgment of limited emancipation unless otherwise provided by law.[71]

Regardless of the type of judicial emancipation ordered, it is effective once the judgment is signed, and it has no retroactive effect.[72] Additionally, the clerk of court must record the judgment in the conveyance records of the parish in which the judgment was rendered, and the petitioner must record it in the conveyance records in each parish in which the minor child owns property.[73]

Once ordered, the court retains the authority to modify or terminate the judgment of emancipation and does so within its discretion on a finding of good cause[74] typically

---

63. La. Civ. Code Ann. art. 366 cmt. (h).

64. La. Civ. Code Ann. art. 366 cmt. (i).

65. Emancipation of Dupuy, 199 So. 384, 387 (La. 1940).

66. Gaston v. Rainach, 74 So. 890 (La. 1917).

67. La. Civ. Code Ann. art. 366.

68. La. Civ. Code Ann. art. 366. This includes, among other effects, the capacity to incur conventional obligations and to make donations. La. Civ. Code Ann. art. 366, cmt. (b). Note, however, that the donations article was never amended to reflect this, and by its terms, directly conflicts with the revised emancipation articles. *See* La. Civ. Code Ann. art. 1476 (providing the donations rules for minors without exception for those who have been emancipated).

69. La. Civ. Code Ann. art. 366. As explained in comment (c) to article 366, by using the language "'unless otherwise provided by law,' this Article clarifies that laws regulating the conduct of those 'under age eighteen,' are not affected by emancipation." La. Civ. Code Ann. art. 366 cmt. (c). Thus, emancipated minors should still be subject to certain age-restriction rules. For example, they should not be allowed to vote. *See* U.S. Const. amend. XXVI, § 1.

70. La. Civ. Code Ann. art. 366 cmt. (d). *See also* In re Franques, 2011-190 (La. App. 3 Cir. 10/5/11), 74 So. 3d 812, 814.

71. La. Civ. Code Ann. art. 366. The judgment must specify the effects of majority conferred and shall state that the minor retains all of the other effects of minority. La. Code. Civ. Proc. Ann. art. 3995.

72. La. Civ. Code Ann. art. 369 & cmt. As a result, the judgment of emancipation has no effect on the validity or invalidity of acts made by the minor before his or her emancipation. *Id.*

73. La. Code Civ. Proc. Ann. art. 3998.

74. La. Civ. Code Ann. art. 370.

"when the grounds for emancipation no longer exist or circumstances have changed."[75] In such a scenario, the court may choose to modify the judgment to make a full judicial emancipation a limited one, or it may terminate the judgment altogether.[76] If the judgment of emancipation is terminated, the minor child reverts back to the same authority that existed prior to the emancipation unless the court orders otherwise for good cause.[77] In such a case, for example, an emancipated minor who has been operating a business could lose the ability to continue doing so by his irresponsibility.

Any judgment modifying or terminating an order of emancipation has prospective effect only[78] with no effect on acts made by the minor child before the effective date of the modification or termination.[79] To affect third persons, the modification or termination must be filed for registry in the conveyance records where the property is located for immovable property and in the conveyance records of the parish(es) in which the minor child was domiciled at the time of the judgment for movable property.[80] Research reveals no caselaw interpreting these rules.

§ 11:8 Emancipation—Types of Emancipation—Emancipation by Marriage

The second avenue of emancipation is by a minor child's marriage which emancipates the child by operation of law.[81] This is true of both valid marriages, as well as putative marriages.[82]

Under current law, a minor child under the age of 16 years may not marry under any circumstances.[83] A child 16 years or older may marry only after obtaining the requisite approvals of both parents, the tutor over the child's person, or one holding custody over the child; judicial permission is also required.[84] Unlike the pre-revision version of emancipation by marriage, the current version yields a full emancipation for the

---

75. Dane S. Ciolino & Monica Hof Wallace, *Recodifying Emancipation: A Precis of the 2009 Revision of Louisiana Emancipation Law*, 56 Loy. L. Rev. 135, 146 (2010).

76. Dane S. Ciolino & Monica Hof Wallace, *Recodifying Emancipation: A Precis of the 2009 Revision of Louisiana Emancipation Law*, 56 Loy. L. Rev. 135, 146 (2010).

77. La. Civ. Code Ann. art. 370.

78. La. Civ. Code Ann. art. 370 cmt. (c).

79. La. Civ. Code Ann. art. 370.

80. La. Civ. Code Ann. art. 370.

81. La. Civ. Code Ann. art. 367.

82. La. Civ. Code Ann. art. 367 cmt. (b). Given the changes to the law of marriage for minors, it is difficult to conceive of a putative marriage by a minor child. After all, only absolutely null marriages may qualify as putative. La. Civ. Code Ann. art. 96. Additionally, even for an absolutely null marriage, at least one spouse must be in good faith, and only the good faith spouse(s) enjoy the civil effects of such a marriage. *Id.* It is safe to assume that most married minor children know their own age such that they would not be in good faith.

83. *See* La. Civ. Code Ann. art. 90.1.

84. *See* La. Civ. Code Ann. art. 90.1; La. Stat. Ann. § 9:221; La. Child. Code Ann. arts. 1545–48.

married minor child, allowing him all of the effects of majority.[85] Research reveals no reported cases on this issue.

Emancipation by marriage is effective upon the marriage, and therefore, has no retroactive effect (just like judicial emancipation).[86] If the marriage of the minor child terminates, the emancipation is undisturbed; in other words, the minor child remains emancipated in spite of termination of the marriage.[87] For example, in *In re Greer*,[88] a minor female was married and widowed prior to attaining the age of majority, and despite the death of her husband, she remained emancipated. Unlike judicial emancipation, an emancipation by marriage may not be modified or terminated.[89]

§ 11:9 Emancipation—Types of Emancipation—Limited Emancipation by Authentic Act

The third and final avenue of emancipation relies on an authentic act[90] executed by the minor and his parents (if the minor is subject to parental authority) or tutor (if not).[91] While pre-revision law allowed this avenue for a minor child who was at least 15 years old, current law requires that the minor child be 16 years of age or older.[92] As is evident from its name, this type of emancipation is limited. Specifically, the minor is allowed the capacity to make only the juridical acts enumerated in the act unless otherwise provided by law.[93]

Limited emancipation by authentic act is effective when the act is executed, such that it has no retroactive effect (like the other forms of emancipation).[94] Once executed, the parties to the authentic act of limited emancipation may modify or terminate it by making a subsequent authentic act; a court may also modify or terminate it for good cause.[95] One instance in which a court may modify or terminate the emancipation is when the emancipated minor unadvisedly alienates his property or is taken advantage of by others.[96]

---

85. La. Civ. Code Ann. art. 367 cmt. (a).

86. La. Civ. Code Ann. art. 369 & cmt. As a result, it has no effect on the acts made by the minor child before their emancipation.

87. La. Civ. Code Ann. art. 367.

88. In re Greer, 184 So. 2d 104 (La. Ct. App. 4 Cir. 1966).

89. In re Greer, 184 So. 2d 104.

90. An authentic act requires a notary and two witnesses. La. Civ. Code Ann. art. 1833.

91. La. Civ. Code Ann. art. 368.

92. La. Civ. Code Ann. art. 368 & cmt. (a).

93. La. Civ. Code Ann. art. 368.

94. La. Civ. Code Ann. art. 369.

95. La. Civ. Code Ann. art. 371.

96. Dane S. Ciolino & Monica Hof Wallace, *Recodifying Emancipation: A Precis of the 2009 Revision of Louisiana Emancipation Law*, 56 Loy. L. Rev. 135, 148 (2010).

Any modification or termination of a limited emancipation by authentic act is prospective only.[97] Furthermore, it is effective toward third persons only when filed for registry in the conveyance records where the property is located as to immovable property and in the parish(es) in which the minor was domiciled at the time of the act modifying or terminating limited emancipation by authentic act as to movable property.[98]

§ 11:10 Emancipation—Effects of Emancipation

The emancipation of a minor child carries numerous legal effects. As discussed in the following sections, these effects extend to such things as (1) the minor child's capacity; (2) control of the minor child; (3) liability for the minor child's tortious conduct; (4) support of the minor child; and (5) prescription.

§ 11:11 Emancipation—Effects of Emancipation—Capacity of the Minor Child

Per the rules on conventional obligations (i.e., contracts), until emancipated, a minor child lacks the capacity to enter contracts.[99] A contract by a minor child is relatively null and, as a general rule, may be rescinded.[100] The law allows for two exceptions under which the minor child's contracts may not be rescinded. First, contracts entered into by the minor child "for the purpose of providing the minor with something necessary for his support or education, or for a purpose related to his business" may not be rescinded.[101] Likewise, those contracts entered into by a party who reasonably relies on the minor child's representation of majority may not be rescinded.[102] Minor children, after reaching the age of majority, may ratify the promises that they made during minority.[103]

Of course, certain nominate contracts have special rules for minor children. One such nominate contract is the matrimonial agreement, pursuant to which parties may establish a regime of separation of property or modify or terminate the default community property regime.[104] Pursuant to the special rules associated with this contract, a minor under the age of 16 years is not allowed to enter into a matrimonial agreement,

97. Any act made by the minor child before the effective date of the modification or termination is not affected. La. Civ. Code Ann. art. 371.

98. La. Civ. Code Ann. art. 371.

99. La. Civ. Code Ann. art. 1918.

100. La. Civ. Code Ann. art. 1919.

101. La. Civ. Code Ann. art. 1923; *see also* Deville v. Federal Savings Bank of Evangeline Parish, 93-1853 (La. 4/11/94), 635 So. 2d 195, 198 (finding that the minor is not entitled to restoration of funds taken from minor's account if funds were used for the minor's support or education).

102. La. Civ. Code Ann. art. 1924.

103. *See* Ogden v. Ogden, 331 So. 2d 592, 594–95 (La. Ct. App. 1 Cir. 1976) (ratification of partnership); Hanks v. Alexander, 166 So. 175, 178 (La. Ct. App. 2 Cir. 1936) (ratification of contract).

104. La. Civ. Code Ann. art. 2328.

and a minor who is 16 or 17 years old may do so only with judicial authorization and the written concurrence of their father and mother, or of the parent having his legal custody, or of the tutor of his person.[105] In *Wilkinson v. Wilkinson*,[106] the Louisiana Supreme Court held that a matrimonial agreement executed by an unemancipated minor was null, despite the fact that the minor was later emancipated by marriage.[107]

Once emancipated, a minor child enjoys the capacity to enter juridical acts like contracts.[108] They also have capacity to sue and be sued without the assistance of a parent or tutor.[109] Immediately upon emancipation, the minor may be substituted as a party to a pending suit,[110] giving the emancipated minor the legal capacity to sue.[111] Further, fully emancipated minors may sue their parents or tutors.[112]

§11:12 Emancipation—Effects of Emancipation—Control of the Minor Child

Prior to emancipation, a minor child is under the control of his parents or tutor,[113] and per compulsory school attendance laws, a person "having control or charge of any child" between the ages of seven and 18 years must send the child to school.[114] Thus, unemancipated minor children are subject to the attendance laws.

Whether those laws apply to an emancipated minor is a different question. As explained by the Louisiana Supreme Court, once emancipated, the minor is no longer a "child" who falls under the care and control of a parent, guardian, or other person within the compulsory attendance statute.[115] Likewise, the Louisiana Attorney General has opined that emancipation in any form frees the child from the care of another

---

105. La. Civ. Code Ann. art. 2333.

106. Wilkinson v. Wilkinson, 323 So. 2d 120 (La. 1975).

107. Wilkinson, 323 So. 2d at 127. While the Family Court ruled that the contract was absolutely null, Wilkinson, 323 So. 2d at 122, the Louisiana Supreme Court never specifically stated whether the nullity was relative or absolute. It did, however, reinstate the Family Court's judgment. Wilkinson, 323 So. 2d at 127. With that said, typically, contracts entered into by persons who lack capacity (like unemancipated minors) are relative nullities. *See, e.g.*, La. Civ. Code Ann. art. 1918.

108. La. Civ. Code Ann. art. 1922 ("A fully emancipated minor has full contractual capacity."); La. Civ. Code. Ann. art. 1918 ("All persons have capacity to contract, except unemancipated minors, interdicts, and persons deprived of reason at the time of contracting.").

109. La. Code Civ. Proc. Ann. arts. 682, 731.

110. *See* Bonnette v. Flournoy, 119 So. 736, 737 (La. Ct. App. 2 Cir. 1929); Turner v. Standard Oil Co., 1925 WL 3270 (La. Ct. App. 2 Cir. 1925).

111. Jefferson v. Jefferson, 163 So. 2d 74, 77 (La. 1964).

112. La. Stat. Ann. § 9:571.

113. La. Civ. Code Ann. art. 235.

114. La. Stat. Ann. § 17:221.

115. State v. Priest, 27 So. 2d 173, 174 (La. 1946); *see also* In re Goodwin, 39 So. 2d 731, 733 (La. 1949).

person, and compulsory school laws do not apply.[116] Under current law, it seems that minor children who have been fully emancipated via judicial emancipation and those emancipated by marriage are not subject to compulsory school attendance. By contrast, those emancipated by limited judicial emancipation or limited emancipation by authentic act must attend school, as control by the parents or tutor is retained in those situations.

§ 11:13 Emancipation—Effects of Emancipation—Liability for the Minor Child's Tortious Conduct

Prior to emancipation, parents and tutors are liable for the damage caused by their minor child who lives with them or has been placed by them under the care of other persons.[117] However, in some—but not all—scenarios, emancipation relieves the adults of this liability.

For example, when a minor child is emancipated by a judgment of full emancipation or by marriage, the adults are simultaneously freed from liability for damages occasioned by their minor child.[118] However, a judgment of limited emancipation only removes the adult's liability to the extent that the judgment expressly provides as such.[119] The same is not true of limited emancipations by authentic act.[120] While some courts allowed for a notarial act of emancipation to automatically relieve the parents of liability for the acts of their minor child under pre-revision law,[121] under current law, such relief is not allowed.[122]

---

116. La. Att'y Gen. Op. No. 03-0094 (2003) ("The Compulsory School Attendance Act cannot be used to compel attendance of minors who have been emancipated."); *see also* La. Att'y. Gen. Op. No. 1946-48.

117. La. Civ. Code Ann. art. 2318; *see also* Chapters 9 (parental liability) and 10 (tutor liability).

118. La. Civ. Code Ann. art. 2318.

119. La. Civ. Code Ann. art. 2318.

120. La. Civ. Code Ann. art. 2318.

121. Held v. Wilt, 610 So. 2d 1103, 1105 (La. Ct. App. 5 Cir. 1982).

122. La. Civ. Code Ann. art. 2318 & rev. cmt. (2008).

§ 11:14 Emancipation—Effects of Emancipation—Parental Support of the Minor Child

Prior to emancipation, both parents are obligated to support their child.[123] Under pre-revision law, the obligation terminated, as a general rule, once a minor was judicially emancipated or emancipated by marriage as long the minor was 16 years of age or older.[124] The same should be true under current law, which provides that termination of the parents' support obligation occurs upon emancipation "relieving the child of the disabilities attached to minority."[125] As a result, child support is not due to children who are fully emancipated by court order or marriage.

Note, however, that two exceptions exist to allow emancipated children to continue to receive child support.[126] First, the support continues if the child is a full-time student in good standing in a secondary school, has not reached the age of 19 years, and is dependent on either parent.[127] Second, the support continues if the child has a developmental disability, is a full-time student in a secondary school, and has not reached the age of 22 years.[128]

Under current law and assuming an exception does not apply, child support will terminate if a court grants full judicial emancipation or if the child is emancipated by marriage. A judgment of limited emancipation and a limited emancipation by authentic act should not affect the child's right to receive child support under the guidelines. It is noteworthy that a child's ability to receive social security benefits may be affected by an emancipation.[129]

---

123. La. Civ. Code Ann. arts. 223, 224, 232, 235.

124. Former La. Civ. Code arts. 382 and 385, *repealed by* 2008 La. Acts 786.

125. La. Stat. Ann. § 9:315.22(A)–(B).

126. *See* La. Civ. Code Ann. art. 224 cmt. (b).

127. La. Stat. Ann. § 9:315.22(C). *See* Smith v. Smith, 44,663 (La. App. 2 Cir. 08/19/09), 16 So. 3d 643, 658–60 (even if emancipated child is a full-time student in secondary school and has not reached the age of 19 years, child support is only due if the child is dependent on the parents).

128. La. Stat. Ann. § 9:315.22(D).

129. U.S. Social Security Administration, Benefits for Children (June 2022), https://www.ssa.gov/pubs/EN-05-10085.pdf; U.S. Social Security Administration, Determining Capability—Children, https://secure.ssa.gov/poms.nsf/lnx/0200502070 (last visited May 18, 2024).

§ 11:15 Emancipation—Effects of Emancipation—Prescription

As a general rule, prescription runs against minors, unless an exception is established by legislation.[130] Several pieces of legislation do just that. For example, prescription is suspended between parents and minor children, tutors and minors, and caretakers and minors during the period of the child's minority.[131] Likewise, prescription does not run against minors in delictual actions "involving permanent disability and brought pursuant to the Louisiana Products Liability Act or state law governing product liability actions in effect at the time of the injury or damage."[132] Furthermore, actions subject to a five-year liberative prescription are suspended in favor of minors.[133] Similarly, prescription on an action to annul a relatively null contract only begins to run when the minor reaches the age of majority or is emancipated.[134]

Therefore, once a minor is fully emancipated by judicial emancipation or by marriage, prescription that had been suspended will commence to run against the emancipated minor.[135] Because limited judicial emancipation and limited emancipation by authentic act are less extensive and do not confer on the minor all effects of majority, such emancipation should not end any legislative suspension of prescription.

130. La. Civ. Code Ann. art. 3468.

131. La. Civ. Code Ann. art. 3469.

132. La. Civ. Code Ann. art. 3492.

133. La. Civ. Code Ann. art. 3497. Actions to set aside sheriff's deeds are also suspended for minors. La. Stat. Ann. § 9:5642.

134. La Civ. Code Ann. art. 2032.

135. Proctor v. Hebert, 1884 WL 7809 (La. 1884) (full judicial emancipation begins the running of prescription); Arrington v. Gray, 108 So. 790, 791 (La. 1926) (prescription against a minor began to run again when fully emancipated by marriage). Although these cases predate the revision to the law of emancipation, nothing should change their result. *See also* Fred Zengel, *Influences of Minority on the Accrual of Prescription*, 13 Tul. L. Rev. 123 (1938).

Chapter 12

Interdiction

by Vincent B. "Chip" LoCoco[*]

* Vincent B. "Chip" LoCoco is a partner with the firm of Many & LoCoco in New Orleans, Louisiana. The authors would like to thank Mr. LoCoco for contributing this chapter to the treatise.

§ 12.1 Introduction

The law of interdiction is a protective measure that allows a person to be placed under the care of a curator, if that person has an infirmity that renders him unable to consistently make reasoned decisions regarding the care of his person and/or property or communicate those decisions.[1] In the common law, this proceeding is called guardianship.[2] An extensive revision of the law of interdiction,[3] which became effective July 1, 2001, significantly changed dated verbiage, guidelines, and other anomalies.[4] The revision provides the court with two choices—full and limited interdiction.

Full interdiction has the effect of stripping the interdict's capacity to make all juridical acts, including contracts and donations,[5] to sue or be sued,[6] to accept or renounce successions,[7] and even the ability to marry[8] and to vote.[9] Full interdiction, however, is distinct from civil commitment.[10] While a final judgment of full interdiction has been called "a pronouncement of civil death without the dubious advantage of an inscription thereof on a tombstone,"[11] when a person's capacity to care for his person *and* property has diminished and no other less restrictive means can be taken to protect this person, interdiction provides a viable way to safeguard the person and his property. Interdiction is also considered a harsh remedy that cannot be used as a matter of convenience and, therefore, has a stiff burden of proof.[12]

Limited interdiction, however, is more malleable. A court is permitted to craft a judgment that protects the limited interdict from the risks brought about by his infirmity, which affects either the interdict's property *or* his person, but not both.[13]

---

1. *See* La. Civ. Code Ann. arts. 389, 390.

2. A person under guardianship in another state will not automatically be recognized as an interdict in Louisiana. *See* Treadwell v. Treadwell, 41,130 (La. App. 2 Cir. 06/28/06), 935 So. 2d 740 (holding that petitioner husband, who was found to be incapacitated under Arkansas law, had capacity to sue).

3. Act No. 25, 2000 La. Acts.

4. "It rids [the previous law] of many anachronisms, consolidates some formerly disparate statutes, and provides judges and practitioners with more detailed guidelines applicable throughout an interdiction proceeding." It also increases the number of procedural hurdles, which in the author's viewpoint, discourages interdiction. William Reid Huguet, *The New Law of Interdiction: Clear and Convincing Revision*, 47 Loy. L. Rev. 1059, 1059 (2001).

5. La. Civ. Code Ann. art. 395.

6. La. Code of Civ. Proc. Ann. art. 684.

7. La. Code Civ. Proc. Ann. art. 4566.

8. A marriage is a civil contract, and a person must have capacity to consent to marry. *See* La. Civ. Code Ann. arts. 86, 87, 93. A limited interdict may be able to marry if he is able to exercise consent over his personal affairs.

9. La. Stat. Ann. § 18:102(A)(2). A full interdict is ineligible to vote, but a limited interdict is permitted to vote unless that judgment of limited interdiction provides otherwise. La. Stat. Ann. § 18:102(A)(2).

10. La. Civ. Code Ann. art. 389 cmt. (f). Civil commitment requires compliance with standards and procedures set forth in Louisiana's Behavioral Health Laws. *See* La. Stat. Ann. §§ 28:1–28:173.

11. *See* Doll v. Doll, 156 So. 2d 275, 278 (La. Ct. App. 4 Cir. 1963).

12. *See* Interdiction of Lemmons, 511 So. 2d 57, 59 (La. Ct. App. 3 Cir. 1987).

13. La. Civ. Code Ann. art. 390.

A judgment of limited interdiction restricts the interdict's capacity to make juridical acts pertaining only to the property or care that the judgment places under the care of the curator; all other rights of the interdict are preserved.[14] In all cases, whether the interdiction is full or limited, the interdict retains the authority to challenge his status as an interdict.[15]

§ 12.2 Full Interdiction

A court of competent jurisdiction[16] may order the full interdiction of an adult[17] or emancipated minor[18] who, because of an infirmity, is unable consistently to make reasoned decisions about the care of his person and property,[19] or to communicate those decisions,[20] and whose interest cannot be protected by less restrictive means.[21] This article makes eligibility for interdiction dependent on functional inability rather than proof, under prior law, of maladies such as insanity, madness, and the like.[22]

For a person to be interdicted, the inability to consistently make or communicate reasoned decisions regarding the care of his person and his property must result from

---

14. La. Civ. Code Ann. art. 395.

15. La. Code Civ. Proc. Ann. art. 4554.

16. For a Louisiana court to exercise jurisdiction over an interdiction proceeding, the person sought to be interdicted must be domiciled in this state or is in this state and has property herein. La. Civ. Code Proc. Ann. art. 10(A)(3). This article changes and overrules prior case law, which did not allow Louisiana courts to interdict a Louisiana domiciliary living outside of the state or a person who had property in the state, though not a domiciliary. La. Code Civ. Proc. Ann. art. 10 cmt. (d). For more on the specificities regarding interdiction proceedings *See* Frank L. Maraist, 1A La. Civ. L. Treatise, Civ. Proc.—Special Proceed. § 7.1 (2022).

17. La. Civ. Code Ann. art. 29 (age of majority is 18 years).

18. *See* La. Civ. Code Ann. arts. 365–85.

19. *See, e.g.*, In re Interdiction of Jones, 55,235 (La. App. 2 Cir. 9/27/23), 371 So. 3d 1164 (finding full interdiction appropriate due to a diagnosis of mild to moderate dementia and testimony by three medical experts that the interdict could not *consistently* make reasoned decisions regarding his person or property); Interdiction of Yazbeck, 2009-1436 (La. App. 1 Cir. 3/26/2010), 2010 WL 1170632 (finding the trial court's determination of full interdiction was proper due to factual findings of diminished mental acuity and evidence that supervision was necessary to prevent harm to herself or others, particularly her proclivity toward automobile accidents if given the opportunity to drive); State v. In the Interest of Smith, 38,192 (La. App. 2 Cir. 03/03/04), 867 So. 2d 890, 894–95 (holding that the trial court's decision to order full interdiction was not manifest error because any evidence in support of a contrary holding was outweighed by other evidence, including life-threatening medical condition brought on by failure to take prescribed medications, paranoia, and lack of appreciation of the consequences of not taking medications).

20. "A person lacks the ability to communicate reasoned decisions only when he cannot convey his thoughts in an understandable manner to other persons. Thus, a person who can consistently communicate his reasoned decisions through any form of verbal or nonverbal communication is not a candidate for full interdiction." La. Civ. Code Ann. art. 389 cmt. (c).

21. La. Civil Code Ann. art. 389; *see* Kathy D. Underwood, La. Prac. La. Notary Handbook § 14:14 (ed. 2023–2024).

22. La. Civ. Code Ann. art. 389 cmt. (a).

an infirmity.[23] While a person suffering from an infirmity may experience lucid intervals, this alone does not prevent a full interdiction.[24] The threshold consideration of an infirmity involves the evaluation of the proposed interdict's functional ability to make reasoned decisions and to communicate those decisions.[25] Advanced age, alone, is not an infirmity.[26] Nevertheless, if a person's interest can be protected by less restrictive means, the court should deny full interdiction.[27] Although the person may already be protected by less restrictive means, such as a procuration or durable power of attorney, this alone will not render an interdiction proceeding moot.[28]

Before the revision, Louisiana courts used a three-part test to determine whether a judgment of interdiction should be ordered.[29] Not only did the court require a finding that the interdict could not care for his person and administer his estate, but a third prong—actual necessity for the interdiction"—was required.[30] Although the revision did not carry forward the "actual necessity" test, the essence of its application appears in the text of the revision which only permits interdiction "if one's interest cannot be protected by less restrictive means."[31]

For example, in *Interdiction of Constance*, a son petitioned for the full interdiction of his mother, Mrs. Constance, based on a 2020 doctor's evaluation that her memory problems were likely caused by Alzheimer's, especially since her mother suffered from

23. *See* La. Civ. Code Ann. art. 389 cmt. (b). Advanced age alone or caring for one's person and property in an imprudent manner, if not from an infirmity, does not render one a candidate for full interdiction. *Id.* "A decision is not unreasoned merely because it appears risky, unwise, or imprudent." *Id.*

24. *See* La. Civ. Code Ann. art. 389 cmt. (d).

25. *See* La. Civ. Code Ann. art. 389 cmt.(b). Chronic substance abuse may qualify as an infirmity, but advanced age alone will not. *Id.*

26. La. Civ. Code Ann. art. 389 cmt.(b).

27. La. Civ. Code Ann. art. 389 cmt. (e). A person's interest can be protected by less restrictive means if, for example, his interests (1) are currently being protected by other legal arrangements, including a procuration, mandate, or trust, or (2) could be protected by other legal arrangements including limited interdiction. *Id. See, e.g.*, Interdiction of Cornwell v. Cornwell, 97-425 (La. App. 3 Cir. 10/15/97), 702 So. 2d 938 (reversing the trial court's judgment of full interdiction due to insufficient evidence to support that the interdict lacked the ability to care for his estate; testimony established that although his investments were not profitable, he understood them nonetheless; ordering the trial court to fashion a judgment of limited interdiction, rather than full interdiction, since evidence established that the interdict was not capable of taking care of his person because he failed to acknowledge his infirmity, bipolarism, and admitted that he would refuse to take his medication if released from the nursing home).

28. In re Interdiction of Jones, 55,235 (La. App. 2 Cir. 9/27/23), 371 So. 3d 1164 (finding that powers of attorney would not protect the proposed interdict); Womack v. Stephenson, 08-493(La. App. 5 Cir. 01/13/09), 8 So. 3d 1 (remanding proceedings to determine whether or not the power of attorney did in fact protect the interests of the person sought to be interdicted); *see also* Turk v. Conner, 2003-791 (La. App. 5 Cir. 12/10/03), 864 So. 2d 672.

29. *See* Interdiction of Badalamenti, 529 So. 2d 1376, 1377 (La. Ct. App. 4 Cir. 1988) (citing In re Interdiction of Adams, 209 So. 2d 363 (La. Ct. App. 4 Cir. 1968)); Doll v. Doll, 156 So. 2d 275, 276–77 (La. Ct. App. 4 Cir. 1963).

30. Doll, 156 So. 2d at 277.

31. *See* La. Civ. Code Ann. arts. 389, 390.

the disease.[32] In the 2020 evaluation, Mrs. Constance tested in the exceptionally low range in areas of recall, memory, and executive functioning, but she tested within average limits in areas like working memory. Concerning her activities for daily life, the report indicated that she could do things independently without difficulty.[33]

The trial court executed an ex parte order naming her son as provisional curator and her granddaughter as undercurator. Subsequently, Mrs. Constance filed an emergency motion to revoke the curatorship. Thereafter, in an amended supplemental petition, her son sought to have the court appoint a neuropsychiatrist to evaluate Mrs. Constance's alleged dementia or Alzheimer's condition. The trial court granted Mrs. Constance's emergency motion to revoke the provisional letters of curatorship but appointed a new doctor to conduct a neurological evaluation. Subsequently, Mrs. Constance's daughter (the mother of the undercurator) intervened in the proceeding, seeking to have the interdiction dismissed.[34]

At trial, the undisputed evidence showed that Mrs. Constance's mental capacity began to diminish in 2018, a year before her husband died. In addition, her husband owned rental property, and everyone testified that Mrs. Constance did not help manage the property nor was she ever fully employed. The court-appointed physician concluded that she suffered from dementia and had some cognitive impairments; however, he disagreed with the 2020 evaluation that had diagnosed Mrs. Constance with Alzheimer's. He found that two and a half years after that evaluation, Mrs. Constance did not evidence the deterioration that would be expected from Alzheimer's. Thus, he concluded that she did not need to be fully interdicted.[35]

The family's testimony regarding Mrs. Constance's mental capacity, best interest, and need for interdiction were highly disputed. Her son testified that full interdiction was necessary because his mother was unable to administer her estate due to her forgetfulness, and that he wanted to protect Mrs. Constance from being easily manipulated by his sister, who had previously stolen $200,000 from their parents and had moved back in with his mother. In his belief, his sister had moved back to Louisiana because their mother's mental condition made it easy for her to be manipulated, and Mrs. Constance was already paying her living expenses. Mrs. Constance's daughter testified that her mother was currently paying for her living expenses to repay her for quitting her job in Florida, selling her house, and moving back to Louisiana upon her mother's request to help take care of her. Mrs. Constance's neighbor testified that her son was verbally abusive to his mother, and that she feared him. Last, her daughter testified that Mrs. Constance did not need to be interdicted as she managed her daily affairs consistently, but she conceded that her mother needed help with finances and her medication.

The trial court issued a judgment of full interdiction, finding that Mrs. Constance had forgotten important life events, had begun to cancel or miss doctors' appoint-

32. In re Interdiction of Constance, 23-318 (La. App. 5 Cir. 3/22/24), 2024 WL 1224029.
33. In re Interdiction of Constance, 2024 WL 1224029, *12.
34. In re Interdiction of Constance, 2024 WL 1224029, at *2.
35. In re Interdiction of Constance, 2024 WL 1224029, *12–13.

ments, and did not regularly take her medication. In addition, the trial court found that due to her years of reliance on her husband, Mrs. Constance was at a great disadvantage and relied on others to handle these tasks for her. Thus, she was unable to take care of her person or administer her estate, warranting interdiction. However, the trial court found it inappropriate to name her son, daughter, or granddaughter as curator due to familial tension, and instead appointed Louisiana Guardianship Services Incorporated (LGSI) to serve as curator.

The appellate court reversed, finding that less restrictive means than full interdiction was available. The court acknowledged Mrs. Constance's dementia and susceptibility to undue influence, placing her property at risk. However, it found that she could manage her personal affairs and daily life. Mrs. Constance's incapacity extended only to her financial, legal, and medical affairs. Thus, the court granted a limited interdiction, applying only to her legal, financial and medical affairs.

As illustrated by *Interdiction of Constance*, Louisiana courts are reluctant to order full interdiction.[36] Full interdiction is "a pronouncement of civil death," and therefore, before ordering it, no other solution should be available.[37] Full interdiction is warranted only when a person's interests cannot be protected by less restrictive means.[38] Where less restrictive means exist capable of protecting the defendant's interests, including limited interdiction or a procuration, mandate, or trust, the court must deny full interdiction.[39] The Louisiana Code of Civil Procedure now requires petitioners to describe with particularity their efforts to use less restrictive means before seeking interdiction, including all of the following:

(a) The less restrictive means for meeting the defendant's needs that were considered or implemented.

(b) If a less restrictive means was not considered or implemented, the reason that the less restrictive means was not considered or implemented.

(c) The reason a less restrictive means is insufficient to meet the needs of the defendant.[40]

---

36. *See* In re Interdiction of Constance, 23-318 (La. App. 5 Cir. 3/22/24), 2024 WL 1224029.

37. *See* Interdiction of Lemmons, 511 So. 2d 57, 59 (La. Ct. App. 3 Cir. 1987). In *Lemmons*, the court noted the defendant's day-to-day limitations and forgetfulness, but ultimately concluded that interdiction was not warranted because the record was void of any evidence that the defendant was incapable of administering her estate. Although the defendant's health was a concern, "interdiction cannot be used as a matter of inconvenience." *Id.*

38. *See* La. Civ. Code Ann. art. 389 cmt. (e); *see, e.g.*, In re Interdiction of Jones, 55,235 (La. App. 2 Cir. 9/27/23), 371 So. 3d 1164 (finding that powers of attorney in a highly litigious environment would not fully protect the proposed interdict); In re Interdiction of Foster, 2014-1296 (La. App. 1 Cir. 03/06/15), 2015 WL 997155, *10 (finding that the record did not contain any evidence to "rebut the significant evidence of [Ms. Foster's] limitations or to show whether less restrictive means would be available or serve any useful purpose, given her physical and mental limitations").

39. In re Interdiction of Foster, 2015 WL 997155, at *10; In re Interdiction of Fichtel, 2015 1711 (La. App. 1 Cir. 06/05/15), 2015 WL 3546056, 84; *see* Sections 12:17–12:19 for a discussion of alternative options to interdiction.

40. La. Code Civ. Proc. Ann. art. 4541(A)(11).

The burden of proving facts to justify an interdiction rests on the petitioner, and the standard is clear and convincing evidence.[41] For example, in *Interdiction of DeMarco,*[42] the court determined that clear and convincing evidence supported the full interdiction of Mrs. DeMarco. Expert medical testimony revealed that Mrs. DeMarco suffered from major depression and dementia and that she required 24-hour nursing supervision.[43] Mrs. DeMarco argued that the trial court erred in not allowing her to remain in her home with medical care and sitters, rather than placing her in an assisted living facility, as her treating physician did not preclude such an arrangement in his testimony.[44] The appellate court disagreed, finding that even if less restrictive living arrangements may be feasible, their existence is not conclusive of whether interdiction is appropriate.[45] The court found the expert testimony to be unequivocal and, in giving deference to the trial court's factual determinations, affirmed the full interdiction.[46]

§ 12.3 Limited Interdiction

Unlike full interdiction, a person is a candidate for limited interdiction if he is consistently unable to make reasoned decisions regarding the care of his person *or* his property, *or* any aspect of either. One who is unable to dress, feed, clothe, or care for oneself but has the mental capacity to make decisions regarding his or her property is a candidate for limited interdiction. Likewise, one who is able to live on one's own, but is making unreasoned decisions about his or her finances or the disposition of property, could be interdicted on a limited basis, as well. Finally, if one is able to make decisions regarding his person or property, but is unable to communicate them, limited interdiction is appropriate.[47]

Unlike a judgment of full interdiction, a judgment of limited interdiction does not deprive one of all capacity. For example, certain limited interdicts may make a disposition *mortis causa.*[48] The judgment of limited interdiction must confer on the limited

41. La. Code Civ. Proc. Ann. art. 4548.

42. In re Interdiction of DeMarco, 2009-1791 (La. App. 1 Cir. 4/7/10), 38 So. 3d 417.

43. In re Interdiction of DeMarco, 38 So. 3d at 425.

44. In re Interdiction of DeMarco, 38 So. 3d at 425.

45. In re Interdiction of DeMarco, 38 So. 3d at 425. The court noted that law prior to the 2001 revision authorized the trial court to "order that an interdict be attended in his own home, in a hospital, or in any other place...." Post-revision, however, these decisions are left to the curator. *Id.*

46. In re Interdiction of DeMarco, 38 So. 3d at 425. *But see* In re Interdiction of Kiser, 2007-1703 (La. App. 1 Cir. 6/06/08), 2008 WL 2567076 (finding the clear and convincing standard unmet because the caregiver could protect the interests of the alleged interdict without the need for a full interdiction).

47. La. Civ. Code Ann. art. 390 cmt. (b). If he is consistently unable to make reasoned decisions regarding the care of both his person and his property, or to communicate those decisions, he is a candidate for full interdiction. La. Civ. Code Ann. art. 390 cmt. (b). A limited interdict may be a viable candidate for forced heirship if the interdict's infirmity is permanent. *See* La. Civ. Code Ann. art. 1493 cmt. (c).

48. La. Civ. Code Ann. art. 390 cmt. (d); *see* La. Civ. Code Ann. art. 395; La. Civ. Code Ann. art. 1482 (rev. 2000); *see also* Section 12:6.

curator only those powers necessary to protect the interdict and must state that the limited interdict retains his capacity otherwise.[49]

For example, in *Interdiction of Keith*,[50] the court reversed the full interdiction of 18-year-old Cassidy Keith and instead ordered limited interdiction with regard to Ms. Keith's financial matters and medical decisions. Although Ms. Keith suffered from developmental disabilities and had only limited intellectual abilities, the record demonstrated that she understood these limitations. Ms. Keith also admitted that she required assistance with financial affairs and medical decisions.[51] Other than those two aspects, no evidence demonstrated that Ms. Keith was unable to make reasoned decisions regarding her regular care and that her interests could not be adequately protected by a limited interdiction with respect to those two specific areas.[52] The court remanded the matter for a judgment of limited interdiction and the appointment of a curator to handle these two areas.[53]

§ 12.4 Temporary and Preliminary Interdiction

When a petition for interdiction is pending, the court may order a temporary or preliminary interdiction (that is either full or limited)[54] when a substantial likelihood that grounds for interdiction exist and substantial harm to the health, safety, or property of the intended interdict is imminent.[55] Life-threatening medical conditions brought on by failure to take prescribed medications, paranoia, and lack of appreciation of the consequences of not taking medication have all been cited approvingly as valid grounds for temporary or preliminary interdiction.[56]

49. La. Code Civ. Proc. Ann. art. 4551(B); *see* Landry v. Hypolite, 23-635 (La. App. 3 Cir. 3/6/24); 381 So. 3d 977 (after a brain injury, plaintiff had been named a limited interdict for purposes of assisting with the settlement of the personal injury suit).

50. Matter of Interdiction of Keith, 2017-1573 (La. App. 1 Cir. 06/22/18), 2018 WL 3080456.

51. Matter of Interdiction of Keith, 2018 WL 3080456, at *7.

52. Matter of Interdiction of Keith, 2018 WL 3080456, at *7. The court noted that Ms. Keith made certain imprudent decisions, such as ceasing to take medication and becoming pregnant out-of-wedlock. *Id.* Nevertheless, the court found that these decisions were neither unreasoned nor attributable to Ms. Keith's infirmity and that she still made reasoned decisions regarding the care of her person. *Id.*

53. Matter of Interdiction of Keith, 2018 WL 3080456, at *7.

54. La. Civ. Code Ann. art. 391 cmt. (b).

55. La. Civ. Code Ann. art. 391. A judgment of preliminary interdiction granted after an adversarial hearing terminates 30 days after being signed, unless extended by the court for good cause for a period not exceeding 30 days. La. Civ. Code Ann. art. 397. The curator appointed in an order of temporary interdiction shall have no authority to admit the defendant to a residential or long-term care facility in the absence of good cause shown at a contradictory hearing. La. Code Civ. Proc. Ann. art. 4566(I).

56. *See, e.g.*, State v. In the Interest of Smith, 38,192 (La. App. 2 Cir. 03/03/04), 867 So. 2d 890, 894–895.

Temporary and preliminary interdictions parallel the relief available in other injunctive contexts.[57] As such, courts may order a temporary interdiction without notice and without an adversarial hearing.[58] If granted ex parte, the order will terminate 10 days after being signed, unless by motion of the defendant or for extraordinary reasons shown at contradictory hearing, the court extends the judgment of temporary interdiction for an additional period not to exceed 10 days.[59] A separate hearing must be held prior to granting an extension.[60] As for a preliminary interdiction, the relief can only be granted after an adversarial hearing and terminates 30 days after being signed, unless the court extends the judgment of preliminary interdiction for good cause for a period not to exceed 30 days.[61]

The purpose of a preliminary injunction is to maintain a particular status pending a full trial on the merits, and thus, a preliminary interdiction is not a final judgment.[62] As such, a judgment denying it is non-appealable unless an appeal is expressly provided for by law.[63]

§ 12.5 Modification and Termination of Interdiction

A judgment of interdiction may be modified or terminated for good cause.[64] The court on its own motion or on the motion of any person, including the interdict, can modify or terminate the interdiction on proof by a preponderance of the evidence that the terms of the interdiction are currently excessive or insufficient, or that the ability of the interdict to care for his person or property has changed.[65] The court will generally follow the same procedures that apply to an original petition for interdiction, unless good cause dictates otherwise.[66] Interdiction also terminates on death of the interdict.[67] The authors could find no relevant cases on modification and termination of interdiction.

---

57. La. Civ. Code Ann. art. 391 cmt. (d); *see* La. Code Civ. Pro. Ann. arts. 3601–13; *see also* Frank L. Maraist, 1A La. Civ. L. Treatise, Civ. Proc.—Special Proceed. § 7.1 (2022).

58. La. Code Civ. Proc. Ann. art. 4549.

59. La. Civ. Code Ann. art. 397.

60. La. Civ. Code Ann. art. 397 cmt. (a).

61. La. Civ. Code Ann. art. 397.

62. Interdiction of Marceaux, 2006-1328 (La. App. 3 Cir. 2/14/07), 951 So. 2d 1286, 1289 (finding that a preliminary injunction is interlocutory because the judgment does not determine the merits in an action for the injunction).

63. Interdiction of Marceaux, 951 So. 2d at 1289.

64. La. Civ. Code Ann. art. 397.

65. La. Code Civ. Proc. Ann. art. 4554.

66. La. Code Civ. Proc. Ann. art. 4554.

67. *See* In re Interdiction of Shubert, 2017-1738 (La. App. 1 Cir. 9/24/18), 258 So. 3d 808, 810 (finding that the death of an interdict renders the issue of whether permanent interdiction was proper moot).

§ 12.6 Curator

In the judgment of interdiction, the court shall appoint a curator and an undercurator unless an undercurator is not required by law.[68] A person qualified as the curator is best able to fulfill the duties of the office and is chosen by the court in an order of preference.[69] If the proposed interdict articulated a preference in a signed writing when he had the ability to communicate, that person shall be considered first.[70] In the absence of an articulated preference, the proposed interdict's spouse, adult child, parent, or a person with whom the interdict resided for more than six months, are given preference in that order.[71]

A person who is appointed as curator qualifies upon furnishing security[72] by law and taking an oath to discharge faithfully the duties of his office.[73] If the person fails to qualify for office within 10 days from his appointment or within another period specified by the court, the court may revoke the appointment and appoint another qualified person.[74] During the interim between the appointment and qualification of the curator, the court rendering the interdiction judgment may issue any protective order necessary for the best interest of the interdict.[75]

Certain individuals are *per se* unqualified to serve as a curator, including a minor, an interdicted person, and a nonresident without a resident agent for service of process.[76] Other classes of individuals are also unqualified, unless good cause is shown.[77] Regard-

---

68. La. Civ. Code Proc. Ann. art. 4551. The court need not appoint an undercurator when it appoints as curator a nonprofit curatorship program. La. Stat. Ann. § 9:1031(F) states: "Notwithstanding any law to the contrary, in cases wherein the program is appointed curator ..., the appointment of an undercurator ... is not required." La. Civ. Code Proc. Ann. art. 4551 cmt. (c); Interdiction of Constance, 23-318 (La. App. 5 Cir. 3/22/24); 384 So. 3d 1111 (appointment of Louisiana Guardian Services Incorporated without notice to the parties was improper, but the error was harmless and appointment was affirmed).

69. La. Code Civ. Proc. Ann. art. 4561 (C)(1)(a)–(f). Under pre-revision law, the defendant's pre-incapacity choice was given preference only if expressed in a power of attorney. *See* La. Code Civ. Proc. Ann. art. 4561 cmt. (a).

70. La. Code Civ. Proc. Ann. art. 4561 (C)(1)(a).

71. La. Code Civ. Proc. Ann. art. 4561 (C)(1)(b)–(f).

72. For specific rules regarding security, see La. Code Civ. Proc. Ann. arts. 4563, 4101, 4102, 4131–33, 4136. *See also* In re Interdiction of DeMarco, 2009-1791 (La. App. 1 Cir. 4/7/10), 38 So. 3d 417.

73. La. Code of Civ. Proc. Ann. art. 4562(A).

74. La. Code. Civ. Proc. Ann. art. 4562(B)(1). The delay allowed for qualification may be extended by the court for good cause. La. Code Civ. Proc. Ann. art. 4562(B)(2).

75. La. Code Civ. Proc. Ann. art. 4562(C).

76. La. Code Civ. Proc. Ann. art. 4561(B)(1)(a)–(c).

77. La. Code Civ. Proc. Ann. art. 4561 (B)(2)(a)–(d). A convicted felon, a person indebted to the interdict at the time of appointment, an adverse party in a lawsuit pending against the interdict at the time of appointment and an owner, operator, or employee of long-term care institutions where the interdict is receiving care, unless he is related to the interdict, can all be unqualified.

less, the failure of a person to qualify as curator following the judgment of interdiction does not affect the finding that interdiction is warranted.[78]

§ 12.7 Curator— Duties and Powers of the Curator

"The duties and powers of a curator commence upon his qualification. In discharging his duties, a curator shall exercise reasonable care, diligence, and prudence and shall act in the best interest of the interdict."[79] The court may appoint separate curators for the person and for the affairs[80] of the interdict.[81]

A curator over the interdict's person must file an annual personal report describing the location and condition of the interdict.[82] This report must also be filed upon termination of the curator's responsibilities or at any other time ordered by the court.[83] In making decisions, the curator should consider the interdict's pre-interdiction statements made in any preplanning documents, wills, or directives.[84] The curator should also consider the interdict's preferences if known to the curator.[85]

In *Interdiction of Krake*,[86] Allen and Terri Krake, the two adult children of Mrs. Krake, disagreed over who should be appointed as Mrs. Krake's curator, and further disagreed over where Mrs. Krake should live.[87] The trial court appointed Allen Krake as his mother's permanent curator over her person, property, and finances.[88] Terri Krake

78. In re Interdiction of DeMarco, 38 So. 3d at 430 (stating that "[a] factual finding that interdiction is warranted is not predicated upon the *qualification* of a curator, although a curator must be *appointed* as part of the judgment of interdiction").

79. La. Civ. Code Ann. art. 392.

80. The term "affairs" is used throughout the title refer to interest of the Interdict that are distinct from his person. La. Civ. Code Ann. art. 392 cmt. (e). This term includes the interdict's estate, property, and business, but may include other interest as well. *Id.* The use of this term is consistent with the terminology used in the mandate articles, *see* La. Civ. Code Ann. art. 2989 cmt. (d) (rev. 1997), and confirms that interdiction serves to empower the curator to protect the interdict from harm to all his interests. La. Civ. Code Ann. art. 392 cmt. (e).

81. La. Code Civ. Proc. Ann. art. 4561(C)(2). Louisiana Code of Civil Procedure Article 4069 states the procedure and standard—in exceptional circumstances and for good cause shown—for which separate curators may be appointed. *See* La. Code Civ. Proc. Ann. art. 4069.

82. La. Code. Civ. Proc. Ann. art. 4569(A). At the time of filing, the curator shall send copies of any required account or personal report by first class United States mail postage prepaid to the undercurator and any successor curator. *Id.*

83. La. Code. Civ. Proc. Ann. art. 4569(A).

84. La. Civ. Code Ann. art. 392 cmt. (c).

85. La. Civ. Code Ann. art. 392 cmt. (c). Also, to the extent reasonably possible, a curator should encourage the interdict to participate in decisions and to develop or to regain the ability to care for his person, to manage his affairs, or both. La. Civ. Code Ann. art. 392 cmt. (c).

86. Interdiction of Krake, 2017 1352 (La. App. 1 Cir. 04/06/18), 2018 WL 1663143.

87. Interdiction of Krake, 2018 WL 1663143, at *2. Specifically, Allen Krake wished to be appointed curator so that Mrs. Krake would remain living close to him and his family in Louisiana, whereas Terri Krake wished to relocate Mrs. Krake to a nursing home near her in Minneapolis, Minnesota. *Id.*

88. Interdiction of Krake, 2018 WL 1663143, at *2.

appealed, claiming that the trial court erred by failing to consider that she had handled her mother's affairs as her power of attorney for the past eight years.[89] The court disagreed. Terri Krake's power of attorney did not contain any statement that she should be appointed curatrix in the event of Mrs. Krake's interdiction.[90] Further, Allen Krake was qualified as curator as one of Mrs. Krake's adult children.[91] Relocating Mrs. Krake out of state, as requested by Terri, would not be in Mrs. Krake's best interest in light of her long-time residence in Louisiana and her declining mental and physical health.[92] With due deference given to the trial court, the appellate court affirmed Allen Krake as her curator.[93]

With respect to managing the affairs of the interdict, the relationship between interdict and curator is similar to the relationship between minor and tutor.[94] A curator must file an account annually, when his appointment terminates, or at any other time ordered by the court.[95] The curator who owns an interest in property with the interdict is permitted to acquire that property from the interdict with court approval.[96] The curator is permitted to accept donations made to the interdict and place the interdict's property in a trust.[97] The curator is not permitted to donate the property of the interdict.[98] If the curator materially changes the interdict's living arrangements or materially affects the interdict's person or affairs, the curator must inform the undercurator.[99] The curator may not move the interdict out of state, consent to an abortion, or consent to sterilization without prior court authorization.[100] Finally, a curator cannot use the provisions of interdiction to commit an interdict to a mental health treatment facility; the curator or a court must proceed in accordance with the Behavioral Health Laws.[101]

To care for the interdict's person or property, the curator is permitted to spend the revenue of the interdict. With court authorization, the curator can likewise spend the

---

89. Interdiction of Krake, 2018 WL 1663143, at *2.

90. Interdiction of Krake, 2018 WL 1663143, at *3.

91. Interdiction of Krake, 2018 WL 1663143, at *3.

92. Interdiction of Krake, 2018 WL 1663143, at *3.

93. Interdiction of Krake, 2018 WL 1663143, at *3. A trial court's ruling will not be disturbed on appeal unless an abuse of direction to act in the best interest of the interdict is shown. *Id.*

94. La. Code Civ. Proc. Ann. art 4566(A). Specifically, the rules provided by articles 4261 through 4269, 4270 through 4274, 4301 through 4342, and 4371 apply to curatorship of interdicts. *Id.* By contrast, special rules applicable to natural tutors and parents do not apply in the context of interdiction. *Id.*

95. La. Code. Civ. Proc. Ann. art. 4569(A).

96. La. Code. Civ. Proc. Ann. art. 4566(B).

97. *See* La. Code Civ. Proc. Ann. art 4566(B)–(D). For specific rules regarding a curator's ability to make donations on behalf of the interdict, *see* La. Stat. Ann. § 9:1022 (authorization of curators to continue making donations to descendants); La. Stat. Ann. § 9:1023 (donation by curator to charitable and nonprofit organizations); La. Stat. Ann. § 9:1024 (donations by curator to collaterals).

98. La. Code. Civ. Proc. Ann. art. 4566(C).

99. La. Code Civ. Proc. Ann. art. 4566(E)–(F). The standard to be used by the court is the best interest of the interdict. *See, e.g.*, In re Interdiction of Rodrigue, 2005-0061 (La. App. 1 Cir. 11/4/05), 927 So. 2d 421.

100. La. Code Civ. Proc. Ann. art. 4566(F)–(G).

101. La. Code Civ. Proc. Ann. art. 4566(H); *see* La. Stat. Ann. § 28:1 *et seq.*

revenue of the interdict to support the interdict's dependents.[102] Court authorization is also necessary if the curator must expend the interdict's capital for these purposes.[103]

At any time during the interdiction, the court has the authority to appoint an examiner to review the personal report or the accounting made by the curator, to interview the interdict, curator, and undercurator, or to make any investigations.[104] These broad powers are necessary to protect the interdict. Likewise, the court may also appoint an attorney to represent the interdict.[105]

§ 12.8 Curator—Undercurator

In the judgment of interdiction, the court shall also appoint an undercurator unless doing so is not required by law.[106] The undercurator's duties are to exercise reasonable care, diligence, and prudence, and he shall act in the best interest of the interdict.[107] The undercurator's quintessential duty is to notify the court when he has reason to believe that the curator has failed to perform any duties imposed by law, including the duties to file necessary accounts and personal reports and to maintain adequate security.[108] The undercurator shall have no duties, either express or implied, other than those set forth in Louisiana Code of Civil Procedure Article 4565 and in Civil Code Article 393.[109]

---

102. La. Code. Civ. Proc. Ann. art. 4567.

103. La. Code. Civ. Proc. Ann. art. 4567. Court authorization is sought by filing a petition seeking the use of capital and the reasons for such use. La. Code Civ Proc. Ann. art. 4271.

104. La. Code Civ. Proc. Ann. art. 4569(B).

105. La. Code Civ. Proc. Ann. art. 4569(B).

106. La. Civ. Code Proc. Ann. art. 4551. The court need not appoint an undercurator when it appoints as curator a nonprofit curatorship program. La. Stat. Ann. § 9:1031(F): "Notwithstanding any law to the contrary, in cases wherein the program is appointed curator . . . , the appointment of an undercurator . . . is not required." La. Civ. Code Proc. Ann. art. 4551 cmt. (c).

107. La. Civ. Code Ann. art. 393.

108. *See* La. Code Civ Proc. Ann. art. 4565(B)(4). The undercurator's duties also shall include: notifying the court when the curator has failed to qualify timely for office, having free access to the interdict and to all records relating to the interdict relevant to his office, reviewing all accounts and personal reports filed by the curator, approving or disapproving any transactions that require his concurrence, and moving to appoint a successor for a curator who becomes disqualified or whose office terminates. *See* La. Code. Civ. Proc. Ann. art. 4565(B)(1)–(6).

109. *See* La. Code Civ. Proc Ann. art. 4565(C).

§ 12.9 Curator— Undercurator and Curator Liability

Neither a curator nor an undercurator is personally liable for the interdict's delicts solely by reason of his office.[110] Prior law stated that "[t]he curators of insane persons were answerable for the damage occasioned by those under their care."[111] As revised, the law now shields curators and undercurators from vicarious liability for the torts of interdicts in their charge.[112] Nevertheless, although a curator is not personally responsible for an interdict's torts solely by reason of the relationship, the curator may be liable for damages resulting from his own acts or omissions.[113]

§ 12.10 Curator— Removal of a Curator

On motion of any interested person, or on its own motion, the court may remove a curator or undercurator from office for good cause.[114] Unless otherwise ordered by the court, removal of the curator or undercurator by the court is effective upon qualification of the appointed successor.[115] In determining whether or not the removal of a curator is in the interdict's best interest, the trial court has broad discretion and that discretion should not be disturbed unless it is manifestly erroneous or clearly wrong.[116]

Good cause for removal exists when the curator becomes disqualified because he no longer satisfies the requirements set forth in Code of Civil Procedure Article 4561.[117] In circumstances where the curator has absconded from the state, failed to render an account, failed to obey court orders, or has engaged in activities that include gross misconduct, incompetence, incarceration, or abuse of the interdict, a curator may be

---

110. La. Civ. Code. Ann. art. 2319; *see* comment (a) stating that this article changes the law, which previously stated under the Louisiana Civil Code of 1870, "[t]he curators for insane persons are answerable for the damage caused under their care." La. Civ. Code Ann. art. 2319 cmt. (a).

111. *See* La. Civ. Code Ann. art. 2319 cmt. (a); *see also* La. Civ. Code art. 2319 (1870).

112. *See* La. Civ. Code Ann. art. 2319 cmt. (a).

113. *See* La. Civ. Code Ann. art. 2319 cmt. (b). For example, if a curator negligently supervises an interdict in his charge and, as a result, the interdict causes damages to himself or to a third party, the curator may be personally responsible for the resulting damages. La. Civ. Code Ann. art. 2319 cmt. (b).

114. La. Code Civ. Proc. Ann. art. 4568; *see* In re Helm, 2011-0500 (La. App 4 Cir. 11/2/11), 84 So. 3d 601, 604 (removing an undercurator for good cause because of an irreparable conflict of interest preventing the undercurator from fulfilling her duties, including the duty to report the failings of the curator, because the undercurator obligated herself as a legal surety for the curator).

115. In re Helm, 84 So. 3d at 604. Civil Code of Procedure Article 4568 omits any provision establishing a maximum term of 10 years for certain curators. *See* La. Code Civ. Proc. Ann. art 4568 cmt. (a). It also omits cross-references to Code of Civil Procedure Articles 4231–4238 because the substance of those tutorship articles is set forth in the article. *Id.*

116. Interdiction of Stephens, 40,965 (La. App. 2 Cir. 06/02/06), 930 So. 2d 1222.

117. La. Code Civ. Proc. Ann. art. 4568 cmt. (c).

subject to removal.[118] On the interdict's death or termination of interdiction, a curator's office terminates automatically.[119] In such cases, "removal" from office is unnecessary.[120]

§ 12.11 Effects of Interdiction

The harsh legal intervention of interdiction is one of the most powerful operations of law in Louisiana affecting individuals. Thus, a judgment of interdiction is avoidable when less severe means of protection would suffice. When interdiction cannot be avoided, the effects on the interdict's decisional authority depends on whether a full interdiction or limited interdiction judgment was ordered.

§ 12.12 Effects of Interdiction— On Juridical Acts Pre- and Post-Interdiction

Interdiction does not affect the validity of a juridical act[121] made by the interdict prior to the effective date of interdiction.[122] A judgment of interdiction has effect retroactive to the date of the filing of the petition for interdiction.[123] Under prior law, acts made prior to interdiction could be annulled when shown that at the time the act was made or done, interdiction notoriously existed or that the other party could not have been deceived as to the situation of the interdict's mind.[124]

A limited interdict lacks capacity to make a juridical act pertaining to the property or aspects of personal care that the judgment of limited interdiction placed under the authority of his curator, except as provided in article 1482.[125] For example, in *Landry v. Hypolite*,[126] Ms. Landry sustained a brain injury as a result of an automobile accident.[127] Pursuant to a petition for a limited interdiction, a curator was appointed to assist in set-

---

118. *See* La. Stat. Ann. § 9:1025.

119. La. Code Civ. Proc. Ann. art. 4568 cmt. (e); *see also* La. Civ. Code Ann. art. 397.

120. La. Civ. Code Ann. art. 397.

121. A juridical act is a lawful volitional act intended to have legal consequences. La. Civ. Code Ann. art. 395 cmt. (b). It may be a unilateral act, such as an affidavit, or a bilateral act, such as a contract. It may be onerous or gratuitous. *See also* La. Civ. Code Ann. art. 3471 cmt. (c) (rev. 1982) (citing A.N. Yiannopoulos, Louisiana Civil Law System Coursebook § 77 (1977)); Marcel Planiol, 1 Treatise on the Civil Law § 265, at 187 (La. State L. Inst. Trans., 12th ed. 1959).

122. La. Civ. Code Ann. art. 394.

123. La. Civ. Code Ann. art. 396. Whether a pre-interdiction juridical act creates, modifies, transfers, or terminates a personal or real right turns on the substantive law potentially giving effect to the act. La. Civ. Code Ann. art. 394 cmt. (b); *but see* In re Interdiction of DeMarco, 2009-1791 (La. App. 1 Cir. 4/7/10), 38 So. 3d 417, 427 (finding that a full interdict has the right to retain counsel subsequent to the order of interdiction against them, and that the retroactive date of a judgment of interdiction does not of itself operate to nullify the attorney-client agreement).

124. *See* La. Civ. Code art. 402 (1870). "Notoriously" meant that the cause of interdiction was generally known by the persons who saw and conversed with the party. La. Civ. Code art. 402 (1870).

125. *See* Section 12:13. *See also* La. Civ. Code Ann. art. 1482(C).

126. Landry v. Hypolite, 23-635 (La. App. 3 Cir. 3/6/24); 381 So. 3d 977.

127. Landry, 381 So. 3d at 979.

tling the personal injury lawsuit and managing her financial affairs.[128] A settlement was reached, which provided Mrs. Landry a monthly annuity, and Ms. Landry's daughter was designated as the beneficiary if Ms. Landry died before final payment.[129] Subsequently, Ms. Landry began communicating with and eventually married Mr. Hypolite, who was incarcerated. Shortly after they were married, she changed the beneficiary of the annuity contract to Mr. Hypolite.[130] Years later, they divorced, and then Ms. Landry died. In a dispute between her daughter and Mr. Hypolite over the annuity contract, the court concluded that the purpose of the judgment of limited interdiction was to preserve the funds awarded to her and to manage the financial affairs associated with the annuity.[131] As a result, Ms. Landry lacked the capacity to make a juridical act—changing the beneficiary on the annuity contract—because that property was placed under the authority of her curator.[132]

Notably, the rules regarding an interdict's capacity act as an exception to the general rule that natural persons have the capacity to make juridical acts.[133] In addition, article 395 explicitly acknowledges that specific legislation may override this general lack of legal capacity of an interdict.[134] For example, an interdict is specifically given capacity to seek modification or termination of the interdiction.[135]

Nevertheless, interdiction has no effect on obligations that do not arise through an exercise of will.[136] For example, an interdict remains responsible for obligations arising under tort law or family law.[137]

128. Landry, 381 So. 3d at 980.
129. Landry, 381 So. 3d at 980.
130. Landry, 381 So. 3d at 980.
131. Landry, 381 So. 3d at 983.
132. Landry, 381 So. 3d at 983.
133. *See* La. Civ. Code Ann. art. 395 cmt. (a); *see also* La. Civ. Code Ann. art. 28.
134. *See* La. Civ. Code Ann. art 395 cmt. (a).
135. La. Code Civ. Proc. Ann. art. 4554.
136. La. Civ. Code Ann. art. 395 cmt. (f).
137. La. Civ. Code Ann. art. 395 cmt. (f).

§ 12.13 Effects of Interdiction— On Donations

Under current law, to have capacity to make a donation, a person must be able to comprehend generally the nature and consequences of the disposition that he is making.[138] As a general rule, one challenging a donation on the basis of mental incapacity must prove it by clear and convincing evidence.[139] However, these rules are modified for interdicts, because their mental infirmity has been judicially determined.[140] Thus, interdicts enjoy no presumption of capacity; to the contrary, they are presumed to lack capacity.[141] This, in turn, shifts the burden of proof to the proponent of the donation to overcome the presumption.[142]

Under prior law, interdiction alone was not determinative of a lack of testamentary capacity.[143] Under current law, the rules hinge on whether one is adjudged a full interdict or a limited interdict. The rules for a full interdict are straightforward—they lack capacity to make or revoke a donation *inter vivos* or disposition *mortis causa.*[144] For a limited interdict, the rules depend on whether the property being donated is under the authority of the curator (or not). With respect to property under the authority of the curator, the limited interdict lacks capacity to make or revoke a donation *inter vivos* and is presumed to lack capacity to make or revoke a disposition *mortis causa.*[145] As to the other property (i.e., the property not under the curator's authority), the limited interdict is presumed to have capacity to make or revoke a donation *inter vivos* or disposition *mortis causa.* These presumptions, particular to limited interdicts, may be rebutted by a preponderance of the evidence, thereby lowering the burden from the more onerous clear and convincing standard used in the general rule.[146]

---

138. *See* La. Civ. Code Ann. art. 1477. In 1991, this standard replaced the former "of sound mind" standard contained in former Civil Code Article 1475. *See* La. Civ. Code Ann. art. 1477 cmt. (a). *See also* Kathy D. Underwood, La. Prac. La. Notary Handbook § 15:3 (ed. 2023–2024).

139. La. Civ. Code Ann. art. 1482(A). Prior law required proof beyond a reasonable doubt. La. Civ. Code Ann. art. 1482 cmt. (c).

140. La. Civ. Code Ann. art. 1482 cmt. (a).

141. La. Civ. Code Ann. art. 1482 cmt. (a).

142. La. Civ. Code Ann. art. 1482 cmt. (a).

143. *See* Succession of Price, 448 So. 2d 839 (La. Ct. App. 2 Cir. 1984); Succession of Cantazaro, 417 So. 2d 863 (La. Ct. App. 4 Cir. 1982); Succession of Cole, 618 So. 2d 554 (La. Ct. App. 4 Cir. 1993).

144. *See* La. Civ. Code Ann. art. 1482(B); In re Succession of Benoit, 14-546 (La. App. 5 Cir. 11/25/14), 165 So. 3d 1017 (finding that Ms. Benoit lacked testamentary capacity when she executed a purported testament, even though the interdiction judgment was not signed until after she executed the purported testament—the purported testament was executed after the retroactive effect of the judgment of interdiction, and thus, Ms. Beniot did not have capacity to donate).

145. La. Civ. Code Ann. art. 1482(C).

146. *See* La. Civ. Code Ann. art. 1482(C). Under prior law, the burden to rebut the presumption that the testator lacked capacity was borne by the proponent of the will by clear and convincing evidence. *See also* La. Civ. Code Ann. art. 395 cmt. (e) (clear and convincing); La. Civ. Code Ann. art. 1482 cmts. (b)–(c); *see, e.g.*, Succession of Deshotel, 09-37 (La. App. 3 Cir. 05/06/09), 10 So. 3d 873 (holding that evidence of decedent's lucidity at the time he executed his will supported the trial

In a Third Circuit case, *Succession of Deshotel*,[147] the court held that although the testator was presumed to lack testamentary capacity due to the filing of a limited interdiction proceeding prior to execution of the testament in question, evidence supported the trial court's finding that the testator had capacity to execute a final will. The court relied on the testimony that the testator had moments of lucidity in conjunction with testimony that the testator was lucid on the day that he executed the will in question. The court ultimately found that this testimony rebutted the presumption and established capacity by a preponderance of evidence.[148]

§ 12.14 Effects of Interdiction— On Forced Heirship

The law of interdiction informed the law of forced heirship. Forced heirs, among others, can be descendants who, because of mental incapacity or physical infirmity, are permanently incapable of taking care of their persons or administering their estates at the time of the death of the decedent.[149] The double disjunctive "either/or" approach to incapacity or infirmity in forced heirship originated in Act 147 of 1990 and its predecessor, Act 788 of 1989, which provided that descendants of any age who were "subject to interdiction" were forced heirs.[150] The meaning of "subject to interdiction" was unclear because it did not indicate whether full, limited, or both types of interdiction were included. Later, the terminology changed to employ the terms found in the concept of limited interdiction, rather than full interdiction.[151] However, due to concerns that the broad scope of the terms might encourage spurious claims for relatively minor incapacities or infirmities, and also uncertainty whether a temporary, albeit severe, incapacity or infirmity might qualify a child as a forced heir, the Louisiana Legislature added the word "permanently" before the word "incapable."[152] The legislature also requested that the comments to the article note that, as a factual matter, a person can be permanently incapable or infirm but on occasion have a temporary remission.[153] At least one court has noted that it was contemplated that the guidelines courts would

court's finding that decedent had testamentary capacity to execute final will although an interdiction proceeding was pending against decedent).

147. Deshotel, 10 So. 3d 873.

148. Proof by "a preponderance of evidence" requires that the evidence, taken as a whole, show that the fact sought to be proved is more probable than not. *See* La Civ. Code Ann. art. 1482 (b) (citing Prestenback v. Sentry Ins. Co., 340 So. 2d 1331 (La. 1976)).

149. La. Civ. Code Ann. art. 1493(A), (C). Further, "'Permanently incapable of taking care of their persons or administering their estates at the time of death of the decedent' includes descendants who, at the time of death of the decedent, have, according to documentation, an inherited, incurable disease or condition that may render them incapable of caring for their person or administering their estates in the future." La. Civ. Code Ann. art. 1493(E).

150. *See* La. Civ. Code Ann. art. 1493 cmt. (c).

151. La. Civ. Code Ann. art. 1493 cmt. (c).

152. La. Civ. Code Ann. art. 1493 cmt. (c). Also, the time at which the incapacity or infirmity is determined to be relevant is at the donor's death. *See* La. Civ. Code Ann. art. 1493 cmt. (c).

153. La. Civ. Code Ann. art. 1493 cmt. (c).

use in interpreting the forced heirship provisions would come from limited interdiction jurisprudence.[154] Consequently, although the formal definitions of interdiction and forced heirship do not align as they once did, they do represent, as one author as commented, a similar factual test.[155]

§ 12.15 Effects of Interdiction— On Miscellaneous Acts

According to Louisiana Code of Civil Procedure Article 683, a mentally incompetent[156] person lacks the procedural capacity to sue,[157] so except as otherwise provided in articles 4431,[158] 4554,[159] and 4566,[160] the curator is the proper plaintiff to sue to enforce an interdict's rights.[161] Likewise, except as otherwise provided in articles 732,[162] 4431,[163] and 4566,[164] the properly appointed curator is the proper defendant in an action to enforce an obligation against a mental incompetent or an interdict per Article 733 of the Louisiana Code of Civil Procedure.[165] If an incompetent has no curator but is interdicted or committed to or confined in a mental institution, the same article provides that an action shall be brought against him, but the court shall appoint an attorney to

---

154. However, in reversing the trial court's decision and finding the appellant to be a forced heir, the appellate court stated that limited interdiction standards as guidelines were not as appropriate because the appellant's capacity to function with the permanent condition of bipolar disorder varies. *See* Succession of Ardoin, 07-43 (La. App. 3 Cir. 05/30/07), 957 So. 2d 237. For an in-depth discussion on forced heirship, see Kathryn V. Lorio, 10 La. Civ. L. Treatise, Successions and Donations, § 10 (2d ed. 2009); Katherine Shaw Spaht, *Forced Heirship Changes: The Regrettable "Revolution" Completed*, 57 La. L. Rev. 73 (1996).

155. William Reid Huguet, *The New Law of Interdiction: Clear and Convincing Revision*, 47 Loy. L. Rev. 1059, 1069 (2001).

156. The term "mentally incompetent" includes a person who has not been interdicted.

157. *See* La. Code Civ. Proc. Ann. art. 684. If an action is brought by an interdict and the defendant timely objects, the curator must be substituted as the proper party plaintiff. If the plaintiff is incompetent but has not been interdicted, and the defendant objects timely, the suit cannot proceed until the plaintiff is interdicted, and a curator is qualified. *See* Frank L. Maraist, 1 La. Civ. L. Treatise, Civil Procedure § 4:3 (2d ed. 2021).

158. La. Code Civ. Proc. Ann. art. 4431 (foreign tutor may appear in court on behalf of minor when no tutor of this state has been provided).

159. La. Civ. Code Ann. art. 4554.

160. La. Code Civ. Proc. Ann. art. 4566 (management of affairs of the interdict).

161. The exception avoids the conflict with the articles recognizing: (1) the right of a guardian of a nonresident incompetent appointed by a court of another state to act in Louisiana without the necessity of appointment and qualification by a court of this state; and (2) the right of an interdict to sue to terminate the interdiction. *See* La. Civ. Code Proc. Ann. art. 684 cmt. (b). *See also* La. Code Civ. Proc. Ann. art. 4431, 4554, 4556.

162. La. Code Civ. Proc. Ann. art. 732 (unemancipated minor cannot be sued).

163. La. Code Civ. Proc. Ann. art. 4431 (foreign tutor may appear in court on behalf of minor when no tutor of this state has been provided).

164. La. Code Civ. Proc. Ann. art. 4566 (management of affairs of the interdict).

165. La. Code Civ. Proc. Ann. art. 733.

represent him.[166] An interdicted person also lacks the capacity to contract,[167] to vote,[168] and to be an arbitrator.[169]

In *Alonzo v. Alonzo*, the Fourth Circuit Court of Appeal found Mr. Alonzo mentally incompetent after he suffered brain damage from a boating accident, and thus, he lacked procedural capacity to be sued in past-due child support proceedings naming him as defendant.[170] Mr. Alonzo did not have a curator, nor was he interdicted, committed to, or confined in a mental institution, but the court did not appoint an attorney for him.[171] Further, the court found that proceeding against him would violate the prohibition of lawsuits against mental incompetents.[172] As such, the court determined that the solution would be to have Mr. Alonzo interdicted, appoint a curator, and proceed against the curator.[173]

§ 12.16 Effects of Interdiction— On Prescription

Prescription runs against interdicts unless an exception is established by legislation.[174] One such exception where the law suspends prescription is between curators and interdicts during interdiction.[175] There is no suspension of prescription vis-à-vis third persons, and thus, liberative prescription, acquisitive prescription,[176] and prescription of nonuse may accrue in favor of a third person to the prejudice of an interdict.[177]

§ 12.17 Alternative Options to Interdiction

As stated above, full interdiction is a last resort and should not be employed when the person's interests are currently protected by other less restrictive means or can be protected by less restrictive means.[178] Thus, the following alternatives to interdiction may be appropriate depending on the circumstances.

166. *See* La. Code Civ. Proc. Ann. art. 733(B).

167. La. Civ. Code Ann. art. 1918.

168. La. Const. Ann. art. I, § 10; La. Stat. Ann. § 18:102(A)(2).

169. La. Civ. Code Ann. art. 3107.

170. Alonzo v. Alonzo, 91-0124 (La. App. 4 Cir. 03/15/94), 634 So. 2d 54, 56.

171. Alonzo, 634 So. 2d at 57.

172. Alonzo, 634 So. 2d at 58 (finding that a suit against Mr. Alonzo would lose "sight of the fact that the major premise and overriding policy expressed by LSA-C.C.P. art. 733 at the outset is that: 'A mental incompetent has no procedural capacity to be sued.' All else flows from and is subsidiary to this concept").

173. Alonzo, 634 So. 2d at 58.

174. La. Civ. Code Ann. art. 3468.

175. La. Civ. Code Ann. art. 3469.

176. *See* La. Civ. Code Ann. art. 3473 (10 years in good faith and under just title runs against interdicts for immovables).

177. *See* La. Civ. Code Ann. art. 3469 cmt. (c).

178. *See* La. Civ. Code Ann. art. 389 cmt. (c).

§ 12.18 Alternative Options to Interdiction— Continuing or Permanent Tutorship

Interdiction proceedings may only be brought against emancipated minors or those who have reached the age of majority.[179] Thus, whether one seeks to protect a person who cannot yet be interdicted or circumvent the formal proceedings of an interdiction, one alternative is continuing tutorship.[180]

Under continuing tutorship, if a minor above the age of 15 years has less than two-thirds of the average mental ability or adaptive functioning of a normal person of the same age, evidenced by standard testing procedures, the parents of such person or the person entitled to custody or tutorship, may with the concurrence of the coroner of the parish of the mentally deficient person's domicile, petition the court of that district to place such person under a continuing tutorship. If successful, the continuing tutorship does not automatically end at any age but instead, continues until revoked by the court of domicile.[181] The tutorship proceeding may proceed without formal or complete interdiction if the person to be placed under the continuing tutorship has not reached the age of majority.[182] However, if the person to be placed under continuing tutorship has reached the age of majority,[183] the proceeding shall be conducted according to the procedural rules established for interdictions.[184]

§ 12.19 Alternative Options to Interdiction— Durable Power of Attorney/Procuration or Mandate

A person's interests can be protected by less restrictive means if, for example, his interests are currently being protected by other legal documents, including a procuration, mandate, or trust.[185] As a result, an adequate power of attorney may eliminate the need for interdiction.[186]

---

179. The age of majority is 18 years. La. Civ. Code Ann. art. 29.

180. *See* Chapter 10, Section 10:28.

181. *See* La. Civ. Code Ann. art. 355.

182. *See* La. Civ. Code Ann. arts. 354, 356(1).

183. The age of majority is 18 years. La. Civ. Code Ann. art. 29.

184. La. Civ. Code Ann. art. 356; In *Interdiction of Conrad*, the Fifth Circuit found two previous tutorship judgments of Ms. Conrad to be absolute nullities because Ms. Conrad was a major and the parties failed to follow the procedure for interdiction. Interdiction of Conrad, 2017-530 (La. 12/05/17), 2017 WL 6812284. Ms. Conrad was not served with process before the tutorship proceedings, nor was she represented by counsel. *Id.* at *6. Thus, the court remanded the case for further proceedings consistent with the procedure for interdiction. *Id.* at *7.

185. La. Civ. Code Ann. art. 389 cmt. (e).

186. However, it should be noted, as one court found, a power of attorney does not automatically "trump" an interdiction proceeding. *See, e.g.*, Womack v. Stephenson, 08-493 (La. App. 5 Cir. 1/13/09), 8 So. 3d 1. On a different issue—whether a judgment of interdiction was a nullity because it invalidated a juridical act made prior to interdiction—another court held that an interdiction judgment, which invalidated both a power of attorney and testament, was a valid judgment. *See* In re Succession of Wilkinson, 2007-1038 (La. App. 5 Cir. 05/27/08), 986 So. 2d 141.

The term "power of attorney" is, in fact, a common law term; the proper civilian name for such an act would be procuration or a mandate. However, because a "power of attorney" facilitates transactions with common law jurisdictions, it is a commonly accepted term that is used in Louisiana.[187] Generally, the difference between procuration and mandate is that a procuration is a unilateral act, whereas the mandate is a bilateral act—a contract between the principal and the agent.[188] However, both involve one person, who is called the "principal," conferring the authority to act on his or her or their behalf to another, who is called the "representative" in an act of procuration and a "mandatary" in a contract of mandate. For ease of reference, both will be referred to using the common law term "agent" from here forward. The rules governing procurations are subject to the rules governing mandates to the extent that the application of those rules is compatible with the nature of the procuration.[189]

Like curators, agents must act as prudent administrators and are responsible for their acts of fault or neglect.[190] However, unlike many instances for curators, an agent does not need judicial authorization to act.[191] Also, statutory powers of an agent are generally broad, i.e., a general power of attorney confers powers of administration of the principal's affairs, more particularly "to do whatever is appropriate under the circumstances" and to "perform all acts that are incidental to or necessary for the performance of the mandate."[192] Nevertheless, certain powers of the mandate must be mentioned expressly in the power of attorney, including the power to alienate, acquire, encumber or lease a thing,[193] make donations *inter vivos*,[194] accept or renounce a succession,[195] contract a loan, acknowledge or remit a debt, or become a surety,[196] draw or endorse promissory notes and negotiable instruments,[197] enter into a compromise or refer a matter to arbitration,[198] make health care decisions such as surgery, medical expenses, nursing home residency, or medication,[199] and appoint an agent to provide for the care, custody, and control of a minor child.[200] There are also powers that a

187. *See* Kathy D. Underwood, La. Prac. La. Notary Handbook § 8:2 (ed. 2023–2024).

188. Kathy D. Underwood, La. Prac. La. Notary Handbook § 8:2 (ed. 2023–2024).

189. Kathy D. Underwood, La. Prac. La. Notary Handbook § 8:2 (ed. 2023–2024).

190. *See* La. Civ. Code Ann. art. 3001; Kathy D. Underwood, La. Prac. La. Notary Handbook § 8:9 (ed. 2023–2024).

191. *See*, e.g., La. Civ. Code Ann. arts. 2995–97.

192. La. Civ. Code Ann. art. 2995.

193. La. Civ. Code Ann. art. 2996.

194. La. Civ. Code Ann. art. 2997.

195. La. Civ. Code Ann. art. 2997.

196. La. Civ. Code Ann. art. 2997.

197. La. Civ. Code Ann. art. 2997.

198. La. Civ. Code Ann. art. 2997.

199. La. Civ. Code Ann. art. 2997.

200. For a more specific rules regarding this power, which is called Provisional Custody by Mandate, see La. Stat. Ann. §§ 9:951–54.

principal cannot delegate to an agent, for example, the power to execute or consent to a notarial adoption,[201] to execute a testament,[202] and to contract a marriage.[203]

A "durable" power of attorney refers to one that does not terminate if the principal becomes incapacitated, disabled, or has any other condition that makes an express revocation of the mandate impossible or impractical.[204] All powers of attorney are durable unless there is a provision in the power of attorney or another agreement to the contrary.[205] However, although the power of attorney is not terminated by the principal's incapacity, such will terminate upon the qualification of the curator after the interdiction of the principal.[206] Nevertheless, the power of attorney can provide that in case of interdiction, the agent is nominated to serve as the curator. In subsequent interdiction proceedings, the court will be bound to give first preference for curator to this person designated by the interdict in a writing signed by him while he had sufficient ability to communicate a reasoned preference.[207]

§ 12.20 Supported Decisionmaking Agreements

In 2020, the Louisiana Legislature passed into law the Supported Decisionmaking Agreement Act, also known as the Dustin Gary Act.[208] The Act provides adults with disabilities a more empowering alternative over the extreme effects of interdiction.[209] An "adult" is a person over the age of eighteen, or an emancipated minor, who has a disability as defined by the Americans with Disabilities Act of 1990.[210] Entirely optional, a supported decisionmaking agreement (SDA) should be considered a less restrictive means affecting a court's decision to enter a judgment of interdiction.[211]

Importantly, the SDA does not limit the powers of the adult; rather, the SDA empowers the adult to make informed decisions with the assistance of a supporter.[212] "Supportive decisionmaking" is defined as "a process of supporting and accommodating an adult to enable the adult to make life decisions, including decisions related to where the adult wants to live, the services, supports, and medical care the adult wants

201. La. Civ. Code Ann. art. 213.

202. La. Civ. Code Ann. art. 1571.

203. La. Civ. Code Ann. art. 92.

204. *See* Kathy D. Underwood, La. Prac. La. Notary Handbook § 8:11 (ed. 2023–2024); La. Civ. Code Ann. art. 3026.

205. La. Civ. Code Ann. art. 3026.

206. La. Civ. Code Ann. art. 3024.

207. La. Code Civ. Proc. Ann. art. 4561.

208. Act No. 258, 2020 La. Acts; *see* La. Stat. Ann. § 13:4261.101.

209. La. Stat. Ann. § 13:4261.103 (2024); In re Interdiction of Parnell, 2013-1201 (La. App. 4 Cir. 11/13/13), 129 So. 3d 690, 692 ("Interdiction is a harsh remedy. A judgment of interdiction amounts to civil death, it is a declaration that the interdict is incapable of caring for herself or her estate.").

210. La. Stat. Ann. § 13:4261.102(1).

211. La. Code Civ. Proc. Ann. art. 4541(11).

212. *See* La. Stat. Ann. §§ 13:4261.102, .103.

to receive, with whom the adult wants to live, and where the adult wants to work, without impeding the self-determination of the adult."[213] For example, although an adult may authorize his supporter to obtain his own medical records,[214] the adult is likewise free to obtain these records on his own.[215]

The SDA is entered into between the adult and any number of "supporters."[216] A supporter may be any individual who has attained the age of eighteen years old.[217] The Agreement may also designate alternates to act in the place of named supporters "under circumstances specified in the agreement."[218] The supporter acts as an adviser and confidant to the adult and generally supports the adult in (1) decisionmaking; (2) obtaining information relevant to those decisions; (3) understanding the information obtained; and (4) communicating the adult's decisions to the appropriate parties.[219] The Agreement may limit the nature or scope of decisions that the supporter may take part in, and the supporter is prohibited from exceeding that scope of authority.[220] For example, a supporter may not advise an adult on his business matters if the SDA only permits the supporter to counsel him on issues relating to his health.[221]

The supporter owes a duty of loyalty to the adult. The supporter must (1) support the will and preference of the adult over his own;[222] (2) act honestly, diligently, and in good faith;[223] and (3) avoid conflicts of interest.[224] The supporter may not impose his own will over the adult,[225] prioritize his opinion of the adult's best interests over the adult's actual will and preferences,[226] exert undue influence upon the adult,[227] or act outside the scope of his authority.[228]

The supporter also owes a duty of confidentiality to the adult. The supporter must keep the adult's nonpublic personal information privileged and confidential when dealing with such information on behalf of the adult.[229] Unless the adult has otherwise

213. La. Stat. Ann. § 13:4261.102(3).
214. La. Stat. Ann. § 13:4261.201(2).
215. La. Stat. Ann. § 13:4261.208(C).
216. La. Stat. Ann. § 13:4261.102(4).
217. La. Stat. Ann. § 13:4261.102(5).
218. La. Stat. Ann. § 13:4261.205(B)(2).
219. La. Stat. Ann. § 13:4261.201.
220. La. Stat. Ann. §§ 13:4261.202, .203(3).
221. *See id.*
222. La. Stat. Ann. § 13:4261.203(1).
223. La. Stat. Ann. § 13:4261.203(2).
224. La. Stat. Ann. § 13:4261.203(4).
225. La. Stat. Ann. § 13:4261.203(1).
226. *Id.*
227. La. Stat. Ann. § 13:4261.204(1).
228. La. Stat. Ann. § 13:4261.204(3).
229. La. Stat. Ann. § 13:4261.208(B). The Louisiana statute relies on 15 U.S.C. § 6809(4)(A)'s definition of nonpublic information. Additionally, the Act requires the supporter to preserve the confidentiality of protected health information and educational records as protected under HIPAA and FERPA. *See* La. Stat. Ann. § 13:4261.208.

consented, a supporter may not obtain the adult's personal information that relates to a decision or matter beyond the scope of the SDA.[230]

The SDA must be in the form of an authentic act, dated, and signed by the adult or his guardian if he lacks capacity.[231] The only requirements of an SDA include: "(1) The name, address, and phone number of at least one supporter;" and "(2) A description of the decisionmaking assistance that a supporter shall provide to the adult and; if multiple supporters, how they shall work together."[232] The SDA may, but is not required to, provide for more than one named supporter and/or alternative supporters, and it may authorize the sharing of information among the supporters or others named in the agreement.[233] Apart from the SDA, each supporter must sign a separate declaration that sets out (1) the supporter's relationship to the adult; (2) the supporter's willingness to act as a supporter; and (3) an acknowledgement of the duties owed to the adult.[234] An SDA that conforms with these requirements is presumed valid.[235] Nonetheless, an SDA is subject to challenge if the adult signed it involuntarily, while subject to undue influence or coercion.[236]

Termination of an SDA occurs when the adult dies or revokes the agreement.[237] Likewise, if a named supporter revokes in writing his participation in the SDA without naming a successor supporter, the SDA terminates.[238] An SDA will also terminate when the adult signs a valid durable power of attorney, unless the power of attorney expressly continues the SDA, in whole or in part.[239] A court can also order termination of the SDA when, with adequate notice and hearing, the court determines that (1) the adult is found to have lacked capacity to execute it; (2) the supporter has used it to commit financial exploitation, abuse, or neglect; or (3) a temporary or permanent guardian should be appointed for the person or property of the adult.[240]

---

230. La. Stat. Ann. § 13:4261.204(2).

231. La. Stat. Ann. § 13:4261.205(C).

232. La. Stat. Ann. § 13:4261.205(A).

233. La. Stat. Ann. § 13:4261.205(B).

234. La. Stat. Ann. § 13:4261.205(D).

235. La. Stat. Ann. § 13:4261.301. Nevertheless, a party who has actual knowledge that the SDA was not validly executed may not rely on such a presumption. *Id.*

236. La. Stat. Ann. § 13:4261.201.

237. La. Stat. Ann. § 13:4261.207(A)(1)–(2). Revocation is only effective by authentic act, dated, and signed by the adult; the adult must also provide a copy of the revocation to each of his supporters. La. Stat. Ann. § 13:4261.206.

238. La. Stat. Ann. § 13:4261.207(A)(3). A supporter's revocation must conform to the same requirements as an adult's revocation. La. Stat. Ann. § 13:4261.206. A supporter may also resign without revoking the agreement. La. Stat. Ann. § 13:4261.203. Resignation is accomplished when the supporter provides the adult with a written statement declaring the support's intent to resign. *Id.*

239. La. Stat. Ann. § 13:4261.207(A)(7).

240. La. Stat. Ann. § 13:4261.207(A)(4–6). An SDA can continue when a temporary or permanent guardian is appointed for the adult if the court expressly modifies but continues the SDA, which limits the powers and duties of the guardian. *Id.* § 13:4261.207(A)(6)(a–b). A court order terminating or modifying the SDA is only available after notice is given to the adult and his supporters and a hearing is held. *Id.* § 13:4261.207(B).

The Act contains a specific provision that applies if a person who receives a copy of the SDA or is aware of an SDA has reason to believe that the adult is being abused, neglected, or exploited by a supporter. Reports of the alleged abuse, neglect, or exploitation must be reported to any adult protection agency or to any local or state law enforcement.[241] Short of abuse or neglect, the Act fails to provide a mechanism for handling supporter violations. For example, if a supporter obtains confidential medical information without the adult's approval pursuant to the SDA, the Act provides no consequence; the adult is simply empowered to revoke the entire SDA.[242] However, general contract and tort remedies would be available in the event of a breach.

241. La. Stat. Ann. § 13:4261.302.
242. *See* La. Stat. Ann. § 13:4261.206.

Chapter 13

Domestic Violence in Families

*by Brooke C. Tigchelaar and Katherine L. DeBlanc**

* Brooke C. Tigchelaar is a member of and Katherine L. DeBlanc is an associate with the firm of Stone Pigman Walther Wittmann, LLC in New Orleans, Louisiana. The authors would like to thank Mrs. Tigchelaar and Ms. DeBlanc for contributing this chapter to the treatise.

§ 13:1 Introduction

Domestic abuse and family violence are crimes and a pervasive problem in society that challenges members of all race, sex, and economic brackets.[1] Such violence largely is hidden from public view but negatively impacts survivors physically, emotionally, psychologically, and financially. Such abuse may impact all members of a household, especially children who witness domestic and family violence and learn that such behavior is normal and acceptable. As a result, the safety, security, and welfare of communities across Louisiana are forced to expend billions annually to address medical costs, mental health problems, loss of work force and productivity, and intergenerational violence.[2]

It is no secret that the prevention of domestic abuse and family violence must be stopped and effective laws are needed to curb and prevent such abuse and violence from occurring or re-occurring. To that end, legislation was enacted by the Louisiana Legislature to tackle this ongoing problem, by protecting victims in a prompt manner, while providing due process to the perpetrators, and to help prevent future domestic abuse and family violence where discovered. Louisiana has several not only civil but criminal statutes governing issues of family violence or domestic abuse and providing for procedures to obtain protective relief. Orders granted under these various statutes may be temporary or permanent and may generally be obtained relatively quickly.

The Domestic Abuse Assistance Act sets forth procedures for obtaining protective relief by family members, household members, or dating partners who experience domestic abuse. Further, if custody of a child is at stake, the Post-Separation Family Violence Relief Act and other laws ensure a child's safety and best interests are of top priority in situations of family violence. The laws can be independently assessed and applied accordingly. This chapter discusses the rights and obligations pursuant to the Louisiana Domestic Abuse Assistance Act and the Post-Separation Family Violence Relief Act.

§ 13:2 The Domestic Abuse Assistance Act

There is a misconception that domestic abuse has only recently grown to epic proportions. However, abuse and violence, particularly against women and children, is not new. Instead, the history of such is often left unspoken and/or unknown.

---

1. As the 2024 Special Report by Tulane University Newcomb Institute explains, "[i]n 2023, about one in 25 Louisiana women (4%) had experienced physical and/or sexual IPV [intimate partner violence] in the past year from a current or former romantic or sexual partner." Anita Raj, .J. Klugman, Li L, , *The Costs of Intimate Partner Violence in Louisiana,* Newcomb Institute at Tulane University, 7 (April 2024), https://acrobat.adobe.com/link/track?uri=urn%3Aaaid%3Ascds%3AUS%3A57726a10-e353-3034-bb0c-574a16b9b5d6 (last visited 12/1/24).

2. Anita Raj, .J. Klugman, Li L, , The Costs of Intimate Partner Violence in Louisiana, Newcomb Institute at Tulane University, 7 (April 2024), https://acrobat.adobe.com/link/track?uri=urn%3Aaaid%3Ascds%3AUS%3A57726a10-e353-3034-bb0c-574a16b9b5d6 (last visited 12/1/24).

While domestic abuse has existed throughout history, only relatively recently has society begun to address its egregious harm and advocate for better protection of the victims/survivors.[3] In fact, "[i]n the past forty years, domestic violence has climbed from relative obscurity to infamy in American social consciousness."[4] For example, while "the concept of 'wife-beating' [arose] in the early nineteenth century, domestic violence emerged as a social problem in the 1960s."[5] Original protests focused on the issue by attributing a husband's violent actions to "alcohol abuse ... rather than the husband's unrestricted legal authority over his partner and children."[6] Nevertheless, concepts introduced by "feminists in the late nineteenth century [such as] ... that physical, psychological, and sexual abuse of women stems from a husband's legal ownership rights over his wife's body" began to permeate the societal understanding of such abuse.[7]

In 1979, the Louisiana Coalition Against Domestic Violence assembled for the first time with the "goal of ending domestic violence in Louisiana" and "empower[ing] its members and communities through advocacy, education, resource development and technical assistance."[8] In the same year, New Orleans became home to the state's "[f]irst shelter for battered women," the Cresent House.[9] However, despite these efforts, "[t]here was still no way to prosecute abusers or keep them from harassing their targets...."[10] Thus, despite fierce resistance, in part due to ingrained societal perceptions

---

3. There are several terms used to refer to those who suffer abuse or violence, such as victim, abused, battered woman, survivor, and petitioner, for example. These terms will be used interchangeably throughout.

4. Alexandrea Masri, *Equal Rights, Unequal Protection: Institutional Failures in Protecting and Advocating for Victims of Same-Sex Domestic Violence in Post-Marriage Equality Era*, 27 Tul. J. L. & Sexuality, 75, 75 (2018).

5. Alexandrea Masri, *Equal Rights, Unequal Protection: Institutional Failures in Protecting and Advocating for Victims of Same-Sex Domestic Violence in Post-Marriage Equality Era*, 27 Tul. J. L. & Sexuality, 75, 75, 77 (2018).

6. Alexandrea Masri, *Equal Rights, Unequal Protection: Institutional Failures in Protecting and Advocating for Victims of Same-Sex Domestic Violence in Post-Marriage Equality Era*, 27 Tul. J. L. & Sexuality, 75, 75, 77 (2018).

7. Alexandrea Masri, *Equal Rights, Unequal Protection: Institutional Failures in Protecting and Advocating for Victims of Same-Sex Domestic Violence in Post-Marriage Equality Era*, 27 Tul. J. L. & Sexuality, 75, 75, 77, 78 (2018).

8. Louisiana Coalition Against Domestic Violence, *Updated LCADV Training Manual for Domestic Violence Advocates*, StudyLib, https://studylib.net/doc/6923691/updated-lcadv-training-manual-for-domestic-violence-advoc (last visited November 27, 2024); *see also* Louisiana Coalition Against Domestic Violence, *About*, About LCADV, https://lcadv.org/about (last visited November 27, 2024).

9. Louisiana Coalition Against Domestic Violence, *Updated LCADV Training Manual for Domestic Violence Advocates*, StudyLib, https://studylib.net/doc/6923691/updated-lcadv-training-manual-for-domestic-violence-advoc (last visited November 27, 2024); *see also* Louisiana Coalition Against Domestic Violence, *About*, About LCADV, https://lcadv.org/about at 14. (last visited November 27, 2024)

10. Janet Allured, Remapping Second-Wave Feminism: The Long Women's Rights Movement in Louisiana, 1950–1997 143 (The University of Georgia Press, 2016).

of women and men in Louisiana, women spearheaded attempts to address domestic abuse through the law.[11]

"Louisiana was one of the first states to address domestic violence through regulation."[12] In 1982, against the backdrop of "strong opposition,"[13] the Louisiana Legislature enacted the Domestic Abuse Assistance Act (the "DAAA"),[14] presently codified at Louisiana Revised Statutes Sections 46:2131–46:2140. The DAAA attempts to tackle the ongoing problem of domestic abuse, helping to prevent future domestic abuse where discovered by creating an avenue to protect victims through the award of civil protective orders in a prompt manner, while providing due process to the perpetrators. The DAAA sets forth procedures for obtaining protective relief by family members, household members, or dating partners who experience domestic abuse, as well as the legal rights and obligations that stem therefrom for victims, perpetrators, the court system, and law enforcement.

Specifically, Louisiana Revised Statutes Section 46:2131 ("Purposes"), enacted by Act 782 in 1982 and amended once by Act 85 in 2015 (to distinguish between family members and household members and to include dating partners),[15] codifies the legislative intent behind the DAAA:

> The purpose of this Part is to recognize and address the complex legal and social problems created by domestic violence. The legislature finds that *existing laws which regulate the dissolution of marriage do not adequately address problems of protecting and assisting the victims of domestic abuse*. The legislature further finds that previous *societal attitudes have been reflected in the policies and practices of law enforcement agencies and prosecutors which have resulted in different treatment of crimes occurring between family members, household members, or dating partners and those occurring between strangers. It is the intent of the legislature to provide a civil remedy for domestic violence which will afford the victim immediate and easily accessible protection. Furthermore, it is the intent of the legislature that the official response of law enforcement agencies to cases of domestic violence shall stress the enforcement of laws to*

---

11. Janet Allured, Remapping Second-Wave Feminism: The Long Women's Rights Movement in Louisiana, 1950–1997 143 (The University of Georgia Press, 2016). Kim Gandy, Mary Landrieu, Diana Bajoie, Margaret Lowenthal, Connie Willems, Maurice Durbin, Sylvia Roberts, and Ayn Stehr were just some of many women who tenaciously drove the movement towards legislative reform forward in Louisiana. *See id.*

12. Alexandrea Masri, Equal Rights, *Unequal Protection: Institutional Failures in Protecting and Advocating for Victims of Same-Sex Domestic Violence in Post-Marriage Equality Era*, 27 Tul. J. L. & Sexuality, 75, 85 (2018).

13. Janet Allured, Remapping Second-Wave Feminism: The Long Women's Rights Movement in Louisiana, 1950–1997 143 (The University of Georgia Press, 2016).

14. Janet Allured, Remapping Second-Wave Feminism: The Long Women's Rights Movement in Louisiana, 1950–1997 143 (The University of Georgia Press, 2016). DAAA was originally drafted by Kim Gandy, an attorney and the Louisiana NOW President at the time. *Id.*

15. Since its enactment, the DAAA has been amended several times, with most of the amendments aimed at further protecting or easing the burdens on the domestic abuse survivor.

> *protect the victim and shall communicate the attitude that violent behavior is not excused or tolerated.*[16]

The remaining statutes in the DAAA provide what is required to obtain relief, modify the resulting orders, and enforce same.

§ 13:3 The Domestic Abuse Assistance Act—Overview

A person who is or has been a victim of domestic abuse may file a petition for an order of protection against a family member, household member, or dating partner who commits an act of domestic abuse. Under the DAAA, a court may issue an order of protection to a victim of domestic abuse, if the court has jurisdiction over the parties and the subject matter,[17] reasonable notice and opportunity to be heard is given to the defendant/perpetrator,[18] and the petitioner/survivor meets his or her burden of proof warranting relief. The prima facie elements of protective relief under the DAAA are, in general: 1) the petitioner is a victim of domestic abuse; 2) the petitioner is in imminent danger of further abuse; and 3) the defendant is in a familial, household, or dating relationship with the petitioner and represents a credible threat to the safety of the petitioner or another identified family member of the petitioner.[19] The order of protection may be temporary, granted ex-parte without advanced proof or a hearing, or issued as a continuing or permanent protective order in certain cases.[20] The orders may be dissolved, modified, or extended, depending on the circumstances. The proceedings for such relief are civil in nature; therefore, the Louisiana Code of Evidence,

---

16. La. Stat. Ann. § 46:2131 (2015) (emphasis added); *see also* Ferrand v. Ferrand, 2016-7 (La. App. 5 Cir. 8/31/16); 221 So. 3d 909, 942–943 ("the purpose of the domestic abuse assistance act is to provide relief to victims of domestic violence by establishing a civil remedy for domestic violence which will afford the victim immediate and easily accessible protection") (citations omitted); Dvilansky v. Correu, 2016-0279 (La. App. 4 Cir. 10/26/16), 204 So. 3d 686; D.M.S. v. I.D.S., 2014-0364 (La. App. 4 Cir. 3/4/15), 225 So. 3d 1127; Lee v. Smith, 2008-455 (La. App. 5 Cir. 12/16/08), 4 So. 3d 100, 104 ("the purpose behind the entire legislative scheme governing domestic abuse assistance is to provide relief to victims of domestic violence by establishing a civil remedy for domestic violence which will afford the victim immediate and easily accessible protection."); Branstetter v. Purohit, 2006-1435 (La. App. 4 Cir. 5/2/07), 958 So. 2d 740.

17. La. Stat. Ann. § 46:2133 (jurisdiction and venue); La. Stat. Ann. § 46:2136(B) ("A protective order may be rendered pursuant to this Part if the court has jurisdiction over the parties and subject matter and either of the following occurs. . . .").

18. *See* La. Stat. Ann. § 46:2136(B)(2); *see also, e.g.*, Darby v. Duplechain, 2016-2 (La. App. 3 Cir. 5/4/16), 192 So. 3d 258, 259 (reversing a protective order issued against an ex-boyfriend who had no opportunity to be heard prior to the issuance of the protective order).

19. *See* La. Stat. Ann. §§ 46:2135 and 46:2136.

20. This chapter does not discuss protective orders that involve third parties that do not meet the definition of family members, household members, or dating partners. Nor does this chapter address abusive behavior that does not fall within the definition of domestic abuse as defined within the DAAA or family violence under the Post-Separation Family Violence Relief Act.

Louisiana Code of Civil Procedure, and the Louisiana Civil Code and corresponding Louisiana Revised Statutes apply.[21]

§ 13:4 The Domestic Abuse Assistance Act— What Constitutes Domestic Abuse Under the DAA

Pursuant to Louisiana Revised Statutes Sections 46:2135 and 46:2136, a court may issue a temporary restraining order or a protective order, respectively, to bring about the cessation of abuse to a party or the threats of abuse. Domestic abuse is defined in Louisiana Revised Statutes Section 46:2132(3) to identify the prohibited conduct, which "includes but is not limited to physical or sexual abuse or any offense against the person, physical or nonphysical, as defined in the criminal code of Louisiana, except negligent injury and defamation" that is "committed by one family member, household member, or dating partner against another. Domestic abuse also includes abuse of adults as defined in Louisiana Revised Statute Section 15:1503 when committed by an adult child or adult grandchild."[22] Thus, the definition of domestic abuse focuses on the actual conduct itself, as well as the relationship between the involved parties.

The types of conduct included in the definition of domestic abuse has not changed over time. When originally enacted, domestic abuse "include[d] but [wa]s not limited to physical abuse and any offense against the person as defined in the Criminal Code of Louisiana, except negligent injury and defamation, committed by one family or household member against another."[23] While the definition of domestic abuse did not limit the definition of domestic abuse to physical touching, its interpretation in the jurisprudence left open questions of what constituted domestic abuse if not combined with some physical injury.[24]

21. This chapter does not discuss criminal protective orders or the implication of criminal laws unless specifically referenced within the civil statutes within the scope of the DAAA.

22. La Stat. Ann. § 46:2132(3); *see also* La. Child. Code Ann. art. 1563 ("Domestic abuse includes but is not limited to physical or sexual abuse and any offense against the person as defined in Chapter 1 of Title 14 of the Louisiana Revised Statutes of 1950, except negligent injury and defamation, committed by one family or household member against another.").

23. La. Stat. Ann. § 46:2132 (1982).

24. In 1986, Act 459 amended the definition to explicitly include sexual abuse. State of Louisiana: Acts of Legislature, 1986 La. Acts. 459, § 1, eff. July 2, 1986.

Other changes to the statute over the years came in 1993, with Act 402, which added to the definition of domestic abuse the "abuse of adults as defined in R.S. 14:403.2 when committed by an adult child or adult grandchild." Abused Parent or Grandparent—Domestic Abuse Assistance—Protective Orders Act, No. 402, § 46:2132(3), 1993 La. Sess. Law Serv. Act 403, § 2 (H.B. 989) (West). At that time, Louisiana Revised Statutes Section 14:403.2 defined abuse as "the infliction of physical or mental injury on an adult by other parties, including but not limited to such means as sexual abuse, exploitation, or extortion of funds or other things of value, to such an extent that his health, self-determination, or emotional well-being is endangered" and adult as "any individual eighteen years of age or older or an emancipated minor who, because of mental or physical dysfunction, is unable to manage his own resources, carry out the activities of daily living, or protect himself from neglect, or

For example, in 1988, the Fourth Circuit Court of Appeal in *Harper v. Harper*, held that "[f]amily arguments that do not rise to the threshold of physical or sexual abuse or violations of the criminal code are not in the ambit of the Domestic Abuse Assistance Statute. Each case must be reviewed individually."[25]

In 2007, the Second Circuit Court of Appeal, in *Culp v. Culp*, held that domestic abuse does not include general harassment.[26] In *Culp*, the plaintiff "emphasize[d] that the definition [of domestic abuse in La. R.S. 46:2132] uses the phrase 'includes, but is not limited to' and argues that this language expands the scope of domestic abuse to include general harassment."[27] The Second Circuit rejected this argument, reasoning

> that the courts could quickly be overwhelmed if every unpleasant child custody exchange or contentious relationship between former spouses warranted a TRO or protective order.... La. R.S. 46:2131 emphasizes that the purpose of the statute is to equalize the treatment of crimes between family members and those between strangers. It further emphasizes the need to protect victims from violent behavior. Those purposes reflect that the D.A.A. has a limited reach. We cannot agree, therefore, that the statute embodies Plaintiff's claims of general harassment by Defendant, nor do the Defendant's actions as contained in the record constitute an offense against a person as defined by the Criminal Code.[28]

Offenses against the person, as defined in the Louisiana Criminal Code, can generally be found at Louisiana Revised Statutes Sections 14:29–14:50.2 and currently include acts such as homicide,[29] assisted suicide,[30] battery,[31] domestic abuse battery,[32] assault,[33] terrorizing,[34] stalking,[35] cyberstalking,[36] intent to intimidate certain individu-

---

hazardous or abusive situations without assistance from others, and who has no available, willing, and responsibly able person to assist him." Abuse and Neglect of Adults—Reports; Investigations; Services; Confidentiality; Immunity; etc. Act, No. 975, § 14:403.2, 1992 La. Sess. Law Serv. Act 975 (H.B. 1506) (West). In 2010, Act 861 revised the citation to abuse of adults from Louisiana Revised Statutes Section 14:403.2 to Louisiana Revised Statutes Section 15:1503. Various Codal Provisions and Provisions of The Louisiana Revised Statutes of 1950 Act, No. 861, § 46:2132(3), 2010 La. Sess. Law Serv. Act 861, § 20 (H.B. 1467) (West).

25. Harper v. Harper, 537 So. 2d 282, 285 (La. App. 4th Cir. 1988).
26. Culp v. Culp, 42,239 (La. App. 2 Cir. 6/20/07), 960 So. 2d 1279, 1282–83.
27. *Culp*, 960 So. 2d at 1282–83.
28. Culp, 960 So. 2d at 1283.
29. La. Stat. Ann. §§ 14:29–14:32.8.
30. La. Stat. Ann. § 14:32.12 (1995).
31. La. Stat. Ann. §§ 14:33–14:34.9, 14:35–14:35.2, 14.43.1–14:43.3.
32. La. Stat. Ann. §§ 14:35.3–14:38, 14:38.2–14:38.5.
33. La. Stat. Ann. §§ 14:34.9.1, 14:36.
34. La. Stat. Ann. § 14:40.1.
35. La. Stat. Ann. § 14.40.2.
36. La. Stat. Ann. § 14:40.3.

als,[37] cyberbullying,[38] rape,[39] intentional exposure to HIV,[40] female genital mutilation,[41] kidnapping,[42] interference with custody of child,[43] false imprisonment,[44] and human trafficking.[45] Noticeably, although each type of criminal conduct does not require physical acts, courts were originally reluctant to expand the reach of the DAAA beyond physical injury or sexual abuse. In fact, courts frequently cited and relied on the *Harper* and *Culp* holdings to deny protective relief.[46]

In *Fontenot v. Newcomer*, the Third Circuit Court of Appeal "agree[d] with the reasoning of *Culp* that the statute [defining domestic abuse under the DAAA] does not embody claims of 'general harassment' nor actions that do not 'constitute an offense against a person as defined in the Criminal Code.'"[47] In *Fontenot*, the defendants "followed [the victim] and her children around town, attended [the victim's child's] basketball games, and drove by the children's school. On occasion, the alleged perpetrators parked behind [the victim's] vehicle in a parking lot, temporarily blocking her in and preventing her from leaving. However, the record is void of any evidence of physical abuse or verbal threats."[48] Interestingly, the court held that:

> [t]hough these actions by the Newcomers [the alleged abusers] may violate certain civil and criminal statutes for which there are adequate remedies and sanctions, they do not rise to the level of domestic abuse as defined by La.R.S. 46:2132 and the jurisprudence interpreting same. Accordingly, we find that the record contains insufficient evidence that the Newcomers' actions constituted domestic abuse within the purview of La.R.S. 46:2131–2132.[49]

In *Coy v. Coy*, the Second Circuit Court of Appeal found that "the trial court abused its discretion when it granted the protective order"[50] based on the alleged abuser's "excessive amount of phone calls."[51] At trial," [n]o evidence of physical abuse was ever produced."[52] After citing *Culp*, *Harper*, and *Fontenot*, the court in *Coy* held that "the

37. La. Stat. Ann. §§ 14:40, 14:40.4–14:40.5.
38. La. Stat. Ann. § 14:40.7.
39. La. Stat. Ann. §§ 14:41–14:43.
40. La. Stat. Ann. § 14:43.5.
41. La. Stat. Ann. § 14.43.4.
42. La. Stat. Ann. §§ 14:44–14:45.
43. La. Stat. Ann. § 14:45.1.
44. La. Stat. Ann. §§ 14:46–14:46.1.
45. La. Stat. Ann. §§ 14:46.2–14:46.3.
46. *See* Rouyea v. Rouyea, 2000-2613 (La. App. 1 Cir. 3/28/01), 808 So. 2d 558, 561 (citing Harper); Coy v. Coy, 46,655 (La. App. 2 Cir. 7/13/11), 69 So. 3d 1270, 1272 (citing Culp); *see also* D.M.S. v. I.D.S., 2014-0364 (La. App. 4 Cir. 3/4/15), 225 So. 3d 1127, 1137; Lee v. Smith, 2008-455 (La. App. 5 Cir. 12/16/08), 4 So. 3d 100, 106; Dvilansky v. Correu, 2016-0279 (La. App. 4 Cir. 10/26/16), 204 So. 3d 686, 689.
47. Fontenot v. Newcomer, 2010-1530 (La. App. 3 Cir. 5/4/11), 63 So. 3d 1149, 1151.
48. Fontenot, 63 So. 3d at 1152.
49. Fontenot, 63 So. 3d at 1152.
50. Coy, 69 So. 3d at 1273.
51. Coy, 69 So. 3d at 1272.
52. Coy, 69 So. 3d at 1272.

types of phone calls and text messages that Ryan Coy [the alleged abuser] was making and sending are only general harassment, and thus do not constitute not [sic] domestic abuse as defined by La. R.S. 46:2132(3)."[53]

Similarly, in *Shipp v. Callahan*, the Second Circuit Court of Appeal noted that "[i]f the only evidence of domestic abuse in this case were Zachary's [the alleged abuser's] act of filing a groundless coroner's commitment against Debra [the victim], this would indeed be nonphysical harassment and insufficient to support the domestic abuse protective order. As in *Coy* and *Culp*, this court would be constrained to vacate the protective order."[54] However, because there existed some evidence of physical abuse according to the examination testimony, the appellate court ultimately upheld the granting of the protective order.[55]

On the other hand, the Second Circuit Court of Appeal in *Shirley v. Shirley*, held that the alleged abuser's threats over the telephone[56] constituted acts falling under "La. R.S. 14:40.3, Cyberstalking, and La. R.S. 14:284, Telephone Harassment"[57] and therefore, the trial court's granting of the protective order was warranted.[58] Though the alleged abuser "was not charged with committing a crime," the implication is that his acts still constitute domestic abuse.[59]

To resolve the confusion between the statutory text and case law, Louisiana legislators revised the definition of domestic abuse in 2015, thirty-three years after the statute's enactment in 1982. The statute now explicitly provides that "'[d]omestic abuse' includes but is not limited to physical or sexual abuse and any offense against the person, *physical or non-physical*, as defined in the Criminal Code of Louisiana, except negligent injury and defamation, committed by one family member, household member, or dating partner against another"[60] so as to explicitly "clarif[y] that non-physical acts are included within the definition of domestic abuse."[61] Cases since the 2015 revision have more broadly applied the definition of domestic abuse to include assaultive and nonviolent conduct that injures or attempts to injure the victim.[62]

---

53. Coy, 69 So. 3d at 1273.

54. Shipp v. Callahan, 47,928 (La. App. 2 Cir. 4/10/13), 113 So. 3d 454, 456.

55. Shipp v. Callahan, 113 So. 3d at 457.

56. Specifically, the victim "claim[ed] that John [the alleged abuser] threatened telephonically to 'burn down the house with her and their children in it before he would give her a dollar of his money.' She also claim[ed] that John threatened in the same conversation to 'have a crack whore kill her and no one would miss her.'" Shirley v. Shirley, 47,442 (La. App. 2 Cir. 10/10/12), 107 So. 3d 99, 100.

57. Shirley, 107 So. 3d at 101.

58. Shirley, 107 So. 3d at 102.

59. Shirley, 107 So. 3d at 101.

60. La. Stat. Ann. § 46:2132(3) (2020) (emphasis added).

61. Louisiana House of Representatives, Hearing on H.B. 772 Before the Committee on Administration of Criminal Justice, (April 29, 2015), (statement of Kim Sport), (at 1:25:00–1:25:37), https://house.louisiana.gov/H_Video/VideoArchivePlayer?v=house/2015/apr/0429_15_CJ.

62. *See* Oliva v. Jones, 2022-385 (La. App. 5 Cir. 3/29/23), 360 So. 3d 573, 580 (blog posts, social media communications, emails and text messages constitute cyberstalking or a "repeated pattern of verbal communications or nonverbal behavior without invitation" that would cause a reasonable person to suffer emotional distress under the circumstances); Craig v. Bishop, 2019-166 (La. App. 3 Cir.

Thus, in order to obtain relief under the DAAA, the domestic abuse alleged does not require physical injury. Domestic abuse can be strictly nonphysical.[63] As such, crimes or threats of crime against a person not involving any physical abuse or sexual abuse may qualify for relief under the DAAA.[64] Courts must exercise their discretion in determining whether the conduct necessitates relief under the DAAA.[65]

Further, a pattern of behavior over a period of time that amounts to domestic abuse is not required.[66] One instance may be sufficient.[67] The abuse necessary to meet the threshold does not require the abuse to be recent in order to warrant issuance of a

---

10/23/19), 283 So. 3d 521, 535–36 (finding the definition of domestic abuse included but was not limited to the offenses enumerated in the statute and by counseling others to commit murder, wife could have been charged with crimes that qualified as crimes against the person, such as murder, therefore the statutory definition of domestic abuse required the grant of husband's petition for protective order against wife); Pellerano v. Pellerano, 2017-0302 (La. App. 1 Cir, 4/12/19), 275 So. 3d 947, 951 (false imprisonment is sufficient for a protective order); Shaw v. Young, 2015-0974 (La. App. 4 Cir. 8/17/16), 199 So. 3d 1180, 1186 ("Ms. Shaw [the victim] testified that Mr. Young [the abuser] had sent messages to her threatening to release private photographs of her to her friends and co-workers.... Because these acts of Mr. Young constitute harassment within the meaning of the stalking statute, La. R.S. 14:40.2, they also constitute domestic abuse pursuant to La. R.S. 46:2136."); *but see* Carrie v. Jones, 2021-0659 (La. App. 4 Cir. 1/21/22), 334 So. 3d 834, 844 n.6 ("While unpleasant and harsh, name-calling alone does not arise to the level of domestic abuse under La. R.S. 46:2131 et seq.").

63. For example, in Cory v. Cory, 43,447 (La. App. 2 Cir. 8/13/08), 989 So. 2d 85, although the husband had never hit the wife, he had threatened to "whip [her] ass" and would intimidate her by walking toward her at a fast pace or revving the motor on his truck and putting it in reverse while she was standing at the end of the driveway, making her believe that he was going to hit her. In such case, the court found domestic abuse and issued a protective order, among other relief. *See also* Pellerano, 275 So. 3d at 951 (false imprisonment is sufficient for protective order).

64. Harper v. Harper, 537 So. 2d 282, 285 ("Mr. Harper [the abuser], although not a batterer, was legally assaultive. He frequently became enraged while intoxicated, raised his hand and threatened to strike his wife and beat on the door in the middle of the night, all of which placed his wife in reasonable apprehension of a battery. These acts are assaults, constitute domestic abuse and justify the issuance of the preliminary injunction."); *see also supra* note 61.

65. *See e.g.*, Francois v. Francois, 2006-712 (La. App. 3 Cir. 11/2/06), 941 So. 2d 722, 726 ("The trial court has wide discretion in the issuance of protective orders.") (citation omitted); Paschal v. Hazlinsky, 35,513 (La. App. 2 Cir. 12/19/01), 803 So. 2d 413, 419 ("Similar cases involving the issuance of orders, including injunctions and support orders, grant the trial court wide discretion in granting or denying such orders and in fashioning the appropriate relief."); Bettevy v. Bettevy, 2019-327 (La. App. 3 Cir. 11/6/19), 283 So. 3d 1047, 1050 ("The purpose behind the entire legislative scheme in Louisiana Revised Statutes 46:2131, et seq., is to provide relief to victims of domestic violence by establishing 'a civil remedy for domestic violence which will afford the victim immediate and easily accessible protection'.... LSA–R.S. 46:2136 permits a court to grant a protective order to prevent the possibility of family violence, provided a petition is filed requesting the order and the defendant is afforded reasonable notice consistent with due process.") (citations omitted).

66. S.M. v. T.M., 2019-369 (La. App. 5 Cir. 12/26/19), 289 So. 3d 141, 145 ("neither the definition of 'domestic abuse' set forth in La. R.S. 46:2132(3), nor any other provision of the Domestic Abuse Assistance Act requires evidence of a pattern of domestic abuse to obtain a protective order").

67. *See e.g.*, McCann v. McCann, 2009-1341 (La. App. 3 Cir. 3/10/10); 33 So. 3d 389, 395 (though the victim did not demonstrate a pattern of abuse by her abuser but showed that her abuser "str[uck] ... [her] on the arm with her keys," the Third Circuit held that "the trial court [did not] abuse[] its discretion in concluding that Barbara [the victim] proved her allegations of domestic abuse by a preponderance of the evidence.").

protective order.[68] If the petitioner is a victim of abuse and there is an imminent danger of further abuse, the test is met.[69]

Specifically, in determining whether to award protective relief, "[t]he court shall consider any and all past history of abuse, or threats thereof, in determining the existence of an immediate and present danger of abuse. There is no requirement that the abuse itself be recent, immediate, or present."[70] In fact, courts have expressly recognized that there is no statutory timeframe mentioned in the statute or case law indicating when the abuse must occur in order to obtain a protective order under the DAAA.[71] As such, the law recognizes that the perpetrator of domestic abuse may pose a risk of violence long after the last incident of violence has occurred and that an order of protection may be necessary to protect the victim from further risk.

Breaux v. Tipton involved an appeal resulting from the grant of a temporary restraining order against a child's stepfather. The biological father of the child petitioned the court for a protective order, claiming that his son "was subjected to violent behavior, including threats of violence by Mr. Tipton [the child's stepfather]."[72] The stepfather asserted on appeal that the biological father's "testimony [wa]s not credible for several reasons, which include: the allegations of domestic violence were not made until over a year after they occurred...."[73] The Fourth Circuit Court of Appeal in *Breaux*, however, noted that "the alleged abuse itself is not required to be recent in order to merit a grant of a protective order."[74] Furthermore, the court held that the "[e]vidence in the record supported a determination that Mr. Tipton's [the abuser's] actions[75] presented an 'immediate and present danger of abuse' as it related to J.B. [the child]...."[76]

The good cause requirement applicable to temporary restraining orders also applies to actions seeking permanent protective orders.[77] That is, "[a]ny person who shows

---

68. *See* Breaux v. Tipton, 2018-0429 (La. App. 4 Cir. 11/14/18); 259 So. 3d 429 (abuse alleged to have occurred over a year prior sufficient to warrant issuance of protective order).

69. Larremore v. Larremore, 52,879 (La. App. 2 Cir. 9/25/19), 280 So. 3d 1282, 1290 (electronic means of mail and/or communication to harass victim, coupled with uninvited presence at her home amounted to cyberstalking and harassment and justified issuance of protective order as danger was present under La. Stat. Ann. §§ 46:2136 and 46:2132); Harper, 537 So. 2d at 285 ("threats coupled with the present ability to carry out the threats are sufficient when one is placed in reasonable apprehension of receiving an injury") (citations omitted).

70. La. Stat. Ann. § 46:2135(A) (2019).

71. Okechukwu v. Okechukwu, 2013-1421 (La. App. 3 Cir. 5/21/14); 139 So. 3d 1135, 1138–1139 (history of abuse throughout the course of the marriage bolstered the claim of victim's fear and warranted a protective order).

72. Breaux, 259 So. 3d at 431.

73. Breaux, 259 So. 3d at 433.

74. Breaux, 259 So. 3d at 434.

75. The stepfather had taken the following actions: "threaten[ed] Mrs. Tipton [his wife] with weapons, whipping J.B. [the child], and attempt[ed] to remove J.B. from school, which resulted in a police report...." Breaux, 259 So. 3d at 434.

76. Breaux, 259 So. 3d at 434.

77. Craig v. Bishop, 2019-166 (La. App. 3 Cir. 10/23/19), 283 So. 3d 521, 533 (citing S.L.B. v. C.E.B., 2017-978, 2019-979, 2019-980 (La. App. 4 Cir. 7/27/18), 252 So. 3d 950); Bettevy, 283 So. 3d at 1049–50 (all history of abuse, threats, past and present must be considered in determining "good cause").

immediate and present danger of abuse shall constitute good cause" for the issuance of protective relief.[78] For example, in *Craig v. Bishop*, the abuser challenged the protective order issued against her by claiming that "neither David [the abuser's husband] nor Jerry [the abuser's ex-husband] proved an immediate and present danger of domestic abuse, as required by La.R.S. 46:2136."[79] The Third Circuit Court of Appeal in *Craig* rejected this argument and upheld the "trial court's credibility determinations," which led to the conclusion, among other things, that "there was an immediate and present danger of abuse based on Shari's [the alleged abuser's] propensity for discussing her abuse allegations with any person she meets, as shown by all the witnesses who testified during the hearing[, that] [s]he prodded Jerry to kill Mr. Meyers, she prodded David to kill Jerry, and she prodded Mr. Martin and the man at the casino to kill Jerry and David."[80]

§ 13:5 The Domestic Abuse Assistance Act— Relationship Status Between Victim and Defendant

For a protective order to be issued under the DAAA, the definition of domestic abuse also requires that the relationship between the survivor and the perpetrator must fall within the statutorily defined relationships. As originally enacted, the DAAA only applied to "family or household member[s]," specifically defined as "spouses, former spouses, parents and children, step-parents, step-children, foster parents, and foster children, who are seeking protection under this Part."[81] If the parties were not related in any of these capacities, relief could not be granted under the DAAA. Thus, the persons who could seek protection under the DAAA were limited.

In 1986, Act 154 added to the definition of family or household member: "any person living in the same residence with the defendant as a spouse, whether married or not, if a minor child or children also live in the residence."[82] This expanded the scope of persons to include boyfriends and girlfriends if children were involved; however, the hesitancy of the Louisiana Legislature to expand the definition too much beyond the traditional family was palpable, as reflected in the amendment's use of the phrase "as a spouse" and the requirement that a minor child or children must live in the residence. However, being married or presently living as spouses is not a prerequisite to filing a petition for domestic abuse under the DAAA today, but the relationship required between the survivor and perpetrator has evolved over the years.

For example, in 1993, Act 402 deleted the requirement that a minor child live in the residence if there is abuse of a parent or grandparent by an adult child or adult grand-

78. La. Stat. Ann. § 46:2135(A) (2019).
79. Craig, 283 So. 3d at 536.
80. Craig, 283 So. 3d at 536.
81. La. Stat. Ann. § 46:2132 (1982).
82. State of Louisiana: Acts of Legislature, 1986 La. Acts. 154 and 459, § 1, effective July 2, 1986.

child.[83] In 2001, Act 619 amended the DAAA such that an adult foster child could be considered an abuser of a parent or grandparent.[84] Curiously, it did not add adult foster grandchild(ren).

However, more remote ascendants and descendants, besides parents and children, were still not included in the definition of family member, an inconsistency given the addition of provisions on adult abuse ushered in by previous amendments. This meant that aunts, uncles or other relatives were not among the class of persons within the DAAA. Yet, Act 101 of 2020 reconciled this inconsistency by adding all "other ascendants[] and other descendants" to the definition of family member.[85] This expanded the definition for actions between spouses, former spouses, parents/step-parents/foster parents and their children or any family members in general, whether ascendents or descendants, within the scope of the DAAA.

In 1997, Act 1156 explicitly clarified that family or household member includes "any person *presently or formerly* living in the same residence with the defendant as a spouse, whether married or not, if a minor child or children also live in the residence, who are seeking protection under this Part."[86] This revision was meant to address the relationship between partners that were not married but lived together, whether presently still living together or not. However, because the requirement included living together "as a spouse," it specifically excluded roommates from seeking relief under the DAAA.

Act 1200 of 1999 separated the definition of household or family member into two separate classes, defining "family members" as "spouses, former spouses, parents and children, stepparents, stepchildren, foster parents, foster children"[87] and "household members" as "any person of the opposite sex presently or formerly living in the same residence with the defendant as a spouse, whether married or not, who are seeking protection under this Part."[88] The legislature explicitly limited household members to persons of the opposite sex and removed the requirement that a minor child or children

83. La. Stat. Ann. § 46:2132 (1993).

84. Public Welfare and Assistance—Domestic Abuse—Define Household Members, Provide Protective Orders Act, No. 619 § 46:2132(4), 2001 La. Sess. Law Serv. Act 619, § 1 (H.B. 1514) (West).

85. La. Stat. Ann. § 46:2132(4) (2020). For a case declining to address this issue prior to the amendments, *see, e.g.*, Clayton v. Abbitt, 44,427 (La. App. 2 Cir. 7/1/09), 16 So. 3d 512 (pretermitting discussion of whether grandfather is a member of the class of people against whom a protective order may be issued.

86. Domestic Violence—Louisiana Protective Order Registry—Statewide Registry of Civil and Criminal Abuse Prevention Orders Act, No. 1156, § 46:2132(4), 1997 La. Sess. Law Serv. Act 1156, § 7 (S.B. 1425) (West) (emphasis added).

87. Domestic Violence—Temporary Restraining and Protective Orders—Violation; Duration Act, No. 1200, § 46:2132(4), 1999 La. Sess. Law Serv. Act 1200, § 2 (S.B. 393) (West). In 2010, Act 861 added to the definition of family member: "the other parent or foster parent of any child or foster child of the offender." Various Codal Provisions and Provisions of The Louisiana Revised Statutes Of 1950 Act, No. 861, § 46:2132(3), 2010 La. Sess. Law Serv. Act 861 § 20 (H.B. 1467) (West).

88. Domestic Violence—Temporary Restraining and Protective Orders—Violation; Duration Act, No. 1200, § 46:2132(4), 1999 La. Sess. Law Serv. Act 1200, § 2 (S.B. 393) (West).

also live in the residence.[89] While the result may have been unintended, this revision actually narrowed the definition of who may seek relief by requiring the parties to be of the opposite sex, thereby excluding same-sex couples from any relief.

At this time, an individual with an intimate relationship with another, though neither married nor living together presently or formerly in the same residence, could not seek relief under the DAAA. "In one particular case that went before a judge, a woman was denied a protective order three times under the Domestic Abuse Assistance Act because she had been abused by her ex-boyfriend and not someone who was a family member or a household member under the Act itself."[90] In 2015, the legislature responded with Act 85, adding dating partners as a class of individuals to which the DAAA applies.[91] Specifically, the statute defined dating partner as "any person protected from violence under R.S. 46:2151 who is seeking protection under this Part."[92] In 2015, Louisiana Revised Statutes Section 46:2151 defined dating partner as "any person who is or has been in a social relationship of a romantic or intimate nature with the victim and where the existence of such a relationship shall be determined based on a consideration of the following factors: (1) [t]he length of the relationship[,] (2) [t]he type of relationship[, and] (3) [t]he frequency of interaction between the persons involved in the relationship."[93]

Two years after the "legalization of same-sex marriage in 2015"[94] by the United States Supreme Court in the *Obergefell v. Hodges*, 576 U.S. 644 (2015),[95] the Louisiana Legislature redefined household members as "any person presently or formerly living in the same residence with the defendant and who is involved or has been involved in a sexual or intimate relationship with the defendant and who is seeking protection under this Part,"[96] thereby eliminating the requirement that household members be of the opposite sex. Prior to the 2017 amendment, Louisiana was just "one of two states ... [with] the language of opposite sex in ... domestic violence bills."[97] Amending the stat-

---

89. Domestic Violence—Temporary Restraining and Protective Orders—Violation; Duration Act, No. 1200, § 46:2132(4), 1999 La. Sess. Law Serv. Act 1200, § 2 (S.B. 393) (West).

90. Louisiana Senate, Hearing on H.B. 722 Before the Senate Committee on Judiciary B, (May 19, 2015), (statement of Kim Sport), (at 19:15–19:55), https://senate.la.gov/s_video/videoarchive.asp?v=senate/2015/05/051915JUDB_0.

91. Domestic Abuse Assistance Act, No. 85, § 46:2132(4), 2015 La. Sess. Law Serv. Act 85, § 1 (H.B. 722) (West).

92. La. Stat. Ann. § 46:2132.

93. La. Stat. Ann. § 46:2151 (2001).

94. *See* Section 13:2, Alexandrea Masri, *Equal Rights, Unequal Protection: Institutional Failures in Protecting and Advocating for Victims of Same-Sex Domestic Violence in Post-Marriage Equality Era*, 27 Tul. J. L. & Sexuality, 75, 76 (2018).

95. *See* Louisiana House of Representatives, Hearing on H.B. 27 Before the Committee on Administration of Criminal Justice, (April 26, 2017) (statement of Sunny Funk) (at 9:00–9:15), https://house.louisiana.gov/H_Video/VideoArchivePlayer?v=house/2017/apr/0426_17_CJ.

96. La. Stat. Ann. § 46:2132 (2017).

97. Louisiana House of Representatives, Hearing on H.B. 27 Before the Committee on Administration of Criminal Justice (April 26, 2017) (statement of Representative Patrick Connick) (at 7:30–7:50), https://house.louisiana.gov/H_Video/VideoArchivePlayer?v=house/2017/apr/0426_17_CJ.

ute to remove the "opposite sex language" minimized the risk of a future constitutional challenge to Louisiana Revised Statutes Section 46:2132[98] and also sought to provide protection to domestic abuse survivors and to punish abusers the same, regardless of their relationship as homosexual or heterosexual.[99]

Finally, Act 246 of 2020 added to the definition of household member: "any child presently or formerly living in the same residence with the defendant, or any child of the defendant regardless of where the child resides."[100] Clearly, the legislature recognized that children are vulnerable to the negative impacts of domestic abuse, whether the children are the biological children of the perpetrator or not and despite where the children currently reside.

As of today, the definition of domestic abuse attempts to broadly define the persons eligible to seek protection from abuse inflicted by certain individuals and to comprehensively include all of those exposed to risk within a household, familial or dating relationship. Protective relief is available to persons related by blood or marriage, or even unrelated members of a household, that meet the familial or dating relationship required under the statute.[101] Cohabitation is not a prerequisite to filing for relief under the DAAA, and the relationship between the victim and abuser need not be current. Thus, the law recognizes that the notion that abuse does not end when victims separate from the perpetrator, but rather that, some perpetrators escalate their violence after separation, thereby necessitating a broader scope of persons protected by the statute.

---

98. Louisiana House of Representatives, Hearing on H.B. 27 Before the Committee on Administration of Criminal Justice (April 26, 2017) (statement of Representative Patrick Connick) (at 7:30–7:50), https://house.louisiana.gov/H_Video/VideoArchivePlayer?v=house/2017/apr/0426_17_CJ. (statement of Sunny Funk) (at .9:09–9:13).

99. Louisiana House of Representatives, Hearing on H.B. 27 Before the Committee on Administration of Criminal Justice (April 26, 2017) (statement of Representative Patrick Connick) (at 7:30–7:50), https://house.louisiana.gov/H_Video/VideoArchivePlayer?v=house/2017/apr/0426_17_CJ. (statement of Representative Patrick Connick) (at 7:44–7:50).

100. Protective Orders Act, No. 246, § 46:2132(4), 2020 La. Sess. Law Serv. Act 246, § 4 (S.B. 505) (West).

101. La. Stat. Ann. § 46:2132(4); *see also* McCann v. McCann, 2009-1341 (La. App. 3 Cir. 3/10/10); 33 So. 3d 389, 395 (affirming grant of protective order to wife and grandchildren as husband's act of striking wife was domestic abuse sufficient to support protective order and court had discretion to include grandchildren that lived next door to her within ambit of protective order); Paschal v. Hazlinsky, 35,513 (La. App. 2 Cir. 12/19/01), 803 So. 2d 413, 419 (protective order issued against daughter and aunt in favor of mother and grandson for restraining and leaving bruise on mother and for fraudulently seeking commitment of mother while in presence of grandson); Rodriguez v. Claassen, 2016-0610 (La. App. 4 Cir. 12/21/16), 207 So. 3d 490 (threatening life, battery, and false imprisonment sufficient for protective order against father in favor of mother and child for acts against mother while child present).

§ 13:6 The Domestic Abuse Assistance Act—Who May Request Relief

Any adult may seek relief by filing a petition for protective relief alleging domestic abuse by the defendant.[102] Adult "means any person 18 years of age or older or any person under the age of 18 who has been emancipated by marriage or otherwise."[103] An emancipated minor may file on his or her own behalf.[104] Additionally, the legislature recognized that children or incompetents are vulnerable to the negative impacts of domestic abuse, as well. Whether biologically related to the victim or the perpetrator or not, the law also permits petitioning the court for a protective order for a child-victim or incompetent-victim through a responsible adult, such as a parent, household member, or the district attorney.[105]

§ 13:7 The Domestic Abuse Assistance Act—Petition Requirements

The requirements necessary to file a petition pursuant to the DAAA require the name of each petitioner or on whose behalf the petition is being filed if for another (child or incompetent) and the relationship between the filer and the victim, if different, as well as the name, address, and residence of the person alleged to have committed abuse (the defendant or perpetrator), if known.[106] The petition must contain the "facts and circumstances concerning the alleged abuse," relationship between the defendant and the petitioner, a request for certain protective order(s), and request for an interpreter, if needed.[107] The petitioner is not required to disclose the address and parish where the petitioner, or the person on whose behalf the filing is made, resides if the desire is to keep such information confidential.[108] If a restraining order is requested ex parte, the petition must contain a written verification signed and dated by each petitioner, swearing to the truth of the facts and circumstances contained in the petition and made before a witness who is required to sign and print his or her name.[109]

---

102. La. Stat. Ann. § 46:2133(D).

103. La. Stat. Ann. § 46:2132(1) (2020).

104. La. Stat. Ann. § 46:2132(1) (2020).

105. La. Stat. Ann. § 46:2133; *see also* S.L.B. v. C.E.B., 2017-0978 (La. App. 4 Cir. 7/27/18), 252 So. 3d 950 (protective order issued against mother on behalf of the child affirmed).

106. La. Stat. Ann. 46:2134(A)(1). Relief cannot be granted without a petition. The court is not authorized to grant a mutual order of protection to opposing parties unless each party files a petition seeking such relief and proves his or her case by a preponderance of the evidence. *See* Bays v. Bays, 2000-1727 (La. 2/21/01), 779 So. 2d 754 (no protective order can be issued without a petition); Pierre v. Pierre, 2023-574 (La. App. 5 Cir. 9/16/24), 2024 WL 4198163 (motion to modify protective order not the proper mechanism to revise protective order to add new plaintiffs; must file new petition).

107. La. Stat. Ann. § 46:2134(A)(2)–(5) (2021).

108. La. Stat. Ann. § 46:2134(B).

109. La. Stat. Ann. § 46:2134(D) (2021). Prior to 2021, "[i]f the petition request[ed] the issuance of an ex parte temporary restraining order, the petition … [was required to] contain an affidavit signed by each petitioner. …" La. Stat. Ann. § 46:2134(D) (2019). An affidavit requires a notary and two wit-

These statutes require the court to establish assistance programs, in collaboration with community organizations, for victims of domestic abuse and outline the minimum assistance to be rendered, including providing victims with information about their rights, the process, and other available services. Specifically, the clerk of court is required to make forms available when seeking the initial application for a protective order, provide clerical assistance to the petitioner when necessary, advise indigent applicants of the availability of filing *in forma pauperis*, and provide the necessary forms.[110] To further assist domestic abuse survivors in seeking a protective order, "[d]omestic abuse advocates may provide clerical assistance to petitioners in making an application for a protective order in accordance with this Part" if they are "an employee or representative of a community based shelter providing services to victims of family violence or domestic abuse."[111]

The Louisiana Supreme Court has approved family law forms, including petitions for protection from abuse under the DAAA, that may be used in seeking protective relief. The forms, with instructions, may be found at https://www.lasc.org/LPOR-Forms.

§ 13:8 The Domestic Abuse Assistance Act— Jurisdiction and Venue to Obtain Order

A petition for protection from abuse must be filed in the appropriate court. Jurisdiction is proper for requests for civil protective orders under the DAAA when abuse has occurred in this state and in any state court empowered to hear domestic relations cases.[112] This implies that the judiciary handling cases of divorce and incidental matters regarding a family's rights and obligations after divorce is in the best position to address the issues involved in applications for civil protective orders,[113] especially when the relief involves victims of family violence and could impact the court's ultimate determination on other issues, such as custody.[114]

---

nesses to sign. In lieu of the affidavit, the 2021 amendment only requires "a written affirmation signed and dated by each petitioner. . . ." La. Stat. Ann. § 46:2134 (2021). The purpose of this change was to eliminate the burden on domestic abuse survivors and attempt to protect them from further abuse by reducing the need to commute to various offices to effectuate an affidavit. *See* Louisiana House of Representatives, Hearing on H.B. 55 Before the Committee on Civil Law and Procedure, (April 19, 2021) (statement of Representative Aimee Adatto Freeman) (at 8:30–8:55), https://house.louisiana.gov/H_Video/VideoArchivePlayer?v=house/2021/apr/0419_21_CL.

110. La. Stat. Ann. § 46:2138.

111. La. Stat. Ann. § 46:2138 (2011).

112. La. Stat. Ann. § 46:2133(A). Originally, the statute provided that "[v]enue lies: (1) In the parish where the martial domicile is located; or (2) In the parish where the defendant resides; or (3) In the parish where the abuse is alleged to have been committed." La. Stat. Ann. § 46:2133 (1982). Over the years, the statute was amended several different times to expand jurisdiction to additional courts and increase the venue options for victims, thereby reflecting an attempt to lift the burdens placed on victims and make it easier for victims to obtain prompt relief.

113. *See, e.g.*, La. Stat. Ann. § 46:2134.

114. *See, e.g.*, McFall v. Armstrong, 2010-1041 (La. App. 5 Cir. 9/13/11), 75 So. 3d 30, 39 (rendering an award of joint custody reversible error if ruled upon before resolution of pending DAAA claim).

For purposes of jurisdiction for filing under the DAAA, residency of the victim is immediately bestowed within a territory of his or her presence if he or she seeks at least temporary residency at that location. Victims of domestic abuse may relocate for various reasons, whether it be for safety, shelter, or support, and the law does not seek to limit the legal protection drafted for their benefit to the location where the abuse occurred.[115] Quick and easy access to the court system is necessary to protect victims of domestic abuse. Thus, venue is proper in the court of the parish were the petitioner currently or temporarily resides or is domiciled (even if the abuse did not occur there), where the defendant resides or is domiciled, where the domestic abuse occurred, where the marital domicile or household is located, or where the last matrimonial domicile is located.[116] If a divorce case is pending, the petition for protection from abuse must be filed in the same proceeding.[117]

Further, judicial district courts comprised of multiple parishes have the option of transferring cases brought under the DAAA between parishes if such transfer is in the interest of justice.[118] The goal of this section was to allow district courts in parishes with larger populations to permit the transfer of the case to another district court within a parish with a smaller population that could therefore more expediently handle the

115. Because domestic abuse survivors may have to "flee from one parish to another in order to escape further harm at the hands of an abusive partner," amendments to this statute over the years have generally been favorable to domestic abuse survivors, providing multiple permissible venues for filing. La. Civ. Law and Proc. Comm., Minutes of Meeting, H. 849, Reg. Sess., at 19–20 (May 20, 1991) (comments by Ms. Patsy Taylor, representing the Louisiana Coalition Against Domestic Violence). The original venue statute defined three appropriate venues for Domestic Abuse Assistance Act claims: "(1) [i]n the parish where the marital domicile is located; or (2) [i]n the parish where the defendant resides; or (3) [i]n the parish where the abuse is alleged to have been committed." La. Stat. Ann. § 46:2133 (1982). Act 80 of 1984 added as a permissible venue "the parish where the petitioner resides only as to the issuance of a temporary restraining order and protective order directing the defendant to refrain from abusing, harassing, or interfering with the person or employment or going near the residence or place of employment of a petitioner or the minor children or any person alleged to be incompetent on whose behalf a petition was filed under this Part." La. Stat. Ann. § 46:2133 (1984). In 1997, by Act 1156, the Legislature removed the qualifying language from the 1984 amendment such that a permissible venue is "in the parish where the petitioner resides" without any further requirement. La. Stat. Ann. § 46:2133 (1997). In 1991, Act 361 added "the parish where an action for annulment of marriage or for a divorce could be brought pursuant to Code of Civil Procedure Art. 3941(A)" as another permissible venue. La. Stat. Ann. § 46:2133 (1991). In 1997, Act 1156 added the "parish ... where the household is located" as another permissible venue, representing a shift from a traditional focus on domestic abuse within marriage to a focus on domestic abuse occurring outside of marriage or occurring in general. La. Stat. Ann. § 46:2133 (1997).

116. *See* La. Stat. Ann. § 46:2133(B) and La. Code Civ. Proc. Ann. art. 3941(A) ("An action for an annulment of marriage or for a divorce shall be brought in a parish where either party is domiciled, or in the parish of the last matrimonial domicile."); *see also* Jones v. Wen, 2020-0437 (La. App. 4 Cir. 9/22/20), 365 So. 3d 706, 708 (holding that case between minor child's father and grandmother was filed in proper venue "[g]iven that Orleans Parish is not only where a divorce proceeding could be brought [between the parents], but also where the Divorce Action [between the parents] is currently pending").

117. La. Stat. Ann. § 46:2134.

118. Venue in Applications for Protection from Family Violence Act, No. 119, § 46:2133, 2016 La. Sess. Law Serv. Act 119 (H.B. 525) (West).

case.[119] Additionally, increasing the efficiency also benefits domestic abuse survivors by reducing the waiting time to access relief.

§ 13:9 The Domestic Abuse Assistance Act—Temporary Relief That May Be Granted

An ex parte order of protection may only be issued if the court deems it necessary to protect the petitioner/victim. The risks of lethality and recidivism are high in the context of domestic abuse,[120] so the safety of victims may be in jeopardy if they were required to give notice and participate in a full hearing before receiving the legal protection available. Louisiana Revised Statutes Section 46:2135, therefore, only requires the petitioner to make a *prima facie* showing that he or she will be able to prove that he or she is eligible for relief and that the temporary order will protect him or her from potential future abuse before the permanent relief can be granted.

Upon filing, the pleadings are presented to the judge. The judge rules only on the contents of the verified petition and attachments, if any. If the court finds that an immediate and present danger of domestic abuse exists, the court may, without proof or a hearing, grant a temporary restraining order ex parte, pending a full hearing to be set at a later date.[121] The court may also issue such relief as is necessary, including but not limited to: protection from a number of feared activities (abuse, harassment, interference with person or work and alienation of property),[122] but may also award to the victim exclusive use of the home, jointly-owned property such as a vehicle and pets,[123] as well as award temporary custody of the children,[124] and restore possession of separate and personal property.[125] The court may also permit either party the right to return to the family residence to recover personal clothing and necessities, when accompanied by a

---

119. *See* Louisiana House of Representatives, Hearing on H.B. 525 Before the Committee on Civil Law and Procedure, Louisiana House of Representatives; Videotape: Civil Law and Procedure House Committee (March 31, 2016), (Representative Carter as the speaker) (at 18:50–21:16), https://house.louisiana.gov/H_Video/VideoArchivePlayer?v=house/2016/mar/0321_16_CL.

120. Tamika L. Payne, *Domestic Violence Recidivism: Restorative Justice Intervention Programs for First-Time Domestic Violence Offenders*, Walden University, p. 1 (2017) ("Recidivism in cases of domestic violence in the United States occurs at a higher rate than other violent crimes, despite the use of interventions such as protection orders, probation, incarceration, and batterer intervention programs.") (citations and citing references omitted).

121. La. Stat. Ann. §46:2135(A).

122. La. Stat. Ann. §46:2135(A)(1)(2019)("Directing the defendant to refrain from abusing, harassing, or interfering with the person or employment or going near the residence or place of employment of the petitioner, the minor children, or any person alleged to be incompetent, on whose behalf a petition was filed under this Part") and (4) ("Prohibiting either party from the transferring, encumbering, or otherwise disposing of property mutually owned or leased by the parties, except when in the ordinary course of business, or for the necessary support of the party or the minor children.").

123. La. Stat. Ann. §46:2135(A)(3) and (7).

124. La. Stat. Ann. § 46:2135(A)(5).

125. *See* La. Stat. Ann. §46:2135(A)(6), (C), and §46:2136(A).

law enforcement officer.[126] "If the court orders the issuance of a temporary restraining order, the defendant may be cast for all costs."[127] Clearly, the temporary restraining order process creates emergency access to civil orders of protection to afford victims of domestic abuse the intended protections, such as safeguarding from the possibility of escalated abuse, to provide safe shelter to the victim, and curb the behavior of the perpetrator that could impact the employment and personal support of the victim, while also enabling the court to award temporary custody of children to protect them from abuse or prevent their abduction from the jurisdiction of the court, to name a few.

§ 13:10 The Domestic Abuse Assistance Act— Service and Hearing Date Timeframes

If a temporary restraining order is issued without notice to the defendant, the court is required to set a date for a full hearing within twenty-one days.[128] If the petition for an ex parte temporary restraining order is denied, the court will set a hearing on the petition to rule on the protective order within ten days of service of the petition.[129] In either case, the petitioner is required to provide notice or service to the defendant of

---

126. La. Stat. Ann. § 46:2135(C). Originally, only the defendant had this right. Presumably, this amendment was added to address a gap in the law where, if the domestic abuse survivor was not awarded use and possession of the home, there was no explicit right under the prior law for the petitioner to collect his or her belongings from the home with the assistance of an officer. As to the presence of an officer, the legislature recognized that disputes pertaining to ownership of property when one party goes to collect his or her belongings from another may be reduced or eliminated by the presence of an officer. La. Civ. Law and Proc. Comm., Minutes of Meeting, H. 276, Reg. Sess., at 3–4 (May 14, 1984) (comments by Mike Barnett).

127. La. Stat. Ann. § 46:2134(G).

128. La. Stat. Ann. § 46:2135(B). The timeframe for setting a rule to show cause as to why a protective order should not be issued has changed over the years. As originally enacted, section 46:2135 provided that "[i]f a temporary restraining order is granted without notice, the matter shall be set within ten days for a rule to show cause why the protective order should not be issued...." State of Louisiana: Acts of Legislature, 1982 La. Acts 782 § 2. In 1999, Act 1200 increased this time requirement to twenty days. Domestic Violence—Temporary Restraining and Protective Orders—Violation; Duration Act, No. 1200, § 46:2136(F), 1999 La. Sess. Law Serv. Act 1200, § 2 (S.B. 393) (West). In 2006, Act 777 reduced this time requirement to fifteen days. Domestic Abuse Assistance Act, No. 777, § 46:2135(B), 2006 La. Sess. Law Serv. Act 777 (H.B. 849) (West). In 2009, Act 427 increased this time requirement to twenty-one days. Temporary Restraining Orders in Domestic Abuse Cases Act, No. 427, § 46:2135 (B), 2009 La. Sess. Law Serv. Act 427 (H.B. 629) (West). Debates as to whether the time requirement should be extended or reduced revolved around competing interests of protecting defendants from being removed from their homes while awaiting a hearing on frivolous claims and giving petitioners time to prepare their cases. *See* Videotape: House committee on Civil Law and Procedure (April 10, 2006)(at 38:10–38:42), https://house.louisiana.gov/H_Video/VideoArchivePlayer?v=house/2006/apr/0411_06_CL. Additionally, as originally enacted, the ten-day time requirement in section 46:2135 presented an issue for "judges[, who] experienced a real problem with getting these cases docketed within that period of time." Videotape: House Committee on Civil Law and Procedure (April 10, 2006), (Ayn Stehr as the speaker) (at 34:20–34:40), https://house.louisiana.gov/H_Video/VideoArchivePlayer?v=house/2006/apr/0411_06_CL.

129. La. Stat. Ann. § 46:2135(D). In 1983, Act 407 added a time limit to "set the rule for the hearing" for a rule to show cause when a temporary restraining order has not been granted to "within ten days from the date of service of the petition." State of Louisiana: Acts of Legislature, 1983 La. Acts.

the temporary restraining order within twenty-four hours, if granted, and in advance of the hearing date, if ex parte relief is not granted, so that defendant can appear and be heard.[130] If there is no service on the defendant within the time prescribed by law or the hearing is continued, the order will be extended until the next hearing date, not to exceed fifteen (15) days.[131] Thus, temporary orders do not impede the rights of the perpetrator in that the orders have a limited duration and thereafter, require the victim to proceed to court to prove his or her case as outlined in the statute.

§ 13:11 The Domestic Abuse Assistance Act—Protective Order Hearing

At the hearing, the judge reviews the allegations in the petition, takes testimony,[132] reviews any evidence presented, and makes a ruling.[133] The petitioner must be a victim of domestic abuse or have reasonable cause to believe the petitioner is in imminent danger of becoming a victim of an act of domestic abuse and be related to the defendant in the appropriate manner, both as defined in the statute as discussed above.[134] Proof is required by a preponderance of the evidence.[135] "Proof is sufficient to constitute a preponderance of the evidence when the entirety of the evidence, both direct and circumstantial, shows that the fact sought to be proved is more probable than not."[136]

After notice and a hearing, if the court finds that an immediate and present danger of domestic abuse exists, the court may grant a protective order including such relief as is necessary. The court can affirm the relief awarded in the temporary restraining order, if applicable,[137] including protection from a number of feared activities (abuse, harassment, interference with person or work and alienation of property),[138] and award

407, § 1. Previously, there was no time limit on when this could be set. State of Louisiana: Acts of Legislature, 1982 La. Acts. 782, § 2.

130. La. Stat. Ann. § 46:2135(B). Since the enactment of section 46:2135 in 1982, the Legislature has grappled with the timeframe for service of process after the issuance of the temporary restraining order. In 1983, Act 406 eliminated the "within twenty-four hours of the issuance of the order" language completely. State of Louisiana: Acts of Legislature, 1983 LA. Acts. 406, § 1. In 1997, Act 1156 re-added "within twenty-four hours of the issuance of the order" to section 46:2135. Domestic Violence—Louisiana Protective Order Registry—Statewide Registry of Civil and Criminal Abuse Prevention Orders Act, No. 1156, § 46:2135(B), 1997 La. Sess. Law Serv. Act 1156, §7 (S.B. 1425) (West).

131. La. Stat. Ann. § 46:2135(E).

132. S.L.B. v. C.E.B., 2017-0978 (La. App. 4 Cir. 7/27/18); 252 So. 3d 950 (neither the DAAA nor case law requires the child-victim to testify in order to obtain protective relief).

133. La. Stat. Ann. § 46:2135(I) (allows "hearing officers to handle the first rule to show cause in the enforcement of protective orders").

134. La. Stat. Ann. § 46:2135(A).

135. La. Stat. Ann. § 46:2135(B); Pierce v. Pierce, 2019-0689 (La. App. 1 Cir. 2/21/20), 298 So. 3d 902, 908 (affirming denial of permanent protective order for lack of sufficient evidence).

136. Oliva v. Jones, 2022-385 (La. App. 5 Cir. 3/29/23), 360 So. 3d 573, 579 (internal citations omitted).

137. La. Stat. Ann. § 46:2136(A)(1).

138. La. Stat. Ann. § 46:2135(A)(1) ("Directing the defendant to refrain from abusing, harassing, or interfering with the person or employment or going near the residence or place of employment of the petitioner, the minor children, or any person alleged to be incompetent, on whose behalf a petition

to the survivor exclusive use of the home, jointly-owned property such as a vehicle and pets,[139] as well as award additional relief, such as temporary custody of the children,[140] and restore possession of separate and personal property.[141] Additional relief afforded by Louisiana Revised Statutes Section 46:2136 includes the ability to order temporary child or spousal support, defendant to provide suitable housing for any dependents, and defendant to undergo a medical and/or mental health evaluation and thereafter attend counseling or other treatment as appropriate.[142] Finally, if the petitioner consents, the defendant may also be ordered to participate in an electronic monitoring program.[143] Under the program, the defendant must wear a device that alerts the domestic violence survivor and the appropriate law enforcement agency when the defendant is within a certain distance of the protected person or protected premises.[144] In such cases, the defendant shall be responsible for all costs.[145]

Mandatory provisions required in a protective order address the possession of firearms by the defendant.[146] If there is a finding that defendant "represents a credible threat to the physical safety of a family member, household member or dating partner,[147] and a protective order is issued, whether after a contradictory hearing or by consent, defendant is prohibited from possessing a firearm[148] or carrying a concealed

---

was filed under this Part") and (4) ("Prohibiting either party from the transferring, encumbering, or otherwise disposing of property mutually owned or leased by the parties, except when in the ordinary course of business, or for the necessary support of the party or the minor children."); Francois v. Francois, 2006-712 (La. App. 3 Cir. 11/2/06), 941 So. 2d 722, 726 (protective order to protect victim from abuse more important than defendant's right to attend church, which was within the prohibited radius pursuant to the protective order).

139. La. Stat. Ann. § 46:2135(A)(3) and (7).

140. La. Stat. Ann. § 46:2135(A)(5).

141. *See* La. Stat. Ann. § 46:2135(A)(6), (C) and § 46:2136(A).

142. La. Stat. Ann. § 46:2136(A)(2) and (A)(4)(a); *see also* Chi v. Pang, 1994-284 (La. App. 3 Cir. 10/5/94), 643 So. 2d 411 (spousal support award permitted under DAAA when divorce proceeding is pending).

143. La. Stat. Ann. § 46:2143(A). This amendment was brought in response to situations where domestic abuse offenders ignored the restraining orders issued against them and caused serious harm or death to the victim. *See* Videotape: House Committee on Administration of Criminal Justice (May 14, 2003) (Tony Dupuis [(Unknown Spelling)] as the speaker) (at 1:48:20–1:48:50), https://house.louisiana.gov/H_Video/VideoArchivePlayer?v=house/2003/may/0514_03_CJ.

144. La. Stat. Ann. § 46:2143(B).

145. La. Stat. Ann. § 46:2143(B).

146. Louisiana Revised Statutes Section 46:2136.3 was enacted to prevent or reduce harm to domestic abuse survivors committed by abusers armed with firearms. Around the time of the enactment in 2014, statistics provided that "80% of women murdered in ... [Louisiana] ... [were] killed by either a husband, a partner, or an ex-partner. 74% of these murders were committed with firearms." Videotape: House Committee on Administration of Criminal Justice, (March 26, 2014) (Representative Moreno as the speaker), (at 1:56:41–1:57:20), https://house.louisiana.gov/H_Video/VideoArchivePlayer?v=house/2014/Mar_2014/0326_14_CJ.

147. La. Stat. Ann. § 46:2136.3(A) and (A)(1).

148. La. Stat. Ann. § 46:2136.3 defines "firearm" as "pistol, revolver, rifle, shotgun, machine gun, submachine gun, black powder weapon or assault rifle," but does not provide a definition for "concealed weapon," and the statute currently remains without such a definition.

weapon. The protective order itself must notify defendant of such prohibition.[149] Any violation of this provision is considered a violation of the protective order and punishable pursuant to Louisiana Revised Statutes Section 14:79.[150]

Much of the relief in the statute is designed to deny the defendant access to the victim to perpetrate the abuse. Because abuse is often accompanied by the use of weapons, the law mandates the prohibition of firearms upon the granting of a protective order. The constitutionality of the statute was challenged, and it was upheld by the United States Supreme Court as constitutional in *United States v. Rahimi*.[151] A trial court's order pursuant to the DAAA is reversible only upon a showing of abuse of discretion.[152]

§ 13:12 The Domestic Abuse Assistance Act—Protective Order Registry

In order to provide a statewide registry for protective orders to prevent domestic abuse, among other violence, and to aid law enforcement, prosecutors, and the courts in handling such matters, the Louisiana Protective Order Registry ("LPOR") statute was enacted in 1997,[153] and "[t]he LPOR was officially launched in April, 1999, when the database was completed and the initial version of the standardized forms was ready for release."[154] The LPOR "encompasses temporary restraining orders, protective orders, preliminary injunctions, permanent injunction, and court-approved consent agreements."[155]

---

149. La. Stat. Ann. § 46:2136.3(A)(2).

150. La. Stat. Ann. § 46:2136.3(C). Louisiana Revised Statutes Section 46:2137 originally provided for the fines and penalties for violating a protective order. Since it was duplicative of Louisiana Revised Statutes Section 14:79, it was repealed in 2018. State of Louisiana: Acts of Legislature, 2018 La. Acts. 367, § 4, eff. Oct. 1, 2018.

151. 144 S. Ct. 1889 (2024).

152. Ruiz v. Ruiz, 2005-175 (La. App. 5 Cir 1/11/05), 910 So. 2d 443.

153. La. Stat. Ann. § 46:2136.2. Since 1997, Louisiana Revised Statutes Section 46:2136.2 has been amended to modify the entities for which the Louisiana Protective Order Registry is available. *See, e.g.*, Social Services, Department of—Safeguard of Information in State Case Registry of Child Support Orders; Access to Information in Louisiana Protective Order Registry Act, No. 213, § 46:2136.2, 1999 La. Sess. Law Serv. Act 213, § 1 (S.B. 815) (West); Civil Procedure—Domestic Violence—Temporary Restraining Orders; Preliminary Injunctions; Uniform Abuse Protection Orders Act, No. 750, § 46:2136.2(F), 2003 La. Sess. Law Serv. Act. 750, § 6 (S.B. 304) (West); Domestic Abuse Assistance Act, No. 674, § 46:2136, 2004 La. Sess. Law Serv. Act 674, § 1 (S.B. 603) (West); Department of Children and Family Services Act, No. 255, § 46:2136.2(F), 2012 La. Sess. Law Serv. Act 255, § 7 (H.B. 389) (West). In 2018, Act 679 required that "law enforcement [and] private process servers" report information to the Judicial Administrator's Office. Temporary Restraining Orders and Protective Orders Act, No. 679, § 46:2136.2(A), 2018 La. Sess. Law Serv. Act 679, § 3 (H.B. 207) (West). Prior to the 2018 amendment, process servers were not required to report service information to the Judicial Administrator.

154. *See* Louisiana Supreme Court, LPOR Overview, Louisiana Supreme Court, https://www.lasc.org/lpor.

155. La. Stat. Ann. § 46:2136.2(B) (2014).

The chief purpose of the LPOR is to expediently[156] provide officers with information about an alleged abuser in an effort to protect victims and witnesses.[157] When an officer arrives upon a domestic violence scene, he or she may need to make an arrest (e.g., if the alleged abuser was in violation of a protective order). The LPOR enables the officer to quickly determine whether there is a temporary restraining order, protective order, preliminary injunction, permanent injunction, or court-approved consent agreement against the alleged abuser and use this information to make an immediate arrest, if applicable.[158] The Louisiana Supreme Court has approved forms that must be used

---

156. The LPOR statute was amended in 2014 to include and/or clarify language demonstrating the intent to expedite the process: "The Judicial Administrator's office shall collect the data transmitted to it from the courts of the state and enter it into the Louisiana Protective Order Registry as expeditiously as possible...." and "[t]he clerk of the issuing court shall immediately send a copy of the order or any modification thereof to the Louisiana Protective Order Registry and to the chief law enforcement officer of the parish in which the person or persons protected by the order reside as expeditiously as possible but no later than by the end of the next business day after the order is filed with the clerk of court...." Domestic Abuse—Protective Orders—Procedures for Filing Uniform Abuse Prevention Orders in the Louisiana Protective Order Registry Act, No. 317, § 46:2136(C), 2014 La. Sess. Law Serv. Act 317 (H.B. 750) (West). Originally, as enacted, the statute stated the following: "The Judicial Administrator's office shall collect the data transmitted to it from the courts of the state and enter it into the Louisiana Protective Order Registry" and "[t]he clerk of the issuing court shall send a copy of the order or any modification thereof to the Louisiana Protective Order Registry as expediently as possible but no later than by the end of the next business day after the order was filed with the clerk of court...." Domestic Violence—Louisiana Protective Order Registry—Statewide Registry of Civil And Criminal Abuse Prevention Orders Act, No. 1156, § 46:2136(7), 1997 La. Sess. Law Serv. Act 1156 (S.B. 1425) (West). In 2023, the Louisiana Legislature amended the LPOR statute such that the deadline for the clerk of the issuing court to immediately send a copy of the order or any modification thereof is now expressed in calendar days, rather than business days. Protective Orders Act, No. 309, § 2136, 2023 La. Sess. Law Serv. Act 309 (H.B. 376) (West). The purpose behind this amendment was "to extend and expedite protective coverage of domestic violence victims over weekends and holidays." Videotape: House Committee on Judiciary (May 3, 2023), (Representative Boyd as the speaker) (at 2:25:15–2:25:45), https://house.louisiana.gov/H_Video/VideoArchivePlayer?v=house/2023/may/0503_23_JU.

Prior to this amendment, "if an individual is assaulted or attacked on a Friday, Saturday, or Sunday, they will not have a much needed layer of protection, not to mention if that Monday is a holiday ... for nearly up to four days." *Id.* Another impetus for the amendment was that "[d]omestic violence ha[d] also increased significantly over the holidays." *Id.* Finally, the LPOR statute has also been amended to eliminate slower forms of transmission of the Uniform Abuse Prevention Order such as mail and to require transmission "by facsimile transmission or direct electronic input." Domestic Abuse—Protective Orders—Procedures for Filing Uniform Abuse Prevention Orders in the Louisiana Protective Order Registry Act, No. 317, § 46:2136(3), 2014 La. Sess. Law Serv. Act 317 (H.B. 750) (West). In 2023, the Louisiana Legislature added Section G to Louisiana Revised Statutes Section 46:2136.2, which provided that "[t]he judicial administrator's office shall develop policies and procedures that provide for immediate entry of protection orders received by the office to include those received the next calendar day. To avoid delays in entry, the office shall have the authority to authorize agencies to enter protective orders directly into the registry when certain conditions or criteria exist." Protective Orders Act, No. 309, § 46:2136, 2023 La. Sess. Law Serv. Act 309 (H.B. 376) (West).

157. *See* Videotape: House Committee on the Administration of Criminal Justice (March 26, 2014) (Representative Moreno as the speaker) (at 1:49:00–1:49:10), https://house.louisiana.gov/H_Video/VideoArchivePlayer?v=house/2014/Mar_2014/0326_14_CJ.

158. *See* Videotape: House Committee on the Administration of Criminal Justice (March 26, 2014) (Representative Moreno as the speaker) (at 1:49:10–1:49:30), https://house.louisiana.gov/H_Video/VideoArchivePlayer?v=house/2014/Mar_2014/0326_14_CJ.

for issuance of temporary and protective order injunctions for domestic abuse.[159] The forms, with instructions, may be found at https://www.lasc.org/LPOR-Forms.

Once a temporary restraining or protective order injunction is issued, the judge shall sign such order (called the Uniform Abuse Prevention Order) and forward it to the clerk of court for filing, all without delay.[160] The clerk is required to transmit the order expeditiously to the LPOR[161] by facsimile transmission or direct electronic input.[162] A copy of the order shall also be sent to the chief law enforcement officer of the parish where the protected person resides within one day of issuance,[163] and the petitioner to notify them "of [the] right to initiate criminal proceedings."[164]

---

159. *See e.g.*, La. Stat. Ann. § 46:2136.2(C) ("Courts of this state shall use a uniform form for the issuance of any protective or restraining order, which form shall be developed, approved, and distributed by the judicial administrator's office, shall be titled the 'Uniform Abuse Prevention Order.'"); *see also* La. Stat. Ann. § 46:2138 (referring to the necessary forms).

160. La. Code Civ. Proc. Ann. art. 3607.1(A) (2014) ("Immediately upon rendering a decision granting the petitioner a temporary restraining order or a preliminary or permanent injunction prohibiting a person from harming a family or household member or dating partner, or directing a person accused of stalking to refrain from abusing, harassing, or interfering with the victim of the stalking when the parties are strangers or acquaintances, the judge shall cause to have prepared a Uniform Abuse Prevention Order, as provided in R.S. 46:2136.2(C), shall sign such order, and shall immediately forward it to the clerk of court for filing on the day that the order is issued.").

161. La. Stat. Ann. § 46:2135(G)–(H) (as applied to temporary restraining orders); *see also* La. Stat. Ann. § 46:2136(G)–(H) (as applied to protective orders). In 1997, the Louisiana Protective Order Registry was created "to provide a statewide registry for abuse prevention orders to prevent domestic violence and to aid law enforcement, prosecutors and the court in handling such matters." Domestic Violence—Louisiana Protective Order Registry—Statewide Registry of Civil and Criminal Abuse Prevention Orders Act, No. 1156, § 46:2136.2(A), 1997 La. Sess. Law Serv. Act 1156, § 7 (S.B. 14250 (West).

162. La. Stat. Ann. § 9:366 (regarding orders issued pursuant to the Post Separation Family Violence Relief Act).

163. La. Stat. Ann. § 46:2135(H) (one business day); La. Stat. Ann. § 46:2136(H) (one calendar day). In 2023, the legislature changed the time limits for transmitting the Uniform Abuse Prevention Order from "business days" to "calendar days" in an effort to more expediently transmit information about abusers to law enforcement. Protective Orders Act, No. 309, § 46:2136, 2023 La. Sess. Law Serv. Act 309, § 1 (H.B. 376) (West). However, the change applied to protective orders under La. Stat. Ann. §46:2136 only and did not update the statute for temporary restraining orders under La. Stat. Ann. § 46:2135, which still reads as business day. Thus, the original fear that "if[, for example,] an individual is assaulted or attacked on a Friday, Saturday, or Sunday, they will not have a much needed layer of protection, not to mention if that Monday is a holiday, then the victim is left with limited protection for nearly up to four days" remains in some cases. Videotape: House Committee on Judiciary (May 3, 2023) (Representative Boyd as the speaker) (at 2:24:30–2:24:59), https://house.louisiana.gov/H_Video/VideoArchivePlayer?v=house/2023/may/0503_23_JU.

Given that "[d]omestic violence has also increased significantly over holidays," the amendment to calendar days represents a needed change to better protect domestic violence survivors. Videotape: House Committee on Judiciary (May 3, 2023) (Representative Boyd as the speaker) (at 2:25:15–2:25:49), https://house.louisiana.gov/H_Video/VideoArchivePlayer?v=house/2023/may/0503_23_JU.

Prior to 2014, the clerk only needed to send the copy or modification of the protective order to the LPOR, not the chief law enforcement officer. *See e.g.*, Department of Children and Family Services Act, No. 255, § 46:2136.2(F), 2012 La. Sess. Law Serv. Act 255 (H.B. 389) (West).

164. La. Stat. Ann. § 46:2135(J) (for temporary restraining orders) and La. Stat. Ann. § 46:2136(I) (for protective orders). The purpose of this amendment was to provide another mechanism to protect the domestic abuse survivor before violence escalates. Videotape: House Committee on the Admin-

The "Louisiana Protective Order Registry [is] administered by the judicial administrator's office, Louisiana Supreme Court. The judicial administrator's office shall collect the data transmitted to it from the courts, law enforcement, and private process servers of the state and enter it into the Louisiana Protective Order Registry as expeditiously as possible."[165]

§ 13:13 The Domestic Abuse Assistance Act—Length of Protective Order

After the contradictory hearing, if the judge grants the request or the parties reach a consent judgment, a protective order will be issued.[166] A protective order generally does not exceed the timeframe of eighteen (18) months, unless there is a contradictory hearing, and it is extended.[167] The only exception to this rule is protective orders that

---

istration of Criminal Justice (April 24, 2019), (Representative Stefanski as the speaker) (at 2:15:00–2:15:25) https://house.louisiana.gov/H_Video/VideoArchivePlayer?v=house/2019/apr/0424_19_CJ. As Representative John Stephanski explained, "when ... [domestic abuse survivors] file a protective order, there's a gap in ... understanding the difference between pursuing criminal charges against that person and filing a protective order." Videotape: House Committee on the Administration of Criminal Justice (April 24, 2019) (Representative Stefanski as the speaker) (at 2:43:30–2:44:14), https://house.louisiana.gov/H_Video/VideoArchivePlayer?v=house/2019/apr/0424_19_CJ. In some cases, filing criminal charges may be more protective, and therefore, the law deemed that knowledge of the right to file such charges is imperative to preventing further violence.

165. La. Stat. Ann. § 46:2136.2 (2018). When it was first enacted in 1997, the LPOR statute required the Judicial Administrator's Office to "make the Louisiana Protective Order Registry available to state and local law enforcement agencies, district attorney offices, and the courts." Domestic Violence—Louisiana Protective Order Registry—Statewide Registry of Civil and Criminal Abuse Prevention Orders Act, No. 1156, § 46:2136.2(F), 1997 La. Sess. Law Serv. Act 1156 (S.B. 1425) (West). In 1999, this list of recipients grew to also include "the Department of Social Services, office of family support, [and] support enforcement services...." Social Services, Department of—Safeguard of Information in State Case Registry of Child Support Orders; Access to Information in Louisiana Protective Order Registry Act, No. 213, § 46:2136.2(F), 1999 La. Sess. Law Serv., Act 213 (S.B. 815) (West). In 2003, "office of community services" was added. Civil Procedure—Domestic Violence—Temporary Restraining Orders; Preliminary Injunctions; Uniform Abuse Protection Orders Act, No. 750, § 46:2136.2(F), 2003 La. Sess. Law Serv. Act. 750 (S.B. 304) (West). In 2004, the list grew yet again with the addition of "the Department of Health and Hospitals, bureau of protective services, the Governor's Office of Elderly Affairs, elderly protective services, [and] the office of the attorney general." Domestic Abuse Assistance Act, No. 674, § 46:2136, 2004 La. Sess. Law Serv. Act 674 (S.B. 603) (West). In 2012, the Department of Social Services was removed from this list and replaced with "the Department of Children and Family Services," Department of Children and Family Services Act, No. 255, § 46:236.1.7, 2012 La. Sess. Law Serv. Act 255 (H.B. 389) (West), as a result of the renaming of the Department of Social Services to the Department of Children and Family Services. *See* Videotape: House Committee on Health and Welfare (March 21, 2012) (Representative Schroder as the speaker) (starting at 2:43:00–32), https://house.louisiana.gov/H_Video/VideoArchivePlayer?v=house/2012/Mar_2012/0321_12_HW. The 2012 amendment also changed the office of family support to "office of children and family support"; support enforcement service to "child support enforcement section"; and removed the "office of community services." Department Of Children and Family Services Act, No. 255, § 46:2136.2(7), 2012 La. Sess. Law Serv. Act 255 (H.B. 389) (West).

166. La. Stat. Ann. § 46:2135.

167. La. Stat. Ann. § 46:2136(F)(1).

direct the defendant to refrain from abusing, harassing, or interfering with the protected person. In such cases, the court may grant a protective order for an indefinite period of time, on its own motion or by motion of the petitioner but must provide the perpetrator with notice of any non-expiring terms at the time of the hearing.[168] The court must conduct a hearing in order to issue an indefinite or permanent protective order and shall hold said hearing concurrently with the hearing for the rule to show cause why the protective order should be issued.[169]

§ 13:14 The Domestic Abuse Assistance Act— Fees and Costs

In domestic abuse cases, the fees shall be paid by the perpetrator.[170] This affords all economic resources and assistance to the victim for any expenses incurred due to the domestic abuse. Any court costs, attorney fees, costs of enforcement and modification proceedings, costs of appeal, evaluation fees, expert fees, costs of medical care, and costs of psychological care for the victim or the children are included.[171] The only limitation is that the fees and costs must be generated "in furtherance of this Part" or necessitated as a result of the domestic abuse inflicted.[172] However, if the court determines that the petition was frivolous, the court may order the petitioner to pay all court costs and reasonable attorney fees of the other party.[173] Failure to appear for the hearing or voluntary dismissal by the petitioner, on its own, does not warrant assessment of fees and costs against the petitioner.[174]

---

168. La. Stat. Ann. § 46:2136(F)(2); *see also* Compton v. Chatman, 2021-0706 (La. App. 1 Cir. 2/25/22), 341 So. 3d 581, 587.

169. La. Stat. Ann. § 46:2136(F)(2)(b).

170. La. Stat. Ann. § 9:367; *see also* La. Stat. Ann. § 45:2136.1(A).

171. La. Stat. Ann. § 46:2136.1(A). As originally enacted in 1997, § 46:2136.1 provided that certain costs, such as "court costs, attorneys fees, evaluation fees, and expert witness fees" are assessed to the "perpetrator of domestic violence." Domestic Violence—Louisiana Protective Order Registry—Statewide Registry of Civil and Criminal Abuse Prevention Orders Act, No. 1156, § 46:2136.1, 1997 La. Sess. Law Serv. Act 1156, § 7 (S.B. 1425) (West). Act 411 in 2008, among other things, added "costs of enforcement and modification proceedings [and] cost of appeals" to the list of costs that the perpetrator must pay. Domestic Abuse Assistance Act, No. 411, § 46:2136.1(A), 2008 La. Sess. Law Serv. Act 411, § 1 (S.B. 264) (West).

172. La. Stat. Ann. § 46:2136.1(A); La. Stat. Ann. § 9:367.

173. La. Stat. Ann. § 46:2136.1(B).

174. La. Stat. Ann. § 46:2136.1(B). In 2022, Act 416 added that "[f]ailure to appear at a hearing on the petition shall not on its own constitute grounds for assessing court costs and fees against the petitioner." Domestic Abuse Assistance Act, No. 416, § 46:2136.1(B), 2022 La. Sess. Law Serv. Act 416, § 2 (S.B. 255) (West). The 2022 amendment was prompted in response to "some judges across the state that were casting petitioners for protection orders with costs for merely not showing up, which would violate the Federal Violence Against Women Act, as well as ... state law." Videotape: Senate Committee on Judiciary A (April 12, 2022) (Morgan Lamandre as the speaker) (at 17:30–18:40), https://senate.la.gov/s_video/VideoArchivePlayer?v=senate/2022/04/041222JUDA.

Acknowledging that there could be many reasons as to why a domestic violence survivor does not appear (e.g., "fear of seeing the perpetrator ... [or being] threatened not to show up despite having a temporary restraining order in place"), the legislature sought to prevent survivors from being finan-

The remedies provided for in the DAAA are not exclusive. The court may impose the remedies provided in the Post-Separation Family Violence Relief Act or any other law when determining a case under Louisiana Revised Statutes Section 46:2131 and vice versa.[175]

§ 13:15 The Domestic Abuse Assistance Act—Violation of Restraining or Protective Order

If the court grants a temporary restraining order or permanent protective order and the other party violates the terms of the order, the defendant can be held in contempt of court. The victim can seek to enforce the order, and the defendant may lose all visitation rights to the child(ren) and may be punished with fines and/or jail time.[176]

Protective orders issued in this state or outside the state are provided full faith and credit and enforced by courts of this state as if they were the original court issuing the order.[177] Presumably, a court of this state would enforce foreign protective orders as written and for the duration specified, even if Louisiana laws would have provided for more limited relief originally.[178] Thus, if a defendant violates an order, he can be held responsible in this state and the penalties for violating an order issued by this state apply.[179]

---

cially punished for failure to appear. Videotape: Senate Committee on Judiciary A (April 12, 2022) (Senator Peacock as the speaker) (at 19:20–19:45), https://senate.la.gov/s_video/VideoArchivePlayer?v=senate/2022/04/041222JUDA; *see also*, Jimenez v. Jimenez, 2005-645 (La. App. 5 Cir. 1/31/06), 922 So. 2d 672 (improper to assess costs to petitioner because of voluntary dismissal; assessment only warranted if there is a finding of frivolousness); Rogers v. Rogers, 2019-0143 (La. App. 1 Cir. 9/27/19), 287 So. 3d 749 (no basis to assess costs to petitioner even if protective order is denied unless petition is frivolous); *but cf.* Boudreaux v. Webster, 2024-0692 (La. App. 1 Cir. 11/13/24), 2024 WL 4762697 (voluntary dismissal for lack of evidence is frivolous, thereby necessitating award of cost against petitioner).

175. La. Stat. Ann. § 9:368; *see also* La. Stat. Ann. § 46:2139.

176. La. Stat. Ann. § 46:2136.3; *see also* La. Stat. Ann. § 9:366(B) ("Any violation of the injunction, if proved by the appropriate standard, shall be punished as contempt of court, and shall result in a termination of all court-ordered child visitation."). If the defendant has been served with the protective order and violates this order, he shall be answerable for the fines and penalties outlined in Louisiana Revised Statutes Section 14:79. La. Stat. Ann. § 14:79.

177. La. Stat. Ann. § 46:2136(C).

178. Because the law directs courts to give credit fully to foreign orders, the courts should enforce those orders as written. However, no case law has interpreted or tested the breadth of this statute.

179. La. Stat. Ann. § 14:79.

§ 13:16 The Domestic Abuse Assistance Act— Modification of Protective Order

An order issued pursuant to Louisiana Revised Statutes Sections 46:4135 or 46:4136 remains in place until it expires or a court modifies it. Due to the time limitations in the statutes, the court orders can expire after the passage of a specified period of time. This leaves the burden on the petitioner to seek court approval to extend the order even if the order remains essential.

On the other hand, the statute does not preclude a defendant from seeking relief to have the court evaluate the continuing need for a protective order or to address the scope of the relief and restrictions. The court has the power to modify a protective order to include items originally omitted or to exclude items and narrow the scope.[180] A defendant may even seek to terminate the order where applicable. In order to do so, the moving party must file a motion. The supplemental pleadings must be served on the other party and a contradictory hearing held accordingly.

§ 13:17 The Domestic Abuse Assistance Act— Use of Law Enforcement

Law enforcement officers are the gatekeepers of the criminal justice system. An arrest can be a critical intervention tool against preventing further violence. Studies reflect that victims are more likely to be assaulted immediately after law enforcement have responded to a call where no arrest is made.[181] Thus, the statutes enumerate the specific duties assigned to officers in a situation where domestic abuse is suspected, articulate when officers should make a presumptive arrest, and give instructions for focused investigation and informed decision-making, while continuing to vest discretion in the officer and offering him or her protection from liability.

Louisiana Revised Statutes Section 46:2140 ("Law enforcement officers; duties") was enacted in 1985 by Act 442 and addressed the methods by which an officer can "prevent further abuse" when he or she "has reason to believe that a family or household member has been abused."[182] Act 750 in 2003 amended the statute to provide that an officer may "arrest the abusive party with a warrant or without a warrant ... if probable cause existed to believe that a felony has been committed by that person."[183] Prior to

180. La. Stat. Ann. § 46:2136(D); *see also* Compton v. Chatman, 2021-0706 (La. App. 1 Cir. 2/25/22), 341 So. 3d 581, 588 (noting that the statutes "clearly gave Mr. Chatman a right to file a motion to modify the effective period of the Protective Order" and court can modify timeframe of protective order upon proper showing).

181. Leigh Goodmark, *Law Enforcement Experience Report: Domestic violence survivors' survey regarding interaction with law enforcement*, https://www.thehotline.org/wp-content/uploads/media/2022/09/2209-Hotline-LES_FINAL.pdf (last visited 11/28/24).

182. La. Stat. Ann. § 46:2140(A)–(B) (2015).

183. Civil Procedure—Domestic Violence—Temporary Restraining Orders; Preliminary Injunctions; Uniform Abuse Protection Orders Act, No. 750, § 46:2140, 2003 La. Sess. Law Serv. Act 750 (S.B. 304) (West).

this amendment, such an arrest could be made on probable cause of an aggravated or second degree battery.[184] Additionally, Act 750 amended the original statute, which provided that an officer may "arrest[] the abusive party in case of simple assault, aggravated assault, or simple battery, whether or not in the presence of the officer, when the officer reasonably believes there is impending danger to the physical safety of the abused person in the officer's absence. If there is no cause to believe there is impending danger, arresting the abusive party is at the officer's discretion"[185] to provide that an officer may "arrest[] the abusive party in case of any misdemeanor crime which endangers the physical safety of the abused person, whether or not the offense occurred in the presence of the officer. If there is no cause to believe there is impending danger, arresting the abusive party is at the officer's discretion."[186]

In 2004, Act 882 added to Section 46:2140, an entire section regulating how an officer should handle domestic abuse situations in which the officer "receives conflicting accounts of domestic abuse or dating violence."[187] Notably, the amendment provides that the officer must determine who is the "predominant aggressor" by using an enumerated set of factors given by the amendment and explains how the officer should handle the predominant aggressor.[188] The amendment defines "dating violence" according to Louisiana Revised Statutes Section 46:2151(C) and "domestic abuse" according to Louisiana Revised Statutes Section 46:2132(3).[189] Act 882 sought to reduce dual arrests in domestic violence cases. As Sheriff Craig Webre of Lafourche Parish explained to the House Committee on Judiciary:

> The existing bill mandates arrest policies under certain circumstances ... as a result of the mandatary arrest policies.... [A]n unintended consequence of dual arrest has occurred. Officers come to the scene of the domestic violence call, they know that the law says that they are required under these circumstances to make an arrest, they don't sort out who was the predominant aggressor, and they arrest both parties. This language in the amendments that are proposed are intended to give the officers guidance in identifying who the predominant aggressor is and to make an arrest in the case of the predominant aggressor to avoid dual arrest, which are usually inappropriate. Nationally, statistics say that only 3% of domestic violence calls are true situations for dual arrest, and if you don't have policies for officers to implement, then often times ... the victim is not only revictimized by the system, she then loses or he then loses confidence in the system and will not call again, so it's important

184. *See, e.g.*, La. Stat. Ann. § 46:2140 (1985).

185. State of Louisiana: Acts of Legislature, 1985 La. Acts. 442, § 1, eff. July 12, 1985.

186. Civil Procedure—Domestic Violence—Temporary Restraining Orders; Preliminary Injunctions; Uniform Abuse Protection Orders Act, No. 750, § 46:2140, 2003 La. Sess. Law Serv. Act 750 (S.B. 304) (West).

187. Family Violence Act, No. 882, § 46:2140, 2004 La. Sess. Law Serv. Act 882 (H.B. 1551) (West).

188. Family Violence Act, No. 882, § 46:2140, 2004 La. Sess. Law Serv. Act 882 (H.B. 1551) (West).

189. Family Violence Act, No. 882, § 46:2140, 2004 La. Sess. Law Serv. Act 882 (H.B. 1551) (West).

> that we have good policies ... to make sure that we don't arrest people who should not be arrested.[190]

In 2014, Act 317 modified Louisiana Revised Statutes Section 46:2140 by separating an officer's response to an abuser's actions based on whether the abuser was acting in violation of certain types of temporary restraining orders, preliminary injunctions, permanent injunctions, or protective orders or whether the abuser was not acting in violation of any of the aforementioned orders.[191] Additionally, Act 317 added an important presumption that "[t]he officer shall presume that the predominant aggressor is the person against whom [one of the aforementioned] order[s] was issued."[192] In 2015, Act 85 expanded the list of protective orders for which an officer must make an arrest if the abuser is in violation, to include those protective orders covered by Louisiana Revised Statutes Sections 46:2171 *et seq.* ("stranger and acquittance stalking"[193]) and Code of Criminal Procedure Article 335.1 (repealed by Acts 2016, No. 613, § 4, eff. Jan. 1, 2017).[194]

As it reads currently, Louisiana Revised Statutes Section 46:2140 requires "a law enforcement officer" to "immediately arrest the abusing party" if the officer "has reason to believe that a family or household member or dating partner has been abused and the abusing party is in violation of a temporary restraining order, a preliminary or permanent injunction, or a protective order issued pursuant to" Louisiana Revised Statutes § 9:361 *et seq.*, § 9:372, § 46:2132 *et seq.*, § 46:2151, § 46:2171 *et seq.*; Children's Code Article 1564 *et seq.*; Louisiana Code of Civil Procedure Articles 3604 and 3607.1; or Louisiana Code of Criminal Procedure 30, 327.1, 335.1, 335.2, and 871.1.[195]

---

190. Videotape: House Committee on Judiciary (May 24, 2004) (Sheriff Craig Webre as the speaker) (at 57:35–59:00), https://house.louisiana.gov/H_Video/VideoArchivePlayer?v=house/2004/may/0524_04_JU.

191. Domestic Abuse—Protective Orders—Procedures for Filing Uniform Abuse Prevention Orders in the Louisiana Protective Order Registry Act, No. 317, § 46:2140, 2014 La. Sess. Law Serv. Act 317 (H.B. 750) (West).

192. Domestic Abuse—Protective Orders—Procedures for Filing Uniform Abuse Prevention Orders in the Louisiana Protective Order Registry Act, No. 317, § 46:2140, 2014 La. Sess. Law Serv. Act 317 (H.B. 750) (West).

193. La. Stat. Ann. § 46:2171.

194. Domestic Abuse Assistance Act, No. 85, § 46:2140, 2015 La. Sess. Law Serv. Act 85 (H.B. 722) (West).

195. La. Stat. Ann. § 46:2140 (2015). Prior to the 2014 amendment, the only requirement was that the "officer has reason to believe that a family or household member or dating partner has been abused" to trigger the mandate that "the officer shall immediately use all reasonable means to prevent further abuse," but it was not required that "the abusing party is not in violation of a restraining order, a preliminary injunction or permanent injunction, or a protective order." *See, e.g.*, Family Violence Act, No. 882 § 46:2140(A), 2004 La. Sess. Law Serv. Act 882 (H.B. 1551) (West).

If, however,

> the abusing party is not in violation of a restraining order, a preliminary or permanent injunction, or a protective order, the officer shall immediately use all reasonable means to prevent further abuse, including:
>
> (1) Arresting the abusive party with a warrant or without a warrant pursuant to Code of Criminal Procedure Article 213, if probable cause exists to believe that a felony[196] has been committed by that person, whether or not the offense occurred in the officer's presence.
>
> (2) Arresting the abusive party in case of any misdemeanor crime which endangers the physical safety of the abused person whether or not the offense occurred in the presence of the officer. If there is no cause to believe there is impending danger, arresting the abusive party is at the officer's discretion.[197]
>
> (3) Assisting the abused person in obtaining medical treatment necessitated by the battery; arranging for, or providing, or assisting in the procurement of transportation for the abused person to a place of shelter or safety.
>
> (4) Notifying the abused person of his right to initiate criminal or civil proceedings; the availability of the protective order, R.S. 46:2136; and the availability of community assistance for domestic violence victims.[198]

Part C of Louisiana Revised Statutes Section 46:2140 provides guidance to law enforcement when he or she "receives conflicting accounts of domestic abuse or dating violence," or claims of mutual violence.[199] Officers are directed to "consider any other relevant factors" to "determine[] if one party is the predominant aggressor[,]" and then the statute enumerates factors that must be considered by the officer "based upon his or her observation"[200] to determine whether the presumption in favor of arrest and charging the other person is overcome by the facts and circumstances.

---

196. In 2003, the Louisiana Legislature amended this statute to provide that one option was to "arrest[] the abusive party with a warrant or without a warrant ... if probable cause exists to believe that a felony has been committed in the officer's presence." Domestic Violence—Temporary Restraining Orders; Preliminary Injunctions; Uniform Abuse Protection Orders Act, No. 750 § 46:2140(A)(1), 2003, La. Sess. Law Serv. Act 750 (S.B. 304) (West). Prior to this amendment, the statute read "aggravated or second degree battery" as opposed to felony. State of Louisiana: Acts of Legislature, 1985 La. Acts. 442, § 1, eff. July 12, 1985.

197. Similarly, prior to the 2003 amendment, this part read "simple assault, aggravated assault, or simple battery instead of "any misdemeanor crime which endangers the physical safety of the abused person...." State of Louisiana: Acts of Legislature, 1985 La. Acts. 442, § 1, eff. July 12, 1985.

Additionally, the 2003 amendment removed the requirement that the officer "reasonably believes there is impending danger to the physical safety of the abused person in the officer's absence" to make such an arrest *Id.*

198. La. Stat. Ann. § 46:2140(B)(1)–(4) (2015).

199. La. Stat. Ann. § 46:2140(C)(1)–(2) (2015).

200. La. Stat. Ann. § 46:2140 (2015). The factors are the following:

(a) Evidence from complainants and other witnesses.

(b) The extent of personal injuries received by each person.

Once the officer determines who the predominant aggressor is, the outcome depends on whether the offense was a felony or misdemeanor. In the case of a felony offense, "the officer shall arrest that person [the primary aggressor]...."[201] On the other hand, if the offense is a misdemeanor, "the officer shall arrest the predominant aggressor if there is reason to believe that there is impending danger or if the predominant aggressor is in violation of a temporary restraining order, a preliminary or permanent injunction, or a protective order issued" pursuant to certain statutes and articles.[202]

In 2014, the Louisiana Legislature enacted Louisiana Revised Statutes Section 46:2141 ("Reporting"), which provides that "[w]henever a law enforcement officer investigates an allegation of domestic abuse, whether or not an arrest is made, the officer shall make a written report of the alleged incident, including a statement of the complainant, and the disposition of the case."[203] This section sets forth the comprehensive written report explaining the reasons for the officer's decision. This requirement can serve as a mechanism to monitor consistent compliance with Louisiana law.[204]

In 1985, the Louisiana Legislature enacted Louisiana Revised Statutes Section 46:2142 ("Immunity") so that "[a]ny law enforcement officer reporting in good faith, exercising due care in the making of an arrest or providing assistance pursuant to the provisions of R.S. 46:2140 and 2141 shall have immunity from any civil liability that otherwise might be incurred or imposed because of the report, arrest, or assistance provided."[205]

(c) Whether a person acted in self-defense.
(d) An imminent threat of future injury to any of the parties.
(e) Prior complaints of domestic abuse or dating violence, if that history can be reasonably ascertained by the officer.
(f) The future welfare of any minors who are present at the scene.
(g) The existence of a temporary restraining order, a preliminary or permanent injunction, or a protective order issued pursuant to R.S. 9:361 et seq., R.S. 9:372, R.S. 46:2131 et seq., R.S. 46:2151, R.S. 46:2171 et seq., Children's Code Article 1564 et seq., Code of Civil Procedure Articles 3604 and 3607.1, or Code of Criminal Procedure Articles 30, 327.1, 335.1, 335.2, and 871.1. The officer shall presume that the predominant aggressor is the person against whom the order was issued. *Id.*

201. La. Stat. Ann. §46:2140 (2015).

202. La. Stat. Ann. §46:2140.

203. *See* La. Stat. Ann. §46:2141. This statute has not been amended since its enactment.

204. Some officers may not arrest or may arrest both parties in response to one complaint, which is not permitted per the law. If the written reports are monitored and reviewed, this could provide a basis for corrective action, where applicable.

205. State of Louisiana: Acts of Legislature, 1985 La. Acts. 442, §1, eff. July 12, 1985.

§ 13:18 Post-Separation Family Violence Relief Act

Family violence is determinantal to children, whether they are a victim or a witness. Prior to 1992, Louisiana law did not provide instruction to the courts as to the appropriate consideration of domestic abuse and family violence in custody cases. For example, various Louisiana laws illustrated the legislature's inconsistent approach to evaluating domestic abuse in child custody and visitation cases. Former Louisiana Civil Code Article 146, codifying the best interest of the child factors used in child custody determinations, did not list domestic abuse by either parent as a considerable factor.[206] Conversely, the "former Louisiana Revised Statute[] 9:574 provided that the court *may* prohibit visitation in … circumstances [of sexual and physical abuse]," while "former Louisiana Civil Code article 133 required the court to prohibit visitation"[207] and former Louisiana Civil Code article 147 "mandate[d] a prohibition of visitation rights whenever the court finds by a preponderance of the evidence that a parent has abused his children."[208]

In 1992, the Louisiana Legislature enacted the Post-Separation Family Violence Relief Act (the "PSFVRA") to resolve the discrepancy and "close a very serious gap in … [the] law which d[id] not require courts to take into account the existence of domestic violence in awarding child custody and visitation."[209] As stated in Louisiana Revised Statutes Section 9:361 ("Legislative findings"),

> [t]he legislature hereby reiterates its previous findings and statements of purpose set forth in R.S. 46:2121 and 2131 relative to family violence and domestic violence. The legislature further finds that *the problems of family violence do not necessarily cease when the victimized family is legally separated or divorced. In fact, the violence often escalates, and child custody and visitation become the new forum for the continuation of the abuse. Because current laws relative to child custody and visitation are based on an assumption that even divorcing parents are in relatively equal positions of power, and that such parents act in the children's best interest, these laws often work against the protection of the children and the abused spouse in families with a history of family violence. Consequently, laws designed to act in the children's best interest may actually effect a contrary result due to the unique dynamics of family violence.*[210]

---

206. La. Civ. Code Ann. art. 146 (rev. 1984); *see also* Chapter 8.

207. Kenneth Rigby, *1993 Custody and Child Support Legislation*, 55 La. L. Rev. 103, 129–30 (1994) (emphasis added).

208. C.F.C. v. J.D.C., 539 So. 2d 47, 49 (La. App. 4th Cir. 1988).

209. Comm. on Health and Welfare, Minutes of Meeting, H. 1056, Reg. Sess., at 8(May 20, 1992).

210. La. Stat. Ann. § 9:361 (1992) (emphasis added); Slayton v. Slayton, 2005-1529 (La. App. 3 Cir. 5/3/06), 929 So. 2d 865 (purpose was to protect the victims from domestic disputes in cases of separation and divorce); State in Interest of A.C., 1993-1125 (La. 1/27/94), 643 So. 2d 719 (intent of legislature was to prohibit possibility of further abuse to child).

Furthermore, without domestic abuse as a consideration in child custody determinations, a woman who experienced abuse by her spouse could be inversely impacted in litigation due to negative connotations associated with "battered women syndrome testimony." "Battered woman syndrome" is a psychological condition associated with a woman's reactions to domestic abuse, notably irrationality associated with fear, anxiety, helplessness, and the feeling of being trapped.[211] Thus, "battered women syndrome testimony stereotypes women as irrational and leads to reinforcing negative images which disadvantages women in child custody battles, child abuse cases, and bar disciplinary proceedings."[212] If a woman displayed signs of abuse, a court may incorrectly attribute these signs as personal flaws as opposed to signs of abuse and conclude that her ex-spouse, the abuser, is more capable of handling the responsibility of child custody.

Louisiana recognized this possibility, and the PSFVRA is now codified at Louisiana Revised Statutes Sections 9:361–9:369. The PSFVRA compels courts and those working in conjunction therewith to consider the impact of family violence on the child when making custodial determinations and elevates the custodial options available to a court where there has been a specific finding of family violence by one parent against another or between a parent and child. Specifically, and as discussed further herein, the law presumes that an award of custody or visitation may not be issued to the perpetrator of family violence in some cases as it jeopardizes the safety and well-being of the victim, whether that is the other parent and/or the child, and provides for other rights and protections.

Overall, "[t]he provisions of the Post-Separation Family Violence Relief Act become operative if the court finds that there has been family violence and that there is a history of family violence."[213] History of family violence may be found by the court 1) if one incident of violence results in serious bodily injury; or 2) more than one incident of family violence has occurred.[214] The laws apply retroactively to cases filed prior to the PSFVRA enactment.[215]

---

211. Erica Beecher-Monas, *Domestic Violence: Competing Conceptions of Equality in the Law of Evidence*, 47 Loy. L. Rev. 81, 113–14 (2001).

212. La. Stat. Ann. § 9:361 (1992) (emphasis added); Slayton v. Slayton, 2005-1529 (La. App. 3 Cir. 5/3/06), 929 So. 2d 865 (purpose was to protect the victims from domestic disputes in cases of separation and divorce); Erica Beecher-Monas, *Domestic Violence: Competing Conceptions of Equality in the Law of Evidence*, 47 Loy. L. Rev. 81, at 114, n. 160 (2001).

213. Nguyen v. Le, 2007-81 (La. App. 5 Cir. 5/15/07), 960 So. 2d 261 (PSFVRA becomes operative if there is family violence or a history of family violence); *see also* Dufresne v. Dufresne, 2008-215 (La. App. 5 Cir. 9/16/08), 992 So.2d 579, 585–86 (citing Michelli v. Michelli, 1993-2128 (La. App 1 Cir. 5/5/95), 655 So. 2d 1342, 1346); Garcia v. Hernandez, 2021-338 (La. App. 5 Cir. 4/11/22), 339 So. 3d 61, 70.

214. La. Stat. Ann. § 9:364(A) (2018); Petsch v. Petsch, 2001-0491 (La. App. 1 Cir. 6/22/01), 809 So. 2d 222 (evidence of one single act that did not result in bodily injury is insufficient to find family violence under PSFVRA).

215. Bruscato v. Avant, 1995-0573 (La. App. 4 Cir. 7/26/95), 660 So. 2d 72.

§ 13:19 Post-Separation Family Violence Relief Act—Requirement of Family Violence

The PSFVRA defines "family violence" as "physical or sexual abuse and any offense against the person as defined in the Criminal Code of Louisiana ... committed by one parent against the other parent or against any of the children."[216] Physical abuse is undefined in the statute, but case law provides several examples of acts that suffice to meet this requirement.[217] Sexual abuse is specifically defined as including but not limited to acts prohibited by Louisiana Revised Statute Sections "14:41 [rape], 42 [first degree rape], 42.1 [second degree rape], 43 [third degree rape], 43.1 [sexual battery], 43.2 [second degree sexual battery], 43.4 [female genital mutilation], 78,[218] 80 [felony carnal knowledge of a juvenile], 81 [indecent behavior with juveniles], 81.1 [pornography involving juveniles], 81.2 [molestation], 89 [crime against nature], and 89.1 [aggravated crime against nature]."[219] Specifically excluded from the definition of family violence is negligent injuring, defamation, and reasonable acts of self-defense utilized by one parent to protect himself or herself or a child from the family violence.[220]

---

216. La. Stat. Ann. § 9:362(4) (2014); *see also* La. Stat. Ann. § 46:2121.1(2) (defining family violence as "any assault, battery, or other physical abuse which occurs between family or household members who reside together or who formerly resided together").

217. *See, e.g.*, Baker v. Perret, 2019-1692R (La. App. 1 Cir. 8/24/22), 349 So. 3d 594, 604 (affirming trial court's finding that "[t]he Defendant-in-Reconvention has an extensive history of physically abusing the Petitioner ... [by] pull[ing] ... [the] Petitioner across the concrete driveway by pulling her hair ... [, going] on a vicious assault on the Petitioner, kicking, punching, and straggling [sic] the Petitioner"); Cockheran o/b/o Cockheran v. Christopher, 2021-0370, 2021-0371 (La. App. 4 Cir. 10/28/21), 331 So. 3d 389, 394 (abuser's threats to victim "to return her to her former sex trafficker" and his other actions such as "slam[ing] her against a wall ... shov[ing] and h[olding] her seven-year-old son ... by his neck, ... hit[ting] her two-year-old son ... on the legs with a ruler so hard that it broke the child's skin" constituted family violence); Laurent v. Prevost, 2018-0126, 2018-0127 (La. App. 4 Cir. 7/11/18), 251 So. 3d 504, 512 (finding that requiring one's children to kneel for, at maximum, thirty minutes "was abusive to the extent it was affecting the welfare of the children so as to require a modification of custody"); Morrison v. Morrison, 1997-0295 (La. App. 1 Cir. 9/19/97), 699 So. 2d 1124, 1126 ("Any intentional use of force or violence upon the person of one's spouse or child, whether the physical contact is injurious or merely offensive, constitutes family violence under Revised Statute 9:362(3)"); *but cf.*, Hollingworth v. Semerad, 35,264 (La. App. 2 Cir. 10/31/01), 799 So. 2d 658, 664 (upholding trial court's determination that "imposition of the harsh consequences of the Post Separation Family Violence Relief Act was not warranted" because "the first acts of violence occurred approximately five years after the divorce, that the child did not require medical treatment of her injuries, and that only three incidents resulted in bruises."); Petsch v. Petsch, 2001-0491 (La. App. 1 Cir. 6/22/01), 809 So. 2d 222, 224 (affirming trial court's finding that "only one incident of possible family violence" is not enough to trigger the PSFVRA and that family violence requires "serious injury to multiple incidents."); Smith v. Smith, 44,663 (La. App. 2 Cir. 8/19/09), 16 So. 3d 643, 651–52 (no family violence where both parties provoked each other into verbal and physical altercations, no serious bodily injury resulted, and father completed anger management and counseling).

218. This statute has been repealed but has not been deleted by reference in the PSFVRA.

219. La. Stat. Ann. § 9:362(6) (2014).

220. La. Stat. Ann. § 9:362(4) (2014); *see* Rouyea v. Rouyea, 2000-2613 (La. App. 1 Cir. 3/28/01), 808 So. 2d 558 (no abuse of discretion for denying protective order to wife in response to husband

In considering family violence, courts assess the number, frequency, and severity of the incident(s), as well as whether family violence occurred in the presence of the children, and to what extent there was provocation for such violence.[221] For example, the court in *Smith v. Smith* did not find family violence pursuant to PSFVRA where it held that both parties provoked each other into verbal and physical altercations from time to time but no serious bodily injury was found and father had since completed counseling and anger management classes.[222]

As originally enacted, family violence under Louisiana Revised Statutes Section 9:362 was distinct from domestic abuse as defined in Louisiana Revised Statutes Section 46:2132. While family violence and domestic abuse both "include but... [are] not limited to physical or sexual abuse and any offense against the person as defined in the Criminal Code of Louisiana, except negligent injuring and defamation,"[223] the two differ in that they apply to different classes of individuals and relationships. Whereas family violence is "committed by one parent against the other parent or against any of the children,"[224] domestic abuse is "committed by one family member, household member, or dating partner against another ... [and] also includes abuse of adults as defined in R.S. 15:1503 when committed by an adult child or adult grandchild."[225] That is, domestic abuse is much broader in scope than family violence with respect to the classes of individuals and relationships it covers, thereby limiting the scope of the PSFVRA as originally enacted.

Hollingworth v. Semerad is just one example that highlights the narrow scope of relationships to which the definition of family violence originally applied. In *Hollingworth*, the abuse occurred between a father and a stepmother. Specifically, the father "brok[e] the stepmother's sternum."[226] Because the definition of family violence "include[d] physical abuse 'committed by one parent against the other parent or against any of

allegedly forcing wife to the ground and holding her there in response to her actions as it was not domestic abuse)

221. Smith v. Smith, 44,663 (La. App. 2 Cir. 8/19/09), 16 So. 3d 643; *see also* Michelli v. Michelli, 1993-2128 (La. App. 1 Cir. 5/5/95), 655 So. 2d 1342 (sporadic events of violence equals history of family violence); Nguyen v. Le, 2007-81 (La. App. 5 Cir. 5/15/07), 960 So. 2d 261 (the fact that one parent willingly allowed the children to visit unsupervised with father before invoking the PSFVRA is a factor considered by the court).

222. Smith, 16 So. 3d 643; *see also* Simmons v. Simmons, 26,414 (La. App. 2 Cir. 1/25/95), 649 So. 2d 799 (occasional incidents of violence in response to claims of adultery do not rise to level of history of perpetuating violence so for that reason and due to insufficient evidence, the court declined to apply the PSFVRA); McGee v. McGee, 1998-1911 (La. App. 3 Cir. 10/13/99), 745 So. 2d 708 (held that two or three slaps over seventeen year marriage and throwing a stool at spouse once does not equate to family violence).

223. La. Stat. Ann. § 9:362(4) (2014); *see also* La. Stat. Ann. § 46:2132(3) (2020) ("'Domestic abuse' includes but is not limited to physical or sexual abuse and any offense against the person, physical or non-physical, as defined in the Criminal Code of Louisiana, except negligent injury and defamation ...")

224. La. Stat. Ann. § 9:362(4) (2014).

225. La. Stat. Ann. § 46:2132(3) (2020).

226. Hollingsworth v. Semerad, 35,264 (La. App. 2 Cir. 10/31/01), 799 So. 2d 658, 663.

the children,'" the court held that the abuse between the father and stepmother could not constitute family violence.[227] The Second Circuit Court of Appeal also remarked that "it is clear that, had the legislature intended to expand the definition of 'family violence' in the Post-Separation Family Violence Relief Act to include a stepparent, it could have done so in a similar fashion [as it had expanded the relationships covered under another Act]."[228]

Prior to 2018, Louisiana Revised Statutes Section 9:364 provided that "[t]here is a created presumption that no parent who has a history of perpetrating family violence shall be awarded sole or joint custody of children."[229] There was thus no presumption in circumstances involving a parent who had a history of perpetrating domestic abuse, and some courts recognized that under Louisiana law, domestic abuse was not a factor in custody determinations.[230] On the other hand, other courts conflated the definitions of family violence and domestic abuse. In *McFall v. Armstrong*, for example, the Fifth Circuit Court of Appeal "f[ound] that it [wa]s imperative for the trial court to render a judgment regard[ing] ... [one parent's] Petition for Domestic Abuse Protection before a custody determination can be made," stating that "[i]n the event a parent is found to perpetuate domestic violence, the trial court is mandated to abide by LSA-R.S. 9:364."[231]

In 2018, the legislature amended Louisiana Revised Statutes Section 9:364 to provide that the presumption also applies to a "parent who has a history of perpetrating ... domestic abuse, as defined in R.S. 46:2132,[232] or has subjected any of his or her children,

---

227. Hollingsworth, 799 So. 2d at 663.

228. Hollingsworth, 799 So. 2d at 663; *see also* MacHauer v. Randolph, 1999-0086 (La. App. 1 Cir. 9/24/99), 754 So. 2d 1042 (abuse between mother and stepfather regarding their child did not implicate application of PSFVA for child of father and mother); Martin v. Martin, 36,860 (La. App. 2 Cir. 12/11/02), 833 So. 2d 1216 (PSFVRA does not apply to fights between father and stepfather or violent acts occurring before birth of child in question); Hudson v. Strother, 2017-1044 (La. App. 3 Cir. 5/2/18), 246 So. 3d 851 (acts of violence between mother and boyfriend do not require application of PSFVRA in favor of father of child as abuse must be between parents or parent and child).

229. Acts of Domestic Abuse—Protective Orders Act, No. 194, § 9:364(A), 2014 La. Sess. Law Serv. Act 194 (H.B. 747) (West).

230. In *Michelli v. Michelli*, the Louisiana First Circuit Court of Appeal explained that "LSA-R.S. 9:364(C) was *specifically* designed to protect the child's interest by restricting the right of visitation of the abusing spouse in families with a history of family violence," Michelli v. Michelli, 93-2128 (La. App. 1 Cir. 5/5/95), 655 So. 2d 1342, 1346 (emphasis added), and noted that "Arizona and Wyoming have enacted statutes similar to LSA-R.S. 9:364(C) which presume that domestic abuse is contrary to the child's best interests and requiring their courts to consider domestic abuse when arranging visitation," *id.*, n. 3 (citation omitted).

231. McFall v. Armstrong, 2010-1041 (La. App. 5 Cir. 9/13/11), 75 So. 3d 30, 40; Lewis v. Lewis, 34,031 (La. App. 2 Cir. 11/3/00), 771 So. 2d 856 (reversible error not to apply PSFRVA where family violence proven); Hicks v. Hicks, 1998-1527 (La. App. 3 Cir. 5/19/99), 733 So. 2d 1261 (reversible error not to apply PSFVRA once applicable).

232. Louisiana Revised Statutes Section 46:2132(3) provides the following definition of domestic abuse: "'Domestic abuse' includes but is not limited to physical or sexual abuse and any offense against the person, physical or non-physical, as defined in the Criminal Code of Louisiana, except negligent injury and defamation, committed by one family member, household member, or dating partner against another. 'Domestic abuse' also includes abuse of adults as defined in R.S. 15:1503 when committed by an adult child or adult grandchild." La. Stat. Ann. § 46:2132(3).

stepchildren, or any household member, as defined in R.S. 46:2132,[233] to sexual abuse, as defined in R.S. 14:403(A)(4)(b),[234] or has willingly permitted another to abuse any of his children or stepchildren, despite having the ability to prevent the abuse."[235] Thus, the legislature responded to cases like *Hollingworth* and expanded the reach of the PSFVRA to include violent behavior between various relationships that come within the scope of the Act. The cases since 2018 reflect this broad application of the PSFVRA.[236]

§ 13:20 Post-Separation Family Violence Relief Act—Injunction Required

If the court makes a determination of family violence, whether or not specifically pled,[237] all judgments involving "separation, divorce, child custody, and child visitation orders and judgment[s] in family violence cases" shall contain an injunction as defined in the PSFVRA.[238] An injunction is "a temporary restraining order or a preliminary or permanent court ordered injunction, as defined in the Code of Civil Procedure, which

---

233. Louisiana Revised Statutes Section 46:2132(4) states that "'Family members' means spouses, former spouses, parents and children, stepparents, stepchildren, foster parents, foster children, other ascendants, and other descendants. 'Family member' also means the other parent or foster parent of any child or foster child of the offender. 'Household members' means any person presently or formerly living in the same residence with the defendant and who is involved or has been involved in a sexual or intimate relationship with the defendant, or any child presently or formerly living in the same residence with the defendant, or any child of the defendant regardless of where the child resides. 'Dating partner' means any person protected from violence under R.S. 46:2151. If a parent or grandparent is being abused by an adult child, adult foster child, or adult grandchild, the provisions of this Part shall apply to any proceeding brought in district court." La. Stat. Ann. § 46:2132(4) (2020).

234. Louisiana Revised Statutes Section 14:403(A)(4)(b) provides that "[f]or purposes of this Paragraph, 'sexual abuse' shall include but is not limited to the perpetration or attempted perpetration of R.S. 14:41, 42, 42.1, 43, 43.1, 43.2, 43.3, 43.4, 46.2, 46.3, 80, 81, 81.1, 81.2, 86, 89, or 89.1." La. Stat. Ann. § 14:403(A)(4)(b).

235. Children Act, No. 412, § 9:364 (2), 2018 La. Sess. Law Serv. Act 412 (S.B. 291) (West); Hill v. Strickland, 2024-0116 (La. App. 4 Cir. 6/12/24), 391 So. 3d 113 (father granted protective order against mother for her failure to protect child from the stepfather's abuse and court awarded mother only supervised visitation).

236. *See* Duhon v. Duhon, 2001-0731 (La. App. 3 Cir. 12/12/01), 801 So. 2d 1263 (father making child sleep on kinder mat in empty room and kneel on rice met test of family violence so appellate court affirmed award of sole custody to mother); *see also supra* note 218. Additionally, Louisiana Civil Code Article 134, outlining the best interests of the child factors, was amended after enactment of the PSFVRA and now specifically includes a requirement that "in cases involving a history of ... family violence, as defined in R.S 9:362, or domestic abuse, as defined in R.S. 46:2132, including sexual abuse, as defined in R.S. 14:403 ... the court shall determine an award of custody or visitation in accordance with R.S. 9:341 and 364." La Civ. Code art. 134(B) (2018).

237. Dufresne v. Dufresne, 2008-215, 2008-216 (La. App. 5 Cir. 9/16/08), 992 So. 2d 579; *see also* Melancon v. Russel, 2018-48 (La. App. 5 Cir. 10/17/18), 258 So. 3d 995 (PSFVRA relief does not need to be specifically pled as long as abuse is raised).

238. La. Stat. Ann. § 9:366 (2014). Notably, this statute is limited to a finding of "family violence" and does not require a "history of" family violence, nor does it reference domestic abuse, sexual abuse, or the failure to stop abusive situations like the presumption in Louisiana Revised Statutes Section 9:364 does. In addition, this statute does not apply to matters involving child support, spousal support,

prohibits the violent parent from in any way contacting the abused parent or the children except for specific purposes set forth in the injunction."[239] The injunction is also required to prohibit the perpetrator of family violence "from intentionally going within fifty yards of the home, school, place of employment or person of the abused parent and the children or within fifty feet of any of their automobiles."[240] The only exceptions are 1) "communications expressly dealing with the education, health and welfare of the children"; 2) exceptions "expressly agreed to by the abused parent"; 3) exceptions necessary for court ordered visitation; or 4) exceptions "otherwise necessitated by the circumstances, considering the proximity of the parties' residences and employment."[241] Such injunctions shall be issued in the form of a Uniform Abuse Prevention Order pursuant to Louisiana Revised Statutes Section 46:2136.2 and transmitted to the Louisiana Protective Order Registry.[242]

§ 13:21 Post-Separation Family Violence Relief Act—Impact on Custody and Visitation

Under the PSFVRA, there is presumption that sole or joint custody of the child(ren) shall not be awarded to a parent that 1) has a history of family violence as defined in Louisiana Revised Statutes Section 9:362, or domestic abuse, as defined in Louisiana Revised Statutes Section 46:2131; or 2) has subjected the children, stepchildren, or household member to sexual abuse; or 3) allowed another to abuse a child or stepchild.[243] "This can be especially helpful since batterers seek custody much more frequently than do non-battering fathers."[244] "If the court finds that both parents have a history of perpetrating family violence, custody shall be awarded solely to the parent

---

or community property partition. For statutory authority involving violence or abuse applicable in those matters, *see* for example, Louisiana Revised Statutes Sections 9:327, 9:374, and 9:375, which are beyond the scope of this Chapter.

239. La. Stat. Ann. § 9:362(5) (2014).

240. La. Stat. Ann. § 9:362(5) (2014).

241. La. Stat. Ann. § 9:362(5) (2014).

242. La. Stat. Ann. § 9:366 (2014). The forms required are located at https://wwwlasc.org/LPOR-Forms. For a discussion on domestic abuse temporary restraining orders and protective orders under the Domestic Abuse Assistance Act, La. Stat. Ann. §§ 46:2135 and 46:2136, *see* Sections 13:2–13:17.

243. La. Stat. Ann. § 9:364(A) (2018); *see, e.g.*, Pierre v. Pierre, 2023-470, 2024 WL 698323, at *11 (La. App. 5 Cir. Feb. 21, 2024) (affirming the trial court's determination that Mr. Pierre's acts of strangulation upon Ms. Pierre constituted family violence and therefore Mr. Pierre is ineligible for sole or joint custody over their child pursuant to La. R.S. 9:364); Merrells v. Dotray, 53,551 (La. App. 2 Cir. 7/8/20), 299 So. 3d 208, 212–14 (finding that the trial court erred in granting primarily custody to the children's father, who had a history of perpetrating domestic abuse against his former girlfriend); Durand v. Rose, 2022-300 (La. App. 4 Cir. 9/15/22), 366 So. 3d 484, 490–91 (upholding trial court's determination that father had a history of perpetuating family violence by physically abusing his wife and threatening her and, therefore, cannot have sole or joint custody); *see also* Chapter 6, Section 6:40.

244. Kathleen Finley Duthu, *Why Do You Need to Know About Domestic Violence? How Attorneys Can Recognize and Address the Problem*, 53 La. B.J. 20, 22 (2005) (citations omitted).

who is less likely to continue to perpetrate family violence."[245] However, the fact that "the abused parent suffers from the effects of the abuse shall not be grounds for denying that parent custody."[246]

If the court finds a history of family violence, supervised visitation between the child and perpetrator is required.[247] The only exception is in cases of sexual abuse. If the court finds by clear and convincing evidence that "a parent has sexually abused his or her child or children," the court shall prohibit all visitation and contact with the child(ren).[248]

Supervised visitation is defined as "face-to-face contact between a parent and a child which occurs in the immediate presence of a supervising person approved by the court under conditions which prevent any physical abuse, threats, intimidation, abduction, or humiliation of either the abused parent or the child."[249] The supervisor may not be a "relative, friend, therapist, or associate of the parent perpetrating family violence."[250] If the abused parent consents, the supervisor may be a friend or family member of the abused parent.[251] The visits may not be overnight and shall not be in the home of the perpetrator of family violence.[252] All costs of supervised visitation are to be paid by the perpetrator.[253]

If the parent is incarcerated, the court order shall include "restrictions, conditions, and safeguards" necessary to protect the "mental and physical health of the child and minimize the risk of harm to the child."[254] The factors the court must consider before ordering visitation with an incarcerated parent include, but are not limited to, length and quality of the prior relationship; whether the child is in need of guidance, enlightenment, or tutelage; preference of the child; willingness of other parent/guardian to encourage a close relationship between child and parent and take the child to supervised visitation; mental and physical health of child and incarcerated parent; length of time child lived with parent prior to incarceration; costs of travel and other expenses; effect upon child and feasibility of alternative technology for visitation; and any other

245. La. Stat. Ann. § 9:364(D) (2018); *see also* Morrison v. Morrison, 1997-0295 (La. App. 1 Cir. 9/19/97), 699 So. 2d 1124, 1127 (upholding the trial court's determination to award sole custody to the defendant, who was least likely to continue perpetrating family violence, even though both parents had a history of perpetuating family violence).

246. La. Stat. Ann. § 9:364(C) (2018).

247. *Id.*; Morrison, 699 So. 2d 1124.

248. La. Stat. Ann. § 9:364(F) (2018); Dean v. Burkeen, 2022-563 (La. App. 3 Cir. 3/8/23), 371 So. 3d 44, 53. As originally enacted, the statute required proof of sexual abuse by preponderance of the evidence. However, the Louisiana Supreme Court struck down the preponderance of the evidence standard as unconstitutional. State in Interest of A.C., 1193-1125 (La. 10/17/94), 643 So. 2d 743. Thereafter, the legislature revised the PSFVRA to its present language requiring clear and convincing proof of sexual abuse.

249. La. Stat. Ann. § 9:362(7) (2014); *see also* La. Stat. Ann. § 9:341.

250. La. Stat. Ann. § 9:362(7) (2014); *see also* La. Stat. Ann. § 9:341.

251. La. Stat. Ann. § 9:362(7) (2014); *see also* La. Stat. Ann. § 9:341.

252. La. Stat. Ann. § 9:362(7) (2014); *see also* La. Stat. Ann. § 9:341.

253. La. Stat. Ann. § 9:362(7) (2014); *see also* La. Stat. Ann. § 9:341.

254. La. Stat. Ann. § 9:364.1 (2014).

evidence or testimony that the court deems applicable.[255] This statute applies even if the parent is incarcerated for reasons unrelated to the child or parent in question.[256]

§ 13:22 Post-Separation Family Violence Relief Act—Overcoming the Presumption

In all cases, no contact or supervised visitation continues until the violent parent can prove by a preponderance of the evidence that the violent parent successfully completed a court monitored domestic abuse intervention program, is not abusing alcohol and illegal psychoactive drugs, and that such visitation is in the child's best interest.[257] The program mandated by the statute requires a minimum of twenty-six in-person sessions comprised of a model designed specifically for perpetrators of domestic abuse.[258] The moderator of the program shall have "experience working directly with perpetrators and victims of domestic violence," "experience in facilitating batterer intervention groups," "training in the causes and dynamics of domestic violence, characteristics of batterers, victim safety, and sensitivity to victims"[259] and be a licensed mental health professional.[260] There is a presumption that any licensed mental health professional who is court-appointed to conduct a custody evaluation in a family violence case shall be deemed to "have current and demonstrable training and experience working with perpetrators and victims of family violence."[261]

The order issued under PSFVRA is interim or temporary. The court monitors a perpetrator's progress in the program.[262] Once the perpetrator successfully meets the requirements of the court-monitored domestic abuse treatment program, visitation with the child, whether supervised or unsupervised, must be in the child's best interest.[263] This involves an application of the custody factors in Louisiana Civil Code Arti-

255. La. Stat. Ann. § 9:364.1; Loya v. Loya, 2017-555 (La. App. 5 Cir. 2/21/18), 239 So. 3d 1048.

256. Loya, 239 So. 3d 1048 (Louisiana Revised Statutes Section 9:364.1 applies even if imprisonment of father is unrelated to his own child).

257. La. Stat. Ann. § 9:364(A) (2018); Barak v. Saacks, 2021-0756, 2021-0757, 2021-0758, 2021-0759 (La. App. 4 Cir. 10/12/22), 367 So. 3d 656, 665; Garcia v. Hernandez, 2021-338 (La. App. 5 Cir. 4/11/22), 339 So. 3d 61 (must meet all criteria under Louisiana Revised Statutes Section 9:364 before any modification in custody).

258. La. Stat. Ann. § 9:362(3) (2014).

259. La. Stat. Ann. § 9:362(3) (2014); D.O.H. v. T.L.H., 2001-174 (La. App. 3 Cir. 10/31/01), 799 So. 2d 714 (treatment program sufficient since psychologist knew he was treating husband for spousal abuse and his treatment consisted of helping husband with his anger management).

260. La. Stat. Ann. § 9:365 (2022).

261. La. Stat. Ann. § 9:365 (2022); *see also* Post-Separation Family Violence Relief Act, No. 1091, Section 9:365, 1992 La. Sess. Law Serv. Act 1091 (H.B. 1056) (West).

262. La. Stat. Ann. § 9:362(3) (2014).

263. Morrison v. Morrison, 1997-0295 (La. App. 1 Cir. 9/19/97), 699 So. 2d 1124 (treatment program completion required before supervised visitation will be permitted).

cle 134.[264] However, once a court determines it is in the child's best interest, appropriate visitation will be ordered.[265] In the case of sexual abuse, only supervised visitation is allowed after meeting the test.[266]

§ 13:23 Post-Separation Family Violence Relief Act—Court Ordered Mediation Not Permitted

Generally, in family law proceedings involving custody or visitation, the court may order the parties to mediate.[267] Mediation is a voluntary process and assumes that the parties have equal bargaining positions required to reach a consensual agreement. However, mediating the issues of violence implies the victim is somehow at fault.[268] Recognizing this imbalance, the law prohibits mediation referrals in such situations. Specifically, in any custody proceedings or any other proceedings for separation, divorce, child support, spousal support, or community property, "no spouse or parent who satisfies the court that he or she, or any of the children, has been the victim of family violence perpetrated by the other spouse or parent" shall be required by court order to participate in mediation.[269] There is no case law interpreting this statute, and Louisiana Revised Statutes Section 9:363 has not been amended since its enactment in 1992. However, the language is clear that courts are prohibited from ordering or referring parties to mediation if there is a proceeding seeking an order of protection in place.

---

264. For a discussion of Louisiana Civil Code article 134 best interest of the child factors, *see* Chapter 6, Sections 6:24–40.

265. La. Stat. Ann. § 9:3646.

266. La. Stat. Ann. § 9:364(D) (2018).

267. La. Stat. Ann. § 9:332. For a discussion on mediation in child custody cases, *see also* Chapter 6, Section 6:53.

268. Kerry Loomis, *Domestic Violence and Mediation: A Tragic Combination for Victims in California Family Court*, 35 Cal. L. Rev. 2, 7 (1999).

269. La. Stat. Ann. § 9:363.

§ 13:24 Post-Separation Family Violence Relief Act—Remedies

The remedies permitted under the PSFVRA shall not "affect the remedies set forth in Louisiana Revised Statutes Sections 46:2131 through 46:2142, the Criminal Code, the Children's Code, the Civil Code or elsewhere."[270] A case brought under PSFVRA may impose the remedies under Louisiana Revised Statutes Section 46:2131 *et seq.* and vice versa.[271] Costs permissible to be awarded under PSFVRA include court costs, attorney fees, evaluation fees, and expert witness fees, "costs of medical and psychological care for the abused spouse, or for any children, necessitated by the family violence," and "costs of enforcement and modification proceedings, [and] cost of appeal."[272] The costs and fees must be incurred in furtherance of the PSFVRA.[273] Thus, any fees and costs unrelated to family violence would arguably be excluded from consideration.

270. La. Stat. Ann. § 9:368.

271. La. Stat. Ann. § 9:368 (2015) and La. Stat. Ann. § 46:2139 (1982); Buchanan v. Langston, 36,520 (La. App. 2 Cir. 9/18/02), 827 So. 2d 1186 (court not limited to Domestic Abuse Assistance Act or PSFVRA remedies in determining father sexually abused child and court could suspend father's visitation under Louisiana Children's Code).

272. La. Stat. Ann. § 9:367 (2018); *see also* Barak v. Saacks, 2021-0756, 2021-0757, 2021-0758, 2021-0759 (La. App. 4 Cir. 10/12/22), 367 So. 3d 656, 666 (mandating award of all attorney's fees and costs once determination of PSFVRA applies); Jarrell v. Jarrell, 35,837 (La. App. 2 Cir. 2/27/02), 811 So. 2d 207 (attorney fees and interest may be awarded without specific demand for it and fees assessed to perpetuator of abuse even if the abuser is successful in subsequent proceedings to modify the orders).

273. Dufresne v. Dufresne, 2008-215 (La. App. 5 Cir. 9/16/08), 992 So. 2d 579 (remand to trial court to determine which attorney fees were necessitated by violence).

Index